9780691052922

Ambassador
MacVeagh
Reports

Lincoln MacVeagh

Ambassador MacVeagh Reports

GREECE, 1933-1947

EDITED BY
JOHN O. IATRIDES

PRINCETON UNIVERSITY PRESS
PRINCETON, NEW JERSEY

Copyright © 1980 by Princeton University Press

Published by Princeton University Press, Princeton, New Jersey
In the United Kingdom: Princeton University Press, Guildford, Surrey

ALL RIGHTS RESERVED

Library of Congress Cataloging in Publication Data will be found on the last printed page of this book

Publication of this book has been aided by a grant from the National Endowment for the Humanities

Clothbound editions of Princeton University Press books are printed on acid-free paper, and binding materials are chosen for strength and durability.

Printed in the United States of America by Princeton University Press, Princeton, New Jersey

CONTENTS

FRONTISPIECE	ii
EDITOR'S PREFACE	vii
ACKNOWLEDGMENTS	xiii
I. "The Greeks Are My Passion in Life!"	3
II. Fall of a Republic: 1933-1935	10
III. Dictatorship: 1936-1939	67
IV. In the Storm's Path: 1939-1940	166
V. "A Grand Little Fighting Nation"	236
VI. "A Gallant and Suicidal Resistance"	295
VII. Interlude: Iceland and South Africa	379
VIII. Cairo	388
IX. From Liberation to Civil War	591
X. End of a Journey	679
APPENDIX A. LIST OF PRINCIPAL NAMES	735
APPENDIX B. ABBREVIATIONS AND CODE NAMES	747
NOTES	751
INDEX	759

EDITOR'S PREFACE

It is a pity that Lincoln MacVeagh did not write a book about his days as American envoy to Greece and elsewhere. He had a strong and lucid style, detailed diaries and other records to draw upon, his own experience as a one-time successful literary agent and publisher, a keen sense of history, and an important story to cover. Students of contemporary Greece, and of American foreign policy generally, would have been particularly indebted to him for a first-hand account of his diplomatic work over a period of twenty years, beginning with Hitler's rise to power and closing with the consolidation of the Western alliance into NATO.

That he did not choose to write such a book is not, however, surprising. An intensely private man, he was not likely to draw attention to himself or air his views in public. His withdrawal from Greece in the fall of 1947 came as a bitter blow to his pride and left him with painful memories, especially since it coincided with a major personal tragedy: the death of his wife in Athens. Moreover, he belonged to a generation of public servants for whom the publishing of one's memoirs was not quite the fashion that it is today.

Although he was well suited for diplomatic service, MacVeagh was not among Franklin D. Roosevelt's principal ambassadors. A truly cultured man, widely read and travelled, a linguist, discreet and discerning, and with the aristocratic bearing that was once considered important for high diplomatic posts, he nevertheless lacked the wealth, political backing and self-assertiveness needed for the choicer assignments. Above all, however, he was interested in Greece, a country that in the 1930s belonged to the backwaters of American foreign policy and was characteristically consigned to the Department of State's Division of Near Eastern and African Affairs.

But if MacVeagh himself was not a major figure in the Roosevelt and Truman administrations, his papers are a veritable treasure, particularly for historians of contemporary Greece, and for those interested in the development of American policy toward the Balkans and the Eastern Mediterranean during the early stages of the East-West conflict. His despatches, diaries, and letters span a long and unusually turbulent phase of Greek history: the collapse of the Republic, the monarchy's restoration, the Metaxas dictatorship, the "Albanian Epic," the German invasion and occupation, the "Cairo period" of the Government in exile, resistance, liberation, civil war, and the inauguration of the Truman Doctrine. They also shed light on a brief but critical moment of Yugoslav history. A collection of MacVeagh's papers represents, therefore, the raw material for the study of many important and still controversial events and issues.

The purpose of this volume is to preserve this material as far as possible intact and complete. Accordingly, this is not a book about Lincoln MacVeagh, his "life and letters," or a history of the period during which he was the United States' representative to Greece. Rather, it is a nearly-continuous record, almost entirely in MacVeagh's words, of those among his diplomatic activities, reports, and observations which are most likely to prove valuable to historians of contemporary Greece, American foreign policy, and the early phases of the Cold War. Beyond providing a brief historical background, and the necessary chronological continuity, the editor has sought not to interject himself in the narrative.

Although the MacVeagh papers pertain equally to his tour as Minister to Iceland (1941-1942) and as Minister to the Union of South Africa (1942-1943), these otherwise important diplomatic assignments are not covered in this volume. Similarly, his term as Ambassador to the Yugoslav Government in exile (1943-1944) is given here very brief treatment on the basis of his diary alone. His years of service as Ambassador to Portugal (1948-1952) and to Spain (1952-1953) remain entirely outside the scope of the present undertaking.

The Sources

The MacVeagh "Papers" consist of three principal categories: the wartime diaries, diplomatic reports and other official documents, and personal letters. From this vast assortment of private and government documents, a chronological journal has been pieced together on the basis of those among his papers that provide valuable detail and insight into major political events, or offer revealing commentary and contemporary reaction. Thus the primary aim of this publication is to preserve in its original form source material, and to help capture the psychological climate of the times.

Diaries

On October 18, 1939, as the war in Europe threatened to spread in the direction of the Balkans, MacVeagh began to keep a diary which, with one major interruption (from December 8, 1944 to April 12, 1945) he continued until April 30, 1945, when the capitulation of Germany appeared imminent. The diaries, therefore, cover the most critical period of his tours as Minister to Greece, Iceland, the Union of South Africa; his term as Ambassador to the Greek and Yugoslav Governments in exile in Cairo; and his return to Greece after liberation. One of these handwritten notebooks, for the period from October 1, 1941 to April 7, 1942 ("Iceland I") has been misplaced and may be lost. The diaries remain the property of the MacVeagh family.

Partly a pleasant diversion from the pressures of his official duties, the diaries touch on the daily routine of the Legation, the weather, the beauty of the season, staff problems, social events, news items of the day, family affairs, travels, books, and personal thoughts. These long daily entries, usually written late at night, provided MacVeagh with the chance to express himself openly and without restraint, offering relief from the restrictions of his position and persona. However, the bulk of this personal record is a detailed and candid account of MacVeagh's official activities, and a running commentary on local and international developments. Because of the highly sensitive nature of the contents, he treated the diaries as classified documents, and until his departure from Greece kept the more current ones in the Legation's safe. The passages selected for publication here deal almost exclusively with major political and diplomatic events of which MacVeagh had first-hand knowledge, and represent a very small portion of the original manuscript. Omissions of entire diary entries of one or more days are not specifically marked, but should be obvious to the reader from the interrupted sequence of entry dates.

Diplomatic Reports

From 1933 until the end of 1940, when the war disrupted regular courier service between Athens and Washington, MacVeagh wrote several hundred long despatches, covering every conceivable topic of possible interest to his superiors. Many more despatches were drafted by others on his staff, and were subsequently edited and signed by him, with the author's initials appearing on the final document together with the Minister's signature. His highly literate style and wit, as well as his profound knowledge of Greek history and national character, made his reports most interesting reading even for those in the Department who were not concerned with Greece. After 1940, the pressures of war and improved telecommunications contributed to the gradual abandonment of the long and polished but slow-moving despatch in favor of the telegram and of terse, cold prose. Most of these documents are to be found in the files of the Department of State (Decimal Series) that deal with Greek political affairs; few have been placed in MacVeagh's personal folder. Some of his telegrams have appeared in the Department's series on *Foreign Relations of the United States*. All despatches and telegrams quoted here and attributed to MacVeagh were authored by him.

Typically, MacVeagh's despatches to the Department of State are addressed to "The Honorable, The Secretary of State, Washington, D.C.," and begin with "Sir: I have the honor to report that" or "Sir: In further reference to my despatch No. ——— I have the honor to report that ———." In this volume the formal portion of the opening sentence has been omitted and the quotations begin immediately with the substantive part of the first sentence. In every other instance where a particular passage is not reproduced in its entirety, excisions are indicated.

Letters

MacVeagh wrote about seventy letters to President Roosevelt, all dealing with political issues. Several of these have been reproduced in *Franklin D. Roosevelt and Foreign Affairs*, edited by Edgar B. Nixon (Harvard University Press, 1969). He also corresponded with Eleanor Roosevelt and with her brother, G. Hall Roosevelt (godfather of MacVeagh's daughter), mostly about family matters. In return, MacVeagh received many letters from the Roosevelts. Although most of the President's responses were written by White House secretaries and are little more than polite acknowledgments of MacVeagh's letters, some of them show a personal touch and a lively interest in MacVeagh's diplomatic bailiwick. MacVeagh's correspondence with the President and First Lady is now part of the Roosevelt Library collection at Hyde Park, New York. His correspondence with Hall Roosevelt and with friends and colleagues in the foreign service, some of which is quoted here, is in his personal papers now in the hands of his family. MacVeagh's correspondence with President Truman, most of which is preserved at the Truman Library in Independence, Missouri, is formal and without historical value.

Identifications

Names of individuals appearing in the text are divided into three categories:

Persons whose identity, not previously made clear in MacVeagh's or in the editor's text, is important for the understanding of a particular passage. Such names are identified in footnotes when first encountered in the text;

Persons whose identity is explained in the narrative when they are first mentioned, but who are historically important or appear frequently in these pages. Such names are included in the List of Principal Names (Appendix A);

Persons who are too well known to require any identification, or are of no consequence to the narrative, or whose full identity and position cannot be established. Such names are not identified further.

Historical events with which the reader may not be expected to be familiar are briefly identified in footnotes when first encountered in the text. Acronyms, abbreviations, code names, and so on, are similarly identified in footnotes when they first appear, and may also be found in the list of Abbreviations and Code Names (Appendix B). Bibliographical information and document identification may be found in the notes.

MacVeagh's spelling of certain names has been changed to conform to the more modern usage or has been corrected. Thus, Carapanyotis has been changed to Karapanayiotis, Puritch to Purić, Kiosseivanoff to Kioseivanov, Mihailovitch to Mihailović, Saloniki to Salonica, etc. Since MacVeagh did not intend to publish his diary, its language at times lacks the clarity and polish that characterize the language of his letters and despatches. The slight editorial changes that have been made in the diary's text in no way alter his thought or style of expression. In every other respect, materials quoted here remain as found in the original.

ACKNOWLEDGMENTS

IN EDITING THIS VOLUME I have benefited from the trust, support and patience of many individuals and institutions.

I am most grateful to the late Ambassador Lincoln MacVeagh for allowing me unrestricted access to his diaries and personal correspondence, and for giving me complete freedom to arrange these materials for publication. The Ambassador's daughter, Mrs. Samuel E. Thorne (Margaret Ewen MacVeagh), first gave me permission to examine the diaries, provided me with detailed information about her parents' earlier years, and facilitated my work in many important ways. Mrs. Lincoln MacVeagh, the Ambassador's widow, graciously invited me to examine his papers in Estoril, Portugal, brought me in contact with many of his friends and associates, and offered much encouragement and assistance. Mr. Colin MacVeagh, the Ambassador's step-son, took a lively interest in the publication and helped me with many delicate aspects of the work. Although the responsibility for the manuscript is entirely mine, the credit for making this book possible belongs to the MacVeagh family.

Among MacVeagh's associates and friends who responded to my questions the following have been especially helpful: Loy W. Henderson, Foy D. Kohler, William H. McNeill, Col. (ret.) Allen C. Miller II, Karl L. Rankin, and Alexander C. Sedgwick.

My research in government records was greatly facilitated by Mr. Arthur G. Kogan, Historical Office, Department of State, Messrs. James E. O'Neill, William J. Stewart and William R. Emerson of the Franklin D. Roosevelt Library, and Philip C. Brooks and Philip D. Lagerquist of the Harry S. Truman Library. I am also grateful to the National Endowment for the Humanities and to the American Philosophical Society for their generous grants in support of my work.

I am greatly indebted to Mr. Sanford G. Thatcher of Princeton University Press for taking an interest in the MacVeagh journal long before I could produce a manuscript, to Ms. Cynthia Perwin Halpern for her editorial assistance, and to Mrs. Virginia E. Lloyd of Southern Connecticut State College for her expert typing and retyping of what must have appeared as a never-ending endeavor.

Finally, I am grateful to my wife, Nancy, for her forbearance during the many years it has taken me to prepare this volume and for helping me with the manuscript along the way.

Ambassador
MacVeagh
Reports

CHAPTER
I

"The Greeks are My Passion in Life!"

THE AVALANCHE of congratulatory messages that began to reach Franklin D. Roosevelt moments after the results of the November 1932 elections had become known included a letter from the president of Dial Press, a small publishing firm in New York. In what was destined to become the first in a long series of "Dear Franklin" letters, Lincoln MacVeagh sought to convey to the President-elect the joy and admiration of three generations of MacVeaghs: "Ever since old times when you were beginning your career and I was Hall's room-mate and visited you in Albany and Campobello, I have been hoping for this. My mother who is seventy-two, and the widow of a Republican ambassador, remained at her country place in New Hampshire over election-day so that she might cast her vote for you, and my little girl, who is twelve, wouldn't go to bed till she was sure you were elected. That's how we feel about you." The brief letter closed on a rather somber note, characteristic of the thoughts of millions of Depression-frightened Roosevelt supporters: "You have tremendous problems ahead of you. But it seems to me that the high spirit and unparalleled courage with which you have brought your career to this great height will carry you to success in their solution. I earnestly pray, and confidently expect, that the final satisfaction will be yours." (1)

Lincoln MacVeagh had known the Roosevelts since childhood. G. Hall Roosevelt ("Smouch" to his friends), Eleanor's younger brother, had been his classmate and close friend at Groton (class of 1909), and the two had roomed together at Harvard.[1] Hall Roosevelt's wife was the godmother of Lincoln's daughter, Margaret Ewen MacVeagh ("Little Peggy"). Groton and Harvard were logical choices for the son of a distinguished family. Lincoln had been born in Narragansett Pier, Rhode Island, on October 1, 1890. His father, Charles MacVeagh of Dublin, New Hamp-

---

[1] Franklin D. Roosevelt was himself a Grotonite, as were MacVeagh's five brothers: Rogers, Ewen Cameron, Charles, Francis Wayne, and Charlton. The class of 1909 also included William Averell Harriman; another schoolmate was Dean Gooderham Acheson.

shire, had been the U.S. Steel Corporation's general solicitor and, later, President Coolidge's Ambassador to Japan. His grandfather, Wayne MacVeagh, had been Attorney General in President Garfield's Cabinet and had served as Minister to Turkey and Italy. While in Turkey, Wayne MacVeagh had been instrumental in persuading the authorities to allow an ambitious but virtually unknown naturalized American citizen, Heinrich Schliemann, to search for the mythical city of Troy, a project which was to revolutionize archaeology and the study of the classical world. Lincoln's great uncle, Franklin MacVeagh, had been Secretary of the Treasury under Taft; his great-grandmother was a cousin of President Lincoln. His mother, Fanny Davenport Rogers MacVeagh, was a direct descendant of Thomas Rogers, the eighteenth signer of the Mayflower Pact.

At Groton, where "every endeavor is made to cultivate manly Christian character, with reference to moral and physical, as well as intellectual development," MacVeagh had been quite successful. He won a number of awards, including the English Essay Prize, the Greek Prize, the Junior Debating Prize, and was elected secretary of his class and editor of *The Grotonian*. His short stories were often centered around his own experiences in England and Italy, where he had traveled with his family. He was also a good athlete and played quarterback on the sixth form's team until an injury forced him to give up that much-coveted position. Although his family had expected him to go to Yale, MacVeagh had been persuaded by his friend Hall Roosevelt to enter Harvard instead, a decision he never regretted. Throughout his life he felt a special kinship for Harvard men and when his step-son, Colin MacVeagh, who had been raised and educated in Europe, was ready to enter college, it would be Harvard again.

Building on an already solid foundation of classical Greek and Latin, MacVeagh majored in philosophy and took advanced courses in literature, history and the arts. He earned the A.B.—and his Phi Beta Kappa key—in three years, graduating in 1913 *magna cum laude*. As an undergraduate he received a John Harvard scholarship, was chosen editor of the Harvard *Advocate*, and worked as secretary to the director of the Boston Museum of Fine Arts. After Harvard, he spent a year in Paris, studying philosophy and languages (French, German, Italian) at the Sorbonne.

His college training and broad cultural interests did not easily settle the question of a career, and there was no family enterprise he could join. After a year in New York, working for the U.S. Steel Products Co., he became a salesman for the college department of the Henry Holt Publishing Co., visiting campuses throughout the southern and western states and being initiated into the secrets of the publishing world. In

August 1917, he married Margaret Charlton Lewis of New York, daughter of a distinguished linguist and authority on Latin, and herself a serious student of classical languages. She was also strong in modern Greek, and in later years enjoyed reading the works of Stratis Myrivilis in the original. Their marriage was to prove the perfect match of two highly cultured companions: in addition to their many mutual interests the MacVeaghs were to spend endless happy hours taking turns at reading aloud masterpieces of world literature. Although MacVeagh was a life-long student of both classical and modern Greek (he used the New Testament as his text), and could eventually read the Athens newspapers with little difficulty, he never really spoke modern Greek. Their only child, Margaret Ewen, born in March 1920, started learning Greek at the age of nine, and was soon fluent in both the classical and the vernacular languages. She was to develop a serious and lasting interest in Greek literature and culture.

In May 1917, MacVeagh enlisted, and two days before his wedding he was commissioned first lieutenant (Infantry), detailed to the school of trench warfare at Cambridge, Mass. Assigned to the 80th Division, he was soon promoted to captain and on May 22, 1918 sailed for France. He saw action on the Artois, St. Mihiel, and Meuse-Argonne fronts and served as aide (Operations Section) to Major General Cronkhite, commanding general of the 80th Division and later of the 9th and 6th Army Corps. In March 1919, he was transferred to the Historical Section, General Staff, American Expeditionary Force, where he was promoted to major. Returning to the United States in late May, he was discharged on July 4, 1919, having been cited by General Pershing for "exceptionally meritorious and conspicuous services" and recommended by General Cronkhite for the Distinguished Service Medal.

A few months after his return to civilian life, MacVeagh rejoined Henry Holt as head of the trade department, and in 1920 became one of the company's directors. He invited his friend, Franklin D. Roosevelt, then Assistant Secretary of the Navy, to write a book on the growth of the American navy, but Roosevelt had already promised such a manuscript to another publisher. MacVeagh was more successful with literary men such as Robert Frost, who soon became a personal friend, Robert Benchley, and Stephen Vincent Benet, many of whose works were published by Holt thanks to MacVeagh's successful efforts. His search for good manuscripts also took him to England, where he secured Albert Einstein's *Relativity* and Marcel Proust's *Swann's Way*.

Anxious to be completely on his own, MacVeagh resigned from Holt in December 1923, and the following year founded the Dial Press, Inc., while also serving as secretary and treasurer of the Dial Publishing Co., publisher of the *Dial* magazine. His considerable experience, scholarly interests, cultured taste and contacts served him well, and he was soon able to attract to his firm both new and established authors. Among the many works published by Dial Press were Elizabeth Bowen's *The Hotel* (MacVeagh's first best-seller), Marshall Foch's *Foch Speaks*, Prince Kropotkin's *Ethics*, W. R. Burnett's *Little Caesar*, Valentine Kataev's *The Embezzlers*, Michael Ossorgin's *Quiet Street*, Prince Yousoupoff's *Rasputin*, Denis Saurat's *Blake and Modern Thought*, A. E. Taylor's *Plato*, and Herman Finer's *Theory and Practice of Modern Government*. MacVeagh also started the Library of Living Classics, edited *Champlin's Encyclopedia for Young Folks* and *Poetry from the Bible* (Dial, 1925), and wrote an essay entitled *Literature, Art and Mythology* (Dial, 1930).

After leaving Holt and for the next ten years, MacVeagh made his home in New Canaan, Connecticut, commuting to his office in New York by train, usually studying Homer in the original along the way. The MacVeaghs travelled to Europe and Greece in 1929, 1930, and 1931, reading aloud from Herodotus, Thucydides, and Xenophon as they visited the historical sites. But it was not only that small country's glorious past that seemed to fascinate them. "It's a genuine place," he remarked after the 1931 visit, "and when you realize what can be done with reclamation of marsh land, engineering projects and reforestation, there is no limit to its future." (2) He thought that Greece was on the threshold of bold economic and social development. "Its political heritage," he observed elsewhere, "which has contributed in varying degrees to the governments of all modern nations, has at home produced a strong and independent race of people, eager for liberty and capable of great achievement. It should not be forgotten that less than a century ago Greece was a medieval scattering of war-spent states, with no national consciousness and no unity.... The story of modern Greece is really amazing...." (3)

While the MacVeaghs were not politically active, their Connecticut friends included some of the state's more prominent Democrats and Roosevelt supporters. Among them were Archibald McNeill, chairman of the State Democratic Committee, Dr. Edward G. Dolan, Margaret Emerson Bailey, President of the New Canaan Roosevelt Club, Homer S. Cummings, William Baldwin, and State Senator William H. Hackett of New Haven. In the fall of 1932, as a Roosevelt victory appeared quite likely, several members of this group casually suggested to MacVeagh that he might wish to become the next President's envoy to Greece. Later on, Dr. Dolan would take credit for first proposing MacVeagh's name to Roosevelt and his campaign manager, James A. Farley. That MacVeagh himself may have cultivated the idea is suggested by an entry in his diary (October 14, 1942), ten years later, in which he recalled the start of his diplomatic career and marvelled at the "strange consequences to one night's inspiration driving home in the dark from Darien station, when I outlined a possibly fantastic plan to Peggy with which she fell in so loyally and enthusiastically! . . ."

MacVeagh's congratulatory letter to Roosevelt on election night was soon followed by another, indicating that he was more than ready to abandon the pleasures of the publishing world for the vicissitudes of a diplomatic career:

January 31, 1933

Dear Franklin:

I am sending you—whether for your birthday or that of Abraham Lincoln, I can't quite make out—a little book I am just about to publish, entitled, "The True Story of the Gettysburg Address."

It is small, and fits in the pocket, and who should have the first copy of it but the next President of the United States? But if you dare to acknowledge it, even through a secretary, you will be guilty of a high crime and misdemeanor, for you are too busy for such things.

I am writing to my mother in Rome about your acknowledgment of her vote for you. That was a gracious thing for you to do, and graciously said.

It may come to your attention that friends of mine in Connecticut are proposing me as a candidate for the post of Minister to Greece. It seems that such a minor diplomatic appointment would greatly cheer the young Democrats, who are fighting to wrench the State from its entrenched Republicanism. Mr. McNeill and Dr. Dolan would not at all be averse to finding someone whom you would consider. They now know my qualifications for the post, but they cannot know to what an extent my willingness to have my friends mention me in the first place was dependent on my desire to put special knowledge, which I had gathered through years, at your personal disposal. When you have so many things to look after as you have, you can't have too many people working for you who are devoted to you. You would have another pair of your own eyes in Greece if I were there, at the same time that you would please some hard-working party friends at home. That seems to make of the idea what the sports' writers call "a natural,"—so much so that perhaps you will forgive my bringing it up!

I hope you are really going to get some days of rest.

Very sincerely yours,
Lincoln MacVeagh

P.S. I haven't been to Greece every year for the past three years just to look at ruins! It's a fascinating place that has had too much history recently for its primitive economic structure to bear. And it's going to take a lot more knowledge and care to get our money out of it than those people showed who put it in. I'm sure I could help you on this small but vexatious problem, if you ever cared to call on me. *The Greeks are my passion in life!* (4)

Following Roosevelt's inauguration on March 4, 1933, the Department of State received word of the President's decision to appoint MacVeagh Minister to Greece, to succeed Robert P. Skinner. After a routine confirmation by the Senate, Acting Secretary of State William Phillips instructed the American Chargé in Athens (Leland B. Morris) to inquire whether the Greek Government would agree to the appointment. Listing the nominee's qualifications, he pointed out that because of his "lifelong study" of Greece and his several visits to that country, MacVeagh "is familiar with Greek problems and Greek psychology as few outsiders are." (5) On July 19, accompanied by his wife and 13-year-old daughter, MacVeagh sailed for England. After visits in London, Paris, and Rome for consultations regarding his new duties, he reached Athens on September 4. He presented his letter of credence on September 22, and in his first despatch from the Greek capital he described the scene:

[Athens, September 22, 1933]
I have the honor to report that I was today, at noon, received by Mr. Zaimis, President of the Hellenic Republic, at his official residence. . . . At the President's Palace I was received by the Acting Chief of Protocol and was met at the top of the stairs leading to the President's rooms by Mr. Maximos, the Minister of Foreign Affairs, who had just returned from Ankara. Mr. Maximos met me with conspicuous friendliness recalling our pleasant time together when I called on him at Salsomaggiore recently, and led me directly to the President. After I had been formally presented to the President by Mr. Maximos, I read a brief speech in English, as prescribed in the regulations of the Department of State. The President replied in kind, using the French language. The President then engaged me in conversation and I said in French that I was sorry not to be able to converse in Greek but that I hoped some day to be able to do so. I had, however,—I said—written out a few informal words in that beautiful language, and, with the President's permission, would like to read them. I then read a few remarks in Greek. My thought in this matter appeared to please both the President and the Foreign Minister, who thereupon began to talk with some animation. . . . (6)

Years later, an account, most probably provided by himself, reported that MacVeagh "followed the presentation of his credentials with a speech in classical Greek which few of his hearers understood, but all applauded." (7)

Returning from the Presidential Palace the new "Envoy Extraordinary and Minister Plenipotentiary of the United States to Greece" telegraphed his superiors: "I assumed charge today. MacVeagh." (8)

CHAPTER
II

Fall of a Republic:
1933-1935

As Minister MacVeagh soon had occasion to reflect, the country to which he had just been accredited represented a fascinating study in contrasts. Once the fountainhead of western civilization, it was now part of what King Nicholas of Montenegro called Europe's *petite monnaie*, the small pawns of power politics. Predominantly a nation of farmers, fishermen, and small shop-keepers, living in little communities scattered across a picturesque but hardly bountiful land, Greece's destiny remained controlled by persons and events in the capital. Athens itself, with its magnificent historical treasures and cosmopolitan society, its wide boulevards and handsome public buildings, was still a tiny oasis squeezed hard on all sides by refugee settlements, old villages, and farms. Even the sacred hills of the Acropolis and the Pnyx, symbols of ageless beauty and human achievement, rising so close to the spacious Constitution Square with its massive Parliament Building (the Old Palace), the famed Grande Bretagne Hotel, and the sidewalk cafes, were surrounded by squalor, offending odors, and filth. Years later, gentle hints to the authorities from the MacVeaghs, who loved to take long walks around these ancient sites, would be only moderately successful in having the paths and grounds of the Pnyx and Philopapou cleaned up. To the outsider, the very mood of the Greeks appeared to fluctuate between Olympian heights of national exuberance and deep gorges of doubt and despair. Yet beyond these dazzling contrasts, two principal movements were clearly evident: native industriousness, entrepreneurship, and economic reforms (however inconsistently pursued), were bringing about slow modernization and social progress, while politically, the cleavages of the "national schism" continued to keep the country in a state of almost perennial turmoil and uncertainty.

Following the turbulence of the Great War and the shattering of the expansionist dream of the "Megali Idea" (the idea of a Greater Greece), the nation appeared to have turned inward, anxious to forget its recent disastrous foreign adventures, and to concentrate instead on domestic economic priorities, overshadowed by the monumental task of caring for more than one million refugees from Asia Minor who had been abruptly added to the nation's population of six million. After 1928, when Eleftherios Venizelos, the country's greatest political figure in modern times, returned to power once again, and with the aid of large foreign loans, the government had undertaken extensive drainage projects which gradually expanded the rich agricultural lands of Macedonia where most of the refugees were being settled. Better strains of wheat were introduced, farming techniques were improved, and with the help of a newly created agricultural bank, large estates were expropriated and turned into thousands of small private plots. Although indebtedness to the state—and of the state to foreign creditors—had by now become a way of life, there was a substantial reduction in grain imports, and the farmer's lot improved, albeit slowly. New roads, often built partly for military purposes, and a small expansion of the railroad network, facilitated transportation and made overland travel less of an ordeal than it had always been. In their many travels by car criss-crossing the country, the MacVeaghs were pleasantly surprised to discover roads where none had existed, and paved surfaces where gravel and dust had engulfed them only a few years before. Similarly, Venizelos' educational reforms were spearheaded by an ambitious building program, which favored technical and agricultural schools and established the *demotiki* as the language of instruction at the primary and secondary levels. Education improved social mobility and enlarged the nation's skilled labor force. Although the Great Depression put a stop to most of these public works, and the frequent changes of ministers meant that programs were often abandoned as soon as they had been introduced, there was a general and unmistakable improvement of economic and social conditions across the country.

While naturally interested in all these social and economic advancements, some of which were being financed with American loans and carried out by American companies, it was to the country's political arena that MacVeagh soon turned his chief attention. His profound knowledge of the classical world impressed every Greek who came to know him and earned him an exalted place in Athenian society. His language skills, urbane manner, and excellent hospitality made him a valued member of the diplomatic community. His discreet ways and common sense endeared him to political leaders and foreign diplomats who confided in him and sought his advice. To the traditional admiration of Greeks for the United States and things American, his relationship with the Roosevelts added a new dimension, and turned him into a man of prestige and popularity in Athens and, before long, in some of the country's remotest corners. Within a short time he became a well-informed observer and perceptive commentator on Greece's internal and external politics.

Politically, the legacy of the Great War had been a veritable "national schism," precipitated by a mixture of conflicting foreign policy objectives, fundamental constitutional controversies, personality clashes, and sheer emotionalism. Its chief protagonists were two strong-willed men engaged in a power duel accentuated by different perceptions of the national interest: King Constantine I, hero of the Balkan wars and recent ascendant to the throne following the assassination of his father, George I, and Eleftherios Venizelos, the country's Prime Minister and its most powerful political personality.

An admirer of Germany's military might, Constantine had expected the Central Powers to prevail in a protracted war against England and France. Married to the sister of the German Emperor, he firmly believed that the family bond linking the two monarchies should also serve as the catalyst for cordial relations between Berlin and Athens. Nevertheless, he was realistic enough to acknowledge that with England and France dominating the Mediterranean, Greece could not possibly enter the war on Germany's side. Genuine neutrality thus appeared to him to be the only prudent course. In his staunch opposition to Venizelos' schemes, the monarch was also motivated by his resentment of his Prime Minister's stranglehold over the nation's political life and a reluctance to see the Cretan's prestige rise to new heights.

For his part, Venizelos saw the commitment of Greece to the Allies' cause as the golden opportunity for the fulfillment of his personal—as well as the nation's—greatest dream, and the logical extension of the gains made in the Balkan wars: the re-birth of a "Great Greece" astride the Aegean Sea, through the acquisition of territories of the Ottoman Empire which were closely associated with the nation's distant and more glorious past. In addition, he believed that geographic and to a lesser extent commercial realities allowed Greece little choice but to align itself with Europe's great naval powers. In sum, in his own mind Venizelos identified his personal vision with the nation's lasting interests, and impatiently sought to place Greece actively on the side of the Entente Powers.

In March 1915, Venizelos' offer to have Greek troops participate in the Dardanelles campaign was not accepted by the Allies and was repudiated by Constantine, forcing the Prime Minister to resign. However, the elections which followed several months later (June 1915) returned Venizelos to office with an even stronger majority than before, and he immediately resumed his efforts toward bringing Greece into the war. Moreover, he believed that his triumph at the polls represented a solid public endorsement of his foreign policy and a mandate which the king could no longer oppose. In September, having concluded an alliance with the Central Powers, Bulgaria prepared to enter the fighting and Serbia renewed earlier appeals to Greece for assistance. Venizelos now invited the Entente Powers to send troops to Salonica to attempt what the Dardanelles campaign had failed to accomplish: to open a decisive breach through the enemy lines. But Constantine refused to accept this new development, and continued to insist on a policy of neutrality. Venizelos had little choice but to resign once again.

This time, however, the relationship between the two men had suffered irreparable damage. When the king called for new elections (held in December 1915), Venizelos condemned this second dissolution of the parliament in one year and over the same issue as authoritarian action contrary not simply to the popular will but to the constitution. He further ordered his Liberal Party to boycott the elections. As a result, about sixty-five percent of the electorate abstained, the king's supporters formed their own government, and Greece remained neutral a while longer. More importantly, a constitutional controversy involving the monarch's prerogatives had been unleashed, and its reverberations were destined to continue for decades to come. By rejecting his Prime Minister's popular mandate, Constantine appeared to act not as the nation's impartial arbiter, but as the head of the anti-Venizelist camp that, at least for the moment, was a distinct minority. This split left Greece defenseless in the face of the impending direct and highhanded foreign intervention.

In the early summer of 1916, Constantine's government brought upon itself the wrath of the Entente Powers, first by refusing to allow Serbian forces to cross from the island of Corfu to Salonica, and then by peacefully surrendering to the Germans and Bulgarians the most important fortification in Greek Macedonia: Fort Roupel. Hostile to Constantine on general grounds, and concerned about their troops already stationed in Salonica, the British and French governments imposed humiliating conditions upon the Greek king, forcing him to dismiss his cabinet, call for new elections, demobilize his army, and purge key officers of the police. When in September the city of Kavalla was seized by German and Bulgarian forces and its imprisoned Greek garrison was sent to Germany, Venizelos resorted to revolutionary action. On October 9, he landed in Salonica, announced the formation of a "Provisional Government," and declared war on the Central Powers. After blockading the rest of Greece, landing troops at Piraeus, and precipitating a bloody incident, the Allies finally forced Constantine to abdicate in June 1917, leaving on the throne his second son, Alexander. Although Constantine was to return three years later, following the sudden death of Alexander, the victorious Allies had written him off and would not deal with him.

Ironically, his political enemy fared no better. Despite his impressive performance at the Paris Peace Conference and the Allies' initial backing of his expansionist policy, Venizelos was resoundingly defeated in the November 1920 elections, which the death of Alexander had turned into a contest between himself and King Constantine. Venizelos' opponents had been able to capitalize on the people's strong resentment of Anglo-French intervention, their pro-royalist sympathies, as well as on the growing disillusionment with Venizelos' ambitious and costly foreign policy, which threatened to keep the nation at war for years to come. Embittered and in fear of assassination, Venizelos sought refuge abroad. This abrupt change of political fortunes served to widen the nation's division, and incidentally sealed the fate of the Greek expeditionary force in Asia Minor, which Constantine had inherited, and Britain first supported but then gradually abandoned. Defeat at the hands of Kemal's (later known as Ataturk) growing Turkish forces came in the summer and fall of 1922, followed by a humiliating retreat to the coast and the massacre of countless Greek communities, including that of the prosperous city of Smyrna.

In search of scapegoats, a group of disgruntled army officers under Colonels Nikolaos Plastiras and Stylianos Gonatas demanded the King's abdication and the institution of a formal inquiry into the national disaster of Asia Minor. Once again Constantine took the bitter road to exile, having abdicated in favor of his eldest son, George. Six of the King's principal advisers, including Prime Minister Dimitrios Gounaris and Commander-in-Chief George Hadjianestis, were hastily court-martialled and shot on November 28, 1922. Britain's ambassador had tried in vain to pressure the government into calling off the executions. Years later, MacVeagh would find himself in a similarly agonizing situation. A political feud, aggravated by military defeat, had now been turned into a true vendetta.

Not surprisingly, the executions of prominent leaders, whose guilt had been more symbolic than factual, settled nothing. On the contrary, the resulting paroxysm of political passions, encouraged by the activities of obstreperous anti-monarchical elements in the armed forces, organized into the "Republican Officers League," compelled King George II to follow his father into exile. In an attempt to settle the constitutional issue once and for all, enemies of the monarchy proclaimed Greece a republic in March-April 1924, and Prime Minister Alexander Papanastasiou, one of the most active promoters of the change, thus acquired the dubious appellation of "Father of the Republic." And so it was that some nine years later, Minister MacVeagh presented his credentials not to a reigning monarch, but to President Alexander Zaimis, a colorless and vacillating man of advanced age, whose principal political virtue was the fact that he was very probably the only political figure in Athens who was acceptable to all the warring factions for the nation's highest office.

From the outset, the republic had been in serious trouble, buffeted by the same rivalries which had persuaded King George to leave. With the political world unable to find a viable compromise on constitutional issues, domestic and foreign affairs, and personal feuds, the military continued to dominate the political field, thus increasing the level of instability, intrigue and violence in the country. Officers came to identify their personal futures with the fortunes of the Venizelists or the anti-Venizelists, the republicans or the monarchists, the Liberals or the Populists. Cliques grew into conspiracies, which invariably led to thoughts of military coups. As Venizelos' star continued to decline and his self-serving tactics intensified, his Liberal Party began to gravitate around such lesser luminaries among his followers as Themistoclis Sofoulis, Andreas Michalacopoulos, George Kafandaris, and Alexander Papanastasiou. The anti-Venizelist forces centered around Panayiotis Tsaldaris' Populists, and the much smaller but vociferous "Free Opinion" Party, led by John Metaxas. Governments rose and fell in rapid order, interspersed with military coups of varying orientations and having various degrees of success. Thus in June 1925, General Theodore Pangalos seized power, and the following April had himself elected President of the Republic. Imbued with an authoritarian and puritanical zeal, he proceeded, for instance, to regulate the length of women's skirts by having them measured and appropriately altered in periodic spot-checks in the streets of Athens, and to combat corruption in government service by publicly hanging several junior officers. His fiscal policies were no more enlightened, and his relations with neighboring states were truly disastrous. To the great relief of the public, he was overthrown by General George Kondylis, who in a remarkable display of originality and wisdom restored a semblance of parliamentary rule through the elections of November 1926. Shortly thereafter, Venizelos returned to power once more, and despite the drastic decline of his popularity and the growing fragmentation of his following, he succeeded in introducing the significant social and economic reforms already mentioned above. Nevertheless, the unmistakable signs of general improvement could not hide the continuing "national schism": Venizelos now symbolized the preservation of the Republic, while increasingly the more implacable among his many enemies rallied to the cause of the monarchy's restoration.

As the American Government was going through the formalities of obtaining MacVeagh's confirmation, political turmoil in Athens continued to intensify. The elections of September 25, 1932, had been held amid strong indications that the Republican Officers League would resort to force to prevent the formation of a Populist government. However, ballot returns revealed that neither the Populists nor Venizelos' Liberals had enough strength to form their own government, and that leftist groups together with the Agrarians had scored something of a victory by receiving a total of eleven percent of the vote. With characteristic astuteness, Venizelos stepped aside, allowing Tsaldaris to form a government which consisted of some Populists, several dissident republicans (including Kondylis), and John Metaxas. Such a motley array of opportunists was not destined to survive long. Indeed, the moment Tsaldaris had made a feeble attempt to bring Populist loyalists into key military and civil service positions, his cabinet fell apart. New elections were announced for March 5, with Venizelos' Liberals now confident of a landslide victory. Yet the nation had no enthusiasm for either of the major parties, and viewed all political leaders, including Venizelos, with growing suspicion. As a result, the combined Populist, anti-Venizelist and monarchist forces, while far from effectively united, received a substantial parliamentary majority.

There is some reason to believe that Venizelos himself was prepared to accept this popular verdict, at least for the moment. However, his political ally, General Plastiras, was not, nor did Venizelos, to whom Plastiras revealed his intentions, make any real effort to restrain him. With the help of other republican officers stationed in and around Athens, on the day after the elections, Plastiras seized the Ministry of War and proclaimed the establishment of a dictatorship for the purpose of defending the republic against its enemies. But the latest coup was a fiasco. Other senior republican officers, led by Generals Alexander Othonaios and Theodore Manettas, refused to endorse Plastiras, and allowed his rather pitiful forces to be crushed. Soon order had been established by Othonaios himself, and Tsaldaris was thus able to form a new Populist government. Some of its more respected and apolitical members, including Foreign Minister Dimitrios Maximos and the Minister of National Economy, George Pezmazoglou, were soon to establish cordial relations with the new American Minister.

Prime Minister Tsaldaris had wisely favored a general amnesty for those implicated in the March 6 coup. However, in a matter of days it became clear that he had no control over the more vindictive among his lieutenants, who were determined to even the score with Plastiras, and to humiliate Venizelos by publicly condemning him as the instigator of the coup. When a warrant was issued for his arrest, Plastiras went into hiding and eventually fled abroad. Protected by parliamentary immunity, Venizelos chose to defend his innocence in a dramatic speech before parliament, destined to be the last of his brilliant and stormy career. On May 15, as tension in the capital had become almost unbearable, Metaxas opened the debate with a devastating attack upon the leader of the Liberals, and Venizelos then rose to deliver his eloquent defense before a packed and highly emotional audience. Some of the deputies, fearing for the worst, had come with revolvers bulging under their jackets. When Venizelos made a favorable reference to Plastiras' past services to the nation, chaos erupted among the deputies and in the galleries. The meeting had to be adjourned and Venizelos refused to attend further sessions, charging that his freedom of speech could not be guaranteed. Months later, with both Plastiras and Venizelos safely abroad, an amnesty decree was finally approved for the civilian conspirators. The long delayed trial of the military officers involved in the events of March 6 never took place, as it was overtaken by the upheaval accompanying the March 1, 1935 revolution, in which the same senior officers were also implicated. At that time, and despite the desperate efforts of MacVeagh and of his British and French colleagues, three of these officers were to face the firing squad.

The disruption of debate in parliament was only a harbinger of worse things yet to come. On the night of June 6, 1933, the car in which Venizelos and his wife were returning to Athens from the neighboring suburb of Kifissia was machine-gunned by a pursuing vehicle and fired upon from a number of strategic points along its route. Miraculously, Venizelos was not hurt, while his wife sustained relatively minor injuries. One of his bodyguards riding in an escort vehicle was killed and a second seriously wounded. This gangster-like battle along several miles of Kifissia Boulevard, ending in the heart of Athens, brought an already deeply divided public to the brink of civil war. While the efforts of the authorities investigating the crime were anything but vigorous, thus enraging the Venizelist faction even more, it soon became common knowledge that high officials, including the head of the Athens police, were involved in the attempted assassination. A brigand suspected in connection with the assassination plot was eventually arrested by Venizelos' private guards, and turned over to the authorities with appropriate fanfare. Charges and counter-charges and terrible threats from all sides reached an unprecedented level of paroxysm. Venizelos soon left for a much-needed rest in southern France, having given instructions to his most trusted aides to prepare for another coup. In the midst of such dangerous intrigue and explosive political passion, MacVeagh arrived in the Greek capital and assumed his duties.

❖

In his initial report to the President, MacVeagh dealt not with Greek politics but with much more mundane matters. In the first "Dear Franklin" letter from abroad, he sought to persuade the President that the effects of the Depression had rendered the salaries of the Legation's Foreign Service personnel woefully inadequate. Recent cuts in salaries and allowances, the depreciation of the dollar, and the ever-rising cost of living had reduced their purchasing power by more than forty percent of pre-Depression levels. "I have found here a fine crowd," he wrote on November 21, 1933, "particularly happy from the point of view of character, efficient and enthusiastic—a crowd that is giving fine service to our country. But one thing bothers me greatly,—the struggle they are having to get along under present conditions." Aware that in addressing the President directly on administrative affairs he was taking an unorthodox step which might not be welcomed in Washington, he made it clear that he was also reporting the matter of salaries to the Department of State and concluded: "Of course, I know how enormously busy you are but I also have the feeling—correct me if I am wrong—that you trust me to observe conditions for you here personally as well as for the Government, and to report them to you from time to time, especially when they are serious." The President's response ignored the matter of salaries. Roosevelt thanked MacVeagh for "the fine work you are doing," adding: "I rather envy you being in Athens and I wish I could run over to visit you." However, he was preoccupied with other matters: "I wish you would drop me a line to give me your own opinion as to the present and future ability of the Greek government to pay us a little more on the debt. . . ." (1)

MacVeagh's first serious encounter with the Greek Government had to do with the celebrated case of a fellow-American, Samuel Insull, Sr. The Chicago-based utilities tycoon, who had once been chairman of sixty-five corporations and director of eighty-five, had seen his empire of holding companies collapse like a pyramid of cards in the wake of the stock market crash, which had ruined thousands of small investors, and severely shaken public confidence in big business. The specter of wide-spread illegal, or at least questionable, finance practices had prompted Roosevelt to promise that his administration would deal harshly with unscrupulous financiers like Insull. In 1932, Insull had fled to Europe, and by October of that year he had made his way to Athens, armed with substantial sums of money and with the knowledge that Greece had no operative extradition treaty with the United States. However, in a matter of weeks Washington had obtained the ratification of such a treaty, and Insull's extradition was immediately requested so that he might stand trial in Illinois for embezzlement and larceny. At first Insull argued that the new treaty could not be made to apply to him retroactively, but the Greek authorities rejected the claim and ordered his arrest. In judicial hearings tainted with partisan pressures and intra-cabinet rivalry, the appropriate Greek court proceeded to investigate the charges against Insull for the purpose of deciding whether he was to be extradited. After endless deliberations and delays, the court ruled twice that the American Government had failed to prove that Insull had in fact violated federal embezzlement and bankruptcy laws. Clearly annoyed by this development, the Department of State charged that the Greek court had gone far beyond its proper function in the matter by attempting to actually try the case, rather than confining itself to the question of extraditable offenses. Accordingly, the Greek Government was duly notified that the extradition treaty would be terminated.

Appearing to have found safe refuge, Insull, now joined by his wife, gave every indication of planning to settle in Greece, and began promoting incredibly ambitious and vague schemes for the electrification of his adopted country. According to a study highly flattering to Insull, the dethroned king of America's public utilities dazzled his eager business associates in the Greek capital with talk of ventures which "might launch Greece on an industrialization program that would restore it to its ancient grandeur." Insull is said to have concluded an "unwritten understanding" with General Kondylis, and was to have become "a Greek citizen and minister of electric power," had Kondylis not "lost the election to power by 700 votes. . . ." (2)

Despite the efforts of the American Legation's lawyers and the services of a special prosecutor dispatched to Athens by the Department of Justice, the extradition case was lost. It therefore became MacVeagh's delicate task to persuade the Greeks to expel Insull, so that the arm of American law might reach him elsewhere. Gently pulling strings behind the Greek political scene, he missed no opportunity to argue that, despite the court's ruling, permitting Insull to stay in Greece would jeopardize important long-range interests, for which America's good will was essential. In particular, he privately sought to persuade Foreign Minister Maximos that under existing Greek law, a foreigner who was the cause of serious embarrassment to the country could be declared an undesirable alien and expelled. Subsequently, Insull's friends and apologists were to claim that, in putting pressure on Greece to deport Insull, Washington had resorted to a form of diplomatic blackmail, threatening to prohibit the export of remittances by Greek-Americans to relatives back home, thus depriving that small country of much-needed income. (3)

Having permitted the matter to become a political issue, and after repeated and conflicting medical opinions concerning Insull's ability to travel, the Greek Government finally ordered him to leave the country by March 15, 1934. At the same time, the American Minister was formally informed by Foreign Minister Maximos that responsibility for Insull's "possible death or suicide under these conditions" would fall on Mac-Veagh. (4) When the small Greek vessel he chartered (which had slipped out of Piraeus secretly, was ordered back, and then permitted to leave again) finally put into Constantinople for supplies, Insull was arrested by the Turkish authorities, and promptly turned over to American officials who escorted him home. He was eventually tried three times on charges of fraud, breaking federal bankruptcy laws, and embezzlement, and was acquitted each time.

20 · CHAPTER II

But if the court case against Insull was overturned, giving rise to speculation that the entire affair had been politically motivated, the charge that extralegal pressure had been used to get him out of Greece is not supported by the record. In a "Personal and Confidential" letter to the President,[1] dated May 9, 1934, MacVeagh proclaimed that he was "indeed glad to get rid of Insull," and provided the following conclusion to Insull's saga in Greece:

M. Maximos worked with a will, and with great astuteness, to put Insull out of Greece against the determined opposition of several members of the Cabinet, and the spineless indecision of a temporizing Premier. His method was simple, but of necessity slow. He would force the Premier to agree that Insull be expelled, and then announce the fact to me and to the press before the Opposition got in its counter offensive and switched the Premier round. Thus he repeatedly put the Government on record as determined to expel the fugitive, and all that the friends of Insull could do was to secure repeated delays. Finally the State Department, which had all this time wisely kept its hands off, insisting that any decision in the matter must be taken by the Greeks themselves, asked to know when Greece intended to put into effect the assurances so many times given the American Minister, and that did the trick. Insull saw the writing on the wall, and fled.

If our Department of State had not taken the attitude it did, and anything but unofficial pressure had been exerted, the touchy Greek character would certainly have prevented our ever getting Insull out. We never bullied or threatened, and so far as "commercial reprisals" were concerned, we increased the Greek liquor quota at this time five hundred percent! I myself was particularly careful never to appear to push or demand. I indeed supplied much material to the political opposition wherewith to interpellate the Government, but arranged matters so that my part was not known. Similarly in communicating with the Government, it was all unofficial "in the interests of Greece which I had so much at heart." Thus I can report to you truly that in the entire course of this long-drawn out and delicate affair, there arose not the slightest unpleasantness in official relations to hamper the usefulness of this Legation in aiding and protecting American interests. In fact, I feel that we are now better friends than ever. . . .

[1] Roosevelt's letters to MacVeagh reveal no interest in the Insull case. When MacVeagh sent him the text of the Greek court decisions the President simply replied that the matter belonged "under the title '*curiosa*.'" Roosevelt letter to MacVeagh, January 16, 1934, PPF, File 1192. And on April 19, 1934 he wrote to MacVeagh: "You must be glad to be rid of that old man of the sea, Mr. Insull. . . ." Roosevelt letter to MacVeagh, April 19, 1934, PPF, File 1192.

MacVeagh concluded:

I pinch myself sometimes to make sure I am not dreaming, and I shudder when I think what might have happened had the man been even halfway human and given a modicum of the money he spent on his campfollowers to the needy and the sick. The Greeks love a benefactor, and Insull missed the best trick of all by not becoming one. As it was, he got a lot of sympathy. (5)

Ever since it had gained its independence from the Ottoman Empire, the Greek state had been forced to rely for its existence upon loans from abroad. Meager land resources and low productivity, a perennially unfavorable balance of trade, costly wars, and the recent social reforms and resettlement of refugees from Asia Minor had kept the national debt growing. The Depression had aggravated the situation enormously by sharply reducing the national income. By 1929, the public debt had reached $100 per capita, which was more than the average per capita income of Greeks. Ten years later, that debt had become $630 million, with almost ten percent of the national income having to go toward its payment. In 1932, Greece had defaulted on the interest payments on certain portions of its foreign debt, in a manner which appeared to discriminate against the United States. In the ensuing diplomatic exchanges, the Greek Government attempted to link its failure to service its debt to the suspension of war reparations, of which Greece had been a recipient. The Department of State vigorously rejected such an explanation, and directed MacVeagh in Athens to press the Greek Government to honor its obligations. (6) Roosevelt's letter of January 16, 1934, mentioned above, seeking MacVeagh's advice on the question of Greece's ability to resume full payments, had been part of the same effort.

In his long reply to Roosevelt, dated February 12, 1934, MacVeagh showed that he understood the intricacies of the vexing problem and could see both sides of the case. He argued that the question of Greece's ability to pay more on her foreign debt had to be viewed not merely from an economic but from a political standpoint as well. He offered considerable evidence suggesting that business conditions in Greece had been improving steadily in the last several years, despite the drachma's devaluation to forty-three percent of its 1931 gold parity, and even though "current revenues of the central government absorb nearly a quarter of the national income without providing for more than a fraction of the service of the public debt, and can hardly be increased." Therefore, "from a purely economic standpoint there appears to be no reason why Greece should not make substantially larger debt payments to the United States Government during 1934 than in the preceding two years." However, this was only part of the picture: "the political factors are less encouraging":

Since the first Greek loan was floated abroad 101 years ago, this country has periodically increased its foreign indebtedness. Maturing obligations were normally met by additional borrowing, and there was apparently little thought that Greece should ever attempt an actual reduction of its foreign debt. The habit of a century is difficult to break. Greece was for generations a pawn of the Great Powers, and it is not surprising that a general feeling still exists in this country that the world owes Greece a living. When new foreign loans were not available, as at present, Greece played poor and complained of the enormity of its debt burden, as though the latter had never been assumed voluntarily. Whatever the purely economic aspects, the fact remains that any Greek Government which attempted too sudden a reversal of these established policies would scarcely remain long in power.

Reminding the President that Greece "has been for years the largest market in American agricultural and manufactured products in the Balkans and the Near East," he pointed out that American economic interests in that country were substantial, far exceeding the value of the Greek debt to the United States. "Summing up," he concluded, "in answer to your question I would say that Greece has the financial and economic ability to pay us more than she is doing right now, and would probably be able to increase the payments in the future as her condition improves, but that it is highly unlikely that any Greek Government would dare in the face of Greece's other engagements and the temper of her people, which is that of Europe at large, to make any serious attempt to live up to this particular obligation." MacVeagh recommended, therefore, a "fixed settlement in guaranteed cash payments to a greatly reduced total, perhaps based on the true value of the debt today, plus trade advantages which a popular government could accord in return for the maintenance of its credit without flying in the face of the general European prejudice against 'Uncle Shylock'." (7)

Several weeks later, inspired by Roosevelt's unfolding economic measures of the "New Deal," MacVeagh wrote again, offering Greece's "planned economy" as a model from which other countries, perhaps including the United States, might benefit:

Personal   Athens, March 2, 1934

Dear Franklin:

It occurs to me that the following may interest you in connection with your vast program of reconstruction in the United States.

Greece is a small country. Economic experiments here have not the importance of those at home, but just because the country is so small the time-element does not figure so largely and results can be tabulated with comparative promptness. From the American point of view, therefore, the experience of Greece which I am about to discuss may appear as a kind of laboratory experiment, but one which has some bearings upon our larger problems.

We have had in Greece for the past year an example of a country operating almost completely under the principles of a planned economy. The plans and their coordination are of course simpler than with us, but the principle remains the same. Economic and financial enterprise has been subjected to governmental regulation to a degree which has been described by the Bank of Athens as "detrimental to the principle of the freedom of commerce." Yet, on the whole, increased prosperity and national satisfaction have been the result.

By governmental action resulting in the establishment of confidence, the flight of capital from the country has in great part been arrested, and with certain vital exceptions, the importation of foreign articles has been subjected to a vigorous control under a quota system. Clearing agreements, obviating the use of currency in foreign commercial transactions, have been concluded with nearly all the countries regularly and largely trading with Greece. In addition, the great impulsion to domestic manufacture resulting from restrictions on imports has been controlled by a law which prohibits the introduction into the country of machines and industrial tools except under special permission from the Ministry of National Economy. Exports, as well as imports, are now carefully supervised and the production of wheat, which has never been sufficient for the needs of the nation, has been fostered even to the point of a guarantee by the government to purchase any and all stocks remaining on the cultivators' hands. The payment of commercial debts to foreigners, both in foreign exchange and in drachmas, has been drastically regulated, and the sums paid on the foreign governmental debts skillfully reduced to a minimum consonant with the preservation of a national credit-standing at least as high as that of most European States. Altogether, the government has worked swiftly and tirelessly in a coordinated effort to strengthen the economic life within the country; to guide, as well as foster, home manufactures; to diminish as far as safety allows the outflow of exchange; and to bring price levels to a parity with those of the world at large. This last aim should, if realized, eventually make possible the full resumption of payments on the foreign and internal debt, with the consequent renewal of the normal flow of capital.

What has been the result of such interference by the State with the course of free, individualistic competition? The gold reserves of the Bank of Greece have increased to a remarkable degree. Foreign commercial debts have been in large part liquidated. Maritime tonnage laid up has decreased by more than 50%. Average quotations on stocks and bonds have risen considerably and price levels on domestic products have been maintained as against falling prices on imported articles. In addition, owing only partly to meteorological conditions, the wheat crop has taken a great step forward and promises this year to maintain its progress.

The operation of a planned economy such as Greece has never known has thus, beyond any question of doubt, proved itself a material success in one short year. But what of its political and social effects? Greece is in many ways a more individualistic country than the United States. Every man here sincerely thinks himself at least as good as his neighbor. Politics veer and change with the wind. But all signs point to the present policy of national economy being more truly national than any policy in Greek statecraft that I have heard of. No party is shooting at it. Its benefits are too obvious even for the marksmen of the café-table. Looked at from a social angle, therefore, it may be regarded as a national unifier, and for the political party which put it into effect a tremendous advantage.

Leaving aside possible dangers from other aspects of the situation here, which have largely to do with Greece's political history and are emotionally involved, I believe that the more recent experience of Greece demonstrates pretty clearly the efficacy of a planned economy in difficult times, and its acceptability to people of democratic tendencies. In spite of the fact that our problems are vaster, this may seem to you, as it does to me, good news.

Sincerely yours,
Lincoln MacVeagh (8)

Whatever the merits of Greece's "planned economy"[2] as a model for reconstruction, its side effects were clearly detrimental to American trade, because the Athens government would permit imports only if payment could be made by the export of Greek products. This barter policy, coupled with a strict import license system, amounted to a virtual embargo

---

[2] Apparently unimpressed, Roosevelt had responded that he was "delighted to know that Greece seems to be getting on so well through what might be called a planned economy." Roosevelt letter to MacVeagh, April 19, 1934, PPF, File 1192.

on American goods,[3] and MacVeagh missed no opportunity to voice his complaint to Greek officialdom. "Would it not be wise," he wrote Foreign Minister Maximos on May 21, 1934, "to encourage imports from America rather than discourage them, as Greece is doing under the barter system? I need not stress the advantages in our depreciated currency, but I can truthfully say that if Greece would only take a helpful attitude toward our trade with her, there is practically no limit to the expansion of her possible trade with us, for the United States is the largest potential market for Greek products in the world." (9) But although promises to review the matter were dutifully made, no change in the situation appeared to be forthcoming, as the Greeks remained preoccupied with their own economic and financial problems. MacVeagh reminded his superiors (on June 26) that the 1924 *modus vivendi*, under which Greece had pledged most-favored-nation treatment to American products, had been signed by men who were now out of power, adding: "It is a Greek tendency to forget what is inconvenient, and this tendency is only strengthened when what is inconvenient is the work of political opponents. . . ." He thought that a tougher stand was called for:

Finally, it is not to be imagined that the Greek Government is unaware of the tariff powers recently vested in the American Executive, and the present moment would therefore seem a favorable one to elicit a statement from Greece as to her considered attitude toward American trade. To bring her to a fully conscious and perhaps anxious realization of what she may be risking by her present policy, or lack of it, toward our imports, would seem likely to do more to correct the evils from which we suffer than any amount of protests against particular instances of discrimination. (10)

And to Roosevelt, on August 6, 1934:

I have . . . been working my hardest, both with the Department and the Greek Government, to get our position rectified. To the Greek Government, aside from the individual cases in which I have been called upon to protest, I have pointed out that our balance of trade is now so favorable to Greece that restrictions on our imports cannot economically be justified. I have won here a partial victory, in so far as bids for Government contracts will now be accepted from American firms without the restrictions hitherto enforced. The British, whose trade balance is not so clearly

[3] American products most affected by Greek import practices included machinery of all kinds, iron, steel, oil, and automobiles.

favorable, have not yet won such a concession. But in private business there is still the need of constant official protest against discrimination, and our trade is being discouraged and our customers disheartened by all sorts of regulations which countries having recent trade agreements with Greece do not have to contend with. . . . My despatches on this subject to the Department of State therefore always end on the same note, like the speeches of Cato. The Greeks, into whose country we now pour some $25,000,000 more per annum than we get out of it, should, I believe, be made to face the loss of some of this or play the game. A commercial treaty with them was in the cards some time ago but was dropped. I believe the idea should be revived, and that the men who are now handling Greek affairs should no longer be merely called to book from time to time on the basis of letters exchanged in 1924, but should be made to undertake and carry out such explicit arrangements in regard to our trade as we feel to be consonant with the fact that America does more than any other nation today to keep the Greek people alive. I do not mean to imply that there is anything anti-American in the Greek attitude. On the contrary, I think we are rather specially liked, if not by all the ruling or upper class at least by the nation at large, and we get along famously, all things considered. But so long as other nations actively foster their trade while we only protect ours, they can be expected to get the lion's share. I am therefore hoping to see us snap into the game more vigorously. (11)

Responding to this prodding, Washington authorized its Legation in Athens to begin preliminary talks for the negotiation of a new reciprocal trade agreement. It was to prove a most frustrating experience. Burdened with a weak economy, and absorbed in Europe's power alignments, Greece was less than anxious to accommodate American commercial interests.

Throughout the 1930s, American concerns in Greece were mainly commercial and financial, and this is reflected in the work of the Legation in Athens. Yet MacVeagh's natural interest in political affairs is clearly evident in his own reporting. Within weeks of his arrival in the Greek capital, he was at work on what was to become a steady stream of despatches, usually entitled "The Political Situation in Greece," interspersed with personal letters to the President. His observations suggest an impressive grasp of his subject, good contacts in and out of government, and a mild dislike for the aging Venizelos. Thus, reviewing developments since the attempt on Venizelos' life, he observed on December 14, 1933, that the government of Prime Minister Tsaldaris had been successful in consolidating its position, and that Venizelos had "over-reached badly" when he attacked the government as a "band of brigands who should be exterminated ... Messrs. Tsaldaris, Maximos, Loverdos[4] and the other prominent members of the Government," MacVeagh concluded, "are anything but rapacious cut-throats, and they are not even cut-purses. All the world in Greece knows it." (12)

In the field of foreign policy, the dominant issue was the recently concluded Balkan Pact and its possible consequences for Greece's international position. In September 1933, following a diplomatic feeler from Ankara, Greece and Turkey had signed a treaty mutually guaranteeing their common frontier in Thrace, and promising continuous consultation on all matters of mutual interest. Significantly, sea boundaries were excluded from the treaty's provisions at the request of the government in Athens, which feared that Mussolini would regard any such cooperation in naval matters as a threat to the Dodecanese and to Italian influence in the Eastern Mediterranean generally. However, the pact appeared to cover the possibility of an attack upon the guaranteed frontier by a Balkan neighbor assisted by a Great Power. Invitations were extended to other Balkan states to adhere to the agreement, and to turn it into a regional pact of sanctified frontiers, cooperation, and mutual defense. On February 9, 1934, the original signatories were joined by Rumania and Yugoslavia (already members of the "Little Entente") in formally creating the Balkan Pact. A "secret protocol," which became common knowledge in a matter of days, guaranteed existing boundaries and attempted to define the circumstances under which the military aspects of the Pact would be activated. In rather vague terms, the protocol stipulated that in the event of aggression by a non-Balkan Power, in which a Balkan state also took part, the Pact would apply only against the Balkan aggressor. Although Bulgaria was repeatedly invited to join, there was no surprise when the government of King Boris refused: with important grievances and territorial claims in Macedonia and elsewhere, Bulgaria was in no mood to recognize the region's *status quo*. Thus, whether this effect was intended or not, the Pact appeared to encircle Bulgaria, which naturally looked for allies among Europe's revisionist Powers.

This diplomatic activity created great excitement in Athens. While there could be no objection to the improvement of relations implicit in the Pact, there were loud expressions of fear that Greece might become embroiled in foreign quarrels (particularly between Italy and Yugoslavia over Albania), and that the new accord would incur Mussolini's wrath. Venizelos, whose prestige in foreign affairs remained a formidable factor at home and abroad, led the Opposition in attacking the Pact as disastrous for Greece. In and out of parliament he argued forcefully against

---

[4] Spyros Loverdos, prominent banker, and Minister of the Economy.

ratification, unless the arrangement had received the blessings of Britain, France, Italy, and the Soviet Union, and only if Bulgaria also joined. The strategic aspects of the debate were accentuated by Metaxas, who resigned from the government, and warned of dire consequences in the event that Greece were called upon to honor her new military commitments. Faced with almost solid opposition, the government finally gave in. To the ratification instrument a formal "reservation" was attached by Maximos (the text was actually drafted by Venizelos), declaring that under no circumstances would Greece be drawn into war against a European Power. At the same time Maximos attempted to reassure the other three signatories that his government was in fact accepting both the treaty and the protocol. The resulting confusion was to poison the atmosphere in the Balkans throughout the 1930s, as each interested party gave its own interpretation of the pact. Moreover, the old Cretan was all too anxious to exploit the government's embarrassment to further his own narrow political interests. Thus, "while the Pact continues to be the major issue in the local as well as in the foreign field of Greek politics," MacVeagh commented for the Department on April 11, 1934, "Venizelos appears to have the benefit of a clear-cut issue while the Government, on account of the dilemma created by its exterior commitments and the Opposition's moves, flounders in contradictions. It still seems possible that Bulgaria may join the concert of Balkan nations, perhaps by the back door, but Greek opinion apparently is satisfied that peace in this region is now sufficiently secured, excluding the possibility of an upset caused from without, and the eyes of the country are once more focused on the internal situation. Venizelism is thus itself again, and little is now heard of the 'attempt' and the personal rancors which, masquerading so long as political issues, made Venizelos seem *passé*." (13)

In a personal letter to the President, dated May 9, 1934, MacVeagh concentrated on the broader features of the Balkan Pact:

Briefly, it represents a consecration in this part of the world of France's policy of non-revisionism, and a virtual extension and reinforcement of the Little Entente. It draws an iron ring around Germany's old ally, Bulgaria. It ties Greece and Turkey into the Central and Western European tangle, and, as Venizelos has not failed to note, removes Greece from her natural Mediterranean grouping with Italy, if indeed it does not actually commit Greece to fight Italy should the latter move against Yugoslavia through Albania. The immediate reasons which led Greece into the Pact have largely to do with her fears of the Slavic peoples on her Northern frontier, and that she is determined to put teeth into it is evidenced by the mission she has just sent to Ankara, consisting of the Minister of War, the Chief of Staff, and a high official of the Foreign Office. The four

Powers signatory to the Pact are now reported as planning to adopt a common standard of military equipment including guns and ammunition, so as to simplify supply problems in case of war. The Pact has indeed the support of the strong local Balkans-for-the-Balkans sentiment, but it is essentially an extension of the great French armed camp in Eastern Europe down into the Aegean and across the Dardanelles, for whatever this may mean in the ultimate lineup of European forces. Thus, while it would certainly be a guarantee of peace in the Balkans if the Balkans only were involved, its implications outside the Balkans make the Pact really another step in the progressive enlargement of the theatre of possible war. (14)

Several months later, again writing to Roosevelt (August 6, 1934), he was pointing to gathering clouds:

Europe seems more and more clearly to be divided into two armed or arming camps—the French and the German—and this fact is perhaps nowhere more apparent than in this Balkan region where international intrigue habitually blooms in all its luxuriance. During the winter and spring, most of the Balkan nations joined the French groupment, causing considerable excitement here and much speculation. In Greece, the Balkan Pact was severely criticized by the local Opposition. The attitude of both England and Italy towards Near Eastern problems was then uncertain. But the events of the summer brought about a decided change. The French entente with Russia greatly strengthened those who saw security in the French camp, and the skillful maneuverings of M. Barthou[5] in relation to his proposed "Eastern Locarno" did perhaps as much, in its way, to the same effect. Then the murder of Dollfuss[6] and the bringing of England and Italy, particularly Italy, into sharp conflict with Nazi ambitions, has put what seems like the quietus on the critics of the policy of the Greek Government in throwing in its lot with the French. It has shown how definitely the other great European powers are opposed to Germany's first serious attempt to upset the *status quo*. Revisionist Italy has had troops concentrated on the border, ready to move to the defense of Austrian independence, and the British Minister here told me, only the other day, that after the murder of Dollfuss he expected nothing less than the concentration of the English Mediterranean fleet, part of which now lies in the harbor of Athens. There is now undoubtedly a general feeling here that Greece has taken her proper place in the balance of

---

[5] Louis Barthou, French Minister for Foreign Affairs.
[6] Dr. Engelbert Dollfuss, Austrian Chancellor, was murdered on July 25, 1934, by a band of Nazis in Vienna.

power which everyone believes is the only guarantee of peace. There are no pacifists in the Balkans.

While the international ferment is now less active than hitherto in this region, there is some uneasiness felt over Germany's political course of action now that Hindenburg's[7] steadying hand is removed. Herr Goering's[8] recent visit here, during which he made a considerable show of his Prussian personality, has done little to allay this feeling. The Greek Foreign Minister told me after his last visit to Geneva, that he did not expect war in Europe except as the result of the action of some madman. Mussolini recently took a very dangerous step in sending his fleet unannounced into the harbor of Durazzo. The immediate cause was apparently of no great importance, but the consequences might have entailed a general conflagration. Mussolini, however, controls even his wildest actions. He sees and forsees and there is a general impression that he has method in his madness. But this cannot yet be said of Hitler. Indeed, I have no doubt that M. Maximos's remark reflects the attitude of his Turkish, Rumanian and Yugoslavian colleagues, as well as his own, and refers chiefly to the German Chancellor. Certainly the nations of the Near East can now be regarded as fearing more than anything else some inflammatory action on Germany's part. The vexed Macedonian problem is still with us. But a determined effort is being made by the new Bulgarian government to deal firmly with this dangerous question. Furthermore Greece has shown the strength of her good will toward Turkey by acquiescing gracefully in the expulsion of more Greeks from Istanbul, and there seems to be nothing to fear at present at the Bosphorus, Salonica, the Dodecanese or Albania—the chief danger spots of this region. All eyes are on the West. (15)

Predictably, in Athens, preoccupation with international issues very soon gave way to partisan politics. In mid-July 1934, MacVeagh was reporting that ". . . with the advent of the hot weather the political situation in Greece, which seemingly has been approaching a solution, violent or otherwise, during the past two months, now appears likely to remain in suspension until September. Until that time M. Venizelos, the leader of the Opposition, is expected to remain in foreign parts. . . ." With the Balkan Pact no longer a burning domestic issue, "The struggle between the Government and the Opposition now centers around the following two questions: first, the desire of the Government to promote certain

---

[7] Marshal Paul von Hindenburg, President of Germany, died on August 2, 1934. He was succeeded in the presidency by Adolf Hitler, who preferred the title *Der Führer*.

[8] Hermann Goering, Nazi leader, member of Hitler's cabinet without portfolio, Germany's economic dictator after October 1936.

army officers who lost their seniority at the time of the Venizelist triumph in the Great War, and second, the proposition put forward by the Government to revise the electoral law in such a way as to secure certain advantages to itself in case of national elections. Incidental to the latter, the question of selecting a successor to M. Zaimis in the office of President of the Republic has taken on a certain importance." For the time being, the government's control of the national assembly (Vouli) was being maintained through "the precarious method of throwing occasional sops to the allied parties of General Kondylis and M. Metaxas, aided, no doubt, by the fact that these two gentlemen, as well as others connected with the present regime, go in some natural personal fear of a return of M. Venizelos to power." (16)

In September, with elections apparently not forthcoming, MacVeagh reported that Venizelos had returned from abroad, and that "the political ferment is again working furiously in Athens. . . ." Moreover, "during the long absence of the leader of the Opposition, his friends have so advertised the possibility of his standing for the Presidency himself, that what was early this summer a side issue is now a major and a burning one." To block such a development, Prime Minister Tsaldaris was hard at work promoting the re-election of President Zaimis, and doing everything possible to postpone indefinitely the parliamentary elections which, if won by the Venizelists, would provide them with enough strength in both Houses to give Venizelos the Presidency. At the same time, despite the usual rumors that General Kondylis, Tsaldaris' Minister of War, harbored personal political ambitions, MacVeagh observed that "the general feeling seems to be that that strange pair of bed-fellows, Tsaldaris and Kondylis, will not divorce at present, since the General is not strong enough to face the country alone and the Premier, in his mildness, needs just such an iron confederate to face the constant, if perhaps diminishing, threat of a Venizelist military coup. At the same time it is obvious that the Premier is watching his Minister of War very carefully. The control of the Athens constabulary was recently shifted from the War Ministry to that of the Interior. . . ." He concluded: "I have a feeling that the present political situation possibly hides a depth of intrigue unusual even in Greek history." (17)

While the formidable figure of Venizelos continued to dominate the political scene in the capital, MacVeagh's periodic analyses began to indicate that, beneath the surface, the Venizelist forces were seriously weakened. Anxious to obtain a change in the nation's election law, and increasingly unhappy with their leader's high-handed tactics, several leaders of the Liberal Party, including the respected Papanastasiou, quietly approached Tsaldaris seeking an accommodation. As a result, Venizelos' chances for the Presidency soon evaporated, and in October 1934, Zaimis was elected for another five-year term. The move signified a resounding victory for the Populists and the beginning of the end of presidential democracy: Zaimis was too old and indecisive to stand in the way of the monarchy's restoration, which growing numbers of Populists, royalists and anti-Venizelists openly advocated. Zaimis' re-election naturally enraged Venizelos, who withdrew to his native Crete, and in a series of bold editorials launched a shrill attack upon his enemies, real or imaginary. He accused Tsaldaris and the Populists of bringing the country to the brink of civil war through repression, and in a celebrated open letter to a supporter wrote: "If those now ruling Greece continue to think, as they declare, that their rule constitutes a state of things which must not be overturned by constitutional means, their violent overthrow will become an inevitable necessity, and then General Plastiras will be recognized by all as the avenger indicated. I know that several members of the National Coalition think that the tactics up to now pursued by those in power have rendered the necessity of General Plastiras' intervention inescapable. But I continue to entertain the hope, though this hope becomes weaker day by day, that the necessity of an avenger may yet be avoided." Reporting the matter to the Department MacVeagh characterized this outburst as "by all odds the most ominous pronouncement publicly made by the Cretan statesman since he fell from power two years ago," and concluded:

It is so threatening that one wonders whether, as I have already suggested several times to the Department, Mr. Venizelos is not losing that sense of realities which guides successful statesmen and has served him, himself, so notably. After his defeat in the Presidential election by perfectly constitutional means, his remarks do not even possess the plausibility of well-founded complaints, and with his National Coalition none too strongly united after the break in its front, this talk of vengeance over a constitutional question which his defeat has temporarily relegated to the background seems fantastic compared with the actualities of improved economic and fiscal conditions on which the Government is consolidating its strength. . . . (18)

The American Minister's reference to an improvement of economic conditions favoring Tsaldaris' Populist government was based on a careful study of developments across the country, especially in the northern provinces of Macedonia and Thrace, traditional strongholds of Venizelism. With the aid of the Legation's First Secretary and Consul General, Leland B. Morris, MacVeagh reported on October 18, 1934:

The climate for the past two years has facilitated record crops in those regions, and Mr. Theotokis, the Minister of Agriculture, has turned out to be not far behind Jupiter Pluvius himself in securing the resulting benefits to the peasants. This year the Government, with of course the now postponed elections in view, has been buying wheat widely at a good price for cash. Gone for the time being has been the old and still expected method of payment in little cash and much paper. A wave of prosperity has swept over the land causing the people to talk once more of pre-war conditions.... In the Salonica region, and between Drama and Kavalla, road building is again in evidence. Employment as well as agriculture shows a gain, and everywhere there is a lack of sympathy with the Cretan's present attempts to upset a regime so beneficial to the land.

MacVeagh concluded:

Of course what the Government has been doing for the electorate in Northern Greece has been done under political constraint, and is tainted through and through with opportunism. Apparently the time is yet to come when a Greek Government will think and act in relation to the welfare of the entire State. But, though the present government's efforts to please the Northern provinces may be short-lived, and for immediate purposes only, they may bring about a weakening in the Opposition which will orient the course of Greek politics away from the history of old men who cannot forget their past, and so confer a lasting benefit on the country at large. (19)

In the fall of 1934, while political feuding in the capital continued unabated, MacVeagh took advantage of his first official vacation to travel about in Greece. He also visited Turkey, whose efforts at modernization he was anxious to observe at first hand. The family had recently been joined by fourteen-year-old Eleanor Roosevelt, daughter of G. Hall ("Smouch") Roosevelt and niece of the First Lady. As the holiday season approached, he wrote to the President once more, combining personal news with political reporting:

Athens, December 4, 1934

Dear Franklin:
Christmas wishes will be crowding in upon you and Eleanor by the thousands but a few more, husky enough to reach you in good condition from the other side of the world, can't do you any harm. We all send them, including little Eleanor, who, I am glad to say, has come through her operation very well, and certainly seems a happier and stronger child than before the acute attack which made it necessary.
I am just now taking a vacation, but my address, as you see, is un-

changed. We hope to get back home for a vacation next summer, but in the meantime it seems best to use this past year's leave to do and see things in the immediate neighborhood which we have no time for when we are actually "en poste." This idea, however, seems to be so unheard of that the Greek press has taken it up as news, and everyone seems to have read that the American Minister is devoting his precious leave not to going to Paris but to studying Greece! In enjoying ourselves we flatter our hosts, and thus seem to be killing two birds with one stone.

Last week we sailed over to Smyrna on an American Export boat and spent two days there, driving up country to Bergama—ancient Pergamon—and calling on the Consul and the Governor. With our trip to the Dardanelles last Spring, we have now seen a goodly strip of the Asia Minor coast. Here in Greece we hear a great deal about the new Turkey, whose friendship means so much to this country at present. I have the official view of Turkish progress and achievement pretty well by heart. But though the vigor of the Government and the wealth of the land itself seems undeniable, the human material which the Government has to work with is very disappointing to the observer. A huge effort like that of Mussolini, or of Hitler, is being made to construct a great State on the occidental plan, and the population consists of orientals from whom their religion, the only thing that ever galvanized them into action, is taken away! It is a commonplace to remark on the fact that the immemorial businessmen of Turkey have been driven out—the Greeks, the Armenians and the Jews. What I have wanted to see is how the Turks are getting along with only themselves as substitutes. Apparently they have taken to the new bureaucracy like ducks to water. They are a governing race. But now they must do the work of the country as well, and the people's poverty and ignorance are appalling. Taxes are terribly high, and paid because it is the will of those higher up, not because the necessity for them is understood. In Greece every person thinks too much about affairs, so that politics are always in a turmoil. But at least the population as a whole is vitally responsive to ideas. It can be appealed to, as any Western people can be. But, with orientals of the dull psychological type of the Turkish peasantry, to try to make a modern organized State seems very like trying to make bricks without straw. I was very much impressed by the peasants I talked with who were refugees from Macedonia. They all longed to get back even to that unhappy region from a country where they can call neither piastres nor souls their own. As I wrote to Smouch the other day, I wonder whether the New Turkey, the product of the Great War, will not easily dissolve away in any new general conflagration. Or perhaps a recrudescence of Mohammedanism, when the present strong-willed rulers disappear, will do the trick. Certainly when we got to the Greek island of Samos, across a narrow strait from Asia Minor, we sensed a great difference at once. It was the difference between a small people of high vitality and a huge depressed population. The vitality of Turkey is concentrated in the head. In Greece it quivers in every limb of every Greek that breathes. Differences like this are not to be observed in the rooms and corridors of Foreign Offices. But they inevitably influence international affairs in the long run. In talking with the island Greeks who are near to her [Turkey], I find less confidence in Turkey as the Greek rock of defence than is expressed here in Athens. Those long-suffering people doubtless know that by taking a fez off a leopard one does not change his spots. East is East and West is West, and the line still runs where it always has. I am very fond of the upper-class Turks I have met and sympathetic with their problems. But to understand, one must get down to humble realities, and one cannot go about in Turkey without gaining the impression that its future is a huge question-mark.

Meanwhile the international situation in the Near East is very strongly affected by the Greco-Turkish *rapprochement*, however formal or temporary this may be. The Balkan Entente, of which it is the keystone, was further elaborated, along economic lines, at Ankara this fall. As the Balkan Pact stands for non-revision of the Treaties, Bulgaria still refuses to join, but the idea of Balkan solidarity has received such stimulus that in one way or another Bulgaria may yet find a way to take her place beside the others in a regional groupment embracing the entire peninsula. The League of Nations, too, is very useful in this part of the world. By settling the Rhodope Forest dispute,[9] it has opened the way to the composition of other long-standing difficulties between Greece and Bulgaria, and a nasty argument now going on with Albania over the schooling of the Greek minority is also being referred to Geneva.

Greece, like most other countries, was frightened by the assassination of King Alexander,[10] and is watchfully waiting for the League to conjure the dangers inherent in the tempers of Yugoslavia and Hungary. Actually, and for the time being, M. Barthou's death was of more consequence here, however. He had become the active soul of the system in which Greece placed herself, at least with one foot, when she signed the Balkan Pact with two nations of the Petite Entente. The success of the Germans in Poland, and the impression which this created in Rumania (though Titulescu[11] made a quick recovery) has somewhat shaken the Greek

[9] On May 6, 1932, a decision of the Permanent Court of International Justice had settled the issue of Bulgaria's compensation to Greece for certain areas in the Rhodope Mountains which had been seized by Bulgaria.

[10] On October 9, 1934, King Alexander of Yugoslavia and French Foreign Minister Barthou were assassinated at Marseilles by a Macedonian revolutionary with Hungarian connections. Peter II (born 1923) succeeded to the throne, with Prince Paul, cousin of the murdered King, serving as Regent.

[11] Nicholas Titulescu, Rumanian Minister for Foreign Affairs.

faith. On the other hand, the Russian *rapprochement* with France, which was the answer to Poland's defection, means much to Greece on account of the importance of Russia to Turkey, and meanwhile she waits to see what Laval[12] can do in Barthou's shoes with Italy. Indeed, Greece is so completely vulnerable from every side that she literally must have friends. The old game of the balance of power is being played all over again in Europe today, and Greece's hesitations and fears supply a watcher in Athens with an almost daily record of how it progresses. When the next war comes, I believe she will do her best to repeat her accidental success of 1917-18, and stay out till it is perfectly clear which bandwagon she ought to jump on. In this sense, her foreign policy at present is perhaps nearer that of England than of any other power. The eventual actions of these two depend on so many variables as to be practically impossible of prediction.

Internally, M. Venizelos almost forced the Government to go to the people a few weeks ago, but his lines gave way, and when seventeen of his senators went over to the other side, the jig was up for the moment. The Popular (Royalist) party is now even more securely in the saddle, and continues to pursue its policy of economic and fiscal retrenchment, and of temporizing on every controversial issue. Our trade with Greece is growing in spite of the difficulties in its path, and I have awakened the Foreign Minister's interest in our new tariff policy, so that the way is prepared for approaching a commercial treaty should our authorities think one desirable at any time. Financially, the Government's position goes on improving, and Greece has lived up to the agreement made last year with her foreign bond-holders to pay a percentage of the interest due. We have shared in these payments, though Greece in principle still maintains that our Refugee Loan of 1929 is really a war-loan, and her position on war-loans remains unchanged.

I hope I have not written too much about what are, naturally, vitally interesting topics to me. Greece is still beautiful, and I need say nothing about that. Senator Joe Robinson, who seemed to enjoy it, can tell you what it's like. Senator Tom Connally, too, drove about with us a bit, and Representative Cochran, a very likeable Republican, from my ancestral State of Pennsylvania. You will have seen a lot in the American papers about the marriage of Princess Marina of Greece to the Duke of Kent. There is some sentiment, or sentimentality, about that here too. But almost fifty percent of the population of Greece would emphasize to any inquirer that the Princess has no Greek blood and no Greek passport. M. Papanastasiou, Ex-Premier and so-called "Father of the Republic"

[12] Pierre Laval, Prime Minister of France.

(Mr. Morgenthau, Senior,[13] knows him well), told me: "the English Prince would have had far better chance of becoming King of Greece if he had not married that Princess," and intimated that he had no chance at all, anyway. Royalist propaganda is noticeably absent. But, of course, Greek politics shift so quickly that it may spring up tomorrow. (One has to qualify every statement or prediction involving Greeks.)

The results of the elections at home were tremendously encouraging. Smouch ends a letter with a post-script: "These *are* times!" They certainly seem to be, and I'm glad they are times in which you are the boss.

Affectionately yours,
Lincoln MacVeagh

P.S. Your welcome letter of Christmas and New Year's greetings to the Foreign Service has just arrived, in good time for me to relay it on to everyone. (20)

Venizelos' polemics against the Tsaldaris Government, and his thinly veiled threats to resort to force, were no empty rhetoric. Rather, they were designed to create the right psychological climate for drastic action, to be justified as necessary to rescue the Republic from its "reactionary" Populist foes. Underneath the harangue, a plot was being hatched for another Venizelist coup. And when it came, on March 1, 1935, it was not merely one more attempt to seize power by force of arms. Although crushed in less than two weeks, the March 1935 revolt proved to be a momentous turning point in the country's modern history. It completely wrecked the republican forces, and gave their opponents a vitality and unity of purpose which they would not have generated on their own. It unleashed a thorough purge of Venizelists, and republicans generally, from all positions of influence, thus transforming the character of governmental institutions at all levels. It led directly to the Metaxas dictatorship of the following year, and through that regime to the ultimate destruction of the democratic process. Moreover, despite its vigorous presentation as a desperate, last-minute struggle to save the republican form of government, the 1935 revolt had little real ideological foundation. In the words of a competent Greek historian, the revolt represented "the last eruption of El. Venizelos' volcanic temperament, an eruption caused not by any anxiety for the entire political system or for the fate of his followers, but for his own person." (21)

In terse telegrams, the American Legation reported the unfolding of

[13] Henry Morgenthau, former U.S. Ambassador to Turkey, had served as Chairman of the Greek Refugee Settlement Commission following the Greek-Turkish exchange of populations in 1923.

these violent events. Then, on March 13, 1935, still unaware of Venizelos' personal complicity in the revolt, MacVeagh gave a detailed account by despatch:

The movement appears to have been planned with the utmost secrecy, governmental, diplomatic, and financial circles alike being taken completely by surprise. As I have already informed the Department, Mr. Venizelos, the Chief of the Opposition leaders, had for some time past, been talking openly of "vengeance," and accusing the government of unconstitutional actions. Also the Minister of War had been "purging" the army of Venizelist elements, while other ultra-conservative opponents of Mr. Venizelos had been making efforts to force the Premier to alter his moderate attitude. But, on the other hand, Senatorial elections had been announced for April, at which time the Opposition would have a chance to demonstrate its strength with the country, and the Government had at last brought to trial the persons accused of the infamous attempt of 1933 on the life of Mr. Venizelos. Thus truce, if not peace, seemed to be the order of the day. It is true that on March 1st, Mr. Papanastasiou, the so-called "Father of the Republic," issued a call to citizens to resort to arms, alleging that General Kondylis had sold himself to the Royalists. But the question of Royalism vs. Republicanism, so dear to Mr. Papanastasiou, has long been a dormant issue in comparison with Venizelism vs. anti-Venizelism, and Mr. Papanastasiou's manifesto assumed importance only in the light of what followed. It does not seem likely that he was informed of the impending *coup*.

As he was boarding the train for Salonica, to attend a Republican meeting, Mr. Papanastasiou was, however, arrested. This was about 8 p.m. on the evening of March 1st. It appears that the Premier had just been informed that a revolutionary movement was on foot and precautions were being taken to meet it. The Minister of War, General Kondylis, at once summoned the Garrison of Athens to quarters by firing the gun on the hill of Lycabettus at regular intervals—an agreed-on signal. Admiral Hadjikyriakos, the Minister of Marine, called up the Naval Base on the 'phone. Almost immediately a serious situation developed near the Acropolis where half of the crack Evzone regiment was quartered. These and some groups of officers and cadets in two military schools, located in another and outlying quarter of town, had, it seemed, openly revolted. The trouble in the schools was soon over. But against the Evzones, who shot their Colonel when he demanded their surrender, General Kondylis found it advisable to mass overwhelming forces, calling out machine guns, light artillery, tanks, cavalry and infantry. The barracks were then shelled by light guns placed in front of the Odeon of Herodes Atticus and in the precinct of Olympian Zeus, near the Arch of Hadrian, and tanks were ordered to attack the gates. The rebels put up a stout defense, but at about 1 a.m. on the 2nd, they capitulated before the threat of heavier artillery.

Meanwhile, Admiral Hadjikyriakos, the Minister of Marine, had been assured that all was well at the Naval Base. But unfortunately for him, his informant was a rebel! The officer in charge of personnel had cunningly contrived that on this particular night most of the dependable loyal officers of the fleet were on shore leave. Consequently, when retired Admiral Demestihas and about twenty officers appeared at the gates of the Arsenal and shot the sentry, two launches were waiting under steam to take them to the ships, which also had steam up. The Commanding Officer at the Naval Base was beaten into insensibility, and the man in charge of signals and telephones was shot and killed. Shortly thereafter, the rebels were in complete control of several vessels. The rest they rendered innocuous by wrecking machinery and stealing breech-blocks. They then sailed out to Phaleron Bay, facing Athens. The Army fired on them as they emerged, with hastily assembled artillery, but only the innocent little village of Perama suffered in this engagement. The captured fleet then awaited the issue of the revolt in Athens, abstaining from firing on the city. When at last it became evident that the military *coup* had failed, it steamed away to Crete, pursued by bombing-planes.

After listing the warships which had joined in the rebellion, as well as those still in government hands, the report continued:

On paper, the fighting strength of the two sides was thus about equal, but the Government needed time for repairs, an advantage for their opponents [on] which the latter failed to capitalize. Indeed, the inactivity of the rebel vessels, and their sojourn in Crete during the next few days, point to the possibility that Mr. Venizelos took some persuading to accept the present of this handsome but already half-tarnished revolution. When called upon by the Governor General of the Island to declare himself, he merely charged the Government with the unconstitutionality of declaring Martial Law—as it had done—without consulting the Chamber. The Government, however, lost no time in remarking on the fact that he had not disavowed the revolution, as he should have done as a loyal citizen, and declared him a rebel and his ships outlaws and pirates. The scotched revolution thus became a full-fledged rebellion, with a chief and at least a fleet.

The rest of the Army, with the exception of the Fourth Army Corps at Kavalla, and perhaps the Division in Crete—I have no exact information on this score at present—remained loyal to the Government. The Fourth Army Corps captured Drama and Serres and advanced to the line of the Struma, patrols clashing with General Kondylis's advance guard on the hills to the west of that stream. With forces from Larissa, Chalkis, and Athens, as well as from Salonica, the Minister of War rapidly built up an overwhelming superiority in numbers, which was increased with every day of waiting for the weather to moderate. Troops from the Peloponnese took the place in Athens of the reinforcements sent north. Finally, early on March 11th, General Kondylis crossed the swollen stream and flooded marshes of the Struma, and military opposition melted away. On the 12th, General Kammenos, commanding the 4th Corps, took refuge with his staff in Bulgaria. The chief of the Corps Staff is reported to have committed suicide.

On the sea, the rebel ships apparently cruised among the islands, where they re-fuelled and took such supplies and recruits as they needed. These forays were reported as "captures"—the Greek Islands of the Aegean are not fortified. On Saturday the 9th, the cruiser *HELLI* was bombarded by government destroyers as she lay in the harbor of Kavalla, and the next day she was abandoned by her officers and surrendered by her crew. The day after that, the *AVEROFF* was reported to have left Crete, with Mr. Venizelos aboard, bound for an unknown refuge. That same afternoon General Kondylis returned by plane to Athens for a parade and ovation.

During the ten days of active operations, much was reported concerning the activity of the air forces of the Government. Raids on the hostile ships and the towns in their possession in Crete and Macedonia were acclaimed in the press with almost monotonous regularity. At present it is not certain how much damage was done in this way. Apparently some property losses were sustained in Kavalla from shelling and bombing, but in general the reports are almost certainly exaggerated. The Government now seems likely to regain its entire fleet with practically no harm done, and aside from the outbreak in Athens, the land victory seems to have been obtained with practically no loss of life. Reliable information gives two hundred as the total casualties for both sides in Macedonia. The strategy of General Kondylis appears to have been of an unusually high order. By exerting every effort to bring up reserves while he waited on the Struma line, he put himself, when the weather cleared, in a position to end a fratricidal struggle almost without a blow.

A like restraint was shown by other Government leaders here. The threat of sudden naval raids was met by the mining of the principal harbours and the extinguishing of all coastal lights, dangers of which foreign shipping was duly and promptly warned. Though martial law was immediately proclaimed, restrictions on individual action were few, for the most part clearly reasonable, and promptly withdrawn when they no longer served their purpose. So far as this Legation is concerned, the Government, both civil and military, was consistently courteous and helpful. A difficult period in the country's history, happily brief, has thus been passed through with credit to those in charge. There remains, of course, the question of reprisals,—the question whether in victory as in strife the Greek can spare his brother. There will be courts-martial for rebel officers, as is natural. But hosts of people prominent in Venizelist circles are under arrest, and all Athens is asking tonight how far old factional and personal hatreds are to be given rein.

There seems to have been very little popular feeling aroused, either for or against the movement. Some rioting occurred around the Venizelos house here on the day after the outbreak, but our Consul at Patras, Mr. Allen, has continued to report apathy in that Royalist center, while Venizelist sentiment in and around Salonica distinctly failed to crystallize as expected. Some of the calm among this excitable people was no doubt due to the salutary suppression of the Opposition press. But I am inclined to lay more stress on the lack of popular leadership. One cannot work up much enthusiasm for Tsaldaris, Kondylis, or Metaxas. The "Popular" party would be a very different affair with a Charles the First, or even a Constantine, to rally round. On the other hand, the Opposition has no Cromwell, or rather he who should have played that role remained watchfully waiting in Crete when he might have unsheathed a shining sword in Macedonia, and his Rupert of the Rhine (Plastiras of the Riviera) only succeeded in getting himself interned in Italy, while explaining to foreign journalists that this was not "his" revolution! Perhaps a little more success at the outset would have sufficed to bring Mr. Venizelos to Macedonia, where every element of discontent might have gathered round him. As it is, the revolt died a-borning among the officers and never got to the people, who were its only hope after its preliminary failure as a *coup d'état.*

There is not likely to be any more trouble with the Opposition for some time. The Venizelists are stunned, and the Government will have its way. If King George were a different sort of person, this would undoubtedly be his chance to regain his throne. But there is a noticeable lack of interest in him, even among people who support Monarchy as the system best suited to Greece's requirements. As far as the Cabinet is concerned, Mr. Tsaldaris seems likely to continue as Premier, to keep the balance between the jealous Generals,—Kondylis and Metaxas. Rumor slates either Theotokis or Michalakopoulos for the post of Minister of Foreign Affairs. The resignation of Mr. Maximos, which I am told by his family was handed in before the coup for reasons of health (he suffers from prostate trouble), has robbed Greece of a valuable asset both as a far-seeing Minister of State and as a moderate counsellor in home affairs. He is not likely to rejoin the government, even if his health improves, since the ultra-conservatives now in the saddle feel that it was his moderation which nourished in Greece's bosom the nest of vipers responsible for the attempted revolution of 1935. (22)

Four days later (March 17, 1935), in another despatch, MacVeagh asserted again that the failure of the revolt had "abolished the Opposition as a political factor." Venizelos, now abroad, was to be tried *in absentia* for high treason, while most of his prominent aides and supporters were under arrest. Metaxas, who had joined the Cabinet at Tsaldaris' invitation as minister without portfolio, was now demanding the swift and severe punishment of the rebels. A thorough purge of the civil service and of the Navy was also expected, to rid them of all Venizelist sympathizers. The report continued:

Whether a move will be made to bring the King back is another question. The character and history of Kondylis makes it seem unlikely for the present, as does the fact that it would immediately give color to the accusations of Papanastasiou and others, and convince many Republicans of the justice and timeliness of the revolt. Later on there may be a different story to tell. For the present the chief questions before the country are the treatment of the authors of the revolt, and the reconstruction of the Government as a one-party dictatorship *ad interim*, with the promise and perhaps the intention of going to the people later for endorsement. There may be some changes in the Cabinet for the sake of cohesion and unity, but there are not many posts, and no important ones, which would seem to call for strengthening from this point of view, and the Premier is as averse as ever to drastic action. (23)

With all its dramatic consequences for the country, the revolt was not without its complexities in matters of diplomatic protocol. Having been left to fend for himself, the American Minister advised his government on March 18:

Following the quelling of the Venizelist revolt which broke out on the first of March, the Ministers of France, Great Britain, Turkey, Yugoslavia and Rumania called separately upon the Premier and tendered the felicitations and congratulations of their Governments. Italy has not so far followed this lead. The German Minister has informed me that he discreetly expressed to Mr. Tsaldaris his own personal feelings of happiness that a situation so difficult for Greece had been terminated with a minimum of bloodshed. The Bulgarian Minister told me that he was saying nothing whatever.

On the 13th of March a *Te Deum* of Thanksgiving was celebrated in the Cathedral here, which all the high officials of the Church and State attended. The Diplomatic Corps, however, was not invited, as it usually is to such functions, presumably because the victory to be celebrated was one of Greeks over their own countrymen. For this reason, and because of the alacrity of the Press at present to seize upon anything which could be construed or twisted into a semblance of partisanship, I have refrained from making any public visit of congratulation. On the other hand, in our normal contacts with friends in official life, both I and the Secretaries of this Legation have taken occasion to express verbally our satisfaction at the speedy termination of a difficult situation, and at my suggestion, my wife has written Mrs. Tsaldaris a personal note saying how happy we are that order has been restored and that Greece has not greatly suffered, and asking her and the Premier to come very informally to lunch or dinner if and when his duties permit.

In attempting to maintain, in the absence of instructions, an attitude which implies nothing but friendship for Greece as a whole, I have of course in mind the fact that England, France, Yugoslavia, Rumania and Turkey all have a stake in the international situation in the Balkans which might have been endangered by a successful revolt. This fact is brought out clearly in the references to the Balkan Pact in the press comments, foreign and local. I have also in mind the fact that Venizelism still exists in this country and counts among its adherents something like half the total population. Should the present political situation in regard to punishment and reprisals set forth in my despatch No. 571 of March 17th, develop dangerously, I will of course inform the Department, in case it may wish me to take steps to support those here who stand for wisdom and moderation. At the present moment, however, it is precisely such people who appear to be in control. (24)

Hopes that the government might show mercy toward prominent persons implicated in the revolt were dashed when, after *pro forma* deliberation, a court-martial condemned to death retired Generals Papoulas and Kimissis. In a separate trial, a large group of political leaders, including Papanastasiou, Kafandaris, Mylonas, and Gonatas, appeared for a while to be destined for a similar fate. Deeply disturbed, MacVeagh, who knew personally some of these men and their families, urgently cabled the Department of State that his British and French colleagues, acting on standing instructions, were intervening with the Greek government, urging moderation. He requested authorization to join in the efforts to save the lives of the condemned, adding: "... it would be well to instruct me now as under military law execution follows rapidly upon sentence." His plea was too late. On April 24, within hours after sending the above message, he telegraphed the horrible news: "Generals were shot at dawn this morning." (25)

The following day, Secretary of State Cordell Hull telegraphed MacVeagh that in the case of the political leaders facing a possible death sentence ". . . you may in your discretion, and acting solely in your personal capacity and if similar action is being taken by your colleagues, orally and informally indicate to the Greek authorities that arbitrary action in the trial or execution of these men would in your opinion undoubtedly make an unfortunate impression in this country." (26) In a parallel move, and acting on MacVeagh's suggestion, former ambassador Henry Morgenthau, who had served as Chairman of the Greek Refugee Settlement Commission and was a personal friend of Papanastasiou, telegraphed Tsaldaris urging moderation and leniency.

Armed with such support from Washington, MacVeagh worked hard to convince the Greek government that the execution of the political leaders "would create an unfortunate impression on the vast public opinion of my country which it would take years to eradicate." (27) These diplomatic representations, combined with the shock in Greece caused by the hasty execution of the two generals, had the desired effect. Although Venizelos and Plastiras (the general had reportedly tried in vain to enter the country in time to lead the revolt) were sentenced to death *in absentia*, the others received mild prison terms or were acquitted altogether. Much relieved, MacVeagh advised the Department: "It is generally conceded in Athens that this victory of moderation and sanity owes much to our attitude as well as that of France and Britain." (28)

MacVeagh's despatches covering these difficult moments do not betray his personal role in rescuing the accused. Instead, they provide background for a better comprehension of the psychological climate in Athens:

[April 24, 1935]

On Monday, April 22nd, a Court Martial sitting in Athens to try members of the semi-military Venizelist organization known as the Panhellenic Republican Defense, charged with complicity in the recent uprising, returned a sentence of death against two retired officers, Lieutenant General Papoulas and Brigadier General Kimissis, leaders of the organization.

It appears that these officers were not involved in the recent revolt to any degree which would justify the death penalty, and the general consensus of opinion here is that the severity of the sentence is due to their past records. After his removal from Supreme Command in Asia Minor in 1922, General Papoulas, though till then a Royalist, gave testimony which helped in the conviction of his successor, General Hadjianestis, and the rest of the famous "six." General Kimissis was also a witness against the Six and later sat on the Court which condemned Prince Andrew[14] to exile. Neither he nor Papoulas showed any change of heart during the succeeding years, but on the contrary continued to represent in Athens all that was hostile to the royalist interests. In the Greek scheme of things, in which from the earliest times politics has been characterized by deadly feuds, these men were all too clearly marked out for reprisals. This morning at dawn behind the Children's hospital they gave satisfaction to their enemies, the President failing to commute their sentences because the requisite recommendations for clemency were never made by the competent Military Authority.

The execution of these two officers is a disquieting indication of the strength of the extreme reactionary faction in the Royalist ranks. It is said that the moderate Premier, Mr. Tsaldaris, whose health is at present very bad, received a severe shock on hearing the news of the sentences, resulting in a serious set-back to his hoped-for recovery. The Government press announced the executions this morning in the barest factual terms. There seems to have been no really popular clamor for blood and no public expressions of satisfaction because blood has been shed. The general reaction in Athens is rather one of nervousness over how far this thing may go.

The fruitless *démarche* of the British and French Legations to which I referred in my telegram No. 55, was made to the Foreign Minister, Mr. Mavromichalis, who is, as the Department knows, one of the extremist group, and one of the last persons to look upon the object of such intervention with favor. Not a word about it appeared in the Press, and the American correspondent, Mr. Alexander Sedgwick,[15] who obtained knowledge of it from the British Secretary who made the *démarche* during the illness of the Minister, tells me that his telegram reporting it was stopped by the censor. The other Legations here, being without instructions, made no official moves, but I am informed that several let their grave concern be known in strictly informal ways. Through Mr. Aldridge, Second Secretary of this Legation, who has been very helpful, I have conveyed to the entourage of the Premier and the Secretary of War an impression of sympathy with their attitude of moderation, which will serve to reinforce any official attitude of this sort which the Department may care to have me take at a later date if the extremists force the government to extend the death penalty to more important figures of State. (29)

[14] Prince Andrew, brother of King Constantine, had served on the Greek General Staff during the Asia Minor campaign, and together with six political and military leaders had been court-martialled, and charged with responsibility for the Greek defeat in 1922. While the "six" had been sentenced to death and executed, Andrew had been deprived of his rank and banished for life.

[15] Alexander "Shan" Sedgwick, Athens correspondent for the *New York Times*, was a cousin of MacVeagh.

Although the situation remained uncertain, and Greek politics did not lend itself to forecasting, the signs pointed to a turn toward the right, which might well mean the early return of the monarchy:

[April 24, 1935]

With Premier Tsaldaris an ill man and War Minister Kondylis not only ill but apparently in insecure control of an Army which is divided politically, an irresponsible but active group of extreme Royalists has made such headway in controlling events, if not the expressed policies of the Government, that the political situation today is decidedly enigmatical.

There can be no doubt that the moderates in nominal control of the government made every effort to prevent the execution of Generals Papoulas and Kimissis, which took place at dawn today. I am told that even General Metaxas did what he could, moved by the tears of Mrs. Kimissis. But it seems that a small group of officers, led by General Reppas, Chief of Military Aviation, served notice on General Kondylis that unless they were given their way with the Courts-Martial they would take over the Government, and that General Kondylis felt powerless to prevent them. This group comprises Admiral Sakellariou, the President of the Court now sitting in the case of the Opposition political leaders, as well as General Panayiotakos, the Commander of the 1st Army Corps, whose recommendation is necessary before the President can commute sentences passed by Courts-Martial in his area. In addition, it appears that this group is backed by a solid and fanatical group of the old Athenian royalist society, among which the ladies are perhaps especially violent, not to speak of Mr. John Rallis, who is said to be howling for blood. One is reminded in this connection of what happened in 1922 when extremists in the Army, backed by popular feeling, forced the death sentences of the six ministers against the judgment of such authority as existed.

In general, I should like to emphasize the fact that present events here cannot be understood without reference to what happened in 1922. In the Greek view, the abortive Venizelist revolt of last month is only a continuation of the situation created then. The trial of the political leaders now going on takes on added importance from this fact, and the position in which Messrs. Papanastasiou, Kafandaris, Gonatas and other leaders now find themselves is a more dangerous one than any connection of theirs with the events of March last would indicate. In the Greek mind they are tarred with the brush of Venizelism from years back, and in Royalist eyes are guilty of the most heinous of all crimes whether any specific charges can be proved against them or not. Particularly is General Gonatas in a serious situation. He served on the Revolutionary Committee with General Plastiras in 1922. In his case, if any semblance of guilt in this recent affair can be trumped up, the Court-Martial may be expected to be especially severe.

In addition to the problems created by the Courts-Martial and the "purification" of government services, discussed in my previous despatches, the problem of elections is now engaging the attention of the government. It is probable that these may be held before any of the "Opposition" parties have a chance to consolidate or even place candidates in the field. Mr. Michalakopoulos states today that he will not compete unless martial law is lifted at least a month before the elections are held. Mr. Metaxas will probably provide the only opposition with his Eleftherophrones Party, which today he has metamorphosed into the "Royalist Union." Though the recent outbreak of terrorism has somewhat shaken him personally, by all accounts, he remains nevertheless a considerable thorn in the side of the government politically. Only the other day, he distributed hand-bills attacking the Government from the President down. These hand-bills purport to give the text of a letter addressed by Mr. Metaxas to the President, the publication of which was forbidden by the censor. They protest against the alleged decision of the Government to hold elections next month under martial law, and declare the bankruptcy of the Republican regime and the necessity of "a new order." It is not certain that martial law will not be lifted before May 19th, the date set for the elections, and, in fact, if the actions of the Courts-Martial do not cause civil disturbances, it is quite possible that it will. But Mr. Metaxas needs ammunition for his campaign and seems willing to grasp at anything. His tactics may be muddled like everything else in the present political scene, but they are generally taken to reveal one thing clearly, namely that if and when elections are held his candidates will stand on a platform calling for the restoration of the Monarchy. In the meantime the anomalous situation created by the control which I have described, of a government behind the government, may bring about changes unforeseen and unforseeable. (30)

In the early part of the summer, with parliamentary elections scheduled to take place soon (the Gerousia, or Senate, long a Venizelist stronghold, had been abolished by government decree in the aftermath of the March revolt), the star of John Metaxas appeared very much on the rise, and the monarchy's restoration simply a matter of time. MacVeagh reported on June 6, 1935:

The confused political situation in Greece now seems to be developing rapidly towards a partial clarification by way of national elections on next Sunday, the 9th of June. The so-called Opposition Parties are not expected to cast any votes in this election, all their leaders—Kafandaris, Papanastasiou, Mylonas, Sofoulis, etc.,—having decided to abstain and called upon their followers to do likewise. Parties which have split off from the Tsaldaris coalition will constitute the Opposition in these elections. General Pangalos has started a tiny party of his own. In Macedonia there is a new party under the leadership of Messrs. Kotzamanis and Dragoumis. This may grow into something of importance since it aims to represent the interests of Northern Greece. But in the present elections it is expected that the contest will almost wholly be between the forces of Mr. Tsaldaris, the Premier, and General John Metaxas, the leading Royalist. The latter is very loud in his claims. One would think from the stir he has been able to make that he had a serious chance of winning. But all the usually well-informed observers whom I have been able to sound out in Athens, in the Peloponnese, in Macedonia, as well as from the Islands, concede the election to Tsaldaris by a handsome majority.

The activities of Metaxas have forced the question of the régime very much into the foreground, and for the moment the question of the restoration of the Monarchy is on everyone's lips. Mr. Tsaldaris has promised to hold a plebiscite on the question after the elections, but it is likely that if he wins a large majority over the Metaxas party the plebiscite may somehow not come off. As the Department knows, Mr. Tsaldaris is an expert at deferring anything that savors of a definite decision. It is thought here that he is not himself anxious for the restoration, since he has not been a great worker for the King these past years and would probably be pushed aside to make room for more loyal supporters should the latter come back. Also the past of General Kondylis hardly augurs a brilliant future for that gentleman should the Royal House return.

The reasons given by the Opposition leaders for abstaining from these elections are connected, of course, with the recent Venizelist revolt. It is alleged that the Government has not given the leaders time to organize, after holding martial law over the country for so long a time and keeping most of the leaders themselves in jail till very recently. There have also been allegations to the effect that the Government will tamper with the election machinery, and dissatisfaction has been expressed with the decision to use the majority system rather than the proportional. But all this is normal in Greece. If there are to be disturbances during the elections, they are not likely to come from the former Venizelists, but from the Metaxists. Last night a fleet of motor cars passed the house of Mr. Pericles Rallis, the Minister of the Interior, and sprayed it with bullets. The perpetrators are said to be Metaxists, and the method employed certainly reminds one of previous outrages with which his name has been connected. It is said that Mr. Rallis (formerly Insull's attorney and Governor

General of Macedonia during the revolt) sinned by forbidding the display of the ex-King's picture, which nevertheless is being displayed.

Mr. Venizelos has written a number of letters and given a number of interviews in which he has announced his definite withdrawal from politics. But his protestations are so long and detailed that they are having the very opposite effect and slipping him right back into the political scene as a force to be reckoned with, and feared, in the moulding of public opinion. (31)

With the immediate effects of the March revolt already quite evident, MacVeagh cast his eyes beyond the Greek scene to the Balkans and Europe. On May 4 he was writing to the President:

Athens, May 4, 1935

Dear Franklin:

Since I last wrote we have had some interesting times over here, and they are still going on.

First, the Italians began what may best be described as their Abyssinian preparations. This was not without repercussions of alarm in Athens, which is the chief nerve-centre of the Near East. Opinion here is always alive to any manifestations of Italian expansionist policy, particularly in view of Mussolini's persistent development of the Dodecanese Islands. Now it has become evident that the Italians, knowing quite well the value of their attitude in the Austrian question, have forced the French and British into letting them have a free hand in Abyssinia. But such a policy, if successful, may easily develop further, and Greece and Turkey may well fear a similar attitude on the part of the Powers should Mussolini later decide to give rein to his ambitions on the coast of Asia Minor.

Shortly after Mussolini began sending troops to Abyssinia, there came, not without general warning but quite suddenly as to the precise moment of the outbreak, the Venizelist revolt in Greece. . . . Internationally, the revolt revealed some interesting things. Bulgaria's nervousness was promptly exhibited in an appeal to the League of Nations against Turkish military activity in Eastern Thrace, while Italy allowed General Plastiras to get all the way to Brindisi on his way to join Venizelos before she stopped him in the very act of sailing. By that time England had sent a battleship into the Piraeus and publicly announced her support of the *status quo*. Titulescu had spoken to the same effect, and France's diplomatic system in the Near East had shown unmistakable signs of holding firm. A French warship had also arrived in the Piraeus. Then, a week after the others, and only then, did the Italian warships arrive. The Italian attitude seems to have been of a decidedly opportunist character in this affair. . . .

Greek opinion is vividly alive to the possible consequences of Germany's scuttling of the Versailles Treaty. Germany's peaceful neighbors may prevent war from breaking out in the West for some time, but if revisionist nations like Hungary and Bulgaria are encouraged to treat their obligations in a similar manner, there are not the same forceful guarantees in Southeastern Europe to avoid a conflict. I feel that if one thing more than another could cause the Balkans to become again the tinderbox of Europe, it would be Germany's doing what she has done. There is unmistakable anxiety in this part of the world, not over Germany's action but over the actions of which this may be the parent. The papers are full of Turkey's claim to be allowed to refortify the Straits. But that the straits are to all intents and purposes refortified already is an open secret. The guns are ready and the emplacements for them. More important are the sudden moves which panic may bring about. Intentions in this part of the world are doubtless not offensive. I happen to enjoy the friendship of the present Director of the Bulgarian Foreign Office who was long Minister here, and I believe him when he says that his country does not want to make war on its neighbors. But war, of course, does not come out of the blue. It is rather the result of what we used to call in school a parallelogram of forces. In the Balkans these forces come from outside too often for the Balkan peoples to foresee their own fate from any distance ahead.

You may have noticed in the papers a good deal of to-do about a restoration of the Monarchy here. Such a thing is certainly in the cards, but there is no agitation for it in Greece comparable to what the foreign press makes out. There is a small group of Royalists which wants a restoration for the personal benefits to be derived by its members. There is, supporting this, the Greek fondness for change. But in general there is apathy. With the Opposition leaders only just released from jail, royalist votes may win a majority in the coming elections. Or the King may come back by a *coup d'état*. But in any case a restoration would not be significant except locally, unless perhaps England should lend the Duke of Kent. She is hardly likely to do this, however, on account of the ensuing responsibility and its effect on her foreign policy in general. Almost certainly if Royalty returns it will do no good to Greece. Its supporters call monarchy a "stable form of government," but the lot of the Greek Kings has always been a stormy one.

American commercial interests have not been doing too badly here. Figures show that our exports to Greece for the first two months of 1935 increased about thirty percent over those for the same period last year. But Greek exports to the United States increased some hundred percent in the same period. The balance of trade, already against us, is piling up. Germany's commercial policy, being more rigorous and almost coercive, has established her as top dog in Greek imports, in the position we used to occupy. I keep urging the Department to bring Greece to book under our new policy and write her up a new trade agreement more in keeping with present conditions than the present one of 1924. And I have been rewarded by a telegram promising that I am to be instructed in this matter soon.

I have written enough for the present, and can only feebly hope you will have time and patience to read it all. We hope to take a vacation at home this summer, sailing June 14th, bringing little Eleanor along with us. I shall go to Washington immediately on my arrival to talk with those who give me my orders. Maybe I shall have the luck to see you. At any rate, I am always

Yours devotedly,
Lincoln MacVeagh (32)

While the turbulence of Greek politics continued, creating in the capital an atmosphere of seemingly permanent uncertainty and perpetual anticipation, MacVeagh found life in Athens pleasantly busy and rewarding. In addition to never-ending social and cultural events, which brought together foreign dignitaries, government functionaries, and Athenian society, there was always time for quiet reading, archaeological excursions, sports, and for walks and rides in the peasant countryside of Attica. Unlike other diplomats, who seldom ventured outside the city limits, MacVeagh showed great interest in the provinces. Accompanied by his wife and daughter and travelling by car, he criss-crossed the country's various geographic sections, and before long there were few towns and villages in all of Greece that the MacVeaghs had not visited at least once. His Greek friends were soon amazed to discover that he knew their country far better than most of them.

Among his many and varied interests, none gave him more pleasure than the study of classical Greece, perhaps his principal reason for accepting the diplomatic assignment. Already widely read in ancient history and classical literature, he became a serious student of archaeology. In the mid-1930's, under the direction of Professor Oscar Broneer of the American School of Classical Studies, MacVeagh financed a small-scale excavation on the eastern face of the hill of the Acropolis, and worked there himself, between diplomatic activities. Although there were no spectacular discoveries, the "dig" yielded many fragments of pottery, some of which were found to be missing parts of vessels already on exhibit at the National Museum. The local press (as well as the *New York Times* of

February 24, 1936) prominently displayed photographs showing the American Minister, in his office suit, wide-brim hat, and smoking his pipe, handling the archaeologist's knife and obviously happy with his work. A more ambitious undertaking was the restoration of the Lion of Amphipolis, near the Struma river in Eastern Macedonia, a gigantic monument commemorating a major battle of the Peloponnesian War in 422 B.C., in which Sparta's most able general, Brasidas, and the Athenian demagogue, Cleon, were both killed. With the ancient city of Amphipolis long abandoned, the Lion's fragments had for centuries been lying scattered in the brush, in an area inaccessible to the outside world. Impressed by what he saw, MacVeagh set out to have the Lion restored. He succeeded in enlisting the expert help of French archaeologists working at near-by Philippi, and of American engineers engaged in a major land reclamation project. He contributed toward the cost of the undertaking, and solicited funds from friends at home, small contributions coming from Eleanor and Hall Roosevelt. The project, which took several years to complete, earned MacVeagh the respect and affection of Greeks everywhere, and in January 1938 he was made an honorary fellow of the prestigious Archaeological Society of Athens. In bestowing the honor, the Society also acknowledged another "splendid example" of the MacVeaghs' "friendship for ancient as well as modern Greece": a volume entitled *Greek Journey* (Dodd, Mead, 1937), a delightful travel book for children written by the Minister and his wife, highlighting the sites of ancient Greece and their contemporary inhabitants. A frequent visitor to ancient Mycenae, MacVeagh became a friend and benefactor of its modern inhabitants, and helped finance the building of the village's church.

The various private American institutions operating in Greece found in MacVeagh a true friend. He was their frequent visitor, and did his best to offer advice and assistance whenever problems with the local authorities would arise, all along reminding his fellow Americans that they remained in Greece only at the sufferance of the Greek government. He was especially fond of the American schools, such as Athens College, the Junior College for Girls (then located at Hellenico), the American Farm School, and Anatolia College in Salonica, and took a personal interest in their development. In a despatch dated June 6, 1935, he reported: "Anatolia College, which I visited at Commencement last year, I found making excellent progress in its building. I went over the entire lay-out, visited classes, and so forth, and was confirmed in my belief that Dr. Riggs, the President, is an excellent leader. Particularly striking is his ability to work well with the local authorities in sometimes very difficult circumstances. . . ." (33)

✧

In the aftermath of the March revolt, the question of the monarchy's restoration clearly overshadowed every other issue. The King's champions were Metaxas, who in parliamentary debate took an openly pro-royalist position (thereby violating the Assembly's standing rule not to consider constitutional revision), and General Kondylis, the powerful Minister of War. British diplomatic circles were reportedly dropping broad hints that the monarchy was the country's best guarantee of stability and progress. Even Venizelos, from the safety of Europe's principal capitals, was rumored to have indicated his grudging consent to the King's return, in exchange for royal consideration for the Liberal Party.

Elections to a new Assembly were first scheduled for June 2, 1935, but were postponed by Tsaldaris till the 9th, to allow the Opposition parties to organize their campaign. This conciliatory gesture was to no avail. At Venizelos' insistence, the Liberal Party abstained, protesting that its leaders, only recently released from confinement (following their trial for the March 1 events) had had no time to resume normal political activity. To no one's surprise, Metaxas conducted a vigorous pro-royalist campaign, extolling the monarchical principle and implying that the issue was essentially already decided. As for the aging and ailing Tsaldaris, he had no particular desire to see the fires of constitutional conflict rekindled, and was personally content to govern the country under the trappings of presidential republicanism. However, more and more of his Populist followers were being attracted to the monarchy's cause, forcing the Prime Minister to include in his campaign promises a statement that he would hold a referendum on whether the King should return.

With the Venizelists taking no part, the election returns held no great interest. The government forces, combining Tsaldaris' Populists and Kondylis' personal following, received about 65 percent of the vote, the royalists under Metaxas and Rallis 15 percent of the vote, the communists 9.5 percent of the vote, with the rest going to lesser groups. The electoral law favored the strong: out of three hundred Assembly seats, the government won two hundred and eighty-seven, the royalists won seven, and there were six independent deputies. On July 10, as its first order of business, the Assembly voted to hold the referendum on the restoration of the monarchy by November 15. It then declared itself in recess until October 10.

It was not destined to be a quiet summer. With most political figures away from Athens, persistent rumors began to circulate that the military would bring the King back without the benefit of a referendum. Senior officers were said to be conspiring to compel the Prime Minister to cancel the referendum, and to restore the monarchy by decree, a move which was certain to be endorsed by the new Assembly. Royalists appeared to fear that in a fair expression of the popular will, their cause would suffer a humiliation.

Returning from abroad on September 9, Tsaldaris was warned by loyal supporters that a military coup was in the last phase of preparation. But when the Premier sought to foil such plans by transferring from key commands certain suspected officers, General Kondylis as Minister of War vetoed the measures, thus leaving the government at the mercy of the conspirators. Under pressure, the cabinet moved up the date of the referendum to November 3. Undaunted, republican leaders Papanastasiou, Sofoulis, Papandreou, Mylonas, and others prepared to campaign against the monarchy's restoration, and appealed to King George not to consent to be returned by decree, but to abide by the nation's will. Above all they insisted, and Tsaldaris heartily agreed, the referendum must be genuinely fair, and must leave no doubt as to its mandate. They were to be bitterly disappointed.

On the morning of October 10, while motoring to his office, Tsaldaris was stopped on Kifissia Boulevard by Generals Papagos and Reppas and Admiral Economou who "invited" him to return to his residence to discuss certain pressing matters. Once there, the three officers demanded that Tsaldaris declare the monarchy restored by decree. When he refused, reiterating his determination to honor his pledge and hold a genuine referendum, he was informed that the armed forces were seizing control of the country. Tsaldaris appealed to Kondylis to help restore the government's authority, but the General made it plain that his loyalty lay elsewhere. Refusing to resign, Tsaldaris announced that his cabinet had been forcibly overthrown. A new government was promptly formed, with Kondylis as Premier and Minister of the Navy, Papagos as Minister of War, and Theotokis as Minister of Foreign Affairs. The cabinet's first act was to declare martial law, an ominous sign to all those still hoping for a fair referendum.

The new government took the oath of office before the Assembly, which was convened for that purpose on the evening of October 10, and was dismissed immediately afterward. In a dramatic move, Tsaldaris rose to defend his conduct, and to warn that the return of the King by means other than a genuine expression of the nation's will would do irreparable harm to the country as well as to the monarchy. He then walked out, followed by the vast majority of the deputies present. To the remaining deputies, Kondylis declared the dissolution of the Republic, and promised that the referendum would be held on November 3 as scheduled. In case anyone doubted its outcome, Kondylis also informed his cheering audience that in the meantime he was assuming the royal prerogatives.

Advising the Department of these momentous developments, MacVeagh, by now an authority on Greek coups, observed on October 14:

Paradoxically enough, one thing which undoubtedly aided General Kondylis and his henchmen in maintaining order was the apathy and disgust of the majority of the onlookers at this new proof of the ineptitude of self-government in Greece. Even the hoodlums, with whose hired aid Mr. Metaxas is accustomed to fan the questionable loyalties of Omonia Square, failed to rouse much enthusiasm for Kondylis' latest coup. The chauffeur of the American Consul General saw Mr. John Rallis firing off a pistol in the street and shouting "Cheer, you people, cheer!"—but he reports that the people on the pavement merely stared at him, as at one gone mad. I have already intimated to the Department that the prevalent sympathies in Greece are probably republican at the present time. But there seems to be also a feeling very much like shame in the breasts of many Royalists. The British Minister remarked to me at the very moment when, unknown to us, Mr. Tsaldaris was being turned out of office by a Revolutionary Committee of Officers: "They are all savages, and I don't care to live among savages." Perhaps the lack of enthusiasm for a brilliantly executed overthrow of the established order, which some years ago would have stirred to frenzy the Hellenic breast, may indicate an advance in a peculiarly backward portion of the Greek mind which has remained stationary since at least the sixth century B.C. But on the other hand, it may simply betoken a knowledge that—"who overcomes by force hath overcome but half his foe," and disgust over the unwisdom of sowing the wind only to reap the whirlwind. The former interpretation has been pressed on me; I am inclined to vote for the latter.

Since the completion of the *coup d'état*, I have consulted with all of my principal colleagues and ascertained the views of nearly all the others. The consensus of opinion seems to be that the new Government is at present established and may expect to maintain itself for the time being on the basis of the watchfulness of the new Premier and Regent, and the consequent inability of the Opposition groups to meet and organize. At least for the moment we may expect a respite from uncertainty. With the military spirit predominant we may even find it easier to transact business with the various Ministries than has been possible under the procrastinating rule of Tsaldarist politicians. The Government has begun, without losing a moment, to prepare the path for returning Royalty. Court decisions henceforth are to be in the King's name and prayers for the Royal Family have been reinstated in the Liturgy. Citizenship and other rights have been declared as *ipso facto* restored to the Royal princes and princesses, and it is rumored that back salary for the King is to be forthcoming. But still it is not known whether the King will consent to return. His throne is being prepared. Will he sit on it?

The Department may have been puzzled by the fact that the movement, undertaken apparently because of the Premier's insistence on holding the plebiscite instead of recalling the King by vote of the Assembly, resulted in a renewed insistence on the plebiscite method of effecting the Restoration. But General Kondylis' speech quoted above lets the cat out of the bag. He said that Mr. Tsaldaris "manifested no disposition to proceed to a plebiscite." Such a conclusion could certainly not be deduced from any of Mr. Tsaldaris' published words. But his opponents had come to realize that he really wished all along "to postpone the plebiscite in the interest of calm," as he said to me himself, and they knew that the nearest he ever got to saying "no" was to say "postpone." He was therefore removed so that the recall of the King might be a certainty, and the plebiscite method of recall was purposely left in as a part of the program because the King is said to demand such an evidence of the popular will, and because of the better color it lends to the whole proceedings. In other words, Mr. Tsaldaris was not thrown out because he wanted the plebiscite, but because he was suspected, with probable truth, of not wanting it. Let it be his political epitaph that he saw clearly the danger to his country of such an adventure as that on which his zealous erstwhile friends are now embarked, and when pushed to the wall at last, had the courage to refuse to join.

As for Mr. Zaimis, the aged President of the Republic, he faded from the picture, as he has been fading from life itself these past few years, with hardly a word. Called upon by Messrs. Kondylis, Theotokis and Mavromichalis at his home in Phaleron, and informed that he was no longer President, as the Republic no longer existed, he sighed and said: "There is no other way," his words having the oracular sound and inadequate sense of the last words of dying men already half way over to the other shore. (34)

All through the summer and fall there was a great deal of speculation as to Britain's position on the issue of the Greek King's fate. It was generally assumed that London was quietly working to assure his return to Greece at the earliest possible moment. On the other hand, London's Minister in Athens, having indignantly announced to his American colleague that he did not care to live among savages, also gave him a rather strange version of British thinking on the restoration of the monarchy. As MacVeagh reported:

[October 10, 1935]

He said that he was convinced that the return of the King would be a "calmity" and that he was so advising the Foreign Office. He also told me that the King of England, with whom he talked on the matter, told him that he was endeavoring to persuade George II "to be sensible" and not get himself into difficulties. When I asked the Minister what he thought would happen here if the King should not return, he said: "Anarchy for a while," and "Sooner or later the Republicans *must* return to power."

The British diplomat agreed with MacVeagh that there was no strong sentiment in Greece favoring restoration, and that the "agitation for the King's return is the work of a few highly placed people, mostly in Athens Society and in the Army." He predicted that Metaxas would emerge as the undisputed leader of the royalist forces. He volunteered the undiplomatic view that the Greek King was "a thoroughly incompetent person, wholly incapable of uniting the turbulent Greek people." Transmitting his colleague's comments to Washington, MacVeagh observed:

The cautionary attitude which he ascribes to the King of England, and his own very definite opinion as British representative in Greece are both "news" from the point of view of Athens, where it has been thought that the King's relations were pressing him to return and that the British attitude toward the Restoration was favorable. With the British Government and Royal House fully apprised of the situation as it actually exists in Greece, we may possibly witness a refusal of the King to respond even to the handsomest invitation that his friends can arrange. (35)

With the referendum still about one week away, MacVeagh was treated to a full view of the government's intentions and of British diplomatic gyrations. On October 26, in a despatch entitled "The Restoration *ante facto*," he wrote:

Last night, in the course of a conversation at the British Legation, Mr. Theotokis, the Foreign Minister, confidentially informed Sir Sidney Waterlow, the British Minister, and myself that the Government was in receipt of a communication from the King indicating His Majesty's willingness to reassume the crown and requesting to be advised of the Government's ideas regarding the time and method of his return. Mr. Theotokis went on to say that the Government was elaborating a reply, in which Sunday, November 17th, would probably be suggested as the date of the King's return here. According to the Government's plan, he said, His Majesty would be accompanied home by a small delegation, consisting probably of the President of the National Assembly, a Minister representing the Government, and a General representing the armed forces of the nation. He would be met at Brindisi by the cruiser *HELLI* and two destroyers. A simple ceremony would take place at the dock at Phaleron, and the King would then lay a wreath on the Unknown Soldier's tomb in Athens, after which he would proceed to the Palace and receive the members of the Government and the Diplomatic Corps. Mr. Theotokis emphasized the fact that the plan called for the minimum of pomp.

Upon hearing this news, the British Minister earnestly requested Mr. Theotokis to inform His Majesty that his regime would have the full support of the British Legation and of himself personally. He also said that he feared the impression had gone about that the British Legation was against the Restoration. He wished, he said, to correct any such impression, adding that the Legation was interested only in the welfare of Greece. He again prayed Mr. Theotokis to assure His Majesty of his own personal desire, and that of the Legation, to help make the Restoration a success. Mr. Theotokis thanked him effusively for his kind words and promised to inform the King as requested.

Sir Sydney then went apart with me, and said that he had not changed his views on the situation (see my despatch No. 875 of October 10, 1935) but that as it now appeared that the Greeks were going to try the Restoration anyhow, it seemed best to help them make it a success in the interests of peace and quiet. It did not seem necessary for me to make any comment to the Foreign Minister on his interesting announcement, and I made none.

The Department will note that Mr. Theotokis' information reveals complete confidence in the favorable result of the approaching plebiscite, not only on the part of his Government but on that of the King himself, who has been supposed to be awaiting the popular verdict before making up his mind. Considering that the country is normally at least fifty percent Republican and that many erstwhile Tsaldarists have now declared themselves of that faith, nothing could be more indicative of the farcical nature of the forthcoming appeal to the people.

The general situation remains quiet. General Kondylis declared today a national holiday, to celebrate the taking of Salonica in the Balkan Wars, and improved [took advantage of] the occasion to mount a review of the Athens troops. The leading Opposition figures are all under police surveillance, and other individuals who might make trouble are being deported daily, usually on the charge of engaging in communistic activity. It seems highly likely that the Restoration is, as the British Minister said last night, already a *"fait accompli."* But if so, the fact remains that it has been brought about by a Government set up under military pressure by a Constituent Assembly elected by one party only, and irrespective of the result of the coming dubious plebiscite, it may be questioned whether a throne so based can long endure, even with the support of the British Legation. But much will depend on the King himself and what line he takes when he returns. (36)

In a letter to the President dated October 15, MacVeagh turned to the international scene, and stressed the alarming consequences of the recent Italian invasion of Ethiopia:

The Anglo-Italian situation continues loaded with dynamite in this part of the world, while war vessels of both navies prowl around fully equipped for any emergency. The British Minister here, who recently returned from London, tells me he thinks the danger of conflict is less than it was a while ago, but with so many people carrying weapons and nervously wrought up, we can never exclude the possibility of an "incident." The Greeks are acutely conscious of their exposed position, and the temptation which their many excellent harbors would be to both belligerents in time of war. The Italians have already anchored repeatedly in these harbors without asking the Greek Government's permission beforehand—a high-handed policy which they seem now to have abandoned under Greek protest, but which has inflamed the Greek press against them, and increased the normal dislike here, and distrust of Fascist Italy. Consequently Greece may be said to be, at the present moment, not pro-British certainly, but less disposed to criticize England than Italy in the situation which has arisen between them. She is desperately anxious to preserve her neutrality, and quite baffled as to how she is going to be able to do it, if war comes. The Turks seem to be very much in the same quandary. The Turkish Minister here came to see me the other day and bewailed the difficulty of his country's situation.

England has a great fleet, but Italy has converted the Islands of the Dodecanese into a powerful base only a few miles from the Turkish coast. It did not seem to console him to think that Italy is already using up a lot of money and men in Abyssinia. Incidentally, the British out here have quite frankly given Malta up for lost should hostilities break out with Mussolini. On account of the airplane and the submarine, there is a general feeling that Italian lines of communication will be preserved to a greater degree than British, at least at the outset, so that if any of the Near Eastern States join England at the start of an Anglo-Italian war they will risk receiving paralyzing damage before they can make their assistance felt to any great degree. Consequently we should expect them to do their best to remain neutral, at least till some decisive actions had been fought, or until time had made it possible to make a good guess as to the ultimate victor. (37)

As the results of the November 3 referendum were being made public, and with many details still unknown, the Legation telegraphed the

Department that the reported great victory of the royalists "cannot be accepted as a true indication of popular feeling. Many Republicans undoubtedly abstained from voting and plural voting by Monarchists appears to have been widespread, as well as intimidation at the polls, non-issuance of opposition ballots and other means of enforcing the Government's will." (38) Later MacVeagh gave a more complete account of one of Greece's most fraudulent ballots:

[November 9, 1935]

The result, in so far as it represented an overwhelming victory for the Monarchists, needs no comment, as such a victory has long been regarded as inevitable, but there are certain aspects which invite remark.

According to official announcements, the Monarchists received over 97 percent of the votes cast. The figures given are:

> For the Monarchy — 1,491,972
> For the Republic — 36,742

In this connection it may be noted that not only is the Monarchist majority so great as to "prove" Greece practically unanimous in its desire to see the King restored, but the figure given for the Monarchist vote is actually higher than the total vote cast by all parties together in any previous election in Greece, and this by no small margin but by over 400,000 ballots! There may therefore be some truth in the rumor that when shown the returns, General Kondylis, the Regent and Premier, expressed annoyance with his followers for "exaggerating."

Reports from trustworthy private sources indicate that there was widespread abstention on the part of Republicans. Republican leaders are said to have circulated, a short time before the plebiscite, various appeals to their followers not to participate in the voting. Though originally they had announced their intention to participate, these leaders are supposed to have changed their minds when the lifting of martial law was not followed by a restoration of the rights of free speech (see my despatch No. 905 of October 31, 1935).[16] Of course their appeals had to be circulated surreptitiously, and it is not known how many voters they actually reached or influenced. General Kondylis has announced that they "found no echo." But even without them, the conviction that votes for the Republic (colored bright red and clearly visible through the envelope) would be thrown out, and even fear of intimidation at the polls, seem to have been enough to keep a large part of the Opposition public away from the booths on election day, which passed with a notable lack of either enthusiasm or conflict.

On the other hand, plural voting by the Monarchists seems to have

---

[16] Not cited in this text.

been prevalent. As the Department is aware, such a practice is not new in Greece. But on this occasion it seems to have flourished with especial vigor. Conservative estimates place the average at three votes per man, with individual records as high as thirty.

Soon after the plebiscite, the Republican chiefs, Messrs. Papanastasiou and Papandreou, were allowed to return from their temporary exile in the Island of Mykonos, and the censorship of the press was announced at an end, though this must be taken with a grain of salt, in view of the fact that the omnibus decree providing for the maintenance of public order ... is still in force. The Regent has announced: "There are happily no longer any political parties in Greece today. The Greek people, in presenting itself at the polls as a unit, has destroyed them. A new political order began in our land of Greece from the day of the 3rd of November." Yet on the other hand, Mr. Tsaldaris and Mr. Metaxas met together on that very day, and from the accord which they are reported to have struck, and from other indications, it may be that the General's announcement that political parties no longer exist in Greece is at least premature.

The King's return has been expected to take place on the 17th of this month, but may be postponed until the 24th. His route will apparently be either via Belgrade and Split, or via Brindisi, and thereafter by the cruiser *Helli* to the hydro-airport at Old Phaleron. A delegation consisting of General Papagos, the Minister of War, Mr. Balanos, President of the Assembly, and Mr. Mavromichalis, Minister of Communications, has left for London to accompany him on his homeward voyage. The last mentioned, a pompous little man with a woman's hands and feet, told me the other day that he was so overcome with emotion at the thought of his mission that he feared he might break down and *become ridiculous*. It is also said that the King will go to Italy before returning to his throne, to visit the graves of his family among other things, thus giving proof of his piety as well as of an appreciation of his country's present difficult position in the field of foreign affairs. His visit should take place at about the same time that Greece, together with forty-nine other nations, begins to apply economic sanctions against Italy. Financial sanctions are already in force, in the form given them by a committee of the League presided over by Greece's representative. It is apparent that the King wishes to return wrapped in as much goodwill as possible. He has sent a message "To the Hellenes" which cites as his motto: "My strength is the love of my people." This has been the motto of his family for some time, I am told, and in the light of history, would seem singularly inept. But these are days of high Royalist hopes. So far, God has not yet been invoked as the Author of the Restoration. But He has at least been mentioned among those invited to attend.

Mr. Mavromichalis is reported to have said that the ceremonies attending the enthronement will be principally religious, "car les Grècs commencent toujours par Dieu." "The Greeks always start off with God." That word "always" opens up a long vista into the past. Certainly the god Hermes would have delighted in the recent plebiscite. If the potent rule of the Regent is not overthrown in the interim,—and such an eventuality, though improbable, cannot be left wholly out of account in so turbulent a country—it is expected here that the King will begin by accepting General Kondylis's advice. I have already referred to the possibility (see my despatch No. 905 of October 31, 1935)[17] of this advice including the dissolution of the present Assembly. It now seems that General Kondylis is intent on such a dissolution, the reason being that the present Assembly is too Tsaldarist for him to depend on when the King's advent makes a return to at least the semblance of democratic rule advisable. (39)

Reporting further on the attitude of the "British cousins," MacVeagh telegraphed on November 18:

I have been confidentially informed by the British Minister that his Government has instructed him to guide and counsel the King after his return but to do so without becoming involved in the internal affairs of Greece. According to his information from London the King is returning in a frightened condition, wholly at sea as to what line to take among the Greek politicians, and trusting nobody but the British. The Minister said that he would probably therefore have to advise the King in internal affairs although upon his own responsibility. The Minister has not yet decided whom to favor amongst the would-be Greek advisers of the King but stated definitely that Princes Andrew and Nicholas "must not" remain long in the country or mix in affairs. (40)

A few days before the expected arrival of King George, another despatch, dated November 21, 1935, gave a description of the preparations underway and of the mood in the capital:

The day of the King's return has been definitely set for Sunday the 24th of November. The main boulevards have been decorated with flags, and with arches and pylons of white plaster, and elaborate police regulations have been issued to safeguard the person of a monarch whose "strength is the love of his people." Unless the King himself changes the plans made for his reception, he will drive up to Athens from Phaleron

[17] Not cited in this text.

surrounded and accompanied by the military. All house-holders along his route have been required to furnish the names and address of every person expected to be on the premises Sunday morning. It may be that the authorities, remembering the fate of King Alexander in Marseilles, are taking wise precautions against communists, anarchists and madmen. But the whole affair breathes the spirit of the successful *putsch* of October 10th and has not escaped wide comment from this point of view. It is more likely that, having secured control of the Army, usurped the functions of Government, and justified their actions by the forced acclamations of an unrepresentative Assembly and bogus Plebiscite, the extremists of the Royalist Party are bringing back their King with every precaution against interference on the part of the vast numbers of their countrymen who are opposed to the proceedings and have never been consulted in regard to them. *Finis coronat opus.*

As far as this Legation has been able to learn, no one expects any disturbance during this last act of the Restoration Comedy. There is little animosity, or even active dislike, expressed toward George II personally, even in the most rabid Republican circles. He is deprecated, and even pitied, but not hated. But more important to his welfare is the military control exercised over the situation by the Regent and King-Maker, General Kondylis. Until the King is once more on the throne and becomes a factor in the political life of the country, this control seems likely to continue, despite recent signs of weakening. The Opposition press is becoming bolder in the face of summary laws "in defence of the realm," and the Regent has even been attacked with impunity in flaming editorials. But the curiosity of the Greeks to see what the King will do when he returns, and their love for parades and show of all kinds, have entered the lists on the Regent's side, and operate powerfully to keep the populace expectant and the Army quiet until the "sublime day," as Mr. Theotokis called it, has come and gone.

The same despatch, appropriately entitled "Venizelos Redivivus," lent credence to current rumors that Venizelos, the republican leader, still condemned to death, had privately communicated to the returning monarch his willingness to urge his supporters to acquiesce in the restoration. In return, the King would undertake to declare a general amnesty for those found guilty of the March revolt, and to free those who had been imprisoned for it. New elections would then be held, to enable the Liberal Party and other republicans to take their proper place in the National Assembly. Whether the King had accepted these terms was not known. In this connection, it was alleged that Venizelos did not desire amnesty for himself (at least for the time being), and that he had no plans to return to Greece in any event. Nevertheless, in the

American Legation's view, the reported "deal" with the King suggested that even from abroad, Venizelos had "reentered the scene of Greek politics at a critical moment in a manner full of possibilities." In a lighter vein, MacVeagh also passed along the report that Venizelos' desire to secure amnesty for the instigators of the March revolt was "largely because so many of them are now living [abroad] on his wife's bounty, and though her fortune is large it is not inexhaustible. . . ."

As for the King's preference for a government, the matter was far from clear:

> Of course, the whole situation is still on the knees of the Gods, in so far as no one can say what the King will actually do when he returns—whether he will attempt to go ahead with Tsaldaris and a semblance of popular rule based on a fraction of the electorate, or with Kondylis and a dictatorship based on the army and farcical elections, or whether he will throw both of these over and go to the people, as it were, with a non-partisan appeal. But while we await his return, we may do well to remember another factor which is likely to affect his decision in this instance, as well as his future in general. I would refer to my telegram No. 172 of November 18, 11 a.m., in which I informed the Department of the British Minister's instructions and feeling of personal responsibility in regard to advising the King. The British Legation here is convinced of a preponderance of Republican sentiment in the country, as well as of the immense difficulty of reconciling the warring elements among the Royalists. It may therefore be expected to exert whatever influence it wields in the direction of disentangling the King from party lines, and its chances of success in so doing would seem to be opportunely increased by the new Republican policy of tolerance. It may even be that this policy stems back to a common origin with the Minister's instructions, as Great Britain and Venizelos have been mutually helpful before this. (41)

At long last the royalists' "sublime day" had come and gone. With the monarch ensconced in his unpretentious palace a few houses away from the American Legation, MacVeagh dutifully reported:

[November 26, 1935]

King George II returned to Athens yesterday, Monday, November 25, after having delayed his announced arrival a full twenty-four hours on account of severe weather in the Adriatic. The weather was so severe that it may not be true that any part of the delay was owing to the King's fear of being sea-sick, as malicious tongues have said. But there can be no question that the postponement was psychologically unfortunate.

The King arrived and was finally installed in the palace without any incident of an untoward nature. On his return voyage he coasted by the shores of Corfu, and stopped a while in the harbor of Patras, both Corfu and Patras being supposed to be hotbeds of royalism. In Athens he found large crowds, many peasants having taken advantage of the reduced railway fares to see the town, but little enthusiasm. Curiosity and the holiday mood created by the display of bunting and the sound of bands, as well as by the presence of many strangers and a lavish show of uniforms, were the most sharply marked characteristics of his reception. There was none of that popular rejoicing which marked the return of King Constantine under similar circumstances.

The King was met at Old Phaleron at 8 a.m. by the Ex-Regent and Premier, General Kondylis, as well as by the rest of the Cabinet, the President of the Assembly, and other notables, and driven up to Athens with Crown Prince Paul at his side. At the Arch of Hadrian he was presented with the keys of the city by Mayor Kotzias, and then attended a doxology in the Cathedral. After this he laid a wreath on the tomb of the Unknown Soldier and stood for about three-quarters of an hour on the main balcony of the Parliament Building (the Old Palace), occasionally saluting the throngs in Constitution Square with a languid hand but making no attempt to address them. Finally, preceded by a squadron of cavalry and a number of Generals on foot, and followed by a fleet of automobiles, bearing other Generals and the newly created dignitaries of the Court, he and Prince Paul drove to the Palace. As I was privileged to watch him make his entry there from the garden of Mr. Maximos, which is next to the Palace grounds, I was able to appreciate personally the perfunctory nature of the proceedings and the lack of enthusiasm among the populace. By government command, everyone along the King's route had been forced to display a flag, and flags were put in the hands of the school children and the members of the various organizations stationed by order along the way. But the applause was little greater for the King, when he at last arrived, than for the Generals who preceded him. Curiously enough, the biggest spontaneous demonstration of the day seems to have been for Mr. Tsaldaris, in front of his apartment on Kifissia Boulevard some distance from the Palace.

No military review was held, and there was no marching, except by a few civilian royalist organizations (taxi-cab drivers, university students, etc.) and the Mayors of Greece with the immense Kotzias at their head, in high hat and dress-suit, and little Mayors of little villages bringing up the rear in derbies and slickers. At the same time, troops were everywhere, many of them, of course, guarding the line of march, and the extent to which military and naval rank clustered round the King left no doubt as to the power behind the Throne.

In conclusion, I would add that my German colleague, impressed by the listless attitude of the King, prophesied that either he will be out of the country in two weeks or there will be another dictatorship. Herr Eisenlohr may, however, have been reckoning without Mr. Venizelos and the British. Though it must be admitted that yesterday the King muffed a great opportunity to impress his personality on the people, it would appear that he still has a chance of success. By taking the path of compromise, he may yet extricate himself from party toils, and hoist himself, through the medium of a non-partisan Government and free elections, into a position above the *mêlée*, at least for a time. (42)

On December 9, President Roosevelt signed Minister MacVeagh's new letter of credence. Although the text was identical to that of June 23, 1933, this time it was addressed to His Majesty George II, King of the Hellenes, and concluded with the customary "May God have your Majesty in His wise Keeping." (43)

CHAPTER
III

Dictatorship: 1936-1939

As soon as King George had assumed his royal duties, the cabinet submitted its resignation. Before stepping down, Kondylis recommended to the monarch that parliament be dissolved, and that national elections be held promptly, to provide the country with a new legislature and with a government enjoying the confidence of both the electorate and the crown. Anxious to heal old wounds and in an effort to place himself above bitter partisanship, the King urged the outgoing government to proclaim a general amnesty for all those implicated in the March revolt. Such a move would open the way for Venizelists to take part in future cabinets. However, it immediately became clear that the King's wise proposal had powerful enemies among his staunchest supporters. Anti-Venizelist factions, led by Kondylis and Theotokis, the spokesman for an ultra-royalist group of Populist dissidents, warned that a general amnesty would be anathema to the military, who would oppose it by force of arms. Thus, the spectre of yet another coup hovered over the King's troubled head.

The Venizelists, to whom the King turned for support, were even less accommodating. One after the other, Sofoulis, Papanastasiou, Papandreou, and Kafandaris declined the invitation to a royal audience, protesting the manner in which the monarchy's restoration had been achieved. This impasse allowed the King no other choice but to entrust the formation of a temporary government to a politically neutral figure. Early in December, law professor Constantine Demertzis assumed the premiership, and proceeded to proclaim an amnesty for all civilians implicated in the March revolt; military conspirators were given a pardon, thus precluding their restoration to the ranks.

In a vain effort to keep himself in the picture, Venizelos protested from abroad that such a fine distinction between civilians and the military was a travesty of justice, since the convicted officers had merely carried out orders. But the aging Cretan no longer ruled his followers. In Athens Sofoulis promptly requested an audience, and informed the King that he was satisfied with the announced measures, and would support all efforts designed to bring about stability and unity. There was now a ray of hope that the King's program of national reconciliation might be given a fair chance.

The elections of January 26, 1936, based on a complex law of proportional representation, offered dramatic proof that the referendum of the previous year had been fraudulent, and that the nation remained fairly evenly divided between Venizelists-Liberals and their combined opponents. An accurate indicator of political loyalties, these election returns also proved the undoing of the two principal political parties, which, by refusing to collaborate, gave much smaller groups, and in particular the Communists, a disproportionately powerful bargaining position.[1]

With no party holding a clear majority, Sofoulis announced that the Liberals, for whom the constitutional issue was now formally closed, would agree to form a coalition government with the Populists. However, exploratory talks along these lines, which at first appeared to give promise of an early compromise, finally broke down. Still immersed in an atmosphere of mistrust, the Liberals and the Populists could not agree on the premiership, and could not find mutually acceptable persons for the key posts of Minister of the Interior and Minister of the Armed Forces.

In the midst of endless bargaining, the Greek political world was stunned by the sudden death, on January 31, of General Kondylis, one of the country's most politically powerful men. MacVeagh's report of February 8, 1936 captured the nation's mood in all its complexity:

The news spread like wildfire over Athens and throughout Greece. Signs of mourning were conspicuously absent. Many people were openly delighted and there was much talk, some witty and some only crude, about God's providence. As the Department knows, General Kondylis was an

[1] The election results were as follows:

Anti-Venizelists	% of vote	seats
Populists	22.10	72
Populist Radical Union (Kondylis, Theotokis, Rallis, Stratos, Tourkovasilis)	19.89	60
"Free Opinion" (Metaxas)	3.94	7
"Revisionists" (Kotzamanis)	1.40	4
		143
Venizelists		
Liberals	37.26	126
Democratic Coalition (Papanastasiou, Papandreou, Kafandaris)	4.21	7
Agrarians (Mylonas)	0.97	4
Democratic Union of Cretans	1.08	3
"Neo-Liberals" (Botsaris)	0.34	1
		141
Others		
Communists	5.76	15
Union Party (Kanellopoulos)	0.77	0
Independents	1.26	0

outstanding exponent of "direct action" in politics and constituted a standing threat to any government with which he was not in sympathy. In the present confused political situation his personal pique over his treatment by the King, whom he, more than anyone else, restored to the throne, coupled with the existence of a large number of disgruntled persons in the Army and Navy as well as civil life, made his organizing ability and his promptness and efficiency in revolution particularly dreaded. Greece, practically to a man, drew a breath of relief at his passing.

At the same time only the unthinking, or those incapable of thought, failed to realize, once he was gone, that here had been a remarkable man. In this little country General Kondylis was indeed a portentous personality. All the day following his death the Metropolitan Church, where his body lay in state, was thronged, not indeed by "a friendy concourse of the vulgar," but by a subdued crowd of persons of all conditions, who came less in curiosity,—that vice of Greeks and cats,—than in awe and a certain respect for the peasant boy who attained the crown, whose life was one long struggle—literally so—and who died on his feet. And when his funeral procession passed through Athens, such crowds thronged to witness it as have been rarely seen in this city. They watched it, if without weeping, yet with solemnity, not as a spectacle, but as an event.

The funeral services were conducted in the Metropolitan Church by the Archbishop of Athens assisted by a dozen clergy in gorgeous robes. Deputies and officers were conspicuous by their numbers, government officials and cabinet officers by their absence. The Chiefs of the Diplomatic Corps were invited to attend, and all did so except those who were ill or absent from Athens, and the British Minister, who sent his First Secretary to represent him. King George, however, was there in person. Mr. Theotokis, looking pale and ill, provided an anticlimax to the gorgeous and often thunderous Byzantine music by reading, in his cracked voice worn down with recent campaigning, an almost inaudible and much too lengthy allocution to the corpse. The latter lay exposed on a high catafalque between candles and rows of dignitaries, his bold Caesarian nose jutting up, defiant to the last, from among the wreaths. When all was over, the King made his way somehow through the crowd, from the place at the side where he modestly stood, turned for a moment in the open center of the church, crossed himself, and left, the most dignified figure of the most dignified day in Greece's recent history.

Altogether it was a strange ending to a strange career. As might be expected in Greece, dignity departed with the funeral car, which was attached to the Orient Express, taking the body of the hated, feared, ridiculed, and lastly honored man to his burial place in Trikkala, and Athens returned to its political preoccupations. The press started fighting over the General's corpse (a Greek habit at least as old as Homer) before it was cold. The struggle over his political heritage began almost as soon. Fortunately, the latter contest will be of small importance, since the political heritage in question is of the slightest [significance], Kondylis having been rather a party instrument than a party leader during all his years in politics. But the press has outdone itself, balancing outrageous abuse with laudatory pathos indescribable. "The death of Kondylis is a national calamity. History will judge his work and devote golden pages to it." (*Ethniki*). "History has gained a hero, and our political Pantheon a great statesman. But the fatherland and the Greek people have lost a patriot and a tender father." (*Hellenikon Mellon*). Let me close with that last phrase of truly Greek sublimity, and let the abuse be covered by the wreath which the King himself laid on the coffin of this hero of sorts. (1)

Writing to President Roosevelt, MacVeagh described the persistent troubles besetting King George, and expressed sympathy for the monarch's predicament:

[February 29, 1936]

You will remember that the King came back on the strength of a revolution supported by a bogus plebiscite. The British, whom he most admires (he told me himself that "We need more Anglo-Saxon ideas in this country"), are undoubtedly, as I wrote you, taking advantage of his being here for what it may be worth. But it can't be said to be worth much as yet. For in spite of newspaper correspondents, who see the restoration, à la E. Phillips Oppenheim, as a move in the British-Italian chess game, it was really, as I wrote you, a development of local politics, with its roots deep in the soil of recent Greek history, and only incidentally connected with foreign affairs. And it is because of the character of its local origin that it has been teetering on the verge between success and failure for months.

Whatever may have been the motives which led the King to accept the call of the plebiscite, the nature of which he probably understood then and certainly understands now, he has shown himself to be a serious-minded and genuine person determined to do his best as Monarch of the entire country and not simply of one party. He showed his attitude in this regard immediately on his return to Athens, when he insisted on amnesty and pardon for all persons, civil and military, who had been condemned for participation in the Venizelist revolt of last March. At the same time he himself has not gone over to the Venizelists, as his enemies say. He has criticized Mr. Venizelos to me personally and his aides have gone even further, so that I know where he stands. He is trying to be a non-partisan Greek. And it is precisely for this reason, which does him honor, that he has so far failed to achieve that prestige with the country which, among other things, would make him an asset rather than a liability to interested foreign friends. There is still a good likelihood that he will remain here. It would probably mean the ruin of any political leader to be implicated just now in a move to get rid of him. But I have yet to find a politician who will say he is satisfied with his attitude, and all the party chiefs without exception have openly ignored his personal appeal to their patriotism to bury the hatchet and get together. His program of uniting the Venizelist and anti-Venizelist factions and ruling over a pacified people has shown no signs to date of even beginning to work.

As soon as he was settled on his throne he dismissed General Kondylis, and others who had helped to effect his restoration, and who desired to run him in their own interests, and set up a temporary government of non-political personages, headed by a university professor. With this body of men in power he then proceeded to hold honest elections in the hope that the example set by him and Mr. Venizelos in composing their differences would appeal to the people and be reflected at the polls. Honest elections were indeed held, but the result was far from what the King anticipated. The proportion of Venizelist and anti-Venizelist voters was almost exactly what it was three years ago, approximately 50-50. All that had happened in the interval, including two armed revolts, with their aftermath of courts-martial, one bloodless revolution, and a restoration— not counting the reconciliation of King and Cretan—had changed the opinions of hardly a single Greek! One ray of hope, however, seemed to exist in the fact that while the Venizelist front was strongly united about the nucleus of one party, the Liberal, which obtained a large plurality of seats in the Assembly, the anti-Venizelists were broken into several groups along apparently irreconcilable party lines. It was therefore thought that the King might call on the Liberal leader to form a coalition government. The adhesion of only one of the anti-Venizelist groups was, in fact, all that was necessary to that end. But the danger of control by the hated Venizelists promptly drew the anti-Venizelist factions together, and over a month of parleying has done no more than emphasize the essential antagonism existing between the two fronts. Now, the not very hopeful expedient of convoking the Assembly and letting it thrash the matter out itself seems about to be tried. If, as is likely, the deputies reach the same impasse as exists at present between the party leaders, then it would seem we must go on with a government such as the existing one, which is at best a temporary make-shift, and satisfactory to nobody in a country where politics is one and the same thing with government.

Such is the situation. Naturally, the root of the whole trouble lies in fear. A coalition government might be possible if only a government did not necessarily control the army, navy and police! Neither side dares trust the other, even in a sworn cabinet, with these important portfolios—and particularly, it seems, with the portfolio of the Interior. For it is this last which has jurisdiction not only over the police and the gendarmerie, but over the election machinery of the country as well, and matters being what they are, new general elections are already being mooted. The fear, of course, concerns the future consequences of past actions. There is hardly a politician in Greece who has not been exiled or condemned to death, or had friends and relatives executed at the instigation of rivals, or has not done these things to others. And the same thing is true of all the higher officers of the Army and Navy. Such people do not imagine that just because the King, presumably in his own interests, has made it up with Venizelos, their own political enemies will follow suit and forgive past injuries. "Do not trust the false promises of the Venizelists!" cried Mr. Tsaldaris, the most moderate of the Antis, publicly in the last campaign. And so it goes.

As a result of this situation, and of the King's attitude, the erstwhile extreme Royalists are now the Crown's most bitter critics. Before his sudden death, which mercifully relieved the country of its greatest potential trouble-maker, General Kondylis publicly exclaimed that the King should be King of all the Greeks and not only of the Venizelists. On the other hand, Mr. Kafandaris, the veteran Republican ex-Premier and Minister of Finance, complained to me only the other night that the King was not acting properly. He was, so Mr. Kafandaris said, not taking a firm enough stand in opposing the absurd pretensions of the anti-Venizelists. When I said I supposed the King wished to stay apart and above party considerations, he remarked: "But he must take a stand somewhere!" And this, I think, shows where the present situation is really critical for the King. Willy-nilly, and by hook or by crook, the Greeks are trying to make a party man of him, and if they succeed in spite of his intentions, they will cook his goose for years in a repetition of King Constantine's fiasco. He is fighting his battle now to avoid such a fate, and the battle is not going very well.

However serious, Greece's domestic tribulations could not overshadow the uncertainties and dangers existing on the international scene. The latest crisis, precipitated by Italy's invasion of Ethiopia, threatened to engulf Greece in a power struggle from which she could not hope to emerge unscathed:

From the point of view of foreign affairs, Greece has been acting normally—though I would not imply by this that her troubled internal state is abnormal; far from it! Like all the little nations of the Near East and the Balkans, she sets great store by the League of Nations, which has helped her compose her difficulties with her neighbors time and again. In her view, she has simply got to stand by the League, and for that reason she subscribed to the sanctions against Italy, though she has hurt her trade thereby and has as yet received no compensation. For the same reason she answered England affirmatively when asked if she would live up to her military obligations under the Covenant if Italy attacked England as a result of the Sanctions. It is supposed that she has conferred with England as to what support she might render in such an eventuality. Indeed, the British Minister confidentially explained the recent visit of British destroyers here by saying that he had requested it for the purpose of exploring the possibilities of naval cooperation. But there seems to be no grounds for the story that some dicker has been made between the two nations—such as the cession of Cyprus in exchange for the use of Greece's western harbors. The British Minister has denied this to me, and besides there is no necessity for such action on England's part. The Greeks are strongly anti-Italian on the Abyssinian question, and do not forget what the Great War taught them in regard to their dependence on the power which controls the seas.

The recent revival in France of the policy, so actively pursued under Barthou, of encircling Germany with pacts, is causing some interest here, on account of the visit of King Carol to Yugoslavia after his conversations in Paris. It is felt that there may be a move on foot to get Bulgaria to join the Balkan Entente, two members of which, Rumania and Yugoslavia, are also members of the Petite Entente. Inasmuch as Bulgaria is suspected of still cherishing territorial designs, at the expense of Greece, by way of an outlet to the Aegean, Greek public opinion is somewhat restively awaiting clarification of this diplomatic activity. The German threat to the peace of Europe is so great in connection with the already critical Anglo-Italian situation that it is felt France may turn on considerable pressure to make her protective encirclement as complete as possible.

Finally, there was a bit of progress to report on the matter of the Greek debt:

> I was pleased and amused when the Greeks came forward the other day with another payment on account of interest on our Refugee Loan of 1929, which they persist in calling a War Loan. They insist that 35 percent of the interest is all they can pay on any of their foreign debt just now, and there may be some merit in the claim. The question is by no means clear. Certainly it would be political suicide for any government here to pay much more. What really counts in the circumstances is the continued recognition of at least one of their obligations. But I was amused because of

the kudos they have received. Apparently they figured correctly that most people would misunderstand the payment as being on account of war debts, on which Greece is actually in default, and thus she would share in some of the glory that has gone to Finland. Representative Shanley, of my State of Connecticut, waxed truly rhapsodical on the floor of the House in his eulogy of Solon, Pericles, Aristotle, Plato and Socrates. And it wasn't so long ago that we were lambasting the Greeks over the Insull affair! They certainly have a kind of small cleverness which it is hard to beat. But in doing what I believe to be the best they can to keep some shreds of credit, they show an appreciation of their situation which is gratifying. Hundreds of years of oppression have made them, as a people, prone to take quick profits at the expense of credit, and I am always trying to make them see that this is bad business, particularly in international relations with a great friendly country whose past benefits to Greece are as nothing to what the future may hold if they will play the game right.

With all best wishes for your health and success at all times, I am, Affectionately yours,

Lincoln MacVeagh (2)

The impasse caused by the election returns, and the subsequent inability of the two principal parties to agree on a coalition government, continued unresolved. The new parliament met on March 2, with no indication that a compromise was to be forthcoming. On the contrary, the capital was ablaze once again with rumors that the military were preparing to block any attempt to form a government of Liberals with the backing of communist votes. Giving weight to such speculation, General Papagos, Minister of War in the Demertzis cabinet, warned the King that any solution of the political crisis that allowed the Communists a say in the government's composition or program would be resisted by force.

Fearing a coup, the King boldly dismissed Papagos, and with the consent of Demertzis, entrusted the troublesome Ministry of War to General Metaxas. In the aftermath of such determined action, Sofoulis was elected President of the National Assembly, receiving the votes of all Venizelists, as well as the votes of thirteen Communists, and the votes of two former Kondylis supporters. The road now appeared open for a Sofoulis government, supported by the extreme Left. In fact, the King called on Sofoulis to form such a government. But a task that, under the delicate power balance at home would have been most difficult, was rendered impossible by external events. The sudden news, on March 7, of the German denunciation of the Locarno Pacts and the reoccupation of the Rhineland was received in Athens as a harbinger of all-out war. Therefore, an uneasy coalition, which excluded the Populists, now appeared to be an unwise course: the country was in need of a broadly based and strong government that could concentrate on defense preparations. The death of Venizelos in Paris, on March 18, added to the confusion in the ranks of his followers at home, weakening Sofoulis' hand. Left with no real alternative, Sofoulis recommended, and the King accepted, the continuation in office of Demertzis (who also took on the Ministry of Foreign Affairs), with Metaxas serving as Deputy Prime Minister and Minister of War.

Observing the turmoil from close range, MacVeagh, in a report to the Department, credited the beleaguered King with considerable acumen:

[March 10, 1936]

Outstanding in the present situation is the personality of the King. Owing to his courage and determination, he seems to be winning a special position of his own in the nation. He is cold and reserved in public, contrasting markedly in this respect with his father, Constantine. But he seems to be gaining the sincere respect of the people at large, which may mean more to him in the long run than such adoration as Constantine received from half the people while the other half detested him.

The politicians, however, are not satisfied with his attitude, and his immediate struggle is with them. It is obvious that what he is trying to do is to influence them without himself becoming allied with any party. Should they succeed in making a party man of him, he will be sooner or later doomed as King, as his father was. Up to now, he has held an even balance between the factions, but the dislike and distrust of the politicians has been his inevitable reward....

One would like to think that a man who can rise to situations as the King did the other day when faced by the recalcitrant officers will eventually become so strong with the people that he need have no fear of anyone. But that time is distant and the immediate difficulties are great, all the more so as George wishes to be a constitutional monarch, and not, as he showed the other day, a dictator. Constitutional Monarchs, whether they like it or not, must rule through politicians, and the Greek brand is likely to make no end of trouble for one who wishes, to quote the King again, to have "More Anglo-Saxon ideas in this country." (3)

But misfortune evidently was conspiring against the King and his unruly subjects. The delicate balance of political forces, which, for the moment at least, tottered upon the all-important person of an apolitical premier, came crashing down under the impact of the least expected event. On April 13, Demertzis was found dead in his bed, the victim of a heart attack, very probably brought on by prolonged nervous strain and total exhaustion. The King now named Metaxas premier. In doing so he acted on his own, unwilling to consult the leaders of the major parties and the officers of the newly elected parliament. The move, which violated tradition and the spirit, if not the letter, of the constitution, was greeted by a chorus of protests, as the nation was reminded of Metaxas' open advocacy of dictatorship in years past. But dislike for Metaxas was the only point upon which the Liberals and the Populists could agree. Within days they had returned to their favorite game of charge and counter-charge. On April 23, the Populists launched a vicious attack upon Sofoulis, charging him with secretly plotting an unholy alliance with the Communists, to gain their support for the premiership. The bitter debate in Parliament, which ended in a vote exonerating Sofoulis, disclosed that Populist leaders had also engaged in similar negotiations with the Communists. Seemingly bent on mutual destruction, the two parties played perfectly into the hands of their only true enemy. Unhindered by any effective opposition, Metaxas presented a program of governmental action stressing economic and defense priorities, and received an overwhelming vote of confidence. (The sixteen negative votes included those of Papanastasiou, Papandreou, and Mylonas.) Exhausted from the otherwise fruitless debate, the Assembly also voted to recess until September 30, thus, in effect, granting the new Prime Minister extraordinary powers. The door to dictatorship was now ajar. The excuse to swing it wide open would not be difficult to find.

Reporting to the President on Greece's domestic troubles and external dangers, MacVeagh revealed a growing respect for the King, and a willingness to keep an open mind about the new premier. On April 30, he commented:

> Since I last wrote, things have moved along here at a merry rate. You will remember that I described to you the difficulties besetting the King in his attempts to unite the country under his leadership as a constitutional monarchy. Shortly after I wrote, a group of the highest officers in the army, navy and aviation, hearing that a continuation of the King's conciliatory policy would result in reintegration in the army forces of the seditious officers whom they themselves exiled or condemned to death last year, called on the King, and demanded a dictatorship. The sequel shows pretty well the King's calibre. He had no time to ask advice of those who are supposed to be his mentors, such as the British Minister. He replied at once: "Who will be the Dictator?" "You will be," they said, "if you will stand with us."
>
> You may remember what I said in my last letter about the King's greatest difficulty being to remain non-partisan. Here he was faced with it in an acute form.

"Let me think over your proposition, Gentlemen," he said. "Give me twenty-four hours." They agreed and withdrew. Whereupon the King immediately seized the telephone and called up Professor Demertzis, the Premier, and ordered him to secure at once the resignation of General Papagos, the Minister of War, and General Platis, the Under-Minister. The truth was that both these men really belonged to the Kondylis faction of die-hard anti-Venizelists (which the King had turned out at the time of his restoration) but had played a double game, pretending to be the King's men while preparing the way to force him to be their partisan. It was this fact to which the King now suddenly woke up, and they and their bold officers found themselves figuratively in the street. "Send General Metaxas to me," went on the King, and in a jiffy Greece had a new Minister of War and Vice President of the Council; and very shortly thereafter this man became Minister of Marine, and temporary Minister of Aviation, as well.

One might describe the above as a *coup d'état* with a reverse English on it. The ball was struck but went the other way. General Metaxas was formerly King Constantine's Chief of Staff. Latterly he has been only one of the smaller political figures in Greece, eclipsed first by Venizelos and then by Tsaldaris. He has a following of only six deputies in the Chamber. But when the King, in order to come back made it up with the exiled but powerful Venizelos, Metaxas alone among the old Royalists jumped with him. He has proved himself indeed the King's man and has reaped his reward. He is a good soldier and a disciplinarian, and seems now to have the army in his fist. His assumption of the War and other Ministries greatly strengthened the King's nonpartisan government. And when Professor Demertzis died suddenly on Easter Monday, General Metaxas took over the Premiership and the Ministry for Foreign Affairs as good measure—and running over!

At that time, the King's plan was to have his non-partisan government receive a vote of confidence from the Chamber, which would thereafter adjourn till the fall. The inability of the various party-leaders either to form a one-party government or a coalition made this program advisable if not, indeed, inevitable, while the death of Mr. Venizelos seemed to herald considerable political changes, the extent of which cannot be immediately foretold. General Metaxas took over this program, and while he has received rather a vote of tolerance than of confidence— owing to the fact that he is himself a politician and therefore hardly to be called "non-partisan"—he may, according to present indications, run Greece until the first of October, when new elections will be in order. Of course, the Chamber may try to tie some strings to his power before it finally adjourns, but if it gets too rambunctious the King may dissolve it altogether.

In the realm of foreign affairs, Greece is still, so far as Italy is concerned, in England's boat. The King has actually admitted as much to a friend of mine, but the fact is evident and inevitable as long as England controls the sea. Germany's action in flouting the treaties of Locarno and Versailles, has, on the other hand, complicated the general situation immensely. It has caused Turkey to ask permission to refortify the Dardanelles, aroused revisionist ambitions in Bulgaria, and brought sharply to the fore again, in Greek foreign policy, the question of the Balkan Pact.

As you will remember, that pact, signed by Rumania, Turkey, Yugoslavia and Greece, guarantees the status quo of Balkan boundaries. It was conceived originally as an extension of Titulescu's francophile policy and aimed to isolate Bulgaria. On account, however, of the possibility of Italian aid to Bulgaria should the latter attempt to break her bonds, a secret military protocol seems to have been attached to the pact, according to article 3 of which the signatory powers are bound to make war on a non-Balkan power should such a power aid a Balkan power in an attempt to change the boundaries guaranteed.

The existence of this secret protocol, which seems to have been signed in Geneva in June, 1934, has long been regarded among us foreigners as an open secret, and recently the Greek Government in official communiques has actually referred to it and to article 3 (though the Turkish Minister here looked me in the eye and said he couldn't imagine what was meant!). There are *soi-disant* copies of it in our files here and in Washington. It seems to have been this protocol, rather than the Pact itself, which led Venizelos, who dreaded anything tending to embroil Greece with Italy, to launch a terrific attack on the ratification of the Pact by Greece two years ago, forcing the Foreign Minister, Mr. Maximos, to make a declaration before the Chamber to the effect that nothing in the Pact obligated Greece to make war on a non-Balkan State. And it was only on the strength of that declaration that the Government secured ratification.

Recently, only a short time before he died, Mr. Venizelos returned to the question and charged, what has not been denied by the Government, not only that Mr. Maximos signed a document (the secret protocol) at Geneva in contravention of his statement before the Chamber, but that he made no written reservations in keeping with that statement, and that therefore Greece stands committed under certain conditions to fight a non-Balkan power under the provisions of the Balkan Pact. Mr. Maximos replied, rather weakly, that he made "verbal reservations" as to article 3 and so reported by telegram to his Government. But no copy of his telegram exists in the government's files, the Venizelist press has branded him as a traitor, and altogether there has been a sweet to-do!

A secret meeting of the Government and the Party leaders has now resulted in the publication of a statement that all is well, and that Greece stands by the Pact and is not committed in the sense indicated by paragraph 3 (which is often referred to but never quoted!) and the up-shot is that Greece's allies are puzzled as to how one can sign and not sign at the same time, and Mr. Metaxas, the present Premier, is going to attend the meeting of the representatives of the Balkan Entente at Belgrade next week and try to explain his country's position—if he can!

The situation is indeed ticklish for Greece. To have the Balkan Pact dissolve away would be a calamity for her, vulnerable as she is not only by sea but along her northern border. Yet she cannot support a policy which may lead her to cross swords with Italy, if she has only Balkan States to back her. Thus in the face of renewed Bulgarian hopes of eventually reaching the Aegean, which have been stirred up by what is going on in Central Europe, she is trying to have her cake and eat it too, to enjoy the secure possession of Greek Macedonia and Thrace by the help of allies whom she herself is not willing to support wholeheartedly.

All this might conceivably be called a tempest in a teapot. But the Balkan Entente is, as you know, tied in with the Little Entente by the participation of Yugoslavia and Rumania, and the above represents the progress of one of those cross-currents which seem threatening the whole structure of French-inspired regional pacts encircling the danger zone of German ambitions. That the current sets from the direction of Italy may be a sign of the times. Perhaps Greece should be forgiven if her foreign policy seems a bit erratic just now. As I wrote before, it is necessarily anchored to England on the one hand and the *status quo* on the other, and one if not both of these rocks would appear to have come somewhat unstuck. One remembers the wobbliness, and importance, of Greek foreign policy in the first years of the World War.

The Greco-Turkish treaty of friendship does not at present show the same shakiness as the Balkan Pact. As peoples, the Greeks and Turks don't love each other. They could hardly be expected to. But economically the two countries are rather complementary than otherwise, Turkey being more of a producer and Greece controlling the carrying trade. Also both countries fear Italy and Bulgaria. Consequently when Turkey the other day, in gentlemanly fashion (compared with Germany) asked permission to refortify the Straits, the Greek Government immediately expressed its sympathy with the Turkish point of view. The general assent to the Turkish proposition is another sign of the times. Turkish feelers in that direction were not similarly encouraged a year ago. Europe seems rapidly reaching a sort of "scrap-of-paper" stage by mutual consent (or necessity?), and allies are being sought on the basis of "what armaments have you got?" rather than "what have you signed?" Observers here feel that

80 · CHAPTER III

Mussolini has bluffed England out on the Abyssinian question and that the next war will at least not start in that quarter. Eyes are rather on Germany and Central and Eastern Europe.

Economically and financially, Greece is in pretty good condition. Too much of her population is concentrated in Athens, and the housing boom is a cause for uneasiness. But in general she is doing well. The Finance Minister is going to London shortly to discuss with the English Committee of the holders of Greek bonds the possibility of increasing the present percentage of payment. His main argument against doing so is likely to be the necessity of increasing the appropriation for national defense. At the same time, the Greeks don't want to be too intransigent, as they undoubtedly wish to work along gradually towards a general reconsideration, and writing down, of their whole foreign debt. Perhaps the most outstanding recent development of their economic and financial situation, however, is the extent to which they have fallen into the hands of the Germans, through the working of the 100 percent clearing arrangement between the two countries. Germany has for the past year and a half been buying Macedonian tobacco of even the poorest grades (we take the best) at fantastic prices. The Bank of Greece pays the producers in drachmas and gets credit in Berlin in blocked Reichsmarks. This enables Germany to bring pressure on the Greek import trade and flood the country with a lot of poor stuff at high prices, and still, in spite of all Greece can do, the amount of her credits in Germany increases. The Bank of Greece recently tried to take measures to correct the situation, but political pressure from the tobacco regions put a stop to that, and as a result the Government has had to step in and take the responsibility; borrowing the Bank's credits in Berlin and promising to do something to ameliorate the situation when present crops are exhausted!

I have already written too much, and I will spare you other details, such as how the past months of uncertainty have encouraged the Communists, and the great number of strikes which we have had in consequence. In general, we cannot say that the country is badly off, and it plays no observable part in causing the present troubles, but it is so placed that it reacts in some way or other to nearly every current of unrest in Europe today, and as you know there are a lot of these. (4)

To the Department, MacVeagh pointed out that with Parliament in a prolonged recess, governmental authority in Greece was assuming definite dictatorial features:

[May 2, 1936]

In accordance with the wishes of the Government, the adjournment was taken for five months, and full legislative powers were voted to the

Government for the duration of that period "with the assistance of" a parliamentary committee of forty members.

As was expected, the Government's program met with plenty of opposition. The Department is aware that the present "non-partisan" Government has been run as a virtual, if temporary, dictatorship of the King—though, judging from the headway made by the latter in the general esteem, and the weariness of the electorate after a troubled year, it might be qualified as a dictatorship with the consent of the dictatees. The King's program has been to impose his national sedative of conciliation through the medium of his hand-picked government, profiting by the squabbles of the professional politicians to bend if not mould the latter to his will. In obtaining practically a free hand for five months he has now apparently gained a great victory. But to do so he had to use the steamroller. I talked with Mr. Tsaldaris for a moment Thursday morning while the session was still in progress, and he said "I am for the Government, but *it can't have its way in everything*." Propositions were put forward to limit the recess to three months; to make all the government's acts subject to the approval of the Parliamentary Committee; and to make it mandatory for the Parliament to be summoned in session at any time upon the petition of a certain number of members. It was even proposed to free certain parliamentary decrees from the necessity of royal approval. But these struggles of the politicians came to nothing in the end, as there seems to be no question but that General Metaxas had the King's order for dissolution in his pocket all the time, and that he has very definitely consolidated the Army for the time being in support of his Master's wishes.

Under other circumstances, the existence of the Parliamentary Committee might efficiently qualify the plenary powers of the Government. As it is, we can hardly expect the Committee to be stronger than the Parliament from which it springs. It will advise the Government in regard to measures of a dangerously controversial nature, such as those dealing with political amnesty and the reestablishment of officials cashiered for participation in the revolt of last year, and even the officer question referred to so often in my previous political despatches. Thus it seems admirably conceived to form a political buffer for the Government, but that it will have any decisive effect on policy is not to be imagined. As I have already informed the Department, the King "dislikes politicians," and General Metaxas is a glutton for responsibility.

In addition to granting full legislative powers to the Government, and saving its face with its precious Committee, this naughty but finally obedient Parliament established a committee of forty members, including the party-chiefs, to prepare a revision of the Constitution of 1911, now the basic law of the land, to suit present conditions. It also voted by a small majority to maintain the proportional system in national elections.

General Metaxas leaves tonight for Belgrade in company with Dr. Aras,[2] who arrived this morning from Ankara. When the General comes back, after doing his best to explain to his colleagues of the Balkan Entente just how Greece stands in regard to the Pact of Understanding, we shall begin to see what progress, if any, the King can make in giving this country "more Anglo-Saxon ideas." (5)

In retrospect, there can be little doubt that, once in office, Metaxas had every intention of seizing complete control and imposing a personal dictatorship. In this, the "Greek Moltke" was motivated by a life-long contempt for the parliamentary process and, conversely, by a profound admiration for Europe's fascistic regimes. Beyond his contempt for the weaknesses of the democratic way, he was convinced that the tense international situation, which could erupt into war at any moment, necessitated a highly centralized and politically uninhibited authority in Athens, capable of preparing the country for war. He genuinely believed in his personal mission, as the nation's savior from the vicissitudes of representative government, and from the vulgarity of partisan politics. With Parliament in recess, and his traditionally high prestige among the military now tremendously enhanced by his rapid rise to power, he was faced with only one real obstacle: the King's objection to dictatorial rule. But the Hamlet-like figure of the Greek monarch was no match for the wily Metaxas, whom he had eagerly elevated to the highest political office as a guarantor of stability and order. In a matter of weeks, King George concurred with his premier's determination that social unrest in the country, coupled with the growing external dangers, called for extraordinary measures of control. "Proof" that the country was in the throes of "revolution" was provided by a series of strikes, culminating in bloody incidents in Salonica in May.

Early in the month, tobacco workers across the country had gone on strike, demanding that the industry raise their wages under the terms of a 1924 agreement. On May 8, when the government's feeble mediation efforts had failed, about six thousand tobacco workers gathered in Salonica and prepared to march on the Government Building, to present a petition with their demands. The local authorities forbade the march, and when the order to stop it was ignored, the police dispersed it by force, breaking some bones and bloodying a few heads in the process. Although initially the tobacco workers had failed to generate much sympathy for their cause, their treatment at the hands of the police enraged other groups, and by nightfall, railroad men, public transportation personnel, and power company workers had declared a 24-hour sympathy strike.

---

[2] Dr. Tevfik Rüştü Aras, Turkish Minister for Foreign Affairs.

The next morning, in their new march on the Government Building, they were joined by dock hands, bakery and textile workers, and other groups totalling about 25,000. Their mood was ugly, and the canes and sticks in their ranks showed that they were out to even scores. In the face of a mass demonstration, the police authorities took extraordinary measures, and the government ordered Salonica's Third Army Corps placed on alert. A clash was now inevitable. When the demonstrators attempted to storm a police armored vehicle blocking their way, they were repulsed by rifle fire, and mounted police chased the scattering crowds, their sabres slashing about indiscriminately. In a few hours, the bloody count was twelve dead, and thirty-two seriously wounded, all demonstrators. Scores of others received minor injuries. The rage of the police was such that military units had to be moved between the police and the crowds. The government ordered the police confined to their stations, and turned the situation over to the Third Army Corps. For a moment, the move appeared to have been a mistake, as soldiers showed signs of siding with the demonstrators. All authority had now collapsed. Thoroughly alarmed, the government despatched naval units to Salonica, and fresh troops with artillery moved north from Larissa. However, these measures soon proved unnecessary. Order was restored by the local military commander, assisted by Salonica's political leaders, who prevailed upon the angry mob to return to their homes. Significantly, when the Communists attempted to capitalize on the popular mood and introduced revolutionary slogans, their agitators found their audiences unresponsive and dwindling rapidly. This had been a local demonstration of labor grievances and of popular anger against police practices, not the start of a social revolution. On May 11, the government announced that the demands of the tobacco workers had been granted, thus bringing the strike to an end.

Eyewitnesses of the Salonica riots included Minister MacVeagh, who arrived in the city on the 9th (the second day of the troubles), on a tour of Macedonia. In his lengthy report to the Department, based in large measure on the views of the local authorities, of American tobacco merchants, and of diplomats, he attempted to explain the events at hand, as well as their root causes:

[Athens, May 29, 1936]

The morning of May 9th was an exciting one in Salonica. Events moved rapidly to a climax, which arrived when a huge crowd in which Vice-Consul McGonigal and several American tobacco men were caught, attempted to approach the Government House to present their grievances. The *Gendarmerie*, their nerves frayed by constant duty during the minor disturbances of previous weeks, appear to have been deliberately goaded into shedding blood. The rioters were not armed, but the first shot of the day seems to have been fired by an unknown person, neither policeman nor soldier, and was aimed into the heart of the crowd from a window above the street. The British Consul General told me that he personally saw this shot fired and that it was only afterwards that the police opened up. Its sporadic volleys and isolated shots were clearly audible at the hotel where I was staying in company with a number of tobacco men, engineers and archeologists. The presence of communist agitators in the crowd is attested [to] by eye-witnesses, and the prompt use made of the blood and corpses of the "martyrs" in exciting to further riot may likewise point to staff work behind the demonstration. Cries of "Long Live Spain!" seem to have been frequent. The action of the *Gendarmerie* in shooting to kill soon dispersed this, the most dangerous gathering of the day, but caused such bitter resentment that the Army had to be called upon almost immediately, and the strike went on smouldering under military repression for a much longer period than might have been the case if the authorities had not been so slow in realizing the seriousness of the situation and had not exposed the already much-tried local police to overwhelming odds and sudden provocation.

The general strike was almost complete for several days throughout northern Greece. The Government immediately took charge of the railways and kept them running through the time-honored expedient of mobilizing the personnel for military service. Road communications were interrupted, however, all around Salonica, where the strikers barricaded the main highways. Perfect order and a kind of Sunday quiet reigned in Serres, Drama, Kavalla, Xanthi and Kommotini, all of which I visited before the strike was over. The Army was especially in evidence in Kavalla, where the General deemed it wise to give me a troop of cavalry as escort. A belated attempt to extend the strike to Athens failed, but the fact remains that the troubles in the north constitute the most serious labor disturbances in Greece's history and afford a couple of lessons which the Greek Government would do well to heed.

The first of these lessons is the extent to which organization has supplemented mere agitation in northern Greece. The frequency of strikes in that region during the past months has not escaped the Department's notice. It has provided a thorn in the side of the Government here, whose more than customary weakness during a period of "non-partisanship" has provided an unusual opportunity for agitation. But the long strike betrayed evidences of timing and control which could only be the product of a centralized directing force such as has hitherto been rather conspicuously absent from Greek labor troubles. The tobacco men with whom I lived for several days during the strike are also convinced that there was a central treasury involved not unconnected with Moscow; and, incidentally, that capital [Moscow] broadcast bulletins reporting the progress of the outbreak. Greeks are naturally individualists and resist all forms of regimentation. Their labor unions react much in the same manner as their political parties, being more sensitive to personal leadership than to doctrine. There would appear to be very few real communists among them, the name being given rather indiscriminately in this country to labor sympathizers of many shades of opinion. What then has so favored the activities of a few agitators that the country can now be rocked to its foundation at their behest?

The answer to this question would seem to lie, firstly, in the conditions prevailing in the tobacco districts of northern Greece. These conditions differ in one vital respect from those which prevailed in pre-war times. Normally, tobacco and tobacco-picking (i.e., sorting the leaves according to grades of excellence) go hand in hand and are performed by the same elements of the population, the picking being done by the women, children and old men of the tobacco-raising families. After the war, however, and the Smyrna disaster, the Greek Government found it necessary to settle a large number of refugees in northern Greece, and also, of course, to find them employment without delay. Instead of settling them on the land and using them to develop the rich grain fields of the region, now largely let out for pasturage to the wandering Vlach tribes, it chose the easier way of huddling them into settlements in the towns and turning over to them the almost exclusive right of engaging in tobacco-picking. Only those granted special permission—represented by a booklet issued by the Government—can now so engage, and this right is not extended to the agricultural population which formerly carried on, as a side issue during certain months of the year, the essential occupation involved. Today's tobacco-pickers are, in general, well-paid and exceptionally well-housed and protected by health and insurance provisions, but their occupation is definitely seasonal, so that for a large part of the year they are idle. Furthermore, during this part of the year they appear to be left by the authorities to their own devices. There is an old adage that "Satan finds work for idle hands to do," and it can be imagined that his task is made infinitely more easy when the idle hands are crowded together in cities. In the old days, of course, those members of the tobacco families who did the picking, and thus added somewhat to the family revenues, went back for the rest of the year to such work on their farms as they could, in their relative weakness, perform. The present situation presents also the added disadvantage that a large part of the tobacco-picking is at present done, by Government order, by able-bodied but butter-fingered men who are much less efficient at this task than women. Altogether it is a bad situation, the result of a hasty and ill-considered solution to the refugee question, and it explains the apparent anomaly presented by the fact that a group which in many ways is the most favored among the laborers of the region is today the most highly organized and the most troublesome of all.

Secondly, the extent to which the organization of the tobacco-pickers has strengthened them *vis-à-vis* their employers and bettered their economic condition has not gone unobserved by their brothers engaged in less fortunate occupations, particularly in Salonica where a large industrial city is in the making under the eyes of a Government which persists in seeing little else in politics but the spoils and pays little heed to economic factors till these take the upper hand. From the organized centers of tobacco-picking, particularly from Kavalla, it has indeed been inevitable, under the prevailing policy of *laissez-faire*, that communistic influence should extend to the miserably low-paid workers of the textile and other industries of Salonica.

The second lesson of the strike may thus be said to be the danger inherent in the present policy of doing nothing to improve labor conditions in the north. Communist leaders can not only point to a certain amount of betterment in these conditions as a result of their activities, but would seem to be abundantly justified in stigmatizing the Government as neglectful of the people's welfare. In fact, so conspicuous has been the central government's disregard of Macedonian interests except for short periods immediately preceding elections, that there is probably no one in the north of Greece today who is not convinced that Athens takes no interest in the country's most productive region beyond what it can get out of it in the way of taxes and votes. That Macedonia and Thrace are still ruled as provinces and not integrated with the rest of Greece is resented. That the best Governors-General who have been appointed to Macedonia, such as Adossidis, Dragoumis, and now Pallis, have confessed to failure on account of political inertia and even opposition in Athens is a subject of constant comment. Indeed it may be said that the region as a whole feels itself in a hopeless situation, and thinks of Athens in terms of the only two recent interventions of the capital in its affairs, the suppression of the revolt of last year by Kondylis and that of this year's strike by Metaxas. There is still some hope felt that the King will move to help matters but he has not even paid a passing visit to the region although he has been in Greece six months.

Is the Greek Government going to heed these lessons? Or is Salonica destined to become another Barcelona and spread the infection of economic revolt throughout the whole of the rotten body politic of this country? It may be that the King, in his dislike of "politicians" and his desire to see Greece adopt "more Anglo-Saxon ideas," may do something to bring a greater degree of contentment and confidence to his northern subjects. But this is a slim hope. It is, on the other hand, a devastating fact that Athens—and this includes its most enlightened and influential men—appears to have so far considered the general strike only in its political aspects, quarreling over it in terms of Venizelism and anti-Venizelism according to the time-honored formula, and losing sight altogether of its fundamental significance. So far no Daniel has come to read the handwriting on the wall.

In explanation, and in part extenuation of this Athenian attitude, I should perhaps recall to the Department that the Communist Party acquired this spring a new importance in the Greek political line-up. It will be remembered that in the struggle over the Presidency of the Chamber when the Liberal front and Popular front were deadlocked, the Liberals secured the election of their candidate, Mr. Sofoulis, by means of the votes of the Communist deputies. Later, a signed document in the nature of a treaty between Liberals and Communists was revealed and acknowledged, and in spite of the fact that it appears that Mr. Tsaldaris also made overtures to the Communists, unsuccessfully, the opponents of the Liberals have been loud in their denunciations of Mr. Sofoulis as a Communist sympathizer. To them, the general strike has accordingly seemed to be nothing more nor less than a piece of sabotage directed by the Communist friends of the Liberals against a government which Liberals and Communists together had vainly hoped to dominate. Athenian society and the Athenian people are divided over the question as to whether this charge is true, and the fundamental reasons for the outbreak remain unconsidered. Mr. Maximos told me last night that he believed Mr. Venizelos himself counselled Mr. Sofoulis to ally himself with the Communists, but that the Old Cretan counted on being able to check his doubtful allies at any given moment and "would never have gone in for this strike." Mr. Metaxas, whom I talked with about the situation immediately after my return from the affected regions, informed me, almost in so many words, that the important thing about the strike was that it was fostered by the Liberals. Mr. Maximos is one of the most level-headed and judicious of the wealthier Greeks, and Mr. Metaxas, while his eminence is derived from other qualities than these, is Prime Minister.

The truth, of course, is that the Liberal Party has indeed made use of the strike to criticize the Government. But it did not originate the strike. I am informed by the most credible of witnesses that no one in Salonica was more disturbed or more anxious to check the strike than Mr. Zannas, the local Liberal Leader. On the other hand, the Liberals have confined their criticisms to the Government's handling of the outbreak and have not attacked the basic question of its causes any more than have their opponents.

When a Greek has enough to live on, and work to occupy steadily at least a part of his time, he is not likely to fall a victim to the blandishments of agitators. He dislikes violence and loves talk more than any blessings which can only come through bestirring himself at risk of life and limb. But he must at least have half a stomachful of cheese and olives and bread. The Government can still turn the flank of this country's incipient communism by assuring to the poor a modicum of such contentment, but it has got at least to do that. To eradicate communism altogether from the north of Greece it should perhaps take tobacco-picking out of the hands of the refugees and give it back to the planters, using the former for much-needed farm-development and possibly public works—the roads in northern Greece must be among the worst in the world. But so long as it shuts its eyes to starvation wages in Salonica and treats Macedonia and Thrace as despised colonies, milking them of the high tobacco tax which it spends in old Greece, and obstructing the efforts of conscientious Governors-General to develop local government in accordance with local needs, it will run the risk of more and bigger strikes with possible results ugly to contemplate. The sympathetic extension of the recent strike to Athens failed, but even the Greek laborer cannot be counted on indefinitely to sit by and watch his brothers starve. Indeed, the time seems clearly to have arrived when those who direct the destinies of Greece,—which means, in general, the upper class in Athens,—must give up living in the past and face the problems of the present. If they fail to do this resolutely and promptly, they and their country may well be the next victims of the social revolution. This, I fear, is the real significance of the recent strike. (6)

A few days after the restoration of order, King George accepted Metaxas' recommendations for special measures designed to deal more effectively with similar unrest in the future, and to combat the spread of communist propaganda. On May 18, Theodore Skylakakis, a reactionary figure and self-proclaimed enemy of democratic rule, was appointed Minister of the Interior, and entrusted with the country's internal security. The previous day Panayiotis Tsaldaris had died, depriving the nation of much needed temperate leadership, and weakening the forces of the Populist center. The days of representative government were now clearly numbered.

As the 1936 national election campaign in the United States was beginning to gather momentum, MacVeagh expressed the desire to return home to help assure Roosevelt's re-election. Following an encouraging response from Hall Roosevelt, he raised the matter directly with the President. "If you think I can be of any help to you," he wrote in his letter of April 30 cited above, "I shall certainly do my best and am in fact ready to go at the drop of the hat." However, with the Department advising against such trips, the President replied that, as the Balkan scene appeared troubled, "it seems to me that you should not return until and unless the situation quiets down. I do not want to have all the Ministers and Ambassadors here at one time, especially if anything were to blow up at that particular moment." Still, MacVeagh was to use his own judgment, and was encouraged to believe that the trip was not definitely off. "I think you can help in various places in the campaign," the President had concluded, "through your own excellent contacts. Things seem to be in fairly good shape. . . ."(7)

Somewhat embarrassed, MacVeagh responded quickly, brushing off the matter of the trip, and devoting his attention instead to Greek and European affairs:

Athens, June 13, 1936

Dear Franklin:

I have received your letter and wish to assure you that I wouldn't think of asking for home leave this year, unless it was your wish that I return. The general European situation does not clear up. Rather it seems to be becoming more complicated, and armaments are growing at an alarming rate. Furthermore, Greece has a lot of local trouble of her own in which our people may at any time be involved, and the Department has taken away my two secretaries, old hands and experts in Near Eastern problems, and given me in exchange only a youngster in his twenties, who is going to be a very good man indeed, I believe, but who at present lacks experience. Professionally, in regard to the job you have given me, and which I try to do my best with, it seems to me therefore that I should stick around subject to your decision as to whether I could be of better use elsewhere.

As far as my personal contacts are concerned, these are by this time pretty wide among the scattered half-million or so of the Greek Americans, who have astonished me by the interest they seem to take in who represents our country here. They and I seem to find it easy to think along the same lines, on many subjects, and that goes for thinking along Roosevelt lines. I believe there are few Greek Americans who are not Roosevelt men, or unaware of the fact, which means much to them, that your administration is responsible for conducting Greek-American affairs with sympathy and understanding.

The "non-partisan" government which recently gave way to the "King's own," as we might call it, was naturally a timid one and little action, if any, was taken by it in regard to a multitude of questions, some of them of considerable local importance. The present Premier is accordingly swamped with administrative arrears. But his policy for the next few months before the general elections is gradually taking shape. It appears that he will stall on the question of the foreign debt, in spite of the claims of the English bondholders that Greece can well afford to pay more than 35 percent of the interest. He will also, it seems, do nothing about the German clearing, which has resulted in Greece's accumulating a dangerously large credit in blocked Reichsmarks. But he is actively working to strengthen the country's military defenses, and increasing the naval forces, and is continuing the King's conciliatory policy toward the Venizelist revolters of last year. Preparedness and unity would thus seem to be his watchwords. As he told me himself, his Government, with probably only a short life ahead of it, has to deal with a thoroughly disorganized country and must not try to do too much at once if it wishes to achieve results. . . .

In foreign affairs there seem to be some big decisions coming in the near future. The French Minister has just been summoned to Paris and tells me that the new French Foreign Minister plans to see every one of his Chiefs of Mission in Europe personally before he goes to Geneva. The French Minister is confident that the Blum Government will prove definitely Anglophile and Sanctionist. We shall see. Today's press reports that d'Ormesson and Pertinax, two of the best known editorial writers on foreign affairs in France, are now emphasizing the dangers of a German-Italian-Polish *entente*. Of course, we all have long been aware of these, but the emphasis in the French press does seem to be new. Is the French nation as a whole going to wake up at last to the facts, which its General Staff makes no bones about, that the one enemy it has to fear is Germany and that England and France have a common frontier on the Rhine? Meanwhile Greece is much impressed by Mussolini's *de facto* conquest of Abyssinia, and is trying to be very polite indeed to the Italians, while noting almost pathetically every rumor as to the immensity of England's efforts in rearmament. The Greeks fear Italian ruthlessness, which was exhibited in Corfu not so many years ago,[3] and they are familiar with a certain Italian point of view which regards small Mediterranean nations as having no right to exist. She is under the spell of the British Navy, but desperately afraid of the Italian air force, as well she may be. And she knows that Italy's real army is still in Italy, that the Straits of Otranto are held in an Italian vise, that Albania is being rapidly developed in a manner perfectly adapted for service as an Italian bridge-head in the Balkans on the flank of Yugoslavia, that Malta is no longer of any use to the British, who have not yet developed Cyprus and possess a doubtful friend in Egypt, that the Dodecanese

---

[3] In August 1923, following the murder of several Italian members of a Greek-Albanian frontier international commission, Italy bombarded and occupied Corfu. The incident, which was subsequently shown to have been fabricated by Mussolini, was settled by the League of Nations.

Islands are fully equipped to form an Italian base in the Aegean on the flank of Turkey, and that Bulgaria is a possible Italian ally, and militarily stronger than either Greece or Rumania. All these facts would, as you may imagine, make her position intensely difficult in the case of a European conflict in which Italy and England were on opposite sides. No one here expresses the idea that Mussolini actually intends himself to start such a conflict. But there are grave doubts as to the limits of his imperial ambitions, and a very general fear of some spark, probably in Central Europe, setting off the whole fireworks as soon as Germany is prepared.

Ever yours affectionately,
Lincoln MacVeagh (8)

In Washington, aware of his friend's disappointment at not being able to take part in the campaign, Hall Roosevelt interceded with the White House, and MacVeagh was permitted to make the trip home after all. On August 5, 1936, in mid-Atlantic, he learned that the previous night, Metaxas, with the King's consent, had suspended the constitution, declared parliament dissolved, and in effect established a personal dictatorship. The official explanation was that these extreme measures were needed in order to combat Communism, which threatened to overthrow the existing social order and to destroy the Greek nation. At dockside in New York, MacVeagh commented to reporters that Greece was "one of the most democratic countries in the world and that, while a Fascist or Communist regime was always a possibility in the present temper of the people," it was highly unlikely that such a regime could last long. (9) It was not to prove one of his more fortuitous predictions.

After a brief visit with his mother in Dublin, New Hampshire, he sought to meet with old friends, and with the country's larger Greek communities, speaking primarily about Roosevelt's prudent course in foreign affairs. Sailing back to his post on August 29, he scribbled a note to the President:

[August 29, 1936]

Dear Franklin:

I am going back to my job after a considerable swing around the country. Your peace talk at Chautauqua seems to have filled the bill to such an extent that smaller fry aren't much in demand on that subject. Neither the Department nor the Good Neighbor League got me any bids, though I got myself all prepared. But, as I thought, the Greek-Americans *wanted* to see me and I gave them the opportunity. We had a big crowd in St. Paul from all over the country, and my speech was enthusiastically received and will be published in their journals. I got some peace talk in with the reporters. In Detroit I got together with the leaders of the Greek colony. In Boston I spoke again, and the speech will be distributed to the Greeks throughout New England.

In general our Greeks are sober, serious, independent men, nearly all devoted to you, mostly for the New Deal, and can be counted on I think to pull at the polls. I hope I have helped to cement their friendship and ideas for the cause.

Affectionately yours,
Lincoln MacVeagh (10)

And following Roosevelt's re-election:

Athens, November 9, 1936

Dear Franklin:

The result of the elections has caused the greatest rejoicing, not only to me and to those about me here in the Legation, but all over this country. The Greek papers all emphasize the sweeping nature of your victory and the tremendous endorsement given to you personally and to your policies, which they unite in praising. Privately, I have been "congratulated" on all sides, with evident enthusiasm and genuine pleasure. Flowers, letters, telegrams have multiplied with the passing minutes, Greeks as well as Americans joining in an extraordinary and spontaneous chorus. Mr. Maximos, who was the Foreign Minister with whom I fought out the long-drawn Insull affair, called me up before the election to express his warmest sympathy with your cause and tell me of his hopes for your success. The British Minister wrote me: "I cannot refrain from saluting you today with my warmest and most heartfelt congratulations on the victory of Mr. Roosevelt. I feel this is a great thing not only for America but for the world." The King, the Dean of the Diplomatic Corps, the head of the Foreign Office (but not yet our local Dictator whom I saw but for a second at the Palace before his trip to Crete, where he now is) have all congratulated me warmly. A friend in England who is a great pro-Greek, writes from London: "It does an outside onlooker like me no end of good to see such a thing happen in this dictator-infested world. I've looked into several papers today, morning and evening, and one and all have acclaimed the Great Man's victory as the victory of common sense, generosity, and freedom. The world badly needed a tonic like this." I like those words—common sense, generosity and freedom. Adding a touch of romance, there came a telegram from Mycenae, ancient home of the dictatorial Agamemnon, where I have helped to build a Christian church in the tiny modern village. The telegram was signed by Greek peasants. It seems that all over the world, down even to the simplest of those who love common sense, generosity and freedom, there is rejoicing over your victory, and the belief that under your guidance America is the greatest force existing today for peace, stability and progress. It would be an anticlimax to speak of my own feelings after all this, but then they have been caught up and expressed perfectly in the biggest vote of confidence and admiration that anybody ever got. And my feelings for you and your family personally put me a long way ahead of the majority in my happiness.

I have not written you about affairs here since my return because you have been so busy and the European volcano has not been actively erupting in these parts. We feel the shock of Spain[4] in the impulse given to fascist ideas and in the repressive measures taken by the Government. There has been little actual communism in Greece heretofore, but the small royalist group which, with the help of the army, bagged the power last August on the excuse that Greece must be saved from the fate of Spain, is now treating all its critics as if they were reds, and with censorship of the press, castor oil, and imprisonment and exile, seems in a fair way to turn all the liberals in the country into radicals and alienate many of the conservatives besides. The King has thrown in his lot with the dictatorship, and is now backing General Metaxas in all he does, contributing personally the only popularity which the regime enjoys, and that, apparently, a fading one. You will remember that the King came back on the basis of a faked plebiscite but promising to rule as a constitutional monarch. His *volte-face* has cost him dear. But I believe his early professions were genuine enough and that he only changed his mind through inability to make anything of the wrangling politicians. He came back with English ideas which he couldn't work out, and now has gone frankly fascist, giving free rein to his German nature, which has little use for democracy. It seems to be generally thought here that if and when the Greeks turn Metaxas out the King will have to go too. Meanwhile the Government seems really trying to put some efficiency into the public service. The seamy side is still the under-side of the new mantle Greece is wearing.

King Edward's good-will tour of Dalmatia, Greece, Turkey, and Bulgaria this summer, followed by the usual visit to Athens of England's Mediterranean squadron, has done, it appears, a good deal to restore whatever prestige England may have lost in these parts after her failure

[4] The Spanish Civil War, which began with a revolt of generals in Spanish Morocco on July 18, 1936, was to end on March 28, 1939, with the surrender of Madrid and Valencia to the forces of General Francisco Franco.

to check Mussolini in Ethiopia. The financial agreement between England, France, and the United States made a strong impression here, and Greece promptly tied her drachma to the pound sterling. But economically she is still in the throes of the German clearing, and we have to fight for everything we get.

Affectionately yours,
Lincoln MacVeagh (11)

After the eventful summer of 1936, and for the next four years, MacVeagh's principal task was to observe the Metaxas dictatorship at close range and to comment on its possible durability. Gone now was the traditional excitement of Athenian politics, with the ever-present likelihood of sweeping change. As viewed from the American Legation, the new régime, while abhorrent in principle, was not without its redeeming features. In addition to unprecedented stability, which made life much "simpler" for Greeks as well as for foreign diplomats, the régime of the "Fourth of August" was genuinely believed to have rescued the country from revolutionary unrest, fomented, if not actually created, by the Communist Party. Thus, soon after his return to Athens, MacVeagh was reporting to the Department:

[September 19, 1936]

In an interview given to the Athenian newspaper *VRADYNI* on September 16th, the Premier, Mr. John Metaxas, made the following statements (I translate from the French of the *REVUE DE LA PRESSE ATHENIENNE*):

"I may declare, without going into details, that Greece will be organized in the future into a Corporative State. It is towards this form of Government that our efforts and our acts are tending. I do not say that the Communists would have proclaimed the revolution on August 5th; that they would have prevailed and taken over the power immediately. But I do say that they would have created such an overturn in the great bourgeois centers, spreading their influence gradually to the smallest centers, that we should have entered, without knowing it, a revolutionary atmosphere from which we surely could not have emerged without bloodshed." After going on to show that parliamentarism, as practiced in Greece, was powerless to deal with the Communist menace, he said:

"The Communists trembled at the thought that my government would enact laws providing for compulsory arbitration and a minimum wage. The last thing they wanted was to have a non-communist government take action in behalf of the working class. It was a matter of *clientèle* and the Communists could never pardon having their clients taken from them."

Mr. Metaxas thus claims to have stolen for his Government the material out of which the Communists in Greece were building their menace. It is he who will now save the unhappy working man. If the Department will refer to my despatch No. 1195 of May 29, 1936, on the General Strike of last Spring in Salonica, it will appreciate the cleverness of the Premier's move and the justice of his claim. For while Communism as a doctrine has not been wide-spread in Greece (a Communist party boasting 15 deputies out of a total of 300 cannot be regarded as impressive), the presence of Communist agitators offering to large groups of miserable people the only help in sight constitutes a real danger to the social order. Mr. Metaxas has now turned the eyes of the indigent to himself rather than to Moscow, and in that sense, and to the degree in which he puts adequate welfare measures into force, may be considered as a savior of the country.

The cleverness of his coup thus resides in the fact that its excuse is something more than merely plausible, and the willingness of labor and business alike to let him go ahead, and even to back him up for the time being, derives from the same source. At the same time it has not escaped the constitutionally sceptical and critical Greeks that essentially the coup was a political move. This explains the lack of enthusiasm attending the inception of an order from which most people think they may obtain benefits, and also the reservations which attend most current judgments of the King, Mr. Metaxas, their busy functionaries, and the manifold activities of the new regime. It is too widely rumored that the political chiefs had at last reached a basis of agreement, and that Mr. Metaxas was going to have to step down in October in favor of a Coalition Government, for any reactions except those of the Government itself to be jubilant. The attitude seems to be: "This may turn out to be fine for us, but it is certainly fine for Mr. Metaxas, so let us wait and see."

In regard to an agreement between the political chiefs, I have it on trustworthy testimony that Mr. Sofoulis and Mr. Theotokis, representing the Liberal and Popular fronts, reached a basis of understanding a few days before the Metaxas coup, and that Mr. Sofoulis went to the King and told him that he respected the five months' mandate given to Mr. Metaxas, but that at its expiration it would be up to the King to call him, Mr. Sofoulis, to form a government. It is presumed that it was the relaying of this conversation from the King to the Premier which pulled the trigger firing Greek politicians and Parliamentary Government into the discard. At any rate, his friends say that Mr. Sofoulis is very bitter in private over the King's "treachery." He may not realize, but others certainly do, that his own private agreement with the Communist Party when he was running for Speaker of the House, made him particularly vulnerable as an opponent of Mr. Metaxas at the present time.

While the present regime is now tolerated, it may be said that its future, and probably that of the Monarchy with it, will depend upon its acts. It has no party organization or group of shirts, black or brown, to back it. That it hopes to build up such an organization is clear, beginning with the youth. But an enterprise of such a sort is a long-term affair, and meanwhile the popularity or unpopularity of the daily acts of the Government will inevitably affect it for success or failure. The Army, which appears now to be in favor of the new regime (though reports differ as to how much) is also open to the winds of doctrine which sweep through the families of the officers and men, or, in other words, the nation at large. If the Government carries out its reforms in such a way as to alienate any considerable portion of the nation, the Army cannot be relied on, in a country where the well-timed and carefully organized *coup d'état* at the hands of a minority is so well-tried and so popular. The backing of a bourgeois militia would indeed seem to be necessary for the success of such an enterprise as that of Mr. Metaxas,—granted that he really means to make a Fascist State. But can he get it in a country where real Communism is not widespread and the democratic spirit is ingrained?

Though Mr. Metaxas has no colored shirts to back him, he has, in Mr. Skylakakis, an active Minister of the Interior, who, through the Under Secretariat of Public Safety,[5] is already running a young G.P.U. It seems to be a fact that castor oil has been freely administered by the police not only to suspected Communists but to incautious talkers in cafés. Interference with the right of free speech and strict censorship of the news, coupled with the rise in the price of newspapers, would seem to be measures well-calculated to defeat any proselytizing the regime may attempt. The Premier and founder of the Regime has also to contend with his own record. He has not come on the scene as a new leader of a new movement, but has a past which makes him personally as welcome to many Greeks as Satan himself, and these people naturally distrust him bearing gifts.

If certain half-baked, omnibus measures, which the Government has already passed, and had immediately to modify, are examples of the kind of thing to be expected of the Metaxas Government in the future, it may be said with assurance that a reaction is due, at no distant date, from this liberty-loving and critical people. But Mr. Metaxas is no Pangalos to trip on the length of a woman's skirt. He enjoys [the] acquiescence of the country now, and if, together with the program of a Mussolini or a Hitler he has considerably less to work with than they had, we can only

---

[5] Headed by Constantine Maniadakis, Metaxas' principal associate in matters of domestic security.

say of him and the King what the majority of the Greeks are saying today: "By their fruits ye shall know them." (12)

Conditioned to regard Greek dictatorial regimes as passing phenomena, that serve as abrupt transitions between various political arrangements, both native and foreign observers at first tended to see nothing especially unique or lasting in the new order of things. Thus MacVeagh commented to the Department:

[October 17, 1936]

If I may be allowed to refer to the "political situation" in a country where politics has been "abolished," I would respectfully report that the political situation in Athens, while remaining generally quiet, presents certain aspects of interest to the close observer. The Government is making a great bid for popularity by providing, at least on paper, for the public welfare in a dozen different directions. Decree laws regulating gambling, assuring financial assistance to the indigent, establishing festivals, protecting and improving the merchant marine, reorganizing health resorts, zoning the capital, beautifying the Piraeus, etc., etc., are published daily. Relaxation of some of the most onerous of the Government's early and hasty measures is also to be observed. A decision of the Council of National Defense was announced today to lift the 20,000 drachma exit tax for Greeks traveling abroad, and as reported in my despatch No. 1361 of October 11, 1936,[6] certain privileges in regard to dealing in foreign exchange have been restored to the banks.

It would seem that Mr. Metaxas has at least some idea of the real danger of interfering too much with the smaller liberties of the Greek people. At the same time, he is running a dictatorship, and there are some things which he cannot allow. One of these is free speech. Side by side with numerous evidences of his paternalistic benevolence and forethought, today's papers carry the following:

> "According to the Prime Minister's order, severe steps will be taken against people spreading rumors. Every person spreading rumors against the Government will be subjected to an inquisition in order that he may divulge the origin of his information and establish the truth of his charges."

Thus early in the new dictatorship have the doors been opened to the malodorous regiment of informers. The town is full of irresponsible talk, guarded, indeed, for fear of castor oil or worse, but still omnipresent in private. Today the papers carry the following item:

[6] Not cited in this text.

"Last midnight alarm exercises of the military and police forces of Athens and Piraeus were held by order of the Ministry of War and the Sub-Ministry of Public Safety."

The popular interpretation of this seems to be that it masks an actual attempt at a *coup d'état*. General Reppas, who has been removed from active command, and who is known to be both bitter and rash, is in some quarters credited with the premature move. Thus, while it cannot be said that the King, and the Army in general, have as yet withdrawn their support from the regime, and certainly no large body of opposition can yet be detected as crystallized, the seamy side of dictatorship is much in evidence. Two Americans of long experience in Greece were talking with me tonight. One said: "I give the regime a year." The other said: "I give it a few months at best." The second speaker, incidentally, was the more experienced of the two. The new French Minister said to me: "I understand Mr. Metaxas makes five hundred enemies a day,—and some days five thousand." Indeed, the general consensus of opinion seems to be that if the Premier's large and drastic program for moulding Greece nearer to the King's ideal of efficiency succeeds, it will be a miracle. On the other hand, Greece has been immemorially a land of miracles.

The present situation is, I believe, one of the most interesting and puzzling in Greek history. For it is not only the foreigners who are puzzled. The Greeks themselves are realizing the truth of the facetious popular song of last year which began: "Oh, what a mystery is Hellas!" The erstwhile Liberals are puzzling over whether the King can really be genuine in his support of Metaxas after having accepted the olive branch from Venizelos; and the erstwhile Royalists, equally removed with their old opponents from the center of things, are puzzling over "what price Royalism now?" It may very well be that Venizelism and anti-Venizelism are at last passing out of the picture, as new issues arise where they have been least expected. When an opposition crystallizes again, I think we may look to find it comprising members of both the old camps, united as anti-Metaxists, and (who knows?) perhaps as anti-King. In this connection I may repeat the widespread story that the office of the old Royalist newspaper, *PROIA*, was wrecked recently because its owner-editor, Mr. Stephen Pezmazoglou, refused to publish a governmental attack on Mr. Theotokis without giving Mr. Theotokis a chance to reply; and the other equally widespread story to the effect that when the King refused to see Mr. Theotokis, the latter remarked: "Never mind, I shall soon be seeing the President of the Republic." The Pezmazoglous, the Theotokises, the Mavromichalises, the Reppases, etc., of the Kingdom, strongest of the old Royalists, are now on the outside looking in, and almost rubbing shoulders with the Mavrocordatos, the Papanastasious, and the Kafandarises.

It is said that Mr. Papanastasiou said to the King: "General Metaxas brought your father to ruin and he will do the same to you." Though the voice was the voice of Papanastasiou, the words might have been those of his bitterest enemies of last year. The cure for the Venizelist-Antivenizelist strife which has been so far applied by George II would thus seem leading less toward unity than toward another cleavage.

I give the above, which is at best a tentative reading of the dubious signs of the times, in order that the Department may not be surprised should the Greek dictatorship not develop according to its widely published plans. At the present moment, in the first blush of unchallenged regulation, some real improvement is to be noticed in the efficiency of the Government services, and the reiterated promises of the regime fill its dawn with a rosy light. (13)

Five months later, the future of the "4th of August" regime was still seen as uncertain, as MacVeagh reported to the Department:

[February 5, 1937]

The difficulties of the Metaxas dictatorship seem to be increasing. A propaganda trip to Macedonia on the part of gigantic Mr. Kotzias, Minister-Governor of Athens and "strutting trumpeter" of the regime, has disclosed the fact that the numerous veterans in that district are not showing the discipline and obedience expected of them. Together with unrest in the Military League previously reported, this may be significant of the personal support Mr. Metaxas may expect if matters should ever come to a showdown. It is understood that Prince George,[7] who left Greece the other day, did so because of definite dissatisfaction with the continuance of the dictatorship. Mr. Passaris, the Under-Minister of Aviation (as the Department knows, Mr. Metaxas is his own Minister of Aviation) resigned yesterday, apparently over a question of military personnel, and finally Mr. Metaxas is reported to have excused himself from attendance at the Palace for several days past on the plea of illness but really because the King has at last informed him of his intention to abandon the dictatorship in favor of a return to some form of parliamentary government. . . .

In connection with the question how far the King may be aware of the dissatisfaction which exists over the dictatorship, I have been able to see a copy of one of the petitions mentioned in my despatch under reference.[8] This petition was presented to the King by Mr. Sofoulis and is dated December 29th last. My informant kindly allowed me to keep his copy

---

[7] Prince George, brother of King Constantine and uncle of King George II.
[8] Not cited in this text.

long enough to extract pertinent portions, and I here quote them for the Department's information. If the King has actually read this document he can hardly claim ignorance of the point of view of at least the Venizelists, who may amount to half the country. In this connection it may be worth noting that Mr. Sofoulis actually describes himself as "the political head of a great party" in spite of the abolition of parties proclaimed by the dictatorship:

> The new sad adventure from which the country is suffering is unique and inexplicable from the historical point of view. It cannot be considered a logical evolution of our political life, nor as the result of a revolution, nor as corresponding in any way to a change in the popular psychology. On the contrary, this adventure bears the aspect of an obvious plot for the subjection of the Greek people to the all-powerful and uncontrollable will of one person, himself deriving from the political world now so defamed by those in power. To open a path for the satisfaction of a personal lust for power, it has been judged necessary to abolish the regime and eliminate all the guarantees on which the free political life of the country was founded.
>
> In the hope of finding a new basis for its existence and a new organ for its tyrannical power, the dictatorship threatens to transform Greece into a corporate state. In Greece, however, such an idea is Utopian and chimerical to the highest degree, necessitating a reconstruction of the life of the people so complete as to be impossible short of a generation of organized political re-education, and demanding systematic and painful effort the very conception of which is an example of irresponsible thinking.
>
> The justifiable discontent of the Greek people caused by the abolition of its rights is accentuated by the fact that the dictatorship has not shown by any of its actions that it possesses the slightest creative ability. Its whole existence is summed up in expensive exhibitions and forced meetings to give the impression of strength. Except for these things, it presents us with a complete blank, a thorough vacuum of thought, and an abundant harvest of empty words.
>
> The 4th of August was the beginning of a new era of slavery for the Greek people. The Premier proclaims that his dictatorship will continue forever. But his hope is vain. Greece lacks the principal factor guaranteeing longevity to the Italian and German dictatorships, the heroic legend enshrining the names of two great chiefs, the Duce and the Fuhrer. These men are veritably worshipped by their partisans. I dare not pose the question whether a similar situation exists here.
>
> According to what history teaches without exception, it is not diffi-

cult to guess what will be the end of the Greek dictatorship, as of all regimes based on force and tyranny. If this situation continues, the discontent of the people, deep and inarticulate, will be transformed into overt effort, and uncontrollable anarchy will succeed to tyranny. We have kept silence for five months, sure that the providence of the Throne would restore to the people its constitutional rights and liberties. But as time goes on without such action, our silence might be construed as negligence, and I myself would bear some of the responsibility as the political head of a great party.

Sire:

Amidst the dangers of today—of which international dangers are not the least—we are being dragged to a precipice overhanging the abyss. It is for Your Majesty to put an end to the affair while there is still time. Only the Royal foresight, opportunely brought to bear, can obviate the woes and dangers fermenting under the continuance of the dictatorial regime.

To this and similar petitions, His Majesty has as yet made no reply. In my despatch No. 1393 of October 23, 1936,[9] I expressed my belief that the King, besides being a loyal person and an old friend of the Dictator, personally favors a dictatorial regime for the turbulent Greeks. This, together with his natural fear of renewed parliamentary bickering, sufficiently explains, I believe, his support of Mr. Metaxas to date. What he will do if the tide of discontent and criticism continues to rise, nobody knows. He does not seem to be such a person as would easily sacrifice his beliefs and friendships to save his throne, but he may have become genuinely convinced that his experiment with Mr. Metaxas has been a failure, and this I think must be the explanation of his remark to my colleague quoted in my despatch No. 1504 of January 22nd,[10] that he desires a return to parliamentary government. What is giving him pause now would seem to be the question of how to guard against a renewal of the political impasse of last year, and to a certain extent what to do with Mr. Metaxas. The latter does not seem strong enough to fight him, even should he wish to do so, but no doubt the King desires to save the Dictator's face, particularly as in the circumstances it is to so great an extent his own face also. He would thus appear to be seeking a formula. Whether events will let him go on seeking in silence much longer is another question. The opposition to the regime still appears to be unorganized, though it is doubtless widespread and growing. The spectre of anarchy evoked by Mr. Sofoulis is almost certainly exaggerated, especially as regards its imminence. But as there is no doubt that the King is the most important

---

[9] Not cited in this text.   [10] Not cited in this text.

person in the country today, so there can be no doubt of the desirability of his coming to a decision one way or the other at an early date. This is true from the point of view of Mr. Metaxas as well as from that of his opponents, since as things stand the dictatorship is hampered by the King's moderation at every turn while the exasperation of the opposition increases from day to day. Finally the King's indecision is a drawback to his own popularity if not as yet to his prestige. Count Mercati[11] told me the other day that the King's strength lies in the fact that while many people tell him their ideas, they none of them know what he himself is thinking. But the country wants a leader and is chilled by an attitude which begins to look like indifference. I am told that at a large cinema recently the King's picture was thrown on the screen before 2500 people and not one applauded, and last night at the opening of a new theater which he and the Crown Prince[12] both attended, the only applause which greeted the royal entrance came from a few scattered handclappers in the balcony, the whole of the orchestra maintaining a stony silence.

Last week Mr. Mylonas remarked to a friend of mine, "soon we shall have freedom," and Mr. Sofoulis said to a journalist of my acquaintance: "This is the weakest of all dictatorships. Here am I sitting on my chair, when I ought to be in exile." And Mr. Michalacopoulos, at a reception in this Legation, spoke openly and loudly to his friends in criticism of the Dictator. It is the King's moderation which is at the bottom of these manifestations, and the Dictator's lack of popular support which allows the King's moderation to be effective. In these conditions the country hardly knows where it is at, but there is a general feeling that something is due to happen soon. It would appear that the King might ease some immediate tension by reverting to parliamentary government, but that this will cure the Greek political disease, which is rooted in the Greek character, is a belief to which perhaps nobody but a Greek politician will subscribe. (14)

With political life at a standstill, there was little to do in Athens but shift through the endless barrage of governmental hyperbole on the one hand, and the hysterical handouts of the rumor mills on the other. Starting in late 1936, and continuing throughout the following year, MacVeagh undertook a series of travels that eventually covered every important region of the country. While mostly concerned to report on political and economic conditions, and to assess the new regime's successes and failures, his lengthy despatches provide a colorful panorama of Greek life, and offer details that only an experienced observer and student of Greece's past could capture. After a tour of the Salonica district, the Struma

[11] Count Leonardo Mercati, aid to King George II.
[12] Crown Prince Paul, younger brother of King George II.

valley, Serres, Kavalla, and the Kassandra peninsula (where the Monks-Ulen companies were working on a number of major irrigation and other projects), he reported to the Department:

[December 8, 1936]

The political situation in Macedonia is quiet, but there seems to be less tolerance of the Metaxas regime, and a greater willingness to criticize its acts adversely than was the case some weeks ago. This is of course in line with the general fickleness of the Greek character. The general reaction to the coup of August 4th was, as I have reported, one of relief. Labor troubles seemed about to be cured and prosperity under a strong hand appeared just around the corner. Though free speech and political action were proscribed, people said of Mr. Metaxas, "Give him time." But in spite of the fact that he has shown commendable energy in trying to introduce efficiency into the public services and correct manifest errors of administration, and has appointed an honest and active Governor General, the time consumed in his approach to the millennium now appears to be working against him. Everyday seems a year to Greeks who have no free press and no political parties. They are now asking, "Well, what has Metaxas accomplished, after all?" And the King who backed him suffers with him from this impatience. Indeed, the King's popularity in this region is distinctly less than it was a month ago. No one seems to think that a *coup* is yet possible against the regime, but in the popular vision of the future such an eventuality is by no means excluded, and though the Government has apparently no intention of proposing anything of the kind, a return to parliamentary government seems to live on in the people's hope. (15)

Following a sweep through western Macedonia, with stops at the towns of Edessa, Florina, Kastoria, Kozani, Verria and Naoussa, he wrote of much building activity and general progress, and concluded:

[May 29, 1937]

It is clear that Macedonia is no longer subject to the traditional neglect of the Government at Athens. It is receiving a great deal of attention from Mr. Metaxas, and absorbing a vast amount of Government expenditure. But the attention is along certain lines only, two, to be exact, of which the first is military, and the second may be classed under the head of nationalist, and incidentally Metaxist propaganda. And the expenditure along these lines, reflected in the rising budget, is at least partly responsible for the increase in the cost of living, and a direct cause of certain elements of taxation which weigh heavily on farmer and factory-worker alike. The unrest and discontent of the Macedonians, their feeling that their problems are not considered in Athens, has not been lessened by the Metaxist measures. The construction of roads for military purposes, and the erection of fortifications, please those who are directly dependent on Government pay. The mass of the people get no use from these things and count every penny of the cost. Efforts to make the Bulgarophones and Slavophones speak Greek please nobody, for Greeks imbibe *laissez-faire* in such matters with their mother's milk. The dictated publicity for the regime which fills the controlled press is equally distasteful to a race which prides itself on knowing a thing or two. While people read of the great benevolence of the Government in regulating the settlement of farm debts, they listen with suspicion to hints of new taxation conveyed by the grapevine route. General Metaxas and his Government are thoroughly disliked and distrusted throughout the whole region, and the King who supports them is coming to share more and more in their unpopularity. That there is uncertainty as to how it is to be accomplished does not lessen the popular feeling that somehow the present regime has got to be temporary, and not, as the Dictator says, perpetual.

Much of this criticism and resentment is certainly unfair to Mr. Metaxas. He has definitely improved the country's defenses and raised the morale of its forces, and though this latter achievement may be to his own advantage, and that of his master, the King, it cannot be said to be against the interests of Greece. He is making the country pay for his regime, but at least some of the ways in which he is spending the money he raises—road building, for instance—are real contributions to progress. I was favorably impressed by the Army officers with whom I talked on this trip. They seemed to me efficient and capable. The soldiers, too, had a firm and confident air, without braggadoccio, particularly the sergeants and corporals. I was reminded, curiously enough, considering General Metaxas' training, of the French army, and remembered that under intelligent and devoted command the Greek army has proved itself on many occasions of the finest fighting quality. Since Constantine wrecked the army which the Allies trained at Salonica, the typical Greek officer has been the lowest form of reptile life, a creature who lived for promotion to be wormed out of influence in political antechambers and drawing rooms, interested in nothing as little as in his own troops. Under such men the intelligent and responsive Greek soldier becomes undisciplined, falling back from possibilities of heroism, called out by comprehension and trust, upon his own native individualism, just as in the days of Xenophon. Every people has its own brand of discipline, and the Greek brand is nowhere more perfectly exposed than in the *Katabasis* of that writer, who shows to what extent the Greeks, even veterans, depend on their relations with the command. Even though General Metaxas does no more for Greece than this, he will still have deserved well of his country if he turns the Greek officer away from private concerns to professional interest and devotion to his men.

Against the rise in the cost of living and the fear of new taxation (Mr. House of the Farm School[13] spoke of a possible tax on farm products, whether sold or not, amounting to 15 percent on gross income), may be set the possibility of a banner wheat crop, of which I saw encouraging evidences, and of an olive crop of more than satisfactory proportions. People in Athens, where the Government has not been slow to trumpet it, speak of this as almost sure to recommend the regime most strongly to the country at large. It is a fact that Governments in the past have profited or suffered from the vagaries of crops and weather, but the condition of the poor is so bad today, that such improvement as now seems promised is hardly likely to do more than partially cure the ill, leaving the Government still held responsible for what remains. General Metaxas will doubtless appropriate to himself the thanks due to a rainy Zeus, but it is probable that with partially-filled stomachs the Greeks will go on hating a regime which is distasteful to their most fundamental instincts and which, with its demands for greater and greater financial sacrifices, pinches them in their most vital spot. (16)

And, after a visit in Eastern Macedonia and Greek Thrace, in the company of American executives of Ulen-Monks and of tobacco concerns:

[June 25, 1937]

The Americans I talked with all seemed pleased with the Government's strong measures in regard to communism, which in this part of the country is a real menace. The best opinion seemed to be that the present regime, and particularly the personality of the Dictator, is not popular, but that prosperity combined with stability is keeping this favored corner of Greece quiet and attentive to business. Certainly there is considerably less overt criticism and restlessness in this region than in Salonica, with its large population dependent on underpaid industries, where the conduct of local affairs by a new Governor General and a new Mayor, who are mere rubber stamps for Mr. Metaxas, stands out like a sore thumb. In that city it is more the military strength of the regime which insures the public peace. (17)

But if the traditionally Venizelist and republican north had no love for Metaxas, the southern regions, while quiet, were only slightly less repelled by his regime. In July 1937, returning from a tour of south-central Greece and the Gulf of Corinth, where travel conditions were still found to be primitive, MacVeagh reported:

[13] Charles House, head of the American Farm School in Salonica.

[July 29, 1937]

The whole region visited on this trip gave evidence of the momentary prosperity conferred on it by the good wheat, raisin and olive crops of the present season. People everywhere seemed busy and contented, while it was very noticeable that the dictatorship at Athens has had little success in changing their undisciplined habits. . . . Greece is still Greece, slowly modernizing out of its backward depths, busy with agriculture and small shipping, happy in a good summer, and inveterately disobedient and individualistic whenever immediate and constant pressure is not applied. (18)

And the following January, after several excursions through Phocis, Orchomenos, Kyme, Thebes, and Chalkis:

[January 7, 1938]

The local population in central Greece seemed to me to be quiet and contented, as is always the case when crops are good and current weather conditions not unfavorable for the future. Since that time, however, the winter has become more severe, and as there is no particular attachment to the dictatorship in the district in question, or indeed anywhere in Greece, and only a lukewarm acceptance of the monarchy, much would seem to depend on how Zeus acts during the coming months as well as upon the actions of the King and Premier. (19)

Although the country's sullen attitude toward its self-proclaimed savior showed no signs of abating, Metaxas' regime was no longer viewed as just another ephemeral dictatorship. With the first anniversary of its establishment only days away, MacVeagh observed that ". . . rumors dealing with possible reaction against the regime have grown noticeably fewer as time has passed. . . ." (20) Assessing the situation at the close of 1937, he wrote on February 18, 1938: "If a people without history is happy, 1937 should have been a happy year for Greece, for the kaleidoscopic changes usual in Greek political life were totally missing. The dictatorship of General John Metaxas was in firm control, but the Greek has no love for such control, and found the second year of dictatorship increasingly distasteful." Although it was generally admitted that the King was not the prime mover behind the new order, "The fact is that he gave it so much support that many people now believe his fate is bound up with it, and that when the Dictator goes, so will he. . . ." (21)

The history of the Metaxas régime, not as yet written, will reveal that a host of factors contributed to the dictatorship's durability. Undoubtedly, the ruthlessly effective police measures, and the resulting paralysis of all forms of protest, had much to do with the lack of serious opposition. The sorry record of party politics shortly before the summer of 1936 had cast doubt on the ability of Greece's political leaders to provide the country with good government, thus numbing the nation to the excesses of the new régime. Under Metaxas, there were undeniable signs of improvement in the performance of the civil service and of the economy. More importantly, for its own reasons, the army, so often the decisive factor in the country's delicate power balance, and now clearly staffed by royalist senior officers, chose to remain loyal to the dictator. But no matter how decisive, these domestic factors are not enough to explain Metaxas' ability to survive: external dangers appeared to play into his hands, and to strengthen the argument for an opposition-free government. Developments in the Balkans and in Europe's power politics, increasingly dominated by German and Italian aggression, made Greece extremely sensitive to the threat of war. There appeared to be a real possibility that the Slavs to the north might resolve their differences at the expense of Greece, and Italy was clearly out to dominate the Eastern Mediterranean, destroying Greek independence in the process.

Under these circumstances, a strong government in Athens, which would concentrate on improving the country's chances for survival in the event of attack, was viewed by some as absolutely essential. Since no such government was likely to be formed by the existing political parties, perhaps a dictatorship was the price that had to be paid for that defense. Whatever else might be said about him, General Metaxas appeared to offer the country's best guarantee that the frontiers would be defended, and that the armed forces would be made equal to the task. In short, Metaxas' oppression was tolerated, however grudgingly, in the interest of national defense. Of course, whether, in fact, the dictatorship was such a necessary solution to the nation's problems is an issue which will divide Greeks for decades to come.

Although fully aware of its unpopularity and of its sinister side, MacVeagh had little difficulty in accepting the dictatorship as a necessary evil. This is often implied in his letters to the President, in which he continued to stress heightening international tensions, and Greece's mounting insecurity:

Athens, February 17, 1937

Dear Franklin:

What is going on in Spain and in other parts of the world must throw this region pretty much into the shade, but as the political situation in Greece and in the Balkans generally is getting more and more complicated, I will venture another letter. I can only hope you won't find it stale and unprofitable.

Old racial and national jealousies keep the possibility of war always very near the surface in Balkan affairs, but it seems that the question of war never crops above the surface so easily as it does when a new peace pact is signed! The phenomenon has made its appearance several times since I have been over here. This time the cause is the pact of peace and friendship just concluded between Yugoslavia and Bulgaria.[14] This pact is being interpreted here widely (though not, of course, officially) as covering a secret understanding for the partition of northern Greece. I am informed that even the Premier-Dictator, General Metaxas, has had his moment of panic, and told his Legation at Sofia that if his government had to resign it would be the Legation's fault. Officially the Government has done what it could not help doing. It has accepted the pact at its face value as a good thing in the cause of peace. But at the same time it has announced that the completion of its own re-armament program will be greatly accelerated, and military maneuvers on a large scale are expected in the spring along the northern frontier. German munitions are flooding into the country, incidentally reducing Greece's blocked credits in Berlin, and I have it from Americans in the district who have actually seen the works in progress that great activity is being displayed (supposedly in secret) in the fortification of the Bulgarian frontier. Of course, this latter work has been going on for some time, and re-armament has been part of the present Government's plans from the moment it came to power last August. Also it is by no means beyond the Greeks to re-export a lot of the German equipment they are now getting to Spain. Some airplanes seem actually to have gone through that way already, and the British Intelligence Officer here told one of my secretaries only the other day that he was sure that some such plan lay behind the recent great increase of Greek armament purchases abroad. Nevertheless, the announcement that Greece would complete her six-year re-armament schedule in one year has served as a reply to those who claim the Government was caught napping by the Bulgars and the Yugoslavs. Greece could hardly oppose a peace pact between its neighbors. But if those neighbors plan aggression, this is her answer. As a face-saving maneuver it would seem to be a good one, as well as necessary in view of the nervousness (always in evidence regarding Bulgaria) which gives otherwise partisan criticism its cutting edge.

But what of the reality of the menace? I am told that many people in Bulgaria, as well as in Greece, believe that the peace pact is a blind, and covers an agreement whereby Yugoslavia and Bulgaria are to attack Greece, the one taking Salonica and the other the exit to the Aegean she has so long desired. Greek nervousness and Bulgar truculence are known factors in the creation of "information" of this sort, and can be dis-

[14] On January 24, 1937, Bulgaria and Yugoslavia signed a Treaty of Friendship and Perpetual Peace.

counted. But we should be careful not to trust our own ideas too much in judging these people. It may seem to us incredible that any statesman could believe in a localized, and as it were private, Balkan war after the lessons of 1914. But those who direct these nations today fought in, or at least lived through, the Balkan Wars of 1912-13, which did not spread to the rest of Europe, and I believe them capable of regarding such a thing as a possibility again, and of starting a new war among themselves if the immediate temptation is great enough and their strength sufficient. Furthermore, Balkan history would seem to justify little faith in the ability of the Balkan Entente to check a sudden access of cupidity on the part of one of its members. Indeed, all those who attribute sinister designs to Yugoslavia blandly assume that the Balkan pact would be no bar. Finally, if the Great Powers, who all have axes to grind here, are counted on to halt hostilities, we have history again to caution us. One has only to read the story of the Greeks in Asia Minor after the War to see what may come from counting on the Powers with their conflicting interests. And finally, in a part of the world hardly yet freed from brigandage and still in the vendetta stage, private wars seem natural. Much as I should like to think otherwise, I am afraid that another Balkan War is indeed a possibility, particularly so long as Bulgaria and Yugoslavia feel they have something to gain by a change in the *status quo*. Considerations which we would think deterrent do not appear the same in the light of Balkan history and character.

The question becomes, accordingly, whether an attack on Greece by Yugoslavia and Bulgaria is likely in the near future, rather than whether it is possible. I am inclined to doubt it, but the question opens up some interesting vistas. Balkan statesmanship may be myopic from our point of view, but it sees very clearly what it sees. The regional pacts fostered by the French some years ago to enclose Germany, have failed of their purpose. The ring was never completed, and Germany has tunneled below political lines and become economically dominant even in the Little Entente, not to speak of the less compact Balkan groupment. These things these people see, and though the Council of the Balkan Entente, meeting this week in Athens, may herald unanimity of purpose and identity of view, as heretofore at other meetings, the fact remains that this Entente is not strong. The feeling is abroad that bilateral pacts with one's strongest neighbors are better guarantees than multilateral agreements embracing doubtful factors. The Yugoslav-Bulgarian agreement seems conceived along these more realistic lines. Greece has enjoyed a similar agreement with Turkey, and it is this agreement, based fundamentally on the fact that it suits the Turkish book to have the weakest of the Balkan states (if we except Albania) as her only neighbor in the Aegean, that appears to be the best guarantee against Slavic aggression in

Macedonia and Thrace. When the abortive Venizelist revolt took place here in 1935, it was the Turkish concentration in Eastern Thrace, rather than the Balkan Pact, which prevented Bulgaria from trying to turn it to her advantage. So I believe that now it is Turkish friendship, or rather Turkish interest, which agrees with Greek interest in preserving the *status quo*, which is the real guarantee of Greek territorial integrity (and to this extent, of peace in the Balkans and perhaps in Europe) rather than the Balkan Pact or German armaments. The Yugoslav-Bulgar *rapprochement* would thus seem a threat to Greece in the event of a general conflagration, in which all question of the *status quo* would disappear, rather than an immediate danger.

But, behind the Yugoslav-Bulgarian agreement there are, of course, other forces. For instance, suppose that Italy has been pressing Yugoslavia to agree to an alliance of such a nature as to free Italy of all fears in that quarter while she embarks on an adventure further afield. (I am supposing a situation actually suggested to me by my British colleague.) Such action, if really taken, would amount to an invasion of the freedom of action of the Little Entente, and would certainly be resisted by Yugoslavia if she felt strong enough to do so. Now some of my other colleagues are presuming that behind the Yugoslav-Bulgar pact lies the influence of England. The two suppositions "march together" as the French say. If Yugoslavia resisted the Italian pressure and the Italians counted on Bulgaria to aid her to keep Yugoslavia in line by threatening the latter's back door,—and hitherto Bulgaria has played the Italian game, —the pact is a definite check to Mussolini. Such considerations as this tend to overshadow the relatively minor question of Greek security.

The question of what Italy is planning is really what exercises the best informed foreign observers here. Even my Hungarian colleague, whose country tries to keep in with Italy without loving her, tells me that he is puzzled and afraid. The gentlemen's agreement between England and Italy has done much to quiet Greek fears for this country's exposed position in the Mediterranean. But as the poem has it, "One rubber plant can never make a home!" Living near Mussolini is like living on Vesuvius. One would therefore expect English influence to be exerted here toward an increase of Greco-Turkish cordiality. But unfortunately England, though still relied on by the Greeks to save them in a pinch, seems none too influential in the immediate conduct of Greek affairs. The influence of Germany is strong with the King, the Kaiser's nephew, and with General Metaxas, who was trained in Germany, and Germany has much to gain and little to lose from trouble in the Balkans as well as in other parts of Europe. The Greeks certainly do not seem to be cultivating the Turks as much as they should for safety's sake, and their persistent internal political difficulties, which they cannot hide from their anxious friends, are, to say the least, not calculated to impress the latter with their reliability.

In regard to internal affairs, I may say that the Metaxas dictatorship is weak and unpopular. It is weak because it relies on the King and the army for its support, rather than on popular enthusiasm and a fascist party, and because the King is a moderate and will not allow a free use of extremist methods. It is unpopular because the Greek people are democratic, and the King will not or cannot completely bar repressive action—censorship of the press, and the occasional use of castor oil, exile, and ice. Nearly all the public men of any consequence are now in opposition, and even in the army, loyal to the King as it is, there is beginning to be evident, particularly in the north, a growing discontent with the régime. Some observers believe serious trouble is due to break out in the spring, others that the régime can carry on some time longer, because the opposition is not organized and no alternative is apparent except anarchy. We shall see; but there can be no doubt that there is widespread uneasiness here as concerns both internal and external affairs.

It seems that war-talk and fear-talk come into the conversation whenever diplomats get together in these days. One of the Czechoslovak secretaries asked me last night what headway the German propaganda against his country is making in America! I did not know there was any, but it appears that Hitler has been calling names, the chief of which is "communist," and that's as bad as "j'accuse" was to Mr. Dooley.[15] The Czechoslovaks seem as convinced that Germany is going to hop on them as others are suspicious of Italy or Bulgaria. Everyone seems to agree that Germany and Italy are not strong enough economically to stand the strain of a European war such as even the most modest armed aggression might precipitate. Nevertheless, it is a fact that the nervous condition of such people as ought to be well posted out here in Greece is very bad. Perhaps we can take consolation from the fact that Europe has cleared some pretty high hurdles recently in the cause of peace, and every one of these that is cleared gives us hope for the next.

Ever yours affectionately,
Lincoln MacVeagh (22)

And several months later:

[15] "Mr. Dooley," fictional character created by American humorist Finley Peter Dunne (1867-1936), appearing in the *Chicago Evening Post*. "Martin Dooley," a saloon keeper, provided incisive and humorous criticism of American politics and society.

Athens, June 7, 1937

Dear Franklin:

The following little digest of Athenian news may interest you under two heads, local and international. To begin with the first, General Metaxas still carries on with his dictatorship. The heralded "Youth Movement," through which he hoped to construct for himself a kind of ultra-nationalist or fascist party, has so far failed to get going. Industrial, commercial, agricultural and other "corporations" have also failed to take shape. The Dictatorship continues of a strictly military type and government is carried on by royal decrees concocted by the Dictator and his advisers. Because of the unpopularity of such a regime in an essentially democratic country, really competent persons are not numerous in the cabinet. The secret police is accorded a wide scope and there has been a certain amount of summary arrest, imprisonment and exile, often on the slightest grounds and sometimes accompanied by considerable brutality. The result has been to keep the opposition cowed and scattered but to add resentment to unpopularity. Since the censorship keeps anything but praise of the Dictator and his policies from appearing in the press, the opposition has found its best expression in the columns of sympathetic liberal newspapers abroad, particularly in England. It seems to be the official British attitude, however, to favor the regime so long as it has the support of the King. The latter would doubtless prefer a parliamentary regime, and is certainly losing in personal prestige from his connection with a government which has to use spies and coercion to keep itself in power, but remembering his experience of last year, he still hesitates to turn the country back to the inefficient mercies of quarreling politicians. Faced with the old dilemma of the devil and the deep sea, he is still siding with what a lot of people would call the devil.

The internal situation is thus not a very happy one. General Metaxas would appear to be trying to improve the condition of the country in many ways, and to run it efficiently, but in his eagerness, to be setting perhaps too high a standard for Greece in this regard. His "legislation" is often hasty and ill considered. The cost of living is going up rapidly, the new budget shows large increases in many items and altogether reaches an all-time high, new taxes are announced nearly every day, and a wide use is being made of what our newspaper men call the "shakedown," the forcing of capital and labor alike to make "gifts" to the Government for this or that patriotic purpose. That the alleged reasons for so much government expenditure are good, that improvements in the army and navy, in roads and frontier defenses, in veterans' relief and pensions, in land reclamation and flood control, etc., are greatly needed, is not to be disputed. But whether Greece can afford the cost of the present regime's large and hasty projects in all these ways at once is a question. Some good observers think not, and that the cost of this dictatorship will eventually wreck it.

In the Near Eastern international field, the complicated peace machinery set up since the war has suffered considerable strain during the past year, and under danger of breaking down has had to be patched up in several places. The fundamental framework is, of course, composed of the Petite Entente, linked with the Balkan Entente and the Greco-Turkish pact of friendship. The new patches, which at first seemed likely to tear the old machinery apart, are the bi-lateral Pacts between Yugoslavia and Bulgaria and between Yugoslavia and Italy.[16] These now appear to be working in quite nicely with the general scheme, but to insure this result it has taken a new factor in the situation, namely, the rise of British prestige based on re-armament. French influence, which accounted for the creation of the Petite and Balkan ententes, has waned since the death of Barthou and more particularly since the advent of the Blum Government,[17] and it is England which now appears to be inspiring the two most important Near Eastern countries, Yugoslavia and Turkey, and to be the active element cementing the alliances preservative of the *status quo*.

For example, to quiet the fears expressed here that the recent Bulgar-Yugoslav agreement nullified the Balkan Entente and isolated Greece— a fear which my Italian colleague gleefully reported to me as being well founded—General Metaxas recently invited the Premier of Turkey[18] to stop here on his way home from the Coronation in London. On his way down Ismet had a long talk on the train with M. Stojadinović, Premier of Yugoslavia, and my Yugoslavian colleague has informed me that it was with the approval of London that the Turkish leader accepted the Greek invitation. On his arrival here he confirmed in no uncertain terms the solidarity of the Balkan Entente and of the Greco-Turkish friendship, and during the dinner in his honor conveyed to General Metaxas a telephonic message from Kemal[19] personally which read in part as follows: "I am happy to tell you that it gives me pleasure as a man and a soldier to declare to you that our frontiers are the same and that the forces which defend them are one and inseparable. The frontiers of the allied Balkan states constitute a single frontier. Such as may have designs on this frontier risk exposing themselves to the burning rays of the sun and I

---

[16] On March 25, 1937, Italy and Yugoslavia signed a five-year Treaty of Non-Aggression and Arbitration. The agreement guaranteed each country's frontiers vis-à-vis the other, and provided for educational rights for the Yugoslav minority in Italy.

[17] On June 5, 1936, Leon Blum, leader of the French Socialist Party, formed France's first "Popular Front" government.

[18] Ismet Inönü.

[19] Mustafa Kemal Ataturk, President of Turkey.

advise them to be careful." These are strong words. Some of the more sly among my colleagues have opined that Kemal was drunk when he uttered them, but it is quite certain that Ismet was sober when he relayed them to the Greek Premier and the Greek press. I am informed that a recent military demonstration in Bulgaria featuring placards with the names of Greek and Turkish towns coveted by the Bulgars got under the Turkish Dictator's skin. In any case, he generally means what he says, drunk or not, diplomatic or the reverse, and that he timed his outburst to coincide with Ismet's Athenian visit would certainly imply calculation and coordination.

Thus, the picture I would leave with you is that of a somewhat uncertain dictatorship continuing in Greece, and of a revived British prestige repairing and supporting the recently weakened framework of peace in this part of the world.

Affectionately yours,
Lincoln MacVeagh(23)

After another brief return to the United States in the summer of 1937, during which he visited the President, MacVeagh reported (in a letter dated November 10, 1937), that he found little change in Athens and in the Balkans:

The dictatorship remains in the saddle, with the hope expressed by many that the King, who still seems to control the army, may at some future date revert to a parliamentary régime. He told one American friend of mine, who had remarked to him that Americans don't like dictatorships, that they should make an exception in the Greek case, since unlike the Fascist and Nazi régimes, the Metaxas dictatorship is neither supported by a party nor permanent. On the other hand, the Dictator himself, it should be remarked, rules as if he quite intended his régime to be permanent. There is little liberty which the Greeks are permitted just now except the liberty to hope,—and to talk when they are confident there are no secret police near at hand. . . . In regard to the international situation, you told me last summer that you believed the German urge to be toward the East and that you felt the Germans would make some move in that direction within the next ten years. Confirming this, the best opinion I can gather around here is that the present talk of colonies is to some extent a smoke screen; that Hitler still believes, as he wrote in *Mein Kampf*, that Germany wants no colonies which she cannot defend. The breakdown and absorption of Czechoslovakia, Austria, and Hungary in a triumphant progress to the Ukraine is regarded in these parts as Hitler's real program. But for the present I am told that, whatever the party may think about it, the German army, powerful as it is, is not prepared for so large an order. Republican Czechoslovakia is regarded as strong enough to resist alone for say three months, and longer with such help from outside as Loyalist Spain is receiving. Furthermore, people here believe that she can count on the full support of France, which could hardly afford to see Germany enlarged and the last liberal regime in central Europe go under. The help of France is of course the crucial question. Krofta[20] appears to believe he has it absolutely assured. So a good observer from Czechoslovakia, who has talked with him, told me only yesterday. If France came in, England could hardly stand aloof, and for Germany to lose another war would be disastrous for her—she would almost certainly go Bolshevik. Such is the reasoning given to support the belief that Germany, at least for the present, is blocked before Prague. As for Austria, it is pointed out that Germany needs Italy these days, and Italy wants an independent Austria. Some people think Germany may move against Poland, the latter having somewhat alienated France. But this would be stirring things up with a vengeance and one hears less of it than of the danger to Czechoslovakia and Austria where German "penetration" is already pretty well advanced.

Closer to home we have the Greeks cementing their friendship with Turkey which is a potent influence against trouble in the Balkans, at least trouble of a local origin. The prestige of the British would seem to be rising—their fleet, their re-armament program, and their constant preoccupation with the preservation of peace, are apparently drawing more and more countries into their orbit. Turkey, with one eye turned to Russia, is looking more and more to England with the other. Yugoslavia is, they say, more impressed with English diplomacy than of yore. The kings of both Bulgaria and Greece have just gone to London.

No wise man cares to prognosticate in such circumstances as prevail today, but I should say there were more people who dared to hope for an indefinite prolongation of peace than there were last year. It interested me greatly to hear one of the best informed Greeks of my acquaintance say only the other day that your recent speeches had contributed greatly to this end. Incidentally, this man came from Macedonia, so in addition to all the other things you have done, you would seem to have answered the cry which sounded in Paul's ears, "Come over into Macedonia and help us!" (24)

In the fall of 1937, with political life essentially frozen, and the dictatorship's drabness permeating everything, Athenians sought diversion in following—and fabricating—reports that Crown Prince Paul was planning to take a wife. Although hardly a popular figure, the tall, hand-

[20] Kamil Krofta, Czechoslovakia's Minister for Foreign Affairs.

some, and athletic brother of King George was believed to be at odds with Metaxas over the leadership and dogma of the national youth organization (E.O.N.), which was pledged to defend the Prime Minister's regime "to the death." As a result, and in addition to its natural sensational quality as a great social event, the contemplated wedding was viewed as politically significant, as a subtle indicator of the royal family's attitude toward the dictator's whim. Throughout the summer months, there had been persistent rumors, discounted by MacVeagh, that the bride was to be the daughter of a prominent Greek family, and therefore a commoner. The suspense was finally dispelled by the official announcement, on September 27, of Paul's engagement to Princess Frederika Louise of Hanover, daughter of the Duke of Brunswick, and granddaughter of the Duke of Cumberland, and thus a distant relative of the British monarchy. To the politically super-sensitive Greeks, the complicated family ties of the petite princess were full of special (if hidden) meaning, and there was endless speculation as to the impact of the approaching marriage upon the country's international position. Aware of the guessing game, the Metaxas government used the controlled press to emphasize that while German, Frederika was closely related to the English royal house.

For the diplomatic community in the Greek capital, the Crown Prince's wedding was the cause of much excitement, accompanied by no few problems in protocol. In December, after informing the British ambassador, Sir Sydney Waterlow, that the United States Government had no plans to send a wedding gift, MacVeagh reported to the Department on the contemplated "international aspects" of the affair:

[December 30, 1937]

I duly communicated the gist of the Department's message to my British colleague, at whose instance the inquiry was made. Sir Sydney expressed appropriate thanks, and then informed me that he had heard from London that his government also would make no special gift to the Royal couple. He added, however, that the King of England would send a personal present and that it was his information that the President of France would do likewise.

The Duke and Duchess of Kent (Princess Marina of Greece) are expected to attend the wedding, the date of which, the 9th of January, is now freely given in the Greek press. An official reception is to be held at the British Legation as well as the German. Reports from London state that there was a meeting of the British Privy Council last Sunday at which King George VI gave his formal consent to the marriage. It seems that this action was necessary because of a British law of 1772 regarding the marriages of the reigning house, of which, as the Department knows,

Princess Frederika of Hanover is a somewhat distant member. Wide publicity has been given to these reports here. Indeed, officially and publicly, both by the British and the Greek authorities, much is being made of the British angle of this alliance. But the man in the street, whether Greek or foreign, generally asserts that he is not being misled. He sees the wedding as primarily a Greco-German affair, and busily circulates rumors accordingly. One of these rumors is to the effect that when the great day arrives every Greek will be compelled to display not only the Greek banner and the emblem of the bride's family, but the Nazi flag as well.

The wedding of the Crown Prince of Greece would naturally require a show of politeness on the part of the Powers, the Greek Royal Family being so integral a part of the European Royal network. But there exists an eager anxiety about taking first place, or at least not being eclipsed, which would seem excessive in the case of a tin-pot ceremony in a marginal near-eastern petty state. If England sends a Kingly gift, must not France send a Presidential one? Both England and France have an uneasy eye on the possible action of Italy, and under the gaze of all, Germany gets away with the prize, the wedding itself! It was not necessary for Prince Paul to choose a German bride, or even to marry at all at this time. The royal marriage-market is not glutted with possibilities, but it is not flat either, and no one has yet risked ridicule by suggesting that the Prince is marrying for love. Neither can the bride's considerable fortune, based as it is on German mining shares, be the main objective of a Royal Prince with plenty of perquisites. The Greek Government is more generous to its Royal Family than to its foreign bondholders, and the Civil List makes ample provision for the Heir Apparent. No, it would seem quite fair to lay this wedding at this time to foreign policy, and to that alone, and to see in the fuss and feathers made over it not only a recognition of this fact on the part of England, France, Italy and Germany, but an indication of an interest on the part of all these powers in who rules the roost in Greece. The four [England, France, Italy, Germany] divide here in Greece, as elsewhere, into two fronts, the democratic and the dictatorial powers. If French influence in Greece has waned, that of her partner has maintained itself. Fear of Mussolini as a ruthless opportunist is ever present, but here again it is the partner who commands the larger share of respect. Germany or England, which is it to be? As reported in my despatch No. 1990 of November 30, 1937,[21] it is General Metaxas's desire to follow Kemal's lead and try to keep out of any entanglement with one or other of the western groupments. But "Things are in the saddle and ride mankind." Metaxas must reckon with his host. All the great European powers are interested in the Mediterranean question and have high stakes to play for in the region where Greece lies

[21] Not cited in this text.

exposed. When King George came back to Athens, recalled by the most fantastic of bogus plebiscites, England gave him her blessing, and considered herself in charge of his destinies (see my telegram No. 172 of November 18, 1935). Now Germany has contrived to thicken still further his family's heavy dose of German blood. In the light of this outstanding fact, the goings-on of the British over this wedding take on a certain significance. Hitherto they would seem to have had the edge on their opponents. Now they may have to fight to hold it. Inevitably a spectator's thoughts turn back to Constantine and his German wife, and the situation before the Great War. General Metaxas is pro-German in sympathy and the King is half German in blood and wholly in character. Little is known here of the character of the young Princess who is coming. On her influence over Paul, who, unless all signs fail, is as amenable to such influence as his father was, much will depend.

But there is something more to be added to this picture, from the Greek point of view. Greece is not a mere *corpus vile* to be dragged this way or that wholly at the will of others. Her own action will count for something, if only a little, in the net result of the parallelogram of forces of which she is a part. Both King George and General Metaxas are genuine patriots, and what they do in any given crisis of foreign affairs will be done because they think it in the best interests of their country. That they believe that neutrality in a general European war, or in a struggle between any of the great powers, or at least neutrality till it becomes clear which side will win, is the only possible policy for Greece, I feel sure now and have previously reported. Whether they like it or not, their country's weakness and exposed position demand that they play the game safe, if they can, to its inglorious end. Theirs not to do and die, but do their best to save their country's hide if Europe burns. This means nothing to the great powers, who will undoubtedly use Greece or abuse her as their own policy may dictate, even as they are assiduously softsoaping her now. But to Greece herself it means that whatever she does in anticipation of a catastrophe, she must have a backdoor of escape. The choice of a German princess as the bride of the Crown Prince undoubtedly indicates the present Greek reading of the signs of the times in Europe, where the German band-wagon is the big noise. But the choice of a Princess of Hanover, a descendant of Queen Victoria, whose wedding must be "consented" to by the King of England, means something too. In fact, it keeps the way open to neutrality and preserves that attitude of Mr. Facing-Both-Ways which, while it may puzzle and exasperate the Powers, and probably will prolong *ad nauseam* their competitive blandishing of this tiny nation, marks her policy in the matter of this royal wedding as fundamentally and essentially not pro anything but Greek. (25)

And on January 9, there was sent another despatch in MacVeagh's unique style, combining the light touch of a society column with a flare for political reporting:

> Crown Prince Paul of Greece and Princess Frederika Louise of Hanover, who will now call herself Marguerite,[22] were married today in the Metropolitan Church of Athens. The wedding was a brilliant one, perfectly carried out, and the singing of the Orthodox marriage-service something to be remembered for a lifetime. The bride is a charming little person, strictly brought up by an admirable if stuffy family. She is shy, very naïve, and of course wholly inexperienced, and at the present time no estimate can be made of what influence she may eventually have on her husband, who appears gross beside her, and on the fortunes of the monarchy in Greece.
>
> The ceremony took place in the crossing of the church at 10:30 in the morning, and was performed by Archbishop Chrysostomos, assisted by other bishops and archimandrites, to the number of about forty, who made a brilliant show with their jeweled robes and crowns against the gorgeous choir-screen. Besides the King, there were present the Prince Regent of Yugoslavia, the Crown Prince of Rumania, the Duke and Duchess of Kent, and a flock of lesser luminaries, all more or less royal. The Hohenzollern connection was represented by Prince August Wilhelm and Princes Hubert and Oscar of Prussia. Denmark, who gave Greece her royal family, sent Prince and Princess Knud, Prince Erik and Princess Axel. Czarist Russia was there too, in the person of Grand Duke Dmitri, who is supposed to have helped Prince Youssoupoff kill Rasputin, and, incidentally, looks quite capable of being in that galley. There were also, of course, the Duke and Duchess of Brunswick, parents of the bride, with their various offspring, and finally, completing a group which it took twenty automobiles to accommodate, numerous Hesses, Bades, Mecklembourg-Schwerins, Hohenlohe-Langenbourgs, Torring-Jettenbachs, and minor members of the houses of Prussia, Hanover and Greece. The body of the church was filled by a host of military and civil functionaries, and the Diplomatic Corps occupied a raised platform in the left transept, facing the Government, which was similarly situated on the right. . . .
>
> In connection with my despatch under reference,[23] discussing the international aspects of this wedding, it may be interesting to note that the German Chancellor sent congratulations by telegram, while the Duke of Kent came as a special representative of the King of England. Despite

[22] Contrary to MacVeagh's report, the future Queen of Greece retained the name Frederika.
[23] MacVeagh despatch 2030, December 30, 1937, cited above.

prognostications, the German Legation is not giving any reception. But tomorrow night the British Minister is entertaining most of Athens, from the King down, in honor of the Duke. Thus the wedding is still in balance, as it were, between England and Germany, the one making up in emphasis for the other's numbers. But the staying on of the Duke of Kent, with the official reception for him tomorrow, and the banquet which will be offered to him Wednesday night by the Anglo-Hellenic League at Greece's leading hotel, may quite well make it appear in the end that the Crown Prince of Greece has but married a German princess to make a British holiday.

Incidentally, the Duke's coming spelt bad news for the local diplomats. Presumably because Athens boasts a limited supply of top-hats (I am informed that the import quota on this commodity was specially increased for the occasion) the Court decided last Thursday that all Chiefs of Mission and their wives, and not only the German and British Ministers concerned, should go to the station to meet the bride on her arrival. The Chiefs were according convoked, and ranged along the platform as a kind of Gilbert and Sullivan chorus to the Royal greetings. Following this as a precedent, they were likewise convoked the next day to meet Prince Paul of Yugoslavia. Obedient to the dictates of their profession, Brazilians, Chileans, Argentinians and Bulgars, Egyptians, Swiss, Swedes and Americans, Russians, Dutch, Poles, Turks, Albanians, Austrians, etc., etc., all turned out again in full dress uniforms or "fracs," in the bitter cold. They thought, and indeed they said, this in the end; nothing further can be demanded of our politeness. But as the Roman poet sings or says:

"Of further woe they had no thought,
When a horrid message to them was brought!"

The Duke of Kent, so ran the word, would arrive an hour later, and the Corps must be on hand to greet him too. Indeed, the British Minister had been to the Palace that very afternoon to fix it all up, and after the Prince Regent of Yugoslavia had been met and escorted uptown in his armored car, we settled down to a long wait while Sir Sydney ranged the whole personnel of his Legation at the head of the line of foreign plenipotentiaries. The Duke, it seems, was actually on the same train as the Prince Regent nearly all the way from Belgrade to Athens, but found it impossible to arrive at the same time because of considerations of rank. ("They're drawing pretty fine distinctions," said the Italian Minister.) So the train was divided at Thebes, and the Regent was given an hour's start, thus allowing King George time to go home and change his Yugoslavian decoration for an English one before greeting the British Duke. Meanwhile, suppressed indignation, by raising the blood-pressure, probably saved the diplomats from freezing.

Great care is being taken of the Regent, who appears to be a very nervous and suspicious man—probably with reason. He has brought his own chauffeur and bullet-proof limousine, cunningly designed so that it offers no running-board or door-handle for any assassin to catch hold of. By special order, not only hotels but every private person who has a foreigner staying in his house must report the fact to the police with full particulars. The streets are lined with police and soldiery wherever the Regent goes, and when he goes, he goes as they say Stalin goes in Moscow, hell bent.

The crowds along the way, both for the receptions at the station and for the wedding itself, and the gala performance at the Royal Theater last night, have been singularly undemonstrative. The bride, who rode to and from the cathedral in a coach drawn by six white horses (to find which the absurd Ypsilanti, the Royal Equerry, is said to have combed the kingdom) received a fair amount of hand-clapping and cheers. But the King has been greeted with silence and the Premier with feeble and scattered applause. The King's princely uncles have driven at salute along the troop-lined boulevards without a single answering gesture or sound. It is plain that the populace has turned out to see rather than to demonstrate, and of course, all the world loves a bride. But perhaps the King's coldness towards his people is finding an answering coldness. Certainly for his German relatives there is indifference, while much indignation is felt over the lavish expenditure devoted to this wedding by a state in which so many people are so desperately poor.

The King appears well and the rumors of his having cancer seem quite unfounded. But he does not seem to like being King of Greece, if his grimness at last night's gala performance, his indifference at the recent meeting of the National Academy, and still more his private conversation, are any sign. He told me that his stay in London was too short and that it was good not to have to see any Greeks for a while. Incidentally, he expressed at the same time considerable dislike of Fascist Italy, too, and complained that the Italians today seem to have no sense of humor. He said that in his interview with Count Ciano, the Italian Foreign Minister, the latter boasted of his courage and seemed to think that because his plane in Abyssinia had received two bullets through the wing he was the bravest of the brave. "In telling me this he got up and walked about thumping his breast," said the King, and added, "I couldn't help thinking of Tarzan of the Apes."

The King's trip to London may have been good for his spirits, but it has not helped his popularity in his own country, where the national temperament is ill-suited to his offishness. It may be true, as some people say, that he has been urged in France and England to get rid of Mr. Metaxas, but while he has been away the latter has been working night and day, not only on various civilian groups, such as labor and agriculture, with special legislative measures in aid of their condition, but on the army as well, with promotion and pay. If it should come to a showdown between the two men, and Mr. Metaxas should not want to be removed, it may be questioned whether the King would now find himself as able to go to the people over the head of the General as he was last spring. Mr. Metaxas has now at last started his long-projected youth movement, with the enrollment in Athens and Salonica of battalions whose oath of allegiance makes no mention of the King—surely a fact of some significance,—and he is constantly operating the press in such a manner as to give him the first place in the public mind. In this connection, the King's unfortunate reserve has been accentuated by his failure to issue a message to his people on New Year's Day, while the Dictator made no such omission. Furthermore, Mr. Metaxas has apparently been at no pains to conceal from the public the high cost of the royal wedding, and his control of the foreign correspondents, who have been prevented from telegraphing all but the barest outline of the festivities, has robbed the King of a fine chance for publicity abroad. The stupidity of the King's Household, which is no match for the Dictator in any contest of wits, has played into his hands in this matter, as correspondents have uniformly been given the cold shoulder at the Palace and referred to the Ministry of Press and Tourism. If the King doesn't want soon to see himself clinging to Mr. Metaxas as the latter has so far been forced to cling to him, it would seem that he should make some move without delay to occupy that place in the love of his people which his motto says is the strength of his House. (26)

In a letter to Eleanor Roosevelt, devoted largely to family matters, MacVeagh casually revealed that the royal wedding had not been the only cause of excitement in the Greek capital:

Athens, January 24, 1938

Dear Eleanor:
... We have just had a Royal Wedding, which was something to remember. Some forty bishops in full regalia and the most divine singing. Afterwards, by way of variety we had the threat of a new *cinema*, as the Greeks call a revolution. It seems to have been snuffed out with a number of arrests and banishments, but it provided a little local excitement to spice the general world unrest.
 We all got hot under the collar looking at the movies of the Panay in-

cident.[24] More and more I feel we are lucky to have Franklin where he is. I like his restraint,—and his naval program! He has made America's influence felt abroad as no President has ever done, without compromising us, and all for the good. Here the Government cuts out of his speeches all mention of democracy vs. autocratic regimes, but it doesn't let the people know this, for they all adore him. He has made the world realize that while we have a giant's strength, and know it, we do not wish to use it like a giant, and in consequence we enjoy a genuine respect. What this means to an envoy working for American interests in a part of the world which thinks in terms of armaments and hardly ever sees an American warship, or even an American Military Attaché, you may imagine.

I read about the "recession" at home and wonder what our people would think of real economic stress such as these countries over here labor under all the time. We are the favored people. I'd like to show some of my New York friends a whole country in desperate straits keeping a high heart nevertheless and making something out of life.

My very best wishes always to you both.

Affectionately yours,
Lincoln MacVeagh (27)

The threat of a new revolution, which the American Minister dismissed so lightly in his letter to the First Lady, was, in fact, a pathetic show of resistance to the regime, brought on indirectly by the wedding festivities. It succeeded in revealing, as nothing had before, the dictator's determination to tolerate no dissent, however innocuous.

To insure that all political activity had ceased, the government had ordered many prominent party leaders confined to their respective districts, away from Athens. When John Theotokis, the influential Populist, was allowed to travel to the capital to attend the royal wedding, he contacted several leaders of the Liberal Party. In a rare display of unity, Theotokis, Sofoulis, and Kafandaris wrote, clandestinely printed, and circulated, a proclamation denouncing the regime for usurping power, and for maintaining it through terror tactics. Perhaps the most telling portions of the statement were those reproducing the texts of earlier protests, delivered to the monarch by respected national leaders, charging Metaxas with the destruction of democracy in Greece. Having failed to respond to such previous warnings, the King was made to appear as

---

[24] On December 12, 1937, following a number of incidents in Chinese waters, Japanese bombers attacked American and British warships near Nanking. The U.S. river gunboat *Panay* was sunk, with a loss of two lives and with thirty wounded.

the dictatorship's accomplice. However ill-conceived, the move was designed to publicly pressure the King into withdrawing his support from Metaxas, thus opening the way for the restoration of parliament.

While the King maintained his silence, the government cracked down on the country's major political figures, regardless of whether they were involved in the preparation and distribution of the offending leaflet. Although Theotokis was simply ordered back to his native Corfu and Sofoulis given a stern warning by the security police, others, including Kafandaris, Mylonas, Papandreou, and Michalacopoulos, were imprisoned and eventually exiled to various desolate corners of Greece, where they were destined to remain until Metaxas' death in 1941. Whereas for most of these men this experience was painful, for Michalacopoulos it proved fatal, and soon MacVeagh was reporting to the Department the death of his Greek friend:

[April 4, 1938]

Taken from his bed, where he was lying ill of sinus infection, and forcibly exiled to the island of Paros, this elderly and distinguished person was housed there in a small, drafty, country hotel, lamentably lacking in heating and sanitary facilities. On or about February 24th, the Chief of Police at Paros telegraphed to the central authorities at Athens that his important charge had contracted pneumonia and that he could not assume responsibility for his health. This information was given to Mr. Michalacopoulos' immediate relatives who begged the Minister of Justice,[25] then acting Prime Minister, to transfer him to a hospital in Athens. Mr. Logothetis agreed, but the Minister for Public Safety, Mr. Maniadakis, held up the permission for 24 hours, until Mr. Metaxas, the Premier, then in Ankara, could be consulted. When Mr. Metaxas had finally given his permission, Dr. Lorando, one of the heads of the Evangelismos Hospital in Athens, was sent to Paros. [Having] arrived there, he advised against the patient's transfer to Athens on account of his extremely serious condition, but Mr. Michalacopoulos was nevertheless returned to Athens on a boat chartered by his family.

The Greek press has not at any time been permitted to refer to the arrest and exile of Mr. Michalacopoulos, but for several days prior to his death and after the arrival of a specialist from Vienna, who came by plane to Athens at the expense of the family, it published bulletins regarding his physical condition. From these bulletins, as well as from private information, it appears that after a long illness, during which double pneumonia was followed by double pleurisy, he died on Sunday, March 27, at 1 p.m.

[25] George Logothetis.

The funeral was really amazing. Daily papers are not published on Monday morning in Athens, and therefore the news of Mr. Michalacopoulos' death spread throughout the city only by word of mouth. The press has stated that the obsequies were a national affair, sponsored by the Government on the scale fixed for former Prime Ministers, despite the wish of Mrs. Michalacopoulos that the ceremony be small and private. Yet there was no notification sent out to the foreign Legations, as was the case when General Kondylis, Mr. Papanastasiou, and Mr. Tsaldaris were buried. People appear to have got their advance information as best they could. I happened to be with Mr. Metaxas at luncheon at the Rumanian Legation that day, and ascertained from his secretary, Mr. Androulis, that the staff of the Foreign Office would attend, to do honor to a former Chief, and that foreign diplomats were expected to go if they desired to do so. Meanwhile, the Legation had been informed only by an anonymous telephone call of the place and hour,— 4 p.m. at the Metropolitan Church. I attended, as I was genuinely fond of the old gentleman, and there was no reason not to do so. My Turkish colleague told me at luncheon that he would lend his presence because "Mr. Michalacopoulos was the possessor of a Turkish decoration." No preparation was made to receive us and our ilk. This "state funeral" was a free-for-all, and if the Government thought that by rushing it through unheralded it might avoid attracting popular attention, it must have been sadly disappointed. The Metropolitan Church was packed literally to overflowing. My French and Rumanian colleagues never got through the portals. My wife and I penetrated about 15 feet into the nave, helped by the kindness of friends who crushed themselves against their neighbors to make us a little room. Everybody who is anybody in Athens seemed to be there, no matter of what political faith. I saw Prince Ypsilanti and Countess Capodistria[26] as well as General Gonatas and Mr. Sofoulis, not to speak of moderates such as Mr. Roufos[27] and Mr. Tsouderos,[28] Mr. Varvaressos[29] and Mr. Constantine Tsaldaris. I am told that somewhere up front was Colonel Levidis, the Master of Ceremonies, and that he presented the King's condolences to Mrs. Michalacopoulos. Mr. Metaxas did not attend this state funeral of a former Prime Minister, but on the other hand a number of cabinet officers were present, whom the press later described as "personal friends" of the deceased. A strange

---

[26] Countess Capodistria, friend of the royal family of Greece.

[27] Kanakaris Roufos, prominent Venizelist politician and former Minister of National Economy.

[28] Emmanuel Tsouderos, prominent financier and Venizelist supporter, and the former Governor of the Bank of Greece.

[29] Kyriakos Varvaressos, prominent financier, former Governor of the Bank of Greece.

atmosphere brooded over the crushed assembly, many tears were in evidence, but what impressed me most was a kind of resentful and sullen apprehension. Police and plain-clothes men were everywhere, both in and out of the church. A small attempt at a demonstration in the square at the back was quickly squashed, and a shower of rain came opportunely as another evidence of the continuing favor of Zeus toward the powers that be.

The next day the Government saw to it that obituaries were published in all the papers, extolling the deceased and laying emphasis on his long service as Minister of Foreign Affairs, a post which he held for the greater part of the time between 1924 and 1933. Uniformly these obituaries laid his death to an alleged and disputed heart ailment of long standing, without further mention of his overwhelming pneumonia and pleurisy,—a weak maneuver on the part of the censorship which has increased rather than decreased the tendency of many opponents of the regime to qualify, in private conversation, the death of Andreas Michalacopoulos as nothing less than murder.

This unfortunate end to the career of one of Greece's last remaining public men of eminence is exactly the kind of thing which the King and the Dictator aimed to avoid when they refused to exile Mr. Sofoulis and sent Mr. Kafandaris to the salubrious island of Zante. It will not help Mr. Metaxas in the eyes of his countrymen that he was apparently not the direct cause of the injudicious ruthlessness which so clearly brought about Mr. Michalacopoulos' death. He will certainly be held responsible for the acts of his Minister of Public Safety at whose door the fault directly lies. The King also, who signed the law under which the Minister operated, a law permitting immediate exile without a hearing for anyone suspected of opposing the regime, will not escape undamaged. The incident has added a tone of righteous indignation to the opposition's expressions of dislike. It may not bring about the fall of the Dictatorship any more than the death of the Duc d'Enghien destroyed Napoleon, but there are many Greeks who regard it as likely to do something comparable, on the small scale of this country, in discrediting the regime and popularizing the cause of its opponents. It is indeed quite possible that we have not heard the last of this affair. (28)

The ill-fated proclamation of Theotokis, Sofoulis, and Kafandaris was the final whimper of a national political leadership that now lay prostrate before the all-powerful "Leader." Fittingly, however, the last spasm of active resistance came from Crete, the Venizelist stronghold and the cradle of several major uprisings in the nation's troubled history. Although a pitiful affair without a chance of success, it was received by the suffocating nation as a precious breath of fresh air, as MacVeagh reported to the Department:

[August 3, 1938]

Early in the morning of July 29, 1938, a revolt against the Metaxas regime broke out in Chanea, the capital of Crete. Amounting really to little more than a smartly executed coup on the part of a small band, it found no active support, though evidently much sympathy, elsewhere in the island and the rest of Greece, and was quickly quelled. But for a moment it seems to have shaken the confidence of the Government, and has been aptly termed an explosion. . . . The facts as at present known may be briefly summarized. Profiting by a reduction in the numerical strength of the garrison, which the central government has been hard put to it to explain, a number of persons, perhaps as many as four or five hundred, under the leadership of one Mitsotakis, a brother-in-law of Venizelos but an old henchman of Kondylis, and other local leaders, including a former mayor of Chanea named Hadjiangelis, took possession of all government buildings and unseated the Governor General, Mr. Sfakianakis, after the time-honored and bloodless fashion of most Greek revolutions. Direct communications with Athens were cut off, and remained so for about 24 hours, but the news of the revolt apparently reached the capital via Heraklion without much delay, and a Cabinet meeting was hurriedly held in the forenoon, a new acting Governor General, Mr. Markellos, appointed, with his seat at Heraklion, and troops, airplanes and naval units dispatched to the rebel city with all speed. The Prime Minister then issued a proclamation, featured in special editions of the press, calling on the people of Crete to show their loyalty. At the same time he is said to have informed the King in Corfu of the measures being taken to restore order, and later to have received assurances of the Royal satisfaction in this regard.

In what manner the revolt was actually quelled is not yet known, the censorship in connection with this affair remaining unusually strict, even now. First reports stated that all was over before the arrival of the military, while the Government admitted that three men were wounded in a fight with the *gendarmerie*, who were engaged "in the process of clearing out the armed bands." Later, however, equally official press reports indicated that the airplanes sent from Athens arrived in time to play a decisive part in convincing the revolutionists that their case was hopeless. All reports are to the effect that the leaders escaped from Chanea, and no indication that they have been captured in their hideouts has yet been forthcoming. A *Te Deum* was ordered to be sung in all the churches of Crete to thank God for saving the regime, and the press has been printing daily, ever since, a flood of telegrams congratulating the Premier on the happy issue of the affair.

It would appear significant that in the Government's communiques and press editorials the revolutionists are always referred to as "armed bands of rioters," or "armed citizens," etc., undoubtedly to emphasize the fact, if it is a fact, that none of the military or *gendarmerie* took part. The keynote in this regard was struck at once in the proclamation of the Premier, which I quote below in translation from the *ATHENAIKA NEA* of July 29, 1938:

"To the People of Crete":

"At a moment when I was preparing to depart from Athens in order to sign a foreign agreement of the greatest national interest, armed rioters entered Chanea and took possession of the city. I am determined to put down the rioters by all means, in order to impose the force of the law and insure peace and order to the Cretan people.

"Relying upon the patriotic sentiments of the Cretan people, as well as upon the proofs of confidence which they have shown me, I invite the entire Cretan population to deprive the rioters of any support and to manifest to the Greek people that Crete stands by the side of and is mutually responsible to the rest of the nation as a whole.

"Everywhere in Greece order and peace prevail and the people stand by the side of the Government."

J. METAXAS

This proclamation, particularly in view of the passing of the trouble like a summer cloud, has caused glee among the opposition, which sees the doughty Premier quailing at the report of a pop-gun as if it were the crack of doom. But the opposition has also had cause to realize that a frightened dictator is hardly a pleasant phenomenon. While order was being restored in Chanea, our local Fouché, the Minister of Public Safety, took prompt occasion for another round-up of reported malcontents in a nation-wide drive. Among those taken into custody at this time were General Gonatas and General Theodore Manettas, both distinguished officers, and the former, as the Department knows, one of the most illustrious, if partisan, of the modern patriots of Greece. Mr. Vlachos, local correspondent of the Associated Press and of the *Daily EXPRESS* of London, was also arrested, as reported in my telegram No. 48 of July 30.[30] The Legation's investigations on his behalf have brought out that he was charged with nothing more than remarking to a colleague over the telephone that in his opinion

---

[30] Not cited in this text.

there was more in the revolt in Crete than meets the eye! The British Legation has also made inquiries in his case. I am informed that under the wide powers which he enjoys, the Minister for Public Safety has insisted on condemning Mr. Vlachos to a year's imprisonment, but the Under-Minister for Press and Tourism[31] believes he may actually be kept in custody only for a period of about 10 days. The incident reveals the jumpiness of the regime as well as a strange disregard for foreign opinion.

The revolt quelled and the demands of public safety seen to, the Premier left Athens for Salonica, in order to sign the pact to which he refers,[32] with wounded but cryptic paternalism, in his proclamation (see my despatch No. 2397 of August 3, 1938).[33] That he was correct in estimating this pact as important to the Greek people, even his enemies admit. But these have also taken heart from the abortive little affair in Crete as supplying possible proof, in a bursting bubble, that the watched pot is coming to a boil. (29)

And a few weeks later:

[September 27, 1938]

It would seem that the Cretan revolt was by no means intended to be the isolated affair it actually became. I have been most reliably informed that similar outbreaks were planned to take place simultaneously in many of the principal cities of Greece, including Athens, and that the movement involved leading personalities both civil and military. These leaders, however, having learned that their plans were known, appear to have held back at the last moment, and nothing overt occurred except in Crete, where, as was the case when Mr. Venizelos misjudged the success of his revolt in 1935, lack of information precipitated a catastrophe in the form not of drama but of farce. On the face of it, the most serious thing about the affair has been the heavy punishment meted out to the rebels in Chanea, many of whom have now been caught. Though the ringleaders are still at large—and happily they are the only ones to have received sentences of death—the Courts-Martial have condemned many subordinates to terms of ten, fifteen, and twenty years, and even life imprisonment, at forced labor. These sentences have been given wide publicity in the press, in proof of the Government's long-expressed intention to visit

---

[31] Theologos Nicoloudis.

[32] On July 31, 1938, the members of the Balkan Entente and Bulgaria signed in Salonica a Treaty of Friendship and Non-Aggression (the "Pact of Salonica"). Bulgaria's right to re-arm was recognized, in return for a Bulgarian promise not to attempt to change by force the existing frontiers and to submit to arbitration all future disputes with the other signatories.

[33] Not cited in this text.

sedition with severity. But more significant would seem to be the disproportion between the small importance of this local disturbance and the overwhelming means employed to quell it. This disproportion perhaps gives the measure of the fears inspired in the Government by its knowledge of the wide-spread nature of the revolt as planned.

A former Governor-General of Crete, and close friend of Mr. Venizelos, who has hitherto been most guarded in his remarks to me concerning the present political situation, now assures me that the movement, of which the Cretan fiasco became the only outward and visible sign, was definitely connected with, and indeed based upon, the growing dislike of the military for the present dictatorial regime. I have previously reported other manifestations of this dislike (see my despatch No. 2378 of July 25, 1938).[34] It has little to do with Venizelism, since few Venizelist officers remain now on active duty. It derives rather from the cold aloofness of the King, who more and more clearly lacks all popular appeal, and from distrust of the Dictator, whose creation of the Youth Movement on quasi-militia lines has caused both doubt and resentment. In this latter connection, the army has always been the controlling factor in the political life of this country, whether for good or evil, and has no intention of being supplanted by a "party" of the Nazi or Fascist type. Finally, there is the characteristic Greek love of change, which easily comes to the surface in the absence of enthusiasm for the thing of the moment.

That the Government is worried would seem clear not only from the extraordinary measures taken to suppress the little Cretan outbreak but also from its subsequent actions. Banishment for cause or "on information received" has now been supplemented with banishment on frankly indefinite suspicion. . . . The precautions taken by Mr. Metaxas during his recent "cure" at Kamena Vourla, near Thermopylae, where he slept every night aboard a warship, are also in point. These precautions, together with the statement of Mr. Nicoloudis, Under-Minister for the Press, made on the eve of August 4th and since repeated with suspicious insistence, to the effect that Mr. Metaxas is "Dictator for life," give a fairly adequate nutshell summary of the present situation of uncertainty and strain.

More of the uncertainty than the strain may appear in the following story, which is undoubtedly true as well as typically Greek. According to one of his best friends, Mr. Pericles Argyropoulos, ex-Minister for Foreign Affairs and Mr. Papanastasiou's successor in the Balkan Conference, was implicated (his friend assures me, actually implicated) in the recent planned revolt, and ordered into banishment on some more or less noxious isle. He is related, however, to Mrs. Nicoloudis, and the latter secured him a personal interview with Mr. Maniadakis, the Minister for

---

[34] Not cited in this text.

Public Safety. At this interview Mr. Maniadakis graciously said that he would revoke the decree of banishment if Mr. Argyropoulos would consent to leave Greece voluntarily and never come back. "Put in your application for a passport," he said, "at once, and I will see that it is acted upon favorably. Only remember you must never come back to Greece." Mr. Argyropoulos, much relieved, replied that he would do as directed, and when he took his leave he thanked Mr. Maniadakis for his consideration, and added: "When we come to power, I'll remember this." "Thank you," replied Mr. Maniadakis, "I'm counting on that." And neither of them cracked a smile.

On the other hand, the strain on the Government may be detected in many of its public utterances. Not only does it harp continually on the perpetual nature of Mr. Metaxas' personal rule (me thinks it doth protest too much), but a shrill note has made its appearance in many of its references to the opposition. No longer is the press denouncing merely "the former party chiefs in cooperation with agitators and common criminals," as in the editorial quoted in my despatch No. 2088 of February 5, 1938.[35] It has now been moved to point its finger at a bigger bogey, and has uttered the name *Plastiras* with a shriek....

At the present moment there reigns here one of those unnatural calms, not wholly to be accounted for by the general anxiety over European affairs, which may be, as so often before in Greece, what Yankees call a "weather-breeder," a calm before a storm. The number of Mr. Metaxas' henchmen and spies remains impressive, but if leadership has really been added to the daily increasing numbers of those who are sick and tired of this rule, the present potentialities of trouble may issue in the real thing before long. At least, if it does so we should not be surprised, since few if any of the Greeks will share that emotion.

The King has come back from his vacation in Corfu, and nothing could better express his position as a cipher, though an expensive one, in the life of the country, than the indifference with which both his going and his coming have been received by the people. At the same time his influence with the Government seems also to have waned almost to the vanishing point, which confirms the suspicion that he can no longer sway the army. Indeed, without that weapon to his hand, and without "that love of his people which is the strength of his house," his value to the Dictator can be little more than that of a buffer or scapegoat....

Even more significant, along the same lines, would seem to be the King's remarks to my Brazilian colleague[36] when the latter called on him a few days ago to take his leave. His Majesty said he could easily understand the attitude of many liberals throughout the world who are being

---

[35] Not cited in this text.
[36] Julio Augusto Barboza-Carneiro, Brazilian Ambassador to Greece.

called "communists" today when in reality they are only disgusted with the regimes of the extreme right, because he feels that way himself. He said, "I have been in Italy and Germany, and know and hate the oppression that exists there, and I resent (sic) the position in which I find myself of being considered responsible for the same thing here." He said that the claims of the Metaxas *regime* to being permanent are "ridiculous," but he gave no indication of being able to do anything about it, or even of being willing to try. Meanwhile he is drawing a great deal of money out of the country and salting it away in England, where lives a mousy lady (whom he introduces as "Miss Brown," but has not brought to this Legation) and several children, so 'tis said. He is spending practically nothing here, and there is a story that he has mortgaged the Tatoi estate (which I believe), and another that he has sold the Palace (which I don't, at least not yet).

On the financial side, the Government is still performing the same miracle of keeping the ship of state afloat that has been accomplished now for years by other and even more bankrupt countries, and which, so far as I know, has never yet been explained. It may even keep on doing this long enough to render the financial question only a contributory, rather than the main cause, of its ultimate overthrow. At the present moment the Finance Minister confidentially expressed hopes of reaching a settlement with the foreign bondholders. . . . Meanwhile, popular rumor, repeated by gentlemen of real fiscal standing and experience, continues to affirm that the Government's finances are about as bad as bad can be.

The weather has been propitious, and the fall crops promise well, indicating that no trouble may be expected from the farm population this year. On the other hand, business men in general are none too pleased with the continuance and reinforcement of the Goverment's tie-up with German trade, and feel that in view of the possibility of war in Europe Greece should rather be seeking better commercial relations with the countries which control the seas. Such considerations as these, however, have always been less important in Greek political life than the desires and ambitions of individual leaders, and the interplay of civil and military combinations in search of place and plunder, and I see no reason to believe the future will be any different from the past in this respect. (30)

While the Near East Division of the Department of State might be expected to be interested in MacVeagh's informed despatches on Greece's latest political convulsions, there was little point in reporting the same events to a busy President. For him, it was the mounting international tension that was truly newsworthy, and although not in the center of things, the Balkans were a good listening post, ablaze with rumors about real or imagined crises. MacVeagh's letters to Roosevelt provide a running account of the diplomatic rumblings in his particular corner of the globe:

Athens, May 20, 1938

Dear Franklin:

I have not bothered you with a letter for some time as things have been taking a more or less quiet, if not exactly normal course in this little country, while the affairs of the world have been exceptionally troubled, as you know probably better than anyone.

In external affairs, Greece remains particularly afraid of Italy, and not too confident of England's strength. She thus has welcomed with relief the recent accord between the two.[37] The German menace to Czechoslovakia still seems somewhat remote to her, in spite of her link with the Little Entente through the Balkan groupment. But the *Anschluss*,[38] coming as and when it did, shocked her. It is recognized that the appearance of the Germans at the Brenner, being a menace to Italy, may have facilitated the Anglo-Italian agreement, and to that extent helped to conjure Greek fears in the Mediterranean. But the creation at the same time of a German-Yugoslav frontier is not regarded as good news. As the situation in central Europe has grown more dubious, what has heretofore been the closest alliance in the Near East has been drawn even tighter, and Greece, possibly egged on by England, has made concessions to Turkey in order to cement more firmly the union with that more powerful country. Under the terms of the Greco-Turkish treaty signed the other day in Athens,[39] Greece agrees to prevent, by force of arms if necessary, any third power from crossing her territory in an attack on Turkey from the West, while Turkey agrees to maintain a similar attitude if Greece is attacked from the East. The Greek dictator explained to me that the treaty is nothing more than an extension to the naval sphere of the Greco-Turkish treaties already in force, binding both countries in the Aegean as already they are bound in Thrace. But Greece is hardly likely to find a foe in the hinterland of Asia, whereas the extension westward of safeguards aimed hitherto only at isolated Bulgaria would seem to point directly at Italy, and the undertaking by Greece of commitments she can

[37] On April 16, 1938, Britain and Italy signed an agreement aimed at reducing tension between them, particularly in the Mediterranean and the Near East, and preserving the *status quo*.

[38] On March 12, 1938, German forces invaded Austria, and the following month, Austria was formally incorporated within the Reich.

[39] On April 24, 1938, Greece and Turkey signed a "Supplementary Agreement" to the Treaty of Ankara of October 30, 1930, providing for mutual support and cooperation in matters of diplomacy and defense.

never carry out without naval help on a large scale smells of British collusion, if not of British impulsion. In other words, the Turco-Greek alliance in its completed form looks very much like a part of the British defensive net against any dangerous eastward sagging of the Rome-Berlin axis. Diplomatically, such a net does seem to be in preparation. My Egyptian colleague tells me that the British are now actively wooing Islam in competition with the Duce, though they operate less crudely, and he assures me that it is no idle rumor which maintains that for some time past they have been anxious to tie up Egypt with Greece and Turkey in an anti-Italian bloc. If so, their diplomacy outruns their military preparation, for my Military Attaché tells me that they have done nothing to fortify Cyprus, and that their forces in Palestine, Egypt, and the rest of the Near East are negligible.

British and German propaganda in this country, not to speak of French and Italian, is now more active than at any time since the war days. Particularly noticeable is the development of the British propaganda. It made splendid use of the Duke of Kent (who married a Greek princess) at the Crown Prince's wedding. And recently, Lord Lloyd, President of the British Council, visited Athens and gave his encouragement and that of the funds at his disposal to the local British effort. The British Minister tells me that if he is to go on doing all the propaganda work required of him, his Legation should be doubled. Meanwhile the Germans are not taking all this lying down. Following the visits of Goering, Goebbels[40] and Schacht,[41] a whole flock of minor officials visited here, and we have seen a big development in German archaeological activity and have been treated to a host of lectures and expositions. This activity is all very reminiscent of the days of King Constantine. We have a new German Crown Princess in place of the old German queen, and the Dictator is the old pro-German chief of staff; on the other hand, the country is probably as democratic as ever at heart. But, and this is a great difference, there is no Venizelos.

In internal matters, the dictatorship continues, and it is this very lack of a Venizelos, or anyone else of his caliber, which seems more than anything else to be keeping it alive, in spite of plenty of opposition. Mr. Metaxas is quite the ablest man in Greek political life today, even if we count in the politicians he has exiled. After the deaths, in quick succession, of Kondylis, Tsaldaris, Venizelos, Papanastasiou and Demertzis, the King really had no one else to turn to half as promising as the rotund little general now in power. And so he gave him the reins, and is letting him drive. The general trumpets that he has the mandate of the people,

[40] Joseph Goebbels, Nazi politician, Minister of Propaganda.
[41] Dr. Hjalmar Schacht, Nazi financier, President of the Reichsbank, and the Minister of Economics until November 1937.

which is not true, and that he will not lay it down, which on the other hand is probably quite correct, if it depends on him. He is intelligent and active and vigilant, and though the kind of regime which is foisted on the country is out of keeping with its spirit there is no one in sight around whom the scattered opposition can get together. If a revolution occurs, as so many wish, it must produce a man. On the other hand, if Mr. Metaxas should die, the position would also be difficult in the extreme. I have canvassed his own entourage as well as the King's, and have heard not a single hopeful suggestion as to who could replace him. (31)

Athens, August 22, 1938

Dear Franklin:

You have been having a wonderful trip since I last wrote. It must have been grand on the "Houston," and reviewing the fleet in San Francisco Bay! In Athens we have followed your every move around the circle.

I am happy to say that the latest big news in Greece and the Balkans generally has been of a peacemaking nature. You may have noticed the recent signing of the Pact of Salonica, which has not only removed some persistent war clouds from this immediate region, but would seem to have a significance even for the general European situation. In its preamble, it speaks of "relations de bon voisinage." Do you recognize the parentage?

The history of this latest Balkan peace pact falls, as I see it, into two parts, the first retrograde and the second progressive. I think I have written you about the fear which the Greeks have so long felt for the Bulgars, a fear that was pretty well justified, all things considered. After the World War, if the other Balkan powers did not fear Bulgaria as Greece did, they were still worried about her as the one revisionist nation in their midst, and this despite the fact that the Treaty of Neuilly[42] had cut her armaments, on paper, to a minimum. Consequently in 1934, egged on by France, who was then bolstering up the *status quo* with "regional pacts," the lot of them—Turkey, Greece, Yugoslavia, and Rumania— ringed her round with an agreement called the Balkan Entente. Being dedicated to the preservation of existing mutual boundaries, this was hardly a pact she could afford to join, despite their invitation. She therefore remained in coventry, an outsider, or rather an uncomfortable *insider*, a possible source of trouble, and undoubtedly regarded hopefully in that light by Germany and Italy, who both of them have long-handled irons in the Near Eastern fire. Indeed, it may be that Italy, viewing the Balkan Entente with disfavor, was partly responsible for what followed. Cer-

---

[42] Signed on November 27, 1919, the Treaty of Neuilly was imposed upon Bulgaria following her defeat in World War I. It deprived Bulgaria of an exit on the Aegean Sea, reduced her army to 20,000 men, and imposed on her substantial reparations.

tainly, Bulgaria was willing enough to take a chance at breaking out. In 1935, a move on her part down into Thrace, when Venizelos raised the standard of revolt in Greece, was only forestalled by Turkish concentration on her flank and the collapse of the revolt itself. Later, in 1937, Kemal, speaking by telephone to Ismet in Athens, thought it well to give her another warning. Anyone attempting to change the existing inter-Balkan boundaries, he said, would "expose himself to the full rays of the sun," he, Kemal, being presumably that luminary. Since that time the Greco-Turkish alliance, regarded by most people as being an even stronger guarantee of our local peace than the Balkan Pact, has been strengthened and enlarged. Furthermore, since 1936, when he came to power, Mr. Metaxas, the Greek Dictator, has been feverishly strengthening the Bulgarian boundary with a "little Maginot line," which my Military Attaché tells me is now probably strong enough to hold the Bulgars at any point where the difficult terrain renders attack feasible. On the other hand, it is common knowledge that Bulgaria's armaments far surpass the restrictions set upon them by the Treaty of Neuilly.

Here, then, is the first part of the picture. The second is contributed by the Anglo-French reaction to Mussolini's advance in the Mediterranean, and Hitler's expanding threat in central Europe. This reaction has expressed itself in this region in revived diplomatic vigor. I wrote you in my last letter of what seemed the effort of the British to construct a defensive network against any possible sagging eastward of the Rome-Berlin axis. The French have now joined them. After a period, under the Blum Government, of complete diplomatic ineptitude, they have waked up with Daladier[43] to a sense of their situation. The British weaned the Turks away from Schacht economically. The French have now collaborated politically with acquiescence in the Sandjak affair.[44] Furthermore, they have sent into the bay of Athens the strongest French naval force that has ever been seen in these waters, and the effect has been electric. The Balkan powers, all except Bulgaria, chiefly want to keep what they have got, and at present seek nothing more, if we except Turkey's designs in Syria, to which France is pandering. They therefore fear the upset of a general war, and when Great Britain and France show strength, they rally naturally to that side, the only one evincing any doubt at present, if we leave out Albania, being Rumania, the most remote in terms of allied sea-power.

With the British already tightening up, it seemed, even as early as the

---

[43] Edouard Daladier, Prime Minister of France, succeeding Blum on April 10, 1938.

[44] On July 3, 1938, France and Turkey agreed to collaborate in the supervision of elections in the Sandjak of Alexandretta, thus ending a serious feud between the two states.

beginning of 1937, that the position of Bulgaria might eventually come in for some redefining, in her interests as well as those of her neighbors. Consequently, with British knowledge, the Yugoslavs,—those "Jugs" whom my British colleague is never tired of praising,—extended to the Bulgars the hand of friendship at that time and it was firmly grasped. Greek opinion, always sensitive to the menace of panslavism, naturally became somewhat alarmed over this. But Kemal's warning about the sun was calculated to dispel mistaken notions, and Prince Paul of Yugoslavia made it his business, at the Crown Prince's wedding last January, to prove to the Greek leaders the value of this move to all the Balkan states. Other things being equal, it could not be denied that the Balkans might go to war again among themselves, but under existing circumstances in Europe it would be tantamount to insanity. Furthermore, to make the Balkans count as a force for peace they must be united. Therefore, in some way or other,—short, of course, of sacrificing Greece,—Bulgaria must be appeased, and the way, the Yugoslavs felt, could only be through a show of friendship and understanding to a proud and smarting people. England was certainly back of this idea, but my Yugoslav colleague tells me that the Greeks did not wholly lay aside their fears even so. However, when France came back into the picture, as I have described, and in addition her bankers even offered Sofia a loan, which has since been realized to the tune of 375 millions of francs, the advantages to Bulgaria of no longer standing aloof became too apparent for even the Greeks to doubt of Slavic *bona fides*. A way was then quickly found for saving her face, and letting her in with the Balkan Entente forces on the ground floor, at least as far as the vestibule. Briefly, in return for the abrogation by her neighbors of the armament provisions of the Treaty of Neuilly, she has now agreed with all of them to a mutual renouncement of aggression. By some observers it is even thought that she will shortly enter the Balkan Entente itself. But it does not matter whether she does this or not, the essential has been achieved, if only from the negative side. For in the tightening network in this region which makes for the preservation of the peace, she no longer presents a gap for disruption or encroachment. Rumania may still be a doubtful quantity. Turkey, for one, seems to regard her leanings toward Berlin and Warsaw with suspicion and dislike. And of course Albania is definitely in the Italian orbit. But none of the countries comprising the heart of the Balkans can any longer be counted on to help in upsetting the apple-cart of Europe. This would seem to be the real meaning and the most important result of the Salonica Pact.

In Greece, the opposition has now scrupled to charge surreptitiously that Mr. Metaxas has paid for Bulgarian non-aggression with a secret promise of territory. But this charge I believe is as groundless as it is malicious. So far as local affairs are concerned, the Dictator continues to rule more effectively and efficiently than has been customary in Greece, at least in my time. There is plenty of opposition, because no dictatorship can be popular in this country, but Mr. Metaxas keeps the opposition scattered. A recent unsuccessful revolt in Crete has raised the hopes of his enemies, but has not yet led to any other manifestations. The Dictator maintains that he is Dictator for life, and this may well be the case, from present indications. Unfortunately there is still no sign anywhere on the horizon of a man capable of being his successor, should he die or be otherwise removed from the scene which he now dominates. His entourage is second-rate, and the exiled politicians seem a feeble folk. This is perhaps the worst aspect of a regime which has many things against it but has done a good deal for the country on the whole.

Affectionately yours,
Lincoln MacVeagh (32)

Athens, November 22, 1938

Dear Franklin:

... The internal situation here remains very much as when I last wrote. The King and the Dictator are still unpopular and still in control of the army, the press and whatever else may be necessary for their purposes. But foreign affairs and the economic situation may call for some comment.

In Athens we have, of course, been witnessing events in Europe rather than playing a part in them. But we have been witnessing them from no great distance, and it is quite obvious that the Greeks are thoroughly scared.

Italy has for a long time been the great bugaboo of this country. But now the shadow of Germany is creeping toward the Balkans, and so far the British and French have done nothing to stop it. Against this new menace the Greeks must console themselves somehow, and they are doing it by reflecting that the German advance threatens Italy too, and imagining that sooner or later the Rome-Berlin axis must break and Italy join hands with France and Britain.

To the Greeks, revisionism is naturally a disease, and they dread its proving contagious. Their joy over the periodic Anglo-Italian rapprochements of the past years has always been connected with their fear of Mussolini's supporting Bulgarian pretensions to a part of northern Greece. Whenever the Duce veers toward London they feel definitely safer. Hence the latest Rome-London agreement has been praised here to the skies. But things are not what they were before Mr. Chamberlain went to Munich.[45] Boundaries fixed by the Peace Treaties have now fallen before

---

[45] On Septerber 29, 1938, at the Munich Conference, British Prime Minister

1. Athens, November 15, 1938. With John Metaxas, Greek Prime Minister and Foreign Minister, signing Commercial Agreement.

the same plausible arguments which were used to justify their creation. The Greeks have emptied their parts of Macedonia and Thrace of most of the non-Greek population; but some still remains. Is this enough to implement with plausibility a Bulgar-Yugoslav move for exits on the Aegean? There are rumors in this connection which the Greeks officially refuse to consider, but the Political Director of the Foreign Office[46] has told me privately that they have recently furnished new data to all their Legations with which, if necessary, to justify Greece's intransigence in this matter before the bar of public opinion.

Of course, under prevailing European conditions, a small country like this must always be afraid of diplomatic isolation. The Balkan Entente has never been a very strong union, and it is weaker today than ever, with Rumania playing its own game, Kemal dead, and Ismet a question.[47] I wrote you of how delighted the Greeks were over the Pact of Salonica, whereby the Entente agreed with Bulgaria not to use the hatchet, al-

---

Neville Chamberlain, as well as Daladier for France and Mussolini for Italy, accepted Hitler's demands on Czechoslovakia, leading to her partition, and to her final destruction by Germany the following year.

[46] Andreas Delmouzos.

[47] Following the death of Kemal Ataturk on November 10, 1938, Ismet Inönü became President of Turkey.

though they did not exactly bury it. More recently the Premiers of Bulgaria and Yugoslavia have had another of their love-feasts, this time at Nish,[48] and the Greeks are wondering what it is all about. Should their northern neighbors gang up, as the saying is, to apply the formula of Munich to Greece's northern provinces, and should Ismet regard the Greco-Turkish friendship in a different light from Kemal, and England go on washing her hands of continental affairs, what can keep this little country from finding itself out on a limb?

Fear, then, has become the order of the day here as elsewhere. It is a time for looking to one's alliances, making new ones or patching up old. The Greeks can expect Germany to support Bulgaria's pretensions if and when she puts them forward, and by the same token, they must hope and pray that England and France will resist them, and that Italy will at least stay on the fence. Accordingly the Greek King is in London right now. His visit is a most important one for the Greeks, and was made at the very moment when the birth of an heir to the throne was being momentarily expected and when normally the King would not leave the country. But perhaps the visit has some importance from the English point of view as well. At the Greek Foreign Office I have been told, "We will fight rather than give up one inch of territory" (how often one hears that!), "but some Great Power must tell our neighbors to stay within their boundaries." This puts Greece's position in a nutshell, and it is easy to see what Power is meant. On the other hand, we find England clapping the Garter on the King of Greece, and as the British Minister told me today, considering an appeal to its manufacturers to order more Greek tobacco "on patriotic grounds," as he said, the aim being to break the German control of the Greek economy. Indeed, England's present plan of campaign, at least in this part of the world, would seem to be to fight the German advance with money, as witness her recent loan to Turkey, and large purchases of agricultural products in various Balkan states. One thinks of Pitt and Napoleon, the old game being tried under new conditions. Last year Mr. Metaxas's proposal that England buy Greek tobacco was treated as "ridiculous" by my British colleague. Thus if Hitler has succeeded in turning the German clock back to the Middle Ages or earlier, he may also have succeeded at Munich in turning the clock of English continental policy back to the 18th century.

To throw Greece and England closer together would therefore seem to be a first result of the fear engendered here by the accord of Munich and its aftermath. On the other hand, it is absolutely necessary for Greece to

---

[48] On October 31, 1938, the Prime Ministers of Yugoslavia (Milan Stojadinović) and Bulgaria (Georgi Kioseivanov) met at Nish for secret talks. In a joint communiqué, they proclaimed total agreement between the "two brother nations," and their determination to "deepen and widen their cordial collaboration."

explore at this time the dispositions of Turkey's new President, since equally with the English fleet the Turkish alliance has been a mainstay of her security. Mr. Metaxas has gone to Kemal's funeral, and it is certain that he will do his best at Ankara to see behind merely formal assurances and determine what new orientations, if any, may be expected in Turkish policy. According to official statements, of course, the Greco-Turkish alliance stands at present much stronger than the rock of Gibraltar.

In regard to economic matters and dollar (or pound) diplomacy, it may be said that England's plan to check German pressure by using her financial strength is likely to find harder going than her financial foreign policy of Napoleonic times. For one thing, it is handicapped by the fact that Germany, though so much weaker in finances, has already been playing a very clever economic game here for some years. Without financial resources of her own to speak of, she has got the economic life of Greece almost in the hollow of her hand, by providing an assured market for Greek agricultural products against her own manufactured goods, and thus freeing much of the foreign exchange gathered by Greece from immigrant remittances, the merchant marine, the tourist trade, and a favorable trade balance with the United States, for purchases of that foreign wheat of which she stands in need. Against such tactics, neither a British loan, to be repaid by buying British manufactures, nor nibbling at the tobacco market, can make much headway. If Britain should offer to pay sterling for really large quantities of Greek tobacco, the result would doubtless be more encouraging. But when I asked the British Minister what his country could do with Greek tobacco, he said, "I don't know. Throw it into the sea, I imagine."

As I have probably told you before, our own trade with Greece has suffered a good deal the past few years as a result of these same German tactics. During this time we have generously tolerated the working of an import control system, framed according to the exigencies of this country's difficult position under her clearing agreements with Germany and others, and protested only flagrant discriminations as these arose and could be proved. This has kept us busy indeed, as I can testify. But by 1937 the balance of trade, and even more the balance of payments, between the two countries, had risen in Greece's favor out of all bearable proportion, and it appeared that the whole Greek system would have to be revised if we were to be properly served. Accordingly, we have, after some lengthy negotiations, concluded a new *modus vivendi* in commercial matters which accomplishes what is tantamount to just such a revision.[49] Every word of this agreement was written in the Department of State, and

---

[49] Text of the Provisional Commercial Agreement between the United States and Greece, signed in Athens on November 15, 1938, in *FR, 1938*, II, 535-40.

though in essence it provides for nothing more than the old most-favored-nation treatment, it calls the spade a spade and specifically outlaws each and every one of the methods, administrative or otherwise, which experience has shown us operates under the existing Greek system to discriminate against our trade. The Greeks have given little publicity to the signing of this agreement, for it is really a thorough capitulation on their part. They were led to accept it, of course, by the fear that we might otherwise take restrictive measures of our own, and they know not only that we are the goose which lays the golden eggs, in the shape of the dollars they need so badly, but that the American market is by far the best in the world for anything they can produce. The war scare in Europe has also, I think, tended to make them look more closely to their relations with us. Accordingly they have promised to be good, dotting the "i's" and crossing the "t's" in every particular we suggested. How they will live up to what they have promised, and what new methods of evasion they may devise, remains to be seen, but in the near future, at least, our exports to Greece should increase. What they buy from us, of course, they have to pay for, but the stuff which Germany dumps here under the clearing is in general so inferior to our products that among the many fears which the Greeks feel at present, the one we have thrown into them should be good for them, as well as for us, in the long run.

With best wishes and regards as always, I am

Affectionately yours,
Lincoln MacVeagh (33)

While the nation's political life had been effectively stilled by the dictator's heavy-handed tactics, a new issue suddenly rose to national attention. In a despatch entitled "The Archbishop is Dead. Long Live the Archbishop!" MacVeagh was quick to observe that the death (on October 22, 1938) of Archbishop Chrysostomos, Primate of Greece, had created a void with clearly political overtones:

[October 24, 1938]

The death of Chrysostomos removes the last Venizelist to occupy a commanding position in the Greek state. Many Greeks who had no personal experience of his saintly character or erudite attainments, and who give no service but lip-service to their national church, regret his departure on political grounds. For they regard it as almost certain that his successor will be more sympathetic with the monarchy or the government, or both, than was this representative of New Greece, who was born near Constantinople, studied in Russia, served his apprenticeship in Asia Minor,

Palestine and Egypt, and was appointed to the See of Athens by the revolutionary government of Plastiras.

Speculating in the same despatch that the Government would "not lose the opportunity of fastening its clutches more firmly on the country by securing the election of a candidate of its choice," MacVeagh quoted Metaxas as having declared that "The episcopate must not be influenced in its choice of the proper person, having also all the responsibility in case its choice turns out not to be a happy one. . . ." To the American diplomat these words had "all the ring of a *caveat*." It was particularly significant that the new archbishop was to be chosen by the country's sixty-two Metropolitans, under the supervision of the Minister of Education, Constantine Georgakopoulos. This gentleman, wrote MacVeagh, "is an ex-soldier, and in his official position, a creation of Mr. Metaxas. He also enjoys the confidence of the Court, and the Grand Chamberlain mentioned him to me only recently as a possibility for the premiership should anything happen to his chief. He will undoubtedly impersonate the latter's 'all-seeing eye' . . . at the approaching election, and it is well known that in the case of our Dictator, what the eye sees the brain does not forget." (34)

Although MacVeagh's prognostications were all too accurate, the situation was not without its surprises. On November 14 he was reporting to the Department again, this time in a despatch entitled "The New Archbishop: To Be or Not To Be":

The election of his successor to the Primacy of the Orthodox Establishment in this country was duly held as announced, on the 5th of November in the Metropolitan Church of Athens. The only two candidates voted on were the Metropolitan of Corinth, Monseigneur Damaskinos, and the Metropolitan of Trebizond, Monseigneur Chrysanthos. The voting was by secret ballot, in the presence of the Minister of Cults and Education, Mr. Georgakopoulos.

All this, as the Department will observe, followed the program envisaged at the time I wrote my despatch under reference.[50] But the result of the election has been, to say the least, surprising, and what has happened since would seem to be causing consternation and even dismay in interested quarters, which means approximately the whole of Greece. Indeed the situation at present existing contains all the elements necessary for a first-class row.

Briefly, the facts are as follows: Though there are 62 Bishops in Greece,

[50] MacVeagh despatch 2525, October 24, 1938, cited above.

only 61 were present at the election, the Bishop of Lemnos being too ill to attend. Trebizond, being the representative of the Ecumenical Patriarch in Greece, and thus not, technically, a member of the national establishment, was not eligible to vote, and was not present, in spite of his being a candidate. The most careful precautions were used to see that each voter inscribed his ballot secretly and deposited it free of all interference in the urn provided for the purpose. The result was thirty-one votes for Corinth and thirty for Trebizond. But as thirty-one is not a majority of 62, which, as I have said, is the whole number of bishops in Greece, it was required by law that two more ballotings be held, after which, the results being precisely the same, the majority of the bishops present was held to determine the election, and the Minister of Cults proclaimed Monseigneur Damaskinos Primate of Greece. The Government later prepared the proper decree proclaiming the new Archbishop and sent it to the Palace for signature.

So far, of course, so good. But it seemed curious, to say the least, that in the press, following the appropriate eulogies and personal histories of the new Primate, there should appear similar matter devoted to the defeated candidate, at even greater length. What this might portend was at first dark, but became clearer a few days later when all the newspapers carried accounts of protests being made to the Council of State by two separate groups of citizens against the validity of the election. These protests are based on the inclusion among the voters of the Bishop of Dryinoupolis, against whom a decree of dethronement, as a result of an ecclesiastical trial for simony, is awaiting the royal signature pending a decision on appeal. It is the claim of the plaintiffs before the Council of State that the conviction of the Bishop, whatever the result of his appeal may be at a later date, technically disqualifies him at present from participation in an ecclesiastical election, and if this claim be allowed, the election of Corinth becomes void. It is easy to see that in such circumstances a new election, with the participation of the Bishop of Lemnos who was previously too ill to attend, might result in the election of Trebizond by the same margin of one vote which has now spelt his defeat. Furthermore, to make matters worse, I am now informed that the Bishop of Phthiotis, who, as I have reported, is Primate of Greece *ad interim*, is himself making a protest to the Council, along with the Bishop of Samos and the Bishop of Mytilene, while Corinth, together with all the thirty bishops who voted for him, are threatening to resign if the protest is sustained!

Numerous and contradictory rumors make interpretation difficult. But if one reasons only from uncontested facts, one may perhaps attain some comprehension of what is going on. That the Government should have given such publicity in its controlled press to Trebizond, after his apparent defeat, and that it should have widely published the news of the protests to the Council of State, alike seem incompatible with the idea that it is pleased with the results to date. That it promptly prepared the decree elevating Corinth and sent it to the Palace for signature is taken by some observers to mean that Corinth was in fact its candidate. But we should remember that it has for weeks made every effort to convince public opinion of its impartiality. In preparing and forwarding the decree, therefore, it may well have acted only with the technical correctness demanded by its previously adopted attitude. The decree itself has by no means yet been signed. Furthermore, a rumor, as authentic as any other, describes the King as having left word, on his recent departure for England, that he desired the election of Trebizond, and this invites belief on account of the latter's personal appearance and charm, as well as his cultivation and diplomatic skill. Some people think that the fact that the protests to the Council of State have been made by private citizens and ecclesiastics, and not by the Government, proves that the Government itself is satisfied. But it would surely be more consonant with the Greek character, as well as with the Government's necessities under its "hands off" policy, to regard this fact as a blind. Under such an interpretation, the Government would now be seeking to upset the election without appearing to have anything to do with it; and in this connection, I may say that I was recently considerably amused when Madame Metaxa told me that her husband was holding a conference on the question of the choice of the new Archbishop, adding quickly, "Il ne s'y mêle pas."

If such is the case,—and it certainly seems the more probable interpretation,—the question of how the Government came to be misled about the way the Bishops would vote on November 5th requires an answer, since no one in Athens seems to doubt that Mr. Metaxas canvassed the situation very diligently in advance. But perhaps no one will ever know exactly what happened in the church, and the secret is locked in some ecclesiastical breast. For after all, a bold bishop may dare to double-cross a dictator if a wily one can stoop to simony. The absolute secrecy of the balloting, which the Government was at such pains to insure, may thus have been its undoing.

The hearing before the Council of State is announced for November 16th. No one doubts that the decision of this body will be the Government's own. But will the Government dare to risk a major schism to gain its ends? How much confidence does it feel in its ability to avoid such a catastrophe while still getting what it wants? How far is the professedly "independent" church of Greece really in bondage to the Dictatorship? All these are important questions, the answers to which hang in the balance. Meanwhile there is so much excited interest on the part of the public that one suspects the Greeks are secretly delighted with the situation, for tempests in the teapot have been rare since politics were banned and the Greek people love nothing better, as the Department knows. (35)

Ten days later, MacVeagh's despatch, entitled "No Archbishop," reported that Damaskinos' election had indeed been voided by the Council of State, that Minister Georgakopoulos had resigned, while his subordinate, who had actually handled the election, had been exiled. (36) Several months were to pass before MacVeagh could submit his concluding chapter on the sordid affair, this time under the title "Archbishop's Elba":

[March 6, 1939]

As the Department knows, the Metropolitan of Corinth was elected Archbishop of Athens, and Primate of all Greece, in a duly convoked and competent assembly of the Bishops, by the margin of one vote over the Metropolitan of Trebizond, but subsequently the Council of State declared the election invalid on the ground that a certain Bishop had participated who was at the time under charges of simony before an ecclesiastical court. Instead of the Bishops being convoked again, however, the law governing the selection of a Primate was then radically changed. The matter was taken out of the hands of the College of Bishops entirely, and only recommendational powers were vested in the Holy Synod, a much smaller body, while the King was granted the power to nominate the Primate from among the candidates recommended. As a result the Metropolitan of Trebizond obtained the Primacy.

So much has already been reported. The Metropolitan of Corinth, however, appears to have adopted the attitude that he was duly elected by the Bishops and is, in fact, still Primate of Greece, the secular power having no right to decide an ecclesiastical matter. He was accordingly offered the archbishopric of North and South America, a position of great dignity and influence, but well removed from intimate contacts with the Establishment. He refused. He was then ordered to return to his see. But he again refused, and the authorities, faced with the embarrassing situation of having two archbishops in the capital, turned again to the law and passed a decree, general in its application, but obviously aimed in the first instance at him. This decree declares that an ecclesiastic who absents himself from his post contrary to the orders of his superior in the hierarchy is subject to punitive action by the State in the form of confinement to such locality as may be indicated by that superior. What follows was witnessed by the wife of my Swedish colleague[51] who lives next door to the house occupied by the Metropolitan of Corinth in the Athens suburb of Psychico.

[51] Sven Allard, Swedish *Chargé d'Affaires* in Greece.

On a certain afternoon a truck drove up to the Metropolitan's door, bearing a squad of gendarmes who entered the house. Shortly thereafter furniture began to emerge, carried by the servants and the gendarmes. With this the truck was piled high. The Metropolitan's four cats were then coralled and set on top together with a small flock of turkeys, and last of all the Metropolitan himself assumed his perch together with his captors, and the whole over-loaded contraption bumped off in the direction of the main road to the city.

The tall, black-robed, stove-pipe-hatted figure of the gray-bearded and bespectacled but still youthful and determined prelate has not since been seen on the streets of Athens. He was taken to a monastery on the island of Salamis, there possibly to await, like the Emperor on Elba, a suitable opportunity for the reinstatement of his fortunes. Defeated he is for the moment, but he knows, as everyone else knows, that he did actually receive the ballots of a majority of the bishops of Greece, and by his attitude of defiance, in whatever cell he may be forced to maintain it, he still remains a force to be reckoned with in the life of the nation.

The appeal of the Bishop of Dryinoupolis, whose vote offered the Government its opportunity to void the election (see my despatch No. 2562 of November 14th, 1938), has now been heard before the superior ecclesiastical court, and his conviction for simony sustained, but a curious fact in this connection has recently come to light, namely that his vote was actually cast, not for Corinth, but for Trebizond! Incidentally, the kind of thing for which he was convicted appears from papers which have just come across my desk in the attempted fraud case of one George Pappas, who apparently obtained false documents from His Holiness in return for 3000 drachmas and a fountain pen (see attached copy of a statement sworn to before Mr. Dunham, American Vice Consul at Athens).[52] God save the Greek Church!

In concluding my remarks for the present on this subject of the election of the Primate of Greece, I should perhaps refer to the informal comment made on January 19, 1939, by the Division of Near Eastern Affairs on the Legation's despatch No. 2614 of December 20, 1938.[53] The Division desires to know the grounds for Mr. Metaxas's strong preference for Trebizond over Corinth, provided it is true that the Dictator was really interested in individuals in this case. The answer is that Trebizond was the King's personal candidate, as a more house-trained individual and a tried diplomat who, whatever his former views and associations, has acquiesced gracefully in the Restoration, and that Mr. Metaxas desired to please the King in this matter, particularly as Corinth not only remained, in the Crown Prince's reputed words, "a damned Venizelist," but was suspected

---

[52] Not cited in this text. [53] Not cited in this text.

of being over-ambitious and stiff-necked. That Trebizond is pliant, despite his reputation for integrity, appears well enough from his acceptance of the Primacy under pressure when he had previously said he would decline; and that Corinth's character is exactly as Mr. Metaxas feared, is also abundantly proved by his recent actions and present attitude. It is not suggested that the regime desired a "stooge" at the head of the Church; that would be too crude even for it. But it did want, and contrived to get, the better man from its own point of view. (37)

MacVeagh's prediction that Damaskinos remained "a force to be reckoned with in the life of the nation" was to come true: he was destined to serve not only as the head of the Greek Church, but as Regent and Prime Minister as well. MacVeagh himself was to play a small role in the process that saw Damaskinos assume the highest office of the Greek state.

While always interested in domestic developments, MacVeagh's main attention remained fixed upon Greece's foreign relations. Fully aware of Britain's privileged position in Greek affairs, he sought to assess the role of his British colleague, Sir Sydney Waterlow, and to discover his attitude toward the Metaxas regime, and toward the Greek King. Thus, he reported to the Department on January 23, 1939:

Following the King's return from his visit to London on December 25th, without bringing with him any assurances of a loan to the Greek Government, or even of a large British order for Greek tobacco, the British Minister has taken up a distinctly altered attitude toward the Metaxas regime. The Department will remember that at the time of the King's restoration, Sir Sydney was instructed to watch over his political fortunes and guide his steps aright. . . . Since August 4th, 1936, when Mr. Metaxas abolished parliamentary government with the King's consent, he has consistently supported the dyarchy of King and Dictator. As late as October 1937, he was actually enthusiastic about it. . . . The other day, however, he said to me at dinner, in a loud voice and in the presence of several Greeks, that he had changed his point of view and is now against the dictatorship, while still in favor of the King. He characterized one of Mr. Metaxas' recent speeches as a "tissue of lies," and expressed the opinion that he is no longer of any importance, being a mere cat's paw for "a bad lot" of supporters.

The British colony in Athens, which is almost uniformly anti-Metaxas, is naturally saying that "His Majesty's Monster" has waked up at last. But it cannot be supposed that the British Legation has been ignorant all this time of the character of the group about and behind the Dictator,—Drossopoulos, of the National Bank, Kanellopoulos of the

Youth Movement, Diakos[54] the "éminence grise," Maniadakis, the sardonic reincarnation of Fouché, Bodossakis,[55] the arms merchant, *et al.* Furthermore, the British Legation as a whole must also be aware, whatever may be said of Sir Sydney himself, that Mr. Metaxas is no mere cat's paw in this country, but very nearly, if not quite, the cat's whiskers, if I may be permitted a slight levity. Therefore, though the voice is the voice of Sir Sydney,—the words, I think, must be understood as those of the Foreign Office, which incidentally is rumored to have told the King in London that the British could see no way of justifying a loan to a government like that of Greece at present, and that he could expect no financial aid unless he first got rid of Metaxas.

In the realm of foreign affairs, this British *volte-face* may be connected with a desire in London to have Greece adopt a less neutral attitude and undertake some commitments in regard to assisting England in case a general war develops in Europe. Traditionally England has not exerted any pressure of this kind on Greece, in times of peace, trusting to her naval superiority to force Greek compliance once the war is on. But times have changed, as the Department knows, and even Greece may be worth lining up, while as I have previously reported many times, Mr. Metaxas is not only a German sympathizer personally, but politically a confirmed believer in the advisability of neutrality for his country vis-à-vis the Great Powers. Current rumors as well as the logic of the international situation as springtime approaches make this interpretation a possibility.

In regard to the internal situation, the British government may have become convinced at last that reaction within the country will soon attain such proportions that Mr. Metaxas will be forced out, and may wish to take time by the forelock in dissociating the King from a sinking ship. Reports of the recent wholesale resignation of cabinet officers and the reasons therefor (see the Legation's despatch No. 2603 of December 10, 1938)[56] could perhaps have had this effect. But in this connection I would attach more importance to the new British attitude as a factor in the future evolution of the political situation here than as an interpretation of present conditions, for Mr. Metaxas appears still to be pretty firmly entrenched, with no leader yet in sight who could capitalize [on] the widespread discontent. It is rather the heartening effect of the new British attitude on this discontent, and its possible aid in calling forth a leader, either the King (poor fellow) or another, which makes the

[54] John Diakos, private secretary and personal aide of Metaxas.
[55] Bodossakis Athanassiadis, generally known by his first name, a leading Greek industrialist and arms manufacturer, believed to be politically influential behind the scenes.
[56] Not cited in this text.

change perhaps the most important event in local politics since the dictatorship began. (38)

A few days later, MacVeagh returned once again to the question of Britain's policy—and influence—in Greece, and reported on a new talk with his British colleague:

[January 31, 1939]

To begin with, I may perhaps say that Sir Sydney is a large, pink-cheeked, walrus-mustachioed, bureaucratic martinet, whose aspect recalls the Major General of "The Pirates of Penzance." As might be expected from this, he is also thoroughly flat-footed and tactless in diplomacy, but it is impossible not to have a warm spot in one's heart for him, since among the wily Greeks he often appears like some bewildered old bear, badgered by a lot of naughty boys. He is cordially disliked by his colony and laughed at by many people behind his back, but the natives respect him to his face, as the local blunderbuss of the British Raj. He reached the retirement age last year, but was given a year's extension and is now expected to retire this summer, to go and live with the other "scarlet majors at the base." Meanwhile his opinions and doings are of the first importance locally.

It would appear from our conversation that his efforts, predicted in my despatch under reference, [January 23, 1939] to cut the Gordian knot, or sever the Siamese twins, or in other words to dissolve the dyarchy of King and Dictator in this country, have already begun, without, however, attaining any great measure of initial success. He said that Mr. Metaxas shows every sign of persisting with his program of turning Greece into a fascist state, and that he, Sir Sydney, has "done his best to circumvent him." In this connection he said that he saw the King immediately after His Majesty's return from England last Christmas, and told him frankly that he is getting himself into a "dangerous position" by his continued support of the Dictator. Reminding His Majesty of a conversation he had with him a couple of years ago, in which the King said that he cared nothing for popularity, and even thought it might be a handicap, but that the respect of the people is absolutely essential to a monarchy, Sir Sydney told His Majesty that he has now not only lost all claim to popularity, but has also forfeited the respect of the people by allowing himself to be dictated to. "But," Sir Sydney said, "it is not too late. You can still save yourself if you will make some gesture to show that you, and not Mr. Metaxas, are the master of the situation. Such a gesture is awaited by the British public."

Surprising as the concluding words of the above may seem, they are quoted literally. Perhaps they may best be understood in connection with the failure of the British Government to grant the King a loan when he was last in London. With the Government of Greece growing more fascist every minute, such a loan might indeed be hard to justify to the British people.

I asked Sir Sydney what the King said during their conversation and he replied, "Very little. He let me do all the talking. But I have the impression that he isn't going to play. I even suspect that he went and told Mr. Metaxas everything that I had said." Sir Sydney laughed uncomfortably, and then went on: "I don't think I am very popular at the Palace these days! But I am glad I said what I did, because if anything happens in the next year or two it will be on record that the British Minister was not in favor of the Metaxas dictatorship, as people have been saying. And I never was, you know!"

In this connection I suspect the Minister of attempting to cover up. For the past speaks for itself, and if His Majesty is in the fix Sir Sydney thinks he is, the fault must certainly be laid, at least in part, to Sir Sydney's own door. He should have sounded the tocsin earlier, in keeping with the doubts he was beginning to feel a year ago. In the penultimate paragraph of my despatch No. 2088 of February 5, 1938,[57] I reported that the British were beginning to sour on the dictatorship, but that Sir Sydney's confidence in His Majesty and estimate of his personal influence and ability ran far ahead of anything I would care to hazard. Now he is beginning to reap the fruits of his credulity and procrastination. Indeed, in the light of the record, his attempt, under instructions (see my telegram No. 172 of November 18, 1935),[58] to guide the King in his choice of advisers, takes on a decided aspect of the blind leading the blind. As the Department knows from past history, British intervention in Greece's internal affairs has often been astonishingly inept, and it appears to be maintaining its standard in this respect.

In regard to Balkan matters, Sir Sydney said that the main question at the moment is the fate of the Balkan Entente. "Is Yugoslavia going to get out? I have been doing a lot of work on this. We have been telegraphing a great deal between capitals, and the general opinion seems to be that she isn't. Of course her doing so would make a lot of difference, but Mr. Metaxas tells me the British-Greek-Turkish combination will hold firm in any case." He agreed that Greece makes a very vulnerable center for such a combination, and that sea-power can hardly save Greece from breaking under any real pressure from the North, such as would threaten if Yugoslavia joined the Axis, but he was inclined to

[57] Not cited in this text.   [58] Not cited in this text.

belittle the possibility of a Yugoslav-Bulgar combination. He said the most obvious way of solving the Bulgar question was to give the Bulgarians the southern Dobrudja in return for renunciation of all other territorial claims. In this connection, I may say that for one who has been so long in the Balkans, he seems strangely unaware of the dangers to Greece in the recent rapprochement between Belgrade and Sofia, probably because he wished to be unaware of it. He is personally a Bulgarophile and sure that all Bulgars are good boys—i.e., good British boys.

I asked him whether he thought Greece would stand with England in a war against Germany and he said that he had no doubt of it whatever. He said that Mr. Metaxas had repeatedly assured him of the fact, as well as of his belief that England would be the victor. He said he could not believe Mr. Metaxas would say such things "to a Minister," and not mean them, reminding me of the noble lord who put his money on a horse he was sure would win,

"For someone who was in the know
Had confidently told him so."

On the other hand, he admitted that Greece is evidently "truckling" to Germany, and said that if the former goes on becoming more and more of a fascist state, "things may become very difficult." Greece, he informed me, is now going to order all her armaments from England and France. But when I asked where she would get the money to pay for them, he could only say that some small loans for the purpose were under discussion, bewailing the fact that his government is so slow to wake up to necessities and that "Whitehall is always behind the times." In this connection, I am informed that Greece is actually ordering some airplanes from England and France, and this may be an entering wedge, but it is certainly far from being anything like what the phrase, "all her armaments," implies.

I feel that the foregoing may seem confused and inadequate, but I have done my best to report accurately Sir Sydney's pronouncements. Do these perhaps give us the mental background of the famous British process of muddling through? Thus, to sum up, Sir Sydney appears to feel that the King is Anglophile at heart, and that Mr. Metaxas will side with Britain if war comes, but on the other hand he fears the former will do nothing to stop the latter from turning Greece into a fascist state, which will mean trouble. He consoles himself with the possible defection of Yugoslavia from the Balkan Entente with the idea of a British-Greek-Turkish combination, the center of which can only be bolstered by hopes for the best. And he talks confidently of weaning Greek trade away from Germany while admitting that any real means of doing so are not in sight. Speaking of the Germans, who seem to be logically carrying out the program of "Mein Kampf," and at least to know what they are doing, Sir Sydney repeatedly said "They are devils," and perhaps it is no wonder they appear so to a representative of diplomacy which only God can save.

In conclusion, the Department may be interested in a side remark of Sir Sydney's to the effect that Mr. Metaxas is always urging on him that Britain ought to adopt the same attitude toward Greece which she holds towards Portugal, namely, benevolence toward a mild dictatorship, thus securing for herself a prop at either end of the Mediterranean. Apparently the British aren't biting, but the Premier's suggestion of a *quid pro quo* in this matter would seem to indicate that his attitude toward England remains fundamentally more neutral than Sir Sydney's wishful thinking, if one can call it that, admits. (39)

Minister MacVeagh's unflattering opinion of his British colleague, and of London's policy toward Greece, is evident in one despatch after another. Thus, on February 20, 1939, he commented:

It is hardly to be supposed that the King does not realize the danger of allying himself too closely with Mr. Metaxas's government, or with any government. But the kind of pressure which the British seem to be putting on him, which makes little allowance for circumstances they themselves let him get into, and none for his psychology, may prove a boomerang to their policy. He gave me clearly to understand the other day that he is not at all pleased with Sir Sydney, whom he characterized as "having an unpleasant habit of thinking aloud," and whom he also described as being a "philosopher," implying that he has little sense of the realities. The next day he made a last-minute decision to accompany Mr. Metaxas to Salonica, on the first lap of the latter's voyage to attend the meeting of the Balkan Entente at Bucharest. When I asked Sir Sydney why on earth he should do that, he replied morosely that it was the King's reply to the British press articles, a public demonstration of his confidence in the Dictator. That Mr. Metaxas himself has understood the gesture in this sense is shown by the acclamations it has received in the local press.

The first fruits of Britain's late awakening to the King's position have thus been, through maladroitness, to make it worse. Fearing that he might be becoming the Dictator's man, they have actually made him more so than ever. Sir Sydney seemed to be expressing astonishment when he said to me the other day, "I don't think the King is going to play." But there is a stubbornness in the King's character which is abundantly sufficient to lead him contrary to even his own interests if he suspects he is being bullied, and as a genuine aristocrat he is quite capable of taking a chance, even on Mr. Metaxas, rather than listen to a bore. Not to have realized these things, and acted accordingly in their efforts to guide him in the difficult task he assumed at his restoration, constitutes a mistake which it will be difficult now to rectify. More pressure of the same kind might even succeed in alienating entirely the very affections which made him a monarch acceptable to the British at the outset, and which have been the reason for desiring to insure his independence from Mr. Metaxas. In that case conditions in Greece would closely approximate those which obtained at the outset of the World War, without, however, the important factor of a Venizelos on the side of the Entente.

When I wrote, in my despatch under reference,[59] that the change in the British Minister's attitude toward the régime was the most important thing which had occurred in local Greek politics for a long time, I expected it to affect the Dictator's position adversely, and it may yet do so. I certainly did not expect the first round to go to Mr. Metaxas, as it has so clearly done. The next round will be interesting to watch. (40)

Reporting on a closely related power contest, the American diplomat entitled another of his despatches "King and Dictator: The Fight is Called on Account of Rain":

[May 15, 1939]

As the Department knows, the King is liberal-minded, and regards his support of the Dictatorship as temporary, in a country which has been politically divided against itself for years, and needs reuniting. Mr. Metaxas, on the other hand, believes in dictatorship as a mode of government, and has been busy for several years organizing a bureaucracy, a secret police, and a youth movement, in direct dependence on himself. By the end of last year, indeed, this activity on his part had gone so far and been so successful that the British Minister attempted to persuade the King to divorce himself from Mr. Metaxas without delay, and reestablish here an internal order of things more in keeping with the British point of view. But after some skirmishing had taken place, the growing danger of a general war in Europe apparently made it seem unwise to risk troubling local waters at this time (see my despatch No. 2962 of April 15, 1939),[60] and now Greece is actually carrying on in the anomalous guise of a fascist state under a British guarantee of assistance. I have rea-

[59] MacVeagh despatch 2695, January 23, 1939, cited above.
[60] Not cited in this text.

son to believe that the King is no more pleased than before with having, as he thinks, to continue to support the Dictator. But from the Dictator's point of view a difficult situation has fortuitously been weathered with success, and as a result he is cuddling up to the Royal Family. I have watched him in action with the King and the Princess the last few days and the expression is hardly exaggerated. Worried as he is over the international situation, he practically prances when he thinks of the indefinite future which this holds open for his personal rule, and in pouring out a flood of eulogy on the most cherished of the King's household gods,[61] to whom in life he was himself a devoted servitor, it is as if he were telling the King in triumph, "As we were together before, we are together still, and nothing can ever drive me from your side." But the King, as usual, only looks a little grim. At present I would only emphasize that in the ideological struggle between the King and the Dictator, the former's British managers would seem to have called for the issuance of rain checks at the end of the second round. (41)

In another of his "Dear Franklin" letters, MacVeagh sought to describe the disquieting effect of Europe's darkening clouds upon Greece and its neighbors. Regional defense arrangements gave little promise of successfully resisting outside pressures, while Britain's role appeared to be both central and largely ineffective:

[March 6, 1939]

The Eastern Mediterranean has still its old importance, and Greece, enlarged by the peace treaties, is even more in it than ever. She is allied to Turkey and is a member of the Balkan Entente. The latter is now unquestionably feeling the disturbing pressure of the *Drang nach Osten*. Two of its members, Yugoslavia and Rumania, are full of minority problems and even more dangerously involved in central European politics than before the *Anschluss* and the Munich settlement. On the other hand, Turkey and Greece, the southern members of the group, remain exposed only to Mediterranean dangers. If more pressure is turned on by Germany in the north, either directly or through Hungary, it is not impossible that the Entente will fly apart. I know that the British have been fearing this result even as things are, and were pleased that the recent meeting of the Entente's Council at Bucharest resulted in at least another expression of lip-service to Balkan unity and independence. Tur-

---

[61] In the spring of 1939, the Metaxas government issued and greatly publicized an album in memory of King Constantine, father of King George II. Metaxas had been Constantine's aide-de-camp and close personal adviser on military matters. The reference ("the king's household gods") is to King George's late father.

key and Greece, however, are relatively removed from the threatening frontiers of Germany, and have no minority problems to speak of, and nothing against each other except historically. Their alliance may consequently be regarded as solid and likely to endure even should the Balkan groupment shortly follow the Little Entente into the Miltonic limbo of the Paradise of Fools.

In the Greco-Turkish alliance, this country is unquestionably the weaker party and the more exposed. Should war break out in Europe with Italy on the side of Germany against England and France, neutrality would seem her wisest policy. As I have written you before, I am convinced that this is the opinion of her leading men. But recent events seem to make it equally certain that such an attitude, while it might be acceptable to the Central Powers, does not satisfy Great Britain. The latter, perhaps understandably, would not welcome any share-alike policy in regard to Greece's multitude of harbors in the Aegean. She would prefer therefore to tie up Greece in advance, definitely, upon her side, and would appear to be putting pressure on this country in consequence, both directly and obliquely.

Directly, she is attempting to extract the King from under the domination of his fascistic Frankenstein, the German-trained General Metaxas, and through a revival of the Royal prestige check what influence the totalitarian states may have acquired with the dictatorship. For though Greece is, in general, more favorably disposed toward the democracies than their opponents, Munich has terribly frightened these small nations, and General Metaxas has once before been sufficiently impressed by the power of Germany to back her to win in a general war. So far, just as in 1914, the British have not played their cards very well. By attempting to bully the King, whom they might have more safely counselled before he got himself so deeply committed to General Metaxas, they have for the moment only driven him to commit himself still further. But they are persistent. Obliquely, it would appear that they are using Turkish influence. The Turks are impressed with British sea power, and financial power, quite as much as the Greeks, but are of course less dangerously exposed to Italy. They can be on the British side, as I am informed they are, without the reservations which geography recommends here. Furthermore they have tremendous influence over the Greeks, since Kemal more than once saved Greece from possible Bulgarian aggression, and anxiety lest Inönü fail to continue such benevolence is something which keeps the Greeks awake at night. The Turkish Minister for Foreign Affairs has just been here, declaring to the press that "the Greco-Turkish friendship is the basis of Turkish foreign policy." If that policy includes ante-bellum commitments to Great Britain, the British may feel that the foreign policy of this lesser partner in the alliance may be influenced to do the same.

There are many aspects of the involved international question out here, and I do not wish to go on at too great length. But the main outlines would seem to be as given above. Germany has now the power and may find the opportunity to crack the Balkan groupment wide open at the top, but Britain has a chance of holding it firm at the bottom. In the latter respect, Greece is at present more problematic than Turkey, British naval power and the influence of the Turkish alliance having to contend with exposure to Italy and enhanced German prestige and power on land. Complicating the matter are the King's divided family affiliations, the dictator's Germanic propensities, the country's penetration by German economic influence, and its need for financial assistance, which only Britain can supply, and so forth. So far as the game has gone, Greece still appears safe for democracy as a sympathizer, but not yet as an actual ally.

I listened to your speech before Congress the other night, getting a great kick out of it, and I would like to say here what I have already reported to the Department, namely that the prevailing impression here in official and unofficial circles is that if war is averted in Europe this year it will have been in great part owing to the attitude of the United States. It is felt that those who might start such a war have been warned in timely fashion of what risks they would themselves be running in thus putting our entire civilization in jeopardy. (42)

MacVeagh's concluding paragraph displayed much of the wishful thinking that characterized the diplomacy of the western democracies. Neither Hitler nor Mussolini appeared particularly impressed by the "warnings" emanating from London, Paris, and Washington. Early in March, the Munich accords were finally scuttled, when Germany annexed the remnants of what had once been Czechoslovakia, and Hungary seized Ruthenia. On April 7, Italy invaded and conquered Albania, thus bringing the sounds of war directly into the Balkans. A few days later, President Roosevelt addressed a much-publicized letter to the German and Italian dictators, proposing the convening of an international conference, with American participation, to discuss regulation of armaments and international trade, and requesting assurances that no aggression would be undertaken against thirty-one specified nations. MacVeagh's reaction was a valiant effort to put a good face on what had been, from the outset, an empty gesture:

Athens, April 17, 1939

Dear Franklin:

I want to tell you personally what I have just wired the Department, namely that your message to Messrs. Mussolini and Hitler has made a most profound and excellent impression here. Early hopes that it might, by a bare possibility, find acceptance on the part of those gentlemen are fading this afternoon as reports come in from Germany and Italy, but it is strongly felt that by their now expected refusal they will stand more than ever condemned at the bar of world opinion.

The Government here, which rightly fears both Hitler's economic grasp and Mussolini's growing army in Albania, does not dare to let what the people really feel appear in the papers. There is no press comment as yet, and when it comes it will probably be mealy-mouthed and ambidextrous. But your message itself has been printed in its entirety, and there's not a Greek today who doesn't know about it.

The local situation has somewhat changed since I last wrote, in that England has apparently realized that Greece's position precludes her making pro-British declarations *ante-bellum*, and the English guarantee to aid Greece if attacked has consequently been given unilaterally.[62] If this country was shocked by the collapse of Czechoslovakia, it has been scared to death by the Albanian affair, realizing that its head now is right in the jaws of the advancing axis powers while its feet dangle in the Mediterranean where Britain is still powerful. Isn't this being between the devil and the deep sea with a vengeance? Meanwhile, popular feeling is more than ever on the side of the democracies, while the form of government is Fascist! Neutrality is the watchword, but how long can it be preserved? Even if Greece doesn't give England the use of her harbors, England will use them, and that will almost certainly bring retaliation from the Italians. My guess is that if war comes, Greece will suffer heavily but, in the interests of her cherished independence, will pin her hopes to the ultimate victory of England and France.

I must stop now, as the courier is leaving and we won't have another for two weeks. But I can certainly send along with this letter the cheers and heartfelt thanks to you personally of millions of people here who realize fully what you are doing for the peace of Europe and the world.

Affectionately yours,
Lincoln MacVeagh (43)

[62] On April 13, 1939, following Italy's conquest of Albania, Britain and France guaranteed Greece's independence and territorial integrity.

By late spring, the dwindling number of optimists, who believed that war in Europe would be averted, did not include the Greek dictator. MacVeagh informed the Department on May 15:

In view of the threatening concentration of Italian forces in Albania and renewed fears of Bulgarian invasion, Greece appears to be taking measures to put her standing army in a position to defend her frontiers to the utmost, enlarging her cadres, and perfecting her machinery for mobilization, but is doing all this with the greatest secrecy and caution, in order to avoid, in the words of Mr. Metaxas quoted in my despatch under reference,[63] any "gesture which would be interpreted as a mark of hostility" by those of whom she stands in dread.

During the past year Greece has purchased through the German clearing a good deal of mechanized equipment, and for training in the use of this she has mobilized a number of classes of reserves in special categories. She has recently purchased from England a number of pursuit planes, and this has necessitated similar action in the air service. While calling up this year's class of recruits, the simultaneous leaves of absence usually granted to others at such a time have been withheld. A new army corps is being formed to take over the Albanian frontier, hitherto held only by one division. And little by little, as more troops move to the border, the military center of gravity of the country is being shifted to the north. But, outwardly speaking, there is little in the everyday life of Greece, except in the provinces of Thrace, Macedonia, and Epirus, to betray that anything out of the ordinary is being done, and the painstaking efforts of a board of generals to determine how many of the cashiered Venizelist officers in the country can safely be recalled to the colors at this time have been effectively masked under an announcement that new promotions are being considered.

Psychologically speaking, on the other hand, the situation is bad, and more than the usual crop of alarming rumors flourishes in the cafés. These rumors have to do chiefly with Italian and Bulgarian intentions, and are not infrequently supported with facts and figures concerning alleged border incidents. In no case has the Legation been able to substantiate any of the latter. But in regard to the intentions, it may be said that Greek fears find some excusable grounds in the conversation and songs of Italian troops in Albania and the Dodecanese, and in popular demonstrations in Sofia. The competent authorities discount such things, feeling that an invasion of Greece by either Italy or Bulgaria is most unlikely except in the case of a general European war, when they consider that both Turkey and Britain will be their allies. Furthermore they know

[63] Not cited in this text.

that the British fleet is strategically concentrated in the Eastern Mediterranean. But the people at large have heard little of this fleet, on account of the Government's censorship of any news that might be "interpreted" as a mark of hostility to Italy, and have actually seen nothing of it, while the new Anglo-Turkish arrangement[64] has been given no more publicity in the press here than the proposed new alliance between the Axis powers. Thus the average Greek feels that his country's exposure is acute and its possibilities of succour vague and remote. Even Cabinet members, outside the Foreign Office and the Defense Ministries, have been heard to ask whether Britain's guarantee is not perhaps only an empty gesture after all. Under these conditions, it appears not unlikely that a British vessel or two may be seen shortly in Phaleron Bay. As the British Naval Attaché puts it, there are a million people here in Athens who crave some reassurance. (44)

In June, the MacVeaghs took advantage of the Minister's regular leave to return home, where they were reunited with their daughter Peggy, a student at Bryn Mawr. He divided his time between vacationing with his mother at the family country home in Dublin, New Hampshire, and consulting with his superiors and associates at the State Department, including George V. Allen, the former Consul at Patras and now head of the Greek-Turkish desk, and Assistant Secretary Adolf A. Berle, whose responsibilities covered the Near East. With the President, MacVeagh talked mostly about world tensions, and about American efforts to defuse Europe's ticking time-bomb. While reviewing recent developments in the Balkans, MacVeagh apparently hinted that he would welcome a transfer to Turkey, whose strength and diplomacy in the dangerous years ahead he regarded as more important than that of Greece. He took up the same idea with his boyhood friend Hall "Smouch" Roosevelt, the President's brother-in-law. While the question of such a transfer remained open, he received little encouragement. In a handwritten letter on July 29 from Boston, where the family had boarded the Europe-bound *Saturnia*, MacVeagh sent the President "a word of farewell," and added: "Smouch . . . spoke about expenses connected with the post in Turkey, but I told him I had this figured out. As a matter of fact, Athens is a much more social capital than Ankara, and also keeps a court. It is in other ways that the Turkish job is bigger, and if I could handle it to your approval as I would seem to have handled the Greek, I would have no end of what Francis Bacon somewhere calls 'satisfaction for a man's self. . . .'" (45)

Once in Athens, MacVeagh returned to the much more pressing issues

[64] On May 12, 1939, Britain and Turkey signed a mutual assistance agreement, in the event of war in the "Mediterranean area."

of rising international tensions. On August 21, the day when the Nazi-Soviet Pact's impending conclusion was made public, he wrote:

[Athens, August 21, 1939]

Dear Franklin:

All's well that ends well, and despite my worries I got back to my post without having to go round by the Cape of Good Hope. Here I find military preparations still going on quietly but efficiently, and though there is perhaps more scepticism than when I left as to whether peace can be maintained, there is noticeably less nervousness and jitters. This is partly owing, perhaps, to the fact that the British fleet has been visiting in these waters. But it is also partly owing to a certain fatalism induced by the long drawn-out threat of war. I understand there is something of the same attitude in England and France.

As soon as possible after my return I had a long talk with the Premier (our Dictator), General Metaxas. I wanted him to tell me just where Greece stands, and he did, in terms he has never been willing to use before. "We are with the Western Powers, because it is to our own interest, and because of our allies (the Turks)." This is what I have been reporting for some time, but I never got it so unequivocally from the horse's mouth. He went on to explain that Greece cannot take this attitude openly, for fear of provoking the Italians and annoying the Germans, who have such a hold on Greece's economic life. "But this attitude will last just so long as peace is maintained and no longer." He stated that the Turks understand the reasons for Greek caution, and even applaud them, since an attack by Italy on Greece would inevitably involve Turkey too. He said he has 80,000 men under arms. Most of these are along the northern and northwestern frontiers. There has been no general mobilization, again for reasons of caution, but "Greece will defend her independence to the last man."

A sudden and, at the outset, secret visit of the Permanent Under-Secretary for Foreign Affairs[65] to Turkey just before I landed has caused people in Istanbul to surmise that Greece was fearing a sudden Italian attack. But the Premier's cheeriness, and still more the fact that *the King is still in Corfu* make me doubt this. The Greeks are obviously angling for all the aid from Turkey they can get; but eventually, not now. In fact, General Metaxas told me he thought that war is not immediately imminent "because the Italians don't want to fight, and particularly don't want to fight for Germany; and because the armaments of the Western Powers are so much more powerful than they were; and finally because of the

[65] Nikolaos Mavroudis.

propitiatory propensities of Mr. Chamberlain." But of course we must remember that, in the present state of tension, when a European statesman says "immediate" he means just that, today or tomorrow, and not even next week. Incidentally I see that Ham Fish[66] prophesied the War would break out today, "and I know what I'm talking about." Such are the dangers of contemporary prophecy.

Do you remember telling me about the danger of graft under dictatorships? Well, this danger seems to be rising up round the Greek régime. There are rumors of serious financial scandals in the air, and these all center around one group, that of the National Bank (not the Bank of Greece), which has little by little placed men of its own in key positions in the Cabinet. They have the portfolios of Finance and National Economy and Social Welfare, among others, as well as the collaboration of a sinister and shadowy figure, or *éminence grise*, named Diakos, whom no one ever sees but who is rumored to be the Premier's *alter ego*. General Metaxas is no grafter. His one besetting sin is ambition, if that is a sin. But to pay for his grandiose schemes, and finance the country's rearmament at the same time, he would seem to be going into debt to an unscrupulous and greedy crew, with all that that may mean for the future. While I was home they finally got their hands on the Bank of Greece itself, whose independent-minded Governor was shelved under suspicion of being a revolutionist. . . .

The papers report you in Campo Bello. Oh, happy days! I hope you enjoyed every minute.

Affectionately yours,
Lincoln MacVeagh (46)

And to the Department, MacVeagh reported on August 19:

Immediately on my return from leave in the United States I called on the new British Minister, Sir Charles Michael Palairet, to return the call he had paid me just before my departure, and to learn if possible his views on the present situation of Greece both as regards foreign and home affairs.

Sir Michael is a much less considerable person than his egregious predecessor, Sir Sydney Waterlow, to whom he compares as a .22 caliber target pistol to a bellmouthed blunderbuss. He will not commit the clumsy mistakes so characteristic of Sir Sydney, but neither will he make the same ponderous impression as an embodiment of British power. He also finds himself handicapped at the outset of his mission by the loss of his

---

[66] Hamilton Fish, Congressman from New York, and an old adversary of Roosevelt.

naval attaché, Captain Packer, and still more by that of his able first secretary, Mr. Hopkinson, who has been given a post in London. His commercial secretary is of fairly recent arrival, and for guidance among the devious channels of Greek political and social life he must depend on a very junior third secretary of tender age.[67] He himself is a career diplomat of long experience and has the local advantage of having served once before in Athens, as secretary of Legation, but against this must be set not only his somewhat diluted personality, but an intellectual equipment of apparently small capacity and range.

Sir Michael appeared bored at being called upon by his American colleague, but such a reaction in a Britisher may easily be misleading. Though what comment he vouchsafed on current affairs at this meeting had to be pried out of him, it may very well be that he will be volunteering information when he feels we have met often enough to establish the intimacy of acquaintanceship. In answer to my questions, he expressed himself as satisfied with the attitude of the Premier in foreign affairs, but less so with that of some of those about him.

I asked him whom he meant precisely, and he named Mr. Nicoloudis, Minister of the Press, and Mr. Kotzias, Minister-Governor of Athens. It is true that Mr. Nicoloudis has a wife who is a hater of the British, and that Mr. Kotzias has been greatly flattered by his receptions in Germany. But it would appear that Sir Michael is mistaken if he attributes any great influence on the conduct of foreign affairs to those two gentlemen. Sir Michael said he thought the Greeks would turn out Mr. Metaxas in a minute, if they could, because of the loss of their liberties, just as (he said) "they once turned out Mr. Venizelos because he became dictatorial." But he thought the present régime had done Greece a great deal of good and that it is fortunate that Mr. Metaxas is in the saddle now, because he is a good soldier and organizer. Furthermore, he thought it would be a great disaster for Greece to have a domestic upset in the present state of European affairs. Thus his Legation will apparently continue the policy latterly followed under his predecessor. In this connection, the Department may remember that after going so far last year as to press the King to divorce himself from the Dictator, the British early this year swung around to the opposite attitude, feeling it unsafe to swap horses while crossing a stream, even though the horse they had to ride was unpleasing to the democratic temper (see my despatches No. 2715 of January 31, 1939, and 3040 of May 15, 1939). Sir Michael further said that he had no idea of why Mr. Mavroudis, the Permanent Under-Secretary of State for Foreign Affairs, has gone to Turkey (see my despatch No. 3309 of August 19, 1939)[68] but is "sure he will do us right" whatever may be the reason.

[67] Harold Caccia. [68] Not cited in this text.

I remarked that the Turks seem somewhat put out with the Greeks for not declaring their attitude more unequivocally in the present circumstances (see my telegram No. 128 of August 14, 1939),[69] and Sir Michael remarked that he felt they are a bit unreasonable in this, as indeed he said, they are also unreasonable in feeling the same way about Yugoslavia, since they themselves are in a much safer position strategically, and by no means so thoroughly in the economic grip of Germany as these two countries. He said Mr. Mavroudis had told him that his Government was deeply grateful to the British Government for not pushing it too hard in its present difficult situation, and he evidently thought the Turks ought to show the same eminently diplomatic understanding and restraint. In regard to Italy, he said things have been quiet along the Greco-Albanian border. He was obviously uninformed of recent trends and events in western Macedonia (see Political Notes No. 70 of August 10, 1939, from the Vice Consul in Charge at Salonica).[70] Apparently co-operation between the British Legation in Athens and the British Consulate General in Salonica, co-operation which was practically non-existent in Sir Sydney's time on account of the diplomatic high-hatting and consular jealousy, is no better today. More generally, on the subject of Italy, Sir Michael said the Italian people are increasingly against the alliance with Germany, and are trusting to their Duce to keep them out of war. Count Ciano he characterized as "dangerous."

As regards home affairs, Sir Michael said he felt no change has occurred worth mentioning in the two months of my absence. The régime, he feels, is still securely in the saddle. He made no mention of the financial situation, and is still apparently in the primary state of knowledge of this country's condition, accepting the importance of such ostensible figures as Nicoloudis and Kotzias and ignoring the vast underground power of the Diakos group, as well as the possible significance of the Tsouderos incident (see the Legation's despatch No. 3268 of August 1, 1939).[71] Neither did he mention the recent British loan to Greece of £2,000,000 (see the Legation's despatch No. 3225 of July 20, 1939),[72] but this is perhaps understandable in view of the fact that this loan was decided on in principle months ago.

[69] Not cited in this text.   [70] Not cited in this text.

[71] Not cited in this text. The "Tsouderos incident" was the last significant plot against the Metaxas dictatorship. In the summer of 1939, the prominent Cretan, Emmanuel Tsouderos, former Governor of the Bank of Greece and a friend of people in prominent political and financial circles in Britain, was chosen by a conspiracy of Greek leaders to become Prime Minister, upon Metaxas' overthrow. In July, the plot was discovered by police agents, and Tsouderos was packed off to Syros, while others in the conspiracy were imprisoned. Tsouderos was destined to become Prime Minister several months after Metaxas' death (on Januray 29, 1941), leading the first government in exile.

[72] Not cited in this text.

To sum up: Sir Michael is a slight, handsome, rather lackadaisical person, who should do well in drawing-rooms, if he will put himself out, and British diplomacy will gain a great deal in grace, if nothing in force, by his substitution for Sir Sydney Waterlow as Minister in Athens. This diplomacy is now handicapped by at least a temporary weakening in the ranks of the Legation's subordinate commissioned personnel. Furthermore, it is not too well-informed at the present time of local goings-on. But it is definite, and appears well-grounded on two essential points. It is satisfied that continued support of the régime of General Metaxas, despite this régime's dictatorial character, is the best local policy under present world conditions; and while it finds it politic not to force him so to declare, it is supremely confident that the Dictator will bring Greece to England's side in the event of general hostilities. (47)

Hours before the troops of Hitler's Germany invaded Poland, launching World War II, MacVeagh wrote hastily and in his own hand:

[Athens, August 31st, 1939]

Dear Franklin:

Our courier service has been interrupted, and we are sending our pouch off on the Export Liner due to leave this afternoon, not knowing exactly when we'll have another opportunity. She will also take scores of Americans whom we have been working day and night to assist in departing. This is just a note to say we are all right, in our small corner of this agitated world. The Greek government is being very good to us despite its own anxiety and the difficulties caused by the mobilization of many of its people. Some hope is still expressed that war may be averted, in general, and that Italy may stay out, in particular. Meanwhile the Greeks now have forces on the Albanian front which can be expected to make Italian penetration very difficult if not impossible, and appear to be cooperating smoothly with their allies the Turks, whose concentration in Eastern Thrace should discourage the Bulgars from moving, at least just yet. I am informed from Salonica that Greek morale is excellent in that critical region. Here there is an outward calm which is remarkable, perhaps influenced by that of Italy. You certainly put the Dictators on the spot with your messages! Private comment here is, of course, universally favorable, and publicity has been good, though comment in the editorial columns has been either non-existent or very guarded.

Best of luck always,

Yours affectionately,
Lincoln MacVeagh (48)

CHAPTER
IV

In the Storm's Path:
1939-1940

DESPITE BRITISH AND FRENCH DECLARATIONS of war on Germany, and Soviet attacks on Poland and Finland, the conflict at first appeared to be confined to Europe's northern reaches. As long as Italy remained neutral, there was little likelihood that the fighting would spread southward to engulf the Balkans and the Eastern Mediterranean. Somewhat listless, in "my small corner of this agitated world," MacVeagh provided the President with a running commentary on the ever-changing scene. Time and time again, he tried to confront the issue uppermost in his mind: if war should come, would Greece stand up to the aggressors?

[Athens, September 16, 1939]

Dear Franklin:

I have the honor to report briefly as follows:

I had another long talk with the Premier, General Metaxas, the other day. He spoke more warmly than ever of Greece's attachment to Great Britain, and when I asked about his own Government's position, he read aloud to me the statement of Turkey's attitude recently made by the Turkish Prime Minister before the Grand National Assembly! From other sources, I learn that Greek and Turkish military plans are coordinated for the defense of Salonica and Thrace; and from General Metaxas, as well as his competent Under Minister, that *Greece will make no move in foreign affairs without England's approval.*

I gave the Premier a copy of your neutrality proclamation and asked him whether he intended also to declare neutrality. He said "no," that it wasn't necessary, and that he desired "to give umbrage to no one," a delicate way of saying he will keep in line with the Turks, who not long ago were cross with him for what they thought a *too* neutral attitude on his part. Meanwhile the attachment to Great Britain is apparent in action as well as confidentially expressed. Greek cargoes destined for Germany have been turned back by the British control, and the matter has been kept dark by the Greek Government. The Premier told me that he would not renew the Greco-German clearing agreement without England's consent, and actually, though initialled in Berlin two weeks ago, the renewal remains unsigned.

The Premier's handling of the foreign situation has the approval of the country at large. For the moment foreign affairs overshadow domestic issues, and as there is virtual unanimity on the one, the danger of dissension arising from the other is lessened. Greece faces the second world war in far better condition than she faced the first.

The question of Italy's neutrality is the question of the hour here, and contributes to the continuance of the "war of nerves" in this region. Is this neutrality genuine? General Metaxas says he thinks it is, in the sense that Italy is genuinely undecided as to which side offers her the greater advantages; and the British Minister says he thinks London has decided to find Italian neutrality "acceptable" for the time being. On the other hand, the Under-Minister for Foreign Affairs sagely remarks, "The measure of Italy's neutrality must be the extent of her disarmament." Hence certain negotiations which appear now to be in progress between Athens and Rome for a reciprocal decrease of forces on the Albanian frontier not only promise some local appeasement but may afford a first justification of England's policy.

An interesting sidelight on present Greek nervousness comes from the Palace. When I asked to see the King on my return, he sent me word that while he would very much like to receive me, and wanted specially to hear of my talks with you, he thought it best not to, for the present, since if he received me it might also be necessary,—in the words of the Grand Chamberlain who gave me the message,—"to receive the Polish Minister and other persons!"

Affectionately yours,
Lincoln MacVeagh (1)

And ten days later:

[Athens, September 26, 1939]

Dear Franklin:

Most of what I write must be ancient history before it reaches you, and of course I am telegraphing the Department frequently, but coming events sometimes cast long shadows ahead, and so I'll keep on with the Greek record, just in case it may contain something illuminating somewhere. One of your secretaries can always call me off if I become a nuisance.

Immediately after I wrote you last, the Russians moved in on the Poles, and threw even people as far away as Greece into a temporary panic. The Foreign Office was, of course, aware that such a thing might happen. But a *fait accompli* is a very different thing from a *fait envisagé*. The immediate anxiety concerned British reaction. Would England declare war on Russia, and if so, what would be the effect on Turkey? When it became evident, in a day or so, that the British had no intention of honoring their obligation to Poland in the case of this second aggressor, there was a noticeable let up in the tension here. But, on the other hand, fear is increasing that Russia may now move to recapture Bessarabia from the Rumanians.

In this connection, the Under-Minister for Foreign Affairs said to me the other day that Russo-German collaboration could not survive an attempt by either power to penetrate the Balkans, where their interests clash today as they always have in the past, and that therefore he thought there was a good chance Rumania might be left in peace. Since that time, however, the Russians have advanced so far west in Poland, and their position there is so strong while Germany is occupied with France and England, that they may feel the present moment offers an opportunity not to be ignored. Under the circumstances of England's guarantee to Rumania and her alliance with Turkey, it is not to be wondered at that the Turkish Foreign Minister is in Moscow today seeking a clarification of the situation!

The question of whether Italy will stay neutral remains, however, the question of the hour here, because the issues involved appear more immediate for Greece. The Greeks and Italians have agreed, on Italian initiative, to reciprocal withdrawal of troops on the Albanian frontier, and the first Greek editorials on any phase of foreign affairs since September 1st record satisfaction and a perhaps unwarranted degree of hopefulness. It is rumored that Italy may now withdraw some of her forces in the Dodecanese, and thus extend her policy of appeasement to Turkey. But the Turkish Military Attaché here suspects that the Italians are planning to join Hitler if the allies continue to reject the latter's peace proposals, and are now attempting to appease the Balkans only as a protection for their rear in case of a joint Italo-German attack in the south of France. In this connection, a recent telegram from Mr. MacMurray[1] says that the Turkish Foreign Minister also feels that the existing Italian neutrality is only for the time being and for strategic purposes. The British, on the other hand, seem still to take this neutrality at its face value, and the Turkish Ambassador in Athens[2] (who is an old friend of mine, since he was Minister here when I came out six years ago) feels the same way. He thinks Italy

---

[1] John V. A. MacMurray, U.S. Ambassador to Turkey.
[2] Akayayen Enis (Enis Bey).

"cannot afford" to join Germany, for whom victory over England is "impossible." When such a conflict of opinion exists in supposedly informed circles, you can imagine the rumors that fly about.

   I have seen the King, and given him your thanks for his message of appreciation of America's cultural and philanthropic help to Greece. I also gave him your message that America had always been a great friend of Greece and intends to remain so. Obviously he was enormously pleased to have this interchange with you, even though it was confined to amenities. I then, without drawing the bow too pointedly at the situation in this country, told him what you said about the danger of graft under dictatorships, and, as luck would have it, that very afternoon the news broke of the enormous fortunes put away in foreign countries by the Nazi leaders! Referring to the concluding paragraph of my last letter, I may say that I was amused to see that immediately I left the audience chamber, the Polish Minister popped in.

   The King told me stories of his visit to Italy this summer which confirmed the impression that the House of Savoy is definitely opposed to the pro-German policy hitherto followed by the Fascist Party. But more interesting than royal audiences, and second only to the possibilities of actual involvement in the war, are the economic problems which have arisen here since hostilities began. The British sea blockade is effective, but rail communication is open with Germany, and the Germans are trying to convince the Greeks that barter trade with them can go on as usual. Shipment by rail, however, is complicated and expensive, since neither Germany, Yugoslavia, nor Greece, will allow their rolling stock to cross their borders. Furthermore, the Greek authorities are very doubtful of Germany's ability, under war conditions, to supply her with anything but highly manufactured articles, and these she can neither eat nor use for fuel. The goods she herself produces she wants to trade for necessities, or for foreign exchange, of which her stock is desperately low. There is a tendency, therefore, to refuse barter, even on the most favorable terms which the Germans can invent. I am informed today that the British will not object to continuance of the Greco-German clearing so far as tobacco is concerned, but that the Bank of Greece itself is objecting and demanding the cash which Germany hasn't got. Altogether the signs indicate that carrying on economic warfare in this region is by no means a hopeless one [case] from the British point of view.

                                                         Affectionately yours,
                                                         Lincoln MacVeagh (2)

A few weeks after the outbreak of World War II—on October 18, 1939 —MacVeagh began to keep a diary. Intended as a highly personal and confidential record of news and impressions of the war, it records political and diplomatic activities and legation work; it reports on speculations and rumors, recounts family affairs, and describes assorted private thoughts. It was continued without interruption through the long days of the "phony war" and the "Winter War," the Albanian War, and the German conquest of Greece. It covers his tour as Minister to Iceland (1941-1942), to the Union of South Africa (1942-1943), to the Greek and Yugoslav Governments-in-exile in Cairo (1943-1944), and his return to Athens immediately following the German withdrawal. This long and fascinating manuscript ends abruptly, two weeks after President Roosevelt's death: the last entry is dated April 30, 1945.

As mentioned in the Editor's Preface, MacVeagh's diary is much too lengthy and personal a manuscript to reproduce fully in print. The passages which have been chosen to appear in this publication deal almost entirely with events of historical importance and, together with his letters to the President, despatches and telegrams, they have been woven into a near-continuous political journal.

October 19, 1939, Thursday

The war so far is a queer one. The allies are letting the Germans do all the attacking—by land, sea, and air,—and seem chiefly concerned with saving lives rather than taking them. Are they counting on a revolution in Germany doing their work for them? Or on the blockade to exhaust German strength? Or on the latter to bring about the former? If any or all of these, it would seem that they may have a long time to wait, defending themselves all the time against most able opponents. . . .

Chief item in the day's news is to the effect that the Anglo-Franco-Turkish mutual assistance pact was due to be signed at Ankara this afternoon. The British radio is confident in its announcement. If true, this is a real strengthening of the allied position. This war has so far been like a football game in which the whistle should blow before the lineups have been completed. We are only beginning to see the composition of the teams. I have been informed by the Turkish Military Attaché that the British are beginning to press the Greeks somewhat for a mutual assistance pact here as well. But won't the Greeks first want to be sure of Italy's intentions? Some interesting and important developments should follow shortly on Turkey's exhibition of firmness toward Russia and confidence in the allied cause, and the least of these should be a strengthening of the peace party in Italy, particularly if the Turkish assistance extends to the west, as expected. The logic of the situation is all on the side of the Italians joining the allies to protect the Mediterranean from

German or Russian domination, eventually, if not now. But are they gamblers or logicians? That is the question.

October 20, 1939, Friday

Usual conference in the chancery at 10, with all officers present. . . . Then I drove over to the Foreign Office and had a long talk with Mr. Mavroudis. He expressed satisfaction with the Turco-Anglo-French mutual assistance pact,[3] which was signed yesterday as announced. He said that what broke up the Moscow talks[4] was the Russian demand that they be not obliged to help Turkey if the latter were attacked by Germany. Since they were also asking the Turks to close the Dardanelles to allied shipping, the Turks thought that they were not getting enough of a *quid pro quo*. Apparently the Russo-Turkish mutual assistance was to be unilateral on the side of Russia, and the Turks said no, thank you! More interesting was the information that this demand was at first withdrawn by the Russians, with Stalin's approval, but reintroduced into the conversations later, after Germany had apparently brought pressure to bear. . . . The Minister also told me that Italy has asked Greece whether she desires to renew the Pact of Friendship and Conciliation of 1928, which expired October 1st, and that with the consent of the British the Greeks have agreed in principle, deferring formal action to a later date. Mr. Mavroudis said he thinks Greece could very well formally renew the thing at once, since she cannot be anything but friendly and conciliatory toward Italy unless the latter attacks her. But he said the Government felt a bit embarrassed in regard to the British position. On the other hand, when asked, the British gave the Greeks *carte blanche* to do as they pleased, urging only that every care be exercised to save Italian feelings in the matter! . . . Does the above explain the rumor mentioned yesterday regarding a new Italo-Greek agreement under British blessing? . . . Mr. Mavroudis said the allies are doing everything to keep Italy neutral, and that Italy also desires to remain neutral (he mentioned no doubts as to Mussolini). But he said the Italians have been worried lest the new pact with Turkey create a situation which would necessitate their going to war. He himself tried to calm Grazzi[5] the other day, saying such a pact would be in favor of peace and could not affect Italy adversely unless she should be an aggressor; and he believes that the British will present the completed

---

[3] On October 19, 1939, Turkey concluded a fifteen-year pact of mutual assistance with Britain and France.

[4] From September 26 to October 17, 1939, Foreign Ministers Molotov and Aras discussed in Moscow a possible Soviet-Turkish pact of mutual assistance. The talks failed to produce an agreement.

[5] Count Emmanuel Grazzi, Italian Ambassador to Greece.

affair in this light at Rome, and that Italy will accept the explanation. He expects no adverse explosion from the Italian press. . . . Incidentally, he remarked that the Pact of 1928 above mentioned, which was signed by Venizelos, had been "somewhat lost sight of recently!"

Last night it was reported on the radio that the Bulgarian Cabinet had resigned. Mr. Mavroudis credited the affair to Russian attempts to spread their influence in the Balkans. He said that while the King is willing to listen to anyone who promises support to Bulgaria's territorial claims, he is also fearful of Bolshevik patronage and desires a government strong enough to resist it. The problem is to get the benefit of Russia's help and not fall into Russian hands—a poser for a small power. Kioseivanov may be retained as Premier to form the new cabinet, as announced. But Mr. Mavroudis' information from Sofia gives this as uncertain. The King is consulting with various political leaders, of whom K. is one. . . . Mr. Mavroudis denied that the British are in any way pressing for a mutual non-assistance pact here. He said they know the Greek position too well and are satisfied with having obligated Turkey to assist if the British unilateral guarantee to Greece is called into play.

October 22, 1939, Sunday

I have been working for hours on a despatch on "Greece and Recent Developments in the Near East." Here is my summary: "Greece finds her dependence on England and her trust in Turkey increased and strengthened by the recent developments in the Near East, and the government is using the idea that these will promote the peace and security of this region to augment the confidence and tranquility of the people. Meanwhile the government itself remains doubtful of Italy's neutrality and suspicious of her intentions, and while seeing Russia as having received a check from Turkey, regards the former as definitely on the march, with designs in the Balkans which will require careful watching."

November 3, 1939, Friday

The papers carry the exchange of notes between Mr. Metaxas and Grazzi. The terms are exactly as stated by Mr. Mavroudis two weeks ago —agreement to be guided by the spirit of the 1928 Pact of Friendship and Conciliation, while hoping that conditions will allow of a more concrete expression soon.

November 7, 1939, Tuesday

Went alone to the Soviet Legation's reception to celebrate the 22nd anniversary of the "October Revolution." A large crowd present. The

British Minister was there, together with the German and French Ministers, but I saw no meeting of belligerents. . . . [Metaxas] seems quite pleased and proud over Greece's present position, with Italy a friend and Turkey an ally. He doesn't think that Germany will drive to the Dardanelles because Russia would come across her path. He admitted there is a tendency to form a neutral bloc in the Balkans but went no further than that. He laughed over Bulgaria's being in a pickle because as a kingdom she daren't accept gifts from the Bolsheviks. He said Greece's present problems are mainly economic. England he said ought to help her by buying the tobacco which she can no longer sell to Germany. If only Greece could sell her tobacco, her position would be all right, he said. "When I used to talk about England buying our tobacco to Sir Sydney Waterlow he seemed not to hear," he added, but now the British are at least beginning to think about it. The idea that the British might be *beginning* to think pleased him mightily. I asked him whether they had not offered to charter some Greek boats, and he said "Not *some*, but 50 percent!" and he went on to say that the offer could not be accepted because the British wanted to limit the profits to what their own ships are allowed at present with their country at war, whereas the Greek shipowners can make a lot more independently. (Of course the British were offering certain advantages in the way of fuel, insurance, etc., but nevertheless they are obviously out for the best bargain they can get from Greece's difficult position.) . . . Mr. Metaxas was inclined to doubt my "information" that the Germans are better off economically than the British admit. . . . I asked him to lunch and he said he would suggest a date through Mr. Androulis. He said that there are some places he doesn't like to go to,—possibly meaning the Legation where we were drinking champagne at the moment, drinking each other's health!—but that ours is not one of them. . . . Mrs. Metaxas spoke most appreciatively of our contribution to the soup kitchens, and I was able to tell her how much we admire the work.

Athens, November 8, 1939

Dear Franklin:

You may have "seen by the papers," as Mr. Dooley used to say, that the Greeks and Italians have exchanged notes agreeing to abide by the spirit of their pact of Friendship of 1928 which has just expired. The event has made a bit of a stir in these parts and has not only a queer history behind it but an importance beyond its immediate significance.

As to the history, the Pact of Friendship between these two countries had become so far a dead letter last spring, that when Mussolini decided that he had no intention of attacking Greece (understand Corfu), he forgot to mention that he was already bound to her in friendship and gave "assurances" entirely *de novo*, while the Greeks themselves never noticed the omission!

As to the importance, the facts are that the initiative was Italian, that the Greeks consulted the British before agreeing, and that the Italians knew it. This exchange of notes—it is hardly a "pact" but may grow into one—thus throws a bridge of sorts between Rome and London. Whether any traffic will cross the bridge remains to be seen, but the practical wisdom of the Near East is asking what is a bridge for? The position of Greece is of course greatly improved. When I talked with the Premier last night he was positively radiant. He has now the friendship of Italy, an alliance with Turkey, and the guarantee of Britain. But the fate of Greece amounts to little in comparison with the implications of this new development, if they are what they seem.

The sequence of events is interesting. Late in August, Germany made her pact with Russia, and on September 1st attacked Poland, without the assent of her Axis partner. On September 12th, Italy officially "remembered" her pact of friendship with Greece, and on September 20th, announced the withdrawal of her troops from the Greco-Albanian frontier. Is *post hoc*, in this case, also *propter hoc*? It looks very much like it.

Greek opinion tends to see Italy veering away from the Axis toward a more neutral policy. This involves the consolidation of the Balkans against Russian, and perhaps also German aggression, and the eventual protection of Italian interests in the Mediterranean against powers far more ruthless than England and France.

I am informed here that the countries of southeastern Europe would probably not wish to form a neutral bloc under Italian leadership, but that such a bloc may possibly come about nevertheless, since "needs must when the devil drives," and that Italy might be accepted as big brother if not as patron. Furthermore, to the extent that Roman imperialism runs counter to any non-Mediterranean domination of the Straits, Italy would seem to be becoming more and more, as Russian appetite grows, the virtual ally of the other Great Powers with interests in the Mediterranean Sea.

The second problem of the day in this region is, of course, this same Russian appetite. Who was it of whom the Bible says that his maw is never full? Was it the Devil? or Anti-Christ? Though the Finnish business is not yet settled,[6] the Russians have already inquired at Ankara how Turkey intends to interpret her Tripartite agreement with England and

---

[6] In October 1939, the Soviet Union demanded that its frontier with Finland, on the Karelian Isthmus, be moved away from Leningrad, and that Finland allow Soviet naval bases on its territory. Following the rejection of these demands, Soviet forces invaded Finland on November 30, 1939.

France so far as Rumania is concerned, and in Sofia there has been talk of the establishment of a Russo-Bulgarian frontier. According to information from the Greek Embassy at the Turkish capital, the Turks have refused to commit themselves. If they don't intend to help the Rumanians, they are, at any rate, not telling the Russians so. And it now seems established that the Bulgarian cabinet fell because the King wanted to be wholly free of Russian influence in the conduct of foreign affairs. These may be good signs, to some extent, but they are also the smoke which betrays the presence of fire. As to the importance of the fire, opinions differ. The Turkish Military Attaché[7] said to me yesterday: "We know that Russia is not in a position to fight; and we won't be bluffed." But the majority hardly shares this view.

So far as internal affairs here are concerned, I may say that the Premier has gathered some laurels as Foreign Minister, but that the Army appears restless over being held so long on a war footing when there isn't any war, while the difficulties connected with the breakdown of the international barter system and the British control of exports have created seemingly endless economic problems, some of them of a serious nature. In this connection, the Premier said to me last night (at the Soviet celebration!) "America is our hope." Maybe the Greeks will now look on a possible American trade agreement with different eyes than when the German clearing was going strong. In any case, that is *my* hope.

Finally, I would add that though the press has been cautious as usual and allowed no editorials on the subject, the Greek reaction to our repeal of the arms embargo[8] has been generally enthusiastic. Naturally, people here think less of our neutrality in this connection than of the fortunes of the belligerents, and I have been somewhat embarrassed occasionally by the unvarnished phraseology of congratulations received.

Affectionately yours,
Lincoln MacVeagh (3)

November 10, 1939, Friday

Mr. Davis[9] came in about his difficulties with the Government and with his own teachers. On the one hand he is required to give all of each Wednesday to the [Metaxist] Youth Movement, and on the other his young American teachers refuse, on conscientious grounds, to help in any activity smacking of dictatorship! He wanted my advice on how to han-

---

[7] Major Pasakay.

[8] On November 4, 1939, the United States amended the Neutrality Act of May 1, 1937, repealing the embargo on arms and placing exports to belligerents on a cash-and-carry basis.

[9] Homer Davis, President of the American Athens College.

dle them in this matter, and it seemed to me that he should demand their loyalty to the school, which after all must comply with the Government's regulations if it wishes to stay on in Greece. He proposed to explain that he is forced temporarily to be "hypocritical," but I advised against saying anything that, if quoted, could be used against him; but merely to state the school's duty to the state, and the teachers' duty to the school.

Interesting telegram from Mr. Lane[10] in Belgrade to the Department, November 7, decoded today, says the Rumanians are proposing a neutral Balkan bloc, including Hungary and possibly Italy. I saw the Yugoslav Minister[11] on this during the afternoon. . . .

The Minister gave me excellent tea in Crown Derby cups and we discussed European events. He was all agog over the Hitler bomb explosion.[12] In regard to the neutral bloc, he said Greece is considering detailed proposals put forth by the Rumanians, but that Mr. Metaxas tells Djuvara[13] that he can't answer till he has consulted with Turkey—Greece seems willing enough herself. There is no question, in these proposals, of either Italian leadership, or any territorial concessions to Bulgaria. But Turkey may have some reserves on account of her relations with Soviet Russia. . . . The Yugoslav Minister confirmed the withdrawal of Turkish forces from the Bulgar frontier . . . I was struck by considerable evidence, in Mr. Vukčević's conversation, of jealousy of Turkey. He asked me whether I didn't think, since they had signed the Tripartite Pact, that they are "posing" a bit as the leader among the Balkans. I hadn't noticed it, but as a matter of fact, I think their strong and constant policy has done much to give them this position in reality.

November 13, 1939, Monday

Called on the Rumanian Ambassador [Djuvara]. . . . We talked, or rather *he* talked, of the European situation, for nearly an hour. But I got the information I was after. He said that his proposals to the Greek Government were for a *neutral bloc* and not non-aggression. [Foreign Minister] Gafencu[14] has telegraphed him that England confidentially supports the idea, and the French Ambassador in Bucharest[15] [Thierry] said, on instructions from Paris, that France is in complete accord. When, however, Djuvara told this to Metaxas, the latter was most embarrassed,

---

[10] Arthur Bliss Lane, U.S. Minister to Yugoslavia.

[11] Alexandar Vukčević, Yugoslav Ambassador to Greece.

[12] On the night of November 8, 1939, a few minutes after Hitler had left a Nazi assembly in Munich, a bomb explosion killed seven and wounded sixty persons.

[13] M. Djuvara, Rumanian Ambassador to Greece.

[14] Grigore Gafencu, Rumanian Minister for Foreign Affairs.

[15] M. Thierry, French Ambassador to Rumania.

and said that in Ankara the French had expressed themselves as not in favor of the idea,—hence the Turkish hesitation, and consequently, the Greek too. Djuvara attributes this French ambiguity to the unwillingness of certain *Quai d'Orsay* officials to give up the idea of winning Russia over to the allied side. He thinks such an idea fantastic. Russia is far closer to the Germans than to the French—to Nazism than to Democracy. She may eventually fall foul of the Germans, but this will come about through a clash of imperial interests (the kind of thing that is always happening in the Baltic region) rather than through love of the French or any fundamental opposition of an ideological kind. Went back to the office and drafted a telegram.

November 14, 1939, Tuesday

Long office conference in the morning, after which I saw Mr. Mavroudis. [He] didn't mention the Rumanian proposals for a bloc in Southeastern Europe until I showed by a brief question that I was *au courant*, and then he discussed them quite freely, saying he felt they would not come to anything because they have been hastily framed in a time of panic at Bucharest, without sufficient basic study, particularly as regards the possible reactions of the Great Powers. Germany, he said, at first saw in the idea a reinforcement of her policy to keep the Balkans out of war as a source of needed supplies, but now suspects the bloc might be used as an instrument of her enemies against her, and has withdrawn her approval. France, while agreeing at Bucharest, has advised the Turks to go cautiously. (This confirms what Djuvara said to me, but Mr. M. does not believe the French ambiguity is due to her Russian policy, but rather to her jealousy of a possible increase in Italian prestige.) The Russians have not replied at all, and the Italians, so said Mr. Mavroudis, while basically in accord, are now themselves proposing objections, so as not to appear to receive a check if for other reasons the plan does not go through. Mr. Mavroudis thought that a more hopeful approach to the same objective might be made through the already existing Balkan Entente, especially if the rumored rapprochement between Italy and Turkey becomes a fact. Bulgaria might join to the extent of giving mutual pledges of neutrality as regards the present hostilities anyhow, and the Great Powers could hardly object to an expression of policy on the part of an Entente which they have already recognized, though the formation of a new one arouses their mistrust. Note: there are rumors current here that Mr. Metaxas is shortly to go on a trip somewhere unknown, and the Bulgarian Legation believes a meeting of the Balkan Council will soon be called. Even before the Rumanians took up the idea of a neutral bloc (probably taking the idea from Italy, as Mr. Lane reports in his telegrams), the

178 · CHAPTER IV

Yugoslavs tried to get the idea in motion via this same Entente route, and Mr. Vukčević saw Mr. Metaxas twice in an attempt to get him to hold out to Bulgaria some hope of recovering the Aegean exit. But Mr. V. told me that the Premier decidedly set him down on this. He believes that it is chiefly the *Turks* who stand in the way of Greek compliance in this matter. I believe that the neutrality bloc idea will not go through, even on such a basis as Mr. M. suggests, unless two conditions are met: 1. the idea of Italian leadership must not appear, and 2. no concessions to Bulgaria, of a territorial kind, must be promised, or even hinted at.

Athens, Greece
Monday, December 3, 1939

Dear Franklin:

Things move so fast these days that my letters, which take so long to reach you, ought to be cast in the mold of prophecies. But I feel rather handicapped as a prophet. It may be true that coming events cast their shadows before, and that a good observer should note them. But when one's whole sky is clouded, with storms on every horizon, there are no definite shadows, and all is more or less dark.

The Mediterranean situation was certainly much improved by the conclusion of the Turkish Pact with England and France, and Italy's continuing neutrality has been no less reassuring, marked as it has been with concrete evidences of pacific intentions, at least for the immediate future. Thus, Italy has given "winter leave of absence" to many of her troops, and has resumed the sailings of the Adriatica Line to the Piraeus, Izmir, and Istanbul, and I am told, is exploring Turkish reactions to a possible extension of the *Ala Littoria Air Line* from Salonica to the Bosphorus. So far as I can find out, she has not withdrawn any of her forces from the Dodecanese, and without that there can hardly be any real Italo-Turkish *rapprochement*, as conditions stand. But feeling is certainly less tense than it was between these two countries, possibly because both realize that they are alike menaced by the threat to the Straits inherent in Russo-German collaboration.

Against this improvement in the local situation, however, which has allowed Greece to reduce her mobilized forces to about the numbers on hand last August, must be set the feeling here that Russian pressure on Rumania is likely to follow promptly on the Finnish business, and that Germany and Russia are encouraging both Hungary and Bulgaria in their claims to the lost provinces of Transylvania and the Dobrudja. I have talked only this evening with the Under-Minister for Foreign Affairs on this subject. He has no proof that an agreement exists between Russia and Germany regarding zones of influence in the Balkans, but he feels such a thing not unlikely, in view of the way the two have been working together in the north. He feels they may not get on so well in this region, since for both there is really only one prize here, namely the Straits. But though there may eventually be some double-crossing between them, preliminary joint maneuvres bringing both within grasping distance of the goal are not to be excluded. In this connection, he mentioned German concentrations on the Hungarian border as possibly meant to encourage Hungarian exploitation of a Russian move against Bessarabia. Both Russia and Germany are known to be actively intriguing in Sofia, but the reduction of Rumania still seems first on the list of agenda. How far it is intended to impair Rumania's independence is a question, but her shearing and humiliation would make Russo-German influence supreme in the Balkans right down to the Greek border, and from the Turkish point of view this would probably be intolerable no matter where the two powers drew the line dividing their zones of influence. It is the Under-Minister's idea that Turkey will fight rather than let any great power control the territory which used, as "Turkey-in-Europe," to constitute the western bulwark of the Straits, and the Turkish Military Attaché confirms this by saying that when Turkey fights it will not be in Turkey but in Bulgaria. All this, of course, constitutes a forecast dependent on a number of unknown factors, but it has sufficient verisimilitude and urgency to cause the Greeks extreme uneasiness.

Something like panic in the Rumanian breast has been the cause of our most recent diplomatic dust-up here. After the repeated failures of the last few years to draw the Bulgarians into the fold of the Balkan Entente, and thus make possible a solid Balkan Bloc, the Rumanians, apparently encouraged at first by Italy (always anxious to play a leading role), proposed the idea that southeastern Europe, that is, the Balkan nations plus Italy and Hungary, should unite in taking the pledge of neutrality. There was to be no question of mutual assistance, or anything like that, but the idea itself would create a bond capable of being developed. The Rumanian Ambassador here informed the Greeks that all the great European powers were pleased with the idea, and it is undoubtedly true that Germany expressed her accord to begin with. The French, however, soon showed themselves jealous of the prestige to be acquired by Italy in such a combination with lesser states, and when Germany heard that England was favorable she withdrew her consent. The Under-Minister of Foreign Affairs added tonight that Russia also was against the idea and that she used her influence with the Germans to help destroy it. Finally, Italy withdrew her support as soon as she saw the plan might not go through. Thus, regardless of the willingness, or otherwise, of the majority of the states immediately concerned, the idea has come to exactly nothing. The Greeks very sensibly say it was too hastily launched and not sufficiently studied in advance as regards the conflicting policies of the Great Powers. Now they say that Mr. Gafencu is thinking of restricting the pledge to the Balkan Entente countries alone. But this could hardly have the same effect. The fact is that the neutrality or the non-neutrality of the Balkan States is not theirs to dispose of, and can never be until they unite on things more fundamental than neutrality alone.

While Greece waits for the storm in northern Europe to roll southeastwards, her most pressing problems remain economic. Like most of the neutral countries, and like all which have been subsisting for years largely on German barter, she is deeply resentful of the British blockade, particularly the new blockade of German exports. Frankly, her leaders tell me that they don't see how she is going to live unless England does something—they know not what—to compensate her for her loss of trade. No protests have been made to Germany in regard to the Greek boats sunk by German submarines and mines. The Under-Minister for Foreign Affairs has told me that this will be done only "when we receive accurate information as to the circumstances in each case." But the British are hearing from the Greeks every day about the blockade. This may seem a little unfair, but as one wit remarked, "Greek ships carry good insurance." So far, the French and British have promised to buy some Greek tobacco, but more than this will have to be done. The French member of the International Financial Commission tells me that the Commission's receipts from the monopolies it controls—salt, customs, matches, tobacco, etc.—have gone down $33\frac{1}{3}$ percent since September 1st, and the movement of shipping in the Piraeus, normally the second or third port in the Mediterranean in this respect, has gone off by 50 percent in the same period. The Greek tramp marine, the second in the world, is making a good profit, as it did in the last war, but is being more heavily and efficiently taxed than it was then to make up for Greece's losses in other ways. The Greeks get meat only three days a week now and are rationed in sugar, coal and gasoline. The bread has been debased (being partly made of beans) and numbers of imported manufactured articles have totally disappeared from the market. But this after all is the common lot of Europe in these days. Though struggling, Greece is still keeping her head above water and is favorably situated still, as European countries go. Also, as far as she deems it safe, she is still on the side of the Allies. She congratulated Hitler on his escape from the Munich bomb, but in so doing she only sent the Director of Protocol of the Foreign Office to call on the German Minister. The incident may serve as a parable of her attitude.

Affectionately yours,
Lincoln MacVeagh (4)

December 29, 1939, Friday

Drove out with the two Bunnies [Mrs. MacVeagh and daughter Margaret] to Tatoi [Palace] at 4:30 for tea with H.M. Found him all alone in a house not yet furnished with rugs or pictures, but with the steam heat turned on and decidedly comfortable in the essentials. He has completely remodeled the inside, put in a lot of bath rooms, and done a beautiful job all round. He took us all over the house, right up to the servants quarters on the top floor, which are admirable and *humane*—a new thing in Greece! The house is an English country house, large and handsome within, though the outside is not remarkable, and the grounds need redoing; there is practically nothing in the furnishings to remind one that one is in Greece! But the view over the Attic plain clear to the sea is very fine and very Greek. . . . H.M. was in golf trousers, and went about opening doors and windows, and turning on lights, showing an interest in, and a knowledge of, every gadget in the place. He said he had only been in the palace for a couple of days, for the first time, and is enjoying it hugely. We had a very pleasant tea, he doing the pouring, no servant about, and he let us out the door himself, getting a good bark and growl out of Souf, when he came near the car. But Mummy said, "He's only saying Zeto."[16]. . . H.M. said that he loves the old palace at Corfu and is going to take it over once more for his own use. He used to live there when he was young, with the family, just as he used to live at Tatoi, and he apparently has a great feeling for continuity, as well as for family—a new Pius Aeneas, in fact, with a love for his household gods and ancestral hearths. Also, as we have noted before, he has a lot of taste. . . . Conversation after tea was lots of fun, as H.M. is full of humor and doesn't mind giving it free rein at such times. He'll look grim enough at the *TeDeum* next Monday! . . .

January 8, 1940, Monday

News in the Radio Bulletin from Rome of the new [American] diplomatic appointments. . . . I guess Smouch's congratulations to me when I left the U.S. last July, "Good luck old man, you've got it" (i.e. Turkey) were a false alarm.

January 13, 1940, Saturday

Saw the Premier in the morning. . . . [He] said that he had telegraphed London that Greece would not pay above the 40 percent of the interest in her foreign debt now being offered. Showed some resentment toward the

---

[16] Greek for "hail."

British on this score, who "seem to want to squeeze a small and friendly country at a most difficult time," and commented that the French, in their new "clearing" with Greece, made no stipulation as to the debt.... Despite his resentment over the British linking of the debt problem with that of aid to Greece in the crisis caused by the blockade, he said "we shall have British and French help if we have to fight.".... He spoke of the war as one of attrition, with odds all on the side of the allies, because of their superior resources, but thought it would take a long time. He thought it impossible for France and England to make peace so long as Hitler's government is in power in Germany (*right*, I should say); asked rhetorically "How to get rid of Hitler?" and then said that when Hitler goes, it will be the communists and not the "right" who will come in. I was very much interested in what he volunteered about the Nazis. "They are practically communists—began as socialists, you know—Between them and communists there is hardly any difference." Somehow this hardly sounded like the Metaxas of old, the imitator of Nazism! It ought to have been heard by those who call him pro-German.

Athens, January 17, 1940

Dear Franklin:

Thank you for your note of December 1st,[17] which reached me in the last pouch. How do you manage to remember us all?

The situation here has not greatly changed, except that the Russian menace is more clearly in men's minds. If Soviet Russia is really started on the Imperialistic quest of the Czars, the Straits are certainly in her thoughts, and from the point of view of Grand Strategy the path in this direction is open to her as never before. A good deal must depend on how much she is weakened by the Finland affair, of course, but while the new Italian tie-up with Hungary[18] may discourage a German push into the Balkans, there is little to stop Russia moving south along the Black Sea coast, with the French concentrations based on Malta and Alexandria. The Greek Premier, General Metaxas, who is an excellent strategist trained in Berlin, where they called him the "Little Moltke," said to me the other day, however, that he thinks Russia is "preparing" an attack on

[17] The President had written: "Dear Lincoln: Just back from Warm Springs in the midst of this dreadful rape of Finland. I find yours of November eight on my desk, twenty-two days from Athens. All that you say is tremendously interesting. Continue to keep me in touch. I wonder what the next Russian plan is? As ever yours. F.D.R." Roosevelt letter to MacVeagh, December 1, 1939, PPF, File 1192.

[18] On January 6-7, 1940, the Foreign Ministers of Italy and Hungary, Counts Ciano and Czaky, held talks in Venice which gave the appearance of improving relations between the two states. Czaky gave assurances that his government would take no initiatives in the Balkans that might help spread the war in that region.

the Straits, which will be more direct and allow no chance at all for British warships to get into the Black Sea. He thinks that her present great efforts to capture public opinion in Bulgaria are with a view to drawing that country on to her side and getting her to attack Istanbul in conjunction with the Soviet air force and fleet. The Turkish forces are practically nonexistent on the sea and in the air, and in mechanical equipment are very weak indeed at present. A squeeze on Rumania would probably take place at the same time, but the main effort would be securing the Straits before help (except from the Greeks) could arrive. Once astride the Bosphorus the Slav might be hard to dislodge even by a large coalition. Incidentally, he thinks the King and the Premier of Bulgaria are fighting a losing battle against the rising tide of Russian influence in their country.

General Metaxas didn't press these ideas, but they will show what Russian activity in Bulgaria and the present stalemate in warring Europe are causing wary people to think in these parts. The General did stress the fact that Germany's dependence on Russia for vital supplies puts her in an inferior position towards her new friend, and he said, both at the beginning and the end of our conversation, that the outstanding feature about the present European situation is that of all the Great Powers Russia alone enjoys the opportunity of initiative.

Ever yours affectionately,
Lincoln MacVeagh (5)

January 27, 1940, Saturday

The radio in the morning announced that the British had reached an agreement with the Greek delegation in London, and that the latter had agreed to pay 40 percent of the current interest on their foreign debt. This last appeared interesting, particularly in view of what the Premier said to me on January 13. So I went to the British Legation, where Sir Michael confirmed the news. He said he had no other details, but from his careful phrasing I gathered that so far as the debt question is concerned, the British told the Greek delegation that if they wouldn't raise the ante at least a little, they might just as well go home. This may have been the foundation of the rumor told last night by the Egyptian Minister that they *were* coming home with nothing accomplished. I asked Sir Michael about the rumors too, telling him the ones I had heard, and put the question concerning Metaxas: "Are you people trying to turn him out?" He answered "By no means." He said the British are naturally annoyed from time to time by the way things go here, particularly small things. Maniadakis, Nicoloudis, and Kotzias, are not always to their taste. But in the matter of general policy they are satisfied with the government. Sir Michael also said he thought it would be bad to have an overturn at this time because there is no one in sight who could take over the Government. I said that I was very glad to have his confirmation of what I had been reporting all along as the official British attitude, despite the rumors. He added that the French are supposed to be urging the Dictator's dismissal, and that though they are not doing so, M. Maugras does feel somewhat more doubtful of the Dictator's loyalty to the allies than the British do; Maugras, he says, thinks Metaxas cannot possibly look forward to continuing his dictatorship if the democratic powers win. But "Why not?" asked Sir Michael. "We certainly aren't going to turn Salazar out of Portugal if we win the war, or interfere with the virtual dictatorship of the Government in Turkey. So why should we bother Mr. Metaxas here?" The answer to all of which is "quite,"—to speak in English.

Athens, January 30, 1940

Dear Franklin:

I have written you recently about the danger of Russian aggression in the Dardanelles area as viewed from here, and this remains perhaps the chief source of local anxiety. But as spring approaches and Italy still plays possum, while Russia seems to have caught a genuine Tartar in Finland, another most interesting problem for this region has arisen in the possibility of the creation of an Eastern Front. Of what is said in London and Paris on this subject you must be well informed, but out here on the ground, as it were, we are observing widespread signs of preparation. The French concentrations in Syria seemed at first to be in anticipation of Italian action, and this, was confirmed by the fact that they lost *tempo* as the Italians gave no indication of "belligerency." But they have recently speeded up once more, and Weygand[19] has arrived in Ankara again, almost at the same moment with a large shipment of British gold. I am informed that military communications between Egypt and Syria have been improved by the metaling of the highway clear to Beirut, and that the British are looking into the future even so far as to envisage the use of Greek islands for hospital bases. That they can be contemplating an attack on Germany with forces concentrated in Syria seems out of the question. But on the other side of the fence, Germany has made an arrangement with Russia whereby she now has a common frontier with Rumania, thereby greatly increasing the latter's jeopardy. Furthermore, Germany seems to be massing troops in Galicia and there is no country in the Balkans, perhaps least of all Rumania, which could withstand for an instant the lightning-like methods of her mechanized forces. Bulgaria would probably not even try, as her Premier has admitted. Under these conditions, if Germany should be the one to attack, there would seem to

[19] General Maxime Weygand, commander of the French forces in the Near East.

be little or nothing to check her advance before she meets with the French and British, who, however, must transport their troops a long way and organize bases on the European coast. Thus the Eastern Front, if it comes, would seem likely to depend on German initiative, and likely to run pretty close to such possible allied bases as Istanbul and Salonica. Whether Germany is able to make a drive in this direction under present conditions, both at home and in her newly conquered provinces, and whether she would dare to do so in view of possible complications from Italy and Russia, are other questions. But it seems clear that one of the reasons frequently urged against her invading the Balkans, namely that such action would destroy one of her main sources of economic supply, is based on a misconception as to where the only really effective resistance could develop.

With threats to Balkan peace on all sides, well-informed people here will watch the approaching conference of the Balkan Entente at Belgrade with considerable interest, though not, I think, much hope. This groupment has never been very strong, and the Premier the other day, in explaining to me his own modest expectations of a conference which he will himself attend, described one of the reasons for this fact. Yugoslavia and Rumania, he said, are oriented towards central and northern Europe, but Turkey and Greece toward the Mediterranean. Their interests consequently tend to diverge on all really important issues of foreign policy. He might also have pointed to the existence of an enigmatic and always dangerous Bulgaria in the very heart of the peninsula. But of course, the real cause of Balkan disunion lies in the stresses and strains set up here by the Great Powers. In the last analysis, their interests will control the approaching conference, and what it develops should accordingly indicate to some extent in what direction the European tide will flow regarding the Near Eastern question, or whether the present dead water is to continue to prevail.

To add to our worries, there is always the local political situation. The Dictatorship is flourishing to all outward appearances. I believe that, despite rumors to the contrary, England has no interest in unseating Mr. Metaxas at this time, and I have got this confirmed by the British Minister himself. He says Britain is satisfied with the Greek Government's loyalty, up to a point. The French are not so certain, but neither France nor England wants trouble here just now, and neither can see the possibility of a change being anything but from the frying pan into the fire. Nevertheless, the hatred of tyranny in Greece is ingrained, and whereas with luck, intelligence and determination the present regime is carrying on, the more the people submit to it the more they dream of overturning it. There is a widespread belief that it cannot survive Greece's entry into war. I am not sure that I share this belief, but its existence must be kept in mind.

The Greek Minister to Germany[20] has just been here for a few days. He appears to be an intelligent fellow and has occupied his present post for six years. He says the Germans are confident that their superiority in the air remains overwhelming, and that they honestly think they can destroy London and knock the British out of the war with bombs. Furthermore, he is sure they intend to try to do this at no distant date. He is very much afraid.

Always affectionately,
Lincoln MacVeagh (6)

February 6, 1940, Tuesday

Went to the F.O. at noon and asked Mr. Mavroudis about the Balkan Conference. He said he would know more when Mr. Metaxas comes back but that now he could only give me his "impressions" of what he called the "cream" of the affair. He said the conference was a great success, because the other nations were able to determine that Yugoslavia is much more decidedly inclined toward the Allied cause than they thought. She wants peace, he said, but if she has to fight, will fight on the side of England and France. Since Stojadinović began to flirt with the Nazis, the other Balkan nations, he said, have been uncertain of her position, despite her change of government. On the other hand, Yugoslavia was pleased to note that Turkey and the others are not in favor of the constitution of an Eastern Front as a means of *attack* against Germany, since under such conditions she herself would be the first to suffer. In general the conference was favorable to allied policy so long as this is restricted to defense against aggression in this area. It revealed also that the possibility still exists of doing something with the Rumanian proposals for a neutral bloc—under a different form,—and that, without making any actual military accord at this time, the Balkan Entente members are all eager to consult together in case anyone of them should be attacked from without. Furthermore, the talks showed that confidence is increasing not only in Bulgaria's declarations of neutrality, but in her throwing in her lot with the rest of the Balkan nations if war comes. Mr. Mavroudis was specially pleased with the clarification of Yugoslavia's attitude. He thinks the Finnish business makes a Russian attack on Rumania unlikely, and that the Germans really do not want to attack in this region; while Italy remains chiefly anxious to maintain her neutrality till the moment comes when she can ask a big price for continuing to do so. The Balkans, on the other hand, he says, do not want the Allies to attack Germany through their territory. He thinks it more likely that they will move on Batum and Baku than that they will start things in Rumania, but

[20] Alexander Rangave.

he thinks Turkey is against taking any initiative against Russia, since she feels she is not sufficiently equipped. . . . Gyppie [the Egyptian Minister] told me that Tambacopoulos, the Minister of Justice, . . . had recounted to him his talk with Hitler. H. said to T. that he admired Greece and T. said to H. that he admired H. He said that just as there are only straight lines in Greek art, so Hitler's policy is wholly straight. H. then took both T.'s hands in his and thanked him warmly for his appreciation, while the dictator's staff stood by and marvelled at the friendliness shown to the visiting Greek. I remarked to Gyppie that in his remark Tambacopoulos showed that he knew little either of Greek art or Hitler's policy, as there are no straight lines in either.

February 9, 1940, Friday
When I got to the office, Major Fortier, our Military Attaché at Belgrade, was waiting to see me. He has been on an official trip "incognito" to Syria, Palestine, and Egypt, to find out what he could about military preparations of the Allies in those regions. At Beirut he found that the G3[21] of General Weygand was an old friend of his, his erstwhile instructor at the *École Supérieure de Guerre*. Weygand, he says, has vitalized the French forces in Syria to a high degree. The offensive spirit is pronounced, and the state of preparation and training excellent. There are plans prepared for at least eight or nine possibilities, but all depend very largely on Italy's not joining Hitler, and thus what Italy will do, which is still unknown, is of capital importance. In fact it remains the most important question for the Near East today. The troops in Syria amount to about five divisions of 16,000 men each, plus extras, in all about 125,000 men. They are Moroccans, Senegalese, Foreign Legionnaires, and Metropolitan troops, well equipped with artillery up to 155 mm (including the new 105 mm gun). Ammunition is plentiful. On the whole, the force is to be characterized as a good attacking force capable of leading the way for large concentrations to be brought from France and North Africa. But planes are restricted in number and there is little mechanized transport. The staff plans include an attack on Baku, and this Major Fortier thinks is Weygand's favorite, "if the politicians will allow it." They count on being able to transport 5000 troops per day across Turkey to the Caucasus. The lack of planes is due to the fact that Germany (so his G3 friend told him) is still twice as strong in the air as both France and England combined, and till the latter can catch up in this respect, they do not dare send many planes away from their own territories. . . . In Palestine the Major found only about 20,000 men and practically no planes, with little offensive spirit and seemingly no object in view but to

[21] Staff officer for plans and operations.

keep the peace between the Arabs and Jews, as usual. . . . In Egypt the British have about 40,000 men, and again the offensive spirit is low. He could get no information about the Dodecanese. He thinks the French don't want to start anything, but if the Russians attack Bessarabia, they are very likely to take a shot at Baku, whether the British help or not. . . .

The radio announced that the President is sending Sumner Welles[22] to "observe at first hand" in Rome, Paris, London, and Berlin. He will bring no propositions from the President, but on the other hand what the European Governments tell him will only be known to F.D.R. and Mr. Hull.[23] I doubt if Sumner can add much in a few days to the observational powers of Phillips,[24] Bullitt,[25] Kennedy,[26] and Kirk.[27] So *that* would seem to me [to be] camouflage. But he might, by the extraordinary nature of his visit, evoke some feelers, or even some propositions from the others, and he undoubtedly has something to say to them which is carefully left unspecified in the President's description of the mission. *One doesn't have to make propositions in order to invite confidences.* Sumner will sail with Myron Taylor,[28] which definitely marks the boat as a peace ship. What a couple! Two of the ablest stuffed shirts in existence.

February 11, 1940, Sunday

[Received] telegram "Confidential for the Minister," instructing me to tell the M. for F.A. that the President is considering approaching neutral governments on the best way to go about the solution of reconstruction problems after the war, and ask his opinion as to the best method of initiating diplomatic interchanges on this question at this time, etc. This appears to be part of the same plan which includes the sending of Sumner Welles to Europe. Does it mean that the President really thinks peace can come this year? I wonder! But it certainly tends to put us very much in the picture at present, judging from the press reactions printed in the press here from all European capitals. Welles seeing the belligerents and the President seeking direct expressions from the neutrals in postwar problems—people are bound to see that America's interest in European affairs is both deep and active, and these gestures, backed up by our naval and economic strength, should give us some influence over their development. At least these gestures will remind people over here that we have

---

[22] The U.S. Under-Secretary of State.
[23] Cordell Hull, U.S. Secretary of State.
[24] William Phillips, U.S. Ambassador to Italy.
[25] William C. Bullitt, U.S. Ambassador to France.
[26] Joseph P. Kennedy, U.S. Ambassador to Britain.
[27] Alexander C. Kirk, U.S. *Chargé d'Affaires* in Germany.
[28] President Roosevelt's personal diplomatic representative to the Vatican.

a great weight to throw into the scales, and show them that we know it, and are prepared to use its potentialities of persuasion to the limit, without waiting for actual war, which we aim to avoid. Using our giant's strength, and the respect and fear which that commands, to promote peace is, I suppose, the idea. What Mr. Metaxas can say at this time about postwar reconstruction is another matter altogether; I suppose he can't say much, but will find fitting words.

February 14, 1940, Wednesday

The Egyptian Minister came in to see me. . . . He has seen the King, to say good-bye. . . . He told me the King talked of local politics, and showed himself fully cognizant of current dissatisfaction, but said he couldn't find anyone capable of taking over from Metaxas. He spoke of Kotzias, but didn't think he would do despite his popularity. The King even spoke of rumors that he himself would be put out, and mentioned the notion of some [people] that Prince Peter would do well to replace him with. . . . Gyppie said that there is an idea among the opposition that bad trouble could be avoided by having Metaxas step aside and Papagos and a group of Generals take over: they would be unable to run the government, and little by little, and one after another, the old political leaders would be called in to strengthen the cabinet, until at last full constitutional life would be restored. Sounds like a pipe dream.

February 15, 1940, Thursday

Went to the Foreign Office at 12 and had a conversation with the Premier. He told me that he and his government were "profoundly touched" by the President's "magisterial" initiative in regard to the questions in my letter, and that he hoped I would so inform my Government. Meanwhile, he said, he is studying the questions personally, and will communicate his views to me in writing. . . . I so telegraphed the Department later. Mr. Metaxas told me (in confidence) that the Balkan Conference had decided to extend the guarantees under the Pact to cover the eventuality of attack by outside powers. He said this transforms the entire pact, and in fact it does. I asked him whether it was put in writing or merely agreed on verbally, and he replied, "We always put our decisions down in *precis-verbaux*." "So it *has* been put in writing, then," I said, and he replied with a raise of the eyebrows and a smile and shrug. Undoubtedly there is a commitment, then; though not perhaps a protocol, it may take the form of *minutes* of the meeting, recording a verbal understanding. Mr. Metaxas spoke of this understanding as making the Balkan Pact a barrier to German or Russian aggression and said the "obligation" of

Greece and Turkey to go to the aid of the northern members of the group is not dependent or contingent on anything Bulgaria may do. . . . I telegraphed all this to the Department together with the Premier's estimate of the present situation. Briefly, he sees Russia as now in the hands of Germany, on account of the ill-success of her Finnish adventure (*he* called it a defeat): also he thinks Germany will prevent Russia from moving against Rumania. Italy he thinks genuinely neutral now, and altogether he regards the Balkan situation as improved and "safe for the moment."

February 23, 1940, Friday

The Rumanian Ambassador . . . told me that Gafencu and Metaxas have expressed (the latter to him personally) the feeling that the recent fall of the Bulgarian cabinet[29] was due, in part at least, to external causes. Metaxas, he said, pointed out that when there is a difference between a Minister of Agriculture and a Premier, it is usually the former who goes out. The feeling seems to be, said Djuvara, that Kioseivanov went too far in his approaches to the Balkan Entente for the majority of other political leaders in Bulgaria, and that these, representing the old revisionist feeling and favored by the political intrigues of the Minister of Agriculture, who had got a lot of his henchmen elected to the Chamber, brought about an untenable situation for the Premier. Djuvara admitted that Bulgaria's foreign policy is controlled by the King, who did not give the task of forming the new government to those who engineered the fall of the old, but chose an innocuous middle-of-the-road candidate, and that this policy will probably not be changed, at least ostensibly at present. But he thinks the lesson which the King and everyone else must draw is that Bulgaria is not ready to follow very far on Kioseivanov's path. She is still her old myopic self.

February 24, 1940, Saturday

Received a long first-person note from Mr. Metaxas in reply to the President's questions which I submitted on the 12th. It seems to me he made a good reply, saying that the Greek Government is ready to collaborate in an effort to find a way of approaching the problems of post-war economy and to exchange its views thereon with other interested governments; that it believes the interchange could be effected by the normal diplomatic channels under the auspices of the USA; and that

[29] On February 15, 1940, the cabinet of Prime Minister Georgi Kioseivanov resigned and a new one was formed under Bogdan Philov.

it is ready to associate itself with any move toward disarmament which may be initiated in association with the principal great powers. . . .

The Italian Minister came in to see me, to ask whether I had approached the Greek Government on the question of an exchange of views on postwar problems—the press had reported, of course, that the American Government intends to consult with the neutrals as stated, but as the Department labelled its instructions "confidential" I could only tell Grazzi that I thought if there was any intention on the part of my government to have me approach Greece, the question had better be asked in Washington where its policy is better known in its entirety than here. I also said that I had no doubt that his own government would soon be able to determine for itself what the attitude of the United States is in regard to neutral policy, since Sumner Welles will soon be in Rome. . . . He denied that recent rumors of Italy's intentions to disturb the peace have any foundation, and said, on the contrary, that she will not go to war unless her vital interests were threatened. (But I suppose she could easily invent a threat to suit her purposes, even so, à la Hitler!) He told me that he had had occasion to inform the Under-Minister for Foreign Affairs recently that Italy is determined to oppose any nation which should disturb the peace of this region. I asked: "Including Germany?" and he said yes, and added that he had included Turkey, too, for Mavroudis' benefit! He thinks this Italian attitude is likely to keep the Near East out of the war, and that victory must be sought by the belligerents in *the West*, that side winning which is able to hold on to the defensive. He said he thought Italo-American relations have recently improved on the basis of a realization on our part that Italy is genuinely peacefully inclined. Perhaps!

February 26, 1940, Monday

Went over to the Foreign Office at noon for a talk with Mr. Mavroudis. He told me that . . . Grazzi had *not* made the statement to him about opposing Germany if she attacked in the Balkans, as Grazzi told me he had last Saturday. He told it to Politis, the new Minister to Rome, who relayed it to Mavroudis. People are certainly talking loosely these days! Anyhow Mavroudis appeared to attach considerable importance to it.

Athens, February 27, 1940

Dear Franklin:

Before this letter can reach you, Sumner Welles will probably have brought you a lot of information about things we can only guess at out here. Nevertheless, I will go on with the local reporting which, if we all do it, gives you, like Argus, a hundred eyes.

Concerning Sumner's visit, one of the Greek papers writes today that the peoples of Europe are anxious to see it crowned with success, "and though the leaders may simulate indifference to the pacific purposes of his mission, public anxiety is greater than that of Noah waiting in his ark the return of the pigeon." Rather nice, that! But the leaders of Greece are by no means indifferent. They think that the trip cannot fail to influence both the war and the peace which must follow, and it is with genuine seriousness that they have expressed their willingness to follow your lead in the matter of an "exchange of views" on post-war problems.

Public anxiety is, of course, very great with us, and seems growing with the conviction that something must happen soon. Italian concentrations and troop movements are again on everyone's tongue, and there are persistent rumors of an approaching Franco-Turkish attack in the Caucasus. However, the Greek Government does not seem much alarmed by the former, and the Turkish Ambassador and his Military Attaché both tell me that Turkey will not lend herself to offensive action. In this connection, the Ambassador points out that as long as Italy's stand remains doubtful, Turkey's main value to the Allies is in helping to maintain the *status quo* in the Mediterranean, and that if she is involved in a war with Russia this value will largely disappear. This seems to be reasonable. Furthermore, Weygand's forces in Syria amount to only about 125,000 men, despite widely current reports of half a million or more, and though they are apparently good shock troops—Moroccans, Senegalese, Foreign Legion—they hardly constitute a sufficient force with which to start a distant and difficult war, particularly with a potential enemy in their rear.

Regarding Germany, people here still feel she is averse to extending the war in this direction, and will neither do so herself nor allow Russia to do so, unless Allied influences cut her supplies off too effectively, especially her supplies of Rumanian oil. In that case she might conceivably feel forced to attack, but must fear the possible destruction of the oil wells in advance of her reaching them. Good informants say that she is pleased with Turkey's stand at present, and with the results of the recent Balkan Conference which ostensibly dedicated itself to nothing but the maintenance of local peace.

All that the four Foreign Ministers of the Balkan Entente said to each other in their secret meetings at Belgrade has by no means been published. It seems generally to be thought that they took no new decisions. But Mr. Metaxas, who is one of the four, has told me in "strict confidence" that they decided to extend the application of the Balkan Pact to cover attack from outside. Hitherto, as you know, the Balkan Pact has been held to involve mutual assistance against Bulgaria only. If what he told me is true, and the Entente now forms "a barrier to a descent into the Balkans by either Germany or Russia," the Conference certainly took a step forward, as I lost no time in remarking. Furthermore it is a step which must be pleasing to allied policy so long as the latter contemplates only the defense of this region, and may even be an indication of what that policy is.

Almost as exciting for this region as the Balkan Conference was the fall of the Bulgarian Cabinet, which followed it almost at once. Reports from Sofia assert that internal politics were the cause. But foreign policy may also have contributed. Mr. Metaxas told me that one of the best things that happened at the Conference was the receipt of assurances from the Bulgarian Premier that, without wishing to join the Entente, Bulgaria would follow a "parallel policy" with her neighbors. He thinks this was going too far to be popular in Bulgaria and that it gave the Premier's enemies just the edge necessary to unseat him at this time. The Rumanian Ambassador tells me that Mr. Gafencu holds the same view, and the Italian Minister has also expressed it to me. The new Cabinet has not been entrusted to the men who ousted the old, but to persons more in the King's confidence. They declare Bulgaria's foreign policy will not be changed. The Minister to Belgrade is now Foreign Minister, and the Minister to Greece, his second-in-command. But the incident calls for caution in estimating the chances of any further *rapprochement* between Bulgaria and the Entente.

Finally we come to Italy,—for the Greeks seem to feel that Russia is out of the picture as a potential aggressor now that she is so tied up in Finland. Italy is still a cause of anxiety to the Greek public, but the Government feels satisfied that she will start nothing, at least for the time being, and probably not till she is fully satisfied which side is going to win. She is moving new recruits to Albania,—about 2,000 have recently arrived there,—and she has sent five thousand or more to the Dodecanese these past few days. But this seems to be no cause for great alarm. The alarm comes from the exaggerations popularly based on the more sober facts. The Italian Minister says—and apparently has been told to say—that Italy will attack no one unless her interests are vitally menaced, but that she will oppose any country, even Germany, which attempts to disturb the peace of the Near East. How reassuring that sounds! One hates to remember the lies which preluded the seizure of Albania, and to think how easily a totalitarian government can fake a "menace" to its interests. But for the time being such protestations do seem to agree with Italy's logical strategy, so far as an outsider can judge of it. So perhaps they may be believed "in so far forth" [sic]—as the Under-Minister for Foreign Affairs tells me the Greek Government is doing.

Locally, three classes of "specialists" have just been called to the colors, but by individual summons, without public announcement. I am reliably informed that the Premier told the staff officers in Salonica, on his return from Belgrade, that "if any Balkan state is attacked, Greece will have to fight." This is in accord with what he told me of the Conference's decisions, and would justify any refurbishing of his army which he may undertake, even if no attack seems immediately imminent. For the moment, there is no talk of internal political trouble,—a bad sign in this country where revolutions are never so likely as when the political scene is quietest.

Reports reaching here from Germany indicate, with somewhat remarkable uniformity, that the Germans expect the war to end this year. This, and the apparently growing unlikelihood of anyone's attacking in this area, as well as the fact that to end the war by a flanking movement would, for either side, probably take several years, all seem to point to the Western Front as the coming battleground. The Italian Minister says he is sure the war will be won in France, and by the side which does not attack. The Turkish Military Attaché says the same thing. This gentleman came in to my office this morning and began, "We are probably soon to see terrible things." But I go back to my thought at the beginning of this letter, namely, that you will have heard, before you get it, from those who are cooking the broth, and will know far better than we can here what we shall have to drink.

Affectionately yours,
Lincoln MacVeagh (7)

March 14, 1940, Thursday

Greek public opinion has been greatly shocked by the Russo-Finnish peace,[30] and is inclined to blame England and France for allowing it, rather than Germany for bringing it about. The prestige of England as the protector of the small nations has received a severe check, and fear of what Germany and Russia may do next is widespread.

Athens, 26 March 1940

Dear Franklin:

On rereading my last letter to you, dated February 27th, I find there is little to be changed or added as a result of the events of the past month. The best opinion here continues to regard the extension of the war to this region as unlikely, at least for the present. It is still supposed that

[30] On March 12, 1940, after three months of valiant resistance, Finland was forced to accept the peace terms imposed by the Soviet Union. Finland ceded the Karelian Isthmus, the city of Viborg, a naval base at Hangoe, and territories totalling more than 16,000 square miles to the Soviet Union.

Germany desires no disturbance of the Balkans and that the Allies will not assume the offensive here so long as Turkey remains averse to such a policy. Russia, of course, no longer has one of her hands tied in Finland, and the possibility of her taking the imperialistic path toward the Straits still exists. But it is felt here that she will almost certainly not attempt such an advance in the near future. Germany is supposed to be against it, for one thing, and aside from that, military men say it would take Russia at least three months after the close of the Finnish campaign to organize a new operation on another front with any chances of success. In the Caucasus I am informed that the Russians have only seven full divisions, with four or five skeletonized ones in addition, and that this is only one division more than they had at the outbreak of the war.

The outcome of the Finnish campaign shocked public opinion in Greece severely and it was felt here, as apparently elsewhere, to be a setback to the Allies. But in official circles I have found this attitude less marked than in the cafés and drawing rooms. The Under-Minister for Foreign Affairs expressed to me only the other day the greatest confidence in England's determination and tenacity. "Having made up her mind to fight the war in 1941," he said, "she is now preparing to do so with telling effect." He was more immediately concerned with the effect of the Finnish peace on France and regarded the fall of Daladier[31] with some dismay.

Italy continues, of course, to be watched with the greatest care. She has increased her reinforcements in Albania by 10,000 men and done the same in the Dodecanese, but trustworthy reports state that these troops are all new recruits. In this connection the Under-Minister for Foreign Affairs said to me, "Italy is less of a menace to us this year than last, because her pretensions have grown so much larger. It is no longer a question of, let us say, Corfu, but of hegemony over the entire Balkans." Doubtless this fact, together with Britain's guarantee, make it less necessary now than formerly for Greece to fear a *coup de main*. Nevertheless, a serious attack by the Italians toward Salonica, combined with German pressure on the northern Balkans, in a joint effort to bring the peninsula promptly and definitely under Axis control, is still to be reckoned with, and, as I have reported to the Department, has not escaped the Greek General Staff, as at least a possibility.

This Legation was deprived only a few months before the war began, and over my protest, of even a part-time military attaché. But I have been able to secure some help from other military observers here, and I have just sent in a report on the present status of the Greek army. If this country becomes involved in the war, you might care to know that while Greece can muster 600,000 men she is prepared to equip only about 20

[31] On March 20, 1940, French Prime Minister Edouard Daladier resigned, and a new cabinet was formed under Paul Reynaud.

divisions, or about 320,000 men; that it will take her ten days to mobilize completely; that her artillery is predominantly of the mountain type; that her airplanes number less than 100; and that she has no tank corps. As it stands, it would seem of questionable value for fighting outside of Greece, though it might give a good account of itself in defending Greek territory, where the terrain does not favor the advance of mechanized forces.

Affectionately yours,
Lincoln MacVeagh (8)

April 9, 1940, Tuesday

News came that Germany has invaded Denmark and Norway. The Danes made no resistance and the entire country passed into Germany's hands as quickly as her troops could take over. Norway resisted, and declared war on Germany, the British thereupon declaring that they would send all help possible. The Germans said they made the move to protect these two neutrals from the designs of the Allies. But evidently Norway, at least, didn't believe them. The poor Danes had no means of resisting. . . . Greek public opinion is profoundly shocked, but it is too early to determine what, if anything, is the official attitude. The fate of Denmark, however, will not leave the King indifferent. As the Swede[32] said tonight, for a Greek he is a very loyal Dane, and of course is already anti-Nazi and pro-British in sentiment. . . . The war seems to be beginning—or at least the side shows are coming nearer home!

April 10, 1940, Wednesday

Saw Mr. Mavroudis in the morning. . . . He was very much afraid that the profound impression caused by Germany's rapid invasion would cause the Germans to be more positive in their protests here against compliance with the British control, and render Greece's position between the devil and the deep sea more difficult than ever. He said that he saw no particular danger yet of the war extending to the Balkans. . . . Public opinion is obviously very worried about Italy, and there are many rumors current, such as that they have mined the entrance to the Adriatic and bottled up a British fleet. There are also new rumors about Mr. Metaxas's illness, but Mr. Mavroudis told me that he is now practically well once more and that all he had was a touch of intestinal grippe.

April 20, 1940, Saturday

Went over to the Foreign Office and saw Mr. Mavroudis, who feels more encouraged at present over Italy's attitude. He thinks she is defi-

[32] Sven Allard, Swedish *Chargé d'Affaires* in Greece.

nitely averse to fighting England now. But if Germany attacks in the Balkans, and achieves the easy victories there which are hers for the asking, it may be different. In any case, Mr. Mavroudis agrees with Maugras that after the recent British naval successes, an attack on Greece is not likely except as a second phase to follow successful operations further north on Germany's part—with possible action to "protect her interests" by Italy on the margin of the German advance. Yet Mr. Mavroudis said, too, that he thought it would be very difficult for Italy to cooperate with Germany in this way without getting into war with England, since the Yugoslav army is largely Serbian, and would almost surely resist, attracting aid from the Allies and possibly also the Balkan States as a whole, in view of the check received by Germany and her obvious need to re-establish prestige. And I think the Greeks are right. There is real danger Hitler will come down this way, and if Italy tries any monkey tricks, "she will suffer in the end," as the King said the other night, "but meanwhile we in Greece shall be badly knocked about."

May 2, 1940, Thursday

The radio news tonight is very bad. The British seem to be giving up the Norway expedition, being unable to land their heavy equipment under the air attacks of the Germans. They have already evacuated the region south of Trondheim and it seems they will also evacuate their other forces (perhaps not those at Narvik just yet), if one can judge by the tenor of Mr. Chamberlain's speech this evening in the House. At the same time the Italian situation continues to grow more threatening. The British seem definitely to have told their boats to use the Cape of Good Hope route to the east, and to have sent naval reinforcements to the Mediterranean. It is unofficially stated that Mussolini told Mr. Phillips that he will not abandon his non-belligerent attitude for the present, and the *Rex* has apparently sailed for New York. But who is to put much faith in such assurances nowdays? And the *Rex* may hope to escape like the *Bremen*.[33] The Italian Minister has come home from his "holiday" in Italy, and assured the Greeks in the same sense as his master. And the Greeks seem to believe him! I may have noted before that if part of his mission here has been to put Greek suspicions to sleep—and God knows the Greeks are prone enough to suspect Italy—he has been remarkably successful. Maugras commented the other day on this point. At the Foreign Office one often hears "Grazzi says this," or "Grazzi says that," as if it must be true.

---

[33] The German liner, *Bremen*, had succeeded in evading the British blockade, travelling from New York to Murmansk, where it arrived on September 6, 1939.

May 3, 1940, Friday

The Brazilian Minister came in and reported a conversation with Delmouzo in which the latter still expressed confidence in Italy's remaining non-belligerent. The Greek Government yesterday called *10* classes of reserve officers to the colors for 1 month's training, about a third to report May 15, and the rest in July and August. Mr. Delmouzo (like the morning papers) said this has nothing to do with the international situation, and is a matter of routine training. Nevertheless it is clear that so many being called up can only be for precautionary purposes. The dates are interesting, indicating a belief in a Balkan crisis to arise during the summer. But of course the dates can be changed if needs must.

May 4, 1940, Saturday

Mr. Mavroudis still feels that Italy will not move unless Germany does. He quoted assurances brought by Grazzi from Rome and given to Mr. Metaxas and Mr. Mavroudis on Monday: "Italy will not enter the war for the present, and in any case has no intention of disturbing the peace of the Balkans." He seemed to draw some satisfaction from this, but I'm damned if I see it. . . . To the station to catch the 8:05 Royal Train. . . . We had three first class compartments in the wagon-lit attached to the Royal cars, (2 of them, one for the King and the Prince, and one for kitchen and attendants, luggage, etc.) H.M. very kindly asked the three of us to dinner and we had a very pleasant evening with him and the Crown Prince.

A long, tiresome ride around by Lake Doiran, Siderocastro, and Serres brought us to Myrvini, where the King drove the last spike into the rails of the new branch connecting the main line with Amphipolis and the new strategic port at the Struma's mouth, Tsayesi. The day was cool, with sun and clouds. A bishop sanctified the new line, while we stood by, behind the royal pair, with the notables and several hundred peasants. There was a band, and a lot of Neolaia[34] girls, etc. The King came into the diner for lunch, and had Bun [Mrs. MacVeagh] and me at his table while little Peggy sat opposite the Crown Prince on the other side of the aisle, and appeared to get on very well. The train stood in the new Amphipolis station for lunch, and then chugged round to the bridge, where we all got out and I showed H.M. the Lion, which looks very well. It is fenced on three sides with a low, barbed-wire fence, outside of which a lot of evergreens have been planted. But the enclosure seems to me too big, and the open side along the road of course destroys the purpose of the fence completely. The goats will get in! and the boys etc.

---

[34] "Neolaia" (Ethniki Organosis Neolaias or E.O.N. = National Youth Organization), the Youth Movement of the Metaxas dictatorship.

who write names on monuments and scratch or break off pieces of marble. Doubtless something better will be done later on. . . . I said to H.M., "I wish to thank you for the opportunity you have given me to present to you personally the Lion of Amphipolis, which I now do in the name of all those friends, Greek and foreign, who have contributed to its restoration." He replied with some friendly appreciation, but we did this privately. I felt there should be something said for the *donors*, but there was no preparation for a ceremony, and few if any who could understand except the K. and the Crown Prince. There was a crowd of peasants gathered from God knows where, about a thousand strong, and one of them stepped forward and read the King a speech as soon as even he got across the bridge! After we had walked about a bit and looked the Lion over from all angles, we went back to the train and trundled down to the new port beyond Eion. . . . After seeing this (Mount Athos stood up most grand and clear) we got back into the train and had tea with H.M. and C.P.

Athens, May 4, 1940

Dear Franklin:

Since the German invasion of Scandinavia, we have been living here under the sword of Damocles, as you better than anyone else, I think, can realize. The Greek government, however, has maintained a remarkably calm attitude, and after a talk with the Permanent Under Secretary for Foreign Affairs this morning, I can report that it still holds the same view it adopted three weeks ago, namely that Italy will not adventure into the war on her own initiative, but may very well move "to protect her interests" if Germany attacks in the Balkans, or even join Hitler as an openly confessed ally if the latter achieves some really convincing success.

Greek timidity, the timidity of one of the least among the neutrals, still leaves a pretty clear field for German propaganda, and while I am informed from Salonica that some three hundred Germans per month have recently come into Greece from the north, I have heard of no expulsions such as are now being reported from Rumania. There may be now some five or six thousand Germans in the country, and it is certain that all of them are in close touch with the very active German Legation. In addition, the French Minister declares that besides several cabinet ministers who are known to have pro-Nazi sentiments there are numerous minor officials in Germany's pay. But all this may not be so dangerous as it sounds. Both the French and British Ministers have expressed to me only recently their satisfaction with the Dictator's policies and actions, and the Dictator is still, despite rumors arising from a brief illness on his part, firmly in control of the party in office, while the opposition is very largely Venizelist and pro-Ally. Add to this the fact that the King, though he has not much of a following, is also decidedly pro-British in the present struggle. Consequently, the "fifth column," though it is undoubtedly at work here as elsewhere, seems not as likely to succeed in softening up the national resistance as in some other places. Mr. Metaxas is the only Stojadinović available, and he remains, it appears, pro-Greek though German-trained, while the other leaders who might make trouble are not only in exile but quite as anti-German as they are anti-Metaxas. An interesting situation.

Greek timidity, the fear of provoking powerful aggressors, is also responsible for the fact that in the past few weeks this country has taken few additional military precautions. A few submarines and destroyers were sent to the west coast when fears arose for Corfu after the news arrived of Germany's invasion of Norway. More recently some thousands of reserve officers have been called up "for training." But the forces on the Albanian frontier are no greater than the Italian forces facing them, and the chief of the General Staff has explained to the Turkish Military Attaché that calling up new classes would only lead Italy to do the same and start a race which Greece could not hope to keep up. Quiet work continues to be done on the defenses of the northern frontier, however, and on roads, and on perfecting the machinery for mobilization.

My canvassing of Greek, Turkish, Yugoslav, British and French opinion at this post would lead one to expect no war in this region at least for a month. Nobody seems to expect Italy to move alone. Germany, of course, in incalculable, but the Turkish Military Attaché remarked this morning that she has been forced to spend so much of her petrol supply in Norway that an invasion of the Balkans, which would have to depend greatly on airplanes and motorized transport, can hardly be contemplated for the present. Russia is regarded as genuinely out of things for the time being, recuperating her strength and preparing to take an opportunist course later.

Much interest has been aroused, and much encouragement gained from Mr. Phillips' reported talk with Mussolini, apparently at your behest. The Italians here (when scratched) betray a feeling that the United States is going to join the Allies sooner or later (perhaps I have mentioned this before) and this appears to frighten them, though nothing else does, their heads have grown so big. "Moi aussi," said the little Italian Minister, running to catch up with the French and British Ministers in a parade not long ago, "Moi aussi je suis une grande puissance!"

Affectionately yours,
Lincoln MacVeagh (9)

May 9, 1940, Thursday

I went to see the British Minister at his Legation. He seemed very calm. Confirmed that there has been no "influx" of British aviators here and that the Allies are not pushing the Greeks to any offensive action. . . . In regard to the Balkans said that he did not regard the situation as particularly threatening. He had not heard the reports which had reached us of Germany's asking Rumania for leave to pass troops through on the way to Bulgaria.

May 10, 1940, Friday

News came that Germany invaded Holland, Belgium and Luxembourg in the early hours. . . . Appointment at the Foreign Office with Mr. Mavroudis . . . He continues to think that Italy will make no move—take no serious military and economic risk—unless her hand is forced by Germany's invading the Balkans or the Allies show greater signs of weakness than they do at present.

May 14, 1940, Tuesday

Went to the Foreign Office to see the Director General about the international situation. He said that there are no signs of an Italian military or naval concentration directly threatening Greece, but that he had a telegram from Switzerland, which he read me, saying that a German attack there is feared with Italian cooperation. He maintained, in regard to the 5th Column here, that there are actually in Greece less than the number of Germans here when war started, about 3,000, and that all are being watched by the police. The question arises, of course, how trustworthy are the police. Athens is full of rumors regarding this matter. . . . It seems almost certain now that Mussolini will enter the war on Hitler's side.

May 15, 1940, Wednesday

The British Minister asked me yesterday . . . whether we had instructions about taking over his Legation in case of necessity and I said we had had a circular to this effect. This morning he came in and I gave him a letter saying I am authorized to take over his interests in whole or in part at his request, provisionally and subject to confirmation upon request of his government to Washington. . . . This shows that the British have in mind the possibility of a *blitzkrieg* in this direction. . . . The morning's news is that Holland's army has surrendered. Developments now will be great attacks on England by air, and [the] extension of the war into the

Mediterranean and the Balkans,—or so it seems.... Vukčević saw Metaxas yesterday and reports that he again stated that Greece would fight if attacked, and expressed the opinion that if any Balkan state is invaded, all will be involved. He seemed somewhat less confident, according to V., that the Italians will stay out of the war, but still hopeful. Vukčević added that he believes Metaxas is "loyal" and it was clear that he was favorably impressed all round by the conversation.

May 19, 1940, Sunday

At ten o'clock Mr. Churchill made a radio speech.[35] . . . Churchill warned that the mechanized forces which routed Holland so quickly are now free to be thrown into the balance against France and England. Is it possible that Mussolini will hold his hand now any longer? The Allies seem to be reeling under the German blow and isn't this just the chance he has been waiting for? I think there will be a big increase of defeatism here in Greece tomorrow.

May 23, 1940, Thursday

Called on Mr. Mavroudis at the Foreign Office. He has no new information about Italy. It seems likely she may come in any day now. He said that rumors in Berlin make it the 24th. Count Ciano is now in Tirana—or rather was yesterday—and will be back in Rome tomorrow. So as not to miss the great day? There are Russian concentrations on the Rumanian border, and some facing Germany. Is Russia going to take advantage of Germany's preoccupation in France and steal a march on her own account? The Rumanian army is fully mobilized. Captain Johnson[36] reports that Greece's new class, called up for the 25th, will add from 30 to 40 thousand men to her present 80,000 under arms, making a total at most of 120,000, out of the 320,000 which she can mobilize, according to the Turk. Thus she is lagging considerably behind the other Balkan states in her preparations and it may well be that she foresees no great opportunity for resisting a serious attack from Italy. . . . I spoke to Mr. Mavroudis about police cars here carrying "U.S.A." numbers, and he said the practice would be stopped, pretending rather feebly to be ignorant of the meaning of those letters and that the police likewise did not know their meaning!

[35] On May 10, 1940, the day that Germany invaded the Low Countries, Prime Minister Chamberlain resigned and was succeeded by Winston S. Churchill. Seven days later Germany invaded France. On June 17, the government of Marshal Henri-Philippe Pétain, who had replaced Paul Reynaud as head of the French government, capitulated to the Germans. A new French government, under Pétain, was established at Vichy, while much of northern France remained under German occupation.

[36] Captain Max S. Johnson, temporary U.S. Military Attaché in Greece.

May 24, 1940, Friday

Went over to the Foreign Office to see Mr. Metaxas. He told me that he had no information one way or another on Italy's intentions, and reiterated his belief that she is unlikely to attack in the Balkans, giving as a reason his conviction that an agreement as to zones of influence in this area between Russia, Germany and Italy has not been made and cannot be made. He also restated his position that Greece will fight if she is invaded. I asked him what resistance he thought she could make to heavy modern attacks, from the air, *etcetera*, and he answered simply, "It will be war." . . . I brought him an *aide-memoire* about falsifiers of American passports and asking for effective action from the Greek authorities. He seemed to take a properly serious view of the matter, and may do something about it. In fact, I was rather surprised by the *empressement* of his reaction. . . . Saw the Italian Minister for a moment. He said he has been sick. Well, it's only tit-for-tat if an Italian is sick nowadays, they are making the rest of the world sick enough.

Athens, May 24, 1940

Dear Franklin:

It seems absurd to be writing when events move so rapidly that a letter becomes ancient history by the time it reaches you. But even ancient history may sometimes throw some light on the puzzling present, and if Italy goes to war you might possibly find a little illumination for dark corners in the following estimate of Greece's attitude before the fact.

That attitude has recently somewhat altered as a result of German successes and their demonstration of the power of mechanized armies. Facing Italy across narrow seas and sharing, too, with her a land frontier, Greece has been thinking fast. The press of course remains editorially colorless but the news columns are full every day of striking pictures and vivid descriptions of tanks and planes in action, and as Greece has no tanks and only one hundred planes, there is being brought home to even the most ordinary citizen that resistance to Italy can only be a relative affair if the latter is minded to put forth here even a portion of her strength. People in the Government still maintain that Greece will resist if attacked, and even talk, though less confidently, of going to war if any Balkan state is invaded, but one senses more than a little bravado in what they say, while the man in the street is at least more honest. You can hear it said in the cafés that all Greece's expenditure for defense, which is enormous for so small and poor a country, has been just so much money thrown away. Such comment of course ignores the insurance aspect attaching to that expenditure in connection with possible limited and local wars, but it correctly expresses a certain resignation to the inevitable which appears to be the most widespread reaction here to the lesson of the German victories.

So far as the military authorities are concerned, this reaction is betrayed by a listlessness which, if its opposite could do any good, would be culpable. Though the international situation is quite as threatening as it was last September, the military precautions being taken by this country are considerably less than they were at that time. Athens has had no black-out for months and the army remains only sketchily mobilized at a moment when every other Balkan state bristles with bayonets. The Turkish Military Attaché pointed out the other day that the reason given by the Government, namely not to provoke a powerful neighbor, is hardly a valid one. For if Italy is decided not to go to war, he said, such a small thing as Greek mobilization will hardly cause her to change her mind. Whereas if she is decided to do so, it is the duty of Greece to be as well prepared as possible. But the Greek attitude seems based on psychology rather than on logic.

In Government circles the change is also marked and foreign policy has undoubtedly been affected. Greece may yet play the part of Leonidas, but at present I am betting on Ulysses. The Foreign Office feels that Italy may go to war now fairly promptly. With France reeling under Hitler's blows, what better opportunity could present itself for a stab in the back? But it feels, too, that this is encouraging for the Balkans if it means that Italy's effort will be concentrated in the west. More than once in the last few days I have caught Greek thoughts turning to the possibility of remaining non-belligerent in case Italy goes to war with England and France and even Turkey. Her coasts and islands may be fought for, but she has always the possibility of submitting—to both sides. Such a policy finds a precedent in Greece's conduct during the first years of the last Great War, when she "balanced herself on a knife-edge," to use a phrase of the King's, and made money at the same time with her tin-pot but abundant merchant marine. Today she may not be able to follow this program if Italy takes it into her head to control the whole country rather than only a few isolated harbors. But the chance lies in Italy's preoccupation elsewhere, and the wits to take advantage of it are not lacking here. My Swedish colleague asked the Director General of the Foreign Office the other day how Greece could stay non-belligerent if Turkey fulfilled her pledges to the Allies, and that clever son of Laertes replied, "Greece's obligations to Turkey arise only if Turkey is attacked, and not if she attacks others in fulfillment of her own obligations"! Technically, he is right, but I have a feeling that this remark, if repeated in Ankara, might go far to dissolve a famous friendship. It justifies suspicions the Turks have had for a long time.

Of course, while Hitlerian warfare has impressed the Greeks and made them more than ever wary of Mussolini's planes and mechanized divisions, the defeats recently suffered by France and England have also had their effect. A Greek said to me today, "The prestige of the Allies is gone forever." That is not true. The Greeks are a mercurial people, and a recovery by the Allies would bring back their prestige here in a jiffy. But, altogether, recent events have made the Greeks acutely aware of their own helplessness and exposure. The old expectation of maintaining non-belligerency as long as possible and thereafter forming a firm front with England, France and Turkey is gone, and I look now rather for a more two-faced policy of token resistances balanced by *pro forma* compliances, of explanations and apologies, and every shift necessary to save the skin. It doesn't sound heroic, but it cannot be called unintelligent, and it certainly is Greek.

Affectionately yours,
Lincoln MacVeagh (10)

May 25, 1940, Saturday

No news today regarding Italy, except a report from New York of great diplomatic activity in Rome. It would seem to be the last chance for the Allies to avert the spread of the war to the Mediterranean, for the signs certainly point to the 25th being Mussolini's D-Day, and zero hour the speech he is scheduled to make. . . . Things will probably not happen this way, but as I see it, Mussolini could now get a high price from the Allies for his continued neutrality, and by accepting that price he could save Italy. His own maneuvers have brought him an opportunity which can make him indeed a Father of his country. But if he doesn't grasp it, if he continues on the path he has made it appear all along he might take, and really joins Hitler in the war, he runs a good risk of selling his country out forever. For if Hitler wins, with or without Italian help, the status of Italy in years to come will inevitably be that of a vassal to the Great Reich. . . . Now, as things stand, to save the future of Italy as well as of France and England and every other European country which values its liberty, the Allies could well afford to offer him immense concessions: recognition of his Empire, extensions of it all around the map, financial aid, an offensive and defensive alliance for fifty years to preserve all that Western European civilization stands for, the civilization of Rome and Christianity. They can afford now, in their straights, to make up, and more, for all they didn't do for Italy after the last war. For moving troops from the Italian border now might win the battle, and eventually the war itself. Accepting such terms would win for the Duce a prestige, and a future for Italy, that winning with Hitler could never do. But their own past and their own pride and blindness will probably prevent the "statesmen" on both sides from taking any such action as it seems to me plain common sense prescribes. The Allies will not offer enough and the Duce will not see far enough for such a fruitful compromise. The single greed of Germany will divide and conquer the varied greeds of the other powers —with France and England down, Russia will collapse at a single push, the Balkans will disappear down the German craw, and Italy which helped will in the end suffer the same fate, as all the rest, her empire only a dream—or a satrapy.

May 28, 1940, Tuesday

Captain Johnson feels that the Italians will not attack in the Balkans as they have more important objectives in the allied navies and land forces, and their strongholds in the Mediterranean, and why mess up another area unnecessarily. The German Military Attaché told him that he expects Italy to come in now, but not to attack in the Balkans, and especially not here, as the strategic advantages which might be gained are only secondary, and besides, the Germans don't want them to. How far the Italians may consider German wishes in consolidating their own position in an area which they regard as peculiarly their zone of influence, is another question. That the Italians and Germans are not agreed in regard to the disposition of Greece may be seen in their propaganda, both of them carrying on as if Greece were their own particular meat irrespective of the other. The Germans have just sent several new secretaries down here for their Legation, and their "pouch" gets bigger and bigger. Would they be going to all this expense if Italy was to be the beneficiary?

May 31, 1940, Friday

I expect he [French Ambassador Maugras] is going to ask me to undertake representing France if he has to move out. The Department has telegraphed authorization for the Belgians in this connection. I'll probably soon hear about Holland, and with England already authorized, and France coming in, it looks as if an invasion of Italy would give us a lot to do. The Brazilian came in this morning, and I told him that by all indications when we come into the war ourselves, I'll have a nice packet to hand over to him!

June 2, 1940, Sunday

Dinner with the British Minister and Sir Stafford Cripps[37] and staff. Talked a long time with Sir S. after dinner. He is waiting for instruc-

[37] *En route* to Moscow, where he was named British Ambassador to the Soviet Union.

tions from the F.O. Said he had wired F.D.R. to please release U.S. planes —i.e. those ordered for or in use by our army—to the allies. . . . The British radio stated that if Italy wants war England is ready. A salute of 101 guns announced the birth of a son to the Crown Princess.[38]

June 5, 1940, Wednesday
Mussolini is scheduled to speak "to the nation" tomorrow and it seems certain that he will now strike France in the back. If he doesn't risk that, he will go on doing as he is now, practically the same thing, that is, hold French troops on his border while the Germans overwhelm those in the north. A pretty picture, but worthy of its maker, just as shooting down defenseless women and children becomes the Bosche. . . . Today the news came that Sir Stafford Cripps has been accepted by Moscow as British Ambassador. It seems London meant him first to be a special envoy, but Russia said he'll have to be all or nothing. I don't envy him his task, but it *may* be that the Russians are beginning to repent of their pact with Germany, and are veering toward the Allies in a belated attempt to restore the balance.

June 6, 1940, Thursday
Mussolini made no speech!

June 10, 1940, Monday
Listened to the radio at 8:00, which described Mussolini's declaration of war on France and England. . . . The news of the battle in France becomes steadily worse, as the Germans, alive to their mistake of last time, throw in more and more troops without allowing any opportunity for French maneuver . . . . Mussolini comes in just at the critical moment when France is reeling and his own risk is least.

June 11, 1940, Tuesday
The British Minister gave me a copy of a note which he was instructed to hand to Mr. Metaxas expressing the British Government's *hopes* that no country would place any assurance in Mussolini's assurances given yesterday—when he said Greece, Turkey, Egypt, Yugoslavia and Switzerland have nothing to fear from him and warned them to take note of the fact. . . . Palairet also expressed no belief whatever in the rumor current

[38] Prince Constantine, second child of Crown Prince Paul, and the future King of the Hellenes.

in Turkey to the effect that Greece and Italy have a secret pact. He said further that unless a change in policy has taken place in London without his being advised of it, it will suit Britain if Greece stays out of the war even if Turkey goes in, and that he believes Greece will fight to keep Crete and other of her possessions from falling into foreign hands, while England will certainly not be the first to lay hands on them. . . . I went over to the Foreign Office later and saw the Director General. Mr. Delmouzo said that there has been no change in Greece's policy as a result of the Italian declaration. He agreed with General Papagos[39] that there is no reason at the moment to doubt Mussolini's assurances, but indicated again that Greece is not blindly trusting, and said once more that she will fight if attacked. He talked a long time and said he cannot conceive of the allies losing the war—being obviously sincere in this. Palairet told me that Mr. Metaxas said that if Germany wins, Greece will be a slave like all other countries. But in this case one wonders about the sincerity. Perhaps the truth about him is that while he likes dictatorships, he prefers his own to any other.

June 13, 1940, Thursday

It was seven years ago today that I was appointed Minister to Greece. Thus I have spent seven years of the best of my life being a diplomat, —and who would have thought it?

June 17, 1940, Monday

The French have asked for peace. . . . All thunder-struck by the news, but to me it seems just another era beginning, another era of force and barbarism to be endured and lived down by suffering humanity. . . . In one campaign of short duration—May 10 to June 17—Hitler has conquered France. He now has two months in which to bring England to her knees and yet remain within his schedule.

June 20, 1940, Thursday

A telegram arrived from Mr. MacMurray according to which the Turks have decided not to go to war at present in fulfillment of their obligations to England and France. . . . The British radio tonight announces that the Italians have sunk and bombed five or six Greek ships in the past few days. More and more the Greek position seems analogous to Norway's before the German invasion and it would seem that she can

[39] General Alexander Papagos, Chief of the Army General Staff.

only escape Norway's fate, at the hands of Italy, by a miracle of patience and compliance, while if taking her will be of any strategic use to the Italians she will suffer it, whatever caution she employs.

June 21, 1940, Friday
[Captain] Johnson was asked by the Chief of Staff, who summoned him to his office for the purpose, whether he would ask if the War Dept. or American industry can supply Greece promptly with a certain amount of guns, tanks, etc. and accordingly I sent off a telegram, but had to add that the request looks funny in the light of present non-existent transportation facilities, and I suggested that as German influence is growing here, the General might possibly be lending himself to some German maneuver such as bespeaking our extra equipment ostensibly for neutral countries but really to forestall further allied orders.

June 22, 1940, Saturday
Called on the Premier at the Foreign Office. . . . Regarding the international situation Mr. Metaxas said, just as Mr. Mavroudis did yesterday, that the danger point in this region is once more the Straits. He thinks Russia is not anxious to fight Germany, but that both she and Italy would oppose any attempt by the latter to come to the Dardanelles, and that Russia's recent military movements in the north are to gain position only. Germany, however, is continuing to arm Bulgaria, and he can see no reason for this unless it be to prepare that country to act as a spear-head for a German advance south-east. I found that he knew about the Chief of Staff's request of Johnson yesterday and asked him how the material could reach Greece. To this he replied that it could come to Lisbon (presumably by the *Nea Hellas*) and be transhipped from there in smaller Greek craft. He said he felt sure the British and Italians would let these craft proceed with their precious freight—but the thing still looks doubtful to me. I asked him why he wanted war material from America now, and he answered that he can no longer get it delivered by the Allies while Germany seems not so willing to supply Greece in this regard as she is Bulgaria. He confirmed that the Italians continue to manifest the best intentions toward this country—for what that may be worth. And he said that Greek trade must of necessity increase with Germany now, though Greece still remains "loyal" to Great Britain,—which he feels can resist a direct German attack, thus turning the war, under present circumstances, into one of long duration.

June 28, 1940, Friday

The morning's news confirmed the Russian ultimatum to Rumania.[40] The Soviets want Bessarabia and northern Bukovina. Roughly this makes their frontier the line of the Pruth rather than of the Dneister. . . . Press and radio reports state that there are excited discussions going on now between the Italians, the Germans and the Hungarians at Budapest. This makes it seem possible that the Russian move was not foreseen, at least at this time, by the Axis. Also Delmouzo told me that he has reports from Belgrade to the effect that the German and Italian circles there have been very much surprised. Well, one never knows! There seems to be a slim chance that the Russians are finished cooperating with the Germans and that this new move is not part of a pre-arranged Russo-German plan but intended wholly to improve Russia's defensive position vis-à-vis the Reich. But it seems to me most likely that it is both: that the Germans have agreed to it—so far and no farther; and that the Russians are doing it with their eyes open to a possible conflict with Germany later. In this view, Russo-German collaboration continues, but only up to the completion of this move, which marks the last step in Russia's repossession of her pre-war territory. After this, a new phase of Russo-German relations begins.

Athens, July 2, 1940

Dear Franklin:

Since my letter of May 24th, Italy has come into the war as expected, and France has collapsed contrary to expectations. So far as Greece is concerned, Italy has continued to manifest peaceful intentions, and Germany has sent a trade delegation, which is busy securing from this country what the British "control" has recently held up. This delegation will probably succeed in tying Greece even more tightly into the German economic system than was the case before the war, but on the other hand its activity here appears to support the idea that Germany, as well as Italy, wants no disturbance in this region for the present.

On the basis of this idea, and the fact that the Allies can no longer expect to form an Eastern Front, the Greeks now seem less apprehensive of being immediately involved in the war than they have been for some time past. Of course, they must envisage possible difficulties over the use of their islands and harbors so long as the naval war goes on in the Mediterranean, but so far neither side has put their tight-rope-balancing qualities to the test, and hope springs eternal.

Meanwhile, a more remote source of anxiety has once again cropped up

---

[40] An ultimatum issued on June 26, 1940. Soviet troops occupied Bessarabia and northern Bukovina on June 28.

in the Russian occupation of Bessarabia and northern Bukovina. It is felt here that this move may have had advance consent from Germany, but that from Russia's point of view it represents not only the completion of her campaign to repossess her pre-war territory, but an improvement of her strategic defensive position in case of German aggression eastwards. The Greek authorities do not believe that it presages an immediate Russian descent to the Straits, but they evidently feel greatly relieved that Turkey did not declare war on Italy when the latter entered the conflict, since Turkey's consequent preoccupation might have seemed to the Russians to offer an opportunity too great to be ignored.

As I duly telegraphed the Department, the Turkish Ambassador here predicted to me just a week ago that Rumania would cede Bessarabia to Russia "peacefully and soon." The Director General of the Foreign Office told me yesterday, however, that Greece was surprised by what has happened. I find this last hard to believe. Certainly there is a general awareness here of Russia's increasing interest in the Balkans. The Premier told me recently that he cannot see why Germany continues to furnish arms to Bulgaria unless she has thoughts of herself making use of that country, presumably in a drive toward Constantinople, but at the same time he let me see that his thoughts are also very much occupied with Russian policy. As for public sentiment, it seems about equally divided between hopes that Germany may soon find herself involved in a war with Russia and fears that hostilities in such a war might eventually extend to the whole of the Balkans, including Greece.

I believe that Greek sympathies remain, for the most part, pro-Ally even today, though German influence in responsible circles has naturally increased enormously since the collapse of France. On the other hand, having feelings and expressing them are two different things, and you will appreciate that bowing in the house of Rimmon is a gesture which has long been familiar to the Greeks. At present, barring a general Near Eastern conflagration as a result of a Russo-German war, our friends here think their lives may be spared, but they are under no illusions as to the place likely to be allotted to this country in a new Europe of German fashioning. If they were, their eyes would be opened by the kind of literature which the Foreign Office spokesman told me yesterday is now being circulated here by German "propagandists," based on ideas ascribed to Schacht's inventive genius. According to this literature, the *Führer* has decided that Greece is an agricultural country and must be content to remain such. Consequently, she is to get rid of her industry and supply Germany with the fruits of the soil, receiving in return all the manufactured goods of which she stands in need, or which may be dumped upon her. But during the past fifteen years Greece has built up, relatively to her size, a vast amount of local industry which it would be difficult to scrap without serious social upheaval, and in addition, the idea of exclusively raising agricultural products for foreign masters against such recompense as the latter may decide to accord, revives memories of the Ottoman domination too vivid for enjoyment.

Affectionately yours,
Lincoln MacVeagh (11)

July 5, 1940, Friday

Meeting of the officers, including Johnson[41] of Salonica. He said the army up there is obviously expecting an eventual cession to Bulgaria of her long-denied exit to the sea. The officers, he said, feel Greece could fight to the end if faced by Bulgaria alone, but with Germany and possibly Italy and Russia behind her, Bulgaria presents a power too great to be opposed. This is of course a direct result of the collapse of France, whose power, combined with that of England, has been the principal prop of the *status quo*. Johnson agrees with me in thinking that the Bulgarian question is not likely to come up immediately, however, despite the nervousness he reports in Salonica.

July 10, 1940, Wednesday

The British have been violating Greek neutral waters, by having an oiler refuel destroyers in the bay of Nauplia, off the Southern Capes, and near the northwest coast of Crete—three separate times, recently, and each time the Greek Government has asked Admiral Turle, the British Naval Attaché, to protest to the C-in-C of the Mediterranean fleet.[42] He has done so—he told Captain Johnson—on each occasion, but has gotten nowhere with the C-in-C! On the first occasion Admiral Turle himself went to Nauplia to get the oiler to go away. Apparently the British navy is going to take the same practical attitude toward Greek neutrality that it did in the last war, and this naturally fills the Greeks with apprehension regarding what Italy may do in her turn! The places where the oiler has been refuelling the destroyers are all on a line, and seem to indicate that constant patrolling is on foot across the direct path between the Dodecanese and Messina.

August 10, 1940, Saturday

Mr. Mavroudis summoned me to the Foreign Office and said Greece wanted to pay what we demanded on the debt, but would like not to do so till January 1st on account of various reasons—she has the money now,

---

[41] John D. Johnson, U.S. Consul at Salonica.
[42] Admiral Sir Andrew Cunningham.

he said, but is being called upon to pay for her prime necessities in cash while she can sell her products only for barter (not strictly true, since as Allard pointed out to me later, she sells her tobacco to Sweden still for foreign exchange.) He asked me whether the American Government would object to payment being made so late. I replied I could make no statement on that matter. He then asked my advice and I said my advice would be to pay at once, but that if the Greek Government genuinely felt it unwise to do so in its present state, he should make his reasons perfectly clear and trust the American Government to recognize his loyal spirit in the matter. He thanked me for giving him an idea, which was to promise to pay soon, and in any case no later than Dec. 31, 1940, and when I left thanked me again, this time for being a real friend who clearly did not want to cut Greece's throat! I said that of course we had no idea of doing any such thing. But if Greece's throat hasn't been cut over this affair, her Government has been made to eat some pretty humble pie.

August 13, 1940, Tuesday

The Italians have started a violent press and radio campaign against Greece, alleging complicity in the murder of an Albanian so-called patriot, and also maltreatment of the Albanian minority in Epirus. All without any grounds whatever. I went to see Delmouzo and found him at a loss to explain the maneuver; he said at once, "Ils nous cherchent querelle, et nous ne savons pas pourquoi." It seems that they have been excited by the German-won revisions (or soon to be won) in the cases of Hungary and Bulgaria to attempt an aggrandizement of Albania. Or maybe there is something more behind the affair connected with the coming grand attack on England in all parts of the world. . . . I got Paşakay, the Turkish Military Attaché, to come. He was pessimistic and predicted that the war would soon come to the Balkans. He said he thought the Germans are annoyed with the Greeks for the recent exiling of pro-Germans and that they are giving the Italians a free hand here. Also that the Turks would go no further than to keep Bulgaria from profiting from the occasion, and that Yugoslavia would not help Greece either. Thus he saw Greece practically facing Italy alone at this time, though Delmouzo told me he thought Germany would not let the Italians start a war that might, as he said, spread to the whole peninsula. Paşakay did not anticipate an ultimatum from Italy just now.

August 14, 1940, Wednesday

The Italian radio extended its charges against Greece last night to include "insincere neutrality." It alleged that the Greeks have permitted the British to use Cretan harbors. It also stated that the Metaxas Government is weak and has had to exile many army officers, who objected to its foreign policy. This makes the situation appear even more serious. Possibly what Italy is really after is not a settlement of the Albanian boundary question—this and Corfu are hardly very important at this time—but concessions in regard to a more vital area. The Yugoslavian Minister, with whom I had a long talk, suggested Crete in this connection, and it does seem to me that this may be the real explanation—and [an] attack on Egypt might be greatly helped, and control of shipping in the Aegean disputed with the British far better than at present, if Greece could be used by the Italians as a larger Dodecanese. Crete could provide air and sea-plane bases for operations to the southeast, and her harbors and those of the mainland could provide shelter for Italian submarines and surface craft sent out to cut up British convoys now passing through these waters with little difficulty. The present Greek Government maintains it will resist any pressure put on it at the point of the sword, and the attention the Italians are now giving to internal dissension—which they perhaps magnify—would seem calculated to sap the strength of this resolution. . . . There are rumors current that Germany has a secret agreement with Italy, giving her Gibraltar, Corsica, part of Egypt, Corfu and Salonica. The possibility must be faced that in the plans of the Axis, Greece is to be an Italian Czechoslovakia, and that when Italy decides the moment has come for the complete reduction of this country, Germany will step aside. Is this moment the present one, when control of Greece might favor the prosecution of Italy's war against England?

August 15, 1940, Thursday

The axe may have fallen on little Greece today, or at least the Axis seems to have done so! After luncheon [Gallagher][43] called me up and told me that the Foreign Office had communicated to the correspondents (there are no papers today), that the Greek cruiser *Helli* (the one that shelled Kavalla in 1935) was sunk this morning at Tinos by an unidentified submarine—she had taken officials to attend the rites of the Virgin, which annually attract many visitors, particularly because miraculous cures are supposed to take place, and was lying bedecked with flags some way off the quay. The submarine fired three torpedoes; two missed and hit the quay causing civilian casualties. The other sank the *Helli*, with the loss of one officer and about thirty men. Apparently the news reached here early, and about 10 a.m. Cannon[44] saw the Premier racing to the Foreign Office with his guards. A conference with military

---

[43] James W. Gallagher, correspondent for the Associated Press.
[44] Cavendish W. Cannon, Secretary of the U.S. Legation in Greece.

and naval leaders was held, but there is no news yet as to what, if any, decisions were taken. No Greek seems to doubt that the Italians are responsible. One Yugoslav correspondent, talking to Cyrus Sulzberger of the *New York Times* who has just come in, and called on me this afternoon, described the affair as designed to "create the proper atmosphere" for demands that are to come. A telegram arrived from Reed[45] in Rome repeating a message he had sent to the Department reporting "reliable" information to the effect that Italy will soon demand the cession of Albanian-occupied Epirus, Corfu and "neighboring islands." I don't know what the neighboring islands may be, but I should imagine the Italians want a control over, or perhaps rather the use of, the Aegean islands and Crete. We shall see. Stephen Pezmazoglou, the Editor of the *Proia* called and asked what news we had—it being a holiday, he had not been to his office, evidently. He told me that the Italian Minister, Grazzi, was away in Spetsai when the Italian press campaign began and that he came back in a hurry and went to Mavroudis, the Under-Minister for Foreign Affairs, to ask him what it was all about! Either suspicions are correct that he has regularly been kept in the dark as to the true designs of his Government—as Eisenloher was in Prague—or he is a merry actor, indeed. Got off a telegram about the *Helli* incident, I hope in time to reach the Department this afternoon, and FDR, if he asks for news from Athens. I have an appointment to see Mr. Mavroudis tomorrow morning, and hope he doesn't now put me off!

Reed[46] has just come back from the Golf Club where he had a talk with the Yugoslavian First Secretary Gavrilović, after the latter had been talking earnestly with Graziani, one of the Italian Secretaries. Gavrilović said the Italian remarked, without admitting that the submarine was an Italian, that the trouble is that the Metaxas regime is not neutral—page the Italian press—and has been far too favorable to England. "It needs to be taught a lesson." Gavrilović thought that what the Italians want here is a régime which will do as the new Germanophile régime is doing in Rumania, and throw the British out, as it were; and that for this reason the next move may be an internal movement in favor of Mr. Kotzias or someone else more inclined to favor the Axis. Unfortunately, Greece is still a maritime country, and Britain is still more powerful at sea than the Axis. If Greece goes pro-Italian the British can sail in here anyday and exact punishment. The question is not clear cut. Nevertheless it is quite possible that internal pressure may now be turned on, and in this connection, the fact that when Italy struck at Tinos she hid her hand may mean that the writing on the wall is meant, at least for the present,

---

[45] Edward L. Reed, Counselor of Embassy, U.S. Chargé d'Affaires in Italy.
[46] Leslie E. Reed, First Secretary of the U.S. Legation, and Consul General in Athens.

for the Government only. So far it is not Italy vs. Greece, but [the] indication is that it may come to that if warnings are not heeded. Add to this the harping of the Italian press on the existence of a large body of opinion here, especially in the army, which does not agree with the Metaxist foreign policy. Add to this the lack of reinforcements to the army in Albania; altogether there is a good deal to support the view that the Italians hope to gain their concessions here by forcing a change of government in the country rather than by actually making war. Whether the hope is one that can be realized in actual practice is another thing, since Britain is by no means as helpless here as in Rumania.

August 16, 1940, Friday

Talk with Mr. Mavroudis at the Foreign Office. He said no official demands or word of any kind has come from Rome, and the Greek Government is keeping very quiet under the rain of accusations and assaults. He said that it is still unknown what is behind the Italian actions. Admitted that Mussolini may be following a policy in cahoots with Hitler aiming at establishing Axis control over Greece and her islands as a means of getting at the British in Egypt and Suez and Palestine more easily than is possible at present. But he thinks himself that the aim is more limited, and that a growing conviction that the war may last a long time, and end not too successfully for the Axis, may have determined the Duce to go after what can be gotten now. In that case the Germans may not back him to the point of actual war, but only so far as he may go in his ends in Epirus and Dalmatia by intimidation and bluff. He granted that a change in the Greek Government appears a part of the Italian program but doubts whether their pressure will do Mr. Metaxas much harm, in view of the dislike and distrust felt here almost universally for the "spaghetti-eaters." It might even reinforce Mr. Metaxas rather than weaken him with the Greek people. Mr. Mavroudis said "There are a lot of Germanophiles here, and a lot of Anglophiles, and many who care neither for Germany nor England in particular, but there are no Italophiles in Greece." He went on to say that Greece will fight, even though she may be defeated, in defense of her integrity and independence, and will never, never abandon her friendship for England, nor the guarantee (as Rumania has done) which England gave her last year.

August 20, 1940, Tuesday

Saw Mr. Mavroudis. . . . As to the Italian situation, he said there is nothing new. The Italian Minister has not been to the Foreign Office, and still the anti-Greek press campaign goes on. He said he thought it possible that Berlin is calming the Italians down, not being anxious for an extension of the war, and that the attitude of Turkey, the firmness of the Greeks themselves, and the reaction of the British press, which shows that England will do her best to implement her guarantee, has had the effect of postponing, at least, the Italian plans, whatever they may have been. But he added that whether this postponement is for a day or for weeks, there is no way of telling.

August 22, 1940, Thursday
Went to see Mr. Melas[47] at the Foreign Office. No developments except that the Italians continue to move troops to the Greek border from the Yugoslavian one, and continue to charge the Greeks with all sorts of crimes. Today, the Greeks are supposed to be arming bands of irregulars to terrify the Albanians on both sides of the border. The Greek Government issued another statement in denial, through the Athens Agency. Am forced to telegraph nearly every day now, because of the rumors which get into the press and need substantiation or denial at home. Also a lot of my time is being taken up by the correspondents, who drop in at all hours for a chat.

August 24, 1940, Saturday
Went to the Foreign Office and saw Mr. Mavroudis. He said the situation appears calmer, because the Italian Government told various diplomats in Rome yesterday that the whole affair is one of the press. From Stefani Agency reports too, it seems that the Italian Government intends, if it does not attack Greece, to have the "Albanian Government" make demands, and thus start diplomatic action. . . . However, he said that Italian concentrations on the Greek border still continue, as well as press attacks, and this keeps the situation disquieting. He said he thinks the Germans and Italians have agreed that an extension of the war into the Balkans is undesirable, but that the Italians now want a victory of some sort, and will not hesitate to take up arms if they can shift the responsibility. Hence Greece must be careful not to give the slightest provocation. He spoke of the task of the Greek Government, in facing out a menace without preparations to meet it, as a positive martyrdom. . . . Though the Under-Minister for Foreign Affairs told me that Greece is still making no military moves which might provoke Italy, the Foreign Office informed all Legations this afternoon that the entrance to the Gulf of Arta is being mined. "Dangerous to navigation" after noon tomorrow, was the phrase used. Apparently the idea is to increase the difficulty

---

[47] George Melas, Under-Minister for Foreign Affairs.

of taking Preveza, which is supposed to mark the southern limit of the Albanian claims. Whatever may be the danger of provocation involved, apparently even the worm will turn. . . . Allard told me "on absolutely trustworthy authority," that immediately after Rumania repudiated the British guarantee,[48] Greece was sounded out for the same purpose by the Axis, with negative results. This probably explains the "never, never" of Mr. Mavroudis' remarks to me on August 16. He also said that he had it on equally good authority that the Greeks asked the Germans to intervene and hold the Italians back. Sulzberger had the same story tonight: he said that after a meeting early this morning (between 2 and 4 a.m.!) the Greek Government called up its Minister, Rangave, in Berlin and told him to make the request. No results were reported by either Allard or Sulzberger. The thing seems possible, and from Mr. Mavroudis' remarks to me it also seems likely that no assurances are forthcoming in reply. In this connection, a story from Miss Gault in the Consulate is interesting. She said she had talked with Stephen Pezmazoglou, the editor and owner of the *Proia* newspaper, who reported that in a talk with the German Minister the latter said that Greece ought to take a lesson from the case of Denmark, which he predicted would be the happiest country in Europe after the war, having lost nothing. Pezmazoglou replied that Greece must consider her honor, and that in addition, if she joined the Axis, England would surely attack and take her ports and islands. A reasonable reply, which I should think the Axis might in reason consider. But then, I thought that reason dictated Italy's staying out of the war, and look what happened! I fear as things are developing now, that we may expect the worst. However, Sulzberger reported that the Italian press has now found an Albanian patriot murdered by the Yugoslavs! If the present campaign is really extended to Yugoslavia, it may mean that war is not intended after all, since Italy would have a hard time with the Serbs, if not with the Greeks. What a confusion!

August 26, 1940, Monday

Went to the Foreign Office and saw Mr. Melas. . . . [He] confirmed . . . that the Italians are concentrating more troops on the border, about 6,000 having arrived from Italy in the past few days, ⅔ of whom went to the southern part of Albania. He said that despite the eased tension due to Italian denials and the information coming in "from all sides" that the Germans have acted to restrain Italy, the Greek Government is remaining "vigilant". . . . The Yugoslav Military Attaché told Foy Kohler[49] that

---

[48] On July 1, 1940.
[49] Foy D. Kohler, Third Secretary of the U.S. Legation, and Vice Consul in Athens.

Greece has managed to mobilize almost completely on the quiet. Full mobilization is complete in the Ionian Islands, Crete, and Epirus. 3 divisions (one of them mobilized) are facing the Albanian frontier, and there are 6 in Macedonia. The navy, the air-force, the anti-aircraft defense, the heavy artillery, and the engineers are all fully called up.

August 29, 1940, Thursday

Called on Mr. Metaxas in the forenoon. Found him looking fairly well. He said at once, when I asked him about the "situation," that Greece isn't putting her faith in any more assurances; that tension has lessened but the Greek Government is remaining vigilant, and if attacked will fight "to the last man, the last woman, the last child." He wouldn't be drawn into any prediction about the future. When I asked him whether he might not be invited soon to Vienna to settle the Albanian problem, he said such a conference would have to consider all minority claims involving this country, and asked me in return if I thought the Italians would care to discuss the Greek minority in Albania or the Dodecanese. His attitude appeared to me to be pessimistic and intransigent at the same time. Pessimistic because Italy as well as Germany is clearly on the march to redraw boundaries and extend her imperialistic control, and intransigent because of the support of Turkey and Great Britain,—support which is of course lacking to Rumania. Possibly also pessimistic because the intransigence may subject Greece to a gruelling experience between the upper and the nether millstones. . . . He said he had talked with Erbach[50] about the Italian menace but that he had asked nothing of him because "Greece is no beggar." This prevented me from asking, as I wished to do, whether he had not, as a matter of fact, made a plea for intercession in Berlin. Regarding German assistance, he said "The Germans say they have brought influence to bear in Rome to preserve the peace," and restricted his own expressions of opinion to "the Germans have understood better" than the Italians the risks involved in the Italian pressure and "the Italians under-rated Greece's morale and capacity for defense." I gather that he did not want me to think that Greece has placed herself under obligations to Germany in this affair. . . . As to England, he denied rumors that Greece has asked for her assistance, saying that he had not discussed the matter with the British at all, as it is only too obvious that they will do all they can. . . . As to Turkey he spoke of the sympathy for Greece and the approval of her attitude evinced by the Turkish press, and stated that "should Bulgaria join Italy" in a war on Greece, Turkey will attack her. . . . I took up with Mr. Metaxas the question of the passport falsifiers; thanked him for his attention to the matter, but expressed my surprise at

---

[50] Victor Prinz zu Erbach-Schönberg, German Ambassador to Greece.

learning that they had been exiled for 7 months only, instead of the year (the maximum) recommended by the competent Commission. He said "never mind about the 7 months: it means nothing, because when the 7 months are over, we shall simply exile them again!" I also spoke about our debt, and suggested that a small payment now, when America knows about Greece's difficult position, would get more favorable comment and create more good will for Greece in America than many times that sum under normal circumstances. His reply was that Greece appreciated American good will, but at present Greece's finances are in a bad way and she is faced with danger to her very existence. "America" he said, "can do nothing for us. By the time you get into this war, Greece may not exist. It is the Italians who will pay your debt!" I told him that of course he must decide and that what I said was only my private idea, but that nevertheless I felt it worth his consideration, since American sympathy is certainly something. He said he would consult the Finance Minister, and I took the opportunity to rub in that the last note I handed in, (which was, I said, justifiably critical in my opinion,) had been aimed at the financial policy of his Government. I wonder if he likes Apostolidis[51] or whether the man is saddled on him by his financial suppliers of the National Bank. He certainly must cause him many headaches!

Athens, August 30, 1940

Dear Franklin:

Since I last wrote, and beginning about two weeks ago, the Italian press and radio has violently attacked this country, alleging hostile Greek designs and actions against Albania, as well as un-neutral conduct in connection with the war. At the same time, Italian troops have been concentrated along the Greco-Albanian frontier, and Greek war and merchant vessels have been bombed by Italian planes and a Greek cruiser sunk by an "unidentified" submarine. You may have read about all this in the papers, as I understand it has been given some publicity at home.

The Greek Government has received no official notification of Italian demands or desires, and ostensibly relations between the two countries remain on the basis of the pact of friendship renewed last November. Nevertheless, the Greek Government has been very much alarmed, and as a result, while cautiously refraining from overt mobilization, which might be construed as provocative, has covertly called many reservists to the colors and made such dispositions of its effectives to meet the menace as has seemed possible without attracting undue notice. Its extensive precautions along these lines lend credence to the reiterated statements of officials that Greece will resist if attacked.

[51] Andreas Apostolidis, Minister of National Economy.

Within the past few days, the Italian authorities have denied privately to diplomats in Rome and publicly through the semi-official Stefani news agency, that Italy has any intention of taking military action. They have explained that the whole affair has been one "of the press" only. In consequence, tension here has been somewhat relieved. But the Greek Government is remaining vigilant and the Greek public retains its apprehension. The Italians have not taken back even the most absurd of the charges they have been so busy making, and if these are not used as a basis for official demands at present, they still remain available for that or other purposes later on.

So far the chief result of the Italian campaign has been to create a wholly fictitious "Albanian problem" out of local minority and border issues of small importance and long desuetude. Should the question of Bulgaria's claim to an exit on the Aegean be revived, as it very well may be if and when Germany gets the present Danubian problems regulated to suit herself, Italo-Albania will be in a position to say "Me too." There are some observers here who see this as all that the Italians have aimed at from the start, and regard the present lull as marking the successful conclusions of the first phase in a drive for limited objectives. But certain aspects of what has been going on appear to indicate that there may have been a larger aim in view. It would seem unnecessary, for instance, in order to establish claims for settlement at a future conference, to accompany propaganda with distinct provocations to conflict, as the Italians have done repeatedly these past two weeks; and in addition, the Italian propaganda itself has not been confined to the Albanian question but has attacked the local government directly with charges of un-neutral conduct and indirectly with incitements to disaffected persons to revolt. Accordingly, it seems more likely that the Italians really started out with the idea of forcing Greece to adopt an attitude in foreign affairs more in conformity with what they term the "New Europe" than the strict neutrality she endeavors to preserve at present, and that they thought that this could be done easily by the undermining and intimidating methods employed. That they have abandoned these methods for the present may have been due in part to a realization that they had misjudged this country's morale and capacities. This point of view was expressed to me yesterday by the Premier himself, who is justly proud of the extent to which his policy of combined caution and determination has rallied the personal support of even his bitterest political enemies. But behind Greek determination in this matter lies the new confidence which British resistance to the Axis has inspired in both Greek and Turkish breasts. Neither this country nor Turkey is yet willing to regard the issues of the war as definitely decided, particularly in the Mediterranean region. The Turkish press has been warmly approving of the Greek attitude under the Italian menace. The British press has emphasized that Greece is not without friends. Under such circumstances an Italian clash with Greece, far from being a localized push-over, might easily develop into a considerable extension of the European war, and once this became unmistakably apparent, a more canny and less provocative policy seemed indicated if the general Axis aim of no-war-in-the-Balkans was to remain undisturbed. As to which member of the Axis first took alarm, the Premier said to me yesterday, "The Germans have realized the situation better," and despite his statement that "Greece is no beggar," I am reliably informed that Berlin brought a restraining influence to bear on Rome on receipt of a petition from Athens which revealed that the situation had reached the point of danger.

Today the Italian press and radio appear to have forgotten Greece, and Balkan eyes are riveted on negotiations in Vienna over the Transylvanian problem,[52] but the Italian Minister says "The Albanian minority question will have to be settled some day." Meanwhile, of course, the larger question of neutrality of this interestingly placed little country, with its head in the Balkans and its feet in the Mediterranean, may pop up again at any time but apparently awaits a turn of events elsewhere, perhaps in the English channel.

Affectionately yours,
Lincoln MacVeagh (12)

September 2, 1940, Monday

Dinner here for Prince Peter.[53] . . . He thinks being in the army here is more interesting than in Denmark. There the discipline and dress is better, but the army is small and without either real problems or experience. Told me that when Dawes[54] arrived at the palace in London to present his credentials, having been taken thither in a coach, as is customary, he said to the King: "Thanks for the buggy ride!"

September 3, 1940, Tuesday

Received today a note from the Foreign Office in reply to my last about the debt. This note repeats the Greek arguments regarding the economic situation here and resulting financial difficulties, but adds that to show

---

[52] On August 30, 1940, having been forced to cede southern Dobrudja to Bulgaria (the Treaty of Craiova, concluded August 21, signed September 7, 1940), Rumania was pressured by Germany and Italy at Vienna to surrender northern Transylvania to Hungary.

[53] Prince Peter of Greece, cousin of King George II.

[54] Charles C. Dawes, U.S. Ambassador to Britain (1929).

its seriousness etc. it will make a part of the overdue payments at once, and has, in fact, ordered the payments in Washington of the amount owing for 1938—about $87,000.00. This seems to follow directly on my talk with Mr. Metaxas in relation of *post hoc, propter hoc,* and it represents a little triumph for me, in a way, since I once had to hear Mr. Mavroudis explain that Greece had no intention of paying us the 43 percent she promised to England because "no discrimination was involved," and that as for not paying 40 percent, the omission of such payment in the past constituted a "precedent." Now the Greek Government has fully eaten every one of its words, and started in with cash to make good its derelictions.

September 6, 1940, Friday

Called on Mr. Mavroudis at the Foreign Office.... [He] is like everyone else pessimistic about the future, if relieved for the present. Italy is still keeping her troops on the Greek frontier, and for the first time Mr. Mavroudis admitted that Greece is reinforcing hers, but carefully stated that there is nothing like mobilization going on here,—which is an untruth. The whole country is on a war-footing, pretty much, already. In regard to the story Allard told me about the German Minister's saying that the Axis had intimated to Greece that she had better copy Rumania and renounce the British guarantee, he said that intimations had been made, but nothing formal. He said that the next time real pressure is put on Greece, he expects it to be by the Axis in conjunction, and not by Italy alone. At present the Italians are keeping their anti-Greek campaign alive by pinpricks such as the recent Albanian charges that the Archbishop of Jannina is forming armed bands on the border.... A telegram came in from the Department expressing commendation over my work in the debt case.... The news of the day is King Carol's abdication.[55] I suppose he had to go on account of the loss of Transylvania, while he was practically sole ruler of the country. In that connection he could be regarded as having failed. Nevertheless he seems to me to have been a pretty able king, though unfortunately placed. Mr. Mavroudis said that he had information to the effect that the resignation followed a demand that he send Madame Lupescu away (she has been not only a scandal but is a Jewess, too) and perhaps this played a part in the drama, though I should think a minor one. General Antonescu[56] has called back Queen Helen,[57] and the promptness of this adds some credence to the story.

[55] On September 6, 1940, succeeded by his son, Michael. On the same day Rumania withdrew from the Balkan Entente.
[56] General Ion Antonescu, Prime Minister of Rumania.
[57] Queen Helen of Rumania, mother of King Michael.

224 · CHAPTER IV

September 11, 1940, Wednesday

Drove out with the two Bunnies at 4:30 for tea at Tatoi with the King at 5:00 o'clock. Others there were the Crown Prince and Princess Frederika, Princess Catherine,[58] and Miss Athenogeni.[59] Tea on the terrace. Very pleasant, but Peggy finally had to get up as the King gave no signal. It was 7:30! And even then the King kept us on a while, showing us the house. I am very sorry for him and the others too. Evidently he is just as much in the dark as to Italian designs as we are, and very anxious. The example of King Carol must bring home to him once more how slight is the tenure of kings in these days! . . . Much talk on the radio of the damage to London. The King seemed greatly concerned and more pro-British than ever, even in the presence of Princess Frederika. The latter brought out her little girl[60] for the company, chubby, but pale.

Mr. Churchill broadcast a brave speech, in which he warned the nation that it must now expect invasion at any moment. He revealed that the "concentrations of barges" at the Channel ports are collections of transports going under their own steam, and that the concentrations exist in Norway and in the Biscay ports as well.

September 12, 1940, Thursday

The Germans and Italians are doing so little that it enhances the impression of a beast crouching to spring.

September 17, 1940, Tuesday

Called on the Turkish Ambassador [Enis Bey], who is just back from Ankara, and from a vacation in Istanbul, where his wife, our useless *doyenne*, is still recovering from her illness of last year. He expressed himself as pleased with Greek intransigence toward Italy, and with the way in which resolution has replaced defeatism here under the Italian menace. He thinks the Greeks will surely fight if Italy attacks them, and predicted that Bulgaria would join Italy and that Turkey would then come in. He thinks the Germans, if checked in Britain, are very likely to attempt to get at the British next through the east, and wouldn't be surprised if Russia connived, receiving an exit to the ocean by way of Persia in return for letting Germany have the Dardanelles. Germany might, he said, invade Africa from Spain, or attack through Libya, but he thought the first too remote from any vulnerable British position, and in regard to the second, stated that Libya is a country very difficult for large-

[58] Princess Catherine of Greece, sister of King George II.
[59] Mary Athenogeni, member of an old Athenian family, and a lady-in-waiting.
[60] Princess Sofia.

scale operations. He said his people know it well from experience. Hence he foresees Germany's descent into the Balkans, if she can't win across the Channel; and he thinks it will be a hard undertaking to invade Turkey, even for the German army. There are no good roads and the mountains are many and rugged. Mechanized equipment would be of little use, and the Germans would have to fight the local defenders in their own fashion (except, I might have reminded him, for planes).

September 18, 1940, Wednesday
Dinner here for the Crown Prince and Princess, on the terrace. Others present Mr. Allard, Count and Countess Leonardo Mercati.... The party really went off very well. The Crown Prince told Jones[61] that he was originally responsible for the Neolaia, or Youth Movement, but that it had been taken out of his hands by "the Dictator." The Prince wanted to make it a larger Boy Scout movement, reaching all classes of the people, but "all it does now is listen to talks about the 4th of August!" However, he said he thought there are "signs of the wind changing," by which he may have meant that he is to be allowed to have some influence in the organization, of which he is the titular head. Though he is married to a German, and is supposed to be Germanophile, he spoke to me rather bitterly of Nazi propaganda which makes out that its enemies are "plutocrats" while the Nazi leaders amass amazing personal fortunes.

September 19, 1940, Thursday
Invitation from the King for all three of us to come out and spend Saturday night and Sunday with him at Tatoi.

September 20, 1940, Friday
Took Major Baker[62] to see the Premier at 12. Mr. Metaxas was very cordial. After I got back I sent a telegram of which this is a paraphrase: "I was informed by the Prime Minister this morning that he is hopeful of successful resistance to invasion by the British; however, in this event the war clouds might come east. Regarding Greece, he said that an Italian or Bulgarian invasion, or both, is a possibility at any time, although he would not say it is probable, and therefore he has to continue preparations for defense. In this regard, he spoke of the continuing criticism of this country in the Italian press, which he said the Bulgarian papers copy

---

[61] G. Lewis Jones, U.S. Commercial Attaché in Greece.
[62] Major Joseph K. Baker, U.S. Military Attaché in Greece.

without mentioning the point of view of the Greeks. However he said, with a certain amount of pleasurable excitement, "That Turkey will intervene if Bulgaria makes a move is now sure." He said, when asked if the Germans might not, in the long run, be expected to protect this country, "It all depends upon us. We may escape, if we are determined to resist invasion to the utmost," adding (I believe correctly) that this country has such determination, and that at present there is not a dissenting opinion in this regard in Greece. The Prime Minister further stated that he has received no advice with regard to the aim of von Ribbentrop's[63] visit to Rome, but has learned "from several capitals" that the attitude of the Soviet toward the Axis has become distinctly cooler because of the Rumanian guarantee, about which he is sure Russia was not consulted beforehand. During the past few days competent observers have reported considerable movements of troops in the direction of the Bulgarian border.

September 21, 1940, Saturday
Luncheon at the house and rapid packing, leaving at 3:30 for Tatoi.... The King was very courteous and charming. We talked a great deal of nothing, but there was some serious conversation after dinner, and his bitterness against the Italians (who have been attacking him on the radio, saying he cannot speak Greek and needs an interpreter to communicate with his own Ministers!) was much in evidence. Also his dislike of the Nazis, and their methods of warfare, as well as his contempt for their so-called reconstruction plans for Europe.... We found the house and grounds perfectly charming, and much reminded us of Dublin.[64]

September 22, 1940, Sunday
Again bright and warm. We spent the forenoon (after breakfasting in our sitting room) walking with the King and Princess Catherine and her friend over the estate, or such part of it, rather, as is near the house.... Then we walked to the royal cemetery and saw the graves of Prince Nicholas and Prince Christopher,[65] and the Mausoleum the King is making in Byzantine style, for his father and mother.[66] The place is on a hill which was also fortified by the Spartans, like Katzimidi, in the days of the Peloponnesian war. The King has made a lovely burial place of it,

[63] Joachim von Ribbentrop, German Minister for Foreign Affairs.
[64] Dublin, New Hampshire, summer home of MacVeagh's family.
[65] Prince Nicholas of Greece and Prince Christopher of Greece, uncles of King George II.
[66] King Constantine and Queen Sofia.

grassy and woody, not a bit formal. The mausoleum is a little gem,—or will be when it is completed. . . . Princess Nicholas[67] has planted crocuses and cyclamen in the grass round her husband's tomb, and the spot had a spring-like appearance which was wholly delightful. . . . The King is thinking a great deal about England these days, and wondering how he can get word from his friends about their safety. He told me the Greek Government prevented his sending an open telegram of congratulation to the King of England on his escape from bombs, but that he managed to send the message privately, through the British Legation. In talking of his uncle George's dislike of the Germans, which he thinks renders his position in France just now rather delicate, the King said "You know our family has always hated the Prussians for what they did to Denmark long ago." I notice that this hatred didn't prevent Constantine from marrying the Kaiser's sister—H.M.'s mother incidentally! But I suppose a little exaggeration may be forgiven at this time, especially when he is talking to people who are well aware of his lineage as well as of his present sentiments. A sort of *apologia pro sententia sua*. . . . The King said "If the Axis wins, I can't think what is going to happen to this country," and it seems to me that since he could very well feather his own nest for the future by advocating a policy here similar to that of Denmark in this war, he is being truly courageous. It isn't as if he could be sure of England's victory. Nothing is sure today. England would probably forgive him a policy which he could plead [was] forced on him by circumstances, should she eventually win, and his present attitude must therefore be set down to his belief that Nazi policy is detestable, on the one hand, and that this country is genuinely menaced by it. His own fate appears secondary in his mind. I give him credit for that. He is a dutifully minded man: it is his duty to be and act the Greek, and the royal Greek at that, and this he will do to the end. What is the country's good he considers his own,—though he has no great regard for his fellow Greeks, whom he refers to constantly as "these people."

Athens, September 30, 1940

Dear Franklin:

While your campaign is going on at home I want you to know that our hearts and prayers are with you, and with the United States of America to which your victory is of such concern. I have already written to Smouch about what I can best do. Meanwhile the hearts that are with you over here are generally in our mouths. Everything points to this country's being determined to resist any pressure the Axis may put on her

---

[67] Princess Nicholas, Grand Duchess Helen of Russia, widow of Prince Nicholas of Greece and aunt of King George II.

so long as Britain remains undefeated or suffers no serious blow to her power in the Mediterranean. King, government, and people are all united in this decision, and military preparations are going on ceaselessly if quietly. If the Axis decides to risk a battle royal in the Near East, as of course it may, Greece will suffer and perhaps go down in the hope of rising again when all is over. Rumors are current, though unconfirmed, that she will soon be invited to throw in her hand. But she is banking on the hunch that at least Berlin wants no extension of the war to this region. The Premier said to me the other day, "If we show clearly that we are determined to resist, we may escape."

Public opinion here is very mercurial. It has been depressed by the Dakar incident[68] and the pact between the Axis and Japan.[69] More recently Rumania's withdrawal from the Balkan Entente has depressed it still further. But a few German planes brought down over England can bring such spirits up again. The British Mediterranean fleet remains in the background of every Greek's consciousness. The more intelligent observers point out that the pact with Japan adds nothing to an already existing situation, and that Greece is in a very different position from Rumania. The only part of the Balkan Entente that was ever really solid —the Greco-Turkish Alliance—is still in operation. Turkey, the Premier tells me, can be counted on to take care of Bulgaria if war develops. And then there is also Russia. The Turkish Ambassador feels she may still be willing to play with Germany, and accept an exit to the ocean via the Persian Gulf in lieu of the Dardanelles. But people round the Premier— though he himself has said nothing of the sort to me—appear to believe that Russia will oppose any further Axis move in the direction of the Straits, including an Italian attack on Greece. Such considerations would seem to justify my use of the term "battle royal" to describe the risk attending too great Axis pressure in this region at this time.

German propaganda seems rather nervously anxious to have people round here swallow the idea that the new order in Europe is already established. But, to quote part of a Turkish proverb, the bears are still roving the woods. So we are going through an anxious period of waiting and preparing for the worst while trying to believe, on the basis of what appears good sense for all concerned, that the worst won't occur.

With my best regards and best wishes to you, I am as ever,

Yours affectionately,
Lincoln MacVeagh (13)

[68] During September 22-25, 1940, an Anglo-French expedition attempting to seize Dakar in French West Africa was repulsed by forces of the Vichy government.

[69] On September 27, 1940, Germany, Italy and Japan concluded a military alliance providing for mutual assistance in the event one of the signatories became involved in war with a state not then a belligerent.

October 2, 1940, Wednesday

It appears that at the performance of "Antigone" in the Herodes Atticus Odeon on Monday night . . . Mr. Metaxas received a remarkable and *genuine* ovation. He deserves it, certainly, but to be popular must be a strange thing for him!

October 3, 1940, Thursday

Had a talk with Mr. Delmouzo. . . . [He] said there have been no *démarches* of any sort on the part of the Axis regarding a conference with the Greeks, as persistently rumored, but said he thought an "invitation" not impossible. He stated once more that Greece will not give up the British guarantee. All she wants is to stay neutral and as she has given no concessions to Britain in return for her guarantee, so she is willing to be guaranteed by the Axis, but also without making concessions! He said the Italian troops in Albania are now perhaps as numerous as 200,000, and admitted that Greece has a considerable force of her own in Macedonia. The Italian concentrations are making the Government here quite nervous, but it has no news of anything having been decided so far as actual action against this country is concerned. He said that he had information from Rome stating that the Spanish have decided not to join the Axis in the war, and not to allow passage of German troops through their territory—this the result of Senior Suner's[70] trip to Berlin and Rome. In consequence, he thought that Mussolini and Hitler may have agreed at the Brenner[71] to extend the war to Africa via the eastern end of the Mediterranean, which puts Greece in the picture once more. He had nothing new on Bulgaria, but thought Russia might prevent her moving in the Axis' interests, and denied the recent rumors according to which the Greeks in Bulgaria have been receiving bad treatment.

October 7, 1940, Monday

The real news of the hour . . . is the sending of German divisions to Rumania. This came today over the British radio. The reasons for this action are not clear, nor [are] the actual number of troops being sent. More will be heard of it. It seems likely to be the first move in a development of the war in this direction agreed on by Hitler and Mussolini in their recent talk.

[70] Ramon Serrano Suner, Spanish Minister for Foreign Affairs and brother-in-law of Generalissimo Franco.

[71] On October 4, 1940, Hitler and Mussolini held talks at the Brenner Pass.

October 14, 1940, Monday

Called on Mr. Delmouzo, the Director General of the Foreign Office, and then on the Turkish Ambassador. The former thinks there will be no drastic action by the Axis in the Balkans this winter, and the latter agrees. It appears to be their idea that the Germans will consolidate their position in Rumania, and develop it in Bulgaria during the coming months, to be ready in the spring to attack either Greece and Turkey or possibly Russia. At least the Director General is quite confident that to attempt to go through Turkey as a present aid to the Italian drive on Egypt[72] is not possible, and that German efforts in this matter will be made through Italy. He also said that military opinion here considers a passage through Asia Minor against Turkish opposition impracticable in any event, even for the German army, though this does not mean that the Germans themselves think so. The Ambassador was disposed to regard seriously the possibility of its being tried, but claimed the passage would take a long time, perhaps longer than Germany can afford. Both thought that the slow tempo adopted in moving troops into Rumania, and the lack of any large-scale preparations for taking over Bulgaria and Yugoslavia at present, indicate that the use of force is not projected by the Germans in this area before it gets too cold for favorable fighting conditions, and as to Italy, the Director General stated that reinforcements do not seem to be moving into Albania in such numbers as to make it seem likely that the Italians intend invasion this fall either.... The Ambassador said that Turkey has 400,000 men (all the district will hold) in Eastern Thrace at present, and when I asked him whether Turkey would help Greece if the latter should be attacked by Italy (the old question!), he replied, to my surprise, that Turkey regards a threat to any part of Greek territory as vital to her own interests. Up to now he and his Military Attaché have always dodged this question by saying that there is no binding treaty, or that it would all depend on what Bulgaria does. There seems to be a new strength of resolution going about, apparently based on satisfaction over Britain's continued resistance, and perhaps on hopes of Russia's entering against Germany. Even the Yugoslav worm has slightly turned, the Premier there having made a speech yesterday declaring his Government's determination to preserve the integrity, at all costs, of Southern Serbia, a district to which both Albania and Bulgaria nurse pretensions. I asked Mr. Delmouzo whether Greece would continue her present intransigence in the face of German pressure added to Italian, and he said, yes, since that is the only way in which a country with pride and an honorable history behaves. But I am wondering if the Government here could swing the people against the united Axis. There are many of

[72] On September 13-15, Italian forces invaded Egypt from Libya.

the poorer people, especially, who are afraid of Germany, as they are not afraid of Italy. The more well-to-do, and the Government itself, of course, are aware of the extent to which Greece's wealth is concentrated in England and her possessions, and in the United States, and consequently might prefer to go down fighting and keep that wealth for future possible resurrection—like Holland—[rather] than give in to Germany and lose it all, perhaps for good. The future will tell. Meanwhile the old question of whether and when full Axis pressure will be put on Greece is always with us. The need for registering a victory may push Mussolini into war with this country, even though this victory would gain him nothing else so long as England controls the seas. On the other hand, if the Germans intend to cross the Straits, their flanks on the south must be protected, as well as on the north. They have taken care of the latter by occupying Rumania, and Macedonia and Thrace is the logical next conquest, to prevent a recurrence of the Salonica catastrophe of the last war. . . . Accordingly, we ought, I think, to be ready now for an Italian attack, with German permission, at any moment, for reasons of prestige, and next spring for an equally possible, but no more certain, amputation of the northern provinces by the united Axis and Bulgaria. You pays your money and you takes your choice.

October 19, 1940, Saturday

No particular news on the radio, except that a statement was made by the British to the effect that Axis menaces against Greece continue and that the British stand ready to give the latter assistance. This will make the Greek authorities lie awake all night from nervousness, I have no doubt.

October 21, 1940, Monday

The Belgrade correspondent of *The London Times*, Mr. Patrick Maitland, came in to see me. He has been in Rumania recently. . . . According to his information the Germans are putting the pressure on Turkey while Mussolini plans to grab Greece, or the northern part of it. In Berlin, he says, officials are talking of breaking the blockade by moving east to the Persian Gulf, and he admitted that Russia might facilitate this plan, though at present her concentrations in the west would seem to indicate that she has not yet agreed to do so and is watching Germany with anxiety. He thinks the Italians in Albania, who are now billeted in small villages in the mountains, or under canvas, will soon have either to go back or go forward, and that their numbers indicate rather that they will do the latter—i.e. an Italian invasion is to be expected without much further delay. Mussolini told Hitler at the Brenner—according to one story he had heard,—that he must have a victory soon or make peace, and that Hitler then agreed to keep Turkey back (the purpose of his penetration of Rumania) while Mussolini moved on Greece. . . . The Brazilian told me that Grazzi, the Italian Minister, has sent out invitations to a performance of "Butterfly" next Saturday, and a big reception afterwards. We have not been invited, so perhaps we are on Grazzi's black-list already, on international grounds. Personally he can have no complaint, though we have never made any particular fuss over him. Puccini's son is said to be coming over specially for the occasion. . . . The Italians may feed the Greeks, but the way to their hearts is not through their stomachs, but through their self-esteem, which the Italians are always wounding. Hence the Greeks will only eat his food and hate his guts, as previously, no matter how big a party he throws. . . .

October 22, 1940, Tuesday

Went to the Foreign Office to see Mr. Mavroudis. He said there is nothing in the British stories about "demands" of the Axis on Greece. There have been, as yet, no such demands. He thinks the stories have been put about purposely in order to excite Russia regarding possible Axis maneuvers in the Balkans. In this connection, he pointed out that Reuters and other agencies have been circulating false rumors about Rumania as well. . . . Who knows? In any case, Mr. Mavroudis said that officially the relations of the Axis powers and this country are easier, if anything, just now, than they have been for some time. The troops in Albania are still a menace, but he thought their concentration was made in anticipation of Hitler's cracking England this summer, when exploitation in the Balkans would have been easy, and he quoted a remark of Grazzi's to the effect that if Italy wanted to attack Greece she would have done so earlier when the going was good, not waited till now. . . . Mr. Mavroudis agreed with the British and Yugoslav Military Attachés that the weather from now on will make the position of the Italian troops on the border very uncomfortable, but he thought them more likely to move back than forward, not only because of opposition, but on account of the extent of the disturbance in the Balkans which such a move would make.

October 25, 1940, Friday

Called on Mr. Delmouzo at the Foreign Office. Greece has officially requested the British not to praise her fortitude too much or talk too much about the possible aid of the British fleet (as the British press has been doing) lest this give the Axis a wrong impression of Greek neutrality—

and attract the lightning. Mr. Delmouzo said Lord Halifax[73] has expressed an understanding of Greece's position in this matter, and that a recent editorial in the *Times* reflects his reaction, stressing Greece's desire to stay neutral though she is arming for any eventuality. He said there are rumors in Rome of an attack on Greece to be launched between the 25th (today) and the 28th of this month, but that there are no indications in Albania of an attack being imminent. . . . The Italians are giving a big party for the Greek officials and society tomorrow, and have invited some diplomats too, but the Turk has not been invited, nor have we. Mr. Delmouzo called the giving of the party at all at this time "maladroit." . . . It is a kind of effrontery which the Greeks of all people are well calculated to resent.

October 26, 1940, Saturday

Saint Demetrius's Day, and a great holiday in Greece. On the last great holiday this year, the feast of the Dormition, the Italians anonymously sank the Greek cruiser *Helli* and bombed two Greek destroyers "by mistake." Yesterday I remarked to Mr. Kohler that we should be on the look-out for what the Italians would do today. (One may remember that Albania was attacked on Good Friday.) But as all seemed quiet and there was no news and no telegrams in the office, Mummy [Mrs. MacVeagh] and I took Mr. Cannon to Mycenae. . . . We didn't know that the Stefani Agency in Rome was launching reports, allegedly from Albanian sources, of Greek attacks on Albanians and Italians in that country. The Agency has reported (falsely) Greek attacks on Albanians before, but never has it charged that Italians were involved. This time the "post" of the Italian Captain of the Port at Santi Quaranta is said to have been narrowly missed by these bombs, and the "Greek or British" perpetrators of the crime are being sought for. . . . Besides making it appear that the Greeks are attacking Albania (which Italy must of course "defend") the Italian propaganda is obviously now aiming at tarring Greece with being unneutral and the ally of England. Recent Italian press comment has stated that only Greece and Turkey now remain (of European nations) in the British camp. Such bogus affairs and bold, unsupported statements of responsibility as the above will now supply the "proof."

October 27, 1940, Sunday

The Stefani Agency reports about Greece are printed in the Greek press today together with prompt denials from the Agence d'Athenes. The

[73] Edward Wood Halifax, British Minister for Foreign Affairs.

British radio says that the Greek and Italian local commanders are getting together over the matter. Perhaps this is just another "threat" to keep the Greeks in line, as Kohler tells me tonight it is thought here by the various diplomats he has talked with today. But it may also be the opening of a campaign to establish a *casus belli*,—though as Bunny says, why the aggressor nations feel they have to have reasons for their aggressions any more is a mystery! I noticed as we drove by this evening at 8:00 that the Foreign Office was lit up—I specially noticed Mr. Mavroudis' window, and many cars were parked outside.

October 28, 1940, Monday
I was waked up at 4:15 this morning by a call from Shan Sedgwick ... who said that at 3 o'clock the Italian Minister handed Mr. Metaxas an ultimatum, expiring at 6 a.m., demanding the right to occupy strategic points in this country because of Greece's unneutral attitude in favoring Great Britain and her fomenting of troubles in Albania. I called up the British Minister at once, who said he had been called in consultation already by Mr. Metaxas and was even then engaged in telegraphing to London. He confirmed Shan's statements and added that when Mr. Metaxas asked Grazzi what points Italy demanded the right to occupy, the latter replied he did not know. Unless Greece yielded, the Italian troops were under orders to advance at 6 a.m. I called up Kohler and he said he had heard the same news from Ben Ames of the United Press, and was trying to get it confirmed before calling me. We both dressed and went to the chancery, where I arrived only a minute before he did. The town was completely blacked out. Staff cars and diplomatic cars, side-cars and motor cycles dashed dangerously through the darkness. . . . At seven the 1st air-raid alarm began, the sirens making a dismal noise. No planes seem to have come over at this time. . . . At about 10 the first planes came over Athens, dropping bombs on the Tatoi air field, with little effect. There were a great many interruptions and conversations during the day, and I can't remember them all, but I saw the Director General of the Foreign Office before luncheon and the Yugoslav Minister in the afternoon. England is promising help, but Turkey and Yugoslavia are holding off. The Italian drive appears to be against Greece only, south of the Yugoslav border. The Major [Baker] saw the Chief of Staff in the morning, and the military intelligence people in the afternoon. . . . All day the streets were full of demonstrating crowds, which attempted to storm the Italian Legation and actually wrecked the premises of the Ala Littoria Air Line.

Delmouzo gave me the story of Grazzi's ultimatum. He went, it seems, at 3 a.m. to Kifissia and got the Premier out of bed to hand him the note! Officially, Mr. Metaxas is said to have replied "I must consider this a declaration of war." Grazzi, in explaining late in the morning to Mr. Mavroudis why he had not asked for his passports, said that no "declaration" was made and that Mr. Metaxas had not used that term! The Premier told Mr. Mavroudis (as I have learned from the latter since) that he may not actually have used that word, but that he certainly said, "C'est la guerre,"—and so it was, and the Italian's quibbling only disgusted the Greeks. I have learned later from other sources close to the Premier, that Mr. Metaxas said also "It is now 3:30 and this gives me till 6. Why, Mr. Minister, I couldn't turn over my house to you in that time, much less my country!" Bravo!

The Chief of Staff told Baker that actually the Italians began firing on the Albanian front at 5:30. Evidently, from the manner of the ultimatum, the Italians wanted to give no chance to the British to bolster Greek courage, and counted on the Greeks caving in if they had to make a decision of their own at once. But again their psychology was at fault. At 6 a.m., the Greek Government declared general mobilization and later martial law was proclaimed throughout the country, while the Premier and the King issued manifestoes, the Premier's being especially dignified and inspiring in its simplicity and appeal. . . . It became evident during the day that more men were reporting than there was equipment or transportation for, and there were jams about all the barracks and army parks —one of the latter being right opposite our house. Several of our servants left, as well as a couple of the Legation messengers. Requisitioning of trucks and private cars began, while Greek-Americans made a path to our door seeking exemption from the draft.

CHAPTER

V

"A Grand Little Fighting Nation"

MINISTER MACVEAGH's direct access to the highest levels of the Metaxas Government and to diplomatic and military circles in Athens, his interest in contemporary military history, and his familiarity with the terrain of Epirus, all serve to render his diary a valuable daily progress report on the "Albanian Epic," which began in the early morning hours of October 28.

October 29, 1940, Tuesday

Major Baker went to the General Staff and was informed that the main forces on the frontier have not yet come into contact. There is still no news of either Turkish or British assistance. The weather here is cloudy, and Johnson reported by phone that it has been raining heavily in the north, which probably accounts for the delay in operations. However, it seems the Italians are massing along the border particularly at Argyrocastro and Koritza. Larissa and Jannina have been bombed, and it appears that an Italian push down along the coast to isolate Corfu is in progress, though it has not reached the main defensive line of the Greeks on the Thyamis river. Martial law is on, here, and general mobilization is continuing under considerable handicap due to lack of uniforms and transport. There was no bombing around here.

October 30, 1940, Wednesday

Cloudy again. There was a brief air-raid warning last night, but this seems to have been a false alarm. People are beginning to hope that the Italians will not bomb Athens for fear of the reprisals on Rome which the British have threatened. . . . Patras was brutally bombed again, with a good many innocent victims. A Sunderland flying boat paid Phaleron a brief visit, but otherwise there are no signs of British aid. I saw the Under-Minister for Foreign Affairs, where the Foreign Office has taken shelter (at the Grande Bretagne) along with the General Staff. He told me the story of the ultimatum once more, and said Grazzi would soon be going, and perhaps the Germans. . . . Grazzi is staying with Erbach at Psychico, and the Italian Legation is full of members of the colony. Mavroudis told me that Turkey has agreed to keep an eye on Bulgaria, but he does not anticipate she will lend military assistance otherwise. Later I saw the Turkish Ambassador, who said his Govt. is conferring with the British, and that he has had no answer yet to the inquiry he made on Monday, at the Premier's request, as to whether military aid can be expected. He thinks himself that Turkey should have moved at once when Italy attacked Greece, because now [that] Bulgaria has made a declaration of neutrality, Turkey can be blamed for aggression if she does anything, —and if she doesn't, the Axis plan of dividing and conquering makes another step forward. He thinks the Germans knew about the Italian plan, but were surprised by the Greek decision to resist, and that now they have to revise their ideas somewhat. He thinks now that they will let the Greeks take a drilling from Italy and realize how unable England is to help them, and that at a certain moment they will then step in and recommend a settlement, with "justice" to both sides, the Greek Government of course going out and a new one coming in under Axis domination. All would depend, in this plan, of course, on what the British really do. Only they must do it soon, if they do anything. Both Mavroudis and Enis said that the Turks are now discussing with this country how they can best lend economic assistance, Enis mentioning wheat and coal.

October 31, 1940, Thursday

Patras was bombed again, and Naupactos also. The Italian radio denounces as a malicious British lie that Italy would even think of bombing one of the great cities of civilization's history! . . . We shall see. . . . Salonica reported no bombing despite clear weather last night. . . . Jones went over to the British Legation in the morning and found the gloom there very dense. He was told that British reconnaissance planes over the Peloponnese had been fired on by the Greeks, and that the latter explained the incident by saying they were not familiar with the silhouettes of the British planes. This shows rather a lamentable lack of liaison between the allies, but also helps to disprove the Italian charges that the British and Greeks have been cooperating militarily in the past. The slowness with which British help is arriving also disproves these charges—no British planes on any of Greece's airfields, no British ships in her harbors. . . . The Axis propaganda has not been slow to assert, on the basis of this slowness, that England intends to let Greece struggle alone. Greek morale is still high, but if England delays to put in an appearance, at least much longer, it may begin to sink. Also if the B.B.C.

gets in many more of its bloomers! This morning Air Marshal Joubert[1] said over the broadcast that Greece is very far away, but the Greeks are a brave people and though they can't win, will go down fighting! The British Legation has protested again and again against this kind of thing from the B.B.C., which complicates its mission here tremendously, but without effect. Today they have cabled for at least one plane to demonstrate over Athens, for the psychological effect. But what does London know or care about the psychology of the Greeks? It is thought there that the greatest compliment Greece can receive is the statement that the ancient Hellenes taught Britain her valor.

November 1, 1940, Friday

Melas told me that he "supposes" the British are making their dispositions. Let's hope so. The Turkish President made a speech defining Turkey's attitude. She will not go to war at present "but remains faithful to her commitments and her friends." There goes one Greek hope (though not a very reasonable one, still a hope that was pretty strong here recently). Will the British go next? . . . Another remark made by Mr. Melas this morning was to the effect that Russia has Greece's future in her hands now, to a large extent, in that she can, by threatening Turkey, nullify her action against Bulgaria should the latter enter the war against this country. . . . The Britisher [Blunt][2] has asked Baker to tell Washington that Greece needs 50,000 rounds of anti-aircraft ammunition of a certain type, and that the British Government will probably be asking the U.S. if it can supply [them]. He thinks our people might make a canvas of the situation before the inquiry comes. We'll pass this on for whatever the Dept. may wish to do with it, but I doubt any success: the stuff is Krupp ammunition. Thus the Greeks are already beginning to feel the effects of "buying German" in times past, to cut down their credits in Berlin. . . . The Brazilian Minister came in . . . to chat and exchange ideas. He has seen Djuvara, who is of course close to Erbach and Grazzi now. Djuvara, he says, expects Germany to come in with Italy now very soon, and that that will be the end of Greece's resistance. It seems to me, however, that though it may mean the loss of the north of Greece, the Greek Government might hold up and the nation continue to exist as "Old Greece" and the islands, if the British support amounts to anything at all. To march down through Thessaly, Phocis, and Boeotia would hardly be worth the candle to the Axis, particularly while the Aegean remains in British hands. Of course if Britain collapses in the Mediterranean, then the loss of Macedonia and Thrace is almost

---

[1] Sir Philip Joubert de la Ferte, British Air Chief Marshal.
[2] Lieutenant Colonel J. S. Blunt, British Military Attaché in Greece.

certain to unseat the Government here and bring in a pro-Axis régime. I continue to think that what interests the Axis—and that means Germany,—is the possession of the northern Aegean littoral as a flank protection for a drive to the Dardanelles, while Mussolini wants a victory, such as the conquest of Salonica, and points thereabouts and in Epirus, would give him, chiefly for home consumption. Unless the Greeks are more timorous than they appear, or are completely deserted by Britain, I don't see them totally submerged yet awhile.

November 2, 1940, Saturday

There is little news from the Albanian front. The Greeks have made an advance in one place, capturing some officers, men and animals, but the Italian effort is obviously slow in getting started owing to the bad roads and weather. The Greeks are immensely pleased with their showing so far, but it is too early to crow! Athens had a brief air alarm this morning. . . . Some British officers arrived in a hydroplane last night from Cairo, and the plane flew low over Athens this morning, arousing much enthusiasm. The British haven't done much for this country yet, but they are evidently starting to get started, so to speak. It is reported that their planes took part in a bombardment of Tirana, and they plastered Naples for the 1st time yesterday, dropping bombs on the oil plants and near the station. Whatever happens to Greece, the British seem to have in mind not losing the opportunity now afforded to bring the war closer to Italy than it has heretofore been. . . . Yesterday, the Italians raided many places in Greece—Corfu, Corinth, Megara, Metsovo, etc. and killed many women and children. In this respect they seem apt pupils of the Bosche.

November 3, 1940, Sunday

Major Baker saw G2[3] and reported that the Greeks are holding their advanced positions in Albanian territory, which they took yesterday, and shelling Koritza from the commanding heights. The Italians are complaining of "torrential rains" (Stefani Agency) but the Greeks say their trenches are dry! Only relatively, I guess. Greeks are used to Greek weather.

November 4, 1940, Monday

A long telegram came from Ankara (a copy of one sent to Washington) giving reasons for Turkey's non-belligerency. Since Bulgaria did not move, it was thought wiser not to incite her to do so with an expedi-

[3] G2: the Intelligence Section of the General Staff.

tion across her front to Macedonia—the actual military help Turkey could give Greece, aside from holding Bulgaria in check, would necessarily be small. Better to keep forces concentrated where they could do the most good, releasing Greek troops on the Thracian border for use against the Italians (all her plans made long ago, as a matter of fact. The only decision come to now is a decision not to change a decision!). I believe the strategy a wise one and have been pleased to see that Greek public opinion has accepted it splendidly. Apparently people here, not to speak of the Government, appreciate the aid that Turkey's position is giving Greece in discouraging a Bulgarian exploitation of the latter's present trouble. I only hope they are not also misled by early successes into overestimating their own unaided ability to defeat the Italians! The first week of frontier warfare has been decidedly favorable to the Greeks. According to Blunt, whom Major Baker saw this evening, the Italians have now more than made preliminary contact with the main defensive line, and the Greeks have captured the heights dominating Koritza. But the main test of strength is still to come. . . . The best we can, or should hope for, if we don't wish to be disappointed too greatly, is that the winter will find the lines stabilized in the mountains. Much may happen before the spring in other theaters of war to affect later developments here. . . . Delmouzo told me that the Greeks could probably capture Koritza now if they tried, but that Mr. Metaxas is anxious not to have them over-extend themselves on the basis of early and illusory successes—like the French in Lorraine and Alsace in 1914—good man if this is true. . . . The twenty British pursuit planes that were supposed to have arrived here yesterday —and to have been seen by excellent witnesses—now seem to have boiled down to nine bombers! I give up!

November 5, 1940, Tuesday

News from the front continues to be favorable to the Greeks. The press reports say they are threatening to surround an Italian division north of Koritza, but the official communiqué is more sober. Johnson reported that a few Italian prisoners were coming in to Salonica, and that their morale is bad, while that of the Greeks is "extremely high" despite the bombings.

Athens, November 6, 1940

Dear Franklin:

Since I last wrote, you have won the election and we have got into the war. Hurray for you, and alas, for us! The Greeks are enthusiastic over your victory. They feel, and rightly, that a change in our Government now would be a calamity for the world. But also your personal prestige is enormous in this country, both for the stand you have taken and stuck to since the war began, and for your humanity and liberalism. It has been a joy to see the joy they have manifested today.

Greece was not surprised that Italy attacked her. She has been seriously preparing for such a thing for a long time. But she was surprised when the attack came. It appeared that it was getting pretty late for mountain fighting in the Balkans, and despite the concentrations in Albania and the constant accusations against Greece in the Italian press, it was felt likely that no war would occur here till next spring. When I asked the Under-Minister for Foreign Affairs, on October 22nd, whether he thought the Italian troops on the border would move forward or back, since obviously they must move somewhere for shelter when the rains came, he said he thought *back*. Later that same week the Italians made some more absurd charges of Greek subversive action in Albania, but on Sunday night, the 27th, the Government went to bed in full confidence that the commanders on the frontier were settling the affair amicably as the mare's nest that it was. But at 3 a.m. the next morning the Premier was aroused at his house, ten miles out of town, by the Italian Minister, ultimatum in hand.

Greece is putting up a gallant show, and there are signs that England may provide some effective aid in spots. Turkey is doing a lot in watching the Bulgars, and freeing a great part of the Greek forces, normally held in Thrace and Eastern Macedonia, for use against the Italians in the west. But what Greece's resistance can amount to if Germany moves in this direction is another matter.

Like the poet, we can see things now "only a step ahead across a void of mystery and dread," but it seems to me that the prizes in this theatre of war are first the Straits, and second, Salonica. If Germany moves to the former, the latter must be secured to prevent the formation of an attacking force on her flank (as happened in the last war.) Her flank along the Danube is secure; the next move must be to take over the north Aegean littoral. In such a campaign, Greece south of Olympus would be of little or no importance, and in any case it falls naturally into the zone controlled by sea-power. If, therefore, as Axis pressure is applied, either through Yugoslavia or Bulgaria or both, the Greek armies can fall back unbroken to Thessaly, there is a chance that the Kingdom may survive as long as England does. If her armies break, it may be another matter, but even so, if Britain controls the Aegean it is hard to see the value of Athens to her enemies, and there are many mountains and few roads between here and Macedonia.

I hope you will forgive my writing in longhand. We have a courier by miracle—it took him four days to reach Athens from Belgrade, 30 hours from Salonica!—and he leaves early tomorrow morning. There is no use reporting daily events—you know them from the press, and if the press goes wrong, you can, if you wish, see the telegrams I send every day. But by way of comment on the present situation here, I would say that Greece has saved her honor by taking up arms against Italy, and has also saved her investments, which are mostly in the British Empire and the U.S.A. The Greeks have always been ready to fight when they could be noble and sensible at the same time. You can read it in Xenophon. In addition, if Greece had knuckled under to the Axis, what would have happened to her far-flung merchant fleet? Now the plan is being considered of putting it entirely in British hands for the duration of the war, with the understanding that Britain will see to Greece's supplies. There is hope now for cargoes under convoy instead of the starvation of blockade. It may be ungracious to think of such things while the Greeks are fighting back courageously against Italian aggression on land and sea and in the air. But it is all a part of the picture, and a vital part of it, at that.

Good night to you. This has been a happy day. The air-raid sirens haven't dampened the pleasure of those election returns!

Affectionately yours,
Lincoln MacVeagh (1)

November 7, 1940, Thursday

The Bulgarian Minister came in to see me. He wanted to inform me officially of his Government's declared intention to stay out of the war. We talked the whole situation over. He thinks Greece cannot hold up under the weight of the Italian attack, and that Germany will hold aloof from at least this phase of development, though he admitted that a big plan may be on foot for a German drive to the Dardanelles. I can't make out whether the Bulgars think that others believe them when they say they want to stay out of the war! He said Bulgaria wants the Aegean corridor, but by negotiation, not war. I replied that if she is to get it that way she must do something for Germany to merit it. To this he said that Bulgaria *is* doing something for Germany in keeping Turkey in check! I said: "That's what the Turks are saying about England: they are helping her, and Greece, by keeping *you* in check." ... Major Baker saw G2 and while he only got the usual communiqué, he feels all is not too well with the Greeks on the front. Apparently they are holding their advanced positions and shelling Koritza at long range, but all along the front the Italians are bombarding them and in the Pindus and in Epirus (along the coast) they seem to have given back somewhat. In the Pindus, it appears to be true that several thousand Alpini broke through entirely between two Greek formations and went off south to cut the Larissa-Jannina road to Metsovo. Italian planes dropped supplies at that place for them but so far they have not reached it, and appear to be lost somewhere near Samarina (Mr. Wace's Vlach village) near Mt. Smolikas, the second highest peak in Greece. Meanwhile the Greek front has closed again behind them. I imagine the "lines" in that region consist of consolidated heights in liaison with each other, dominating and enfilading the passes. When one or more are blasted out by artillery fire or captured by assault, the others have to be abandoned to right and left. But there should be excellent opportunities for maneuver and surprise, especially by night, on the part of trained mountain detachments. . . . Count Mercati called me up and said the King would see me at 4:30. Just had time to walk home, get into striped pants and grey coat and walk over to the palace. The King was alone, and we had tea together in his study, having a very good time. He seemed well and very courageous and dignified as regards the situation. He discounts loose newspaper talk (especially Reuter's reports!) and said that Greece must expect reverses and that there is a long and hard road ahead. As we were talking he said "Listen, that's a British pursuit plane passing overhead." There was a humming sound but I had not noticed it. Later Mummy said she had seen the plane, a long silver fighter flying very low. . . . The King expects military objectives in the outskirts of Athens to be bombed, and "wouldn't put it past the Italians to drop a bomb on the Acropolis." He said the Yugoslavs have assured the Greeks that they will not let the Italians pass, but have evaded the question as to what they will do if Germany presses them too. He thinks the Yugoslavs have been too obsequious to the Axis, and has told Prince Paul (the ex-regent) so. He said they are in a difficult situation, and must be polite to their neighbors, "but they don't have to lick their behinds." He told me that Greece has asked the USA for 60 planes and that the reply was that England should have the first call; and he wondered if I couldn't do anything to help. I said that now [that] Greece is England's ally, the latter should be induced to release the planes. . . . He said the Germans are talking in Berlin about getting rid of him *and his brother* (the last added, I thought, expressly lest I might have heard the talk that the Crown Prince, with his German wife, is the Fuehrer's candidate for the throne here) as well as the Government,—when all would be well and the war could be stopped. But he went on to say that he had heard from many of the old political chiefs endorsing his policy and that of Mr. Metaxas. He thinks, and rightfully, that Italy's crude psychology, in recent months, has united this country as nothing else could do. . . . I asked him whether he was going to the front, and he replied not just now, since troop concentrations are not yet completed and he must be at the post of command. The concentrations, he said, will not be completed for four or five days yet. I mentioned the troops convoyed recently to Salonica, and he said that many have gone up that way without once being molested by the enemy, though he woke up the other night during the air-raid in fear lest they were being caught in the Euripus. He said a British cruiser arrived today at Phaleron with more British officers, and that the ship had characteristically selected the shortest course though it meant passing through a narrow channel in the Dodecanese. Not an Italian was seen, on or under the sea, or in the air.... The King also spoke of the election at home, adding that one bad thing about a change of administration was that it meant a change of diplomats, "which is always a bore." I suppose this was his shy way of indicating that he is glad that I am to stay, but I didn't get it till later. He asked if he could come round to our house to tea sometime as it is so near, and I said, of course, that he could any time he so wishes.... Pindar Androulis called up to say the Premier wants to see me tomorrow at 11:30.

November 8, 1940, Friday

The Premier received me promptly. He expressed great enthusiasm over the President's re-election and asked me to send him his personal congratulations. Then he asked if I could telegraph the President about 60 pursuit planes that Greece wants but which have been refused because the British have priority. I said I could and would, at his request and the King's but added that they should really arrange with the British about the matter. He replied that he knew that and that the British Minister is also telegraphing; also Simopoulos, the Greek Minister in London, and Diamandopoulos, his counterpart in Washington, have been advised. I asked Mr. Metaxas to give me a memo in writing on the basis of which I could proceed.... We spoke about the new bombing of Monastir and he said that the Greeks are holding and therefore the Italians want to extend the front—to get around the line in the north and strike for Salonica across the Greek communications. He said—as the King did yesterday,—that the Yugoslavs have assured the Greek Government that they will not permit the passage of Italian troops. I asked "What if the Germans put pressure on them too?" and he answered, "If they yield, it will be the greatest betrayal in history." Apparently the Yugoslavs have committed themselves pretty far, in this matter, to the Greeks.... Prince Paul came dashing through, but I didn't have a chance to speak to him. On my way out, I saw the King, and told him I would telegraph about the planes. Everybody was evidently very anxious over the Monastir business. ... Androulis brought me a signed message from the Premier to the President, and a list of war material, besides the 60 pursuit planes, which the Greeks want to buy at home. I was somewhat taken aback by all that, and said the Greeks would have to telegraph the list to their own Legation—it would hardly do in a wire to the President! I promised to explain the affair, however, to F.D.R. and include a translation of the Premier's message, and this I did.

November 9, 1940, Saturday

Mr. Apostolidis, the Minister of Finance, came in to tell me of Greece's difficulties in obtaining dollars to purchase supplies at home, and [to] request that I cable in support of giving credits to Greece. Rather ironic (as Jones pointed out!) after all my experiences with the man. I asked him to send me a memo of his talk on which I could base a message. The British have given, or lent, or advanced £5,000,000 to Greece, but this can't be used outside the Empire. I should think the two allies would now pool their orders from us, and the British could buy for Greece along with themselves on whatever basis they are using, and adjust Greece's part of the cost direct[ly] with Greece. I doubt whether Greece can get any credits with us on her own: Apostolidis spoke of Finland's case, but Finland was exempted from the Johnson Act *because she paid her debts*. He wanted to know if he could get wheat sent over in American vessels, because the convoy system from Australia is so slow. I told him, of course, that this would be impossible on account of war zone restrictions. . . . He talked about the winter wheat coming in when men and animals have gone to the war and said Greece will be in great need; she has had recently to buy Russian wheat at "double the price," etc. . . . The military situation remains practically in *status quo*. The Italians say they have reached the Acheron River, way south of Corfu, and have turned east on the Gumenitza road. The Greeks say they are "holding" in this sector and have advanced a little more in the north. After tea Count Mercati called up and said the King wanted me to help him draft a telegram of congratulations to the President. After some talk I finally wrote out the following for the King's approval: "Accept my warmest congratulations on your re-election to the Presidency of the great and friendly American nation, and my earnest wishes for your continued success in the fulfilment of your high mission."

November 10, 1940, Saturday

It is reported in the press that Molotov is to go to Berlin and probably meet Ciano as well as Ribbentrop there. What will come of that? I suppose they will try to bribe them to let them have their way in the Balkans. . . . It is confirmed, says the B.B.C., that the Italians are changing their commander in Albania. An admission that things have not gone as expected! But the new commander is *not* Marshal Badoglio.[4]

November 11, 1940, Monday

The Greek communiqué, as though in celebration of the first two weeks of the war, announced the destruction of the Italian 3rd Alpine Division in the Smolikas region, where it had broken through on October 28th, attempting to reach Metsovo and turn west to Jannina, while the advance down the sea coast turned in eastwards. Apparently many of the Alpini were captured, many killed, and some are escaping back to Albania through the mountains where the Greeks hold the heights. Early in the Italian advance they seem to have had some support from reserves sent up from the Albanian coast, but these also were involved in the debacle caused by Greek reserves coming up on three sides. The communiqué is fairly long but not bombastic, and though the people, press and radio talk of a victory, the authorities put the thing in a proper perspective. What it amounts to is the destruction of a serious threat to the Greek rear,—and what we have really learned today is how serious that threat was, and how good the Greek soldiers must have been to get the upper hand of it.

November 12, 1940, Tuesday

Baker saw the General Staff spokesman as usual, and reported that the Italian division supposed to be surrounded in the Pindus is filtering back across the border, and that a salient of several miles' depth still exists where it came through. But it appears to be established that the division was not only one of Italy's best, but a "reinforced" one of about 24,000 men. In Epirus, Italian troops who are supposed to have reached the Acheron seem to have withdrawn to the Kalamas again and the Greeks for a time lost contact. "Reconnaissances in force" on the Koritza front seem to indicate that the new Italian commander may seek to regain prestige lost by his predecessor by attacking seriously at the one strategic point in a campaign for Salonica.

November 13, 1940, Wednesday

The General Staff takes the attitude today that the first phase of operations is over on the Albanian front, and that both sides are reorganizing their lines, but Baker learned from Captain McNab, recently British Military Attaché at Bucharest, that the Italians have just brought in 4 new divisions from Italy and that two more are expected in 48 hours. Ap-

[4] Marshal Pietro Badoglio, Supreme Chief of the Italian General Staff.

parently they are not going to take their defeat in the first phase lying down (and it *was* a defeat). . . . I cannot imagine why there has as yet been no pronouncement from the USA regarding the aggression against this country which is surely one of the most arrant monstrosities of even this war. Yesterday the Department cabled "You are instructed to inquire of the Greek Government whether it considers itself in a state of war," and I got an immediate reply from Mr. Mavroudis that Greece considers herself at war since 5.30 a.m. on October 28, at which time she was subjected to an unwarranted attack by Italy. . . . Apparently the Department is thinking of protocol rather than reality if lack of advices has impeded a pronouncement. Let us pray "for all good souls lost in the dark" of red tape! If I had been the President, and Greece had been invaded as she has, I would have gathered my cultural tags and rapped out a manifesto to shake the world. Perhaps the election had something to do with our being forgotten: the President can't think of everything: but the Department does,—everything that is petty-fogging, besides some things that are not. . . . [H]elped Kohler with a long message we must send tomorrow about Apostolidis and his desire for credits in the USA. He sent me today, not a memorandum, but a 5 page letter, asking me to convey its contents to Washington, with a "favorable report" of my own. The Greek Minister in Washington will be instructed to furnish details. In my opinion, he should also do the sounding out—I am a third wheel in the business. But it seems the Greek Government wants the moral support of my philhellenism! God help them if they think I have any influence with the Department or the President. I've never seen it myself, if I have, though I've worked hard for them for seven years and done commendably for the Government in several instances. . . . Kohler condensed the Minister's five pages to a viable telegram and together we worked out a presentable framework of preamable and conclusion. The Greeks certainly can't get any credit in the USA, but they might be able to secure some indirect assistance—through the Export-Import bank, or through the British. I sincerely hope their requests are explored with sympathy, and said so.

November 14, 1940, Thursday

Went with the Minister of Public Welfare, Mr. Krimbas, and Bunny, to see the results of the bombings in the Piraeus. Most of the bombs fell in the poor quarter on the promontory south of Zea, and it was there, and not near the Railway Station, as I had supposed, that the market was being held when people were killed. A little, local market in a dusty square. Two bombs fell in the square, one of which was a dud. Out of four bombs in the vicinity, two were duds! Mr. Krimbas is an engineer and we particularly examined the effect of the bombs on various types of structure. A 50-kilo bomb on a typical rubble and plaster three-story house left twenty people on the ground floor unscathed, with the floor of the story above them unbroken. The roof fell in and the bomb wrecked two stories, but not the ground floor. A similar bomb, on a reinforced concrete house, knocked a piece of the roof off—a small piece,—and sprayed the street with fragments, but that was all. The conclusion would seem to be that except for direct hits by fairly large bombs, 100 kilos or more, and near hits by heavy bombs, the cellar of a three-story house, especially if it contains some reinforced concrete, is a safe place, but that the street is decidedly unsafe in all cases.

November 16, 1940, Saturday

The radio announced that President Roosevelt (at last) has issued a declaration on the Greco-Italian War, extending the neutrality law to Greece. He made no comment, it seems. I still feel badly over the fact that our Government, which has expressed itself in no uncertain terms about other examples of unprovoked aggression, has passed over in silence what Italy has done to Greece. Some day I may find out the reason. Meanwhile I understand that public opinion is decidedly sympathetic at home. . . . Went to a movie. . . . Topics of the day contained a flash of the Premier, and he got a hand! This is the first time that I have heard him spontaneously applauded, and I was happy to join in myself. . . . How times do change! But if anyone ever deserved his popularity, Mr. Metaxas does so today. . . . When we came out of the theatre at about 6:00 we found the town in great excitement. Apparently five British warships had arrived at Piraeus and were debarking troops—infantry in battle dress, several thousand of them, with more expected tomorrow. The Greeks are ecstatic.

November 17, 1940, Sunday

The Department wants me to inform the Greek Government that following its declaration that it considers itself at war with Italy, the United States has proclaimed its neutrality, but that this does not in any way mean a diminution of its traditional friendly feelings for Greece. . . . Apparently Athens is to be an important advanced base for the British air offensive against Italy. British troops are all over town, and I must say it is nice to see them, though I hate the thought of such decent and white looking boys getting killed by the Germans or Italians. . . . The way the Italians are taking a lacing these days, and reacting scarcely at all, and the silence of the Germans, who are, in addition, doing practically nothing but sending night bombers over Britain, makes us anxious. The two of them must be cooking something up, and doubtless Molotov was informed of it, and his blessing on it asked, if not obtained. . . . The Greek communiqué about the new Monastir bombings was printed in the *Messager* this morning. It says that Italian planes circled over Greece and approached Monastir, to drop their bombs, from the direction of Florina. This afternoon the Italian radio accused Greece of the bombings. I wonder if this stupid and transparent maneuver will deceive anybody? The Yugoslavs are apparently saying nothing, though their anti-aircraft guns fired on the raiders all night. Their Military Attaché was with Baker last night when the British radio announced the affair, and he obviously had no previous knowledge of it. Not knowing what to say, he treated the matter lightly. But something is going on that is far from being a joke. The Italians are pretending to be Greeks in order to say that the Greeks are pretending to be Italians in an effort to embroil Italy with the Yugoslavs. Meanwhile, they bomb the Yugoslavs and presumably either frighten them, if they don't believe the planes are Greek, or get them sore with the Greeks, and thus pave the way for their letting the Italians through to attack the Greeks, if they do! Rather complicated, but the game is played with bombs, and while armies are ready to fight at the drop of the hat. The question is, can the Italians make the Yugoslavs really believe that the Greeks have been bombing them? If they can, then Yugoslavia may allow Italy to come through, and Greece's whole line is turned. (Note: the Greek official communiqué, as it is printed this morning, does *not* say that Monastir was bombed "for the third time" as reported on the British radio last night. Moral: don't believe everything you hear even on the B.B.C.!)

November 18, 1940, Monday

Went to Headquarters (at the Grand Bretagne) to see the Premier, and handed him the Red Cross draft for $10,000,000 with a letter explaining its purposes,[5] and an *aide-memoire* for himself in the same sense. . . . I also gave Mr. Metaxas the President's thanks for his message, and explained that the Department is glad to have the Greek Minister in Washington collaborate with the British Purchasing Commission, in the matter of supplies, as the authorized Greek agent in touch with the President's liaison committee, thus cutting out annoying private agents. I told him that the President had given instructions to the competent authorities to help the Greeks all they can, and he was very appreciative. I also informed him of our neutrality proclamation, and of the extension of the neutrality law to Greece, adding, as the Department suggested,

[5] A contribution of the American Red Cross to the Greek Red Cross, for the relief of children.

that this makes no difference to our sympathy with Greece in her present trials. All this matter was covered in three "first person notes" which I handed to the Premier at the end of our conversation. Mr. Metaxas told me that the Italians are now holding up the Greek advance with a concentration of bombers and dive-bombers—as many as 500 being used yesterday, and more today. He said that the Greek airforce is rapidly becoming exhausted and that he is very anxious to get (and pay for) the 60 pursuit planes he spoke of the other day. He hoped I would emphasize this need to my authorities at home. Greece is holding on, he said, but gave me to understand that she cannot do so long if this overwhelming air attack continues. . . . I said that it would take some time to get planes from home, and suggested that he get the British to provide planes for the immediate emergency, replenishing their supply from us as time goes on. Clearly he knew very well, and had not forgotten, that no planes bought in America now could be expected to help in the battle for Koritza; I suspect he was "turning the heat on" so far as I was concerned, to make sure that his request for the 60 planes, for use later, gets the best possible presentation I can give it. He said that he is doing his best to get British planes from Egypt at once, and that he has even telegraphed Mr. Churchill in the matter. With a hundred and fifty fighters and bombers he believes he might definitely turn the tide in the present struggle. As regards the repeated bombings of Monastir, he said he thought the Italians are mistakenly attempting to intimidate the Yugoslavs, but that if they succeed in making the Yugoslavs go to war with them, Germany may feel forced to come in too, in which case Greece would be lost. So far, the Germans, he said, have not helped the Italians either with troops or planes.

November 19, 1940, Tuesday

Mr. Archer[6] came in and talked about relief questions. . . . Archer said that some of his Albanian friends are beginning to fear that if Italy is beaten, Greece will try to hold on to Koritza and other parts of Albania. It seems to me that if the Greeks are wise, they will kill any suspicions of this sort at once, since in the unequal battle they are fighting, the help of the Albanians behind the Italian lines, and even in or alongside the Greek forces, may be very precious. . . . Berry[7] got the news tonight from Sebastian, the British consul, and Sir Thomas Blomefield, the Assistant Naval Attaché, that the British have 180 planes,—fighters and bombers,—already at Eleusis, and expect more. Most of the 180 came by air from

---

[6] Laird Archer, head of the Near East Foundation in Greece, had spent many years in Albania.
[7] Burton Y. Berry, Second Secretary of the U.S. Legation in Greece.

Egypt or in the big convoy which arrived today. The Premier's plea seems to be bearing fruit! . . . German diplomatic activity continues. . . . But there is no word of any summons to the Yugoslavs. Does this mean that what is going to happen is going to be at their expense? . . . The Italians are reported to have dropped leaflets in Montenegro, calling on the inhabitants to shake off the yoke of the tyrant Serbs. . . . The Yugoslavs are being subjected to exactly the same treatment as the Greeks were before the war, and are doing just what the Greeks did, trying to maintain a dignified neutrality. Will they be any more successful? Incidentally, their neutrality may be purer than that of the Greeks, but their dignity under the Axis bullying is considerably less.

November 20, 1940, Wednesday

Called on Mr. Mavroudis at the Grande Bretagne. According to him, the massed airplane attacks have not broken the Greeks. Their offensive is still going on, though slowed up. The British have been able to bring up a few fighters, and these brought down nine Italian planes yesterday while the Greeks brought down eleven. Mr. Mavroudis stressed, just as the Premier had done to me, the great need of aviation here. He said planes had been ordered in England and diverted to Finland at the time of the Finnish War. Then they had been ordered from France, and never delivered. Now the hope is America, but like the others (the King, the Premier, the Finance Minister) he seemed to put little faith in the idea that the British Purchasing Commission in the U.S. will release anything to Greece, unless we put on some sympathetic pressure. He agreed that the best thing would be for the British to send planes which they now have to this front, and replenish the supply from the USA. But he doubts whether they will. Meanwhile he praised the cooperation they have been giving so far, citing the raids on Italy's embarkation ports and on Valona and Durazzo and communications in Albania. Regarding the political scene in Europe, he expressed anxiety over King Boris's visit to Hitler,[8] saying it may presage an attack by Bulgaria, or by German troops passing through Bulgaria, toward Salonica. Militarily as well as geographically this would be the best way to help Italy at the moment, since Yugoslavia might resist passage through *her* territory. He was sure she would resist any Italian attempt, and thought her likely to oppose Germany as well. . . . Mr. Mavroudis said that the Greek Ministers in Berlin, Belgrade, Berne, Sofia, and the "Ambassador" in Ankara all report that it is unlikely that Hitler will make a military move to help Italy now, but the German

[8] On November 17, 1940, King Boris and Bulgarian Foreign Minister Ivan Popov traveled to Germany for talks with Hitler, who had just been visited by Soviet Foreign Minister Molotov.

Legation here is so quiet and even docile as to be positively a cause of suspicion. The German Minister has not been to the Foreign Office since war broke out on the 28th of October, and only went then at Mr. Mavroudis's request. In routine matters the Germans have accepted everything the Greeks have done, without a single protest. "It looks as if they are waiting for something to happen soon," said Mr. Mavroudis. I asked him whether he thought Turkey would attack Bulgaria if the latter attacks Greece, or even if she lets German troops come through her territory to do so, and he said he is confident of it, in either eventuality. Regarding Russia, he said he thought Mr. Molotov told Hitler that Russia still regards herself as interested in Balkan affairs. If this is true, then Turkey will probably not be threatened in the Caucasus as part of a German plan which would mean the exclusion of Russia from the Near East, and her satisfaction elsewhere.

November 21, 1940, Thursday

Went to see the Turkish Ambassador.... Said that he has no information from Ankara as to what would be Turkey's attitude in case of an invasion of Greece by Germany, passing through Bulgaria. Such a move, if countered by a Turkish attack on the latter, would be an astute way of putting Turkey in the bad position of being an "aggressor," but nevertheless he felt that Turkey is likely to fight over any impairment to Greece's northern frontier. Even if Russia should menace Turkey in the Caucasus, he felt that Turkey would act to safeguard her vital interests in the Balkans. But he was very careful not to say these things categorically. They were given as his impressions only. He cited the radio and press reports of the blackout now being enforced in Turkey, and other war precautions, as evidences of a feeling there that war is inevitable. I was interested in what he had to say about Yugoslavia. He thought she would very likely resist if Germany applied too much pressure on her, and that she might give way gradually before the Germans while helping the Greeks to clear Albania of Italians. Then she might join up her lines with the Greeks, and if Bulgaria attacked, with Turkey also, theirs constituting an "Eastern front" once again, resting on the British control of the sea. This is exactly the same picture as Sulzberger of the *New York Times* drew for me the other day. Sulzberger is a great Yugoslavophile.... Enis Bey thought, however, with the Under-Minister for Foreign Affairs and the Yugoslav Minister, that Germany is more likely to attack Greece through Bulgaria, and in this connection not only seemed to envisage Turkish aid to Greece, but great difficulty for even a German attack under Macedonian winter conditions.

November 22, 1940, Friday

Today Earle[9] sent another copy of a message telegraphed to the Department, according to which he had seen the Foreign Minister, who went to Berchtesgaden with King Boris. The Foreign Minister told him, in brief, that Hitler gave no signs of wanting to make any military move in the Balkans at this time, they being his best granary at present. He offered Boris, however, a ten year economic agreement, offering to take all Bulgaria's products on the barter basis. Bulgaria would then join the Rome-Berlin-Tokyo Axis. The Foreign Minister also told Earle that he thought Hitler would not at this time offer to help the Italians against Greece, on account of their pride. Earle got the impression, for the first time in his talks with this Minister, that he believes in the ultimate victory of Germany. Apparently nearly everybody does who gets received by Hitler! Earle went on to say that there is no indication yet as to whether or not King Boris will accept the German proposals, which Hitler told him are in line with a policy for Europe which will bring peace for a hundred years.... Perhaps all this talk to Earle, however, is camouflage. The Turks are clearly taking no chances and seem today to be considering placing the Straits in "a state of siege."... Meanwhile the news of the day is the taking of Koritza by the Greeks.... Early in the afternoon the Prime Minister personally announced it from a balcony of the Grande Bretagne to large crowds gathered in Constitution Square. The town was promptly decorated with flags and people went about singing and calling out to each other the good news.... Colonel Blunt, the British Military Attaché, ... said the victory is a major one and the Italian withdrawal fraught with danger as well as difficulty. He said that now is the time to strike a serious blow at Mussolini while Hitler is still making up his mind whether and how to help him. For that purpose more planes are badly needed, and though the British are bringing up all they can spare from Egypt, more must come from America, and without delay.... The Greek communiqué on Koritza, to judge from the British broadcast (we shall see it in print tomorrow) is apparently very measured and conservative. It is to be hoped (and I think it can be expected of Mr. Metaxas) that the army will develop its success in the same spirit, not overextending itself too far. The Italians will have a hard time reconstituting an army broken at several points and retreating on few roads through the mountains; meanwhile the international situation calls for watchfulness on the Bulgarian front, and ability on the part of the Greeks to shift troops in that direction at any time. Whatever happens in the future, however, the Greeks have already shown themselves, at Koritza, in the Pindus, and in

---

[9] George H. Earle, U.S. Minister to Bulgaria.

Epirus, to be a grand little fighting nation, and Lord Halifax was right (it is practically the only part of his yesterday's speech unattacked by the German broadcaster tonight) when he said, "never has Greece stood so high in the eyes of the world as today, and never has Italy stood so low." One thing made me laugh today: a Greek cartoon showing the Rabbits of the Pindus protesting to Mr. Nicoloudis, the Minister of the Press, against the libels on them in the Greek papers.

Athens, November 28, 1940

Dear Franklin:

I sent you a cable on your re-election, but such messages must always be cold and formal in comparison with one's real feelings. Personally you know what these are, anyhow, so far as I am concerned. Otherwise, I am not a bit behind our Greek friends, who from King to bootblack have been congratulating the world in general and thanking their lucky stars that you and not another will continue to guide our ship of state.

Recent news about this country has probably been well covered at home. The army has done excellently and appears to have established a moral superiority over the enemy, but its equipment is inferior and it particularly needs pursuit planes and antiaircraft ammunition. The British were cautious about coming here at first, but are now giving some valuable assistance to the Greeks in the air and exploiting the opportunity afforded to them themselves to bring the war home to the Italians. In this connection, General Parry, who has been here coordinating the British and Greek efforts for the past couple of weeks, told one of my officers, the night before last, that the British General Staff changed its mind about aiding Greece as a result of the Greek successes in the early days of the war. He also paid a tribute to the military "genius" of General Metaxas and said the Greek dispositions at the beginning of the conflict were "exceedingly clever." He further added that it is impossible to overemphasize the importance of the Greek success, since "after all it is the first and only success of the Allied armies on land." My latest talks with Foreign Office officials indicate a belief on the part of the Greek Government at present that the British attacks on the Albanian ports will effectively prevent serious Italian reinforcements from arriving, while the Greek army can handle what is there already.

Of course, the question of international complications has been bothering the Greeks a great deal. Their right flank is now badly exposed to attack from the north. That Germany should bring military pressure to bear to restore Axis prestige has appeared inevitable, and that she should do so through Bulgaria rather than through Yugoslavia has seemed the more likely. However, in the past few days, a stiffening attitude on the part of Yugoslavia and new indications of Turkey's determination to "protect her vital interests" have encouraged Greece, even as her successes have perhaps encouraged them. The Director General of the Foreign Office told me yesterday that he thinks Germany wishes to localize the Greco-Italian conflict just as far as may be possible. Nobody here knows exactly what Russia has been up to behind the scenes, but it is suspected that she has not abandoned her freedom of action in regard to Balkan questions and that this may be fundamental in the present situation.

Local political affairs have taken an amazing turn. When Italy began menacing this country, politicians of all shades of opinion rallied behind the Government, instituting a kind of "era of good feeling" for the duration of the emergency. But when General Metaxas accepted the Italian challenge so simply and fearlessly in the dark hours before the dawn on October 28th, he spoke words which have positively endeared him to the Greek people. He now represents the whole country as perhaps no one has ever done at any time in its history ancient or modern. The "era of good feeling" has become an "union sacrée." As I have cautioned the Department, this condition may not survive a long and hard struggle calling for solider qualities than enthusiasm, but it represents an unexpectedly good start and should help tremendously no matter what the future holds.

Affectionately yours,
Lincoln MacVeagh (2)

November 30, 1940, Saturday

The King came to tea, walking over from the palace all by himself, in uniform.... Regarding the fighting on the front he said the Italians are fighting well, but that he is encouraged rather than otherwise by the progress of the Greeks, "only I hope it doesn't last too long. I don't say this generally, because I don't want to discourage people. But I am thinking not only of the soldiers but of the morale at home." By "it" I suppose he meant the tough battle now raging.... I have had no news from the Department either about Red Cross aid, or about military supplies, despite my part in forwarding Greek requests. But from Melas I learned that we have promised 30 (half the number asked) planes, out of the British quota, to be shipped in January. The King said too, that there has been news from the Greek Minister in Washington about other supplies.

December 4, 1940, Wednesday

The line in Albania seems now to have straightened out on a front leading from Santi Quaranta northeast to Lake Ochrida. The Greeks are evidently pressing on the ridges running northwest toward Klissoura, but snow is hindering operations, and maybe the difficulty of getting up all sorts of supplies is also having its effect. . . . The British don't seem to be developing their offensive against Italy as seemed possible when this phase of the war began. Apparently they are shy of the straits of Otranto. The Italians are mobilizing more men. It hardly seems as if they needed a larger army at this time, with so many idle troops already on hand in Italy. Can it be that they want to draft possible malcontents into the army where they can be held under discipline?

December 5, 1940, Thursday

Tompkins of the *Chicago Daily* and *News* told us of some of his experiences and observations at the front, mainly in the Argyrocastro sector. Nothing new, so far as I was concerned, but it was delightful to hear another unprejudiced observer pay warm tribute to the Greeks. Like Sulzberger, Stevens, Gallegher, *et. al.*, he was full of amazement at the spirit and toughness of the troops, their ability to go on attacking height after height with practically nothing to eat day after day, and told how they sing at their work of repairing roads, or on their long night marches. The thing which most struck him was the bitterness of the Italian prisoners against Mussolini personally. . . . Had a long talk with Colonel Brower and Major Craw,[10] the two American Air Corps observers with the R.A.F. who have just come over from Egypt. They pictured the British pilots as amazing for their skill and spirit, but said the British equipment is far below the American standard. Their bomb-sight is primitive (so that their accuracy is low) and their planes (here and in Egypt) are antediluvian (*Gladiator* pursuit planes can't catch up with the Italian bombers, for instance, though they are good in defense, when the enemy carries the fight to them, since they are heavily armed, and maneuver easily). In numbers of planes the Italians both in Egypt and Greece have a 10 to 1 advantage. They said that there is a perpetual struggle going on here between the British who want to use their few planes for strategic purposes behind the Italian lines (to cut communications and bomb ports and dumps) and the Greeks who want them to help defend the troops from Italian planes, i.e. use them purely tactically. He said the British are gradually getting the Greeks to see their point, but only gradually, and that every day some planes have to be detached for tactical purposes. The Greek air force started out with just over 100 and has now just about 30 left! They want British planes as they come in to be allocated

[10] Major Demos T. Craw, U.S. observer (with Colonel Brower) attached to the British Royal Air Force (R.A.F.), was to serve as Assistant Military Attaché for Air in Greece.

to their force, and their pilots are very good, but the British realize that if this happens they will be used up very quickly on front line work and in any case will be lost for the wider strategic aims. Probably some sort of compromise will have to be reached here too. Meanwhile the British have here four squadrons, averaging after recent losses about 8 planes apiece. They hope to fill these squadrons up to 16 planes each, and they think that this is about all they can use advantageously on this front. The other British here are all connected with supporting these (at present) 32 planes! About 4,000 men,—pilots, air men, ground men, anti-aircraft men, hospital workers, supply men, and guards! Of the squadrons one is mixed, two are bombers, and one is pursuit. . . .

Colonel Brower said that the command in Egypt was against sending any force at all to Greece, on the theory that it would only prove another Norway. Mr. Churchill, however, ordered the move himself. At first it was decided to send 8,000 men (presumably 8 squadrons, then) but the Air Force cut this down by half, saying it would rather have to evacuate 4 than 8! Thus we have been right in suspecting here that there was reluctance among the British even to try to implement their guarantee to Greece! Now, however, they seem to want to cull some *kudos* out of the Greek victories which they haven't earned; for besides mentioning the excellent help given by their few squadrons, the British radio is mentioning "troops" supposed to be fighting on the side of the Greeks, and the British press is publishing pictures of British tanks rolling through the Greek countryside. Colonel Brower confirmed that though there are "troops" of the British army here, they are *all* connected with the air force, so the B.B.C. is misleading; and that British tanks may be here indeed, but they are tanks bought by the Greeks and run by them! . . . He said that General Heywood[11] is here, not in command of anything but on a special mission to arrange for the sending of military supplies, such as ammunition, guns, etc., and to advise the Greeks about the use of this material—also, Colonel Brower added, to advise the Greeks how to fight the war. This would be very British; but all present, including Major Baker who was sitting in on our talk, opined that the Greeks, who have won the only victories the allies have yet seen on land, might better be sending advisers to the British *to teach them*! According to the Colonel, too, there is jealousy between the British Air Force and Army to such an extent that the Air Force here suspects Heywood will advise that army units (as distinct from supplies only) be sent to Greece so that the Air Force will not get all the credit at home (for the Greek victories!). Oo, la-la! With this kind of thing going on and the Greeks and British

[11] Major General T.G.G. Heywood, chief military representative of the British armed forces in Greece.

at cross purposes on the use of the R.A.F. it is evidently only good luck and the courage of the individual pilot and *Evzone* [foot soldier] which will save the situation.—Except that there *is* a wonderful spirit of cooperation on the part of the Greek authorities responsible for the reception and installation of the British here. The Colonel and Major Craw both said that the British cannot say too much for the helpful kindness and the efficiency, too, of the aid given them on their arrival here, some of them with nothing to their names, straight from the Western desert.

Other remarks by these observing airmen. The Middle East Command expected big shipments of planes in September. None have come, and none can now be expected before the end of this month. The failure of the overwhelming Italian air force in Egypt to bomb the British forces off the map is incomprehensible. The Tatoi aerodrome is not big enough to accommodate even the two squadrons of British planes now located there. Its field is too small for proper scattering of the planes in case of a raid, and is now being enlarged. The buildings are badly camouflaged. With the waxing of the present moon heavy bombing attacks on this field are confidently expected.

December 6, 1940, Friday

The news of the day is that Marshal Badoglio has been replaced as Chief of Staff of the Italian Army. Comment over the London radio is guarded, referring to his age (69) and saying otherwise only that his going deprives Italy of one of its best thought-of generals "who probably has not seen eye to eye with Mussolini in the conduct of the war." That, I think, goes without saying—or without repetition—at this time. It looks to me more like a big success for the Greeks: either Badoglio's advice has not been taken and he has retired to escape being tarred with a defeat which is not his fault; or else he has been removed because he has failed. In either case, it's an admission of failure for Italian arms. Generalissimos don't get canned for successes. . . . The Greeks seem to have captured Santi Quaranta today, and their front now appears to run on almost a straight line from there to Lake Ochrida via Premeti and Moschopolis. The Greek advance threatened now north of Premeti toward Klissoura and Tepeleni makes the Italian position at Argyrocastro precarious and if pushed still further may spell the doom of Valona. But how long can the Greeks keep up this pressure, and will their ammunition hold out? The British can help with a lot of supplies, but as Blunt told Baker, with ammunition they are hampered by the fact that the British and Greek guns are of different calibers. The British Middle East Command might supply guns of its own for use with its own ammunition, but *it has no artillery to spare*.

December 7, 1940, Saturday

During the morning I had a talk with Mr. Metaxas, at his request. He asked that I forward pleas to Washington, and to the President personally, for credits for war purchases and for airplanes. In regard to the first of these matters, he said that Greece must go on driving the Italians hard in order, if possible, to get them out of Albania this winter. "Let us not fool ourselves," he said, "the Germans will attack in the spring, undoubtedly. If we can get through with Italy in Albania by that time, we can reform to protect ourselves, and Yugoslavia, Turkey, and *perhaps* even Bulgaria will be encouraged to resist the German pressure. If not, the whole Balkans are likely to collapse. Thus this present war may be a turning point, and it may even be *the* turning point in the whole war. But our supplies of munitions are not sufficient to last us over an unremitting offensive lasting many months. Nor can the British supply us with enough. We must apply to America, where the material can be bought. But our dollars are low. I believe it is in America's interest as well as our own that supplies should be sent here to help us be victorious." I told him about the Johnson Act once more, and he said he fully understood the difficulties, but repeated that he thought something might be done to enable Greece to get what is so necessary for her and for all who cherish freedom. I suggested that owners of American securities might turn them over to the Government in exchange for Greek, and that the dollars thus obtained could be used by the authorities for the purpose in view (as I understand has been done by the British) but he said that the Greeks who have money in America are mostly American citizens, and that the rich Greeks here have largely placed their investments in Britain. He gave me a memorandum of his situation in this matter, expressing hope that the American nation would not leave Greece to her fate, and this I promised to forward together with his remarks to me, earmarked for F.D.R. and I did so by cable during the afternoon. The other problem, regarding planes, he exposed as follows: when Greece asked some time ago for 60 planes (see my entry of November 8) the President personally took an interest and the Greek Minister in Washington telegraphed that Greece could have 30 planes from those being manufactured for the American army. This, however, was premature, since American aviation authorities blocked the idea, and Greece was told she could get her order from among planes being furnished to the British. Yesterday afternoon, word came from London, in response to Greece's request, that *the British can spare no planes at all*. So Greece is back where she started from! The Premier said he wished to lay this situation before the President personally and beg his further assistance. I replied that I would be glad to expound the matter to the Department and send, through the Dept., any message he personally might draw up for F.D.R. He promised to send me a memo and a message for this purpose, but it didn't arrive today.... Meanwhile, over the British radio tonight we learned that in an exchange of telegrams with the King, the President has assured H.M. of American aid. So what? Is it all going to be just words?

December 8, 1940, Sunday

Androulis came in ... with a long letter about credits and planes from Mr. Metaxas, and I spent the rest of the evening drafting a long telegram, in two parts, while Mummy obligingly translated a letter which the Premier had written in French for transmittal to the President.... The news of the day is the capture (at last) of Argyrocastro. It was announced just after dark, and for a moment the blackout was lifted, as the King and Metaxas stepped on to the balcony of the Grande Bretagne to say a few words to the crowds. Great rejoicing in the streets all evening to the accompaniment of church-bells and whistles. The Greeks have now captured the two bases from which the Italian invasion started. But their progress in the Albanian mountains is slow and painful. The Italian Naval Chief of Staff has now resigned ("relieved of his duties at his own request") as well as Badoglio and Vecchi, the Governor of the Dodecanese, and there are rumors of more "resignations." Mussolini is certainly cleaning house, and of course it is possible the new men may be more successful than the old. I don't see what can be done for the Dodecanese, unless the British fleet is defeated (and maybe the new men will try to do just that), but in Albania it [there] is still time, as the Italian radio contends that though pushed back, the Italian line has not been broken. If the Greeks can get up enough fresh divisions for a heavy attack in one place, to make a gap somewhere and pour through it (perhaps at Tepeleni-Klissoura), now would seem to be a good time for such action, the Italians being shaken and not yet on any fortified line of resistance. But the terrain is so difficult that it may not be possible to operate according to Hoyle.

December 13, 1940, Friday

Mr. Adossidis[12] and Mr. Stevens[13] came in, and the former told me that the Government has ordered the amalgamation of the Greek Red Cross with the Youth Movement. He was very much excited and from what he told me it is clear that many Greeks will see in the move a prostitution of Relief to partisan politics. The Premier may attempt to

[12] Alexander Adossidis, former Governor-General of Macedonia, and Director of the Greek Red Cross.

[13] Gorham P. Stevens, Director of the American School of Classical Studies in Athens, and representative of the American Red Cross in Greece.

justify it by pointing out the theoretical value of centralizing all philanthropic effort, the Youth Movement being now chiefly used for relief purposes. But the Youth Movement is only momentarily a relief organization. Essentially it is a recruiting organ for the dictatorship, and as such it is bitterly opposed and detested by all former Venizelists and other liberals, as well as by the army. It will now not only be able to dominate the activities of the Red Cross—its leaders being young, vigorous, and supported by Mr. Metaxas, while the Red Cross leaders are old and of the opposition, for the most part—but it will have the disposition of Red Cross funds. Mr. Metaxas has long shown that he intends, for his political purposes, that there shall be only one Santa Claus for the Greek people, if he can have his way . . . and with this move he stands to make a very big step indeed in this direction. Normally the Red Cross does not attract much attention, but wartime is different. I think there can be no doubt that Mr. Adossidis and his friends are right, both about the fundamental purpose of this new move, and about the effect it will have in awakening the old opposition to Mr. Metaxas which his splendid action so far in this war has laid so happily to sleep. The Greeks, who got together by a kind of miracle at the moment of danger, will now start squabbling again, when the danger seems not quite so acute. As in the case of Mr. Venizelos, internal policy will wreck the gains of foreign policy, and Mr. Metaxas who has done so well is on the point of spoiling all! I advised Mr. Stevens and Mr. Adossidis to talk with Mr. House,[14] and later all three came up to talk with me. Mr. House sees the danger in the move, but agrees with me that we Americans must lie low in the matter until we find out what Greek reaction may accomplish. The American donors of charitable funds do not, of course, want them used for political purposes. But it may be that things will take a different turn in a few days, and in any case we may be able to save in some way the American share of Greece's relief funds for use in the manner we want. To report the matter as it seems to stand at present might lose Greece many precious dollars, and we don't want to do that, of all things.

December 14, 1940, Saturday

Talked with Mr. Melas and with Mr. Mavroudis at the *ersatz* Foreign Office in the Grande Bretagne. . . . The Under-Minister said he thought the Hungarian-Yugoslav pact of friendship is fundamentally a German move to counteract the growing influence of the Soviets, particularly in Bulgaria. In connection with rumors of an approaching Bulgaro-Turkish pact, he said he was quite sure the Turks will agree to nothing requiring

---

[14] Charles L. House, head of the American Farm School in Salonica, and recently named Executive Director of the American Red Cross in Greece.

the removal of their army from Eastern Thrace, where it is now concentrated. In other words if they agree to "friendship" with Bulgaria, they will not be too trusting.... The King said yesterday that he thought the move toward a Bulgaro-Turkish *rapprochement* has its source in Soviet policy. Mr. Mavroudis said that he thinks the Bulgarian Government is glad to have the two powerful trends, German and Russian, crossing at Sofia, because Bulgaria can itself remain neutral better that way than if there were only one pushing her. But he said that whichever side invades her first she will join. He thinks the Hungarian pact with Yugoslavia, which to a certain extent knits the latter now into the system of German protectorates, gives some assurance that if and when the Germans move in on the Balkans, it will not be through Yugoslavia, but through Bulgaria; and if this is so, the King may well be right in thinking that the Russians are pushing for a Turco-Bulgarian tie-up, to prevent the whole of the Peninsula going over to the Germans....

Colonel Brower and Major Craw in to report after a flight to Larissa and Jannina and a thorough inspection of the Greek fighter and bomber commands. They had had a risky flight over the Pindus, with the ice-ceiling at 6,000 ft. But though Major Craw was frightened for the first time in years, the skill of the pilot was equal to the occasion. The Greeks are using men who have been flying the mail-route over the Pindus for a long time and our officers said that no one else could have negotiated the difficulties they encountered today. Both were highly pleased with the inspection, and praised the Greek pilots and the Greek organization. They think the force, which now disposes of about 45 planes for active operations, could handle a hundred more light bombers and pursuit planes, and they stated that after what they have seen here they believe that it would be well worth our while to give them that number out of those we are building for our army. Of course the Greeks would pay for them, but the point is that these very astute and judicious observers feel that the use Greeks are capable of making of these planes is so good at the present time, that to put them in possession of them would be more to our own advantage than keeping the planes at home for our own air-force now at peace.

Sent off a telegram on my talk with Mr. Mavroudis and the general situation. It seems that the latter, despite the heavy weather, may be pointing up to a strong Greek attack in the Klissoura region. The Colonel and Major said that they heard of operations in that sector today, and saw Greek bombers go out in support—and return in safety to Larissa. In the Pogradetz sector, the Italians appear to have counter-attacked heavily and though the Greeks still claim to have the upper hand, they have advanced very little. Colonel Melas, of G2, told Major Baker in confidence yesterday that the Greek plan is now to hold Pogradetz as a pivot and swing up from the south. Whether this is the plan or not, it represents what seems to be happening. The biggest Greek advances these past few days have been along the coast and north of Argyrocastro, toward Tepeleni, and there have been moderate advances in the central mountains. News from Egypt confirms big advances by the British toward the Libyan front and many thousands of prisoners, but the actual positions of the opposing forces cannot be determined as yet.

December 16, 1940, Monday
Mr. House has talked with General Pallis (now Chief of Staff, since Papagos became Army commander) about Red Cross regulations and the inadvisability of merging the Greek Red Cross with the Youth Movement, at least so far as to render its collaboration with American agencies unfeasible—and maybe if and when the King gets hold of the same idea, and others too begin to realize it, the Prime Minister will see that present plans are revised. . . .

Major Craw said that the Greeks are expecting the Germans to attack through Bulgaria and want planes of ours very badly, for that eventuality even more than for pursuing the Italians,—thus confirming what the Premier said to me the other day (see my entry for December 7). He said there appears to be a good chance now that the British will release some of their American planes to Greece, and spoke of the British sending up here a lot of the equipment captured in Egypt. Also that many of the guns the Greeks are taking from the Italians themselves shoot the same ammunition the Greeks are using. So that as the Greeks have at least as many troops as the Italians in Albania at present,—15 to 16 divisions,—and their material is likely to improve, their chances of going on driving the Italians back look favorable.

December 17, 1940, Tuesday
Mr. House had an audience with the King, Levidi calling me up to arrange it. H.M. didn't mention the question of the Government's "taking over" of the Red Cross, so of course Mr. House couldn't mention it himself. From what I hear now, however, the Government has left medical, first aid, and nursing problems in the Red Cross's hands, which are its proper concern. Here in Greece there is no Y.M.C.A., or Salvation Army, or Knights of Columbus, etc. and in consequence the Red Cross has taken on the distribution of clothing and the organization of canteens in addition to its usual functions. It is these things which the Government has now placed in the hands of the Youth Movement. The latter is by no means yet organized to do such work efficiently, and the enthusiastic

Red Cross people, who have acquired some training in it, naturally criticize the Government's decision, and are also, of course, disappointed to have their own efforts arrested. But it seems to me that theoretically, and irrespective of charges of a political motive inevitably incurred by the Premier in so doing, the removal of these functions from the Greek Red Cross and their placement in the hands of what corresponds here now to the Y.M.C.A. etc. is quite proper and may prove, as time goes on, to be in the interests of efficiency as well. The latter point depends on the seriousness, of course, with which the Youth Movement takes hold. So far as the contributions of the American Red Cross are concerned, I do not see that the situation has been altered, as these are purely along lines still left in the Greek Red Cross's hands.

December 18, 1940, Wednesday
Mr. House told me about his talk with the King yesterday. In connection with the Prime Minister H.M. said: "Most politicians, you know, aren't gentlemen. But this one is." . . . The Italian radio, speaking of Albania, says "Time is on our side." It might also have said, "So is the weather."

December 20, 1940, Friday
I received telegrams from the Department about the Greek pleas for credits and planes. I am to explain to the Premier that while the President has read his letter with sympathy it is impossible under existing legislation to extend financial assistance to the Greek Government; and that the request for war supplies (for which Greece can pay, of course) will be given every consideration. Not a very cheering reply, but perhaps actual negotiations with the Greek representatives in Washington are proceeding better than is necessary or proper to indicate in a formal note. The second telegram is apparently only for my information, and states that the 30 planes "accorded" by us were not specified originally; that the Greek Government specified the type desired; that this was a type wholly earmarked for the British; and that this being the case, Premier Metaxas agreed to a British proposal to take, in exchange, 30 planes of a different type, to come from some which the British already have in Egypt.—A wholly different story from what the Premier gave me of the affair! . . . Well, no matter who is right, I hope the Greeks get some planes! . . .
A telegram came in from Belgrade—copy of one sent to the Department—reporting a conversation with a "high official" who said the Albanians are dissatisfied with the Greeks and British for not declaring that they will liberate Albania. There is growing suspicion, this official said,

of Greek designs. . . . I have already talked with Mr. Mavroudis, Mr. Delmouzo, and Count Mercati several times about the possibility of it being a good idea to present Greece to the Albanians a little more clearly in the light of a liberator, and so obtain more cooperation against the Italians. But Mr. Delmouzo said today that there is not much value to be gotten out of the Albanians; they are divided into factions among themselves, they are poorly armed, and able to do very little. Mercati spoke of how untrustworthy they are. Furthermore, it is a fact that Mr. Metaxas has clearly stated that Greece is fighting "to liberate Albania"—in his radio speech of November 23, after the fall of Koritza. It looks to me as if Italian propaganda runs at the bottom of the dissatisfaction reported, or at least of a large part of it. The official spoke of a desire in Albania to see an Albanian Government set up in Koritza, as a proof of Greek intentions. But obviously the Greeks couldn't allow a foreign civil administration behind their advancing lines;—and if they could, they couldn't find a group to satisfy the Albanians themselves. Obviously the Greeks want to wait till they have won before they take up this question of Albania. But the local inhabitants, a mixture of Illyrians and Slavs, of Orthodox, Mohammedan, and Catholic, most of them bandits and nomads, illiterate and incapable of any but tribal organization, make a fertile field for trouble making. Some of them have been aroused against the Italian invader by the Greek invader, and the Italian is probably trying to turn the tables.

December 21, 1940, Saturday

Arrival of a second part to the Department's telegram about planes, advising me, if the dispute between the Greeks and British about P-40 and Defiant planes is not settled, to do what I can in my discretion to persuade the Greek authorities to give up their desire for the P-40 and take the British offer of immediate delivery of Defiants. But I must make it clear that this is only our advice and that we have no intention of going back on our assurance of helping them to get planes in the USA. The reasons for our advice are also given, namely that it may be a long time before we can deliver P-40's (Curtiss-Wrights); that these ships are hard to maneuver and have actually been given up by our air force, though the British are ordering them, and have indeed bespoken our whole production,—which accounts for their offer of the Defiants, if the Greeks will forego their 30 P-40's. And finally it is clear that the lack of mechanics trained in the P-40, and of spare parts, may turn these very fast but tricky machines into liabilities here rather than assets at an early date. . . . I found out through Major Craw that the Gladiator planes recently sent here from Egypt have nothing to do with this controversy, and intend to see Mr. Metaxas and put the problem before him according to the Department's instructions. Major Craw is in full agreement that the P-40 is likely to be much less useful to the Greeks, for their kind of fighting (necessitated by the mountainous front) than the Defiants, but says he thinks the Air Ministry still wants to press for the P-40's because of their great speed. He has flown the ships and knows their quality. Meanwhile he told me in a long conversation this afternoon that the British Air Officer Commanding is against more planes being sent here at this time on account of the weather and the lack of suitable fields. The Larissa field is snowed under, and the only practicable fields left are around Athens, except for the small one at Jannina where it is difficult to land. The British also want to concentrate as much as possible in Libya at present. The Department says Mr. Metaxas has signified his willingness to take planes *from Egypt* in exchange for the P-40's, but Major Craw says the British now have fewer planes there than here—I think this is doubtful, but they certainly haven't got many. I take it he (Mr. M.) is willing to do this, if it can be done, for the sake of getting something soon, but otherwise as between Defiants from England and Curtiss-Wrights from America he still wants the latter, and it is my job to persuade him to change his mind without letting him think that we are going back on our word. For the Dept. expressly states that we *did* assure him of 30 pursuit planes.

No particular news. The Italians have been bombing the Greek front lines heavily and the R.A.F. has been working with the troops loyally—the score today being 9-0! The Greek advance appears to be continuing, but very slowly, around Chimarra and the Klissoura defile. Nothing said about the northern front. The Greek navy sent some ships through the straits of Otranto and met no Italians.

December 23, 1940, Monday

Called at Headquarters in the morning and gave Mr. Androulis an *aide-memoire* for the Premier setting forth the Department's arguments for the purchase by Greece of the Defiant rather than the Curtiss-Wright P-40 planes, and offering Major Craw's expert advice (as one who has flown the P-40) if desired. I felt it would be better to let the Premier read this first and see me afterwards if he has anything to say, rather than ask him to listen to my explanation and read the summary afterwards—and as a matter of fact this proved a lucky idea, as the news of the fall of Chimarra came just as I was going to Headquarters and the Premier was with the Cabinet, everybody being very excited. Androulis told me that a whole battalion of black shirts, 800 strong, with 30 officers, had been captured in Chimarra, and this was later announced in the press. Whistles were blown and bells rung to celebrate the victory. As a matter of fact, the Greek troops are well beyond the town by this time. As in other instances, they have waited to take the town until enemy artillery has been driven out of range. They are now pressing over the southern end of the Acrocerannian promontory, and threatening to cut in between Valona and Tepeleni, which has probably also been evacuated by the Italians though still being under their fire. . . . The King telephoned me himself from Tatoi at lunch time and asked if he could come to tea. He arrived promptly at 4:45 and stayed for what was to us a very pleasant visit by the fire. He gave each one of us a 100 drachma piece of silver from the issue struck recently in commemoration of his return to the throne. I told him the whole air-plane story of the P-40's, but he didn't seem to know much about the background, if anything, so I got no comments or information of value.

December 24, 1940, Tuesday

Allard arrived back from Sweden. . . . He said his Legation in Berlin told him that Hitler never knew about the Italian invasion of Greece until he arrived at Florence just after it had started. The Italians, he said, even delayed his train so as to be sure he would not arrive before it was known that the attack had been launched. He was furious. However, tonight the German papers are all talking about the Axis as an invincible bloc once more, ignoring Mussolini's defeats, and laying into Mr. Churchill for his speech of last night (which we heard clearly over our radio, and a wonderful speech it was). The German Commander-in-Chief has told the German troops in France that they can invade England, and will do so as soon as the Fuehrer gives the word, overcoming the Channel as easily as they did the Maginot Line. This last was *turned*, not taken by direct assault. Will the Channel be turned in like fashion, by an attack on Ireland, perhaps, or the north of England? Who knows.

Athens, Christmas Day, 1940

Dear Franklin:

I hope you are having a happy Christmas at Hyde Park. Our first courier in nearly a month arrived this morning and we are busy getting out a pouch that would stagger Santa Claus. Somewhere in the bag I hope there will be a place for this letter, though I may not be able to tell you much that you do not know already. Locally we live an intensified life under war conditions, but many of our windows on the world outside have been darkened since hostilities began.

If you have had time to read what our American correspondents have been sending out about Greece's war effort—and I know you don't miss much in the news of the world,—it would be gilding the lily for me to describe it. Correspondents like Leland Stowe, who know what they are writing about and have seen other wars, even the most recent, are doing full justice to what is in many respects a remarkable show. You may be interested, however, in the following words, not written yesterday but appearing in the Official British History of the War of 1914-1918 (Operations in Macedonia, Volume II, p. 189): "The British underestimated the quality of the Greek troops, whose dash and drive astonished them."

The Greeks, after advancing for the better part of two months over territory which an American observer with the R.A.F. described to me as resembling the worst parts of the Rocky Mountains, are now facing reinforced Italian resistance on the last and best strategic line covering Valona and the coastal plain. The next week should show whether they still have enough "dash and drive" to carry them forward another step, with possible momentous consequences. If so, it would seem that the next Official History will have to add endurance to the catalogue of the Greek soldier's surprising qualities.

Of course I have been as much surprised as anyone by the Greek successes. Explaining miracles is perhaps a thankless business, but it is human to try one's hand at it. Thinking this one over, I remember a remarkable essay by William James on "The Energies of Men." Something has released an energy in these people of which none of us had any suspicion. Patriotism may be part of this something, as well as hatred of the Italians, and resentment over their insults and threats. But more important than these, I believe, has been the consciousness of unity which the nation suddenly achieved in the dark dawn of October 28th. The history of ancient Greece is at least 50% discord, and there was plenty of it in the Greek Revolution, while the whole life of the modern Greek State has been factious almost beyond belief. But from the moment Mr. Metaxas rejected the Italian ultimatum, there has been only one party, one class, one purpose in the whole of this small land. Such unity is in itself a force, but the realization of it by a people which has never known anything like it has created a kind of national intoxication to which the traversing if not the removal of mountains is a thing to be taken in one's stride.

At the present moment, the Greek Government seems satisfied that despite the possibilities inherent in the Greco-Italian war, in which England is actively assisting Greece, there will be no further extension of hostilities in the Balkan area before the spring. The Turkish Ambassador here takes the same view. It is thought that Hitler was genuinely put out by his friend Mussolini's untimely adventure in this direction, and is all the more content not to give him military assistance in this region because of indications that his other friend, Stalin, is keeping a jealous eye on Balkan developments. In this connection, Bulgaria is seen as wooed by both Berlin and Moscow, and likely to remain neutral, balancing the one against the other, at least until Berlin becomes too exigent. Meanwhile a purely Bulgarian attack against Greece is regarded as out of the question if Turkey maintains her present concentrations in Eastern Thrace, as the Greek Government is confident she will.

The big events of the winter are looked for in the west. But that Germany may attack in this direction in the spring is something which the Greeks, engaged in a campaign which leaves their northern flank badly exposed, cannot afford to forget. "Let us not fool ourselves," General Metaxas said to me the other day, in connection with his urgent plea for planes, "Germany will attack us when the winter is over, and consequently we must drive the Italians out of Albania, if we can, before that time." Greece is also aware, of course, that if England brings enough forces here to menace Germany as well as Italy, Germany will come down through the Balkans winter or no winter. Fortunately, from this point of view, the British now have here only five squadrons operating with the Greeks. But there is also a military mission now in Athens engaged in studying possibilities of future action, and this too may have a bearing on what the spring brings forth.

The courier has brought a note from you acknowledging, in your usual miraculous manner, a telegram of congratulations received among many thousands after the election. The note has taken just six weeks to make the voyage from Washington![15] So perhaps, though this is only Christmas, it may be timely to add here my best wishes for the Inauguration.

Affectionately yours,
Lincoln MacVeagh (3)

December 26, 1940, Thursday

[A]s I sat in my study after dinner, a messenger from the Foreign Office brought me a note from Mr. Metaxas, with a long "notice" attached, in reply to my *aide-memoire* of last Monday on the air-plane question. The Premier says he cannot accept our suggestion that the Defiant planes be taken by Greece in lieu of the P-40's. Not that he wants the particular

---

[15] In a letter dated November 18, 1940, Roosevelt wrote: "Dear Lincoln: I have only just received your letter of September 30 and want to express my appreciation and thanks for your kind message of support during the campaign, which is now fortunately over. Events in Greece have moved fast in these intervening weeks and this country has been greatly heartened by the heroic resistance of the Greek Army. No one can yet tell how significant may be the results of this intensified Mediterranean campaign. I can appreciate that these are difficult days for you but have been relieved to note that you personally in Athens have so far escaped the perils of intensive air warfare. With kindest personal regards, Very Sincerely Yours, Franklin D. Roosevelt." PPF, File, 1192.

model P-40 so much, as that he wants a fast pursuit plane as soon as possible in view of the likelihood that soon he will have to contend with German as well as Italian opposition. He makes a very strong plea for planes of this sort, of the latest type being supplied to the American army, and begs that we delay no longer to fulfill our promise to let Greece have them.

December 27, 1940, Friday

Allard came in for a talk. . . . I brought him up to date on what has occurred here in his absence, letting him see some of my despatches, and he told me that the German Minister, to whom he is related by marriage and whom he sees frequently, said to him the other day that Germany regards the Greco-Italian war as only Italy's business, not hers, and that he has been instructed to stay here. He said Germany has not attempted to mediate and has no intention of so doing. Furthermore he said that he knew in advance nothing of the plan to serve Greece with an ultimatum, and that the first he heard of the matter was at 3 a.m. on October 28th when Movin (the Italian Military Attaché) arrived at his house, on the Italian Minister's orders, to acquaint him with the fact, and to tell him that even then the ultimatum was being served! If this is true, one can understand the Germans here being somewhat annoyed.

December 28, 1940, Saturday

Cy Sulzberger dropped in with his dog, just back from Belgrade. He drove alone from Monastir to Athens *in one stretch*! The most interesting thing he had to say was that he found well-informed people in Belgrade, Sofia and Bucharest, all three, who expect a Russo-German war in the spring. The idea is that if Germany can put England out this winter she will be all set to use her army for the move which is to make the Reich economically complete, the conquest of the Ukraine; and if she can't, she will invade Russia by force of necessity, to be able to go on against the British blockade, as she figures, indefinitely. Sulzberger said he found little if any belief in the idea that Germany will invade the Balkans. She is getting all there is to be had out of this region already, and to save Italy is no object with her. . . . Enis is worried over the reports of German forces moving into Rumania on a large scale. He doesn't trust the Germans not to come down this way. On the other hand the papers today announce that Bulgaria has again decided against joining the Axis, and what appears to be going on is a tightening up of the Balkans as a result of the Greek victories and Russian influence. More and more it seems that Russia is playing an anti-German game in the Balkans and that Germany is playing an anti-Russian game. The moves so far are, on the one hand, a growing strengthening of Russo-Turkish relations, with the possibility of extension of the Russian hand of friendship through Turkey to England, and Russian anti-Axis intrigues in Bulgaria and Rumania behind the front which Germany has built up against the Soviets from Poland to the Black Sea. On the other hand, there is the German domination and infiltration of Rumania, the increasing German ascendancy over Hungary, and Hungary's new German-inspired friendship with Yugoslavia. In the background there are the huge Russian concentrations in the Ukraine and those of Germany all along her eastern marches. The attitude of the Communist Party in Greece and other Balkan states is also of interest. It seems that it is instructed to support local regimes against the Axis. I spoke to Sulzberger about this and he said he was aware of it and would try while here to get some definite information.

The news of the day was the announcement by the Greek Admiralty that on Christmas Eve a Greek submarine in the Adriatic sank three Italian transports and damaged a fourth vessel, probably a tanker, convoyed by planes and destroyers. The transports totalled about 23,000 tons. The submarine, the *Papanicolis*, commanded by Milto Iatridis, was not damaged and has regained its base. Smart work!

December 29, 1940, Sunday
Cuza Hotta, who is to stay here as Rumanian Press Attaché, his *remplaçant* having been recalled almost as soon as sent, told Kohler that Filotti, now Rumanian Minister in Sofia, is sure that *pourparlers* of some sort are going on between Greece and Bulgaria. It seems that talks have been in progress between the latter country and Turkey for some time. The Ambassador said yesterday (to Allard) that they have come to nothing, Bulgaria asking the withdrawal of Turkish troops from Thrace and Turkey asking Bulgaria to promise to let no foreign troops pass through her territory—both in vain. Nevertheless, the fact that such talks have been going on at all, plus Bulgaria's refusal to join the Axis,—or rather the Three Power Pact,—and articles appearing in the Turkish press about the advisability of a new order in the Balkans which will make the "Balkans-for-the-Balkans" a reality, all seem to point one way, and a way which would make a Greco-Bulgarian *rapprochement* seem a possibility. Certainly, if Turkey will withdraw objections to Bulgaria's having an Aegean exit, and England and Russia join to bless the project as an inducement to the Bulgars to join a new Balkan Entente, it would seem that Greece might be willing to agree in order to remove the threat of a stab in the back which she now feels so acutely, and the Metaxas Government, strong in the popular support it now has as a result of its victories

over Italy, might be able to reverse traditional Greek policy in this regard. A Bulgarian corridor between Greece and Turkey would not be objectionable to the Turks or to the British if it were certain that it did not also mean an Axis corridor; and to accord it in return for security on her northern frontier,—the laying of the Bulgar bug-a-boo by a pact of union between Turkey, Bulgaria, Greece and perhaps Yugoslavia,—would be far from a concession on the part of the Greeks; it would be a real triumph, particularly at a time when they need all their strength to fight Italy. It would be interesting to find out if Greece is really sounding out the Bulgars! Recent Bulgar press articles have agitated the "exit" question once more, attacking this country in the old, traditional manner. (Metaxas, of course, will cede no territory to Bulgaria under menaces.) But this may be a blind, if it is true that an attempt to form a new Balkan bloc favorable to Russia and England is brewing. The Italian Minister is reported to have paid a long call at the Sofia Foreign Office yesterday as a sequel to the new announcement of Bulgaria's decision not to join the "Three Power" alignment, and it is obvious that any brewing that may be on hand must be very secret indeed. . . . In this connection, Mr. Delmouzo's remark about Greek war aims to Allard the other day is interesting. He said "Greece aims to drive the Italians out of Albania *for the sake of the entire Balkans,*" and hopes to retain Southern Albania and to regain the Dodecanese for herself; the rest of Albania remaining independent. The Greek Government thus conceives its present war, which began as self-defense only, as a constructive effort in the interests of the Balkans-for-the-Balkans, and through this fact the question of her war aims ties in with the possible and even probable ideas of both Russia and England regarding a method of stopping Hitler in the Near East. The old Balkan Entente was fostered by England and France; a new one seems likely to arise as a result of the necessities of England and Russia; and in both cases the aim is the same, to contain Germany within bounds. The former has passed away and France has fallen with it. Will the latter be formed, and Russia go down too? If Germany defeats England before turning against the Ukraine, there will be no question of any bloc here or elsewhere in Europe being formed to oppose her. But if not, the Germans risk having to attack Russia; if they do attack her, [they will do so] with not only a rear open to the British assaults and under continued blockade conditions, but with a right flank exposed as well, unless they take some action first to prevent the crystallization here of a Balkan union containing Bulgaria as well as Greece and Turkey. Will they let Bulgaria elude their group? And is not the Turkish Ambassador right, and Metaxas also, in fearing a military descent of the Germans to the Aegean and the Straits next spring? Personally, I should think the Germans very foolish to attempt a Russian war (if England is not beaten first) before dominating not only

Rumania, as has already been done, but the rest of the Balkan peninsula as well. The same reasons which I believe would make them take Salonica before driving to the Straits would operate to make them take the Straits before attacking in the Ukraine—while England still holds out. So that unless the invasion of Britain is successfully accomplished this winter, I think a German attack in the Balkans will precede one on Russia, whatever the wiseacres in Sulzberger's collection may say.

December 30, 1940, Monday

Went to the Foreign Office and had an hour's talk with the Director General. He would not admit that any approach has been made, official or unofficial, by the Germans in regard to mediation. But he said that there have been "rumors in Berlin" of such a thing. Going on with the subject he said that mediation is impossible now, in any case, on account of the fact that Greece is in the position of victor and could only accept a victor's terms—territorial readjustments and a large indemnity. It would also have to be taken into account that Greece cannot force England to leave the territory here which she has taken for bases against Italy (Crete, for instance). . . . I asked him about this matter particularly since the Department had relayed to me a telegram from Morris[16] in Berlin to the effect that an unofficial but important German had suggested to the Greek Minister in Berlin that as England is sure to be defeated very soon, and Italy will be able to impose terms on Greece, it might be well to mediate the Greco-Italian war now, and that Germany might be able to get Greece good terms. The fine performance of her army would not be forgotten, he said, and he added that Greece could apply to the German Government through either Yugoslavia or Turkey. The Greek Minister replied, according to Morris, that it is not for the victor to request mediation, and that anyway Greece feels she is doing something for Germany in this war by removing the possibility of embarrassing Italian pretensions in the Balkans. Also Greece thinks that Hitler will not be too hard on her if he defeats England, on account of his admiration for her culture and the manifest justice of her claims to Northern Epirus and the Dodecanese, claims which she is sure he will recognize, etc. etc. From the prompt reference of Mr. Delmouzo to the fact that a victor doesn't ask for mediation, it would seem, despite his denial of anything but "rumors," that Morris' report is true; and from the astuteness of the Greek Minister's reply in Morris's story I suspect the fine hand of Metaxas. . . . In any case, Morris's story has a verisimilitude which is very convincing in itself—the statement about the fine performance of the Greek Army—against Germany's dear ally—for instance! . . .

[16] Leland B. Morris, U.S. *Chargé d'Affaires* in Germany.

I took my cue from Delmouzo's reference to territorial adjustments to ask him what are Greece's war aims. I said: "You didn't have any war aim when you were attacked—nothing, that is, besides defending yourself. But now you are fighting on foreign soil and must be presumed to have war aims like everyone else." He laughed and replied that he could not speak officially, but that surely it is clear, as Greece successes grow, that the nation is thinking more and more of the return of Northern Epirus and the Dodecanese. I then asked him about Bulgaria—trying to sound him out in the matter of the rumored secret *pourparlers* at Sofia. But he was not to be drawn, and to my suggestion that this might be a good time to compose differences with Bulgaria and give her her greatly desired exit to the Aegean, merely said that she has no right to such a thing; and he added that the Bulgars can't be trusted. He has lived there several years and knows the country and people well. To give them the exit would only whet their appetite to enlarge it. . . . If talks are going on, it would appear that the Foreign Office is anxious indeed to keep the fact dark, for he gave me not only the old traditional point of view, but with a vengeance!

December 31, 1940, Tuesday

I called on Mr. Mavroudis this morning at the Grande Bretagne and asked him the same questions as I asked Mr. Delmouzo yesterday, with similar results. He also referred to "rumors" of mediation in Berlin. Here, he said, there have not even been rumors. The German Minister has called, but at Mavroudis' own invitation, and about another matter,—a complaint the Greeks wished to lodge about some nasty article in the German press. Dealings with the German Legation, outside of this question, have been chiefly concerned with commercial matters. Regarding Bulgaria, Mr. Mavroudis said that it is not the time to talk of getting her into a Balkan Entente. For one thing, Turkish suspicions are too strong to allow for anything like a genuine pact of friendship to be made between the two of them. These suspicions will keep Turkish troops in Eastern Thrace, and thus the situation resembles that which obtained recently in regard to Greco-Italian "friendship" while Italy retained her concentrations in Albania. . . . In regard to President Roosevelt's "fireside chat" of Sunday last, Mr. Mavroudis said, "It just about discards the last vestige of neutrality." I telegraphed the delighted comments made by the Greek press on this speech, but omitted Mr. Mavroudis' candid remark. It hits the bull's eye all right, but might be understood in a different sense than that in which it was meant. Mr. Mavroudis is by no means an Axis sympathizer, and if he didn't add expressions of joy to his comment, it is only because he has long taken the attitude that we must inevitably come in. The speech, he feels, is only another indication that he is right.

January 2, 1941, Thursday

Major Craw, just returned from the front, spoke very interestingly of his experiences. He watched an attack in the Tepeleni area and took part in one north of Chimara. He was heavily bombed at Santi Quaranta and elsewhere, and shelled by warships at Spelia. . . . It seems that the Greek artillery is very good, that the mountain 75's are carried up incredible heights, that the Greek infantry shoots poorly but attacks brilliantly with bomb and bayonet, that the Italians are making constant use of their overwhelming superiority in the air and resist very well up to the final attack with the bayonet, and that they have everything that is needed for modern warfare, and use it too, while the Greeks have very little but courage and pertinacity. Somehow the advance goes on under these conditions, a daily miracle. More disturbing was the Major's statement that he saw no supports or reserves anywhere. . . . The Major was loud in his praise of the dash and toughness of the Greek soldier, contrasting his qualities along these lines with the rather flabby listnessness of the Italian prisoners with whom he talked. But the picture he gave of Italian resistance based on the terrain and the control of the air, as well as superiority of equipment, was not encouraging from the Greek point of view. Some of the planes he saw he believes were German *Stukas*.

Tonight the radio reported that German air forces have arrived in Rome (officially announced there, it seems). This adds another and overwhelming hazard in the Greek path. Can the Germans lend their air-force to Italy for use against Greece and yet remain at peace with this country? Stranger things have happened. It could be said, for instance, that the newcomers were not attacking the Greeks but only their British allies! But, on the other hand, Germany *might* admit war with Greece, and recall her Minister, without creating any of the Balkan difficulties she is supposed to wish to avoid at present, if she confined her attacks to the Albanian theatre. It is only if she comes through Yugoslavia or Bulgaria that complications are likely to follow. . . . So I see no reason to suppose that the Greeks will not have to contend with some of the German airmen now being sent to Italy in the near future, just as Mr. Metaxas has been fearing. . . . The question of the effect on opinion in Italy of having German troops come in to help the Duce out of a hole is another question, and more difficult to assess. Wickham Steed, in one of his radio talks some time ago, said that Italian pride would never stand for such a thing. But "needs must when the devil drives," and apparently the Italians are in sore need of stiff reinforcement. I believe that the appearance of German planes and pilots over Albania would greatly encourage the morale of the Italian forces there, whatever might be thought of it at home. And on the other hand, with the Greeks now so hard put to it to advance against Italian resistance, the mountains and the snow, the arrival of even only a few Germans might change their morale also, for the worse. The British don't seem able or willing, or perhaps both, to send more planes to Greece than are here already, and we have let two whole months go by without selling the Greeks a single one of ours. If the Germans come flying over to Italy's aid now, it may indeed be not too late to turn Italian defeat into victory, despite what some competent observers have written. It might have been better to come earlier, but the psychology of the present situation seems to me to offer still an opportunity to turn the tables. It will certainly, in any case, be a shocking discouragement to the Greeks to have to face hosts of dive-bombing Stukas just now.... If the Germans don't help the Italians in Albania, but only in Libya (as is, of course, possible), it may be owing to continued Hitlerian displeasure with Mussolini for embarking on the Greek venture; but to bet on this would hardly be wise. Rather I think the advent of German air forces in Rome proves Metaxas once more a military prophet of sorts.

January 4, 1941, Saturday

Had a long talk with Mr. Delmouzo at the Foreign Office, to ask him principally whether the Germans here have shown any indications of a more hostile attitude or said anything at all regarding their air-plane reinforcements of Italy.... Mr. Delmouzo said that there have been no indications whatever of any changed attitude toward this country on the part of Germany, and that Erbach's visit to the Premier was a week or ten days ago and had to do with commercial matters. Whether true or not, this answer was given in a manner which clearly showed that the Greeks are not any more anxious now than they have been in regard to Germany, and that's what I wanted to find out. I take it too, that the German Minister's visit was the same one discussed by Mr. Mavroudis last Tuesday, though I was not told then that he had seen the Premier.... While we were talking, Mr. Marketis, lately Greek Minister in Moscow, dropped in and we discussed recent press stories of growing uneasiness in Russo-German relations. Both Marketis and Delmouzo thought the stories exaggerated, and the former emphasized that Russia is afraid of Germany as she is of no other power. She will not precipitate a war with Germany, you may be sure, he said. This leaves the question aside of whether Germany will precipitate a war with Russia. Both gentlemen fought shy of this, but seemed to think it certain that Germany will have a go at the Ukraine *if* and *when* she defeats England.

January 5, 1941, Sunday

Found a telegram from Smouch reading OK GO / HALL. Rather cryptic, but it *might* mean that the appointment to Ankara is decided on and that his advice is to accept it. Anyhow, I replied, "Cheering message received. Thanks. Love from all, and Happy New Year," for I suppose the message is meant at least to encourage. Otherwise why send it at all? . . .

Major Craw came in. . . . He hopes soon to go to Salonica and after that to fly back to Egypt and go down to the Sudan. He thinks he has learned about all he can here, and a British Intelligence officer has told him that an insurrection is expected soon in Abyssinia. As to Greece, he thinks the British have arranged to let the Greeks have 30 P-36 planes instead of the P-40's, and that some of these have already arrived in West Africa. Perhaps the very cordial tone of the Premier's two recent notes to me reflects this success, though no official announcement has been made. . . . Major Craw said further that the bombing of Elvasan these past two days has been due to failure to reach Durazzo because of bad weather. The British planes are so old and have such a short cruising radius (Major Craw said no American instructor would let his charges fly about an airfield in such antiquated "crates") that reaching and returning from Durazzo is always a close thing by the roundabout route from Athens. Hence the R.A.F. is trying to substitute the Larissa approach, as shorter. Elvasan is on this route and is given as the second objective if finding or reaching Durazzo is impracticable. The British radio has made these bombings out to be connected with an imminent Greek attack on Elvasan, but the Greek lines are nowhere near that town yet, which is an Italian corps headquarters. It is possible, according to the Major, that the R.A.F. may now give up some of their "strategic" bombings of distant objectives in favor of short range work on the front line troops and close concentrations—as the Greeks have wished them to do all along. This would not be strictly according to the book, but in such warfare as is going on in Albania, with the odds so greatly against the Greeks in the air and in nearly every other respect except morale, it may be the thing to do, nevertheless. Major Craw didn't think so at first, but he does now. He hopes that some work of this kind will soon be done,—not sporadically, as in the past, in response to isolated and desperate Greek appeals, but systematically, and says that results should soon show whether the Italians can take it. If they can't, then continuation of this tactic will be indicated. News on the afternoon radio was to the effect that the Italian authorities began today to prepare the public for the possible fall of Bardia, admitting, too, that it would be a serious blow. In the evening, the news came that the whole of the position has fallen, with the exception of two forts. There are 20,000 prisoners!

January 6, 1941, Monday

The Yugoslav [Minister] is much insensed over the treatment of his nationals by the Greek police. He said they are practically regarded as enemies, and he told me some outrageous stories. He regards Mr. Maniadakis with special detestation, though he doesn't know him. I said that I realized many things are happening now in regard to foreigners which ought not to happen, and that it is not the Yugoslavs only who have to contend with suspicion. But I said, too, that I thought the Greek police has done a fine job in general in keeping down the elements which might lead to disorder in war-time,—"5th Columns" and the like. He had to agree to this, but added weakly (if properly) that he had to take cognizance of cases where his nationals are not treated rightly. . . . He is a nervous and fussy man. . . . Regarding the interior situation, he spoke of growing dissatisfaction in the army with the way the Government is handling—or mis-handling—relief and supply at the front, and also of the unpopularity of the regime, particularly of the Royal Family. He confirmed that the Crown Prince was booed on his recent trip to the front, and added that Prince Peter was too. Metaxas is accepted, and to a certain degree popular, even, on account of his strong stand; but his reference the other day to the 4th of August as the source of Greece's united resistance was "a mistake." The Minister thinks this statement was put out rather by Nicoloudis or Papadakis as a counter-blast to the growing unrest and criticism of the regime (coincident with the slowing down of the advance in Albania) but that it will only make things worse. I agree. There are too many Greeks who feel that their own willingness to forget partisanship for patriotism at this time is responsible for Greek unity, and by no means the 4th of August which they hate. To keep Greece unified now, in the face of the enemy, it would be better not to mention the 4th of August at all! . . . I asked the Minister his views on eventual Balkan unity, and as usual he stated that Yugoslavia has in the past been the only Balkan power sincerely to desire this. But he showed suspicion and dislike of each and all of the other Balkan nations! . . .

General Nicolaidis confirmed to me that Greece has been allowed to buy 30 P-36's. . . . A telegram had come in from the Department stating that the President has not accepted my resignation and wants me to stay here. So what did Smouch mean by "OK GO?" Well, I guess I must resign myself to one more disappointment, and of course there are many compensations. There is no place in the world we love being in more than Greece.

If she can keep her independence the next four years may be good ones for us.

January 7, 1941, Tuesday

Major Baker told me that he had had a long talk yesterday with Prince Peter, who is now chief of the Greek Staff's liaison section. The Prince gave him the first pessimistic view of the situation which we have had from Greek sources. He didn't deny that the Greek forces are still making small gains here and there, but he stated that the Italians have been successful in reinforcing their troops to a great degree, so that they have now nearly double their original numbers of troops in Albania,—upwards of 350,000 men. The British bombing of Valona and Durazzo has thus proved quite ineffective. He showed Major Baker a staff map of Valona, with the hits registered on it, and buildings appear very little damaged and jetties practically not at all. Hits are scattered all about in open spaces and even in fields. Evidently the British planes, which have no adequate bomb-sights, have been too few; to be really useful they would have to attack *en masse*, with their haphazard layings of sticks of bombs across the target. The Prince also said that the Italians have profited by the delay caused the Greeks by bad weather and insufficient transport to prepare heavily fortified positions, to which they have gradually retreated and on which they are now resisting, all along the line, with great tenacity. Meanwhile, the Italian air supremacy is causing great damage, particularly in the areas immediately in [the] rear of the Greek front lines. . . . Thus the picture he drew differs little from that given by Major Craw the other day, but coming from Greek headquarters it has special significance. The Greeks are obviously very much "up against it." I hope the British can rush over some much-needed material from Africa soon. Some of that Italian booty would help—particularly trucks.

January 8, 1941, Wednesday

Rumors came in all day to the effect that German concentrations are increasing. Also that some of these concentrations are on the Yugoslav border, while more Germans are now facing the Yugoslavs on the Austrian frontier. An attack on Yugoslavia by Germany at this time hardly makes sense. However, I did what I could to confirm these rumors. . . . It apears that the reinforcement of German troops in Rumania is a fact, and also that they have sent there a very important general who was one of the leaders in the *blitzkrieg* against Poland. But the Yugoslav Minister denied the concentrations against his country. Regarding the increased numbers of German troops in Rumania, he told me that the Premier asked to see him the other day and discussed the situation. Mr. Metaxas said that if these troops come south, he is 100 percent sure that, no matter whether the Bulgars ally themselves with the Germans or only allow the passage, the Turks will attack Bulgaria. He also said that he is 50 percent sure that Russia will move to prevent the Straits falling into German hands. On the other hand, he thinks the Germans may be planning to strike at Russia without dragging in the Balkans, from which they are now deriving economic benefits which war would destroy, at least for a time. He said, and Vukčević agreed with him, that Germany's ultimate aim in this region is the conquest of the Ukraine, and that her position enables her to move against it directly, without fear of attack from the rear—by Britain, for instance, or Turkey,—provided Bulgaria and Yugoslavia can be counted on to remain neutral. He looks for German action soon in any case, either north or south from Rumania. . . .

Considering these remarks it strikes me that several things appear to support the hypothesis that Russia will be the one to be attacked. The King of Rumania has recently spoken of "hopes" for the new year and intimated that his country can expect to be enlarged. It is hardly likely that he looks for aggrandizement in the direction of Bulgaria, or of Germany's other satellite, Hungary. Where else, then, than in Russia? And his speech becomes comprehensible if we suppose that Germany will seek to drag Rumania along into a Russian war by promising the restoration of Bessarabia. . . . Then there has been a recent declaration by King Boris of Bulgaria, that his country intends to preserve its neutrality. . . . In addition, there is the condition of the roads in Bulgaria, especially those leading to the Greek frontier, which is very bad, and not being improved, as would seem natural if armies were expected soon to move along them. . . . There are observers here, however, who think that all this talk about a growing conflict between the Russians and Germans in this region is merely British wishful thinking transformed into rumor.

January 9, 1941, Thursday

Worked on a telegram on the internal situation. The first flush of enthusiasm having worn off, the Greeks are back at their game of criticism and politics, and German propaganda is busy spreading the evil, so as to undermine morale. There is dissatisfaction over the amount of assistance rendered by the British, and over the superior feeding, lodging, and clothing of the British troops; over Mr. Metaxas's failure to form a coalition government and taking all the *kudos* of Greece's resistance for himself and his regime; over the turning over of so much relief work to the fascist and incompetent *Neolaia*; over the dismissal of Generals at the front, etc. etc. The "era of good feeling" is a thing of the past,—though doubtless all this doesn't spell disaster yet awhile. Morale will continue good so long as the Greek troops can go on advancing—and they are still doing a little of this. But the regime has failed to endear itself to the people, though it had a grand chance to do so after winning admiration and respect in the first days of the war. Now we can expect, even if Greece wins, to revert to the old internal struggle; and if there are reverses, the position of the Government, and the dynasty, too, may become very difficult. . . . When the Crown Prince and Prince Peter visited the front they were actually booed in certain instances, and elsewhere treated with indifference. I wish for the King's sake he had gone instantly to the front. Now it is too late.

January 10, 1941, Friday
The news of the day was the fall of Klissoura. Apparently the Italians have lost the mountain immediately behind it, and their forces in Tepeleni are in a badly exposed position, while the Klissoura defenders are retreating northwest toward Berati. The news comes at an opportune moment to bolster Greek morale. With the slowing down of the advance in Albania there has been a noticeable break-down in the "era of good feeling" and criticism of the Government on many counts has been going the rounds of the cafes.

January 12, 1941, Sunday
Note from the British Minister saying that Colonel Donovan[17] would arrive here from Egypt on Wednesday in care of an English Lt. Col. and that both of them would be staying with *him*. Also that Col. D. wants to see the King but that doubtless I can arrange that later! I immediately asked the British Minister and Col. Donovan, *and* the Lt. Col. *and* Lady Palairet, *and* Miss Palairet, *and* the Dunsanys[18] . . . to lunch on Thursday and asked the King too. I don't care whether any of them come, but it rather gets under my skin to have a man on special mission from the U.S.A. come to Athens and not only stay with the British Minister but let the British Minister be the first person to know of his coming. It is true that Johnson[19] in London telegraphed some time ago that the Colonel intended to visit the Near East and hoped to come to Athens, but

[17] William J. Donovan, hero of World War I and friend of Secretary of the Navy Frank Knox, travelling as Roosevelt's personal representative to assess Britain's needs against the Axis.
[18] Lord Edward John Dunsany, English author and lecturer, on a visit to Greece.
[19] Herschel Johnson, U.S. *Chargé d'Affaires* in Britain.

since then I have had no word whatever of his plans, except through Sir Michael. Part of the embarrassing position this puts me in may be covered up by my prompt invitation, since the King may not realize that I have been informed through Sir Michael and not direct. But I'll just have to stand the Colonel's staying at the British Legation! (Not that we want him here, but it will appear queer to many, I am positive). And last but not least our prompt invitation shows that *we* know what to do, anyway, if *he* doesn't.

January 13, 1941, Monday

Rumors kept coming in all day of German troops in Bulgaria—started by a statement from the Tass Agency in Moscow, over the radio, to the effect that "if there are German troops in Bulgaria, it is not with Russia's consent, since she has never been consulted," etc. Question: *are* there troops there? And if not, why deny the knowledge of it? . . . The Bulgarian Premier has made a pacific sort of speech, saying that Nazism, Fascism and Communism may be good for Germany, Italy and Russia, but that they are not for Bulgaria. She is apparently resolved to remain neutral and herself. The Cabinet members have likewise made speeches around the country, to quiet the alarm of the people, who don't want to go to war. But all this may be an elaborate throwing of dust in the eyes: an effort to convince Turkey, particularly, that if German troops come through Bulgaria, it is not the latter's fault. . . .

According to Greek Staff information, given today to Major Baker by Prince Peter, the German air assistance to Italy amounts now to 300 planes, all concentrated in Sicily and the toe of the boot, for attacks on British shipping. Evidently, a strong beginning has been made. . . . Another interesting item in today's news is the relinquishment of his command in Albania by General Soddu,[20] "for reasons of health," and his replacement by General Cavallero,[21] who retains his position of Chief of the General Staff. The British radio interprets this as another confession of failure, but it may equally well be that if Germany is coming in on the Greeks' flank and rear, and the Italians expect to make a *retour offensif* in the near future, they are merely making the shift of Generals which usually precedes such action. Troops don't often respond well to a general who has done nothing but retreat!

January 14, 1941, Tuesday

Major Craw had a meeting with Mr. Metaxas about aircraft, and told him his reactions on the question of air-fields and the little work being

[20] General Ubaldo Soddu, commander of the Italian forces in Albania.
[21] Count Ugo Cavallero, Chief of the Italian General Staff.

done on them, especially on holidays, when all the Greeks seem to knock off, despite the war. Mr. Metaxas said there is a shortage of labor, but seemed impressed by the criticism—which certainly is well taken—and said he would look into the matter himself.

General Wavell[22] and Air Marshal Longmore[23] flew over from Egypt for a meeting of strategists here tomorrow. A number of new planes for the British air force are also expected to arrive tomorrow. Received a telegram from Mr. Fish[24] in Egypt saying Colonel Donovan is coming over and will stay with the British Minister. Better late than never!

January 15, 1941, Wednesday

In the late afternoon Colonel Donovan, who had just arrived by plane from Egypt, came in to see me, and we had a long talk. He is representing the Secretary of the Navy, unofficially, and is observing and talking with all and sundry, especially in the Near East and Mediterranean, with an idea of finding out what is being prepared here and how we can help, and incidentally also to carry assurances that the United States means business. This last should be helpful to the British in the Balkans.... The Colonel, despite his nick-name of "Wild Bill" is a man of well ponderated judgment, of considerable intelligence, wide interests, and pleasant and rather restful manners! ... A fine type of American, who has made himself an important person by his intelligence and charm, a natural gentleman. I take it the "Wild Bill" must have been an affectionate appellation, probably due to the pride his soldiers took in his courage, for he is anything but "wild" in manner and appearance. He is the only American to have won the Congressional Medal, the D.S.C. and the D.S.M. A stunning record. Yet, since he is getting a bit stout, one might think him a mere "bon papa," if it weren't for those bright blue eyes!

Discussing his recent trip, he said that when he saw Churchill the latter was talking of "taking" the Irish bases. Donovan said, "If you do that, you will lose America," and advised him to wait till we begin sending convoys over, when *we* could ask and the Irish might yield. Rather good.... He told me that it is thought at home that Weygand may be induced to come in against the Italians in Africa, and he hopes to see him on his way home, if it can be managed unofficially. But he said the trouble with Weygand is that he has always been a second man, not a first, and may not be able to act without Petain when it comes to the point.... He confirmed my suspicions that Kennedy "ran out" on the British, being con-

---

[22] General Sir Archibald P. Wavell, British Commander-in-Chief, Middle East.
[23] Air Chief Marshal Sir Arthur Longmore, Air Officer Commanding-in-Chief, Middle East.
[24] Bert Fish, U.S. Minister to Egypt.

vinced they cannot stand up to the punishment much longer and that we are wrong to waste our substance in helping them. "It's what you might expect from Jim (sic) Kennedy," he said. "He's always been accustomed to selling short. Made his money that way." The Colonel himself emphasizes that wars are won by the imponderables, it takes heart, and this he thinks the British have got,—determination and valor. This, too, he said, is what is losing for the Italians. He has seen them fight in Abyssinia and now at Bardia and Tobruk. "It is overdone, this talk about their not fighting. They do fight, and fight well. But their heart isn't in this war." I think he has put his finger on it, at that. . . .

British industry, he said, has been slowed down perhaps 15 percent by the German attacks so far, but the proportion will have to be 50 percent to be effective. The next six months will tell the tale. German strategy is to press on Britain's jugular vein—her sea communications—and soften her up at the same time with air bombardment, till she is in no condition to resist invasion. British strategy, on the other hand, should be to make Germany extend herself and fight in many places at once, to use up her supplies of oil and stretch her communications to the limit, hitting her here, there and everywhere all the time. For this reason, and because the British realize it, he thinks a war here is inevitable, with Germany as well as Italy, and advisable too. He says, besides, that it is time to realize that avoiding provocation will never prevent attack from the aggressor states, which act in strict accordance with what they want, and make up provocation if it doesn't exist. Consequently Britain—and Greece—should take their own line, irrespective of any danger of attracting the lightning. Making Germany fight in the Near East would serve British interests by extending the Germans and making war on two fronts, which Germany doesn't want, and Greece should fall in with the grand strategy involved, risking her near future for the sake of the final aim, etc. etc. All pretty tough for the Greeks, but the Colonel says that to present this point of view here is the reason, principally, for Wavell's visit, and that the British Mission now in Ankara is likewise trying to get the Turks to come into the war without further delay. The British have their eyes on Salonica and on the Dardanelles. They know a move toward these places on their part will bring the German troops thundering down, but they think the Germans will come down this way, in any case, if it suits them to do so, and besides, it couldn't suit them more than the British to have the war extended; such, in a nutshell, was his talk.

January 16, 1941, Thursday

Luncheon at 1:30 for the King, Colonel Donovan, Lord and Lady Dunsany, Sir Michael and Lady Palairet, Col. Dykes, Major Craw and

Major Baker.... Col. Dykes comes from the British War Office and is escorting Col. Donovan around. The party went well, Colonel Donovan having a long talk with the King, which was the purpose of the luncheon.... I introduced Colonel Donovan to Mr. Metaxas at Headquarters, after he had had a talk with General Papagos.... The Greek front is practically inactive these days, unless it be that the Italians are getting the upper hand at last, and the Greek communiqués won't admit it!

January 17, 1941, Friday

Colonel Donovan came in to report on his talks with Mr. Metaxas and General Papagos. The former told him that he expects Germany to come to Salonica in the spring, and he replied with the point of view set out in my entry of Wednesday, also impressing on him, as he did on the King yesterday, that America means business in connection with helping the democracies. From General Papagos he got a list of the things Greece most badly needs, and we sent it off in a telegram "personal from Col. Donovan to Colonel Knox." I also sent off a long telegram of my own on the conference between Wavell and Longmore and the Chiefs here, based on Col. Donovan's information but not naming him directly. He O.K.'d it before I sent it. It spoke about the inability of Wavell to send more supplies up here from Egypt just now, chiefly on account of transportation difficulties, and also of the pressure being put on the Greeks to cooperate in operations, defensive or otherwise, as circumstances may dictate, against the Germans in this region. Also of the efforts of the British at Ankara. It is sure the Greek decision will be greatly affected by the Turkish attitude, but meanwhile the Greeks have yielded sufficiently to allow British reconnaissance in the north, which they haven't permitted so far for fear of exciting the Germans. It appears, too, that discussions turned on establishing British administrative control here of the Greek Army's transport and technical services, aiming at greater efficiency and coordination, and facilitation of an extended effort later. I mentioned, too, that the American attitude is having some weight here, but made no predictions. Finally I reported what the *Christian Science Monitor* man, Stevens, told me the other day on his return from Crete, that the British now have a whole division in the island, besides air forces.

January 18, 1941, Saturday

The British Minister called at the house about Colonel Donovan's plans. He said he and General Heywood felt that, in order to be most effective, he should go to Sofia and Belgrade at once, and I concurred absolutely. Only the Colonel had said he wouldn't go unless I agreed—hence this rather unnecessary visit. . . . In our talk in the forenoon he [Donovan] told me that Metaxas has agreed not only to allow British reconnaissance of Salonica, but has agreed as to the advisability of preparing an expeditionary force complete with transportation, to come to Salonica the minute the Danube is crossed by the Germans. In other words Greek caution has no objection to the British making preparations outside the country! But we mustn't be unfair. Greece is in a hot spot and knows it. To try and hold Salonica against the Germans with a handful of newly-landed British and a tired Greek flank and rear guard seems a desperate idea. On the other hand, if Turkey will strike on the east with a large and fresh army, the British might be able to stay long enough to get a firm foothold, and the "eastern front" might become a reality. It might even attract the Yugoslavs into amalgamation with it, to the ruin of the Italians. But the British seem now to feel that the Yugoslavs won't fight. As to Russia, Colonel Donovan told me that Cripps has advised London that the likelihood of intervention from that quarter becomes less every day, the Russians showing a tendency to believe now that a German drive to the Aegean would be more deleterious to the British than to them. . . . What we may see, indeed, in the near future (Colonel Donovan thinks by March 1st) is a clash between the British desire to extend the war and make Germany expend her forces in efforts on far and widely separated fronts, and the German desire (now that Italy seems unable to do it) to press down harder and harder on the vital communications of the Empire. The clash may coincide with a German assault on Britain, and with a British move in Abyssinia to free the southern flank of the Red Sea route. According to the papers, the war drums of Haile Selassie are already throbbing.

Athens, January 19, 1941.

Dear Franklin:

I wish to thank you for the kind words with which the Department recently refused my resignation. That resignation is and has been, of course, always yours to accept at any time, owing not only to the terms of the appointment but to the loyalty of the appointee. In addition, let me say that this is Inauguration Eve, and that our thoughts are with you and with the future, so much of which we are happy to know is in your hands.

On re-reading the pertinent paragraphs of my last letter, of Christmas Day, I find the present general situation here remarkably similar, only intensified. Things appear to be "hotting up." The most outstanding developments from this point of view are the coming of German airforces to the Mediterranean and the subsequent visit of General Wavell to Athens. In the former connection, it seems that Germany has decided to take over Italy's job of pressing on Britain's life-line in this section of the world, and if so, a move on her part to Salonica would make sense as a step toward securing bases in the Eastern Mediterranean to supplement those she now has in southern Italy and Sicily. Thus, new weight is given to the Greek Premier's opinion, which I have already reported, that a German drive southward from Rumania may be expected soon. On the other hand, British strategy must not only be prepared to meet this threat, but has always contemplated forming an Eastern Front, if possible, in order to extend and exhaust the enemy within the circle of the blockade. Consequently, immediately after expelling the Italians from Egypt, General Wavell has come to Athens not only to discuss with the Greeks the problem of supplying their army, but to seek their aid in the prompt preparation of Salonica for action against Germany, either defensive or offensive, as circumstances may dictate. At the same time, a British Military Mission now in Turkey is trying, I am told, to influence that country to enter the war on Britain's side without further delay. And this also makes sense in the premises, whatever be the success achieved.

To go on with the story, German forces in Rumania are increasing, though perhaps not to the extent alleged by British propaganda, and General Wavell's mission, while disappointing so far as concerns insuring immediate and adequate supplies to the Greek army (hence the continued appeals to us!), has overcome part of Greece's natural caution regarding giving provocation to Germany to set these forces in motion. The British argument in this connection seems to have been that in dealing with the Dictators it is no use not provoking them, since they will follow in any case what they conceive to be their interests, and if no provocation exists, will invent it, as Italy has so recently done with Greece; and that consequently the best policy is to "fear God and take your own part" rather than to fear Hitler and neglect opportunities. As a result, General Metaxas has consented to allow British reconnaissance of the Salonica district—hitherto barred to all members of the British forces—and, I understand also, to begin discussions aimed at bringing the Greek army administratively under British control, to facilitate supply and the operation of technical services as well as to prepare for eventual cooperation on an increased scale. In addition, I am told that he has concurred in the advisability of the British amassing forces immediately, and preparing transportation, to proceed to Salonica, the moment the Germans cross the Danube. Whether he agrees to anything more than this later, will doubtless largely depend on what Turkey decides to do.

Colonel Donovan has just left here for Sofia after a visit of three days, during which he did a grand job. He flew over from Egypt at about the same time as General Wavell, and stayed at the British Legation with the General, but I had him to lunch with the King and introduced him to the Premier, and without my long and repeated talks with him, both before and after his conversations with the authorities, I could have written little of the above, and none of it with so much confidence. He has been particularly useful, not only as a prominent American fresh from home, but as a Republican, in impressing these people with the unanimity as well as the importance of our attitude toward the war. (He conquered me at once by frankly giving you due credit for your leadership in this matter.) He has shown tremendous interest and a quick grasp of our more important immediate problems, and will certainly know whereof he speaks when he gets back to the United States. I hope you will have a moment to ask him about Greece. He was planning to go to the Albanian front, but the British Minister and General Heywood, Chief of the British Military Mission here, were anxious to rush him up to Sofia and Belgrade without delay, believing that the present moment is truly critical and that he might help to give the leaders in those capitals a very timely steer. When asked my advice on this matter, I fully concurred both in the change of plan and in the reasons for it. The Colonel now intends to visit the front later, before going on to Ankara.

As to the war in Albania, the papers are probably keeping you posted fairly accurately. Neither bad weather nor difficult terrain, nor enemy reinforcements, nor inferiority of equipment, nor deficiency in transport, nor lack of airplanes has yet halted the Greek advance. But these things have, taken all together, slowed the advance down, and it now seems definitely out of the question that the Italians can be ousted this winter. All the more reason for the Greeks to dread the future, with their flank and rear exposed to possible German onslaught! But the country at large knows nothing of the Government's previsions in this regard, and is quite unaware of British plans and even of General Wavell's visit. The morale of the people, as well as of the Army, remains remarkably high, God bless them both! The young Foreign Service Officer who brought our pouch down to Athens today from Yugoslavia, and who saw, *en route*, the destruction in Salonica caused by recent bombing, was astonished at the smiling faces he met with. I only hope they may still be smiling when this letter reaches you.*

Affectionately yours,
Lincoln MacVeagh (4)

* It has taken just 2 months for your last note—of Nov. 18th—to reach me.

January 20, 1941, Monday

Just after noon the Italians came over with two waves of 4 and 5 bombers each and strafed the Piraeus, obviously aiming at the 21 cargo ships in the harbor which arrived in convoy the other day—the biggest convoy to arrive so far. They dropped a lot of heavy bombs, rattling the windows even as far away as Athens. One empty cargo vessel was hit, and I am told the Greek coasting vessel *Chios* also, but most of the bombs fell in the poor quarter near the custom house, on the Castella, and in the sea. British pursuit planes came on the scene late because, though they were expecting the raid, the Italians concealed their approach in the clouds.

January 21, 1941, Tuesday

Salonica was raided again,—the Italians aiming at the oil installations along the shore, and the bombs all dropping in the sea. A hospital at Preveza was destroyed from the air, and a lot of workmen's houses at Volos.

January 22, 1941, Wednesday

Col. Donovan has seen the King of Bulgaria and will go to Belgrade tomorrow. He is getting plenty of publicity for his visits to the northern neighbors, and I imagine this is with his consent; quite in line with his purpose. The British radio now calls him actually "President Roosevelt's special emissary to Europe"!

January 23, 1941, Thursday

Mr. Melas told me of a Reuters report from Sofia to the effect that Colonel Donovan's papers have been stolen. Another similar report from Belgrade adds the information that he arrived there without a passport. The thing therefore has a look of being true. Mr. Melas was worried about what he might have had in his papers about Greece, and I said I knew he had a paraphrase of a telegram he had sent from here. He asked whether this contained anything which might be damaging to Greece, and I said "No"—but not very confidently! All I could remember was that it discussed supplies—which is all right. When I got back to the office, I looked up the paraphrase in question, and found that at the end, where the Colonel expresses his hope that the President may send supplies to Greece, he adds that this might help to bolster morale here for defense or *attack*. This might sound suspicious to the Germans, though they are not mentioned in any close connection. At the beginning of the message it is said that Metaxas thinks the Germans may come down this way and that in that case the Bulgars and the Yugoslavs might not resist. All in all, the message is not informative, in the sense that it tells what the Germans are not likely to know already. It *is* informative to Col. Knox and F.D.R. as emphasizing a situation which I and doubtless others have been reporting—and coming from him may be of special value. . . . Nevertheless, if he has lost it and the Germans have got it, it doesn't help any, and that's a fact, not to speak of the memoranda he may have made on his talks here and in Egypt! I telegraphed Mr. Lane in Belgrade for information at once, Mr. Melas advising against the telephone. We'll see what we see, but I'm afraid it's bad. As Cannon said, the affair illustrates the risks of having these unofficial officials trotting round loose.[25] . . . The news of the day continues to be the fall of Tobruk. The British indicate, too, that the Italians are about to launch a big counterattack against the Greeks in the northern sector. Cavallero is about to prove himself! The sector is well chosen, as a success here would move the Italians along the shortest road to the frontier and Salonica as well as compel the Greeks to give up their pressure toward Valona and Berati. I wonder if the latter have enough troops to withstand a big push.

January 24, 1941, Friday

Mr. Lane telegraphed from Belgrade that the report of Colonel Donovan's having had his "papers" stolen is untrue. He lost, says Mr. Lane, only his passport and wallet. I telephoned this to Mr. Melas and he was much relieved. So was I.

January 25, 1941, Saturday

There are no new developments. The Italians are counterattacking, and one may be allowed to suspect that they are having some success, the Greek reports are so laconic. However, the Greek Staff says it thinks the Italians are in no condition to mount a really serious offensive and Major Baker is inclined to agree. . . . The Staff talks between the British and the Turks in Ankara have been terminated, and the press and radio report complete agreement, as usual. However, the British here don't seem very happy while Enis Bey appears quite content! So I deduce the Turkish point of view prevailed, and there will be no Turkish entry into the war at present. Enis said that the Turks feel (1) that England should hurry up and finish the campaign in North Africa promptly, so as to dispose of greater forces here than are now available, and (2) that it would be a mistake to provoke Germany in the absence of any sure indication that

---

[25] According to one authoritative source, the "loss" of Donovan's papers in Sofia was a ruse, planned by British and American intelligence to deceive the Germans. See William Stevenson, *A Man Called Intrepid* (New York, 1976), p. 208.

the latter's troops in Rumania are otherwise than defensively intended. Just as he left, I asked him once more whether Turkey would attack Bulgaria in case the latter allowed the German troops to pass through against Greece, and once more he said that he has no information but supposes that his Government would regard such an action as threatening Turkey's vital interests, and would decide to fight at once rather than later.

January 27, 1941, Monday

News came from various sources that Colonel Donovan has gone to the front—Koritza and Jannina—and will not arrive in Athens till tomorrow or the next day. No radio news to speak of. London has had a whole week without air-raids, which certainly looks queer,—and sinister. . . . About 30 prominent Germans here are said to have left the country in the last day or so, and this also has a bad look. Anyhow it frightens the Greeks. Mr. Metaxas has been sick at home for a week and the rumors are now very alarming. Today I heard that he has had three blood transfusions. However, H.M. nodded most cheerfully as he passed me in his car this afternoon and didn't look a bit as if he were expecting his Premier's demise.

January 29, 1941, Wednesday

Poor Mr. Metaxas died at 7:00 a.m. His illness had too many complications for his fighting spirit—Androulis told me, when I saw him this evening, that the last three days have been hopeless, but the old man fought on, and everyone hoped for a miracle. The poison from his throat infection apparently spread and an old ulcer of the intestine broke and caused an internal hemorrhage, weakening him beyond repair. . . . The King acted quickly to keep the government going, and by nine o'clock Mr. Korizis[26] had taken the oath as Premier. Proclamations by him and the King assured the people that there would be no other changes and that the policies of Mr. Metaxas would continue to be followed. . . . The appointment of Korizis was a great surprise to everyone, but also apparently a very clever move on the King's part. He is a respected and experienced financier and administrator, a public man without being a politician, a member of the group which has supported Metaxas but with friends outside that group, a royalist who is not hated by the Venizelists. In addition, he is the King's man—has no pretensions to having restored

---

[26] Alexander Korizis, prominent financier, and Governor of the National Bank of Greece.

the King to power or kept him in it, or anything of that sort, so that the old dyarchy of King and Dictator is now a thing of the past, and the King is at last head man! If now the war is not lost and Greece continues free, the King's success in the future will probably depend on how he goes about restoring certain liberties to the people. . . .

Colonel Donovan came in and told me about his trip to Sofia and Belgrade, where he had a most interesting time. He saw both King Boris and Prince Paul[27] and talked most frankly to them about American aid going to the countries which do not join or assist the Axis, and not going to those which do. He also had a tour of the front on his way back, going to Koritza from Salonica, and coming on down to Athens by Jannina. . . .

In the afternoon, Mr. Metaxas's body was moved to the Cathedral, for lying-in-state. The procession passed the chancery—mechanized caisson, gun and coffin draped in the Greek flag, the new Premier walking bareheaded behind, then the Government, troops, Youth Movement, and leading citizens, all in the cold drizzle half rain and half snow. . . .

I took Colonel Donovan round to the Palace, where he had a talk with the King, who told him that the appointment of Mr. Korizis was his own idea, and that Mr. Metaxas had never been willing to discuss the question of a successor. He also said that the new Premier will not be swayed by German pressure or intrigue (the British had expressed some fears to the Colonel on this score). Later I took Colonel Donovan to call on the Turkish Ambassador who went so far as to say that his country regards both Bulgaria and Greece as lying within her "zone of security." But this is almost a catch phrase now. More interesting was his statement to the Colonel that he believes Germany has already lost the war. . . . I then took the Colonel on to Headquarters and introduced him to Mr. Korizis, who was very tired and brought the conversation to a close rather rapidly, after asking a few questions about Bulgaria and Yugoslavia and expressing a hope that Greece may receive some needed supplies from us.

January 30, 1941, Thursday

Colonel Donovan came round to the office to say good-bye in the forenoon. . . . He thinks that Germany will not attack in the Balkans if she is sure of the united resistance of Bulgaria, Yugoslavia and Turkey, and that though these states are divided on many counts, a common desire for American economic and moral assistance now and after the war might lead them to get together to resist further German aggression or demands, if the President should propose it. He also thinks that Germany may

[27] Prince Paul, Regent of Yugoslavia.

decide to defeat Greece and drive Britain out of her stronghold here not by passing through Bulgaria, which might precipitate war with Turkey, but by reinforcing Italy in Albania.

January 31, 1941, Friday

Left the house at a little after three for the Cathedral, with only the officers of the Legation, as ladies were not invited. . . .

The church service was not as impressive as requiems used to be under Chrysostomos, largely because Chrysanthos has altered the music, and partly, I think, because some of the best singers have been mobilized. The King, Crown Prince, Prince Peter, Prince Philip,[28] and Princesses Catherine, Nicholas and Alexander, and the latter's mother, Mrs. Manos, were also there. The German Minister did not attend. He sent two secretaries only (his Military Attaché is in Berlin, doing something nefarious for Greece I have no doubt), and for himself alleged an indisposition. After the ceremony there was a long wait and great confusion at the front door before the cortège got started for the cemetery, and when it did get going was very listless and straggling. We heard no music, though the diplomats walked immediately behind the Government and could see the coffin on its gun-carriage not far ahead of them. I was told later that there were three bands far out ahead. The streets were deeply thronged and the windows full of spectators, looking white and unhappy, but only a few hysterical people wept. The people seemed more shocked and apprehensive than sorrowful. At the cemetery, which I entered for the first time (catching sight of the Sleeping Lady,[29] really an excellent piece of work), there was a band at the portal playing Chopin's funeral march, none too well. Evening was coming on by this time. We walked a long way, almost to the cemetery's other end, before the head of the procession reached the Metaxas family plot. The paths were narrow, so the diplomats were halted a good way from the actual grave, and very near the platoon of soldiers which suddenly let off a very ragged but ear-splitting volley. Two more better ones followed, but there was no bugle, and I don't know why the shots were not fired actually over the grave as is customary. On leaving the cemetery we found the cars were all clustered in a great dusty parking place outside the portal, and the scramble to find one's own in the hundreds that were there reminded me of experiences at New Haven after a foot-ball game. It took all the feeling of solemnity out of the occasion.

[28] Prince Philip (Duke of Edinburgh), son of Prince Andrew and cousin of King George II.
[29] A monument by the Greek sculptor Halepas.

February 4, 1941, Tuesday

Drove out with Mummy to Kifissia to call on Mrs. Metaxas. . . . Mrs. Metaxas was wonderful,—practical and clear-eyed. She was sitting on the green sofa where Grazzi and the Premier discussed the Italian ultimatum on the fatal morning of October 28th and told us how the servant had announced the French Minister, instead of the Italian; Mr. Metaxas couldn't think what Mr. Maugras could want at 3 a.m. but went downstairs in his dressing-gown, nevertheless. Mrs. Metaxas heard loud voices, and finally her husband came upstairs again in a hurry, saying "It's war." That was the first time she knew it was the Italian who had come.

CHAPTER

VI

"A Gallant and Suicidal Resistance"

As MacVeagh soon reported to the President, Metaxas' death appeared to "decapitate" the Greek state, leaving King George "all the dictator that there is...." With each passing day, a German drive southward appeared more and more certain, with disastrous consequences for Greece. The MacVeaghs prepared for a possibly hasty departure from Athens.

February 8, 1941, Saturday

Another telegram from Earle, sent yesterday, said that the British in Sofia are expecting the Germans to come through Bulgaria soon. The road to the Greek border (the big one down the Struma valley) is being repaired, and it is estimated that the Germans can cross the country in less than ten days. The British Military Attaché in Sofia (our old blustering friend, Ross) told Earle that he is packing to leave—which I don't think is true. (He can kid as well as bluster.)

Major Baker hadn't been able to see Blunt, so I went over to the British Legation and had a talk with Sir Michael. He said he had no such alarming news from Bulgaria, but admitted to being apprehensive about the situation there. He could see no logic in the Germans attacking Salonica —no good to be gotten out of it for them. But he could see their wanting to fix things so that the British can't go there. This the military occupation of Bulgaria would do, and by not taking the initiative against Greece, the Germans could avoid risking a war with Turkey. As to Turkey's attacking Bulgaria if the Germans do come through against Greece, he said this is still only likely and not certain, and he hoped Colonel Donovan's talks in Ankara helped to stiffen the Turks.... The Minister asked me what I thought of the internal situation here. He himself is worried. He said the King told him the day before Metaxas died that he intended to broaden the Government, but now he is afraid that the King has given this idea up. I asked why he thought that, and he said Maniadakis had told Bowman (the owner of the marble quarries of Penteli) that there will be no cabinet changes. I said I thought this was merely repeating the order of the day, as it were, and that gradually and in due time changes will be made. But Sir Michael said he feared Mr. Maniadakis' ambition and that the country which stood for him with Metaxas would not stand for him alone. He said he intended to put the matter up to the King this afternoon when he came to tea. . . . The King has been to the front at last, and at rather a psychological moment. The papers are fulsome in their reports. Later on, I have no doubt, we shall get the "low down". . . . Incidentally the first change in the Metaxas regime has already occurred. Mr. Kanellopoulos has been relieved of the command of the Youth Movement and replaced by an Army officer. Immediately after the Dictator's death, a proclamation included the Youth Movement among the things that would suffer no change. I reminded Sir Michael of this, but he still was pessimistic. Personally, I think that once the King gets an idea he sticks to it, and he certainly thinks the Metaxas cabinet can be improved. . . .

February 9, 1941, Sunday

I went round to the Turkish Embassy and had a long talk with Enis Bey, about the Bulgarian situation. He said that all his recent information tends to indicate that the Germans intend to pass through Bulgaria, and that they will start the movement before the end of this monh. He also said that he thinks the Turks will strike at Bulgaria as soon as this movement starts and will not wait to see what happens, i.e. whether the troops stop in Bulgaria or go on to Salonica. He said, "Of course the Germans may inform us and the Greeks that the move is not in anyway intended against us, but who will believe them?" As to Russia, he seemed not to have had the information of his Military Attaché—told to Major Baker yesterday—that the concentrations on the Caucasus front have been increased recently. But he still feels that the Germans may have seduced the Russians by offering them the bears in the Persian and Indian woods in exchange for a free hand at the Dardanelles, and he expressed a belief that in spite of the certainty that if she wins the war, Germany will attack Russia next, the present leaders of Russia are quite capable of falling for the bait, since they are "not normal, but half crazy." He has been in Russia, *en poste*. . . . Enis also thinks the British will start coming to Salonica the moment the Germans begin their movement, as Colonel Donovan told me Mr. Metaxas agreed to their doing. He doesn't think the Yugoslavs will do anything to help. . . . His attitude was somewhat fatalistic, as usual. . . .

February 10, 1941, Monday

The Greeks are apparently stymied in Albania but report beating back another Italian counter-attack today. They keep up their courage remarkably well.

February 11, 1941, Tuesday

Craw reported that, for the past 3 days, German planes have been reconnoitering the country east of Salonica. . . . There was an alert about one o'clock, but the plane which caused it got no nearer than Marathon. . . . I went to the Grande Bretagne to see the Prime Minister, at his request at 7:30 just as another alert was sounded. He gave me a long letter conveying a new appeal for supplies, chiefly planes. We refuged in the cellar of the G.B. where we found the King, Prince Paul, Prince Peter, General Papagos, General Papademas,[1] Count Mercati, Mr. Mavroudis, Mr. Tambacopoulos, Mr. Maniadakis, etc. I had a long talk with the King. He had a fine visit to the front, but came back hurriedly on account of news from Bulgaria. He says he is almost certain the Bosche will come right through against Greece. But Greece will resist, even though the British so far have offered no help but one regiment of artillery, and the Turks are a doubtful quantity still. He said the Yugoslavs show a curious lethargy, like a rabbit fascinated by a snake. . . . Greece will push the Italians back to the Skoumli [River] if they can, and then hold that line with a part of their forces and send the rest back to face the Germans. In northern Greece now he has only three divisions. . . . He seemed tired, but spoke like a gallant leader, who will not let his country's honor and loyalty go down, even if she must suffer. . . . I admired him a lot. Metaxas's death has obviously deprived him of a great source of reliance and confidence. Also he trusted him to handle the Germans if and when need should arise. He himself, he said, is hated by them, because they once thought his having served in the German army would keep him at least neutral in this war. . . . The air-raid lasted about 45 minutes. . . . After dinner I sat up late concocting a telegram about what the King said, and trying to frame it in such a way as to give some effective support to the pathetic appeals of the Greeks for supplies. So far they have got precious little out of us, and they are by no means behind the British, or any one else, in heroism and devotion to the very ideals we ourselves love best.

[MacVeagh's telegram concluded:]

No less than Finland this country is fighting in civilization's front line and she faces even far greater odds today than those she met so stirringly

---

[1] General Nikolaos Papademas, Under-Minister of the Army.

last October. I trust our authorities will not be insensible of such heroic resolution. Greece's failure to obtain any planes whatever from the United States of America after 3 months of effort has been heartbreaking. (1)

February 17, 1941, Monday
Got a letter from "Wild Bill" Donovan . . . saying that the Germans prevented his going to Syria and Morocco—doubtless by forcing the French to refuse visas. Too bad, as he was particularly hoping to see Weygand. He promises me a copy of his report on his trip, with his estimate of the Mediterranean situation, which he says has been read and "concurred with" by General Wavell and Admiral Cunningham. . . . The Greek advance, if any, is slow. Their radio is growing expert at saying nothing in high-sounding phrases. The situation remains that the bulk of the Greek army is fighting deep in Albania while the German preparations to occupy Bulgaria with a powerful force continue, and Turkish and Yugoslav action in such a case remains undetermined. In addition, despite what the King and Korizis say privately—which is probably the truth—there are many Greeks who doubt whether Greece will not be prevailed upon to make a separate peace. . . . At 10:45 p.m. the British radio announced that Turkey and Bulgaria have signed a joint declaration expressing their adherence to the policy of non-aggression. The Germans are already, according to the radio, saying that this means that Turkey will not move if German troops enter Bulgaria. I am reminded of what the Bulgar told the Brazilian last Thursday, that Turkey had given Von Papen[2] assurances that she would not fight unless attacked! If this means that the Germans can come on down to the Greek frontier with a Turkish *laissez-passer*, it is bad news, indeed.

February 18, 1941, Tuesday
Went to see the Turkish Ambassador. He said the declaration is not significant, and ill-timed. Some time ago a peaceful gesture toward Bulgaria might have been a good thing, but not now. He believes his Government has made a psychological error. He talked a lot about how the Bulgars cannot be trusted, and again reiterated his belief that Turkey must come into the war to prevent German domination. He said he saw Mr. Mavroudis at 7 o'clock last night, and that Mr. M. said over and over again that the Greek Government is fully confident that Turkey will fulfill her obligations. These obligations, Enis Bey pointed out, have been expressly mentioned in the declaration as not affected by its terms; and he again stressed Turkey's knowledge of the danger inherent for her in a

---

[2] Franz von Papen, German Ambassador to Turkey.

German occupation of Bulgaria, and cited the Turkish press. He said the only really important sequel to the declaration would be the necessity of explaining it. He seemed quite unhappy about it, but my question is to what degree he is representative of his Government's feelings. It may be he is expressly kept in ignorance of these in order to keep the Greeks in the dark more easily.... He told me that Mr. Mavroudis denied that the Germans have made any representations here regarding peace or mediation. The German Minister *did* call on Mr. Korizis, but it was only his formal call on the occasion of the latter's assuming the Premiership. During their conversation, however, Mr. Mavroudis said, the Premier told the German Minister that he intended following Mr. Metaxas's policy in foreign affairs to the letter, adding that he hoped Greco-German relations would continue undisturbed as heretofore.... After seeing Enis Bey, I went to the Foreign Office and had a talk with Mr. Delmouzo. He did not seem to be disturbed about the declaration, which he said did not affect the situation fundamentally, since Turkey is still obligated under her pacts with Britain and Greece. He thought the declaration was an attempt to pour oil on troubled waters, but that while it is well-intentioned, it has been made at the wrong time, and will probably only incite the Bulgars to receive the Germans and not discourage them. The Turkish Ambassador said that the British were responsible for the move, and that it is just another instance of their misunderstanding of how to treat the Bulgars. When I pressed him, he said "Well, at least the British could have stopped it and didn't." Mr. Delmouzo, on the other hand, said that the British Ambassador at Ankara advised against the draft as finally drawn up, since it might be misunderstood, but Mr. Saraçoglu[3] went ahead, saying he thought the Bulgars would refuse to sign anyhow, because of the reservations regarding existing obligations. Then the Bulgars not only signed, but did so with gusto, obviously because they saw a chance to claim a diplomatic achievement, and the Turks are left with the necessity of explaining. He said he thought the chief harm would be the encouragement which the seeming aloofness of Turkey would give to the elements in Bulgaria which are working for the Germans, but that essentially the situation in the Balkans remains unchanged.... The British radio tonight insists that England was kept *au courant* of the Turkish talks with Bulgaria (which appears to be true) and that Turkey will remain true to her obligations, which may or may not be, though I think it would be very un-Turkish to sell out an ally.

[3] Sükrü Saraçoglu, Turkish Minister for Foreign Affairs.

February 20, 1941, Thursday

Called on Mr. Mavroudis at the Grande Bretagne, to talk about the Bulgar-Turkish declaration. He said he thought the Germans helped to put it over, and that it is a defeat for British diplomacy, constituting a kind of public notice to Germany that she can occupy Bulgaria without risking trouble with Turkey. Essentially, he said, he can't see it changes anything, because he feels the Turks would never have attacked Bulgaria anyway, just to stop the Germans entering. The Turks still hold to their actual obligations. But the psychological effect here and in England, too, is deplorable. ... He thinks occupation of Bulgaria will now follow, but holds to his idea that Germany will not attack Greece, since this would really force Turkey's hand and by bringing her into the war give the British a chance to form an Eastern Front. ...

February 22, 1941, Saturday

I forgot to note in this diary that the other day I received a very warm letter from the Premier stating that the American Government has now promised to let Greece have 30 Grumman planes during the month of March. He thinks my efforts are largely responsible for this, and I shouldn't be surprised if my last telegrams did jog it along. I don't know what Grumman planes are, but Major Baker says he thinks they are a fairly recent type.

Athens, February 23, 1941

Dear Franklin:

As you certainly know, and as my telegrams have emphasized, developments since I last wrote have been uncomfortable for this country. German concentrations in Rumania have reached an imposing figure, and German troops may already be entering Bulgaria. Greece's great friend Turkey has chosen this of all times to show an undetermined attitude (to quote a euphemism of the King's), and Great Britain has apparently made no preparations "to come to Salonica the moment the Germans cross the Danube," as I wrote the Greeks hoped she would. It is consequently felt here almost unanimously that a German military occupation of Bulgaria is due to be realized very soon without opposition from anybody. But as to what will happen next there is a noticeable difference of opinion among informed persons.

The Under-Minister for Foreign Affairs thinks Germany intends to stand on the defensive in the Balkans and to occupy Bulgaria merely as the best means of closing Europe's back door. He thinks she has no wish to attack Greece, for the reason that this would infallibly bring Turkey into the war and give England the chance to form the Eastern Front she is supposed to desire. He expects diplomatic pressure on Greece to force her to make peace with Italy, but for the present at least, no assault. On the other hand, both the King and the Greek Staff regard a German drive as overwhelmingly probable. They interpret the heavy present German concentrations as offensively designed, and see no reason why Salonica should not be among the objectives. In fact, they foresee a tremendous development of the war here this spring, with Germany taking the initiative.

Clearly, anything like inside knowledge of German plans is lacking here, or responsible opinion would not differ so widely. As to Greece herself, the situation is less obscure, though unpromising. Whether she is to be faced with pressure merely, or with an attack by the dreaded German army, she is certain to find herself handicapped by the recent death of General Metaxas, her one available "strong man." His passing has, as it were, decapitated the State. The King is now the dictator, or rather, all the dictator that there is, the new premier being only a competent administrator. The King's policy is now to carry on from where General Metaxas left off, in foreign as well as domestic affairs. The latter had planned to resist any German aggression exactly as he resisted the Italian, in the belief that honor requires it and that, in any case, England is bound to win the war with America's help. The King has told me that he has decided to continue with this plan. But whether he can carry the people with him is a question. I believe that if the Germans attack this country brusquely, he has a chance of doing so, at least to begin with; Greece is still in her heroic mood. But the King's character is hardly the kind to keep a volatile people united in a long struggle against odds. On the other hand, if the Germans refrain from attacking and, with their troops at the border, begin one of their well-known campaigns to soften up and disorganize the country with a war of nerves, his leadership, which is now resting almost wholly on the character and achievements of a dead man, will offer an ideal target for intrigue.

I am afraid Greece is in for some bad days whatever happens. Meanwhile she is trying to force the Italians in Albania back to a shorter line in order to free some troops to face the Germans, if need be, in the north. To man her lines there she has now only three divisions and some "fortress troops." Helping her in Albania, where the weather and fortified mountains 6,000 feet high still impede her advance, she has at present seven squadrons of British planes. This modest figure may be worth your notice. North of Crete, there are no British troops whatever in Greece with the exception of this air force and its groundlings. Today's paper, in connection with Anthony Eden's[4] visit to Cairo, quotes the London *Times* as

---

[4] Anthony Eden, British Minister for Foreign Affairs.

saying, "The immediate role of Great Britain should be the intensification of material assistance effectively given to the valiant Greeks." One wonders whether this is another case of being too late. . . .

Affectionately yours,
Lincoln MacVeagh (2)

February 24, 1941, Monday

Mr. Pezmazoglou (Stephen) came in and told Kohler that Anthony Eden came to Athens Saturday and was here most of yesterday. I called on the British Minister to find out if this is true. He said he could only tell me that Mr. Eden is *now* in Cairo. But it was clear from his hesitation and embarrassment that the story is correct. Sir Michael's attitude apparently was that it is for the Foreign Secretary himself to reveal his movements if he wants them known. However, the story is all over Athens. . . . Mr. House was told in addition, that General Wavell came too, and that the General and Mr. Eden had a two-hour conference with Korizis.

February 25, 1941, Tuesday

The Germans do not seem to have begun their drive into Bulgaria yet, but many continue to come in in civilian clothes. The British radio again spoke of the improvements to Bulgarian roads under German supervision. . . . Mr. Saraçoglu's statement about the Turco-Bulgarian "pact" which the British are lauding to the skies, seemed to me rather equivocal, but Mr. Delmouzo (with the Turkish Ambassador standing by) said he could not be more definite since that would be convicting himself of making a meaningless move altogether. Perhaps. Personally, I believe that Mr. Mavroudis is right, and that the Turks have simply made explicit the fact that they do not intend to attack Bulgaria for letting the Germans enter their territory. But I also think it very *likely* that the Turks will fight if Germany attacks Greece thereafter. They could, of course, allege, if the Bulgars refrain from moving, that the Greco-Turkish pact does not apply in such circumstances. But the Anglo-Turkish accord is another matter. I find it hard to believe in Turkish bad faith. It would have no precedent that I know of. As the Turkish press is saying today, stung by some of the Axis propaganda, Turkey is not Italy! At any rate, I shall go on believing that if Germany drives to Salonica, the Turks will fight, giving Britain her chance of coming to the Dardanelles, and as the British Minister said yesterday, attacking the Rumanian oil fields from Turkish bases.

February 26, 1941, Wednesday

Went to see the Premier, and gave him the $2,000 check for the Red Cross,[5] and then talked about the situation. He said he is *"plus que sûr"* that if Germany occupies Bulgaria she will come on to Salonica, and that in that case Greece will resist even if she has to resist alone. On the other hand, he feels certain that Britain will send aid, which Greece's resistance will give her time to do, and that Turkey will fulfill her obligations to Great Britain. Furthermore, he said, news from Yugoslavia these past few days has been distinctly more encouraging.

February 27, 1941, Thursday

Was received by the King in his office at the Grande Bretagne. He told me—asking me to keep it absolutely secret—that Eden, Dill[6] and Wavell did come here last week-end, but that few people in the Government know about it. They are expected to come back again after their visit to Turkey is over, and will make *that* arrival openly. The Greeks will receive them as if they had not come before and as if the coming was on the spur of the moment, as it were, and not premeditated—all this, I take it, because when they were here last week they talked military plans for defense against Germany in anticipation of their talks with Turkey, while visiting Athens *after* Ankara may appear natural and less compromising to the Greeks in German eyes. Or perhaps it is felt that *two* visits, necessitated by the fact that what is going on is joint planning between the three countries, would give this fact away too clearly. Anyway them's the facts. The British, he said, are going to send troops here in anticipation of German attack, but so far only three divisions are contemplated with accessories. Some troops are already *en route*. They are coming to the Piraeus and will be considered as auxiliaries to the air-force, so as not to reveal their true purpose to the Germans. They are not being sent to Salonica because British troops there might provoke Germany (and couldn't be so easily camouflaged as air-service auxiliaries, either) and also because unless Yugoslavia comes into the war on Greece's side, the King thinks it would be impossible to hold Salonica against a German drive through Bulgaria. Against such a drive the Metaxas line could not hold, and the Struma line might be turned on the north. Consequently, the Greeks are thinking of holding the Vermion line west of the Vardar; the troops in Albania to carry on as long as possible against Italy. If Yugoslavia, which so far has said only that an attack on Salonica would have to

[5] A contribution from the Greek-American community of Roanoke, Virginia, for the Greek Red Cross.
[6] General Sir John Dill, Chief of the British Imperial General Staff.

be considered as vitally affecting her interests, really agrees to resist such an attack on Greece's side, then, of course, the Struma line (Lake Doiran —Amphipolis) might do.... H. M. said "I'm afraid I was rather excited when we talked last" (see the entry for February 11th) and I replied "No wonder you were." I think he now thinks the situation is just as grave but that Greece herself is not so badly off for friends as she seemed. He is a most decent and likeable soul....

During the forenoon the Brazilian Minister paid me another of his visits.... He told me that he has news from the Swiss Legation that German officials here are packing. We have heard this before, but that is no reason for doubting it now.

March 1, 1941, Saturday

News came early in the forenoon that Bulgaria would sign the Tripartite Pact at Vienna, and the British radio at 3 P.M. announced that she had done so. Telegrams came in from Sofia and Bucharest confirming still further the impression already existing that Germany is about to enter Bulgaria with armed forces....[7]

Weather in Albania is very bad indeed, but the Greeks hope to continue to push the Italians back when conditions improve.

March 3, 1941, Monday

News on last night's late radio was to the effect that Eden did arrive during the afternoon, and was immediately received by the King.... The Bulgarian Prime Minister told his Parliament that the German troops to enter Bulgaria would only be a few and that they would only come in for the sake of Balkan peace and would soon be withdrawn. (This would seem to be another way of saying that they are only coming in to force Greece to join the Axis.) Also, he said, the Germans are not asking Bulgaria to do anything not in keeping with her friendly relations, which she intends to maintain, with all countries. Most of the deputies gave him the vote of approval he wanted, but it is said that some twenty voted "no," and about five who wanted to speak were howled down, and a row was going on when adjournment was taken.

Today the British air force has news that there are already five German divisions in Bulgaria, and several hundred planes. Greece has now about five divisions in the Salonica area, one of them recently organized; the British may send three, but it may take two months to get here! The holding up of the Greek offensive in Albania means that no troops can be

[7] German forces entered Bulgaria and occupied Sofia on March 1, 1941.

withdrawn from there. Altogether the Greek ground forces plus British are desperately inadequate to hold back both Germans and Italians. They may give a good account of themselves in the mountains if they can fall back in good order. But the overwhelming German air-power is likely first to destroy the R.A.F. on its few and poor landing-fields in Greece, second [to] smash all the vital centers of command and supply, and finally [to] disrupt communications and terrorize the troops. It will take superhuman qualities for the Greeks to bear up long under that kind of punishment. They may have such qualities and the British may be able to give more help than seems now to be likely. But we should not give way to wishful thinking. A march through Greece is not easy for any army against guerrilla resistance, but the Germans are tough and the blitz from the air may be truly overwhelming. . . .

Just after breakfast, the British Minister called up to say that Mr. Eden would like to see me, and we fixed on 11:30 for me to be at the Legation. . . .

I found Mr. Eden very easy and pleasant, a sartorial symphony with a definitely sixth-form dating, but not at all silly though also not particularly impressive. I liked him at once and felt he was on the ball, though perhaps at the moment the ball is between his pony's legs and he doesn't know how to get at it with his mallet. . . . He said he was very pleased with his reception in Turkey, and that the Turks are fully loyal. They want more military equipment of all kinds but are generously willing to admit that Greece should have priority at present. They realize Germany's menace to them, and are not taken in by Von Papen. He then went on to say that he believes what Germany is after is to reduce Greece to subjection, peacefully or by arms, in order to get use of her territory for air and other bases. If she attacks Greece, it will be in about a month's time, however, because of the bad weather and roads in the Balkans. During that month the usual diplomatic and other "pressure" will be applied. But he is confident that Greece will stand firm. Britain will send Greece all the aid she can, too, beginning with planes, and for Germany to come through Greece will "not be very easy." I said "You will send troops" and he replied that he is making no such statement to anyone, and that what comes will be considered as connected with the air-force (what the King said the other day; nevertheless I understand that the troops and tanks already arrived). He was so transparent in this matter that we both laughed while dropping the subject. Perhaps more interesting was his comment that even if the Germans occupy Greece it will be of no particular effect on the war, since Britain by that time will be "sitting pretty" in Africa. To fight her way to the domination of the whole Balkans will do Germany no good, since she will be enclosed in the circle of the British blockade, and as he put it "playing football in her own cabbage-patch." Regarding Russia, he said Sir Stafford Cripps had reported to him in Ankara that the Soviets are not likely to make any move at this time. Yugoslavia remains unable to make up her mind. This he said he believes is what underlies the inability of the Turks and Yugoslavs to get together. I gave him a paraphrase of a message received this morning from Mr. Lane. This message told of conversations with the Yugoslav Premier and the Turkish Ambassador, and carried forward a subject which Lane had discussed already with Mr. Campbell, the British Minister in Belgrade who is now here, namely this same inability of the Turks and Yugoslavs to achieve a meeting of minds over the question of opposing German aggression. Mr. Eden said that in Ankara he had run across the same thing, and that Mr. Saraçoglu had said to him that whenever he met the Yugoslav Minister there, there was a *malentendu*. Mr. Eden called Mr. Campbell in to where we were talking (in Sir Michael's study) and they discussed the problem for awhile and decided that they had better try to establish a bridge, as it were, between the two, through the medium of Campbell in Belgrade and Knatchbull-Hugessen[8] in Ankara. Just about this time, I left, but not before Mr. Eden had expressed his belief that sooner or later Greece, Turkey, and Yugoslavia would all three be fighting against Germany, but that there would be a lot of shifts and hesitations before that happened....

As I left the Legation I was waylaid for pictures and movies.... Then on to the Grande Bretagne to see Mr. Mavroudis. He was very gloomy, in marked contrast to Mr. Eden. He asked me to find out confidentially from Washington whether the U.S. would consider taking over Greek interests in Bulgaria and Rumania if relations should be broken.... I asked him whether Germany had yet made any demands here, and he said no. But he fully expects this to happen soon, and stated, as before, that Greece would have to refuse. He mentioned (this for the first time) that there would probably be a certain section of Greek opinion favoring acceptance of any German terms, but he said it would be only among business men anxious to preserve their affairs, and that there would not be much pro-Germanism as such. In any case, he added, this kind of thing is not organized here, and the army will stand firm.... Then he went on, seeing that I was not taking my leave, to volunteer some comment on Mr. Eden. He had no idea I had just seen him, and said, "I can tell you little about Eden. But it appears that his visit to Turkey has not been a success, despite all his optimism. He determined that the Turks remain loyal to the extent that they will resist German aggression. But there is nothing new in that. The only new thing he has brought back with him is the certainty that if Greece is attacked, she can expect no military as-

[8] Sir Hugh Knatchbull-Hugessen, British Ambassador to Turkey.

sistance from the Turks." . . . Went back to the office and drafted several cables. . . . I had quite a talk with Vukčević, finding him even more defeatist than usual. According to him, not only has Eden's trip been a failure, but it is useless to try to do anything against Germany now. It is too late. Germany won when France fell, and is now the master of Europe, etc. He left early in order to keep an appointment with Campbell. I wonder what the latter will make out of him, but anyhow I prepared him for a disappointment when I saw him this morning. . . . Back again at the office. Major Baker came in with an interesting report from Craw on a conversation with Alex. Argyropoulos who, as the Premier's aide in matters dealing with supply (he is Economic Director of the Foreign Office), had been present at a conference of H.M., Korizis and Eden. According to what he heard in this conference the British will need two months to get three divisions into Greece, while in the two days, March 1st and 2nd, the Germans poured five into Bulgaria, together with 400 planes. . . .

March 4, 1941, Tuesday

The news of the morning was Russia's rebuke to Bulgaria for signing the Tripartite Pact. . . . The Boston radio tonight opined that it means a Soviet strengthening of Turkey in an effort to get the Turks, *and* the British, to preserve the Straits from falling into German hands, Russia herself taking no risks in the matter. Personally, I doubt whether Russia is ready to fight Germany, but at the same time this is the first expression of official Russian dissatisfaction with Germany's expansion, and I think this fact should be given weight. Russia may not be going over to England, but she has shown at last that she is not indifferent to what takes place in the region of the Straits, and I think we can abandon the idea that she and Germany have agreed to barter the Dardanelles for Persia, or anything like that.

The news of the evening is that Hitler has sent a special envoy by plane with a personal message to President Inönü. The evening broadcast from London said the Turkish Cabinet, together with the Chief of Staff, has met to consider it, and Ismet has sent his personal thanks to the Führer for his gracious gesture. Mr. Eden told me yesterday that he was informed before leaving Ankara that this gesture was about to take place, and that he was sure the Turkish authorities would be neither impressed nor mislead. I wonder! I have, and cling to, a belief in the genuineness of the Turks, but I must admit that Ismet has always seemed to me to be a doubtful quantity. If only Kemal were alive, I think Turkey would have entered into the game squarely long before this.

March 5, 1941, Wednesday

In the afternoon I spent several hours at the office trying to work up a despatch on the war during February. Then, feeling that Mr. Eden might be leaving before I had a chance to see him again, and that the Dept. would like some news, especially about anything he might have attempted to do *in re* Yugoslavia, I called up the British Minister and asked if I might drop around. He said yes, and when I did so, whom should I find in his study but the Great Man himself. The three of us sat and talked, being joined after awhile by Air Vice-Marshall D'Albiac.[9] Mr. Eden said he had sent Campbell back to Yugoslavia with a note to Prince Paul stating very clearly the British intentions here. He added that he thinks there is a chance that the Yugoslavs will fight if Salonica is attacked, but that they are trying to persuade themselves that this won't happen. He spoke again of Turkey's being likely to declare war and give Britain her facilities if Germany invaded Greece, and told me that the Turks have already agreed to the Greeks removing their troops from Eastern Thrace, on the Turkish border, thus leaving a vital spot open on the Turkish flank —the implication being that the Turks will cover the gap themselves. A Greek suggestion that the Turks move into Greece in order to do this better is actually being considered by the Turkish Staff. "So you see," said Eden, "that the Turks stand just where they always did." He said that Hitler's letter to Ismet was a lengthy protestation of friendship, and so forth, with no menaces, and maintained that the Turks would not be impressed. In regard to his visit here, he expressed himself as very pleased. The Greeks are determined to resist, but he found them rather fatalistic and hopeless in the matter, and trusts that he was able to cheer them up. He asked me, "You do think it was a good idea, my coming, don't you?" And of course I said yes,—has done a vast amount to buck them up, and all that sort of thing. . . . With D'Albiac he talked about planes coming from Africa, and obviously contemplated pretty well stripping that continent. Opposition there, they both seemed to think, is just about ready to fold up anyhow. I felt that they have in mind making a real resistance here, and are convinced that enough can be done to make things hard for the Bosche, while such a fight might well encourage the Turks and Yugoslavs to throw in their lot too. Eden struck me again as rather at sea in a difficult situation, hoping for the best and trusting to luck. He went off after about half an hour to say good-bye to the King. Sir Michael and I stayed behind, of course, and I started to take my leave but Sir Michael said to stay a while longer, and just then the British Air Attaché came in, and we talked about Turkish assistance, the Attaché saying that Turkey has ten good, British-constructed air fields, with more building, which

[9] Air Vice-Marshall John D'Albiac, British Air Officer Commanding in Greece.

would be most useful if she comes in. Sir Michael had just told me that he understood that Turkey had no air fields worth anything, and that the Greek are better! He seemed rather discomfited of what the Attaché said (the latter is also accredited in Athens, and I can't quite see how Sir Michael had failed to inform himself from him as to so important and elementary a matter!).... Earlier on, Sir Michael replied to my question—why do you think that Greece can be held against the Germans? by telling me that "it is the considered opinion of Wavell and Wilson."[10] This is very interesting, if true. But . . . ! However, it seems clear that considerable British forces are coming over—or at least considerable convoys with as many troops as they can bring,—and with General Wavell commanding. I can hardly think another Norway is being planned. . . .

Major Baker went to the Piraeus this morning with two Greek officers. . . . He saw some cargo ships being unloaded, and learned that 4,000 British troops landed from four British warships (one of them the *Ajax*) on March 2nd. Only 700 of these are R.A.F., the rest being infantry. They are now in barracks at Voula. Rumors state that others went at the same time to Salonica and Volos, but the Major couldn't get this confirmed. The British are very tight about this business of troops coming, lest the Germans start to bomb their convoys, and the Greek ports, before they can bring what they want in. . . .

Mr. Eden told me that he is leaving tomorrow on the plane—the arrangement was actually made with D'Albiac while I was there—from Scaramanga tomorrow at 8, for Cairo. D'Albiac said, "It will be overcast and there will be no danger of your being intercepted, whereas if you left tonight there might be some risk in the departure since it is rough as well as dark." In Cairo, Mr. Eden said he would meet General Smuts[11] who is coming up from South Africa for the purpose. Also the Iraqi Foreign Minister. He went off cheerfully and after my "Bon Voyage!" turned both thumbs up in the air to signify what he thinks of the chances out here, and said "You tell 'em," which I promised to do, "Thumbs up." Eden is likeable on the surface, boyish and superficially sympathetic, but I should say lacks imagination and depth. I feel his nature to be somewhat hard and thin, but I may be wrong, of course. Two talks can't be conclusive! Only when one thinks of Cordell Hull one appreciates the difference between a great man and one who has had the greatness externally added to him, like his clothes.

[10] Lieutenant General Sir Henry Maitland ("Jumbo") Wilson, deputy British Commander-in-Chief, Middle East (under General Wavell).
[11] General Jan Christian Smuts, Prime Minister of South Africa.

March 8, 1941, Saturday

Major Baker saw Col. Blunt, the British Military Attaché, last night and I sent off a digest of his report—rather a lengthy matter. The new portion was to the effect that the British troops already landed here are engineers and signal corps only, though armed like the infantry. They are to prepare the way for divisions to arrive, which will be mostly motorized. There are no British troops in Salonica now, and none will be landed there, in view of the ease with which the port can be bombarded from Bulgaria.

The British Minister came in and said that the situation is critical in Belgrade, and that Mr. Lane has been taking a great interest in having Yugoslavia decide to do the right thing. At the suggestion of Mr. Campbell, he asked whether I would telegraph Lane that the Greeks will fight and that the British are sending early and useful assistance. This I did, since I know the Greek attitude, and I had the Department's confidential telegram of yesterday to back me up if necessary on the score of British plans. . . .

Went over to the Foreign Office to see Mr. Mavroudis. He said that the Germans have made no *démarche* here yet and he is glad of it, since proposals might start people arguing, and weaken resistance. . . . Mr. MacMurray had telegraphed me that he had information that proposals had been made. . . . Mr. Mavroudis said also that if the Germans propose terms to avoid invasion, there are some members of the Government who could propose counter-terms, such as that the Germans evacuate Bulgaria. He gave no indication that anything would be agreed to that would be against British interests. What he expects is an ultimatum coincident with attack, as in the case of Italy's action against Greece. He said the stories of proposals having been made probably emanate from the Germans, as part of a campaign to undermine morale here. He said that warnings to Greece are common in the conversation of German officials now-a-days, chiefly in Ankara and Belgrade. . . . Mr. Kohler had heard from Cuza Hotta, the Rumanian Press Attaché, that a couple of Turkish papers have printed advice to Greece to yield to German demands! I queried Mr. Mavroudis, and he said it is true. The Turkish Government, he said, has taken steps to see that there is no more of this kind of thing, and the papers will not be allowed to come into Greece. But the fact is not encouraging, to say the least. Mr. Mavroudis regards the articles as expressing a very real desire in Turkey to conjure the danger she sees approaching,—our old friend "appeasement" raising its head again. I must say that the Turkish attitude becomes more and more disappointing. A few weeks ago the press there was breathing fire over any encroachment on Turkey's zone of security. Now the strongest statement is that "if they come this way, they will find out how Turkey can fight." But "they" are already on the Turkish border.... Mr. Vlachos, in the *Kathimerini*, published an open letter to Hitler saying in sum that Greece having learned how to live, will now learn how to die. An oratorical hymn to the spirit of Thermopylae. Greeks of all classes have been much impressed.... There are no flies on the courage of this country just at present! (*Pourvu que ça dure!*) Over a thousand Italians were taken prisoner yesterday. I told the President, "Greece is still in her heroic mood."

Athens, March 8, 1941

Dear Franklin:

"Leg-over, leg-over, the dog went to Dover," and country by country the Germans have come to Greece. They are now on the border both of Greece and Turkey, and it is confidently expected here an attack toward Salonica will develop very shortly. Even the hitherto optimistic Under-Minister for Foreign Affairs now thinks it unlikely that Germany is merely on the defensive in this region.

Greece is still determined to resist, and the Germans have so far made no officer of terms which might create dissension. The country is still in its heroic mood. Meanwhile, since my last letter, the British have apparently decided not only to help Greece as a gesture but as a part of their own strategic plan. They seem clearly to be intending to bring in considerable forces, mostly motorized, as quickly as transport can be arranged. These forces will be landed south of Salonica, to avoid the obvious risk from air raids at that port. (The story that there is a Canadian division there already is such a poor lie that I wonder the Germans bothered to put it out.) About a brigade's worth of engineers and signal corps arrived in the Piraeus promptly when the Germans crossed the Danube, and there now seems to be a race going on to see which side can concentrate for the struggle with the greater dispatch, the advantage being with the Germans because of the nature and length of the British communications. In addition, whatever the British bring, the Germans are sure to have the advantage of numbers. But the advantage of the terrain will be decidedly on the side of the defenders. When I asked the British Minister what reason his people had for thinking the defense of Greece possible with the forces available, he replied, "It is the considered opinion of Generals Wavell and Wilson."

The Greeks at present do not intend to withdraw in Albania, fearing the morale effect and the difficulty of retreating with their poor transport facilities. The Italians have close to half a million men in Albania but the Greeks are definitely the better soldiers and believe they can hold. To face the Germans they have some five divisions of their own available and may, with British help, eventually have all the force that can be used to advantage on a short front in mountainous country. At the outset it seems that there will be an attempted resistance at the frontier and then perhaps on the line from Lake Doiran to Amphipolis, where the Allies had their positions in the last war, and finally along the mountain barrier running north from Olympus along the Yugoslav border, giving up Salonica but still protecting both Greece proper and the rear of the army in Albania. Much will of course depend upon the ability of the Royal Air Force to keep the more numerous German planes from utterly disrupting communications and demoralizing the defense, and of course if Yugoslavia joins the Axis and the Germans get the use of the Monastir gap, these well-laid plans will go a-gley. On the other hand, if Yugoslavia decides to fight rather than see herself further encircled, there will be a different story too, but this seems to people here to be definitely unlikely, however desirable.

The Greeks in general are beginning to realize the facts outlined by Mr. Eden to the Government (and incidentally to me) in his recent visit. The Turkish army is not equipped to take the offensive and furthermore the Turks are convinced that Turkey and not Greece is the principal objective of the German drive in the Balkans. Turkey may possibly declare war if Greece is attacked, and give Britain the use of her airfields, but Greece can hardly expect any direct assistance. Yugoslavia, on her part, is wavering as to whether or not to take up arms even in case Salonica, which she maintains to be within her zone of security, is attacked. In between the two, Greece will have to bear the brunt of the first shock, and the British will give her all the assistance they possibly can, in the hope that a show of successful resistance here may hearten the others and finally bring about an Eastern Front stretching from the Bosphorus to the Adriatic. Mr. Eden said to me, "I think eventually the Yugoslavs, Turks and Greeks will all be in the fight, but there will be a lot of slipping and sliding before that happens." Obviously, right up to the very last minute, the British have failed to get a line-up established and are still living on efforts and hope. Mr. Eden himself did not seem to be too cast down about this. He said to me, "Even if Germany succeeds in overrunning Greece, I don't see how this will help her. By that time we shall have cleaned up in the Middle East and be sitting pretty in Africa. In making war in the Balkans, Germany is only playing football in her own cabbage patch."

Mr. Eden of course looks at matters from the Empire point of view. If he can't win a victory here, he can console himself with thinking that Germany's victory will be a Pyrrhic victory, but the Greeks have their own fate to consider and were definitely distressed by the news he brought them from Ankara. However, he did his best to cheer them up with assurances that England's effort will be a serious one, and with Wilson here and troops obviously coming, they certainly have something to go on.

Affectionately yours,
Lincoln MacVeagh (3)

March 9, 1941, Sunday

The King came and stayed about an hour and a half. . . . [He] said that the Yugoslavs are worrying him to death. He has little faith in the Prince or the Government, but said that in Serbia public opinion is strong for resistance to German pressure. Regarding British assistance, he confirmed that General Wilson is here, in command (though he is never mentioned publicly), and also that what British troops have arrived are only advance specialists. He said the British command seems confident, but that he can get no statement as to when troops will arrive. Despite the seven or eight divisions spoken of by the Department, and the three the King talked of the last time I saw him, he said this afternoon that only two divisions can be sent for the time being, one of them motorized. . . . Major Craw, who came in after the King had gone, told me that the British divisions, of the time of whose coming the King could get no information, are already arriving at the Piraeus. It is all very confusing; combining what really appears to be confidence on the part of the British authorities (or they wouldn't take the risk) with considerable anxiety on the part of the Greeks, and of the British officers whom Craw sees, as to whether the assistance can get here in time. . . . The amount of British motor transport that one sees in and around Athens these days is impressive, but probably not much more than is needed for a division in addition to the air force present. . . . The Greeks yesterday took another thousand prisoners, and today, according to the King, beat back some very serious counter-attacks in the region north east of Tepeleni. Craw says Tepelini will fall in a few days, but we have heard that before! If it does, it will bolster morale here tremendously at a critical moment. The King expects German proposals about the 15th of the month, and that they will be made to him personally, a thing he dreads!

March 11, 1941, Tuesday

The British Military Attaché said that there are no British troops in Salonica and that it wouldn't be good policy to send any. . . . Absurd rumors still fly about concerning the number of British here. . . . Colonel Blunt told Major Baker that he couldn't give him any estimates, but had telegraphed to London to find out just how far he is to trust the American Military Attaché with secret information of this kind! It seems to me to be somewhat strange that we should be the Arsenal of Democracy but yet not trusted by those we help! . . . There are rumors about Athens today that [Yugoslavia] will not knuckle down to Germany after all, and the morale of the "cosmos" has gone up for the moment. However, I am very pessimistic about the Yugoslavs, and fairly so about the Turks. Tomorrow, on which date the Turkish Prime Minister is expected to define his country's foreign policy, and the Prince Regent of Yugoslavia will hold a Crown Council, will probably show if I am right. The mentality of these small nations when they are brought face to face with Germany shows a remarkable sameness, and Yugoslavia is now practically surrounded by Germans, and Turkey faces, according to British information, even more German troops on her frontier than does Greece. I expect both will continue to say they will fight if attacked, and go on watching what England and Greece can do against Italy, Germany and (probably) Bulgaria. If the former are beaten then there will be no resistance at all on the part of Turkey and Yugoslavia. We'll see. Tonight, any other expectation seems to me pure "wishful thinking," though miracles do happen.

March 12, 1941, Wednesday

Called on Count Mercati in connection with a request from America for the King's autograph. The Count thinks (and so do I) that it is certain the Germans will bomb Athens so long as the British use it as at present for headquarters of all sorts. He thinks the British should move out. But where would they go? They will have to go on using the Piraeus, of course, for landing. Perhaps a G.H.Q. could be set up in the country somewhere, as was the case in France in the last war. But there is no sign that they have yet thought of the idea. The King George Hotel is now practically devoted to British officers. . . . The fighting on the Albanian front keeps on, very heavy. G2 told Major Baker that the Italians have tried hard (in one instance putting on an attack on a 30 kilometer front) but have been unable to take any ground, and that the Greeks remain confident. . . . Some German pressure is apparently being put on Spain to let planes go through to Africa, but so far Suner and Franco have not agreed to the idea—or so the papers say. . . . With the British here, little Greece doesn't have to worry over what she is going to do—only over what she is going to suffer!

March 13, 1941, Thursday

Major Craw has been told by a British source, which he thinks trustworthy, that the Italians, who now fear a bombardment of Rome more than ever, on account of the state of morale in Italy, have prevailed on Hitler to agree to no bombing of Athens, lest this result in British retaliation on the Eternal City. This may explain the confidence with which the British are crowding into Athens these days!

March 14, 1941, Friday

[A] British R.A.F. officer named Namen Smith came in to see Kohler. He said the British know that the Germans have a wireless sending apparatus in our building[12] and want to spot exactly where it is. He implied that when spotted they expect somehow to smash it, and he tried to get, through Kohler or through one of our journalists (Sulzberger), an introduction to our landlord, Mr. Stephen Pezmazoglou, who lives on the roof. Kohler refused to help, and Sulzberger, when consulted, did likewise, and Smith left, with Kohler believing that he would try to make his way to the roof with the aid of the British Cable and Wireless Company on the top floor. He asked Kohler to keep a package for him till this afternoon. . . . When I was told this story, I said that our Legation must not be involved in this sort of thing. Kohler opened the package in my presence and found a listening-in apparatus. I told him to take it back to its owner at once, and then went over myself to the British Minister, to whom I protested. Sir Michael understood at once and said he would put a stop to the affair, and that he is constantly having trouble with enthusiastic young men. . . . I think he'll do something about it, but also have no doubt that in one way or another the British will get at the offending wireless—though I should think it would pay them better to leave it alone, since Smith told Kohler that they have broken the code used and can read the messages sent. I mentioned this aspect of the affair to Sir Michael, who seemed to share our view. But there it is. It will be most embarrassing for us if the British and Germans start to mess it up right in our building, and I hardly relished the idea of a spy (Smith said he had a journalist's card and would go up to see Mr. Pezmazoglou in civilian clothes) using our office to store his paraphernalia. As I told Sir Michael, we may love the British, but there are limits! . . .

March 19, 1941, Wednesday

Mr. Plytas, the Mayor of Athens, came in with a telegram he wanted to send to F.D.R. It announced that the City Fathers of Athens in Council assembled have decided to make the President an Honorary Citizen of the City, and to name one of its principal avenues after him. The ave-

---

[12] Sections of the United States' and German Legations in Athens were housed in the same building.

nue in question is Academy Street. Mr. Plytas asked if I should send the telegram or whether it ought to go direct. I said send it direct. He then asked about the sheepskin of Honorary Citizen, and I said it should go *via* the Greek Minister in Washington. A nice gesture, I think. But Mummy's comment was, "How long do you think Academy Street will be called Franklin D. Roosevelt Boulevard?" One has recent street changes in Paris to remember, I suppose.... The *Gloucester* ... arrived today with a battalion of Australians who fought in Libya. Two more battalions are coming soon. Here are combat troops at last, and with a vengeance!

March 20, 1941, Thursday

Sent off three telegrams, two on the British troops and movements here so far as we can tell what they are—and that's not very much!—and one on the honors given to the President by the City of Athens. I asked [that] the President be informed that Athens has never before named a principal avenue after a foreigner. It seemed possible that people at home might not give him quite the right perspective on this thing, and I do want a polite acknowledgement, at least, for the Greeks. They have made the best gesture in their power.... Allard and his wife returned with Enis Bey from Turkey and came to tea this afternoon. Allard has seen a lot of the Germans in Ankara, from Papen down to journalists and what-nots. He says the Germans expect to come through Greece in a fortnight, and to start as soon as the weather improves. Probably about the end of the month. They have seven hundred thousand men echeloned back of the Greek border all the way into Rumania, which they can devote to this attack, and dispose of new weapons which they want to try out, as well as of a whole division of parachutists. Their aim is to occupy Greece, take Crete with their parachutists, and then cut Turkey off from England progressively, until, with the application of a little pressure, they feel sure she will fall unresistingly under their domination. Yugoslavia will simply be surrounded and, as it were, digested by the Axis. No mention in this of Italy's aspirations.... Driving down through Greece he met British light tanks and much transport, but nothing east of the Vermion range. He thinks there are only a few in Salonica.... The Turks, he said, are scared to death, and will do nothing except sit behind their fortifications. He gave Kotzias (whom he saw in Thrace) the credit for being fully patriotic and for quelling a serious incipient panic in that province. He said Kotzias told him that when the Greek troops withdrew from Thrace and Turkish troops did not, as was hoped, take their place (Mr. Eden, when I saw him last, spoke of this hope as his also), the people became so wild with fear that they rushed for the sea-coast and in many cases threw themselves, actually, into the sea. To make them go back to their villages he had to threaten to cut off their supply of food everywhere except at home, and forbade the restaurants to serve anything to refugees. Mr. Allard scouted the idea that Mr. Kotzias could have been sent to Thrace because of his pro-Germanism. . . . No world news today, except that London had its worst raid of the year last night. Will the day ever come when the British can repay? They go on banging at factories and goods yards—to what purpose? The German army is today as strong, if not stronger than ever; the German fleet is growing; the German submarines are an increasing menace, etc. But retaliation on the German people might have some effect on morale. It is a card to play, anyhow. Will the British keep on holding it back till the game has been lost?

March 22, 1941, Saturday

The news of the day was that some of the Yugoslav Cabinet resigned in protest against signing a pact with Germany, and the army is also supposed to be protesting against signature. Lane sent an outline of the proposed pact, containing the shameful provision that as part payment for Yugoslavia's neutrality (and her joining the Tri-Partite Pact, new order in Europe, etc.) the Germans will give consideration after the war to her aspirations in the Aegean area (i.e. her desire to have Salonica.) Only a little while ago, Yugoslavia was one of the Balkan Entente allies, and her General Staff consulted with that of Greece on questions of common defense. Now she appears willing to accept a part of Greece as payment for deserting her! Hitler has a devilish magic, which consists in appealing to the worst in others as well as in his own people. It seems clear that most of the Yugoslav politicians, a feeble folk, are ready to take the bait. Only the Serbian army—if rumor can be trusted,—stands between Yugoslavia, which owes all she is to allied victory in the last war, and complete disgrace.

March 23, 1941, Sunday

Apparently the Yugoslav Government has not yet signed on the dotted line. Perhaps signature is being postponed till the Japanese Foreign Minister arrives in Berlin. It would provide a good opportunity for staging an impressive reception. Took Major Baker and the Bunnies [Mrs. MacVeagh and daughter Margaret] to Corinth for the day. The Major got the necessary permissions by rapid work at headquarters. . . . When we were stopped at the bridge over the Corinth Canal on the way out and asked to show our papers, a Greek soldier said "Is this MacVeagh?" and kissed me on both cheeks! Luckily for me, he smelt neither of garlic nor retsina, and though I wouldn't choose to be saluted so, the naivete of the gesture was rather charming. Mummy, Bun and Michali,[13] in the car ahead, were convulsed with laughter. The Major reserved his till later. . . .

March 24, 1941, Monday

Telegram from Lane in Belgrade saying that the Yugoslavs will join the Tripartite Pact after all, with guarantees from the Axis that their boundaries and independence will be respected and that they will not be required to lend military aid. . . . Went over to see Mr. Mavroudis at the Grande Bretagne. He said he had the same information from Belgrade, but added that the Yugoslavs will permit the passage of German supplies and wounded. He pointed out, in connection with the "wounded" that it ought to be specified which direction they are allowed to travel in: if both ways, there can be little doubt what the Germans will use this clause for! . . . I asked him if he knew whether the Yugoslavs are to be obliged to demobilize their army. He said he didn't know, but that this is of course the crux of the whole matter. He was very much depressed. . . . Got a long letter from the Premier saying that the Grumman planes promised by our Government are now being held up: the British want to take them over against Hurricanes from Egypt. This sounded O.K. in Washington, but the Greeks here know that there are no Hurricanes in Egypt for such a purpose! It is just another trick, and a shameful one, of the British Purchasing Commission to get more for themselves. After $4\frac{1}{2}$ months of effort, the Greeks are exactly where they started from so far as getting our planes is concerned. And these planes they are ready to pay cash for, too. . . . Sent off a telegram on this at once, and may it bring good luck, better than its predecessors! . . .

March 25, 1941, Tuesday

Greek Independence Day. Yugoslavia signed the Tripartite Pact, betraying her Balkan allies and selling her birthright for a mess of potage. I say her birthright for she was born of the victory of the British, the French, and the Americans in the last war, and the mess of potage is the poor vestige of "independence" she will enjoy under the Germans—little short of slavery. But at least she hopes to live. Compared with Greece, who took up arms against a power six or seven times her size without hesitation, [of] what ignoble stuff these Balkan peoples are made up! I shouldn't be surprised to see the Turks give in next without a fight. They

[13] The Greek chauffeur of the U.S. Legation.

say they will defend their independence, but so did the Serbs, only to sign it away without fighting! . . . The news, which came in the afternoon, greatly depressed the Greeks and British in Athens,—since it probably means that Germany and Italy can now command the whole northern frontier of this country, and the army will have to fall back in Albania, and Salonica be given up. But in the morning there was still hope that Yugoslavia would stand firm. . . . Worked on despatches and a letter to the President.

Athens, March 25, 1941
Greek Independence Day

Dear Franklin:

Re-reading my last letter, I find that there is no need to alter the general picture there given of the Greek situation. Recent important developments have been few, and mainly along lines already indicated. The picture is becoming more definite, if more uncomfortable.

Yugoslavia has joined the Axis today. The terms are not yet known here, and there may be reservations. But it is the first step which counts, when one gives in to Germany. Turkey's attitude, according to diplomatic friends recently returned from Ankara, has become increasingly offish and timid as regards helping Greece and Great Britain, and Yugoslavia's action is likely to make it more so. Britain, on the other hand, continues to pour in reinforcements here. The British authorities are giving out no information whatever as to the real extent of this effort. This is in keeping with Mr. Eden's remark to me, "I am saying nothing on that question, not even to the United States, or to my own Minister in Athens." But of course we can see with our own eyes the ships coming in, trucks and troops crowding the roads, and camps in all the outskirts of the city. The Turkish Military Attaché estimates that there are now 120,000 British in Greece. He may be right, but Major Baker, of this Legation, thinks 80,000 would be closer. Meanwhile, the Greeks have fought an Italian counter-offensive to a standstill, but have themselves been unable to progress toward the desired shortened line in Albania which would permit the withdrawal of divisions to face the Germans. The weather in the north is improving.

Following the settlement with Yugoslavia, and the packing of a huge German force on the Greco-Bulgarian frontier, it is expected here that German demands will be made of Greece very soon, probably in the form of an ultimatum. Von Papen recently told my Swedish colleague in Ankara that the Greeks can expect far less favorable terms now than they might have had last January, if they had asked for them. But now the British are here in force, and the decision is out of Greek hands. Public opinion has been frightened by Yugoslavia's defection, but the die is cast, as the Government and the army as a whole well realize.

Indications, such as the presence of ammunition dumps and transport parks, would seem to confirm what the King told me some time ago, namely that it is the intention of the British and Greeks to make their principal resistance in the Olympus region. It is clear that a development of the German attack through southern Yugoslavia, which is now more than ever possible, would not turn a line there as it would one established further east. As stated in my last letter, the terrain of Greece greatly favors the defense, particularly against mechanized advance. On the other hand, the discrepancy in numbers between the present opposing forces is enormous. Perhaps the best that the Allies can look forward to is a succession of Thermopylaes. The German airforce, according to recent estimates, will take the place of the Persian arrows, darkening the sun, and British tenacity and Greek devotion will fight in the shade.

It is possible, of course, that the Germans will not press their attack against Greece proper but content themselves with Salonica, and then switch off against the Dardanelles, leaving a British force cooped up here which might have been used to advantage elsewhere. The Turks appear to be afraid of this, but the idea is not supported by apparent German dispositions in Bulgaria. Meanwhile, recent indications of Soviet willingness not to molest the Turks if they defend themselves are not regarded here as meaning any shift toward Great Britain on Moscow's part, but only a desire to let others fight Russia's battles for her.

There are still some dubious points to be cleared up, but we are doubtless on the eve of drastic clarifications.

Affectionately yours,
Lincoln MacVeagh (4)

March 26, 1941, Wednesday

Went to Headquarters for a talk with the Premier. He said that despite the defection of Yugoslavia Greece would resist. He said that she made up her mind last October, and would resist both the Germans and the Italians even if the British were not here to help. Regarding Turkey he seemed thoroughly disillusioned, and said that she sends telegrams of admiration for Greek determination and courage, but will do nothing else. . . . He told me that the Government has just received news that the U.S. will let Greece have the planes she wants—perhaps my telegram did some good. I gave him a couple of formal replies to his notes on the air-planes and the general supplies.

March 27, 1941, Thursday

During the morning rumors began to come in of a revolution in Yugoslavia, and by evening it was known that the military turned the Government out in the early hours, setting up a new "national" Cabinet. King Peter has taken over, and the Regents have resigned, the Prince [Paul] and Princess Olga leaving the country. The former Premier etc. are in prison.[14] The British are delighted and the Greeks have been in holiday mood all day. No news as to how Germany is taking it, or whether the new Government will repudiate the signature of the Tripartite Pact. . . . Craw says he has seen D'Albiac's plans for air operations against the Germans and Italians combined in this area, and that they are based on hopelessly small forces. . . . A lot of British trucks, artillery, and even some infantry arrived in Athens this afternoon, the people, happy over what they hope will prove good news from Yugoslavia, cheering and waving from the windows. . . . Major Craw says that a German patrol in Greek territory, after several warnings, was fired on by the Greeks today, and a German officer was wounded. Here is an "incident," if the Germans want one to begin with. . . . Allard called up to ask if I had any news; said he was having the German Minister to dinner and would tell me about it in the morning.

March 28, 1941, Friday

Telegram came in from Mr. Lane during the morning which said that the Under-Minister for Foreign Affairs in Belgrade had told him that the policy of the new Government is peace and neutrality, and that the change has been only in the direction of achieving national unity. The German radio announced that the *coup d'état* was a matter of internal politics only and had nothing to do with foreign affairs! The Italian radio said nothing at all about it! Greek opinion is greatly cheered. The whole atmosphere in Athens is changed. But still there is no indication as to whether the Tripartite Pact will be repudiated. . . . The Swedish Chargé came in and told me of his dinner with the German Minister last night. The latter said he had as yet received no instructions in regard to any *démarche* to be made here. . . . The Albanian front is very quiet. . . . Mr. Eden is supposed to have arrived today from Cairo, so I asked to see Sir Michael, and got an appointment for tomorrow morning at 10. . . .

March 29, 1941, Saturday

Went to the office and found a telegram from Earle in Sofia to the effect that German plans for an attack on Greece comprise a sudden blitzkrieg

[14] Yugoslavia's new Prime Minister was General Dushan T. Simović, Chief of the Air Force.

from the air against Greek and British planes on the ground, probably at dawn. I took this (which gives us nothing new, but confirmation from a source near to the enemy) and also Lane's telegram of yesterday, over to Sir Michael. Asked him how he saw the situation, and he volunteered that Eden is here, and went out and asked the great man if he would see me. Eden came in from the garden. He said Lane's telegram states just what his people have reported. He thinks England and America have somewhat overestimated the meaning of the Yugoslav coup,—at least for the present,—and he is here to see what may be done to develop it into an understanding or general policy of cooperation with England, which can then be presented to the Turks. Campbell in Belgrade is seeing the new Premier there and will send someone down here today by plane to report on how the land lies. Eden said his stay here will depend on what develops. He and the Palairets and the D'Albiacs will lunch with us tomorrow. He himself, he said, may have to leave tomorrow morning, but it isn't likely.... He was much excited over a reported sweep of the Italian fleet in the Eastern Mediterranean which turned into a flight as soon as the British were sighted, but seemed to know nothing of the attack on Suda Bay (and sinking of a British cruiser) being reported on the Italian wireless.... He took great interest in Earle's blitzkrieg telegram, and called in D'Albiac, who said that the air force here expects such an attack, and also the landing of parachutists behind the front to cut communications etc. Eden said to me before D'Albiac came in that some more fighter planes are coming here. (I hope, soon!) I asked him whether Prince Paul of Yugoslavia has come to Greece, and he showed considerable annoyance with the B.B.C. for speculating on the matter, causing, as he said, embarrassment to the King of Greece. But he himself would not say whether the Prince is here or not.... Just as I was leaving, Sir Michael brought in word that General Wilson would like to see me, and D'Albiac took me out into the garden and introduced me to him and to Sir John Dill. Wilson bespoke my aid in keeping American correspondents from giving away too much about British movements, and I said that I would do what I could in appealing to them, but at the same time made sure that he understood there is no control of the press possible on our part except in such a manner. I gathered that he understood, and was only speaking to me as a counsel of perfection, to leave no stone unturned. He knows the Germans can see just as much as we can here. He spoke of our correspondents hanging round the King George bar, and perhaps was thinking that his own officers may be letting out a thing or two!... Both Eden and the military men think the Yugoslav business has postponed German attack on this country, which D'Albiac said he was sure was set for yesterday in conjunction with the Italian naval sweep....
I talked a bit to Dill and Wilson about the possibility of flooding the

Vardar plain in the Verria region by cutting the canal that runs along the western mountains. Wilson said he had seen this canal recently and that there was no water in it, but I told them that when the snows melt it will be full. It always has been in the past. They said they already had taken cognizance of the possibilities offered by the Kerkini weir in the Struma plain. Wilson said he thought it might not be so easy for an army trained and equipped for the roads and plains of France and Poland to fight its way through the mountains of Greece, against opposition of any serious sort. . . . Went over to the Palace offices and talked with Mercati, who admitted that the Prince Regent and his wife are here, staying with Princess Nicholas at Psychico. I asked for an audience with H.M.

March 30, 1941, Sunday

Warm, bright, a perfect spring day. I had a nasty chest cold coming on, and stayed in bed most of the morning . . . Got up in time for lunch. Mr. Eden came, and Sir John Dill, and the British Minister and Lady Palairet came somewhat late from her hospital. General Wilson gave out at the last minute and we had hurriedly to rearrange the table. There were the three of us and the Kohlers. Mr. Eden was very much excited over the news of the naval battle in the Ionian Sea. He had talked with a captain who had returned from it, and it appears that several cruisers and destroyers of the Italians were sunk in a *night* engagement, one being blown almost out of the water at the range of 70 yards! No casualties at all on the British side—almost incredible. . . . Before lunch, Mr. Eden talked about this, but also told me that he felt some encouragement over the situation in Yugoslavia, though he obviously is not wholly confident. It seems the Premier is ready to fight if the Germans attack Salonica, but the other Ministers are not yet known quantities. He told me that it isn't excluded that he may go up to Belgrade himself secretly. After luncheon the other guests sat on the terrace, while Mr. Eden took his cigar, coffee and brandy out in the garden, where he and I sat in the sun and had a long chat on many phases of the war. He told me he had come here from Malta and that the morale there is excellent; damage to the port is not great. There was a convoy in the harbor when he was there; as the result of a German raid, one ship had its bridge destroyed. . . . This interests me, about there being a convoy there, since Craw insists that the Mediterranean is "dominated" by the German planes. I doubt if the British tell him everything, though he certainly collects a good deal of information. However, though the domination may not be complete, the British are evidently using the Cape Route to the Middle East chiefly. Mr. Eden spoke of the length of this route and the great need of shipping, and suggested that we might send stuff in our boats at least as far as the Red Sea.

... I asked him (to see what he'd say) "How soon will you be wanting manpower from America?" He squirmed a little, and I got the impression that he thinks that sooner or later it may come to that. But what he said was that there is plenty of manpower in the Balkans, and that what is wanted is motorized transport, anti-tank artillery, airplanes, etc. In regard to planes he said a dozen Hurricanes were due to arrive today, and that more will be coming soon. Mr. Eden made a polite and pleasant guest, chatted in a free and friendly fashion with Mr. Kohler, admired the house and garden, liked Greece, etc., and in general put on no airs at all. . . .

After the guests left, Kohler and I went to the office for a while, and then I had to rush back, as H.M. came to tea. Major Baker got back from Salonica just about that time, and I brought him along. . . . The King, Major Baker and I sat on the terrace till the sun set over the house-tops and it began to grow chilly. The King said some interesting things. He is keeping his fingers crossed on the Yugoslav situation, since, though the Premier is all right, the rest of the Cabinet doesn't seem to him to give any very strong guarantee that German influence will not continue in the country. He said he would like to see some generals in charge of the Interior and Public Safety, for instance. However, it seems that the Italians, at least, are worried about what the Serbs may do, for the King said that there are indications of troop movements in Albania toward the Yugoslav frontier. The Greeks have been making patrols to determine whether the front has been so weakened by this movement that a resumption of the Greek offensive would be justified at this time. The patrols met strong resistance in the Tepeleni area, but surprisingly little in the north, near Pogradetz. . . .

On the war in general, the King said that German movements show that preparation is going on for a large scale attack against Russia, which he thinks will be coincident with the attack in the Balkans. Pressure is being put on Sweden and Finland to facilitate German plans, and work on roads in Poland around Cracow and Warsaw is being rushed. According to him, whatever may be his source of information, the Germans' first objective is the Ukraine, and if that proves an easy conquest, they intend to go on as far as the Urals. He said the German General Staff is urging Hitler to decide whether England is to be attacked directly, but he cannot make up his mind. As the King had just come from a long conversation with Prince Paul of Yugoslavia, I believe that the latter gentleman is his source. He spoke with a great deal more assurance than is his wont, of things in which he himself is not directly involved, and as if he has just heard something from the horse's mouth. . . .

"A GALLANT RESISTANCE" · 325

April 1, 1941, Tuesday

April Fool's Day, and meeting of Mussolini and Matsuoka[15]—so the B.B.C. is never tired of repeating! . . . The Greeks took another important and strongly defended height on the central sector of the Albanian front, in a brilliant local operation. They still have some sting left!

April 2, 1941, Wednesday

Went over to the British Legation and saw Sir Michael. The Italian and German radio stated this morning that Mr. Eden went to Belgrade yesterday, but Sir Michael told me he is still here, and while I was talking in his study, sent a telegram out to the garden for Mr. Eden to read. Yesterday Mr. E. was received in audience by the King, and spent the afternoon on Pendeli with the Minister. Yet American newspaper correspondents swore up and down to Kohler this morning that he went to the Yugoslav border yesterday and conferred there with two Cabinet Ministers! . . . Sir Michael had no news. Thinks the Yugoslavs are playing for time, and said that General Papagos made the statement that the Germans themselves aren't ready, in a military sense, to cope with the new situation. Mr. Eden will probably stay on here until the situation clarifies. The British Ambassador in Ankara reports that it is no use pushing the Turks,—it only makes them stubborn,—but there seems to be at least the beginning of an understanding developing between them and the Yugoslavs. "We tried," said Sir Michael, "to knock their heads together and failed. Now they seem to be doing it for themselves." He said that Gavrilović,[16] now said to be in Ankara, has for a long time past advocated a closer understanding between his country and Turkey. Sir Michael asked me whether I had heard any criticism of the King for harboring Prince Paul here, and I truthfully said no: but I can quite imagine there being some, just the same. . . . Saw Allard, who told me that Zu Erbach still has no instructions, and remains so nervous he cannot sleep. . . . Saw a whole truckload of German printed matter being unloaded and carried into the German Commercial office in our basement. What can this be for, at this late date? The Brazilian came in and told me among other things that the Yugoslav Minister received yesterday a telegram from his Government, according to which the new Foreign Minister called in the German Minister and made him a declaration on Yugoslavia's position. I then went round and saw Vukčević, and got the thing from him direct. He took out of his pocket a copy of the telegram and translated it into French for me. Yugoslavia remains faithful to the

---

[15] Yosuke Matsuoka, Japanese Minister for Foreign Affairs.
[16] Milan Gavrilović, Agrarian Party leader, Minister of Justice.

principle involved in honoring treaties already signed, and this covers the signature of the Tripartite Pact. But, at the same time, she insists that she remain neutral in this war, because of the feelings of her people which demand this attitude, and that she maintain friendly relations with all her neighbors. In addition, her Government, while of course deeply concerned in the Pact mentioned, must and will attend to safeguarding the essential interests of the nation. . . . Vukčević said he could only regard this statement as an effort to gain time by proposing to let the signature of the Pact become a dead letter, rather than to repudiate it, a maneuver which he felt would not fool Hitler but might allow of further talk, at least. The Minister seemed more convinced, even, than he was the other day that Germany will attack his country. It is only a question of time. But at present there have been no demands made, and it is untrue that the Italian Minister has left Belgrade. Only the German has gone to Berlin "to report." Vukčević has seen Eden, and was not favorably impressed, since the latter replied to all his questions with one invariable answer, "Your Government is informed." I explained that the Foreign Secretary doubtless desires to avoid the danger of misunderstanding by not talking to too many people, and by going direct through his Ministers to the Governments concerned rather than roundabout through their Ministers to other Governments. But I still think, if this is the case, it would be better at least to pretend to take these people into his confidence. Clearly, Vukčević thought him brusque and rude. . . . Incidentally, I was told by Sir Michael that Mr. Eden saw Enis Bey last evening,—after getting my memorandum. I hope this last helped to orient the conversation in a useful direction. One can never tell. . . . Kohler told me that Sulzberger, after leaving Greece last week, promptly telegraphed a lot of material which he had gathered here and would not be allowed to send out, and that this material comprised secret information, or at least information as yet unknown to or only suspected by the Germans, who have picked it up and broadcast it, claiming that now they have proof of British troops being in Greece, not to speak of good indications as to exactly where they are now and where they may go! In this way has "Cy" repaid the confidence of Greeks and British alike, who have given him (because of his position as Balkan Manager for his paper, and because of the reputation of the paper itself) exceptionally fine treatment. I can hardly believe it, and feel I should wait till I hear more before passing any judgment. But this evening Colonel Melas complained about the matter very bitterly to Major Baker. It seems the Greeks may fear to take action, such as barring Sulzberger from reentering the country, lest he take it out on them and the British by revealing more! . . . A pretty kettle of fish!

April 3, 1941, Thursday

Communicated to the Premier a message from the Dept. saying that the 30 Grumman planes have been definitely allocated to Greece, and some of them have been crated already and will soon be despatched *via Suez*. That, I'm afraid, will mean a long time in coming. Wonder why they couldn't be sent to West Africa and flown over. . . . Major Baker sent off a telegram on his trip north. Estimates that part of two motorized divisions and a mechanized brigade are in the Olympus region, no more. Craw says that the British now have about a hundred planes in Greece. Also that most of these have been kept away from the Greek-Albanian front, preparing for resistance to Germany, but that if no German attack develops before the 10th they will assist a Greek drive scheduled for April 10th. . . . .

April 4, 1941, Friday

Craw came in and reported that the British air-force is convinced that an attack on Greece is imminent and had sent a hurry call to Air Vice-Marshal D'Albiac in Belgrade, to come back at once. . . . I went over to see the British Minister and found him calm. He doubted whether anything drastic would be done by the Germans yet awhile. I asked him about Mr. Eden, and he said he went the day before yesterday to the north of Greece to be "near" a military conference taking place between the British, Greeks and Yugoslavs at the border. He is expected back today.

April 5, 1941, Saturday

Went over to the British Legation in the morning and had a final talk with Mr. Eden. He thinks the Germans will not attack Yugoslavia, till they are ready to make a large-scale attack, which may not be for some days. But there is always a chance that they may elect to make a swift thrust at Greece combined with one through Southern Serbia. He spoke of the advance of the Germans in Cyrenaica as strong, and comprising at least 100 tanks—perhaps a whole armored division plus two mechanized ones. He had received a wire from Churchill saying that there is a lot of material now available for the Middle East, but he stressed the time factor to me, and said that our help in the next two months will be of paramount importance. In this connection he was encouraged by the reports of President Roosevelt's statement that with the elimination of Eritrea it may become possible for the Red Sea to be opened to American shipping. . . . About Turkey he was still rather doubtful. She appears uncertain,—

doesn't want to stick her neck out. If England could give her more materiel of war it might be different.... He spoke of Prince Paul's having told the King here of remarks by Hitler against the Russians: the Führer is supposed to have said that he must go against Russia to get the raw materiel he needs. I replied by giving him what the King said about German preparations against Russia, which it appears certain that he got from the same source. Mr. Eden said he would leave this afternoon, and would not make this public lest opinion in England should be further alarmed in connection with Benghazi's fall. . . .[17] Craw said that the British air force is convinced that war is imminent: "The balloon is going up." Major Baker came in and said that Colonel Melas and the rest of the Greek Intelligence did not feel so sure of it, but that they have observed signs among the Germans here which would indicate it: burning of papers, and the grouping of all the clerks in the officers' houses to sleep, as if it was felt they might be at any time subject to seizure or attack.

April 6, 1941, Sunday

The balloon has gone up! Allard, the Swedish Chargé, called me up before 7 o'clock and said he knew it for a fact. . . . Told me that the German Minister called him over to his house at about 6:15 and said he had just been to see Mr. Korizis. Apparently Erbach phoned the Premier at about 5 and was received at a quarter to six. He read Mr. Korizis a statement declaring that Germany considers Greece to have been unneutral ever since the war began, but especially since she allowed the debarkation here of large numbers of British troops. Consequently Germany must put aside the Greek forces on the border and enter Greece to strike at the British, though this does not mean that she is inimical to Greece or the Greek nation. The Minister then asked for his passports. . . . Allard told me also that Erbach asked him to take over German interests here. . . .

We put the flag out at the chancery to avoid being mixed up in any attack the crowds might work on the German premises in our building and next door. There were crowds outside, making considerable noise, when we did so, but as the flag was unfurled, they cheered, and I got the first of several little ovations when I stepped out on the balcony. . . . I called up the Brazilian Minister and gave him what information I had, and he told me that he had just heard the Germans are attacking north of Xanthi and on the Struma (probably Koula). . . .

[17] Following the defeat of the Italian forces in Cyrenaica by the British in January 1941, German armored divisions under General Erwin Rommel arrived in Tripolitania and began a devastating counterattack which threatened to push the retreating British back to Egypt. The port of Benghazi was evacuated on April 4-5.

At about 7:30 this morning the air-raid sirens were sounded repeatedly to indicate that the war had begun. At 10:30 there was an alert lasting for about half-an-hour, but no firing or bombs were heard. Major Craw said he thought the raiding would begin tonight,—there is a good half-moon, on the increase. He also told me that the British packed a lot of Hurricanes on a boat for the Piraeus, instead of flying them over, and that this boat has been sunk by a German dive-bomber! What awful luck,—and rather a stupid affair too, it seems to me. He said British morale is very high; they say "The Germans have opened the way, and now we can go get them." They plan raids tonight on Bulgaria and Rumania, especially the oil fields. . . . Of course they are hopelessly outnumbered, but the Yugoslav air-force will make a difference, at least to begin with. The British radio, at 8:15, said that the Germans are at war against Yugoslavia too, and there are rumors that a drive against her in the south has already begun, as predicted yesterday by Mr. Eden. Hitler's quarrel with the Yugoslavs is said to be with their "usurping" Government. . . . The news of the evening is that Belgrade has been heavily bombed at least twice today, and all communications with that city are cut. Craw called up to ask if our Legation had any news from there—the British air force was anxious because they themselves could not get in touch. The Greeks repulsed the first push of the Germans at Roupel (Koula). . . .

Air-raid warning at 9:30 in the bright still moonlight. It is going on now, as I write. . . . (Later) The raid was a very heavy one, apparently on the Piraeus, and lasted till 11:45—the "all clear" is now sounding. We could see the search lights (very faint in the light of the moon) and see the great flashes of the explosions from our upstairs terrace, also hear the planes overhead. Some of the explosions shook our windows, though the Piraeus is four miles away!

April 7, 1941, Monday

There was an air-raid in the forenoon, probably a German reconnaissance to photograph the damage caused by last night's bombing of the Piraeus. This appears now to have been considerable, less from the actual bombing than from the subsequent spread of the fires and several huge explosions of ammunition and explosives. A vessel with 200 tons of TNT still aboard her (she was supposed to be all unloaded yesterday, but the British stuck at the Sunday prices asked by the stevedores!) blew up at the end of the Free Zone dock. The Free Zone is a wreck. Craw, who visited the harbor this afternoon reports 19 ships burnt out or still on fire, with lighters blazing and floating about setting fire to other craft, and practically nothing being done about it. Apparently the authorities never thought of moving the shipping out of the harbor, even the ammunition boats, before the raid came,—or if they did, thought it wasn't worth while; and after things occurred were too shocked to take any action....

News from the front was that the Germans have entered Komotini, and have taken a fort of the Metaxas line west of Roupel, but elsewhere have been held. At least on the *first* day they didn't "brush the Greek forces aside." Craw says they landed 200 parachutists behind the Greek lines and that the Greeks captured 70 of these and killed or wounded all the rest....

The Allards are much excited over the way the German Legation is being treated, but I couldn't be very sympathetic! Apparently all the members of the Legation and their families that are not staying in the Minister's house, have been cooped up in the chancery with few if any facilities. Their servants, nurses, etc., have been arrested and taken elsewhere. It appears, too, that they were lured to the chancery by assurances that the Minister was there and wanted them there also! Allard is right in protesting to the Foreign Office against this treatment of diplomatic personnel,—he says, too, that some of the houses were "entered" and furniture destroyed. But I had just heard from Craw of the barbarous bombardment of Belgrade, where "90 percent of the population were caught unprepared." Craw said this news came from a British Secret Service man who escaped from the city and was able to set up a wireless sending set of his own. There is still no telegraphic or telephonic communication.

April 8, 1941, Tuesday

Got to the office to learn that Johnson had telephoned saying the Germans had broken through the Yugoslavs and had crossed the Greek border at Gevgheli, thus turning the Struma line. (The Greeks held on to the Metaxas fortifications as far east as Xanthi for 36 hours and then the Germans came through Roupel, where 150 Greeks held them up all that time and died to a man!—but this we learned later in the day.) With the Germans coming down on Salonica from the north, Johnson said the military authorities were leaving the town. Also all the Americans, except Mr. and Mrs. House. They should all get here all right, by car, provided they find the Vardar bridges still standing. Craw and Baker got the news confirmed from R.A.F. and Greek headquarters respectively. Apparently the Germans have pushed deep into southern Yugoslavia from Bulgaria, taking Skoplje (Uskul) and Veles. They have now a clear road to Monastir, Florina, and Koritza! The Yugoslavs are pecking at Fiume and Zara instead of throwing themselves southward in force to join up with the Greeks and British! The Germans are doing just what they did in France, striking around the end of a fortified line at a point where three allies (Greeks, British and Yugoslavs this time, not French, British and Belgians) fail to coordinate. And it is working again! . . .

Very busy all day with telegrams. Called on the Mayor of Athens at the City Hall at 11 a.m., with Calligas,[18] to present a letter of thanks for the President's having been made an honorary citizen and had a street named for him. . . . Got an ovation from a crowd as I came away. Poor people! . . . In the afternoon called on the British Minister. . . . He was preoccupied, quite naturally, since he had just been talking with General Wilson, and wanted to see the King at once. He made his appointment with the latter while I was with him, and I drove him over in my car, thus getting what Wilson had said. This was that the Yugoslavs have been pushed back and Salonica must be allowed to go, but that the British are moving to hold the Monastir Gap, and have some hopes of doing so, since the Germans have no great force at present at this point and the terrain is a difficult one. The situation is pretty bad on account of the failure of the Yugoslavs to concentrate southwards as the British have urged all along that they do, but apparently Wilson doesn't think it is wholly hopeless yet. . . .

It is certainly a terrible thing to see a country we love so fall once more into slavery. . . . The Turks are not moving. MacMurray telegraphed that he expects them to do nothing unless attacked, or *possibly* if Bulgaria invades Greece. But this forenoon a rumor went round that Turkey had declared war on Germany, and there was a great cheering around the Turkish Embassy. Afterwards, what a let-down! The police arrested some of the leaders of the crowd on the idea that they might be 5th Columnists. . . .

April 9, 1941, Wednesday

Lively morning in the office. Craw brought in a report stating that Marshal D'Albiac had told him certain things to be telegraphed at once to our State and War Departments. Some of these seemed to me to be of a startling nature, and I therefore went over and saw Sir Michael, to ask him if he wanted the State Department to be so advised—the opinions ascribed to the Marshal were of the most pessimistic kind. Sir M. went through the roof, and called D'Albiac in, who denied having seen Craw! It then turned out that Lord Forbes, the Air Attaché, had given Craw the interview, and Craw had passed it on as coming from D'Albiac. Of course Forbes was to blame chiefly, but so was Craw for not telling his true source to me. D'Albiac then called both Craw and Forbes to his office and gave them a dressing down, and 'phoned me afterwards to thank me for having brought the matter up, and, as he said, "saved his

---

[18] Stephen Calligas, MacVeagh's personal secretary and interpreter in Athens.

career." I take it that though D'Albiac denied holding anything like the opinions expressed (about the hopelessness of the present situation here) it *does* represent what he thinks and what he doubtless told Forbes, and that what he means is that *officially* he doesn't hold them, and is in no position to ask that anything be relayed to a foreign government. It is for his superior in the Middle East Command to do this, Marshal Longmore in Cairo. . . . Craw is greatly cast down, and feels that his usefulness with the British is impaired,—and I guess it is, for the time being, at any rate. . . .

The Polish Minister came in and said he had heard from Mrs. Papastratos, who is close to Mr. Korizis, that the latter feels quite hopeless, and believes the Government must soon move to Crete. . . . I tried to cheer the Pole with talk about difficult terrain, etc., and it is true that according to the British Minister, neither Wilson, nor Papagos, nor the King share this utter hopelessness. But many people do. Athens is a sadly subdued and apprehensive city. You can *feel* it, the gloom is so dense. . . .

The Brazilian Minister came in and asked me again what I intended doing if the Government leaves. He said he would follow my lead in the matter. I said that I would probably take the Department's wishes in Lane's case as a precedent and follow the Government, if possible, leaving a senior officer in charge here. . . . Salonica has been taken, probably some time today. . . . An armored division followed by mechanized units swept down from Doiran. The British now expect an attack across the plain against Verria and Katerini, while they themselves have had to extend northwards to stop the Monastir Gap against armored forces descending from Prilep. The Italians are attacking in order to make a junction with the advancing Germans, and according to Sir Michael, General Papagos is considering refusing his right flank in Albania in order to link up with the British. This would mean a severance of the Greeks and British from the Yugoslavs. However, the latter are said to be driving down from the north in the rear of the Italians. The situation is therefore confused, but it looks now as if Southern Serbia would be cut through and occupied by the Germans, and Yugoslavia encircled and reduced, while the Germans and Italians will pinch in on the Greeks and British in the Pindus-Olympus region. . . . In Eastern Macedonia and Thrace, isolated Greek forts on the Metaxas Line still put up a gallant and suicidal resistance. The Greek fighting along this front appears to have been some of the finest in history,—but to what end? The Germans have broken through the line in several places, chiefly in Thrace, where there were practically no defenders, and they are now moving west against Kavalla in the rear of the main Metaxas fortifications. According to the Greek Staff there have been only one division, plus fortress troops in all this region— 15,000 men!

Another moonlight raid, apparently with a lot of planes, over the Piraeus tonight. . . . I hope they scattered the boats this time, but I guess they didn't bother, and I shan't be surprised tomorrow to learn that the big anchorage in the Salamis straits is strewn with wrecks. The Piraeus, of course, will be completely ruined with this raid so close on the heels of what happened the other night. . . .

Sir Michael told me today that Admiral Turle (who was having a party for the captains of some of the ships when last Sunday's raid took place) assured him that the port would be restored to 60 percent efficiency in a week. But even if that were possible this morning, it won't be now. Sir Michael also said that British convoys are now using Eleusis, Chalkis, and Volos. . . . But the most depressing thing that happened today was Churchill's speech in the House of Commons (I think it was in the House) during which he made it clear that Greece's decision to fight for her independence was her own, not Britain's, and that the latter's assistance to the Balkan nations must of necessity be limited. I imagine that the Prime Minister wanted to reply to the German charges that Britain had pushed Greece into war, and leave the onus of the attack where it belongs, on the Germans themselves. But the way he put it was characteristically British in its lack of tact, and will, I am sure, impress people here as a kind of washing of the hands so far as British interest in Greece is concerned, and a warning of no more help to come. He said, "British troops will stand in line with the Greeks," but he might have heartened them differently. The rest of the speech, too, was none too encouraging. The admission of huge shipping losses added to the statement that the Germans launched heavy armored forces against the British in Libya "before the British command thought it was possible for them to do so," does not make good news. Add to this a news item following in the same broadcast to the effect that the British are fortifying themselves in *Tobruk*—miles behind the mountain line that was talked about only the other day! Then Churchill sounded the warning that a difficult task lay ahead not only to defend Cyrenaica *but to defend Egypt*! It appears that five or six German armored divisions in the Balkans, and one or two in Africa, may win the war. What is the matter with the British? "In the money" as they have been and are, can they not create armored divisions too? They have had a year now since they learned the lesson of modern warfare. . . .

After I had talked with Sir Michael today about Craw's misdemeanor, he showed me his most recent telegrams to London, and I learned the amazing fact that the British forces here consist of no more than $1\frac{1}{2}$ divisions, plus a mechanized brigade and some anti-aircraft units. Of course there is also a lot of transport, and hospitals and labor troops, etc. But all this hardly makes an "Imperial Army" such as the British radio has been speaking of! The Turkish and Yugoslav Military Attachés have put the British strength at 150, or 120 thousand, and Major Baker thought he was conservative at 80,000! Weeks ago, he estimated *four* divisions. And now behold the truth! I have pooh-poohed the idea that Wavell and Wilson would let themselves in for another Dunkirk; but if they haven't done just that, they will be running things pretty close. . . .

April 10, 1941, Thursday
 Another day full of bad news. The Germans have taken Monastir and made contact, it seems, with the Italians in the region north of the lakes, and thus the Yugoslavs are completely cut off from their allies. . . . The Greeks must now try to draw back their right flank in Albania and establish a line with the British. This may involve giving up Koritza and Florina, and running the line from near Moschopolis to Edessa, using high ground, and leading thence along the Vermion range to Verria and Katerini. . . . However, the Germans have crossed the Vardar in a swift move from Salonica and are reported already at Verria! There is still a small Yugoslav offensive going on in northern Albania but probably the Germans will arrive in time to save their allies from destruction at this point. Too bad the Yugoslavs could not have begun their concentrations earlier and been really ready for the fray! As it is, they are cut to pieces, with mechanized columns running rings around them! . . . In the Struma valley, the Germans have at last taken the Roupel fort and the valley is open; Greek troops are trying to get out via the sea—I suppose at Tsayesi, under the eyes of the Lion, if he is still standing. . . .
 The day began for me with a long talk with Wallace[19] of the British Legation about Sulzberger. He is in the "dog house" all right, but Wallace thinks he will be forgiven his sins, not because of any justification for his actions, but because of the standing of his paper. He asked me to tell Sulzberger just that, and I did so by means of a letter to Shan [Sedgwick]. . . .
 Went to the Foreign Office (in the Grande Bretagne) and saw Mr. Mavroudis. Told him of the telegram we had received from Ankara according to which the British and Yugoslavs have both asked the Turks to break off relations with Germany, at least, if not to enter the war. Mr. Mavroudis showed me a telegram he had just received to the same effect, only adding that the British Ambassador was rather cold in talking with Mr. Saraçoglu (I don't wonder!) and that the latter had only said that he would refer the matter to the Council of Ministers. Von Papen told the Turks at the same time that the attack on Greece and Yugoslavia is not aimed at Turkey and that Bulgaria will not take part. But Bul-

---
[19] David Wallace, British Press Attaché in Athens.

garian troops are said to be going along with the Germans in Serbia. Mr. Mavroudis has no hope left that the Turks will do anything. In the end it has proved to be they and not the Yugoslavs who have been fascinated by the snake. They will make his next meal, peacefully or otherwise! Mr. Mavroudis said no plans have yet been made to evacuate the Greek Government (wherein I think he lied) and promised to let me know when this happens, and that passage will be provided for such diplomats as want to go along. . . . As the decision, if and when taken, is likely to come suddenly and give us very little time, we are packing a couple of bags each so as to be ready on short notice. We are also trying to get some packers in to do up our books, papers, smaller pictures, and odds and ends, so as to leave the house ship-shape for whoever has the task of closing out finally. . . .

Major Baker came back about six from the Greek Staff with news that the Germans may be sweeping round the lakes north of Koritza, to join the Italians; and that that town will be abandoned as the Greeks draw back was confirmed by news Mr. Kohler got later. . . . But the worst news of the day is that the British are so hard pressed in Cyrenaica that they have lost 2,000 prisoners and three generals, including General Gambier Parry who was here some time ago when the British first began to explore the military possibilities of this front. The Germans must indeed be superior in strength, and perhaps also in skill, to catch 2,000 of the men who drove the Italians from Sidi Barrani to Benghazi. The foreboding is ill! The B.B.C. tonight dilated on the capture of Addis Ababa and last night's raid on Berlin, but it couldn't sweeten the pill. I hazard the prediction that the British will lose Greece (and all those fine Australians and New Zealanders!) this spring, and will be thrust back into Egypt, if they don't lose that also, this spring as well. The Germans have better equipment and more of it, and know how to use it just as well if not better,—and that's the story. Man to man the Australian or New Zealander is a better soldier than the German, I still believe, but they are so few! . . . The Greeks have just shown themselves great fighters, too, far surpassing on the Metaxas line what they have already done against the Italians. Perhaps they, in the plenitude of their amazing spirit, are the finest fighters of all. But again, how few! The hordes of the mechanized barbarians are too numerous for the few free peoples brave enough to fight for their freedom. The men in the Metaxas forts all knew they must die—like the Spartans of Leonidas—and were all volunteers. The Americans back from that front all testify to a morale beyond praise. . . .

April 11, 1941, Friday

Meeting of the officers during which we decided that if the Greek Government should leave Athens, I would go with it, and take Major Baker, Berry, and two clerks. . . . Talk with Sulzberger about his troubles. He is hiring a caique and thinks of smuggling himself out of Greece. "The Germans will shoot me if they catch me, and after what has happened, I won't ask the British for any help in getting out." . . .

Went and saw Sir Michael, who assured me that the King has promised to tell him when the move to Crete is decided on.

April 12, 1941, Saturday

Sulzberger came in and I advised him to give up the idea of smuggling himself out of Greece. Told him it would do him no good in the future to have done such a thing. He is not a fly-by-night reporter, but the Balkan representative of the *New York Times*. Said I thought it would be better judgment for him to go to the British and get accommodations above board, regarding what has passed as passed, and being dignified about it. He seemed to agree, and I hope he will get over his sophomoric pet. He and the British don't agree about his recent article, but that is no reason for him to act as if he were a criminal escaping from justice. . . .[20]

The news is that the Greeks and British are in contact with the Germans and Italians on a line comprising the present Albanian front and a new front running probably south of both Koritza and Florina to Edessa and the sea. But though the Germans and Italians appear to have established contact north of lake Ochrida, they have not yet started any offensive southwards. The Serbs are isolated, but trying to pull themselves together for an effort. . . .

Dinner at the Allards . . . Allard quoted the German Air Attaché as saying that the Germans intend to bomb only the Piraeus and Eleusis. Tatoi is too poor an air-field to demand attention (though Craw says it is the best *all-weather* field in Greece) and Phaleron will be wanted intact by the Germans themselves! . . . Packed up for departure, with two suit cases, at a moment's notice.

April 13, 1941, Sunday

There is very little news here today. Nobody seems to know what the Yugoslavs are doing, if anything. It is unconfirmed that they have reached Durazzo. The Germans have trumpeted that they have joined forces with

[20] In fact, as the Germans approached Athens, Sulzberger left for Turkey in a small chartered vessel (*caique*), having obtained permission from the authorities with MacVeagh's assistance.

the Italians—and state also that the population of Salonica welcomed them with open arms! This last is probably about as true as the Britisher's statement that when he left Salonica at the last minute before the Germans entered, "it was in flames." The truth may be that he saw the Shell and Socony installations "going up," and that a few Germanophiles and a lot of Germanophobes demonstrated when the conquerors arrived. . . .

The British are sending a lot of their colony, mostly women and children out in the cargo vessels used as transports. The evacuees include some of the Legation people. . . . At the same time, however, British troops continue to arrive. Twelve ships came in yesterday, with a couple of destroyers and have been unloading what Major Baker thinks is infantry all day. . . .

Sir Michael informed me that General Wavell has been here, and left again today. "The situation is bad, of course, up north, but not too bad, and General Wilson is quite confident." "If the Florina line cannot be held, the positions further back can, and there is always the Thermopylae line." I pointed out to him how there are no roads south through Greece west of Thermopylae until one reaches the even narrower pass along the Gulf of Arta; the Karpenisi-Agrinion road is still unfinished, and even un-begun, for forty kilometers through the wildest country. Against good opposition, to penetrate this barrier comprised of Orta, Oxia, Tymphrestos, Kaliakonda, Chelidona, etc. would be impossible. But the British would have to keep their forces from being chewed up and swallowed on the retreat from up north. "Oh, I don't think that would happen," said he. He also told me that the British have laid magnetic mines in Brindisi harbor, and "Bari will be next, I fancy." Perhaps the British are hoping for something from the Yugoslav descent along the Albanian coast. . . . Sir Michael said he had heard that the Greek Government planned to go to Crete tomorrow, so he rushed over this morning to see Mr. Korizis, who replied "That's a damned fifth-columnist lie." Sir M. then told him of Wavell's views, and he "crossed himself with emotion." Sir Michael said to me that the Greeks have had a "Good Friday depression" but are feeling better now. . . . Of course, the fact is that preparations *have* been made for moving (and ought to be) and that this (as well as such things as the British Legation's own action in evacuating its people) have led to exaggeration.

April 14, 1941, Monday

Major Baker could get no information from the Staff—a thing which always happens when the news is bad. So I called up Count Mercati and asked to see the King. Was told H.M. would see me at 3 o'clock at the palace. . . .

Dressed up after lunch and was received by the King as arranged, in his library. He told me that King Peter was expected here at 5 o'clock, coming by plane from Paramythia, where he arrived this morning with no prior announcement. He said he is sorry for the boy, whom he described as a 17 year old with the mind of a child of 12! Also said that the Yugoslav General, Simović,[21] has told all commanders they can follow their own initiative from now on—the army is no longer acting as a unit! The claims of the Yugoslavs to have captured Durazzo have been punctured by Greek planes which flew over that port and saw no signs of them anywhere. But worst of all, while the Greeks have been falling back from Pogradetz, the British this morning withdrew their armored forces south of Florina and the Germans have come through between them and the Greeks, advancing this morning as far as Ptolemais, branching off toward Kastoria. Perhaps they are as far as Kozani now. This turns the British Vermion line and cuts the allies in two. The King seems to think it quite possible that German motorcycles and light cars will soon be dashing about the country, even if the main body is forced to move slowly. He said he had sent a staff officer north to inquire why Wilson withdrew; it was not a plan concerted with the Greeks and came as an awful surprise to them. They lost a full regiment in trying to stop the Germans single-handed.[22]

We talked about defeatism in the Government and the King told of his troubles and efforts in this connection. He has sent them packing back to their bureaus with the injunction to spread hope and cheer. Naturally, he himself is ready to leave if he has to, but not till it is clear he cannot carry on here effectively. If the Government does go, he prefers Cyprus to Crete, as less exposed to bombing from all sides, and has actually asked Britain to cede a part of Cyprus so that the Greek Government might still be on Greek soil. . . . He said Korizis proposed to ask for the whole island, but that he himself demurred, as he felt the British might well hesitate over an action which might create a difficult precedent. . . . In regard to my going with the Government he said he would distinctly wish it, and that he even consider it "vital"—meaning, I take it, that the prestige of the refugee Government would be bolstered by the presence of the representative of the U.S.A.

[21] General Simović was also head of the new Yugoslav government.

[22] In his memoirs, Eden maintains that the falling back of the British armored forces to the Aliakmon line (Mt. Olympus-Verria-Edessa-Kaymakchalan) had been in accordance with earlier British-Greek plans. See Eden, Anthony, *The Reckoning*, (Boston: Houghton Mifflin, 1965), pp. 234-5. The matter is examined in considerable detail and under the title "Unfortunate Misunderstanding" in John S. Koliopoulos, *Greece and the British Connection* (London: Oxford University Press, 1977) pp. 221-62.

An air raid alert sounded as we were talking, and the King suggested we go to his new shelter in the back garden, where we were soon joined by Princess Catherine, waked up from her nap, and by Count Mercati, who kindly brought me my hat and stick. It appears that 27 planes came over and very ineffectively bombed New Phaleron bay, where the British convoy I mentioned yesterday still lay at anchor. The anti-aircraft fire was intense, and all about the palace was quite shattering. I understand that four planes came down. . . .

The Italians have announced the fall of Koritza—*sic transit* the glory of a great chapter in Greek history! Greece has certainly shown up magnificently in this war,—only to have what she earned snatched from her with a stab in the back. Now, though the army morale remains high, Athens people are grumbling and fearful. Pro-Germans are coming up for air with fantastic stories encouraging defeatism. As the King said today, there will be a lot of Quislings in this town when the Germans come! He said Wavell told him (very different from Sir Michael's account!) that all the British can hope for is a resistance of from two to three weeks, after which the allies must be able to take the offensive or perish. . . . The King has talked with Greek soldiers from the Metaxas line, who told him that the German infantry unsupported by tanks is worse than the Italians. The whole thing lies in that word "unsupported." I wrote to the President some time ago of the likelihood of a "succession of Thermopylaes" here, and it looks as if I was right. A Salamis, and even more, a Plataea, can hardly be hoped for.

April 15, 1941, Tuesday

The Turkish Ambassador came in to talk about evacuation of the Diplomatic Corps. I advised him to see the King, as only the King's word now counts, Mr. Korizis being only an administrator. Enis is desirous of doing his duty as dean, but confirmed he didn't like to face the King, on account of the feeling here in regard to Turkey's attitude. However, he promised to see him, after seeing Korizis. I gather he hopes that the latter will fix things so that an interview with H.M. will not be necessary.

Went over to see the British Minister and got the dope on the front. The Greeks and British are back on the Aliakmon with their right (British) on Olympus and their left (Greeks) north of Smolikas. The Germans have taken Kozani and apparently Grevena also. General Heywood came in when I was there. Apparently the communications with the north are difficult; Papagos was going to fly up today to see Wilson. The Bosches have bombed Larissa heavily, and probably cut the wires. They have also bombed and laid parachute mines at Chalkis. Talked with

Sir Michael about evacuation. He said warships (which the Turk thinks should be a *sine qua non* of the diplomats' departure) are unlikely to be sent to take us off. He and his family are going on Lord Forbes' yacht, and said he would be glad to take us three along. My staff, however, would have to go with the regular convoy, as his room is limited. The yacht is a small one, and slow, but on the other hand would make a poor target and might slip away unperceived. The convoy is sure to be spotted, but on the other hand would have some protection in all likelihood by destroyers and perhaps planes. It is a toss-up which to choose, and I am much in doubt whether I should take the Peggies. Mummy is no help, because she just keeps on saying she'll do as I decide! To cross to Crete (which Sir M. says is certainly the first destination even if the King's idea of Cyprus is accepted, and he thinks it won't be, since the British regard Crete as easier to defend) is risky, and we may be marooned there if the Germans take Egypt....

Planes this morning circled a lot overhead, however, and I wouldn't put it past the Bosche to do a Belgrade here. The only hope is that Hitler is against it, on account of some fantastic liking for antiquity, which they say he affects. But that is a slim hope. As for the assurances of the Italian radio and reported understandings on the non-bombardment of Athens and Rome, a fig for that....

The Dept. wired that it approves my plan for going along with Berry, Baker, Ernst and Brewster.[23]

April 16, 1941, Wednesday

Busy morning with many visitors asking for help of all sorts, chiefly in regard to evacuation. At one o'clock went over to the Yugoslav Legation. The Minister had 'phoned me that the Government had arrived and that the Foreign Minister wished to see me. This gentleman[24] proved to be a great talker, and for an hour poured out his soul. Began with asking me to thank President Roosevelt for his encouraging messages. Then traced the recent history of Yugoslavia. Blamed Prince Paul. The latter's government after signing a pact which would never have been ratified and was therefore framed to come into operation upon signature, began demobilizing the army at once thereafter, and the new government had to catch up with this loss in addition to mobilizing later to face the German threat. He was particularly anxious to impress me with the fact that his government tried to avoid war until it was sure that nothing less than the country's independence was at stake. From the moment it saw that

---

[23] Philip Ernst and Daniel Brewster, secretaries of the U.S. Legation in Athens.
[24] Bogoljub Jevtić.

Germany wished to encircle and force Yugoslavia to disarm, war was decided on, but not before. He said, too, that Russia was pushing to conclude a defensive military alliance with Yugoslavia, and the latter's plenipotentiaries actually expected to sign such a pact in Moscow, when at the last moment the Russians decided they wanted only the milder non-aggression affair actually concluded, and he thinks Germany had meanwhile found out what was going on, and promptly menaced and frightened the Russians off.... He then traced the history of the campaign in Yugoslavia. Said the Serbs planned to fall back into Bosnia and Herzegovina, where they could hold out for months. But the Croats treacherously allowed German motorized columns to cross through from the north in the rear of the Serbian armies. Divisions attempting to overwhelm the Italians in Albania were cut off by fast-moving German columns breaking through Southern Serbia, etc....

During the afternoon there came disturbing news that the front near Kalambaka had been broken and Larissa taken by a pincers movement there and at Tempe.... Had a talk with the Turk about evacuation of the diplomats. He complained that no plans were being made.... Went over after dinner to see the British Minister. He said the Government plans to leave tomorrow night for Crete, as a first stop, and that he hopes to get on his yacht then too, asking us three to come along. The diplomatic corps may get a cargo boat, but in any case, arrangements will be by the British, not the Greeks, which is reassuring.

April 17, 1941, Thursday

Sulzberger has just told me that at 8:00 tonight the Government issued a proclamation to the press saying that the King and Government are leaving Greece, but withdrew it almost immediately. Apparently news that the front has been miraculously held for the moment is what delayed the evacuation. Sulzberger said that this shows the Government will go, when it does, without much warning to us ahead of time, and in view of what Mavroudis told Enis at 3:00 I guess he's right. I knew about the plan from Sir Michael last night. Why then did Mavroudis tell Enis that he didn't know when or where? ... The diplomats are being treated as if they were not wanted, and turned over to the British to be handled in any old way. Probably all the planes available (and they are few) are needed for the Greek and Yugoslav Governments. The latter, by the way, is still here. I got a message from Washington to be relayed to it.[25]

[25] The diary entry for April 17 also records that the family dog, "Souf," a mongrel which the MacVeaghs had found and taken in many years earlier, had been taken by Mrs. MacVeagh to the vet and "put away," since "he could hardly be taken on an Odyssey we might undertake—even if only because his health wouldn't stand it."

April 18, 1941, Friday

Went to the Grande Bretagne and saw Mr. Mavroudis. He said the Government could not provide transportation for diplomats and possibly I might stay on here and rejoin it later, through Turkey, perhaps; and that it would, in fact, feel a little more confident in leaving if it knew that the American Minister were here during the first dark days. . . . I sent this off to the Dept. and wonder what they will say. . . .

Archer called up and said that Miss Aravantinos, a great friend of Mrs. Korizis, had just told him that the Premier had shot himself. Evidently his responsibilities were too much for his frail health and nerves. . . . This will be a great shock for the King. Sent off a brief wire. . . . Rumors came in all evening to the effect that a military Government will be set up, Generals Mazarakis[26] and Othonaios being named as possibilities. . . .

The news from the front is better, and it appears that the Germans were unable to break through to Kalamata. The line runs now from Chimara through Argyrocastro to Grevena, Elassona and the sea. Kennedy, the A.P. man, came back from near the front, north of Larissa, and said the slaughter of Germans has been tremendous, but they have, of course, inexhaustible forces. Their aviation dominates the whole battle and continually dive-bombs the roads and even isolated trucks and men. . . . Two air-raids today, one in the morning and one just after lunch. The British sent a few fighters to protect their outgoing convoy, and there was little or no bombing, to judge from the noise.

April 19, 1941, Saturday

The British Minister called me up at breakfast time and I went round to see him at 10. He said that the Premier's suicide followed 5th column pressure and dissention in the Cabinet (particularly involved was Papademas, the Under-Minister for War). The King's efforts to form a new Government resulted only in getting Mr. Kotzias as Vice-President of the Council, the King himself taking the Presidency. I had already seen this in the press, and it struck me as a most inadequate, and even unfortunate arrangement, particularly in view of Mr. Kotzias's past reputation. The British Minister said a military Government seemed to him the only solution, and I completely agreed. Mr. Michalopoulos[27] then came in and

---

. . . Our hearts will be sore for a long, long time for Souffles, and we shall never forget him, for when we have become accustomed to being without his presence, he will be a happy memory. But tonight I am just sick with sorrow. . . ."

[26] General Alexander Mazarakis, Venizelist officer and former Minister of War, in forced retirement during the Metaxas régime.

[27] Michael Michalopoulos, one-time private secretary of Venizelos, the Vice President of the Athens Water Co., and a radio commentator during the Metaxas régime.

read us a letter he had just sent to the King in this sense. It seems he had been asked to join the new Government along with Mr. Kyrou of the *Estia*,[28] and that both of them had felt the arrangement impossible and had decided to ask the King to put a number of Generals in. Sir Michael then discussed with him what Generals. That appears to be the question, particularly. Michalopoulos (whose absence from broadcasting last night is now explained!) mentioned Gonatas among others, but I can't see the King accepting *him*! Finally Sir Michael and I went over and saw H.M. in person, and found him willing to make a military government, but baffled by the question of personnel. He spoke favorably of Mazarakis and Manettas, but wants also to have Maniadakis continue to run the Sureté, and neither of these Generals will stand for that! I can't think what he will do—seems rather in a fog, poor man. But in any case it is clear that something in the way of constituting a firm and unquestionably patriotic government must be done quickly, or discouragement and panic will spread to the front, where morale appears still to be high.... The British Minister spoke of Generals up there, however, who are in sympathy with the defeatists here, and disintegration, if it once sets in, will be rapid.

The strictly military news today is not bad. Wilson is holding and preparing to fall back to Thermopylae. Wavell has telegraphed to hold, and is expected himself today. What the British fear most at present is that the Greek front should collapse, and especially that Metsovo might be taken....

April 20, 1941, Sunday

Mummy and I walked on the Acropolis in the afternoon, between air-raids, of which the day produced seven! The Bosche strafed the Tatoi air-field and burned up 13 planes on the ground.

It was announced early in the day that the Government would be formed by General Mazarakis, as Vice-President of the Council, with the King retaining the Presidency, but later about 5 o'clock, Admiral Sakellariou took up the reins, as the head of a Cabinet including Mr. Tsouderos (the Venizelist ex-Governor of the Bank of Greece) as Minister of Foreign Affairs, and a General Panagakos as War Minister. I went over to see Sir Michael and he told me that the King had fought all day against defeatism, and that Mazarakis and Manettas had given out on him, Sakellariou being chosen (somewhat unexpectedly) because of the firmness with which he has held the navy in hand (Papavasiliou[29] seems to have

[28] Kyros Kyrou, owner of the royalist Athens daily *Estia*.
[29] Admiral Ippokratis Papavasiliou, Under-Minister of the Navy.

gone the way of Papademas). Maniadakis, Nicoloudis, and Dimitratos remain from the old Cabinet.[30] Sir M. said he is satisfied Nicoloudis is not a pro-German, or his wife either. I wonder! And as to Maniadakis, Mr. Theotokis, who came in to see me yesterday morning, said that he had proposed they go together to Crete, so perhaps he does not feel clear enough in his record so far as the Axis is concerned to do a double-cross now! And on the other hand, he has an organization which might, I suppose, make trouble for the new Government if the latter failed to recognize it.... But the Cabinet is certainly a queer one, not least in having Stavros Theofanidis as Minister for Merchant Marine!

While I was at the British Minister's, Admiral Turle and General Heywood came in. The British are very much worried about the situation on the Greek front, and Heywood may go up to Jannina to consult with the Generals there. Tsouderos suggests that he take General Pangalos (the ex-dictator who has suddenly come back into all men's minds) with him. The Admiral remarked to the Minister in my hearing that "we are trying to keep as many boats away from Greece as possible just now." This was anent a request of the King's to send Greek boats back here *pronto*, from Egypt and Suez. It shows to what extent the German air superiority has interfered with British supply plans here—and perhaps with evacuation plans also, though the Admiral wouldn't admit this when I asked him. Wavell is still here, and Blamey[31] of the Australians is expected down to meet him....

Tonight I felt badly in my turn; I was quite sick, physically.... The war of nerves getting in some of its work on us!

Got off a telegram on the chief figures in the Cabinet late in the evening. The only really good thing about the day was our time on the Acropolis, where the camomile is thick and fragrant, reminding us of our first visits, in April eleven years ago....

Kotzias came in this morning and asked me for a visa for the United States—Berry and I told him he had better get a diplomatic passport, and this he went off to do. Mr. Mavroudis called up to speak on his behalf and from what he said it appears *Apostolidis* wants to go too! I dashed over to see Sir Michael about Kotzias and he said that while he felt the man might become a Quisling if he stayed here, he might equally well be quite the opposite in other circumstances. Anyhow the British want to get him out of here and are willing to have him go to Egypt, India, etc., so I guess we can let him come to America. Poor fellow, I am sorry for him. He is pretty far down now, but his native bounce should bring him back!

---

[30] Maniadakis, as Minister of Interior, Nicoloudis, as Minister of the Press, and Dimitratos as Minister of Agriculture.

[31] Lieutenant General Sir Thomas Blamey, Commander of 1st Australian Corps.

April 21, 1941, Monday

The Cabinet was announced in the papers, and later Mr. Tsouderos took over the premiership. There were many air raids, and many rumors. ... Late in the afternoon Mr. Jones came in from the British Legation with the news that the Greek army in Albania had asked for an armistice. I tried to see the British Minister, but he was at Headquarters or somewhere. At dinner time, Major Baker arrived at the house with an account of what he had learned from the British Military Attaché and the Greek Staff. This agreed with Jones' information except that the armistice was not mentioned, only that the Greek troops were not expected to continue resistance much longer. Apparently, the Germans have come into Jannina over the Metsovo pass after pushing the British south in Thessaly. Trikkala and Jannina are said to have been absolutely destroyed by aerial bombardment. The British will attempt to hold the Thermopylae line and block the Messolonghi-Delphi approaches to their rear while arranging to evacuate their forces! What a picture. It would never have come true if the British had seven divisions the Department told me they were planning to. Two divisions and a half! There will be a grand rumpus now in Parliament, and what will Australia and New Zealand say? ... After dinner, the British Minister asked me over, and I had a talk with him, General Heywood and Air Vice-Marshal D'Albiac. They told me that the General in command at Jannina, Pitsikas, had asked yesterday, on the earnest representation of his corps and division commanders, whether the Government would agree to his organizing an armistice of the Germans "to prevent capitulation to the Italians." Admiral Sakellariou replied in the negative, but the reply seems not to have reached Pitsikas, who today went ahead on his own. It is not known whether the Germans are in Jannina, but it is possible that they broke through over the Metsovo pass, where the Greek forces when last heard of had dwindled to two battalions. ...

When I left the very discouraged trio they were on their way to Headquarters to hear some more news, probably bad, or Androulis, who telephoned them to come over, could have told it on the phone. ...

April 22, 1941, Tuesday

The air raids began at 7 o'clock ... continued at short intervals all day. ...

Meeting of the officers, from which I was called by the British Minister, who said that the best information about the armistice is that the Greeks will lay down their arms and disband, and the Germans will interpose themselves between the Greeks and Italians, none of the latter to come on Greek territory. No political arrangements made. ... However, this information is not official. Communications are practically non-existent. ... It appears that Pitsikas himself did not ask for the armistice, but was supplanted by one of his juniors,[32] acting with the Archbishop of Jannina ...

Went over and saw the King. His family—the ladies of it—left by plane for Crete this morning, and he will go tomorrow at the same time (very early, in an attempt to evade the Bosche). The Crown Prince and Tsouderos will go with him. He is very tired (no wonder) but we had a very friendly talk. He said the Germans are now marching south on the Jannina-Arta road; that in flattening the city of Jannina they particularly bombed the military hospitals (they sank two hospital ships last night) and killed many doctors and nurses. Amazing people! He talked again of my staying here for the time being, and thanked me for doing so,—but did not offer to take us off in a plane; only said jokingly that we should have a plane or a battleship, presumably of our own. ... Said good-bye to him. Incidentally, he said that he will not recognize the armistice, but this will do no good, except, I suppose to keep the record clear. ... Talked a bit with the Crown Prince, and then with Mr. Tsouderos, who showed fine spirit. Greece has done her duty and fought bravely against odds for home and freedom, and should be happy not sad, since having done right she can never be the loser in the long run, etc. Said the same things as Mr. Mavroudis and the King about my staying here, but asked if I could send an officer on a warship leaving tonight with some of the Greek Government.

Saw Mr. Mavroudis (now no longer *en fonction*) and he asked me to keep money for him, which I said I could hardly do; and then Mr. Androulis asked me to keep his wife's jewels, which I also had to refuse, as we have done for Mr. Stathatos and Mr. Skouzé. Perhaps these poor people are slightly over-panicky about their private possessions. I have an idea that the Germans will not rob them, but will rather take the attitude of being their friends and liberators, at least at first. ...

A great deal of shooting and banging about during the noon air-raids. ... Went back to the Grande Bretagne at 3 to find Mr. Tsouderos, but had to wait as he was napping. Finally saw him, and told him I can't spare an officer to go with the Government, since the British have turned over their affairs to my Legation, and I am already short-handed. He said he understood, and I stressed that we expect to rejoin the Government soon.

---

[32] On April 20, Lieutenant General John Pitsikas, the commander of the Greek forces in Epirus, was falsely informed by Lieutenant General George Tsolakoglou, the commander of the Greek forces in Western Macedonia, that he, Tsolakoglou, had been authorized by the General Staff to conclude a cease-fire. Later in the day, Tsolakoglou, acting without the knowledge of the government in Athens, signed the capitulation agreement.

... My real reason for not taking up his suggestion is that Majors Craw and Baker, and D'Albiac too, say that nobody who doesn't have to should leave here by sea now, and I don't want to take the responsibility of ordering anyone to go against this professional warning....

Major Baker got very little information this afternoon, but what he did get—that the British on the Thermopylae line are not in contact with the enemy, while preparing their evacuation, agrees with what Sir Michael said later when I went over to see him, that the Germans aren't even sending out reconnaissances in this region. I wonder if what they plan to do is now to shift the whole weight of their aviation against the few British and blast them to pieces as they try to embark without making any further land attacks at all?

Anne Palairet[33] came to tea with Bunny and Mum. She said they are leaving, not in the yacht tomorrow night with the Caccias and the Pole (!) but in the plane with H.M. tomorrow. I went over at once and said goodbye when I heard the news, and saw the three of them just for a moment. He looks completely worn out, poor fellow! ...

Finished the burning of all our codes today except Grey, and all confidential despatches and true readings of telegrams.

April 23, 1941, Wednesday

St. George's Day and the King's name day, but the King, with the Crown Prince, Mr. Tsouderos, and the British Minister and family left Scaramanga at 5 o'clock on a Sunderland flying boat for Crete. Poor King, once more driven out! ....

The air raids began at 7 and continued on and off all day. ...

During the day it became evident that many disbanded Greek soldiers are flocking back to Athens; the streets are full of them, lounging miserably about. The problems of food and lodging and how to keep idle hands from trouble will soon bulk large. ...

The morning papers today still talked about the front holding, and said nothing about the authorities leaving. The King's proclamation, therefore, issued in the early forenoon, caught the people very much unprepared and the effect was stunning. It said that the situation called for removing the Sovereign, the Government and the capital, to a place on Greek soil whence they could continue the fight with the future of the country in mind. It praised the armies for their great fight "against two empires" and the British for their prompt and stubborn assistance. A grand proclamation. But I feel the people's morale is about finished. Things are going soft. Too bad!

[33] Daughter of the British Ambassador in Greece.

April 24, 1941, Thursday

The first air-raid sirens blew at 8:20 and raids went on all day along the coast, with much firing from the Athens guns. . . . The office was besieged by Britishers all day, and Jones and Berry put in a lot of time over at the British Legation, mostly telling people that we can't evacuate them. The last British officials have left, and we sealed up the house last night and put placards on the doors, etc., but there are still a lot of their people un-taken care of. . . .

The Grand Rabbi of Salonica called during the afternoon, and I was able to get him a million drachmas for the Jewish soldiers now stranded here. The money comes from the 20,000,000 handed over to the Legation by the Vanderbilt Committee[34] for relief of Greek-Americans "or other charitable purposes." As the Jews at home have contributed some of the Vanderbilt money there is every reason why it should be used for their people in this great emergency. The Committee is also giving money to the Archbishop of Athens and the Greek Red Cross, but without our intervention (and immediate at that), I doubt if anyone will help the Jews. The Grand Rabbi impressed me very favorably, and has an excellent record in Salonica, according to a whole line of our consuls up there. . . .

George Zalacosta, who works in Greek Headquarters came in at 5:30 with the news that at 6 the Military Governor of Athens, the Prefect and the Mayor would leave for some place unknown to meet German delegates and arrange for the surrender of the city. Major Baker called up Prince Peter for confirmation and the latter said he thought it a mere rumor, but would check up. Later, Zalacosta came in and reported that the scheme had been postponed until the British should have time to leave the city. . . .

About sunset a lot of German dive bombers came over, and we saw them swoop on the Piraeus and heard the explosion of very heavy bombs. Later Mr. Reed telephoned to say he had been informed by one of the unfortunate Yugoslav Attachés left behind by Vukčević that the Greek General Staff had been bombed while embarking and that many people were killed or injured, including the Yugoslav Military Attaché, who was badly wounded. It may be true that the General Staff was on the way out; Major Baker reported this morning that Headquarters was being closed. But why in heaven's name people go about embarking in broad daylight in the Piraeus these days beats me! The nights are dark now, and I can't see the need for committing suicide. . . . The German bombers had the air to themselves, not a British plane to be seen here all day long.

---

[34] The Administrative Committee of American Relief, headed by Harold Vanderbilt and Cleveland Dodge, was engaged in relief work in Greece, as it was in other war-torn countries.

... Allard came in. He said the Military Governor called on Erbach yesterday only as a courtesy and to ask what he could do for him—but even that is extraordinary enough. The German Minister asked—for the privilege of having his electric light turned on again! Allard thinks the Greeks will surrender Athens as soon as the Germans put in an appearance, but knows nothing of any *pourparlers*. . . . General Wilson is still here, and one of his aides told Craw today that he plans to stay to the last and then take to the hills in disguise if necessary,—but that somehow doesn't seem to make good sense. . . . Prince Peter is now with the General as liaison officer. Major Baker found him really glum today, for the first time. He doesn't know how *he* is going to get out, either. . . .

The military situation appears to be that the British are embarking their troops by night in lighters from little ports and roadsteads all along the Boeotian and Attic coasts, and even to proceed along the roads by daylight, and the German planes are making this movement difficult and even deadly. The Empire troops hold the Thermopylae line, where the Germans have not yet attacked them. Perhaps the Germans will attack when evacuation has thinned the lines down, and at the same time raise the bombing of the evacuees on the roads and ships to even greater proportions. . . . Mussolini broadcast today a hymn of triumph over the conquest of the Greeks—by the Italians. Not one word did he say about the Germans! Incredible, but I am assured it is true. . . .

Greece has been having a pretty hard time of it these past weeks: in fact we have been assisting at the death pangs of a wonderfully brave little nation, and we Americans have been in the midst of it all, and shall be sufferers from the consequences, but at no time has the Department of State indicated by so much as a word that it even knows what is going on (it gaily sends us messages to relay to Salonica!) let alone that it is interested. I would never have thought it possible to work faithfully for anyone for eight years and then be so thoroughly ignored with all my people in trouble as I have been by Uncle Sam.

April 25, 1941, Friday

Another glorious sunny day. The roses in the garden are simply bursting with life. The pansies are somewhat past their bloom, but the lantana is coming out on the walls, the calla lilies are still gleaming along the borders, the clover beds are a lively green, and the orange blossoms very fragrant. . . . We were wakened up by the usual sirens, but there was no anti-aircraft firing, and the same was true of the only other raid during the day, late in the afternoon. I guess the planes were after shipping either along the Attic coast or at the Isthmus.

When I got to the office I found a Brigadier named Salisbury-Jones, sent by General Wilson to ask if we could undertake payment of British military bills which might be left over on evacuation. He said they are doing all they can to pay up before leaving but might not be able to make a clean slate. We told him to telegraph London to have us authorized, and we ourselves sent off a wire to Washington. . . .

During the morning I sent Major Baker to see the Military Governor and saw Prince Peter myself at his house. The Military Governor is in full charge here now. The War Minister has resigned, and the coming capitulation will thus not compromise the Government or the King. Karvakos (the Governor) told Baker that the British have promised not to fight near Athens and he expects a peaceful occupation, as at Salonica, where the Germans halted outside the town and gave the citizens time to be shooed into their houses before the entry began. Prince Peter told me that he and General Wilson, General Heywood, Mr. Maniadakis and Admiral Sakellariou would probably leave tonight by flying boat for Crete. The fleet, except for four or five destroyers and submarines lost in the recent raids, has joined the British, he said, at Alexandria. There was a little trouble about it, but Admiral Sakellariou was firm. The Prince said only that he thought the *Princess Olga* and the *Psara* had been sunk: the Marine Ministry refused to say anything to Major Baker: but the "four or five" etc., we got from the British liaison officer with the Greek navy. The Prince seemed fairly cheerful, and our talk (which was at his little house, Jenny Manussi's, in Lykiou St.) was not too gloomy. . . .

I must say that the authorities have been very efficient in keeping order so far. There is a 9 o'clock curfew, and patrols are everywhere along the streets, instructed to fire on trouble-makers if necessary. Public servants who leave their posts do so under pain of court-martial. But in addition to all this, the people themselves are in general showing an admirable calm. The British are supposed to be unpopular, but I have seen the people waving to the boys as they drove by on their way to a dubious exit, and am told that flowers were thrown and the British flag cheered on at least one occasion. . . . This may be the last free night for Greece, or at least for Athens. How many conquests she has lived through! From Xerxes to Hitler, they have all been proud of taking this city of light, which however has never been extinguished. . . . For our own part, our Athens experience has been a varied and compressed lesson in diplomacy: we have faced a Republic, a revolution, a regency, a monarchy, a dictatorship, a war, and an enemy occupation, and, of course, began it all with the most spectacular extradition case on record. The experience has been something; better probably than being a publisher all these years, even if I could have made money, which is highly unlikely! And even if I have now to go home to little things. We have seen many interesting things and played a part, if only a small one, on the world's stage, and have lived at the same time in Greece, in the very heart and home of beauty. It has *surely* been worth while!

April 27, 1941, Sunday

Athens was captured by the Germans.... We were waked about 8:00 by heavy explosions which may have been demolition, or some dumps going up. Went over to the office and saw the first party of Germans come in about 10:00. Immediately afterwards, Berry and I saw the swastika flag hoisted on the Acropolis, and a rocket fired. Then a long train of side-cars, automobiles, a few tanks, and many lorries, came in from Kifissia way, and there were big scenes of rejoicing round the German chancery next door to ours. The Germans were fine looking specimens, but of course very dirty and dusty—including their equipment and vehicles. . . . Learned that the British Legation had been broken into, and went over there directly, with Reed, Jones, and Major Baker. . . . There were sentries at the gates and we couldn't get in, but we saw that our seals had been broken and our signs pulled down and trampled on. . . . Later the butler told me that a party of soldiers and a civilian employee of the German Legation had come, and the civilian had egged on the others till they did the damage. They entered the house but took nothing but some bottles of whiskey, a flag, some keys, and a valuable shot-gun. Having learned from Allard that there was a representative of the Wilhelmstrasse installed at the Foreign Office, I sent Mr. Reed to see him, and after lunch a secretary of the German Legation, Dr. Vogel, came to see me and apologized. He brought two soldiers with him, supposed to have done the deed. Later still, Dr. Vogel brought back the flag and keys and one bottle of whiskey, and at 7 o'clock I went over with him and Jones and Kohler, and a German captain, examined the house, which I found perfectly all right, and re-sealed it. We also examined seals, some damaged and some not, on the Passport, Air and Military Annexes, and on the Consulate General. Vogel was very helpful, I must say, and Jones was able to arrange with him a lot of details regarding the personnel of the British Legation and the property of the staff. . . . Vogel seemed genuinely disturbed about this and the entry into the Minister's house, and I must say the way the few things—including the gun—that were taken were restored showed both decency and efficiency on the part of the authorities. At first I thought the putting of the blame on the military was a ruse; but the butler's description of the footless and aimless entry convinces me that there was no premeditation. . . .

Major Baker had a full day of it too, for when he got back to the office, after our first visit to the British Legation, he found a lot of British stragglers gathered there, and before he got rid of them some time after six—trying, though he was, all the time, to find somebody to take them off his hands,—the number had grown to twenty, including one I sent over from my house. He tried the German Legation, the Greek military, and the Greek Gendarmerie, but only after seeing a German General did he get action. Then a young lieutenant came around with an auto, or truck, and took them all out to the hospital at Kifissia. . . .

The most disagreeable occurence of the day was the taking of pictures in the hall of our office building by both a German officer and a German journalist, showing a crowd of British soldiers up against our official signs,—indicating of course that the Americans were protecting British troops! Major Baker protested to the General in charge of the town, and I to Dr. Vogel, who said he would do his best to get the pictures and give them to me. But whatever he does, I am sure that copies will reach Germany and will serve as excellent propaganda against us, despite the fact that we were loyally doing nothing but the proper thing throughout, and although the hall of the building is by no means a part of the Legation. . . . This has been a hectic day for me, and what I cannot bear is to have to turn over these poor British stragglers to the Germans, or at best to refrain from helping them escape! . . .

All day long the German planes have been zooming low over Athens, but the war has rolled away from here as occupation has rolled in. Now we have new problems—and with a vengeance. . . .

I must go on record as saying that during its first day, at least, the German occupation of Athens has been a model of order, efficiency, and restraint.

April 28, 1941, Monday

Major Baker had a lot of trouble all day with British soldiers, trying to get them taken off his hands. The German officers who came in to Athens yesterday have apparently gone on to the conquest of the Peloponnese, and a new lot are here now. According to Allard, Marshal List[35] arrived today. . . . Mr. Reed and I had further talks with Vogel about representation of British interests. For the time being, we can pay pensions and doles and pay military bills. . . .

Planes kept flying low over Athens all day. The streets, however, are resuming a more normal appearance. The blackout is still in force, for fear now of the British! . . .

Mummy and I listened in on Churchill's broadcast last night. I think his explanation of the Balkan fiasco was not wholly truthful. The British

[35] Field Marshal W. von List, Commander of the German campaign in the Balkans.

"A GALLANT RESISTANCE" · 353

had more in mind than helping the Greeks. They have been trying for a long time to form an eastern front: they labored mightily and brought forth this mess. But in other respects I thought the speech very fine.

April 30, 1941, Wednesday

Drafted another telegram for Reed to try to get through to Washington in German, saying that a new government has been formed under General Tsolakoglou, and that all the usual portfolios are accounted for except Foreign Affairs, the Missions still remaining in Athens being looked after provisionally by the German Legation. . . . Confusion in German arrangements seems greater than at the outset of the occupation, perhaps because more troops have come in. Reed was unable to see Vogel all day, and we began sending formal notes to the German Legation in regard to this and that. I expect soon that things will be put in order and then we shall know definitely what we can and cannot do,—mostly cannot!

The streets in the main part of town are full of soldiers, discharged Greeks and strolling Germans, the latter for the most part ignored by the population. There are many more officers and cars in evidence than before. Houses and flats are being requisitioned from the wealthy Greeks, —as might be expected. But the way private soldiers are allowed to break in and commandeer quarters for themselves is surprising. . . .

Planes keep on zooming overhead. . . . Craw went to Eleusis yesterday and reported today that planes from there are constantly going out to the Peloponnese and Crete with loads of bombs. . . . Stories current here are to the effect that the British evacuation has been "worse than Dunkirk," as the Germans claimed it would be. However, Mr. Churchill declared in the House today that out of 60,000 troops sent to Greece, 45,000 have been safely taken back. In the fighting at Olympus and Thermopylae, 3,000 were killed and wounded; the rest are still fighting to get away. The figures for the safely evacuated appear to all observers here as far too high, and the casualties in the north too low. But I can't see how the Prime Minister would dare to give out what can be proven false.[36] . . . The banks today refused to cash drafts, even government ones. No dollar exchange was quoted. Prices are beginning to soar. . . .

[36] In his memoirs, Churchill gave the following "final evacuation figures for the Army":

> In Greece at the time of attack: 53,051
> Evacuated to Crete and Egypt: 41,211
> Total losses: 11,840

See Churchill, Winston, *The Second World War*, vol. III, *The Grand Alliance* (Boston, 1951), p. 232.

May 1, 1941, Thursday

The German National holiday. Sent my card to Prince Erbach "pour félicités," since it is customary to do so and to omit the gesture at this time might seem pointed and render a difficult situation needlessly more so. . . .

Walked with Mummy back through the gardens from the Temple of Zeus. The Germans have apparently taken over the antiquities for themselves. There were sentries around the Temple enclosure, and when we innocently approached the gate we were rudely waved away. German soldiers are swarming now all over the city—and the people still ignore them. They have taken over nearly all the houses in Kifissia and many in Psychico and Athens—not only the officers, but soldiers being quartered in the best houses. . . .

It is now reported that the new Government, which was announced yesterday to include, besides several Generals, Dr. Logothetopoulos[37] and Professor Louvaris,[38] did not take the oath before the Archbishop of Athens, but before an Archimandrite of St. George Karytsi [Church], and that Professor Louvaris did not appear, but (so the rumor goes on) has gone to Berlin to protest against "the dismemberment of Greece." The latter phrase is used because Italians have begun to appear in Athens, and have occupied both Corfu and Preveza. It is said that a whole battalion is here in Athens already,—certainly there are some officers,—and this is bound to result in bad blood. . . . Mussolini is said to have insisted that he must be represented in the big parade supposed to be coming off. . . .

More British soldiers turned up at the Legation and were taken in charge by Major Baker.

May 2, 1941, Friday

The office is becoming very dull. No political reporting; no telegrams. Major Baker has to take care of an occasional British soldier and see that he gets taken over properly. Mr. Kohler has some routine records to keep. Things are more lively in the Consulate but even there activity has generally diminished. . . . Thorn[39] came in with Mr. Brunnell, of the International Red Cross. We talked about prisoners of war, and the latter said that as this is now to all intents and purposes a part of Germany, the protection of the prisoners properly falls on the American Embassy in Berlin and on the International Red Cross representatives there. Nevertheless he will do what he can provisionally, and I told him that I had

---

[37] Constantine Logothetopoulos, dean of the medical school of the University of Athens, and Deputy Prime Minister under Tsolakoglou.

[38] Nikolaos Louvaris, Minister of Education and Cults.

[39] John Paul Thorn, assistant director of the American Red Cross in Greece.

wanted to get in touch with him, not because we can ourselves do anything in our anomalous position, but because, having been asked by the British to represent their interests, and having accepted to do so, I felt we should at least be in contact with the one organization which can and does occupy itself with war-prisoners in general. I wanted him to know that we had this affair in mind and would certainly help if and when we should be authorized to do so....

The papers announced that the *Germans and Italians* will stage a parade here at nine o'clock tomorrow morning. Everyone ordered to keep off the streets in the center of the town, nobody to appear on balconies, blinds to be drawn. Obviously there is anxiety lest someone take a potshot. A good deal of speculation is going on as to whether the Führer and Mussolini will be present.... Craw came in later. He had had some trouble with German soldiers trying to seize his car at the Tennis Club during the afternoon. Said he has been surprised by the lack of discipline in this occupation and by the poor appearance of the German troops and transport. So have I.... When he left we found a German soldier making another attempt to take his car. We showed him the Major's papers (signed by me!) and he said "gut" and got out....

May 3, 1941, Saturday

Mr. Reed came in before breakfast to tell me that two Greek gendarmes called on him last night to ask him to tell the British to bomb the parade, as nobody would attend it but Germans and Italians. They also said that they could not bear the presence of the Italians, and that there would certainly be some shooting. He did his best, and quite rightly, to dissuade them from anything so foolish.... The parade came off as per schedule, and there was no trouble. Mr. Thorn saw it from the terrace of the Old Palace, just above the Unknown Soldier, and reported no signs of the Führer or the Duce. Major Baker saw it from University Street, where he said the armored and motorized columns charged four abreast down the avenue at 40 miles an hour! He was duly impressed.... I went to the office and saw a long column of Austrian Alpine troops with mules and police dogs. They marched well and sang lustily, but looked dirty and rather out at elbows, though the men themselves were fine, tall blond beasts....

Dr. Vogel came in and told me that the missions here in Athens may stay for the time being and will be given hospitality. He said if we want anything, especially as regards our cars, benzine, etc., we shall be facilitated! Advised against our trying to leave at once, on account of the roads, but promised to help if and when we decide to go. I said I must wait for instructions. Before he came in, I had a long talk with the

Turkish Ambassador, who came round to the house. He said he had wanted to see Erbach yesterday, but when he went to keep his appointment, he found a new minister installed. . . . He is still anxious to get a boat to come and take him—and the Rumanian and also me—to Turkey. But I am less than formerly inclined to go out to the Near and Middle East, with trouble looming,—Turkey, Iraq, Crete, and Egypt! Who knows? . . . I think we ought to try to get out through Europe. If we go into the war, we shall be caught of course. But we shall be caught equally, under such circumstances, if we try to go east, and it would be better, say, to be in Switzerland than in Siberia or Arabia for the duration! . . .

Vogel expressed great distress over the way German soldiers have gotten out of hand, and told me one man had already been shot for flagrant looting. He explained it by saying that after many hard days, with little to eat, the men have somewhat lost their heads on arriving in a city, which seems like Paradise to them. . . . One quite understands. But the fault lies elsewhere, with the officers. . . .

May 5, 1941, Monday
According to the Greek newspapers, the new Greek Government holds the Regime of the 4th of August responsible for the country's downfall and will soon take steps to punish the culprits. I wonder if the country is in for a reign of terror, with Greek political enmities aiding and abetting the Gestapo? No decree deposing the dynasty has yet been issued, though it is rumored imminent. Perhaps they are waiting till the King leaves Greek soil. People whisper that he has already done so, but I don't think it likely, since the Germans would certainly have broadcast such news if it were true. . . .

Went back to the Chancery, where I found all quiet. There are still some British soldiers in the hall, the Germans being very slow about gathering them in. They eat and sleep there, while the Major does his best to get the Germans to take them over! . . . All Greek private cars have now been taken over by the Germans. . . . For the few hours of the parade the other day, they held 12 hostages at the town hall, who were to pay with their lives for any shooting. Luckily none took place; and curiously enough, the fact that hostages had been taken was not announced! These included the head of the local Chamber of Commerce, the Rector of the University, and our friend, A. Stathatos, president of the Touring Club. . . . Everyone has remarked on the apparent lack of control over the German troops. They seem very different from the soldiery of the last war, and almost to have a bolshevik spirit of sorts.

May 6, 1941, Tuesday

Got off a long telegram via the Germans, telling the Department about all the people here who are now anxious to go home, and about the money, visa, and rail difficulties now besetting the would-be traveller. . . . Added to the telegram that I should be grateful if I could be ordered home for consultation or at least given home leave before proceeding elsewhere. I would much rather take the Bunnies home than traipse about the Middle East with them at the present moment, or send them home alone. If the Germans don't garble or alter my message, the Department may comply; but judging by its attitude toward me all these years, I'm not sanguine. We have not had a word from it since the occupation, and that is not because communications are cut. They can reach us at any time through the Embassy in Berlin, and must know that besides wondering what our fate is to be, personally, we have many problems, such as the money problem and evacuation of Americans, the answers to which they know from the past, but which we don't. A reassuring and guiding telegram sometime during the past few days would have done much to relieve anxiety and solve difficulties; but as it is the impression is created (quite correct, too, I guess) that the Department doesn't give a damn about us; and I dare say I'll be told I've been wrong to ask even the questions I have. It's the way you treat a dog only if you are a brute yourself: "Lie down and keep still, till you are spoken to." When I tell people that I haven't heard from the Department since the Germans came in, they don't believe me, or at least they look incredulous. And I don't blame them. . . .

An order of the day to Greek officers and soldiers was today published in the press by the new "Premier," General Tsolakoglou. It states that the German army did not come to Greece as an enemy but as a friend, to oust the British who had been invited here by the criminal Government of the 4th of August. It is the duty of every Greek to show his friendly feelings and to comply with the new order of things, and to adopt the great doctrines and lofty ideals of national socialism, the new political religion created by the enlightened mind and big heart of the Führer, etc. . . . The general, and five other generals now in the Cabinet here have been crossed off the list of the Greek army by the Government in Crete. . . .

In the papers today, the Government again assures the public that it need not worry about the food problem, as all necessary steps are being taken. But Dr. Vogel told Mr. Reed that the German authorities would be glad to see foreigners leave the country, since the food question is already bad, and will be worse! . . . An ominous note in the papers: "Special courts will be set up to try persons guilty of scandalous acts during the past 5 years . . ."

May 7, 1941, Wednesday

Mummy and I walked on the Pnyx after lunch. The hill has several small German camps on it, with anti-aircraft guns. Lorries have also been driven up it somehow and parked near the Observatory. . . . We tried the Acropolis first, but the road near the steps was packed with German cars and trucks, and there must have been near a thousand German soldiers on the Acropolis itself, many in dense groups, probably being lectured to. . . .

The press announced that General Papagos and other important people have been arrested by the new Government, as well as the following members of the Government of the 4th of August: Economou, Kyriakos, Tambacopoulos, Nicolaidis, Arvanitis, Alevizatos (Cooperatives), Mavroudis, Papademas, Papavasiliou, Economakos, Zafiropoulos (Markets), Spentzas, and Polyzopoulos (Posts and Telegraphs); also Prof. Phocas, the son-in-law of Metaxas: charges expected to be filed today. The news has frightened a lot of people here, and the Hungarian Minister came in to see me about it. He said he had spoken with Altenburg, the new German "Plenipotentiary for Greece" and urged him not to let the Greeks go too far, calling to his mind past experiences here. He added, however, to me, that he doesn't feel sure that the Germans quite understand the local situation, or they never would have set up this new government. He asked me whether I thought he should see the German again on the matter, and I replied I thought it would be a good thing to do so, since one never can tell how far things of this sort may go, once they are started, though I thought probably in this case nothing more is intended than to curry favor with the conquerors. The people arrested are not, in any case, those responsible for the war; they are all relatively small fry, whose execution would be manifestly inappropriate, etc. However, I asked him to let me know what he thinks after he has seen Altenburg again. The Germans *can* stop things if they want to, of course. . . .

Mrs. Maximos came to tea. . . . She began talking about the arrests at once, and told me confidentially that the new Premier had invited Maxy, among others, to talk with him this morning about the matter. Maxy advised him to go cautiously and not create a new source of internecine strife, and came away from the interview with the impression that Tsolakoglou is not inclined to press things very far. . . . I don't want to put my oar in when it isn't needed, but if I learn that the situation is really dangerous, I am willing to go see the German Minister myself and say a few words "off the record." We want no more vengeance or causes for vengeance in this unfortunate country, and the Germans can't want it either.

The cabinet last night approved the decree drafted by the new Minister of Justice, Livieratos, abolishing the Royal Regime. We are no longer in the kingdom of Greece but in the Greek State—*Helleniki Politeia.* . . . The Mayor of Athens, Plytas, who has often addressed fulsome remarks to me about the United States and only recently was very officious over the dedication of Franklin Roosevelt Boulevard, has addressed a message to Hitler on behalf of the people of the city thanking him for his chivalrous remarks and expressing the city's gratitude for the way it has been treated by the brave German troops, their gentleness to the inhabitants, etc. . . . An order published in the press states that the Germans have taken over the "protection" of the city's electricity, water, railways, *and artistic treasures.* . . .

The food situation is getting very tight. . . . Beginning tomorrow, the bread ration per person will be cut from 100 to 80 grams a day.

May 8, 1941, Thursday
[T]he Vanderbilt Committee, represented by Archer, Thorn, Shafer[40] and Davis, asked my advice about the disposal of the funds they are turning over to the Greek Red Cross, whether to earmark them for long-term charities or for immediate relief. I advised them, in keeping with their own inclination, to earmark only a certain amount for relief of orphans and the providing of artificial limbs, two long-term projects to which they stand in a certain degree committed, and to give the bulk for immediate purposes, connected with repatriation of the soldiers, and so forth, the reason being that when we leave, as we hope to do soon, there will be no way of making sure that the funds are actually disbursed as intended. The amount in question is over 50 million drachmas. . . . The Hungarian Minister called up to say that he feels less worried about the fate of arrested Ministers after his second talk with the Germans. He was guarded over the phone, and I couldn't tell him of Maxy's interview, which had encouraged me, but I arranged for him to come in tomorrow for a chat. He confirmed that Mr. Mavroudis has been allowed to go to a hospital. . . . In regard to these arrests, it should be remembered that the government of the 4th of August did a good deal of arresting and exiling itself. Remember Michalacopoulos, who died as a result of his treatment, and the exiling of such excellent persons as Kafandaris and Mylonas! Of course, it didn't go in for shooting (largely on account of the King's moderation), but I don't think this new puppet government will do that either. Apparently Tsolakoglou saw, besides Mr. Maximos, a lot of other prominent persons yesterday, to get their advice; among them Pangalos and Othonaios, and Messrs. C. Tsaldaris, Papandreou,

[40] James F. Shafer, executive of Socony Vacuum in Greece.

G. Pezmazoglou, P. Kanellopoulos, Mercouris, and Pericles Rallis. The papers indicate that all these erstwhile leaders side with the present government against the King's but this may be doubted. On the other hand they should have been able to give good counsel as to the advisability of moderation at this time. Or is that only a pious hope? They all have their own brands of vendetta politics and should have no interest in seeing a new one come into being, and in addition I doubt if any one of them is of the type to love a quisling. . . . The bread ration of 80 drams may soon be cut to 60, and has already been so cut for the city orphanages. A Greek laborer normally consumes one *oke* of bread a day, = 400 drams.[41] A Greek child can now have ⅐th of that ration. . . . We all knew the food situation would be bad here if the Germans came, but how bad it would be, and how sudden, we hardly guessed.

May 9, 1941, Friday

The Hungarian Minister came in and reported on his second talk with the German "Plenipotentiary" about the arrested cabinet members. He said that Altenburg denied absolutely that the Germans are involved in the affair, but that he seemed to realize that it would be to no one's advantage to let the Greeks go too far. He thinks the men may be allowed to go to their homes tomorrow, and that the danger of extreme measures is not great. . . . Received a note in French from a German major saying that it is "inadmissible" for a neutral nation to protect the British Legation and demanding that we take our seals off and tomorrow morning hand the keys over to some officers who will call upon me to receive them.

Reed took this over to Vogel, and the result was that he promised to call the officers off, and defer the matter of the Legation till instructions arrive from Berlin. In any case, he understands that I won't take the seals off myself, in view of my instructions, and that any entering will have to be entirely on the Germans' responsibility. . . . Locally, the Germans are commandeering all the Greek boats of over 50 tons along the coast *to carry troops*. The "Premier" had another talk with Gonatas. General Tsipouras has been made Prefect of Attica and Boeotia! The Ministry of Cooperatives has been abolished. The German authorities have ordered the strict enforcement of the blackout and the keeping of all air-raid shelters in perfect preparation. (Is this anti-British propaganda? The British will surely not bomb Athens; but if they bomb Piraeus the Germans are not above dropping a few here themselves and then saying the British did it!)—and finally, Berlin announced that the economic life of Greece is becoming normal again and that in many places in Greece indi-

[41] One "dram" = 3.2 kg.; 1 "oke" = 400 drams = 1,280 kg.

viduals have expressed the desire to go to "Germany for work." I prefer to read romances in the form of novels, and tragedies in books.

May 10, 1941, Saturday

More talk about the lack of discipline among the troops, the looting in the smaller towns and villages, the seizing of all food, killing of cattle, sheep and goats. . . . The Germans have come in without any commissariat, and after eating what they had by way of rations in their cars and trucks on the way down have been turned loose to feed on the country, which in this respect is the poorest in Europe. Carolou, who is interested in the fisheries here, told me that the control of this vital Greek industry has now been taken over by the Germans and that fish caught here, normally a staple reliance of an undernourished people, are being packed to be sent to Germany. . . . Can you beat it?

May 12, 1941, Monday

Mr. Theotokis came in for a chat. He and his family are going back to their estate at Corfu, hoping to live there better than here, where already they find the food problem very difficult. He was Minister for Foreign Affairs in the Kondylis Regency and a great booster for the restoration, but this time he told me that Greece will never take the King back again. He accused the King of letting pro-Germans run the army, who surrendered, many of them without resisting at all. He said he is confident that the Democracies will eventually win the war, and that though Tsolakoglou invited him to confer with him along with other leaders he refused to accept because of the "Premier's" declaration that Germany will win and that Greece should take her side. But at the same time he feels the King should himself have kept closer to the army and should have called in the political leaders to help him. He doubts whether any very serious measures will be taken against the imprisoned government, but regrets that anything was done at all in the circumstances, which he rightly thinks call for the union of all Greeks. I liked Theotokis better in this conversation than I have ever done in a fairly long acquaintance. Seemed sounder and more of a man than I had suspected. . . . The German planes are very active today, and were so all last night—bombers going out and returning from Crete, I have no doubt. Apparently the British have no forces with which to retaliate. These moonlit nights offer every advantage and the air-fields here are crowded with planes and petrol, making magnificent targets. . . . Craw has just been to Megara and saw and talked with Australian and New Zealand prisoners being forced to work there on the new aerodrome. The guards have taken nearly all their clothes, and some are clad only in loin-cloths. They are given nothing to eat but some gruel which they cannot stomach, and if it wasn't for kindly Greeks they would be actually starving. The Greeks working on the field get a hundred drachmas a day, but the British nothing.

May 16, 1941, Friday

Called on Dr. Altenburg, the "German Plenipotentiary for Greece." Found him a pleasant, round, fresh-faced person. His only instructions about us seem to be to allow us to stay but not to allow us to circulate or communicate with the outside world! He asked if I liked Greece, and when I said I love it, he said "Why not stay on here, then? I invite you."

May 18, 1941, Sunday

Learned from Allard that the Swedish Military Attaché in Berlin is here and will go back to Berlin tomorrow morning early, taking mail. . . . I saw Kohler, and together we planned to put before Morris all our troubles. Reed wrote a letter to go with it. . . . I drove out to the Allards and met the Military Attaché and his assistant. Allard said it is settled that the Italians are coming here to take over very soon; the Military Attaché, who has been touring the Greek and Yugoslav battlefields under German auspices (together with the other M.A.'s in Berlin, except the American and the Swiss—why the Swiss?), gave the figures for the British Expeditionary Forces in Greece as 56,000—two divisions and an armored brigade. He also said that the British put up their stiffest resistance on the Thermopylae line, knocking out ten German tanks, and that the attack on Crete will take place in a few days and in any case "before the 25th". He added that the British only have about 12,000 men in Crete now. . . . Rumors continue to go about that the new Greek "Government" is about to fall. It cannot solve the food problem, the responsibility for which the Germans of course have shifted to its shoulders. Furthermore, it hasn't sufficient money for the huge tasks before it. Allard told me that the Germans now say that it will take a year to repair the Greek railway—especially the tunnels—which the British destroyed, and Philon[42] said that the Germans insist that the Greeks pay for the whole thing. He is connected with the State Railways and should know. Incidentally, the Germans have not "recognized" this Government, which they only "allowed" to be set up, but did not actually form, and so it can pass out without compromising them. Possibly they will keep it, or something like it, going till the Italians take over, and what the latter may try

[42] Philon Athanasios, Director of the State Railroads.

to do may appear from recent events in Croatia! Meanwhile the Germans are building new airfields, not only at Megara, but far south in the Peloponnese, east of Gytheion, and many of their men are embarking on Italian boats at Piraeus and Patras, and others are going out on flatbottom pontoon boats towed by Greek caiques, possibly to pass from island to island across the Aegean toward Crete or Syria. How much do the British know about these movements, I wonder! . . .

May 19, 1941, Monday
There was a heavy air-raid during the night, from 2:15 to 3:30. Bombs dropped on all the near-by airfields, but particularly at Helleniko, where there were heavy explosions which shook our windows. . . . General Mazarakis came to the house before luncheon to explain how it came about that he failed to form a government just before the collapse (see my entries of April 19 and 20). He said that the King insisted on having Maniadakis in the cabinet and that he (Mazarakis) objected, but that the real reason why he stepped aside was that the military situation was impossible and that it was clear that all the Government could do was pack its bags and get out. He then went on to criticize the King from the old partisan point of view, saying that he and his father cared nothing for the country, but only for themselves, that the restoration had been made on the basis of a bogus plebiscite (which is true) and that if the democracies win, Greece will become a republic, and will never take back a dynasty which has brought her nothing but disaster. He said the King is a "Bourbon" who never forgets and never learns. His treatment of the political leaders had been a shame, etc. . . . I told him that I hope Greece is not going to give the enemy a spectacle of renewed internal dissention at this time, and that she will keep her soul alive for the future by unity at home; and that regardless of what government she may decide to have in the future, she enjoys a certain strength at present in having a government (in Crete for the moment) which cannot be coerced into signing away any of her rights and which will keep her banner raised pending the final decision. He said people here don't want the King and don't want the people who went with him; but he was very much disturbed lest some puppet government here cede parts of Greece to Bulgaria and Italy; and I pointed out that by holding to the government that has gone, Greece can at least invalidate any cession the puppets may make. He seemed to see the point, but there is a ferocity of partisanship still alive in the oldsters of the Greek political scene which reason never can quell for long. . . . In talking about the hopelessness of the military situation on the 19th of April, when he was asked to form a government in place of Mr. Kotzias, General Mazarakis said that the King called in General Papagos to describe the situation to him, and that he did so briefly. Later

in the afternoon of the same day, Saturday, there was a conference at Tatoi attended by both Generals Wavell and Wilson. The Greek army was at that time being hopelessly exposed on the flank and rear by the withdrawal of the British in Thessaly, and its supplies and communications were becoming doubtful, owing chiefly to the overwhelming air superiority of the enemy. At that time the Greeks and British had no airplanes left at all! . . . An Italian plenipotentiary has arrived, and it is said that this morning he received the "Premier." The "Minister for National Economy," Mr. Hadjimichalis, sent word through one of the clerks in the Legation that he would like to call on me unofficially at my convenience. It appears he wants to get me to appeal for wheat to come here, and thinks his guarantee that the Germans won't take it may carry weight! . . . In speaking of this Government, General Mazarakis pointed out that its chiefs were creatures of the régime they turned against, but such shame does not alter the pity of the present situation.

May 20, 1941, Tuesday

The Germans started their attack on Crete. The British radio said that 1,500 parachutists had landed and some of them established themselves south of Chanea. . . . Formations of German planes, some of them very large, 60 or so at a time, kept going south from here, and returning, all day, and the night bombers are now, this evening, departing every few minutes from Helleniko. . . . The German plenipotentiary, Altenburg, called on me during the morning, to return my visit of the other day, imagining perhaps that that was a visit of courtesy, and not a business call. . . . We had a pleasant enough chat. He again stated that the German Government is not pressing the diplomats here to leave. . . . The Greek "Government" has not resigned, and today issued a circular to the people calling on them to be polite to the Germans, and especially to the Italians, who were their friends before the war and are so once more, etc. The Germans have put up signs round Athens telling how they helped Greece in her War of Independence more than the British did (which is, at least, questionable), and also recalling the fact that King Otto was a German —though omitting that the Greeks of his day kicked him out! . . . Got a telegram from the Dept. at last, through Berlin, and all it says is "Did you send certain funds to the Consulate at Salonica?" Very helpful; and besides, we have no funds!

May 21, 1941, Wednesday

The Archimandrite who presides over Agios Isotheos, outside Megara, came in to tell me that there are some British soldiers in the foothills of

Mt. Geranea whom the nuns at the convent are feeding. He wants someone to advise them what to do—one of their number (they were originally 10) has died. Was wounded in the head, and of course got no treatment. I called in Major Baker and he said he would give the Archimandrite a letter which the nuns could pass on, advising the boys to give themselves up. They are, it seems, armed, and the nuns think will not take *their* advice. The Major has done this before, for other bands he has heard of. He leaves the decision up to the men, but tells them frankly what the situation is so far as possibilities of escape go, and advises them to surrender, either through him or to the nearest German authorities. . . . The news of the day is concerned chiefly with the attack on Crete. Some 3,000 parachutists have been nearly all accounted for, but an airborne division has also attempted to land, and there is no news yet of its success or failure. Boat landings are also being tried. An anonymous informant called up and told Niko that 300 moto-torpedo boats are at Megalo Pevko preparing to leave with troops tonight. Mr. House said that he saw boats of this kind coming through Salonica on trucks. The boats are made of aluminum. There are rumors of concentrations of German troops at many points along the Greek shore, waiting for boats to take them off. It seems, from what Michali the chauffeur picks up, that Kyme in Euboea is one of these points! The Germans are surely making a big effort. They will lose a lot of parachutists—highly trained men—and many soldiers will be drowned; but one division of British and two of Greeks can't hold out indefinitely if the Germans don't mind what they lose.

May 22, 1941, Thursday

There is very little news, but what there is is bad, of course. The British are talking complacently about their resistance in Crete, just as they always do about their "brilliant" failures. What sticks out is their admission that their forces are fighting without air support. They speak of this proudly, but it may well mean the battle is decided already. The Germans, of course, are pouring their bombers, fighters, and transport planes down from here in hundreds. You cannot win a war nowadays without planes, any more than you could win in Napoleon's day without artillery. Aviation is an auxiliary arm, of course, but where it exists only on one side in the battle, it is now so effective as to be decisive. If the British can't send planes to neutralize the German bombers in Crete, their forces there I believe are doomed. As Mr. Churchill said today, neither side can hope to escape from the island; the fight must be to a finish, and the finish looks like another disaster for men who are always too few and always inadequately equipped. If the Germans win this war it will not only be because they prepared before hand, but because they think faster and work harder than their opponents. The attack on Crete has been painstakingly prepared in every detail, it is supple, powerful, full of feints and disguises, and above all professional. The defense is a matter of improvisation, bull-dog courage and the "thin red line," put in order, as Cyril Falls[43] said tonight on the radio, "after we found out that the Germans were preparing the aerodromes in Greece obviously for an attack on Crete." But the Germans began preparing for this affair long before they attacked Greece, and Crete should have been prepared by the British at the same time that Wilson brought his troops here. It should have had an air defense which could not be blasted into nothingness in one day. . . . Falls said that the British are aware that the Germans are regarding this attack as, in part, a rehearsal for the invasion of Britain, and that the British as well as the Germans expect to learn something from it. Let's hope they do. But their capacity for learning,—so far, at least, as the art of war is concerned,—seems low. . . . It is announced that Mr. Lane, with a few members of the Legation in Belgrade, have arrived in Budapest. I wonder how much longer the Department will delay before ordering us out of here.

May 23, 1941, Friday

The news of the day is that the Germans are continuing to attack Crete heavily, but so far are being held off by sea, while only maintaining a foothold gained near Chanea. . . . More men apparently went off by ship today from the Piraeus. And a high proportion of the German troop carrying planes have been destroyed or damaged. I believe the capture of Crete will cost thousands of German lives and that the operation will indicate that an invasion of Britain will be, if nothing else, sanguinary in the extreme.

May 24, 1941, Saturday

Mr. Philon came in to talk about messages he wishes to send to the King concerning his property here, and I suggested he see the Turkish Ambassador, who is going home next week. He then told me of the experience of a Greek captain whose ship—a small coasting vessel—formed part of a convoy carrying German troops to Crete. The boat belonged to a friend of Philon's, and the story is trustworthy. It seems that this boat and the *Calydon* (which used to ferry from Patras to Kryoneri for the Greek Northwest Railway, on the board of which Mr. Philon serves), plus a lot of caiques and an Italian destroyer, gathered at St.

[43] Captain Cyril Falls (retired), British writer and commentator, and a leading authority on modern warfare.

George island off Sunium and sailed from there to Chanea. The boats carried about 200 soldiers each, plus small trucks and ammunition. The caiques had also about 200 men aboard, very crowded. In all, the convoy carried upwards of 4,000 men. The rendez-vous at St. George was effected ten hours late, because many of the caiques came from far-away ports—as far as Corfu—and their captains were not familiar with the coast here (perhaps also they intentionally delayed!). At last it got away, the next day, and when approaching Chanea was suddenly caught in the beams of searchlights from British warships. In a few seconds the escorting destroyer was blown out of the water, and then caique after caique was destroyed by gun-fire. Seeing this, the captain of the Nomikos boat (Nomikos is Philon's friend) proposed to put about and run back to Melos, but a German officer, in command on board, said "No. I'm ordered to go to Chanea, and to Chanea I will go." So on they sailed. But when a searchlight came in their direction the officer changed his mind, and the boat was turned and headed back. According to the captain, the Germans by this time were in a panic. Dawn came up and the captain said he could see ahead of them a battle going on between dive bombers and a number of British ships. The German commander at first wouldn't believe him, but he proved to be right. In this battle no ship was hit, and no plane destroyed. The ships zig-zagged sharply, often so much so as to heel way over, just as the planes would dive. At length the planes went away, and the captain urged the German to take down the German flag and hoist the Greek, so as to avoid an attack by the ships. But he refused. A shell landed near by, and immediately the German commander cried out for someone to raise the Greek flag. A Greek sailor raised one over his head, holding it stretched out between his arms. A shell exploded and took off the top part of his head. The German then cried out for white flags, and the men brought up towels and sheets from below and waved them. But soon a shell landed squarely on the ship and she was blown apart, not a soul escaping but the Greek captain and one or two others, who secured a small boat, and gradually made their way back to Greece. Strangely enough the *Calydon*, which was the lame duck of the convoy, got away scot free and has returned to the Piraeus with all its troops and cargo. Mrs. Delmouzos told us of a German officer quartered in one of the houses in Kifissia of which she knows. This officer appeared homesick; said he had been away from his family now for years; showed pictures of his wife and children. He was particularly fond of talking with the Greek children who would cluster round him and apparently liked him. One day he took them all down to the village and bought them all the candy and toys they could carry, and when they had left him, went up to his room and shot himself. . . . [I] had a long talk in my study with Mr. Hadjimichalis, who now is Minister both of Finance and National

Economy in the new "government." He appears an earnest and honest soul, who wants to do the best possible for the Greek people in their present straits. Most of our talk was taken up with his protestation in this connection, but he wanted also to sound me out as to ways and means of appealing to the U.S.A. and England to get food stuffs through to Greece. Boats laden with wheat from Australia, he said, were on the way here when they were stopped in the Red Sea or Suez. Even a couple of grain ships would be of incalculable use here now. I told him that I am deeply sympathetic with the Greek people and will do all I can to help them when I am allowed to communicate with my Government; at present, I explained, all my messages have to go in German through Berlin, and it is certain that nothing would be forwarded which would give the kind of picture of Greece under German rule which alone would have a chance of moving the Americans to break the existing precedent in regard to feeding occupied countries. I asked him how much of Greece he has jurisdiction over, financially, and he replied all of it up to the Struma. The Italians in the west have only occupied the country militarily (though this is quite contrary to the Armistice terms) and have not (yet) annexed any of it. The Bulgarian occupation is less clear-cut. The Greeks are trying to insist that Bulgaria should be considered in this connection in the same light as Italy; they can't help her troops coming along with the Germans, since the latter permitted it. But she has clearly no rights at present to regard any Greek territory as hers. Meanwhile, the question remains undecided, pending some definite solution from Germany, and the present Greek "government" is not in a position to administer the territory. Mr. Hadjimichalis claims to have done one good thing for the country in setting his fall [?] against inflation; he has, he said, insisted that the German and Italian currency put into circulation here be canalized through the Bank of Greece. He has won his point with the Germans, he says, but still has to fight it out with the Italians. The Italians are calling for an absurd exchange rate of 16 drachmas to a lira! The Germans are more reasonable with 50 to the mark. On the other hand the Germans are calling for a dollar rate here of 125, while I have been told that the Black Market offers as high as 350! These problems make the present "government's" future appear very doubtful indeed. Trade with Germany is to be resumed under an unlimited clearing; but Greece can't live on what Germany can supply. Her agriculture is ruined, her seaborne trade is gone, her merchant marine destroyed, or lost to her. Tinkering with her finances is only scratching the surface of the real troubles since these are only symptoms of what ails the state.... The radio tonight reports that the *Hood*, the world's largest warship, was hit in the magazine in a battle with Germany's new 35,000 ton *Bismark*, and blown to atoms! I fear this will give the British a terrible shock. Also the battle took place off *Greenland,* and this will shock the U.S.A.! . . . Crete is still holding out valiantly. The British claim to be in control of Herakleion and Rethymnon, which they lost temporarily, and that they are making it hot for the Germans on the flying field south of Chanea, where more troops and some artillery have been landed by the enemy. They also claim that no landing in any force has been made by sea. Two large convoys have been dispersed, they say, and the German casualties are very high. R.A.F. planes from Egypt have destroyed some 14 of the Germans' large troop carriers, but air supremacy continues to be overwhelmingly on the German side. The bombers are constantly going and coming from the Athens airports, and doubtless the dive bombers keep busily employed, based on new fields in the Peloponnese. The German attack has not had the quick success expected, but it is continuing.

May 25, 1941, Sunday

Kohler said he had it on good authority that Richtofen,[44] the head of the German flying corps, had been killed in a glider on Aegina last Friday, and Mrs. Skouze contributed the information that some of the German airmen had objected to gliding (one of the methods used to land men in Crete from airplanes) and that Richtofen had said he would show them it was perfectly safe. The rope that was pulling the glider behind the plane broke, and the whole crew in the glider, including Richtofen and his whole staff, was killed. . . . The German planes were again very busy, going and coming. Probably destroying some more poor Cretan villages.

May 27, 1941, Tuesday

The Germans entered Athens just one month ago. . . . Kohler called up before breakfast to say that the Radio Bulletin announces that, according to a statement by the Department to the press, I have been ordered to return to Washington for consultation. Bravo! Apparently my cable of May 6th has been received—and borne fruit. . . . In the afternoon, saw Vogel about going home. He said he would telegraph Berlin. . . . [H]e advised that our best way of exit would be via Berlin, where we could arrange to the best advantage for transportation to Lisbon. . . . The battle of Crete is still going on fiercely. Our friends on the *Gloucester,* which is announced sunk, along with one other cruiser and four destroyers, may have escaped, as the boat sank "near the coast," but their fate is unknown. British reinforcements are being sent, but the Germans have made progress toward Chanea and the great prize of Suda Bay. In the North Atlantic

[44] General von Richtofen, the German commander of the 8th Air Corps.

the *Bismark* has been sunk. Mr. Churchill described the action in the House of Commons, and the Germans have admitted the loss. . . . This is great news, as the *Bismark* is brand new and the Germans have called her unsinkable.

May 28, 1941, Wednesday

Mr. Papandreou came to the house after breakfast and we had a long talk. He said that in his view Great Britain would win the war, with the help of the United States, probably as a belligerent, and that in such an eventuality Greece would take up her freedom once more practically united in the desire for a new régime. He assured me that until that time the Greek people would not recognize any repudiation of the Tsouderos Government or the King, no matter what the Germans or a German-created "government" might say, but that after the war a plebiscite would surely be demanded by popular opinion, and that it was to be hoped that the United States and Great Britain would not seek to impose the royal or any other régime but would allow the plebiscite to be held, possibly under their control to assure complete fairness. Under such conditions he said he felt certain that the people would vote 100 percent for a republic on the American model. I told him that I felt it would be very wise for the Greek people to cling to their exiled government during the war, since this gives them a symbol of unity and is besides the government recognized by the powers through whom alone the freedom of Greece can be restored. But that the United States should thereafter seek to impose any régime on the Greek people against its will, I said I thought unthinkable. . . . In this connection General Frantzis sent me a message through Mr. Bert Hodge Hill,[45] urging me to inform my government that Greece wants to choose its own régime after the war is over and hopes the United States will not associate itself with any effort, presumably British, to bring back the King. General Frantzis was Greek Military Attaché in London during the last war and aide-de-camp to King Alexander. Thus Mr. Hill was able to call him a "Venizelist Royalist."

May 29, 1941, Thursday

Got a telegram from the Department sent on the 16th of May via Morris in Berlin, but forwarded as sent, and signed "Hull." It instructs me to return for consultation "at my earliest convenience"! and adds that formal travel orders follow. . . . At 6:30 I saw Dr. Altenburg, and also Dr. Vogel. The latter showed me a telegram just received from Berlin, saying that when the present military operations are concluded (Dr.

[45] Bert Hodge Hill, American archaeologist in charge of excavations at Corinth.

Vogel said this means Crete, and that the delay now will be only for one or two days more), foreigners will be allowed to travel under the usual passport controls.

May 30, 1941, Friday
Dr. Vogel called up and said that Berlin has signified that it has no objection to our leaving, and that we can have three places as far as Vienna on next Thursday's plane and possibly three places on the same plane from there on to Berlin; the thing must be taken up with the Vienna office, and we may know by Monday. . . . The British radio says that fighting is still going on in Crete and that German claims to have taken Herakleion are "unconfirmed in London." What a delusion and a snare is the B.B.C.! It is clear from the great decrease in German air activity here that Crete no longer counts as a problem in German eyes.

May 31, 1941, Saturday
The type of German soldier here is steadily getting worse—which is saying a good deal. We have now not only an undisciplined, but a shabby, and even filthy mob. . . . Last night the German flag on the Acropolis was torn down mysteriously, and today the Germans have punished the Athenians by declaring a ten o'clock curfew from now on. . . . This punishment is also intended to discourage further manifestations in favor of British prisoners (there was a demonstration of this kind again yesterday, outside the Athenian club), and the "Premier" made a declaration today warning the public against making such manifestations in the future, and saying that he has given orders for the arrest of all such unpatriotic individuals "in the pay of foreign propaganda" who are endangering the whole Greek people! . . . If the Germans don't want hostile feelings here, they had far better feed the people than threaten them.

June 2, 1941, Monday
Mr. Diomedis[46] came in at 10 o'clock and we sat on the terrace. He repeated that he has not talked frankly and openly with me before because he was on the outside of political life and did not want to meddle. Now the situation is changed, and "We have suffered a catastrophe." He said he is not an impassioned person, but he has come to feel very bitterly about the men and the policies which are responsible. The country will never forgive the Metaxas régime for having tried to follow a pro-British

---

[46] A. N. Diomedis, prominent financier, and former Governor of the Bank of Greece.

policy with a pro-German clique, or the British for having allowed such a thing to happen. There is, he emphasized, deep and lasting resentment against the British on this account, and all the sentimental trust of this liberty-loving people is now placed in the United States and its President. He echoed what General Mazarakis had said to me (see my entry of May 19th), that the Greek people will not repudiate the King and his Government while the Germans are in occupation of the country, but that when freedom comes they will never accept them back. He said he had known the Royal Family from King George 1st down, and that none of them think of anything but their own interests, and their strongest characteristic is their miserliness (this is well known, of course, in regard to the two Georges). There is nothing Greek about them. Like General Mazarakis, he clearly wanted me to understand that he fears that British policy which was so stupid as to support a fascist régime here in a war against fascism, may again ignore its true interests and seek to restore the crown, which by keeping all the most experienced generals and most capable political figures in exile or retirement these past five years, prepared and smoothened the way for collapse. He indicated, by saying again that all Greece's trust is in America, that he hopes we will not permit this to happen. Incidentally, he told me of a talk he had with Mr. Korizis just after the latter had taken over the Premiership (he could talk to him freely since he had helped Korizis to rise in the Bank). He urged the new Premier to act at once to bring into power the real brains and ability of the nation, and not to "ask" the King about it, as he proposed to do, but to force the King's assent. He urged him in particular to cashier Papagos and bring in Pangalos. But Korizis was too weak to do anything but try to carry on with the third-raters and the scalawags of the Metaxas group, and paid for his weakness with his life. . . . In all this talk of Mr. Diomedis's, the Venizelist bias was clear, but it cannot be denied that British policy has been badly directed here during all the years I have been in Athens. The Ministers have been short-sighted and ill-informed, and Britain's reputation with the people at large has been severely compromised, less by the failure so far, of her war effort, than by the tolerance she displayed toward a régime which stood for everything [to] which she is opposed. We could be tolerant and not compromise ourselves, because we have no stake here. But all the Greeks know, because it is proved every few years, that control of Greece is important to Britain. Yet the British did nothing to keep this country in the hands of their friends. The Metaxists were forced by circumstances to fight on Britain's side, but when things got bad, it was easy for them to surrender to Germany. The shock which the British here experienced that night of April 21st, when they heard of the armistice which left Wilson's divisions to fight it out alone, might have been avoided if the generals had been more representative of the people. Greece could not have won, but the people were ready to fight on, and the army could have gone on resisting under determined chiefs—that is why the British were so surprised. But it was the fault of their own government, from years back, that the key men at the front stood in greater awe of Germany than either the men they commanded, or than the circumstances warranted. . . . Mr. Diomedis is also right, I think, in saying that if Greece gets her freedom she will want (if noses are counted) to decide again on the question of the régime. Good and honest and conscientious as H.M. is, he has not made a record as a leader. Mr. Diomedis said, it is not so much that the Greeks hate him as that they despise him! Only a few old ladies are for him now, he said. Poor King, when you add to his unpopularity the fact that he is persistently unfortunate, I fear there is nothing left for him to stand on with the people "whose love is the strength of his house," as the family motto says. . . . Mr. Diomedis also spoke about the problem of feeding Greece, and suggested that as she has no foreign exchange here, her blocked funds in the U.S.A. might be used to pay Russia for badly needed wheat shipments in the future. He said that the amount of wheat needed here would not be enough to excite the cupidity of Germany, and therefore the transaction would safely be expected to benefit the Greek people. But I am not so sure of this, or of the confidence that would be inspired at home over such a deal. However, Mr. Diomedis knows the economic situation here as few others can, and it is certain that if he says that the need is desperate, such is the fact.

Mr. Constantine Tsaldaris came in for a chat after Mr. Diomedis left. . . . Mr. Tsaldaris spoke, like all the other Greeks, of the barbarity of the Germans, their lack of any understanding of others, their inability to control their locust-like legions, and cases of pillage and even rape. Today the invasion of Crete, which began May 20th, is officially over, and the German Legation declared itself a holiday. The Lufthansa told Mr. Calligas that there will be no answer on my application for three seats in the plane till tomorrow morning. . . . We continue to pack. . . . Here, for the record, is the announcement in the press issued by the German Garrison Commander yesterday:

"On the basis of the facts and ascertainments set forth below, the police (curfew) hour in Athens and Piraeus is fixed at 10 p.m. effective at once.

1. During the night of May 30-31, the German war flag flying on the Acropolis was stolen by unknown persons. A strict inquiry is being instigated and the perpetrators will be punished with death.

2. The press, and public opinion among all classes, is still sympathetic with the British who have been ousted from continental Europe.

3. Events in Crete and atrocities committed against German prisoners in defiance of International Law not only are not discussed with indignation, but are widely commented on with satisfaction.

4. Manifestations in favor of British war prisoners have been observed contrary to prohibitive order. These manifestations are tolerated by the Greek police, which has not opposed them with all means at its disposal.

5. The conduct of the city at large toward the German armed forces has again become less friendly.

6. Profiteering in Athens has exceeded every measure without being suppressed in any way by the competent authorities.

7. Almost all merchandise in Athens is being sold to the German military at considerably higher prices than to the Greeks.

The German military authorities have up to now endeavored to act in every respect favorably to the Greek people. In the event the orders of the German armed forces are not obeyed, the severest sanctions will be regretfully imposed." Athens, May 31, 1941, The Garrison Commander (no signature.)

In regard to the selling of goods to the Germans at "higher prices than to the Greeks," it may be observed that the Germans "pay" for what they buy in special marks which have no value outside of Greece. They are taking goods out of the country, and the "currency" they give in exchange is valueless to bring any goods back in. What they are doing is therefore taking away the wealth of this country under the barest pretense of purchase; looting under another name.

✧

The MacVeaghs left Athens for Vienna by plane on June 5, 1941. Encountering endless travel restrictions and delays, they made their way by train and by car to Berlin, and from there to Basel, to Barcelona, and finally to Lisbon, where they boarded the *Exeter* for New York, arriving on July 21. Describing to newsmen the conditions in occupied Greece as "a progression toward famine," he nevertheless characterized the spirit of the Greeks as "magnificent," adding: "I'm proud of that country. They are not whimpering a bit. They are defeated but unconquered." (5)

During his stay in Berlin, MacVeagh drafted a long report on "The German Conquest and Occupation of Greece," which he sent to the Department and to the White House. After a brief but skillful explanation of German strategy and tactics in the opening phases of the campaign, he attributed the final collapse of the front to the invader's "exploitation of the gap opened up by the rapidly withdrawing motorized British in the plain [Thessaly] and the slowly retreating Greek infantry in the mountains" of Epirus. Nevertheless, the ensuing capitulation appeared to have its sinister side, as "something clearly went wrong at this time with the liaison between British and Greeks." He elaborated:

✧

I was with the British Minister, General Heywood, commanding the British Mission, and Air Vice Marshal D'Albiac, commanding the RAF in Greece, when they received the news of the Greek surrender, and they were obviously taken completely by surprise. It was clear that they did not regard the German penetration in the Greek rear as being necessarily decisive, and there are many Greeks today, including soldiers, who agree with them. In this connection, it may be noted that the armistice was signed not by the Greek Commander in the field, but by some of his subordinates, the leader of whom has since become the local "Quisling." An important Greek said to me just before I left Athens, that General Metaxas had made his greatest mistake in attempting to resist Germany with a pro-German clique, meaning that his cabinet and his generals were largely drawn from King Constantine's adherents in the last war. The armistice certainly appears justifiable on purely formal grounds, but the question of whether more determined leadership might not have brought at least a large part of the Greek Army safely back to the Thermopylae line will probably always be debated. When the rebellious generals were communicating with the Germans regarding an armistice, a mysterious order was issued in Athens dismissing all soldiers in that area to their homes and providing them with pay in drachma bills which had been raised from 100 to 1,000 in value. This order was speedily countermanded, but what appears to have been a plot involving the Ministers of Finance, War and Navy, resulted in not only a wave of defeatism spreading throughout the capital, but in the suicide of the Prime Minister, Mr. Korizis, and the formation of a new government. The British are supposed to have borne down heavily on the Premier for what had happened, and this is probably the origin of certain stories to the effect that they had him put out of the way.

Giving particular attention to the battle of Crete, as well as to the "locust" tactics of the occupation, MacVeagh concluded: "To sum up, Greece is now more pro-British than at any time previously, because she has had the German myth exploded in her face. Instead of civilization, order and discipline, she is experiencing an ill-coordinated and shoddy tyranny, with whose insincerities and inconsistencies she finds it impossible to cope rationally, and under whose violent and uncontrolled rapacity she risks starvation." (6)

In another report, written during the transatlantic voyage, MacVeagh reviewed the political developments in Greece resulting from the German invasion, and paid tribute to the fallen dictator:

It was said of General Metaxas up to the day he died that he was pro-German at heart and was ready at any time to sell out his country to Berlin. The facts, however, utterly fail to support such a charge. At no time during this present war did he let his authoritarian tendencies betray his judgment or sway his actions in foreign affairs contrary to the interests of England. He believed that England would win eventually, and that Greece must stand with her on that account, even though it meant initial sacrifice. He believed also, with the King, that a country with Greece's traditions could not afford to yield tamely to any menace from whatever quarter, and that menace from England was unthinkable. But these beliefs, which I personally know him to have entertained, constituted so complete a reversal of his equally convinced opinions during the last World War, that his enemies could not credit him with holding them, and many of his followers, lacking his courage to defy consistency, could not join him in adopting them. While he lived, the latter, who owed to him their political preferment, followed where he led. But when his leadership was removed, their doubts remained. Furthermore, though General Metaxas was a great enough man to reverse himself when he found his judgment wrong, he was not great enough to pardon opponents and, like Caesar, risk entrusting them with authority and command. Not only the doubting Thomases of his Government, but the higher officers of his army were all appointees of his political machine, organized in the days before he himself had conceived his new beliefs. To many of these men the invincibility of Germany was an axiom, and without Metaxas behind them they were half beaten before the war began.

In sharp contrast to such a eulogy for the architect of the régime of the "Fourth of August," MacVeagh was openly critical of the Greek monarch's personal role: "It did not actually bring about Greece's defeat, which had long been anticipated both by General Metaxas and the King in the event that Germany as well as Italy should attack her, but it had a great deal to do with the way in which her defeat occurred, and it is very likely to affect the future of both King and country if and when Greek independence is restored. Indeed, when that time comes, it is almost certain to be remembered that the King's only answer to Greece's political problems in the past was to install and support a dictator, and that after that dictator's death he deferred his appeal to other leaders till it was too late for anyone to save the situation, and embarked on a crucial war against Germany with a Government, and a High Command, representing nothing more national than the rump of a fascist *junta*." As a result, the monarchy's future was not bright, whatever the war's outcome:

Since Mr. Tsouderos has never been a standard-bearer in Greek life, and the other members of the cabinet are of even more negligible importance politically (unless the crafty Maniadakis should be able to avoid assassination and stage a come-back through intrigue), the King is now practically synonymous with the Government in the minds of all the Greeks whom he left behind. Mr. Tsouderos is honest, intelligent and capable, and if he gets on personally with the King, may be of great assistance to him in the conduct of such affairs as the Government may still control,— foreign affairs, for instance, and the merchant marine. But it is unfortunate that he could not bring along with him any portion of the personal allegiance of the people, of which the King himself, as an unpopular though well-bred monarch, stands in need. Had the King taken only one leading politician with him into exile, at least one important group of Greeks would be praying for his Government's return. As it is, no one is interested but a few stranded members of his court. Greece as a whole wants a government of her own. She will never be happy in bondage, and for Quislings she has only contempt. But her politics are always intensely personal, and there is nothing of this sort now to cement the Government in exile with the country it represents. For the time being, Greek opinion will probably respect the King's diminished and distant leadership, and even be glad of its existence, since it is all Greece has. But when the day of redemption arrives, we should perhaps not be surprised if a demand arises for another government than his. In fact, despite the German occupation, the thoughts of leading Greeks are already turning in this direction, dealing in futures with that boundless optimism which distinguishes their race. Fiery Venizelists, like Mr. George Melas, Mr. Papandreou and General Mazarakis, have urged me to realize that the King can never come back, no matter what happens, and have begged me to tell my Government not to let the British attempt to impose him on an unwilling country. Moderate liberals, and even royalists, of more weighty opinion, such as Mr. Diomedis and Mr. Maximos, have argued to me to the same effect. It is impossible to ignore a view held with such unanimity by competent observers of such varying types, and I am glad that I stayed in Greece long enough to be made aware of it. It is possible, of course, that the King's future conduct may conquer for him an esteem which he could never win previously. But this seems unlikely. Whatever his good qualities, he is no Albert of Belgium to sum up in his person the heroism of a whole nation. It appears more probable that what Greece has against him and his dynasty,—their avariciousness and self-absorption at the expense of the country, but above and beyond everything, their ill-success, —will bulk even larger than it does today when the hour of possible return arrives. In any case, the flight of King George and his crew has marked the end of a strange and remarkably interesting period in Greek history, during which a temperamentally constitutional monarch tried to govern the world's prime democracy through the medium of a dictator, and saw that dictator die in a blaze of glory whilst he himself lived on to reap the reward of dislike and failure. Whether what the future holds for immortal Greece includes another try for King George II, it would be foolish to attempt to predict, but those who are interested in that country of restless political change might do well to keep in mind a growing itch to try a Republic on the American model. (7)

CHAPTER
VII

Interlude: Iceland and South Africa

On his arrival in Washington MacVeagh discovered that a new assignment had already been chosen for him: on August 25, 1941, he was formally commissioned as the first American Minister to Iceland. His appointment was closely related to the dispatch to Iceland of American troops under Major General Charles H. Bonesteel, to assist in the defense of that country in the event of a German invasion. Accompanied by his wife, and travelling to his new post with an American convoy, he presented his credentials on October 1. Returning to the United States early the following February, 1942, for consultations and personal leave, he had long talks about his new duties with President Roosevelt, Army Chief of Staff General George Marshall, Secretary of the Navy Frank Knox, Admiral Ernest J. King, and, of course, with officials of the Department of State. After broad hints from Colonel Donovan and others that he might soon be sent to Portugal, he was back in Iceland in April, only to learn within a few weeks (April 21, 1942) that the President had recommended him for the post of Minister to South Africa.

In Iceland, MacVeagh's principal responsibility was to be a peacemaker between American and British military authorities, and between the American command and the Icelandic Government. He played an important role, settling the endless diplomatic and labor problems that surrounded the construction of the large military airfield at Keflavik and the handling of convoys to Murmansk—including caring for torpedoed seamen, and overseeing the disposition of mutinees onboard American vessels—calming an ever-present Army-Navy rivalry, and advising commanders in matters of public relations and press censorship. By all accounts, he proved himself a masterful diplomat, earning the respect, gratitude, and friendship of those who had to work with him. He was decorated with the Order of the Icelandic Falcon, an honor he was permitted to accept upon his retirement from government service. He appeared to enjoy the intricacies of the country's political situation, and declared in his diary (April 18, 1942): "The Icelanders are really wonderful politicians; as good as the Greeks! . . ."

One of the highlights of his assignment was the arrival, on May 27, 1942, of a Soviet mission headed by V. M. Molotov, en route to London and Washington. After a much-needed nap at the MacVeagh residence, the Commissar of Foreign Affairs turned out to be a jovial and interesting guest. MacVeagh recorded in his diary (May 28):

> M. Molotov asked me at dinner if I had much diplomatic work to do here, and I told his interpreter to explain to him that we have recognized the independence of Iceland but have also occupied her militarily, and Mr. Molotov caught on at once, nodding his head while his eyes twinkled. One doesn't have to tell him much. I then said jokingly that I was here to see that General Hower is a good boy, and he laughed. He knows what a political commissar is, I guess! . . . Later an officer asked him what he thought we could best do—the British and Americans—to win the war, and he poked his fat forefinger out ahead of him and said "Francia." He asked a lot of questions which showed that he is principally anxious to find out whether we mean business ourselves or expect Russia to do all the fighting for us. He thinks this is the critical year, and that if Germany can be defeated, Japan will be easy. Speaking of France, he said "If you can draw away some German divisions to that front we can smash them in Russia, but you can't afford to give them time to consolidate on both fronts. You must attack now." . . . I liked Mr. Molotov, he was so bright and keen about everything. But his staff was obviously very much afraid of him. . . .

The Soviet party stopped over again on June 8, on its homeward journey. MacVeagh recorded in his diary (June 8, 1942) that he found his guest definitely pleased with what he obviously perceived to be the main achievement of his mission to the United States:

> Mr. Molotov looked very well and bright, and was clearly very happy over his visit. His interpreter proudly told me he had seen FDR five times. He said to the General and me, "What would you say if, after my return to Moscow, a communiqué should be issued saying that the President and I had reached a full understanding on the question of a second front?" . . .

Seeing Molotov off at the airport on the same day, MacVeagh gave the Russian, "for good luck," a silver coin of Alexander the Great:

> He asked what he should say to such a gift? I replied that Alexander was a great *conqueror*. Quick as a flash he came back: "Russia wants no conquests but only to defend her own." So I said that "perhaps the best thing

one can say for Alexander is that he defeated the *barbarians*." And to this he replied, "the barbarians of today will be defeated too." He seemed quite pleased with all the attentions we have shown him.

MacVeagh's assignment to South Africa caused him to reflect, as he was to do often during his years in government service, on the apparent ineptitude of the State Department bureaucracy, and its seeming lack of consideration for the convenience and personal feelings of its representatives abroad. On April 21, he received word from the Department that the President hoped that MacVeagh would accept the new post. He responded immediately, indicating his acceptance and appreciation. One month later, having heard nothing more on the matter, he read in the press that his name had in fact been submitted to the Senate for confirmation. Then, on June 9, still without any information from his superiors, he read in the *Congressional Record* that the Senate had indeed confirmed him on May 21. He wrote in his diary on June 9, 1942:

I can't see why I have never heard a word about it from the Dept. (either before or after the confirmation), unless (1) they can't find anyone to take the job here, or (2) the shootings [of several Icelanders by triggerhappy American sentries in isolated incidents] are being laid to my door and I'm being penalized. Or perhaps it's a bit of both, a would-be Minister to Iceland is hard to find and at the same time it is inadvisable to swap horses while a stream (even a small one) is being crossed. In any case, the uncertainty is damned disagreeable to me, and the discourtesy involved in saying not a word all this time is almost (but not quite, in the case of the Department) unbelievable. . . .

Finally, on June 22, MacVeagh received a personal message from the Department inquiring as to the date of his departure from Iceland. He replied that, lacking instructions, he had been unable to arrange for transportation. On June 26, he received telegraphic authorization to leave Iceland, and after frantic efforts and the helpful intercession of Navy officials, the MacVeaghs were able to sail the next day. Some time later, the papers of his recall and assignment to South Africa reached the Icelandic capital, having been sent there by surface mail.

In Washington, the MacVeaghs were reunited with their daughter, who had gone to work for the Department of the Navy soon after the family's return from Greece the previous summer. "A very satisfactory child," he wrote in his diary (September 26, 1942), "and one can be proud of her as well as love her. . . ." After a brief rest in Connecticut and New Hampshire, the new Minister to South Africa set out to learn about his duties.

It proved to be a frustrating experience. The President complimented Mac-Veagh on his work in Iceland, and asked him to convey his regards to General Smuts, "whom he remembers with great admiration and esteem from having met him in Europe after the last war" (entry for September 29, 1942). But Roosevelt had little to say about American objectives in South Africa, other than to indicate his strong support for the government of Prime Minister Smuts. Secretary Hull had no advice or instructions to issue either, and Assistant Secretaries Adolph Berle, Dean Acheson, Howland Shaw and Breckinridge Long could offer little more than generalities. Only Sumner Welles, an old friend, seemed interested in discussing fully the South Africa assignment. The most useful contact from the Department was to be Herbert Feis, the Department's principal economic adviser, who patiently explained to MacVeagh the problems of stockpiling strategic materials and of trade relations with Pretoria. In Washington, and subsequently on the long voyage to his new post, MacVeagh read everything he could find on the Union of South Africa and cheerfully concluded: "I have certainly been picked for a messy place this time! . . ."

On September 21, 1942, MacVeagh and his wife sailed from Staten Island on the *Aquitania*, in the company of seven thousand British troops bound for the Middle East. They reached Rio on October 3, and sailing again three days later, arrived at Capetown on the 13th. Their first impressions were rather mixed. "Stuffy little place" he recorded (October 13, 1942), "full of lower middle class British of the Victorian vintage, set in a magnificent and somewhat exotic landscape. . . ." After a two-day rest and consultations with consular officials, they left by train for Pretoria, arriving there on October 17.

While in Iceland, the war had been an ever-present reality; in South Africa, its impact was muffled and diverse. Although the loyalty of the Smuts government to the allied cause was not in question, the country's contribution to the war effort left much to be desired, and the political climate in Pretoria remained very sensitive on the subject of South Africa's commitments to the allies. Indeed, neither Britain nor the United States could count on many outspoken supporters in a state where business considerations appeared to be paramount. In certain quarters, pro-German sentiment was barely concealed, while enemy agents were believed to be operating with little hindrance from local authorities, and acts of sabotage were not uncommon.

Under these conditions, MacVeagh's assignment was hardly an easy one. In addition to the customary duties of diplomatic representation, he had to persuade the South African Government to reduce its production of gold, which was not essential to the war effort, but which constituted the country's most lucrative export commodity, and to concentrate instead on such raw materials as coal, copper, asbestos, chrome and vanadium. This shift in priorities could have generated embarrassing economic and political consequences for a government which the allies were anxious to keep in office. There was also the need to reorganize the Legation, to expand and to coordinate the work of the many American agencies operating in South Africa, to establish direct telecommunications between that country and the United States, and to supervise efforts to initiate broadcasts in *Africaans* on American radio programs. Not the least of his problems was developing an effective working relationship with Smuts, who regarded virtually all American activities in South Africa as manifestations of economic, commercial, and cultural imperialism. While trying to allay such fears, MacVeagh lost no opportunity to support the expansion of American commercial interests, and to encourage efforts to undermine Britain's economic supremacy in that country. He travelled extensively, usually as the guest of prominent South African leaders, and became a serious student of the country's complex political, racial, and economic problems. He took special interest in reports that communism was spreading rapidly among the population's non-white groups. Once again, Washington appeared entirely satisfied with his work, and both Roosevelt and the Department congratulated him for his successful dealings with the South African authorities, and for his excellent reporting.

Smuts' entourage included members of the royal family of Greece, who had taken refuge in South Africa, while King George himself remained in London, to be closer to the center of action and to the Tsouderos Government. Although Crown Prince Paul, the King's younger brother, appeared to shun the limelight, his wife, Frederika, was Smuts' frequent companion. The old warrior and the petite princess shared a strong interest in mysticism, and there were rumors that Mrs. Smuts, who had suffered a stroke and was confined a good deal of the time, was critical of Frederika for taking so much of the Prime Minister's valuable time.

MacVeagh chose to remain politely distant from the Greek royalty, quietly sharing the scepticism of Prince George that his nephew would ever be returned to his throne. On the other hand, the MacVeaghs were often the guests of honor of Greek communities across the country, and Mrs. MacVeagh occasionally attended the gatherings of Frederika's relief organization. There were also cordial messages from Greek leaders elsewhere. Thus, MacVeagh's diary for December 22, 1942 reads:

Received a Christmas telegram from M. Tsouderos, the Greek Prime Minister in London: "I send you and Mrs. MacVeagh my best wishes for Christmas and the New Year. May God grant that my fellow countrymen before long may be able to show you in freedom all their gratitude for your unfailing sympathy toward them and your faith in Greece's future."

This unexpected message pleased me very much, and I replied: "I appreciate your kind message and reciprocate your wishes most heartily. Nothing your country's friends can ever do will begin to express their love and admiration, and we believe in her future as in the rising of the sun."

The MacVeaghs had been in South Africa for less than one year when Tsouderos' wish appeared destined to be fulfilled. On September 29, 1943, MacVeagh was informed that Roosevelt had chosen him for a new assignment: ambassador "near the Greek and Yugoslav Governments in Cairo," and representative on allied councils responsible for Balkan political affairs. "I am pleased," he wrote in his diary, "that it isn't merely a *pro forma* appointment back to Greece but evidently a job...." And the next day, September 30: "Sent off a telegram in the morning to say that I thank FDR and will do my best to merit his confidence, and that I shall be ready to leave 'on confirmation *and receipt of the Dept's instructions*.' I don't want to go through the Iceland experience again when they sent me my instructions to go to South Africa and addressed them to me *in the Dept*. where they remained for weeks as in a dead letter office...."

Although delighted with the news, MacVeagh had had nothing to do with the decision to transfer him to Cairo. The move had been prompted by impending military operations in the Eastern Mediterranean, which, coupled with the surrender of Italy (on September 9, 1943), raised the hope in many quarters of an early liberation of the Balkans by allied forces. In turn, that prospect necessitated the establishment of more direct and effective contact with the Greek and Yugoslav governments-in-exile. Since their arrival in Cairo, the United States had been dealing with these governments through the American Minister to Egypt and Saudi Arabia, Alexander Kirk. And even though military plans were soon to undergo drastic changes as a result of the failure of British forces to capture the islands of Kos and Leros in September—and were in fact abandoned following the decisions reached at the Teheran Conference in December—the Department was beginning to display a growing interest in the political difficulties facing both Balkan states. There could be little doubt that these difficulties would complicate allied plans for the liberation of these countries and might be the prelude to civil war. Washington's attitude was further influenced by the anti-royalist and, by extension, anti-British, sentiment of Greek-American organizations whose views were being communicated to the White House in increasingly loud terms. In addition, OSS men in the Middle East, and behind enemy lines in Greece, many of them Greek-Americans, were generally critical of Britain's support for the Greek King, and of British efforts to stifle the political ambitions of the leftists in the resistance movement. OSS circles in Cairo were unhappy with Minister Kirk, blaming him for what they perceived to be American support for British policy regarding Greece. Influential Greek-Americans in the OSS worked behind the scenes to have MacVeagh brought from Pretoria to Cairo, in the hope that his well-known affection for Greece might encourage Washington to dissociate itself from British plans to restore the monarchy and to suppress the forces of the Left.

The news of his impending reassignment once again heightened MacVeagh's interest in current Greek affairs. On October 5, he was disturbed by German claims to have repulsed a British invasion of the island of Kos: "How they could do this with our air and sea superiority in the Mediterranean, I can't understand, unless 'somebody blundered.'" He also recorded in his diary (October 5, 1943) a report that six leaders of the Greek resistance had arrived in Egypt, demanding the abdication of King George and the resignation of Prime Minister Tsouderos, with George Papandreou to be named Minister of Interior in a new govenment. "Evidently they are good Venizelists!" he mused, adding: "I fear there is lots of Greek trouble ahead—and shall I be in it? . . ." Meanwhile his own situation was once again unclear and he began to worry:

October 21, 1943, Thursday

The Department still gives me no word about my supposed appointment—it is now three weeks since it telegraphed "would I be ready to go at once"! Rather hard to bear, from my personal point of view. If something has gone sour I think they ought to let me know. Meanwhile, I have given up this house to be ready, as asked, and if nothing eventuates after all, we'll be badly stuck for some place to live! But unless one is rich or has political pull—neither of which conditions is fufilled in my case—the Department is no respecter of persons, even among its Chiefs of Mission.

October 22, 1943, Friday

Got a wire from "Stettinius Acting" saying that "the President sent your nomination as Ambassador to Greece and Yugoslavia to the Senate today." It was in the clear, and dated yesterday. . . . The papers say the Greeks are being told by the Germans that they are being forgotten by the allies. I suppose I shall have to do my share in counteracting this propaganda, and perhaps my appointment itself at this time will help to do it. . . . The British C-in-C Middle East (Jumbo Wilson) has broadcast to the Greeks urging the utmost unity in the face of the Axis. The poor people must be getting tired of oppression on the one side and only words on the other, whatever may be the reasons for our delay.

October 29, 1943, Friday

Much in the papers about strife between various Greek factions, and Yugoslav, too. It would seem as if allied help has been too long in coming. No word from the Department. It looks as if the Senate were not going to confirm my appointment—which will be rather a bitter pill for me, after having had it offered on a platter as it were. But others, of course, have had the same experience, and I must take what comes.

On November 13, MacVeagh received word from the Department that the Senate had confirmed his nomination, and he was instructed to proceed to Cairo. A few days earlier (November 7, 1943) he discussed with the Greek Ambassador in Pretoria the growing factional rivalry in Greece, and the possibility of there being more serious troubles after the war:

He thinks the only solution will be for the allied military to run things there for a time, until people get settled down somewhat after liberation. My own ideas now are not only that this should happen, but that thereafter the Americans should conduct a plebiscite, which would then be above suspicion, as we have no axe to grind in Greece, and the Greeks know it. [Ambassador] Kollas confirmed my belief that the Greeks feel the British are prejudiced on behalf of the Royal Family and may try to force it back on them willy-nilly. The other great power with possibilities in this connection is of course Russia, and here the feeling cannot be avoided that there is also prejudice,—in favor of communism. No, the only outside power which could have a chance of putting things straight in Greece, internally, is the U.S.A. Whether we would wish to undertake this responsibility is another question. . . . Kollas is an old Venizelist, who, however, has served all *regimes*, including that of Metaxas, as a career diplomat. He takes a dim view of the King and his advisers. Agrees the King has a sense of duty, but says he lacks discretion and [the] ability to unbend. "One must be pliable with the Greeks." One must also *like* them, which the King doesn't,—and says so!

And on November 18, three days before his departure from Pretoria for Cairo, MacVeagh wrote:

I talked with M. Kollas about my mission to Greece. He said the various Greek factions will all be running to me for support, and that he is sure that even the King, though perhaps in a roundabout manner, will ask my advice, and added that, as I myself said, I will be lost if I take sides with one group or another. He said that the Greeks now look to America more than to England, which they mistrust, especially since

Churchill has made some unfortunate statements. The Greeks, he went on, don't want to be *told* what they are to do internally. I remarked that I feel I should follow Mr. Hull's policy, to the effect that "Each nation should be free to decide for itself the forms and details of its governmental organization, as long as it conducts its affairs in such a way as not to menace the peace and security of other nations" (His radio speech of September 12, 1943), and that my only interest in Greece would be, as it is, in Greece as a whole, her peace and prosperity. Therefore I feel that unless instructed to do otherwise, I should listen to all, but limit my comments and counsel to the need for unity now to win the war and secure that tranquility for the country in which only it can decide properly of its future course.

In Cairo, MacVeagh was not "instructed to do otherwise." In fact, during his first year as Ambassador to Greece and Yugoslavia, he was hardly "instructed" at all.

CHAPTER

VIII

Cairo

IN THE FALL of 1943, Cairo was an overcrowded city, bristling with war-related activity. As the Headquarters of the British Middle East Command and of the Supreme Commander, Mediterranean (General Sir Harold Alexander), and of numerous other allied missions, agencies, and boards, Egypt's capital offered second-rate and expensive accommodations to countless military officers, diplomats, propaganda specialists, and intelligence agents. It was also the temporary seat of the "exiled" governments of Yugoslavia and Greece, and the home of the Greek monarch, King George II, and his brother and sister-in-law, Crown Prince Paul and Princess Frederika.

After a four-day voyage by flying boat across the length of the African continent, the MacVeaghs arrived at their new post on Sunday, November 28, 1943. The welcoming party included Alexander C. Kirk, the American Minister to Egypt and to Saudi Arabia, as well as to Greece and Yugoslavia; George V. Allen, the Assistant Chief of the Department's Division of Near Eastern Affairs, who was *en route* to Washington from Moscow, where he had accompanied Secretary Hull at the Foreign Ministers Conference; Walworth ("Wally") Barbour, and Andrew Foster, secretaries of the Legation to the governments of Greece and Yugoslavia; and Arthur W. Parsons, special assistant to the Ambassador.

November 29, 1943, Monday
Called on Mr. Kirk at the Legation, and found him very pleasant. . . . We discussed the Greek situation, and he told me that his attitude has been that this is not the time to agitate politics, and that he has refused to see a lot of the Greeks who wished to talk politics with him; others he has simply quelled by expressing his view that such talk is inopportune at the present time. I think he is right, but that I shall do well to listen and be patient rather than turn an unsympathetic ear. I have never known the Greeks to misunderstand our attitude of neutrality in their internal affairs, but they love to talk and hate to be squelched. . . . In the afternoon I called on the Yugoslav and Greek Premiers in turn, and listened to

their very frank *exposés* of their troubles. Kirk had told me that the British haven't kept the Y. and G. Governments advised of either what they know or what they are doing in the countries concerned. He said he thought this a great mistake, and both the Premiers mentioned this fact to me with resentment. They said the British are supporting the wrong people in Greece and Yugoslavia, largely because of their lack of knowledge of the countries. The Yugoslav[1] said that "Tito's Partisans" are pure communists, and the Greek said that the majority of the guerrillas—those calling themselves E.A.M.[2]—are communists too. Mr. Tsouderos added that he felt quite sure that many of the people to whom the British are now supplying arms will not use them as the Britsh expect. . . . Talking of the Greek King's situation, Mr. Tsouderos said that he personally believes the King would do well to wait at least six months after the liberation of the country before deciding on whether to return or not. He said that by that time spirits would be calmer and that the King might even be recalled, but that this could not be expected at once. He also said that there are various members of his cabinet who hate the King (Roussos,[3] etc.) but that he told them not to "brusquer la chose," but to wait developments. "I told them, 'We have already got enough out of him for the present'—his declaration that he will hold elections for a constituent assembly to pass on the question of the regime."[4] . . . Afterward I had a long talk with George Allen about the Moscow Conference. This was after dinner, at which he and Foster and Parsons joined us. He is convinced that the Soviets are not interested in seeing Soviet governments established in the Balkans, since this would involve Russia in the necessity of supporting a "sphere of influence," and what Russia needs is peace. At the same time they don't want any other nation to extend its influence over the Balkans, and if the British go ahead and attempt to control the

---

[1] Bozidar Purić, former Yugoslav Ambassador to France, was appointed Prime Minister on August 10, 1943.

[2] E.A.M. (*Ethnikon Apeleftherotikon Metopon* = National Liberation Front), a coalition of leftist-republican groups engaged in resistance to the occupation authorities, dominated by the Greek Communist Party (KKE). Its military arm was E.L.A.S. (*Ethnikos Laikos Apeleftherotikos Stratos* = National Popular Liberation Army).

[3] George Roussos, Deputy Prime Minister in the Tsouderos Government.

[4] On July 4, 1943, King George in Cairo broadcast a declaration to the people of Greece stating that after liberation the nation "will be invited to decide by popular and free vote the institutions with which Greece must endow herself in sympathy with [the] forward march of democracy." Accordingly, "as soon as [the] security of [the] country is complete and necessities of military operations allow, free and general elections for a constituent assembly will be held and will take place within 6 months as [the] Government has decided. I am confident that no Greek and least of all myself will fail to respect [the] decision of [the] constituent assembly." *FR 1943*, IV, 135.

internal affairs of these countries, all the good of the Moscow conference will be lost, and Russia will revert again to playing a lone hand. He said that at Moscow, the idea of "spheres of influence," "*cordons sanitaires*," and so forth, was abandoned, chiefly at the instigation of the Russians who regard them as breeding wars, but that while he feels that Russia and the U.S. are likely enough to live up to the agreement, he fears the old British imperial habits and complexes may upset the apple-cart. Rather interesting, all this. He said that Mr. Hull is in thorough agreement with this general hands-off policy, and that the Russians trust him, but that the idea has yet to be sold to Messrs. Churchill and Roosevelt. Perhaps this is going on now. . . . George told me a lot which tends to show that British officials—capitalizing on our agreement to let the eastern Mediterranean be their *military* zone—are working to establish a thorough economic and political monopoly of their own in this region also. . . . I think we must be watchful and firm in keeping ourselves in the picture, but we must not be led into bickerings and recriminations against our allies *on any account*. As Peggy said when I told her all this, "The only way to win a war as allies is to work together." If the British pull away from us, or against us, we must be careful to correct the situation without conflict. . . . The Greeks and Yugoslavs and our own people—to judge from the talk of Allen and Foster, both fresh from Washington,—are indulging in a lot of such criticism. I think the Embassy should not lend itself to this, but should follow the President's lead in looking to the larger issue of solidarity, while keeping our friends from going too far, not by criticism—which will only do harm—but by being watchful, and on the spot at all times with the representation of our just claims, in a spirit which need be no less firm for being friendly and good-humored.

November 30, 1943, Tuesday
Received a call from Col. Levidis, the King's Master of the Household. Very friendly. He criticised Mr. Tsouderos for having turned too drastically against the Metaxists, as if all the officers who had fought for Greece under the King and Metaxas had been believers in the Fascist system. They were only obeying the King and doing their duty. Now many of them are in concentration camps, and a lot of the cabinet are actually the appointees of sergeants and corporals who represent mutinous troops of leftist tendencies. He also criticised Mr. Tsouderos for taking Kanellopoulos into the government as vice-premier. The latter brought in the leftist elements, and then Tsouderos turned round, ejected Kanellopoulos, but retained the elements he had brought into the government. He also criticised the British, who, he said, on the one hand say that

politics must not be played at present, and who support the King until peace comes, etc., and on the other, through a choice of inferior agents here, foment the political spirit and raise opposition to the King by favoring anti-royalist elements, etc. . . . Harry Hill[5] arrived from Washington, as a special assistant to me. I think I can use him as liaison with Dean Landis' outfit here,[6] which "coordinates" B.E.W.[7] and other work. He told me a lot of disheartening stuff about the multiplication and telescoping of "agencies" at home, particularly as regards relief and rehabilitation work. It seems that the British are actually ready to step in and reconstruct the economy of the Balkans while we are still making plans on paper and disputing over organization set-ups and personnel. . . . Incidentally, I should note that Levidis spoke very disparagingly of Mr. Leeper,[8] the British Ambassador. He said he knows absolutely nothing about Greece and is consequently of no value in his job (my own people say he is a weak sister, too and carries no weight). He added that Sir Michael Palairet was removed at Tsouderos' instigation, because Palairet refused to intercede for Tsouderos when the latter was banished by Metaxas for his Venizelist plotting; also because Palairet knew well that Tsouderos was going too far in his persecution of all associated with the Metaxist régime. Leeper doesn't know what Tsouderos has done, cannot appreciate his present actions in consequence, and is therefore, naturally, more welcome to the Premier than Palairet who knew too much. I gather from all of Levidis' talk (he is the King's parrot) that H.M. doesn't trust his Premier wholly. And indeed I don't see, from the remarks he has himself made to me and which I have noted in this diary, how anyone could trust him.

December 1, 1943, Wednesday
After lunch Mr. Landis, economic coordinator for the Near and Middle East, called. He told me of his difficulties and his ideas, and I offered to help, but he put forward no constructive ideas, and seemed depressed. . . . My letter of appointment came, together with the signed copy of the credentials, for King George, just in time for the presentation. The letter read that I am appointed Ambassador to *Greece*, and also to serve

---

[5] Harry Hill, special assistant to MacVeagh, had been executive of Socony-Vacuum and Manager of the American Express Co. in Greece in the late 1930's and until the German invasion.

[6] James M. Landis, American Director of Economic Operations in the Middle East, and principal American civilian representative on the Middle East Supply Center (MESC), with the personal rank of Minister.

[7] B.E.W. = Board of Economic Warfare (British).

[8] Sir Reginald W. Allen Leeper, British Ambassador to the Greek Government-in-exile since February 1943, succeeding Sir Michael Palairet upon his retirement.

392 · CHAPTER VIII

concurrently, but without extra remuneration, as Ambassador to Yugoslavia, so that when we go back to Europe, if we do, I suppose I shall go to Athens and some one else take the Belgrade job.... Archer talked a lot about Landis' problems. Archer is head of the F.E.A.[9] organization here and comes under Landis' coordination. The Department wanted three members on a policy committee for Balkan reconstruction here—the so-called A.T.B.,[10]—started by the British (I was to be one of the members). But the British have withheld agreement and gone on planning by themselves. Thus Landis, feeling that the A.T.B. had about finished its work, proposed that we should join, and have the chairmanship of, the operating committee carrying out the A.T.B.'s plans, and got the British to assent, but *the Department* has not assented! So Landis feels himself out on a limb.... Archer feels that the whole scheme of Balkan rehabilitation will probably have to be revised in the light of the Moscow conference, which has brought Russia into the picture, and that the Department is likely waiting on this account. If this is true, the British plans will be included in the revision, and we need not be disturbed at not joining in a dual scheme at present. I hope this is right. Otherwise our hesitation and delay will simply result in the British acting unilaterally, and bringing about a situation contrary to the spirit of Moscow, in which one country will be building up a "zone of influence" in the Balkans. Much depends on what the President and Mr. Churchill decide. It seems that Landis saw F.D.R. when the latter came through, the other day, and hopes to see him again the end of this week.

December 2, 1943, Thursday

Today the news broke of last week's conference here between the President, Mr. Churchill, and Chiang Kai Chek. Meanwhile the second conference "elsewhere"[11] has been finished and the parties are on their return journey. The security people have banned a visit to Ankara, and it is possible that Inönü may come here, but he has telegraphed that if he comes it must be "as an equal, and not simply to receive information as to the decisions taken in Teheran!" From a short-term viewpoint, I hope he does not come, as I want very much to see the Greek question taken

[9] F.E.A. = Foreign Economic Administration (American).
[10] A.T.B. = Administration of Territories (Balkans) Committee (Allied).
[11] Following the First Cairo Conference (November 22-26, 1943) between British, American, and Chinese representatives, Roosevelt, Churchill and Stalin met in Teheran (November 28-December 1, 1943) to co-ordinate military plans and to begin discussions on the peace settlements. The principal military decision was that the "Second Front" would be opened by a cross-Channel invasion in May 1944. At the Second Cairo Conference (December 2-6, 1943), Roosevelt and Churchill discussed mainly the conduct of the war in the Far East.

up by the President and Mr. Churchill, and his visit might prevent that.
... I had a full day, with a visit to Mr. Casey[12] in the morning and to
Mr. Leeper, the British Ambassador to Greece, in the evening. ... I
liked both Casey and Leeper. Casey says he pulls Kirk's leg and that
Kirk rather likes it. "I cut through all the affectation." Leeper is frail
and appears weak, but is not so in reality and has brains and perception.
Both have a good sense of humour. I learned from them that American
cooperation is very much desired both in regard to economic and political
questions in the Balkans. ... Leeper has prepared a memorandum on
the King's situation of which he gave me a copy. It comprises a plan as
follows: The King to make a declaration now that he will not return to
Greece till recalled after a plebiscite; the Zervas forces of guerrillas,[13]
now favored by the British instead of the Communist-Bulgar-Macedonian
revolutionists, to be invited then to become Greek regulars serving with
the government; a local Greek government to be formed, with the King's
blessing, of people who have remained in Greece throughout the war, to
carry on after the Germans withdraw and until elections are held; a leading figure to head this crowd, possibly Archbishop Damaskinos (!);[14]
and finally the resignation of the present government and the formation
on Greek soil of a new one on the basis of elections to be held under
the auspices of the local authorities, and the settlement of the régime
question, with the return of the King or not, as the people may decide.
... This memorandum has been supplied to Mr. Eden and Mr. Winant[15]
already, and it is to be hoped that on the basis of it, Mr. Churchill and
Mr. Roosevelt will personally persuade the King to make the desired
declaration at this time. Leeper says, and I think rightly, that no one
else can persuade him, certainly not his Cabinet, which he despises. The
question is whether at this crowded time the Chiefs will attend to this
question. Also whether Mr. Churchill will agree. He is, said Leeper, determined "not to let the King down." But it would probably be to let him
down to allow him to keep on his present course in view of opinion in
Greece, and would certainly be his political ruination (and perhaps even
his death) to let him go back to Greece before spirits there are calmed.
So far, Leeper. It seems to *me* that the idea is a sound one, and I said so.
What I am against, myself, is any possible attempt to put the King back
by force. It won't come to any good, and I don't want our government to

[12] Richard G. Casey, British Minister of State in the Middle East.
[13] General Napoleon Zervas, military head of E.D.E.S. (*Ethnikos Demokratikos Ellinikos Syndesmos* = National Republican Greek League), a resistance organization. Zervas, a staunch republican, gradually came to support the King's return, and was thus identified with right-wing forces.
[14] Damaskinos had been named Archbishop of Greece by the occupation authorities.
[15] John G. Winant, U.S. Ambassador to Britain.

be associated with it, while unfortunately, as things are, we cannot be disassociated very well from what the British do. I am delighted to see the British, therefore, taking the point of view described, and told Leeper I was very favorably impressed, and would support his ideas as outlined if given the chance. I particularly applauded the clever choice of Damaskinos.... Personally I doubt whether, if the King waits, he will be recalled at all. But also I am sure that not to wait would be fatal to him. The poor man is thus in a bad fix, as I see it, with no future ahead of him as King. But just the same because two alternatives are bad is no reason for choosing the more disastrous.... Leeper decribed to me the history of the "civil war" in Greece. Apparently the British Military decided to support the E.A.M. outfit—the wrong horse—on inadequate information as to its real aims. When they found out that it is more communist than anti-German in character, the British then switched to the "democratic" but smaller forces of General Zervas. Zervas is in the Pindus, around and chiefly east and south of Jannina. The others, supported perhaps by Bulgarian influences, and certainly composed largely of Macedonians, but not, it seems, connected with Moscow, at least directly, are in Macedonia, Thessaly, and even the Peloponnese, with headquarters in Athens itself. This crowd is dangerous for the peace of a liberated Greece, whereas the Zervas outfit, if convinced that the British are not intending to force the King back on them, might be counted on to be loyal to the Government. This is the distinction which governs the policy suggested in the memorandum, and supplies the motive for an open declaration on the part of the King,—to take out of the hands of the Communists the propaganda weapon they are now using to the effect that to side with Zervas is to help enslave the country to a foreign-imposed monarch.... Mr. Leeper bases his forecast of events on the supposition that no allied attack will be made in the Balkan region, and that Greece will be evacuated by the Germans as a result of operations elsewhere. Few British troops will then actually go into Greece, and the local government to be set up will have need of patriot armed forces to avert anarchy. On the other hand, it must be kept in mind that a big effort is being made to bring Turkey into the war, and if this happens there may be an allied front at least in the north of Greece. Under such conditions, I should imagine that internal strife in Greece would pretty much disappear, through gravitation of the patriots in both camps to one side and the others to the Germans.... Sent off a letter to F.D.R. saying that I have arrived here and am at his service if he finds it desirable and possible to see me. Also a telegram, drafted by Foster and Barbour, urging that the Department send us American, and not Greek-American, clerks.... I feel it would be bad for our Mission to be subjected to the suspicions which racial connections and political sympathies inevitably arouse.

December 3, 1943, Friday
Shortly after I arrived at the office I had a call from Kirk who said that F.D.R. wanted to see me at 2:30, and that he would arrange for my entrance to the house (Kirk's house) where the President is staying near the Pyramids. I prepared a brief memorandum on the Greek situation to take with me, covering two essential points: "Firstly, it should be made absolutely clear that the King is not going to be forced on the country against its will; and secondly, the present collapse in Greek morale consequent on the loss of Kos, Leros, and Samos,[16] should be countered with some assurance that winter relief is not also going to fail." I attached to my memorandum, which briefly elaborated on this, the memo which Mr. Leeper had given me yesterday, containing the plan to have the King declare he would not return till called for, and outlining the idea of having Archbishop Damaskinos conduct an *ad interim* government etc., and said I agreed with it thoroughly. I also attached a memo from Mr. Archer on the food situation, showing that grain shipments are already 30,000 tons in arrears, owing to lack of available transportation. . . . Peggy and I had to go and be received by the Crown Prince and Princess Frederika at 1:15 and take lunch afterwards, so I arranged with Col. Levidis to tell them I would have to leave at 2:00 sharp. This he did and they were very nice about it, understanding the reason without my having to give it. Lunch was very pleasant. . . . General Smuts is due to pass through here soon and will take the Princess with him to fetch the children and bring them up here. . . . She cut loose in her usual downright and thoroughly indiscreet way, which gets her disliked, about many people in South Africa. . . . I left at exactly 2 o'clock, and drove out to Kirk's villa, above which the group of the Great Pyramids towers magnificently. Kirk had arranged that I should get through the gates without a pass and this worked, and I was ushered into a large hall where I found George Wadsworth, Consul General in Beirut, who had had an appointment with the President at 2:00 but was still waiting. He told me the whole story of the recent Lebanon affair, showing up the French as having acted outrageously.[17] The President was still hav-

---

[16] Following the collapse of Italy in early September 1943, a small British force attempted, but failed, to capture Kos, Samos, and Leros in the Dodecanese. Although the Italian troops on the islands remained inactive, the Germans succeeded in reenforcing their garrisons from the air.

[17] On November 11, 1943, following a move of the Lebanese parliament to proclaim the country's full independence, the French authorities imprisoned the Leba-

ing lunch, and as we talked Admiral Leahy[18] came out and spoke a few words to Wadsworth as he passed through. . . . As soon as the President was moved out of the dining room he sent for me, somewhat to my embarrassment, as Wadsworth was really first on the list. We sat in a kind of screened-in porch—almost in the shadow of the Pyramids of Egypt—and there I had the longest consecutive and most intensive talk I have ever had with him, lasting about one and a quarter hours,— in my acquaintance of over 30 years. Strange, what things happen. . . . We talked of the Teheran Conference, of the Greek and Yugoslav situations, and of South Africa. He told me that they had settled the post-war fate of Germany, "dismemberment, and the end of the Reich," and that what he and Stalin saw eye-to-eye on, and thus carried through, "came as a bombshell to the British." I take it that the British Foreign Office had geared Churchill to a less forthright and more compromising policy in the interests of the old-time balancing of power idea. The President also said that he liked Stalin, and that the latter was always "ribbing" Churchill, giving him digs and goading him and pulling his leg. "Churchill stood it very well, and didn't say a lot of things about the Russians which he might have said." . . . Most of our talk was about Greece and "Georgie," as the President calls him to his face. He thinks him nice, but stupid. At first the President told me that the King should be treated squarely and allowed to go back to his country with his troops. Then he outlined the kind of constitution Greece should have, in which the monarch would have nothing to do but lay wreaths, attend functions, etc., and be entirely outside of politics. "What's the matter with that?" I said, "Nothing, only the nature of the Greeks." Then he listened very carefully, as he always does, while I tried to explain that "Georgie," for the Greeks, is a man with a whole history behind him, and that the question of how he is to go back in the present condition of the country,— and given the fact that, as the President himself says, there is likely to be no large-scale military action attempted in Greece,—is a most complicated and difficult one. I said my chief concern was that though we must support, or rather go along with our British allies, we should not be concerned [involved] in any forcing of any régime whatsoever on the Greeks (to this he nodded his assent), and that therefore I felt immensely relieved when I learned of the present plans, which provide very carefully for self-determination as regards the régime, and wise restraint in regard to the King's own risk as well, etc. etc. I said I would leave my memoranda with him, and he said he wanted to have them, and promised to see the

---

nese President and cabinet. In the face of strikes and rioting, the French freed the prisoners, and on November 27, France's mandate over Lebanon was formally ended.

[18] Admiral William D. Leahy, Chief of Staff to President Roosevelt.

King personally, if this is at all possible. But he said that as Inönü is coming tomorrow it may be difficult. (So evidently they assured Ismet that he would be "treated as an equal!") I asked the President if he felt the Russians are fomenting or supporting the Greek communistic uprising which is making so much trouble, and he said he didn't think so, "not officially." But he added that you never can tell, since the Russians have a way of acting differently with either hand. This question came up again in regard to Yugoslavia. Mihailović,[19] he said, is acting in concert with the Germans, to some extent at least, and Tito [is] not; therefore we shall support Tito.[20] I asked whether he could be sure of his information in this matter, and he said "no," but it is the best information we can get, and we must act on it. The truth is that in regard to the guerrilla resistance in both Greece and Yugoslavia, the allied policy has been,— and has had to be,—purely opportunist. We are out to defeat the Germans and must use what instruments we can find to hand. If they fail us, we must switch and try others. Of course such methods are dangerous when politics are superimposed, and make a continuous and coherent policy towards the countries concerned, and towards their governments, very hard to frame and preserve. . . . The President said confidentially that he had always felt that Yugoslavia is an artificial creation, and that perhaps the only possible future for it would lie in a loose federation of the component parts, something like America under the Articles. "I said to Peter, 'Peter, which would you rather be, King of Serbia and have at least some quiet hours, or King of Yugoslavia and never have any?' and he said, 'I am a Serb, and I'd rather be King of Serbia.'" The President said that his idea of the best way to handle Yugoslavia and Greece would be to put walls around them and let those inside fight it out, and report when all was over who was top dog! But more seriously, I was interested in his reaction when I queried the Articles of Confederation idea, and reminded him that the weak point in *our* experiment had been the lack of provision for an army and navy to defend the Federation. He flashed at me, "Will it be necessary for these states to defend themselves after this war?" It looks to me as if he really thinks that he and his collaborators have arranged to banish war, from Europe anyway, for good. But why should one quarrel with the faith of the worker in his work? . . . We also talked of South Africa and he referred to my letters which he was pleased to say were "fine." "But I have formed a very depressing idea

---

[19] General Dragoljub-Draža Mihailović, Serb right-wing officer and guerrilla leader, Minister of War and Commander-in-Chief of the Yugoslav government-in-exile. Mihailović's resistance movement was known as the Chetniks.
[20] Tito (Josip Broz), communist leader and supreme commander of the Partisans, a resistance organization that was a rival of the Chetniks. Tito assumed the rank of Marshal.

of the future there." I elaborated on the big and complex problems and the little men of the post-Smuts generation.... Finally, I got up to go, and F.D.R. said that he would be seeing me again before he leaves. He told me his plans about going to Italy. I said that I doubted very much whether he would in fact see me again, but asked that he try his best to see King George, as I felt this would be worthwhile. I explained to him how the King has been advised by so many people, including people he has no use for and despises, such as most of his Cabinet, that now only he and Mr. Churchill can be counted on as having any influence over him. "He will listen to you, I am sure, but to no one else." The President again promised to do his best to see the King, and then called in his aide, Col. Wilson Brown, and said that he wanted to see *me* again before leaving, and instructed him accordingly. But I am quite sure it won't work.

December 4, 1943, Saturday

The news broke today regarding the Teheran Conference,—but nothing [was] said about the decisions taken. Apparently it was expected to hold the matter secret several days longer, but the Russian Tass Agency broke out of line. I am sorry, as it makes the President's stay over here all the more precarious.... Other news is that the Tito Partisans in Yugoslavia have proclaimed a government. There is a President and a Marshal (Tito), just as in Russia.... This will make the Allied policy in supporting Tito with arms and continuing to recognize the Government rather difficult!... Was called on by Mr. Tsouderos, who is exercised over a statement by a State Department official to the effect that the U.S. is interested in preserving the territorial "integrity" of Albania. He wants this corrected because it does not agree with our announced policy not to prejudge boundary questions while the war is on, *and* because Greece has every right to what is called Southern Albania and is really northern Epirus.... Was then called on by Levidis, who said that King George wants to see me at 11 tomorrow morning.... Stevenson, the British Ambassador to Yugoslavia, called me on the 'phone and wanted to see me urgently, so I asked him to dinner.... It seems the British S.O.E. (Special Operations Executive),[21] plans to bring out of a certain country the emissary of a certain well-known leader, who is prepared to do certain acts, and Eden proposed that I join with Stevenson and the newly arrived Russian Envoy, Novikov,[22] in conferring with him. I said I'd be glad to hear what the man has to say, but could not meet with him unless

[21] S.O.E., British wartime agency engaged in intelligence operations, political activity, and sabotage behind enemy lines.

[22] Nikolai V. Novikov, Soviet Ambassador to the Greek and Yugoslav governments-in-exile (Cairo).

instructed,—as obviously the man's principal might afterwards lay claim to having negotiated officially, and therefore the Department should be advised and take the responsibility. Stevenson said he would repeat my reply to Cadogan,[23] and showed me an S.O.E. document on the matter from which it is clear that not only the British but the Russian Foreign Offices have been in on the matter from the start. . . . I stayed up till about 2 a.m. reducing all this to telegraphic form.

December 5, 1943, Sunday

Drove to the Greek Legation at 11 a.m. precisely, and sat with Princess Frederika and Mr. Metaxas[24] in the big hall till the King came. Then we went into a private room and I heard of the King's troubles, and why he doesn't want to make the declaration which the British are now proposing. He says he has already said he will decide about returning as soon as Greece is liberated, and that to make another and contradictory statement, deciding *now*, would appear weak; also that if he says he will stay out till called back, people will say he is a coward, etc. He told me a lot about British agents, MO-4[25] people and so forth, who appear to be against him, and said he sometimes wonders whether the British government itself is not anxious to get rid of him. Poor fellow, he has seen and talked with altogether too many people anxious to advise him and pulling him this way and that in their own, rather than his, interests. Now that the British have a plan for him which does not involve running counter to our principle that the Greek people should decide as to their government, I felt free to advise him personally to stick by them—that is the Foreign Office and the Government, not the services and agents, now here but gone tomorrow. I said that I could not advise him officially as I was uninstructed, and that as he knew, our policy had always been not to engage in the internal affairs of this country. He said he knew this, but went on talking, and I then said that I thought that in his position he should assert himself and tell the British that he is willing to play ball with them, but that they must do the same with him, and if they want him to act in a certain way, they should make it possible for him to do so. I fear, however, that he is afraid of them somewhat. He complains about them, but won't stand up to them. I said that I felt a decision on his part to stay outside till recalled would clear the air, and make it impossible for the communists and others to charge that foreigners are going

---

[23] Right Honorable Sir Alexander Cadogan, British Permanent Under-Secretary of State for Foreign Affairs.

[24] Petros Metaxas, head of the Political Bureau of King George II.

[25] M.O. = Morale Operations, British agency engaged in propaganda and psychological warfare directed at the occupied countries.

to bring him back with bayonets, whereas if he makes no decision now and no declaration, not only are all charges possible, and consequent confusion in Greek opinion inevitable, but when he does go back, uncalled for in the manner suggested, he will have to be supported with troops, on account of the communist menace now growing so rapidly, and therefore charges of *force majeure* will seem justified. All this I put in as friendly a way as I knew how, and indeed I sympathized with most of what he had to say himself, and could genuinely say I was only trying to think out along with him the best path for him to pursue. Finally it boiled down to this, that he should attempt to put aside all the thorny non-essentials of the situation and cling to the one real clue through the maze which is available to him,—the British government's policy in his regard. He should follow their advice, or get them to adopt his own views, but in any case go along with them and damn the torpedoes, as it were,—and altogether, many and cogent as the arguments against it might be, the plan they had for him seemed to me the best for him, probably, in the long run. . . . I must say that the conversation was very friendly, and I don't think he will suspect me of any but genuine motives, but of course one can't tell, as he has experienced so many deceptions he is prone to suspect everyone. At the close of our conversation, which lasted a long time, he reverted again to his doubts as to whether the British government itself, as well as many of the agents it employs, is not against him, and I had to try again to reassure him. . . . Lunch given for us at the Mohamed Aly Club by Col. Levidis. The Leepers and the Metaxases were there. . . . Leeper said he had been with Eden during the morning and the latter was doing his best to get Mr. Churchill lined up for a talk with the King along the lines now adopted. I told him I had seen the President and tried to explain the idea, and had left Leeper's memorandum with him, and felt perhaps that he would support it, though at first he had talked along the lines adopted at Quebec[26]—that the King should

---

[26] At the First Quebec Conference (August 14-24, 1943) the United States and Britain agreed to concentrate their military efforts on the cross-Channel invasion scheduled for May 1944. Operations elsewhere in Europe, including the Mediterranean and the Balkans, while not excluded entirely, were definitely downgraded. It thus became apparent that there would be no "Balkan Front." At the insistence of Churchill, and in response to a telegram from the Greek King, it was also agreed that George should not have to go beyond his statement of July 4, 1943, concerning the future of the monarchy. Specifically, the King would not have to promise to remain abroad until the contemplated plebiscite, as most Greek political factions demanded. Furthermore, the United States and Britain "should continue to support the governments and *régimes* as now recognized by them generally through the period up to the defeat of the enemy." Finally, "the British Foreign Office should reply to the King's telegram, supporting his contention that he was prepared to return to Greece as soon as possible, and submit the question of the Royal House to

return with his troops. "Ah, yes," said Leeper, "but that was when it was still thought that there would be military operations in the Balkans. Now no such plan is contemplated, and that alters the King's situation altogether." This, of course, is the very basis of his memorandum, and makes sense. . . . The King having asked that I do my best to see that he gets an appointment with the President, I wrote a personal note to the latter and sent it out to the Villa via the Legation—to reinforce my verbal suggestions on the subject. Perhaps this will help.

December 5, 1943

Dear Franklin:

King George of Greece told me this morning that he is very anxious to see you and has asked me to convey to you his request for a meeting before you leave.

As I told you the other day, I believed it would be a good thing for you to see him if you can possibly arrange it, as he is distressed in his mind as to whether he should make the declaration which has been suggested to him by the British, and a talk with you could not fail to reassure him and help him come to a decision.

Ever yours affectionately,
Lincoln MacVeagh (1)

December 6, 1943, Monday

Stevenson gave me a copy of the document he showed me Saturday night and said that Cadogan wished me to inform the Department and ask whether it is desired that I meet the Emissary, or send someone to do so for me, or simply be advised of what he has to say. In other words, ask for instructions. I didn't tell him that I had reported the matter at once. . . . Leeper said he had "hopes" that the King may be persuaded to adopt his plan and issue a declaration; he said that Mr. Tsouderos had been to see him and told him that "even the Diadoch[27] has counselled the King in this sense." So perhaps I shall not figure, conspicuously at least, in his black book! . . . Just before lunch I heard from Kirk by telephone that the President would see the King at 4:10, and this I communicated to the latter. . . . In the afternoon I had a long call from Mr. Purić, the Yugoslav Prime Minister, and also a call from Mr. Robert Murphy, our

---

plebiscite. The President said [that] the United States Government would not take any different position." *FR 1943*, IV, 147-48.

[27] Diadoch = Crown Prince or heir apparent (Prince Paul).

2. Cairo, December 1943. With King George II.

man in Algiers who has been given Ambassadorial rank on the Mediterranean Commission—or is it Italian? In any case he deals with de Gaulle and also with Italian civilian problems. He said that it has been decided to unite the whole Mediterranean military command, probably under General Alexander, and that Eisenhower would "go north." This looks like business. Mr. Purić has a sense of humor, or he could never take the punishment. He told me he thought the setting up of the Tito government a good thing in that it has proved what he has always told the British, that the partisan movement is not purely patriotic but political. He said he has seen Mr. Eden this morning, who was "very sweet. Nothing could be sweeter," but who told him the English policy would be to go on recognizing the Yugoslav government and go on supporting Tito! He blamed the British for a lot of things, particularly for allowing the Russians to broadcast to Yugoslavia while preventing the Yugoslavian government from so doing. He said the partisan movement is the "bastard child" of the Tiflis so-called free Yugoslavian radio and the British Broadcasting Corporation, which reproduces the former's news. He said that the British information from Yugoslavia, both as to the aims and the numbers of the partisans, is exceedingly doubtful. What he specially fears is that the support we are giving to the partisans will force the conservative people into the arms of the Germans for protection, when they realize that no allied military invasion of the Balkans is forthcoming. ... He said that though the British press had announced this morning that his government had met and denounced Tito's new move, there had been no meeting and no denouncement! He had himself, however, put out a news bulletin, stating among other things that United Nations propaganda and institutions (Tiflis [Radio] and the B.B.C., that is) were responsible for much that is going on, and this Stevenson had immediately asked him to withdraw or correct. I knew about this, as Stevenson told me at lunch. *He* thought it most inopportune! But the British do seem to me to have been unnecessarily stupid in their handling of both the Greek and the Yugoslav governments,—a little less rigidity, a little more understanding and yielding graciously on small points, a little perspicacity as to what points *are* small and what large, etc., would avoid a lot of trouble. They are piling up dislike and resentment against themselves without reason but with cause, every day, and will regret it later, I am sure.

December 7, 1943, Tuesday
Leeper called at the office at 3:45 and told me that the King resisted Churchill and Eden and refused their combined advice for several hours,—on the strength of what F.D.R. had said to him.

December 8, 1943, Wednesday
Was called on by M. Ilya Jukić, who used to be Under-Secretary for Foreign Affairs. He criticized the Purić government, and said he feels the government should not side with any group fighting in Yugoslavia, but encourage them all, so that the King may be kept above politics; if the King becomes tarred with any one brush, he is lost. But, he said, Purić thinks that there is bound to come a split between Russia and Great Britain and the U.S.A., despite Moscow and Teheran, and is playing his cards in Yugoslavia accordingly. Jukić gave me a letter to the President, signed by himself and Cubrilović[28] and another, in the interests of the federated Yugoslavia idea, which is the Partisan idea now, and about which incidentally, the President spoke to me favorably. ... Ambassador Winant called up and asked me to meet him at Kirk's house at quarter to one. He told me the President had sent me a message before leaving —whispered it hurriedly to Winant at the airport. He thinks the King

[28] Dr. Branko Cubrilović, former Minister of Agriculture.

is having a pistol put to his head by the British and doesn't want me to associate myself with any effort to force the King's decision against his will. Furthermore, he feels I may have gone too far already in this direction! I wonder what the King told him? I said to Winant that the only action I took was to advise the President, as I supposed he would want me to do, and that in talking with the King I had not only told him, to begin with, that I could not advise him officially, as I was not instructed, but had urged him in the end to make his own decision, and if he couldn't accept the British plan to say so frankly and try to get the British to accept a plan of his, but in any case not to distrust his friends as he seemed inclined to do. . . . Called on Dean Landis with Harry Hill, showing him a telegram I had sent backing him up on his plan for a combined British-American economic information bureau here for the Balkans, and talking of his other plans, which he intends to try to get approved at home, to facilitate the speeding up of practical relief operations here. He is leaving for the U.S. on Friday. . . . Drafted a telegram on the Yugoslav situation, and Jukić's views as contrasted with those of the Premier. . . . Called on Winant again at 7:00 at Kirk's house at his request. He wanted to make *sure* I hadn't put pressure on the King.

December 9, 1943, Thursday
Was received by the King of Yugoslavia, a nice, shy young man, younger than his years, but evidently trying to do his best in his position. . . . I gave the King Biddle's[29] letter of recall as well as my credentials. . . . There was a lot of photographing, which the Yugoslavs evidently regarded as the most important part of the affair—"for the record," as one of the aides said to Barbour. . . . There is a rumor to the effect that the unification of the Mediterranean Command may force the British Embassy to Greece to go where the new headquarters are, probably Tunis, and if the Embassy (which is so tied in with the Military—Kirk, who doesn't like Leeper says: has to be watched over by the military!—that it can't be separated from it) moves, then the Government to which he is accredited must move too! I say then the Greek Government should be called "the Government of Greece near H.M.'s Embassy!"

December 10, 1943, Friday
Got a telegram from the Department about the emissary business. It instructs me to join with Stevenson in seeing the man, if the Russian

[29] Anthony J. Drexel Biddle, Jr., U.S. Minister to the Yugoslav government-in-exile (Cairo).

Ambassador is also there.... Called on Stevenson to tell him this, and learned from him that Mr. Churchill told King Peter today that in a short time it is likely that the British will urge him to dismiss Mihailović from the Cabinet. Stevenson thinks this premature, but was unable to prevent it. He said, however, that M. is certainly not active in helping us, and has collaborated with the Germans at least to the extent of letting several divisions pass through his territory unmolested.

December 11, 1943, Saturday

Was called on by Mr. Venizelos,[30] who confirmed a rumor to the effect that King George has signed a declaration, devised by Tsouderos, saying that when the time comes for him to decide whether or not to return to Greece, he will make his decision "in agreement with his government."[31] This pleases the Republican group in the cabinet, of which Venizelos, of course, is one, as it practically puts the King in their hands, and means that he will in all probability do just what he refused to promise when urged by Churchill and Eden, namely, wait outside of Greece till it is decided by the people whether to recall him or not.... Venizelos also said that he had talked with Mr. Churchill and urged the employment of Greek troops in Italy, and that Mr. Churchill had turned to Leeper and said, "This must be done. The Greeks defeated the Italians, and they must enter Rome with the others." Venizelos, however, wants them to engage in the actual fighting; and he is right. It would do wonders not only for the morale of the Greek army, but for that of the Greek people, if the Greek troops were no longer kept idle but went into the front line once more.... Called on by an O.S.S. man, with a Major Farish,[32] who has been in Yugoslavia with the Partisans. He is much impressed by their numbers and their organization.... Dinner at the Leepers; the Tsouderoses and young Wallace and Waterhouse of the British Embassy also there.... Tsouderos was much excited over his success in getting the King to make his declaration—in the form of a letter to Tsouderos which was written, all but the essential clause, last month, and was at that time unacceptable to the Government.... Leeper took me aside after dinner and talked about the situation. He said Tsouderos had shown the greatest ability and craftiness in saving the situation after the King's

---

[30] Sofoclis Venizelos, son of the great Greek statesman, and Minister of the Navy in the Tsouderos government.

[31] In a protocol dated December 13, 1943, essentially reaffirming a pledge given in a letter to Tsouderos on November 8, King George agreed to consult with his government before deciding on the timing of his return to Greece.

[32] Major Linn M. Farish, U.S. Army officer assigned to OSS, parachuted into Partisan territory on September 19, 1943.

talks with F.D.R. and Churchill, and had capitalized on the King's satisfaction with his victory over the British by getting him to sign something which he doesn't understand amounts to practically the same thing as what the British were advising! According to Leeper, the King was so happy and stupid at the same time, that he fell for a trap, and Tsouderos rushed publication so as to prevent his changing his mind.... But perhaps the King realized that it was inevitable that he should delay his entry into Greece, and only sought to save his face, which this new form of declaration allowed him to do.... I said to Leeper, "Do you realize that this means that the King probably never *will* return to Greece?" and he said "Certainly I do." The British have gone a long way since 1935!

December 13, 1943, Monday
Had talk with Hill and Foster on the economic situation in Greece. Suggested that Levinson of Landis's office come and talk with me about how we can go about getting more cooperation with the Greek government on technical matters,—it seems the Government has very few experts here who know anything about conditions in Greece, agricultural and economic, even before the war. They are all, like Varvaressos, in London or Washington. I suggest we tell it [the Greek Government] what we want, and get it to help us turn up, or get out of Greece, the kind of man necessary to advise us.... Got off my letter to F.D.R. It gives my *apologia* and *defensio* for "forcing the hand of the King," which of course I never did; and though I have been pretty sore at his telling off Winant to reprove me, I made the letter goodhumored as well as clear.

Cairo, December 13, 1943

Dear Franklin:
You did get away from Cairo just as I thought you would, without seeing me again, but you saw the King of Greece, as I hoped, and that was more important.

In this connection, you may remember that you sent me a message through Ambassador Winant, to the effect that you desired me not to associate myself with any effort to force the King to a course of action against his will, and also that you felt I had perhaps already gone too far in doing just this.

I should like to reassure you, if possible, regarding the second half of this message, as I should hate to have you think me so ignorant of my business after all these years as to associate myself with any foreign policy but our own, without instructions.

Actually, my whole initiative in the matter of the King's decision was limited to my conversation with you and the memorandum I left with you. Having been told by the British Ambassador that a plan he had worked out would be brought up to Mr. Churchill and to you, I secured a copy of it, and gave it to you with my most considered reactions, as I presumed you would wish me to do. But I went no further. When the King asked me to come and see him, and led the conversation on to the question of what should be his policy, I explicitly told him that I could not advise him officially, as I was not instructed. I also reminded him of our own policy, as it had existed all during my time in Greece, of not taking part in the internal affairs of the country. He expressed his thorough understanding and agreement on these points. If you understood from him later, at the meeting I asked you to accord him, that in this conversation I associated myself in any way with a British attempt to force his hand, I fear I must say that he misled you—probably unintentionally, since his mind was much disturbed. He wanted my opinion, and I could hardly refuse to give it when he put our conversation on a friendly and unofficial basis. Furthermore, as you know, that opinion was to the effect that the British plan was a good one and in the King's own interests. But in view of his inability to appreciate this, harrassed as he has been by advice from all sides, I also told him just as clearly as you can have done that he should make up his own mind, and if he couldn't accept his friends' proposal, then he should tell them so squarely, and perhaps evolve with them some other plan that would suit.

A good diplomat shouldn't have to make explanations, so I close off these of mine in some embarrassment, only hoping that you will take them as they stand for the truth they are. Actually, the King, after receiving your advice, has now done what I told him personally he should do in any event. He has made up his mind, and having told the British squarely that he could not accept their proposal, has settled on a plan which apparently pleases both himself and them, as well as his own government. This plan was worked out by his Prime Minister, Mr. Tsouderos, and involves a declaration by the King to the effect that when the time comes for him to make his decision whether or not to return to Greece, he will do so "in agreement with his government." I have not seen the King since Mr. Winant delivered your *caveat*—and spanking— nor have I made any inquiries of my British friends as to what occurred between the King and Mr. Churchill, or anything else connected with the matter. But the mountain has come to Mahomet since Mahomet would not go to the mountain, and I have not been able to avoid being informed. Between you and me, I am told that the King is very happy over having been able, with your support, to make up his mind, and stick to it; that his republican-minded government is as happy as he is, because in his happiness he has agreed to agree with it; and the British Ambassador looks like the cat which has swallowed the canary. Some observers are already saying that the King has been outwitted, and that he should never have signed his new declaration, which ties his future decision to that of his government. It is pointed out that the Prime Minister published the pertinent paragraphs within a few hours of signature, though the document is antedated to early last month to avoid ostensible connection with recent controversy. It is alleged that this haste was due to anxiety lest the King retract and escape a trap. But however that may be, and such early interpretations are always dubious, this time the affair would appear to be of wholly Greek inception, and this, and the fact that I never heard of it till it was all over, leads me at least to hope that no one will tell you that I was involved in it!

Affectionately yours as always,
Lincoln MacVeagh (2)

December 14, 1943, Tuesday

Stevenson came in at 6:15, and gave me (at my request) copies of recent telegrams he has sent, and which he first discussed with me in detail. One of these reported Churchill's talks with King Peter and Mr. Purić, and others outlined a plan which Stevenson is suggesting to the Foreign Office, to get the Yugoslav Government to dismiss Mihailović as War Minister and Commander-in-Chief, and urge his followers to collaborate with Tito. The plan of course included Churchill's decision to switch military support wholly to Tito, if Mihailović muffs a last chance that is being given him to collaborate, by blowing up some vital communications. . . . Stevenson said that pressure on the Government to dismiss Mihailović will result in its resignation, as Purić and his friends regard M. "not as a man but as a symbol of Serbian resistance." He thinks Cubrilović would then come in, with Jukić as his Foreign Minister, and that this new government, which does not share Purić's phobia regarding Russia and Communism, would not be averse to contacting Tito and seeing at last what could be done to collaborate with him. This would give the King a chance, and later on, he might appear over Yugoslavia as a bomber, and after that perhaps join the Partisan forces as a junior officer. *Pourvu qu'il ne soit pas trop tard!* In the papers today, the Russians announced that they intend sending a Military Mission to the Partisans and declared also that Mihailović must be regarded as of no use to the cause. Stevenson says this decision was reached some time ago (at the Moscow conference?) and that the Mission will come through here and get supplies for Tito from the British and us; I guess, Lend-Lease.

December 15, 1943, Wednesday

Stevenson told me last night, in connection with the new allied combined Mediterranean Command plan, which I got from G2, that the Balkan Support Command may have to stay here in Cairo on account of the Mena radio station here, which is used by the allied services (such as O.S.S.) and would take three months to replace elsewhere. In that case the Embassies would remain, and the Governments.

December 16, 1943, Thursday

In the morning Mr. Heinemann and another O.W.I.[33] man came in and told me of the movie, radio, and publication program being worked up for Greece after the liberation. I told them to be careful of the Greek translations they put out, and found they had little idea, if any, of the language problem in Greece. I also said I hoped their work would be rather in the direction of making American stuff available—in which case I was sure it would be eaten up—than in that of regular propaganda. They said this was their idea exactly.... A United Press man called, and in the afternoon an Overseas Agency man, to whom I talked as well as I could, mostly generalities "off the record." A lot of people seem to be wondering what our "policy" is in regard to Greece and Yugoslavia. I wish I knew! But I say, with only Mr. Hull's general statements and past experience to guide me, that it is hands off internal questions. As the Overseas man, and Cy Sulzberger, both have said to me, America could help both countries enormously if she would step in and take the straightening out of their affairs on her shoulders. She would be listened to, because she has no axe to grind. But while this would help the little states and get us loved by them—as Woodrow Wilson was and is loved in Czechoslovakia—what about our big allies who do have axes to grind? Are the American people ready to take on the commitments which direct intervention in Balkan affairs would create? I think all that we can do is to exert our influence without seeming to, and help to bring about a world order, if this is possible, which will no longer include the strains and stresses of Great Power influences which have hitherto made it impossible for the Balkan states to work out their own salvation.

December 17, 1943, Friday

H.M. was very friendly, so much so that it seems impossible that he complained of me to the President. I am more and more inclined to think that the British emphasized my support to a degree which made the President imagine I might be pressing the King, when I wasn't.... There

[33] O.W.I. = Office of War Information (American).

is a rumor that Tito's government is "demanding recognition" by the allied governments. . . . I shall have been here three weeks tomorrow, and in that time I have received no more from the Department regarding its views on the Yugoslav situation than I did after my appointment and when I was still in South Africa,—and that was exactly nothing. . . . As to Greece, I have had only Wallace Murray's[34] letter, dealing with the problem of the King's return.

December 18, 1943, Saturday

Called on the Yugoslav Prime Minister at 11 a.m. He told me that he had been informed by Stevenson that he might soon expect pressure from the British *and American* governments to dismiss Mihailović from the Cabinet, and outlined a long telegram which he asked me to send to Washington. This contained his pro-Serb, anti-communist views about as stated to me previously, summed up in the criticism that the British proposals are "fantastic and dangerous." He doesn't object to our present policy, as stated in a press report and credited to Mr. Hull, to the effect that we recognize the Yugoslav Government but will continue to give military support to all groups fighting the Germans. However, he would like more help given to Mihailović! It seems to me that Stevenson went pretty far in mentioning *us* at this juncture, and I told Mr. Purić that I had no information that our policy is changed in any way from what I also understand it, from the papers, to be. (The Department has simply not communicated with me at all regarding its policy, and so here I am faced with discussing it daily, with O.W.I., O.S.S., the British, the Serbs, and the Greeks, on the basis of no knowledge whatever beyond that of the man in the street!) Wally Barbour told me of a British Ambassador who was sent to Mexico without any instructions or previous knowledge of the country. He telegraphed home for some directives, and the Foreign Office replied "The policy of H.M.'s Government regarding Mexico remains unchanged." . . . Mr. Purić told me he had asked Stevenson to telegraph his reactions to the Foreign Office (and Stevenson sent me a copy of his wire tonight), and also that he had telegraphed Fotić, the Yugoslav Ambassador to Washington. . . . During the afternoon I drafted a telegram as he requested, and added my view that the only way to clarify the situation in Yugoslavia and Greece as between the genuine patriots and other elements would be to set up an allied front somewhere in the Balkans. We'd know then who are our friends and who not. But as this is not apparently to be done, I think to take sides with one or the

---

[34] Wallace Murray, Director of the Office of Near Eastern Affairs, Department of State.

other of various warring parties within these countries is a matter which the Department may want to consider most carefully, as likely to lead to future embarrassments for us. It looks to me as if the British were rather rushing us into supporting their plan, and I doubt strongly if it is in our interests to do so. . . . In the afternoon, Tsouderos asked me to come and see him! He wants me to support his desire for Greek military participation in the Italian campaign, and told me that Mr. Churchill had expressed his agreement but had added that realization depended on Eisenhower. Wilson had *not* been willing to allow Greek troops to come into Samos in any numbers, he said, and evidently felt that the only hope for effective and prompt generosity toward the Greeks lies with the Americans. . . . I think the effect of Greek participation in the Italian fighting would be to relieve much of the political tension among the inactive Greek forces and thus help the political situation, and would also do much to help raise Greek morale in the home land. . . . The Premier is also fearful that the British are planning to send too few troops to Greece when the Germans withdraw (as everyone seems to suppose they will!), to cope with the state of civil war and communist terror and usurpation now being created by the E.A.M., with German connivance and even support. I am afraid I agree with him, and in fact provoked his remarks on this point by my questions, which were suggested by my talk with General Hughes[35] the other day. I feel the British will have to send in a substantial force if anarchy, or even a reign of terror, is to be avoided after Greece is freed. Tsouderos added the just remark that since the British helped the E.A.M. to power with supplies and ammunition (when they thought it would fight the Germans) they ought now to help Greece protect herself against it. . . . He said to trust this task to the Greek army principally, as the British told me they think of doing, would be worse than useless, as the Greek army would simply split up into factions and add to the confusion. . . . Regarding the King, Mr. Tsouderos said he seemed today to be again worried over his declaration. He had been told that Mr. Roosevelt and General Smuts feel he should not have made even such a statement as he did (to "decide in agreement with his Government"). I wonder how his informant knew what the President thinks! It is too bad so many people can get at the King to trouble his peace of mind! . . . The O.S.S. has received a message from the Tito outfit, sent through their liaison man, hailing the United Nations and asking support for the United Yugoslav people etc. It is addressed to Mr. Churchill and Mr. Roosevelt. . . . At the same time we got, and passed on, a long blast from the Tito Government demanding recognition and damning the King's present government and the monarchy. . . . All

---

[35] Major General Ivor T. P. Hughes, General Officer Commanding British Liaison Headquarters, Greece, head of the Allied Military Mission (AML), Cairo.

this tends to thicken the gruel!.... With a copy of his telegram about his talk with Purić, Stevenson sent me a letter reporting a talk between a Foreign Office representative and the Soviet Ambassador in London, in which the British expressed their Pollyanna hopes that after dismissing Mihailović they can get the Partisans and Chetniks to cooperate like good children.

December 20, 1943, Monday

Stevenson came in and told me that he has revised his ideas as a result of the Partisans' broadcast and declarations, which now reveal them as definitely revolutionary against the King and Government. He is accordingly now recommending an attitude, to be concerted with us and Russia, very similar to that we have taken all along—military action in support of elements fighting the Germans, and postponement of all political issues till after the war is over, when the people should decide for themselves! He is recommending therefore that the idea of forcing the King to remove Mihailović from the Cabinet be dropped.

December 21, 1943, Tuesday

[Visited by] the Russian Ambassador, Novikov. Talks fair French, and is not impressive-looking, but may be intelligent. He said that in his opinion Germany should be "punished" and made to suffer for what she has caused others to suffer, and that afterwards the dismemberment of the Reich, to prevent recurrence, is "probable." He thought Poland might be given some German territory to compensate her for territories "in the East"! . . . Then Mr. Metaxas called on behalf of the King. H.M. asks that I send the President a memo he has drawn up stating that the King has made no declarations about returning to Greece—no public statement at all since his July 4th speech. He has been queried by General Smuts about his letter to Mr. Tsouderos, and wants to tell him and F.D.R. that he has followed their advice. Unfortunately he cannot—and of course does not—deny the letter, but he says it adds nothing to the situation since he would naturally not act without reference to his own Ministers, and anyway, it wasn't a public statement! Pretty thin, since he allowed Tsouderos to publish it, and as to not being a "declaration," he may not have meant it so, but the Greeks have so accepted it, and Mr. Tsouderos mentioned it tonight over the radio along with the 4th of July speech. . . . Sent off a telegram on the Greek guerrilla situation drafted by Parsons. It seems the ELAS and EDES bands want to amalgamate now against the "security battalions" formed by the Germans and Pangalos—these battalions are said to be formed to keep order after the country is liberated, but are otherwise quite actively employed at present. ... The Department sent a telegram to inquire what was the reason for the British government's change of attitude toward the King—from supporting his return with his troops to trying to persuade him to wait outside till called! This change occurred before I came, and of course surprised me too, when I arrived. Parsons says he saw it coming, in the attitude of the British Embassy here from day to day, but that despite his urgings, Barbour and Mr. Kirk did not report it. What happened was, of course that Leeper (and probably Casey) brought Eden round, and the latter convinced Mr. Churchill—and stood over the latter when he talked to the King lest he forget he had been convinced! But all the various reasons, except seeing the facts of the situation in Greece, are obscure to me, and I therefore handed the drafting of a reply over to Barbour.

December 22, 1943, Wednesday

Worked over a long telegram Barbour had drafted[36] explaining to the Department that the British attitude toward the King has not changed, so far as fundamental policy is concerned, but that their tactics as to the best way of helping his régime to survive have altered since allied strategy has decreed that no large forces are to be sent to Greece, and since civil war and a threatened state of anarchy, to follow German withdrawal, has supervened in the country. The Department's telegram which caused this explanation revealed that it was puzzled by the counsel given the King by Leeper, Eden and Churchill so soon after he had been told

[36] The telegram of December 22, 1943, read in part: "From conversations with the British Ambassador and from confidential documents which he has made available to me, it seems clear that British policy continues to be based on the hope that the King will be restored to his throne as a constitutional monarch by the will of his people. However when Allied strategical plans were so changed recently as to make it seem unlikely that any large military force would occupy Greece upon evacuation by the enemy, it occurred to the British Embassy here, which was advised of the growth of anarchy within the country, that the King's early return with only the small forces envisaged would be inadvisable. In the circumstances, as I saw them, which appeared to necessitate a certain lapse of time before conditions of tranquillity could be obtained, requisite to the determination of the people's will regarding the régime, it felt that the most hopeful procedure would be to secure some suitable person who had resisted the Axis in Greece and who might be expected to command general respect such as the Archbishop of all Greece to be appointed by the King to head a Regency committee to exercise constitutional authority during the immediate post-liberation era, the King remaining abroad. This idea was as I am convinced conceived purely with a view to giving the Royal régime the best possible chance of survival though it is true that many employees and agents of the British Government now working on Greek affairs both within and without the country are personally anti-royalist in sentiment. . . ." *FR 1943*, IV, 158-60.

from Quebec that he should "go in with his troops." And I don't wonder. I was puzzled myself, though pleased, when I heard Leeper's plan the first time. . . .

Cairo, December 22, 1943

Dear Franklin:

The enclosed memorandum[37] has been sent to me by the King of Greece for personal forwarding to you. I am sorry to say that he is unhappy again, this time concerning the developments covered in the last part of my letter of December 13th. He is very anxious to assure you that he has really strictly conformed to your advice not to make any more "declarations," and is afraid you may have seen some erroneous press reports concerning the letter which he wrote to his Prime Minister, published after you left. Furthermore, although in the approved text of that letter he said "that when the desired moment of liberation arrives I will establish the time of my return to Greece *in agreement with the Government*," he does not conceive that this constitutes any "public statement" on his part, and denies that it adds anything new to the situation, since he would naturally, in any event, consult his own appointed Ministers when making an important decision.

I have of course told the King that I will transmit his memorandum to you and convey his assurances. But for your information, since I know you to be personally interested in his fortunes, I think I should add that his own Government is not taking his point of view in this matter—which is perhaps the real reason for his anxiety rather than the erroneous press reports, which were quickly corrected. The Government clearly considers his letter as a public statement, quite on a par with his declaration of July 4th, in which he promised that a constituent assembly would decide on the future regime in Greece, and this was shown only last night, beyond a peradventure, when the Prime Minister said in a radio broadcast to the Greek people, "the King has already given an example of unity by his declaration of July 4th *and subsequently by his letter of November 8th*." It would appear to be the Prime Minister's view that since not only the present Government, but any Government which the King may be able to form prior to his return, is likely to be against his returning in advance of an expression of the people's will, the King has now practically bound himself to await such expression. The King doesn't want to recognize this, but unfortunately he allowed his letter to be published.

In all this, it seems possible that the King may have given us another example of his inability to think as fast as his subjects, but in any case,

[37] This memorandum has not been located.

if there are any further developments in this matter, which Gilbert and Sullivan might be tempted to call a pretty kettle of fish, I shall not fail to let you know.

Affectionately yours,
Lincoln MacVeagh (3)

December 23, 1943, Thursday

Mr. Leeper came in at 10 o'clock. He said that the Greek Prime Minister wants to broadcast another appeal to the Greek guerrillas to get together and would like to get some word of agreement to his plea from the U.S., British, and Russian Governments to which he could refer in his talk. He has asked his foreign representatives to take up the matter, and Eden has agreed. He thinks Eden has also telegraphed to Molotov, and that Halifax is seeing Hull. . . . We talked of other problems. He is going to recommend to the Allied Defense Council that a committee be formed to advise it on civilian affairs in the Balkans, composed of a British, a Greek, and an American member—he to be the British and I the American. This seems to me in agreement with the Department's ideas as set forth in its first telegram to me about my appointment here, but not referred to since. . . . He agreed with me that the British forces now envisaged for the occupation are too few, but felt we should wait awhile before taking this up. . . . He told me that General Eisenhower has turned down Tsouderos's plea that Greek troops be used in Italy, because Alexander doesn't want them there, and because there are no ships to transport them. . . . After he had left he rang me up to say that the Foreign Office had advised him that Halifax saw Hull, and that the latter agreed to the idea of supporting the Tsouderos broadcast, and would instruct me accordingly. I have as yet heard nothing from Washington about this. The Department always seems to lag behind the Foreign Office in its communications. . . . Col. Moore came in and talked about the situation of the Greek forces and their morale. He feels that if the 1st Brigade isn't used in active operations soon, there will be trouble like that which occurred in the 2nd Brigade last March,[38] and ruined its effectiveness for good and all. But he supports the idea that the Greeks shouldn't be used in Italy, on account of their hatred of our "co-belligerents." . . . Mr. Joyce of the O.S.S.[39]—who handles the Yugoslav desk—came in and we had a prelimi-

---

[38] During March and April 1943, senior officers of the Greek forces in the Middle East had been removed from their commands by Tsouderos, following attempts to stage a royalist mutiny.

[39] Robert P. Joyce, Foreign Service officer on loan to OSS, and head of secret intelligence operations in Yugoslavia.

nary talk on the Yugoslav problems. He promised to come in during the afternoon for a continuation. He seems to think the Partisans are the boys to play with, but he recognizes the dangers of cutting out Mihailović. . . . [Later:] Tsouderos began to talk to me of his broadcast idea, and I said I thought I would have good news about it soon, from our angle. . . . He said he thought some Greek troops—a company—might be sent to march in the entry into Rome, if and when this happens, but was very much cut up by Eisenhower's refusal to use Greek troops in the fighting. I don't wonder; it would help his own position so much if this could be done. Unfortunately very few military men can see issues beyond their own narrow sphere. . . . Joyce also stayed a long time. The situation as we agreed to see it is that the Partisans have about everything there is on their side at present in the Mihailović controversy, but are beginning to play their hand too high politically just at the moment when the British are about to help them effectively, and thus they are causing the British to draw back. He had some very interesting information from an American observer to the effect that the paucity of effective help from the British and Americans is causing many Yugoslavs to lean toward Russia and communism who would not otherwise do so. However, more effective help is certainly on the way, and will arrive, unless Tito continues to tempt Nemesis by attacking the King and demanding political recognition. In my opinion, if he would make some gesture toward the King he would get all the support the British can give him—and be damned to Mihailović—pronto! . . .

December 24, 1943, Friday

Sent off a telegram saying that in my opinion some use of the Greek forces (1st Brigade) should be made, to avoid political trouble in the army, and boost Greek morale in the home land. Doubtless the Department will not feel like tackling the army authorities on this matter, but that is not my problem, which ends with telling what I see to be the situation.

December 26, 1943, Sunday

Leeper says he wants me to join him on an "informal committee" (what is that?) to advise the Greeks on their conduct of affairs, particularly as to the reconciliation to be brought about, if possible, between the guerrillas in Greece. It seems his previous larger proposals [for Anglo-American cooperation in Balkan affairs] have boiled down to this, "which you need not get permission to join." I said that I could see no reason for a committee, since we are all here together and can talk to each other whenever we wish. He says that he proposes we should talk not with Tsouderos but with Venizelos and Karapanayiotis,[40] so as to ease the position of Tsouderos, who is always being accused of acting without the knowledge of the rest of the Cabinet. I think this is a good idea, especially as Leeper has discussed the matter with Tsouderos, who prefers it, and as he will, he says, at all times keep Tsouderos informed of what is said. But as to *my* participation, I left it that I would ask the Department (which, I am sure, will prefer, as it usually does, that no "joint action," even of an "informal" nature, be entered into without its knowledge and instructions), and that in the meanwhile Leeper will keep me informed of what he does.... I think I shall tell the Department that this effort to get me to join in advising the Greek Government doesn't attract me. The British want to guide the Greeks in their internal politics. They say they don't, but they do, putting the matter as "helping them to help themselves," and in case they come a cropper in so doing, they want us associated with them in some manner so as to share the blame,—or shift it. I do not see that we have any business advising the Greeks, though of course we would like to know what the British do. Just as in the old days, when Waterlow was told to keep the King on his throne.... But of course the Department may see things otherwise.... We got Secretary Hull's message to Tsouderos today, supporting him in his efforts to end fratricidal strife in Greece by appealing to the partisans of all parties....[41] This, however, seems to me something different from having our representative join with the British, even on an "informal" committee, to advise the Ministers of War and Navy! Also this breezy approach to such a matter, verbally between cocktails, doesn't go down very well with me, and I think I shall ask Leeper to let me have his proposals in writing—"so that I may be sure to express it as he would have me express it" etc. I have a hunch that his larger idea—about a civilian committee on Balkan affairs (see my entry for December 23rd) has faded out of the picture and been replaced by this much less grandiose "informal" affair—because I did just that, namely, asked him for a statement in writing, and it might happen again. All of which doesn't mean that I think we should not

---

[40] Byron Karapanayiotis, liberal politician, and Minister of War in the Tsouderos government.

[41] Secretary of State Cordell Hull's message of December 23, 1943, read in part: "Reports of fratricidal strife within Greece have shocked the American Government and people to whom the heroic and united resistance of the Greek people against Axis aggression and occupation has been a constant inspiration. We earnestly hope that the Greek resistance groups will no longer dissipate their strength in internal quarrels but will promptly unite among themselves and with us in the struggle against our common enemy. Such united collaboration will speed the day of victory and liberation when the Greek people, proud and honored, will again be masters of their own destiny." *FR 1943,* IV, 164.

work with the British. Far from it; but I do think we should be careful of their attempts to jockey us, pleasantly, into positions where we do not want to find ourselves.

December 27, 1943, Monday

Joyce called, with some memorandums for me on the Yugoslav question. One of the Tito people here had been talking of the idea of having the U.S. Government make a loan to the Partisan Government. So their ideas are going pretty fast, it seems! . . . We went over to see Tsouderos and gave him Mr. Hull's message, which he can use as he sees fit. He plans to broadcast on New Year's Eve and call on all the Greek forces of resistance to unite. . . . Called on Mr. Leeper and told him I can't go in for his "informal committee" idea. Explained that in my view a committee can hardly be informal, and that as our policy regarding Greek internal affairs is not that of the British, the latter being concerned as we are not, it might create a wrong impression among the Greeks if we joined together in advising them. He said he realized this, but obviously would have been glad of my support if I had agreed, and wouldn't have worried over whether I would be slain by the Department as a result, or not! I like Leeper a lot. He explained that he *has* to occupy himself with Greek internal affairs, though he thinks he ought not; he said the Greeks have become accustomed to relying on him (the British, i.e.) and come to him about everything; also he has the S.O.E. people working in Greece in liaison now with the Foreign Office, and what information the Greeks get they must get from him. I said, Go ahead. No reason for him not to advise them, but I would keep out. The Greeks do not come to *me* to know how to form their cabinets or what to do in this or that emergency —I have never given them the opportunity to form such a habit, and don't intend to begin now—unless by some miracle, the Department changes its point of view, and instructs me. . . . We talked about Greek relief. I do like Leeper: he is not only extremely intelligent and well-informed about Greece, though not from personal acquaintance with it, but has his heart very much in the right place in relation to his job. He is deeply concerned over the very likely eventuality that with no front in the Balkans, and a "second front" started in northern Europe somewhere, the shift of effort will carry relief work largely away from this area. The shipping and the food will be diverted from forgotten Greece and sent to France, or where have you. . . . He told me that Mr. Eden will send Tsouderos a message like Mr. Hull's (drafted by Leeper himself, as a matter of fact) for Tsouderos to use in his New Year's Broadcast along with the Secretary's, but that Molotov has refused to do a similar thing, saying that he doesn't know about affairs in Greece and therefore hesitates to say anything about it. He would appear to have some doubts as to allied plans and as to whether there may not be some "Mihailović" in the Greek mess! . . . Mr. Eden has wired that he proposes to "have another go" at Molotov, sending him a copy of his own message; and Leeper is sending the Secretary's, the hope being that when Molotov sees exactly what is intended, he will join in for the general good in the spirit of Teheran! Leeper doesn't think that Tsouderos' broadcast can do much good, but we agreed that it is in the right direction. He feels, just as strongly as I do, or General Hughes, that the British troops planned for the eventual occupation after German withdrawal, are far too few for effectiveness. . . . Incidentally, I wonder about this German "withdrawal." If Germany doesn't collapse, the withdrawal, if made at all, will be very gradual and spotty, to secure reinforcements for more threatened fronts. To occupy the places vacated under such conditions will be a real military operation, and will gradually end, *must* end, in a "front" in Greece. If, on the other hand, a sudden central collapse occurs, there will be no withdrawal, and the Germans will simply be left stranded in the Balkans and the islands—and again there will have to be military forces to cope with them. I think we are nowadays envisaging the future in a way which will never occur. . . . Arthur Parsons came to dinner, at the hotel. He agreed with me that the time to encourage subversive action in occupied Greece, now that no front there is envisaged, is over, though good information agents are always useful. Leeper feels the same way,—it has no value militarily, as Greece is no longer a strategic spot; it is positively deleterious economically, as we shall have to repair the damages caused; and it is only useful psychologically. He asked me the other day whether I thought Tsouderos ought definitely to advise the guerrillas to give up the fight now, and I said "no," since many of them are fine chaps who are giving their all, and it would be most discouraging to them to think it is not appreciated. The spirit of the Greeks must be kept up. Leeper said tonight that he had telegraphed Eden what I said, and Eden has replied that he was glad I felt that way as it was his idea also! What *can* be done, however, is to keep our secret agents from going on being so active with their incitements that feeling against the allies will continue rising as realization increases that we ourselves are not coming to help. That is rather complicated, but there is no doubt that the Greeks are suffering a severe deception as they see no Balkan front being formed, and that they must resent, under these circumstances, having our people urge them all the time to greater sacrifices. If what they could do would affect the course of the war, it would be different, but it can't.

CHAPTER VIII

December 29, 1943, Wednesday

Stevenson came in. Opening a subject I had meant to leave untouched, he explained that what he said to Purić was simply that U.S. and British policy must coincide. But he was embarrassed when he made his explanation, and I guess he has been at pains to find a formula to explain matters to the Foreign Office, and knows very well that I know he gave Purić to understand just what Purić afterwards told me. . . . This was only an incident, however, in a long and most interesting talk. He brought along his dossier of telegrams exchanged with the Foreign Office and went over them with me, allowing me to make notes. Against his strongest advice, he has been instructed to send a liaison officer (Brigadier Maclean)[42] to Tito, to sound out the latter regarding the King's joining the Partisan forces! Stevenson is sure the scheme will not succeed, Tito will refuse, and grow only more arrogant. But the Foreign Office (not itself in love with the idea), thinks "it ought to be tried." Maclean has gone to Yugoslavia, and Stevenson has sent the text of his proposed orders to London for approval—which is all that is needed now. . . . Stevenson also told me that Mihailović has asked the British to mediate between him and Tito, but the F. O. has refused this "deathbed repentance" as it calls it (I saw the telegram), and suggests that M. do the contacting himself. . . . Another item of news was to the effect that to Purić's suggestion that negotiations be started between his Government and Russia for a treaty like that just signed by Russia and Czechoslovakia,[43] the Soviet Foreign Office replied that it was interested in general, but that first the Yugoslav Government ought to compose the differences existing within the country. . . . Stevenson said this sounded like a hint to Purić to get together with the Partisans! . . .

December 30, 1943, Thursday

Got off several long telegrams to the Department, on the new Yugoslavian move of the British, and about the British tendency to regard "informing" us as the same thing as "associating" us in their schemes. Said I thought the Department's action as regards Stevenson will help, but that I don't anticipate the efforts will cease altogether, and therefore I would urgently request the Department to find out the true facts from me before believing anything they may hear about uninstructed Anglo-American consultations at this post! I let them know that I suspect Leeper

[42] Brigadier Fitzroy Maclean, head of the British Liaison Mission to Tito.
[43] On December 12, 1943, the Czechoslovak government-in-exile, under President Eduard Beneš, signed with the Soviet Union a Treaty of Friendship, Mutual Assistance, and Cooperation.

of having given the impression that I had associated myself with British "pressure" on the King, and also told about his attempts to get me to join an "informal committee" to discuss and advise on Greek internal affairs. But I emphasized that all this has not harmed my friendly and I hope useful relations with two excellent men. . . . One must speak for oneself, sometimes. . . . Sent a copy of this telegram to London—for Winant; I hope he'll see it, and am sure he will understand, if he does. . . . In the afternoon called on Prime Minister Purić. He confirmed what Stevenson told me about the Russian answer to his suggestion for a pact; and he made the same comment. . . . He knows nothing about the British plan regarding the King, and thinks that it is too early now to consider having the King return to Yugoslavia—maybe later will be all right, when the Germans are defeated or are withdrawing from the Balkans, but not now. . . . Stevenson had told me that P. wants to go to London to be present should allied discussions take place regarding policy toward Yugoslavia, but Purić said tonight it may be premature to go just yet. I gather he thinks the anti-Mihailović situation is easing somewhat due to criticism at home and in England of the pro-Russian policy now being followed by the Foreign Office. I wonder what he'll think when he learns the latest! But it is true that the military have given Mihailović a couple of weeks more to prove his good faith—in which one Brigadier liaison officer, Armstrong,[44] believes as strongly as the other, Maclean, disbelieves.

1944

January 1, 1944, Saturday
The Department has sent me a message in answer to my request for any confidential advices or background information it can give me on the Yugoslav situation. Hitherto, as noted before in this diary, it has sent me not a word on this subject. It now says that in a following telegram it will give me a statement it issued to the press on December 9th.

January 3, 1944, Monday
Purić said he understands the British are contemplating the formation of an "International Brigade" to fight with Tito, and some of his people are being seduced to join it, though Beaumont-Nesbitt[45] denies the whole thing. Actually, I have heard from Moore, Joyce, *et al.* that many of the

[44] Brigadier Charles Douglas Armstrong, head of the British Liaison Mission to Mihailović.
[45] General Beaumont-Nesbitt, staff officer for the British Commander-in-Chief, Middle East, General Sir Bernard Paget.

regular Yugoslav soldiers and officers are now straining at the leash to go over to Tito, now that they see where allied support is going. A few have actually done so, and others will follow suit. . . . The second-in-command of the Yugoslav army here has resigned, though there is nothing (as yet) to connect him with the movement. . . . I went over to see Leeper. He said that Eden had had his "other go" at Molotov, but the latter had still refused to make a statement for Tsouderos to use January 1st along with Messrs. Hull's and Eden's statements,—on the same grounds as previously —he is not sufficiently instructed as to the situation in Greece. However, Leeper says, and I agree, that it is highly unlikely that Molotov is not fully aware of the Communist movement in the Balkans and that it is not confined to Tito's Partisans but has ramifications in Albania, Bulgaria, and Greece also. Though Molotov would make no statement, the Moscow radio [did] broadcast [on] New Year's Eve a long appeal to the Greeks to unite. However, it reads rather like an appeal to E.A.M.—the Greek "Partisans"—than to the people as a whole, and is full of praise for the Red Army. . . . Stevenson says the "emissary" may reach here any day, and I asked the Department for further instructions, as to who is to meet with him, since Novikov says a special man will be sent from Moscow, and Stevenson talks of appointing a Mr. Steel,[46] who is the Foreign Office Representative with the M.O. crowd here. This would make my being our representative rather out of place, and the Department may wish me to appoint someone as deputy. . . . The situation in Greece looks to me nastier and nastier. If and when the Germans pull out, it will not be a clean-cut operation, but gradual, and in the regions liberated there will be a condition of anarchy. The British have armed the more active guerrillas, both in Greece and Yugoslavia, and naturally these have been the people most accustomed and skilled already in underground work—the Communists, Macedonian Irredentists, and so forth. It will be *they* who are around when liberation dawns, here and there, and they will naturally seek to impose themselves and rule each locality as the enemy withdraws. The better elements will *not* be armed, and if we send in only a few troops to guard our supplies for the starving, they will be attacked either by the Communists or the Germans near-by, or by both, and the supplies looted. Yet there are no plans to send in large forces! Thus there *will* be a Balkan front, though only spottily here and there, with the odds all against us, and at the same time confusion worse confounded in the country we have freed! Meanwhile we go ahead with large plans for relief and rehabilitation, as if we were going into a country, starving indeed, but thoroughly tranquil under a regime of law and order! . . .

[46] Christopher Steel, Foreign Office liaison with SOE, Cairo.

January 4, 1944, Tuesday

Joyce sent in a memo regarding a conversation between the O.S.S. and Dr. Beneš, after his visit to Moscow, in which the latter defined the Soviet attitude toward Yugoslavia. Attitude very much like ours in many ways, but he included the statement that the Soviets would not deal "under any conditions" with the Government-in-exile. This I think inaccurate, as if this Government should succeed in making things up with the Partisans and getting rid of civil strife in the country—a big "if"!—the Soviets would deal with it all right, while at present they keep an Ambassador near it, and only today the papers published a cordial reply to Purić from Stalin himself, on the subject of New Year's wishes. Not much,—but still, just as we are doing, the Soviet Government is "recognizing" the Government-in-exile.

January 5, 1944, Wednesday

Was waited on by a committee of Samian members of the E.A.M., who call themselves the "staff" of the Samian E.L.A.S. army. They wanted me to see to it that they are allowed by the Greek Government and the military to continue as a unit and not be drafted into the regular Greek army. I had coffee served and explained to them as nicely as I could that the Americans are for Greece with all their hearts but that we cannot take part in purely internal affairs. We want to help the whole people, and as such are their friends, but if we began interfering in their internal affairs we would become friends only of some of them and enemies of others. In my position, also, I had to deal with the external affairs of Greece so far as they concern America, and cannot professionally tell the Greek Government or the military what to do in domestic matters. Etc. . . . The priest, among others, kissed me when they left! . . . Molotov has now agreed to support the Tsouderos appeal for unity. I suspect his delay in deciding (he says he could not do so till he was informed by the British Embassy!) has been due to a desire to have the Soviet pronouncement made by itself and not along with ours and the British,—thus giving it more importance. The Soviet Foreign Office can hardly be "uninformed" of Greek matters, in view of the great communist activity in the Balkans generally.

January 7, 1944, Friday

Ambassador Stevenson came in to discuss various Yugoslav matters, and brought with him Mr. Steel, the Foreign Office Representative here with the SOE. . . . Stevenson said that the Tito "revolt" in the Yugoslav regular forces is spreading, and gave some figures. Some two out of the three hundred men, mostly Slovenes, in the Cairo "depot" of Yugoslavs, have opted for Tito, and yesterday 10 of the 11 men of the King's guard, also Slovenes, likewise "revolted." Stevenson proposed to Purić that the British now take over the administration as well as the operation of the Yugoslav army (putting the Yugoslav G.H.Q. out of business!) but the P.M. naturally refused, and at his suggestion the British will probably segregate the dissenters from the royalists. . . . He also had a lot to say about an attempt which he has heard of through the Foreign Office on the part of M. Fotić in Washington to get the O.W.I. to broadcast secret code messages to Mihailović. He thinks this would be very dangerous, as likely to give away allied plans to the enemy, Mihailović being in his view by no means to be trusted, and the Yugoslav Government not as strong, perhaps, in discretion as it might be. He said Colonel West[47] of the O.S.S. agrees with him. Colonel West handles the operations branch of the O.S.S. here. . . . We also talked about our famous emissary. It appears that the Germans may know what is afoot, and therefore that it behooves us to be very cautious if *pourparlers* take place. The Department has authorized me, if it seems necessary, and the others have military advisers, to get the theatre commander to attach a military man to whoever represents the U.S., and Steel thinks there may be a sudden cropping up of armistice terms, if Russia continues to advance,—a kind of repetition of the Italian business. So you pays your money and takes your choice, at present! It may be an enemy "plant" to find out if possible what are our plans, or it may be a move actually toward unconditional surrender. But the chances are it is neither, and merely what it purports to be, a feeler on the part of the emissary's sender. . . . All this made material for several long telegrams to the Department, and there were airgrams too, on the Greek situation. (Tsouderos' broadcast, and a decree of the Greek government depriving the chief Quislings, Tsolakoglou, Logothetopoulos, and Rallis, of their citizenship.) Also about the efforts being made here to build a fleet of caiques for inter-island transport after the war. . . . Joyce came in twice, to talk about Mihailović and the O.W.I. messages; and I got him to see West, who confirms that he agrees with Stevenson. . . . Colonel Toulmin of the O.S.S.[48] also came in, bringing General Donovan, who had just arrived from Moscow, where he has seen Molotov and others. The General is particularly interested in Bulgaria, where, by arrangement, the O.S.S. is taking the lead in subversive operations, just as S.O.E. is leading in Yugoslavia and Greece. He does not agree with the British method of encouraging minorities, which has got them tied up so badly with E.A.M. and Mihailović. He wants to work directly on the Bulgarian Government, at least to start with, trying to suborn and seduce it against the enemy—

---

[47] Lieutenant Colonel Paul West, head of special operations, OSS, Cairo.
[48] Colonel John E. Toulmin, head of OSS, Cairo.

turning to the minorities only if necessary, and later. . . . Regarding Russia, he said the same thing as George Allen, and almost in the same words. The Russian government, he said, does not want to have a zone of influence around it, or "cordon sanitaire," with the commitments this would involve. It wants the blessing of friendly governments, not the responsibility of satellites, on its frontier. Furthermore, it is tending towards nationalism rather than internationalism. If the Communist elements in the Balkans think they will be supported in any effort to form Soviet Republics under Moscow's aegis, they are in for a great shock,—if Donovan *et al.* are correct.

January 8, 1944, Saturday

Call from General Osmun, of JICAME.[49] He wanted to know what I think about acceding to a request the Greeks are going to make (he thinks) for equipment for four armored divisions, to be used in Greece and probably recruited there, when the Germans begin withdrawing and the Allies move in. (A Colonel who called on me yesterday talked very much the same thing, but less definitely.) General Osmun believes the British are not looking with favor on the idea. I said that I felt, first, that we should not make any promises which we are not sure we shall be able to fulfil. We have done enough of this with the Greeks already, and our standing with them has suffered—so has that of the British, to an even greater degree, for the same reason. Secondly, I thought that we should not discourage the Greeks, either, but should say that we would consider the matter carefully, and then point out the uncertainties of the future in this connection, and insist on definite information as to how the divisions are expected to be formed and trained, and how the equipment, if supplied here, is to be transported to Greece, and so forth. I cautioned him in regard to the political factors which might be involved, the possible desire of the Government here to use the promise of the equipment as a sign of its strength, without really believing it could, when the time comes, either raise or train or use the personnel. Also I pointed out the likely political divisions in the Greek army when it goes back, quoting what Mr. Tsouderos has himself said to me to the effect that it would be folly, as the English propose, to leave a large part of the pacification of Greece after the occupation to the Greek army, since this would only split up into factions and add to the confusion. All these things, I said, should be given careful thought before any decision was reached, and that meanwhile no promises should be made and also no discouragement offered. He replied that this "made sense" to him, and went off apparently

[49] JICAME = Joint Intelligence Committee Army, Middle East (Allied).

pleased. At first blush, it seems to me that a demand by the Greek army for equipment for four armored divisions is fantastic. If granted, how would they use it? And if they couldn't use it properly, and left it lying round, the danger of a lot of it being gradually dispersed in Greece in the hands of various opposed groups would be great indeed. Furthermore, the loyalty of the officers to the Government—any Government which might be set up at the outset—is doubtful, as is also the ability of such a Government to recruit in Greece a sufficient force of able-bodied soldiers after the dissensions that have broken out there and the terrible effect on the physique of the nation which the German occupation has had. But if good answers can be given to these questions and a loyal and efficient army can clearly be raised and officered, then there may be some justification for the demand. It all depends!

January 10, 1944, Monday
Mr. Tsouderos has had news that the Greeks are turning away from the E.A.M. and leaning toward the Government, whose return, they think, will favor security and tranquillity. Leeper has heard from Churchill that the 1st Brigade is to go to Italy. Bravo! So far, the news is to be given to the King only, and not to the Government,—until details have been worked out by the Command.

January 11, 1944, Tuesday
Mr. Leeper came in for a long talk on Greek affairs. He said Mr. Eden wants him to keep both his Soviet and American colleagues informed of the British plans and operations in Greece. He said that he is giving M. Novikov his information *in writing*, because of the latter's poor English and limited background in Greek affairs. He promised to give me copies of any memoranda so furnished, so that I might be advised of what the Russian knows. He then described the latest British plans for Greece: (1) reconciliation and coordination among the guerrillas, and (2) the setting up of a secret committee in Athens to deal with the guerrillas and act generally in the name of the Government to prepare its return; the head to be a personage "above the *melee*" such as Archbishop Damaskinos.... I let the Department know about this plan somewhat in detail, by telegram.... Ambassador Stevenson came in and said that Brigadier Maclean (Fitzroy Maclean) has not yet gone to Tito, and final instructions have not yet come from London as to what he is to say when he does. The reason for the delay is that Maclean was summoned to see Mr. Churchill, and what he says will depend to a certain extent on whether and what Mr. Churchill decides himself to send to Tito on his

own behalf. He is having his son Randolph accompany Maclean, in any case.... I sent the Department word about Maclean's delay, but nothing about Mr. Churchill, as Stevenson wanted that part kept private (perhaps his people think he doesn't know!)

January 14, 1944, Friday

Sent off a telegram about the Russian word to Tsouderos about its support of unification of the guerrillas against the common enemy. Tsouderos will not broadcast it, because that might give it too much publicity as against the coordinated statements of Hull and Eden,—which is, I think, just what the Soviets were aiming at by their delay! Instead he has sent it to Greece by telegram to be bruited about by the agents, and get the effect that way. It has also been published by the papers.

January 15, 1944, Saturday

Harry Hill came in and said he needs to get in touch with the Relief people in General Hughes' Liaison Force (which will be the force to go into Greece to begin with, when the Germans get out, and will have the first shot at relief and rehabilitation in consequence). I said I'd fix it up with the General.... Took lunch with the General and his staff at Maadi Camp, and found them all most cordial. Brigadier King, a fine big New Zealander, is the Relief man, and I arranged with him to come and see Harry Hill. I liked his ideas on the reconstruction angle,—using relief to get reconstruction started by the Greeks themselves. General Hughes explained the plan and showed me his charts. The military will advise and assist the Greeks, but not attempt to run the country, and if the relief it brings is abused by warring factions, it will be stopped—that will be the handle used to control the situation.... Sent off a telegram on Roussos' resignation.[50] It has been accepted, but not announced publicly here, perhaps so as not to stress disunity in Cairo when everything is being done to promote unity in Greece. It seems the resignation was presented because Roussos despaired of pushing Tsouderos any further along the path of republicanism in the face of the King and the British, and was accepted because Tsouderos felt that he had done enough for the Republicans at present in making the old man Vice-President of the Council and suffering him as such so long.

[50] On November 16, 1943, Deputy Prime Minister George Roussos had written a letter to Tsouderos, attacking his policy on the issue of the monarchy and submitting his resignation. After a number of exchanges between the two men, Roussos' resignation was accepted on January 19, 1944.

January 16, 1944, Sunday

Berry told me, in regard to the Bulgarian situation, that the story the Bulgars have been giving our people in Turkey is that they would be willing to evacuate all the foreign territory they have occupied, as part of the peace settlement, provided Bulgaria as she was before the war remained intact and independent. Otherwise, they intimated, the Allies should realize that Bulgaria "has never broken relations with Russia," i.e. they will move into the Soviet orbit if we don't treat them right. They are certainly cute rascals,—since if Germany wins, their policy will give them conquests unfought for by them, and if she does not, they lose nothing through having joined her! I am inclined to feel that the recent bombings of Sofia are among the most deserved drastic measures of the war.

January 17, 1944, Monday

Ambassador Stevenson showed me a copy of the letter Churchill has written Tito, and the Foreign Office's comments, and his own. Churchill stated: "I am resolved not to send any more assistance to Mihailović, but only to you." The F.O. is considering advising King Peter to drop Mihailović, and Stevenson says that if this is done, *and* Purić falls, and *if* the King then asks British advice, H.M.'s government should then advise the formation of a government publicly committed to support all resistance units of whatever political color. He said the Department is being advised of all this, and the Soviet Foreign Office too, but I sent off a telegram just the same, in case some of what I saw and learned might not get to the Department. . . . Stevenson also gave me figures on the spread of disaffection in the Yugoslav armed forces in the Middle East, and those I also forwarded.

January 18, 1944, Tuesday

Ambassador and Mrs. Leeper came to dinner, out at the Mena House. He looked better than I have seen him so far, and talked with some animation. He told me that E.A.M. has congratulated Tsouderos on his attitude toward the "Security Battalions" and has suggested that the Government and E.A.M. confer on political unity. Tsouderos has replied saying that first of all there should be reconciliation among the guerrillas, and then, when this is secured, he will have someone in Athens who will be authorized to talk about the political problem. Everything now indicates that the Government's prestige is rising in Greece as the population becomes more and more disillusioned with the warring guerrillas and their pretensions. If Tsouderos is able to capitalize on this fortuitous emergence (which Leeper told him has come to him "by process of elimination!") and if the liberation of Greece is not deferred too long, the situation facing the Government after the war and its chances of taking over the country more or less peacefully, may be better than we have hitherto anticipated. I think Tsouderos should now keep up his radio talks, and especially impress on the Greeks that the Government is being active with relief and rehabilitation plans. Up to now the Greeks have been taught to think of their eventual salvation too much in terms of the British and Americans (or Russians, if you like) and not enough in terms of their own government, which has thereby lost a most important trick which it should now try to win back.

January 19, 1944, Wednesday

The King of Greece told Larrabee[51] yesterday much the same thing that Tsouderos told me the other day, about his anxiety over the O.S.S. work in Greece, which he thinks, as does Tsouderos, is giving too much help to E.A.M. My question has been how far it is *helping* and how far merely reporting on what E.A.M. is doing. Parsons told me that he thinks there is some aid going to a few of the E.L.A.S. bands (controlled by E.A.M.), which are beyond question working against the Germans, but not to others.... During the afternoon I had a visit from Colonel West of the O.S.S. and Rodney Young.[52] I wanted to find out from them to what extent the O.S.S. are really supporting E.A.M. in Greece, on account of the anxiety on this score expressed to me by Tsouderos, and to Larrabee by the King. West said that the British counterpart of O.S.S., under the direction of the Foreign Office, is taking the lead in secret work in Greece and Yugoslavia (as I was told by General Donovan himself), and also with Zervas as well as the E.A.M. These men, so far as E.A.M. are concerned, have for the past few months been observers merely, and no military supplies of any sort have been sent in. Rodney Young added that for one group, in Euboea, food and medical supplies may be sent soon in exchange for some information it is hoped this group will be willing to furnish, but there will be no arms nor munitions included.... West said that sometimes American airmen are shot down over Greece, on their way to Bulgaria or elsewhere, and that they then are rescued by EAMites and become partisans of those who rescued them—he instanced a certain young man named Huling, who is now stumping the country making

[51] Colonel Sterling L. Larrabee, Military Attaché of the U.S. Embassy to the Greek and Yugoslav governments-in-exile.

[52] Dr. Rodney Young, head of the Greek desk of Secret Intelligence (SI) of OSS, Cairo. Before the war, Young, an archaeologist, had been at the American School of Classical Studies in Athens.

speeches for E.A.M. But such men are not O.S.S. agents and the O.S.S. is doing its best to get them out—including Mr. Huling. (Of course this may happen with young aviators shot down bombing Greece as well, if they happen to fall in with guerrillas. But it is more likely in the outlying regions than near the great airports which are the specific Greek targets.) I think the King and Tsouderos may have got hold of the Huling story, or may have been expressing anxieties formed on the basis of the British practice of several months ago, when arms *were* being given to E.A.M. At any rate, I am pleased to have the direct statement that no encouragement is being given in the way of guns, etc., to groups the Greek government feels so strongly are inimical. On the other hand the presence of our officers among them, if only for intelligence purposes, may help to influence these groups in the right, and away from the wrong, direction. West said that he thinks no direct aid is being given to Zervas either, just at present. Emphasis is of course on reconciliation of the various bands. . . . West said that while he has not seen the evidence the British claim to possess incriminating Mihailović as a collaborator with the Germans, he is convinced that he is not collaborating with us, that there are many things he could have done to interfere with German communications which he has not done, and that certainly some of his lieutenants, whether with his knowledge or not, have actively assisted the enemy. . . . Larrabee got a query from the War Department saying that it has heard a rumor that Tito has been wounded, and may be dead, and asking for confirmation. A hard thing to confirm here, where the rumor, even, is unknown, but the Colonel is going about it to find out.

January 20, 1944, Thursday

Tsouderos had asked Parsons to come and see him, so at 6 o'clock we both went over to the "Foreign Office" in Tsouderos' house. . . . Among other things, the Prime Minister said that he is trying to sell the idea to the British that a "secret army" can be organized in Greece out of the demobilized officers and men of the forces which fought in the Albanian war. These men are not now involved in the guerrilla bands, for the most part, but are living quietly in Greece awaiting liberation. His agents tell him they can be reached and would be glad to enroll in an army of national character under the Government, to strike the Germans immediately the latter begin to move out, and take over the country thereafter in the interests of national security. He showed me one of the British secret agents' reports which confirms this view. . . . He also told me a fantastic tale about this same British agent, a certain Captain "Don" of the British Military Mission. I think, from the man's signature, his real name is D. J. Stott.... At any rate, the story is connected with the recent charges made by the Moscow *Pravda* to the effect that the British have been in touch with Ribbentrop,—charges based, according to *Pravda* on information emanating from "Greeks and Yugoslavs in Cairo." Mr. Tsouderos said that though he told the Russian Ambassador today at lunch that he knew of no such information being current among "the Greeks in Cairo," and that he wondered very much what it was all about, he does know something about it, and would tell me personally now in strictest confidence. Especially he does not want to have the British told what he knows. He got it from four separate persons, all of whom have recently arrived from Greece, and who tell stories which agree.... According to these stories, in December last this Captain "Don" was several times in touch with Germans, holding conferences with them in the house of the Quisling Mayor of Athens; at the last conference, a secretary of Ribbentrop's was present, having come all the way from Berlin for the purpose. Captain Don had as his secretary the daughter of Rallis, the Quisling Prime Minister. At this last conference, too, he wore his British uniform, and when he left Greece he was escorted across to Turkey by the Gestapo, for his protection! It is supposed that he discussed, not peace terms, but the evacuation of Greece; but however that may be, the fact of his conferences was speedily made known in Athens, it seems expressly so, by the other British agents in the country, and when the matter was thus "blown," Captain Don, on arrival safely at his base, was cashiered from the service! ... The interpretation given Mr. Tsouderos to this amazing tale is that the Captain put something over on the Germans; having got them to discuss with him, and reveal things the British want to know, on the basis of his being an emissary of the British sent to treat of peace or what have you, he arranged to have himself discredited as such an emissary and ostensibly dismissed for failure to keep under cover, thus masking his real purpose, and success.... Perhaps! In any case, the daring and positive effrontery in the face of death of such a man, is astounding.... There is always the possibility that the fellow went out simply to have a fling on his own, and was genuinely disgraced for posing as a British emissary. But it is also possible, of course, that Mr. Tsouderos is right, though I am inclined to doubt it.... In that case, as Mr. Tsouderos also suggested, it may be that the Russians really know all about it, and that the *Pravda* article is merely another dodge to keep the real meaning secret, and keep the Germans confident that the mission failed and that the Allies feel they have got nothing from it.... There are some nice elements in this story which should appeal to future Oppenheims and Edgar Wallaces—particularly that touch about the uniform. "Captain Don" is described, too, as being tall and blond of a true

British type—Bulldog Drummond to the life. Or perhaps what I am really thinking of is John Buchan....[53]

January 21, 1944, Friday

Harry Hill told me that the Greek Government has printed its new drachmas already, in England. It will take thousands of the present drachmas to buy one of the new, I suppose, but luckily since the people who have [the] most of [the] present currency are those who have collaborated with the Germans, it is they who will suffer most of the loss in exchange. The others have already been despoiled by the invader.... The Department some time ago instructed our Minister in Stockholm to associate himself with his British colleague in inviting the Swedish Government to continue relief work in Greece after the war. Then it appears to have reflected that Greece, after all, goes for something in this set-up, and instructed us the other day to advise the Greek Government, "as it will doubtless wish to associate itself with this move." It seemed to Barbour, and to me when he brought me the telegram and the note he had drafted in compliance, that it is rather strange to inform a Government of something which is to be done by outsiders on its own territory "in case it may wish to associate itself in the affair." So I advised that we point out to the Department that the Greek Government may be expected to feel that it, not we, should invite the Swedes in the first instance, and also that it is possible that the Greek Government may have ideas of its own as to what agency is to control relief distribution in Greece after the war (it may desire to assume the responsibility itself), and to ask the Department to give us other instructions—perhaps to consult the Greek Government as to its ideas in the matter. We worked on a telegram to this effect, but I am not yet satisfied. In any case the action now being proposed seems to me an extreme example of the disregard of the Governments-in-exile which has been so common, particularly with the British, and which not only infuriates the Governments concerned, but which increases to a great extent the difficulty they are under in acquiring and maintaining prestige at home.

January 24, 1944, Monday

Larrabee learned today from OSS that the Russian Mission to Tito has arrived here and contains a Lieutenant General, two Major Generals, and

---

[53] The traditional explanation for Captain Donald Stott's activities in Athens is that he had in fact entered into secret talks with German authorities without the knowledge of his superiors, and that he was recalled from Greece for that reason. Stott, a New Zealander, was presumed killed in 1945 in the Pacific, when the submarine carrying him to a sabotage mission behind Japanese lines was reported lost.

several Colonels, with many other officers. JICAME knew nothing about it, but I confirmed the fact from Stevenson, who agreed that it looks as if the Russians were trying to steal the British thunder with Tito by sending so much rank (the British mission is headed by a Brigadier!). But he added that after all the Russians can't give Tito the actual supplies he needs and the British can. . . . Larrabee says the British Military however, are furious over the Russians stealing such a march. . . . Stevenson added that the Russians know so little of the situation in Yugoslavia that they were thinking, before this mission got here, of having it go on from Tito's Headquarters to those of Mihailović, and that they expected to be taken in to Yugoslavia in a normal way, and to have the red carpet laid down for their arrival. Actually they may all have to parachute in, as Maclean has done, and Randolph Churchill too. . . . Maclean has reported his and R.C.'s safe arrival and that Tito has been cordial after receiving Churchill's letter, but that his reply will not be forthcoming till after further conversations.

January 25, 1944, Tuesday

I had a visit from M. Smiljanić, who is going to Algiers on the Mediterranean Commission, for Yugoslavia. He is a Serb, and did a lot of talking on the political situation, without giving me any new ideas. Everything which these people say confirms me in the belief that the federative idea for Yugoslavia is the only one which has any promise of success, and even it is doubtful, since so much blood has been shed, especially between the Croats and the Serbs, and there is such a lust for domination in both of these peoples. . . . The President's idea of building a wall about the country and letting the factions fight it out among themselves, and tell us later who is top-dog at the last, would surely seem to be the only way for us to treat the question if we don't wish to get hopelessly committed and involved! But of course what we are going to do is to try to give relief to the whole people without prejudice toward one faction or another, and the military aid we are now giving to the Partisans will result in our being in touch only with them when the war is over, and in their being the only people capable of receiving and distributing the relief. In consequence we shall relieve only a part of the population, since the Partisans will distribute only to the Partisans, and the result will be that both with military aid during the war, and with civilian aid after it, we shall be supporting only one section of the country, and discriminating politically in fact if not in intention. But I don't see how it can be helped. . . . Lunch at the Mohamed Aly Club for King Peter of Yugoslavia. . . . In the afternoon, Kirk took me to an audience with King Farouk. This King is taller than I thought and not so fat. Speaks excellent English and has a sense of humour. Kirk was very courtier-like and the King swallowed it. The palace (in town) is large and not in bad taste—Louis XV decoration everywhere and flunkeys in fezzes much in evidence. The King is kept well advised of his visitors in advance, so that he can speak to them about themselves, and evidently prides himself on knowing things. King George is good at this, too, but King Peter hasn't yet developed that far in his business, and I doubt if he ever will. He is more boyish still than his twenty years would justify, and there may be something in what King George said once to me that he is a case of arrested development. At present he is a bright lad of fourteen or fifteen, interested in everything mechanical, particularly in airplanes, guns, and so forth, tanks, jeeps, and whatnot, and practically nothing else. . . . Stevenson came in later in the afternoon in connection with several questions. He said the Russian military mission will probably stay here a couple of weeks, waiting for a landing-strip to be made near Tito's Headquarters so that they won't have to parachute in. He also said that Maclean has telegraphed Tito's reply to Churchill's letter, but that it is difficult to decode and not yet readable, but he thinks it is just what he expected, noncommittal. . . . During the morning, Parsons had told me the EAM has agreed to a truce and *pourparlers* with EDES, and the British Chief Liaison officer in Greece has been instructed to arrange a meeting between the two parties.[54] . . . Leeper confirmed this and was full of hope, which I trust may be justified. The next move, if this is successful, will be to set up a committee under the Archbishop in Athens to discuss plans for National Unity with the various factions, and try to get a few representatives chosen by all of them together to come out and join the Tsouderos government-in-exile. There are obvious recommendations for such a plan, and difficulties to be surmounted in its realization which are equally obvious. . . . Leeper also told me that the British difficulties with Karapanayiotis, the Minister of War, have come to a head in a struggle with General Holmes of the 12th Army. The British are running the Greek army operationally, as they are the Yugoslavs. But Karapanayiotis has insisted on changing his officers under Holmes' command, without consultation with the British, and for political motives. Finally one such order for a change in high place was countermanded by Holmes, who couldn't stand this any longer, and Karapanayiotis appealed to Leeper "on a matter of principle." Leeper told him that it was a practical matter, rather, and that the Greek army *must* get on with the British, if it hopes to be used effectively in this war, but Karapanayiotis still felt he was in the right. So

[54] In October 1943, friction between ELAS and other resistance organizations erupted into serious fighting. Following appeals by the Allies in January 1944, British Liaison Officers under Colonel C. M. Woodhouse succeeded in arranging a cease-fire on February 4, 1944.

Leeper went to Tsouderos and said that he would get Holmes to rescind his order if the Prime Minister would get rid of Karapanayiotis. It looks now as if K. would be shifted to Aviation (a more or less inactive Ministry) and Venizelos would move to the War Office, with the Aviation Minister, Voulgaris, going to the Marine.

January 26, 1944, Wednesday
Sent off a long telegram, drafted by Barbour and myself, on the impossibility of controlling the news about relief plans and shipments, and advising that the Department give us the official information to have broadcast by the Greek government in the first instance. Worked on a despatch along the same lines, arguing that the Governments-in-Exile have lost prestige through being so much overshadowed in the relief picture by the Swiss, the Swedes, the British, and ourselves, and that they should now be associated with us, not just as also-rans, but as leaders and prime-movers in fact, for the sake of their standing with their peoples when the hour of liberation comes. They should not be allowed to attempt to go back as mere suppliants for doubtful votes, and otherwise as do-nothing governments with no record behind them but of political bickering abroad, but should go back bearing the gifts their countries have a right to expect of them,—supplies obtained from their allies, and fully formed plans for reconstruction. Around such governments the leaderless and divided nations might gather. Otherwise they will continue to be simply distracted in a state of anarchy or civil war, and the Allies will have to run the show, with far greater military forces being required for that purpose than present plans provide for. . . . Stevenson called up and said he had some news, and could I come over. So I did, Barbour coming along to call at the Soviet Embassy on Solod, the Counsellor. Stevenson showed me Maclean's reply about the Churchill letter. Tito was pleased with the letter; but though he is willing to refrain from attacking the King, since he does not wish to embarrass the Allies, whose point of view he understands, he does not wish to discuss politics, and thinks that at present the main thing is to kill Germans! Stevenson has asked Maclean to report whether, in spite of this reply, there appears that later there may be a chance of further messages, and of Tito's getting together with the King—of some contact being made between them—which is what H.M.'s Government principally wants. If the reply to this is again negative or noncommittal—which amounts to the same thing,—Stevenson has advised the Foreign Office that it should seek to secure an agreement with Washington and Moscow on a common attitude, involving very much our own present attitude of military support to Tito plus political recognition of the King's Government, but with the addition of publicly announced

withdrawal of military aid to Mihailović on Britain's part, it being made clear that only Britain is involved, but after consultation with the principal Allies. I told Stevenson that I have still no instructions as to our policy beyond the background given the press "confidentially" on November 9, 1943, but that personally I had a feeling that the Department will not want to go so far as to throw over Mihailović completely—withdrawing our Liaison officers and publicly announcing the action, as Stevenson proposes—though we may not give him any supplies so long as he is not fighting the Germans, and in fact are not doing so now. I wondered, too, whether this would not be the Russian attitude also, if it is true that this military mission now here had planned to go on to Mihailović after visiting Tito. . . . Stevenson said that he too felt that we might hesitate to go so far as his plan calls for, and that we might "stick at half-way house." However, the future will tell, but neither Barbour nor I can quite see the Department going so far at present along lines of interference in "internal affairs." It would be more like it to preserve at least a semblance and last shred of correctness combined with watchful waiting. . . . Barbour said that the Soviet Counsellor told him that only about fifteen of the Mission will go into Yugoslavia, the others staying here as a rear echelon, and that the head man, the Lieutenant General, is one of the fighting Generals of this war. I didn't see Larrabee all day, and so don't know what he may have secured from British sources about this matter, but I hope to have a picture of the Mission, its composition, purpose, and plans, in a day or so, which will be closer to the facts, though probably less romantic, than what we have heretofore had.

January 27, 1944, Thursday

I wanted to find out whether the Army Headquarters, or General Royce[55] personally, has seen the Russian Military Mission. . . . Larrabee came back before lunch and reported that there has been no contact with the Mission whatsoever. I learned later on, through Larrabee, that JICAME too has not been in touch. Only the OSS, of the Americans, has seen the Russians so far. This seems amazing to me, since there is nothing to prevent our Military from making contact, and the Mission is the most interesting as well as the most important thing that has come this way since the President and his party. The military mind just seems not to have caught on to this, that's all. . . . In the afternoon I had a long talk with Colonel Bellm, the economic man of Headquarters who has been to Algiers along with General Hughes and other Britishers to find out whether the military part of the relief problem in the Balkans—the 1st phase—is to be a joint Anglo-American affair, or wholly British. He

[55] Major General Ralph Royce, Commanding Officer, U.S. Middle East Forces.

said that General Wilson wants it to be joint, but that the matter cannot be decided until the War Department says its say, which it has not yet done. On the other hand, he told me that he has plans all completed similar to those of General Hughes, and also providing for a joint setup should this be decided on. Hughes believes this will be the decision, but has not yet made such joint plans. . . . I found that Bellm's ideas of the method of entry, and of the distribution of food and other supplies, now being contemplated by the British, were distinctly erroneous, and tried to set him right. He thought that the British (and we also) intend to recognize no government in Greece whatever when we go in, while at the same time the British intend (and he asked, did we also?) to "screen" the distribution of supplies according to the political opinions of the recipients. I therefore told him of the present situation as regards King and Government and the efforts being made to form a national organization in Greece to work with the Government-in-exile, and when the time comes, provide for the transfer of Government without a break into the country itself, the Allies recognizing this national front only, and postponing politics until later, when normal conditions should be more or less restored. We discussed also the ways in which American association in the military operations could help make things run smoothly, and he told me of the alarming possibility that the British may select Indians or other colored troops as occupation troops. Surely, if this is really proposed, it must be prevented at all costs. In many ways, I fear, the British tend to treat the Greeks like "natives," and this won't do. . . .

January 28, 1944, Friday

Went over to Headquarters to see General Royce about the Russian Mission. He said that he has not had any contact with it, and since the Russians are said to feel they have not been made enough of here, I suggested that he contact them. This he said he would be glad to do, but he didn't seem to think there was any special reason for it,—and he a soldier and they also soldiers fresh from the principal front! I like Royce, but he certainly has the Military Mind! He said that he is perfectly free to contact the Russians, since he has sent a telegram himself to Tito; furthermore the OSS is under his command, and they have agents with Tito, and are engaged in sending supplies to the Partisans. For the Embassy, which is accredited to the King and Government, it is of course different, and we must get our information and contacts with the Partisans secondhand. I explained this to the General. But in truth he is not much interested. . . . Stevenson called up and I stopped in to see him on my way home. He has received another message from Maclean promising an early reply from Tito to Churchill's letter, but suggesting he be authorized to put the question to him in writing: "H.M.'s Government, whilst confirming that they have no, repeat no, wish to force on the Yugoslav people any form of Government not, repeat not, freely chosen by them, are anxious to see as many national elements as possible united in a common struggle against invaders. They take a personal interest in the fortunes of King Peter who joined forces with Great Britain at a time when she stood alone in the field against the Axis, and they would be glad to learn whether Marshal Tito would be prepared to enter contact with him with view to common prosecution of war." Maclean suggests that this be presented to Tito "if possible jointly with U.S.A. and Soviet Governments." Stevenson supports this suggestion in a telegram of his own to the Foreign Office, and says, "It would be obviously desirable if the United States and Soviet Governments would agree to support such a communication to Tito," but he told me that he doubts whether the United States will do so, and thinks the Soviets will prefer to wait till they can hear from their own Mission. This last, he said, has received orders from Moscow to leave here on the 31st (Monday), and will go, he thinks, either to Algiers, to contact General Wilson, or direct to Bari, there to wait till it can fly in and land at Tito's headquarters. Novikov, the Soviet Ambassador, invited me to a dinner for the Mission to be given Sunday night—evidently hurried by this new order to leave promptly. . . . I had Barbour say over the 'phone that I was out, and would reply tomorrow morning, but I am pretty sure I shall have a previous engagement. Doubtless, my going could be explained on the basis that I was only going to a colleague's house, not calling on the Mission itself. But explanations should not be necessary, and I feel the Department's attitude and my position with the Yugoslav Government make it better to stay away. Stevenson told me he will go (though he will not call); but then his position, as director here of all the operations now going on with Tito, is somewhat different from mine. . . . Maclean's description of the Partisan attitude at present is interesting, and not particularly reassuring as to prospects of success for Churchill's plan: "Attitude of Tito and Partisans in general extremely friendly. They show greatly increased appreciation of help we are giving them, and of our share in the war. On the other hand, conversations and publications and statements made during my absence show distinct hardening of attitude toward King Peter, Yugoslav Government, and Mihailović, and tendency to link all these more closely than ever." Stevenson, in his message to the F.O. says he regards this as indicating a favorable atmosphere (!) and adds that the "comparative failure of the latest German offensive may have contributed to it." Is he kidding himself, and hoping against hope, since he has been forced into a policy against which he himself protested all along? "I do not think," he says, "that Brigadier Maclean would have put forward the proposal contained in his telegram unless such an atmosphere did exist"—i.e. Stevenson himself doesn't really see it as existing!—"and I would therefore be in favor of taking advantage of it in the way he suggests." Meanwhile, of course, Tito's answer to Churchill's letter, which Maclean says he promised to give "tomorrow" (i.e. the 27th) may be so definite that no further questions need be or can be asked. . . . All this simply goes on with another chapter of the amazingly fumbling foreign policy characteristic of Eden, and reminds me of his "direction" of affairs in the last days before the German attack on Greece, when like a beaten quarterback in the last few minutes of a game lost by his own faulty strategy to begin with, he resorted to passes in all directions, and had no final answer but a turning up of his thumbs with an appeal to hope—"are we downhearted? no"—the collegiate gesture and attitude in which I last saw him as he passed out through Palairet's door. . . . Mr. Hull's foreign policy, which sticks by a few principles, and for the rest is content to wait and see, has the strength of Gibraltar compared with this nervous grasping at any line of action on the chance that it may be a good thing to do. . . . Got off a long telegram on the Greek situation. It appears that a number of political leaders—Mylonas, Gonatas, and Chloros,—this last a representative of Theotokis (still, I suppose, in Corfu) have signed a protocol expressing their willingness to discuss a National Government with Mr. Tsouderos. There certainly appears to be a growing desire on all sides in Greece to find some principle of unity, and a growing tendency to crystallize around the Government-in-exile which is both new and encouraging.

January 29, 1944, Saturday
Archer came in with an airgram he proposed sending to Washington (to Lehman),[56] pointing out that estimates drawn up by MESC (the Middle East Supply Center), and other British organizations here (e.g. ATB) for the agricultural requirements of Greece and Yugoslavia, are being sent in for presumable final acceptance by UNRRA without having been shown to the Greek and Yugoslav governments! I altered his message in several instances but specially provided a statement: "The Embassy believes that no estimates of specification should be adopted without first being cleared with the Governments of the countries concerned." I don't see how we can justifiedly go on acting toward these countries as if they were our own possessions, or savage territories we intend to occupy.

[56] Herbert H. Lehman, a former Governor of New York, and the Director of the Office of Foreign Relief and Rehabilitation Operations, Department of State.

January 31, 1944, Monday

Ambassador Stevenson came in and showed me Tito's reply to Churchill's letter. As expected, it was extremely noncommittal on the main question of entering into relations with the King,—recognizes, understands, etc. that the British have commitments there, and doesn't want to embarrass them, and then switches off to generalities. The Ambassador said he would probably now suggest to the Foreign Office that Maclean go ahead and pop the definite question proposed the other day. . . . I telegraphed a summary of Tito's message. . . . The Ambassador also said that the Columbia Broadcasting System here wants to broadcast a talk by a wounded Partisan officer named Lt. Col. Dedijer,[57] who was brought here by the British for the treatment of his wound, but who has become a "focus" for anti-Yugoslav Government elements. Stevenson said that militarily the broadcast is unobjectionable, but that it is political and if made would embarrass the British Government. He therefore asked me to join him in preventing its being made, but I said that I had no reason to believe that the U. S. Government would be embarrassed. After all, the papers at home are constantly publishing stuff on one side or the other of the political Yugoslav fence. I pointed out that as the British control the censorship here anyway, my joining in is not necessary, if Stevenson is to stop the broadcast, and this he admitted—so that it became clear that what he wants is for me to share the responsibility, should criticism develop! But I did tell him that if he stops it, and the Columbia people appeal to me I will not support them against him unless the Department instructs me to do so. If the matter is one involving embarrassment to the British Government, I am sure I should not, on my own, take an opposite line. Altogether, I feel strongly that in the execution of our somewhat different missions here, my British colleagues and I should, as representing Allies, not take any openly conflicting actions unless we are clear that our Governments desire it. . . . Lunch at the Mohamed Aly Club for King George of Greece. . . . It seems that though the headquarters of EAM and EDES have expressed willingness to parley, their forces have just opened the severest campaign of the "civil war" against each other, somewhere along the Achelous!

February 2, 1944, Wednesday

We continue to get no word from the State Department, and to hear what we do occasionally hear from there through others,—generally the

[57] Vladimir Dedijer, former journalist, and close wartime associate and biographer of Tito.

British. Today Warner[58] of the British Embassy to Greece (the "consumptive mosquito") called up and said that his Ambassador had been instructed to associate himself with us in suggesting to the Greek Government that it ask the Swedes to continue their relief work in Greece after the war. So apparently the Department has taken notice of my telegram on this subject, but we have to hear of it through the British first!

February 4, 1944, Friday

I had an interesting talk with Colonel Toulmin, head of the local OSS, who came over to see me at my request. Colonel (General) Donovan had promised to let me see a report he wrote, and Toulmin was to give it to me, but had forgotten. Now he promises to let me have it promptly. We talked about the Greek and Yugoslav situations, and I found that he had only a sketchy idea of recent developments as regards Tito; so I read him my recent telegrams. He said that the British Military are annoyed over Brigadier Maclean's political activities ("He reports only to Mr. Churchill, not to us") and the OSS, for the same reason—politics, in which it is not interested—now wants to divorce itself from the leadership of "Force 133"[59] in the Balkans, lest it become involved too deeply in Britain's schemes. What I told him only convinced Colonel Toulmin the more, he said, that such a course is advisable. . . . In regard to Greece, he outlined to me the "Noah's Ark plan"[60] of the British, which OSS is following along with, apparently. This plan is to suspend all activity of the guerrillas for the time being;—a cessation of the ELAS-EDES hostilities, which have gone on despite previous attempts at a truce, till Zervas is now in real danger of being wiped out on the Achelous and northward, has been arranged for tonight. Thenceforward a force of about 12,000 ELAS and 3,000 EDES warriors is to be kept ready in nine different regions, to take action against communications as soon as the Germans begin to move out—"that mythical date," as Colonel Toulmin put it. And to facilitate the action of these bands, each of which will be nucleated around a British Force 133 or OSS man (or several men), a lot of high explosives are to be flown in, beginning, I think he said, in March. . . . This is of course the operational part, in detail, of Leeper's plan, which involves also the setting up of a secret governmental committee in Athens to coordinate all patriots of whatever party, and take charge of running

[58] Edward Warner, senior political officer of the British Embassy to the Greek government-in-exile.
[59] "Force 133," designation of SOE forces in the Balkans with headquarters in Cairo.
[60] "Noah's Ark," code name of the allied plan for the liberation of Greece.

the country, with the King's authority, on the "mythical date." But this part of the plan we didn't discuss. . . . Toulmin also told me that the British high-up military authorities here are all against the plan to invade Europe from England, direct into France. They are all, he says, "Easterners," to use the expression of the last war, and have not forgotten that the German collapse in 1918 began at Salonica. They feel the establishment of the "Western Front" will be too costly and fail, though they admit that if successful, it will bring the war to an end more quickly than anything else. He said they still hope, at this late date, that Eisenhower may decide finally against it, but have little expectation that their hopes will be fulfilled. When I expressed surprise that anyone could think at this time that any other plan than an attack from England could be adopted—the preparations having gone so far—he said that there will be three months yet before an invasion of France can be set on foot. The "Overlord Plan," which is the Western Front plan, was practically adopted at Quebec, he said, but finally so at Teheran, owing to Stalin's insistence. I am reminded of Molotov at Reykjavik, after dinner at Camp Pershing, when in answer to a question from one of our officers: "What do you think we ought to do to help win the war?" he stuck out his pudgy forefinger in a prodding gesture, and said shortly in his funny lingo (he speaks no foreign language but got the idea of the question like a shot from his interpreter) "Francia"! . . . Got a telegram from the Department expressing "appreciation" of the Embassy's view that if the Swedes are to be asked to continue their relief work in Greece after the war, the Greek Government ought to do the asking, and instructing us to approach the Greek Government with the suggestion. It adds that the British have been instructed by their people to associate themselves with us in this *démarche*. It is not often the Department appreciates a correction from the field.

February 5, 1944, Saturday
Called, at his request, on the Yugoslav Prime Minister, who gave me a copy of a telegram he sent last night to Mr. Eden, through the British Ambassador, who told him that if he sent it at all, he had better send it quickly! It appears that Purić had learned from an article in the *Observer* of London, of February 1st, and other notices in the British press, that the British are discussing, in London, the cutting off entirely of supplies to Mihailović and an announcement, publicly, to this effect. This is of course what Stevenson has told me, and presumably the Foreign Office has told the Department, but Purić was not informed. He called Stevenson who admitted the truth of the reports, and when he said he would be sending the British Government his views today or tomorrow,

Stevenson kindly advised him that the matter was hot and if he wanted his views considered he'd better move more quickly. So the telegram went off last night. Then Purić shrewdly bethought himself of the likelihood that the British would not do anything so drastic unless we agreed to it, and asked me to help him make sure that Washington as well as London knows what he thinks. . . . I sent off his text this morning, following an explanatory telegram. Purić says that he and the King are both morally bound to stay [stand] by Mihailović, and therefore if the British announce that they are abandoning him, it will be virtually a declaration of war against Yugoslavia! But, he added, he and the King won't budge, nevertheless; and when he suggested to the King that they might be sent to a concentration camp, the King said "All right, let's go!" Purić also told me that when he said to the King that in such a matter he must make up his own mind and not be guided by a mere Prime Minister, who could be changed at any time, the youngster replied, "I'm not being guided by you. I'm simply thinking along the same lines as you." . . . In my covering telegram, I told the Department that it is the publicity part of the proposed action which seems to be particularly objected to. Said Purić, "The BBC will be broadcasting five times a day to the Yugoslav people" that Britain is severing its relations with Mihailović, who is the Yugoslav Government's Minister of War. But as Britain (and the U.S.) has already practically ceased sending Mihailović any supplies, there is nothing new about that angle. So I suggested to the Department that in view of the strong reaction of the King, perhaps the best thing to do would be simply to go ahead on military grounds cutting Mihailović out, but to keep the action purely military, and not give it the political aspect that the proposed publicity would entail. I also added that my talks with Stevenson made me think (and they ought to have made the Department think so too, if they don't already know it directly from the Foreign Office) that a British aim in this matter is to bring about the fall of Purić and his replacement by somebody more likely to cooperate in approaching Tito; and I suggested that the King's firmness might make it seem wiser to attempt this on grounds less closely connected with Serbian national sentiments. In other words, they might seek to oust him on grounds such as his handling of finances, or other administration, or even on his lack of cooperation with them in general, rather than because he refuses for their sake to abandon a "Serbian national idol." In the sequel, should the British take the action they propose, there is certainly a possibility of Mihailović's forming a Government of his own, in opposition to British policy, and a great increase of bitterness towards the British (and us too, since we are allied with Britain) on the part of a large part of the Serbian population. It seems to me that it would be folly to take the risk of such consequences—which would extend into the future far beyond the close of this war—when it is unnecessary to do so, and it is certainly possible to continue the policy, which the United States, at least, has been following so far, of keeping military action and politics distinct and separate. This policy cannot, doubtless, be carried out practically so far as the results of our arming one group rather than another are concerned; but it can be carried out ostensibly, and in such a case as the present the results would be practical, in a negative way—very practical indeed, in avoiding rendering confusion worse confounded, and starting trouble we don't need to have. . . . I don't know what the Department may think of all this, but in view of its expression of policy to the Press on November 9th, which is the last word it has given on the subject, I cannot well conceive how it could encourage the British to go ahead with their plan. . . . Letter received from Mr. Groth in Cape Town, and a pleasant letter from F. D. R., marked in his own handwriting "Secret," and very chatty about the King of Greece. It is obviously a kind gesture to make me feel better, and to take time out in order to dictate it was after all something to do on the part of perhaps the world's busiest man. The essential part of the letter is "I fully understand about the Greek matter." So that is that.

[The President had written:]

January 15, 1944

Dear Lincoln:

This is the first chance I have had to write to you, as I have been laid up with the "flu." I wish I could have seen you again before leaving Cairo.

I fully understand about the Greek matter and I merely want to let you know that the King had a long talk with me and felt (strictly between ourselves) that he was being "railroaded" or "blackmailed" by the British. He felt that nobody can tell just when the Allies will get back into Greece or when the last Germans will depart and that, therefore, it was premature for anybody to make a final decision as to whether he should return or not. I like George very much—in fact, I call him by his first name—but, of course, he is not a very strong or convincing person, as he has not had the opportunity of conducting a Presidential campaign.

Making all due allowances, however, I told him that if I were in his place I would, at the proper moment (not yet), tell the people of Greece frankly that as a constitutional monarch he had gone a bit too far in the Metaxas case even though his intentions were of the best, i.e., the peace of Greece; that, however, he had learned his lesson and that if he continued as King he would do so in a strictly constitutional manner—and not get caught again at playing with a dictator.

I will bet you a good dinner that if I were in his place—and wanted to do so—I would find ways of returning as King of Greece. Actually, however, I can assure you that I have no such ambition! But if I did want to go back I would not do so by going to Bermuda and telling the United States of America that if they really wanted me as President they could jolly well elect me.

When I saw him he was, as you say, much disturbed. He had been getting too much advice and did not seem to be able to make up his own mind.

I wish you would write me and give me your own slant as to what is the best form of government Greece could have. My own mind runs to the idea that a tiny spot in the Mediterranean, like Greece, has its reputation enhanced if it has a constitutional monarch, but with certain provisos:

(a) He should take absolutely no part in government except to open county fairs and give entertainment to visiting firemen.

(b) That the country (and Parliament) should be allowed to have only three parties—a primary confined to perhaps five parties or six parties, and a general election confined to the three top parties in the primary. Most Latin or Eastern countries would benefit by this.

(c) A Prime Minister elected for a specific term—two, three or four years—thus making for continuity and an approach to the republican form of government.

What a mess your two bailiwicks are in! I am inclined to think Yugoslavia, in the long run, will be more of a mess than Greece. I think I forgot to tell you that when I saw Peter I asked him why he did not marry the girl, take a month's honeymoon, ship her back to England, and go to the front in person—visiting both Tito and the other fellow (his Minister of War) whose name I cannot spell.

If you see the Crown Prince of Egypt you might tell him how very much interested I was in meeting him. He is an interesting old globetrotter—a thorough reactionary I think—but well versed in the ways of all civilizations.

With my warm regards and all good wishes for the New Year,

As ever yours,
FDR (4)

February 7, 1944, Monday

In answer to my query whether, in view of the possibility that the Foreign Office is now keeping the Department informed of all its Yugoslav negotiations, the latter desires me to continue reporting on these from here, and thus perhaps duplicating information, the Department sent me a message which indicates that information from London on this subject is not yet as full as it might be. The Department is giving careful consideration to what attitude it should take toward the Yugoslav resistance movements (personally, I hope it doesn't change much from its present one, which seems to me to be, all things considered, about the best possible in the circumstances—which doesn't mean perfect, either), and it says it has "found your telegrams on this subject exceedingly valuable. Please continue to report all information of this kind.". . .This is encouraging, and perhaps indicates that my latest long ones will not come amiss. . . . In the evening, I went round to Leeper's office and had a long talk on the Greek situation. Tsouderos had told me that the Greek politicians (chiefly Kafandaris and Sofoulis) are now making difficulties about a *rapprochement* with the Government-in-Exile, which had recently seemed a possibility. They want an "interpretation" of the King's letter of November 8th, and apparently an interpretation which will make it clear that the King will definitely *not* go back to Greece till called. Tsouderos is against this, he says, because it is impossible to foresee exactly what conditions will obtain when the time comes, and from the point of view of the politicians as well as of the King the question should be left open. Leeper was inclined to lament the fact that no agreement can apparently be reached among the Greek factions, but I said that perhaps it is just as well, since no agreement reached now could possibly last until liberation—on account of the very nature of the Greeks. It will be the best time to reach an agreement a week or so before we go in! He then told me of the latest proposals of the EAM, which is apparently jockeying to get control of all the resistance forces, and by setting up a united resistance front dominated by it (on account of its numbers), with headquarters in the mountains, to create a kind of Tito situation in Greece. The British are insisting, to avoid this, that when an arrangement is made between EDES and EAM to cease fighting and unite against the enemy, further talks *on political grounds* regarding the setting up of a National Unity Front, or what have you, shall be held in *Athens*. Leeper then went on to tell me that the Military (the United Chiefs of Staff) has turned down the proposals included in the "Noah's Ark Plan" for a diminuation of resistance effort in Greece for the time being, and insists that the Greeks be pushed to continue sabotage at present to the utmost of their power, regardless of consequences to them. The theory seems to be that everything counts now, every German killed, and every bit of material damage caused to the Germans is something gained, and no matter how little it may be it is worth while for the war effort. Leeper thinks this a great mistake, and that the Greeks are at the end of their strength now, and that to push them to further exertions can have only a minimal effect on the war, while it will have a very great one in further depressing the population and creating a worse situation for the allies when they do come in eventually.

February 8, 1944, Tuesday
Colonel Toulmin called in the afternoon and told me some interesting things. There appears to be a movement northward among the German troops in Greece, perhaps to replace the four or five divisions which are or have been moving from Yugoslavia to Italy. This accounts for the British Military wanting the sabotage efforts of the Greeks not to be let down at this time. Unfortunately for Force 133, however, Churchill has become "naughty" again, and taking a sudden interest in the efforts of French Partisans has ordered Wilson, by wire direct, to switch to France the planes he was planning to use in Greece! . . .

February 9, 1944, Wednesday
Last evening, on my way home, Stevenson showed me Churchill's reply to Tito, and his own telegram to the Foreign Office, commenting on Purić's message to Eden. He gave me a copy of his telegram and I made a digest of Churchill's and got off messages of my own this morning. Churchill's blast was by way of asking Tito to say whether or not he would accept the dismissal of Mihailović as a *quid pro quo* for a *rapprochement* with King Peter, and in addition states that he has called on the Mediterranean Command to start amphibious operations against the German-held Dalmatian islands. According to Toulmin, the British Military higher-ups are peeved over Churchill's thus butting-in directly on strategic matters for diplomatic ends, and Stevenson commented on the message as a whole, "We shall burn our fingers." I told him I didn't see why the Purić Government couldn't be turned out by some other maneuver than the public repudiation of Mihailović, which would certainly alienate many loyal Serbs from Britain (and the U.S. too, I fancy) for years to come. Why not object to Purić's handling of finances, or administration of some sort. To this he replied eagerly "Why not?" He suggested that the British might simply insist on the recognition of all fighting groups equally. The Government would have to resign if they pressed for that, as it is committed against the Partisans. Then Mihailović would fall automatically as War Minister, and a new Government could be formed which would recognize his movement and Tito's on an equal basis under the King, and the Serbs who support Mihailović now could not claim that he especially had been pilloried, as they could do were he to be publicly disowned. It would be a question of saving the Serb element

from entire disaffection—or that part of it, the size of which we cannot tell but may be very large, which idolizes the Serbian leader. Why slap it down if it is unnecessary to do so? And there are plenty of Serbs outside of Yugoslavia, here and elsewhere, who would be glad to join in a middle-of-the-road Government. Mr. Churchill says that he has hesitated to press for the dismissal of Mihailović so far because it would probably mean the resignation of all the King's ministers and the loss by him of "his only adherents." If by this he means all the fanatical Serbs, he is right. But why drive so fine a group unnecessarily into indignant opposition? . . . Stevenson's comments on Purić's message ended by pointing out the complexity of the situation and claiming that this supports his contention that the Mihailović problem should be treated wholly on the military plane. I called the Department's attention to this. . . . Other information he gave me was to the effect that Tito is asking for war correspondents to be attached to his Headquarters. Maclean has suggested one man each from Reuters and the A.P., but Stevenson has "counselled stalling" until the political situation is clarified. He also told me that the Foreign Office has been "embarrassed" by the Czechoslovak Government's desire to send a Military Mission to Tito. Everybody's doing it! But the F.O. thinks this would start a dangerous precedent and that Tito would only use the Mission for his own political ends. . . . I advised the Department of both the above matters, and personally think the British are right in both. . . . Patrick Hurley, ex-Secretary of War,[61] called, and talked to me for about an hour, largely about himself. He has been impressed by the trickiness of our British friends and the "English" they always put on the ball, and most of his talk was about how he personally has told them off. In general I think his point of view sound—the British have been doing the Empire stuff for several centuries and are at it still. If we, or anybody else, don't cotton to their curves, well, that's too bad and it's *sauve qui peut!* All's fair in love and war—and foreign affairs! No need to get mad about it; only watch out. Really, of course, now that the British need us so badly, they should modify their trickiness somewhat in our behalf for their own interests; but it's in the blood. I feel that we must be understanding as well as watchful, but that fundamentally the aim must be to let nothing ever prevent the collaboration of the English speaking peoples: otherwise all we both stand for,—all the decencies we both prize, and nobody else does—will be lost from the world's life. . . . The General (Hurley was made a Major General only yesterday, from Brigadier, and carefully informed me that the President had made him an Ambassador, "the highest rank I ever attained") has been particularly annoyed by British attempts to belittle the value to them of Lend-Lease.

---

[61] On special mission as the President's personal representative in the Near East and Iran, to assess regional problems in relation to American interests and concerns.

Also it annoys him to have them think we are impressed by their titles. He is very proud to relate how he has told them that we think so little of Lords that we relegate them to our comic strips; "Lord Plushbottom in the funnies" etc. . . . I guess nothing about the British in my mild letters will ever shock the President after he has listened to his globetrotters, Hurley and Donovan!

February 10, 1944, Thursday

I was summoned by the King of Greece to talk with him. He told me that he is going to London next Monday, but not to say anything about it "for security reasons.". . . He is happy over the 1st Brigade's going to Italy. "Winston has lived up to his promise." But he clearly doesn't know that the British plan to use the Greeks only in the rear areas and on communications. I didn't enlighten him, but I did suggest that when he gets to London he should urge that enough allied troops be assigned to the Liaison command here to enable our relief movement into Greece to be a success. He thoroughly understands the reasons for this necessity, and we agreed on all the aspects of the matter. But I fear he has too little weight with the British to cut much ice, even if he does say something. Most of his talk was very excited, about his difficulties with his cabinet (which he could avoid if he would assert his authority and pick his men occasionally himself), and his fears that we and the British may go too far with EAM. He knows that the British are now thoroughly against this "resistance movement" and that we are taking no part in internal affairs, but he still has fears, and must blow off steam. He wants me to see the OSS about a Greek agent they are making use of whom he believes to have communist connections and tendencies. He also told me that the EAM is sending out to Cairo fifty officers, whom the British say they cannot do anything to repress if they get here, and whom he is sure that Karapanayiotis, his War Minister, will somehow or other get into the Greek Forces to corrupt them. What he thinks of Karapanayiotis is nobody's business, and the same of Roussos. Venizelos he feels kinder about, but says he can't keep his mouth shut, and that to tell him anything is to broadcast it. He said that he felt my efforts to give the Greek Government a proper place in its own affairs,—in planning for Greece, etc.,—were "touching," but asked "What is the use, when the Government itself is uninterested?" I was sorry for him as usual, and liked him very much.

February 14, 1944, Monday

General Royce brought in Lt. General Eaker, commanding our air forces in North Africa. We talked about the bombing of Bulgaria and

Greece. It is true that raids on Bucharest have been called off for a short period pending talks with "emissaries," but if these lead to nothing, it is likely that the raids will be resumed with increased intensity. General Eaker said the greatest care would be taken not to harm the civilians in Greece more than necessary, but defended the recent Piraeus raid. He said he had seen the photographs, which show a high degree of accuracy on the targets, and he asserted that there was a lot of shipping in the harbour including some fairly large vessels and a German destroyer.... The King of Greece left this morning for England by air, taking Mr. Metaxas and Colonel Levidis.... Ambassador Stevenson came in and told me that a reply from Tito has been received to the questions Maclean was authorized to put to him in writing, and while the message is so garbled that it may take a day or so to decipher completely, the gist is clear. What Tito proposes is that if the King will dismiss Mihailović, dismiss his Government, and recognize the provisional government of the Partisans, Tito will consider discussing his future status! To this the Ambassador feels like replying that the cart is before the horse, and that discussions should take place before the King is required to take any action, not after. He also points out that what the King would gain by casting aside his only supporters would be nothing more than the opportunity of further talk.

February 17, 1944, Thursday
Called on General Royce to see how he feels about a recommendation I want to make about having the Military Command, in the 1st phase of Balkan relief operations, in American hands. Toulmin and Bellm came in at my request and I read them part of my letter to the President dealing with this question, as well as a telegram I propose to send "to the Secretary or Undersecretary." They agreed to all I said, and General Royce this morning did too. I suppose I am sticking my neck out a long way in making this recommendation, unasked, in the highest places. But in my belief it would be a great error not to secure the cooperation and allegiance of the Balkan peoples in our reconstruction efforts, and under British command this will be difficult, if not impossible, owing to the bitterness, suspicion, and distrust which British mistakes in this war have aroused. We don't need to have all the troops or all the staff, or even the major portion, but if the operation were known to be American in its direction and control, a thousand things would go straight which might otherwise not. There are also future considerations as between British and Russian zones of influence in the Balkans, which I put into my letter to F.D.R., and which I feel most important. Of the three great powers surviving here after this war, the one which has no self-interest in the

Balkans should take the lead to keep the others apart so that new wars may not be bred here.

Cairo, Egypt
February 17, 1944

Dear Franklin:—

It was awfully good of you to write me as you did—your letter of January 15, which I have before me now. The King of Greece, whom I have seen several times recently, seems to be feeling better for the moment. At least, the problem of his return is not so acute at present, while the principal efforts of our British friends, and of the Greek Government, with whose affairs and prospects they are everlastingly busy, are being directed to securing some sort of *rapprochement* between the guerrilla forces in Greece, the political leaders there, and the government itself here in Cairo.

These efforts so far seem to have had some success. The guerrillas have declared a truce to their internecine warfare, and their leaders, together with the local politicians and the Government's spokesmen in Athens, seem to be headed toward some sort of conference, the aim being a national unity front. All is not perfectly clear ahead, of course. The most powerful guerrilla group (ELAS) seems dominated by an inner ring (EAM) mainly composed of Macedonian communists and others not nationally minded from the Greek point of view, and is probably aiming at swallowing up the rival groups and forming a kind of Tito movement to face the Allies with a *fait accompli* when liberation occurs. The idea seems to be that, with headquarters somewhere in the mountains, and control of the main towns, it could be in a position not only to dominate the distribution of relief brought in from the outside, but even perhaps also to accept or reject, as it might please, the returning Government. The present efforts of the British, therefore, are being directed to preventing this possibility, and to jockeying the guerrillas into a "union now,"—and in Athens, not in the mountains,—with the Government's representatives. Should these efforts be successful, there is the further prospect that representatives of the union so formed may be brought out from Greece to Cairo and taken into the Government here, thus facilitating the latter's eventual re-entrance to the home land as a government truly of, and by, as well as for, the people.

You may feel that this is a somewhat complicated plan; but then the situation itself is complicated. Doubtless it will not go through in all its details, and I mention it only to show how things are shaping up at present. There has also been a military plan devised for Greece,—likewise complicated,—and this was recently presented to the Allied Chiefs of Staff as "the Noah's Ark Plan"—why the name, I do not know. Briefly, the British here ("Force 133" plus the Ambassador) have conceived that the Greeks should not be urged, in their present exhausted and febrile state, to continue sabotage operations while Greece is no longer a strategic area. Rather they should now compose their internal differences, and live quietly without incurring any more reprisals for damage which the Germans have plenty of time to repair. At the same time, however, small forces of them—about 15,000, all picked men trained by Force 133 and our OSS,—should be prepared to take action against communications, et cetera, once the Germans begin to withdraw. At that time it is conceived that a strategic situation would again have arisen, and the Greeks should be ready to meet it. This might seem reasonable, and those who know Greece best feel it in many ways desirable, but the Allied Chiefs of Staff have turned down the idea of any but the shortest respite, and this to be only for the purposes of the "reorganization" of the guerrilla bands. They say the military situation requires unceasing action against the enemy, to hold him and to harry him, and thus the Greeks are not to be allowed to rest, let the consequences to the depressed and exhausted country be what they may.

This military situation, superimposed on the terrible misery existing in the whole occupied region, is what is likely to make all our relief plans very difficult in the early stages. Plans have been made to bring relief in "when the Germans go out." But the Germans are clearly not going out all at once, nor could they do so if they wished. Consequently "liberated areas" will be found existing side by side with "occupied areas" for some time at least, and relief will have to go in armed, to begin with, not only in view of the anarchy certain to prevail where the Germans have evacuated, but also to parry possible attack from any enemy still in the vicinity. The British have a so-called "Liaison Force" established here, under a Major General Hughes, to take charge of the opening phase of relief operations, and the economic section of our Theatre Command, under a young colonel named Bellm (note the difference in rank and experience), has for some time been maturing plans for a similar unit, should we be called upon either to perform in the same manner or to conduct a "joint operation." The British blue-prints I have seen are splendidly developed and most imposing, and the British already have a force consisting of some 150 officers assigned to the task of advising and guiding the local authorities from the moment of arrival in Greece. But troops are lacking, and obviously if there are no authorities to be found, or if these "authorities" are only local bandits who have terrorized the population, while the enemy still has forces here and there eager to seize the supplies we bring in, troops in some numbers will be necessary. General Hughes, even as late as yesterday, has been profoundly pessimistic as to his chances of receiving an adequate force, and on our side, not only do the commissioned cadres so far merely exist on paper, but they include only "20 or 25 Civil Affairs officers to participate on a combined basis with the British to supervise and control distribution of civilian supplies," while Secretary Stimson has written to Secretary Hull, under date of December 21, 1943, "It is the present policy of the U.S. Joint Chiefs of Staff not to divert troops from military operation for the purpose of supporting the administration of civil relief in the Balkans."

Two thoughts would appear to recommend themselves in this matter. The first is that though it may indeed be impossible on other grounds to divert American troops to the support of Balkan relief, the idea that such relief can in its early stages, be regarded as a wholly civilian affair is untenable. As long as there are any German troops in the area at all, there will be a "front" in the Balkans in the true military sense; and as long as such a front exists, the liberated areas involved in it will be no man's land but his who has the force to police and guard it. *Ergo*, military operations in the Balkans should be considered more seriously than seems to be the case at present, if relief, in which so many of our people are so deeply interested, is to get started. Secondly, if enough American troops cannot be spared to share at least equally with the British in this matter, our military authorities should satisfy themselves thoroughly that the British are going to devote enough strength to it to ensure success before we associate ourselves with it in any way. Our old habit of attaching observers to foreign enterprises may be useful under certain conditions, but we should be careful to avoid its leading us into the appearance of responsibility in vital matters over which we have no effective control. You know, doubtless far better than I, the British habit and skill in putting "English" on the ball. The "English" in Balkan affairs right now is this, that through our association with British schemes we can be handed an equal portion of the blame if these go wrong. Some Americans would even say that a way will be found to hand us a major portion, but I don't believe in being picayune. Sufficient unto many days ahead is the evil of this matter. Let me give you an instance of what I mean, though I feel it may be unnecessary. By agreement between the British SOE and our OSS, the British secret services have the lead in Yugoslavia and Greece, while ours have it in Bulgaria and Hungary. In the latter countries, the British have not wholly played the game with us, but in Yugoslavia and Greece, we have faithfully observed the pact. Yet while our OSS remains strictly under military and not State Department control, and is operating for purely military ends, the Foreign Office has taken over the guidance of the British agents and has immersed them deeply in political maneuvers. This throws our agents, "by association," into a similar position, and despite the fact of our carefully disinterested attitude toward internal political matters in these countries, involves our government, in the eyes of every Greek and Yugoslav, in responsibility for all the British schemes. If you saw as many Greeks and Yugoslavs as I do, you would realize how far this has gone already. It is America and Britain together who are universally regarded as being responsible for what are actually purely British actions, and unless we do something to correct this misinterpretation, we may expect it to continue, since it barks right up the British tree. Actually, as far as concerns the military phase of Balkan relief, the British here are already talking of "joint operations" though all we have suggested so far is the minimal collaboration above noted.

It wouldn't be so bad, of course, if the British were not playing a game out here which is very different from what we perhaps ingenuously conceive to be the agreed-on program for the post-war world. British policy as it is being worked out in the Near East—I say nothing of how it may be expressed in high phraseology for world consumption—is essentially today what it has always been, just as I believe the Russian policy as regards Pan-Slavism and the Mediterranean remains unchanged. It is directed primarily at the preservation of the Empire connections and the sea route to India. People complain of its many apparent contradictions, but all such are easily resolved when the essential is understood; they come simply from the application of the trial and error method to the end in view. In Greece, the British have tried backing the EAM; they have tried backing the EDES; and now they are trying to back the two together. They have tried persuading the King to go in; they have tried persuading the King to keep out. In Yugoslavia they have tried Mihailović, and are now trying Tito. In answer to the Ambassador here, who protested that putting Tito and King Peter in harness together would be impossible, the Foreign Office replied, "It is something we think we ought to try." And so forth. This is short-term opportunism, if you like. Nevertheless it all shapes up to finding where Britain can secure the firmest vantage ground for the preservation of a stake in the Balkans—obviating total control of Southeastern Europe by any other great power. It is very far from a policy aimed at the reconstruction of the occupied countries as free and independent states, friendly to all others but under the influence of none! But such as it is, it explains many things, including attempts to make American assistance, Lend-Lease or otherwise, appear as British, and, what is more germane to my subject, this itch to exploit for British uses what must seem the God-given collaboration of a people like ourselves, presumed to be inexperienced in the realistic business of international affairs.

Perhaps the cure in this whole matter would be to prove ourselves more realistic than we have hitherto been considered. I may be over-bold to say so, but I am personally very strongly in favor of America's taking the lead in the coming Balkan operation in all its phases, including the military, whatever may be the short-term reasoning against it. This does not mean that we should contribute all the troops, or even necessarily the major portion. We might actually have but very few. But it does mean that the command should be American. I say this with all the earnestness in my power, not merely because we shall be saddled with the responsibility anyhow, if we let our allies take the lead, but because both sentimentally and practically our leadership is required. The countries we are going into are not merely devastated as by flood or earthquake, they are demoralized, in the full and awful sense of that word, by years of barbarian occupation. Furthermore, they have been profoundly disillusioned by the repeated ineptitudes, political and military, of British policy and action in this region. As my Military Attaché has put it, two things stand out in Balkan psychology today, distrust of England and fear of Russia. Under such circumstances, the extent to which America is being looked to cannot be overestimated, nor can the salutary effect of our guidance, if we will give it. There is hardly a Greek or Yugoslav today who does not think of America first, despite our involvement in current British errors, whenever he dreams of his country's rehabilitation. Superficial observers might perhaps be tempted to put this aside as sentimentalism, but there is good reason behind it. Even in its earliest phases, and perhaps chiefly then, our coming Balkan operations are going to prove critical in what will remain after this war, whether we like it or not, a critical area for the peace of the world. Here was a focal point for the imperialisms of Russia, Germany and England in the past, and to a certain extent of Italy and France as well. Now only two of these nations remain as great powers in Europe, but have they changed their spots? Realism requires that we consider not only the "bitterness, suspicion and distrust" which General Donovan in a recent communication to the Allied Chiefs of Staff has described as characterizing Greek feeling towards Great Britain today, but also the consequences of this feeling along with other factors, and chiefly the likelihood that if Great Britain remains in the forefront here, playing her old game of power politics with inadequate means, while we remain aloof, the whole area will eventually fall under the dominating influence of the only other great power in the vicinity, namely Russia. To keep Russia and Britain from eventually conflicting in this region, the Balkan States may be reconstituted as genuinely free and friendly to both sides. But this is not likely to be done by either interested power, and only we are sufficiently trusted by all concerned (still sufficiently trusted, I believe) to undertake it. Present military strategy may well be against our diverting troops to the Balkans, but surely the grand strategy of world peace hereafter counsels that what is done to reconstruct this region be done under our direction. Are we to fight a war and sacrifice for victory the aims we seek to win? Where then will be the victory? To save precisely that for which we all have made such sacrifices, the one disinterested power among the three left standing should take the initiative where the interests of the other two clash. The Balkan peoples' sentimental instincts run true to expediency in this matter, where expediency and sentiment coincide on the highest plane. They want to be saved by America, knowing well that the preponderance of power in Europe will certainly drag them to Russia's side if we sell them down the river to the British. I would say then, give us an American commanding general, whatever be the decision about the number of American troops and the constitution of an allied staff. Let it be known that America is running the job, and our operations will benefit from a popular allegiance which no other tactics can secure, and without which only a relative success, which in so important a matter must be tantamount to failure, can possibly be foreseen.

I think this should be enough for one letter, considering that it is written to the world's busiest man! I have not forgotten your request that I write you my ideas about what is the best form of government Greece could have, and will do so, but at another time. For the present, the question seems to pose itself as to whether Greece, and Yugoslavia too, for that matter, is likely to be able to have any government at all, after this war, which will correspond to the essentially non-communist predilections of its people. You are probably right in thinking that in the long run Yugoslavia will prove more of a mess than Greece. Its blood-feuds and mixture of races and religions seem to make this almost certain. As to what we can do in the matter, I don't see how we can escape our present policy of giving military support to the faction which is fighting against the Germans, but this should not blind us to the truth that in so doing we are, indeed, arming a faction, and that evil will come of it later as sure as shooting—Yugoslav shooting. Furthermore, the current British tendency to mix political with military support to Tito, of which you as well as the Department are doubtless aware, seems calculated to increase the dangers of future trouble. I doubt whether anybody yet has an adequate idea of how the Serbian people, still the vast majority of the Yugoslavs, would react if the King were to sell Mihailović out and adopt the Partisan Government as his own. However, I shall say no more about this here, as the Department advises me that its attitude toward "the resistance movements in Yugoslavia" is actually under review. Personally, I have felt that the Department has been most wise so far in keeping our involvement strictly on the military level.

Affectionately yours,
Lincoln MacVeagh (5)

[And to the Department:]
MOST SECRET February 18, 1944

For the Secretary or Undersecretary.

In connection with the initial or military phase of Balkan relief and reconstruction, I understand that plans are being made for "joint operations," in which, however, American participation is to be on a minor scale. The idea in Washington seems to be at present that the British will provide both the troops and the command, to which some 20 or 25 "Civil Affairs" officers of ours will be attached (see the Department's Greek 19 of February 10, 5 p.m.).[62] Thus the operations envisaged are to be "joint" only so far as concerns responsibility and not repeat not control, which would be in British hands.

I feel very strongly that to allow such a plan to go through would be to commit a great error not only as regards relief and reconstruction but as regards the political future of this whole region. Whatever may be the decision about our sending troops—and the studies made here by General Royce include American troops—that we, and not repeat not the British, should have the command, I believe to be so important that it cannot be exaggerated. Bitterness as regards the British, resentfulness of their lack of tact toward smaller peoples, distrust of their capacity to devote sufficient means to any project, and suspicion as to their political intentions, are so wide-spread as to be practically universal among the Balkan peoples today. These feelings constitute the inevitable aftermath of repeated disillusions in this war, and as things stand, it is beyond the power of the British to conduct any Balkan operation with the same chances for winning Balkan collaboration and allegiance as we. Yet if such collaboration and allegiance are not repeat not secured, and secured promptly, in the operations we are about to undertake, not only will our relief and reconstruction become a farce, but the forces of communism already seeking to profit by the demoralization of the occupied territories will be the certain inheritors of our failure.

I would urgently and emphatically recommend that, whatever joint arrangements may be made as to troops and staff, the supreme command in this matter be given to an American General. In my view, his appointment alone would be worth the sending of many troops, because it would obviate much of the necessity for their presence, and the mere announcement of the decision to nominate an American at the head of things would do more now to raise the morale and promote the unified resistance of the oppressed peoples than any amount of costly propaganda.

This recommendation is the result of careful study since my arrival here last December. I have found the British deeply disturbed over the way

---

[62] Not cited in this text.

they are regarded in the Balkans and by no means eager or confident in regard to this particular phase of coming operations. I believe they would accept our leadership. General Royce has given me leave to quote him as concurring completely. He has himself made a similar recommendation to the War Department in connection with the "favorable atmosphere" necessary for success. Colonel Bellm, in charge of the Economic Section of USAFIME, is also wholly in accord, and last but not least, as being most closely in touch with actual conditions in the occupied areas, Lt. Col. Toulmin, head of the local OSS. I mention these men as the most important examples of competent American opinion, which so far as I have been able to determine is all on the same side. I have read them this telegram, to all of which they agree. Though coinciding, their views and mine have, for the most part, been formed independently.[63]

MACVEAGH (6)

February 21, 1944, Monday

Stevenson told me that Col. Bailey,[64] second-in-command to Armstrong of the British Mission with Mihailović, has come out from Serbia, and that our Captain Mansfield (OSS)[65] has also come out. Another American, Lt. Col. Seitz,[66] has got into Partisan territory, but our third man, Lt. Musulin,[67] is still with Mihailović, and, under General Donovan's present orders, will stay there, though all the British go. He said that the OSS and the SOE have discussed this matter and the British feel it would be a mistake to give Mihailović the chance of exploiting a difference of opinion between the British and us, and thus putting what is strictly a military decision (to withdraw the British liaison officers) on the political plane. I asked Toulmin to come in and he confirmed that he has put this matter to General Donovan, but has recommended—since his job is to gather information—that Musulin stay with Mihailović regardless of what the British do. Political aspects, he said, must be considered by others, not by him. I telegraphed the Department, and said I thought it might well desire to consider these aspects! I also paraphrased and sent to the Department a telegram of Stevenson's to the Foreign Office giving the

[63] MacVeagh apparently attached particular importance to this telegram and kept a copy in his personal papers. Years later he wrote along its margin for the benefit of a researcher: "Amb's plea for U.S. Command in Balkans. No luck with suggestion which if taken might have saved all that which followed."

[64] Colonel S. W. Bailey, SOE, senior Liaison Officer with Mihailović.

[65] Captain Walter R. Mansfield, U.S. Marines, assigned to OSS, was parachuted into Serbia in August 1943.

[66] Lieutenant Colonel Albert B. Seitz, U.S. Army, assigned to OSS, was parachuted with Brigadier C. D. Armstrong into Chetnik territory in September 1943.

[67] Lieutenant George Musulin, assigned to OSS, was parachuted into Chetnik territory in November 1943.

views of Colonel Bailey on the prospects of the Partisan movement in Serbia. He thinks it will not be able, even with British help, to do much against the Germans in Serbia proper, and that after the war there will be a disastrous civil war in that territory, because Mihailović will have about 40,000 fairly well-armed troops backed by the sentiment of most of the peasantry, who will oppose the Partisans bitterly, in the belief that these latter are out to liquidate them, as happened to the Kulaks in Russia. This idea is being fostered by both German and Mihailović's own propaganda, Mihailović himself being convinced that the Chetnik-Partisan struggle is essentially Serb-Croat in its nature, and consequently making a point of constantly coupling the Croats and the Communists in his public utterances.

February 24, 1944, Thursday

Long talk with the Russian Ambassador, whom I went to see at 10:30 to get his views on recent Balkan affairs. We had Turkish coffee together in his hideously rich Egyptian house by the Nile, and he said some interesting things. Particularly I noted his remark that Turkey's neutrality was of definite value to the allies when Russia was weak and retreating, but now that Russia is strong and advancing, it is of definite value rather to Germany. This he said "officially and confidentially" is his Government's view. He emphasized that Turkey "ought to come into the war now, as such action on her part would be of the greatest strategic value," but he admitted that he had no idea of what her intentions may be. Curiously enough, since the Russians—one would think—ought to be informed, he asked me whether we and the British intend taking any large-scale military action in the Balkans. Regarding Yugoslavia, he smoothly said that Russia's policy is the same as ours, to recognize the existing Government and to give military aid to those elements engaged in fighting Germans, and he described the current Moscow press attacks on the Purić government as being merely "opinion," pointing out that our press also prints things which are not connected with the official attitude! He thinks, however, that Purić is being upheld rather by the influence of our attitude (in not taking sides politically) than by his own character and tenacity of temperament, and that eventually his refusal to face the fact that the Partisan movement represents the people will bring him down, while there are plenty of Serbs available who would be willing to form a "popular" government.

February 25, 1944, Friday

Colonel Toulmin came in and told me that while he has received no word from Donovan about withdrawing Lt. Musulin from Mihailović if the British get out (and he has recommended that Musulin be kept in for information purposes) the British C.-in-C. (*Jumbo* Wilson) has ordered *all* allied officers out at once, and this is being flashed to Armstrong at Mihailović's Hq. As Musulin is under Armstrong, he must now come out whatever OSS thinks about it—and thus the British, who want us to act in concert with them in this matter, have "pulled a fast one" to get their way. . . . Purić talked me dizzy about the Yugoslav problem. He is satisfied with the Churchill speech[68]—more or less—, and clearly thinks the nigger in his woodpile is the Moscow government, to the pressure of which he feels sure that the British are yielding. All through his talk the animosity against the Russians and Novikov was apparent. Incidentally, he told me that his Ambassador in Moscow is a "red" and he expects him at any time to resign and join Tito. To Purić, the Tito-Mihailović struggle is essentially one over the issue of Bolshevism, whereas Colonel Bailey told Stevenson that it is essentially one of Croat vs. Serb. But Purić told me he has seen Colonel Bailey and approved of his ideas, which he is to lay before Mihailović in a few days. . . . One thing stands out about Mr. Purić, he is determined. Novikov underestimates him in this respect. And he has an ascendency over the King. I feel that if his government is to be got rid of, it must be forced out; it will not resign. Regarding recent press attacks on him by the Soviets, and falsification of news—as about dissident soldiers said to be arrested by the Purić Government and kept from joining the Partisans—he said he would make no reply, lest he give the Soviets a word of which they could take advantage as giving them offense. "But under normal circumstances, you can imagine what I'd say!" . . .

February 26, 1944, Saturday

Colonel West brought in Captain Mansfield of our Marines and the Mihailović Mission. Mansfield talked with me alone for a long time and I got opinions from him very similar to those of Colonel Bailey. He thinks the trouble in Yugoslavia is primarily racial, not ideological, but that the ideological factor has been brought in and overlaid. There is great resentment in Serbia proper, he said, and even hatred of the British, whose policy is now thoroughly distrusted. Mihailović is a "Messiah" in North Central Serbia, and the rest of Serbia is devoted to his cause, if not in the same degree to him personally. The King is held "sacred," but the Government-in-Exile is despised for living in ease and safety and doing noth-

---

[68] On February 22, 1944, Churchill made a statement in Parliament on his Government's position with regard to Yugoslavia, Greece, Italy and Poland. He praised Tito, in whom "the partisans have found an outstanding leader, glorious in the fight for freedom," and, on the other hand, charged that certain of Mihailović's commanders were collaborating with the enemy. *Parliamentary Debates, 5th Series, House of Commons,* Vol. 397, cols. 692-99.

ing for the people. Evidently the people don't know what championship Purić has tenaciously exercised on Serbia's behalf against foreign pressure. England is regarded as "selling Yugoslavia down the river to the Russians" by the aid she is giving to Tito, but America is still popular, as having no axe to grind. . . . Called on Mr. Leeper, and had a long talk about Greek affairs. [He] said that the latest information is that the truce between warring elements in Greece still holds, though the leaders don't seem to make any progress on getting together. We agreed that "solutions" aren't much good in Greece, since they never hold for long, and that the main thing is that the fighting is stopped, and while they talk may stay stopped! . . . General Royce sent me over documents—copies of telegrams from him to Washington and from the combined Chiefs-of-Staff to General Wilson, this last approving the plans made by Leeper pushing Greek military and political unity; practically agreeing to the Noah's Ark plan; and knocking General Wilson down on proposals of his to back EAM and ELAS further against Zervas and EDES. This represents quite a triumph for Leeper and common sense. Wilson has been out of touch with developments in Greece for some time, and his plan would clearly be a mistake at this time.

February 28, 1944, Monday

Got a letter from Lord Moyne, the new British Resident Minister (in Casey's place), outlining a plan he proposes for U.S. and U.K. coordination in the Balkans and asking me to help set up immediately a Balkan Relief Committee composed of British civil and military authorities, and American ditto. I asked Colonel Keith and Mr. Landis to come over and we had a talk, with the result that Landis will draw up some suggestions of our own. If Lord Moyne agrees to these, we can then ask the Department and the War Department whether they concur in our going ahead. Landis feels the Committee would be helpful if we can get it constructed on the lines we want—i.e. not too much British preponderance, and a secretariat which will represent us both, not the British only. . . . Called on Stevenson before dinner and gave him Mansfield's reaction, somewhat edited from my telegram to the Department, to read. He told me that King Peter and Purić have been "invited" to London, where they will be "given advice." I asked whether pressure will be put on the King to remove Purić, and Stevenson said "Undoubtedly." When I told Peggy of this, she said: "Right in the Hitler tradition." Personally I think they'll have a hard time getting Peter to give up Purić, and the latter has the stubbornness of a mule. So if Churchill wants to gain his point he may indeed have to Hitlerize his unfortunate guests! Stevenson is going along on the party, which will be ready to go "any time after Saturday," and may actually leave early next week. Meanwhile Stevenson has been authorized to signal Armstrong to withdraw all the liaison officers—though he has heard that Donovan has taken up to the combined Chiefs-of-Staff the question of retaining Lieutenant Musulin at Mihailović's headquarters. And at the same time Stevenson has been authorized to serve his proposed note on Purić, telling him of the action taken "by direction of the C.-in-C." and saying that no publicity will be given to this "purely military move." He said he supposes the Yugoslav Government will desire no publicity itself in the matter, and he hopes it will advise Mihailović, too, to keep quiet. He can't see what advantage the latter would gain by letting the facts get out, but who knows? The whole thing sails very close to the political line, and it will be a miracle if it doesn't cross that line sooner or later.

March 2, 1944, Thursday

Had a visit from Stevenson, who told me that the Rumanian "emissary" from Maniu,[69] Prince Stirbei,[70] has come out and is in Ankara with his nephew, the Rumanian Ambassador; also that the C-in-C, Mediterranean, (Wilson) wants to be in [on] our Bulgarian talks, if these come off. . . . Tsouderos talked mostly about the mistakes of the British in dealing with the Greeks, and particularly the Greek Government. He said the Greeks everywhere have felt that Churchill's recent speech dwelt too much on the strife among a few and gave no credit to the courageous resistance of the nation as a whole, or the Navy and Army which have done so well. Also that he should not have talked about Italy, Yugoslavia, and Greece on the same level. Doubtless, Mr. Churchill did not mean to give offense, but it is a matter of what I call "the psychology of alliance." The Greek National Day is coming (March 25th) and Mr. Tsouderos is suggesting to Churchill that the wounds he has dealt unwittingly to the sensitive Greeks may be cured on that occasion by a few well-deserved pats on the back. The "civil war" in Greece is not the whole Greek picture by any means, even if ELAS did kill a British officer once! . . .[71] Mr. Tsouderos harked back to the British habit of ignoring his Government on all occasions, never telling it what goes on in Greece, and so forth. This situation is better now, he said, but just the other day he heard from the press that

[69] Iuliu Maniu, leader of the Rumanian United Opposition Parties, was plotting to overthrow the government of General Ion Antonescu.
[70] Prince Barbu Stirbei, former Rumanian Prime Minister, and Maniu's secret emissary to the Allies.
[71] On October 14, 1943, during a nighttime ELAS attack on an EDES-held village, First Lieutenant W. A. Hubbard, a New Zealander attached to EDES, was killed, probably by accident.

a successful coup had been pulled off by the guerrillas (derailment of a train in the Peneus Gorge), without any previous word having been passed on to him by the British, which would have been so easy. A lot of this is, of course, simply the traditional British lack of graciousness in dealing with allies, particularly small ones. But it is a costly kind of error when multiplied indefinitely and makes and keeps a large part of the world anti-British! Mr. Tsouderos's recent speech about what Greece has done in the war,—a good speech,—was not noticed in a single British paper, and here was actually banned by the censor, till he himself protested. Yet the British are supposed to be supporting the Tsouderos Government, and Mr. Churchill himself asked Mr. Tsouderos not to resign, when he was here recently, but to carry on for the good of all despite discouragements! Strange, but always with us, is this British characteristic of ignoring the feelings of others while still expecting their friendship and assistance. I told Mr. Tsouderos that we also suffer from this kind of thing —the British still tend to treat us as a kind of British colony which somehow got lost, rather than as an independent nation. But we have to remember it is just their way, and represents no evil intentions in our regard.

March 7, 1944, Tuesday

Toulmin told me that Donovan has telegraphed that he agrees completely with my idea about the desirability of an American heading the Balkan relief operations, and wants to know what I wrote the President. I showed Toulmin my telegram to the Secretary (again) and read him (again) the pertinent parts of my letter to F.D.R., and he said he thought that would enable him to give the General all the ammunition necessary. He took the number and date of the telegram and the date of the letter. I said I didn't see how I could give out copies of a letter to the President, even to the OSS, and he agreed. . . . Novikov told me that his instructions as to the Bulgarian and Rumanian emissaries are the same as mine and Stevenson's, to listen to what they may say, and report to his Government. He is suspicious regarding Prince Stirbei's mission. As the Prince is reported to be making the presence of British and American troops near the Rumanian border a condition of action, Novikov sees him as rather the agent of Antonescu than of Maniu, the peasant leader, and he thinks he may be coming out not really to arrange terms for unconditional surrender but simply to find out from our reactions how the land lies and what the allies are planning. In this connection, one should remember that the Germans probably as yet are not at all sure that we may not be intending to make a Balkan offensive, and that if Antonescu could find out definitely whether this is so or not he would have information of incalculable value to Germany. Novikov may be wrong in his suspicions. Stirbei in the last war was instrumental in bringing Rumania in on the allied side. But nevertheless it behooves us to be careful.

March 8, 1944, Wednesday
Before lunch Mr. Tsouderos came in and gave me some documents he has received from Greece,—from the Archbishop, Sofoulis, Gonatas, etc., recommending that the Archbishop be appointed now as Regent to assume office on liberation, with a government to be headed by Sofoulis, and expressing, except for some divergences on the part of the Communists, satisfaction with the continuance of the present Government till that time. He himself (Tsouderos) would be invited to take some post in the new Government. He told me that these documents have convinced him that the King must not go back at once after liberation occurs; that this might be fatal to his throne, but that if he stays away he is sure to be recalled, "perhaps within a year." He asked me to tell the President, as he thinks still that only he and Churchill, and to some extent Smuts, can influence the King in this matter; and he told me he is writing the King his views, and promised to send me a copy of his letter, for me alone,—but I think he would like me to send a copy to F.D.R. He said that he knows there are many royalists in Greece today but they are all 35 years old or over, whilst all the youth is anti-royalist, including his own children.

March 10, 1944, Friday
Lord Moyne's secretary called up and invited me to a conference at his office at 6:30. I went over to the Soviet Embassy and found out that Novikov had also been invited. We figured that either Stirbei has arrived, or Lord Moyne, who is replacing Stevenson as regards the emissaries, desired a preliminary allied conference. . . . Toulmin brought in a Mr. McFarlan, now heading OSS in Turkey. . . . He said Stirbei can't be here now, and later checked this for me, phoning back to Barbour. He described his outfit as not as extensive as the British, but able to do a good deal, and offered to help me with information at any time. . . . He does not think that the Bulgarian emissary flurry is likely to have any early sequel. The Bulgarian Minister has been informed that the Allied Governments are ready here in Cairo to talk, but McFarlan feels that the Minister, though himself probably reliable enough, may not be in close touch with anybody who could act in such a matter. He thinks Bulgarian governmental circles are very much at sixes and sevens at the present time, and that more bombings would do the psychological situation good there,

and crystallize it in favor of some definite move in our direction. . . . Got a long letter from Kohler. He describes my telegram on the Allied Command in the Balkan relief operation as a "Masterpiece," "full of T.N.T.," and says it has had the attention of the highest authorities. But I doubt if it gets us anywhere, for all that! . . . Except perhaps me in a hole. . . . Lord Moyne's meeting turned out to be preparatory, as expected. I took Shantz[72] along, and Moyne is being "briefed" by Steel of the F.O., an old friend of Shantz's. Novikov says he, too, will be assisted by his counsellor. Moyne told me that Stirbei will arrive here next Wednesday, and we shall have a second preliminary talk on Thursday morning, and then perhaps see Stirbei Thursday, at Maadi, where he will be kept for security reasons. After getting back to the office I sent a brief report of this to the Department. At the conference both Novikov and I said we are instructed only to listen to what Stirbei may have to say, and report to our Governments accordingly, but of course we may have other instructions before Thursday. In any case, it will be interesting to see the Rumanian brought face to face with the Russian,—an old rabbit and a young snake! A Department telegram received today says the talks are to be "exploratory," but how much will the Rumanian be able to talk when he sees Novikov in front of him? If, as supposed, he wishes to "explore" how far the British and Americans can be counted on to save Rumania from the Russians (whose armies at Tarnapol are only 100 miles from the Rumanian border) it may be too much for him when he confronts us *tous ensemble.*

March 13, 1944, Monday

The news came in that the ELAS has decided to form a government of its own in the mountains, *à la Tito*.[73] This seems like a bid to blackmail the Tsouderos Government into accepting one of the proposals recently made by EAM that a *joint* government be set up with *some* of the Ministers in Greece. The Tsouderos Government seems certain or rather bound

---

[72] Harold Shantz, Councellor to the U.S. Embassy to the Greek government-in-exile.

[73] On March 16, 1944, an official message from ELAS to Tsouderos announced the formation in "Free Greece" of a "Political Committee of National Liberation" (PEEA) for the purpose of "uniting the national forces for the coordination of the national liberation struggle by the side of the Allies, for the administration of the areas in Greece already free or being freed, and for safeguarding after liberation a smooth and free political life throughout the country." In particular, PEEA would work for the establishment of "the firm foundation of a government of general national unity, interpreting the manifest desire of the people and their armed forces." The message appealed to Tsouderos "to realize the imperative national needs and make an effective contribution to the formation of a government of general national unity." John O. Iatrides, *Revolt in Athens* (Princeton, 1972), p. 44.

to refuse. But will the EAM (which is hiding behind the ELAS in the matter, with a leftist but apparently not communist Colonel named Bakirdzis as titular Prime Minister) then really try to go it alone *à la Tito* with no chance of support from the Allies? Surely the spectacle of Tito's success is encouraging all these people, but the British are far from feeling towards the EAM as they feel toward the Partisan leader. There remains, of course, Moscow. . . . Simultaneously with the news of this guerrilla move, we heard through the British Embassy that the King has told Tsouderos that though his "final decision" must await perusal of the documents sent to London by the Prime Minister, he can say right now that he will certainly not consent to the Regency idea! . . . Leeper came over and we had a long talk. He says that Tsouderos hopes the King will change his mind, otherwise, since the Cabinet and all the "political parties" in Greece have advised him to accept, there will be nothing to do but for the Government to resign. After that the King would find that he can form no Government except from among the old royalists or Metaxists in exile (there are none vocal, apparently, in Greece), and that would be followed by revolts in the Army and Navy. Then, indeed, EAM would be sitting pretty, and its government would be the inheritor of the show. The King also said to Tsouderos that he would be consulting "friends,"—doubtless meaning Mr. Churchill. He might also cable Franklin Delano Roosevelt and so this evening I gave up the idea of telling the latter about Tsouderos' message by airmail and sent off a telegram, giving simply the gist for his information in case he should be consulted and wonder what it's all about. No *advice* this time! My previous letters should give him the background, and I did say in my letter that this time the question lies between the King and his own government and not between him and the British. . . . Colonel Toulmin came in and told me that General Wilson has issued orders putting the Yugoslav and Albanian divisions of Force 133 under the Command of Algiers rather than Cairo, thus taking control of secret operations in Yugoslavia out of Stevenson's hands. . . . He apparently has displeased Mr. Churchill by his constant advice against plunging into internal Yugoslav affairs on the Partisan side.

March 14, 1944, Tuesday

Archer brought in Mr. Jackson, Governor Lehman's deputy, who has just arrived. The Governor himself is expected Friday or Saturday. . . . We talked UNRRA problems, particularly the first or Military phase, and I learned that when Jackson left the States,—not so long ago,—the War Department was absolutely categorical about not sending troops, and about lending only 25 Civil Affairs Officers to help the British. "The

Balkan operation is not a military one, and will not help to win the war." Whether or not it may help to avert a future war, or may even, if badly handled, help to bring on future conflict, short-term military thinking leaves out of the picture; and the typical soldier seems to pride himself on being so short-sighted. "It won't help to win the war." Granted; but what are we going to win the war for? . . . Jackson shares Archer's doubts about Landis's Balkan Supply Council, and Moyne's proposed Balkan Relief Committee. They seem to feel that these things in some way may hamper UNRRA . . . or steal its thunder, or duplicate its responsibility. We tried to figure out the necessity for the Council and failed, and I must say that I cannot see a *necessity* for the Committee either. . . . Sent the Department a wire about Wilson's order on the secret operations business, commenting on Stevenson's apparent punishment at the hands of the Great Man, and also asking what it means that political affairs as regards Yugoslavia will be handled in Algiers, under arrangements to be made with the British and American "Resident Ministers." I wonder where the American Ambassador to Yugoslavia comes in—or whether the Department is allowing Mr. Churchill to bowl me out as well as Mr. Stevenson. Incidentally, the Department has sent me a wire saying that Mr. Churchill has informed Mr. Roosevelt that Mr. Macmillan[74] in Algiers will handle the British side of talks with Bulgaria. There is another of Stevenson's jobs gone! I begin to wonder whether he will come back here,—to do what? Be, like me, a messenger-boy for his Foreign Office perhaps and a well-spanked one into the bargain? We shall see.

March 15, 1944, Wednesday

Had a long visit from Admiral Vasiliadis,[75] who said he had met me in Athens at the house of Mrs. Alexandris (wife of the ex-Foreign Minister). The Admiral was aide to Koundouriotis[76] and a devoted follower of Venizelos. He has just escaped from Greece. . . . He talked a good deal about politics, and I have learned from an OSS report that he expects to "work on me" because of my "weakness!" So I told him I was glad to have his views, and praised his report, but made it clear that the United States Government does not take, and never has taken, since I have been connected with it, any sides in the internal affairs of the country. . . . In the afternoon I went over to Mr. Tsouderos' office for a talk, and Parsons went to the British Embassy to Greece. The confirmation has come in of the EAM's new "government" having been set up, and the text of a

[74] Right Honorable Harold Macmillan, British Minister Resident, Allied Forces Headquarters, Algiers (1942-1944), Caserta (1944-1945).
[75] Admiral Gerasimos Vasiliadis (retired), liberal politician.
[76] Admiral Paul Koundouriotis, President of the Greek Republic, 1924-1925.

proclamation, which will not be officially broadcast, Mr. Tsouderos told me, till it "seeps out" otherwise. Parsons got the text from Waterhouse. The Prime Minister talked about the King's situation and emphasized that this new development makes it all the more desirable that the King accede to the Regency proposals, as a rift between the King on the one hand and his Government and the political parties in Greece on the other would give the new "Government" a fortuitous strength it would otherwise lack. He also said that if the King refuses, he does not see how he, Tsouderos, can "hold" his Government, and if he can't, he will have to resign himself. The King would then be faced with the necessity of forming another government, which he might do with political non-entities, or non-politicians, in London, but hardly otherwise; and thus he might fall into the position of King Peter at present: the British would go on recognizing his Kingship, but would also have to recognize that the situation in Greece presented only one opportunity for continuing resistance to the Germans, and consequently would adopt ELAS as they have done Tito! Parsons said he believes Leeper put this possibility into Tsouderos's head, and it looks like something with which they might be able to scare the King. . . . Clearly the situation as it stands today is critical for the King's chances. . . . Learned from Lord Moyne's office that Stirbei has arrived. Conversations will begin Friday, and we may have a preliminary meeting tomorrow afternoon again. The British are hoping for further instructions from London.

March 16, 1944, Thursday

Chester of the AP came in in the morning and told me that the secrecy of the Stirbei mission has been "blown." Articles about it have appeared in the London papers (also, I hear, the BBC broadcast the "news") and in consequence General Paget[77] at a Press Conference this morning told the correspondents confidentially all that we know about the matter, which of course is not much. At the same time censorship on outgoing reports from here has been clamped down, so that the boys, even if one of them would wish to violate this confidence, cannot answer the queries they are getting from their home offices. . . . Lunch with the Leepers at their apartment. Mr. Leeper told me that the Stirbei story was broken by some journalist in Ankara, and that the British have felt that the only way to handle it now is to treat it openly as another one of these stories of peace moves which are so common today and not try to conceal anything but the actual conversations themselves. We talked, of course, of the Greek situation, and he said that Tsouderos has told him definitely that he will resign if the King refuses the Regency proposal, and that he,

[77] General Sir Bernard Paget, British Commander-in-Chief, Middle East.

Leeper, has so informed the Foreign Office. Late in the afternoon there was another preparatory conference on the Stirbei matter at Lord Moyne's office. The "aged emissary" has been lodged in Gezira, since there were too many stairs to climb at the house in Maadi. We were given the address and the hour, 11 a.m. tomorrow.... I had a long talk with Lord Killearn[78] about the Egyptians and his difficulties here. He is a hearty cheerful satrap of the old school, with no patience for the follies of incompetence and backwardness.

March 17, 1944, Friday

Conference with Prince Stirbei at Soliman House in Gezira. Lord Moyne and Mr. Steel, Novikov and his counsellor, Shantz and I and Colonel Masterson, Secretary of the group, all sat about a table with pads and pencils and listened to the courtly prince, who is said to be the father of several of Queen Marie's children. We carried on in French, for Novikov's sake. No handshaking, merely bows, to begin with and to end the "conversation." Stirbei was asked by Lord Moyne whether he had anything to say about unconditional surrender, and he then read a statement about what his friends would be prepared to do, and what assurances they would like to have. Then he was told that we would communicate his proposals to our Governments, while he remains here. To this he replied that he can't go back to Rumania anyway. He did not seem to notice Novikov any more than the rest of us, and clearly showed that he recognizes that the Russians are the only ones who are likely to be able to enter the country with any force, though, should the Rumanians come over to us, or make a *coup d'état* with that in view, British and American air support would be expected as well as sabotage operations in Bulgaria and Hungary, if these latter countries should attack Rumania. The minutes of the meeting will be drawn up by the British and gone over and o.k.'d by Novikov and me, but meanwhile I sent the Department a preliminary report from my notes, briefly as follows: Stirbei represents only Maniu, but knows Antonescu's ideas, and the Government and the King and the Opposition all desire a change of front. The Government under Antonescu, who "knows the war is lost" and would "like to save his own skin," could best conduct the movement, as it could organize it secretly under the noses of the Germans, by whom it is trusted, and thus get perhaps ten or fifteen divisions into the fray. But Maniu will make a *coup d'état*, if the Allies want something immediate, and even if not very successful this would doubtless have a good effect in dislocating German defense against the Russian advance. Only, the Rumanians would like assurances that (1) their independence will be maintained and (2) their

---

[78] Sir Miles Lampson (Lord Killearn), British Ambassador to Egypt.

territorial rights respected. (3) They want assurances, too, that we shall accept them as co-belligerents (disastrous effects of that Italian nonsense!)[79] and (4) help them against Hungary and Bulgaria if these attack. The Russian asked, "What do you mean by territorial rights" and Stirbei replied, "That covers Transylvania," but added that the Bessarabian question should be settled later, no matter what has to be ceded now (probably up to the Pruth line), by a plebiscite; and that Rumania has no claims to the part of the Dobrudja ceded to Bulgaria in 1940. He said also that the Germans have only 40,000 troops in Rumania at present, but that these control all strategic points, air-fields, and the railways on the Bessarabian side of the country. . . . At the end he said he could communicate with his principals through Cretianu, the Rumanian Ambassador in Ankara. . . . When he had left the room the Russian expressed the view that all that he had to say amounts to very little, but Steel and I said he had gone further than we expected. Doubtless there is nothing final about his demand for assurances, and a couple of them should not be difficult to give—the independence one (No. 1) and No. 4. . . . Call in the afternoon from Mr. Venizelos, who wanted to emphasize that it is most important that the Government-in-Exile be supported vis-à-vis the new "Provisional Government" of EAM. He wants no military supplies to be sent to that outfit for the present, and has seen Leeper; but I wonder if Leeper can control the Military! The situation begins to take on a Tito-like aspect, and this will become definitely so if the King turns down the Regency proposals of the Archbishop and the political parties. Venizelos and Tsouderos both spoke of the reply sent by the latter to the "Provisional Government," which had asked the Cairo Government to amalgamate with it. The reply, as I reported in a telegram yesterday, was that the political parties must be consulted. This seemed a good reply to Leeper, and Tsouderos is delighted with himself. It gains time, and prevents a rift opening between the parties and the Government, which is doubtless desired by the EAM.

March 18, 1944, Saturday

The Department cabled some information about Stirbei's being in touch with Antonescu, which we knew already. But it added that it would like me to give any reactions of mine or my colleagues. This will mean another telegram on my part. The British reaction is that they feel Stirbei's

[79] Following the capture of Sicily and the allied landings in southern Italy on September 2, 1943, the government of Marshal Pietro Badoglio at Brindisi, which had replaced Mussolini's régime in July 1943, surrendered "unconditionally." However, at Churchill's insistence, the Brindisi government was allowed to function as the Government of Italy and was accepted as a co-belligerent.

talk went somewhat further toward meeting us than Maniu is really willing to go, to judge from their reports from their agents; while the Russian feels that he said nothing which gets us any further. Steel expressed today a good deal of annoyance with the Russians. If they would only put forward some terms of capitulation, or armistice, or what not, he feels the Allies could make use of them in breaking down the whole Balkan set-up, but as it is they are blocking developments which might greatly help the collapse of Germany before we have to lose too many lives in a Western offensive! But he said, of course they don't care about that.

March 20, 1944, Monday

Because the Department had telegraphed me for the comments of my colleagues (and my own, incidentally), I called on Novikov to see what he might say about Stirbei's performance the other day. He said he thinks the thing lacks practicality—Stirbei has no credentials even as regards Maniu, and his connection with Antonescu is even more tenuous. Furthermore, Stirbei admitted that a *coup d'état* would be speedily quelled by the Germans. Therefore it seems that only an approach on Antonescu's part could really mean anything. In addition he ridiculed the Emissary's talk about Allied landings at Constanza, saying that this would present the utmost difficulties, since Russia's naval bases are in the Caucasus, and those of the Allies even further away.... Went over to see Lord Moyne, and found him more optimistic than Novikov about the Stirbei affair. He thinks we need not worry about the Emissary's lack of credentials, and that if we sent word back that should the Rumanians "work their passage," their independence will be all right, though we can't talk boundaries now, this might lead to Antonescu's getting out "to save his skin" after turning over the government to Maniu for the purposes of the required *volte face*. However, Lord Moyne has yet made no comments to London, as he is awaiting General Wilson and Mr. Macmillan, who are expected today, and they may have some views.... Worked up two long telegrams, on the Rumanian and Greek situations. My own views on the Rumanian matter, I said, were rather like Lord Moyne's than Novikov's. It seems to me there may be a chance, at least, of our capitalizing on the present defection in Rumania—and this must be pretty strong to bring together such "strange bedfellows" (Lord Moyne's expression) as Maniu, the Peasant Leader, Stirbei, the liberal, and Antonescu, the reactionary. In any case I said I thought our conversations so far had elicited two facts, that defection is common to all parties, and that a *coup d'état* does not promise anything like equal results with a reversal of the government (on the Badoglio model). This would appear to be something gained, even if it is decided not to pursue the matter further here. . . . The other telegram, on the Greek problem, was drafted by Parsons and worked over by Shantz and me. It gave the gist of the messages to and from Tsouderos and the new *Political Committee*, and of Tsouderos to Sofoulis. Tsouderos returns a soft answer to the Committee, which called upon him to take it into partnership, as it were, and passes the buck to the politicians. Meanwhile the Committee has been given charge of the ELAS forces by EAM and has issued a proclamation establishing the People's National Army of Liberation. It is all very Tito-esque. And now we shall see whether the King will refuse collaboration with the politicians, and thus throw his Government, and the politicians too, out of the picture, which will then be all EAM!. . . I managed to get my letter to Franklin Delano Roosevelt into typed form at last, but it can't go off till tomorrow. I hope he will understand, from my explaining the entirely internal nature of the Greek Government versus King problem, that he should not advise "Georgie" to do anything but listen to his own advisers and decide for himself. But who knows how the King may put the matter up, and how the President's sympathies may be aroused.

Cairo, March 17, 1944

Dear Franklin:—

I was sorry to bother you again about the King of Greece—and this time by telegram.[80] But the Prime Minister himself requested it, coming to my office with hat in hand. Now I have been able to get hold of a copy of his letter to King George, to which my telegram referred, and enclose

[80] On March 13, 1944, MacVeagh telegraphed Roosevelt that Tsouderos wished the President to know that "on the basis of widespread advices from political leaders and other competent persons in occupied Greece" he had advised King George that "he should certainly and at once authorize the appointment of a Regent to exercise Governmental powers in Greece from the moment of liberation until a plebiscite may determine the question of the régime." Archbishop Damaskinos was being proposed as Regent. Moreover, "The Prime Minister wants you to know this, he says, because he believes you to be interested in the King's fate and he emphasizes his hope that the King will consent. If he does not the Prime Minister believes the cause of the monarchy will be lost in the situation now prevailing which he describes as being 'controlled by Leftist elements and the armed guerrillas in the mountains.'" MacVeagh concluded: "It is clear that the Prime Minister fears that the King may again appeal to you this time in a question which lies not between him and the British as was the case when you were here but between him and his own Government. The Prime Minister said to me that the only people to whose advice the King will listen are you and Mr. Churchill and to a certain extent General Smuts. As the King is in London he will probably be consulting Mr. Churchill presently." *FR 1944*, V, 87-88.

it herewith[81] feeling that even though you may not care to read it, you may like to have it in your files as an example of how Prime Ministers write to Kings,—Balkan style.

On the other hand, if you have time you may find it interesting to glance at. This new flare-up of the king problem in Greek affairs was, of course, foreshadowed in my letters to you of last winter. In the hands of the Prime Minister it has become a purely internal problem, and what is at issue now is the King's taking advice, not from the British but from his own Government, based on a wide survey of opinion recently made within the country. The counsel now given to him to set up a Regency to administer affairs in Greece from the moment of liberation until a plebiscite can determine the question of the regime, comes from all the political parties as well as from military and other leaders canvassed by the Archbishop of Athens. It happens to run contrary to the King's feeling that the "plebiscite" of 1935 gave him a mandate from his people, and so his first reaction, in answer to a telegram from the Prime Minister, has been to indicate that he will refuse. But he is postponing his final decision against receipt of the Archbishop's and other documents, and the outcome of conversations with "friends."

Should the King accept the solution offered him, the Prime Minister professes to think that eventually, and perhaps even very soon, feelings will change in Greece, as so often happens, and the King will be recalled at the popular desire. But for the present he underlines strongly the unwisdom of trying to oppose "the existing situation" and to stem a "mistaken tide" of opinion dominated by "leftist elements and the guerrillas in the mountains."

Should on the other hand the King refuse, the Prime Minister, who with his government has given full support to the proposed solution, has told me that he would not be able to keep his Government from resigning and that he himself, in consequence, would have to go too. This, he added, would leave the King with no possibility of forming another Government which would have any effective support either within or without the country, while there would be trouble in the Armed Forces, and the "Political Committee" which is now aspiring to emulate Tito in Greece, and which is certainly controlled by Communist elements, would be the gainer.

The Prime Minister is therefore hoping that the King will play ball, and that the political parties and the Cairo Government can achieve the desired solidarity against the subversive elements now dangerously active in the country. The State Department is fully advised of the situation,

---

[81] This enclosure has not been located; the text of Tsouderos' letter to King George, dated March 8, 1944, can be found in E. Tsouderos, *Ellinikes Anomalies sti Mesi Anatoli* (Athens, 1945), pp. 87-91.

which we are closely watching. So far as Greece is concerned, we are mostly busy here, of course, with the relief picture, while we observe and report on the politics of the hour. I don't wish to burden you with details, but this whole little drama, insofar as it may (if played badly) cost a king his throne and a whole people some agony, has something moving about it, which I am sure you will appreciate.

Now, as to your suggestions regarding the proper constitution for Greece. I entirely agree that a King "above the melee" is desirable if a King is to be had at all, and also that the three-party limitation you outline for the Parliament would be most helpful in avoiding some of the worst consequences of the political instability of the Greeks. Indeed, this latter suggestion might even be adopted, and work. But as to the "constitutional monarch," while such a position might be written into the constitution even more clearly than it is today, it could never be filled satisfactorily in Greece except by the rarest of individuals. The trouble is that no Greek will ever believe that a "head man" can't do things if he wants to, whatever may be the rules, and no such "head man" can survive in Greece unless he is accessible. Therefore a successful Greek king, no matter how "constitutional" he may be on paper, must have a very special character if he is to get along successfully with his subjects. He must, in fact, know how to be affable and reserved at the same time, and must combine Nordic strength with Mediterranean tact and indirection. The present King's grandfather was such a man, and reigned successfully for 60 years. But he was a case of sheer luck,—in every sense a "sport,"—and what is wanted is a system which will work normally. It may be, as you say, that a tiny country like Greece acquires prestige abroad if it has a king, though I am inclined to think that Greece is somewhat of an exception and will always have a peculiar prestige of her own which many great empires have risen and fallen without acquiring. But for her current well-being, given the character of her people, I would be inclined to favor a republican system on the American model, which allows of the "head man" being changed periodically, though not every day. So far as I know, this is the only system that has not been tried in Greece at some time or other since the ancient Greeks began the discussion of political theory which continues to this day.

One word more, regarding Yugoslavia. The developments which I have been able to see and report from here, however partial in the whole picture, have included some remarkable British maneuvers leading up to what looks very like positive intervention in internal affairs of the country. If indulged in, such intervention is likely to have repercussions long after the war is over, and whatever one thinks of it—my last word from the Department is that our policy is still "under review"—it will make history. It would seem to be as true of folly as of evil that it lives after us, and therefore it is to be hoped that it is not folly to run so counter to the idea you expressed to me here, of letting the Yugoslavs fight their internal differences out among themselves while keeping our own action on the purely military level against the common enemy. However, you are so much better informed about this matter than I am that I can have few if any coals to bring to your Newcastle.

Not to make this letter too long, I will only add that I have indeed met your friend the Crown Prince of Egypt, and found the "old globe-trotter" delightful, sartorially as well as personally. I gave him your message and he volunteered that you appeared to him "neater" than Mr. Willkie, and that you talked and acted like a gentleman,—which seemed to me pretty good coming from one so little removed from the dubious Albanian origins of the great Mohamed Ali. Finally, for your amusement here is a South African Press cutting, sent by one of my "boys" down there, who for some reason thought it gave him cause for congratulating me! It is from the Pretoria *News* of January 22, 1944.

"Lieut.-Colonel E. A. Biden, of Johannesburg, formerly Commanding Officer of the S.A.A.F. tactical reconnaissance squadron, has returned to the Middle East for duty after a protracted stay in the United States, says Sapa's special correspondent in Cairo.

"Lieut.-Colonel Biden was sent 'on loan' to the United States Army Air Force to instruct and assist in the opening of a big fighter reconnaissance and army support school.

"During his stay in the United States, he was invited to the White House. President Roosevelt asked him many questions about South Africa, and he was amazed at the President's vast knowledge of the Union."

Affectionately yours,
Lincoln MacVeagh (7)

March 21, 1944, Tuesday

General Giles[82] brought General Chickering (out from Washington with the UNRRA people on a look-see trip for "Civil Affairs") and Colonel Breckinridge along to my office for a meeting which Landis wanted, on UNRRA matters, before Lehman's arrival. But Lehman has broken his knee-cap now, and won't be coming. However, we had a lot to talk about, and I asked Harry Hill and Mr. Shantz to sit in. The chief subject discussed was the manner and extent of American Military participation with the British in the coming Balkan relief operation. It seems clear that my suggestion of American command will not go through, as the Department says, "for strategic reasons." But General

[82] Major General Benjamin F. Giles, Commanding General, U.S. Armed Forces, Middle East.

Giles suggested a joint system whereunder we would have equal authority as well as responsibility in all matter touching policy—leaving the British to look after the mechanics of the operation, and if this can be put through against [the] possible objection of General Wilson and others, it should answer the requirement I had in mind, at least to a great extent, that we should not be saddled with responsibility for a job over which we have no control.... Giles is going to talk with Wilson about this matter, and then refer his suggestion to Washington. I am naturally strongly in favor, but I could see that Landis doesn't like sticking his neck out. He wondered if our ideas don't run counter to policy decided on already. But I feel that should not deter us if we think we are right; and it is our duty to say what we think.

March 22, 1944, Wednesday

I had calls from Mr. Chester of the AP in the morning, and from Mr. Joyce of the OSS who has just come back from Bari. He says the Partisans are getting "out of hand" in Italy [brought there for medical treatment and other purposes] presuming to act as an "independent" group and not follow orders from the Allied Command. One of them said to him: "We are a sovereign state." They profess to be planning a democratic Yugoslavia after the war, with free press, free elections, private property, and individual enterprise, but actually they operate among themselves very closely on the Russian model, with commissars, secret service, and liquidation all complete. Obviously Britain's support to Tito has gone to the heads of his followers, if not to his own. Joyce said that the OSS and SOE in Italy are now quite unable to handle them and that an Allied Military Mission will probably be set up to keep them in order there.... Lunch with Mr. Macmillan at the *Auberge du Turf*. Leeper, Broad,[83] and Macmillan's secretary were the others at our table.... Our lunch was very pleasant, but hardly of a "business" nature, though I found out that Macmillan feels as I do about the "short term" military view in Balkan affairs. Also that Leeper feels he has killed the British idea of using native or Indian troops, and that Broad's belief is that the London talks will prove the impossibility of getting the King and Tito together. "The only thing likely to be gained is perhaps a new Government which will not be always obstructing us."... The Department answered my cabled query about General Wilson's proposal to have the political side of special operations in Yugoslavia handled by "the British and American Resident Ministers in Algiers." The Department says it presumes this has to do with an advisory "Committee" on which General Wilson would

[83] Philip Broad, Counsellor to the British Embassy to the Yugoslav Government-in-exile.

have a representative from the offices of such Ministers, but that the matter is being discussed with our Mr. Wilson, now in America, and that in any case "close coordination" would be maintained with me! Not very satisfactory, and I don't think the Department felt very easy in sending this message. But the whole situation is confused. When I asked Macmillan if he thinks Stevenson will come back here, he replied that he is wondering whether the Yugoslav Government itself will do so. Perhaps we are now at the beginning of the end of my Yugoslav mission.... Macmillan told me a nice story about Churchill. When he was asked whether he did not think this was a great improvement over World War I, in the sense that we now have the benefit of joint Chiefs-of-Staff and joint operations all along the line, he grunted: "No, I don't agree. If you put together in one room the most gallant sailor, the most intrepid soldier, and the most daring aviator, the result of their deliberations will be the sum of their fears." ... To conclude, Macmillan substantiated what Joyce told me about the behavior of the Partisan Yugoslavs in Italy, and remarked that he feels our strictly military policy in the Balkans is getting us into a lot of trouble. It was all right when there was doubt of final victory, but now we should begin to think and act for the future. If he means by our "strictly military" policy the policy now being pursued by Churchill with Tito, and the old MO-4 policy toward the Greeks, now being continued to some extent by General Wilson against Leeper's better judgment, I agree. He thinks the Russians are trying to divide the British and Americans in order to profit themselves from our confused counsels.

March 23, 1944, Thursday
Dinner at Lord Moyne's, "for men only," Peggy staying at home. General Wilson was there, and I had a few words with him about old times in Athens.... General Giles told me that he has got nowhere with General Wilson on the matter of an independent joint American authority in the Balkan relief operation. Wilson told him squarely that the American officers would be under Hughes's command and would do as Hughes told them, serving in such positions as he might determine. If this idea goes through, Giles sees no use in having the Americans in the show at all. They will only serve to make the affair Anglo-American in name, and give us the co-responsibility without any measure of control—which is what I have been against all along. Giles wants to talk to Hughes, and after that, plans to put his views before the War Department.

March 24, 1944, Friday
Steel came in and told me that the British had news from Moscow that Molotov has taken the same view of Stirbei's Mission as Novikov did,

namely that the emissary represents no one and the only useful contact would be with Antonescu direct. However, a word from Antonescu came in to Stirbei the day before yesterday: he has been summoned to see Hitler and must have some answer as to what the Allies are ready to do. So, as the time was short, the British got Wilson in on the matter, and as Allied Commander in the Mediterranean, the latter sent a message back to Antonescu not to go to Hitler, but to get busy and throw his lot in with the Allies; "only results will count," and the German position in South Russia is very serious indeed just now, so that results might be obtained. . . . I informed the Department of this move at once; though it did seem to me rather queer that the British consulted with neither Novikov nor me before they made it, still Wilson is an *Allied* Commander, and there is no question that "time is of the essence" just at present. However, this afternoon Novikov came in to see me in considerable dudgeon. He had just learned from the British of Wilson's message, and obviously he wanted to find out if I had been ignored too. I told him of my surprise but that I figured the message could do no harm, as it said nothing which would compromise the Allies while at the same time it urged action favorable to us. However, Novikov remained sore, and highly conscious that the right procedure had not been followed. Furthermore, he pointed out that though Wilson might be Allied Commander-in-Chief in the Mediterranean, the Rumanian front is in the Eastern, not the Mediterranean, theatre. . . . Something in that!

March 27, 1944, Monday

Long talk with Robert [Richard] Weil,[84] the OSS man, in the morning, with Joyce and Shantz joining in. Weil feels that we ought to give Tito more support, and that his movement is spreading throughout Yugoslavia and will eventually control it. We ought, if not to recognize Tito diplomatically, at least to grant him some sort of political contact, and encouragement, as the British have done, and the Russians, if we don't want to lose out with the Yugoslavs. Tito complains that he has had correspondence with Churchill and Stalin, but not with Roosevelt. . . . Weil's talk was very interesting on the military side, but on the political he seemed to me to leave the big questions unanswered. How strong is the Serb opposition to Tito, and to what extent is it rooted in nationalism? His idea that the other groups in Yugoslavia will just naturally throw in their hands and join Tito if they see him getting the support of all the great powers, is perhaps too easy. In any case, he didn't convince

[84] Major Richard Weil Jr., OSS, attached to Tito's Partisan headquarters at Drvar (February-March 1944).

me that our policy should be other than hands off internal problems....
[Saw] Governor Lehman at Kirk's house in town, at 4 o'clock. He is in bed with his leg in a plaster cast, but mentally is very fit, and eager to get at UNRRA problems. I told him what I know of the situation, which isn't much. I advised him to get the Russians more into the picture, and certainly to see Novikov. Also to see Leeper, particularly as regards the choice of a man to head the UNRRA here.... Shantz went over to see Steel and brought in the news that Molotov has now told the British that while his Government takes a dim view of the Rumanian Government, which is "even worse" than the Finnish and Hungarian Governments, it is willing to "explore Antonescu's status," whatever that means, and believes that Wilson's message was O.K., but should be added to. The Rumanians should lay down their arms and refuse to fight the Russians, and those who do this on the front, in the Ukraine and the Crimea, will be sent round to Marshal Antonescu to fight for him against the Germans in Rumania; then, too, the Rumanians should concert action with the Russians in detail, using for this purpose an emissary to the Russian command, or perhaps a General from among those now in captivity in Russia.... When Lord Moyne and Steel got the message, Saturday afternoon, they again went ahead and without letting us or Novikov know, or Wilson (now back in Algiers), telegraphed the whole thing in to Maniu, as a message from "HMG"! Only today have they informed us. Again, it seems to me that the need for prompt action justifies what they did, but I shouldn't be surprised if Novikov is again having a fit. A message from his Government to pass right under his nose through British hands and he not know it! ... It appears too, from what Shantz reported, that the two Antonescus went to see Hitler as summoned,—the message from Wilson against compliance not having been received in time. But also it appears that they have got back to Bucharest safely and without having, as yet, turned over the country to the German military. This, from secret messages the British have received.... Got off a long telegram on all this to the Department, and another giving a statement broadcast by Mr. Tsouderos last night, on the new Committee in the mountains and the exchange of messages it had had with the Cairo Government. This only puts into the public domain what we have known for some time. The buck which Bakirdzis passed to Tsouderos, the latter has now passed on to the politicians in Athens. Meanwhile time is gained as decisions are deferred.... The King is doing the same thing, apparently, as regards his own problem. He has made no answer as yet to the letter Tsouderos sent him, and the Archbishop's and other documents. "Stalling," Leeper calls it. But according to Leeper there is no evidence of his having yet consulted Churchill or the FO, "and until he does this we won't offer any advice." *That* is decided.

March 28, 1944, Tuesday

The British received word from London that Molotov approves their having passed his letter on to Antonescu, and also approves of its being communicated to Maniu, should the latter decide to pull his coup. General Wilson has also added his approval. Thus Stirbei is for the moment side-tracked and the whole effort is in military channels and oriented towards Moscow rather than London and Washington. But Stirbei has been useful in getting the thing started, certainly, while any hopes that the Western Allies might be used as protection against the Soviets have been dashed for the Rumanians. . . . We duly advised the Department.

March 29, 1944, Wednesday

Conversation in the morning with two young naval officers who have been with the Greek guerrillas in Euboea; also with Commander McBaine[85] of the OSS. The two boys went in to Euboea to see if they couldn't arrange with the guerrillas for freer exodus of persons desired by the Allies. Such people have had difficulty because most of the Euboea guerrillas are EAM people and have been affected by the prevalent EAM antipathy to the Tsouderos Government and the British. They seem to have accomplished their mission and to have come out with the belief that most of the "andartes" in Euboea are genuine patriots of all parties who have no idea that they may be in the position of being manipulated by a communist clique. . . . They say that German propaganda has brought a lot of Greeks into the Security Battalions who genuinely think that they are fighting Communism now but later will be able to turn against the Germans (!) and are totally misled about the activities of the British and Americans in the country. And they urge that more leaflets be dropped giving the real facts to guide the dazed people. . . . Commander McBaine had a message from Venizelos and Vasiliadis for Sofoulis and Gonatas which Venizelos has asked the OSS to transmit. He wanted my advice on sending it. The message urges the political parties to get together with the Cairo Government, even at the cost of some concessions, and suggests that emissaries come out. The gist of the message is not contrary to Tsouderos' policy at present, and McBaine said it would be "embarrassing" to OSS to refuse despatch. So I said I thought it would be all right, though I could take no responsibility in the matter, and if queried would have to deny all knowledge of it. But I do think that, whether in pulling together or apart, this Greek practice of cabinet officers and premiers (Tsouderos often sending messages through the British, of which his cabinet is in ignorance) acting inde-

[85] Lieutenant Commander Turner H. McBaine, Secret Intelligence section, OSS, Cairo.

pendently of each other on political matters is something to which we should lend no support. Even doing it unofficially and through an organization like the OSS bristles with possibilities of involvement in internal squabbles. McBaine says he will come to me in all future cases of this kind, and I feel the utmost caution is in order, perhaps to the extent of having him make a general rule of "no messages accepted unless they come from the Government itself, and not merely from an individual," to be broken only in the most exceptional cases. . . . A telegram from the Foreign Office to Lord Moyne indicates that the Department is still considering instructions to me on the Stirbei proposals, but meanwhile the soldiers, Russians included, are moving away with the ball. . . . I had a conference with Landis and young Kermit Roosevelt,[86] at the Department's instigation, about relationships with UNRRA. The Department wants to be very careful not to have any impression given that the United States dominates or seeks to dominate UNRRA policy.

March 30, 1944, Thursday

Governor Lehman asked me to come round for another talk at Kirk's house. I found him sitting up in a chair by the window. We talked about the whole subject of the UNRRA Balkan operation in all its phases, but what he wanted particularly to ask my advice about was a visit he is expecting from Major Weil. It appears the Major has a message for him from Tito, who wants UNRRA men to come in to the Partisans now and study relief needs, particularly medical. . . . I told the Governor all I know about Weil and advised him to see Colonel West (the head of OSS here in the absence of Toulmin) before making any decision. I said I thought that Weil is a clever observer, and wants to be impartial, but that he doesn't know the whole picture in Yugoslavia by any means; and furthermore, that while medical help is certainly needed badly in the Partisan area, as elsewhere in the Balkans, Tito's desire for UNRRA people is perhaps not unconnected with his desire for wider contacts with the Allied Powers for political reasons. The Governor seemed to feel that as there is at present no specific territory which can be counted on to remain under Partisan control continually, while the guerrilla war ebbs and flows, the kind of advance information which UNRRA desires might better continue to be gathered by officers such as Weil himself rather than by civilians. . . . He is very anxious to keep out of political entanglements, of course, and I wonder whether sending UNRRA men to Tito and not to Mihailović would not please the former particularly as a kind

---

[86] Kermit Roosevelt, grandson of Theodore Roosevelt and professor of history at the California Institute of Technology, on special assignment with OSS.

of public endorsement of his claim to have established a responsible regime,—if not as yet quite a "sovereign state," as his followers in Bari claim!

March 31, 1944, Friday

Tsouderos came in during the afternoon, and told me that while he feels the new Committee in the Mountains lacks strength with the Greek public (he has received another message from it asking that some sort of amalgamation with the Cairo Government be effected), the news of its formation has excited liberal circles in the Middle East, particularly in certain marginal military and ex-military circles, and he fears that unless he can get some answers from the King, about the Regency, and from the politicians, the commotion may spread to the regular forces. The 1st Brigade is preparing to go to Italy, but still must wait two weeks. To have to take repressive measures would be most unfortunate in the circumstances. He has therefore again cabled the King to give him some reply (though he also advises the King not to return at this time, lest his coming merely add to the turmoil), and he is doing all he can to get the politicians to reply also. Papandreou has acceded to his suggestions but he hears that Sofoulis and Kafandaris are "intriguing." And so the ball goes merrily on! The people who are agitating here now, calling on the Prime Minister to recognize the Committee, are, he said, mostly young officers of leftist tendencies and "old enthusiasts" who have not been retained on active service but infest Cairo with their presence on the loose, and officers and men of the depot battalions which have been formed out of "untrustworthy" elements. But Tsouderos points out that "there are slogans which catch on quickly," and he wants to be able not merely to make radio broadcasts but to do something in the way of promoting a get-together of all parties before this excited criticism goes too far. The thing makes sense. It is clear from four young men who came in to see Parsons today, carrying the petition they gave to Tsouderos, that all the Prime Minister's critics are by no means low-down rabble. However, their enthusiasms if left to boil up in a vacuum, can do much harm.

April 1, 1944, Saturday

The Greek affair took a turn through the arrest of 6 of the 14 officers who called on Mr. Tsouderos yesterday. The others are being sought for. It appears that the Council of Ministers made the decision after Mr. Tsouderos left me yesterday, and the reason given is that the officers exceeded their military authority in presenting political demands to the

Prime Minister. I tried to see Leeper, to get his reaction before telegraphing the Department, but he was seeing Lehman (which I was very anxious for him to do) and Parsons talked with Waterhouse, who said that the British feel the Greek authorities had no choice but to act as they have. The danger is of course that the officers will become, in some sort, martyrs, and that their cause will be joined to the EAMist enthusiasm of the men in the depot battalions and spread to the 1st Brigade,—though the latter's expectations of going to Italy soon may discourage interest in politics at this time. . . . Meanwhile Venizelos broadcast an appeal to the Greeks for unity last night, and it is in all the papers today,—speaking for his "colleagues" and repeating what Tsouderos has already said on the desire of the Government to achieve the broadest possible representative basis. . . . I informed Lord Moyne the other day that the Department thinks his Balkan Supply Committee will not do anything which the Military and UNRRA are not already set to do, and he now replies that he has noted my Government's view but that the Supreme Commander, Mediterranean, has approved his proposals and he has asked his Government for permission to make them to me "formally," which he hopes to do soon. You can't keep an Englishman down!

April 3, 1944, Monday
Got the news from the British in the morning that the Soviets would issue a statement saying that they want no more of Rumania than Bessarabia and Bukowina, and will not interfere in her social structure. The way they put it is that they have no designs on Rumanian territory. But then they consider the 1940 line as the boundary! The announcement was duly broadcast and appeared in the afternoon papers here. Under all the circumstances it is a very fine statement indeed, and should have some effect if anything can in bringing Antonescu over. The British sent him a message this evening again urging him to act, and mentioning this statement as an answer to Rumania's desire for territorial assurances, but adding, too, that while we can help with air support if he comes over to our side, if he doesn't, there will be immediate bombing of all Rumanian communications—as has already taken place in Bulgaria. . . . The message referred to "a clear and generous" statement of Molotov, but when Steel asked me if I saw any objection, I asked to have the "generous" taken out. I think in the circumstances it *is* generous, but I gather from a long background telegram I received this morning that the Department wants very much to avoid commitments on territorial questions, if this is at all possible at this time, and to praise the Soviet statement, which presumes that Bessarabia and Bukowina will become Russian again for good and all after this war, would be in a sense to give assent to a territorial settlement

in advance. It also seemed to me that Antonescu might not feel the statement so "generous," and the telegram would be stronger without a possibly arguable word. So I got Steel to say he'd leave it out. . . . Early in the afternoon I heard that Tsouderos had resigned, and went over to see him, coming in after the local grand Rabbi, who was calling to thank the Prime Minister for the statement about the Jews which we got him to make in support of the President. So Tsouderos said it was my fault that I had to wait a few minutes! . . . He then told me that he has resigned and urged the King to call Venizelos. Since yesterday morning, he said, defections in the military, the navy, and the merchant marine, all stirred up with enthusiasm for the "People's Committee," have multiplied, and by this morning what seemed to him on Saturday an inconsiderable and scattered movement had got quite out of hand. The arrested officers were freed by their own guards this forenoon, and a new Commander of the Garrison took over, while army friends of the Premier's called on him to tell him the situation was hopeless. The 1st Brigade is keeping quiet so as not to lose its opportunity of going soon to Italy, but it too is ready to revolt if the "movement" should need its support. Then, at a cabinet meeting, Tsouderos sensed that his own colleagues were against him! They suggested that he go for a rest to Palestine, or fly to join the King, but in any case made it clear that they would take over. He told me he thinks that they may not have started the "movement" but that they have known about it and have fostered it and used it for their own ends. Now he thinks they may become its servants, and he fears not only the lack of experience and force of Mr. Venizelos, but some stupid action on the King's part. If the latter should say "no" to this resignation, Tsouderos thinks there may well be an anti-royalist outburst, and maybe the declaration of a republic. In any case the EAM will make hay enormously out of what it will regard as a victory over the Cairo Government and the conservative elements. . . . Leeper is sick in bed, so I couldn't see him this afternoon, but Parsons reported that the British Embassy, as much surprised as anybody, thinks the "coup" was engineered by Admiral Vasiliadis, in cahoots with Venizelos on behalf of Sofoulis and Gonatas, in whose interests he recently came out of Greece. It sounds possible. In any event, here is another case of the successful Greek revolution which is always a surprise. The "movements" talked about in advance never work. Personally I regard it as merely the latest phase of the steady swing to the left which began right after Metaxas' death. Tsouderos slowed it down in the interests of a sane middle-of-the-road policy accepting both democracy and King. But the momentum was too great to be stopped. In this view both EAM and the intriguing politicians are merely the external accidents of the reality below. EAM is communist and thoroughly non-Greek essentially, but ostensibly it is a sign of the liberty-seeking trend of the times and has the allegiance of many non-communists and good patriots. Venizelos is a trumpery politician, but anyone of that name would be thrown up as a leader by the advancing wave of anti-Fascism. What the King is going to do now with a Government of the Venizelos ilk, or what he is going to do if he refuses to accept it, remains to be seen. He was impatient and suspicious of Tsouderos, but in losing him he has lost the last leader in active public life among the Greeks of the post-Metaxas reaction who is likely to put up any fight at all on behalf of the Crown.

April 4, 1944, Tuesday

Call from Mr. Theofanidis, the Greek Minister of Merchant Marine. He was alarmed over developments and told me of how his colleagues have been barred from their offices by soldiers requiring them to sign statements of adherence to the "People's Committee" in Greece. British soldiers apparently straightened out this situation later and I heard that when Theofanidis got to his office he had "protection." The British are of course in charge of military security here and the operations of the Greek armed forces, as they are of the Yugoslavs. . . . General Giles called, along with General Chickering, to talk relief arrangements. He has worked out a scheme with UNRRA and the AML[87] (British Liaison outfit) which is satisfactory all round, providing for the coordination of the American Civil Affairs officers with the British in the "first phase" of the Balkan relief operations. Now he is going to Algiers, on the first leg of a long swing by air round the continent, and will try to sell the scheme to General Wilson. He will give me a typed copy later, but meanwhile assured me that it provides for freedom on the part of American officers to present their minority opinions to higher American authority. Without that we should indeed have "responsibility without control." Now, if their opinions are sound, the War Department can know of them, and take measures accordingly,—which gives us some opportunity of control, at least. . . . We also talked about Moyne's proposed committees. I explained the state of suspense in which the "Balkan Relief Committee" stands at present, and that the "Balkan Affairs Committee" has not yet been made the subject of approach to us. We agreed that such a committee should be small, composed only of top men out here, and make its recommendations to the Governments at home for approval and transmission to the military, rather than to the military direct,—otherwise the Generals concerned might find themselves with conflicting directives

[87] AML: Allied Military Liaison.

from uncoordinated sources. However, I advised him not to worry about this Committee as it is very nebulous at present, and will be well vetted in Washington before it takes form. I am sure the interests of good military functioning will be taken care of as well as other aspects. . . . Had a long talk with an enthusiastic Greek Committee, made up of lawyers and ex-deputies from Chios, Mytilene, Chalcidice, and Thessaly, as well as Egypt, some of them liberals, others democrats, and one communist. All convinced that EAM represents the fighting people of Greece and not any one party, and all believing that the Government should be composed of men who have taken part against the Axis, and not of the old-line politicians, who have some of them collaborated with the Security Battalions, and none of them done anything active in the defense of their country. A good crowd, though they may be a bit sanguine about the EAM! They wanted to protest against the British action in arresting people these last days, but I told them that this is a matter for the Governments concerned, (British and Egyptian) and got them to talking about their own ideas, which is what I was interested in. . . . Harding came in and I advised that he should go to Alexandria to see what is going on, or not going on, in the Greek Navy. . . . Called on Leeper in the afternoon and learned that the British Military have put several hundred Greek officers and men under "preventive" arrest. Leeper is very angry with the Greeks and his mild demeanor was lost as his eyes flashed fire, once or twice. "We wouldn't allow this in England, and we won't here!" While I was with him, his Mr. Warner brought in the news that the King has said that he will talk about Tsouderos's resignation when order is restored, and meanwhile instructs Venizelos to come to London and explain the situation! Rather clever, but Leeper said that any Greek will say that the King is "funking his job" by not coming straight back to Cairo in this emergency. The King also asked Agnidis, the Greek Ambassador in London, to request the British to intervene for order's sake. Of course the British have done so on their own already, but I doubt if this move of the King's will be made public by Mr. Tsouderos. The Greeks are too sensitive about his turning to foreigners at every juncture, and this, like his turning to Churchill and Franklin Delano Roosevelt for advice last fall (still a secret) is something well calculated to sink him even further than he finds himself already in their affection and esteem. . . . Leeper also told me that Mr. Venizelos has been so frightened by the forces he has attempted to exploit in this crisis that he today begged Mr. Tsouderos to take back his resignation, and asked for a British guard in Alexandria, where he lives, and where the head of the Greek Seamen's Union has threatened to beat him up! . . . Stirbei has sent a message to Maniu saying that if now, after all the allied messages and Molotov's declaration, he still cannot do what is expected of him, then he, Stirbei, must presume that some forces of which we know nothing are impeding him, and conclude that his, Stirbei's, mission has been a failure! I sent this on to the Department without comment.

April 5, 1944, Wednesday

Shantz told me that the Greek Navy has revolted. Harry Hill has seen the Premier on another matter early this morning and got the news. . . . I went over and saw Mr. Tsouderos as soon as I could. . . . Tsouderos had just had another cabinet meeting, at which, as he told me, the Ministers all resigned. Venizelos, Karapanayiotis, Voulgaris,[88] and Sofoulis declared that the King's answer was "dictatorial and unsatisfactory," and the others, Dimitrakakis[89] and Theofanidis, just resigned. In addition, Venizelos refused to go to London at the King's behest. The four principal ministers were quite determined and united. However, in the background, Mr. Tsouderos said, there is old Roussos, who is strongly anti-Royalist and has had some connection with EAM for a long time, but who, Mr. Tsouderos thinks, feels he is too old now for office and only wants to direct from outside. Before the meeting, all the commanders of the Greek war vessels in Alexandria,—about 70 percent of the Greek fleet—called on Mr. Tsouderos and told him that practically all the officers and men of the Greek navy want a government which will collaborate with the People's Committee and that they want Mr. Venizelos for the Premiership. Accordingly Mr. Tsouderos again telegraphed H.M. urgently, telling him that it is absolutely necessary that he call the little man to form a government. Tsouderos said that undoubtedly the movement is out to get the King, and himself for being "too royalist," but that essentially it has been engineered by EAM for its own aims, and that he thinks it quite likely that after a few months the EAM will seek to remove the Republican Venizelos for someone still further to the left. . . . This present move is just another step in the leftist advance which has gone on for a long time, ever since the death of Metaxas, in fact,—not the first, nor is it intended to be the last. . . . He hopes that some strong Republican figure such as Mr. Papandreou may come out of Greece to guide affairs here before the leftist swing goes too far. . . . Harding came back from Alexandria and confirmed that the situation in the Navy remains quiet, but barely so, while the officers and crews await developments in favor of their chosen leader, Mr. Venizelos. . . . I worked with Harding and Larrabee to get their information (and telegrams) coordinated with mine. . . . Worked a very long time on a very long message of my own.

[88] Petros Voulgaris, Minister of Aviation in the Tsouderos government.

[89] Stelios Dimitrakakis, Minister of Justice and Labor in the Tsouderos government.

...[90] The British appear not to have been very severe or careful in their detention of their Greek prisoners here, and some have escaped. In Alexandria, arrests among communists of the merchant marine have been carried out by the Egyptians at British request, but in one case, when the Egyptians attempted with 4 men to arrest 20 Greeks, they themselves got arrested!

April 6, 1944, Thursday
Had a long talk with Major West, now running OSS here in Toulmin's absence in the States. I told him the Greek political situation as far as I know it, and he told me of OSS plans in connection with Greek operations. It appears that the "Noah's Ark plan" is to go into effect about the middle of May, and that commando units (some of them the Greek-Americans who recently came over, among whom was Mr. Tsouderos's son) will be landed at various points to attack communications, with, it is hoped, the help of the *andartes* or guerrillas. West doesn't think much of the guerrillas, and has the feeling that they are hoarding arms against the day of liberation for the purpose of then attacking their countrymen and securing control of Greece. He said that, repeatedly, ragged fellows came forward for arms and ammunition to whom the OSS knows that such has been issued previously. He also thinks it is certain that the Germans will leave suicide troops—Bulgars, Poles, and other "satellites," not Germans,—behind when they go out, and that these will cause trouble, and prevent the first phase of our relief operation from being the peaceful affair now apparently being planned for. In other words, he agrees with what I have been saying all along, that there will be a "front" in Greece, whether we like it or not. He says that already German troops are being withdrawn and *ersatz* troops sent in to take their places. He told me that Tsouderos's son has been sent to Italy till it is decided whether to use him in Greece along with his companions, and he asked me whether I thought it would be dangerous for him, being the son of his father, to be sent in among the guerrillas. I replied that I'd think it over, but that at first blush I didn't think so. It seems to me that the Greeks don't visit the sins of a father's politics on the children—they don't carry blood-feuds into their political quarrels like the Yugoslavs. Parsons agrees with me on this, and I think I'll tell West to go ahead and let the boy do as he wants—he is crazy to go in. . . . General Kallergis of the Greek Army, now *en retraite* and recently arrested (and released) for his participation in the present coup . . . curiously enough, expressed exactly the same view about the EAM and the part it is playing at present

[90] Text of MacVeagh's telegram of April 5, 1944, in *FR 1944*, V, 92-94.

as Mr. Tsouderos. . . . I liked him as I do all Greeks on all sides of the political question! Of course I think they are being very foolish to pull a revolution in the midst of a war and ruin their reputation abroad, but I understand the feelings of the anti-royalists, and how so many have been taken in by the EAM propaganda about the people in the mountains being the ones who should have the say; and I sympathize too with the blind King, though not so much with his blind followers, and with the wily Tsouderos, the most capable of the politicians, whose praiseworthy and noteworthy feat of keeping a government going for three years under almost impossible conditions has made him distrusted by all! . . . Called on Mr. Tsouderos in the afternoon, and learned that Mr. Venizelos has definitely turned tail before the difficulties ahead, and that he and his companions have insisted that the King appoint Roussos as Premier. The principal ministers all met again and this time Roussos was with them. They told Tsouderos that the Navy now wants the old man, and practically dictated a telegram to be sent to the King to this effect. . . . As old Roussos was the man whom Plastiras sent to tell the King to leave the country in 1923, I wonder how H.M. will take this latest suggestion! However, Waterhouse told Parsons that the British Embassy has supported it in a telegram to the Foreign Office, as a temporary matter to quiet things down. Last night and this morning the fleet has been behaving badly, throwing officers into the sea (mostly royalists as well as anti-EAMites) though not mutinying against their duty, as naval men, to fight the enemy—the Greeks think there is a difference! The British have restored order without the use of force, for the time being. There has also been some trouble in the 1st Brigade, and the British have segregated some 200 officers and men. . . . Tsouderos showed me a telegram which he got from Mr. Churchill asking him to stick to his post, until the King gets back "next week," at least. He also came around to the office later and gave me a copy. He will not show it to his cabinet or to any Greeks for fear that it would excite passions further, as a proof of British interference. It speaks of orders issued to the C.-in-C., Levant Fleet, to prevent political outbreaks in the Greek Navy, and to General Wilson to hurry up and get the 1st Brigade to Italy. When I read the message at Tsouderos's house I particularly noted the phrase "our ally, the King." But when I got the copy from Tsouderos at my office, this phrase had been left out! He also gave me a copy of his reply, which explains the situation but promises that he will not do anything unconstitutional, but will stick to his job until the crisis is given a legal solution. He warns Churchill, however, that if the King waits till his return next week to make his decisions, it may be too late. . . . I worked on a long telegram to the Department but in the middle of this was called away to see the Crown Prince of Greece. He wanted to know if the Greek politicians in Athens had sent a message to Venizelos and Karapanayiotis through my Embassy, as he had heard a rumour to this effect. I found out for him that such a message had come through OSS—not the Embassy—from Sofoulis and Gonatas. It said that the Government here should have nothing to do with EAM and should not be too hard on the "Security Battalions"—the Quisling guards! Evidently the politicians' fear of Communism has got the better of their loyalty. . . . When I got back to the office to look into the matter and complete my telegram, Mr. Tsouderos came in with his documents. The Crown Prince had told me that the King is coming soon—he got the message, actually, while I was with him. Tsouderos said he also had news—but rather in the form of a rumor—to the same effect. He said it would be a calamity for the King to come back now, he has nothing to take charge of any more, at this juncture at any rate, and his presence would only make things worse—add "fuel to the flames." . . . Tsouderos's solution would seem to be to have the British take over the Greek armed forces entirely, cutting out the General Staffs and the Ministries, and thus deprive the politicians of the weapons of revolution, in the interests of the war effort. He says he suggested this seven months ago, as a preventive measure, but though General Wilson was agreeable, Admiral Cunningham balked. Now "it is not too late," he thinks, but he doesn't want to *ask* the British now, on account of his position under fire, as it were, but he has "suggested" it again, to Leeper. . . . The Crown Prince confirmed that the idea had been put forward before, and also favors it. His view of the present situation is that the whole trouble is "the old Venizelist clique." "It is always the same people who do these things," he exclaimed, and then complained, "Nothing is ever *done to them*!" How nice it would be to see things as clearly and simply as Royalty sees them. The Royal Highness greeted me with the words, "Well, the Navy has gone *bolshie*!" . . . In the midst of all the above, there was another telegram to get off, on the Rumanian matter. Stirbei got another inquiry—from Mihai Antonescu,[91] this time—about Russian armistice terms, and accordingly posted off to the Russian Embassy, where Novikov told him that there can be no armistice while fighting goes on with mixed Germans and Rumanians on Rumanian soil, but that sufficient terms have been offered, amounting to co-belligerent status, in the message sent to the Marshal by H.M.'s Government several days ago, and agreed to by the allies, and that assent must be given to these before further talks can be had. . . . Meanwhile the news states that Marshal Antonescu is cooperating 100% with the Germans and has offered them the help of a million men! Is it the greatest bluff in the world, or the double double-cross? We should know in a very few days.

[91] Mihai Antonescu, Deputy Prime Minister and Foreign Minister of Rumania.

April 7, 1944, Friday
Mr. Archer, ... told me that Governor Lehman left last night, and that Matthews[92] has accepted the headship of UNRRA for the Balkans. Archer will be sub-chief for Greece, and during the planning period, for Albania as well. ... No one has yet been selected for Yugoslavia. Lehman, Giles, and Hughes have signed an agreement about the participation of UNRRA in the Military Phase of relief, which Giles and Hughes have taken to Algiers to sell to General Wilson. Archer gave me a copy. ... There are many rumors that the King is arriving presently. ... On the other hand, Parsons was told at the British Embassy this morning that the Foreign Office is doing all it can to prevent his coming. ... *Later*: Got the news from the British Embassy that the King has telegraphed (so apparently he is not arriving so soon as all that!) that Roussos is unacceptable, but that he accepts Venizelos, and the latter is now forming a government, with himself holding the Ministries of War, Navy, and Air, Roussos as again Vice-Premier, Politis as Foreign Minister, and a man named Mouratiadis as Finance Minister. The last named is a banker here, head of the local Greek Red Cross, and favorably known to Harry Hill. There is a certain Skoufopoulos (name uncertain) said to be appointed Minister of Merchant Marine, who would seem the only bad appointment so far—or at least doubtful—if one excepts the weak little Premier himself. News from Port Said is to the effect that her crew has taken over the *Averoff* to put her at the disposition of the Political Committee in Greece when its representatives arrive in Egypt, but meanwhile they will obey the British orders and remain loyal to the war effort, thank you very much. I wonder how many more acts there will be before "the comedy is finished." *Still later*: I have just completed a telegram on this new development. Practically the whole of the Greek armed forces have now gone over to the revolutionists, but there has been remarkably little real trouble. Some shootings last night in the 1st Brigade, whose chance of going to Italy is probably now lost.

April 8, 1944, Saturday
Novikov called up urgently, and brought me in a copy of the armistice terms which the Soviets would be willing to give Rumania. At the same time I received a copy of a telegram which the Department sent to Harriman,[93] largely on the same subject. Looking over the Russian terms in the light of the Department's instructions, it seemed to me that they could and should be agreed to, so as to lose no more time,—except for a political

---

[92] Sir William Matthews, Chief of the UNRRA Balkan Mission, and former head of the Middle East Relief and Refugee Administration, Cairo.

[93] Averell W. Harriman, U.S. Ambassador to the Soviet Union.

clause about Transylvania. The Russians say they regard the Vienna award as unjust and are willing to fight with the Rumanians against the Hungarians and Germans with the object of restoring Transylvania or the major portion of it to Rumania. We can't tell here what our Governments may have in mind about Hungary, so both Lord Moyne and I cabled to get assent to the terms before replying to Novikov. But surely time presses! . . . During the afternoon, we had word that the trouble in the 1st Brigade had become much more serious, and I went over to see Leeper. He confirmed this, and said that the British War Office and Admiralty have now taken over direct charge of the Greek forces, cutting out the Ministries of War and Marine. He hopes that bloodshed between Greeks and British may be avoided. . . . In addition, he told me that the King is returning now with all speed, and that Venizelos this morning took back his proposals of yesterday and that, though Leeper sent a telegram to the King for him proposing a cabinet, he now wants to remain for the time being under Tsouderos. All the Ministers are now "remaining at their posts," and the responsibility is shifted to H.M. to settle everything on his return. Leeper was justifiably scornful of the "revolting cabinet" (as I have called it to the Department) in his remarks to me. Meanwhile, the British Military, assisted by the Egyptian police, have continued their arrests of civilians, as well as members of the Greek armed forces, and resentment among the Greeks here is growing hot. Today, Mr. Valtikos, the nice little Cairo attorney who headed the delegation which visited me the other day, was arrested without warning, and those who arrested him refused to disclose the charges or tell his wife where he was being taken. In talking about this kind of thing to me, Leeper said he was aware that his association with it might make it impossible for him to go to Greece after the war, but that nevertheless it had to be done. Great Britain is committed to the Egyptians to keep order among the Greeks and other refugees which she has asked Egypt to accept, and if she didn't take action to prevent it, the Greeks, who are genuinely engaged now in one of their periodic revolutions, would be shooting each other on Egyptian soil. He said civilians like Valtikos, who get up committees and sign manifestos, incite the armed forces, and must be treated accordingly. . . . I believe, however, that he is missing a trick, in not making greater efforts to explain his reasonable point of view to the Greek public, which, in the lack of such explanation, is tending more and more to accuse the British of tyrannically oppressing the expression of democratic ideals and of supporting the King and Mr. Tsouderos. . . . Regarding the King's return, Leeper said he is not opposing it any more, in view of the Cabinet's latest *volte face*, but he thinks it will create a very difficult situation. He fears the King will be sour and stubbornly dynastic in the face of this new liberal outbreak, whereas he should be "reasonable."

... It seems to me that the King would put himself "on a good wicket," as the British say, if he should at once declare (1) that as a Constitutional Monarch he has nothing to do with any one party, but is the King of all the Hellenes; (2) that in normal times he is bound to accept a Government representative of the majority of the electorate, but (3) that as under existing conditions elections cannot be held, a Government representative of all parties is the only one possible, and (4) that he will, as the People's King, accept and support only such a "Government of National Unity," to function until the liberation of the country renders the old system of majority rule again a possibility.

April 10, 1944, Monday

Ralph Kent[94] brought in his Ensign Johnson (real name Giannakis!) who told Shantz and Larrabee and me about his visit to the Greek Brigade on Saturday. He also gave me a lot of documents—copies of orders, et cetera—which the officers of the Brigade asked him to bring out, to prove the excellence of their intentions. They told Johnson that they had only wanted to declare their opposition to the Tsouderos Government, which as Greeks they feel they had a right to do, but that after they had done that, and had a little 24-hour "strike" to show their sympathies with the "movement" and were all ready to go on with the war, the British suddenly appeared and told them to lay down their arms. This, of course, they could not do, and a hysterical soldier actually committed suicide at the thought, and now they are all blockaded in the camp, with British tanks round about; they get no food, and when they send emissaries out to parley, these never come back! ... I got young "Johnson" an appointment with Leeper, so that the latter could hear the story and get the documents. ... Harding came in and said the Naval situation remains bad. The ships are all being run by committees of their crews, and the British are sending into Alex. [Alexandria] a six-inch [gun] cruiser and some smaller vessels. ... Question: How long will this uneasy situation go on before someone looses off a gun? ... A messenger brought in from Lord Moyne's office a copy of the British reply on the matter of the Rumanian armistice terms, in the form of a telegram from Churchill to Molotov, saying H.M.G. agrees, but suggests that as regards Transylvania's being restored, there should be a qualifying clause about the approval of the Peace Conference, and also adds that we presume that the Russians will allow the British and Americans to have political representatives in Rumania during the Armistice period, just as the Russians

---

[94] Lieutenant Ralph Kent, on the staff of JICAME, Cairo, and former assistant director of the Athens College.

are allowed to do now in Italy. In conclusion, it expresses complete confidence that Russia will act in the interests of all the Allies, and says go ahead metaphorically, and God bless you.... I got off a telegram on the Greek situation, warning the Department of its seriousness as regards a possible British-Greek clash, or clashes. No news of any political developments, except that the Communist party in Greece and the EAM have both telegraphed to Tsouderos (not Venizelos) that they regard a Government of National Unity as essential and accept his invitation to send emissaries to Cairo for its formation. The Communist Party's signer is also its representative on the People's Committee, so this last is also tied in, though Tsouderos has heretofore taken the attitude that he will not deal with it, as being a one-party organization.

April 11, 1944, Tuesday

Call from Colonel West about various things. He says "Noah's Ark" will start with three parties as soon as this moon is gone, in about ten days. He also says that he has stopped the OSS practice of carrying political messages for the Greeks.... The Greek King returned this morning, "very tired," according to Leeper, from his trip.... Captain Foskett and Admiral Alexandris[95] called with a typed proposal to have the British and American and Russian Governments make a joint statement to allay Greek political excitement, saying that we are all united behind the British in their attitude that order and discipline must be kept, and calling on the Greeks to fight the common enemy, leaving politics aside.... The statement would, it seemed to me, be unexceptionable to the British and ourselves, but the Russian, when I showed it to him, said he did not agree with the British action in this affair! He said all the Greeks want to do is change their Government; and to surround them with tanks and refuse them food is unjust. I gave the document (which was of course drawn up by Alexandris) to Leeper. It *might* do good to issue such a statement if the Russians came in on it, but not otherwise—in fact it might do more harm than good to put it out without the Russians. The Moscow Press, incidentally, is underlining the difference between the Russians and British in this matter by attacking the Tsouderos Government and blaming it for the repressive actions which, of course, it is the British who are taking! ... When Novikov came in, shortly after Foskett and the Admiral, it was principally to talk about the Rumanian affair. He has heard from Moscow that the British suggestions are acceptable. I told him of our own message received this morning, and assured him that I would immediately let him know on receipt of the promised further

[95] Admiral Constantine Alexandris, Chief of the Greek Navy in the Middle East.

instructions. On the Greek matter, he predicted that British action would result in the loss of the Greek army ("30,000 men") to the Allies, and he strongly criticized British policy as regards Yugoslavia, as well. "They took the whole responsibility for Yugoslavia, and it is their own fault that the Purić Government is now absolutely washed up. And now it is the turn of the Greek Government! Their policy has been petty and uncertain throughout." . . . I then went over to see Leeper. He thinks that the King must absolutely make a political statement right away to quiet the Greeks and make them feel that something will really be done now to broaden the Government. H.M. brought such a statement with him, which Leeper saw, but it was dead and utterly uninspiring in its tone. He is seeing Tsouderos tonight (after a cabinet meeting which is going on right now), and tomorrow General Paget, Admiral Cunningham and Air Marshal Sir Keith Park[96] will see him together. Leeper hopes to brief those gentlemen first. The idea is to get H.M. to say something satisfactory regarding present Greek demands, in his own interests but also in theirs—his Allies. . . . Today, Paget is meeting a deputation of the 1st Brigade. That is good news, if it is handled properly. I advised Leeper that one can only succeed with the Greeks by talking; threats and even shooting will not do. They will only remember Messolonghi, if not Thermopylae, and bare their breasts! . . . Harding tells me that Commodore Rawlings[97] went out in a boat in Alexandria harbour and spoke to the Greek fleet through magnifiers, telling the Greeks that they must obey orders or they will lose their ships—the British will take them away from them. That sounds like the military mind, all right; the result, if this kind of thing is really proposed, is likely to be that the Greeks will simply scuttle the vessels. . . . I believe that further dangerous developments and regrettable incidents may be avoided if, as the Greeks want so badly to have happen, this affair should be taken on to the political level, and the word spread about by press and radio that a large reorganization of the cabinet is to take place. The situation in the armed forces would at once become less tense, tongues would wag again and fists relax. The British, too, should save Greek "face" by taking back their order to surrender their arms. Gradually, the whole movement would die down, and no harm would have been done, while all eyes would be focused on the process of the Government's enlargement. But Leeper says that the armed forces have mutinied, and that this cannot be overlooked, that the British have other things to do than to talk with the Greeks, that at any moment Paget may be asked from London why he "doesn't get on with

[96] Air Marshal Sir Keith Park, Commanding Officer, British Forces, Middle East.
[97] Admiral Sir Herbert Rawlings, Commanding Officer, British Naval Forces, Eastern Mediterranean.

it," and whether he is incapable of handling the situation, and finally that the British cannot make statements for the Greek Government and that only the King is in a position to speak now. So, while there is growing immediate danger of impatience and misunderstanding bringing about an explosion, the whole hope of settlement is being placed in a King who is notoriously inept at speaking to the people.

April 12, 1944, Wednesday

Little news during the day about the Greek situation, except that the King has been interviewing the political leaders. As the British afternoon *Gazette* puts it, he saw "Kanellopoulos, Exindaris,[98] *Pericles* and *Argyropoulos*."[99] Let us hope that some of Pericles' wisdom will be found available. . . . We finally got the Department's authorization to agree to the Russian armistice terms to Rumania, and I so informed Novikov. He had already, however, given the word to Stirbei that we are all in agreement and the message, which will go via the Rumanian Ambassador in Ankara, is now on its way, with some additional hopeful urgings on the part of Stirbei personally. . . . Late in the afternoon we got the results of the King's deliberations, in the form of a statement to be published tonight. He reiterates his old statement that after the war, and when calm is restored, he will abide by a plebiscite on the régime, and for the time being says that a Government of national unity must be formed, to be composed principally of representatives of the people who have remained in Greece and suffered with her in the cities and villages "and in the mountains." In addition, he calls on the Greeks to unite in prosecuting the war against the common enemy. . . . Not bad for the King, but it lacks all warmth or emotional lift. . . . Meanwhile, conditions in the armed forces are, if not better, at least no worse. . . . The 1st Brigade has been given food, and Paget had a long pow-wow, without results. . . . Under existing circumstances "no worse" is "better," certainly, and it seems possible that if there is no relapse, and no shooting starts because of impatience and short-sightedness, the danger may blow over with the passing of the first flush of revolutionary enthusiasm. Some officers and men deserted the revolting units in Port Said today.

April 14, 1944, Friday

The news this morning is that Venizelos has started to form a "service government" to tide over the interim period, and he came in today to

[98] George Exindaris, prominent member of the Liberal Party.
[99] Pericles Argyropoulos, career diplomat, and former Minister for Foreign Affairs.

tell me of his plans. He will have a very small group of "technicians" and hopes that emissaries will come out of Greece soon enough to get a "Government of National Unity" within two weeks. During the morning I advised the Department of the likelihood of this move, and in the afternoon gave the names of the Ministers whom Venizelos named to me. Mantzavinos in London has accepted Finance, and General Zanakakis, a Cretan who was C. of S. [Chief of Staff, Greek Army, Middle East] here for a short time after the Government came to Cairo, has accepted Social Welfare and Labor. Venizelos has asked Admiral Demestichas to take the Merchant Marine and Mr. Kaclamanos to serve without portfolio, presumably to help Venizelos with Foreign Affairs, which he will himself assume along with National Defense. . . . I advised the Department that Russian interest in this Greek business, as shown by Novikov's attitude, and attacks on Tsouderos and his Government in the Moscow press, has caused many Greeks here to wonder whether Russia now intends to supplant Britain in Greek affairs. . . . It would appear that in this business, as in the Russian support of Tito, and the Russian appointment of an Ambassador to Badoglio, we may be witnessing the beginnings of Russian exploitation in the Mediterranean of the Soviets' new-found power, and the shadow cast in advance of an eventual British-Russian clash along the Imperial highway to the East. . . . No change in the Greek naval and military situations. The question of "face" is coming into the picture, as the British have given orders "to lay down your arms" which the Greeks resent as an insult and which the British feel they can't rescind!

April 15, 1944, Saturday
Tea with King George. He talked a long time and less nervously and unhappily, I thought, than when I saw him before he went to London. He said that the President has sent him very kind and friendly messages through Biddle and asked me to acknowledge them for him. I wonder whether he confuses the President's friendship with support by the American Government of his political position. He always seems to understand me when I mention our policy of keeping hands off internal affairs. I rang in on our conversation today Mr. Hull's statement that we have no interest in the governments freely chosen by the liberated countries, unless they should menace others—just in case! . . . He is convinced that the present movement has been fostered and directed by enemy agents, who have cleverly organized and timed it to interfere with allied operations at a critical time. He knows of the Russian attitude toward the movement, but does not think that Moscow is directly having anything to do

with it; rather, he feels that the communistic aspect, revealed in the EAM propaganda and all that, has been worked up by the Germans through Sofia. He is fully aware, however, of the Russian influence pushing itself down into the Mediterranean. . . . We talked of plans for liberated Greece, and I told him of my ideas (now killed so dead)! for American command and the reasons for them, with which he agreed to such an extent that he asked me to tell the President that he is in accord completely. He wants American troops, at least some of them, too. But I explained the Military veto which has been imposed. He saw King Peter in London, of course, and believes that he is opposing strongly any pressure to dismiss Mihailović unless they can prove to him that M. is or has been collaborating with the Germans. But the British go on saying that though they have proof they cannot show it! He spoke to Winant about the Yugoslav question, and the Ambassador said "Please don't talk about it, it's too hot!" . . . About Greek matters,—he thinks Venizelos is too easily influenced and is approachable by too many people (this last from the King is good!) He fears that V. will insist on dealing with EAM about the new Government and that the politicians coming out from Greece will oppose this and create another difficulty. This seems likely. He hopes it can be arranged not to have the conferences about the new Government held here in Cairo, but in Syria, or somewhere like that, so that it can be done in peace and quiet without the influence and disturbance of excited groups. . . . He thinks it possible that the present slight defections from the ranks of the mutineers may increase and finally leave only the responsible agitators, who can then be dealt with. . . . He confirmed (from the British Embassy, he said) that the Tass agency here is using the Russian official channels to get news out. . . . And finally, he spoke several times of Mr. Tsouderos with approval, and not at all as I expected from what I had heard of Colonel Levidis' remark on landing at Cairo: "See in what a mess Tsouderos has got us!" I dare say that this was the way he felt when he arrived, but that he has learned a good deal from the old fox since he got here. . . . No telegram tonight, as there seems nothing to report. Tomorrow is the Greek Easter, and we'll see what that and Easter Monday may bring forth among the Greeks for good or ill. Parsons remarked that while the King may be right regarding the forces that have pulled the strings in this movement, he does not appear to recognize to what extent anti-royalist feelings have been appealed to, how widespread these are, and where he now stands in consequence. Personally, though I like him quite as much as F.D.R. does, and know him far better, I must say that if I were a soothsayer asked to tell his future, I would say at present, "I see another term of exile ahead." The omens are too much against him.

April 17, 1944, Monday
Ensign Johnson of JICAME came in again and told of another visit to the 1st Brigade. Apparently the Brigade is determined to resist the British "to the last" and will not admit that it is in the wrong. At Alexandria, in the Navy, there is worse trouble, with several hundred ratings bottled up in the Naval Barracks without food or water, and with trench mortars mounted on the roofs! The ships, too, can't get any food, but the revolting crews are standing by their loaded guns. It seems very few deserters are getting away, though the British are convinced that both in the Navy and the Camp there is only a small minority which is really recalcitrant. ... The appeals of the King and Mr. Venizelos have largely fallen on deaf ears, as the rebels say they have had enough of statements and now want action.... Lunch with Mr. Kirk and about twenty, all men, to meet General Sadler,[100] Giles' new deputy.... General Paget, the local British C-in-C, sat on Kirk's right. He told me that the British are not giving the 1st Brigade any food (despite my earlier information from Parsons), and that "one doesn't issue rations to mutineers." ... In the afternoon I called on Leeper to learn about the Greek situation, and feel that British patience is running out.... Later, Harding reported that the British navy expects that a showdown will have to come this week. The Greek ships are too badly needed for convoy work.... Harding said that two of our "Liberty" ships have just been "got" by a submarine off Tunis, and that the British reaction has been that this wouldn't have happened but for the Greek defection.... Leeper feels the British army cannot compromise,—it is British military "face" now versus Greek "honor." ... Got off a long telegram on this subject, and another about Rumania. Lord Moyne has received a message for Stirbei from Maniu proposing terms of his own, and suggests that two stern messages be sent to Maniu and to Antonescu calling their attention to the Russian armistice terms and demanding a prompt reply. He thinks it time these people realized where they stand.

April 18, 1944, Tuesday
Colonel West came in and asked whether he could have the Rumanian armistice terms to give to an American OSS "team" which is going in with a British Force 133 "team" to Rumania in a couple of weeks. He said he thinks the British will give their men this document so that they may be well-informed, and that they will also be supplied with some sort

---

[100] Brigadier Percy L. Sadler, U.S. Deputy Commander for Relief and Rehabilitation, Greece (Cairo).

of document from Novikov, for protection should they fall into Russian hands. I told him to get exact information as to what the British really will do, and that I thought that then I might possibly help him, but that I would have to ask the Department about the armistice terms before I gave them out to anybody.... He told me that Noah's Ark is due to start in "about two days." Also that the British sent 150 officers into Crete recently on a rumor that the Germans there are surrendering. I wonder if they sent so many as that, and certainly nothing has come out about their surrendering! We talked about the present Greek situation, and he said that Force 133 feels that if the British start shooting the Greeks here, their agents in Greece will none of them survive.... There is little news of this situation today. Exindaris said that the British have given Venizelos a few days more to settle things, and that he is trying to get a loyal force together to deal with the naval mutineers especially. The idea is if blood must be shed, it is better to keep it in the family.... Some Greek loyalists are going to the Brigade to try their eloquence on the recalcitrants there. Later I heard that Mr. Voulgaris has gone to the Naval people in Alexandria to try the same thing. Monday next is said to be the British deadline before shooting starts.... Larrabee, who is very emotional about the Partisan-Mihailović controversy, now is greatly stirred by the Greek affair, and wants to telegraph the War Department that I should mediate! He doesn't realize that to mediate one would have to satisfy the Greeks on political matters, and make statements and promises which would put the U.S. definitely into the Greek political picture, where we have no place and want none. One would have also to persuade the British to take back their orders, at least to some extent. The Department already knows the situation and will doubtless instruct me if it desires me to do anything, but meanwhile I don't see it stepping forward either to hold the British baby or to undertake commitments as an arbiter in Greek internal questions. If I could guarantee to the Greeks that they would get the government they want, and persuade the British to let bygones be bygones and take the Greeks back into service without disciplinary action or any laying down of arms, I think I could arbitrate. But neither is possible, and the proposal is foolish—though flattering as an evidence of Larrabee's confidence.... Meanwhile it seems to be getting clearer every day that, unless something of the sort is done, the "ugly outcome" envisaged by Leeper is a certainty.... Yesterday young Johnson gave me some leaflets which the British dropped on the 1st Brigade calling on them to surrender or take the consequences, and these were marked (in Greek) "Distributed by the British *and American* air forces"! I asked OWI whether they knew about these, since they handle all our leaflet propaganda, and they said "NO." So I told Leeper about the matter, to his confusion, and the OWI

took the matter up with PWE,[101] who explained, with apologies, that it was due to "inadvertence" that we had been included. But a lot of other leaflets, already printed and about to be distributed, were then found with the same notation! These were destroyed. So Johnson's action has had a good effect.... The Greeks in the Brigade who gave the pamphlets to Johnson said, "We know, of course, that the Americans are not in this thing, and that it is simply another British trick." But a lot more leaflets, all with the same notation, might soon enough carry conviction....
Colonel Bellm's visit was chiefly about a communication the USAFIME[102] has received from Lord Moyne saying that all the committees (Balkan Affairs, Balkan Operations, Balkan Relief) which he recently proposed to us have been now set up under authority of General Wilson. USAFIME is included, but not the Embassy—due to the Department's attitude, which was *anti* the Relief Committee as being unnecessary, and reserved toward the Balkan Affairs. Bellm was very critical of the terms of reference of all the committees, and said that Lord Moyne is mistaken in including USAFIME. I can hardly understand Moyne's assuming to do so, as the Department has told me that the War Department shares its views. Anyhow, Bellm says that USAFIME will not sit on any of these proposed bodies, and promised me copies of Lord Moyne's communication and his reply, which he is writing today. Bellm is very strong against the BSC[103] and thinks it serves no useful purpose but to give jobs here to Landis and his crew, and it does seem to me that it is hard to explain what it is for. So much is this true, that the Russians are positively suspicious of possible hidden motives. It is hard to believe that any sensible government would maintain so large an organization without *some* purpose to fulfill!

April 19, 1944, Wednesday
After lunch, called on Leeper at his flat, meeting Kanellopoulos in the hall, coming away. Leeper said that no term has been fixed yet as to British patience in connection with either the Greek navy or the Greek army, and confirmed that Alexandris has been replaced by Voulgaris. He doesn't think this is a very hopeful change! Venizelos was told by Admiral Cunningham that the Greeks should quell the Naval revolt themselves, and Voulgaris is in Alex. now trying to get a group together to take over a couple of the rebel ships. The British think this shouldn't be too difficult, but determined leaders seem lacking among the Greek authorities. Leeper thinks the King should get a stronger man than

[101] PWE: Political Warfare Executive (British).
[102] USAFIME: United States Army Forces Intelligence, Middle East.
[103] BSC: Balkan Supply Center (Allied).

Venizelos, and has told him so, even for this interim period. Two EAMites and one Zervas man are going to come out from Greece, and the meeting for the purpose of forming a National Government if possible, will be held somewhere away from Cairo, perhaps at Brumana in Syria. As to the revolt, I asked Leeper if he thought we could help in any way, and he answered, "I think not. We have the military responsibility and must go ahead. As to mediation, we can't have that." This settles that idea! He said the Russians are behaving "outrageously" with their open sympathy for the rebels, and the Tass articles (which he believes go out from here through Novikov's cypher), and the Soviet broadcasts in Greek. If they wanted to, they could stop the mutiny in a minute, he said. Churchill has telegraphed to Molotov, explaining the trouble here and protesting against the Russian reports and broadcasts. No reply yet. He has also wired to F.D.R., whose reply (very garbled) he showed me.[104] The Presi-

[104] In his telegram to Roosevelt of April 16, 1944, Churchill reviewed recent developments among the various Greek factions and quoted his instructions to Ambassador Leeper: "Our relations are definitely established with [the] lawfully constituted Greek Government headed by the King, who is [the] ally of Britain and cannot be discarded to suit a momentary surge of appetite amongst ambitious *émigré* nonentities. Neither can Greece find constitutional expression in [a] particular set of guerrillas, in many cases indistinguishable from banditti, who are masquerading as saviours of their country while living on local villagers. If necessary I shall denounce these elements and tendencies publicly in order to emphasize the love Great Britain has for Greece, whose suffering she [has] shared in a small measure, being alas not then armed as we are now. Our only desire and interest is to see Greece a glorious free nation in the Eastern Mediterranean, the honoured friend and ally of victorious powers. Let all therefore work for this objective and make it quite clear that any failure in good conduct will not be overlooked." After asserting that "All the time I have been planning to place Greece back high in counsels of victorious nations," Churchill returned to the issue of the Greek monarchy. "The King is the servant of his people. He makes no claim to rule them. He submits himself freely to [the] judgment of the people as soon as normal conditions are restored. He places himself and his Royal House entirely at the disposition of the Greek nation. Once the German invader has been driven out Greece can be a republic or a Monarchy entirely as the people wish. Why then cannot the Greeks keep their hatreds for the common enemy who has wrought them such cruel injuries and would obliterate them as [a] free people were it not for [the] resolute exertions of the great Allies." *FR 1944*, V, 96-98.

Roosevelt replied on April 17: "—With you I join in the hope that your line of action toward the problem may succeed in bringing back the Greeks into the camp of the Allies and to a participation that will be worthy of the traditions established by the heroes of the history of the Greeks against the barbarians. As one whose family and who personally has contributed by personal help for over a century to Greek independence, frankly I am not happy over the situation as it is at present and hope that everywhere Greeks will retain their sense of proportion and will set aside pettiness. Let every Greek show a personal unselfishness which is so necessary now and think of their glorious past. If you want to, you can in the above sense quote me." *Ibid.*, pp. 98-99.

dent sympathizes with Churchill's efforts to end the revolt and hopes he may be successful in calling the Greeks back to their old glorious traditions, etc., all in such general terms that, though Leeper is authorized to use the message here, he can't see where it would do any good! . . . After seeing him, I had a visit from Papandreou, who evidently remembered me and said "We haven't met for three years!" though I don't remember him at all, except as a name. He was very intelligent in his talk, wholly against the mutinies and sympathetic with the British in their fix. "One cannot behave this way in war time." He had had a talk with Solod at the Soviet Embassy and suspects that the Russians are not only sympathetic with but may have had a hand in fomenting the trouble. In Greece he says that recently EAM has switched from being a political to being a revolutionary movement, and that it represents communist tyranny. Therefore, he is against it, though a leftist democrat himself. He wants political and social *freedom*, not slavery. According to him (and he has, of course, just come from Greece), the EAM began as a patriotic resistance movement, but has recently, under the control of Communist elements, turned against the Greeks, and is now an armed minority, thoroughly hated and feared, engaged in the attempt to foist its rule on the unarmed majority. He was himself once asked to be its head, but because of its Communist aspect, refused. If a National Government is to be formed (by which he understands a Government is which minorities are represented), he thinks EAM should be included. But he thinks that, if it joins, it will be with the purpose in its own mind of dominating the whole show eventually. He is a tall, grey-haired, straight-looking fellow, who seemed specially pleased when I spoke of Mylonas, among others, as being a friend of mine. He said Kafandaris is seriously ill and has been in bed for 10 months, but that Philip Dragoumis is likely to come out, and is well. Gonatas also. Theotokis is still on Corfu, and has not come to Athens. I liked him a lot, and agree with Leeper that he is several cuts above the petty figures we have had here, like Karapanayiotis and Venizelos. Something might be done with him to get the Greeks together.

April 21, 1944, Friday

The uneasy lull in the Greek situation continues, with nothing to report but an ineffective public appeal on the part of Mr. Venizelos to the mutineers to abandon their sabotage of the common war effort. . . . The Brigade sent a demand to Venizelos that it be turned over to the Russians to fight on their front, since it is convinced the British now won't use it in Italy! This "demand" probably won't go very far or be given publicity (we got it from OSS), but is interesting as showing the Russian sympathies of the mutineers. . . . Received a telegram from the Department asking for information about Lord Moyne's new Balkan Affairs Committee, and drafted and sent off a long telegram on this and the other committees he has now set up under General Wilson's authority. I couldn't help showing that I take a very dim view of these committees, both as to the necessity for them and their composition and terms of reference. Behind the British insistence on having them is maneuvering, I am sure, by the Middle East Supply Center, and perhaps Landis also, in order to keep their hand in on the Balkan matter which threatens to become absorbed by the Military and UNRRA. . . . Heard from the Department that it approves our stimulating Maniu and Antonescu through Lord Moyne's proposed telegrams, but prefers to leave off the closing threat, in the one to Antonescu, that if he doesn't act he will be held to be a war criminal. A telegram from Maniu dated the 20th states that the armistice terms have been received and that he will be glad to send out "another emissary" and "start negotiations" along these lines and those of his own recent proposals! What can you do with such people? Another telegram from the Department says that Rumanian contacts have been opened up through Gafencu in Switzerland, but that the Department prefers to keep negotiations in the Cairo channels, which have proved satisfactory so far.

April 22, 1944, Saturday

I called on Mr. Venizelos in the morning and he expressed himself as more hopeful than he has yet been of attaining a settlement of the Naval mutiny without calling on British assistance. He said that Admiral Voulgaris has gone to Alexandria and is organizing loyal elements to attempt to recapture the mutinous ships. Later in the day, I saw Ambassador Leeper, and he was less sanguine, speaking of the "weakness" of Venizelos and Voulgaris, and stating that it is becoming more and more clear that the King must replace Venizelos with a bigger man, like Papandreou. . . . The British have received word that the People's Committee in the Mountains of Greece has been broadened to present a kind of popular front, after the analogy of Tito's "Government." Professor Svolos, a Socialist, has replaced Colonel Bakirdzis at the head of it. At the same time, the London and "Free Yugoslavia" radios report long and warm interchanges of messages between Bakirdzis and Tito. Mr. Leeper told me that he has received an anxious wire from London about these developments, and added: "Greece is now at the crossroads. This movement has ceased to be an internal affair. The question is whether Greece will move into the Russian orbit and lose her independence, or remain a Mediterranean country under British influence." He said he finds it very hard to express his views on the Russian angle to his Government as Mr. Churchill is now directly handling Greek affairs, but this inquiry from London will give him a chance to say something pretty outspoken. He asked me whether I could not give the Department some idea of what is going on, and I said that I had already done so many times. He thinks that, despite Churchill's relations with Tito, he and F.D.R. must now take cognizance of the way the Russians are extending their "zone of influence."

April 23, 1944, Sunday
Parsons learned from OSS that at 2 a.m. this morning loyal Greek parties boarded the Greek ships in Alexandria harbor and recaptured them all except the repair-ship *Hefaistos*, with a loss of nine dead and over forty wounded. British action was avoided. No word as to the effect of this on the Brigade or on the naval units at Port Said. . . . Went to the office and Parsons and I got off a brief telegram on the above, which was confirmed by Captain Foskett in Alexandria through Harding's office. Meanwhile, the Russian attitude remains unchanged.

April 24, 1944, Monday
News arrived early that the Brigade of Greeks has surrendered, and when I arrived at the office there was a note on my desk that General Smuts wanted to see me at 11. I went over and saw Leeper at once, who confirmed the report about the Brigade. It seems that Paget ordered a British move toward the Greek camp last evening, and that a ridge overlooking it was occupied. One British soldier was shot. Other details are lacking, but Leeper thinks the British did not fire on the Greeks. The Brigade sent word that it would surrender when they saw the British held the ridge. . . . Leeper told me that he saw Smuts last night and would see him again this noon. He said that the General is greatly concerned over the Russian aspect of the Greek affair and the Russian problem generally. . . . Leeper also told me that Venizelos has resigned (which Leeper has wanted all along) and that Papandreou will probably form a Government. . . . I went over to the Residency and talked with Smuts, whom I found in friendly form and apparently well as usual. He talked at once of the Venizelos resignation. Has no use for V. any more than Leeper has, though he admired V.'s father. Said the King had asked him to help persuade V. to stay in the cabinet under Papandreou, but that he thought he would stay out of the affair. He asked some questions about P. which I could answer in a general way favorably enough, but he indicated that he didn't want to mix in Greek internal politics, and I said that we were in the same boat. Then he turned to the growth of Russian influence which he attributed to the Soviet military successes, and said:

"There is something very serious going on in the Balkans." Russia is coming into the Mediterranean picture through the spread of Communism, by-passing the old barrier of the Dardanelles completely. He said he thought the extent to which the British have been playing up Tito has been a mistake, as was also the British support to EAM. I gathered that he was briefing himself somewhat from Leeper, and would urge on Churchill in London that the situation be taken in hand. . . . When I got back from seeing Smuts, Venizelos called and confirmed that he had resigned, but the real reason of his visit was to complain of Leeper, who, he said, had acted "unfairly" to him in forcing his resignation after the responsibility he took for fixing up the naval situation. He said he would not join any cabinet under Papandreou now, though later he might join a Government of National Unity if such were formed. . . . Later in the day, Mr. Metaxas called up for the King, to ask me to see Mr. Venizelos again and try to persuade him (as Smuts was asked to do), but I said please to tell H.M. that I would love to do as he asked, but that I cannot take any part in internal Greek affairs He said that H.M. thought that as Leeper would do as he asked, I might too, but I explained that Leeper's position and mine do not absolutely agree in such matters. . . . After I saw Venizelos, Novikov came in and showed me a message he had just received from Moscow, saying that the Soviet Government has taken note of my explanations that in making reservations about boundaries (to be settled at the Peace Conference) in connection with a possible move of Maniu to Russian-held Moldavia, there was no intent to refer in any way to Bessarabia or the 1940 line already agreed to in the Russian Armistice proposals. On this basis, the Russians agree with us and the British that Stirbei can suggest to Maniu that he go to Russian-held Moldavia and set up a Government in opposition to Antonescu, if he thinks the situation warrants it, and will have the same terms granted him as have been put forward to Antonescu should the latter make the revolt against the Germans. . . . Novikov also said that the Russians now agree to sending Maniu and Antonescu the prodding messages, practically ultimata, suggested by Lord Moyne, leaving off the threat to Antonescu that if he doesn't act, he personally will be held to be a "common war criminal." We have proposed leaving out the words "and will take no excuses" also, and Novikov has no particular objections, though he doesn't see the necessity. Perhaps he feels we may "take excuses,"—who knows? and why be so definite. . . . Regarding the Greek situation, Novikov said that the British will "show an ignorance of their own interests" if they take Papandreou as Premier, as "he is not the man to make a success of the Greek situation." This contrasts oddly with the Russian professions of last January that they lacked knowledge of Greek affairs and needed to be advised by the British. They have come a long way—

with their victories and the appetite for influence which these have caused, and doubtless seem to warrant from their point of view. . . . Later: Harding called up to say that he has just heard from Port Said that all the naval vessels there are in line again and only two merchant vessels are standing out.

April 25, 1944, Tuesday

Got a cheerful and facetious letter from F.D.R. in answer to my letter of March 17th. He never has referred to my longer and more serious effort of February. He says: "Your letter of March 17th is a joy and I think you are wholly right." That refers, I guess, to what I said about the Greeks and the possibility of their having a really constitutional monarchy. . . . I spent most of the afternoon trying to answer, with a condensation of the recent Greek revolt into a paragraph, to lead on to the serious international aspects involved in the Russian attitude. . . . Mr. Papandreou is supposed to be about to take the oath as Premier, but wouldn't do it today, as Tuesday in Greece is unlucky!

[The President had written:]

Dear Lincoln: April 1, 1944

Yours of March seventeenth is a joy and I think you are wholly right. I am rather sentimental about Greece. My great grandfather and great uncle, Messrs. Howland and Aspinwall, got a frigate for Greek independence. and I myself, in early 1914, got two battleships to save Greece from Turkey. Surely there must be a third occasion.

I think you might go up there at the first opportunity, raise an army of brigands, decapitate the Germans, declare yourself Autarch—which translated into modern English means a self-winding dictator—run the show for a couple of years, get thoroughly bored, and finally abdicate in favor of George II. If I were as young as you are I would do just that!

If you don't want to be so strenuous I will put you in touch with some excellent moving picture people and for the next year or two you can get out some real movie thrillers in Greece and Yugoslavia. The public is ready for something new but on the line of Graustark.

I am glad that you and Mohamed Ali have become chummy. Of all the Princes, Potentates and Powers whom I met in Cairo, Teheran, etc., he appealed to me most. A milder mannered man never scuttled a ship!

As ever yours,
FDR (8)

April 26, 1944, Wednesday

Papandreou has taken the oath as P.M., but can't get a political government together (the politicians are all sore at British dictation and are supporting Venizelos, with Bodossakis in the background!) so he is asking the Directors General of the various ministries to serve as temporary Under-Secretaries. . . . Waterhouse of the British Embassy is going to Syria to prepare a place for the Conference of National Unity. . . . The *Averoff* is said to be the last of the Greek vessels in Port Said to be holding out for the mutiny, and its food supply has been cut off.

April 27, 1944, Thursday

I had a long conversation with Mr. Leeper, principally about the Conference of the Greek politicians in Syria. He assures me that it will be a wholly Greek affair, and that the British are concerned in the arrangements only from the point of view of security. He will be at Beirut himself during the conference "in case things come up concerning the guerrilla bands," with whose operations the British are concerned, and also to advise the Greek Prime Minister if requested. I asked him if he had told Novikov, and he said, "No." He has given up sending Novikov information, since the use which has been made of it in the Moscow press has made him feel that he was not dealing with a "good ally." As regards present Greek politics, he said Papandreou is going to take his job seriously and show initiative, and he thinks that the other politicians will join him as he begins to have some success. He now believes that behind the jockeying of the little liberals has been Bodossakis all along, and he lays the political side (at any rate, if not much more) of the recent trouble at his door.

April 28, 1944, Friday

I went over to call on Mr. Papandreou, and got him to clear up some doubtful points in his "program" published this morning in the press. He confirmed that the publicity given to the coming conference would be after its termination, not during the session and from day to day. . . . Mr. Papandreou said he plans to use the program as the basis for the agenda of the conference, and that he is sure that all the delegates except the Communists will accept it at once, and thinks the Communists may do so, rather than be held up to the Nation as having refused something so reasonable, though he has no illusions as to their actions afterwards. Declarations and actions are two separate things in Communist practice everywhere, he said, but he is not afraid of what they can do in Greece if they give their public assent to such a truly national program as his. . . .

He said the great problem of our time is "How far will Stalin go?" . . . His personality has completely revolutionized the Greek Foreign Office, which now has something vital and expansive in it. On the purely temperamental side it is like the change from Tsaldaris to Metaxas.

April 29, 1944, Sunday

I had a long call from Mr. Papandreou in the morning, and also a visit from Mr. Massock, the new A.P. man, a very satisfactory and serious correspondent. Papandreou said he wants to send the President a message urging that the U.S. give Greece its "moral support" for the avoidance of civil war after liberation, in case a Government of National Unity is not formed before that time. He pointed out, as so many of the Greeks do, that the Allies armed EAM and must bear some of the responsibility of seeing that it doesn't impose a tyranny of the Communist Party on the Greek people. He also talked of the importance to the Western Allies of the avoidance of such a catastrophe. He knows we can't send troops, but some expression of policy on our part would do just as well, he thinks. I told him that he ought to send his message not to the President, but to the Department, through the Ambassador at Washington, and this I think he will do, if he does anything. He is certainly right in thinking that the Greek situation is today part of a world situation, and that we shall not be looking after our own interests if we ignore it. What he said was right up Edgar Mowrer's street, and General Smuts', and Ambassador Leeper's, and mine. We all see grave possibilities of trouble ahead in the unchecked advance of Russian interests and influence across the British Imperial lifeline. But it is almost impossible, it seems, to make people at home see the importance of the Balkans from this or any point of view, much less its importance to us. Yet American soldiers may have to fight another war to pay for such indifference. . . . My letters and telegrams on this subject have all gone unanswered, and today an "information" telegram from the Department shows that it was quite cold to an inquiry from the Greek Embassy as to our attitude on the Russo-Greek matter and Churchill's telegram to Mr. Molotov. I keep thinking in this connection of Cy Sulzberger's amazing and significant remark, "My paper isn't interested in the Balkans." Who is, but the Ambassador on the spot? . . . Another telegram from the Department today shows that we haven't changed our attitude regarding Yugoslavia yet, and that's a good thing. The British, having "burned their fingers," as Stevenson predicted, in their failure to put the King and Tito together, are now coming back to our point of view, and Stevenson's. Oh, la, la! . . . Harding came in and said the British have got hold of what appear to be two members of a central Cairo committee which controlled and perhaps planned the revolt. I wonder. . . . Mr. Venizelos has come out with a statement supporting Papandreou in his efforts to form a National Government, but Venizelos and the other "little liberals" here are not personally reconciled to Papandreou, but call him a "tool" of the British, and resent vocally (in Shepherd's hotel, mostly) the forcing out of Venizelos at Leeper's hands. . . . Parsons says the British are thinking of "exiling" Bodossakis and Vasiliadis from Cairo.

May 1, 1944, Monday

Long talk with Mr. Leeper in the morning. He is going to give out the President's message to Mr. Churchill about the Greek revolt, since Churchill presses for some use to be made of it, and Papandreou thinks it will strengthen his hand. However, Parsons and Kent both feel strongly that it will have the effect of making most of the Greeks confuse even further than ever American policy with British, and we shall have to take the responsibility with them for their efforts in regard to Greek internal affairs. On the other hand, on the highest level, where the President speaks, the Greek Army and Navy cannot be considered as anything but an Allied force, under Allied Command, and the issues in this revolt are greater than Greek internal policies. . . . I got off a long telegram on Molotov's reply to Mr. Churchill about the Tass reports. Molotov says, as he did last winter, that he is "uninformed about Greek affairs," but agrees to tell Tass to verify its information more closely! Of course, the Russian Foreign Office is very well informed on Greek affairs, and Novikov has shown me recently that he considers that he, at least, is quite an expert as regards them! . . .[105]

May 2, 1944, Tuesday

Conference with Lord Moyne and Novikov at the former's office on the Stirbei matter. We agreed that there is nothing more to do as regards Antonescu, whose 72 hours have expired, and that as regards Maniu's new emissary, all that we can hope is that he can give us some idea of conditions in the country; the terms to Maniu are clearly stated. Steel, Shantz, and Solod were at the conference, and Steel said he thought it evident that Maniu can do nothing in Rumania now, and that his transfer to Moldavia is the only really hopeful solution. . . . Steel told Shantz and me that Molotov has complained to London about the parachutists the

[105] In his telegram of May 1, 1944, MacVeagh commented that Molotov's protestations of ignorance regarding Greek affairs were difficult to believe. Nevertheless, Moscow was apparently contributing to "some immediate easing of the situation. . . ." *FR 1944*, V, 105.

British have been sending in to Rumania, and evidently suspects the British of independent negotiations with Antonescu! He gave us a copy of Molotov's message on this subject. Evidently the British have not made the Russians very close confidants in what they have been doing, and while I don't think there is anything in the idea of separate negotiations, the Russians always suspect what they don't understand. Misunderstandings are inevitable when you have such opposed types as Moyne and Steel on the one hand and Novikov and Solod on the other. I agree that these unkempt young men are hard to swallow socially, but it should be the business of diplomats to take the rough with the smooth. To my way of thinking, the British and the Russians should practically live in each other's houses at this juncture in history. Only mutual knowledge has a chance to create mutual trust. As it is, they are getting more and more into each other's hair!

May 3, 1944, Wednesday
General Paget spoke of continuing trouble in the Greek forces. A unit in Palestine is now in revolt, has barricaded itself in its camp and dared the British to "come and get them." The General said he is thinking of "exiling" Karapanayiotis to the Sudan, and is very dubious concerning Bodossakis.

May 4, 1944, Thursday
Call from Lieutenant Colonel Hellowell, G-2 of USAFIME, in the afternoon. He reported that the Greek unit which Paget told me had revolted is the Greek Armored Regiment (500 strong) at or near Tripoli. It laid down its arms at 10 a.m. today, and is reported quiet. Hellowell showed me some complete G-2 reports on the Greek mutinies, based on British information, and said he would send me such material, as well as the minutes of Special Operations meetings, hereafter. He said that, up to now, his information on Anglo-Greek doings has been defective, but that he hopes in the future it will be better. "It has taken nine months to crack the British unwillingess to tell us what is going on." Another remark: "British H.Q. in the Middle East can't sleep at night for thinking about Russia." He said one Britisher had shown him a map marked, "Where the next war will start." It had four places marked on it,—the Danube, the Dardanelles, the Suez Canal, and the Persian Gulf. ... Later, Mr. Skeferis[106] came in with a message from Mr. Papandreou. The latter is unhappy over the publication of Mr. Roosevelt's message,

---

[106] Ambassador Pericles Skeferis, Director General of the Greek Ministry for Foreign Affairs (Cairo).

which he says the Greeks are interpreting as being *against him,* in that it reproves "the Greeks" under his Premiership! I told Skeferis that I had had nothing to do with the publication, but that Leeper had told me that it was published with Papandreou's consent, and that in any case the message clearly relates to the mutinies and scores only those Greeks who have sabotaged the common war effort, contrary to the great Greek tradition, etc. He admitted this last, but said that he hoped the President might say some words of encouragement to the loyal Greeks at some future date. How impossible these Greeks are, hyper-sensitive, ego-centric, and likeable, all in one, like children! Skeferis almost wept when I said that Americans at home so far away and concerned in a great war, cannot,—no matter whether I wear myself out explaining!—be expected to consider all the intricacies of Greek politics, but will see in the recent revolt only the fact that the Greeks have done harm to our common cause, and will judge them accordingly.

May 5, 1944, Friday

Massock of the Associated Press ... told me that Leeper, at a conference about the coming Greek meeting in the Lebanon, expressed doubts as to whether the meeting would be a success. To me, Leeper has always expressed his "hopes," rather than his fears, and Parsons is inclined to doubt whether he really does hope for success. Hellowell spoke yesterday of British operational plans to "knock EAM out!" If the meeting in the Lebanon is a success, this cannot of course be done. So perhaps there is something in Parsons' feeling. But I am inclined to believe that the British have, as usual, no settled long-range plan, but are simply continuing to try any and all expedients to keep their influence paramount in Greece as Russia looms....

May 6, 1944, Saturday

Long talk with Leeper about the arrangements for the Lebanon meeting. The British have flown the EAM and People's Committee delegates to Bari, and will fly them from there to the Lebanon. There will be over twenty delegates in all, and I got most of the names and sent them to the Department.[107] It would seem that the main groups at the Con-

[107] The official delegates to the Lebanon Conference were as follows: *Social Democrats*: G. Papandreou, Th. Tsatsos, L. Lambrianidis, Ch. Zgouritsas. *Liberals*: S. Venizelos, C. Rentis, G. Exindaris, G. Vasiliadis. *Populists*: D. Lontos. *National Populists*: S. Theotokis. *Progressives*: G. Sakalis. *Agrarian Democrats*: A. Mylonas. *National Unity Party*: P. Kanellopoulos. *Union of Leftists*: J. Sofianopoulos. *Socialists*: D. Stratis. *Communists*: P. Roussos. *PEEA*: A. Svolos, A. Angelopoulos, N.

ference will be the leftists on one side and the liberal party people on the other. In between there will be a few royalists, popular party men, and delegates from anti-EAM resistance groups. The hopes for agreement rest on the fact that the leftists have selected fairly high-grade representatives, such as professors in the University, with whom the liberal politicians feel they can talk. A real danger lies in the fact that the liberal politicians —Venizelos, Exindaris, etc.—are now obviously controlled by money interests,—e.g. Bodossakis. . . . Leeper is going up to Beirut and hopes to visit Damascus as well, with Mrs. Leeper. He will not attend the conference himself. Personally, I think he would do better to keep away even from the vicinity, as his being there will certainly give rise to the story that the British have "controlled" the meeting, or tried to, whatever happens.

May 8, 1944, Monday

The USAFIME office of G2, sent me in some excellent British reports on the Greek revolt, very secret, and an account of a recent meeting of the sub-committee on Special Operations which shows that while the British are openly supporting "unity" via the conference in the Lebanon, they are secretly trying to build up Zervas to knock out ELAS! . . . West said that though Leeper told me the other day that the ELAS/EAM delegates flown out to Bari would be flown thence *direct* to the Lebanon, actually Sarafis[108] of ELAS was brought here and put on the carpet in the office of General Paget's Chief of Staff this morning. West was asked to be present,—surely to impress on Sarafis that we support the British! They then asked him to withdraw the 24th Regiment, which is blocking off British supplies to Zervas (who is inland), and he refused. They could do nothing with him. This will certainly not help "unity" at the conference, where the Leftist elements will surely "smell a rat" as to British designs, and probably be less willing than ever to show a cooperative spirit. Doubtless the British planned to show ELAS that it has no hope of liquidating Zervas, and thus render it obedient to "toeing the line" at the conference. But since they were unable to convince Sarafis that their support of Zervas means very much (he knows there is not much force to back up "Force 133" in its schemes), they may expect the opposite effect. . . . I am sorry for Papandreou, pushed out ahead as he is by his British backers while they fumble the ball behind him!

Askoutsis. *EAM*: M. Porfyrogenis, S. Sarafis. *EDES*: K. Pyromaglou, S. Metaxas, A. Metaxas. *EKKA*: G. Kartalis. *National Dynamic Organizations*: C. Ventiris, A. Stathatos. Philip Dragoumis attended as an independent.

[108] Colonel Stefanos Sarafis, republican officer, and commander-in-chief of ELAS.

May 9, 1944, Tuesday

[I]n the afternoon a visit from Mrs. Karapanayiotis, whose husband was arrested yesterday by the British—just in time to send the liberal party delegates off to the conference of "National Unity" in a fury! The British have certainly done all they could to make the task of their man, Mr. Papandreou, difficult, and it certainly does look now as if they really do desire the conference to fail! . . . The Greek situation is certainly very bad on the eve of the great conference. A good summary of our position in it all is given by the OSS. "It is worth noting that both inside Greece and in Cairo the British convey the impression that the United States is in full agreement with their Greek policy. As matters stand at present, the United States shares equally with Britain the responsibility for allied mishandling of the Greek problem. In fact, however, the United States does not have the resources to enable her to share equally in the actual direction of policy. Allied policy towards Greece is strictly British policy for which the United States will be held responsible."

May 10, 1944, Wednesday

Harry Hill and I attended General Hughes' first informal meeting on Balkan relief. The General prefaced the meeting by saying that of course he has full responsibility for the military phase but would like us all who are interested in the Balkan affair to know his plans and give him advice as we might wish. Brigadier Eves spoke on organization and plans for operations, and Brigadier King spoke of the present stockpile position. The Yugoslav operational plans are obviously extremely speculative owing to the political situation, the Greek somewhat less so, but still not wholly clear. Developments will determine a lot in this regard. The stockpile position is bad, particularly as regards fats and clothing, including blankets. I feel the meeting was very useful, and hope there will be others at regular intervals and that they will be kept on the same informal level. There is a rumor, which I asked Harding and Parsons both to verify if possible, that Bodossakis has been arrested, as well as Karapanayiotis.

May 12, 1944, Friday

The Department sent me a telegram authorizing me to "attend the conference between the Greek Government and the politicians" in the Lebanon, or send a representative. In reply I sent my reasons for thinking it inadvisable to go there, and explaining that no outsiders have been invited in any case. I do feel that for us to have anybody, not to say the Ambassador, hanging round the outskirts of the conference would only create a false impression and encourage the Greeks to think that we are with the British in their attempts to manipulate Greek internal affairs. Most of the time we can't dissociate ourselves sufficiently from our allies to counteract the impression, which they naturally like to foster, that British policy in Greece is Anglo-American, but surely here is a situation where we can. I have asked Wadsworth and the OWI in Beirut to let us know of anything they may hear "without showing undue interest," but essentially what this Embassy wants to know is the results of the conference, and its day to day conduct (if any of this is made known to outsiders) can be left to the journalists,—and of course to British intrigue. . . . We got some more news as to the identity of the delegates, and believe the conference has started. . . . Wally Barbour learned from a good source (SIME—British Secret Intelligence, Middle East) that Bodossakis was arrested last night on Mr. Churchill's personal order,—"arrest him and I will take the responsibility." Another bombshell for the Liberals at the Conference. Surely it ought to have been exploded long ago, or not until the conference was over.

May 14, 1944, Sunday

After lunch Lord Moyne held a solemn conclave with Novikov, Steel and myself on the subject of the Stirbei Mission. It appeared that the British wanted to send another back-up message to Maniu, in the shape of an ultimatum: You have our terms. Now go ahead, pop over to Russia, unfurl the flag of Russian cooperation with us, and get our good terms. But if you don't do this, these terms will no longer be available to you, and so forth. But Novikov pointed out that Stalin, in his May 1st speech, and the Three Powers in a later address to the Satellites have already emphasized the need for something to be done promptly, and he thought it would be "weak" of us to put in another oar now. . . . Steel then asked us whether we would agree to the British sending in another radio team (2 men) and set to Maniu, as nothing has been heard from him direct for some time and it would appear that something has happened to the men and the set we have hitherto been using. I said I saw no objection, and Novikov said the same, only he would have to ask his government. The British have had such nasty messages from Molotov (so Moyne said to Peggy at lunch) on the subject of their unilateral operation of secret communications and intelligence in Rumania, that they are now falling over backwards to allay suspicion! . . . Steel explained how in the absence of radio communication the British still can communicate with Maniu though they can't get replies the same way or as quickly. It was really ingenious.

May 15, 1944, Monday

Call from a Mr. Queen of the OWI who showed me the plans for circulars and leaflets which OWI is carrying out on behalf of AML. A most ambitious program. We shall have to be careful not to treat the Greek peasants as if they were Americans. I spotted a case in point: "You have a veterinary inspector in your district. Go to him. This means you!" etc. . . . I called Harry Hill in, and we arranged that all copy, before being finally o.k.'d for printing, will pass through our hands. We may thus be able to keep absurdities out, but whether the whole campaign of colored posters and other printed matter will not seem odd to the Greeks, and therefore suspicious, is another thing. . . . Warner of the British Embassy came in with a message from Leeper. The Delegates of the People's Committee have sent messages to Churchill and Roosevelt. We passed the one to F.D.R. on to the Department.[109] . . . The Delegates agreed, said Leeper, to the publication of the one to Churchill, and he was himself very keen for this, since, to his surprise, it contained a severe condemnation of the recent mutinies. . . . Wadsworth telegraphed that the Conference in the Lebanon has been deferred, because Papandreou is ill, probably till tomorrow. . . . I got a telegram from the Dept. explaining its previous telegram authorizing me to go to the Lebanon. This, it appears, was only in case I desired someone to be there with a knowledge of Greek affairs, and was not, despite its form, a "travel order" in any sense. . . . Worked a long time on my letter to F.D.R., which because of the complications of the present situation and the continued need of being, nevertheless, both brief and clear, has been perhaps the most difficult of the series to date.

---

[109] The PEEA message to Roosevelt, signed by Svolos, Porfyrogenis and Roussos, read as follows: "We, the representatives of Fighting Greece at the Conference for National Unity, wish to express to you our respectful admiration and gratitude for the friendly interest which you take in our country.

The Greek people, who are fighting in the towns and in the mountains against the most barbarous of tyrannies, will never allow themselves to be withdrawn from the camp of the Allies and of the United Nations who are fighting for freedom and amongst whom your great country occupies, under your illustrious leadership, so glorious a position.

Though the desire for national unity has led to actions as melancholy as the late mutinies in the Middle East forces, actions deplored and condemned by all, we can assure Your Excellency that the Greek people, by their struggle of yesterday, today and tomorrow and by the help of their great Allies, will succeed in rubbing out that dark page.

We rely on your sympathy which you have so often shown towards our country and we assure you that we will do our utmost to achieve that national unity which is an indispensable condition for the liberation, peace and well-being of our country which has endured so much from Italian, German and Bulgarian aggressors." *FR 1944*, V, 108-109.

Cairo, May 15, 1944

Dear Franklin:

Thank you very much for your letter of April 1, written in the full spirit of that date. Though I should love to watch you playing "autarch" in the Balkans, and am sure you could make a success of it if anyone could, you may believe that I am happy, with millions of others, that fate cast you for a different role.

Since I last wrote, the situation here has not failed to become even more interesting and complicated. In my letter of February 17, I had a good deal to say about Russia and her growing influence in this region. Recently, she has made even more rapid advances than seemed likely a few months ago. This has been true, not only in the territory reoccupied by her armies, but in the thoughts and fears of men. The chief intelligence officer of our forces here said to me the other day, "British Middle East Headquarters can't sleep for thinking about Russia," and he then told me of a map which a Britisher had shown him, entitled, "The next war begins here," with four places marked on it, namely, the Danube, the Dardanelles, the Suez Canal and the Persian Gulf. You may remember the acute British fears of Russia when we were young—Kipling's "Man who Was" and his "Bear that walks like a Man." These fears are all coming back now with a vengeance, and will doubtless be intensified when Russia is no longer simply one of the great powers but the only great power remaining on the European continent. The British Ambassador to Greece recently said to me, in regard to developments in that country, "Greece is now at the cross-roads, the question being whether she is to move into the Russian orbit and lose her independence, or remain a European country under British influence." Our Consul-General in Istanbul is here to confer with me. I asked him what he thought of the various Communist-inspired organizations now operating as "resistance groups" throughout the Balkans under various guises of democracy and nationalism. His reply was that there can be felt in Istanbul a powerful Russian surge into the Balkan area at present —"but underneath." Finally, General Smuts, posting through here on his way to London, said to me, "Something very serious is going on in the Balkans." He had no doubt that recent British efforts to deal politically with Tito, and the British handling of Greek affairs to date, have been unfortunate.

In this connection, the British have now apparently failed to sell King Peter to Tito, and having somewhat "burned their fingers" in the attempt, as their own Ambassador here warned them they would, seem to be edging back to our firm position of supporting the latter militarily and the former politically until such time as the liberated people may choose its own regime. At the same time, we have had a political crisis in Greek affairs and a revolt in the Greek armed forces, with the results almost exactly in keeping with the Prime Minister's predictions which I quoted in my last. You will remember that Mr. Tsouderos told King George that if he did not agree to certain proposals, the government would fall and the King "would find himself with no possibility of forming another government which would have any effective support either within or without the country, while there would be trouble in the armed forces and the Political Committee which is now striving to emulate Tito in Greece, and which is certainly controlled by Communist elements, would be the gainer." In the event, King George characteristically deferred action, and he now has a new Price Minister without any Cabinet at all, while negotiations are in progress for the formation of a Government of National Unity in participation with the People's Committee which has been exchanging notes with Tito. Thus, in Yugoslavia a Communist marshal has rebuffed a British attempt to bring King Peter back into the local picture, and in Greece leftist elements have stepped into a position in the national councils which they have never before enjoyed.

The Greek revolt falls somewhat disturbingly into this picture. As an overt mutiny, it has been quelled, at least for the time being, but politically it is still a force and socially it still simmers. On the surface, its causes have all seemed similar to those of other Greek "movements" known to us in the past. As I once misquoted to the Department years ago, "In the Spring an old Greek's fancy lightly turns to thoughts of revolution." By this Spring, the Tsouderos government had been in power for all of three years, and was consequently widely unpopular with the unstable Greeks. The Army, being traditionally "in politics," was of course the normal instrument with which to upset the government, and therefore the lining up of the politicians with a group of Army officers was no occasion for surprise. Furthermore, the issue of royalism versus Venizelism being still paramount in the Greek political mind, and the King having supported the Fascist dictatorship of Metaxas, it was natural that the movement should be on the "liberal" side. A new and disturbing factor was of course injected by the necessity of staging the movement on foreign soil. The British, who are the guardians of security in Egypt, and operationally in charge of the Greek forces, said, "You can't do this!" while the Greeks replied, "It's our affair," and thus some very bad interallied complications arose, which have done some harm to the war effort and threatened to do more. But there was something else which was new in this movement, something which sets it aside fundamentally, and not merely on the surface, from all previous Greek "revolutions," and which soon took it out of the control of the politicians and their high-ranking officer friends, placing it squarely in the general international picture created by the Russian advance. This was the existence and activity in the forces, both afloat and ashore, of Communistic committees and cells. In addition, there has been open support of the movement from Russian sources, expressed by the Ambassador here in criticism of British repressive measures, and by the Moscow press and radio in repeated attacks on the "Fascism" of the Tsouderos régime. I have been informed that after Mr. Churchill protested to Mr. Molotov about the Moscow press, the latter called in the Greek Minister and told him that the Soviet Government is "not interfering" in the Greek internal situation. Recently, too, the Russian radio and press reports have been less provocative than formerly. Nevertheless, like Truthful James, "I state but the facts" when I say that, beneath all its traditional Greek trappings, the revolt was inspired and maintained by an ideology especially associated with Russia, and that while it lasted Russian sympathy with it was openly shown, despite its dangerous implications for the Allied cause. Incidentally, there are also some grounds for suspecting that while the Greek politicians and officers probably were not aware of the nature of the ferment in the rank and file which they attempted to exploit, the Germans had agents here who were, and that the fifth column played some part as a catalyzer in the precipitation of events at this critical time.

Though ostensibly quelled, this revolt has played its part in bringing the forces of the extreme left into the national Greek councils, and from that point of view must be regarded as having succeeded. Furthermore, as I have said, its spirit is still simmering, and it is doubtful whether a substantial part of the Greek armed forces can be counted on for further service in this war unless present efforts to achieve "national unity" result in a government satisfactory to those elements. The new premier, Mr. George Papandreou, who has just come out from Greece and who, while not exactly in the top political flight, is a much more potent figure than any of the politicians who have been in the government-in-exile these past three years, is a social democrat and strongly opposed to the "resistance movement" known as EAM, which the Moscow Press has been supporting. The Soviet Ambassador has informed me—though only a short time ago he expressed complete ignorance of Greek affairs—that Papandreou is "not the man" to achieve national unity in Greece. On the other hand, British influence has made him premier, and the British are backing him to effect a settlement which will still preserve their paramount influence in Greece. It seems hardly likely that he can succeed. In choosing him, the British have bitterly offended the "liberal" Cairo politicians and have probably alienated what remains of the old Venizelist party in Greece. At the same time, on the very eve of the conference, their military has cracked down heavily on some of these same politicians, and their friends, arresting them for being implicated, even if only through negligence or folly, in the outbreak and political conduct of the recent revolt. Mr. Papandreou is therefore going to the conference in the Lebanon with the assured enmity of the liberals as well as of the left, and since the King and the royalists are nothing to count on nowadays on account of their recent connection with the Metaxas dictatorship, is without visible means of support except for the British and his own eloquence. A miracle may happen, of course, and I hope it will, so that Greek "unity" may be obtained now, but otherwise the outcome would appear almost certain to be more confusion, more resentment over British interference as a cause of Greek frustration, and more turning of the eyes towards Moscow.

In view of all this, and should nothing worse occur, I believe that when Athens is restored we may look to see a diplomatic game there (as well as in the rest of the Balkans, Eastern Europe and the Middle East) similar to that which we saw in the past, only this time not between Great Britain and the Axis but between her and the Union of Soviet Socialist Republics. Can this be prevented from becoming more than a game? If it leads to war, I suppose we shall again be involved. To keep it from doing so would seem, therefore, to be in our most vital interests, and "to achieve harmonious action during the period of peace," as Mr. Hull says, to be the only way. Just now, however, the drift does not appear to be towards harmonious action. This is not true on the highest level, of course, but it may affect that level later through the sowing of suspicion and distrust. In my letter of February 17, I suggested that we might take the lead in the coming Balkan relief operations in order to cushion off the impact of British and Russian pressures. That suggestion, which I also made to the Department, was apparently out of line with the short-term, strictly military policy of the hour. On the other hand, much is being done here in the way of economic planning for the Balkans during the so-called military period, in regard to which the Russians are only occasionally being advised, if they are being advised at all. This, which to their minds may very easily appear as masking an attempt at establishing a post-war zone of influence, may be just as dangerous to future harmony as their own propaganda practices which annoy and alarm the British. Perhaps what is needed is closer consultation on all vital subjects having to do with this region. In any case I feel, and am so recommending to the Department, that the Russians should be brought more closely into all our long-term planning hereabouts. Meanwhile, our efforts here to maintain an independent balancing policy, are being heavily handicapped by our good cousins. Though we stand aloof from the interior problems of small states, the British, who do not so stand aloof, "convey the impression that the United States is in full agreement" with their maneuvers, if I may borrow some words from a recent OSS report. It is difficult to combat this advantage which they are taking of our being their faithful allies without damaging our all-important wartime solidarity. While the process continues, however, we are more and more being committed by implication to one side of the local struggle for influence which, though it may not involve the higherups, is nevertheless going on right merrily. Perhaps the false impression given may be rectified when the war is over, though it would be better if there could be no delay. As General Smuts said the other day, genuine buffer states in this region are a necessity, but if the trends which are now observable under our very noses are continued for long, such states are certainly not likely to be realized.

To turn to happier things, your new Minister to South Africa, General Holcomb, is here (held up for a few days by an illness of his wife's). I have seen a lot of him and we have had long talks about "the Union." I think you have made an absolute ten-strike in picking him, and that the South Africans ought to eat him up, while his shrewdness will never lose sight of the interests of Uncle Sam. "My" people in South Africa, I know, have been somewhat alarmed over the advance publicity and grim photographs of the former head of the Devil Dogs. So I sent our Chargé a wire the other day, as follows: "Please tell all the boys I have had some long talks with your new chief and have found both him and his wife delightful. He is simple, kindly, humorous, intelligent and interested, and with your cooperation should make a great success in South Africa. Best wishes to you all." That, together with letters I have given the General to South African public men, and the diplomats, closes a fascinating chapter of my life for which I am indebted to you.

Ever affectionately yours,
Lincoln MacVeagh (9)

May 17, 1944, Wednesday

The Greek conference is supposed to have begun today. Leeper has been at a hotel in the Lebanon, seeing the delegates who have called on him and talking to the press. To this last he continues to emphasize that the conference is purely Greek and that he is "not interfering." What is the Greek for *eye-wash*? It must be heard quite frequently in Beirut these days. . . .

May 18, 1944, Thursday

I got a shock yesterday when I received an "Information Bulletin" from the Department in which my reports on the Greek situation were handled in such a way as wholly to miss all the points I was trying to make! The method followed appeared to be to take striking statements out of their context and string them along in sequence. There was only one factual error, but the paragraphs all succeeded in giving quite a false impression of what was reported on. . . . So I wrote Foy Kohler a letter today pointing this out. I only hope the trouble came from the work having been turned over to somebody incompetent, and that it has not arisen from inability on my part to make competent people understand. I also gave Foy a resumé of what I feel to have been the important things to cover in a resumé of the period treated (1) that the Greek revolt was quelled without a clash between allies, (2) that the movement differed from all previous movements by being staged on foreign soil and by the presence of communist ferment in the forces, (3) that Papandreou was put into the Premiership by British influence with a view to the coming Conference of National Unity, and (4) that Russian disapproval of British handling of Greek affairs was openly expressed during the revolt. All these things were missed completely in the Information Bulletin, though I thought my telegrams, if read with care, would bring them out. . . . The Greek Conference began today, and Mr. Papandreou made an opening speech putting it up to EAM to show by dissolving ELAS and regrouping it in a National Army that it does not intend trying to foist a tyranny on the people. "The Greeks are averse to tyranny of all kinds," he said, almost repeating the "speech" he made to me about EAM some weeks ago and which I then reported to the Dept. . . . The list of delegates is given in the papers in full—no more secrecy. Perhaps the delegates now feel the Germans know about their absence anyway, and there is no use trying to protect their families, and their own future movement, anymore. Their return to Greece, anywhere but in the mountains with the guerrillas, is now impossible.

May 19, 1944, Friday

Received a most interesting long message from the Department on the subject of Lord Moyne's Committees. I am to tell him that my Government is "much disturbed" over these having been set up without prior consultation with it as to its views, particularly as I had already told him of its disapproval of the Balkan Relief Committee and its expectation of further advices on the Balkan Affairs Committee. The Department's idea now—which I am to communicate—is that the Operations and Relief Sub-committees should be dropped altogether, and only a Balkan Affairs Committee of "top men"—me, Landis and Giles (as an observer) and similar Britishers—retained for advisory purposes only, not day to day operations. All this is in strict accord with the ideas I suggested, and I know that Giles feels the same as I do. The Department says the War Department concurs in its message. So now we'll see what the Lord has to say! Incidentally, Murphy has been instructed to hand the same message to

Wilson, and copies have gone to London and Moscow. This last is included because the Department suggests that the Russians should be invited to join, or at least attend the meetings of the Balkan Affairs Committee—"to avoid suspicion and distrust,"—again (which makes me feel quite happy) in line with my feelings, and the telegram I recently sent. ... The news from the Lebanon is of more talk, this time of Venizelos, in condemnation of the recent mutinies. It is amusing to recollect how he tried to exploit the "unrest in the armed forces," at least in the early stages!

May 20, 1944, Saturday

Got a telegram from the Department with a reply from the President to a message sent him the other day by the leftist delegates to the Lebanon Conference, Svolos, Roussos,[110] and Porfyrogenis,[111] and relayed this at once to Wadsworth in Beirut.[112] The British think the Conference will be over today, but the message is a good one, on the general subject of Greek unity and how much we hope for it, and so I see no reason why it should not go through whether the Conference closes or not. The Department asked my advice on releasing it for publication, and I said "yes," since it might be misquoted. It also asked whether the names of the men addressed should be given, or whether they should be described simply as "certain delegates to the conference." But I thought that as the Greeks will all soon know who got "the message from the President," there would be no use in keeping its addressees officially anonymous, while to do so might well give some offense. I suppose the Dept. was doubtful of the wisdom of the President's sending a message to the leftists in particular (as it would appear), but after all he did it, and a cautious lack of candour hardly goes well with a generous gesture! ... Wally Barbour and Shantz fixed up a letter to Lord Moyne embodying the Department's instruction, and I called in Mr. Landis and read it to him. He said it was "all right with him" and that his previous objections to the Department's attitude were based wholly on its lack of any definite directions, but that

[110] Petros Roussos, member of KKE's Central Committee.

[111] Miltiadis Porfyrogenis, Secretary-General of EAM.

[112] The President's message, dated May 19, 1944, read as follows: "I have received your welcome and reassuring message. We Americans are firm friends of the Greek people, who have fought so valiantly and suffered so direly during the course of the war, and have therefore been profoundly distressed by the recent disunity in Greek ranks. But we remember that the Greeks have always shown the capacity to submerge their differences and rally together in times of real national crisis. The occasion and the opportunity exists again today and it is our earnest hope and prayer that the Greek leaders assembled in the Near East will make of the current conference a new landmark of purposeful unity in Greek history." *FR 1944*, V, 109-110.

now he felt differently. I told him of my feeling that Lord Moyne's office is not acting correctly in handling the informal meetings under AML. The AML is an allied affair, stemming from AMHQ which in turn comes under the Allied Commander in Algiers. Lord Moyne's office is not "allied" in any sense, and should not be calling AML's meetings for it and preparing its agenda! He saw the point and said he'd speak about it, but I think I had better see General Hughes myself. I also discussed with Landis the handling of UNRRA here, and Matthews' habit of writing as UNRRA chief on Lord Moyne's stationery. I said I thought the Resident Minister's office showed a tendency to try to get its hand on everything going on here. In the case of UNRRA I didn't see, however, what I could do about it, as I could in the case of AML, since the Department wants us all to keep aloof from UNRRA affairs. Landis agreed that the trouble with UNRRA is that it hasn't got a big enough man to handle it here, a man who will see the point of the organization's international character, and hold out for its realization. In the absence of such a man, he said, national attachments and allegiances will persist. As I see it, the danger here is that UNRRA will operate so clearly as a British affiliate that it will breed suspicion, especially among the Russians (as the BSC has already done) of its being only another mask for British imperialism.

May 22, 1944, Monday

The news on the Greek Conference is that it ended Saturday, just an hour or so before Wadsworth got the President's message to Svolos and the others. Apparently the climax was a general signing of Papandreou's original program, and a rather emotional scene of mutual congratulation. But it does not yet appear whether any agreement was reached as to the composition of the "Government of National Unity" which was the aim of the Conference, or as to whether the guerrilla bands are to be reorganized as a National Army. Mr. Papandreou has sent messages on a triumphant note to F.D.R. (through us, today)[113] and Mr. Churchill, and as his secretary (young Frantzis) says, "to others"—Stalin?—and has come back to Cairo to present his resignation to the King, obviously in the expectation that H.M. will then entrust to him the formation of the

[113] Papandreou's message to the American President, dated May 22, 1944, read: "Great was the distress of our beloved Fatherland caused by the recent mutiny of the Greek Armed Forces in the Middle East. I am happy today to announce, Mr. President, that the Congress of Greek Delegates in the Lebanon has put an end to the internal strife and determined the national unity against the barbarian invaders who are violating the sacred soil of our Fatherland. The United Greek nation looks with complete confidence to the noble people of the United States and to their great leader and invokes their full support for the realization of the struggle for national liberation." *FR 1944,* V, 111.

new Government. Papandreou is very correct,—"The New Government will be formed at the bidding of superior authority" etc. But unless he has a mandate in his hands from the delegates, and the King accepts this and directs the formation of the Cabinet accordingly, there is likely to be trouble, as all the delegates are now coming to Cairo! Going to the Lebanon was of course decided on to begin with to keep political shenanigans away from here. . . . Leeper has not come back and Parsons tried all day to find out whether the Conference really came to political decisions or not, but without result. Meanwhile I forwarded Papandreou's message to the President via the Department together with the thanks of Svolos *et al.*, and sent a telegram of my own describing the present undetermined state of affairs. . . . Had a long talk with Col. Toulmin, who recently returned from the U.S.A. His Yugoslav and Albanian sections are transported to Bari, and he has been directed to go to Turkey and bring the office of OSS there (under MacFarland) more closely under Cairo's control. It hasn't been running smoothly. . . . Toulmin told me that Skouras[114] has been forced out of OSS here at last—described him as a "hot potato." The reason Skouras wants to stay here, and he got a job now with the Greek War Relief (of which he is a director), is that he is under indictment in the USA! . . . Toulmin also told me that "Overlord" will come between the second and fifth of June. . . . The news from Italy is that the American advance continues, with the capture of Terracina. . . . The Russian front has been quiet for 29 days, practically a month now. . . . In Greece, the Germans have made more arrests of prominent persons, including the Archbishop, and are seemingly indulging in a new orgy of terrorism. Caused by the escape of the delegates, or the growing knowledge that they have lost the war and must soon leave their conquests behind, or both? Toulmin says they are not moving any troops out, but that their morale, especially in Crete, is reported very low.

May 23, 1944, Tuesday

Lord Moyne replied to my letter conveying the Department's remarks about his committees. He sees no justification for so serious a message! I wrote a letter in rejoinder, but destroyed it, and hope we can have a talk. He is all wrong, and the Department, which his action has "embarrassed," is right, but there is no need to descend to acrimonious discussion! His office has tried to sidetrack Washington in this matter, and has been caught out in the attempt. We'd better now concentrate on joint action for the future, not rub in the past. Harold Shantz and Wally Barbour both take this view, and after I had said what I wanted to say in my

[114] George Skouras, Director of the Greek War Relief, brother of Spiro Skouras, President of Fox Films.

letter, I did too, and the letter was destroyed. Lord Moyne's foolish missive stands, however, in the record. Abe Lincoln's policy about destroying angry letters,—but writing them first, so as to get the bile well out of the system, is wise. . . . Papandreou has been told by the King to form a government, and it appears that its composition was decided on at the conference. Nearly everybody will be in it,—about 16 portfolios and some 11 parties and organizations represented. Mr. Tsouderos called this morning and said he felt the Conference had succeeded up to a point, and that a step has been taken in advance, but that several knotty points were left undetermined, on which the new cabinet may well split as time goes on: the question of the King's return and the question of disbanding the guerrillas and reforming them as a national army. In regard to the second of these, he said that Allied Hq. Middle East had served notice that ELAS was not to be tampered with, as it needs it in its business. Leeper has of course been gunning for ELAS, and through it, EAM, so here was a check to him as well as to Greek "unity." Papandreou has had to agree "for the time being," but his task with a cabinet divided between anti- and pro-EAMites will be difficult. As to the King question, it is too bad that something definite was not agreed on, since sooner or later, the cabinet members will begin seeing everything in relation to it, as of old. . . . Another question, Mr. Tsouderos said, which was left unresolved was that of the punishment of the mutineers. Practically the only achievements of the conference were to agree to agree while all the members were in the Lebanon, and to have everybody represented in the new Government. Beyond these two things the field was left open. . . .[115] Received news from Steel that the new Rumanian emissary is arriving, and a conference is to be held day after tomorrow at Stirbei's place in Gezira.

May 24, 1944, Wednesday

The formation of the new Greek cabinet has been held up while the leftist delegates from Greece await word from home as to whether they may or may not participate. Papandreou, meanwhile, is stressing his interest in relief and rehabilitation—a good idea, since Tsouderos has been

[115] The announced "Agreement" reached at the Lebanon Conference included the reorganization of the Greek armed forces and the unification of the guerrilla organizations "under the orders of a single Government"; the end of the "reign of terror" in Greece; provision of adequate relief; punishment of "traitors and those who have exploited the misfortunes of the people"; and the satisfaction of national territorial claims. On the issue of the King's return the "Agreement" stated: "On the question of the sovereign power, the political leaders who have joined the Government of National Unity are understood to retain such views as they have already expressed." Iatrides, *Revolt in Athens*, pp. 294-95.

criticized widely for doing so little, i.e. saying so little, since there wasn't much he *could* do. Papandreou is also putting out the idea that Greece has contributed her blood and glory, and now the allies should *give* not *lend* her their aid! . . . I sent a wire off on this, and on the things the recent conference failed to do, so that the Department may see that all is not roses in the path of the new Government of National Unity. . . . Lord Moyne came in to see me about his committees. His office thought I should go to him, but as things stood on this question—he having "embarrassed" my Government, I thought my office would be the proper meeting place, and Wally Barbour arranged it. As a result of our talk, he took back the letter he had sent me, which expressed "surprise" and betrayed annoyance, and told me to take no official cognizance of a long *aide-memoire* he had brought with him. I explained just what had occurred (his ideas were very hazy!) and why the Department had written as it had, and then got him to say that he will draw up his views on each of the Department's present proposals and send them to London, with a copy going to General Wilson. He is obsessed with the idea of *committees*, whereas I stressed again the desirability of informal consultation, leaving the chain of responsibility clear, in the hands of the military and civilian operating agencies. As to Russian participation on the Balkan Affairs Committee, he said he would give no views. He thinks, however, that it would be inadvisable, as there would be too much likelihood of misunderstanding and misrepresentation, for language, and also for other reasons. He said, "The Russians don't tell us anything they are doing or let us in on their committees, so why should we reciprocate?" I pointed out that this was not the question, but rather whether we might not gain by seeking to disarm suspicion. . . . We talked also of the new emissary, and he read me an instruction from London to the effect that since the Russians have shown so much suspicion and distrust in the matter of de Chastelain and other British agents in Rumania, he should tell Novikov that the initiative in regard to all dealings with the new emissary is his. The message also said that Moyne is not to press Maniu in regard to the plan of going to Moldavia, and that the Foreign Office has never believed in the plan anyway, but only fell in with it because the Russians took it up so strongly. . . . It seems, from what Lord Moyne said, that Mr. Churchill's explanation of the doings of de Chastelain and other agents in Rumania failed to satisfy Molotov, who returned another nasty message, and Mr. Churchill is now very angry indeed with his ally, and disgusted in the bargain. . . . Got a long message from the Department about the amalgamation of OWI in the PWB,[116] in reply to mine. It appears that my suggestions as to clearance with us on political questions,

---

[116] PWB = Psychological Warfare Board (American).

and on the entrance of OWI along with the Diplomatic Missions when we go into the liberated countries have found favor with OWI and the Department both. There is to be a policy committee here, with a representative of "the Ambassador" on it, and the OWI section of the PWB will follow its own directives from home, "marrying" them here with the British PWE directives and then submitting the marriage to the Committee. Complicated as usual; but perhaps we can get it working.

May 25, 1944, Thursday

Meeting at Stirbei's apartment with him and Vishoianu, the new emissary from Maniu. Lord Moyne, Novikov and I, with Steel, Shantz and Solod were present, and a couple of British—Stirbei's "jailer" and Masterman, the secretary, who, I found out from Toulmin later, spilled the story of what went on to OSS, just as he did with our first meeting! Vishoianu made a very poor impression, a small, shifty-eyed person. However, he did little but mumble some comments, and Stirbei did the talking for the Rumanian side. He read a prepared memorandum in French, and then explained it and answered questions. The gist was that Antonescu has failed, being under German control, and that the number of German troops in the country has so increased that a *coup d'état* by Maniu, as proposed, is now impracticable. However, Maniu is willing to try to stage a revolt in the army, with the help of General Nicolescu and some others, and the consent of the King which has been obtained. Only this will be difficult as the army is now in the line, or that part of the army which can be used—the rest being too much under German control in the interior of the country—and what is in line is sandwiched between German units. Maniu wants the allies to advise as to how, when and where he should make his attempt, in order to offer the maximum advantage to the allied cause under these conditions. After discussion, we told Stirbei that Maniu should send someone through the lines to the Russians, and fix it up with them. Lord Moyne turned the initiative over to Novikov, but offered to help him in the matter of communications, if asked. It was arranged that Stirbei should draft his message in consultation with Novikov, and the British would see that it gets to Cretianu in Ankara. The emissaries said that Maniu wanted also to present some views on the armistice terms, but Novikov, with our concurrence, said it is now up to the Rumanians to act, and that details of the terms, the main lines of which have been laid down, can wait. He also reminded the emissaries that by not acting at once when the terms were presented the Rumanians have helped to bring about a situation in which what they can do to "earn their passage" is a good deal less than it was. . . . I had

CAIRO · 529

long calls from Masseck of the A.P. and Barboza-Carneiro, the Brazilian Minister, both on the subject of Greece and the recent conference. A few cabinet officers have been selected, and sworn in,—Venizelos as Vice-President of the Council, Kartalis[117] (representing Kafandaris) without portfolio, and Philip Dragoumis as Under-Secretary for Foreign Affairs. The Prime Minister has appointed an old associate of his as *chef de Cabinet* with rank of Under-Minister,[118] the most interesting thing about whom is that he is said to be Russophile. It seems that it isn't only the delay in hearing from EAM and the rest of the leftists in Greece that is holding up the formation of the Government, but also jockeying (about Shepherd's foyer) for positions. It was decided at the Conference who would be in the Cabinet, but not in what posts. So happy days have come again, for the Greeks, who have agreed to agree, but by no means exactly how.

May 26, 1944, Friday

Toulmin said that as a result of the Molotov-Churchill fight over British secret operations in Rumania, all these operations have now been stopped, both British and American, and there is also a stop on such operations except *intelligence*, and sabotage operations already projected, in Bulgaria, Hungary and Greece. Toulmin is discouraged, after all the work he has done in organizing and instructing "teams." . . . He also told me that Skouras, whose resignation he secured, is not now to resign after all, since a message came in today signed "Marshall" forbidding it and saying that the War Department and OSS both want him to stay on and are much interested in some plans he has, etc.!

May 27, 1944, Saturday

Sent off my telegram on the psychological warfare activities (in the Balkans) which fall outside our control. . . . It is impossible for us to enlighten the Balkans as to what American policy really is so long as powerful propaganda and news agencies like the BBC and Reuter's continually distort it. . . . Ensign Johnson (Giannakis) of JICAME came in with Ralph Kent and gave me his story of the Lebanon Conference which he attended (on the outside) for that organization. What he had to say confirmed our previous impressions here. Leeper was nearby throughout, and was visited at one time or another by practically all the delegates. His constantly reiterated statements that though he was exerting no

[117] George Kartalis, republican politician, and representative of EKKA.
[118] Lambros Lambrianidis.

influence on the conference the delegates should come to an agreement in the best interests of Greece and in accordance with the wishes of HM's Government, and of the United Nations, acted as a kind of steam-roller on the conference, and though many delegates came in a critical, and some even in a recalcitrant mood, none finally dared to stand out against Papandreou with this backing behind him. They therefore all signed his general terms, but at the same time no specific results were achieved, these all being left open for subsequent settlement here. . . . Dinner at the Mena House for the Leepers and their daughter, who has just come out from England. Arthur Parsons came along. Leeper talked to me about the conference and confirmed that he had talked with practically all the delegates and advised them. Also he showed that he knows very well that we can, from now on, expect a lot of intrigue and maneuvering here in Cairo. He told me that Friday night the British sent Sarafis back into Greece, not only to get the EAM/ELAS crowd to agree to have their representatives in the Government, but to start negotiations for the disbanding of the guerrillas and their reformation into a national army. The British Military, he confirmed, stopped this movement at the Conference, because they want a guerrilla group to be functioning in Greece when the Germans withdraw, but they don't want more than 10,000, and as the ELAS says it has 30,000, the disbanding of two-thirds of this force can begin at once. Zervas has promised that with his much smaller group he will do the same thing, and Sarafis said not only that he would carry the British proposals to EAM but that he would himself urge their acceptance. This sounds pretty rosy to me. . . . During the day we got a telegram from the Department conveying F.D.R.'s thanks to Papandreou for *his* thanks for F.D.R.'s reply to Svolos *et al.*, and giving a new expression of American hopes for Greek unity.[119] I passed this on at once in a personal note to Papandreou. . . . Mylonas has taken the oath as Minister of Marine, and Petros Rallis as Minister of Air. The Prime Minister, for the time being, will be War Minister (doubtless a good move at this moment.) . . . Leeper, when I told him of Mrs. Karapanayiotis' visit to me and her complaints about the way her husband was arrested, showed no sympathy whatever. I don't blame him as to Karapanayiotis, himself, but the lady did make some points which may be hurtful to the British from a propaganda viewpoint. However, Leeper, who said he saw this, said that it could only do harm in the Liberal party circles, which he affected to regard with disdain. "I tell Venizelos that I don't like his

---

[119] "The President and the American Government and people have learned with the utmost pleasure the good news of the unity agreement reached in Lebanon, which they are confident will help speed liberation and restoration of Greece." *FR 1944*, V, 112.

friends, and I don't. And he replies, 'they're not my friends, really they're not!' But he goes on playing around with them." Leeper was particularly critical of Exindaris as a trouble maker, and spoke of having some "serious words" to say to Lambrakis, the editor of the *Eleftheron Vima*, who was not allowed to go near the conference though he came out at the same time as the delegates. I feel there is something decidedly schoolmasterly about Mr. Leeper, and wonder if he'll survive as Ambassador to Greece after the country is liberated.

May 29, 1944, Monday
Long talks with General Giles in the morning and King George of Greece in the afternoon. The rest of the day was spent on telegrams and despatches. . . . Prepared with Parsons a long telegram on the Greek situation. Pessimism about national unity seems to be growing. . . . The Venizelists and the leftists both seem to be regretting that they let Papandreou get away with the Premiership, and to interpret the division he is making of the chief ministries as "knuckling under to the British." . . . Shantz and Wally Barbour had a great time going over a "policy" telegram I drafted in connection with a blast sent in to the Department by Murphy. It seems to be Murphy's idea that we shouldn't stress any differences in policy between ourselves and the British, lest the Germans make capital out of our lack of unity. But I think the time has come when we should risk this for the sake of the future. If we go on giving the impression that our policy is the same as Britain's right up to the moment of liberation, we shall have little chance of getting the record straight thereafter, when we shall be wanting to exert an influence of our own in keeping the peace between the conflicting interests of Britain and Russia in this region. . . . While the war was hot out here, it would have been a mistake to take any line separately from our allies, but now the time has come to be ourselves if we want to count in the future; and the future, the after-the-war future, is coming more and more into the picture here everyday, with its ugly possibilities of World War III, which we are in the best position to help avert, but only if we act independently. . . . The Department sent some very interesting "information telegrams." One of these was about Yugoslavia. The new Government has not yet been formed! Discussions are still going on, with the chances now that a three-man Cabinet, a Croat, a Slovene, and a Serb, will be set up, and that Mihailović will remain as C-in-C, and that he and Tito will be invited to send representatives to a Military Committee, which will work with the Government. A long way from the original Churchill proposals of getting Tito to "accept" the King! And while all this goes on, Purić still seems to be Premier, though the British press had him cashiered long ago.

May 30, 1944, Tuesday

Averell Harriman came in about six thirty and at eight I took him over to General Giles's, where he dined, leaving Cairo late at night by plane for Teheran. I went on back to the hotel, and we had Colonels Toulmin, West and Larrabee to dinner, a jolly party. West said that the British are preparing something in regard to Crete, but he doesn't know exactly what it is, and Toulmin told us that the Germans have tried to round up Tito and his entire headquarters by a surprise attack of glider-borne troops. The latest news is that they failed, but our correspondent Pribichevich,[120] and an OSS photographer are reported missing. . . . Harriman had also heard the news about the Tito raid. I had not seen him since 1913, as far as I can remember. He has hardened a lot, and is a capable, thoughtful man. We talked about European politics, most of the time, though as we drove off together to Giles's he spoke of home affairs and politics. He thinks the President was really ill and said that even after his recent vacation he looked wan and weak, but that now he is fully himself again. He thinks the President will run again, and will be elected. Dewey[121] has taken a "me too" attitude on foreign affairs, and as for domestic issues, the overwhelming interest of the war will keep them in the background. Dewey will reach his zenith at about convention time, and after that will fade. The Republicans with whom Harriman has talked recently all said they thought their party had an even chance, and the Democrats were all confident of about a 4 to one victory. But one can never tell, etc. . . . Harriman expressed interest in Russian doings in the Balkans, and I told him what I could. He asked me to write and said he would reciprocate, but prepared me for little in this line, as he added, "I'm not very good at writing." He feels that Russia is genuinely anxious to see the Moscow agreement carried out and to have the states on her borders genuinely friendly, though not under her active control. Stalin knows that after the war is over, his people will expect him to see to the country's reconstruction, so he doesn't want bothersome commitments outside. The border states should therefore have "democratic" governments friendly to Moscow, and looking to Moscow for their protection; they must not be ruled by groups antagonistic to Moscow, or communism, or things Russian, and must not be under the influence or "protection" of any other power—to such a situation, Russia would react immediately. In regard to England, Harriman said the higher-ups, as distinguished from the Foreign Office officials, and the civil servants and military in the field, are now disposed to play with Russia along these lines, and he told me that the annoyance of Churchill and his Govern-

[120] Stoyan Pribichevich, correspondent of *Time* magazine.
[121] Thomas E. Dewey, Governor of New York, and Republican presidential nominee.

ment over the Rumanian matter has now abated. In fact, when he left London, hope there seemed higher than ever of Russian collaboration and cooperation. The Russians he said genuinely want to work with England and America,—always with the reservation that we respect the above conditions regarding the border states. He said he thought that Beneš has provided the example to be followed in dealing with Russia now, and was inclined to support the Russians in regard to the Polish question. Russia wants two things in connection with Poland,—the Curzon Line (with possible slight modifications in Poland's favor) and the elimination of the officer and aristocratic elements from the Government, which must be democratic and look to Moscow rather than to London or elsewhere for its guidance and support.... We also talked somewhat about England, and he said that he thinks the Conservatives will continue in power for a couple of years after the war, and that then Labor may come in. He said he recognized the danger that nervousness over the security of their Imperial connections might cause the British to make moves in this or other regions which would provoke corresponding moves on Russia's part, but reiterated that British high policy is against this. Our hands-off attitude in the Balkans must be restricted to internal affairs; in regard to the Great Powers, we have an active role to play in helping to avoid conflict.... Specifically as regards Yugoslavia, he said that the Russians have given up Mihailović for good, and all will support Tito 100%. This differs from the Foreign Office notion reported recently to the Department, to the effect that there may later be a switch back to M., or at least to the Serbian element, on Russia's part.

June 1, 1944, Thursday
Col. Moçarsky of OSS, ... brought me messages received through Bari about the raid on Tito's Headquarters. Pribichevich seems to have escaped, but Tito lost most of his equipment and all his radios, and after fleeing from Drvar to Potock, he is now being attacked there by three German columns of 2,000 men each. All this in the very heart of his own territory, which Partisan propaganda has been calling "liberated"! The British papers play up the capture of Talbot, a British correspondent, but soft-pedal all the rest of the affair, and the public has not been allowed to know that Tito is really in a serious position.... Leeper came in to tell me that the British and Russians have agreed that in Rumania the Russians shall be allowed the "initiative," and in Greece, the British, to avoid divergencies of action and policy. Each is to support the other in the other's field, though of course not abandoning its own legitimate interests. Molotov has insisted that American assent to this arrangement be secured, and Leeper asked me if I had any advice on the matter from

Washington.[122] The answer, of course, is "no," though I suppose I shall hear in due time. I think we shall want to agree on something which puts our allies in a good frame of mind toward each other and may tend practically towards greater unity, but I wonder how far we want to support British maneuvers in Greek internal politics,—as for instance, if they should, under Churchill's guidance, really go all out to restore the King. . . . Leeper has seen Novikov on this matter, and feels, he said, that Novikov has had some instructions and will not now continue to criticize British doings to the Greeks who come to see him, at least not to the extent he has done this in the past. . . . Turning to Greek affairs specifically, Leeper said that Sarafis has been held up in Bari by bad weather [and] is still there. He hopes that the Leftists in Greece will agree eventually to join the Government,—which their delegates here all want done,—but if they won't, then he thinks the Government must go on being formed without them. The Prime Minister could broadcast that the failure to include them was due to their own refusal and thus place the onus squarely on them; but the situation would be unsatisfactory, as the Government would still remain a Government-in-Exile, and not a truly national representative body—representative of all organizations, that is —which is what is desired. Leeper explained to Novikov that a stable government is desired so that there may be a stable army and navy, and Novikov, he said, saw the point. "Talk realism to the Russians every time," he said, "that is what they understand." So he is getting the idea! Meanwhile, as long as no word comes from the Leftists in Greece, Papandreou can't go on dishing out ministries to other delegates here, waiting to get on the pay roll, and intriguing is going on apace while the expectant Ministers have nothing to do. Leeper spoke specially bitterly in this connection of Exindaris, Vasiliadis, and Lambrakis. Venizelos, he said, is "behaving pretty well, but is afraid of such men as Lambrakis." Tsatsos[123] has received word from Sofoulis, in Athens, that Papandreou must be supported, so this may help in keeping the Liberals in line. But the situation, while it remains thus tentative and unclarified, cannot be regarded as good. . . . At the conference in Lord Moyne's office it was decided to consult our governments over the advisability of telling Stirbei that Maniu's latest telegrams show the uselessness of further conversations, and that therefore our talks must be considered at an end. . . . Novikov asked Lord Moyne what about the Balkan Supply Center, which his Government had told him was being set up here and would be

[122] Texts of memoranda of conversations and messages exchanged between Churchill and Roosevelt beginning on May 30, 1944, on what became known as the Anglo-Soviet "percentages agreement" of October 9, 1944, can be found in *FR 1944*, V, 112-134.

[123] Themistoclis Tsatsos, liberal politician and close associate of Papandreou.

explained to him in detail by the British and American authorities. He asked who he should see to get this explanation, and Lord Moyne said that the BSC is still under some discussion, though technically set up, but he would tell Novikov about it when matters were all straightened out. This seemed to me not calculated to encourage collaboration among allies temperamentally disposed to distrust, so I told Novikov, afterwards, to come around to see me, and I'd show him all I have on this subject including the terms of reference of the BSC, as communicated to the Greek and Yugoslav Governments, and the telegrams I have reporting exchanges of view with Moscow. I think he should be able to get a good idea of the whole thing from these.

June 2, 1944, Friday

Novikov came in and I explained to him what we know of the Balkan Supply Center, which is only what we have already told his Government (namely, its terms of reference), and the fact that it has been set up. That we have not told him about it (as opposed to telling his Government) as yet, has been due to the fact that while we have been instructed to inform him of its work, it has not yet begun to function. As a result of our talk, he will get in touch with the heads of the center, through his counsellor, when the thing does begin to operate, and I will tell him in the meantime of anything we may learn further about it. . . . A call at the office from the three principal leftist delegates to the Lebanon Conference, Messrs. Svolos, Roussos, and Porfyrogenis. The last named represents EAM and was bitter because at the Conference EAM was attacked for its misdeeds and never once praised for its fight against the Germans, until, on the last day, Papandreou admitted that this had been of some value. Roussos is a typical young and humorless Communist. Svolos, a professor of law, who represents the Committee in the Mountains, is gentle and learned. . . . We talked a long time, Arthur Parsons being with us, and what they had to say was interesting. They claimed that the parties of the left are the true patriots of Greece, and that they never made *coups d'état*, as the people of the right have done repeatedly. Nor do they wish to do so now. They want a true democratic régime without tyranny of any sort—it might have been Mr. Papandreou himself talking. And all that! Svolos mentioned that it was a pity that the conference didn't go on record about the King. The others agreed, and all insisted that the great majority of the Greeks don't want him. They said a plebiscite cannot be held "in his presence" and therefore he must not come back to Greece before it is held. Also they don't trust his declaration that he will decide this matter in agreement with his government, and want another and more categorical assurance on his part. . . . I told them that the United States hopes that the Greeks will achieve real political unity among themselves for the sake of all, and that our interest is in all the Greeks, not in any one party, and in helping them to restore their devastated country. This, I pointed out, we can do better if they do not fight among themselves.

June 3, 1944, Saturday

Long talk with General Giles in the morning, chiefly about relations with the British. He has put out a splendid order forbidding criticism of our allies by members of our armed forces here, and General Paget, seeing this, was so pleased that he issued a similar order to his people. I brought up with General Giles the complaint made to me by Leeper, about OSS agents talking to the Greeks and expressing criticism of the British, and said I thought our people should be told that their duty as Government employees engaged in gathering information is to keep their ears open and their mouths closed, and that this is particularly true as regards allied policy, since anything they should say would be immediately construed by foreigners as having an official quality, however personally they might mean it. If they have to express views regarding the doings of our allies, it should always be favorable in speaking to outsiders, though of course in confidential reports to their superiors their duty is another thing altogether. General Giles said he agreed entirely, but that he could not control the OSS, or the OWI either, in the handling of their operatives. However, he promised to talk with Colonel Toulmin (without mentioning me) on the basis of his order, and to call his attention in that connection to the aspects of the matter I had raised. Later in the day, I asked Colonel Toulmin to come and see me and said the same things to him, and later still had a similar talk with Mr. Snedaker of OWI. Both saw the point at once and agreed to take steps to keep their men in line. OWI, curiously enough, seems quite as active here in Cairo in gathering information of a political character as OSS, though its job is strictly that of a propaganda agency. I suppose it helps them to make up their minds what propaganda is needed to have contacts of their own of this kind. . . . Got through with several despatches, and telegrams on the Greek and Yugoslav situations. Sarafis, after being held up at Bari by bad weather is now in Greece, and the answer as to whether EAM, the Communists and the Political Committee in the Mountains will agree to join the new government is anxiously awaited. If they agree, the Political Committee will disband, and the EAM and the Communists will have two portfolios each, perhaps including the important one of Finance. If they don't agree, however, it will throw the whole situation back very near to where it was before the recent troubles, with division between the organizations in Greece and what will still be, though enlarged and more widely representative, a Government-in-exile. . . . In regard to Yugoslavia, I reported the reaction here to the Subašić appointment,[124] adding that the Government here had not yet been informed of the appointment, or of Purić's resignation. But later in the day we heard that this information had come through. Subašić is said, in a telegram the British got, to be going at once to Bari and thence to Yugoslavia, for the purpose of uniting *all* resistance groups. But the impression given by Churchill's recent speech and subsequent British propaganda is that his mission is principally to Tito and that he aims to swing the whole of Yugoslavia behind that gentleman. . . . Toulmin promised to give me promptly any further news he may get of the German drive to capture Tito. It would certainly be a joke if Subašić had to telegraph back to Churchill that the Marshal can't be found! He also said that he has heard that the date of "Overlord" may have been deferred, but that it can't be later than the 8th or 10th of this month, or it will have to go over until July.

June 4, 1944, Sunday
The [British] Ambassador told me that the reply from the leftist organizations and the Communist Party in Greece has come in, and insists that the delegates of these outfits keep out of the new government unless there is a clarification of the Constitutional Question, i.e. unless the King declares squarely that he won't go back to Greece before the plebiscite. The organizations also want more portfolios in the new government than they are getting,—Leeper said they want half the number,—so it looks as if "national unity" were still very much around the corner! I asked Leeper if he saw any hope that the King might yield on the matter of a declaration, and he said no. . . . Alexander Mylonas came out to dinner; it was fine to see him after all these years. Thinner, but apparently no older despite his exile under Metaxas and the German occupation. He told me that he would have preferred to take Reconstruction rather than one of the Service Ministries in the new Government, but couldn't refuse when they put it to him on patriotic grounds. He did turn down the War Ministry, urging Mr. Papandreou to take this most important post himself for the present. Then they urged the Marine, and he agreed. His task will be a thankless one with 3,000 arrested mutineers to deal with. All the more credit to him. The man is one of the best anywhere, with no personal

---

[124] Ivan Subašić, former Ban (Governor) of Croatia, living in the United States, was appointed Yugoslav Prime Minister to succeed Purić in late May 1944. King Peter had acted under pressure from the British government, and in an attempt to bring about a *rapprochement* between the Yugoslav government-in-exile and Tito.

vanity or small ambition for himself. And the Greeks in the Navy and in the Nation are lucky to have a man so gentle, just, and wise at a critical post,—though I dare say they will show their appreciation in strange ways! . . . He told us about life in Athens and his escape from Greece in a caique. Also discussed the political situation. Said he had urged the Conference to settle the constitutional question, because he foresaw that the extreme left might make use of its present slightly—though only slightly —equivocal condition to make trouble; and now they are doing it. He urged on the King the other day, repeatedly, he said, to make a clear declaration that he would not return before the plebiscite,—urged him to do it in his own interests. But the King as often returned no answer on this particular point, though he was very friendly and considerate in his reception. I suppose the King always has in mind that Churchill may back him at the end through thick and thin, and F.D.R. likewise. Certainly the Greeks suspect "the British" may do so. And Leeper and I both have the uncomfortable feeling that "authority" in the end may ignore the fine points of the Greek situation.

June 6, 1944, Tuesday

Got the news of the invasion of France over Wally Barbour's radio in his office in the forenoon. Thus "Overlord" has arrived practically as predicted by Col. Toulmin on May 22nd. Went over to General Giles' Headquarters and took him to see King George for his first audience. . . . I talked to both Giles and Leeper of the advisability of our getting together with the British now in connection with plans they have been formulating for a long time for an agreement with the Greek Government covering the activities of the AML. Since we are now definitely included (to the extent of 63 officers) in the coming operation, we should have something to say from the start as to the basic charter under which it will function, otherwise later we might perceive objections and valuable time at a critical moment might be lost getting things straightened out. Up to now the British have been very secretive about this business, and I don't know why. Both AML and Leeper's Embassy have drawn up plans and avoided (never refused) letting us see them. Harry Hill has been much disturbed, but now I think is not only the time for us to say something about it (AML being now definitely "allied") but also the time when we can expect to be listened to. Leeper promised to get me the material together and have a talk with me soon, when his man Warner (the "consumptive mosquito") comes back from leave. And Giles will send his legal man on the AML staff over to see Hill before talking with his British counterpart. . . . At lunch today, Mr. Leeper turned to me and said, "The edifice of Greek Unity constructed at the Lebanon is cracking."

CAIRO · 539

June 7, 1944, Wednesday

Philip Dragoumis, the new Greek Under-Minister for Foreign Affairs, came in to pay his official call. He told me of his escape from Greece, and of conditions there. We discussed the EAM problem. He thinks that the question of the King's return can best be handled by the King and the Government when the moment of liberation arises, and that the EAM is only using it now as a pretext to cover up its real reason for not wishing to join the new government. This he sees as an unwillingness to abandon control of the guerrilla situation by sinking ELAS in a national army, and thus lose the chance it now has of emerging on liberation as the *de facto* government of Greece.

June 8, 1944, Thursday

Eight new ministers were added to the Greek Cabinet, none of them of much personal importance except Kanellopoulos, who becomes Minister of Finance, but the whole list has been carefully chosen to give representation to all the groups at the conference, except EAM and the Communist party, for which, however, five ministries are still left open, including the Interior. Papandreou issued a statement calling attention to the fact that EAM and the Communists have not yet been included because of their own refusal to join, and expressing the hope that they may change their minds. He also made it clear that their delegates had *agreed* to join, but his statement was sober and took no offensive tone.

June 9, 1944, Friday

Markham of OWI has gone to Bari, and sent me a telegram to say that Velebit[125] for Tito, and Topalović[126] for Mihailović, are there, presumably to hold conversations with Subašić with a view to getting the factions together under the King. Markham points out that Tito's recent defeats, and his present utter dependence on Anglo-American support, should make him more amenable than he has been hitherto to compromise. Markham hopes that we can do something to promote the success of the conference in the interests of Yugoslavia as a whole. I talked with Shantz and Barbour, and we all think that we might send Markham's message on to the Department as it stands, by airgram. We know that the Department played no part in the substitution of Subašić for Purić, and has not been "pressing" the King in any way. But on the other hand, the present mis-

[125] General Vlatko Velebit, Tito's representative with the Yugoslav government-in-exile (London).

[126] Dr. Zivko Topalović, former president of the Yugoslav National Democratic Union, and leading figure in the Chetnik movement.

sion of Subašić to Bari rather closely parallels Papandreou's *hegira* to the Lebanon, and the Department might possibly consider supporting in some public way at this time the idea of National Unity in Yugoslavia, without reference to the individuals concerned (and certainly without giving countenance to Churchill's idea that Tito should be the dominating personality).

June 12, 1944, Monday
Learned from the British Embassy to Yugoslavia that it has received orders to close up here, "in view of the setting up of the Yugoslavian Government in London . . ." Got a long telegram from the Department about British efforts in Washington to enlist our support of Papandreou, and saying that the British claim to have information that Papandreou is supported by the great majority of the Greek people. The Department's reply was that it has little information (!) but in the meantime follows its policy of supporting no one group or party, though it is instructing me here to consult with my British colleague, etc. . . . I drafted a reply to all this to assure the Department, if it needs such assurance, that I am trying to keep in close step with Leeper within the limitations of our policy, and cited my conversation with Svolos and his friends in which I spoke for Greek "unity" along the lines laid down by the President's message to the leftists at the conference, and my more recent efforts with Giles, Toulmin, and Snedaker, to stop anti-British talk on the part of American "agents" among the Greeks. . . . Maniu sent a message saying that he accepts the armistice terms and will soon move to implement them. He added, however, that he is confident that the terms will be ameliorated "as promised by the allied representatives" if he does move. We don't understand this at all, since we have made no such promise, and have only reiterated that if he doesn't move the terms may get worse! He says he is sending out some more "emissaries" to contact Prince Stirbei. As the Russians have not joined the British, and our Government is agreeing to calling off the conversations, we are letting these people come, but in dealing with them the British feel that Novikov should take the initiative (as in the case, recently, of Vishoianu) and I have agreed. . . . Dinner at the Mena House with Mr. Mylonas and Harry Hill as guests. Mr. Mylonas looked very tired. He told us, however, that at the first Greek Cabinet meeting, held today, the question of the date of the King's return had been taken up—and settled! He referred to his talk to me on this subject the other night, and said that the whole Cabinet had signed a statement to the effect that in their view the King should not return before the plebiscite, and that then Papandreou had seen the King, and he had agreed. Now he pointed out, the EAM's pretext for not joining the Government has been taken

away from them, and they must either come in and share responsibility, or give other reasons, which may be difficult for them to find if they wish to keep a large following. The real reasons,—which he said are to keep control of the ELAS bands which the Government wants to incorporate under General Othonaios in a "national army," and to keep aloof from responsibility in connection with the approaching trials of the mutineers,—are hardly such as they can avow openly. . . . If this news, about the King's return, is true, it is a great step forward in Greek affairs, since it will make it impossible for anyone any longer to say that the British seek to impose the King on the Greek people, while it will undoubtedly help the Government, as expected, in dealing with the communists who will no longer have a "bogey" to hand. But I wonder if Mr. Mylonas may not be a bit sanguine as to the King's acceptance of the solution arrived at. He has not made any declaration, Mr. Mylonas said.

June 13, 1944, Tuesday

Talk with Col. Toulmin in the morning, who brought me a message to the effect that King Peter came with Subašić as far as Malta, but has been detained there by the British while Subašić has gone on to Bari and Vis. The idea of Mr. Broad, now representing the British in Bari, is that the King should not go there, or further, till preparations for his reception and protection are completed. Meanwhile, the Yugoslav Government here remains sublimely ignorant of the whereabouts of its King and Prime Minister! It seems to me that the British are going pretty far in their attempts to cover up their maneuvers to "swing Yugoslavia behind Tito" *quand même*. . . . Called on Mr. Papandreou to get the story of yesterday's developments. He told me that he had persuaded the King to accept the Cabinet's declaration by pointing out how necessary it is now to deprive EAM of a pretext for sabotaging the work of the Lebanon Conference, and by arguing that from the King's own point of view it would be better for him not to stick on a small question like that of his residence at home or abroad for a few months, but rather to show that he is a supporter of national unity and not an obstructionist. In addition, he told the King that he would have to resign if the declaration was not accepted, and he impressed on me that the fact that he is still Prime Minister proves that acceptance was given. A declaration of the King, he said, is not now necessary,—and this pleases the King, who has all along objected to making further statements of his own on this subject. . . . Mr. Papandreou also said that he thought a regency during the interim period in Greece, before the plebiscite can take place, would not be necessary. The Government would move in and function as the King's Government, while he would remain the Chief of State, residing abroad and keeping contact with the great allies. . . . Parsons obtained from the British a copy of the declaration, which is an amazing document, reading, as Cy Sulzberger said this afternoon, like a portion of one of Plato's sophistic dialogues. After some hard reading one can just get an inkling of what it means, but after all, that meaning is there, subtly insinuated. One wonders at the Greek mind. . . . Lunch with Mummy at the Mohamed Aly Club. She had been all morning at her new Yugoslav work-shop, and had heard there from Mrs. Sandberg that the BBC broadcast this morning that the King had assured his cabinet that he "would not return to Greece before the plebiscite." Evidently somebody in England, or the English service here, has taken pains to prevent any change of heart on the King's part leading to an appeal to Churchill. . . . I suspect Leeper, this time, of making use of the BBC, which he is usually so annoyed with. . . . Last night I said to Mylonas that some Greeks suspect the British "and Mr. Churchill" of supporting the King, and he looked at me with a twinkle and said, "and Mr. Roosevelt too!" So cats do get out of bags.

June 14, 1944, Wednesday

Long talk in the afternoon with Ambassador Leeper, about the King's return question and other matters. He feels that Papandreou has handled the King in a masterful manner and that the situation is now definitely improved, particularly as regards EAM and the Communists, who must now join the Government or allege some other excuse for not doing so. It seems hardly likely that they will adduce their real reasons for wanting to stay out, but they might perhaps insist that the Government's declaration on the King's return is not enough and that he should make a declaration personally. I wonder about this. Leeper, however, isn't bothered by this possibility. He has reported to the Foreign Office that Papandreou's tactics have been masterly in saving the King from embarrassment, pointing out that the present position secures to the King a possibility, at least, of a change, in that the Government might, without loss of face, later reverse itself, whereas if he himself declared he would not return before the plebiscite, he could not take this back later, even under altered public conditions, without incurring the charge of being unstable and not knowing his own mind. I told Leeper I thought he must have had in mind, when he wrote this report, the possibility of Mr. Churchill's seeing it, and he laughed and said I was quite right. . . . I asked him whether he thought the King had really accepted the Government's declaration, or had merely let it pass, with the idea that he might somehow get his own back later, and he said he was having the King to dinner tonight and would endeavor to find out just what his reactions are. . . . I brought up with Leeper the question of AML's preparations for a monster leaflet and poster campaign on all sorts of subjects connected with relief, and my impression that these preparations are not being very well adjusted to Greek conditions. I said I thought he and I should get together, and possibly see General Hughes, and agree on some sort of control. I told him that some observations I had already made on this matter had been treated very cavalierly by AML, and that I really felt it a serious matter that we should not let things happen at the hands of AML which would get the British and Americans generally into a position of ridicule and possibly dislike in Greece. He said he felt the same way, and even more so, on this subject, though he has less information than I have just now regarding it, and I am hopeful of results from combined efforts on our part. . . . After our conversation—and cutting it short, so that I had to leave out another subject I wanted to discuss (an excursion by an AML officer into Albanian boundary questions!) Mr. Porfyrogenis, of the EAM came in, to take leave of Mr. Leeper before setting out to Greece, where he will try to persuade his principals to join the Government; on the basis that the King's return question has now been settled. He and his associates seem genuinely anxious to have their signatures honored, but I doubt if their principals care much about this. They are more likely to be worried over keeping control of the ELAS bands! . . . During the day, I got a telegram, repeated from Algiers, which Murphy had sent to the Department, quoting (in paraphrase) an instruction sent by Wilson to Paget. This instruction said that Wilson is against Papandreou's plan to disband the guerrillas and form a national army, because the disbanding of ELAS would cause confusion in the ports and endanger the allied military missions operating in and out of them. Furthermore, it brands Papandreou's efforts in this connection as "political." I showed Leeper this telegram and he said "It is just like Jumbo," and is "premature and exaggerated." . . . He pointed out that the plan (of which Larrabee, incidentally, has secured a draft in its present stage) is only tentative, and can't be put into effect unless and until EAM joins the Government, which it may not do. And he also said he was sure the higher-ups in London would support his own decided view (which is mine, too) that from now on political matters in Greece should get the preference over fading military considerations. "Jumbo" is a great believer in the continuation of sabotage efforts in Greece despite the small present strategic value which these have and the terrific reprisals they bring on the Greek people. No one quite knows why! Sabotage at the right moment—when the Germans start to move out—would make some sense, of course. Or if an invasion of the Balkans were to take place. But not now. And it is a part of Papandreou's plan to get a well-coordinated National Army constructed for the express purpose of eventual effective sabotage on German withdrawal. But "Jumbo" continues to insist on present ineffective and (to the Greek people) disastrous methods.

June 15, 1944, Thursday

Called at the Greek Legation at 6:00 for an audience with King George (at my request, and I got no tea!). The King looked very badly, and is obviously distressed over his position again. His talk was incoherent and spotty, but I made out that he regards himself as having accepted the Government's solution of the return question merely temporarily and because Papandreou told him it was necessary at this time to disarm EAM of its chief pretext for not joining the government of National Unity. He thinks that EAM represents virtually the whole opposition to his return to Greece before the plebiscite, and thinks that Papandreou himself told him this! In consequence he thinks that later, when a new situation arises, either by EAM's joining or refusing definitely to join, there will be an opportunity for a new decision on his return. He is in a mood now in which he talks of taking the bit in his teeth and going to Greece "as a private citizen" at his own discretion, or accepting an appointment as commander-in-chief of a Balkan invasion force (what force?). He said that many people have been to see him these past few days to protest about the way he has been treated and urge him to assert himself. "But if I dismiss this Government, where will I get another?" Even Venizelists (he said) have taken this line—defection from *national unity* already beginning? Royalists, he said, now feel he has let them down. However, today's *Phos*, the royalist paper here, takes the line editorially that he has agreed not to return before the plebiscite, and praises him for it.... He started to ask me if I couldn't explain to the President what his position is, but stopped himself with a laugh, saying that he supposes it is too complicated for anybody to explain. I said at the end of our talk, "so the position is this, that you have allowed the Government to make this declaration at this time in order that you may not stand in the way of efforts to achieve unity, but you believe that the Government may later change its mind, either of its own accord, or led to do so by you," and he agreed. Incidentally, his talk revealed that Mr. Papandreou *did* present his resignation, if the King refused to accept the declaration, but it seems also clear that he did not wholly understand all his eloquent Prime Minister said. For he reported that Papandreou told him that besides the EAMites and the communists the only people at the Conference who wanted him not to return before the plebiscite were Mylonas and Sofianopoulos.[127] "I asked him who these men represent, and he answered, Mylonas represents himself and his daughter, and Sofianopoulos represents his own writings. Is that a large section of the Greek people,—one daughter?" The King is nearly always quite accurate in detail in what he says, but things get loose from contexts, because he rarely listens more than half a minute consecutively

---

[127] John Sofianopoulos, socialist leader.

to anybody. Somewhere along the line Papandreou probably made the remarks above cited, either cattily about his rivals or forced into a cynical admission that the old parties are today defunct. But that they were made in the sense given them by the King is another matter. . . . The poor man is really a sad case. He said he wants to go to Algiers and on to Italy to see the front, but fears to leave Cairo because another crisis may arise when EAM makes its reply. His life is just one crisis after another, tied together by periods of depression, during which he chews the bitter end of wondering whether he did right or not.

June 18, 1944, Sunday
I drafted a telegram suggesting that I be called home for consultation, and after that couldn't sleep, so worked on a letter to the President till about 4 a.m., much to Mummy's disgust.

June 20, 1944, Tuesday
Had a long talk with young Colonel Woodhouse,[128] who has been the head of the British Military Mission in Greece and hopes to go back there soon. He asked to see me, for some reason, and Col. West brought him round. He said that there is an inner ring of Communists controlling the EAM, which will not, in his opinion, allow the latter to join the Government. These men, he says, will go on making one excuse after another, playing for time, and he thinks that Papandreou should also play for time, keeping his offers to them open, and not attacking them, which would only strengthen their position in Greece. He said that the majority of the Committee in the Mountains are now just waking up to the fact that they are being led by the others for Communist purposes, and are unhappy and alarmed about it, but dare do nothing, as there is a kind of police, or budding Gestapo, which watches their every movement. He thinks that when the allies get back to Greece, the enthusiasm of the people will relegate EAM and all the troubles of the present to a position of absolute unimportance, and that British (and American) mistakes of the past years will be forgotten immediately. Some bandits will remain in the mountains, undoubtedly, but there will be no organized resistance to our forces, which will only have to parade with bands. On the other hand, he thinks the Germans will not abandon the Balkans unless they are forced to, and that the allies will have to overcome the resistance of suicide groups of satellite soldiers, led by a few German officers.

[128] Colonel Christopher M. Woodhouse, Chief British Military Liaison Officer in Greece, from 1943 to 1945, following the recall of Brigadier E.C.W. Myers.

June 21, 1944, Wednesday

Leeper came in to the office early and we had a long talk on Greek affairs, particularly on the need for an understanding between our Governments and the Greek Government as to the authority to be given to the AML. When we get that, we can deal with the AML's present tendency to act as if it were going to run the country in every way and without reference to the civil authority. I showed him a lot of the propaganda leaflets and posters which it is having PWB prepare, and Harry Hill explained to him the manner in which a lot of this could rub the Greeks the wrong way. Leeper took the very sound view that control of this sort of thing must be in our hands, and he promised to appoint someone in his Embassy, possibly Balfour, to collaborate with Hill in checking on it in detail. We agreed that we should urge our Governments, meanwhile, to draw up an overall charter for AML, preferably as brief as possible—I had in mind the President's exchange of letters with the Premier of Iceland,—and that we should do this simultaneously and soon. He said he wanted a few days to get his views in order and would talk with me again on the subject. . . . Robinson of the OWI came in for our O.K. on a Greek edition of *Victory*, and we suggested that pictures of Yugoslavs at war be taken out in favor of some pictures of the Greek-Albanian war, and that articles emphasizing the abundance of food and miracle-working medicines in the U.S.A. be dropped. . . . On instructions from the Department I got Mr. Papandreou's consent to inviting an Italian observer to the Monetary Conference at Bretton Woods.

June 23, 1944, Friday

Mummy and I dined at the Mohammed Aly Club with the Colonel [Larrabee] and Lt. McNeill,[129] also Miss Theron and a British Colonel Hobbs, of the Allied Liaison. There was some talk of the Greek mutinies and the courts-martial, and Hobbs showed a contempt and dislike for the Greeks which would seem to me to make him entirely unfit for liaison work. His organization deals also with Poles, Yugoslavs, and other nationalities, comprising part and parcel of the United Nations forces in the Middle East, and it is to be hoped he has greater sympathies with some of these. He speaks no language but his own, however, and seems to understand no other point of view. He is the kind of man calculated to make any Greek revolt, which would not mean that the Greek would be right, —only understandable. He got under my skin to such a degree that I made a most undiplomatic remark, considering our desirably close rela-

---

[129] Lieutenant (later Captain) William H. McNeill, Assistant Military Attaché to the American Embassy to Greece.

tions with the British, and when I should have said that it was "unfortunate" that the Greek brigade had been left in idleness so long—which led to its mutiny, in great part,—I said it was *"outrageous!"* This is, of course, what I believe, and we are the allies of the Greeks as well as of the British. But I am not here to argue with colonels, or to criticize allied policy to anybody but the Department, and certainly not to my juniors! Toulmin told me today that Paget had asked him if *I am anti-British*. His wondering this probably arose from the fact that I have had to support our views as against the British on various occasions. I caught Stevenson out using our name in vain; I have refused to join Leeper in advising the Greek Government in supporting particular Greek politicians and internal policies; my caution as to proper consideration of the Department's views has held up the "marriage" of PWE and OWI; and I have implemented the Department's views regarding Lord Moyne's committees. Toulmin explained quite properly that I can hardly be called anti-British just because I am not pro-British in everything, and that I am merely following out here the policies of my Government. But if I allow myself to be goaded by silly officers into using strong words, I may give real cause for being suspected of an attitude which in general I do not personally hold at all, and which it is not good that anybody in my position should hold while this war continues.

Cairo, Egypt
June 23, 1944

Dear Franklin:

I forgot to tell you in my last letter that King George of Greece wanted to thank you for [the] comforting messages you sent him when he was in London. He, poor man, is again in a bad way, psychologically, over the question of the timing of his return to Greece. He seemed to have benefited from his visit to London, but since this matter which bothers him so much has come up again, he appears to be once more in the grip of uneasiness and anxiety.

In my last letter I said that I doubted whether anything but a miracle could get the Greeks together after their recent troubles here in the Middle East, and behold, the miracle took place promptly after I wrote, proving once more the difficulty of latter-day prophecy. However, like most if not all modern miracles, this one was somewhat less miraculous than it was advertised to be. The water turned into wine all right, but the wine proved only synthetic. Everybody at the Conference in the Lebanon agreed to practically everything in principle, but details were left to the Government of National Unity which it was decided should be immediately set up here in Cairo. Then, when the delegates all adjourned here for that purpose, the communist-controlled organizations in Greece, —the so-called EAM and the Committee of Liberation "in the mountains," as well as the Communist Party itself,—refused to allow their delegates to participate, despite the fact that these last had come out from Greece with full powers and had agreed to join. The real reasons for this breakdown are still obscure, but it is surmised that the organizations in question do not wish to relinquish control of the guerrilla bands, through which they hope to control the situation within the country after the German withdrawal, and that they are shy of being connected with a Government which must now proceed with the court-martialling of the recent mutineers. In any case, however, the only reason which they themselves alleged was that the question of the time of the King's return to Greece had not been settled at the Conference, and here we have the origin of the King's present unhappiness. They said that unless and until it was made clear that the King would not return before the plebiscite, they could not join any Government—except presumably one of their own making. Accordingly, Mr. Papandreou decided to clarify this point immediately and once for all. It is true that nothing had been decided about it in the Lebanon, but much had been said, in one way or another, and the general opinion of the Conference had clearly been that the King should await his people's call. Therefore Mr. Papandreou passed a unanimous declaration through his cabinet (composed almost entirely of former delegates to the Conference) stating that such was the Government's opinion also, and furthermore that since the King had accepted the Government in full knowledge that its members held this opinion, he had himself signified his assent to it. Mr. Papandreou then went to the King and told him that this declaration would have to stand or he would have to resign, and he also pointed out how desirable it was to make such a declaration at this time in the interests of unity, in order to deprive the Communists of their pretext for not entering the Government. To this the King replied that he obviously could not get another Government if this one, composed of all parties but the Communist, should now resign, and that in any case he could not wish to stand in the way of national unity. He therefore allowed the declaration to stand, and it was published forthwith. He himself has argued to me, in a long conversation which I had with him subsequently, that nothing absolutely decisive has been done. He emphasized that he has made and will make no declaration of his own, which it would be difficult for him to take back, while if circumstances change, the Government is always free to reverse itself. Furthermore he thinks that circumstances may very well change, being convinced that royalism is still strong in Greece and may become even stronger if the Communists are unmasked and the people realize the danger of a leftist dictatorship. But unfortunately for his peace of mind, public opinion appears not to be sharing his opinion. Even the royalist Cairo newspaper, *Phos*, has editorially congratulated the Premier on his definite solution of a vexed question, and praised the King fulsomely for his patriotic action. Consequently the King cannot quite convince himself that despite his logical arguments he hasn't somehow closed the door on himself politically, and is miserable as a result.

I write so much about this because the King himself practically asked me to explain it to you, checking himself, however, with one of his shy laughs and saying, "I suppose it's too confusing to explain to anybody." Personally, in view of the political instability of the Greeks, with which I have plenty of reason to be familiar, I would not say that he has no chance at all of coming back to Greece with his Government's consent before the plebiscite, but the political tide is certainly running against his hopes in this matter just at present, and there may not be much time ahead for circumstances to alter. He seems to think that keeping quiet, which is what he is doing, is his best line just now, and it may very well be that, as Mr. Papandreou told him, it will favor his chances in the plebiscite not to show too much eagerness to return. Incidentally, the declaration makes it clear that in the interim period the Government will continue to be the King's Government and that while remaining outside the country he will "care for our national interest with our Great Allies, as Chief of the Greek State." Perhaps a regent will be appointed, though at the moment the Premier thinks this may not be necessary. Meanwhile, the new Government has taken over the reins in other matters with equal initiative and determination. It is proceeding to the courtmartialling of the mutineers, and has set up new ministries of reconstruction and supply to collaborate with our efforts and those of UNRRA for relief and rehabilitation. There is much more vitality in it than in its predecessors in exile, which would seem to be a good sign. Without any pretensions to working miracles it is setting its hand soberly to the plough and making some headway with it.

Yugoslav affairs continue in a condition somewhat similar to the Greek, with the British trying to engineer a national unity campaign from outside. But in this case they are playing perhaps a more difficult game, the Yugoslavs being more emotional and less supple politically than the Greeks. The British have already been able to get rid of a Pan-Serb premier and to replace him with a Croat, thus giving a less intransigent character to the Government-in-Exile. But they would also seem to have set themselves to bringing all the resistance groups within the country, as well as the national forces outside it, under the supreme command of Tito, which may well prove impossible. As in the Greek business, a measure of success in the present negotiations may be achieved at the outset, and doubtless there will be a flood of propaganda announcing a fuller measure than has been achieved, the British believing in the Virgilian maxim "possunt quia posse videntur." But actually the Serbs who object to Tito constitute a far stronger portion of the nation than do the Communist hold-outs in Greece, and it would seem that an agreement between the new premier and Tito giving the latter command of all the forces will be far from popular in Serbia, where unpopularity on such a subject is serious. It also seems that Tito, though in a chastened mood after his recent collapse, and feeling himself forced to a greater extent than formerly to eat out of British hands, is boggling over "accepting" the King for fear of what his followers may think. Thus on both sides of the radical division in Yugoslavia there are to be considered the essential attitudes of the followers, and not only those of the leaders, if the civil war is not to continue unabated. Furthermore, playing favorites is hardly ever a successful form of intervention in troubled households. A leader without affiliations with either side might raise a standard in Yugoslavia to which mutually antagonistic groups could repair, and do much to get rid of internal dissension, at least for the time being, by calling on all patriots to join him against the Germans. Thus, an American General with even only a small expeditionary force might eventually gather the whole weight of the various resistance movements behind him. This is doubtless an extreme instance of what would seem to be required. But to pick the Partisan leader of one of these movements to lead the whole nation is a procedure too clearly political in its implications to do other than risk perpetuating civil strife. It will be interesting to watch developments.

Regarding the recently disturbing Russian attitude toward Greek affairs, I am happy to report that some improvement has clearly occurred. Following exchanges on the subject between London and Moscow, the Russian press and radio has confined itself now for some time to stressing the desirability of unity, as well as of continued resistance to the Germans, and the British Ambassador told me the other day that he has sensed a new spirit of cooperation in our Russian colleague, which he has no doubt has been instructionally inspired. However, this same colleague has not yet seen fit to call on the Greek Prime Minister, which keeps tongues wagging to some extent. The Russians have had some protests to make, too, against the British in recent weeks, in the matter of British secret operations in Rumania, and I am informed that London and Moscow may come to an agreement to recognize each other's "initiative" in Greece and Rumania respectively, without of course abandoning their own legitimate interests in these countries. This kind of thing may be only patchwork to cover up the rifts of fundamental suspicion and distrust, but it is all to the good so far as it goes, and the easing of tension here for the moment is marked.

In conclusion, I would say that I am enclosing herewith for your stamp collection some specimens sent out of Serbia by General Mihailović especially for you. They are stamps of a new issue he has put out. Not being a philatelist myself, I can describe them no further, but have attached the rubric which came with them into my hands, and I hope this will mean something to your expert knowledge.

Affectionately yours,
Lincoln MacVeagh (10)

June 24, 1944, Saturday

I had a long talk with Major Wines, the Senior American Liaison officer in Greece, who came out with Col. Woodhouse, and will now be replaced by Col. West. He is a very sensible fellow. In general, he agrees with Woodhouse's views on the situation. Sees no hope of EAM's joining the Government, and thinks that the proper (and only) way to handle the situation is to assume that EAM has patriotic motives and keep offering it chances to come in, not to attack it, as Papandreou has started to do. Eventually this way, it will have to reveal its true colors as a selfish party organization concerned only in strengthening its grip on the country, or participate in national unity at last. But to attack it will only give it more opportunity to fight back with its customary charges of Fascism, etc. . . . He also remarked in passing, "one meets very few royalists in Greece. They don't want the King back. . ." . . . Long talk with Ambassador Leeper. He read me a telegram from the Foreign Office, to its Embassy in Moscow, dated June 19th, according to which the U.S. has agreed to the proposal for the mutual recognition by London and Moscow of British and Russian "initiative" in Greece and Rumania respectively. I asked him for a paraphrase, and he sent me a letter of which the following is the essential part: "Arrangement discussed between H.M.G. and the Soviet Government was a purely practical wartime one, *viz.* that Rumanian affairs would be mainly the concern of the Soviet Government while Greek affairs mainly concern of his Majesty's Government, each Government helping the other in respective countries. Matter was then referred by his Majesty's Government to the United States Government. It was pointed out that there was no question of dividing the Balkans into spheres of influence or excluding U.S.G. from formulation and execution of allied policy towards these countries. In no way did this arrangement affect rights and responsibilities of the Three Great Powers at Peace Conference and afterwards in regard to Europe as a whole. Arrangement is purely to prevent differences with Soviet Government from developing during war period. After some delay U.S.G. agreed on condition that it should not extend beyond circumstances for which it was devised and should not lead to division of Balkans into spheres of influence. This has been agreed between [the United States and] his Majesty's Government and to make doubly sure it is agreed that arrangement should be subject to revision after three months. In this form proposal has now been put to the Soviet Government. No reply has been received. . ." On my return to the Embassy I found the code room deciphering an "information telegram"—i.e. a circular—on this subject, but there has been no direct word to me about it yet (and it looks as if there will not be) despite the fact that it is of particular interest and application here. The message being deciphered seems to be only part two of a long message, which, after the manner of information telegrams, may touch on several subjects.

Leeper is very anxious that this proposal should go through, as he can then, perhaps, count on some support from Novikov in his efforts, through Papandreou, to bring the EAM into the Greek national unity picture. He thinks such support would be practically decisive, and I agree. Just at present, Novikov's new cooperative spirit has gone no further than a purely negative and aloof attitude. The Russians are not any longer criticising the British, but they are not helping them in any positive way either, and Leeper says that when, in accordance with his instructions to "consult" with Novikov, he goes to see him, he himself does all the talking and Novikov merely listens. In addition, he told me that N. still has not called on Papandreou, and the latter has telegraphed the Greek Ambassador in Moscow, to bring this peculiar diplomatic behavior to the attention of the Soviet Foreign Office. . . . Regarding Greek affairs, Leeper confirmed that there is a recrudescence of intrigue in the Cabinet, the Liberals agitating for the release of Bodossakis. In particular Mr. Venizelos is contemplating resigning over Papandreou's determination to take the control of the Hellenic Intelligence Service out of the hands of the Vice President of the Council. This Service is largely functioning in Greece through contacts in the industries, now German controlled, which formerly were owned by Bodossakis, and the personnel are to a great part his men. Leeper says the Service does good work, but the tie up with the Liberal party exclusively is not good. He complained of the party being now practically the party of big business, and interested only in itself and its political prospects—at this moment in world history. . . . Bodossakis is being kept in custody by the Military, and Leeper thinks it is a good thing.

June 26, 1944, Monday
Got the full text of the Department's information telegram,—several pages,—on the British-Russian proposed accord for Rumanian and Greek affairs. From this, dated June 22nd, several days after the telegram from London to Moscow which Leeper read me, it appears that Churchill and F.D.R. have had exchanges on the subject, and that, based on a long memorandum from the Department, the President did not agree!. . . I called up Mr. Leeper and he came over at once and I read him the message. He has had nothing further, but will see Novikov this evening and ask him if he has had anything from Moscow. Meanwhile the Department's argument is that fundamentally the proposal is one for the formation of spheres of influence, despite its careful limitation to the war conditions of the moment. I wonder whether perhaps a further exchange between F.D.R. and W.C. may not have taken place after the Department's telegram was drafted, in which the 3 months trial period was proposed and accepted. In any case, I sent off an inquiry to the Department this morning based on the contradiction between the British Embassy's present information and ours. Conference with General Hughes and General Sadler here in my office, at which I asked Harry Hill and Shantz to sit in. Sadler is Hughes's American deputy, in the place of Chickering whom we tried but failed to get. He doesn't seem bad, but is clearly not as familiar with his job as Chickering. The two Generals had just seen Leeper and took up the question of the agreement with the Greek Government to cover the AML operation. We decided that they should draw up as quickly as possible the AML's views as to what this agreement should cover, and in what manner, and give these views to Leeper and me. Leeper thinks he won't have to refer to London, but I am sure the Department will want to know our best thoughts on the subject here before final decisions are taken in Washington, after consultation with the British. We also decided that plans should be made for dealing with a Yugoslav Government on the same basis as with the Greek Government, despite the fact that the political position in Yugoslavia is more nebulous at present. As to Albania, I explained that this Embassy is not accredited there, but I advised them to seek a clarification from London and Washington respectively of the procedure they will be expected to follow in that country,—where the governmental question is even more nebulous than in Yugoslavia. We then talked about relations here with the new Greek Government. Sadler expressed some doubts as to whether it could be considered "permanent" and I pointed out that it should at least be considered so, as it is certainly the reorganized Greek Government now, and if it should be changed, its successor would carry on in relief matters from where it left off. If there were no successor

and anarchy should supervene, then of course, all bets would be off. But meanwhile taking the Government into AML councils will have another good effect, that of not only being correct, but of strengthening the Government itself, one of the chief things against the Tsouderos Government having been its obvious unrelation to anything being done for Greece.... Had a call from Professor Angelopoulos,[130] one of the Political Committee's delegates to the Lebanon Conference, and an accomplished economist. He asked me to transmit a memorandum he had written on financial reconstruction to Mr. Varvaressos. He, like Svolos, spoke hopefully of EAM's agreeing to join the Government. But later, in the afternoon, I saw Leeper, while both of us were waiting to call on General Smuts, and he said that word had just come that the leftists in Greece want (1) Papandreou, whom they hold personally responsible, to call off alleged new attacks by Zervas against the ELAS bands, and (2) Papandreou to denounce the Security Battalions which are making trouble for EAM. This second demand is astute, since the Security troops were set up by the Rallis Government, and are quislings, but because they have been fighting EAM, Papandreou and the British have stopped all propaganda against them recently. This gives the EAM a chance to say that the Government is more interested in fighting Communism than the Germans—with sufficient reason to make the story very powerful as propaganda. In general, however, these new excuses of the leftists for not joining up are clearly pretexts, like the King's return argument, to keep the ball going, and themselves distinct from the rest. Their idea remains to create in Greek minds a distinction between the Government-in-Exile (it cannot be one of National Unity without their participation) and the Government-in-Greece, namely their Committee in the Mountains. In reply to this, Papandreou must try to show as many people as possible in Greece that the Government of National Unity is actually formed, all except for the adherence of the Communists, and that there is no division in Greek ranks except what these are making for their own purposes. He may do this by constant offers to them over the radio, and constant harping on the theme; but meanwhile he will have to fight impatient politicians in his own ranks here, just as Tsouderos did, and also the underground propaganda in the Middle East which will grow stronger with every day that passes during which he fails to reach a solution. He can only win out in the end if liberation occurs before these factors together amount to sufficient [force?] to unseat him....

Called on General Smuts at the Residency at 6:15. He wanted to talk a little about the Greek situation, and I confirmed his impression that

[130] Angelos Angelopoulos, Professor of Economics at the University of Athens, and representative of PEEA.

Mr. Papandreou is showing some ability and vitality, and that the situation is better, at least psychologically, than it was when he was here last, though by no means settled. He asked if I saw much of the King and if I thought he got along alright with Mr. Papandreou. I said, yes, I saw quite a lot of him, and yes, I thought so, though I felt he was not happy. I emphasized that the whole Greek situation is an unhappy one, and inevitably so, after these past years, and that we should try to understand and make allowances. He spoke strongly of his belief that some sort of operation—even a small one—should be undertaken in Greece, which would have the effect of bringing patriots together and curing present difficulties. We then recalled his belief after the fall of Sicily that a Balkan operation should be undertaken at once and talked of how that would have avoided all the troubles now so rife on the peninsula. Regarding Yugoslavia, he said that Tito has had "a hard knock" and that this has resulted in reducing his "swelled head," so that there is at least a chance for Subašić to succeed. He thinks Subašić knows very well that the Serbs ("to whom Mihailović seems to mean a lot") must be given their due share in any union that is formed. He said the Prime Minister (Churchill), after Tito's retreat to Vis and British protection—over which Smuts laughed considerably—told Subašić to "go on down there and fix things up. Now's your chance." So apparently Churchill is aware of his great and good friend's hard knock and of the intentions and aspirations which it has had the effect of reducing. . . . The General talked a lot about the second front, which he says has so far greatly exceeded expectations. He is against the Anvil plan,[131] which has now been largely abandoned, and thinks the allies may be able to drive the Germans far enough back in Italy to enable a push to be put on through northern Yugoslavia in the direction of a tie-up with the Russian front, which strategically would be much better. . . . In France he sees a development southward to include the port of Brest, if we are to get a broad enough base for effective operations. Meanwhile he thinks the Germans will resist everywhere to the utmost, losing heavily but stubbornly in a thoroughly unsound strategical manner, while their lack of petrol will greatly hamper them everywhere. Already, he said, this lack is affecting the Luftwaffe, whose refusal to fight can only be accounted for on this basis. . . . Finally, we talked somewhat of the relief problem in the Balkans, and I told him of how good the AML planning is, and how indefinite the supply situation, and how this must improve if we are to be effective. . . . Our conversation was very pleasant, very general, and if the Greek situation was the cause of his asking to see me, it figured very little. It was the most friendly meeting and parting I have had with him, and he said he wanted to keep up the

---

[131] ANVIL: code name for the allied invasion of southern France.

old contacts. There is not much that is human in him; he has the Wilsonian trait of attracting personal allegiance and giving none of his own except in the realm of ideas. But he can at times switch on an irresistible charm which makes his companion think, for the moment, that he is very human indeed, which is no inconsiderable weapon in his varied and powerful armory.

June 27, 1944, Tuesday

Dino Tsaldaris came in to see me. He has just come out of Greece, but looks much as usual, though he says his wife has lost much poundage (that won't hurt the fair Nadina). He said that he is head of the *Partie Populaire Légitimiste*, and that this party was not represented at the Lebanon though the Democratic wing of the Popular Party was, and is now represented in the Government by its leader, Londos.[132] He himself wanted to come out, but means were not given him to do so, and he implied that this was the Government's fault "on purpose." However, he said that he long ago circulated a letter in Greece proposing the very same unity program as that adopted at the Lebanon, and he is in full accord with what is now being done,—only he thinks that his group should be represented in the cabinet along with the others, and he also thinks, as a "legitimist" that the King should not await the plebiscite (which according to him ought not to be held till the war is over) but go in "with his troops." I take it that he will try now to work on Papandreou and Leeper to get into the Cabinet, and that in airing his views on the King situation he will play his small part in making things difficult, along with the Liberals, who are following their own line in this direction.... The Department sent me a long message according to which Lord Moyne has censored some of Sulzberger's despatches and has stated to London that Sulzberger said that the information on which these despatches were based came from *me*. I am always very frank with the pressmen so that they may understand what they write about, and not mislead the public. But I expect them to respect my confidence, and while being guided by what I tell them, not to cite me in connection with it. So I called Cy in, and he denied that he had ever given me as the source of these reports, and also stated that his information had come to him from many sources.[133] So I asked him to tell Lord Moyne of this, and also

[132] Dimitrios Londos, royalist leader, Minister of Welfare.
[133] Sulzberger's despatch, dated June 19, 1944, had dealt with the Anglo-Soviet understanding concerning their respective responsibilities in Greece and Rumania. According to Sulzberger's published account, his source had in fact been MacVeagh, who was "furious" and "wanted the news of this private deal between London and Moscow, dividing up Eastern Europe, to be known." C. L. Sulzberger, *A Long Row of Candles* (New York: Macmillan, 1969), p. 241. There is no evidence that

to advise his New York office to tell the Department. He promised to do both. The Department doesn't seem to be angry in the matter, as it does not believe in political censorship, but I want to keep the record clear, and disabuse the British of any thoughts which might keep them in the future from passing information on to me.

June 28, 1944, Wednesday

Professor Svolos came in for a talk about the Greek situation. He is very fearful lest Papandreou in his radio talk tonight close the door finally on negotiations with EAM, following the latter's recent presentation of further excuses for not joining the Government. He thinks this would be the worst thing that could happen just now, and seems still to believe in the intentions of EAM to join, if they can do so without sacrificing their principles, etc. This last, of course, does not jibe with British ideas, and Leeper told me again this afternoon, when I went over to see him, that he does not believe for an instant that EAM/ELAS have any idea of joining, no matter what the Government may do. I reiterated to Svolos that the United States wants very much to see Greece united, particularly since we cannot be effective in bringing her the aid she needs unless she is. But as to how she is to achieve her unity, that is not for us to say. He went off saying that he had thought that he should make his position clear to me. I don't know that he did this, exactly, but he left me with the impression that he is very unhappy over the failure of his mission, and very anxious to convince himself that the organization to which he has sold his soul is sincere. Another thing on his mind is the certainty that there will be many death sentences handed out by the current courts-martial. Three men were condemned to death from among the 16 tried of the crew of the *Ierax* at Alexandria yesterday. He thinks there should be "no more shedding of blood." Apparently he is not one of these who would condone the mutinies, but he wouldn't punish them either, not, at least, as such acts are punished in armed services the world over, and though murder was done by these men, he thinks it should be treated as murder with a difference because it arose from politics, and politics with which he sympathizes. All this is muddy thinking, but thinking in which so large a part of the Greek people indulges that for the sake of the latter's future internal peace, I too hope there will be clemency exercised, even for rats who deserve none! . . . Went over to see Leeper at 7:15 and he gave me a copy of Papandreou's radio speech, which will be delivered

---

MacVeagh was opposed to the Anglo-Soviet agreement as reported to him; on the contrary, he appeared to welcome it as evidence of improved cooperation between the Allies.

tonight. It had just been translated by Waterhouse, and well done, too, considering he had to dictate it! As expected, the speech leaves the door open, but blames EAM for preventing the completion of the unity program agreed on by everyone, including its own representatives, at the Lebanon. As to the alleged attack of Zervas against ELAS, it says that information here indicates that ELAS did the attacking, but that in any case the way to stop this kind of thing is for EAM to join the Government —a point well taken. The Security Battalions are not mentioned, but here too, as Leeper pointed out, if a full national unity were secured, these Battalions would soon find themselves impotent, and unable to recruit. Still, I do not like the present British policy of tenderness towards these quisling outfits. It gives EAM much too good a chance to point the finger, —and though what Leeper says about unity being the best weapon against them is true, this also is true and is of immediate importance while the other is theoretical. It is amazing to see the British practically condoning the Security Battalions in Greece and damning the Chetniks in Yugoslavia—where the case as regards collaboration with the Germans is much less clear. But this is only one of the anomalies of British Balkan policy today.

June 30, 1944, Friday

In the morning I had a long call from Mr. Exindaris, who still thinks he may be replacing Mr. Politis shortly on the Mediterranean Commission in Italy. He wanted to tell me how badly he thinks the British are treating Mr. Lambrakis of the *Eleftheron Vima*, whom they are forcing to leave Egypt for Syria. He thinks the political antagonism of Lambrakis and Papandreou is to blame, and that the British have acted on the latter's request, and he emphasized that Lambrakis has always been pro-British, and that this action against him, which Leeper has told Exindaris (and me, too, incidentally) has been taken by the military on security grounds, will do much to increase resentment against the British among the Greeks. He hoped I might say something about this to Leeper, off the record. He then went on to sing the praises of Venizelos and to express the opinion that Papandreou's antagonistic attitude toward EAM will result in perpetuating the civil war rather than stopping it. He thinks the Premier's speech too severe and unyielding. "The Leftists are in a certain sense mystics, and you can't coerce mystics; you must persuade them." If Venizelos were premier, there would be a better chance of achieving unity because he is reasonable and trusted, etc. Not that there is any intention to upset Papandreou, he said. Nevertheless he gave me to understand that the Liberal Party opposition within the present Government is growing, and this is not a happy state of affairs. Their personal grievances are multiplying—Karapanayiotis, Bodossakis, Lambrakis, all persecuted! ... I used the occasion to tell Exindaris again what the American policy is toward Greece—to support her independence, and her right to choose her own régime, provided she does not interfere with the liberties of others, etc. And I emphasized that if the Greeks quarrel among themselves we can't be as effective in helping with relief and reconstruction as we want to be. He complained about British "interference" in Greek internal affairs, and I pointed out that much of this comes from the Greeks themselves asking for it, and I said that if they themselves unite behind one leader and stick to him, during the period before liberation, I felt sure they need fear no interference from outside. ... In the afternoon, Major General Deane,[134] of the U.S. Military Mission in Moscow, called, with messages from Harriman. I told him of my doubts as to whether the Subašić-Tito arrangements, as we know them now, are likely to cure civil strife in Yugoslavia, unless some new developments in the way of concessions to the Serb element are in the cards.... Dinner at Shepherd's Hotel with Mr. and Mrs. Kanellopoulos. The Polish Minister to Greece and his wife (he is an "Ambassador") and Mr. Rendis[135] and Mr. Tsatsos of the Greek Cabinet were the other guests. Rendis spoke to me about Lambrakis much as Exindaris had done, and indicated that the Cabinet is much disturbed, and there may be some resignations. Rendis is without portfolio, and Tsatsos is Justice. ... What is behind this Lambrakis business I cannot tell. I have asked Leeper and he side-steps every time, merely saying that the man is a bad influence, etc. I do not believe Papandreou has made the silly political mistake of asking the British to remove him. But their silence as to what they have against him is damaging to Papandreou as well as to themselves. I have gone as far as I can in suggesting—in this case and that of Karapanayiotis—that what the Greeks feel with some justice to be Gestapo methods in dealing with Greek politicians can do no good, and that a reasonable openness and frankness could be combined with firmness, avoiding suspicion, distrust and resentment. The British could well feel in regard to interference on our part that as we take no responsibility in these matters it is not up to us to criticize.

July 1, 1944, Saturday

Received at last the Department's orders to return for consultation. Called General Giles over, and he promised to give us No. 1 priorities on 10 hours notice.

[134] Major General John R. Deane, chief of the American Military Mission to the Soviet Union.

[135] Constantine Rendis, prominent liberal politician, and Minister-without-portfolio.

560 · CHAPTER VIII

July 3, 1944, Monday

Calls of farewell on Leeper and the King during the afternoon. . . . Leeper said he has had further confirmation of the 3 months arrangement with Russia on Greece and Rumania. But I still have no answer to my request for enlightenment on this subject. . . . The King seemed to me to be thinner and more worried than ever, and again talked disjointedly. He wants me to tell the President how deeply he appreciates his friendship, and that Anglo-American policy should be more effective in support of a national army in Greece and against EAM, to whose atrocities he referred repeatedly, commenting that they have drawn no word of rebuke from us or the British. . . . Parsons reported that Svolos told him that he and his friends will not join the Government unless EAM consents, but Leeper said that he thinks Angelopoulos may be an exception, as "he wants to be Finance Minister." While I was in Leeper's office, he told me that a message to Papandreou from Sarafis and Porfyrogenis had just come in, accusing the Premier of violating the Lebanon Agreement on no less than seven counts! Woodhouse commented, according to Leeper, that probably neither Sarafis nor Porfyrogenis ever saw that telegram! . . . EAM is trying to carry things with a high hand, but a message from Murphy quotes Maclean as reporting that Tito has recently turned a very cold shoulder to EAMite approaches, saying that EAM is not fighting Germans. . . . Messages from Algiers continue to confirm that the Tito-Subašić agreement has not extended to any concessions to the Serbs, and one received today says that Maclean has impressed on Tito that he must go in and take over Serbia, as HMG doesn't want a civil war! Murphy adds pointedly "comment would seem unnecessary."

July 4, 1944, Tuesday

In the morning I called on Lord Moyne . . . and Mr. Novikov to say good-bye, and received a call of courtesy (on the occasion of July 4th) from Mr. Papandreou and Mr. Dragoumis,—which I was able to use for a farewell visit! . . . Also got a telegram from the Department saying that with the President's authorization it is proceeding to appoint Schoenfeld[136] in London Chargé d'Affaires *ad interim* to Yugoslavia, and to "relieve me of the Yugoslav assignment." At the same time it wants to maintain my organization here to deal with important problems affecting Yugoslavia during this period and coordinate with other agencies dealing with them, as heretofore. I think it well to go home and find out just what this means in terms of actuality. . . .

Lord Moyne was very pleasant and friendly this morning, and we talked

---

[136] Rudolf E. Schoenfeld, Counselor of the U.S. Embassy to the Yugoslav government-in-exile (London).

over the problems we have in common, agreeing that London and Washington must settle the committee question and the BSC Question. We can give our views, but the decisions must come from higher up, and till that happens we must remain somewhat at a disadvantage locally, since he continues to think that the committee method is the best way to handle many of our Balkan problems, and I do not. He sees the BSC in the guise of a big committee, and argues that as the committee method is working in Italy and Algiers it is appropriate for Balkan purposes also. I feel that the existence of recognized allied Governments of Greece and Yugoslavia, and of diplomatic missions accredited to them, makes a tremendous difference, and that no conclusions can be drawn from experience in enemy territory. The military in the Balkan relief operation has a definite and restricted task which must be subordinated to the civil authority of the sovereign states it is to assist. It is not going into the Balkans (presumably) to set up a military state on its own! In addition, therefore, to the fact that committees tend to weaken the authority of the command by taking away some of its responsibility, we must remember that the command in Yugoslavia and Greece will have the British and American and Russian Missions, plus the local governments and their appropriate services, at hand to guide and advise,—super-committees, one might call them, which will not take away any of the responsibility of the military in its allotted field but will supplement and reinforce it rather. It is to my mind pure Jumbo-ism to see even the military period of the Balkan operation purely in terms of the military. If one takes this point of view, then I can see how one might incline to Lord Moyne's idea of committees as a method of exerting some control in the interests of political and economic policies, but if one realizes that the military is only a part of the Balkan show from the very start, then the committee idea cannot even have this to say for it. . . .

Novikov was also very friendly and chatty. He remarked,—which may be indicative of a new Russian attitude,—that he thinks Greek unity has already been achieved, namely by the Lebanon Conference, and that he cannot see why the organizations in Greece don't recognize it! . . . How glad Leeper would be if Novikov, or any official Russian, would say this publicly! Perhaps this may happen if the new "3 months" arrangement regarding initiative is really agreed to. But Novikov has had no reply to his request for enlightenment on this matter just as I have had none. It remains a mystery. . . . On the other hand, Novikov remarked, when I asked him how things are going between him and our British colleague, "We are not here representing our Governments to the Greek Government, but to Mr. Leeper. He is the real Prime Minister of Greece." Some truth in that, as well as bitterness! But I told N. that I felt the British would not be running Greek affairs to the extent they are if the Greeks themselves didn't ask for it. The trouble with them is that instead of setting their house in order themselves, they constantly run to the great powers to do it for them, and the British, who are particularly concerned that order should prevail in Greece, are forced to do something about it. I have watched this going on for years. . . . Novikov asked what our policy is, and I said (again) that it is to promote Greek unity, but to leave the means of achieving it to the Greeks themselves, while making it clear that our great aim to help reconstruction in the country cannot succeed if the latter remains divided. . . . Arthur Parsons brought in from the British Embassy a new long telegram from the leftists in Greece to Mr. Papandreou, giving the terms on which they will join the Government. These include a statement by the King himself that he will not return before the plebiscite, and several other apparent impossibilities. I doubt if the Government can accept. Another of the terms is: no executions for the recent mutinies, and a general amnesty in regard to them, to follow EAM's joining the Government!

July 5, 1944, Wednesday
Col. West of OSS called and said that he is going into Greece shortly, to be chief American Liaison Officer there. He doubts whether Col. Woodhouse, the Britisher, will go back. He asked me how he should act as regards political affairs, and I said I thought that as he represents the military he should keep out of them, but that if he had to say anything, he should say the same things to all Greeks regardless of their party or group; namely, that we want to see them united in order better to fight the enemy, and the better to facilitate our efforts to relieve and reconstruct their country, but that the way in which they should achieve this unity is not our business. I said I thought this differed in no way from what OSS has been doing right along, for the most part, very successfully.

The MacVeaghs left Cairo's Payne Field by military plane in the small hours of Thursday, July 6, and after brief stops at Tripoli, Casablanca, the Azores, Newfoundland, and New York's La Guardia Airport, arrived in Washington, D.C. in the early afternoon of the following day.

July 7, 1944, Friday
I put in an appearance at the Department and stayed till 7 o'clock! I called on Wallace Murray first and found Foy Kohler with him. They were actually discussing the matter of the Anglo-Russian agreement on "initiatives" in Greece and Rumania. It appears that what I thought was

true, namely that after the President had accepted the Department's views as expressed in our "information telegram," Mr. Churchill wrote, or telegraphed, directly to his Great and Good Friend, and the result was that we have agreed to the 3 month trial period. . . . I then spent the afternoon mostly in Kohler's office, talking over Greek affairs, and specially the BSC. It seems that Mr. Kohler and Mr. Dort[137] of the Liberated Areas Division quite share our views and those of Linebaugh and Scott,[138] and there may be a chance that BSC may be killed and some device adopted to deal with Balkan supply problems in the post-UNRRA period which will be more appropriate in the circumstances. I gave Mr. Kohler the documents which Barboza-Carneiro had given me dealing with the MESC. Both Landis (whom I met in the hall) and Jackson of the MESC are here, and can be counted on to do their best to maintain the BSC at all costs. . . . On the plane this morning, I had a long talk with Steinhardt,[139] and he and I agreed completely as to the urgent need of our having, and following, a policy of our own in the Near East from now on. Later, in talking with Wallace Murray I was able to develop this idea somewhat, and happily found that he too (and Foy, most certainly!) has been thinking along these lines. . . . The matter is just as important (and even perhaps more so) in regard to Yugoslavia as in regard to Greece and Turkey.

July 8, 1944, Saturday
All day in the Department. Talks with Cavendish Cannon[140] and Nathaniel P. Davis, the Director of Personnel, and a conference on the BSC with Charles P. Taft, of the Division of Wartime Economies, and Mr. Mitchell, head of the Liberated Territories Division and Mr. Dort of the same Division and Mr. Kohler. They seemed to want my ideas, and I supported the Linebaugh and Scott report, and suggested that the way to go about reconstruction after the war is through the Balkan Governments and the Missions of the Great Powers attached to them. Instead of an outside, over-all regional supply center to screen and adjust requirements for the whole area, the screening should be done by the various countries themselves in association with the missions of the supplying countries (on the idea of the South African Supply Council) and regional adjustments should be encouraged between the component states. This encouragement could take the form of suggesting that if Greece and Rumania, for instance, should agree to do their best to supplement each

[137] Dallas W. Dort, Adviser, War Areas Economic Division, Department of State.
[138] Walter K. Scott, Communications Officer, Department of State.
[139] Laurence Steinhardt, U.S. Ambassador to Turkey.
[140] Cavendish W. Cannon, Chief of the Division of South European Affairs, Department of State.

other's deficiencies out of their respective surpluses, the great powers would do their best to make up what might still be left over in both cases. This last was an idea of Mitchell's who saw in it a practical way to start economic reciprocity in the Balkans leading possibly to greater political stability. I added that not only did it seem inappropriate to the actual conditions in the Balkans,—when the whole territory is not enemy territory, and where none of it after the war will be in the state of *vassalage* vis-à-vis the Great Powers which Jackson talks about,—to attempt to administer its economic life through a wholly foreign agency like the BSC, but that it appeared to me important that whatever was done by the British and Americans to enlist the Balkan Governments in a rational campaign of mutual reconstruction should be shared in by the Russians at the start. Starting something and then telling them about it afterwards is a sure way to incur their ever-ready suspicion. I do not know that Russia will help much in fact, but certainly if they are not in sympathy with what we are doing they are in a fine position to wreck it.... In my talks with Cannon, both morning and afternoon, I was happy to note that he has exactly the same views on the Yugoslav political situation that we have in Cairo—and perhaps even more so! He said that there is no news of any *rapprochement* with the Serbs, that the Topalović talks apparently led to nothing, and that British instigation to Tito to go in and conquer the Serbs in what is believed to be their very weak present condition seems to be a fact. He expressed the idea that the British may be thinking that there is no longer any possibility of securing a united Yugoslavia, and that as the Russian influence is bound to extend down through Rumania, Bulgaria and Serbia, it is to Britain's interest to secure for her own influence at least the Adriatic territories. Hence her frantic support of a movement which is strong principally in Dalmatia, Croatia and Slovenia, and her apparent willingness to abandon the Serbs. Incidentally, this idea dovetails rather nicely into that of Joyce, to the effect that the British hope by uniting as many resistance groups as possible under Tito to make it impossible for his government to be a communist one. The program would then appear to be to make Tito at once an ally of Britain and the overlord of the whole Dalmatian-Adriatic coastal region (and as far inland as possible) while at the same time drawing the teeth of his communism by building up his strength out of non-communist elements. ... I told Cannon that I think this presupposes considerably more foresight on the part of British policy than it has shown in this region in recent years, where a nervous and sometimes almost frantic opportunism has, as it seems to me, been its chief characteristic—based of course on lack of strength to be anything different. The bull-headedness of Mr. Churchill may count for more in the present tenacious and exaggerated support of "Marshall" Tito than any far-reaching calculations as regards the relative strength of Russian penetration south-westwards and the preservation of the British Imperial life-line. But these speculations are at least interesting, and it may be noted as a fact that British opportunism in the Near East, which so often appears contradictory on the surface, is always true to one fundamental principle, the preservation of the imperial lines of communication. Mr. Churchill, therefore, may not be consciously far-seeing in what he is doing, but what he is doing, if only by a Britisher's instinct, is aimed at the same target as it would be if he had thought the whole thing out. . . . Granted now that the British are going to push Tito to the conquest of Serbia, or as much of it as possible, so as to make the British Adriatic zone a state of considerable size, the question arises as to whether we may not see the Russians abandoning Tito as a broken reed for their purposes and shifting their attention to the Serbs. British abandonment of, and what amounts really to treachery against, the men who, of all the Yugoslavs, put up the best fight against the Axis, may carry the Serbs on the rebound into the Russian camp, particularly if the Russians play the game of national and racial rather than economic or party blandishment—as they know well how to do.

July 10, 1944, Monday

More talks with Cannon and Kohler. Met Eric Biddle in the latter's office. Both Kohler and Biddle feel (it is Foy's idea, really) that we should strengthen our participation in the MESC or get out altogether. If we strengthen our participation we may be able to control its activities better and keep them more in line with our policies (which I gather are mainly, in this case, to restrict MESC to what it was originally set up to do!), and also to see to it that MESC ceases to function when the war is over and its *raison d'être* disappears. . . . I am afraid Lord Moyne would be quite unhappy if he could hear many of the things being said here about his pet organization! . . . Kohler told me that the question of the Balkan Affairs Committee has been given some attention, and that a proposal is going forward to London that it be constituted in Cairo with a very small high-level membership. He thinks that what will eventuate will be in accordance with my ideas. This, however, brings up the subject of my status in Cairo, and I had a long talk with Cannon, urging that we cannot in Cairo perform duties in connection with Yugoslavia, as desired, unless we have some standing other than that of Embassy to Greece,—and this remark extends to the whole Balkans, if I am to serve on the Balkan Affairs Committee. I suggested that I stay on as Ambassador to Yugoslavia, with Schoenfeld as Chargé *a.i.* [ad interim] in London. If the Yugoslav Government goes to Italy or Malta, it will be easy to appoint another Chargé there. Meanwhile the Embassy to Yugoslavia would remain essentially undisturbed, in touch with AMHQ and UNRRA etc. in Cairo, till the final move back to Belgrade. Cannon said he thought this could not be done as the President is planning to have the Missions to the other exiled Governments set up there independently (not all lumped under Schoenfeld as now), and would not wish to see Yugoslavia treated differently—though I pointed out that the Yugoslav situation, with nothing settled in it from our point of view, or that of the British, but the position of the King, to whom the Ambassador is accredited, differs greatly from the secure governmental situations of Norway, Holland, etc. Cannon's suggestion is that I lose the Ambassadorship but continue to do the bulk of the Embassy work, which must remain in the Cairo area at present, but that to cover this and other Balkan activities required of me, I be given some such title as "Administrator of Balkan Affairs." I said I don't care what solution is adopted so long as I be given a position consonant with the functions I am required to perform, but I still think my suggestion the logical one, and quite feasible in the circumstances. . . . Talk with Mr. Stettinius in the afternoon. He is no expert in foreign affairs like Sumner Welles, and all he had to tell me was how proud he felt of having got the halls and rooms of the Department swept and washed, and the Negro attendants put into clean uniforms. Sumner would at once have gone into the difficult problems we have to face in the Near East and attempted to get from me anything I might have which would tend to clarify them in his mind. But "Big Ed" only talked of mutual friends he thought we might have. . . . It is certain that the new "streamlining" of the Department for which Mr. Stettinius is largely responsible, has been a good thing, particularly the feature which extends the signing privilege down to Assistant Chiefs of Division. But this would not be such an improvement if we had an Under-Secretary who personally read all the non-routine telegrams, as Sumner did, and took a personal interest in all aspects of our policy. At present there seems to be no initiative in policy-thinking above the ranks of the desk officers in the divisions. Above that there is of course decision in the form of consent or denial, more or less in accord with the broad principles of Mr. Hull. But the fast well-informed thinking necessary to deal with events before they develop into insoluble problems is all in the hands of the youngsters, who are terribly handicapped in the presentation of their ideas by indifference and ignorance in the higher ranks. Foy Kohler gave me a summary of the present Greek situation, describing the impasse which has resulted from the refusal of the Papandreou Government to accede to the demands of the EAMites. This he intended as a *brief* for his superiors in the Department, and he asked me to go over it. It had to be short, or they would not read it, he said; it had to be clear for the same reason; and when I used the word "ecumenical" to describe the Government, he said I would have to take it out as they would not understand it! As a result, I fear that the understanding of the Greek situation, which is a critical one in a critical region of the world, will be but very summary and inadequate on the part of the Department's "policy makers"—the Under-Secretary, the Assistant Secretaries and the Office Directors. *But they don't want it otherwise.* They have neither the time nor the inclination (nor the belief that it is necessary) to understand anything well. I often resent the criticism of the Department in the press, but when you get beyond certain men in our missions in the field and the desk officers in Washington, the good correspondents, such as Cy Sulzberger, are, I fear, far ahead of any personnel the Department can boast of in their knowledge of foreign actualities.

July 11, 1944, Tuesday

My talk with Mr. Hull was interesting. He asked me how long I am home for, and I said only for a short time, to familiarize myself with the Department's ideas on my area, a thing which I had felt to be particularly necessary since I went to Cairo some six months ago direct from South Africa without having the opportunity for prior instruction in the Department. I said I wanted to "touch base." He then asked me if I had brought home with me any points of view other than those I had already reported from my post, and I said no, that I was anxious rather to learn the Department's views on the mess I had in hand. I said that Greece, of course, always would be complicated politically but that the Yugoslavian mess is more serious than the Greek because of the different nationalities, religions, *et cetera,* involved, as well as the long history of massacres and so forth. Mr. Hull asked what is going to happen there now, and I replied that I felt it impossible to say, since we (or at least I) do not know how far the British intend to go in pushing their present pro-Tito policy. He smiled at this and said that the Russians seem to be to blame for what the British have been doing since they supported Tito to begin with, and then the British thought they had to follow suit. But I replied that so far as I could see the Russians have done very little in regard to anything in Yugoslavia. It is true that they sent a high-powered military liaison group to Tito's headquarters, but this was *after* the British had begun to take him up. I said I thought the British policy was motivated rather by nervousness over what Russia might do than by any actual Russian move to date, and that I thought the Russians have behaved very correctly, and will not seek to extend their exclusive influence unless they see the British doing so. Mr. Hull continued to smile and evidently liked this kind of talk. He then asked me about the Anglo-Russian exchange of initiatives in Rumania and Greece, and I told him of its genesis in the Russian suspicion of British secret operations in Rumania and British resentment of Russian criticism in connection with the Greek mutinies. He said the Department had been against this exchange as leading to the establishment of zones of influence, and when I said I understood it had now been accepted for a three months' period, he said, "Yes, but that wasn't our fault, it came from across the street,"— with a gesture over his shoulder. He asked me if I saw any signs of Russian preparations to extend Soviet power over the smaller states, and I said no, though there are plenty of signs that the Russians are feeling their oats as a result of their recent victories and that they desire to have a say, at least, in everything that goes on in the Mediterranean region. He nodded his head at this and seemed to be fully aware of what I had in mind. He told me of how he himself had reminded the Russians of the old adage about the giant's strength. "Do you want to be respected by all, or do you want to make enemies for yourselves everywhere?" I then told him of the fear, which is so obvious along the British Imperial Life-Line, of Russia as being now the only great continental power, against which no "balance" is possible in Europe—which means we may be called in again to defend England unless by foresight we can get the British and the Russians to avoid the clashes of policy which little by little lead on to war. I told him that I thought we should get the Russians in with us on the ground floor, together with the British, in connection with all our Near Eastern planning, just for this reason, though I doubt if they would be of any great practical assistance at this time. He asked me whether I saw any signs of growing trust between the Russians and the British, and I said that things seem improving but unfortunately it is almost impossible to get Britishers and Russians to meet as man to man in the way the Russians and Americans can do. In this connection he told me of how he talked straight from the shoulder and "just like one politician to another" to Molotov, and I told him of Leeper's complaint that he can't collaborate with Novikov since when he talks to him the Russian never says anything! We then branched on to the supply picture, and I told him of the uncertain basis as to tonnages, *et cetera*, on which all our extensive planning is being built, and he urged that I talk about all this sort of thing "to Mr. Dunn,"[141] and said that he himself would always be at my disposal. "We are so busy that sometimes we don't tell each other enough." I told him of my feeling that as the war is leaving the Balkans, we are able to see there the beginnings of the reconstruction problem which will later effect all of Europe, and I emphasized that this problem differs in Yugoslavia and Greece from what it has been in Italy

[141] James C. Dunn, Director of the Office of European Affairs, Department of State.

since the former are allied and not conquered states. He seemed to agree thoroughly that this difference is a cardinal one and must not be lost sight of. This ended our conversation. Mr. Hull appeared definitely older and somewhat weaker than when I saw him two years ago, though when I complimented him on his appearance he said, "I am doing very well." How he stands the strain of his official life, I don't know. He had a continuous stream of visitors all afternoon and while I was waiting to see him the Vice President came in without an appointment and kept him a full hour.

July 13, 1944, Thursday

Was summoned to see Mr. Stettinius at 12. . . . Stettinius (the second time I have seen him) clapped me on the shoulder and called me "boy." He then said he wanted to talk with me "in case there was anything we left over the other day." As we discussed nothing the other day, this seemed superfluous. He asked me what I thought would be the reaction on my territory if "we should get Turkey to enter the war," and got up and looked at the map, saying "they have 18 divisions." I said I thought that if the Turkish move against Bulgaria were a success it would have a profound psychological effect in my area, certainly, but it would have to be a success, and I referred to the terrible let-down in Greek morale following the Dodecanese-Samos fiasco. I asked Stettinius if he thought the Turks can defeat the Bulgars, and he said that "the British tell us so," and "yes, if they get enough tanks." I said that Steinhardt had told me that the Turkish decision rests on whether the British decide to give the materiel they want. Stettinius then showed that he thought we had talked long enough, and our brief talk ended with my saying again that the Greek situation is complicated, but the Yugoslav is worse than that. He nodded, saying "It is bad. It is dangerous," and I had to be content with hoping that he knows what the words mean. At least he used them, and as they correspond with the reality, that is useful. It seemed to be very much on his mind how busy he is. . . . In a talk with Cannon which I had both before and after seeing Stettinius, I learned that the new Yugoslav Cabinet is composed, besides Subašić, who is Prime Minister, Minister for Foreign Affairs and War, of (1) Prof. Streten Vukosavljević, a Serb, Minister of Agriculture, Supply, Mines and Forestry; (2) Dr. Juraj Sutej, a Croat, Minister of Finance, Trade and Industry; (3) Mr. Sava Kosanović, a Serb, Minister of Home Affairs, Social Welfare, Health, and Public Works; (4) Prof. Izidor Cenkar, a Slovene, Minister of Education, Posts and Telegraphs, and (5) Mr. Drago Marusić, a Slovene, Minister of Justice and Communications. Sutej and Subašić are members of the Croatian

Peasant Party, Marusić is a Tito nominee, a lawyer, former Governor of Slovenia and leader of the Slovene Peasant Party. Cenkar is Yugoslav Minister to Canada, a former Catholic priest, member of the Slovene Clerical Party and Prof. of [?] at Lubljana University. Vukosavljević, another Tito nominee, is Professor of Sociology in Belgrade. Neither he nor the other Serb, Kosanović, have any substantial Serb following though the former "is said to be popular in the Sanjak and Montenegro." (All the above is from Winant's telegrams.) The King is trying to bring the Serbs into the picture under Tito's overall command by replacing Mihailović with a Lt. General Glišić,[142] and summoning M. to come out of the country. The F.O. believes M. will obey, and that the Serb people are so loyal to the dynasty that they will accept his replacement by Glišić. . . . A new meeting between Subašić and Tito has been arranged by Wilson, to take place at Caserta. It seems that all is not settled yet! But the latest news is that Tito has told Maclean he will not go to the rendezvous, since "the reactions throughout the country and in particular in Croatia and Slovenia to the recent agreement with Subašić have not been favorable, and if he went abroad at this juncture it would have an even more unsettling effect on public opinion and would react unfavorably on his prestige." The London Embassy further reports that Tito was "deaf to all Maclean's arguments" that his refusal would make a "deplorable impression" and do his cause great harm. Mr. Churchill is sending him a letter asking him to reconsider. Later: a message has come in from Murphy saying that Wilson may insist that Tito "come to Caserta tomorrow as planned" (dated July 12). What a kettle of fish! Even the Britisher's favorite will not play the British game, and what about the others? Do they indeed so cling to their beloved dynasty that they will take *his* [the king's] going over to the Partisans whom the British are instigating to attack *them* [the Serbs]? Well, doubtless we shall see. . . . My lunch with Berle was very interesting in this connection. He at least is on the ball, and though his lack of humor is depressing, his eager concern in all vital problems is refreshing. He is thoroughly sound both on the Yugoslav and the Greek situation,—and that includes the King question! He knows that the return of King George to Greece is important only as it may be mishandled, and that it can be mishandled if foreigners attempt to decide the matter. Otherwise the question is as nothing compared with the great economic questions of reconstruction. In Yugoslavia he sees clearly the dangers of the present British policy, which is likely to increase rather than put an end to civil war. He confessed himself baffled by British policy in the Near East, and I said that 80 percent is political opportunism based on inadequate strength to take a line and keep it,

[142] General Djordje Glišić, Serb royalist officer.

and 20 percent commercial policy to capitalize on victory. . . . Governor Lehman called up and said he wanted to talk with me about several decisions he is being called upon to make just now, and we arranged that I call on him at 4:15 tomorrow. I told him that Saturday I hope to get away from here, and he kindly changed his appointments to fit me in. . . . No word from General Watson, so I figure I shall not see the President till I get back. The Democratic Convention is about to start in Chicago. . . .

July 14, 1944, Friday

Had a long talk with Wallace Murray, lasting till nearly one o'clock. We covered a wide range of subjects, but mostly we talked of the problems of the Near and Middle East, particularly as regards the future; the growth of Russian power, the persistence of the British imperial idea, and what must be done,—what *we* must do,—to keep the two from clashing. He referred to a memo which had been sent to the Secretary by the Joint Chiefs of Staff, and which seems to have made a big impression in the Department, as I have now heard about it from many sides. This memo seems to have sounded a warning that in the next war the United States might possibly be able to save Britain from being conquered *in her own islands*, but that it will be out of the question for her to count on us for more than this. . . .[143] It is encouraging that so many people in the Department—from the Secretary down—realize the Anglo-Russian danger. A third world war would about finish the Western World, and there is no place where it is more likely to get started than in the Near and Middle East. But forwarned may be forearmed, and the diplomacy of the coming generation must somehow contrive to make the Lion and the Bear lie down together, and the Eagle has his role to play in this likewise. . . . Lunch with Cannon and "Chip" Bohlen[144] at the Hay Adams House. Bohlen has only recently returned from Moscow,

---

[143] The memorandum of the Joint Chiefs of Staff, dated May 16, 1944, explored the possibility of future conflicts among the great powers and asserted that ". . . it is apparent that any future world conflict in the foreseeable future will find Britain and Russia in opposite camps." In view of the "recent phenomenal development of the heretofore latent Russian military and economic strength," the memorandum warned: "Having due regard to the military factors involved—resources, manpower, geography and particularly our ability to project our strength across the ocean and exert it decisively upon the continent—we might be able to successfully defend Britain, but we could not, under existing conditions, defeat Russia. In other words, we would find ourselves engaged in a war which we could not win even though the United States would be in no danger of defeat and occupation." *FR 1945, The Conferences at Malta and Yalta*, pp. 106-8.

[144] Charles E. Bohlen, Chief of the Division of Eastern European Affairs, Department of State.

where he served some time. He thinks that Tito's reluctance to play further with the British may be owing to word from Moscow. . . . Long talk in the afternoon with Governor Lehman, of UNRRA, at his office in Dupont Circle. After a while, his Mr. Jackson joined us. The Governor is being pressed by the Russians to extend UNRRA aid to Tito, and is told that there is "liberated territory" in Yugoslavia where such aid can be administered to the people. I said that I feel that "liberated" is a relative term in this connection, that parts of Yugoslavia are free of Germans, undoubtedly, but that so far none of it can be regarded as definitely liberated, since the Germans can and do push in anywhere they like and at any time they choose to do so. In any case I advised him that as Tito is now represented in the Yugoslav cabinet by at least two ministers, he might ask the Yugoslav Government about liberated areas and ports, and so forth. He could tell the Russians that he was doing this, and so escape any further embarrassment on that score. But why did he need me to suggest anything so obvious? He is obviously very much in the dark as to what is really going on in Yugoslavia. I advised him most earnestly to go slowly at present, and to wait until he could clearly see that the situation contemplated for UNRRA action has really arrived, before he commits his organization to anything in that country. Between our military authorities and the Yugoslav Government, he should be able to get some adequate information. . . . We talked about the UNRRA work in Cairo and I urged that more good American personnel from the voluntary agencies be secured and sent out as soon as possible.

Between July 15-30 the MacVeaghs were on vacation, visiting the Ambassador's mother at the family summer home in Dublin, New Hampshire, and enjoying a few restful days at Greensboro, Vermont. He returned to Washington on the 31st.

July 31, 1944, Monday
Spent the morning with Foy Kohler, in his office for the most part. . . . The principal news from our part of the field is that some members of the Russian Liaison Mission to Tito somehow managed to fly into Greece, landing on a secret British air-field there.[145] They are proceeding to the headquarters of the Political Committee in the mountains, and it seems to be expected that they will advise EAM to join the Government of National Unity. Novikov's remark to me the day I said "au revoir" in

[145] On July 1944, a ten-member Soviet military mission, under Colonel Gregori Popov, arrived at ELAS headquarters in Thessaly. It had been transported by a Soviet plane that had picked up the group at Tito's headquarters, after flying there from Italy. British authorities were surprised and disturbed by this development.

CAIRO · 573

Cairo, to the effect that he saw no reason why this joining should not now be effected, in view of the fact that National Unity has already been accomplished at the Lebanon Conference, comes back into my mind in this connection. . . .

August 1, 1944, Tuesday

Had a long talk with Kohler on the agreement with the Greeks in connection with AML's functions. The AML has submitted a draft, and the British Embassy to Greece wants a second agreement specifically dealing with possible military operations as distinct from relief and reconstruction. Kohler thinks the British had better make the agreement or agreements with the Greeks, subject to our approval, along the lines they desire, and that we should make a *separate* agreement associating ourselves with the British-Greek understanding so far as relief and reconstruction are concerned. This will keep the limitation of our responsibility clear, and at the same time put us on public record as being concerned in the relief work for which we shall probably be contributing most of the supplies.

August 2, 1944, Wednesday

Lunched on sandwiches in the office, and worked the rest of the day on a condensed report on Greece and Yugoslavia to be presented to the Policy Committee at its meeting tomorrow. Just got it finished in time to be typed this evening. . . . The writing of my report was difficult because not only of the necessary brevity but of the fact that many members of the large committee, which includes all the Assistant Secretaries and the heads of offices and Divisions, have very little if any knowledge of the subject matter, to start with.

August 3, 1944, Thursday

I attended the Policy Committee meeting. Ambassador Braden[146] was there also, to report on Cuba. He sat on the right of Mr. Stettinius, who presided, and I on the left, next to Berle; Shaw, Long, and Acheson were there, as well as ex-Ambassador Grew,[147] and Stanley Hornbeck,[148] Hawkins[149] of the Economic Division, Paul Alling,[150] and numerous

[146] Spruille Braden, U.S. Ambassador to Argentina.
[147] Joseph C. Grew, Under-Secretary of State.
[148] Stanley Hornbeck, Adviser on Political Relations, Department of State.
[149] Harry Hawkins, Chief of the Division of Commercial Treaties and Agreements, Department of State.
[150] Paul H. Alling, Deputy Director of the Office of Near Eastern and African Affairs, Department of State.

others. Mr. Long took over a half-hour discussing a new policy regarding the continental shelf and fisheries. Then Mr. Braden reported on Cuba, and I had to mind the clock. So I briefly introduced my report, and read it rapidly. Mr. Dunn asked how I would propose to correct the false impression I mentioned as being given to the Balkan peoples in regard to our policy, and I answered, chiefly through correction of the radio propaganda being put out. I said that I felt no propaganda at all would be better than misleading propaganda, and there was general assent. Mr. Stettinius asked whether the matter could not be taken up at once with OWI, and I said a conference has been arranged for next week. Mr. Stettinius then adopted Mr. Braden's report and mine for the minutes, and later he sent me a note to say that he had sent my report to the Secretary.

[The report was as follows:]

1. The problems in both Greece and Yugoslavia today are less military than economic and political. It is currently predicted that as the Allied pincers in Poland and France close on Germany, the Germans will withdraw their forces from the Balkans, and Allied military action is planned at present on this basis. In both countries it is contemplated to use the local guerrillas to sabotage German withdrawal, and to confine actual Allied military operations chiefly to the facilitation and protection of the initial stages of relief and rehabilitation.

2. Plans for relief and rehabilitation are far advanced. They cover two periods, a military one, in which UNRRA will assist the military in the distribution of the supplies brought in by the latter, and a so-called UNRRA period to follow, in which that organization will exercise full responsibility. A military organization called the Allied Military Liaison, commanded by a British major general, has been set up in Cairo, and is now adequately staffed, though no troops have yet been assigned to it. On the staff there are some fifty or sixty American civil affairs officers. American participation in the functioning of this mission is strictly limited to collaboration in relief and rehabilitation problems. Should military action be found necessary, either to preserve order or to subdue remnants of the German forces remaining in the country, American forces will take no part in it. The chief unsettled questions in connection with the work of this mission, aside from the assignment of troops, are how to assure sufficient supplies to meet the anticipated needs, and how these supplies are eventually to be paid for. In Greece the currency question is especially acute, the pound sterling having risen from between four and five hundred drachmas to well over a hundred million.

3. In the political field both countries have suffered from the fact that their governments, which went into exile on the approach of the Germans,

were newly and hastily formed affairs, while both their kings, and in particular the Greek King, enjoyed only a limited popularity with their people.

(a) As regards Greece, the Government-in-Exile is now formed of a coalition of all parties except the extreme Left, but has a strong republican complexion as a result of popular reaction against the Fascist dictatorship of 1936-1941. This situation has forced the King to agree to a plebiscite on the question of the monarchy, to be held after liberation, and also to agree not to return to Greece unless and until called for as a result of the plebiscite, or previously at the desire of his government. At present his government is against his returning before the plebiscite, but the King continues to hope that it may change its view before the hour of liberation comes. He thinks it possible that continued refusal on the part of the Communists, now controlling the largest of the guerrilla organizations in Greece, to join the Government of National Unity may bring about a popular demand for his presence which his government would have to heed. However, his notable lack of personal qualities as a leader is against him, as well as his long association with the recent tyranny of the extreme Right.

(b) As regards the Kingdom of the Serbs, Croats, and Slovenes, the political question is complicated by profound divisions within the country which do not exist in homogeneous Greece. These divisions have long been played upon from the outside, particularly by Italian and German diplomacy, and were acute at the time of the German invasion, which the Serbs resisted wholeheartedly, while the Croats and Slovenes in general did not. On the other hand, the most successful anti-Axis guerrilla movement in the country is Croatian and Communist in origin and character, rather than Serb and Royalist, and with military aid from the Allies, granted primarily for the purpose of war against Germany, this movement now seems on its way to attempting to force its domination over Serbia and thus bring an end to the primacy which the latter has enjoyed in the conglomerate state hitherto.

4. Internationally, the Balkans remain a potential region of conflicting pressures. The war is eliminating the Anglo-German conflict of interests, but is replacing it with Anglo-Russian. Communist ideology holds no great appeal for the Balkan peoples, largely composed of peasant landholders, but the success of communist-led resistance movements in disorganized and demoralized territories supplies a dangerous opportunity for the imposition of Communist Party dictatorship. Refugees from Dalmatia, now to be seen in increasing numbers in Italy and North Africa, present unmistakable signs of indoctrination and regimentation with this end in view. Russia's interest in the Communist resistance movements of Tito in Yugoslavia and the EAM in Greece has also been clearly

shown, particularly by the Soviet press and radio, though Russia continues officially to recognize the Greek and Yugoslav Governments-in-Exile, and there is no evidence that her own government is directing or financing these movements, which stem rather from the international Communism of 1917, than that of present-day Moscow. The British are intensely anxious as regards the Russian attitude, and this explains much of their activity in connection with the internal affairs of both nations. In Greece they have switched from supporting the EAM to opposing it, and in Yugoslavia they have abandoned Mihailović and are trying to hitch the Tito movement to the car of British policy, possibly with the idea that a great accretion of recruits under British influence will overbalance and destroy its present Communist character. Evidences of growing mutual suspicion between London and Moscow have not been lacking. Shortly after Mr. Churchill began his personal correspondence with Tito, the Russians sent the latter a large liaison mission, headed by a lieutenant general, far outranking the local British brigadier. And when the British took strong action to quell the Greek mutinies in Egypt, which were led by adherents of the EAM, the Russian Ambassador in Cairo was outspoken in his disapproval. Further evidence of this sort was forthcoming when the Russians recently expressed displeasure and surprise over British secret operations in Rumania. This last affair has led to an attempt by London to establish a division of zones of interest in the Balkans, though only temporarily, for the war period. The attempt seems doomed to failure, largely on account of the Department's doubts as to the advisability of such action in connection with decisions taken at Teheran. But it shows that London, at least, recognizes the dangers inherent in the present situation if suspicions are allowed to grow.

5. The Rumanian peace feelers made in Cairo by an emissary of Maniu, the peasant party leader, have so far come to nothing, owing partly to a continued hope on the latter's part that the Allies could be split and negotiations carried on with the Anglo-Americans separately from the Russians, but also, it would seem, because of genuine impotence on Maniu's part to move against the Germans, whose control of the country up to this time has been exceedingly watchful and thorough. Bulgarian peace feelers, which have been rumored for months, seem now to be imminent, and here, a hope of getting special consideration out of the supposed leniency of the Americans is clearly apparent.

6. As the war seems to be drawing to its close, post-war territorial claims and aspirations are coming more and more into the picture in the Balkans. In Yugoslavia, the Tito group is naturally the one most heard from so far. It appears to nurse dreams of domination not only over the whole of Yugoslavia, but also over the vague region known as Macedonia, including parts of Greece and Bulgaria. More serious, perhaps, are the views of

the Greeks, who merit consideration for their unquestioning resistance to the Axis from the beginning. All the Greeks who have talked to me on this subject realize fully that any territorial acquisitions beyond the prewar boundaries of the country must await decisions to be made at the peace conference. But they are nevertheless letting it be known that they regard Greece as entitled to the Dodecanese and Southern Albania, on ethnical grounds, as well as to a boundary with Bulgaria running north of the coastal range, for strategic purposes. It can hardly be questioned that the Dodecanese Islands are predominantly Greek in their population, as well as in their history, while the strongly Greek character of that part of Northern Epirus which is now called Southern Albania, including the towns of Koritza and Argyrocastro, is also undeniable.

7. American policy towards Greece and Yugoslavia is briefly, as I understand it, not to intervene in internal affairs while giving military support, during the war period, to such resistance groups as actively oppose the common enemy. British policy seems to be to insure the establishment of post-war governments favorable to British interests. Russian policy appears, generally speaking, to be similar to the British from the Russian viewpoint. The British are very active in their direction and manipulation of the Governments-in-Exile. My Russian colleague in Cairo complained to me that the real Prime Minister of Greece is the British Ambassador. On the other hand, the Russians, while critical and suspicious of the British, appear for the most part to be holding aloof in the belief that repeated British mistakes, coupled with none on their part, will infallibly orient the sentiment of these distressed countries toward Moscow. So far, this belief may find some justification in the low ebb to which British prestige has fallen owing to the opportunist shifts of British policy toward the resistance movements, the repeated British military fiascos in Greece, Crete, and the Dodecanese, and the many mistakes in psychology which the British have committed in their handling of the Greek military and other problems.

Conclusion: Under the circumstances, I would recommend no change in American policy, but would point out that it might be made more clear to the peoples concerned. At the present moment, owing to faultily married propaganda-directives and the often loose employment of the term "Anglo-American" for activities purely British in character, American policy tends to be confused with British throughout the whole Balkan region, and we are rapidly incurring the same dislike, suspicion, and distrust which the Balkan peoples are increasingly feeling for our cousins. In addition, I believe that, in view of the great dangers for the future peace of the whole world, including ourselves, which the Balkan region continues to present as a crossroads of empire, we should maintain and even intensify our present salutary efforts to associate the Russians together with the British in all Balkan planning and activity of whatever character, from the ground up and in complete openness and confidence. Lord Moyne, the British Resident Minister in the Near East, told me the other day, that he would not recommend associating the Russians with an Anglo-American Balkan Affairs Committee, and other bodies of this sort which he was proposing, because "The Russians themselves never tell us anything." It seems to me that such an attitude can do nothing to remove suspicions already existing, and if persevered in, will infallibly produce more, with evil results.

After the conference was over, I gave Mr. Kohler and Mr. Cannon copies of the above, which they approved. The part about the post-war claims of Greece was, in fact, included at Mr. Kohler's wish. The Greeks are going to need some help to get justice after this war is over, because of the fact that their contribution was an initial one and tends to be forgotten, while there is no doubt that Bulgarian intrigues to get out of the war, and Turkish maneuvers to get in it before the curtain comes down, will secure for these countries, perhaps at the expense of the Greeks, more consideration at the peace table than they really deserve.

August 5, 1944, Saturday

The days have been passing rapidly, and I have not given much attention in this diary to the great events of the world. Turkey has broken relations with the Axis[151] and the Americans have swept around the left end of the Axis line in Normandy and seem about ready to over-run the whole of Brittany. Today I had a visit from Col. Aldrich, who will take Toulmin's place as head of the Cairo OSS, with Turkey also under his command for the time being. . . . Foy Kohler brought in Mr. Argyropoulos (Alexander) who has been here attending the Bretton Woods conference. The Greek Government, through Mr. Varvaressos, who has returned to London, has approached us for a loan of $25,000,000 "to run their Government-in-Exile and have something over for the early stages of reconstruction." Most of the expenditure is for the armed forces, of course. However, Foy said that it was understood some time ago that if we looked after Greece's *dollar* needs, the British would take care of what they want in *pounds*, and it does not appear that what they need in dollar exchange now is anything like the sum requested. So Argyropoulos was asked for further information along this line as well as a detailed statement of the present position in both pounds and dollars.

[151] On August 2, 1944, Turkey declared war on Germany.

When I last saw Leeper, he said Kanellopoulos, the Finance Minister, had said that the Government was against contracting a loan in exile. But I guess needs must when the devil Penury drives.

August 7, 1944, Monday
News from my bailiwick abroad is to the effect that Jumbo is backing a plan to have AML HQ move to Bari from Cairo, together with that part of AML (and UNRRA) which is concerned with Yugoslavia and Albania. The Greek sections would remain in Cairo, but all would be under the direct orders of the Mediterranean Command rather than Middle East. An exception to this last is *Dodecanesian* affairs. Neither Kohler nor Cannon think much of this plan, which seems partly owing to Jumbo's personal imperialism, and partly to the British desire to have easier sailing in their control of Balkan affairs than they have found possible in Cairo hitherto. The Department will consult with the War Department on the matter, but if I am any good as a prophet, Jumbo will have his way, and I shall be still further handicapped in my efforts to represent the American viewpoint in Balkan affairs. Neither Murphy nor Kirk knows or cares anything about them, and the British doubtless feel correctly that they will be easier to take "into the fold" to use Paget's phrase, than I have been!

August 9, 1944, Wednesday
Long conference in my office with Kohler, Cannon, Reams and others of the Department.... on the question of what can be done to correct false impressions now being given the Balkan peoples as to our policy, particularly as distinguished from British policy.... We decided that for the war period we must get along with the British, both because we are allies and because they control most of the means—radio and printing—through which propaganda is issued. But a closer check should be kept on so-called allied propaganda to keep it from being too much British under the name of Anglo-American, and on the positive side, we should do more in the way of publicizing our own point of view on Balkan problems, without criticism of our allies. It is a very difficult and delicate line we have to follow. As soon as we go into the Balkan countries, however, the situation should be eased, and at that time, when we shall associate the local OWI offices directly with our diplomatic missions, we can more clearly appear as following a separate policy of our own. The war effort in the countries concerned will then be finished, and we can devote ourselves wholly to the post-war problems. The trouble now is that post-war problems are already coming to the fore in the Balkan

regions—with the British trying to establish the government which the countries are to have—while the war is still going on there. I figure that we can't wholly cure the present situation, in which our policy is confused with the British, but we can and should do something to make it better. . . . Col. Goodfellow showed me a report emanating from Col. West in Greece, to the effect that the Russian Mission with the Greek Committee in the mountains seems to emanate from Tito, though it is too low in rank (the head is a Lt. Colonel) to be anything but a scouting expedition in all probability. It expects to stay in Greece for some time and to see something of EDES as well as ELAS! The idea that it may have gone to Greece to persuade EAM to join the Government of National Unity is not mentioned by Col. West, but if the story is true that Tito has been critical of the EAM for not really fighting the Germans, there still may be something in it.

August 14, 1944, Monday

Talk with Cannon, who undertook to get me an appointment with Dunn, and who wants me to see Matthews, and promised to try out the White House. The President is not yet back, and there is some division of opinion as to when he will be. . . . I told Cannon that I shall be returning to Cairo with the satisfaction of knowing that I think exactly as the Department does on the Yugoslav situation, but also with the knowledge that nothing will be done about it. He remarked on the difficulties of the Department when it does not share the views of the Prime Minister of an allied country who "will not tolerate" opposition. In connection with Tito he said again, "Mr. Churchill will not *tolerate* opposition to what he is doing," and this I think about puts it in a nutshell. But I think we might at least let it be known that we don't go along with him in his policy—speaking for ourselves!

August 15, 1944, Tuesday

Call from the Secretary's office. The great man was seeable, and I took the opportunity to go say goodby to him. He has been on a vacation, and looked much better than when I saw him last. Speech and reactions not so slow. He said he had read my report to the Policy Committee and gave me a chance to emphasize my views on the danger of the present British one-sided policy toward Yugoslavia, and the desirability of our making it clear that we are not in accord. I think he has been roused by the way the press has played up the presence of General Somervell and Mr. Patterson (Asst. Sec. of War) in Rome with Churchill and Tito, making it appear that we are going along with the British policy. He asked me what I would think of his making a statement to the effect that our policy toward Yugoslavia has not changed. I said I thought that would be fine, but we ought to say at the same time what the policy is. To this he replied that it might be good to make people look it up, but I ventured to stick by my idea that some "recapitulation" at this time would be useful. I feel that our policy being largely negative, has tended to get itself forgotten while the positive British interventionist policy has stolen the limelight. It seems the Secretary is just about ready to do something and as I expect to lunch with Mr. Dunn on Thursday, and Mr. Hull trusts a great deal to his advice, perhaps I can contribute the little push at this time which may be all that is necessary. Anyhow the Secretary spoke of possibly "talking Turkey" to the British, and said (actually he said it) that he felt my coming home has been a good thing. He said I had done "good work" and asked me to watch the situation abroad in my area "very carefully" and not hesitate to write him and telegraph him about what I saw. Regarding Greece, and the Near East in general, he rightly said that everything that is being done is "British policy" and that the President hadn't been willing to admit this till he went to Cairo, but that after that he came home seeing little else! I told him of what someone had said here (Cannon) about Mr. Churchill's being unwilling to "tolerate" any interference in his Yugoslav campaign, and he replied that he felt the British haven't understood us so far. He told a story of the American diplomat who told his foreign colleague that now "he would talk turkey to him," and when he got through the colleague said, "But you haven't said a word about Turkey." Obviously the old man is feeling now like making himself clear to the British, but whether he will do so is something else again. I feel a little encouraged about the prospects, but.... Another encouraging thing is that the Secretary's attitude should make it possible to approach him with some prospects of success in the event that Mr. Churchill attempts to force King George back into Greece, taking personal charge and swinging the Foreign Office into line with his views, as he has done in the Tito matter.... Visit from the Greek Ambassador, who showed me a note he was just about to give Stettinius on the Greek attitude toward Albania, and the points which should be covered in the peace terms to that country. The note, on instructions from Papandreou, said that Albania had declared war on Greece concurrently with Italy, but both Diamantopoulos and I are skeptical as to whether there was such a declaration. He has cabled Cairo for clarification. He then asked me my advice as to the policy of bringing Greece's postwar territorial claims before the Department at this time. He is preparing very thorough-going statements with supporting material. I said I thought it could do no harm, and might even be a good idea to have this material in the Department's hands at an early date, but I emphasized that much would depend on the way it was presented, and that he should make it thoroughly clear that the matter was brought up at this time with no idea that any commitments could be made before the Peace Conference, and purely for the Department's information. . . . The news from Greece is that the British have sent word to the Greek Government that they will not allow Papandreou to resign (as EAM demanded) and that Venizelos and other Liberals (including Mylonas) have sent EAM another plea to join the Government. Venizelos told Shantz that if this plea is not successful, he and his friends may have to quit the Government. The problem lies no longer he said "between the Government and the mountains but between Mr. Eden and the mountains"—referring to the British support of Papandreou personally.

August 18, 1944, Friday

Conferred with Cannon and Kohler about my return. Cannon said that word had come from the White House to the effect that the President can't see me till next Thursday or Friday, but that "Jimmy" Dunn feels I ought to wait over and see him. Cannon asked whether I am in a hurry to go back to Cairo! I said my only anxiety was not to stay longer than the Department wanted me to. Kohler then said that he would be glad if I stayed, also. He himself will be gone on a short vacation next week. So I decided to wait over "indefinitely," with the expectation of getting away early the week after next. Kohler said he would cancel the plane arrangements for next week, and make a new application later. Cannon said that the President has got a new letter from Churchill, about the latter's recent talks with Tito. I wonder what the President thinks of it all, and myself cannot conceive how, after the Moscow agreement to work together for the avoidance of any clash of interest between the Great Powers, Churchill could have started out on a purely unilateral course of action in the highly critical Balkan region almost immediately! Both in his support of Tito first, and later of Subašić and Papandreou—neither of whom he is now allowing to resign!—he has taken no counsel first with either of his allies. The Russians, who have shown, again and again, that they want from now on to have a say in everything which concerns the Near East and all regions within striking distance, as it were, of their borders cannot like this, and will undoubtedly feel it justifies their acting unilaterally themselves elsewhere. Thus the very fabric and foundations of the Moscow accord are already undermined. I remember that we feared they might be, by British unwillingness to play the game though they helped to lay down the rules. Now Mr. Churchill is evidently trying to persuade F.D.R. that he has done well. He tells him that the Subašić-Tito accord is working out successfully for the unification of

Yugoslavia, which he knows the President is interested in. Brigadier Maclean has of course told Mr. Churchill that things are fine. But will the President swallow this, when information from other sources is to the contrary? The British are amazing! Markham's recent complaint that American war materiel was being used by the Partisans against the Serbs was sent to the Combined Chiefs of Staff, and as a result queries were made in Italy. Yesterday Murphy wired that Maclean reported that all materiel supplied to Tito has been British, though perhaps a few items have been made in America and been so marked. Today we get another message to the effect that General Donovan, in talking to Tito, took pains to impress him with the fact that *all the equipment sent him was American*! Yesterday also we learned that while the British call their policy one of unification and prevention of civil war, the Partisans, whom they support, now claim they can't resist a new German drive in Croatia because they have sent three divisions into Serbia! But enough of this hypocrisy, for the present. . . .

August 24, 1944, Thursday

Received a summons from the White House to see the President for 10 minutes, at 12:10. Actually I think we talked for about 15. Not much time, that, in which to discuss the whole Balkan situation, and unfortunately the President did a lot of repeating of what he had said in Cairo. When I came in he said at once that he had something to tell me "which you won't like." He then said emphatically that the United States will not use any troops in the Balkans for any purpose whatsoever, the reasons being that they are not available, and if they were he doesn't want to commit them where it might be difficult to get them out. In this connection he spoke of the tendency of the British and Russians to come into conflict in the Balkans. "It isn't so bad now, but may become worse, and I don't want our men to be involved." Besides, he went on to say, our troops will not want to stay in Europe after the war is over. Already he is being badgered by the British to take over the French part of the post-war military problem in Europe—to cushion them, he said, against trouble—and he can't see how he is able to do that. "Perhaps I can get replacements over, to let the men who have done the fighting come back." So, as far as the Balkans are concerned, he has told Mr. Churchill to go right ahead and run the show. I told him that the British are pursuing an active interventionist policy in Yugoslavia and Greece which is the very opposite of our policy, and he agreed. I told him that much which the British are doing is bound to excite Russian suspicions, and he agreed to that, too. I said I thought that the British are over-sanguine in thinking that their policy in Yugoslavia is succeeding (Churchill has recently sent him a message to the effect, as I learned from Cannon yesterday), and, somewhat surprisingly, he agreed also to this. But when I asked whether something could not be done to make it clear that we are not supporting this policy, or the British puppet Governments in Greece and Yugoslavia, he said nothing. On the other hand, he did not say that we should not try to clarify our position, and I believe that if the Department proposes to make some statement now as to what our policy is, he will not object. He seemed even more impatient and critical as regards the Balkan peoples and their dissensions than he was in Cairo. If he can't do it in reality, he is putting a wall around them in his own thinking. He spent some time re-outlining to me his idea of how the Europeans (the French, and even more, the Balkan peoples) should reorganize their political systems,— adopting the primary and electing premiers for a set time—and when I asked if he had any directives for me to follow from now on in Cairo, said no more than that I should proceed on the basis that we are not going to let ourselves be involved in Balkan matters, and that I might talk up this political suggestion! . . . His illness of last spring has clearly cost him much in weight and vitality. He is thinner in face and form, and lacks that old robustious bounce which was so marked, even in Cairo last fall. Hitherto, each time I have seen him, usually at long intervals, since 1933, he has seemed to be enjoying being President. Today, not. . . .

Before I left I managed to tell him of the feeling of the Greeks, both abroad and here, regarding his message to Mr. Churchill at the time of the mutinies, in which he said that he hoped "the Greeks" would return to their allegiance, as if the whole nation, and not just a handful had revolted. He understood exactly what I meant. I added that the head of one of the most important Greek-American newspapers[152] had told me that he is getting letters constantly, complaining that the President had misunderstood the situation (to put it mildly) and he replied that he thought the same man had said something similar to Mr. Stettinius, and that he hoped he could find some excuse to make a new statement setting the thing right. He blamed the Department for the misleading wording of the message, but from what Kohler told me, the Department had nothing to do with it and never saw it till long after it was sent. In any case, I urged that he do say something soon on the matter, saying, "You know the Greeks and how eagerly they respond to a friendly word." I didn't mention the local political angle, but if he didn't get it he is not the politician the world takes him to be. There are half a million Greeks in this country, most of them voters, and the coming election shows every indication of being close. . . . Incidentally, in connection with the Yugoslav muddle, he said that Mr. Churchill had asked him whether, in the event

---

[152] B. Vlavianos, editor of the *Ethnikos Kyrix* (National Herald).

the Yugoslavs should reach an impasse over how to reconstruct their state, he would be willing to arbitrate, and that he had replied, Yes, certainly. I remarked on this that there would appear to be a danger that before that time arrived, Mr. Churchill would have brought things to such a state with his interventions that the President could do nothing. He laughed and said he thought it quite possible. . . .

Our whole brief, cluttered, and rushed conversation was most unsatisfactory, as nothing was considered or developed to any degree,—except that one notice served on me at the start. The meaning of this and of the short time he was willing to give to me on this visit would seem to be that Pilate is washing his hands, or, to paraphrase Bacon, "What are the Balkans? asked jesting Roosevelt, and would not stay for an answer." He has handed over the region to his friend Churchill, and as the latter must take the responsibility, it is 100 percent sure that Franklin will not call a halt to any of his doings. The most we can expect is that he will allow us to make it clear that Churchill's doings are not our doings. And that will be something, though it is far from what our Balkan friends expect. We had said, and repeated, that we stand for the right of all nations, big and small, to run their own affairs so long as they do not infringe on or threaten the rights of others; and it has been thought that we would not remain indifferent to violations of this principle on the part of our allies. But this is what we are doing. We won't force puppet governments on Greece and Yugoslavia, but if England does so it is all right with us. If our Balkan friends feel "sold down the river," who can blame them? And my job seems to be to keep them from feeling this way, which it would take a miracle—a miracle of deception—to do. . . .

After leaving the President I talked a while with "Jimmy" Dunn in the outer office, where he and Stettinius and a number of others were waiting to be received. We talked mostly Yugoslavia, of course, since he heads the European Office, but he did speak briefly of Greece and I explained my feeling that the guerrilla question there is by no means as serious as in the neighbour state, owing to the character and composition of the Greek population. As regards Yugoslavia, I found him thoroughly aware of the dangers the British are running in their all-out support of Tito and neglect of the Serbian element,—danger of intensifying civil war and danger of provoking eventual reaction from the Russians. He too seems favorable to our clarifying our stand toward the Yugoslavs.

August 25, 1944, Friday

I talked for an hour with a Major Thayer,—loaned by the Department to the OSS for the purpose of going in with the new mission to Tito, which will be independent of the British, and headed up by a Col.

Huntington. Thayer asked many questions which neither Cannon nor I could answer, and wouldn't have asked them if he had known anything of the situation. He has seen a good deal of Brigadier Maclean, and said that he is sure that the British have taken up Tito in order to "kill him with kindness," and render him and his Partisans an asset rather than a menace to British influence in the Balkans. But he pointed out that if the Russians have been really counting on the movement to establish their predominance in Yugoslavia, the capture of the leader by the British will not stop them. . . . I feel that if Churchill had talked the Yugoslav problem over with Moscow—what to do with Tito and Mihailović, so as to avoid conflicts of interest which might be dangerous to Anglo-Russian relations, instead of trying to steal a march on Moscow by taking Tito into the British camp, much of the danger in the present situation would have been avoided. As it is, after Churchill has moved "unilaterally" in Yugoslavia, can one blame the Russians for doing the same thing in Poland? . . . The new Rumanian Government seems to command some forces and to be directing them against the Hungarians, thus fulfilling to a certain degree our demand that, before any armistice could be signed, the Rumanians must join actively against the enemy. The armistice will probably be signed in Moscow, with the British and American Ambassadors there representing the Western Allies. . . . Cannon told me today that the Russians want any Bulgarian peace talks to be held in Ankara, not Cairo. This seems reasonable, on account of communications, and perhaps, too, Novikov has not reported very favorably on the dealings he has had with Lord Moyne and Steel. I doubt if there has been much feeling of sympathy and understanding between them!

August 28, 1944, Monday

Conference in the Department with Cannon, Kohler and Dort, who has just returned from Cairo, on AML and UNRRA matters as well as FEA problems. Cannon said that he has been instructed to draw up a brief for the President on Balkan Civil Affairs problems, for use in a forthcoming conference with Mr. Churchill.[153] As far as Yugoslavia is concerned, I said that I feel relief and reconstruction should await the end of civil war conditions, otherwise neither we nor UNRRA can distribute on a non-partisan basis. To send supplies to "liberated" areas now, if any such exist, would certainly not be acting impartially. Though sent in to be distributed under the auspices of a government we recognize,

[153] During September 11-19, 1944, Roosevelt and Churchill held talks at Quebec (the Second Quebec Conference). British attempts to revive the idea of military operations in the Balkans failed, and the Americans refused to participate in military activities involved in the liberation of Greece.

they would certainly not reach any of the opponents of the Partisans. The President might possibly put forward this point of view to begin with if properly briefed, but Churchill now takes the stand that his puppet government is a success and will soon bring all Yugoslavia under its control, and if he should insist on this despite the President's doubts, which I know him to entertain, I think it only too likely that he will get his way. Being in the mood now to let Churchill run the Balkans, FDR is far more likely to take his word than ours as to civil as well as military affairs, and the result will probably be that after arming Tito for the conquest of Serbia we shall feed him as well. . . . Kohler, when I was just about to go home, after our conference was all over, came back with a telegram from Shantz according to which Wilson has made arrangements now to take not only AMHQ and the Yugoslav and Albanian Sections of AML to Italy, but the Greek Section also, plus the Greek Government *and* the British and American Embassies! All are to go by ship on Sept. 3rd and the Government and Embassies will be established at Salerno. Kohler drafted and sent off a telegram at once ordering Shantz not to move until instructed. Later we may hear—and should hear—from the Greek Government. Just at present it looks as if Emperor Wilson had started to extend his empire over the Department as well as the Near East! I talked with Kohler and Cannon, and in view of the possibilities raised by this message we decided that I had better put off my departure, which was set for tomorrow, again indefinitely. . . . The terms to be handed the Bulgarians are now practically agreed on,—and include, thank heaven, her abandoning her ill-gotten gains in Greece. But it is not yet decided whether the parleys will take place in Ankara or Cairo. The Russians want Ankara, and the British are clinging by Lord Moyne.

August 29, 1944, Tuesday
All day in the office. Lunch with Kohler, which was to be our farewell, but it now looks as if I would be here for days. . . . No news on the move of the Greek Government, the reasons for which at this time remain perfectly obscure. . . . Telegram from Shantz saying that Moyne has received a message from London regarding Bulgarian armistice negotiations to be held in Cairo, and asking authorization for the American representative to negotiate along with him, agreeing to clause 3, which should have a time limit of two weeks placed on Bulgarian withdrawal from allied territory, without further reference to Washington and on the basis of advice as to military aspects from Giles or his delegate. The Bulgarian delegate, he says, is expected this week. . . . Another telegram from Shantz states that Novikov, under instructions, is taking Stirbei and Vishoianu (and Major Russell, assistant to Moyne and Steel) to Moscow to sign

the Rumanian armistice. Cretianu in Ankara will give Stirbei and Vishoianu the Rumanian Government's written permission to sign. . . . Regarding the Bulgarian matter, Cannon tells me that it is still undecided, so far as we are concerned, as to whether the negotiations are to be held in Ankara or Cairo, and that if the latter place is chosen the Department may want me to go over quickly. But I think Shantz is capable, and with this Greek matter up, he may have to do the job.

August 30, 1944, Wednesday

Cannon reported that it now looks as if the Bulgarian negotiations would certainly be held in Cairo, but whether I shall get over in time to take part is another question. . . . A telegram from Shantz came in elaborating on the move of the Greek Government to Italy. Apparently several liberals have resigned from the Cabinet, and the move will inevitably present the aspect of a new and outstanding bit of British manipulation, emphasizing British control of the Papandreou Government. Shantz therefore suggests that the Department may not wish to associate itself too closely with the affair. On the other hand, he reports that Leeper has expressed the view that "it is essential" that I go with the Government. "Essential" to what? Obviously, to the British scheme; they want our support, as usual, and if they don't get it—as seems likely, since I think I shall be instructed to stay in Cairo and send such representation to Salerno as I may think proper after I get there—the scheme is so clearly one of Mr. Churchill's own, that the President may get a complaint from his good friend in due course. Consequently I suggested that the President be briefed on the Department's views before his forthcoming conference with "Winnie," and Mr. Kohler said he would certainly see that this is done,—and even had it in mind already. Mr. Shantz's telegram came "most immediate" and has evidently beaten a previous telegram telling of the resignation of the Liberals, and the reasons for it. He says that the Cabinet approved going to Italy, but I wonder whether he means the Cabinet *without* these men, or whether their resignation followed the decision and was made on other grounds. In any case, it is too bad that just after EAM had been induced to come in, these Liberals went out! Where is National Unity now? And won't the Government-in-Exile in Italy be even more clearly a British puppet than in Cairo? Mr. Kohler suggested that this finishes Papandreou's political future in Greece. . . . I have written much in this diary about the desirability of having our propaganda make clear that we are not involved in British interventionism in the Balkans, and I still hope that something can be achieved in this way to keep our skirts clear of involvement, in the eyes of the Balkan peoples, in doings which run directly contrary to the principles we have always followed hitherto and so often expressed. I hope, too,—still hope,—that some clear statement or restatement of our own Balkan policy may be forthcoming. But perhaps my not being sent to London to dance attendance on the Subašić Government, and now my not being sent to Salerno to bolster the equally puppet outfit of the Greeks, may do more in the long run to enlighten the Balkan peoples as to our independent attitude than anything else in our power.

August 31, 1944, Thursday

Last night the Department wired Shantz among other things that "Ambassador MacVeagh will leave Washington tomorrow, and unless unforeseen delays prevent, should arrive Sunday." (This is a paraphrase.) "You are authorized to represent the U.S. in discussions and arrangements in connection with the armistice with Bulgaria, acting as deputy for the Ambassador, who will take over on his arrival anything that may remain to be done." The full text of the Bulgarian terms are being sent to Shantz today, I expect, in the form in which they now stand. . . . It is now known that Mr. Churchill privately advised F.D.R. of his arrangements concluded in Italy, and the President replied that he is in accord with all that Mr. C. is doing, but the Department has not seen the messages and the information has come from Murphy, who got it from the British! Nevertheless, Kohler says the Dept. will advise the President of its plans to have me go to Cairo—particularly as I am wanted there in connection with the Bulgarian matter—and later to decide whether I or a member of my staff will follow the Greek Government to Salerno. The Greek Cabinet, according to a telegram from Shantz just received, has split over the question of Papandreou's going to see Churchill without consulting the Govt. and taking only the King's political adviser (Rossetti). Venizelos, Mylonas and Rendis resigned. The Cabinet decision to go to Salerno was apparently taken after their resignation, and of course the EAMites have not yet arrived. There is a possibility that the British-supported Papandreou crowd will be in Bari and the Liberals and Leftists remain in Cairo! What a kettle of fish! The Liberals accuse Papandreou of planning to make himself Regent as well as Premier, and of insisting that he remain as Premier for six months after liberation. The trail of Greek suspicions of British intent to foist the dynasty back on Hellas lies all too plainly across the scene. . . . Received just as I left a copy of Mr. Churchill's long telegram to the President about sending in a division of troops to Greece on liberation—including U.S. parachute troops. He asks for the President's consent (I don't think he'll get the U.S. troops!)

to planning along these lines.[154] I see nothing against the idea, which may help to avoid anarchy at a critical moment. But Mr. C. says nothing about moving the *Government!* or *moving* the *Embassies*, of course. So that the Department's task in keeping our policy straight may be the easier. I talked with Kohler along these lines as a last thing. . . . Left Washington on the 12:30 B. & O.

After several days in New York City, the MacVeaghs left by plane for Cairo on Monday, September 4, arriving there in the small hours of the morning of the 7th.

[154] Churchill telegraphed Roosevelt on August 17, 1944: "We have always marched together in complete agreement about the Greek policy and I refer to you on every important point. The War Cabinet and Foreign Secretary are much concerned about what will happen in Athens and indeed in Greece when the Germans crack or when their divisions try to evacuate the country. If there is a long hiatus after the German authorities have gone from the city before organized Government can be set up, it seems very likely that E.A.M. and Communist extremists will attempt to seize the city and crush all other forms of Greek expression but their own.

"2. You and I have always agreed that the destinies of Greece are in the hands of the Greek people and that they will have the fullest opportunity of deciding between a Monarchy or Republic as soon as tranquility has been restored but I do not expect you will relish more than I do the prospect either of chaos and street fighting or of a tyrannical Communist Government being set up. This could only serve to delay and hamper all plans which are being made by UNRRA for distribution of relief to sorely-tried Greek people. I therefore think we should make preparations through Allied Staff in the Mediterranean to have in readiness a British force, not exceeding 10,000 men, which could be sent by the most expeditious means into the capital when the time is ripe. The force would include parachute troops for which the help of your air force would be needed. I do not myself expect anything will happen for a month and it may be longer but it is always well to be prepared. As far as I can see there will be no insuperable difficulty. I hope therefore you will agree that we may make these preparations but with staffs out here in the usual way. If so British Chiefs of Staff will submit to Combined Chiefs of Staff draft instructions to General Wilson." *FR 1944*, V, 132-33. In his reply, dated August 26, Roosevelt gave his consent to the British plans, and approved the use of American transport planes in support of the proposed operation. *Ibid.*, pp. 133-34.

CHAPTER

IX

From Liberation to Civil War

IN SEPTEMBER 1944, as the withdrawal of enemy troops from Greece appeared to be imminent, diplomatic activity in MacVeagh's bailiwick intensified rapidly. Despite the facade of national unity, the political feuds that had festered during the war years were now headed for an inevitable showdown, aggravated by social unrest, by demands for revenge, by acts of lawlessness, and by emotional tension. With all the planning, and with the endless committees, preparations for actual relief operations remained woefully inadequate, while the country's devastation appeared to be near total. Thus, the work of the soldier might soon be finished; that of the diplomat was destined to become more hectic. In Cairo, the excitement over the prospect of returning to Greece was mixed with growing apprehension over what liberation might bring to that troubled nation.

September 7, 1944, Thursday
  Very busy day in the office. The main piece of news is that while we were *en route* the Russians declared war on Bulgaria, which promptly (within half an hour!) asked for an armistice. This changes the picture regarding our negotiations, as Russia now figures not as a mere observer but as one of the principals. . . . Steel came in and talked with Shantz and me. He said he thought the negotiations would now be moved to Moscow, that Mr. Moshanov,[1] the Bulgarian delegate here, had better go home, and that in fact he was planning to leave tomorrow. I asked him to bring Moshanov around—he was going to see him this afternoon anyway—and this he did about 5 o'clock. It seemed to me that I ought to get a glimpse of the man at any rate, and hear for myself anything he might have to say before his departure. Steel, at my request, sat in with us,—I am not seeing any of these emissaries alone!—and so did

[1] Stoicho Moshanov, former President of the Bulgarian Parliament, was authorized by the government of Prime Minister Ivan Bagryanov to negotiate a peace settlement with the Allies.

Shantz. I asked Moshanov why he was going back, and to my surprise he replied that he was being *sent* back, and that he himself had not asked to go. Steel then confirmed this and said he had thought it wise to send Mr. Moshanov back because there seemed little likelihood of his mission here being continued, now that Russia has entered the picture, *and because there is an available plane tomorrow for Ankara.* To this I observed that while the chances of continuing negotiations here are doubtless very small, the fact remains that we don't know actually that they are non-existent. I pointed out that we are awaiting instructions from our Governments, and until we get them, we might be making a mistake in taking an action which would be embarrassing if the instructions were other than we expect. I thought, I said, that it would be better to play safe and keep the emissary here till we know definitely he won't be needed. After some talk, Steel agreed, Shantz also agreed, and Moshanov thanked me for my intervention! Apparently he felt that being sent away would be *infra dig.* . . . Later Steel called me up to say that he had just received a telegram from London instructing him to hold Moshanov here for the present! So that is that. Shantz told me afterwards that he thought Steel was particularly anxious to get rid of the man as soon as possible as he is himself expecting to go back to London for another job and is only held here while this Bulgarian thing continues. . . . Novikov has not returned here from Moscow yet, but there are rumors that he is on his way. The Rumanian negotiations in Moscow seem to be proceeding on the basis of the terms handed to Stirbei here and agreed on by the three powers, but details are being filled in, presumably in concert with London and Washington. However, nothing on the subject appears as yet in any of our information telegrams, nor are there any "repeat" telegrams from Harriman concerning it. . . .

Had long talks with Shantz, Barbour and Parsons on developments during my absence, particularly as regards Greece. It appears that the EAMite delegates tried to keep the Government from going to Italy, but yielded finally to the plea of "national unity" and did not carry their opposition to the point of resigning. Parsons says there has been little if any feeling aroused by the nomination of the Crown Prince as "Regent" during the King's absence in London—another development I had not heard about. One might have imagined that the nomination would appear to most of the Greeks as a prelude to a British attempt to force the King back on the country. Perhaps the big majority of the liberals and leftists in the Cabinet has given them a feeling of security in this regard. The reason for the move of the Government to Italy appears to have been principally to have it available for air transport to Athens on the heels of the coming military operations. The British planes are apparently better suited for the flight from Bari to Athens than from Cairo. At the same time, a desire to isolate the newly-formed Government of National Unity from possible infection in the political atmosphere here also figured to a certain point. Having got the Government to "gel," the British are putting it in the ice-box for the remaining days before re-entry into Greece. . . . The Government left by plane last night. . . .

It is the opinion of Shantz and Barbour, as well as my own, that there need be no hurry in our regaining contact with the lost battalion. They are all in a great stew, have left their "services," such as they are, behind them here, and will take a week or ten days to settle down, by which time they will likely be on the move again! Better for us to plan on staying here and rejoining in Greece when the Government gets, at last, established there. If, however, the Government becomes stuck for some time in Italy, I might go over there for a brief visit, or send Barbour or Shantz. Meanwhile, no other diplomats have gone except Leeper, or seem likely to go, and our hastening to do so could only serve the purpose of indicating a solidarity between the British and us on the question of interfering in Greek internal affairs which by no means exists. No wonder Leeper said that my being in Italy was "essential"—essential to the strengthening of his hand with ostensible American approval. But I think it equally essential that we should keep our skirts clear of involvement in the high-handed interventionism which has created Papandreou a puppet Prime Minister, has refused to let him resign when he wanted to go, and is moving him and his cabinet about the map at Churchill's word of command! Didn't the President give it to me as my directive that I should make it clear that we are not going to be involved in Balkan affairs? This is one way of doing it. . . . Worser and worser, I am told that the reason for the hold over the Government which the British appear to have secured so strongly that even the risk of EAMite defection and the ruin of the long-desired "national unity" could not shake it, is owing to their having let it be known that if their behests are not obeyed, Greece's claims will not receive the hoped-for consideration at the Peace Conference. Thus, if this is true, Greece's willingness to submit subserviently to British influence, and not the justice of her claims, is to be the criterion followed by our co-creators and co-proponents which are members of the Atlantic Charter. . . .

September 9, 1944, Saturday

Visits from Cy Sulzberger at 10, and Wayne Adams of the FEA at 11. General Sadler came in at 12, and in the afternoon Colonel Aldrich[2] of the OSS and one of his people. Sulzberger is very pessimistic about the

[2] Colonel Harry Aldrich, head of the OSS mission in Cairo, succeeding Colonel John E. Toulmin.

situation in Yugoslavia, and I don't wonder. Mihailović is beginning to mobilize against the Germans, or says he is, and says that he will fight the Germans if the Partisans get out of Serbia, but is it not too late, with the Russians practically on Serb territory and the British pushing Tito from behind? The Serbs, who form the gallant core of Yugoslavia which resisted German aggression, are almost sure to be crushed between the British who support Tito because they believe his talk about being democratic and not communist, and the Russians who support him because they don't; between the British who want to establish their influence in Yugoslavia so far as possible and the Russians who want to do the same thing; between the Partisans armed by the Western Allies and the Russian hordes. This picture is pretty clear now for all to see, a moving picture,— in two senses,—tending toward the disappearance of the ruling class in Yugoslavia and its replacement by the lower elements in the towns and a sprinkling of fanatical students and so-called intelligentsia, which will impose, with Russia's support, a communist, Gestapo-controlled régime on the peasant majority. Whether this régime will be preferable to that of the small upper, chiefly officer class is perhaps a question. But it won't be what the British, who will have contributed to this *dénouement*, are expecting, and will not be favorable to the maintenance of their influence in the Balkan peninsula. And like most revolutions everywhere, and all revolutions in the Balkans, the change-over will be bloody. . . . Sulzberger is pessimistic also about Greece. I feel the future there is not so dark as in Yugoslavia, on account of the character of the people. But Sulzberger spoke of a spirit of cruelty which has come out in the Greeks during the ordeal of occupation—a spirit not unknown in Greece before and of course common to the Near East, but which was not in evidence in the Greece we have ourselves lived in to date,—and it is possible that dreadful things will continue to occur even after "liberation." We spoke chiefly, however, of the lack of realization in the United States of the supreme importance of the Balkan area for the question of world peace, a lack of appreciation which makes it equally impossible for me to get the Department to do anything but assent to my *Cassandra* talk, and for him to get his paper to give adequate space to Balkan policy. I told him for us to get excited over what goes on in South America, and to ignore the rise of possible conflict between Britain and Russia along the principal life line of the British Empire, is to mistake a symptom for a disease. Nazi-ism in Argentina is dangerous only if Nazi-Germany wins the war. Communism in South America will be dangerous only if Russia takes the place of Germany in bidding for world domination. Let us then be careful of where things start, and work to keep them from developing. . . . General Sadler came in to discuss AML matters. He said that the British task-force operation against the Athens-Piraeus area is due to begin on the 13th, and that he expects to go in with Lt. General Scobie,[3] the British task-force Commander. "Loopy" Larrabee gave me an outline of the proposed operation, which he obtained from Brigadier Benfield of Force 133. The 3rd Phase of "Noah's Ark" (3rd Phase now called "Smash 'em!") is commencing now, and is to increase in intensity as German evacuation proceeds. Reports coming in from OSS show that there has been considerable movement northward in the Peloponnese, and away from the larger islands (except Rhodes) in small boats and planes at night, and that the guerrillas are intensifying their activity. The British, however, have told their agents to forbid the acceptance of surrender lest the guerrillas get the Germans' arms and turn these to the uses of civil war, or even eventually against the British! . . . British plans, according to "Loopy," who got his information from Brigadier Benfield commanding Force 133, include flying an airborne parachute brigade of from 2,000 to 3,000 men, all British, to attack the Athens airfields and neutralize coast defenses. An "independent brigade group," entirely motorized, will proceed from Alexandria to the Piraeus, their landing to coincide with or shortly follow the parachute attack. The strength of this brigade will be about 3 to 4 thousand, again all British. It will be self-contained, with its own field and a.a. artillery, field trains and hospitals—in short, a small division. In addition, there will be some 4,000 technical troops, engineers, etc., to repair harbour installations, dispose of land mines, and fix up damaged plants and other utilities. It is not known whether these will be British, *Indian* or other troops. I doubt if there will be any objection in Greece to colored troops for this kind of work in small numbers, but I hope it won't be tried, nevertheless, as there is always difficulty in the offing, at any rate, when colored personnel is imposed on a white population. Immediately following the task-force operation, which will include the use of British warships and some eight small air-craft carriers, the AML will be moved in on Greek vessels, such as the *Averoff*, the refitted *Adrias*, etc. I am sending Lt. Commander Spencer with the Greek commodore on the *Adrias*, and Lt. Kent of JICAME (assigned to Spencer for special duty and perhaps later, with Griffiths, to be assistant Naval Attaché to give JICA a chance to get into the country) will be on the *Averoff*. The news that the Germans are evacuating the Athens area—which has been confirmed and denied both —will have to be true if the above small force is to succeed. I only hope the British are not going to repeat their characteristic mistake of attempting too much with too little. . . .

Colonel Aldrich came in particularly to ask me whether I would allow

[3] Lieutenant General Ronald M. Scobie, General Officer Commanding British and Greek forces in Greece.

OSS men to go into Greece ahead of the Embassy under the Embassy's *cover*, i.e. as members of our staff. Shantz had already turned him down on this and I did the same. I said that later, if the OSS is attached to us, as it was in South Africa, I would not object provided the activities of the men were such as we could officially countenance, but that I could do nothing now. The Colonel's problem is difficult because the army will not allow the snoopers to go in in uniform, under the decision which has been made to use no troops. In this last connection, I received a copy of a telegram sent by Kirk to Washington according to which General Wilson proposes that the Commander of the Task Force in Greece shall call himself "Allied Commander" since he will command "British, Greek and American forces." It is not a question of the AML, in which we shall have 63 officers. I immediately wrote and sent off a strong protest, on the ground that I have understood that no American troops will participate in military operations in the Balkans, and urging that if we don't want to assume responsibility for decisions and inevitable mistakes, over which we shall have no control, this misuse of the term "allied" be prevented at all costs. "Anglo-Greek" might do, but not "allied" which implies our participation. I also mentioned the drawing up of military proclamations to be issued in connection with the task force operations without consultation with this Embassy, as an example of what we might expect as regards any reality attaching to the term "allied" in connection with military operations in Greece. The proclamations have been written by Brigadier Smith-Dorrien and shown to and approved by the British Embassy and the Greek Government, but we only heard of them by chance, and secured copies of them after they had been sent on to AFHQ!

September 11, 1944, Monday

Colonel Toulmin came in. He has just returned from Italy, and will stay here a week or so while Aldrich is away in Istanbul. He brought me a summary of recent reports by one Lt. Col. McDowell[4] now with Mihailović. According to these reports aggravated civil war conditions are imminent in Yugoslavia. Mihailović is really getting under way with his mobilization. Toulmin is pessimistic about the situation,—things have gone too far now for it to be likely that anyone will pull back. In regard to the coming Anglo-Greek operation he expressed fears that the forces being used are not sufficient. He criticized the plan to take only the Athens-Piraeus area, leaving the rest of Greece to be liberated by the guerrillas and only about 400 secret operations troops. He feels that the British antagonism to ELAS, which persists despite EAM's joining the

[4] Lieutenant Colonel Robert H. McDowell, U.S. Army intelligence officer in Chetnik territory.

Government, will react against them under these conditions, and that ELAS will get arms from the Germans and then attack EDES with them, and perhaps also attack the British and try to drive them out of Greece! He thinks that if the British are going to keep on with their antagonism to ELAS they should occupy all the important points in Greece themselves and carry the war to the retreating enemy on a regular basis and not leave so much to be done by the Greeks themselves.... He told me that at Pyrgos (Elia), recently evacuated by the Germans, the ELAS first fought the Security Battalions and then massacred women, children and men indiscriminately in a frightful holocaust.... I sent a telegram to the Department reporting this and Toulmin's views, as I am not sure that it realizes quite to what an extent the British attitude to the ELAS is likely to influence coming events.

Snedaker of OWI came in and reported that following my talks in Washington orders have come out breaking up PWB so far as the Greek operation is concerned. In other words no "allied" propaganda is to be taken in with the British task force. The AML propaganda is its own, and as such allied, but it has only been prepared by OWI and will not be issued by PWB under the aegis of the task force commander, but under that of the Allied Military Liaison. Snedaker says that some of the British with whom he has been working are furious over this last-minute decision, and feel that we are letting them down. But this can't be helped. I am glad that the decision has been made as it has, even though at the last minute, because it keeps our skirts clear of entanglement and allows us to proceed on our own line of policy. Snedaker asked me whether I would approve his sending in a couple of moving picture men with the liberating forces, to avoid the likelihood that PWE would sew up the motion picture exhibitors with British contracts before we get there, but I told him that all OWI activities should await the Embassy's entrance into the country and be connected with the Embassy's OWI section which is presumably to be established soon under Barclay Hudson,[5] and that he need have no fear of the Greeks tying themselves up exclusively to the British motion picture industry. They know too much about their business already, and have had too many contacts with the United States producers, such as Skouras brothers, to do any such thing, and they and the Greek audiences know too well the difference between Hollywood films and British!

September 12, 1944, Tuesday

The King of Yugoslavia has issued the long-expected proclamation calling on all true Yugoslavs to join Tito, but not mentioning Mihailović

[5] Major Barclay Hudson, head of Greek Section, OWI, Beirut, and later Athens.

by name, though denouncing those who collaborate with the Germans. "Loopy" tells me that he has Yugoslav officers in his office nearly everyday complaining of being sold out by the British. As the Partisan-Russian pincers close on Serbia, I suppose the poor King felt that he could do no other than accept the inevitable but I shall be surprised if many of the Serbs do not now feel he has betrayed them. Recent reports of conversations between Churchill and Tito show that the latter still insists that the matter of the *régime* must be deferred till after the war, and obviously there is little support for him [the King] on the Partisan side. If this final repudiation of the Serbian patriots as collaborationists throws them against him, there would seem little hope indeed for his eventual return. It all depends on how many of the Serbs have remained genuinely loyal, and it seems probable that the majority of them have done so. Under such circumstances, the King might even come in for assassination some time as a result of this final capitulation to the forces engaged in strangling his people....

General Sadler ... came in. He said that the latest information indicates no great movement of the Germans out of the Athens area, and he would not like to be in the shoes of the commander of the task force operation. He said there are some 200,000 German troops still in the Greek-Yugoslav area, and that though it is unlikely that they can get out, it cannot be said that they will all surrender like lambs. I suppose that much depends on the fanaticism of their leaders and how many S.S. troops there may be among them. Brest and St. Malo might be repeated at Athens under certain conditions, and to meet such conditions the present British preparations are certainly not adequate.

September 13, 1944, Wednesday

Mr. Tsouderos called. He said he thinks that the Papandreou Government cannot survive long after getting back into Greece, since it will find many leaders there, with the support of various groups, who will make the going too difficult. He thinks a small "service" government would be the solution, to prepare elections. He also thinks the people ought to be consulted as to whether they want a plebiscite on the régime before this is undertaken, and perhaps this could be done by having elections as soon as possible and letting the deputies decide on the question. His royalism dies hard,—a royalism which he never had in Greece but which has grown in him since he served in exile and has come to feel more and more that one can't tell from outside what the Greek people want. Perhaps it is less royalism than the conservatism of age and a banker's training. He's a wise old owl, but inclined to hedge in action....

Parsons reported that Admiral Vasiliadis, the Greek Minister for

Merchant Marine, returned several days ago from London and after talking with his liberal friends, Venizelos, Rendis, and Mylonas, had added his resignation to theirs. I doubt if this deals any great blow to the Government, which still has a couple of "liberals" in it to give it color,— though they are not important men. What the big shots are after is to be ready on the side-lines to make a bid for power when the Papandreou Government commits its mistakes in Athens, as they count on its doing from the start. . . . Archer brought in a number of his colleagues during the afternoon, including "Doc" Wright. The AML stock-piles are only 50 percent of requirements, and plans for onward movement and distribution are very uncertain. It becomes more and more certain that when liberation occurs, not only will it occur spottily as the Germans withdraw from this place or that, but it will find our relief organizations in no position to take the immediate action expected. . . .

General Giles came in at noon and we talked about the Greek operation. He is more sanguine than Sadler, and said that his reports indicate the Germans are rapidly evacuating Athens, so that he thinks there may be little resistance. He knows of no agreement between British and Germans in this regard. But there are rumors that the Germans have agreed to spare the city by withdrawing to Boetia before the British come in. On the other hand, there are also—and have been for a long time—rumors that they will blow up the Marathon Dam, and I understand the British Navy is to bring in a great quantity of water for the troops, and plans are all made to tap the Hadrian Aqueduct far up the line (not near Athens, where it may be blocked) and pipe the water into the city along the ground. At Kalamata, which the Germans have recently left, the main installation there, the flour mill, was destroyed. . . .

Reported to the Dept. that Steel favors Moscow for the Bulgarian negotiations rather than Ankara, as there is no British Ambassador at Ankara now, and anyhow things move faster when the Russian negotiators are right under Molotov's thumb, and the Russian delegates don't always have to consult by telegraph. On the other hand, I said I could see no objection to the British preference for Cairo if the terms are not to be discussed but merely signed after being drawn up and agreed on by the three Governments elsewhere. . . . Under such conditions, I think we might consider the natural pique of the British over Russia's sudden entrance into the affair at the last minute, and their desire not to be pushed around!

September 14, 1944, Thursday

Mr. Tsaldaris called and tried to enlist my support for his program, which is, much like that of Mr. Tsouderos,—for a service government and a proposal to the people to declare for or against the plebiscite before the latter is taken. . . . He is of course a royalist, and I think he feels, and many like him feel, that royalist sentiment is still strong in Greece, and likely to become stronger as confusion grows.

September 15, 1944, Friday

Long talk in the morning with a Mr. Dimitrov, a Bulgarian Macedonian who has been many years in the British Secret Service in Bulgaria and done his best, even to being condemned to death, for the Allies. However, he wanted to plead Bulgaria's cause, saying that the people never wished to follow the pro-German policy of the dictatorial group in power. He talked a lot about the exit to the Aegean (which Russia may obtain for the Bulgars, I suppose, though he didn't mention this) and about the atrocities in Greece being exaggerated, as well as about the desirability of making an independent Macedonia. He said Bulgaria will be glad to cede her share of Macedonia for this purpose, but I pointed out that for Greece the matter is much more difficult if, as he claimed, Salonica, Greece's second city, is "Macedonian." He could not tell us where are the boundaries of "Macedonia" nor when such a state ever existed since Alexander's time. In fact, it is a geographical expression, about as vague as our "Middle West." Barbour and I made plain to him that Bulgaria had been at war with us and that she should not expect to win from us in her defeat what she expected to win by joining the Germans. He admitted that "historically" Bulgaria has been in the wrong but maintained that in her heart she has always been on the right side, and went away with the conviction that despite our stern views as expressed, America will in the end be good to Bulgaria and not let her lose the benefits for which she went to war on the German side! It is incredible. And I have a hunch that he may be right. America has always been especially lenient and "understanding" to the most consistently double-dealing of all the Balkan states! . . .

In the afternoon, the Under-Secretary of Foreign Affairs in the Subašić Government[6] called, and Mr. Kekić[7] sat in on our talk. Mr. Gavrilović knew Kekić in Belgrade, and our talk was long and interesting. He is quite sold on the "democratic" intentions of Tito, whom he thinks (Gavrilović is quite a polyanna) a very fine man. He sees no communist danger in Yugoslavia, and thinks that Mihailović does not represent Serbia, and that his movement can easily be liquidated. He did not talk of the Russians at all but did state that the Subašić Government and the

[6] Milan Gavrilović, former Agrarian Party leader and Minister of Justice.
[7] Emil A. Kekić, Special Assistant to Ambassador MacVeagh and secretary of the U.S. Embassy to the Yugoslav government-in-exile, Cairo.

Committee of National Liberation are not yet by any means united, and intimated that unless Subašić can get more supplies of all kinds for the Partisans out of Britain and America, his Government will fall. In other words, Tito is trying to use Subašić for his own purposes, to strengthen his movement with aid from outside, and if this aid is not enough in the view of Tito's followers, he will ditch him, and look elsewhere—Russia, of course. . . . The British operation in Greece is clearly postponed indefinitely. Spencer and Kent sent word that they will come back from Alexandria Sunday. Information from OSS and Force 133 is to the effect that the island evacuation of the Germans has crowded the mainland, including the Athens area in particular, with troops. There must be some 40,000 in Greece still, mostly round the capital, Thebes, Larissa and Salonica. Imagine the British taking in one small division now! . . . The Peloponnese is said to have been evacuated except for its northern strip. EAM depredations and massacres in the "liberated" areas continue. Chios, liberated, has asked for food, and the AML and UNRRA are of course not ready, and may not be for a couple of months. We have sent out an urgent suggestion that the Greek War Relief send some food from Turkey to Chios and the adjacent islands without delay. Harry Hill had a long talk with the UNRRA and AML people; an "advanced party" is all *they* propose, to go along with an officer of the British Military and assist the new Governor of the Liberated Islands, appointed today by the Greek Government. This Governor, who will have so little to work with, is Mr. Bourdaras, an ex-deputy and associate of Mr. Kafandaris. . . . The danger is, of course, of anarchy and EAMite terrorism in the islands, as on the mainland, when no allied help comes in to replace the Germans. In Chios, the Metropolitan has taken charge, and though he is an EAMite himself, this would seem a good thing, and may perhaps provide a precedent for other places. The British procedure seems to be to warn the EAM and the ELAS of dire consequences if they do not behave properly, thus antagonizing them further,—and meanwhile to do nothing about the situation otherwise. Doubtless they have too few troops, but it was possible to prepare for this situation—there has been plenty of time, and this Embassy has long foreseen that the German evacuation would be gradual and the resulting situation messy. I have always said so, and others, who have the authority, might have been equally foresighted, *and prepared*. Now neither the military, strictly speaking, nor AML, nor UNRRA, are able to do a thing. If the Russians move their armies into Northern Greece to catch the retreating Germans at the bottleneck and restore order to the country, who can blame them, in the absence of any British action? I am reminded of the Greek Revolution, and the Czar's final move, putting a term to British indecision by sending an army toward the Straits and bringing the struggle to an end at last. We have gone through an orgy of planning here, and now that what we have been awaiting is upon us, no one is ready to do anything. What a mess! And the British will have only themselves to thank if Russia really liberates Greece a second time. This is so plain to see that I am told that even the young King of Egypt said the other day, "The British had better hurry up, or the Russians will do their job for them."

September 16, 1944, Saturday

Information from London is to the effect that the Russians want a Russian General to sign the Bulgarian armistice, not Wilson, as was proposed when the negotiations were simply with us and Great Britain. Also they want the thing signed in Moscow. From another telegram it seems the Department is boosting for Ankara, and, from what Steel told Barbour yesterday, the British still want Cairo. Meanwhile the European Advisory Commission is re-writing the terms to include Russian suggestions along lines finally adopted in connection with the Rumanian armistice. . . .

Sent off a telegram, which I got Parsons to write, reporting the official Greek announcement that the Government in the Mountains has ceased to exist following EAM's adherence to the Government of National Unity. . . .[8] Got a telegram from Washington to the effect that the British (Lt. General Scobie now in command, instead of Paget, of the forces for Greece) have informed both ELAS and EDES that as part of the Greek national forces they are under the supreme command, M.E., and warning ELAS that they must cease killing Greeks, and doing anything which will make more difficult the successful harassing of the German withdrawal. . . . In connection with a telegram from Kirk which reported that the Greek Sacred Brigade—made up of elements which have hitherto remained loyal but are now becoming restive,—would be attached to "Force 140" probably for use in occupying the evacuated Greek islands, I was able to confirm this from local sources, and so advised the Department.

September 17, 1944, Sunday

Received a telegram from the Department saying that it will not ask the Greek War Relief to help with supplies to Chios and the Islands as

[8] On September 2, 1944, EAM's leadership formally agreed to enter Papandreou's government of National Unity without conditions. The leftist coalition received the following posts: Minister of Finance (Svolos), Communications (Askoutsis), National Economy (Tsirimokos), Labor (Porfyrogenis), Agriculture (Zevgos), Under-Minister of Finance (Angelopoulos).

this is "the responsibility of the Military." Alas, I had explained that the military cannot fulfill this responsibility! So we are going to stick by formalities and ignore dire suffering and need till these can be complied with. Well, then, we must not be surprised if allied prestige suffers some more in this area, from the cruellest of deceptions, and anarchy and communism take a big jump ahead in Greece.

September 18, 1944, Monday
   Call from the Polish Ambassador to Greece, who thinks of going to London for a brief visit, and hopes he can get there and back before the move to Athens comes. He is very much perturbed over possible Russian intentions in Greece. The news this morning is that Russian troops have penetrated to Argyrocastro *en route* to Salonica, but there is no confirmation. If the Russians come into Greece and attack the Germans there, cutting off their retreat northward, and then pose as the liberators of the country, the English can have only their own hesitancy and feeble policy to thank for it. The Russians will then have—or at least will be able to insist on having—a leading say in the composition of Greece's Government, just as they have had recently in Bulgaria. No wonder not only the Pole but all the Greeks here in Cairo are as nervous as cats over the present situation. . . . Spencer came back from Alexandria. The operation is indefinitely postponed, but the ships are all in harbor loaded with troops. The Greek ships will take AML in after the British operational forces have established a bridgehead, and they will also take several thousand British soldiers, I suppose of the engineers and special services. Meanwhile there are signs of trouble again in the Greek navy, and handbills signed "EAM" call for the killing of Admiral Voulgaris and others connected with the quelling of the recent mutiny. It is feared that the Greeks plan to throw their officers overboard on arrival at Piraeus and take the ships into the crews' hands,—though this might be difficult with British troops aboard, Greek fanatics are quite capable of trying it—and thus a British-EAM war would start right in the port of entry! A pretty kettle of fish. . . . The Papandreou Government has sent proposals to Venizelos and the other Ministers of the Liberal Party, asking them to rejoin the Government, and Parsons has heard that they will demand as conditions that Prince Paul stay out until the plebiscite, as well as the King; that Papandreou refrain from staying in as premier for six months, as it is his rumored intention to do, and that the Government resign immediately on arrival in Greece; and that the portfolios of War, Navy and Foreign Affairs be now turned over to the Liberals. I don't see such terms being accepted. In any case Venizelos wishes to come in and see me tomorrow.

September 19, 1944, Tuesday

Colonel Toulmin came in. He brought me a telegram giving an eyewitness account of mob violence in Kalamata—the lynching of a lot of cooperationists by a crowd of men, women and children. Rather awful, but the quislings have asked for it, and the manner of the "executions" is due to the lack of civil authority, for which their German friends' withdrawal is responsible.... Toulmin also brought me a report from an OSS man in Rumania, according to which the Rumanian Government is aghast at the armistice terms added in Moscow requiring control of Rumanian commerce and industry, and also the press, radio and movies, during the occupation period. However, the only comment I see applicable is *Vae Victis!*—and Rumanians just naturally hate being the *victi*, but they are.... We talked as usual about the British-Russian affairs in the Balkans. As to our relations with our British allies in the Middle East, he told me that the British have recently broken the codes of the Saudi Arabian Government. Our OSS people learned of this and informed the Saudi Arabians, who are now revising their codes! Our action would doubtless have been difficult if the British had taken us in with them on the secret, but one thing leads to another, and I don't see how the British can object logically to what we have done, since the first deception was theirs. But the picture is not pretty, particularly in its augury for the future....

Mr. Venizelos came in at noon and told me of the latest developments in his position and that of Mylonas and Rendis, who recently resigned from the cabinet with him. He said that Messrs. Tsatsos and Sgouritsas— "nominal" Liberals still members of the cabinet,—did bring a message from Papandreou urging that they rejoin, and that they are replying with conditions. If the Government will appoint a Regent *in* Greece (which means they will not stand for the Crown Prince, any more than the King, going back before the plebiscite) and agree to resign at once on reaching Athens, in favor of a government of all parties and organizations to be formed there at that time, they will give it their "full support" in the interim. But to rejoin the cabinet now themselves, they must first have a statement from Papandreou that he admits his position is dependent on his cabinet and the parties represented in it. They feel that hitherto there has been too much "personal" rule on his part. They are still very much annoyed over his going to see Churchill in Italy without consulting his cabinet, and his taking Rossetti, the King's Minister, along with him also rankles. He told me also that he has received from the Premier's *chef-de-Cabinet*, Lambrianidis, a feeler as to his possible willingness to go to Crete at this time, to help with the settlement of affairs there on German withdrawal. He said he would be willing to do this, staying in Crete until the Government moves to Athens, but only as a private person, "as Venizelos,"

FROM LIBERATION TO CIVIL WAR · 605

and not as Governor, since that would mean taking office under the Papandreou Government. Mr. Venizelos did not ask me anything, perhaps remembering the good advice he got from Mr. Shantz recently, to the effect that the Greeks ought to settle their political problems themselves. But just to keep him on this right track, I told him of my visit to Washington and of our policy, which I had found unchanged, to abstain from interfering in internal Balkan affairs, and not to take part in any possible military operations, except as regards relief and reconstruction, which I said remain our chief interests in the countries concerned. He accepted this, with a certain show of resignation as well as comprehension, but said he still thought I could do much personally in Greece by way of moral support to the people, whatever that may mean. . . . Later in the day, he sent me a copy of a letter he has sent to Sgouritsas, giving the conditions of his group for supporting or rejoining the Government,— a tremendously lengthy document which I handed to Parsons to decipher and summarize. The modern Greeks must be the wordiest of mortals; too bad they haven't studied their own classics to better advantage. . . . After lunch I had a call from Frank Gervasi[9] and Fodor,[10] and a long and interesting talk. Gervasi has been in France recently and was horrified by the brutality of the French in taking revenge on collaborationists and even German prisoners. He remarked that Germany has brought to the top all the worst in people throughout the areas she occupied. All the French people, men, women and children crowd to the FFI[11] executions, scream with delight, and spit and kick on the dead bodies. As to the German prisoners, he is concerned lest news of their treatment at French hands gets back to Germany, and allied prisoners there suffer accordingly. We discussed signs of coming Russian-British conflict along what I call the "dangerous crescent"—from Warsaw to Teheran—and Gervasi said he wished people in Europe might be better informed as to our tremendous contribution to this war. But I said I thought what is chiefly wanted is greater realization at home of our stake in what goes on in this part of the world. We must wake up to the fact that England is going on with the Imperial Game, counting on us to help her out when she gets in trouble, but not consulting us before she does; and to the fact that the conditions of modern war make this game infinitely more precarious than in the 18th and 19th centuries, while Russia is better placed and stronger potentially than any other power to crack the most vital of England's tenuous communications, right in this very region where we still tend to think "trouble in the Balkans" is something to laugh at. Fodor certainly understands all this and though it seemed a bit new to

[9] Frank Gervasi, correspondent for the Columbia Broadcasting System.
[10] M. W. Fodor, correspondent for the *Chicago Daily News*.
[11] FFI (*Forces Françaises de l'Intérieur*), French resistance movement.

Gervasi, I think he got it all right—at any rate he appeared very grave about it. . . . So I go on with all the best correspondents I meet, talking like poor Cassandra of the doom of Troy! But Cassandra was right, and we can, I am certain, avert a worse fate than that of Troy through involvement in a new world war in the more or less near future, only if we will recognize the seeds of trouble as they are sown and destroy them before they sprout, by exposing them to the full rays of publicity, comprehension, and international settlement. . . .

When the correspondents left, I had a call from Ambassador Culbertson,—heading an economic mission to North Africa and the Middle East. He used to be—before the Roosevelt era,—ambassador to Chile, and before that was Minister to Rumania, he told me, for three years. His mission now is to explore, with the appropriate officials of the countries he is visiting, the problems involved in changing over from war-time controls to peace-time economic and commercial procedure, and to see what chance there is of getting this procedure to fall in line with our policies, or rather the policies of Mr. Hull, with which Mr. Culbertson is thoroughly in accord, despite being a Republican. It seems the Mission was started as an FEA affair, but the Department took it over since policy is so deeply involved. It comprises a Department man, Mr. Fox, some FEA people, and a group of prominent business men. At bottom, of course, is the question of exploring the post-war possibilities for American trade, and to lay foundations where possible for the expansion of such trade. Mr. Culbertson said he got nowhere with the French in Algeria, who took a narrow colonial view on the subject, were suspicious to the point of refusing to allow their junior officials to talk at all with the Americans, and were in any case thinking more of getting back to France personally, than of the problems Mr. Culbertson wanted to discuss. He found the same official suspicion in Morocco and Tunisia, but greater freedom and friendliness in practice. Here his work will be to a large extent with the MESC. "I think the British will realize they have an important partner in this region," he said,—and intimated that they had better. He has talked with Commander Jackson here but didn't see Landis before coming out, which would seem to be too bad, as the latter might have given him some valuable orientation on British intentions here and the tightness with which the British oyster is trying to clamp down on the Mid-Eastern pearl. . . .

A telegram came in from Shantz in Italy according to which he found the Greek Government installed in a miserable little village called Cava (hollow!) near Salerno, and Papandreou and Leeper occupying villas nearby. No other diplomats are there or are apparently expected. Shantz recommends we send an officer as liaison to Caserta "frequently," where there is also a British liaison man, but nothing more, and that Papandreou said that though of course the matter depends on the military, he is convinced he will be seeing me in Athens within two weeks.

September 21, 1944, Thursday

The news bulletin today announces that new Ambassadors have been chosen for the exiled Governments of countries being liberated, or shortly to be liberated if all goes well,—Belgium, Norway, Denmark, Holland, Poland, and Yugoslavia. An ex-Secretary of Commerce named Richard Patterson is named for Yugoslavia. I hope we may now soon move to Greece, so that I shan't have to go on functioning for Yugoslavia without any status, according to the Department's genial idea which I argued against in Washington.

September 25, 1944, Monday

Shantz and I drafted a telegram recommending that we keep in touch with the Greek Government through the office Kirk has in Caserta, and if much more delay occurs in the move to Greece, Shantz pay another visit later on. Also recommended that Kekić go to Bari to keep in contact with the Yugoslav branches of ML and UNRRA now there, and be attached administratively to Kirk's mission. . . . The Department wired to have Hulick[12] prepare to go to Rumania. It says that Berry will probably be appointed the Dept.'s representative on the Armistice Commission there, and Hulick will assist him. This disposes of the idea that Berry would come to us in Athens, at least for some time. . . . The gradual fading away of the "MacVeagh Mission" in Cairo received increased emphasis from the orders regarding Hulick, and I accordingly drafted the following telegram of resignation. I shan't send it, because I feel now is not the time to make much of our personal feelings. Let us stick to our jobs, whatever they may turn out to be, during the emergency. But it has relieved my feelings to write it! "When the Department offered me this post last September, it stated in its telegram that in addition to being Ambassador near the Governments of Greece and Yugoslavia then established in Cairo, I would be the United States representative in connection with overall Balkan planning. Advisory functions in regard to the Balkans were, however, subsequently entrusted to Mr. Murphy, and the proposed Balkan Affairs Committee, on which it was repeatedly suggested that I serve, was never set up. Now a separate embassy to Yugoslavia is being constituted, and prior to this, the Yugoslav Government moved to London, while more lately the Greek Government moved to Italy. Meanwhile,

---

[12] Charles E. Hulick, secretary of the U.S. Embassy to the Yugoslav government-in-exile, Cairo.

of the only three Foreign Service Officers assigned to this office, one has been recalled for duty in the Department, another is earmarked for Yugoslavia, and the third is apparently slated for Bulgaria. Of the four auxiliary officers assigned here, one is designated for Yugoslavia, another for Rumania, and the other two are likely at any time to revert to their private occupations. Finally an officer now in Istanbul who I was told in Washington might be assigned to me for service in Athens, is now being sent to Bucharest in connection with the Rumanian Armistice Commission. Thus there is no officer but myself now connected with this Mission who may be expected to serve in Greece, despite the fact that Athens may be liberated almost any day, and is almost certain to be the first capital in the Balkans to be opened to our returning services. Under these circumstances I cannot but feel that the post I now occupy is of small importance to the Department, and since, in addition, when I saw the President for ten minutes in Washington recently and asked him what instructions he wished to give me for my future guidance here, he replied none, except that I should bear in mind that the United States is not going to be involved in Balkan affairs, I see no other course open to me than to offer my resignation. Please be advised that this resignation is to take place immediately, and please also convey my decision and the reasons therefor to the President, together with my sincere regrets based on more than thirty years of admiration and affection for him. I would not take this action if I thought it would embarrass him in any way, but I am sure that it will not be difficult to find someone else willing to accept the rank and emoluments of an Ambassador in return for the discharge of the unimportant and diminishing duties now devolving on this Mission." I read Peggy this amusing blast, and she said it was fully justified, but she agrees it oughtn't be sent. So, in this form at least, my resignation will not get beyond this diary! . . . Loopy's report is that Tsatsos, the Greek Minister of Justice, who came here recently with Sgouritsas, arranged with the Greek military that the mutineers still in detention in Egypt, Libya and Eritrea, are to be kept in detention till they can be returned to Greece, set free, and pardoned. But there will be no general amnesty, and for the time being, of course, no action can be taken.

September 27, 1944, Wednesday
Colonel Aldrich of the OSS came in to talk about the tinned goods (and some clothing) which the OSS has in Cyprus. It is closing down its Cyprus base and is willing to turn over the supplies to the Greek War Relief—perhaps even without charge, though the GWR is willing to pay. So far the ML (Greece) and UNRRA have maintained their indifference

to these supplies, Brigadier King insisting that it would be folly to spoil the Greeks by giving them tinned goods which it will be impossible to continue to supply, and anyhow that the British MA in Ankara is arranging to send supplies to the islands from Turkey. Mr. Curtis of the GWR, however, is willing to take the OSS supplies and try to get them distributed somehow, and I am delighted and told Aldrich I hope his deal can go through. What a piece of folly—practically criminal folly—to pettifog while people starve! The clothes which Aldrich had can be sent to Ismir and get distributed from there through the ML it seems. . . .

I took the opportunity of asking Aldrich what is going to be done with the American operational groups and intelligence groups in Greece once the British go in, it having been decided that we shall use no American troops in Greece whatever except the officers attached to ML for relief and reconstruction. He said it is planned to withdraw these groups as soon as the final phase of "Noah's Ark," called "Smash'em," is concluded. But this may take some time, and meanwhile we shall be acting contrary to our policy, which being so largely negative, has strength only if it is thoroughly consistent. Furthermore, the British operational and liaison groups with which ours collaborate are actively engaged in promoting EDES against ELAS and thus participating to a certain degree in Greek internal strife, and our men must inevitably be regarded by the Greeks as involved so long as they remain with their British counterparts. Aldrich said he saw all this, but that the matter was one for higher authority than his. I am thinking of putting it up to the Department. . . . News from Greece is of continued trouble with the *Andartes*,[13] particularly in the Athens area. There it is said that General Scobie, the new British Commander, has appointed a certain Col. [Gen.] Spiliotopoulos as "Commander of the Garrison" and this man is roundly charged by the leftists as being a friend of the Rallis régime. It is thought that he may disarm the Security Battalions at Scobie's order when the time comes, and then re-arm them as his own police force! It is also rumored that Scobie has told the ELAS to keep out of the Athens area, where the British intend to land, and that ELAS has sent a demand that British troops do not come at all, but that Greece be left to handle her own problems with liberation. Not unnatural, really, since the British have done so little for the Greeks to date, and are now only coming in after the Germans pull out! The London *Observer* states that the Greek Government itself has asked that no British troops be used in Greece, and this has caused a lot of talk here. I doubt if Papandreou would feel able to make so bold a proposal to his "sole begetters," but it may be that under the influence of the Svolos group he has proposed that the British confine themselves to

---

[13] *Andartes*: Greek for "guerrillas."

putting the enemy out and not undertake police or garrison duty in the country....

The news tonight is that the British have landed parachutists and infantry, under cover of naval forces, in Albania, to cut off the retreating Germans and link up "with Tito" and the Russians. I don't think the force can be very large, and it has some bad terrain ahead of it if it pushes inland, but the fact of the landing—near Chimara, in the south—will perhaps encourage the Greeks.

September 29, 1944, Friday

News was received last night by telegraph,—and it is confirmed in the press this morning,—that the Greek guerrilla chiefs—Zervas of EDES, and Sarafis of ELAS,—have met with Wilson in Italy and agreed to serve under his orders and those of Lt. General Scobie, commanding for Greece. Boundaries for Zervas's activity have been agreed on; and the ELAS will not operate in the Athens area. All seems rosy, and the mere fact that Zervas and Sarafis could be got to sit down together and agree to anything, and with Wilson too, is amazing enough. *Pourvu que ça dure!* The British had better hurry on their operations. According to the agreement the Security Battalions are to be regarded as enemies, and there is no confirmation of the appointment of Spiliotopoulos.[14]

September 30, 1944, Saturday

Lambrianidis, now designated as Governor of Thrace and Eastern Macedonia, called me and we had a long talk. A little man, born in Russia, ex-deputy from Drama, he is alarmed over the situation into which he is being thrown as it were naked and single-handed. He anticipates that the chief trouble in his region will come from the Macedonian irredentists and *comitadjis*. About the King, he said his return is "exclus," before the plebiscite, that is, though "some people in England would like to see it." He said Spiliotopoulos is a good republican, despite "a royal background," and his appointment has been accepted by the Leftists.

[14] The principal points of the Caserta Agreement of September 26, 1944 were: that all the guerrilla forces in Greece accept the authority of the government of National Unity and of General Scobie, and "will forbid any attempt by any units under their command to take the law into their own hands." The Security Battalions were denounced as "instruments of the enemy" and, unless they surrendered, would be treated as "enemy formations." EDES would confine its operations in Epirus, with ELAS operating in the rest of Greece except Attica, which was placed under the command of General Pan. Spiliotopoulos. Iatrides, *Revolt in Athens*, pp. 311-313.

A broadcast by Papandreou, published today, announces this appointment as well as the agreement with the guerrilla chiefs.

October 1, 1944, Sunday
Lunch at Lord Moyne's near the Mena House. Some MESC people and generals. I sat next to General Paget.... Paget told me that the British have "salvaged" about 50 percent of the Greek mutineers and are giving them arms since they have agreed to fight for the present Greek Government. This doesn't sound as bad as anticipated only a short time ago. He also said that the Crown Prince has now gone to Italy, but will not accompany the Greek Government to Greece. He himself has tried to explain to the Prince, he said, why this must be. He couldn't go back without in some sense representing the King, and the King has made an undertaking to stay out himself, etc. I was interested in the General's apparent acceptance of the fact that the King is committed.

October 2, 1944, Monday
Calls in the morning from Mr. Hudson and Mr. Frank Shea of OWI, and from Mr. Rankin, and Mr. Sourlas, Chargé d' Affaires of Greece. The last named had some routine messages to transmit. He also required to be comforted regarding certain rumors being circulated concerning Russian and Bulgarian plans to run Thrace and Macedonia with very little assistance from the Greeks until the conclusion of peace. The Turkish press (also, of course, nervous about Russian intentions) has picked these rumors up—decisions have been taken by Russian generals and announcements made by Bulgar ministers etc. Apparently, all the Greeks in Cairo are stirred up. I reminded Mr. Sourlas of the fact that the Bulgarian Armistice terms are still being drawn up, and that meanwhile what any Bulgarian official or Russian general may say can have no permanent validity. The terms will establish what Bulgaria is to do, and Mr. Molotov will see that the Russian generals keep in line. I also said that I felt, from our experience as regards Rumania, that the Russian Government has no desire to be anything but correct in its dealings with its allies on armistice arrangements.

October 3, 1944, Tuesday
Denials are now coming out publicly about the supposed Bulgar-Russian-Greek arrangements in Thrace. The Bulgarian Telegraph Agency "is authorized to deny the news spread by the Turkish Press regarding the *soi-disant* joint occupation of Thrace by Bulgarian and Soviet forces,"

and to "announce that the Bulgarian authorities have withdrawn from all Thracian, Macedonian, and Serbian territories after having handed over the administration to the local population." Simultaneously Mr. Porfyrogenis, Greek Minister of Labor and Secretary General of the EAM Central Committee, has announced in Italy that "the EAM organizations are not competent and have no authority to conclude agreements with foreign governments on any question whatsoever," etc. All this is very well, and I hope may restore some confidence to the jittery Greeks here. ... The President has sent Papandreou a long message assuring him of our wish to help in sending adequate supplies and saying that he has himself sent word to the military urging that the utmost be done. In the message he goes out of his way to speak of the "encouraging evidences of increased unity among the Greek people" and of their approaching liberation from enemy occupation. I think I see in this an attempt to do something along the lines I suggested to him, to repair the ravages caused by his reference, in his message to Mr. Churchill, to the Greek people's returning to their allegiance as if all of them were derelict.

Dinner at General Giles's. The new Minister to Saudi Arabia, Colonel Eddy, and his wife were there, together with Ambassador Culbertson, Miss Winslow, and the Petroleum Attaché and his wife. Eddy was very interesting and amusing about the Arabs. He gave me the explanation of the proposed pipe-line to the Lebanon, to bring the oil where it could be sold outside the sterling area and distributed to Europe and North Africa without incurring the canal tolls and other expenses connected with the sea route from Red Sea or Persian Gulf ports. He is strong for the development of our oil interests, and also believes we should be on a parity with Britain as regards commercial opportunities in Arabia, since on that basis we are sure to develop what is already a lead over Britain in the modernization of the country. He said we should make the British see that to allow, and not attempt to prevent, as they are doing, our building up a big stake in that country is to their advantage, as it will force us in the end to protect our interests there actively, and thus assure Britain of our intervention in case of trouble in the Middle East where her interests are so much greater than ours, and where our help would be so welcome. I think the British ought to see this themselves, but I very much question the extension of our interests in this way into a region so remote militarily from our own bases. Our Chiefs of Staff have gone on record as believing that in the next war we cannot do more for Britain than perhaps to save her in her own tight little isle. Could we save ourselves in Arabia? And if not, ought we to put so many eggs in the Arabian basket? The oil companies doubtless see huge peace-time profits, and will gamble on war-losses. But it has happened before that money invested in militarily indefensible places has led a Government to attempt the impossible, and cost much human life. A developing market for our manufactures, such as Eddy covets in Arabia, is one thing, and a huge investment locally in oil production is another, though they may go hand in hand. The second does not represent such a stake as might involve us dangerously rather than risk its loss, but the first most clearly does. If England is wise, she will do everything she can to aid the interests seeking to involve us in Arabia up to the neck, without any need of Eddy's urging, or that of anyone else. And if we are wise, we shall avoid the trap, no matter whose the greed that is involved. It is a sage imperialism which knows where and when not to be imperialistic.

October 4, 1944, Wednesday

Novikov came in and told me confidentially that he is being transferred to Washington, as Minister-Counsellor to the Embassy there. He is delighted, and said that of all countries Russia admires America most.... We talked about the disposition to be made of his present mission, and he said he thought Yugoslavia would be taken on by the man in London now handling the affairs of the Governments-in-Exile there, and that an appointment for Greece would probably await the solution of the Greek governmental problem after liberation. He had no comment to make on the Yugoslav situation—said he has lost interest in Balkan affairs since learning of his new assignment. But as usual he was critical of British mishandling of Greece. He said it is clear that Britain intends to impose her will on Greece, and when I reminded him of England's natural interest in that country, on account of her position etc., he said yes, but in this war she has shown herself "trop brutal" toward the Greeks, adding that the transfer of the Papandreou Government to Italy has made that Government a laughing-stock. He was pleased with the Rumanian Armistice terms, which he characterized as "fair" (as they are), and I was particularly interested to note that he showed no disposition to regard Bulgarian pretensions to special treatment as being in any way justified. If his Government had any such view, I am sure his attitude would have been different, as he is the perfect mirror of officialdom.

October 5, 1944, Thursday

I had a busy day in the office, mostly with paper-work, though in the afternoon two OSS men came in—Lt. Col. Hoppin and a naval lieutenant named Wood, and brought me a document to read, not keep, giving the instructions issued at Caserta recently to the Greek guerrilla leaders who had agreed to "collaborate." Zervas, according to this document, is to have his headquarters in Jannina, and Sarafis in Lamia. Zervas' "territory" is Epirus, from Preveza northward, and east almost to Metzovo, which is under Sarafis. According to the OSS men, the arrangement is good, in that it gives Zervas some territory where he can operate against Germans—there are some in Northern Epirus still—whereas before, his "territory" was such that if he operated at all it had to be against ELAS. On the other hand, the instructions to both guerrilla leaders, and to Spiliotopoulos, the Military Governor of Attica, forbid the capture of Germans or the arrest of any quislings or collaborators! The British still don't trust the *Andartes*, and want to retain the capture of arms for themselves. This will hardly please the Greeks, and will be hard to enforce, since the British are so slow in putting in an appearance. I asked the two men why, in their opinion, the British act in this way, and Wood said he had heard junior Force 133 officers say openly "Greece is British," and Hoppin said he had heard Britishers say frequently, "Greece is a zone of British influence." Force 133 has certainly been a bad influence from the start, has set the Greeks against other Greeks,—continuing to do so to this hour,—and brought about a dislike of the British and hatred of the foreigner generally where it never existed before. . . .

More and more ministers are coming here from Italy and going on into Greece. Tsatsos and Zevgos are now in Athens. Askoutsis and Tsirimokos and Kartalis are here. The first of these three is to go to Crete and the second to Athens. Kanellopoulos is in the Peloponnese. The reception given the ministers of ELAS has on the whole been encouraging, and the prestige of Svolos in the government and with the British is said to be increasing. He may now be made Vice-Premier. . . .

October 7, 1944, Saturday

I had a call from Commander Spencer, just returned from Alex. He says he will probably stay here now to next Thursday. The landings on the Greek mainland and islands, are all, he said, mere holding attacks and intended to hearten the Greeks into the bargain. The move against Athens is still impracticable because the British haven't force enough to risk it till more Germans pull out. At the same time, successful operations against Germans attempting to make their way to Athens—and thence north—from the islands are slowing this evacuation down. It is an odd situation. . . . The invasion of Albania, which the papers built up into a great attack "on a four hundred mile front," comprised 500 commandos. The occupation force at Patras is about 800 strong, with one RAF squadron, and an RAF "regiment," whatever that means. There are 400 commandos in Northern Epirus, 400 more in Elia, and there have been small commando landings at Kalamata and Nauplia (he said

Argos). The 600 commandos recently landed at Kythera have moved, he thinks, to Poros, along with 500 Greeks (the Sacred Brigade). This last outfit has been bombed, as well as shelled from one of the other islands, I suppose Aegina. Meanwhile there are still about 11,000 Germans left in Crete, and several thousand more in Rhodes, Leros, etc., and Athens is still chock-a-block with Bosches and guns. . . . I sent the Department a message warning it not to expect this Embassy to undertake an onward movement to Athens yet awhile! . . .

Strange how the British seem doomed always to operate in this area with inadequate forces. Here are the Germans all cut off from home by the Soviet move across the Danube to the outskirts of Belgrade, cutting the one railways line from Salonica northward (not to speak of guerrilla action), and the British are too weak to close with them. There seems always to be plenty of British troops in Egypt, and one hears of plenty of them elsewhere in the Middle East. But perhaps it would be too risky to take these away from sitting on the necks of the local populations. Paget told me last Tuesday that the Jews in Palestine have an army of 80,000 men—an underground army all equipped and ready to fight the Arabs and the British too, if they interfere. The Arabs, on the other hand, he said couldn't muster more than 40 or 50 thousand. He thinks the situation very dangerous, and said that the only thing that seems now to be holding an outbreak off is the desire of the Jews to jockey the Arabs into making the first move,—and the Arabs are too coony.

October 8, 1944, Sunday

Last night we learned that Archbishop Damaskinos has asked General Wilson to respond to an offer of the German Commander in Greece to "exchange garrisons" with the British, both in Athens and other Greek towns, so that not only would there be no assaults on these places but there would be no opportunity for civil war in them should the Germans withdraw before the British arrive. The idea would be that, just as happened in Athens in 1941, when the Germans chased the British out, one side would retire and send word that it had gone, and the other, having waited for this word would go in. . . . Indications we got last night were to the effect that Wilson clung to "unconditional surrender," and I was much alarmed. I therefore drafted the following, which, though I didn't send it because we got better news this morning, may be worth preserving as expressing a point of view. "I would respectfully call your attention to telegram No. —— of ——. The course of action for which the Archbishop pleads virtually parallels that taken for the protection of Athens when the British withdrew in 1941, and to expose the city now, with all its priceless monuments, to the risks of becoming a battleground, by continuing to insist on local unconditional surrender, would be to assume a risk before the bar of history which even the Germans in the heyday of their victory refused to accept. In addition, the risks to be run by the Allies in this connection are far greater than those faced by the Germans in 1941, owing to the senseless vandalism and other atrocious tendencies of cornered German troops as repeatedly evinced in this war. I therefore must earnestly urge that this question be not left wholly to military decision but be given consideration by the highest authorities." This morning further messages from Italy indicate that while Wilson has replied to the Archbishop that he can't trust the Germans and if he deals with them must ask for unconditional surrender, nevertheless he, the Archbishop, can be sure that if the Germans pull out, British troops will be ready to come in immediately. This, of course, allows the Archbishop to be in a sense an intermediary, though not officially so, and his telling the Germans what Wilson has said would enable the "exchange of garrisons" to take place in fact if not in theory. Actually, this is what happened in 1941, for it was the Greeks who persuaded the British to go out and a committee of Greeks who went to the Germans with a word that the British would be out at a certain time. The question now will be whether the Germans, knowing they have little chance of escaping from Greece will nevertheless evacuate Athens and put up their resistance further north, or whether they will decide to die fighting (and destroying in Athens) or—last and least likely—surrender *sur place*. The British when they left in 1941 had, after all, a clear escape route open by sea. The Germans have no route open now. Consequently some risk of having to deal with cornered rats must be taken. But I don't see how one can quarrel with Wilson's attitude.

October 9, 1944, Monday

General Sadler came in and discussed ML (Balkans) and the changes that have had to be made because of the way liberation is proceeding—so different from the original plans, which were based on moving to Athens first and radiating relief from there. I take it that the President, in accordance with his recent message to Papandreou, has put some pressure on the military and now Wilson has issued orders to draw up immediately an *ad hoc* plan for relief to the now liberated areas,—the Peloponnese and islands. . . . While we were talking, a telegram from Caserta came in stating that Wilson has instructed Scobie to press Papandreou to move his Government to Patras. Sadler thinks P. may be persuaded, though he would prefer to go directly to Athens. But the move to Athens may still be some time off. As Sadler put it "The British can't afford to risk a defeat now" and they simply haven't got the men available to fight a real action for Athens, which has good defenses, both coastal and anti-aircraft. Sadler expects to go back to Caserta Thursday, but if Papandreou moves before, that will of course speed up his departure.

Saturday night the French press published in full a splendid statement of F.D.R. on Greek liberation, full of sympathy and understanding, the best thing any foreign statesman has yet said so far as its appeal to the Greek people is concerned, and thoroughly true and deserved into the bargain. The British press on Sunday also carried it (though in a brief and niggardly form!) and the OWI broadcast it to Greece on six consecutive programs. Before I left the office I told Wally to be sure and inform the Department of this publicity—so that the President may know it. And I shall write myself later. He told me that when he got a chance to do this, [he would do it] and he did....

General Sadler said he had got a rumor from *JICA* here that there is trouble in the Greek General Staff. I called in "Loopy" and the story seems to link up with what Paget said to me a week ago about "royalist plotting" here and what the Crown Prince said to me even earlier that General Ventiris, the C. of S. is a good fellow. Ventiris, according to "Loopy," though once a republican, is now royalist on account of his hatred and fear of EAM. He has surrounded himself with conservative officers and the feeling that Papandreou has "sold out to EAM" is strong among them. At the same time, I don't see how they can do anything against the Government in Italy just now, and as Sadler suggests, if the Government goes to Greece, they may be still further off base. "Loopy" says that Ventiris has gone to Italy to see the Greek troops fighting with the 8th army. If Papandreou is wise to what is going on, he may not come back, and the staff may return to the hands of the non-political Liossis, or even some EAMite, who knows. A telegram from Caserta today describes plans being evolved by the Greek Government and Wilson for a reconstructed Staff and National Army to be formed in Greece with the idea of taking over all garrison duties there in the Government's name and also forming further units to fight outside of Greece by the side of the allies. Judging from the way things are going now, the EAM will have more to say about this reorganization than the stranded reactionaries in Cairo. But of course we have got to remember that Greek affairs are subject to quick changes, and after being in Italy Sadler is of the opinion, which is undoubtedly sound, that there are still many British who would like to see the King go back to Greece. Who can tell what these British might not be able to do even at the last moment, with Mr. Churchill to guide and lead?... The Crown Prince, allegedly in disgust because the Government is adamant about his not returning to Athens with it, has packed up and taken himself and his ambitious Princess to England. The idea that the

King may be coming here, which "Loopy" picked up from Stathatos,[15] seems to have nothing in it. He does, however, want to go to Italy to see the Greek troops,—and although he has, to my knowledge, wanted to do this for a time, his reference to "being with you soon" in a broadcast message to the Brigade at Rimini, has excited all sorts of nervous speculation here. This is symptomatic of the Greek state of mind at present. The King question is fundamentally of no importance compared with, for instance, liberation, relief, and reconstruction. But it has become a perfect red rag, not only because of the King's past but because of present Greek feelings toward the British. It is profoundly to be hoped he will not be escorted in with Mr. Churchill's bayonets, or he may come out on Greek ones. To my mind, his game must now be to go cautiously certainly, but above all things to *go Greek*.

October 10, 1944, Tuesday

Latest news indicates that there are only a few German troops left in Athens and the Piraeus, and "defense positions outside the city are manned by troops of low calibre." Perhaps the British will now feel it safe to approach.

Calls in the afternoon from Sven Allard, passing through on his way to be Swedish Minister in Chungking, Mr. Tsirimokos, Greek Minister of National Economy, on his way to Athens, and Mr. Hirschman of the War Relief Board. Allard was very interesting about the work of the Swedish Relief Commission. As he represented the Swedish Government in Athens he had general supervision of the work, but resided mostly in Sofia, where he was sent to represent Sweden shortly after we left Greece. He said that he could have done better work with the Commission if he had been able to be in Athens more, but he couldn't send any code messages from there, and reports were constantly being demanded of him which necessarily had to be confidential, while travel between Sofia and Athens was very difficult and time-consuming. He left Sofia for Sweden last December. Harry Hill and Wally Barbour joined our conversation, and Harry asked M. Allard many questions about the Commission's work and his own experiences with the Greek, German and Italian authorities, the answers to which were always promptly forthcoming and to the point. Mr. Allard gave us the names of some undoubted war-criminals, both German and Italian, and told us of various Greeks who have made fortunes out of collaboration, as well as some who, like the Papastratos Brothers,[16] could not very well help working "for the

---

[15] Captain Antonios Stathatos, political adviser of the Greek Royal House.
[16] A principal tobacco company in Greece.

Germans" if they kept their businesses going at all but who will certainly have to bear the onus, in popular estimation, of having "collaborated." He said that the Germans in general behaved squarely with the Commission, but the Italians did not; that the Germans kept business and industry going as well as they could, but wrecked the whole economy of the country by their financial exactions. To pay for the cost of maintaining the army and making their fortifications, they demanded loan after loan, which the Greeks had to print money in huge quantities to supply, and thus deluged the country with currency, leading to the present astronomical inflation. (Harry Hill said that today the gold pound is worth 170 billion drachmas, and that the drachmas in circulation total in the quadrillions!) As these advances were always in the form of loans, it would seem that the Greek state has now a pretty good claim to a share in German reparation payments, if the Allies care to consider the claims of so small a state! Regarding Jacobus of Mytilene, he said that the oil merchants of that island didn't want to sell their oil to the Commission for distribution to the people in Greece, preferring to sell it on the black market for a higher price, and that Jacobus (the church having many olive trees) was in it with them, coveting the money he could thus get for the use of his local charities. When Allard, who admitted that what he offered was not high enough but pointed out that it was a matter of patriotism and humanity, and that the U.S.A. and Canada were *giving* wheat to the Greek people, threatened to have the names of the merchants reported to the Allies for future black-listing, he got an immediate response not only from them but from Jacobus as well. The merchants I have little sympathy with, but this story confirms my belief that the basis of the wide-spread rumor of pro-Germanism on the part of old Jacobus lies in his taking too strictly diocesan a view of his mission as a Greek bishop. About Damaskinos, Allard said that he has won great moral prestige by his daring in opposing the Germans, and that he is a very clever man and politician, but that he is not wholly trustworthy and lied to him several times. His relief organization, which the Germans finally broke up precisely because of its political implications, did good work in connection with the Commission (the only way in which Allard could judge it) but was clearly used by the Archbishop to promote his own political prestige....

Tsirimokos seems to be an intelligent little person.... [T]he purpose of his visit to me today was to tell me of the inadequacy of the ML supplies on hand, and of the great need of the Greek people, and of how they look to America for help, and it wouldn't appear to be very intelligent to think I don't know about these things...

October 11, 1944, Wednesday

It appears now that the Greek Government will not go to Patras but only Mr. Papandreou personally, to make a speech there and return to Caserta, and that the British Military count on moving to Athens soon. . . . Reports from Athens are confusing as regards the temper of the population, but on the whole things look more favorable than we have expected they would in this regard. The EAM seems trying to obey the orders of the Government, but I don't like the continued reports that Spiliotopoulos is using the disbanded members of the Security Battalions to form a gendarmerie, for if this is true I don't see how trouble with the ELAS can be avoided. However, the worst news to come in today is embedded deep in a long report of Smith-Dorrien's on his conversations with Greek Government officials concerning relief questions. In a brief paragraph of that document he states that the Government has established a new crime of "anti-nationalism" for which punishments will range from five years' imprisonment to death, and which will cover not only collaboration with the enemy but *implication in the Metaxas Dictatorship*. It will be hard enough to weed out the true collaborationists from the multitude of those sure to be accused, but what will be the result, when political accusations covering the whole span of the "4th of August" régime are added, who can say? It seems likely that the EAMite and communist members of the Government are at the bottom of this move, which starts the political ball rolling again with a vengeance, in the true sense of the word, and puts not only traitors and war-criminals but the whole extreme right in jeopardy of liberty and even life. Is reconstruction to be complicated with a political terror? Perhaps the word is too strong, given the relative mildness of typical Greek "revolutions," but political revenge to some degree seems, from this action, to have been settled on as a government policy, and can lead to no good. One doesn't have to sympathize with the Metaxists, or to wish to see the King come back, in order to realize this. Extremes are always unwise. I am surprised at Papandreou. But perhaps the report is not wholly accurate. It will be interesting to see the reaction if it is, so many people will [be] affected, from the King down!

October 12, 1944, Thursday

During the day rumors came in to the effect that Athens is already liberated and celebrating—but the Germans still hold the airports and the Piraeus, which would seem to make the "liberation" rather a farce and perhaps a dangerous one, with the opportunities offered for internal strife before the British can come in; that Leeper has left Italy; that the Greek Government will go "to Greece" at once in order to be near at hand to enter Athens as soon as this is possible, etc. More definitely, we heard from Kirk that Papandreou has refused to go to Patras, preferring to await the move to Athens. . . . I got confirmation of rumors to the effect that the Greek General Staff here, under Ventiris, of whom the Crown Prince recently spoke so well to me, is furious with Papandreou for playing so much with EAM, and that it (or rather a number of officers in it) is supported by a group of Royalists and conservative republicans throughout the Middle East. Doubtless this group is too small, too scattered, and too remote from the seat of Government, to stage any coup just at present, but this kind of thing will doubtless make difficult the reorganization of the National Army which General Wilson is said to be planning. Such opposition to Papandreou may also make a lot of hay out of the new "anti-national" criminal law, if reports on that subject are correct. . . . The Department sent a telegram stating that according to reports reaching Washington the personnel of the Swedish-Swiss Commission in Athens may be in danger from the *andartes*, particularly the EPON or Youth Movement of the EAM. In addition to having cabled Caserta to get the Greek Government to take steps, it asks us here to consult with the OSS and OWI to see if anything can be done by those organizations. We did so. OWI is willing to give us any publicity in favor of the Commission which we think might be helpful. OSS will send in word to its agents. But in addition, Harry Hill telephoned Mr. Tsirimokos and Mr. Kartalis, both now in Alexandria awaiting transportation, and they promised to radio an official message in the name of the Greek Government to the EAM in Athens. . . . We have heard of dissatisfaction with the Commission before, and of its stores being threatened, but this is the first report of its personnel being in actual danger. It has done a good work of distribution, on the whole, but of course there has been criticism, since it could not hire everybody, nor feed everybody in Greece, and it has also made some mistakes. Rumors against it have apparently excited hot heads, and anyway one of the relatively few unlovable traits of the Greek people has always been to bite the hands of its benefactors.

October 13, 1944, Friday
The papers are full of the liberation of Athens, and Greek school boys paraded the streets shouting "Zito," but a telegram from an OSS agent in Athens (identified to me by Colonel Toulmin as Rodney Young) confirms my belief of yesterday that so far it is only a German withdrawal from the city proper. Germans were still in the suburbs and the Piraeus this morning though the Swastika was hauled down on the Acropolis yesterday morning at 10:30. Wish I had seen that, as I saw the odious

ensign hoisted on that memorable morning in 1941. Rodney also confirms the rumored rejoicings in the city, of which the papers are making much, but adds that, as I feared, there is apparent friction between various political groups, which may become open conflict if the British delay too long to put in an appearance.... The fleet seems to have sailed from Alexandria all right, but when it will arrive is another matter.... A good story, also received by the OSS, is to the effect that the Germans before leaving Athens paraded before the tomb of the Unknown Soldier and laid a wreath on it. The Greeks kept aloof from the ceremony, but afterwards fell upon the wreath and tore it to pieces.... Eye-witness newspaper reports on conditions in Greece are now coming in. They are, as was to be expected, terrible. Secret agents with the *andartes* have of course only touched on conditions they themselves have known. Now we can see with the eyes of the village populations. British reports from Patras indicate that despite censored reports in the press of peace and harmony, the EAM has been very obstreperous, and this is true also in the central Peloponnese where "Aris"[17] is making trouble, promising to obey orders of AFHQ but not doing so. Still further away from the center of things, the Island of Mytilene, but not Chios, it seems, has been taken over completely by the Communists. We are clearly going into a nest of woe and trouble....

In the afternoon I had a call from Mr. Pappas, the Greek Minister Resident in Egypt. He told me that there has been an earthquake in Chios and Mytilene, and that there are 6,000 homeless people in consequence. Papandreou has wired him to see me and ask urgently for tents and medicine. I called in Harry Hill and we started to try and get the Military "who have the responsibility" to supply these things, but it appears there are no tents available, and medical stores are "in short supply." Later we learned that the Greek Minister of Reconstruction hoped to be able to buy tents in Alexandria. Why can't the Military do the same thing? They seem hopelessly tied up in their rules and regulations. As to medicines, I had just had a call from Colonel Toulmin, who had told me of several tons of medical supplies which OSS has here, and I immediately got Col. Cochrane of ML in touch with him. Pappas also had a complaint about a lot of vitamins—20,000 small boxes—which he said some organization had sent to Greece from America, but which according to his information had been re-routed to France after arrival at Accra. In the shipment there had been a lot of propaganda material addressed to the Greeks, and this had been taken out at the time of re-routing, and he had seen some examples, but his information was so vague I had to tell him to make it

---

[17] Aris Velouchiotis (Athanasios Klaras), chief *capetanios* of ELAS, and a seasoned communist leader.

more precise before I could undertake investigation. Finally he wanted to tell me especially that he had just had word from Moscow to the effect that Wednesday evening Mr. Molotov had summoned the Greek Minister, and told him that Bulgarian troops had been ordered to be out of Greece within fifteen days, and had in addition talked with the Minister in a much more "easy and friendly" manner than had been his wont previously. Pappas was much encouraged by this news.

October 14, 1944, Saturday

Col. Larrabee went to Alexandria to represent the Embassy at the unveiling of a monument to fallen Greek aviators in the Middle East. Mr. Tsaldaris called and said that the Crown Prince arrived last night in Alexandria, and would be present at the ceremony as announced. I ascertained from Lt. Laughlin, of Commander Spencer's office, that the *Averoff* and escorting vessels, Greek and British, steamed out of the harbour of Alexandria yesterday morning, amid scenes of rejoicing and the noisy whistling of all craft present—not much secrecy left! All task force units seem to have sailed several days ago, so "D" day must be just about upon us. The last escorting destroyer, a Britisher called the *Aurora*, with the Greek C-in-C supposedly abroad, waited till afternoon, but the Prince did not sail with her as I figured he might try to do. His coming here at this time can only be connected with his desire to get back to Greece somehow, and as soon as possible, but perhaps he has taken a leaf out of the King's book and has decided just to be close at hand in case communist troubles in liberated Greece result in a call for the dynasty after all. Mr. Tsaldaris told me that he intends seeing the Prince at once in order "to find out what he learned in London, where all decisions are being made." . . .

Late news flashes tonight state that the British troops today entered Athens and the Piraeus. Details are lacking.

October 15, 1944, Sunday

Churchill in Moscow seems to have been making a strong attempt to get some agreement with Stalin on Polish policy. Also perhaps on Yugoslav policy.[18] Tito is said to be going to visit Stalin. I wonder. He

---

[18] On October 9, 1944, during a visit to Moscow, which was principally devoted to Polish issues, Churchill submitted to Stalin his proposal for a division of Anglo-Soviet responsibilities in the Balkans. Under the "percentages agreement," which Stalin appeared to accept, the division was to be as follows:

has recently been closer in touch with the Russians than with the British, and Toulmin told me yesterday that the British in Bari, at any rate, are now frankly disgusted with him. I feel that if Anglo-Russian problems as regards Poland and Yugoslavia had been thoroughly and realistically thrashed out on the highest level months ago, things would have been much better now. Even if an understanding can be reached at this time, the suspicions and animosities aroused by recent cross-purposes must continue to color the relations of the two powers. . . . Later: a telegram has come in from Kirk according to which Shantz left *the day before yesterday* in company with General Sadler, the Greek Government and the British Ambassador. Where he went to and how far the group has gotten on its journey to the capital is still obscure. Perhaps the way this is turning out, from the diplomatic point of view, is not too bad. This Embassy is preserving its contact with the Greek Government, through Shantz, but at the same time it is not entering under the auspices of the British military, Shantz being with the American section of the Relief and Reconstruction Group, and the Ambassador still outside with all other Chiefs of Mission, waiting to come in when the Government is established and Greece, not England, is the host. Wally, at least, thinks this is satisfactory, and I do, too, on reflection, though I should dearly love to be flying in there now and beat Leeper and the Greek Government, too, to the tape. If only the Military had been under American command, as I have always wanted it to be! . . .

Dinner at the *Auberge du Turf* with the Allards, adjourning afterwards to the Swedish Legation, where they are living. . . . He told me two interesting things, one, that in November, 1943, the German "political and economic plenipotentiary for the Balkans," Neubacher, told him in Sofia, where Allard was then stationed, that he had concluded an agreement with Mihailović for joint action against the Partisans; and two, that he had been very friendly with such Bulgarian leaders as Archbishop Stefan, Mr. Stajnov (now Foreign Minister under Kimon Georgiev) and the elder Moshanov, and had got the impression that these men believed Russian policy in the Balkans to intend the setting up, with Tito's help, of a federated Yugoslavia composed of autonomous states of Croatia, Serbia, Macedonia, *and Bulgaria,* with a generous exit to the Aegean comprising Kavalla and perhaps Salonica.

    Rumania: Russia 90%, The others 10%
    Greece: Britain 90%, Russia 10%
    Yugoslavia: 50-50%
    Hungary, 50-50%
    Bulgaria: Russia 75%, The others 25%

In the case of Greece, Britain's share was to be "in accord with the U.S.A." See Winston Churchill, *The Second World War,* VI, *Triumph and Tragedy* (Boston: Houghton Mifflin, 1953), 227.

October 18, 1944, Wednesday
I went on with my letter to the President, which takes as usual much care and revision.... News that the Government has arrived at least off Piraeus came in a flash from Spencer through OSS. No details yet of this situation but OSS got word that the powder factory in Athens, the munitions factory at Eleusis, and the Sparta radio station were blown up or otherwise destroyed. The electric light plant, however, is still functioning....

Cairo, Egypt
October 15, 1944

Dear Franklin:

I feel somewhat overdue in writing this, so much has happened since I last wrote, and since my brief talk with you in Washington. But you will understand that I have felt reluctant to bother you at this time, when you must be even more busy than ever, if that is possible, with this campaign on your hands in which the hopes of all of us are deeply involved.

To my last letter about the Balkans you replied, "What a mess!" As I write now, the Russians have entered Yugoslavia, apparently more as a part of the development of their campaign against Hungary than as a prelude to overrunning Yugoslavia (though that may come later) and the Civil War between Tito's forces and the Serbian irreconcilables under Mihailović seems developing favorably to Tito, who, while accepting such assistance from the British as they have been able to give, is more and more openly turning to Moscow for guidance. It is hard to see what influence in Yugoslavia the British are going to be able to retain when the smoke clears away, if as seems to be the case, they have built up Tito only to have him serve in the end as a Russian tool, and in so doing have favored the Croats, who promptly yielded to Germany at the moment of invasion, and have deserted the Serbs, who did all the fighting at that time. Mr. Churchill, now in Moscow, may agree with Stalin on the composition of a new Yugoslav Government, but it seems certain that such a government will be even further to the left than the present one, and thereafter, if communism makes good its hold in Yugoslavia, Russia need do little more than to stand by and watch the liquidation of the elements in the social structure which are dangerous to her interests. It may be said that the result should be favorable to peace in our time, as enabling the Russians to return their armies to their own country fairly soon, to help in much-needed reconstruction without fear of frontier menace to her way of life; and it would seem that similar results are being sought in other countries, through the clever use of communism as a solvent, all along the critical crescent from Riga to Istanbul. But the experience involved for the small states concerned seems only too likely to be painful in the extreme, and allowing for all differences of geography and national character, we must, I fear, see the future of Yugoslavia somewhat in the light of that of Poland, which is not encouraging to Westerners sympathetic with human suffering. Furthermore (which may touch our Westerners even more closely!), the establishment of such a central and Southeastern European zone as would be, in Russian minds, as friendly to Russia as to other countries, would seem likely, through the probable elimination or suppression of the classes possessed of western trade affiliations, to provide Russia with unparalleled opportunities for commercial expansion; and thus the upshot of the agreement not to establish zones of influence or *cordons sanitaires* along Russia's periphery, may, through the instrumentality of communism, favored by conditions of war-time fatigue and collapse, end in the virtual if not nominal annexation to the Soviet Union of an imperial domain of some hundred million souls.

To turn to Greece, that country is, of course, economically the quite useless vermiform appendix of South Eastern Europe. Our State Department doesn't even regard it as European, and includes it under the Office of the Near East and Africa. The Greeks themselves, when leaving Athens for Baden-Baden or Biarritz, talk of "going to Europe." But it is nevertheless a part of Europe, and its people are definitely European in background and psychology (if not wholly in blood), as I have had occasion to realize forcibly when talking with Greek islanders only a few hours after conversations with Turks in Asia Minor. Greece is now being "liberated" by a few cautious British following up the retreating Germans, and being welcomed by crowds bearing the Red flag. She is not, strictly speaking, on the Russian periphery, and I have no doubt that the realistic Stalin recognizes the realism of Britain's strategic interest in her position in the Aegean Sea. Nevertheless, subversive social forces are continuing to operate powerfully in Greece today, and are receiving the open sympathy of Moscow, if not its active support. I therefore still feel that, however the Russian Government may formally keep hands off, the Greece of the future is going to be very different from the Greece we have known in the past. The social order there has been relatively stable these last hundred years. The great Greek problems of our time have been purely political, revolving almost up to the outbreak of this war around the old issue of royalism vs. Venizelism, which harks back to 1917. All efforts in the 1930's to bring to the polls more vital and immediate questions than this politico-personal cleavage failed dismally. But the war, and to some extent the Metaxist dictatorship which was swept away in it, has now done what aspiring young would-be statesmen could never do. Greece is now clearly conscious of issues which never troubled King Constantine or Venizelos, and Greek revolutions are likely, from now on, to wear, at least to some degree, a social aspect. This makes the question of the King's return a good deal less vital, except to him and his family, than it would have been in times gone by, when the dynasty was of real influence in the country. Russia, probably playing a deeper game, doesn't seem to care whether he returns or not, and even Britain appears to realize that beneath and behind the window-dressing which he represents, the new growth of class-consciousness and proletarianism has altered the whole aspect of the problem of retaining British control. These forces have already raised their heads openly once,—in the recent Greek mutiny in the Middle East,—and Russia may be well content with the strength they then revealed. Again, she has only to watch while the trends of the time work for her,—while forces which the Bolshevik revolution set in motion years ago exploit post-war conditions for the spread of Russian influence. As the Soviet Minister said to me here one day (he was speaking of Egypt, but the parallel is clear), "They are terribly afraid of me here lest I engage in subversive activity. But I intend doing nothing of the sort. I don't have to. Conditions in the country itself will do all that is necessary."

Parenthetically, I realize that Yugoslavia,—and Greece to an even greater extent,—are very small potatoes still in the typical American view of foreign affairs. But I should like to stress once more my belief that eventually what goes on in the Balkans and the Near East generally will have to be recognized as of prime importance to us despite the fact that the countries involved are small and remote. Here both the French Revolution and the Nazi Revolution have made their most dangerous bids to crack England's empire and pick the lock of world dominion. No one can say for certain, of course, that the Empire of the Czars, which has now become the Empire of the Soviets, will make a similar attempt in its turn, but the fact remains that,—as I have presumed to emphasize in my previous letters,—Russian interests are clearly tending to cross with Britain's in this region even now. Nor is this all. Evidence is equally plain right here of Britain's inability to defend alone her Empire against powerful pressure under conditions of modern war. I doubt if in any other part of the world it can appear so clearly as here,—along its principal artery,—that, militarily speaking, the British Empire is anachronistic, perfect for the eighteenth century, impossible for the twentieth. Every day brings its evidence of weakness and dispersion, or consequent opportunism, and dependence on America's nucleated strength. No one, I feel, can keep his eyes and ears open here and fail to believe that the future maintenance of the Empire depends on how far England consents to frame her foreign policy in agreement with Washington, and how far we in our turn realize where that Empire, so important to our own security, is most immediately menaced. British fumbling in the Balkans, fears of what may happen in Palestine, uneasiness as to Syria, doubts regarding Turkey, and alarm over growing Soviet interest in Iran, Saudi Arabia, Egypt and the whole North African coast, together with the fact that it was only through America's productive strength being thrown into the balance that Rommel's threat to this region was defeated, all seem to me to teach the same lesson in their varying degrees.

But let me return to my muttons. I quote below a part of a recent highly recommended report by one of our secret agents of the OSS, which confirms my view of what existing trends are doing to our traditionally political and ideologically dormant little country of Greece:

> "The movement created by EAM can only be regarded as a full-fledged revolution. One cannot conceive the situation otherwise.
>
> The EAM movement dominates. There can be no question of repressing it. The ideology it represents and the interests connected with it are so vital that a compromise (i.e. with the traditional order) is the most that can be hoped for.
>
> British political maneuvering has failed, and it can only be said that the populace will no longer tolerate it. England has lost ground and will not be able to regain it in the future."

It is my belief that the present (Papandreou) Government of Greece, with its social democratic leanings, will attempt to affect such a compromise,—such an accommodation of new wine to old bottles,—as the above report states to be the only hope. But it remains to be seen whether it can do this and survive—or even survive at all, whatever it attempts. As things stand today, immediate developments in Greece can hardly be guessed at, least of all by one outside the country. I hope, however, to be in Athens soon myself, and my next letter may be more definite.

Affectionately yours,
Lincoln MacVeagh (1)

October 19, 1944, Thursday
Word came (in a garbled message through the British) from Spencer in Athens. He said Shantz arrived with the Government, that the Government's resignation "according to agreement" is expected, that the liberating troops got an ovation, but that there have been some shootings ("seven killed") as a result of political disturbances—evidently *before* the Government's arrival. We heard sometime ago that the Liberal politicians were insisting that Papandreou resign on arrival, and so reported to the Department, but his willingness to do so has since been both asserted and

denied in rumors reaching this Embassy and the existence of any "agreement" on the subject has never been confirmed.

October 20, 1944, Friday

General Giles called up and said that the Athens area is open now only for operational flights, but that he would advise me as soon as this restriction is relaxed. Apparently there are still German airplanes too close for comfort. He said that Harriman passed through here last night *en route* to Washington, and that he wanted to fly via Athens, but Giles wouldn't allow it. "I wouldn't want him to take a swim in the Aegean just now." . . .

Spencer reported that Papandreou resigned yesterday and was "reappointed" Prime Minister in accordance with "an agreement with the King made before leaving Italy." He is now forming a new Government, "Sofoulis the only party leader dissenting." This looks as if the Liberals are sticking to their belief that Papandreou must eventually fail and are planning to both speed his fall and capitalize on it by holding aloof from all his endeavors. Spencer also reports that EAM is "contesting control" of Athens, whatever that means, though "order is being kept," and that there are two Russian Laision officers with EAM in Athens! He confirms press reports that the food situation is critical and the currency question is unsettled. Only the former underground newspapers are circulating. . . . An OSS report dated yesterday says the Athens cinemas are open, showing old American films, and the price of entry is "a cake of soap, two packages of cigarettes, or 40 million drachmas." . . .

An information telegram from the Department gives some of Harriman's views on developments in Central Europe which parallel fairly closely what I have been writing to the President. A certain amount of "economic stress" Harriman thinks, would not be unwelcome to the Russians in the border states, "resulting from policies to which the Russians are committed from other causes." This is pretty soft talk to cover some stern realities, but one can see what it means. "There would be a resultant reduction in the industrial and military potential and the standard of living would be reduced to something nearer the Soviet level." In other words, a social revolution is to follow the Soviet advance. "The wealthy and more conservative classes would be affected primarily, and the governments likely to be unfriendly to the Soviet Government would have to take the blame for the decrease in economic security. This would result in governments entirely friendly to the Soviets being set up." The cart is perhaps getting ahead of the horse here, and Polyanna is driving. As I see it there will be no governments in these states from now on for a long time "unfriendly to the Soviets," and the governments which the

Russians allow to come to power will themselves be instrumental in increasing the "economic insecurity" to the point where western commercial affiliations cease and Russia's "standard of living" (i.e. Russia's economic control) takes over. But it all comes to the same thing. Harriman simply sees the elimination of the upper and middle classes as leading to the establishment of "friendly governments," whereas I feel the establishment of such governments, which is beginning to take place right now in Rumania, Bulgaria, and Poland, is a step toward the elimination of the upper and middle classes and [the] eventual Russian absorption into its system of the remaining proletariats.

October 21, 1944, Saturday

We got our first message from Shantz. He has secured our old offices, and has moved into the School[19] where he says we can go too. He says *serious trouble* in Athens can only be avoided if the currency situation is promptly attended to. I advised the Department of all of the above.

I asked Larrabee to see Capt. Stathatos and find out all he could about the Regency situation, and Papandreou's resignation. Stathatos hadn't heard of the resignation, but consulted HRH who replied that the resignation and reappointment of Papandreou to form a new Government had all been arranged with the King before the Government left Italy, just as I thought probable. Stathatos also told "Loopy," very confidentially, that though the Crown Prince is Regent in name, all important decisions coming up to him are decided by the King in London. The Crown Prince's *entourage* thinks there is a serious situation with EAM in Athens already, not just a matter of the currency, and that only the British troops are keeping it from developing openly. But of course the royalist crowd wants this kind of thing, so that a demand for the King's return as a stabilizing factor may eventuate. We continue to hear the most conflicting things from Athens. . . . At the end of the day Barclay Hudson called up with news, unconfirmed, that real trouble has broken out in Athens. What would that mean? There are all sorts of possibilities, of course. . . . And in the midst of all this I got a telegram from the Department asking for detailed reports under 12 different headings of official reactions to the proposals of the Dumbarton Oaks Conference![20] I replied that the Greeks aren't in any condition now to be making comments on these proposals but that I felt sure they would, when conditions stabilize in Greece,

[19] The American School of Archaeological Studies in Athens.

[20] From August 21 to October 9, 1944, representatives of the United States, Britain, the Soviet Union and China discussed at Dumbarton Oaks the establishment, the structure and the functions of the new international organization (the United Nations Organization).

have opinions to express, and that the Embassy would not fail to report what it might hear. But imagine!

October 22, 1944, Sunday
   Received at the office, from Shantz, a couple of messages repeating reports made telegraphically on Oct. 20th and 21st by Sadler and Sir Francis Rugman to the War Department and the Foreign Office respectively. These stress the extreme necessity of fixing some exchange rate "otherwise there may be strikes and civil war." Sadler says that the food situation in the country is critical and more supplies must come forward, but destitution is not evident in Athens. Wired the Department suggesting that it may be interested in these messages. It ought to be.

October 23, 1944, Monday
   Toulmin and West came in, the latter to tell me of conditions in Athens, which he described as "safe" for our staff but exceedingly difficult as regards nearly all the conveniences of life,—money, food, transport and the like. Everything is terribly expensive, and the army rations being handed out not really sufficient for living comfortably. Good meals can be bought, but cost about $20. a meal! The poor people are starving and unemployed. About eight supply ships are in the bay, but can't discharge, owing to the fact that docks have been blown up and the British brought no lighters. If these supplies can be brought to town, prices will go down, and if the currency can be stabilized industry can start up again, but meanwhile crowds of hungry idlers and the presence of subversive elements and armed "patriots" must remain a threat to security, particularly, of course, in the slums and suburbs. West says that for the moment Papandreou's prestige is high, and he may do a good job for the country, but that he cannot succeed personally very long. The "cleverest man in Greece" is Siantos, the Secretary of EAM, who West thinks will play with the Government till the British troops withdraw, and thereafter will really go out for control. "Papandreou is a marked man." . . . Messages from Shantz and Spencer confirmed the general picture drawn by West. Spencer says that the reorganization of the Cabinet is expected to include Siantos and General Mandakas, both original members of the Committee in the Mountains, and General Othonaios. . . . Harry Hill reported word from UNRRA to the effect that two of the best office buildings in Athens, on which UNRRA had its eye, have been taken over by EAM and the Communist Party respectively. More and more it looks to me as if Greece were in for a 4th of August Dictatorship again, but in reverse. . . . West says nobody has any interest in the King's return any more, and he thinks it quite likely that he would be killed if

he should come back now. West's opinions are of course not always very considered or necessarily sound, but he has been about. . . .

The following remarks from a resumé of the Soviet press, circulated secretly by our Embassy in Moscow, fall in so closely with what I have been thinking, and trying to express for so long, that it is worth quoting here in paraphrase: "Subject to variations to fit local conditions, Soviet policy seeks to set up, along Russia's western border, régimes favorable to Russia but not necessarily to impose communist system, social or economic. Though refraining in an ostentatious manner from any overt interference in local internal matters it is the policy of the Soviets in the border countries to encourage the local communist parties and parties sympathetic with the Left to demand prompt arrest and trial of all who have been associated with anti-Communist or pro-Nazi tendencies, and to seek sweeping changes, particularly in land reforms. Terms of armistice covering immediate and large deliveries of supplies in kind to Russia and the setting up of Control Commissions under the chairmanship of Russian generals to see that these terms are enforced, are means used to insure Russian influence over the national economies of the states concerned. Under such circumstances economic upheaval and political foment appear unavoidable. These are recognized in orthodox Marxist ideology as conditions ideal for the development of revolutionary movements, and the active communists in the countries concerned, who make up the only groups there now which appear to have a well-defined program and strong backing, may well be expected to turn this situation to advantage and obtain for themselves a controlling voice in the Government when the moment is propitious." Here the cart is definitely before the horse and the whole thing makes sense.

October 25, 1944, Wednesday

General Ritter called up and said all is clear now with AFHQ, and General Giles plans to take us off at 6 a.m. day after tomorrow. . . . Kirk wired that Eden, who stayed here after Churchill left the other day,[21] is going to Greece today. He has not invited me to call, and I have not asked, as I feel I must still carefully keep it clear that we are not involved in either the military operations in Greece or the internal political problem. My arrival in Greece at the time of Eden's visit (he is said to be taking Lord Moyne with him) I can't help, and don't much care about. He should get there and the tumult and the shouting should have died down, anyway, before we arrive. . . .

News from Athens is to the effect that the currency inflation has now

[21] On the return trip from the Moscow Conference, which ended on October 17, 1944, Churchill's plane stopped at Cairo.

quite reached the German stage of collapse after the last war, and nothing has been done about it. Wilson suggests that BMA notes be circulated (if this is possible!) more widely, backed by "assurances" from the British and Greek Governments. But it may be imagined how much weight these assurances will have, as the British steadfastly refuse to commit themselves to backing the notes with sterling or in any way making any financial advances or commitments to the Greek people who gave their all in this war. The Greeks are being treated in this matter as if they were conquered enemies, quite. It won't be at all wonderful if they turn *en masse* against the western allies, who must appear to them to be allies only when there is something to be got for it, and fall into Russia's arms. Not that they would get anything more from Russia. . . . The more I see of the coming job in Greece, the less I like it. Colonel West said that he was asked on all sides when we were coming back, that we are being eagerly awaited, and that he admired our courage! Allard said that he learned after the occupation and the diplomatic corps had left that Peggy and I were by far the most popular diplomats in Athens. All right. But Col. West's remark about the courage surely applies, though it isn't courage (except in Peggy's case) but only fate. Because we have some popularity, we are being sent back to spend it—it will soon enough be spent—and with nothing else to offer the Greeks but a policy of "no involvement" while the British blunder and the Russians advance. I figure that we shall end up disliked far more than we have been loved in the past. Well, we can only do our best, as I told the Colonel, and *that* we shall.

October 26, 1944, Thursday

Col. Aldrich called and brought me a couple of pyreth bombs to take to Greece. . . . The Colonel told me that the OSS "operational groups" and "Special Operations" men are going to be withdrawn from Greece as soon as possible. West is not going back, and Major Wines is taking his place for this evacuation business. Intelligence agents and "teams" will, however, continue in Greece for awhile if not indefinitely, and Colonel Aldrich asked my opinion of their value and proper status at this time. I told him I thought that now that the country is liberated and the Government established in Greece, the OSS there ought properly to function under the control and authority of the Embassy, and that as I think in addition that OSS intelligence work should be very useful for some time to come in Greece, perhaps it would be a good thing if the Department and the OSS should get together on the appointment of a Special Assistant to the Ambassador. Aldrich said he would report my views to General Donovan, and I myself sent a wire to the Department.

October 27, 1944, Friday

Bright to begin with, then cloudy as we moved west in our plane—General Giles' private DC3, the *Sheba*. . . . We are going roundabout via Benghazi to avoid Crete where the Germans still have anti-aircraft defenses. . . . After stopping a short while at Benghazi and being treated there to a "breakfast" of egg sandwiches and hamburgers, coffee, tomato juice, etc., we flew on to Greece. . . . Shantz and Sadler, with Spencer and, to our great joy, Calligas, met us on landing. . . . Greek friends began to call or send cards and even flowers, and Shan Sedgwick came in after dinner and talked excitedly for an hour or more.

October 28, 1944, Saturday

Today is the anniversary of the entrance of Greece into the War—the Italian ultimatum and Metaxas' famous "No." A *Te Deum* was held in the Cathedral, and Mummy and Shantz and I attended. Leeper and Mrs. Leeper were there with their staff, and the French Delegate and the Swedish-Swiss, together with some naval and military personnel, including "Jumbo" Wilson. The Cabinet faced us across the church, and there was a crowd of privileged civilians as usual, but very few faces among them which I recognized. Damaskinos officiated, leaving out the prayer for the King and the Royal Family, and Papandreou was the only one to kiss the cross at the end. Music very good. Papandreou waved his hand to me across the church with smiles, but afterwards greeted Wilson before anyone else. Outside in the square there was some shouting during the ceremonies and the whole place was packed with delegations of EAM, KKE, and so forth, bearing banners calling for "Death to Traitors." The streets were lined with screaming youngsters—paid, I am told, to demonstrate—repeating over and over again the slogan "Laos, Kratia," [Laokratia]—"people, power." But order was kept pretty well by the police. . . . I spoke with Mantzavinos and Zolotas, the new Governor of the Bank of Greece—Varvaressos has resigned—in the church. Mantzavinos has been in London all the time and looked sleek. When I said I hoped that something could be done soon about the currency—the gold pound is worth now some six trillion drachmas—they said, virtually, "that depends on you," meaning, I take it, the Anglo-Americans. I let them see that I didn't subscribe wholly to this idea, but I am sure we must help, or there will be chaos here shortly. The currency question is closely tied in with the supply question, and both are at the root of the widespread unemployment. Unfortunately very little has been done regarding these matters to date. There is no complete, coordinated plan in operation, only tinkering, and the situation is becoming riper and riper from the Communist point of view. It is even suspected that the communists are sabotaging such tinkering as is being done. . . . In the afternoon there were more calls, cards and flowers. Our arrival has not been publicized but our friends have heard of it somehow, and their welcome is very touching. All we can do for them is to say how glad we are to be back, give them little gifts of soap, cigarettes and candy, and above all, listen to their stories. . . . Dinner at the British Embassy with Mr. Eden, Mr. Macmillan, and others, including Mr. Mitchell, the Chief of the Division of Liberated Areas in the Department, who has flown over here from Italy on a brief visit. Mr. Eden was very cordial, but when I stated that the military has unloaded only 2,000 tons of food for the Greek people in the last 15 days at the Piraeus, he became much excited and insisted the figures were all wrong. Harry Hill had just given me these figures during my talk with Sadler. When the smoke cleared away it appeared that Eden was talking about military as well as relief supplies, and naturally our figures differed! He has aged noticeably since I saw him here last in 1941. His hair is grey instead of auburn, but he seems the same old play-boy, the Noel Coward of diplomacy, taking the same opportunist attitude toward affairs, trying to cure grave situations with haphazard expedients. It seemed clear, too, that he felt his presence here constituted in itself a great concession, which should do much to set things right. Both before and after dinner, which was served in the main hall (the dining and reception rooms still being full of stored furniture) and consisted of dolled-up army rations, he held frantic and hasty conferences with British and Greek officials, and told me with pride that [he] proposed telegraphing to London and Cairo to have 300 trucks sent at once, and a lot of luxury articles such as coffee and cosmetics shipped in here by air for sale by the Greek Government to augment its revenues; and, finally, that on the financial side he had arranged for a new expert from London to come here post haste (a Sir David Waley). Of a coordinated economic and financial plan which would give the currency the backing it needs and build up speedily a supply situation which would break the black market and provide work for the unemployed, he seemed not to be thinking at all, and certainly there are no other signs of any such plan being in contemplation.

October 29, 1944, Sunday

Got off my first telegraphic report, sending it via Caserta through General Sadler, as the Cable and Wireless Company will at present take only journalists' messages. In conclusion I said that I could not too strongly emphasize that the economy of Greece has been completely broken down, that its people are in a feverish condition of undernourished excitement on the verge of another winter, and that there are no reserve stocks of supplies anywhere to be had, the supplies offered at fantastic prices on the Athens market being only a drop in the bucket of the nation's need. Unfortunately, and despite repeated warnings, the ML has counted on certain supplies being available here and as a result of what turns out to be the case, it cannot provide a minimum ration of 2,000 calories as planned. What supplies it has been able to unload have remained on the docks. Barter is the usual mode of exchange in the country districts, and already has begun to be employed in Athens, while the drachma continues to be issued in notes of astronomic denominations, prices to sky-rocket and morale to sink. Unless the terrible experience of the winter of 1941-1942 is to be repeated here, and a situation demanding the despatch of more troops to keep order, together with relief on a scale beyond anything yet contemplated, energetic action must be taken now, I said, to increase supplies and accelerate their distribution. I have little hope that much will be done, however, and I foresee a worsening of the situation which will bring actual uprisings and bloodshed both in Athens and in the country districts. The Department will, I am sure, heed my warnings, but "military responsibility" and lack of British willingness to contribute sufficient supplies and troops from what they have in the Middle East to cure the demoralized condition here, will do the trick. . . . Leeper came around to see me. He said that as a result of Eden's visit, a new committee is to be set up (how the British love committees!) to advise General Scobie on ML matters. It appears Scobie is now in charge of these here, as well as of operations, and Hughes is sidetracked in Italy. The committee is to have a financial and a supply expert, and a political adviser (our old friend Harold Caccia!) representing Macmillan, the adviser to General Wilson. Lord Halifax is to be asked to approach the Department with a view to our appointing similar members to this Committee "to preserve the Anglo-American character of ML." I telegraphed the Department that we would welcome a U.S. treasury expert at this time, and recommended that one be attached to the Embassy; he and Harry Hill (for supplies) could then be delegated to sit on the Committee, if the Dept. wants us to join it. But I said I wouldn't recommend that any such official come here unless attached to the Embassy, and in particular I felt strongly that the political man on the Committee should represent the Embassy to Greece.

November 1, 1944, Wednesday

The Government is planning to stabilize the currency within a week or ten days, and is putting in a plan whereby corporations and private businesses can issue promissory notes with the endorsement of the Bank of Greece to be discounted (heavily no doubt) on the stock exchange for the payment of salaries and food allowances. This will save the Government a part of its present enormous expenditure on such allowances and cut down the necessary printing of money. Of course most businesses will not be able to redeem the notes, and they will then issue stock which will be taken over by the Bank of Greece for the account of the Government, thus taking control out of private hands—a procedure right up the Socialist street. Mr. Svolos told Harry Hill that the Government would not hold the stock but would sell it to the public. But that remains to be seen. . . . He complained to Hill that the Americans do not seem interested in helping Greece in these troubles, and Hill promptly replied that we are here and will be glad to give our advice and counsel if asked, but will not intrude it on the Greeks. As a result Angelopoulos, the Under-Minister of Finance, called me up this evening and invited me or my representative to attend tomorrow's big conference of the Government, the Military and Sir David Waley, the new British Treasury expert just arrived. I replied that I have already told Harry Hill to attend, as I understood Mr. Svolos to have expressed a wish to that effect. . . . During the afternoon I had a call from Sir David, who is a very nice and simple and even humorous man, hoping he can help here, but extremely poorly informed on Greece. He said and repeated (till I caught him up, but really I couldn't let it go!) that all the Greeks need to live on is bread and olive oil.

November 2, 1944, Thursday
Brief talk with Mr. Archer, who tells me that the Swedish-Swiss Commission, which has consented to distribute ML supplies in the Athens (and Thessaly) area, now wants to terminate the arrangement as of Dec. 15. He is discouraged over the supply setup and is thinking of recommending that the UNRRA withdraw completely during the Military Period, as he thinks the ML may be trying to put UNRRA out in front to take the blame for its own mistakes. Spencer brought in the ML Major who is "in charge" of the Athens district. Name of Glafka. He said that the chief trouble with unloading supplies comes from the fact that the Germans provided the dock-workers with food, which was distributed at soup-kitchens and canteens in the port, and that as the British won't do that, the workers, who often have to come miles to their work barefoot, or in ruined shoes and hungry into the bargain, naturally strike. They don't want money because they don't know what its value may be next day, and they need nourishment. However, the policy of ML which goes right back to the CCAC,[22] is not to feed one category of workers if others can't be fed. . . . Leeper held a press-conference of British journalists

---

[22] CCAC: Combined Civil Affairs Committee.

this morning and excluded the Americans because he was going to talk about "things they wouldn't understand." Incredible, but apparently true enough, and are the Americans mad! . . . Telephoned the Foreign Office and asked young Matsas to tell the Premier that I am at his disposal to come and see him any day at any hour if there is any way in which he thinks I can be of help in the present difficult situation of the country; that, so far, I have waited for him to let me know if he wanted me, because I knew how busy he is, etc., etc. My idea, of course, has been not to put myself forward, but to let the British hold the stage, in order to make it fully clear here from the start that, as the President said, "we are not involved." Now I think I have let our cousins get out far enough ahead to permit me to take my normal course. . . . Harry Hill came in and told me that the long financial conference this afternoon came to nothing, but will be continued tomorrow.

November 3, 1944, Friday

General Scobie called at 5 o'clock, bringing with him another General, who is a supply Chief on Wilson's staff. Scobie has been made commander of the district of Attica, and has the Athens police, *gendarmerie*, fire brigade, and Evzone Guard directly under his orders. The local authorities are thus strengthened for the keeping of order. The justification of course is that Greece as well as her Allies is still at war. The decree was issued by Papandreou in his capacity as War Minister. Scobie gave me a lot of information which may be interesting to the Department. He said that the 4th Indian Division is to be used not only in the Salonica area, but in the Peloponnese, and perhaps also, later, in Crete as well. It contains, he said, a lot of white officers and men; all the gunners are white, and the Division is the "best disciplined" of the Indian outfits, and very tired, so that he feels it won't make any trouble (!). The Greek Mountain Brigade, which has been fighting in Italy, will be brought over to Athens at once, without its heavy equipment (to save transport space) and the first of the new classes to be called up, the 1935 class, is expected to be already equipped with British arms and uniforms (green battle dress) by the third week of this month. This new force will be called the "National Guard" and as soon as it is on foot, the guerrilla forces will be ordered to disband, as being no longer necessary to the nation's security. Scobie said that the brigade coming from Italy is very "rightist" in its politics, but on the whole the Government and he think its coming will be useful in the circumstances. He intends to warn all the officers that politics will not be permitted. This sounds fine—makes sense to a Britisher. But to a Greek? I fancy if soldier politics aren't indulged in while Scobie and his troops are around, they won't delay to appear when the field is clear.... All these arrangements are clearly being made to confront and discourage the communist influence in the country, now so strong on account of unemployment and lack of supplies.... Then Harry Hill came in, and Mr. Svolos, and we three had a talk on stabilization and the food situation. I told the Minister of my repeated efforts to acquaint my Government with the seriousness of the situation here, and when he left he thanked me "for what you *are going* to do." The possibility of getting a large amount of sesame seed oil from Egypt and Turkey, owned by the U.S. and U.K. Governments, is still open, but people are putting difficulties in the way. To get this oil here to supplement olive oil supplies is most important, and I asked Harry Hill to draft a telegram about it. Svolos said the stabilization plan which Harry showed me is the Government's plan, approved by Sir David Waley, with a few basic observations of his own added. It is hoped to put it into operation next Friday. Small notes of the new currency are being printed here and big ones in England. A certain amount of the latter will be flown here, but as the whole amounts to many tons, the bulk will have to come by ship later. The old currency will be called in for exchange against the new at banks and post offices before a certain date, and meanwhile sufficient supplies of basic commodities will have to be made available in the country so that prices on them can be fixed in terms of the new currency without danger of the cost of living sky-rocketing again and the value of money falling in proportion.

November 4, 1944, Saturday

Conference with Sandstrom[23] of the Swedish-Swiss Commission and Archer of the UNRRA. Sandstrom said that the Commission's task of helping the civil[ian] population to live under the German and Italian occupation is now over, and the political situation here now is not such as to facilitate its efforts to assure distribution without discrimination. It therefore seems the time [for the Commission] to cease functioning. On the other hand the Commission wants to help the Greek Government in its task of switching over to a new method of distribution, and therefore it is willing to continue to help the Government and ML for a while. The date of Dec. 15th has been set as that on which the Commission would relinquish responsibility, and until that date it will distribute in the Athens area and the provinces naturally supplied from Athens, including Thessaly for the time being, but only till the military can take charge there. After that and until the 15th December, the area will be roughly east of the central mountain range from Thessaly to Corinth.

[23] A. Emil F. Sandstrom, President of the Swedish Greek Relief Commission.

In addition, delegates of the Commission will act in advisory capacity, and even in some cases, where the Government is at present unable to function, as at Patras, to supervise distribution temporarily. Sandstrom particularly emphasized that in order to assure non-discriminatory distribution, not only in the provinces but in Athens as well, it will always be necessary to have a foreigner on every distributing committee.... During the morning a large delegation besieged the Prime Minister's office bearing exhumed bodies and crying "Death to the Traitors." A pretty sight, and one indicating the need for Scobie's authority over the police, which are helpless to stop such things. Immediately following this gruesome delegation was another of neatly dressed school-boys and girls demanding the reopening of the schools. As Hudson remarked, truly an anticlimax!

November 5, 1944, Sunday

I went over to the British Embassy and had a long talk with Leeper, who promised to get Scobie to protect our Consulate in Salonica for the time being. We discussed many things. He said the Government here has just let the regency question go by default, for lack of interest and because of the pressure of other affairs. The King operates exactly as he would if he were on a voyage to London, and Leeper supposes that when the new ministers took the oath in the presence of Papandreou and the Archbishop, the former had authority from the King to represent him for the occasion.... Leeper said he is advising Papandreou to concentrate on getting things started in the capital, and not to worry too much about the provinces, recalling to him the method used by Lenin and Trotsky in dealing with a country "in dissolution." Secure the capital first and move outwards from there. Scattering efforts in the provinces cannot be nearly so successful. He said he thinks that the Communist Party is going to lose gradually its support from the socialists, and that as order is restored through British influence, many parties will start up leaving the communists relatively weak and isolated, though he also thinks the old parties are now substantially defunct. The problem of the King is now not exciting anyone, isn't, in fact, practical politics for the time being, but he thinks that fear of communism is perhaps strengthening royalist sentiment at the expense of the old line Venizelists and republicans. I agree with all this, and Siantos's recent statement about his party being for "democratic solutions" and there being no more need for partisan forces now that a National Guard is to be formed, falls in with it. For the moment danger of a red terror seems to have been removed, with communist leadership turning to political maneuver rather than direct action—and this will certainly be a losing game for that leadership in Greece. However, the danger is not far removed. Starvation and disorganization are what may bring it right back again, and we have just begun to bring in supplies and to start up the country's economic machine once more. A bad hitch in our efforts, such as a failure of the stabilization now proposed, might cause a worse collapse than anything the country has yet seen, and the general feebleness of the Government augurs ill for its ability to impose the regulations and restrictions necessary to a successful conversion of the currency with its concomitants of price and wage fixing, exchange control, *et al.* Despite the cooperative attitude of the communist leaders, and despite Scobie's assumption of police power, demonstrations still take place in the city and the suburbs are unsafe. Thus the social waters are still cloudy and easily to be disturbed still further.

November 6, 1944, Monday

Harry Hill reported that Scobie was depressed this morning over the Government's continued weakness. Yesterday the *gendarmerie* and the police together staged a jail delivery [unauthorized freeing of prisoners] of some 700 prisoners, and tomorrow the communists are threatening to attack the Averoff prison and lynch the political prisoners [collaborationists] found there, apparently in celebration of the Soviets' "October Revolution." Scobie thinks he can defend the prison all right, but has been told by the Government that they can do nothing to control the communists. Yesterday, according to Larrabee, there was some shooting right across from our Embassy, and some supposed fascists in the apartment house on the corner were casualties. The police arrived promptly, but let the little battle take its course. Scobie's position is certainly unenviable, with so few troops of his own to support him, and the Greeks proving unreliable at every turn. I wonder if the Government is going to be strong enough even to impose the regulations which must accompany the stabilization, now being planned for next Friday. Without the confidence of the people and without strength to enforce the law, it will certainly have a hard time, even if ML gets in enough supplies to make the stabilization feasible,—which itself is doubtful. . . . Sasserville, now Deputy Director of the WSA[24] for Greece, came in. . . . He said that American vessels cannot be expected before a month or six weeks. There is a shipping bottle-neck just now owing to the intensification of the Pacific War. . . . In the afternoon Rodney Young brought in Capt. Else, who is to take his place directing OSS here for the present, Rodney devoting himself from now on mostly to UNRRA. Else said Col. Aldrich may come over, but not before the 8th. The movement of evacuation of our O.G.[25] people

---

[24] WSA: War Shipping Administration (American).
[25] O.G.: "Operational Group," a team of agents operating behind enemy lines.

is under way, and there are already some twenty "commando" men in Athens. I hope they don't stay long, and that as few more as possible come to the capital. We are trying so hard to keep it clear that militarily we are "not involved" here,—and the departure of the O.G.'s is due to that very fact. Yet the Greeks seeing them around the streets will easily, too easily, conceive that the American Army is coming—not going!

November 7, 1944, Tuesday

General Othonaios has been made C-in-C of the Greek Army (I understand Plastiras was offered the post some time ago by Papandreou but refused it, being unwilling to take the oath to the King). The ELAS has been adopted into the official ranks by being made the guardian of security throughout the country (except in Zervas's area) from now until Dec. 1st when the class of 1935 now being called up will take over and be the National Guard. Then, on Dec. 10th, the guerrilla bands will be disbanded.... The *Gendarmerie*, which is now being displaced by the ELAS because it simply isn't functioning, will be reorganized and purged, and then absorbed into the army. In the Athens-Piraeus area, the local police will not be changed, apparently, at least for the present. General Scobie, at the meeting today of his advising committee, said that he has forbidden all demonstrations today in honor of the October Revolution, except a celebration scheduled at one of the theatres, and that he thought he would be able to see that his orders in this connection are obeyed. He also feels that the EAM will not oppose the disbanding of the guerrillas on Dec. 10th. On the other hand, it is doubtful if the disarming of the guerrillas—and all other Greeks who have been able to obtain arms during the occupation—will take place for a long time.... I got off a telegram to the Department on all this, and as a matter of fact, Scobie's predictions have been in part fulfilled, for the day has passed without any particular trouble. There was no attempt, as feared, to storm the Averoff prison and lynch the Quislings.... Got a telegram from the Department, sent on November 1st (through AFHQ) stating that the British have been assured by the Turks that they will not oppose Greece's claims to the Dodecanese.... That is all well and proper,—and good news.... Harry Hill advised me of the Government's decision to put off stabilization from Friday to Sunday, on account of the impossibility of getting the new currency printed in time for the former date, and delays in forming the necessary laws and regulations. Mr. Maximos called me up and said that Mrs. Rallis, wife of the Quisling Prime Minister, now awaiting trial, wants to see me, and suggested that I come to his house tomorrow afternoon, where she will be. I said I could not be involved in the matter of her husband's fate, but agreed to go to his house at his request since he is such an old friend, and tell the lady myself that I can't interfere. Not a very pleasant task. The man made his bed and must lie on it now, but it isn't very agreeable to have to tell a panic-stricken woman that one can't help her! I am reminded of the days following the 1935 "revolution," when I had to turn down the last minute appeal of General Kimissis's wife and daughter. . . . It is said that tomorrow the Mountain Brigade from Italy will arrive and parade through Athens. As this outfit is supposed to be very much on the right of the fence, it will be interesting to see what happens. It is to be quartered at Goudi—which lies between Psychico and Hymettus.

November 8, 1944, Wednesday

Called on Leeper and discussed with him the question of the Quislings. He said that he has not spoken with Papandreou about it, and thinks he will do nothing unless the Government asks him, when he will consult London. I pointed out that it is not a purely Greek matter, and the Quislings everywhere are falling into the same position, and he mentioned that his government has not interfered in France. We then discussed the present "state of the Nation" and he described it as "anarchy pure and simple." He thinks Papandreou could be much more exigent with the EAM ministers without risking their leaving the Government, and he is constantly pressing the Prime Minister in this sense. . . . Leaving Leeper's I went to see Maximos, and told him that after our talk on the telephone I had thought the matter over and believe it would be best for me not to see Mrs. Rallis, but that he might tell her he had talked with me, and that I cannot take any initiative, though I would consult my Government if the Greek Government should express a desire to have the opinion of its allies on the general question. Mr. Maximos showed himself quite understanding, and said he thought he could tell her, too, that it would not be to her advantage to bring foreigners into the affair. This is so true, in view of the jealous nationalism of the Greeks, that it might actually prejudice her husband's case fatally, and I applauded Maxy's suggestion. We all know how British interference precipitated the execution of "the Six. . .". Commander Spencer came in and said that he has word from the outlying districts in the Salonica area that if British troops arrive there (and they are on their way) they will be met with antagonism by the local bands, if not the inhabitants in general. I have had reports before of anti-British, mainly communist, sentiment in Kavalla. . . . By noon I was already receiving *written* congratulations on F.D.R.'s election from Greeks, but no really trustworthy or significant returns. At 3 p.m. the B.B.C. announced that "President Roosevelt has been reelected" and on the basis of its reports from New York stated that he would carry New York, Pennsylvania, Illinois and California, without which it would seem clear that Dewey cannot win.... The United States may be showing some of its famous horse-sense at this critical moment. ... Shantz told me how Lord Moyne was assassinated the other day,— we only had brief news by radio. Two members of the "Stern" gang in Palestine came specially to Cairo to kill him, hid in the entrance to his Gezira house, and shot him and his chauffeur as they were returning from the office for lunch. The *aide-de-camp* escaped. Only a few days previously Lord Moyne, a peaceful, inoffensive old gentleman if ever there was one, had asked that there be no guard on his house in the day time! He was hit three times and died sometime after eight in the evening. His assailants were chased and caught by an Egyptian motorcycle cop, who braved their fire as they fled away on their bicycles, wounded one and rode the other off into the ditch. The King (of Egypt) has decorated the cop, and indeed such Wogs must be rare....

November 9, 1944, Thursday

The Mountain Brigade returned from Italy and paraded through the streets of Athens, passing our windows in the office. Peggy was below and watched along with "Loopy" from his office, and he became so overcome with enthusiasm that he insisted on breaking out a bottle of Greek wine.... There were no incidents in connection with the parade, but much public enthusiasm. However, it seems the EAM is already spreading the rumor about that the royalists intend using the brigade to mount a *coup d'état*.

November 10, 1944, Friday

Called on Mr. Papandreou in the forenoon. He is optimistic, but says the crisis is coming when the days arrive for demobilizing the guerrilla bands,—Dec. 1st and 10th. He spoke of his difficulties in trying to establish government in this demoralized country "by political means only and without force to impose it," and again asked my aid in insuring the necessary supplies and credits. He thinks fear of communism is reviving royalist sentiment, particularly in "old Greece," but didn't betray any feeling, either *pro* or *con* in this connection. The Liberal Party, he said, though participating in the government, is providing at present his only political opposition, but this he thinks is not very important, and the old parties no longer have much influence.... From other sources, I believe he is right regarding royalism—and it seems to be spreading even among erstwhile liberals, as a *pis aller*. But this is far from saying that the King would win in a fair plebiscite.... Papandreou emphasized that the whole north of Greece is "democratic"—and we have always known this to be the case. At no time since I have been in Greece would a fair plebiscite have favored the dynasty "whose strength is the love of its people," and since 1935 there has been the connection of the King with Metaxism which has sunk his cause incalculably in popularity.... I asked Mr. Papandreou whether the Quislings are going to be shot, and he said "there will have to be some executions. Otherwise the communists will take things into their own hands, and the Government's prestige will suffer, and probably also injustices occur." I asked him whether he would lump Metaxists in with the traitors, and he said no law has yet been passed against those implicated in the régime of the 4th of August, and that perhaps none would be, but that Greece has suffered too much from that tyranny for it to be overlooked: "That is why we must have a plebiscite on the régime. If the King hadn't supported Metaxas, this question would never have arisen."... Maynard Barnes... is going to Bulgaria as the U.S. Government representative, with the rank of Minister.... He feels that the job he has been given may not last long, that the Russians are likely to push so hard for arrangements in the Balkans in accord with their own individual interests that the British and Americans, so weak in this part of the world, will be unable to hold them off, and that the end may be that a South Slav state, consisting of Yugoslavia plus Bulgaria will be set up, isolating Rumania, which will then become virtually a part of the Soviet Union, and inevitably Greece will be pried loose from contact with Turkey. He said that the feeling of the Department as regards Russia now is that no matter how one deals with her she cannot be trusted, that at the very moment when her statesmen are talking reasonably and openly with you they are engineering unspeakable things behind your back; and that Harriman himself has recently come to feel the same way, and is now said in the Department to have been actually Americanized by his Soviet experiences. I should like to check this in a talk with Averell. It doesn't sound like his remarks to me reported in this diary, but Barnes says his change of heart has occurred since the latest Churchill visit to Moscow.

November 11, 1944, Saturday
Lunch at the Grand Bretagne, given by Papandreou as a farewell to Sir David Waley. Men only,—those who have been working with Sir David, mostly; Bank of Greece men, ML, Government finance men and their advisers. Papandreou, Sir David, and Macmillan made speeches.... Though the speeches at lunch today were marked by optimism, both Waley and Macmillan cautioned that we cannot be sure that the stabilization begun today will succeed, and after lunch Hill told me that the

Government is doing nothing to get rid of its vast over-stock of paid employees, while as yet it has no adequate revenues in sight! Apparently Papandreou is shy of bearding the communists, whose Minister of Labor, Porfyrogenis, is the source of this trouble, and wants the Allies to put such pressure on him as may be necessary! Hill also told me that the Greek Government has heard from Diamantopoulos in Washington that our Government is willing to let a certain amount of emigrant remittance money come over, but the Bank of Greece is planning to grab it and not let it go to the intended recipients. If this is the case, I doubt if we shall let it come after all.

November 13, 1944, Monday

Mr. Archer came in and told me of the new arrangement as regards the Swedish Commission and UNRRA. Stockholm has advised the Commission that if the Swedish ships are to continue to bring supplies, some members of the Commission must stay here to guarantee non-discriminatory distribution; so Sandstrom is staying, along with several others, and ML and UNRRA are planning a "policy committee" to include the Swedes, which should be acceptable to the Greek Government. The last named, after Dec. 15 (the date when the commission is to cease functioning as such) will handle distribution with the aid of ML and UNRRA, under guidance of the Committee. UNRRA is bringing over a lot of personnel to take part in distribution, and the Committee will advise on the problem of what Greek personnel to retain out of the Swedish-Swiss organization which has become so unpopular. Meanwhile the Swiss have not been consulted, and are very sore about it. Deglutz, who has gone to Geneva, may seek instructions, and it is possible that the Swiss will demand representation on the Committee—or they may withdraw altogether. The Swedes and Swiss get on together like cats and dogs, and both similarly with the Greeks, though recently the Greek Government has taken pains to express its proper thankfulness to the Commission and protect it against popular demonstrations of antipathy.

November 14, 1944, Tuesday

Visit from a group calling itself the Council for Eastern Rumelia. The head man read me a lengthy document claiming the ancestral right of Greece to a large part of Bulgaria. I feel it is hardly practical politics to press such claims today, but much which was contained in the document was perfectly sound and ought to be heeded. If justice is to be done to Greece, she must be compensated for what Bulgaria has done to her— not once but repeatedly—and must be protected in some way from further aggression and atrocious spoliation. But will justice be done? Despite lip-service given to Greece by statesmen, and the devotion of philhellenes in all countries, which has influenced leaders to give her praise and even promises, the Foreign Offices of the Great Powers have for years past, consistently favored Bulgaria, for whose treacherous conduct on repeated occasions not the feeblest justification can be found. This is true of our own Department of State. The phenomenon is a curious one with us, but it exists, and I fear will continue to do so, while with England, her claims in the region of the Straits have always ruled her policy here. Only Russia has at times (as for instance, after Navarino) supported Greece. But now her interests too are drawing her to overlook Bulgaria's most recent treacheries. Given the Department's traditional preference for Bulgaria (never in accord with the feelings of the American people but due, I am told, to abler diplomatic representation on the part of Bulgaria) and the selfish interests of the other Great Powers, it will be lucky for Greece if she gets the barest recognition of her most elementary rights after this war, and if she becomes impertinent to an impractical degree, she may not get even that. Nevertheless, I shall forward the document presented me by my over-sanguine friends pointing out the justice of most of it, which needs, God knows, to be emphasized. . . . General Hughes came in for a formal call. He expressed himself as pleased with the development of the supply situation. He said it is now going according to plan, but admitted that the plan should be enlarged. He also said that the recent visits of big-wigs—Eden, *et al.* had somewhat distorted the situation, but that now it was settling down and good work is being done. He and Sadler are both now deputies to Scobie, for ML. Sadler will have his Hq. here, but Hughes will have some work to do in Italy—not much at present,—for Albania and Yugoslavia. Actually the great test of ML and UNRRA too, which is more important, is coming in this country. . . . Mr. Delmouzos paid his formal call as Director General of the Foreign Office. He confirmed my understanding that the Crown Prince's regency has lapsed, now that the King gets all the decrees to sign. On urgent matters his consent is requested telegraphically to have his signature affixed here. Delmouzos "believes" that the Constitution of 1911 provides that in the King's absence the Government acts as a regency council, and that this provision may have covered the recent taking of the oath of the new Ministers in the presence of Papandreou.

November 15, 1944, Wednesday

In the afternoon the OSS counter-espionage man came in and told me that the British CIS[26] has telegraphed Wilson that the EAM and ELAS

---
[26] CIS: Counter Intelligence Service (British).

3. Athens, November 17, 1944. Arrival of Greek Air Force units from Italy. From left: Lt. Gen. Ronald Scobie; Gen. Alexander Othonaios; Ambassador Reginald Leeper; Adm. Charles E. Turle; Ambassador Lincoln MacVeagh; Greek Air Force officer.

may try a *coup d'état* to forestall the disarming of the guerrillas due to take place on the 10th December, and asking urgently for reinforcements, including tanks, to protect strategic localities and installations. I doubt if the leftists want really to risk all on a fight with the British and Greek regulars, but they may wish to frighten the Government in their campaign to force concessions. Or they may want to provoke action from the right, to which they could reply as a democratic movement and thus cement in their support the elements which have been helping them so widely under the occupation. On the other hand, hot-heads may try anything at such a time as this, and in reporting to the Department I emphasized that the situation will bear watching. . . .

There continues to be a lot of shouting, with megaphones, in the streets for EAM—apparently paid agitators of the KKE or Communist Party, and there were a number of shots fired in the town again tonight. . . .

November 17, 1944, Friday

Two squadrons of Spitfires and one of Baltimores (36 planes in all) belonging to the Greek Air Force arrived from Italy, and the British put on a ceremony at the Kalamaki airfield to receive them, which I attended as well as Mr. Leeper, and Buelen, the French Minister. Papandreou, and Fikioris, the new Minister of Air, addressed the Greek troops. Among the "distinguished visitors" besides our rudimentary diplomatic corps, there were Generals Scobie and Othonaios, and Admiral Turle. I was glad that I went, despite the fact that the British as usual ranked the American Ambassador below the military and naval staff, even including the American Colonel Norcross, because I had the chance to meet General Othonaios after all these years. A slight but very soldierly looking figure. They say that he is not pleased with the British plans for reorganizing the National Army, feeling they are too favorable to the royalist party, but when Leeper asked Scobie if he had resigned as rumored, Scobie answered "No. Otherwise he wouldn't be here this morning!" But Scobie added that he is being kept "in the background for the next few weeks,"— i.e. I suppose, until the attempt is made to demobilize the guerrillas the British don't want to complicate matters with politics. . . . Leeper told me that he is much concerned over the lack of cooperation between the extreme left and other elements in the cabinet, and that Scobie yesterday summoned Zevgos and Porfyrogenis, and Siantos, the head of the Communist Party, and told them that unless more cooperation on their part is forthcoming, particularly in such matters as the fixing of wages at levels in keeping with the stabilization plan, and the maintenance of order, he will have to impose martial law. . . . Later Leeper saw Papandreou on the same subject, and this morning there was a long cabinet meeting at which (Papandreou coming to the review late, and confiding the result to Leeper briefly) it appears that the leftists decided not to break away from the Government at this time, which Papandreou told them they would have to do or collaborate more closely. At the same time, I understand they have told Scobie that they couldn't give him any assurances unless they know more clearly what is exactly the position of the British in this country. The civil affairs agreement between the British and Greek Governments—to which we are to adhere by a special protocol so far as relief and reconstruction are concerned—has not yet been signed. The Greek Government has been suggesting changes in the text agreed to in London and Washington. But Leeper said that he has persuaded Papandreou to sign now, and in view of the Communist attitude this may be a good thing. From other sources I learn that in addition to signing, the Greek Government will express the reservations it would like to make in the form of an accompanying letter. But the main thing is to get this matter settled, of exactly what rights in Greece the British and the (ML) Allied Forces have, as, incidentally I have been urging that it should be settled for many months past. Now it is being found damned inconvenient to have it hanging in the air! . . . The lack of collaboration in the Greek

Government, and the weakness which this causes is certainly a complicating feature in the present situation. Captain Else of the OSS came in and said that the first result of the British CIS appeal to Wilson has been orders for AFHQ to put a blockade around Athens, allowing no one who is armed to come in. At the same time, Calligas tells me that he has learned from friends that ELAS is concentrating in the Mandra area south of Eleftherae, and Mr. Karapateas, who has come from Kalamata for a few days here (we were able to give him some relief money and some food and other supplies out of Mummy's stores) said that the *andartes* in his region are all moving north. One still cannot say whether EAM will risk a showdown, but their movements are threatening, and Scobie's actions in reply are not only necessary to preserve order but are more and more verging on the kind of thing which might be pointed to by the leftists as savoring of foreign interference with Greek liberties— imposition of dictatorship by foreign force, etc. The EAM and the communists may be scheming not to make a *coup d'état* but, in advance of a plebiscite (which they doubtless want soon, if it is to be held at all) to put the rightists in the Britishers' pocket in the eyes of all Greece and benefit themselves from the reaction. . . . Worked on a long telegram to the Department trying to make this conjectural position clear, as well as reporting facts to date. . . . I hear that the ML has at last waked up to the possibilities of the 1,500 or so condemned trucks in Egypt which we tried weeks ago to get the UNRRA to buy, and they have become positively frantic over the necessity here for roofing materials and timber, which we have said for months would be necessary. On the whole, I don't think that anything could have been worse handled than the relief problem in liberated Greece up to this point. Between the planning of men who knew nothing about the country they were planning for, and refused to listen to those who did, and the jealousies and squabble of brigadiers, managers, directors, etc., all jealous of their authority, the real needs of the Greek people have gone unseen or been lost sight of. Now these needs face the reliefers on the home ground, and there is panic.

November 18, 1944, Saturday

Long talk with Mr. Kanellopoulos, now Minister of Marine. He admits the Government is weak, in the sense that the *bona fides* of the supposedly collaborating (yesterday's "crisis" he said is over) leftist ministers is not as clear as that of the Prime Minister and the others. But he strongly defended the Government's Fabian policy as the only one possible in the circumstances. Civil war must somehow be avoided and normal political life resumed. But he criticized the Liberals for acting as if parliamentary activity was already possible, and forming an "opposition."

FROM LIBERATION TO CIVIL WAR · 651

November 19, 1944, Sunday

Big parade of the communists to celebrate the 26th anniversary of the Party. Many Soviet flags, some British and American. Orderly marching, with cries of "What the people wills!" and "Plebiscite! Plebiscite!" This last a good omen perhaps, as showing that the chiefs, who dictate these slogans, are turning their followers' attention to political solutions. . . . I got a nice telegraph from the President which read in clear as follows: "At this time when your letters of recall as Ambassador to Yugoslavia are about to be presented in London by your successor, Mr. Richard C. Patterson, Jr., I desire to express to you my sincere and hearty appreciation of the splendid services you have rendered in a difficult and exacting mission. I thank you for the devotion and skill with which you have used your fine talents in performing the dual functions as Ambassador to both Yugoslavia and Greece. In your continuing capacity as Ambassador to Greece the problems of your office will be many and complex. With full confidence in the success which your leadership portends for this mission I send the greetings of old friendship and esteem." Selah!

November 21, 1944, Tuesday

Large parade of the communists and a mild speech by Mr. Siantos from a balcony of the Grande Bretagne. Good order preserved throughout. But the KKE with their signs and slogans and "megaphone boys" are getting on the nerves of the ordinary citizen. . . . Mr. Archer and Mr. Gustensang wanted to talk about UNRRA affairs in connection with ML. It seems still to be a moot point between the two organizations how far UNRRA is to operate, during the military period, as a separate entity. UNRRA maintains it is to be subjected only to policy control by ML, and the latter tends to try and absorb UNRRA into itself.

November 22, 1944, Wednesday

Finally got off a telegram concerning 5,400 tons of sesame seed and 6,000 tons of sunflower seed held in Turkey by the USCC[27] and the UKCC. The seed can be used here for pressing to make oil, badly needed. The delay has been due to ML discussions, but it has now decided to ask for this stuff, and I hope the Department may help. . . . SACMED[28] wired Scobie that he is prepared to recommend the raising of the calory ration here to 2,000 if the Greek Government will comply with Scobie's recommendations as to the fixing of wages here and the collection of

---

[27] USCC: United States Control Commission; UKCC: United Kingdom Control Commission.
[28] SACMED: Supreme Allied Commander, Mediterranean (General Wilson).

Government revenues from the sale of supplies to those who can afford it, and if Scobie can assure him that effective measures have been "satisfactorily arranged" to implement these two undertakings.

November 23, 1944, Thursday

Capt. McNeill, just back from a trip to Salonica, turned in an excellent report to the War Department which I summarized in a telegram. The ELAS is in complete control, but is cooperating with the British, though no love is lost on either side. . . . Colonel Larrabee reported that the Government's mobilization of one class (now the 1936 class, not the 1935 as previously stated) is liable to be only a very limited success, if a success at all. I said "slow and spotty" in my telegram to the Department. It starts tomorrow, and is to go in two stages, each one accounting for a certain number of districts. Whether and where the ELAS will obstruct are questions, and the Colonel reports that the Government has practically none of the necessary administrative machinery ready for the operation! . . .

Mr. Fodor has been to Macedonia and reports conditions substantially as seen by McNeill. He says there has been no trouble over the "color question" as regards the Indian troops. Says they are more "popular" than the British, and he thinks this may be because the Greeks have heard that the Indians resent British rule and therefore suppose the Sikhs in Salonica to be sympathetic with their own views in this connection. He said that in a recent "Free Macedonia" movement around Florina, fomented by the Germans and Bulgarian Communists, Greeks of all parties united under an EAM General to drive the Bulgars out.

November 25, 1944, Saturday

The British exchanged notes with the Greek Government on the functions of the British military in Greece. It had at last become necessary to hurry up this long delayed matter, which I urged on Leeper and the Department long ago in Cairo, because the Communists have been refusing to agree to the Prime Minister's proposals for the reorganization of the Army unless they first knew the exact status here of General Scobie and his troops. We are to associate ourselves with this agreement by a separate exchange of notes, so far as Relief and Reconstruction are concerned.

November 27, 1944, Monday

Lt. Kent . . . had written a very good report on the general situation which I sent to the Department with comments. The EAM he points out is not the menace its opponents claim, nor the pure patriotic organization its supporters call it. The thing is mixed. The communists do count for something in it, and are manipulating it to a certain extent. On the other hand, many members are real patriots, and in some places the organization has creditably supplied government when no government existed.

November 30, 1944, Thursday

The present government has been going through a series of crises, and in a telegram written last night and despatched this morning, I told the Department a major crisis may be impending. The leftists continue to view with suspicion the retention of the Mountain Brigade as a separate organization in the proposed new national army. They want to break up guerrilla and government cadres equally and reform the whole with a mixture in equal proportions. Failing that, they threaten to resign. The Government is attempting to palliate them by giving them a brigade of ELAS, to parallel the Mountain Brigade, but of course there would be an EDES formation too, and the air-force, and the Sacred Regiment, [Battalion]—so the rightists would predominate on the whole. Suspicions are understandable! But the British want the Mountain Brigade kept, saying that it is the only trained outfit of its size the Greek army has at present and should not be lost to the Allied Nations. To which the leftists reply: "Then why don't you send it back to Italy where it came from and where it can be used for the war effort? Why keep it here?" At the same time, it seems that Papandreou tries to be "a fixer,"—as Leeper said to me, —not a leader, and always agrees with the leftists when they ask for things, laying on the British his inability to comply! . . . The latest small crisis was over the appointment of officers for the new National Guard. It seems the leftist ministers were to be consulted, but Lambrianidis, the Under-Minister for War, and Papandreou's "man Friday," consulted them only in connection with a few names, and published the whole list nevertheless. Lambrianidis has been dismissed—kicked upstairs as Minister without Portfolio,—and General Sariyannis, an erstwhile Liberal who "went to the Mountains" when PEEA was formed, has been put in his place. Also General Ventiris, the Chief of Staff, also an ex-Liberal but one who has been "going royalist" in Egypt (the Crown Prince spoke to me of him in satisfied terms), has been relieved of his post and sent to London as M.A. . . .[29] These concessions to the left have infuriated the right, and Leeper has had (he told me) to work hard to keep Liberal ministers from resigning forthwith. But the chief crisis is coming over the terms of

[29] M.A.: Military Attaché.

the decree organizing the new Army, as above stated. Papandreou (backed by the British) is sticking by his guns. The Communists (Askoutsis and Porfyrogenis) will probably resign. The question then will be what will the EAM ministers, headed by Svolos do? If they go out with the Communists, it may mean that there will be no obedience on the part of the ELAS to Scobie's demobilization orders, and the leftist *"coup d'état"* which the British Military have so long been expecting for the 6th of December (and to meet which they have been asking for reinforcements) may not come in the guise of a *coup d'état* so much as in that of a civil war. . . . News about the first phase of the mobilization of the National Guard is more favorable than seemed likely at first. It has not been the success Papandreou said it was at dinner the other night. (He is always an optimist!) But many recruits have reported. Whether on Dec. 1st they will be able to take over arms from the ELAS guard, however, remains to be seen. I very much doubt it, myself. At best, there may be disbanding, but not disarming. I told the Department long ago that I did not believe Greece could be disarmed for many years, and I still think so.

December 3, 1944, Sunday

A big demonstration of the EAM was scheduled, and then last night, forbidden by Government orders. . . . Nevertheless, crowds gathered and attempted to force their way into Constitution Square. The police fired, and some people were killed, mostly women and children and other quite innocent paraders pushed on from behind. . . . Elsewhere, as for instance in front of Papandreou's apartment near our offices, and directly under my window on the corner of the Gardens and Herodes Atticus Street there was rioting and shooting, the police, however, firing blanks for the most part. I watched this business from my balcony, and heard bombs go off near the officers' club on Regillis Street, and near Constitution Square, and these I believe were thrown by the instigators of the riots and not by the police, but I cannot be sure. The crowd was not supposed to be armed, and I saw no arms in their hands. . . . The most remarkable thing I noted was the extreme youthfulness of the crowds, both male and female. There were many banners carried featuring "death to the traitors" (i.e. the collaborationists) and one I saw said "Death to Gonatas." The General is now in the black books of the KKE with a vengeance. He is accused of having favored the Security Battalions, but singling him out especially from among others who saw some value to the country in those questionable formations, may be owing to his connection with Plastiras, whose rumored recall by the Government might constitute a threat to the extreme left, in the sense that his known republicanism might wean away many now supporting the communists and diminish their present "cannon-fodder", built up so sedulously by propaganda, about the King's return and so forth. By discrediting Gonatas the reds may figure they can discredit Plastiras too. But this is drawing a long bow. . . . Other banners carried by the crowd were Soviet and American, and even British (!) flags. . . . Everywhere there were young men bellowing slogans through paper megaphones and waving the crowds on to face the police bullets. As I could see, these agitators whipped the people, especially the girls, into a perfect frenzy, and some of the latter ran out into the street and shook their little fists in the rifles' mouths. . . . One got the impression inevitably that here was a riot deliberately brought about and exploited by the leftist leaders to secure "martyrs" for their cause, and place the onus of ensuing trouble squarely on their opponents' shoulders. The mistake made by the Government in first trying to call off the demonstration too late, and then in not handling it with calm and the approved methods of control—fire-hose, night sticks, tear gas etc., and last but most important by the obvious means of breaking up the crowds at their source and not after they had all reached the entrance to the square—played into the leaders' hands. . . . After all this was over, I received a call from Mr. Maximos on the telephone, who said he wanted very much to see me. So I walked around to his little house in Lykiou Street. He said he had an idea for the solution of the crisis and would like to lay it before Mr. Leeper, but unfortunately he did not have his acquaintance, and so far had been prevented by mourning from making a call. The idea was that the Archbishop should take over the premiership, and call in all the real leaders of the political world to help him. Papandreou might stay in the cabinet in some capacity, but obviously not as premier after all that has happened. Mr. Maximos thought his own party, the Popular [Populist] Party, would agree to the idea. He has been, he said, offered the leadership of that Party, but refused, preferring to stay out of politics from now on. . . . I went back to the office and called Leeper, who said he would see Mr. Maximos at 5:30. I then walked back and told Mr. Maximos, and offered to send my car for him at that time, —not going myself, since we are "not involved." Of course, poor Maxy has no car of his own just now and his health is frail. . . . Drove out with Mummy to lunch with the Dragoumises in Kifissia. Family party, except for us, and very pleasant. The ELAS is in full control of Kifissia, with their warriors strolling about the streets and the little square. On the way out I saw a machine gun nest on the left of the road facing Athens and manned with helmeted ELASites. . . . Our electric light is cut off, but our water still runs and the telephone is working. Curfew has been declared for 7:00, and a general strike has been called for the Athens-Piraeus area tomorrow. No one is doing much work here now, of course, but this will mean the closing of the shops added to the breakdown of electric power, and perhaps water and telephone will also fail. Who knows? General Scobie issued a proclamation saying that he will "support constitutional government by all means in his power until free elections can be held..." The "means in his power" are not very great, and "free elections" have nowadays a very utopian sound!

December 4, 1944, Monday
Bleak and cold. . . . The general strike is on. . . . Long talk with Mr. Svolos, who came in to make his *apologia* for his resignation[30] and previous record in the government. The burden of his talk was to the effect that he has always tried to steer a moderate course, and keep the extremists on the left side in line, but that when, on the question of disbanding the Mountain Brigade, Mr. Papandreou told the communists that he was personally in accord with their views but that the British wouldn't let him comply, his (Svolos's) influence over the communists was gone for good. He blamed Mr. Papandreou's "weakness" for much of the present trouble. As regards the shooting affair of yesterday, he said that the Government's refusal to allow the demonstration in Constitution Square came too late at night (about 10:30) to make it possible to advise most of the prospective participants, and that he himself did his utmost to get it revoked for this reason. As regards the British, he made the best remark I have heard for a long time, though I wonder if he himself knew how good it was: "The British must give the Greeks at least the impression that they are a free people..." After his visit, Fodor and the correspondents of *Time* and *Overseas News* came in. They said that the leftist press published today a story to the effect that I had written a letter to Mr. Leeper protesting against British intervention in Greek affairs; that he had then come to see me and that I had reiterated my protests. All, of course, a pure invention. . . . After they left, Mr. Dragoumis came in, sent by Mr. Papandreou to inquire about the truth of this story, and I authorized him to issue a denial. But of course, as usual in such matters, the denial will never catch up with the story, and those who see both will simply believe whichever fits in with their own wishful thinking. . . . Mr. Hill came back from his ML conference and said that Caccia, Macmillan's representative here, has spoken of Mr. Maximos's visit to Leeper and had said that Maxy's proposals had made a real impression and that the British were grateful that I had sent him around. Sporadic shooting (sniping) in the streets all day, and by evening young battles seemed developing between ELAS reserves and the government

[30] The leftist Ministers, Svolos, Askoutsis, Tsirimokos, Zevgos, Porfyrogenis and Angelopoulos, resigned on December 2, 1944. General Ptol. Sariyannis, Under-Minister of the Army, resigned on December 4.

police in various spots—Omonoia Square, Philopappos, the Stadium. Phaleron and most of the Piraeus, except for the Naval Headquarters and the Cadet School at the tip of the promontory, and the actual dock areas being used by the British, are in ELAS hands. Harry Hill's car, parked in front of the Embassy, had a window broken by a shot from a sniper in the Royal Gardens, but luckily there was nobody in the car at the time. A stray bullet also came through Spencer's window on the top floor.

December 5, 1944, Tuesday
Called on Mr. Leeper in the morning to discuss the situation. He said that he had been much impressed by Mr. Maximos, who seemed to have no personal axe to grind. His suggestion that the Archbishop form a cabinet was a good one, too. Leeper had told him that he thoroughly agreed, and that Papandreou should step down but that the Greeks must make their own arrangements and that he, Leeper, should not appear in the matter unless they came to him. He is getting the idea that "the British must give the Greeks at least the impression that they are a free people." Maximos gladly undertook the task of seeing the Premier and the Archbishop, and both agreed. However, both the Liberals and the royalists had ideas of their own, and Papandreou then came to Leeper for help. Of course he could do nothing with Petros Rallis, who was simply downright against the Archbishop idea, but there seemed some chance of persuading Sofoulis. Leeper asked him to come round, and talked to him at length. The outcome: Sofoulis wants to be premier himself! At 84 years of age, too. Maximos said he thought this was at least a solution of sorts—not as good as getting the Archbishop, but at least something, and Leeper sent a telegram to London urging that Papandreou should step down in favor of a new deal. . . . Mr. Maximos [came in] to tell me of his talk with Leeper, and thank me for my part in putting them together. He seemed very hopeful of a solution, and while still feeling the Archbishop would be the better choice, said Sofoulis would do, in his opinion—though he couldn't see how any man at 84 would want the job. . . . The Greek police and the ELAS continue their civil war, and the latter are infesting the Royal Gardens with snipers. There was a lot of firing from the Evangelismos Hospital near the School (and our house). The hospital attendants are all armed it seems, and "communists" to boot. . . . We moved all the staff, except the naval attaché's people, radio operator, and messengers, home to Loring Hall, as the streets are no longer safe. . . . The story is that the British are "going into action" tomorrow, in their effort to "preserve order and protect constitutional government." We have only some very bad Cairo candles to light us, and must be very chary of these, as they are few and burn fast.

December 6, 1944, Wednesday

We are attempting to work at the School without files or codes or safes. Every now and again I can let one of the boys go to the office, where I have put Commander Spencer in charge, when there is a lull in the shooting, but this is rare. Clearly, the codes at least will have to be brought up here if fighting continues much longer. I can't let any of the girls go out in the streets. The battle is going on spasmodically all about us. The British have "come in." They have placed what we think to be a half-battery of 4.5's in the Infantry Barracks compound a few hundred yards from our house, on Kifissia road, and have already opened fire on the "Communist" suburb of Kaisariani. About four o'clock, British planes began machine-gunning the same locality, as well as the "dasos"[31] between it and Kifissia road, and the Stadium and the Ardettos, where the ELAS clearly has a powerful strong-point, whence snipers infiltrate into the Gardens. Snipers are all about us, and infest all the streets, so that circulation is very dangerous. . . . Americans who go about do so in cars with American flags, or on foot with flags sewn to their sleeves. When the flags are seen, the carriers are generally respected, but as the police fire in all directions, and the snipers too seem rather more "trigger-happy," as the saying is, than purposeful, the stray bullet is more to be feared than the aimed. . . . For me the day was too cluttered with talks and decisions on this and that to be detailed here. Peggy writes in her diary that "Snipers just back of the house shot down to the boulevard all day. Miss Capart, a Swiss Red Cross man and a girl brought in a letter from the EAM appealing to L. against the British." I imagine this will become a fairly frequent occurrence, through one channel or another.

December 7, 1944, Thursday

Very disturbed night with artillery, machine gun and rifle fire. Desultory firing continued all morning. Kaisariani, Pankrati, and Byron are strongholds of the insurgents, who have thoroughly entrenched themselves on and around the Ardettos and along the Ilissos southwestward across Syngros Boulevard to Kallithea. They also hold the lower parts of the town from there northward through the Agora and clear out Patissia from Omonoia Square, and around up Alexandra Boulevard back to Kaisariani. The British hold Constitution Square and Kolonaki, where we are, but little else. The Plaka is being bitterly contested. Sniping still in the Royal Gardens. The Prime Minister and others of the Government are at the Grande Bretagne, with the chief British officers. British Hq. is located a few buildings down University Street. . . . Our gar-

---

[31]*Dasos*: Greek for "woods."

den is frequently crossed by snipers' bullets, and we keep the staff indoors as much as possible. Trips to and from the office are made in cars with American flags, by officers only for the time being. . . . Collected all our water today from the pump in tins, as the town supply no longer reaching us. There has been some cutting of the mains, and the Hadrian Reservoir has been drained, but our trouble seems to be that we have been dependent, situated as we are fairly high up, on electric pumps to hoist the water, and these of course are no longer in operation. . . . Much firing all afternoon by 25 pounders installed by the British in the infantry barracks about a quarter of a mile from our house. The military barracks opposite on the right side of the boulevard extending out to the Goudi barracks, home of the Mountain Brigade, are furnishing the chief bone of contention nearby, but the guns shell Kaisariani and the Ardettos also. . . . Col. Hobbs said that a German officer has been caught (named Werner) firing an ELAS machine gun, and that the guerrillas have been gouging out the eyes of captured members of the Mountain Brigade. . . . During the evening I started a letter to the President expressing my views on the struggle that has now broken out. . . .

December 8, 1944
Athens, Greece

Dear Franklin:

As I have feared for many months,—it almost happened in Egypt, as you know,—the disciplinary British and the unruly Greeks have at last come to blows. Moreover, in trying to do what they aim to do here, namely, to "keep order" and "protect constitutional government" with the small forces at their disposal, the British would appear to have got a bear by the tail. Fighting has been going on between the British and the guerrillas since early morning the day before yesterday, and the British staff thinks the operation may last a long time. If it does, I very much fear for health conditions, as many of the dead are not being buried, and not only are relief supplies held up, but water-rationing has been abandoned and the Marathon Lake, already dangerously low, may soon be drained. In the higher parts of town there is already no municipal water, for lack of electricity to run the pumps, and the few old wells available are not safe. Meanwhile, areas around and in Athens which were cleared of guerrilla bands yesterday must be cleared again today because of reinfiltration during the night, and snipers are everywhere. Two men of the "loyal" Greek Mountain Brigade, taken by the guerrillas, were recaptured yesterday morning with their eyes gouged out (this is not a rumor, but the statement of a member of the British staff). A German named Werner was captured firing a heavy machine gun for the guerrillas, and other Germans, Italians and Bulgars are among the few prisoners taken.

Though German and communist instigation and leadership exist in this affair, however, and though primal and ugly Balkan passions have risen again to the surface here (as witness the eye-gouging), there are other factors which are of greater importance and bode worse for the future. There can be no question that thousands of the ELAS and EAM are genuinely convinced,—misled, if you will, but convinced,—that they are fighting for liberty and independence, like their ancestors, and in this they are fanatical. They believe that Mr. Papandreou and the British, who set him up as Prime Minister and are supporting him through thick and thin, even to the point of not letting him resign, intend to force the King back on the people together with the dictatorship for which they hold him personally responsible. Nothing the British say to the contrary in regard to this belief will these "patriots" even take seriously, and unfortunately little that the British actually do belies it. As Professor Svolos, the head of the EAM, said to me the other day most aptly and moderately, "The British *must* give the Greeks at least the impression that they are a free people." But this they have not been either deft enough or understanding enough to do, and I greatly fear that the opportunity which their attitude gives the communists (and just now the Germans too) to spread the idea among the Greeks that in opposing the British they are standing for freedom, opens the door to trouble which will not be terminated by "restoring order" or "defending constitutional government," but will last for years, with wide-spread bitterness and enduring disturbance, perhaps affecting British relationships with the peoples of all the Near Eastern countries. It is possible that the present outbreak might have been averted for the time being if Mr. Churchill had let the Government be reformed as suggested by his Ambassador here. Psychologically, a political new deal might have provided a palliative for the moment. But at bottom, the handling of this fanatically freedom-loving country (which has never yet taken dictation quietly) as if it were composed of natives under the British Raj, is what is the trouble, and Mr. Churchill's recent prohibition against the Greeks attempting a political solution at this time, if a blunder, is only the latest of a long line of blunders during the entire course of the present war.

Of course there are suspicions on the other side of the fence here as well. Not only the old royalists, but now also not a few of the old liberals who have vested interests (the intelligentsia are mostly leftists) are quite as convinced as the guerrillas of the correctness of their own point of view; and the rightist view is, of course, that behind the guerrillas' libertarian program lies an intention to impose a communist dictatorship. Many people are now wanting the King back not because they like royalism but because they fear communism. But the truth is that neither pure royalism nor pure communism has many followers in Greece today, while each enjoys accretions of strength, none the less dangerous for being fundamentally fictitious, from suspicions which are rife and growing among democrats with possessions, on the one hand, and among democrats without possessions but hungry, homeless and armed on the other. Mr. Svolos sadly commented to me, "At the bottom of the whole thing lies the King question." Dozens of old Athenian friends have similarly told me, "Communism is the fundamental issue." But the Greeks will never be quiet under any dictatorship, or suspicion of dictatorship, from either right or left. Therefore, I feel that a hopeful solution for the present situation must involve removing any such suspicions. There is much talk here of a plebiscite on the regime, which might solve the problem if properly handled. But any settlement here must not only be impartial, but accepted as impartial, if it is to be successful and civil peace ensue. This question of general acceptance is the crux. After what is now taking place, any settlement proposed by a British-installed government would never be accepted as impartial by the other side. Equally, one proposed by EAM, if by peradventure the guerrillas should win the present struggle here in Athens (though I don't see how the British could accept defeat) would never be regarded as impartial by the partisans of the right. Consequently it would seem that a neutral agency is indicated, and I believe that a commission on which British, Russian and American members should all sit, to guarantee impartiality, would do the trick. Let me repeat that fundamentally it is mutual suspicion that is the trouble in Greece today. It has led to the present fighting, and will lead to more, no matter how successful Mr. Churchill's undoubtedly benevolent severity may prove for the time being. Disarm such suspicion on both sides, however, and there is enough soundness left in the Greeks, despite all they have gone through, to warrant some hope that they may settle back to their relatively harmless normal state of political instability with the passage of time, the restoration of communication and the provision of food and shelter. Otherwise, communism will continue to exploit its present marvelous opportunities for still further collapsing the social order and creating a "Greek problem" to plague Britain, and us too in the background, perhaps for many years to come. Of course, I realize that to set up an International Commission is a serious affair, presenting many difficulties. But I give you the suggestion advisedly, believing that the problem to be solved is also serious. If Britain herself could be got to propose it, to save her "face" which is now deeply involved, this might go far towards setting her back on a "good wicket," even if it were never actually put into effect, but for success in composing Greek differences it would have to be implemented.

I have talked personally with the British Ambassador along these lines and he said that similar ideas had "come into his mind." He agreed fully as to the fundamental nature of the clash of suspicions here, and that something must be done "after the present battle is over" to disarm these suspicions. He said that he didn't want to see his government "associated with another dictatorship in Greece," and spoke of the possibility of a tripartite Commission of the three great powers to guarantee an equitable settlement of the nation's problems, mentioning the "precedent" of the three "guaranteeing powers" after Greece's war of independence. He said he would communicate these ideas to his Government, but added that he feared to go too far on the matter himself and thought the person most likely to succeed with Mr. Churchill would be you.

I am writing this letter under conditions of some peculiarity. Where I live there is now neither light, water, heat nor telephone, and around the office bullets fly about the streets so that I am forced to keep the staff away from there, except on missions warranting risk to life and limb. However, I would like to add that among the many thousands of telegrams which you received on your re-election, the one from my wife and myself was by no means the least heartfelt. In addition, I should like to tell you that my mother, in New Hampshire, got herself over to the voting place, where her age and illness hardly let her climb the steps, to vote for you. This I mention because I think you appreciate the gallant actions of spirited old ladies.

Affectionately yours,
Lincoln MacVeagh (2)

After December 8, 1944, the hazards and hardships brought on by the fighting in Athens, as well as the pressures created by the need to provide Washington with a running telegraphic account of the bloody events, caused MacVeagh to abandon his diary. He returned to it briefly on April 13, stunned by the news of Roosevelt's death, and finally gave it up following his entry for April 30, 1945.

Throughout the December revolt, during which his numerous telegrams to the Department gave full details of the vicious street fighting all around the city, MacVeagh concentrated on the possibilities of arriving at a compromise settlement. On December 11, he reported that the proposal to establish a regency under Archbishop Damaskinos, an idea which he had favored while in Cairo, was now receiving serious attention in Athens.[32] The next day, with Harold Macmillan and Field

---

[32] In the same telegram, MacVeagh also reported that the British forces in the capital were "insufficient to assure the defense of a city of this size" and that "Savage battles continue in many parts of Athens and suburbs today." *FR 1944*, V, 146.

Marshal Alexander in the Greek capital to review the situation, he telegraphed that the crucial decisions would have to be made in London: ". . . I am reliably advised that especially in connection with the safety of the city during the next few critical days General Scobie as well as the British Embassy is counting heavily on London's being persuaded to let the Archbishop assume the Regency."(3) And on December 15 he wrote:

According to the British Ambassador with whom I have just talked, the King has replied from London that he must have the advice of his Ministers before agreeing to the proposed Regency. Papandreou is already in agreement with the proposal and the British expect that the consent of the others can be obtained today. They feel that the solution proposed is most hopeful of success in stopping the civil war as the Archbishop is confident that he can deal with ELAS. His program if he is named Regent is to proclaim at once that if arms are laid down (1) there will be a general amnesty, (2) the British Army will see to it that no reprisals against ELAS occur, and (3) he will constitute a new government of all parties and resistance movements represented in the recent coalition.

I asked Mr. Leeper if there is anything that we could do to help bring the present dreadful conditions in Athens to an end and he said "I hope the American Government will support this effort as it constitutes the only reasonable hope of saving the Anglo-American (*sic*) position here." I personally feel that the effort is as well conceived as anything could be under the present circumstances, in which compromise and moderation appear essential, though the amnesty regarding which ELAS is reported to be particularly anxious, and the reacceptance of the Communist Party into the Government, are bound to be very unpopular with the extreme Right. Meanwhile, the British are continuing to bring in reinforcements and should have all of their two new divisions here today or tomorrow. Their plan according to the Ambassador is to show themselves strong enough to face any eventuality while at the same time attempting conciliation and placing the settlement of internal political questions squarely in Greek hands. (4)

But the political haggling continued, and the government and British troops were soon able to take the initiative. MacVeagh reported:

[*December 16, 1944*]:
British Ambassador has just told me that while Sofoulis as head of the Liberal Party telegraphed the King yesterday supporting the proposal to name the Archbishop as Regent . . . Papandreou unexpectedly failed to

concur, and persuaded the Cabinet that a better idea would be to have a regency council of three composed of the Archbishop, Plastiras and Dragoumis, present Under-Minister for Foreign Affairs. A telegram carrying this recommendation has, therefore, also gone to the King. It is obvious that if this council of three were to be set up it would strengthen Papandreou's chance of retaining the Premiership since it would remove the possibility of competition from Plastiras, and the naming of the Royalist Dragoumis would appear to have been included as a bait to secure the King's acceptance. However, both Leeper and Macmillan are much alarmed as well as disgusted at this recrudescence of political maneuvering at this critical time and believe—as I feel correctly —that passions can now be calmed only by the appointment of a single Chief of State enjoying the confidence of the people and by an act which will completely and clearly remove the King question from the present picture. They have, therefore, telegraphed Churchill that he should at all costs and today, if possible, persuade the King to appoint the Archbishop as sole Regent. (5)

Aware that Churchill continued to hope that his declared policy of "no peace without victory" would ultimately succeed, the Greek King refused to give in. MacVeagh informed the Department:

[*December 17, 1944*]:
The King's reply to his Government, received yesterday, was to the effect. . . . that he is not convinced that a Regency is necessary. This reply appears to have been owing, at least in part, to the fact that the Cabinet's telegram included, along with the suggestion of a council of three, a statement (unknown to the British Ambassador yesterday) that the Ministers were themselves not in favor of a regency and were making their suggestion only because the British desired such a solution. On receipt of the King's answer, Mr. Leeper and Mr. Macmillan conferred last night with the Archbishop and Mr. Papandreou, and the last-named promised that he would telegraph the King again today stating, this time, that it is the Greek Government's desire that the Regency be conferred on the Archbishop. Mr. Leeper is hopeful that this will have the desired effect, but telegrams which I understand on good authority that the King has sent to other persons here, including Mr. Kafandaris and even General Plastiras, would appear to indicate that he is once more in one of his characteristic moods of fatal indecision. (6)

In London, Churchill would not pressure the Greek monarch; in Athens, the main obstacle to Damaskinos' regency appeared to be the

Populist (royalist) Party. "This group," MacVeagh reported on December 20, "and the King's stubborn preference for the interests of his dynasty over all other considerations in this country seem threatening now to extend indefinitely the present deplorable struggle." (7) Indeed, there remained the possibility that the Populists would attempt to exploit the military situation in order to crush the republican Left in other parts of the country as well: "Mr. Leeper says that with [the] appearance of British reinforcements, the leaders of the Right here seem to be hoping that [the] British will carry their battle for them throughout [the] whole of Greece, but he emphasized to me that [the] British intend only to protect Athens and thereafter by all means possible to effect conciliation. . . ." (8)

However, the King's principal foreign supporter was beginning to alter his course. Advised by Alexander and others that the Greek problem could not be solved by military measures, Churchill telegraphed the American President on December 26 that together with Eden he was flying to Athens "to see what we can do to square this Greek entanglement. The basis of action:—The King does not go back until a plebiscite in his favour has been taken." Churchill urged Roosevelt to direct MacVeagh "to make contact with us and to help all he can in accordance with above principles." (9) Churchill's dramatic descent upon Athens, his willingness to formally postpone the King's return and to accept Damaskinos' regency, together with the arrival of more British troops, all combined to produce the desired result. MacVeagh attended the hastily-convened meeting of the leaders of the warring factions, and reported to the President that Churchill had sought to reassure the Greeks that "Britain wants nothing here for herself but only the welfare of the country, the continuance of Anglo-Greek friendship and most-favored-nation treatment for her trade," and that "whether Greece has a republic or a monarchy is a matter for Greeks alone to decide." (10) After a private talk with Churchill on December 27, MacVeagh informed the President that the Prime Minister "is clearly deeply disturbed over the situation here, and its dangers for British prestige and his own position, but is also determined to persist in military operations until Athens and its surroundings are cleared. . . ." He continued:

After that, he appears to be thinking of the possibility of composing matters in the rest of Greece through the medium of a commission of the three great powers, somewhere along the lines of my suggestion to you in my letter of December 8. He showed himself to me, both yesterday and today, to be resentful of American press criticism of his Greek policy and deeply disappointed over what he feels to be our Government's lack of understanding of his attitude and its failure to support him. I asked him if he wanted me to send you any message and he replied "Tell him that I hope he can help us in some way. We want nothing from Greece. We don't want her airfields or her harbors—only a fair share of her trade. We don't want her islands. We've got Cyprus anyhow. We came in here by agreement with our Allies to chase the Germans out and then found that we had to fight to keep the people here in Athens from being massacred. Now if we can do that properly—and we will—all we want is to get out of this damned place." (11)

When MacVeagh told Churchill that he had already suggested to the President the establishment of an international commission to help solve Greece's current problems, the British leader indicated that he welcomed the idea. Indeed, Churchill appeared willing to go a step further. At a press conference on December 27, he warned the Greeks that unless they stopped their fighting, he, Roosevelt and Stalin would have to resort to drastic measures: "if you cannot get a satisfactory and trustworthy democratic foundation, you may have to have for the time being an international trust of some kind or other. We cannot afford to see whole peoples drifting into anarchy...." (12)

Upon his return to London, Churchill pressured the Greek King into accepting the regency formula. On December 31, in a brief ceremony attended by Ambassador MacVeagh, Archbishop Damaskinos took the oath of his new office. Yet the shooting had not stopped, and the political crisis was far from over. MacVeagh telegraphed on January 3, 1945:

General Plastiras has undertaken to form a government and if he is successful it seems likely that some clarification of obscure questions here will not delay to follow. With the King removed from [the] immediate picture and with the Archbishop and Plastiras at the head of affairs, some practical proof will have been supplied in addition to Churchill's repeated verbal assurances that no danger of a forced return of royalty and possible re-establishment of a Fascist dictatorship menaces the Greek people and it will then remain to be seen whether Republican Greece will (1) be satisfied that a continuance of hostilities can be of advantage only to the Communists and (2) can express such satisfaction, this last depending on how far the Communist leadership of the revolt has been able to make a genuine Red Army out of ELAS. [The] Archbishop's plan is so to administer the cleared territory and such islands as have remained loyal to the government that Republican Greeks hitherto fighting on the insurgent side for Greek liberty and independence will gradually gravitate to the government, leaving only the relatively few Communists supposed to exist in Greece to get here with such irresponsible banditti as have been inevitably produced by the times to carry on the struggle for the breakdown of the country's social and economic life. In this plan British Ambassador tells me that the Archbishop will have [the] full support of the British as it seems the only alternative to an undertaking on the latter's part to clear the entire country after the fashion now being employed in Athens. Considerable speculation would appear to be involved but Department will realize that there is room for little else in Greek politics at present. (13)

After strenuous negotiations and continued recriminations on all sides, hostilities were finally brought to a halt on January 15, and on the same day MacVeagh wrote what was to prove his last letter to Roosevelt:

Athens, January 15, 1945

Dear Franklin:

It is just over a month since I last wrote, though it seems a year. Recent experiences here have been tough for anyone who loves this country and its people and at the same time has a old and deep-rooted affection for our British cousins, but I need not bother you with personal matters. Officially, my path has had to be very straight and narrow to keep this Embassy from becoming involved, and I hope I have got through all right so far. But I know how the locomotive felt in Kipling's story when it "took the eighty foot bridge without a guard-rail like a hunted cat on top of a fence."

You will have appreciated from my previous letters, I am sure, that this affair in Greece is not the simple black and white proposition which so many of our newspaper correspondents represent it to be. Such persons, with little or no background knowledge and pressed for a "story" every day, may perhaps be forgiven for over-simplifying, but in so doing they inevitably do poor service to the truth, which lies, as we know, at the bottom and not on the surface of the well. This attempted revolution in Greece represents no clear-cut struggle between liberalism and despotism with England lined up on the side of the latter. It is rather a bastard offshoot of the traditional line of Greek revolutions, composed of social as well as political elements and fathered by international communism on a country economically ruined and politically distraught. The British have only played the part of midwife in this affair. It was not their fault that the child was conceived, but they have certainly lent themselves with astonishing ineptitude to its delivery, and have only themselves to thank if, in trying to retrieve their error by doing away with the child, and thus, as it were, adding murder to abortion, they have effectively stolen the limelight in a case where the chief criminals are obscurer elements in the world's view. The swing to the Left in Greek politics following the

Metaxas dictatorship, the exploitation of this by the communists, and the ripe conditions for social revolution created by the German occupation and fostered by German intrigue, are really the mixed elements fundamentally to blame, and this being understood supplies the key to many things which cannot otherwise be accounted for, and which accordingly the correspondents have not stressed, such as the atrocious character of the struggle between Greek and Greek in the recent conflict here, the many liquidations of "enemies of the people," the looting and destruction of private homes, and the taking and maltreatment of rich hostages without discrimination as to age or sex.

Things being as I described them in my last letter, Mr. Churchill apparently did the best thing immediately possible in the circumstances when he came down here and after approving of the Archbishop personally and putting him in charge of a Conference of all parties, which unanimously recommended his appointment as Regent, returned to London to tell the King that he must definitely accept this recommendation and assure his people, without further equivocation, that he would not return until called for. Before leaving Athens, Mr. Churchill confessed to the British Ambassador, who, as you will remember, strongly urged over a year ago in Cairo exactly the same solution which has now been adopted, "You were right"; and this was doubtless very handsome on his part. But unfortunately it was also very late to realize the mistakes which had been made, and "hence all these tears." For though he was correct,—and recent events would prove it if nothing else would,—in explaining to the Commons that a massacre would have occurred in Athens had not the British intervened militarily last month, the fact remains that if the British had taken the political action a year ago which they have taken now, the communist leadership of the National Resistance Movement would never have been able to spread those suspicions which have made so many genuine Greek patriots their collaborators in an armed attempt against the State. Even as late as last Spring, when the mutiny in Cairo showed such unmistakable signs of close affiliation between the republicans and the extreme left, an overt act on the part of the British to remove all possible suspicions that they intended to support the King's return before the plebiscite (and the possible restoration of the fascist dictatorship for which he is so widely held responsible) might have averted bloodshed by giving a government of national unity, such as Mr. Papandreou's Government aspired to be, at least a chance of success. But as no such act ever eventuated, the suspicions which had already been so sedulously sown by the Communists could still be spread and cultivated, and when the charge was put about that the Papandreou Government was merely a blind to conceal the preparation of a rightist *coup*, this also seemed reasonable to many patriots in the light of what the British did. Actually, the latter insisted, "for military reasons," on the retention in the new Greek National Army of the carefully purged royalist Mountain Brigade, and it was on the basis of the resulting wide-spread suspicion that this was to provide the Government with a kind of Pretorian guard that the showdown came.

Now, though the Archbishop has called Greece's best known republican, General Plastiras, to head a non-party Government of apparently serious individuals who aim to effect national unity rather than to represent it, and though an armistice has been signed with the insurgents,[33] who have had to agree to retire from a part of Greece under British military pressure, so much killing and so many related horrors have been perpetrated that new factors have entered into the situation in the form of bitterness and desire for revenge among the Greek factions, and the prospects for the future cannot be considered as other than dubious still. No hostilities have as yet broken out in Salonica but my latest information from that city is to the effect that communist propaganda is now violently attacking the republican Plastiras as a tool of the fascists, while the British may be demanding more concessions of the insurgents than the latter feel justified by the armistice terms. In addition, the British permitted a "victory" demonstration here in Athens yesterday which inevitably took on a conservative and even to some extent a royalist aspect. Under such conditions, new hatreds are not likely to die down while old suspicions may well be kept alive, and I fear there may be more serious trouble ahead, particularly in Macedonia but perhaps in other parts of Greece as well. Meanwhile, no industry is working, unemployment is almost universal, the Treasury is without revenue, and though a new national army is in the process of formation this will necessarily take some time and there seems to be some reason to fear that the British may withdraw a large part of their troops and equipment before the "constitutional government" which they have "saved" has sufficient forces of its own to render its safety permanent.

Of course few situations are ever completely hopeless, and on the

---

[33] A truce, agreed upon during January 10-11, 1945, became effective on January 15. A wide-ranging political settlement, concluded on February 12, 1945 (the Varkiza Agreement), provided for the restoration of basic liberties, the lifting of martial law, amnesty (except for "common law crimes against life and property which were not absolutely necessary to the achievement of the political crime concerned"), the immediate release of all hostages, the trial of collaborators by competent courts, the organization of a new national army, the demobilization of all armed bands, and the purging of the civil and security services. Finally, the Varkiza Agreement provided for a plebiscite on the issue of the monarchy, to be held during 1945, to be followed by elections for a Constituent Assembly which would prepare a new constitution. Observers of the plebiscite and elections were to be invited from the Allied Powers. The text may be found in Iatrides, *Revolt in Athens*, pp. 320-24.

credit side there are one or two developments here which may be noted too. Thus, while the insurgents here have put up a bitter fight, much if not most of this has been the work of their so-called "urban reserves,"—armed civilians of the communist party, released convicts, and other dependable elements in the class struggle,—aided by some reinforcements of banditti from the provinces, flotsam and jetsam of the German occupation, under well-known cut-throat chiefs such as "Aris" (whose picture *Life* recently reproduced full page in the guise of a hero). Out of the great body of "regular" guerrillas in the provinces, relatively few would appear to have engaged in the battle of Athens, though thousands of them were concentrated a few miles outside the city. This fact perhaps permits of the belief that while the communists have been successful in regimenting republican Greece up to a certain point (and every regular insurgent unit has its political commissar), they have not been quite able to sell their leadership *à l'outrance*, and reports of growing defection from the insurgent ranks, now that the battle of Athens has been lost, confirm it. There are also reports that many of the "regular" forces in Athens bitterly opposed the tactics of the communist chiefs in taking civilian hostages. Apparently they were not prepared for the Red revolution which they saw being actually unleashed here, and would take no part in it, so far as was possible for them under the control which their own credulity had fastened on them. Now it may well be that such insurgents as carry on the war from this point will be much fewer in number than the original forces deployed, as well as less abundantly equipped as to arms and munitions, so much of which has fallen into British and government hands. In addition,—and what may be even more important in the long run,— Russia has given no sign of supporting this movement openly, nor can any evidence be found of her doing so secretly. She has just announced the appointment of a new Ambassador to the Greek Government.

Taking a long view,—and if I aspired to be a prophet, which I don't,— I might hazard that after British intervention is over, the future will show a gradual reduction of the state of civil war here to one of mountain banditry somewhat resembling that which followed the War of Independence against the Turks, and that the duration of this second phase will depend not only on the wisdom and energy of the Central Government in placating honest patriots in the opposition and combatting recalcitrants, but also, and to a great extent, on the efficiency of the relief and reconstruction efforts undertaken. This latter condition will indeed be of critical importance for the country-wide restoration of law and order, since without the importation and distribution of very substantial amounts of supplies, particularly of food and roofing material, during the next few months, financial stabilization cannot be effected, epidemics will almost certainly occur, and public morale will be even less able than heretofore to resist the crude temptations of anarchy and the misleading propaganda of those who batten on it.

In this connection, it is apparently now felt that, owing to the clash which has occurred between the British and the Greeks, the strictly military phase of allied relief control should be terminated as soon as possible and the UNRRA take over. If and when such a change takes place, the leadership of UNRRA will be vested with a truly incalculable influence over the future of this country, and through this country of the whole Near East. Perhaps, therefore, Governor Lehman would be well advised to send here some tried and trusted leader of experience in relief work, possessed not only of the necessary personal prestige and ability to handle a large group of miscellaneous social workers with smoothness and efficiency, but also of the authority to take important decisions locally for the achievement of prompt results. I know the Governor has been worried about the calibre of the directors he has so far been able to get for Cairo and Athens, and certainly, from my observation of the fumbling and lack of discipline which has characterized UNRRA out here to date, the difficulties of the task ahead seem quite obviously beyond the capabilities of these persons. A man like General Haskell, who did such a fine job here for the Red Cross after the Smyrna disaster, might make all the difference between failure and success. The job is a big one and needs a big man to swing it.

Affectionately yours,
Lincoln MacVeagh (14)

Throughout the early months of 1945, MacVeagh continued his running commentary, by telegram and despatch, on the Greek political scene, which remained dangerously unstable, and on the unsuccessful efforts of both Greek and British authorities to deal with the country's chaotic economic conditions. While insisting on a policy of "no involvement" in Greece, Washington soon began to display a growing interest in the possible intervention of the communist régimes of neighboring countries in the Greek crisis. Instructed to investigate, MacVeagh reported rumors that the Greek communists were receiving arms and other support from the north, but stressed that "tangible evidence" was lacking. Reviewing for the Department an assortment of "alarmist and often heresay material" produced by Greek government services, he pointed out that OSS agents tended to regard such reports as "largely tendencious and untrustworthy," although they confirmed that small quantities of weapons from Bulgaria were in fact occasionally reaching Greek communist elements. He also advised that captured communist documents revealed a breakdown between the Greek left and Tito's agents over the question of

Macedonia's future, "the local ELAS attitude in this matter being clearly shown as opposed to any arrangement which would rob Greece of any part of her territory. . . ." (15)

In a lengthy report on February 27, 1945, MacVeagh commented once again on the dangerous political situation, and expressed the belief that as long as British forces remained in Greece, the communists would confine themselves to political activity. However, "Much depends on the methods adopted by the Greek Government for pacifying and unifying the country." In particular, there was pressing need for effective relief and reconstruction programs in the provinces. "The Greeks remain a singularly vital people, even after the experiences of the occupation, and are traditionally adept at running their affairs on a shoe-string. But they must at least have the shoe-string to start with. . . . In its absence, and if tendencies toward renewed rightist dictatorship, such as seem to be foreshadowed in the recent proposal of the Prime Minister to institute a separate Under-Ministry of Public Safety, are not curbed, the 'psychological communism' to which destitute people are prone will continue to provide a dangerous weapon here for the use of the unscrupulous." He reiterated: ". . . to pursue violent action against the KKE could only result in its going underground." Acknowledging that hard-core communists were bound to go into hiding in any event, he asserted that ". . . it is only the truly democratic elements in EAM which can be saved by the Government's showing conclusively that it wishes to find a *modus vivendi* with ELAS. Luckily, these elements form by far the majority. . . ." As for outside assistance to the Greek communists, "There is reason to believe that ELAS' attempt to obtain foreign support from certain of the great allies on the Greek question was decidedly snubbed in precisely those quarters in which ELAS placed the greatest faith. . . ." MacVeagh closed his report by noting that his British colleague, to whom Prime Minister Plastiras had been talking about the Greek armed forces "as usual in a big way," retorted: "The defense of Greece is not your little army but the understanding reached by your allies with the Russians at Yalta. . . ." (16)

Within a few weeks MacVeagh's spirit received a stunning blow, one from which he never fully recovered:

April 13, 1945, Friday
Fair and warm. A perfect spring day. . . . This diary begins again! Since the last entry I have been much [too] occupied everyday to keep up with regularity, and breaking it off as I did during the days of the revolution, when we had no light at night but a feeble lantern and a candle, I have continued to ignore the occasional opportunities which

4. Athens, 1945. With Damascinos, Archbishop of Athens (Primate of Greece) and Regent. Portrait is of Archbishop Chrysostomos.

were given me to bring it up to date. . . . Much has happened in the interim—Churchill's visit to Athens and the establishment of the Regency (which we suggested in Cairo so long ago!), the Premiership of Plastiras, the end of the revolution through the Varkiza Agreement, the fall of Plastiras,[34] and now the death of President Roosevelt. . . .

We were waked up last night at 1:00 by the telephone, and there was Mr. Barbour at the other end, saying Hudson has just called up with the news that the President died at about 4 o'clock this afternoon. Peggy and I got up and turned on the radio but could get neither the USA nor London. But we did hear a band playing the Star Spangled Banner and heard a voice in Italian saying something about the President's death, so we got it confirmed. After that there was little sleep for either of us. Today has been one long reception here, and the town has been decked —I understand quite spontaneously—with flags at half-mast. . . . The Greek Government is to give a memorial mass on Sunday in the Cathedral. Always heretofore the Greeks have let the foreigners do these things for themselves, but for President Roosevelt it is as if he had been one of themselves! The Government has decreed that there shall also be services in all the principal churches throughout Greece, and there will be a further ceremony of a civil character at the University next week. I was asked whether I would broadcast over the Athens radio tonight, but I refused, and the Regent will do it himself Sunday morning. I thought it better not to seem to be using the President's death for propaganda purposes. . . .

The President has died at the height of his fame and glory, within sight of victory, like Moses on the mountain. He has not had to face the organization of the Peace, the Promised Land. His name will always be associated with triumph. But it is a sad struggle we shall have to go through in the aftermath without his inspiring leadership and the prestige he has built up over the years throughout the world. I have tried all day to speak hopefully as well as loyally of Truman, but were he the greatest man in the world, he could not be a Roosevelt yet for many years. At least half the game in world leadership is the trust and confidence of the nations, and this can only be won gradually. It is amazing how F.D.R. was looked up to and believed in by foreigners almost as if he were a god! One after the other this morning my colleagues came in with white, scared faces—the Brazilian, the Britisher, the Pole, the Turk—not to speak of the Greeks. Each seemed to feel that a prop had been pulled out from under his particular world. For myself, I do not realize it as yet. It is a far greater loss for me and my country than for these friends

---

[34] The Plastiras government resigned on April 8, 1945, and was succeeded by one constituted under Petros Voulgaris.

of mine and theirs—so perhaps it is natural that I can't size it up so soon. We may, with a Senator in the White House, return to more orthodox methods of government, and maybe this will be a gain so far as it goes. The State Department may come into its own again and the mushroom agencies dwindle and disappear. But America's influence in the world, and her own ability to see ahead on her own predestined path, will certainly suffer. . . . For me, the personal side of my job is gone, the vitalizing element. The ship will sail on, and I may still be for a while a part of the crew, but *my* captain is gone. As I write in the stillness of midnight I can hear the *koukouvaya*[35] meowing in the Royal Gardens. I have heard him every night since we moved into this house, and felt him to be the evil omen the Greeks say.

April 14, 1945, Saturday

Another day full of calls of condolence, but I managed to put in several hours at the office both morning and afternoon. I received there the Frenchman and the Spaniard, and General Zervas, and General Liossis, among others. Zervas has shaved his beard and abandoned guerrilla warfare for politics. He has founded a party of his own, and told me that our old friend Sikelianos (the ex-Minister to the U.S.) will be around some day to explain its principles! . . . Got a note from the Foreign Office asking us to assign Hill and Patterson (our Treasury assistant) to a committee ("Coordinating Committee") which is advising the Greek Government on supply and financial matters. The committee is now composed of Britishers who advised ML before the latter turned over to UNRRA on April 1st, and our men advising ML used to sit in with it from time to time. However, the Dept. has agreed with me that advising the Greek Government is a different thing from advising ML, and has instructed me not to join with the British in so doing. Knowing this, the British have, I suspect, instigated this request from the Greeks. They are, of course, very anxious to get us in to share their responsibility, while the Department, which is by no means responsible for the Greek Government, as the British most certainly are, prefers to have us "keep in touch" and give advice only informally and as we feel appropriate.

April 15, 1945, Sunday

Requiem mass for F.D.R. in the Cathedral. All our staff went. We were clustered on the right of the ersatz catafalque, where the Government usually stands, facing the Diplomatic Corps. The Government was

[35] Vernacular Greek for "owl."

on the left of the aisle (as one looks down the nave) and the church, but not the balconies, was full. The Regent stood where the King usually does, and he and the Prime Minister each placed a wreath at the foot of the catafalque, which was draped with an American flag.

April 18, 1945, Wednesday

I told Leeper the other day that he ought to make a collection of "Prime Ministers I have tried,"—including little Venizelos, who might have a card round his neck reading "Three times." He protested that he didn't select Voulgaris. But he had forgotten that only a week or ten days previously he told me, "We are thinking of putting Voulgaris in."

April 20, 1945, Friday

Busy day in the office, with Wally planning to leave tomorrow morning. Gave him a memo in regard to a recent telegram from the Dept. which would seem to indicate that we are beginning to change our policy here and to take an interest in internal political affairs. I was instructed to see the Regent, which I did today, and explain that a recent reported statement by Mr. Stettinius to the effect that I had not been consulted about the new change of Government but that the British Ambassador had, was erroneously given in the Press. The Secretary had merely stated the facts as he knew them in answer to a correspondent's question, and the U.S. Government does not object to "internal changes in Greece which are carried out constitutionally and in accord with the Varkiza Agreement." (17) Having in mind that we have never objected to changes of Government here whether constitutional or not, and that we regarded the EAM revolt which ended in the Varkiza Agreement wholly [as] an internal affair *in which we were not involved*, I asked Wally to make some inquiries with a view to my being instructed if indeed we are assuming new responsibilities. In the President's report of March 2nd . . . he spoke of political and economic matters in the liberated countries being the joint concern of Britain, Russia and the U.S., according to agreement at Yalta.[36] Of course, Russia has so far sent no representative here while her press has openly criticized the Government, and Britain has not only not been consulted about the Governments in Bulgaria and Rumania, but along with the U.S. is

---

[36] One of the many decisions reached at the Yalta Conference (February 4-11, 1945) was a "Declaration on Liberated Europe," under which the United States, Britain and the Soviet Union promised to cooperate "in meeting the political and economic problems of liberated Europe in accordance with democratic principles." Assisting in the holding of elections was one specific example of such cooperation.

busily trying to get another solution of the Polish question than that being supported by the Soviets. But perhaps the Department wishes to be ready to cooperate here if and when cooperation becomes possible factually as well as theoretically!

April 23, 1945, Monday

The news is that the Russians are two miles from the Brandenburg Gate and Hitler is said still to be in Berlin. Patton has swung south toward Munich and the British are attacking Bremen. . . .

Got a long telegram from Mr. Kohler enclosing copies of telegrams exchanged between F.D.R. and Mr. Churchill about joint advising of the Greek Government on financial and economic matters.[37] Churchill proposed it—as I had already learnt from Leeper and Caccia,—but the President consulted the Department, which drafted his reply along the lines of the instructions already sent to me in agreement with my suggestions. The Department thinks a bilateral mission would be a mistake, as it would look as if we were ignoring "the Yalta decision for tripartite action in liberated areas" and "might easily be interpreted as indicating that we regard the Yalta decisions as no longer valid," while Mr. Churchill thinks that "at a time when the Russians are firmly excluding both you and us [from] any say in the affairs of Romania, it would be rather odd to invite them unsolicited to assume some degree of responsibility in Greek affairs." This attitude toward Russia is the same as that I noted, and regretted, on the part of Lord Moyne in dealing with Novikov in Cairo.

[37] The messages were as follows: (1) Roosevelt to Churchill, telegram 723, March 21, 1945, proposing an Anglo-American-Soviet commission "for developing the productive power of Greece rapidly by concerted, non-political action . . . . It would not take them long and might have a highly constructive effect on world opinion at this time. . . ." (2) Churchill to Roosevelt, telegram 932, April 3, 1945, expressing doubts "whether this [is] an appropriate moment to bring the Russians in." Instead, Churchill proposed an Anglo-American commission for Greece. (3) Roosevelt to Churchill, telegram (?) April 8, 1945, recognizing "the force of the observations on the Russian angle in your 932 and agree that it might be better not to go forward with a tripartite economic mission at the present time." On the other hand, Roosevelt asserted, "I think it would be a mistake to set up a bilateral mission. This would look as though we, for our part, were disregarding the Yalta decision for tripartite action in liberated areas and might easily be interpreted as indicating that we consider the Yalta decisions as no longer valid. Such is certainly not the case, as you know, and I therefore feel that we must be careful not to do anything that would weaken the effectiveness of our efforts to get the Russians to honor those decisions on their side." While Roosevelt's message of April 8 was in fact drafted by the Department of State, his telegram of March 21 had apparently been sent without the knowledge of the Department. See Roosevelt Library, Map Room Papers, President's Messages to Churchill.

The Russians are suspicious of everyone, and nothing can be done toward getting them to cooperate unless we take the lead in it. If we simply copy their way of doing things, we shall never get together.

April 28, 1945, Saturday

Bright and warm. Started off with Mummy in the car at 8:30, with Michali and Calligas, and drove to Mycenae. Lunch there and then drive to Nauplia and Epidaurus and return [to Mycenae]. . . . As we walked home over the hill in the dusk (by the well path) we stopped to listen to a shepherd piping on an opposite hill. We could hardly make out where he was, but the piping ceased and then went on, and in the interval a voice came to us across the valley, "Yia sou,[38] Kyrie MacVeagh!"

[38] Familiar Greek greeting or farewell.

CHAPTER

X

End of a Journey

As THE DEFEAT of the enemy in Europe was drawing near, and as the Truman Administration began to seriously reassess American responsibilities and challenges in the postwar order, MacVeagh's role in Athens underwent a slow transformation. From an attentive, but "uninvolved," observer of the country's continuing crisis, he began to emerge as an influential adviser of political leaders in and out of government. At first, this change was hardly systematic or deliberate; the British ambassador still dominated the scene, and Washington's instructions to its envoy in Athens remained vague and tentative.

In response to MacVeagh's attempt to elicit a clarification of the Department's attitude toward governmental changes in Athens in light of the much-discussed Declaration on Liberated Europe at Yalta (see diary entry of April 20), Gordon P. Merriam, chief of the Department's Near Eastern Division, could offer many generalities, but little concrete direction. Washington was prepared to take "a stronger line than heretofore on many questions concerning other countries which fall into that twilight zone between those purely international in scope and those undeniably internal." Maintaining order and stability in the "Near East" was essential, as was the need for the major powers "to deal justly with the small countries," if the United Nations conference at San Francisco was to succeed. Also, "in their relations with the Near Eastern countries, the Western Powers will stand or fall together, in the long run." As for the political situation in Greece, Merriam conceded that in the past the United States had not objected to coups and dictatorial régimes, which in any event had not been opposed by the majority of Greeks. However, the current crisis had resulted from the war, "and we have assumed a share of responsibility for the re-establishment of stable internal conditions." Accordingly, Washington would "probably now make known its disapproval if any one unrepresentative group in Greece seized power in an obvious attempt to prevent the free expression of the people on the form of government they desire." Even though it was not possible to determine the precise point at which "an unhealthy internal situation crosses the frontiers and becomes a matter for our practical concern," a principle of sorts was evolving: "In an effort to encourage the establishment in liberated areas of stable and democratic government and of economic conditions essential to domestic peace and recovery, the Department now feels justified in making itself felt in favor of democratic solutions in countries whose outlook has been warped and purposefully demoralized by enemy occupation." For example, any open violation of the Varkiza Agreement, whether by the Left or by the government, would "probably evoke a statement of disapproval" from the United States. Although the "Yalta decision" was not being applied to the Greek case, the Department felt a "moral responsibility to live up to the spirit in which it was made." Specifically, the Department favored consultation with the allies on the eventual restoration of representative government in Greece. Merriam concluded:

> Possibly it all boils down to the fact that, while spheres of military responsibility still persist, as do spheres of interest, our armed forces have done such a splendid job in this war that our military power and capabilities are now, at long last, out in the open for all to see. While there are plenty of situations which require careful handling, and some which require circumspect handling, in a general way I think that we feel freer than we have in the past to go to work on the kind of peace we want. (1)

The Department's Delphic pronouncements offered only a vague promise of an active American role in the management of Greek problems. MacVeagh's attention, therefore, remained focused upon those internal factors that might upset the precarious political balance established in the aftermath of the December uprising. On June 22, 1945, he had a long conversation with Nikos Zahariadis, the Secretary of the Communist Party, whom the German authorities had held prisoner at Dachau, and with Porfyrogenis, political chief of the now dissolved ELAS. They asserted that the KKE, which Zahariadis called "the most conservative" party in Greece, planned to conduct an intensive campaign among the peasants in order to expand its political base. Both visitors appeared concerned about the anticipated elections, which they regarded as indispensable, not only for the creation of representative government, but also for the establishment of political stability and economic progress. They complained that right-wing "domination and terror" rendered the holding of elections problematical, but there was no hint that the KKE might decide to abstain. Although Porfyrogenis was particularly anxious to underscore the persecution of the Left, Zahariadis appeared to be more optimistic. He agreed that the political climate was oppressive but readily conceded that there had been some improvement in the situation.

On the burning issue of territorial aspirations, Zahariadis maintained that his Party fully supported Greek claims, especially those for Northern Epirus and the Dodecanese, but thought that these matters should be settled democratically, and without causing tension with other Balkan states. He particularly objected to the popular suggestion that Northern Epirus should be seized immediately by Greek troops. When MacVeagh speculated that the noisy press campaign on territorial claims might be not only premature but possibly even counterproductive, Zahariadis blamed the whole affair on the Right, which he said was hoping to turn people's minds away from the far more serious issues at home. Nevertheless, the KKE had felt compelled to support the campaign in the interest of national unity. He reiterated the view that all such issues should be settled democratically, and promised that his Party would honor any solution which was acceptable to the "democratic world."

Reporting to the Department on the views of his visitors, MacVeagh commented that Zahariadis' emphasis upon "national unity, constructive effort and sweet reasonableness in general," suggested that, under his personal direction, there appeared to be a definite shift in the KKE's orientation. "Apparently he is finding it salutary to go underground, not only in action, following the failure of last December's attempt to use the resistance movement to establish a Communist régime, but also in agitation and claims." He concluded:

> The lesson would appear to be that, given peace in Europe, and provided that Greek reconstruction proceeds with reasonable celerity with the help of UNRRA and the Allied economic missions, and that no unduly disturbing delays are encountered in securing a return to normal political expression at the polls, this country has little to fear in the near future from any renewed direct action initiative on the part of the extreme Left. On the contrary, under its new leadership, unembarrassed by responsibility for last December's failure, the Communist Party would seem now to be definitely embarked on a long term policy of lulling its opponents to sleep by overtly confining itself to politics, with emphasis on "anti-fascism" and "democracy" while never ceasing to bore from within in the labor movement, the public services, the armed forces, and even among the peasants, with a view to the best possible exploitation of such opportunities as may develop as time goes on.... One of these opportunities—doubtless the one most hoped for if not the one most counted on—would be a war between Russia and the Western Powers. Short of this, the policy would appear well calculated, through its laborious concern with the grass-roots of discontent, to take advantage of any decided extension of Russian influence as opposed to British in this country. (2)

While the local communists did not appear to pose any immediate threat, MacVeagh was becoming increasingly preoccupied with possible Soviet aggressive intentions concerning Greece. In early June, in a letter to Ambassador Harriman in Moscow, he wrote of a menacing Soviet shadow over the Balkans, and solicited Harriman's opinion on the matter of Stalin's postwar objectives in that region. Observing that Soviet press and diplomatic attacks on the Greek Government were intensifying, Harriman, in a letter dated July 5, 1945, characterized such moves as "tactical maneuvers within a larger strategy directed at the Balkans and Asia Minor." Moscow appeared determined to create along its eastern and southern borders a "security zone of Soviet-dominated states," employing different methods and degrees of control according to local opportunities and perceived dangers. As for MacVeagh's own bailiwick, "Greece cannot be overlooked by the Kremlin, particularly in view of certain chauvinistic Greek pretensions to northward expansion; of the fact that Greece can be used as a British springboard into the Balkans; of the fact that, even were the Soviet Union to gain control over the Straits, Greece and [the] Greek islands in the Aegean would still constitute a barrier to the open Mediterranean, and finally of the fact that Greece is the only spot in the Balkans where the Soviet secret police are at present unable to play the dominant role and to satisfy themselves that Soviet interests are not threatened." Harriman concluded:

> For fundamental strategic reasons it seems that Greece and Turkey (now that Poland is disposed of) must develop in the near future as important points of Soviet attention, and possibly of difference[s] between the Soviet Government and the British and ourselves. What we are seeing now in the press and in the diplomatic attitude are, I should say, symptoms of a girding of the Soviet propaganda loins, in preparation for what may be a hard battle.
>
> How far the Soviet Government will attempt to establish its direct influence in Greece is not yet clear and will probably depend on further developments. But it is routine Soviet tactics in areas close to the Russian security sphere to display extreme reserve, if not hostility, to all forces which are not extensively amenable to Soviet influence; and neither the Government nor any other political elements in Greece should expect to remain immune from the application of this rule. (3)

On the immediately important question of Moscow's direct relations with the Greek communists, MacVeagh sought to weigh carefully the evidence and to avoid hasty conclusions. Early in 1945, he dutifully informed the Department that British authorities in Athens attributed KKE's policies, and its seemingly inexhaustible coffers, to "Russian sources," but he characterized such an assertion as a "psychological element" in the prevailing situation; his own intelligence sources could find no evidence of Soviet financial support for the KKE. He thought it more likely that the communists were still drawing upon the large sums of gold sovereigns with which London had supplied the wartime resistance groups. Although Moscow's political influence might be another matter, and more difficult to determine, the only hard proof consisted of documents taken from communist couriers moving between Greece and Bulgaria and all these were of a "relatively innocuous nature." He therefore concluded that "Possibly the Russians, who are showing themselves in these days to be supreme realists, do not feel it necessary, in order to keep the leftist pot here boiling merrily, to do more than fan the flames with a sympathetic press and radio and keep the local communists in a constant state of hopeful expectation of more definite assistance to come." (4)

Meanwhile, the communists' posture appeared to be essentially defensive. MacVeagh reported on July 17, 1945, that, according to British intelligence, the KKE had decided to oppose by force a rumored royalist coup, sending mobs of supporters to demonstrate before the embassies of the Allied Powers and telling its members that assistance from Albania and Yugoslavia could be expected to reach them "within twenty-four hours" of such a coup. He thought that the rumor had been basically correct, but that the danger of a royalist move had subsided because of stern warnings issued by the British authorities. He offered the opinion that the "danger of such an outbreak has been deferred until after the results of elections in Britain have become known, and that possibly [the] Potsdam Conference will cause further delay. Of the fact that [the] extreme right still harbors ideas of an eventual coup no doubt is expressed. . . ." (5)

From the first days of post-liberation euphoria, MacVeagh had attributed the rising level of disorder in Greece as much to economic conditions as to political passions. In view of the trauma of the Metaxas dictatorship and of the violent politics of resistance to the enemy, he regarded a large measure of turmoil as a natural state of affairs, which only time and the prospects of a brighter future could alleviate. However, the country's utter devastation and gloomy outlook for economic recovery fueled the fires of popular unrest, discredited the Government, and prevented the healing of the nation's political divisions. He argued that relief measures deserved to be given the highest priority, and that Greece could not be expected to recover unassisted. But as he reviewed the situation from his Athens office he found no cause for optimism. "Relief and reconstruction here is proceeding awfully slowly," he wrote to a colleague on January 29, 1945, "partly because of the civil war and the small amounts in which supplies are coming in, but partly also, I think, because there are too many cooks and no chef." An assortment of civilian and military agencies and committees, including UNRRA, theater commanders, the British-American "Military Liaison" (ML), the International Red Cross, and a myriad of Greek government officials seemed to be working without coordination, with the result that "too little is being done to bridge the gap between planning and action." To MacVeagh, the basic problems were two: inadequate supplies and lack of central direction. He wrote:

> If ever there was a need for a "czar," it is in this complex problem of relieving and reconstructing a completely ruined country under conditions imposed by a global war. Things can never go "according to plan," and there ought to be one central authority on the spot with the ability and prestige to get something done anyway, even if it isn't perfect, despite hell and high water. Otherwise, with crises arising everyday, what is done to meet these tends to be restricted merely to changing the plans, or even merely to advising their change, and actually this goes on constantly. The winter here is more than half over now and even in such a relatively small matter as the distribution in Athens of the clothing long ago brought in here for relief, plans are still being made and remade while the people go bare. . . . (6)

The American Ambassador's sympathy for the plight of the people did not always extend to official efforts to cope with the worsening situation. When, in January 1945, the Greek Government had requested from Britain and the United States substantial financial assistance to meets its obligations and to expand its armed forces, MacVeagh reported with approval the views of an old acquaintance and prominent Athenian banker, Kyriakos Varvaressos, who found the Greek Government's plan extravagant and ill-conceived. "He is disturbed," MacVeagh telegraphed, "at the apparent attitude of many of the Government officials that their problems are so difficult that only foreign aid can solve them and that what they can do is so small that it is not worth doing." Varvaressos was especially critical of plans to use foreign economic assistance to enlarge the Greek armed forces and provide them with compensation comparable to that of their British and American counterparts: "For the immediate future he thinks it essential that the Allies clothe, equip and provide rations for this army, but he regards as ridiculous the request that the Allies pay the salaries and wages of the Greek armed forces. . . ." (7)

At the same time, MacVeagh remained opposed to any direct and formal American role in counselling the Greeks on economic matters, especially if this were to be done in association with the British. When, in the early spring of 1945, the "Military Liaison" was about to leave Greece, turning over its relief activities to UNRRA, he objected to a British suggestion that the ML's American economic advisers stay on to assist the Greek Government as members of a joint British-American committee. "It will not escape the Department," he telegraphed on March 14, 1945, "that to advise a foreign government is a very different thing from advising an Anglo-American organization such as the ML and before deciding on its course in this matter it will doubtless wish to consider whether it desires to share with the British (already deeply involved in internal Greek affairs) the responsibility for the success or failure of a Greek reconstruction program which cannot fail to become involved in local politics. Should the decision be to start newly (for us) in such responsibility here I believe that the departure from our former policy will be less sharp and apparent the more informally it is effected while our resulting tie-up with any particular Greek Government in the coming months will present less possibilities of embarrassment if our advice is given independently and occasionally as asked for and not in joint committee sitting regularly at the right hand of authority. Our advisers could keep in contact with their British counterparts without forming any special body with them. . . ." (8)

Prompted by persistent reports from its embassy in Athens that UNRRA's work was not having any significant impact upon the country's continuing economic crisis, the American Government decided to take a closer and independent look at the situation. On June 2, 1945, Acting Secretary of State Joseph C. Grew telegraphed MacVeagh that the Department felt "grave concern" over the situation in Greece, and wished to "show interest and assist constructively wherever feasible." MacVeagh was instructed to submit promptly his recommendations "as to what we can do most effectively to make plain our policy and at the same time give more than stop-gap aid to Greece." In particular, MacVeagh's comments were requested on the desirability of sending to Athens a small group of industrialists to assist with problems of production and efficiency. Grew emphasized that the contemplated mission would be purely American. (9)

In his prompt reply, MacVeagh expressed little enthusiasm for such a committee of experts, and sought to draw attention to the broader issues of the Greek crisis, as well as to the disturbing impact of external influences:

> To help effectively with [the] overall problem of Greece's economic recovery I feel any contemplated clarification of policy should take into account [the] political and psychological conditions beyond [the] competence of industrial experts. Such factors as [a] dynamic

Communist movement under Moscow-trained leaders and [the] widespread belief in non-Communist circles that Anglo-Russian conflict is inevitable, placing Greece in jeopardy to Soviet-supported northern neighbors, are largely responsible for local stresses preventing resumption [of] normal activities. Meanwhile US prestige [is] high due to [the] war, but [our] traditional policy, restricted to general benevolence and trade promotion combined with strict nonintervention [in] internal matters, seems ill-adapted [to the] present world situation in which local upheavals even in small countries [are] capable of causing wide repercussions. Furthermore, this policy [is] actually enabling both Left [and] Right [to] claim US sympathy while continuing extremist activities. [I] Realize [the] difficulties of reorienting [a] policy maintained [for] many years, but suggest [that a] clear statement of [our] firm determination [to] discountenance all unilateral solutions whatever in Greek external, internal affairs from now on might provide [a] useful warning to troublemakers and assist [to] restore necessary calm. Leaving aside larger aspects, purely economic causes of local unrest can perhaps best be dealt with by supplying raw materials and fuel to reactivate industry through existing agencies and, particularly, normal channels of trade. Proposed advisory mission of industrial experts could not affect present situation appreciably, but might possibly be useful later in connection [with the] development [of] relatively simple industries after elementary needs [have been] supplied. (10)

Encouraged by the Department's expressions of concern, MacVeagh also attempted to provide an analysis of the political and organizational problems which had tended to render UNRRA's operations in Greece slow and ineffective. He stressed, in particular, the controlling influence of British officials, whose role "represents frank sphere-of-interest politics, in the same manner as recent British action in influencing the making and breaking of Greek Governments," and added: "Whether or not such action happens to be for the best short-term interests of Greece, it furnishes the perfect excuse for unilateral action by other powers elsewhere, and to that degree may be considered prejudicial to a world situation of which Greece forms a part." He concluded that beyond local remedies and unilateral declarations of policy, the problem of Greece called for a clarification of purpose, and better coordination, at the highest levels of the American and British Governments:

I sympathize with the inferior position of the Americans in UNRRA, but I am convinced that a fundamental solution of their problem is beyond the competence of anyone in Athens. With the shifting of various UNRRA functions from Washington to London, . . . UNRRA in Greece seems likely to become more and more an instrument of British policy, in a manner similar to the Middle East Supply Center. That it is British-controlled at present is undeniable, and the whole conception of what UNRRA is and stands for is accordingly at stake. Should the United States parallel British action here with a more aggressive independent policy of its own in supplying official advice and guidance it would only duplicate grounds for objection by other UNRRA members, and in addition create the impression of competition between the Anglo-Saxon powers for benefits to accrue from an enterprise shared in by over forty other nations. What would seem possibly necessary at this time, therefore, is the discovery and institution of practical and effective methods for bringing the UNRRA effort (not only in London and Washington, but here in Greece as well) on to the broadest possible international basis, to save UNRRA's own credit and make clear beyond any question the disinterestedness in this great project of both Great Britain and the United States. (11)

By the end of 1945, the American Government, slowly responding to the steady stream of alarming reports from its embassy in Athens, was beginning to focus its attention more systematically upon the problems besetting Greece. As viewed from Washington, the trouble was largely of the Greeks' own making. "Dept. deeply concerned of late," the Secretary of State telegraphed MacVeagh on November 2, "at [the] unwillingness or inability [of] Greek leaders to work together for [the] urgent needs [of] their country. [The] Impression [is] gaining ground abroad that [the] selfishness and cupidity of Greek public figures are blinding them to all broader issues and that perhaps Greece [is] incapable of running herself and solving her immediate economic problems. . . ." Under such conditions, he implied, UNRRA's work in Greece may have to be terminated, as no more funds would be forthcoming. Nor was the United States willing to step in: "Although US [is] prepared [to] give sympathetic consideration [to] Greek request for loans these must be made on [a] sound economic basis. [There is] Little likelihood [of] credits being made available to [a] country offering as little financial and economic stability as Greece at this time." MacVeagh was asked to suggest ways for making the political leaders of Greece fully aware of the American position on this matter. (12)

Byrnes' communication to MacVeagh had been prompted also by a message from the Supreme Allied Commander, Mediterranean Theater

(Lt. Gen. William D. Morgan), indicating that the British military authorities were seriously contemplating abandoning Greece to her fate, unless the United States were prepared to assume some of the burden in that country. General Morgan complained that Greece's economic crisis was worsening, that UNRRA had been ineffective, and that the "Red Tide" in the Balkans was further aggravating the situation. Under these circumstances, he intended to "state bluntly to the British Chiefs of Staff that in his opinion as a soldier, Great Britain could not carry on alone and that unless the United States decided to play a more active role in Greece the British should get out of Greece completely and take their losses." In addition to sharing the financial burden, he hoped the United States could send troops to Greece, or at least station there substantial air forces. (13)

Responding to Washington's messages of concern, MacVeagh, in a long series of telegrams dealing with a variety of specific issues, took the position once again that the lack of direction in UNRRA's work was as much to blame for the failure of the recovery program as was the lawlessness of the politically divided Greeks. While recommending the appointment, as UNRRA chief, of a "top flight man for top flight job with authority [and] ability to press and guide [the] Ministry of Supply," (14) he also cautioned against the despatch of high-level foreign "mission" that might exercise direct and undue control over Greek affairs. He proposed instead that carefully chosen American technicians, acting as individuals, for specific duties, and responsible to the Greek Government, be sent over at once, allowing matters of policy to remain in the hands of the Department of State and its diplomatic representatives in Athens. (15) In this last recommendation, MacVeagh was obviously motivated by the strong desire to keep American policy decisions channelled through his embassy rather than have them usurped by roving "trouble-shooters," who had no understanding of the Greek mentality and no regard for traditional diplomacy. At the same time, he was consciously searching for ways to encourage Washington's involvement in the economic recovery and political stability of Greece, without in the process undermining the sovereignty of the Greek state.

During the closing months of 1945, in his reports to his superiors, MacVeagh often questioned the wisdom of particular acts and tactics of the ever-changing Greek Government, whose composition was based not on a national mandate, but on the prevailing maze of traditional partisanship and British intervention. He also felt compelled, however, to justify repeated requests for economic assistance, and to defend the Greeks against what he viewed as unreasonable and damaging criticism from British, American, and UNRRA officials. In a long despatch dated

December 15, 1945, he was remarkably outspoken in his response to such detraction:

> Two of the Four Freedoms are taken for granted in liberated Greece—the only Balkan country where such is the case—but the remaining two, involving Fear and Want, are in the mind of every Greek. Fear is inspired by the traditional Slav menace from the north, now far more frightening than even before, with three of Greece's immediate neighbors almost completely under Soviet domination and a dynamic Communist movement within the country under Moscow-trained and directed leadership. In the meantime the specter of Want, due largely to the country's catastrophic shortage of foodstuffs, is an ever-present reminder that only UNRRA stands between Greece and starvation.

He was particularly anxious to dispel the impression that Greece had failed to make effective use of the enormous quantities of relief supplies provided by the military and UNRRA operations: "All but a small portion of the relief supplies sent to Greece," he pointed out, "have gone toward filling the gap between available stocks of consumers' goods within the country and the minimum requirements to sustain life.... Virtually nothing came into the country from abroad for industrial rehabilitation until the middle of 1945, and then only in small quantities, while the effect of military and UNRRA assistance to Greek agriculture will become apparent only after many months," particularly in view of the country's physical devastation and the recent severe drought. He cautioned against the "unfairness of expecting Greece to show really substantial and visible economic recovery until after the 1946 harvest," and stressed again that large-scale relief assistance would be required "simply to provide some measure of Freedom from Want under present circumstances." Moreover, in the industrial sector recovery was believed to compare favorably with that elsewhere in Europe. However, "With the best will in the world Greece cannot expect to bring total agricultural and industrial production back to prewar levels in less than three or four years, not to mention the difficulties of replacing the country's merchant marine and reviving its tourist traffic and export trade, all of which are essential to restoring the balance of payments. How are imports of food and other absolute necessities to be paid for during the interim period after UNRRA leaves? To the Greek mind there is only one answer: foreign financial assistance."

As always, in his analysis of the Greek situation, he emphasized the inexorable link between economic and political affairs, as well as between domestic and foreign considerations:

Most Greeks are not interested in Communism as an economic theory, and all of them have found it associated, in their recent experience, with looting and murder. Fear of what the future may hold for them in this regard is with them an obsession; for what assurance have they that British Labor Party[1] preoccupation with Socialist dogma, or an American lapse of interest in Balkan affairs, may not deliver Greece to Communism in much the same way as Yugoslavia? Therefore, it is scarcely to be wondered at if they are hesitant to take a long-term view in utilizing what liquid capital remains to them in efforts to expand production. A small bag of gold jewelry or foreign currency held in readiness for sudden flight would be worth far more than a large factory under conditions which many Greeks and others regard as by no means unlikely.

The Greek also realizes that the traditional safegards of military alliances or pacts of mutual assistance are of doubtful value, even in the improbable event that the United States and Britain would extend such guarantees under present circumstances. The country's northern frontiers could no more be held against a Russian-supported invasion than was the case against the Germans in 1941. Freedom from Want can not be looked for until the United Nations Organization has become an effective reality. In the meantime Greece must strive to retain the interest and support of her Western Allies during a period of uncertain duration and manifold difficulties. Fear will not be allayed during that period, but hope will remain until it becomes clear whether Greece is to be a sovereign member of a full-fledged United Nations Organization or simply a Soviet puppet.

MacVeagh was especially disturbed by the reporting on the Greek situation in the western press, which he found distorted and harmful:

During the past year Greece has learned that foreign sympathy may be unreasonably fickle. As a reward for maintaining freedom of its press, at the same time permitting foreign correspondents to circulate about the country and report as they see fit, Greece has been misrepresented and maligned in the American and British press in a most undeserved fashion. This flood of abuse from supposed friends, all having the effect of supporting the Communist thesis, has made it even more evident that some tangible guarantees must be sought from

[1] Following the Labor Party's victory in the national elections of July 1945, Churchill's Government was succeeded by a Labor Government under Prime Minister Clement R. Attlee, with Ernest Bevin as Minister for Foreign Affairs. The new Government initiated an ambitious program of socialization.

America and Britain. Direct financial support is again the most obvious answer.

After commenting on the latest Greek request, by the Government of Prime Minister Themistoclis Sofoulis,[2] for foreign credits and gold, which had caused "disillusionment" among Anglo-American UNRRA officials, "whose somewhat Leftist sympathies tend to favor dictatorial methods of government abhorrent to the Greeks," MacVeagh concluded:

> All of the foregoing is not to say that the Greeks have put forth their best efforts to reestablish the country's financial structure or that they should not have done more in the way of rationing and price control. But to the quick Greek mind, impatient of detail often to the point of being superficial, there is little purpose in undertaking drastic and locally unpopular measures, as advocated by the British and UNRRA, against a background of fear which is more than likely to render such measures stillborn. With unassailable logic the Greeks persist in their desire for Freedom from Fear and Want. Financial aid from the United States[3] and Britain appears to them as the only practicable road. (16)

Throughout the summer and fall of 1945, in addition to the problems of relief and economic recovery, the most important aspect of United States policy toward Athens concerned the question of providing supervision for the upcoming Greek national elections. From the outset, there was no doubt that the British, already deeply involved in Greek affairs, were very anxious to have the Americans (the French were to be added later on) share in the responsibility for observing the elections and certifying their results. London expected Moscow to decline

---

[2] The Voulgaris Government resigned on October 17, 1945, forcing the Regent to assume the duties of Prime Minister as well. A new government under P. Kanellopoulos, sworn in on November 1, resigned on November 22, and was succeeded by a Liberal cabinet under the octogenarian Th. Sofoulis.

[3] In Washington, MacVeagh's sympathetic assessment of the Greek situation found a somewhat unexpected supporter. While approving the substance of a State Department note to the Greek Government (on the need to put its finances on a sound basis before American assistance could be considered) President Truman made the following marginal notation: "It is all right but it does seem to me that it is rather harsh, in view of the fact that the Greeks were almost annihilated fighting our common enemy, the Germans, and while they have had some severe internal difficulty and some difficulty with the British, I can't help but feel extremely friendly to the Greeks. This note to me seems to be rather harshly worded. While I am not an expert in the matter, can't we say the same things and implement the same policy in a little more friendly way." *FR 1945*, VIII, 290, fn 50. As a result, some of the "harsher" words were deleted.

a similar invitation which, if accepted, could serve as precedent for tripartite action in the Soviet-controlled countries of Eastern Europe. In addition, London had no desire to encourage a Soviet presence in Greece under any circumstances. For its part, the Department of State recommended, and President Truman concurred, that the United States participate in the supervision of the Greek elections, together with Britain, on the grounds that such an obligation had been assumed under the Yalta accords. At the suggestion of Assistant Secretary of State Dean G. Acheson, and to forestall possible Greek objections to such foreign supervision, it was decided not to solicit an invitation from Athens, but rather to inform the Greek Government that the United States and Britain, as signatories of the Yalta agreement on liberated Europe, "are prepared to participate in the supervision of Greek elections and that they assume the Greek Government will wish them to do so." (17)

There is no evidence that MacVeagh was consulted on this matter, or on the twin issue of the timing of the elections in relation to the plebiscite concerning the King's return, which according to the Varkiza Agreement, was to *precede* the elections. On the other hand, there is reason to believe that until he was advised otherwise by Washington, MacVeagh thought it likely that the Soviet Union would be invited to take part in the supervision of the Greek elections. (18) On September 1, MacVeagh was instructed to inform the Regent, Archbishop Damaskinos, that the United States favored the holding of the elections *prior* to the plebiscite, so that a representative government might preside over the settling of the question of the King's return. He was to make it clear that Washington's "only wish in this instance is to encourage Greeks to reach [a] solution offering them [the] best possible early tranquillization [of the] unsettled conditions obtaining since liberation. We do not mean to dictate or offer gratuitous advice to [the] Greek Govt. but realize [that] this subject is under active discussion by [the] Greek press and [by] political figures, and [a] confidential friendly talk with [the] Regent[4] might offer him encouragement to crystallize Greek thinking into some formula acceptable to most political factions. . . ." (19) In late November, Damaskinos, upset by the composition of the new Cabinet under Sofoulis and by royalist opposition to the postponement of the plebiscite, threatened to resign as Regent. MacVeagh, uninstructed but acting as an "old friend of Greece," interceded with the Archbishop and persuaded him to stay on. In his public statement, Damaskinos credited the American Ambassador with having prevailed upon him to withdraw his resignation. In a rare gesture of approval the Department

---

[4] Damaskinos agreed, and expressed the view that the plebiscite be postponed for a considerable period, possibly as long as three years after the elections, a suggestion which the Department found unacceptable. *FR 1945*, VIII, 151.

complimented MacVeagh "on taking initiative at [a] critical juncture in [the] Greek governmental crisis." (20)

On December 13, MacVeagh was made an honorary citizen of Athens, an honor seldom bestowed upon a foreign diplomat. Several weeks later, he requested permission to return to the United States, so that he could bring home his wife, who was seriously ill. The MacVeaghs left Athens in late January, and he was away from his post until the end of June. During his absence, his duties were assumed by Karl L. Rankin and by Ambassador Henry F. Grady, head of the newly arrived American team of observers who were to oversee the Greek elections.[5] Just before his departure, he called to the Department's attention a long report on the Greek crisis prepared for the War Department by Captain William H. McNeill, the American Assistant Military Attaché in Athens. After a brief summary of the report, he repeated with approval McNeill's contention that "Greece's economic and political problems must be tackled concurrently and that in the long run her salvation as an independent country depends on a balance being achieved between the Near Eastern policies of Great Britain and Soviet Russia." MacVeagh concluded:

> It is indeed always possible for Greece to find a kind of temporary "stability" in what Captain McNeill describes as an "authoritarian" government, "enjoying the support of a violent police and a pliant army." Such a thing has occurred many times before in Greece throughout her very long history, and the present report indicates convincingly that all the essential conditions may now be present for its occurring again once the British forces leave. However, in the present state of world opinion, and particularly of British politics, such an authoritarian government, if issuing from the right, could hardly maintain itself, and therefore the most likely eventuality in case the new government to be produced by the forthcoming elections should prove unviable in the face of a Parliament closely divided between leftist and rightist elements (thus repeating the situation which only a few years ago produced the fascist dictatorship of Metaxas) would seem to be the eventual emergence of a dictatorship

---

[5] The elections of March 31, 1946, held under a form of proportional representation, resulted in a sweeping victory for the Right. Of a total of 354 parliamentary seats, 231 were won by the Populists and other royalists, while the Liberals received only 67 seats, with another 51 going to republican deputies. Of the registered voters, forty-nine percent actually cast ballots. The Left, which boycotted the elections, claimed afterwards that more than half of the electorate had abstained in support of the boycott. Impartial estimates of communist support at the time of the March 1946 elections range between twenty and thirty percent. In the new Populist Government, sworn in on April 18, Constantine Tsaldaris held the posts of Prime Minister and Minister of Foreign Affairs.

of the left, which in turn would infallibly place Greece, like all the other Balkan countries at the present time, under the predominating influence of Russia. Persons interested in world politics and the future maintenance of world peace might do well to consider what such an eventuality would mean, having regard to the critical position of this small country at the oldest historical crossroads of empire. (21)

While in Washington, MacVeagh called on President Truman (on March 1), and had long sessions at the Department of State, discussing the problems of Greece. He concurred with the Department's decision to urge the Greek Government not to postpone the national elections, as the communists, most of the socialists, and, at one point, the Liberals as well had been demanding, and instead, to do everything possible to insure full participation by the voters. "It would be unfortunate," Chargé Karl Rankin was instructed to advise Prime Minister Sofoulis, "if upon the first occasion after 10 years that the citizens of Greece are given an opportunity freely to choose their own Govt. at the polls, the outcome of the elections should be prejudiced by abstention from voting by parties or groups. . . ."[6] [The] Greek people by patriotically going to the polls on Mar. 31 and casting their votes for the parties of their choice will justify [the] faith of [the] American people in [the] imperishability of [the] Greek democratic tradition." (22) Similarly, MacVeagh found "logical" a British proposal that the plebiscite on the issue of the monarchy be held at a "relatively early" date (that is, during 1946, and not a year or two later, as initially envisaged), and that a small Anglo-American mission should supervise the preparation of the electoral lists. "The holding of a plebiscite, as well as of elections," he argued in an office memorandum, "was foreseen in the Varkiza Agreement, and both must be considered parts of one and the same operation undertaken to solve the Greek political problem by recourse to the people. For us to help the Greeks with one part of this operation and withdraw entirely as regards the other would really be going only half way in extending our assistance. . . ." (23)

From Athens, to which he returned in late June, MacVeagh reported that the Communist Party, having boycotted the elections, was now declaring its intention "to participate in, and win the plebiscite." He dis-

---

[6] In a separate and top secret telegram, Ambassador Grady was advised that if, despite the urging, the elections were delayed, the Department was prepared to recommend to the President that the American observers in Greece remain until June 1 at the latest, if the British and French were to do the same. *FR 1946*, VII, 127. However, yielding to British and American pressure, the parties of the center agreed to the March 31 date.

counted the KKE's claim that the national army would disobey "orders for civil war and dictatorship" and pointed out that "these threats are but a faint echo of former truculence"; instead, "the fact is made clear that reconciliation and confidence are now the communist order of the day." He continued:

> Whether the party really wants reconciliation and actually feels confident may, however, be doubted. The actions of the KKE, particularly in connection with armed band activities in the North of Greece have recently been anything but conciliatory, while, as regards confidence, the March elections have supplied unmistakable proof, if such were needed, that only with the aid of large numbers of republican voters can the extreme left hope to emerge on the victorious side in a free referendum. Hence it would seem that, locally, the new conciliatory and confident party line may be aimed to convince republicans of royalist responsibility for the conditions of disorder in the country, while coincidentally a state of chaos is promoted tending to impress on foreign opinion the impossibility of anything like a free referendum here under existing conditions. In this connection, the Department will recollect that postponement of the plebiscite is still a part of republican policy ... forming a strong point of agreement with the Left along with a common fear and distrust of the Rightist extremists in the present Government. An attempt at this time to hang sheep's clothing on the communist wolf (also feared, of course, by the center group) may therefore have appeared to Mr. Zahariadis and his friends as a good idea,—however difficult of success in a country where the wolf is so well known,—while as regards foreign opinion it has every possibility of succeeding, owing to the wide-spread efficiency of Soviet-supported EAM propaganda abroad. (24)

In early August, fighting between communist bands and government troops in the Mt. Olympus area began to reach serious proportions. Reporting on the expanding size of the forces involved in these operations, MacVeagh observed that "Much seems to depend on [the] early success of these forces if conditions of 'civil war' repeatedly mentioned in communist propaganda ... are not to develop." Recalling the KKE's recent conciliatory declarations, he repeated an informant's assertion that the Greek Government was about to launch an all-out offensive against the communists, including the outlawing of the KKE, and that this was the reason for the current "overt policy of 'reconciliation' adopted by communist chiefs." There was, however, another aspect to the situation:

Meanwhile, though strong measures [to] insure law and order undoubtedly carries [*sic*] appeal to large part of population, [the] Government may be making as many enemies as friends on account of [the] growing official tendency (1) to consider all persons Communists unless Royalists, (2) to protect former Metaxists and collaborators and (3) to accept armed assistance from disreputable elements professing royalism. [The] Increasing exasperation of members of all parliamentary opposition groups [is] apparent in this connection, and [the] strengthening rather than weakening of anti-King and even pro-Communist sentiment throughout country [is] not impossible as [a] result of [the] present extremist policy of [the] governing authorities. (25)

On the matter of communist protestations and complaints, MacVeagh was often able to comment on the basis of first-hand knowledge. In late July, he was visited by a delegation of EAM's Central Committee, headed by George Siantos, demanding the intervention of the United States against the excesses of the Tsaldaris Government. Specifically, Siantos charged that the Government's policy of "supporting by force its political purpose to bring back [the] king" was creating a situation which "has almost reached the stage of civil war." After the March elections, this policy was implemented openly and officially, forcing "thousands of democrats" to take refuge in the mountains and to resort to armed self-defense. EAM had in vain urged the Government to convene an all-party meeting for the purpose of insuring the "equality [of] all citizens and [the] amnesty [of] all persons whether left or right who have been forced [to] flee [their] home and take up arms for protection." EAM's Central Committee had therefore decided to request that the United States investigate the situation, and under the terms of the Yalta agreements "intervene to assure equal democratic opportunities" for all in Greece. In his report on this conversation, MacVeagh observed that EAM's move was probably motivated by the communists' "alarm over new government measures" and the desire of the communist-controlled EAM to maintain its reputation abroad as a democratic movement. Moreover, while it was true that the Government's "law and order" measures were "largely in [the] hands of unscrupulous reactionaries with restoration aims,"[7] conditions in the country were not in fact those of civil war.

---

[7] A month later, MacVeagh telegraphed the Department that one of his informants had found in northern Peloponnesus "royalist intimidation" of unprecedented ferocity: "Leading Leftists fled from [their] homes and democratic activity on [the] part of both Liberals and Leftists is at standstill since this produces instant threats of destruction of property or death." MacVeagh telegram 1132, August 28, 1946, *DSR*, 868.00/8-2846. A serious incident of such "intimidation" attributed

As for the Government itself, its royalist complexion was "largely due to countrywide reaction against past Communist excesses." (26)

In a separate despatch a few days after his meeting with the EAM leadership, MacVeagh transmitted to the Department an intelligence report[8] concerning a government plan to purge the armed forces and police of "all persons suspected of membership in or sympathy with the KKE." Greek military authorities regarded the communists as a "fifth column," conspiring with external enemies to destroy the country's territorial integrity, and responsible for recent acts of sabotage and for mutinies in army units. The report concluded that while American intelligence tended to confirm the fears of the Greek military authorities, it was nevertheless "perhaps regrettable that moderation and discretion have not been considered as consistent with effectiveness by the present Government, and one may wonder whether precipitate and ill-considered moves will not do more damage than good in the long run." In his own analysis, MacVeagh endorsed the substance of the report, but pointed out that the charges against the communists were hardly new and had in fact been more valid the previous year. He therefore speculated on the reasons why the Greek authorities were prepared to resort to drastic action at this particular time:

> What is new in the present situation is of course on the Government side of the picture rather than on that of the Communists. A year's intensive training of the Greek army and *gendarmerie* by British Missions has resulted in a much more effective instrument for "law and order" than any Greek Government possessed in 1945. Also the Greek Government itself has changed radically in character since last March. It is now, for the first time since 1936, at least to some extent an elected Government. If it cannot yet claim support of a true majority in the country, it can be sure that it has at least a numerous party behind it, and feels encouraged thereby to use every instrument at hand to consolidate and improve its position. Furthermore, that people menaced ever since December 1944 by the terrors of *sans culottisme* in its most deadly organized modern form should wish to strike back effectively once they have the power to do so, is quite understandable. They can hardly be expected to accept Com-

---

to the royalist organization "X" was the subject of yet another lengthy report: MacVeagh despatch 3017, August 16, 1946, *DSR*, 868.00/8-1646.

[8] The author of the report, Thomas Karamessines, identified as "an Attaché of this Embassy in close and constant touch with Greek and British security authorities," was at that time chief of OSS in Greece and MacVeagh's principal confidential liaison with Greek political leaders. He was to become a key figure in CIA operations in Greece and elsewhere.

munist offers of "reconciliation" at their face value, or even such a "middle of the road" policy as the relatively secure British and American Democracies have been counselling from abroad. All this can be understood and allowed for. But what is less understandable, at least at this time of the world's history, is the positive program only too clearly allied with this defensive reaction. Under the guise of royalism this program actually approximates Fascism at a time when, if anything has been proven by events, it is that Fascism has no place in the modern world. By their policy of continually enlarging their definition of Communism to include all who do not support the return of the King, the extremists of the Mavromichalis type now conducting the Government's crusade against Communism are risking the creation here, by confirming the alliance of large numbers of democrats with the extreme left, of the same sort of ideological civil war which has occurred in Spain. Thus they are promoting precisely the kind of conflict which the Communists themselves have been trying to effectuate here through their past manipulation and present control of the Resistance Movement. Such folly, if continued, can only result in rendering confusion worse confounded in this country, and is the very thing to fit beautifully (in its blindness) with the possible schemes of any foreign power which might wish to make an issue of conditions here before the United Nations.[9]

On August 19, 1946, in anticipation of the impending plebiscite, the Department made public the findings of the "Allied Mission to observe the Revision of Greek Electoral Lists." The Mission was satisfied that "the revision and recompilations of the electoral lists as observed by it attain a degree of fairness and accuracy which justifies their use in seeking the opinion of the Greek people in matters of national import." (27) The head of the Mission's American section, Leland Morris, was therefore instructed to consult with MacVeagh and British officials in Athens on the necessary arrangements for observing the plebiscite. He was also directed to inform the Greek Government that Washington was "somewhat disturbed by recent reports of [a] growing tendency on [the] part of various factions to bring pressure for the apparent purpose

[9] MacVeagh despatch 3010, August 10, 1946, *DSR*, 868.00/8-1046. On August 24, the Soviet Union submitted a formal complaint to the United Nations Security Council charging the Greek Government with the creation of conditions in the Balkans which threatened the peace and security of the area. See United Nations, *Official Records of the Security Council, 1st year, 2nd series, Supplement No. 5*, p. 149. MacVeagh was not involved in the decision concerning the handling of the complaint in the United Nations, or in the subsequent deliberations which led to the establishment by the Security Council of a Special Committee on the Balkans to investigate clashes along Greece's northern frontier.

5. Athens, October 1946. With King George II.

of influencing plebiscite results." Observers' reports of any acts of violence or intimidation would be considered "in arriving at our decision with regard to [the] fairness of [the] plebiscite." (28)

Following the plebiscite, which was held on September 1 and resulted in a decisive vote in favor of the King, Morris reported that conditions had been generally satisfactory, despite many complaints from voters, and despite the established fact that in an unspecified number of voting stations "irregularities" had given "advantage to the supporters of the Government." Morris and his British counterpart criticised the lack of safety and order, especially in the countryside, and dismissed as "unreal" the 94 percent voter turn-out reported by Greek authorities. They added: "There is no doubt in our minds that the party representing the government view exercised undue influence in securing votes in support of the return of the King, but without that influence we are satisfied that a majority of votes for the King's return could have been obtained." (29) Reporting on the final results of the plebiscite MacVeagh observed: ". . . the returns can hardly be regarded as an index to the country's feeling as between royalism and democracy, since undoubtedly many republicans voted for the king's return as a purely temporary expedient against communism, while many communists cast "democratic" ballots as a part of their campaign to confuse political issues. Probably the returns from the plebiscite show that a majority of the voters (all due allowances being made for disturbances at the polls and intimidation both by the right and left)[10] desired, on September 1, the return of King George. But they cannot be made to mean anything more than this." (30)

After the King's return to Athens (on September 27), Washington felt compelled to urge upon the Greek Government a policy of moderation, toleration, and democratic principle. The Department considered asking President Truman to address a letter to the Greek monarch, which might also be made public, "welcoming him back to the throne and at the

---

[10] The Department's own concern over voting "irregularities" was conveyed to the British in informal conversations in Washington. Discussing the possible release of Anglo-American reports on the conduct of the plebiscite, the Department took the position that "Although it is the general feeling of Ambassador Morris and other qualified observers that the majority of the Greek people favored the return of the King, the conditions under which the plebiscite was held were far from ideal and it would be impossible for either of our Governments to issue a statement giving the Greek Government a clean bill of health. At the same time, any public rebuke of the Greek Government would be seized upon and exaggerated by governments unfriendly to Greece. . . ." Baxter Memorandum, October 8, 1946, *DSR*, 868.00/10-846. Reflecting the same concern, Secretary Byrnes took advantage of the Paris conference on the peace treaties to advise Prime Minister Tsaldaris "as to what should be done when the king returned." See Byrnes' letters to William L. Clayton, October 1, 1946, *DSR*, FW868.00/10-846.

same time stating in fairly general terms our hope that his presence will lead to harmony among the various political factions in Greece and to complete restoration of democratic procedures in his country." MacVeagh might also be instructed to express to the King "somewhat more frankly" American dissatisfaction with "some of the disturbing characteristics of the present Populist Government." (31) Although the President's letter was not sent,[11] MacVeagh had his "frank" talk with King George, and reported on October 11, 1946:

> In a long conversation with the King this afternoon I was able to make the following suggestions on the purely personal and informal basis which he seems to invite and appreciate:
> (1) That the King should insist on the political leaders getting together to form a broadly representative govt. and that the possibility of his personally advising the public of any opposition to his appeal might be enough to bring recalcitrants into line; (2) that unity among all nationally minded Greeks is as important now as collaboration among the politicians and that in the country's present dearth of statesmen, *only the crown's leadership can bring this about*; (3) that the only practicable curative program for this country after what it has gone through is one of widespread tolerance, justice and mercy similar to the program of Lincoln after the American Civil War; (4) that in pursuance of such a program all people who have "gone into the mountains" except those subject to definite charges under the Greek code should be allowed to return freely to their homes; (5) that wives and children of fugitives should no longer be imprisoned and exiled as hostages; (6) that in general every Greek should be allowed his or her political opinions and no one be prosecuted except for definite commission of crime. I emphasized my belief that if such programs were put into effect at least 70 percent of the existing banditry in Greece would disappear. I spoke of my belief that certain policies of the present Defense Minister, Mavromichalis, may be "tending toward Fascism" which I felt could not be tolerated again after the Allied Nations have fought a war for its eradication; and I added that whether or not the policy I suggested is the right solution for the present problems I felt sure that in following it the King would have the satisfaction of the approval of his own conscience.
> Somewhat to my surprise the King expressed thorough agreement

[11] Following MacVeagh's conversation with the King on October 11, the Department informed MacVeagh that a letter from the President was no longer considered necessary, particularly in view of the fact that the King had been so receptive to MacVeagh's suggestions. *FR 1946*, VII, 239, fn. 6.

6. Athens, summer 1947. With King Paul.

with each one of the above points. In regard to (1) he said he has already sounded out the politicians and found all of them agreeable to the idea of collaboration in a broadened govt. except Sofoulis who holds out for being Premier. He said he had approved of the politicians going to Paris[12] because they might learn there some things to convince them of the necessity of getting together as well as of the fact that Greek "national claims" must be considered as part of the whole great problem of world peace. Regarding (2) he accepted the idea and showed no tendency to shirk the responsibility of the Crown and in respect to (3) and (4), indicated that he had already thought of attempting to follow the Lincoln example. As to (5) he was emphatic in stating his belief that the present policy only tends to increase bitterness by the addition of resentment and in connection with (6) assented warmly and fully as to this being the general need of the hour. In addition he was impressed by my estimate of the number of non-criminal elements in the band [land?][13] and said of Mr. Mavromichalis that "He is an old playmate of my youth but I think him stupid." Fascism, he agreed, is no longer a possible solution, adding:

[12] A large all-party delegation of political leaders had represented Greece at the Paris Peace Conference.
[13] Probably "bands."

"Dictatorship never agreed with my ideas and I made a mistake to fall in with it."

In comment I would point out that the King spoke as I did purely personally, that he is a lonely and distracted figure and that his happily good intentions are not likely to find much support from the local influences surrounding him.... I therefore intend to communicate the substance of my conversation to my British colleague who in his first audience received only the formal assurance that the King "will act constitutionally" and the impression that he is resentful toward the British for having kept him out of Greece these past 2 years. This last probably true but the British can afford to ignore it and I believe that if they will only make full use now of their position here to strengthen the King's hand in an all-out effort to liberalize the Govt. and unify behind the régime all but the criminal and subversive elements in the country, there is a chance to reduce greatly the dangers of Slavic infiltration and Communist activity and consequently to favor the economic reconstruction now so greatly hampered by widespread dissension and fear. However the time to make use of the King's possibilities as a unifying and constructive agent is now while he still retains some adventitious popularity as a result of his return by the plebiscite. After he has been seen for a while to do nothing or is felt to be falling under the influence of some local group it will be too late....[14]

To an old colleague in the diplomatic service, MacVeagh expressed little confidence that political conditions in Greece would improve, and once again emphasized the need for outside assistance and strong counsel:

Lack of leadership is certainly what principally ails this country at the present time—leadership which can see beyond political problems which are not only local in character but also completely out of date. The five-year Metaxas dictatorship seems to have effectively prevented the rise of a new generation of politicians to take the place of the oldsters, who have now come back into the saddle, for lack of other leaders, and who still think in terms of the old struggle be-

[14] *FR 1946*, VII, 233-35. Emphasis added. In a rare gesture of approval the Department telegraphed MacVeagh a strong message of commendation, adding: "Your ideas expressed to him [the King] show profound understanding of [the] complicated Greek situation and represent [the] finest kind of US advice to [a] head of [a] friendly Allied state whose future is of extreme concern to this Government. You should seek [an] early opportunity to inform [the] King that you have reported [the] substance of your conversation to your Government which is in full agreement with the ideas expressed and gratified to learn of [the] King's attitude towards [the] specific problems discussed." *Ibid.*

tween Royalists and Venizelists, entirely missing the meaning of the developments in Europe and the world which World War II and the rise of Russia have brought about. Small men, old men, and men entirely lacking in the sense of realism which the situation requires, are what we are having to deal with now. In addition, the King, who has been brought back as a "solution" for the problems which the politicians will not tackle, is the same old muddled indecisive figure that he always was. Nobody loves him, trusts him, or believes in him, but he is expected to work miracles. And finally, the British, hampered by the leftist affiliations of their Government, and wanting to maintain their control while fearing to take the steps necessary to that end, seem to be pursuing a dangerously "hands off" policy. I say "dangerously" because, if left to themselves, the King and the politicians are only too likely to repeat their old non-cooperation of 1935-1936 and to run into a similar impasse to that which produced the dictatorship.

Briefly, what seems to be needed now is that King and Government should work together in creating here such a liberal democracy as the Western Powers can support, and that anything which might be construed to savor of a police régime (and there has been too much of this under the Defense Ministry of our friend Mavromichalis) should be avoided. At the same time, everything possible should be done to build up the economic life of the country, which the war has thrown into a state highly favorable to Communist propaganda. But if the British, who I feel really see things exactly in this way, won't step out and use their influence here for all it is worth to secure the first requirements of this program, the whole may very well prove impossible and Greece go down the Soviet drain,—unless, of course, we wish to take the primary responsibility for Greece ourselves.

It is unfortunate that the King has come back in a bitter mood toward the British, whom he considers to have unwarrantedly prevented his return to Greece these past two years, and that he is consequently somewhat disinclined to listen to their advice. To their counsel that he observe "moderation," he has replied only that he intends "to act constitutionally." But perhaps with some backing from us they might move him to exert his influence which should be considerable now, immediately following his return, in a more constructive fashion. It is commonly thought here that Britain and the United States must infallibly support Greece, no matter what line she follows internally. My British colleague (Leeper) was actually told this to his face by Greeks, when trying to moderate Royalist extremism, on a number of occasions. Such misconception, if indulged in by the King himself, would only confirm him in his natural reluctance to make decisions and might very well lead to serious consequences, in view of the character of the present British Government and the tendencies of our public opinion, and I shall certainly support Norton,[15] unofficially and personally, in any attempts he may make to influence the King to abandon his formal constitutionalism in favor of an active liberal policy. But ultimately, I think, I shall have to be instructed officially if we are to be successful in any such capital intervention. The unsupported word of envoys no longer carries conviction as it used to do, say in the days of Stratford de Redcliffe,[16] now that everyone is accustomed to hear over the radio the very voices of our policy-makers themselves "thundering in the index." Of course, if a leader like Mr. Venizelos were alive here today, Greece would not need foreigners to tell her where her only possible future lies. Furthermore, she would have gone to Paris with a clear conception of what was obtainable there, and not annoyed her best friends with crying for the moon. But now she truly seems to be in a position where strong guidance by those friends, however harassed they may be from other causes, is more necessary, both internally and externally, for the security of all concerned, than at any other time in her whole modern history. (32)

MacVeagh's firm but largely ineffective advice to the Greek monarch heralded a dramatic change in American policy toward Greece. In retrospect, it is clear that this new policy was not caused by any significant changes in the situation in Greece, although increasing attention was being paid to the rising level of violence, particularly in the northern provinces. Instead, it reflected American apprehensions concerning the intentions of the Soviet Union and its suspected agents across Europe. Verbal assaults upon the Greek Government in the United Nations and the communist press were now viewed as the prelude to the active involvement of outside forces in the Greek crisis. Accordingly, on October 15, 1946, after high-level consultations between the Departments of State and War and the White House, MacVeagh was informed that a document[17] on "specific steps to implement active US interest in Greece" had

[15] Sir Clifford V. Norton, British Ambassador to Greece, succeeded Leeper in March 1946.
[16] Stratford de Redcliffe, British Ambassador to Turkey (1842-1858).
[17] In its final version, dated October 21, 1946, under the title "Memorandum Regarding Greece," this document, about which the Department informed MacVeagh on October 15, stressed the strategic importance of Greece as "the only country of the Balkans which has not yet fallen under Soviet hegemony," and which, together with Turkey, was "the sole obstacle to Soviet domination of the Eastern Mediterranean." The Soviet Union was providing military assistance to Greece's enemies, both domestic and foreign. The United States should be prepared to as-

been approved in principle by Secretary Byrnes. Because the "strained international relations focusing on Greece may result in [an] early major crisis which may be a deciding factor in [the] future orientation of Near and Middle Eastern countries," a new policy principle had evolved: "It is of importance to US security that Greece remain independent and in charge of her own affairs, and we are prepared to take suitable measures to support [the] territorial and political integrity [of] Greece." While looking for ways to initiate its new policy, the Department remained critical of the continuing political oppression and the "lawlessness of Extreme Right groups." It wished to urge the Greek Government to "distinguish sharply in its attitude towards [the] opposition between those essentially loyal groups which differ with regard to the kind of govt. Greece should have and those groups which are intent on depriving Greece eventually of its independence." It was understood that the inclusion of the communists in the Government was not possible under existing conditions. At the same time, "certain notoriously reactionary Rightists are almost equally to blame for objectionable features of present Govt. policy and should be removed from power for the good of the Greek people as a whole." MacVeagh's comments were urgently requested on a number of specific components of the new policy, "some of which have been in effect for some time":

1. Make clear to world by diplomatic conversations, public statements, or other appropriate means that US strongly supports Greek independence and territorial integrity and actively encourages development in Greece of democracy and peaceable and reasonable policy on part of Greek Govt.
2. Direct US advice to Greek Govt. that policy of moderation in internal political affairs should be followed now that regime question has been voted on.
3. Clear statement by US to Greek Govt. of view that Greek frontiers should remain those of 1939 in interest of justice, peace and stability.
4. Active support of Greece in UN and Security Council when occasion arises.
5. Question of sale to Greece and by what country of sufficient arms for maintaining internal order and defending territorial integrity until UN military forces are prepared to undertake guarantee against aggression has been discussed in general with Secretary but final decision on policy awaits his return in near future.

---

sume greater responsibilities in supporting the Greek Government, particularly in view of the gradual withdrawal of the British forces in Greece, *FR 1964*, VII, 240-45.

6. Recommendation to Eximbank[18] and International Bank concerning economic assistance to Greece provided credits are expended on sound projects which will strengthen economy.

7. Relief assistance following cessation of UNRRA activities. Methods of implementation now under urgent consideration by Dept.

8. Additional credits and if necessary priority treatment, for purchase by Greece of US surplus property both in US and abroad.

9. Make available to Greece appropriate US financial and economic advice through advisers and technicians or through dispatch of US economic mission.

10. Appropriate US action when necessary to assist Greece in finding export markets and in acquiring essential goods in US market.

11. Appropriate action to relieve Greek shipping crisis through sale or charter of vessels.

12. Active attempts to inform American public through press and foreign policy associations of nature of US policy towards Greece and reasons for it. (33)

MacVeagh's reaction to the long telegram of October 15 was one of pure elation. In a personal letter to Loy Henderson, Director of the Department's Office of Near Eastern and African Affairs, he wrote: "I feel now as Cassandra might, had anyone suddenly agreed with her!" He expressed his personal gratitude "for your understanding of what is going on out here." (34) And he telegraphed the Department: "Cannot concur too strongly in revaluated general policy re Greece." On the specific policies enumerated in the October 15 telegram, he offered the following comments:

> Numbers 1 and 12. These seem cardinal for success of entire program and I hope may be fully implemented.
> Number 2. Idea of "direct US advice" is especially apt since weakness of King and pettiness of politicians [are] unlikely [to] respond satisfactorily to advice on merely informal level.[19]
> Number 3. This might be more helpful if mention of "justice" omitted since strong feeling here that justice, if not realism, requires cession of some territory to Greece especially by Albania.
> Number 4. "When occasion arises" might be clarified. Does it mean

[18] Export-Import Bank of the United States.
[19] MacVeagh read the October 15 telegram to Prime Minister Tsaldaris and urged him again to broaden his government and to "dissociate himself squarely and openly from Metaxism and Fascism. . . ." MacVeagh telegram 1441, October 23, 1946, *DSR*, 868.00/10-2346. Similarly, he read the message to the King and reported that, according to the monarch, the only party refusing to cooperate with such a plan to broaden the Cabinet was Sofoulis' Liberals. *FR 1946*, VII, 238-39.

"when occasion warrants"? If latter it might be beneficial so to inform Greece to strengthen Greek morale on the one hand and to forestall intemperate attitude on the other.

Number 5. One of contributing causes of internal disorder is excessive amount of arms already in country and no amount of arms sold to Greece would enable its small army to withstand forces of northern neighbors. Best way to control banditry would seem to be more intelligent employment of armed forces . . . combined with more liberal political policy.

Number 9. Would suggest sending only small economic mission of top flight persons capable of determining and effectively promoting sound practical projects as foreseen in number 6. Believe general advice ineffective but if fear for security can be lifted economy might benefit from foreign technical and financial assistance in connection with realizable enterprises of self-liquidating nature. I am particularly pleased that US has decided henceforth actively to support territorial and political integrity of *Greece* as important to US security; as well as to give governing authorities in Greece such direct advice and assistance as may seem necessary to encourage development there of real democracy in contrast to spurious brand, pressing down from the north. (35)

Throughout the fall and winter of 1946, the Embassy in Athens provided the Department with frequent and detailed accounts of guerrilla activities across the country, and especially along the borders of the north. Beginning as isolated incidents earlier in the year, these attacks on small towns and garrisons gradually took on the appearance of a well planned operation to challenge the ability of the government troops to control the countryside. While large scale foreign support for the insurgents could not be established with any degree of certainty, there could be no doubt that the guerrillas had free access to the territories of Albania, Yugoslavia, and Bulgaria, and often used them as staging areas and supply centers. In late November, MacVeagh telegraphed that the armed bands in northern Greece had declared themselves the "Republican" (or "Democratic") Army, but added that the new name "represents no change in [the] military situation since coordination as well as excellent training and equipment" of the guerrillas had been quite evident in recent months. He thought that the name might have been modeled after that of the Irish Republican Army, in the hope that it would appeal to anti-British sentiment in America and elsewhere. That this "Army" was communist-controlled was clearly beyond question. (36) After a long conversation with Field Marshal Montgomery, who, as Chief of the Imperial Staff, had just visited Greece for a personal review of the military situation,

MacVeagh reported on December 3 that Montgomery had urged the Greek Government to devote the winter months to the training and equipping of its army, especially for combatting guerrillas, and then, during the spring of 1947, to take the initiative and totally destroy the communist bands. The Field Marshal took the view that unless this were done, Greece would be lost to the communists. (37)

Alarmed by the deteriorating situation, and acting in the spirit of the recently agreed-upon policy, the Department advised MacVeagh that an "American Economic Mission to Greece," headed by Paul A. Porter, would soon be leaving for Athens, with instructions to complete its work by May. Its task would be to "examine economic conditions in Greece as they bear upon the reconstruction and development" of its economy, and to consider "the extent to which the Greek Government can carry out reconstruction and development through effective use of Greek resources, and the extent to which foreign assistance may be required." (38) Earlier (on November 8), MacVeagh had been told that as a result of talks between the Secretary of State and the British Foreign Minister at the Paris Peace Conference, Britain was to continue supplying Greece with arms and military equipment, while the United States was to limit itself to economic assistance. Under certain circumstances, American weapons might be provided to the British for delivery to Greece. MacVeagh was to explain to the Greeks that the United States' "reluctance to furnish military equipment direct[ly] is not due to any unwillingness on our part to support Greece in its efforts to retain its independence and territorial integrity, but rather to our feeling that in the world situation the wiser course would be for the Greeks to look to Great Britain. . . ." (39)

The decision to provide Greece with substantial economic and diplomatic support, a move which he had been advocating for years, nevertheless placed MacVeagh in a difficult position. The Department wanted it understood that such assistance was conditional upon the formation of a new, broadly-based coalition government in Athens, from which such right-wing personalities as Mavromichalis and Zervas would be excluded. MacVeagh dutifully and repeatedly conveyed this message to Tsaldaris, to the King, to the King's political adviser P. Pipinelis, as well as to the leaders of the non-communist opposition. When no results appeared forthcoming, he had the unpleasant task of informing Tsaldaris, who was determined to travel to the United States—ostensibly for the purpose of presenting Greece's territorial claims to the Foreign Ministers Conference meeting in New York, but in essence to win for himself Washington's stamp of approval—that while the American Government would "welcome" his visit, it nevertheless felt that "it would be unfortunate for him [to] leave Greece [at] this critical time. . . . It seems to us [that the] task of broadening [the] govt. and endeavoring to strengthen Greece internally is [the] most important one that can face a Greek Pri[me] Min[ister] at [the] present time." (40)

Despite the stern warning, Tsaldaris did visit the United States (December 19-23), and had meetings with Secretary Byrnes and with President Truman. He also appeared at the United Nations to defend his Government against Soviet charges of aggression and political oppression, and to present Greek counter-charges against its northern neighbors. Subsequently, the Department informed MacVeagh that American officials had been "unfavorably impressed by Tsaldaris' lack of precision and by [the] complete absence of any well-prepared data to substantiate [his] exaggerated demands" on every issue discussed. The Greek Prime Minister was not to be permitted to take personal credit for any American commitments of assistance, "and to exploit his success in order to perpetuate his uneasy position in [the] Greek political world." Once again, MacVeagh was to tell the Greeks that "in this critical time, when [the] existence of Greece is threatened by unfriendly neighbors as well as [by] civil strife and economic collapse, all loyal political parties and leaders should unite to form [the] most broadly based govt. possible, dedicated to modernization, [to] all feasible conciliation to [the] loyal opposition, and [to a] sincere determination to institute economic and fiscal reforms even though drastic in their nature." And lest it appear in Athens that American support of Greece in the Security Council's recent discussions of incidents along Greece's northern frontiers (which had resulted in the establishment of a special investigating commission) was unqualified, Tsaldaris was to be advised that Washington was "not sure that [the] Greek Government has been above reproach in [the] manner of instituting and applying recent security measures. . . ." (41) Exploring every avenue of approach, MacVeagh told Pipinelis that "it seems to be felt in [the] US and Britain that [the] time has come for the King to impose his leadership on [the] politicians. . . ."[20]

While meticulous in his role as his Government's messenger, the ambassador also sought to caution his superiors that the failure to improve the composition and policies of the Athens Government was not entirely Tsaldaris' fault: the opposition parties appeared unwilling to participate responsibly in the handling of the nation's many problems and preferred to wait until the Populist Government collapsed. Although British and American remonstrations were justified, and had to continue, he pointed out that "in view of [the] powerful nature of [the] forces making for division and eventual anarchy in this country, we also believe that such

[20] *FR 1946*, VII, 270-71. Pipinelis replied that the King could pressure his government into action, but had no power to compel the opposition parties to cooperate. *Ibid.*

persistent pressure on our part should be given [the] least possible publicity and that every care should be taken, as long as [the] present government remains in power, to prevent [the] growth of disrupting impressions that it lacks Allied confidence and support." (42) This concern for Greek pride, and for Greek sovereign rights that might be damaged by excessive and publicized foreign intervention, was destined to cost MacVeagh his post. The charge that he had come to espouse the cause of the Greek conservative-royalist factions would be heard even long after he had left Athens.

As conditions in Greece continued to deteriorate, Anglo-American presssures for a more representative government gradually had their desired effect. On January 24, 1947, a new coalition government took office, under Dimitrios Maximos, with Tsaldaris now serving as Deputy Premier and Foreign Minister. Although Sofoulis continued to hold out for the premiership, a number of prominent Liberals, including Kanellopoulos, Papandreou, and Venizelos, joined the cabinet which, with a number of alterations, survived until the end of August. Meanwhile, by early February, MacVeagh's reports assumed a more alarming tone than heretofore, and increasingly placed the blame for the Greek crisis upon external factors. After consulting with Paul Porter, head of the Economic Mission, and with Mark F. Ethridge, the American Representative on the United Nations Commission of Investigation, he reported on February 11 that the conclusions and recommendations of the UN Commission were expected to be "satisfactory" to the American Government. Similarly, the Porter mission, "while dealing with the internal problem of preventing imminent financial collapse, is also facing fundamentally the same external threat." He explained: "This is true because among other factors the loyalty neither of the civil servants who have already struck successfully against the Government nor of the armed forces which are already dissident to a dangerously high degree can be expected to withstand another catastrophic inflation, and revolution in this country's present circumstances can mean only one thing, Soviet control." Observing that Porter's recommendations for substantial and immediate American economic assistance were fully justified by the conditions prevailing in the country, he concluded: "If Greece falls to communism the whole Near East and part of North Africa as well are certain to pass under Soviet influence and to prevent this and the world-wide complications it would entail, a premium of not only five but many times 5 million dollars[21] would seem cheap insurance for the US." (43) In another report, MacVeagh expressed the view that the situation in Greece would not

---

[21] The amount being considered by the Department of State as immediate emergency assistance to the Greek Government.

necessarily invite direct Soviet intervention (as the Greek General Staff appeared to expect) "as long as the Russian-controlled forces of the neighboring states are available for such a purpose." (44) On February 20, again expressing also the views of Porter and Ethridge, he urged the Department to act immediately to bolster the Greek Government; otherwise, its collapse appeared imminent:

> 1) We feel situation here so critical that no time should be lost in applying any remedial measures, even if only of a temporary character, within possibilities of US and UK. Impossible to say how soon [governmental] collapse may be anticipated, but we believe that to regard it as anything but imminent would be highly unsafe. If nothing but economic and financial factors were to be considered, full collapse from Greece's present position might take several months. However, deteriorating morale both of civil servants and armed forces, as well as of general public, owing to inadequate incomes, fear of growing banditry, lack of confidence in Government, and exploitation by international communists, creates possibility of much more rapid dénouement.
>
> 2) We believe best way combat explosive situation would be to help recreate confidence in State and in future of Greece as democracy of western type by removing, at least in present acute stage, growing fear of inflation and consequently of increased misery, and by making plain to everyone, including Soviet Union, our determination not rpt [repeat] not to permit foreign encroachment, either from without or within, on independence and integrity of Greece.
>
> 3) We feel that immediate temporary solution to gold problem should be effected, and that this should be followed closely by such heartening attention to Greece's situation as our suggested visit by Secretary would supply. Coordinated practical and spectacular measures of this sort we believe would help to avert at least the imminent danger of explosion, and would "buy time" for eventual application of remedies of a longer term character such as constitute chief concern of UN and Porter Missions. (45)

MacVeagh's top secret telegram No. 243 of February 20, quoted above,[22] had a profound effect upon the Department. On the same day, Henderson reported its substance and immediate background in a lengthy memorandum to Under-Secretary Acheson, who endorsed it and submitted it

[22] In a copy of this telegram, which he kept in his personal files, MacVeagh added along the margin for the benefit of a researcher: "Ambassador's plea for facing up to situation squarely. Answer partly given in President's message" (the "Truman Doctrine" speech).

promptly (on the 21st) to Secretary Marshall under the ominous title "Crisis and Imminent Possibility of Collapse in Greece." The memorandum echoed MacVeagh's argument and expanded upon it: "The capitulation of Greece to Soviet domination through lack of adequate support from the U.S. and Great Britain might eventually result in the loss of the whole Near and Middle East and northern Africa. It would consolidate the position of Communist minorities in many other countries where their aggressive tactics are seriously hampering the development of middle-of-the-road governments." After reviewing current Anglo-American commitments of assistance to Greece, it drew a frank and alarming conclusion: "Under present arrangements Greece will receive neither adequate economic aid from the United States nor adequate military aid from Britain." The time for resolute action had come: "We recommend reconsideration of our policy and [a] decision to assist Greece with military equipment." (46)

A few hours after Acheson had signed his memorandum to Secretary Marshall, the British Embassy delivered to the Department two *aide-memoires* announcing Britain's inability to extend further assistance to Greece and Turkey after March 31, 1947, and requesting immediate consultations for the purpose of shifting to the United States the burden of such assistance. (47) Thus MacVeagh's alarming assessment of the situation in Greece instantly received additional support, importance, and urgency, as Britain appeared ready to abandon that country to its fate. As a result, in a matter of days the initiative for bolstering and guiding the Greek Government shifted dramatically to Washington. The American embassy in Athens was now essentially confined to the task of providing supplementary information which was needed to respond to potential critics of the proposed programs of action, and to the task of implementing such policies, conceived by officials who had only the most general understanding of the real problems besetting Greece. Once the Greek crisis had come to be perceived as the work of the Soviet Union and its agents in the Balkans, the complex realities of Greece's particular situation appeared as minor details in the broader and all-important East-West confrontation. For his part, and before he was swept away by the new spirit of "shirt-sleeve diplomacy," MacVeagh attempted to warn the Department against a precipitous assumption of direct responsibility for supporting an undemocratic régime in Greece. On March 4, once again in agreement with Porter and Ethridge, he telegraphed: "We feel it most desirable that British share responsibility here to fullest extent possible both economically and militarily and suggest US might continue avoid direct military assistance to Greece even if it must grant credits to Britain in this connection. Distinction admittedly narrow, but might have some psychological value in connection Anglophobe feeling in US and argument we being 'left holding bag'." Moreover, MacVeagh argued that American support should be given only if the Greek Government changed its narrow partisan tactics, and stopped exploiting foreign assistance "for political purposes and private gain." Finally:

> Greatest care should be taken to avoid giving impression that US aim at financing Greek "civil war," or maintaining in power an essentially reactionary govt. incapable of developing sound economic program on democratic principles. Perhaps aim might be stated to insure opportunity for broader democratic govt. and greater implementation of political, social and economic responsibility than now is possible. In this connection it might help if Congressional leaders were told privately that present govt. is not representative of nation under normal conditions, having been elected under fear of Communism both external and internal and that our policy will be directed towards liberal changes here at opportune time when this fear removed. (48)

Recalled to Washington for consultations, MacVeagh testified on March 28 at the Senate's Committee on Foreign Relations hearings on the administration's proposed program of aid to Greece and Turkey. (49) Evidently instructed to avoid as much as possible any serious review of the record and character of the Greek Government, he concentrated instead on the issue of communist subversion and of outside assistance to the rebels. Speaking in a casual style designed to appeal to his audience, he reassured the Committee's chairman, Senator Arthur H. Vandenberg, that dealing with armed subversion in Greece would not be especially difficult, and that the way to accomplish it was to have it "beaten at the top." In his view, ". . . the fellow to blame was the fellow who controls the little countries to the north of Greece, the fellow who is backing them, right square back to the Moscow Government." He elaborated:

> I think that the organizers, these fellows who are organizing the unfortunates in Greece, and that is what it amounts to—the unfortunates and miserable have gone into the mountains and are organized and tightened up and being formed into a weapon by an international Communist group. You break down their organization and you chase out or capture the fellows who are organizing them, and you will have a certain amount of banditry in Greece for a great many years, but it will not be [an] organized subversive political movement. It will be just fellows in the hills like Robin Hood, who occasionally come down and carry off somebody for ransom.

He also told the Committee that he regarded the Greek King as "a very good man," who "does not really figure in this struggle at all, except as a figurehead for the people who are afraid of communism." His only problem was that he was "not a public man," in a country which is "like a great big Near Eastern village," where "everybody has to feel he knows him [the King] and that the head man thinks about his problems and likes him." However, King George "regards himself as a constitutional monarch on the pattern of the King of England and sits in his palace and never sees his people. For that reason he cannot win unless he changes his entire attitude. . . ." MacVeagh's earlier political sophistication and his penetrating analyses, especially evident in his letters to Roosevelt, had fallen victim to the Cold War, and to the demands and limitations of Congressional politics.

With the backing of Senator Vandenberg, Truman's request for congressional authorization of his program of assistance to Greece and Turkey was never in serious danger of defeat. Nevertheless, criticism of the Greek Government in the media and in Congress was strong, and the Administration was not insensitive to it. Perhaps no one in Washington felt the barbs more than MacVeagh. On April 11, he telegraphed a secret and personal message to Prime Minister Maximos:

> While every effort is being made here to secure implementation of the President's program for aid to Greece, public opinion is being constantly disturbed by reports of official toleration of rightist excesses and the application of security measures to non-subversive political opponents of the govt. The impression created by these reports is that the President's program aims to assist a reactionary régime with all the earmarks of a police state, which is an idea unacceptable to the American people.
>
> You will remember my concern over this matter expressed to you on numerous occasions. You will also remember your assurance to me that in my absence your policy would be in accord with the President's message. I would now respectfully emphasize again, but with a new urgency born of a critical moment, the advisability (1) of your Govt.'s giving some clear factual evidence of its political tolerance and broad national character by proceeding with equal vigilance and severity against all lawlessness whether of the right or left, and (2) of its giving its actions in this respect the fullest and most persistent publicity. That the Government of Greece is "fascist" in mind and action is the argument which is telling more potently than any other against the President's program and it can be effectively answered only by the observed conduct of that Govt. itself. (50)

7. Athens, June 20, 1947. Signing of Aid Agreement. From left: Ambassador Lincoln MacVeagh; Constantine Tsaldaris, Greek Deputy Prime Minister and Foreign Minister; G. Hatzivassiliou, Director of Tsaldaris' Diplomatic Bureau; Panayiotis Pipinelis, Permanent Under Secretary of Foreign Affairs.

Returning to his post in late April, MacVeagh continued to urge the Greek Government to pursue a more conciliatory policy at home and coached it in all matters, big and small, pertaining to the assistance program. On June 20, he and Foreign Minister Tsaldaris signed the principal agreement for United States aid to Greece. (51) On July 8, MacVeagh and Prime Minister Maximos signed a supplementary agreement providing for relief assistance. The stage was now set for the United States to assume in Greece new and far-reaching responsibilities, particularly in view of the fact that the Greek Government had been compelled to accept effective American controls not only over its financial and administrative practices (which would have involved American assistance funds), but over all of its major domestic activities as well. As if to underscore the new situation, in early July the Greek Government consulted MacVeagh before launching a new wave of arrests, directed against the communists. MacVeagh was reported to have assured the Greek Government that he did not object to the arrests, if they were believed to be necessary for the country's security. On the other hand, he was said to have expressed his "surprise" that those arrested numbered almost four thousand. (52)

One would have thought that in 1947, with American policy in Greece acquiring a definite and ambitious purpose, as well as the means for its pursuit, MacVeagh would have had every reason to feel not merely vindicated, but pleased with his work. In reality, this was for him a most difficult period, as personal tragedy and professional problems conspired to bring him much pain and humiliation. Earlier in the year, his wife fell gravely ill, and during the summer months her condition became hopeless. She died in Athens on September 9, 1947. MacVeagh's own health soon began to trouble him, and he lost his zest and stamina. In the Department, some of his colleagues thought that the shock of his wife's death was so great that perhaps he should be moved to another post, where he might be better able to adjust to her loss; Greece was too full of memories for him. Although no action was taken at that time, the possibility of such a move remained on the minds of those who were responsible for such decisions. Meanwhile, his work became much more taxing, more frustrating, than ever before.

In particular, he was increasingly upset over what he saw as the domineering and high-handed manner in which American policy was being implemented. Although he fully supported the need for effective controls (particularly on the spending of American funds), and expected the Greek Government, to comply with Washington's directives, he was at the same time anxious to preserve at least the image of Greek sovereignty, and to limit American involvement to pressures upon the highest levels of the Greek Government, rather than to have American officials assume responsibilities within the Greek bureaucracy itself. Above all, he wanted to keep American policy clearly and exclusively identified with the embassy in Athens, instead of allowing it to be divided among a number of more or less independent agencies and missions. On the other hand, even considering his profound knowledge of Greek affairs and his perceptive reporting of them over so many years, MacVeagh was not regarded by his superiors as the high-powered administrator needed to manage successfully the enormous economic and military assistance programs about to be introduced. As a friend and appointee of Roosevelt, he carried no weight with the Truman administration, which by 1947 had its own supporters to reward. Finally, his traditional diplomatic style and cautious outlook brought him into conflict with the head of the Mission for Aid to Greece (AMAG), Dwight Palmer Griswold, and this clash led directly to his recall.[23]

A former Governor of Nebraska, Griswold received his new appointment on June 5 and arrived in Athens in mid-July. A Republican of considerable influence, he had been chosen in part to please a Republican-dominated Congress, and as a symbol of bipartisan harmony in the new

[23] This review of the MacVeagh-Griswold conflict is based largely on information and comments provided by senior officials of the Department who were in various ways involved in the matter, and on a long letter which MacVeagh wrote to his brother Charlton very soon after his removal from his post as Ambassador to Greece.

policy of active opposition to Soviet or communist expansion. His prior experience in foreign affairs was apparently limited to his service abroad as an army captain during World War I. Reportedly a man aspiring to national office, and obviously unfamiliar with the people and problems of Greece, he was determined to have his mission viewed as dramatic proof of his own organizational skills and of American efficiency and know-how. His selection had been made without MacVeagh's knowledge, and despite the ambassador's pleas to Acheson and others in the Department that no "politician" be sent to head the AMAG.

Before leaving for Athens, Griswold requested a meeting with the Secretaries of State, War, Navy, and Treasury, and with senior officials of the Department of State. In particular, he wanted to know what his authority would be in the anticipated reorganization of the Greek Government, in facing a possible large-scale invasion of Greece by communist forces, and in his relations with MacVeagh. He told his audience that according to journalists he had consulted, his first responsibility would be to change the Greek Government, and he thought that he might have to be "more firm" than MacVeagh in his dealings with the Greeks. According to a Department of State memorandum on this meeting, Secretary Marshal requested Henderson to respond to Griswold's remarks.

> ... Mr. Henderson outlined the Department's policy with respect to the composition of the Greek Government. Mr. Henderson said that we agreed entirely with Governor Griswold in his feeling that certain changes might be necessary, and that the Mission would probably encounter obstructions or a lack of cooperation from certain officials, who would have to be eliminated. In doing so, it would however be necessary to proceed discreetly, in order to avoid creating resentment on the part of other officials as well as the Greek people. It would be desirable that any changes in the Government which might seem desirable should be effected in such a manner that the Greeks would feel they themselves had brought about the changes. For this purpose it would probably be advisable to establish regular channels of discussion at a high level. We felt strongly that in all matters affecting the political situation in Greece or possible changes in high level Greek officials it would be important for Governor Griswold to have the advice of Ambassador MacVeagh, who is, by experience and familiarity with the problem, in a position to offer sound guidance.... (53)

Following this meeting, and obviously with certain of Griswold's remarks in mind, the Department attempted to clarify its position with regard to the powers and responsibilities of the chief of AMAG. In a long top secret letter to Griswold, dated July 11 and drafted by Henry S. Villard, Deputy Director of the Office of Near Eastern and African Affairs, Secretary Marshall outlined the objectives of American policy in Greece and the proper methods for their implementation. Specifically, he stressed the need to view the Greek situation as the result of a "worldwide Communist effort" to destroy governments which had not already become subservient to Moscow. Accordingly, the goals of American policy were: "(a) Maintenance of the independence and integrity of Greece, specifically to keep Greece from falling into the Soviet orbit; and (b) development of the economy of Greece on a self-sustaining basis as soon as possible." The United States wished to have in Greece a government whose members were loyal and patriotic, and "devoted to the ideal of a free and independent Greece in accordance with the best traditions of their country." Under ideal conditions, which Marshall admitted did not prevail at this time, such a government "should be drawn from the political parties of the left, the center, and the right, but not so far to the left that they are disposed to make concessions to, or deals with, the Communists or so far to the right that they would refuse to cooperate with non-Communists for the good of Greece." If the Griswold Mission found it necessary to have the Greek Government reorganized, or officials removed "because of incompetence, disagreement with your policies, or for some other reason," such changes should be made quietly, discreetly and always after consultation with Ambassador MacVeagh.

On this last point the Department appeared determined to permit no misunderstandings:

> You will have the benefit of the wisdom and practical experience of the American Ambassador in Athens. The external and internal political problems of Greece are of direct concern to the Embassy, and I am confident that the Ambassador, to whom I am sending a copy of this letter, will be ready to lend you every assistance in his power and to consult and advise you regarding your plans and difficulties. The Ambassador should be kept closely informed of the progress of your Mission toward economic rehabilitation and reform in order that he may be able fully to discharge his duties in the political field. This cooperation between you and the Ambassador should extend also to the matter of your first appearance before His Majesty King Paul and other high officials of the Greek Government. The questions which you might touch upon at that time and the opinions which you should express can most appropriately be discussed beforehand with the Ambassador.

The responsibilities of the Ambassador, I may add, include in particular the problem of bringing about changes in the Greek Government, the question of holding new elections, and the matter of amnesty for political prisoners. Your views will of course be particularly welcomed and helpful as your familiarity with the situation grows, but the Ambassador's judgment should be a principal determinant in the formulation of our policy in regard to these and related matters. (54)

In a second message to Griswold, dated July 12, Marshall again attempted to define the division of responsibility between AMAG and the embassy; between Griswold and MacVeagh. After stating that Griswold was to have "on behalf of the United States supreme authority in Greece" over all civilian and military assistance, the memorandum continued:

> Your Mission will operate as an entity separate from the American Embassy in Greece, but the two should work in close collaboration. The United States Ambassador, as the accredited diplomatic representative of the United States, will continue to be in charge of the conduct in Greece of overall relations with the Government of Greece and will continue to have primary responsibility for all aspects of those relations which are not directly related to the activities of the Mission. He will advise you on the diplomatic and political aspects of your activities, and you will seek his counsel on such matters. You will keep him informed of the progress of the work of the Mission and its relations with the Greek or other foreign authorities. It is not believed possible to draw up in advance a formal definition of the respective responsibilities and spheres of action of the Ambassador and yourself; it is expected that you and he will establish a close, mutually satisfactory relationship, keeping in mind that the common objective of both is the furtherance of the policies laid down by the President and the Secretary of State. (55)

It proved to be an unworkable arrangement from the very beginning. While Griswold demanded the creation of a coalition under Sofoulis, MacVeagh advised the Department against applying pressure in favor of the inclusion in the Government of particular parties or persons. "I believe our policy of careful non-interference in Greek internal affairs," he telegraphed on July 21, "to be one of our strongest assets for dealing successfully with the Greek people. . . ." (56) Again, when in early August the British authorities announced that their troops in Greece would soon be withdrawn, Griswold immediately telegraphed the Department that American troops "of slightly greater strength than those withdrawn" should be sent to take their place. He thought that such a move would have the desired effect if it were made conditional upon the broadening of the Greek cabinet in accordance with American wishes. (57) Without openly contradicting Griswold, or opposing the idea of sending American forces to Greece, MacVeagh (who on July 30 received the honorary degree of Doctor of Philosophy from the University of Athens) advised caution. "I feel," he telegraphed on August 5, ". . . that every non-interventional influence at our disposal should be used to secure greater political unity here. . . . [I] Have been hoping and still hope that influence of AMAG's presence and operations here may eventually bring Greeks to realize that working successfully with us requires greater unity among themselves. Should we decide [to] replace British troops, [I] believe [that] this could not fail to help Greek politicians realize [the] utter dependence of this country on us and [the] necessity of cooperating with us." He continued:

> On other hand, [the] Department may wish to consider whether it can afford to make [the] decision to send troops contingent on [a] prior agreement of Greek politicians to broaden [the] Government. As I see it, such [a] decision must necessarily rest in [the] last analysis on considerations far transcending Greek internal problems and involving indeed our whole Near Eastern policy. Furthermore, Greek politicians thoroughly understand this situation and are therefore only too likely to discount threatened sanctions and take their time about uniting, if they do so at all.
>
> Consequently, while providing military assistance might very well strengthen our position here as regards gradually influencing [the] Greeks to improve [their] Government . . . , perhaps we should be careful not [to] put into [the] hands of Greek political leaders any possibility of preventing or delaying a decision vital to ourselves. (58)

By mid-August, Griswold was openly complaining to the Department that MacVeagh did not have the necessary resolve for dealing with the Greek situation. In a letter to the coordinator for aid to Greece and Turkey, George C. McGhee, he stressed the need for the immediate reorganization of the Greek Government, and added that MacVeagh "seemingly is as anxious as anyone to have certain changes made but he continues to use such words as 'gradually' and 'we of course must not intervene' to such an extent that I feel somewhat alarmed. . . ." He concluded: "In my judgment we do not need to be affected by a fear that we will be accused of 'interfering.' That accusation will be made even if we do nothing."[24]

[24] Specifically, Griswold had urged upon MacVeagh the need to remove from

Washington's initial response was to give qualified support to MacVeagh. On August 24, the Department telegraphed the embassy in Athens that while "It is extremely difficult for us at this end to endeavor to give advice as to precisely who should or should not be included at this time in Greek Govt.," the Department agreed that "at least for [the] time being we should continue to pursue [a] policy of avoiding detailed interference in Greek politics at [the] same time emphasizing to Greek political leaders [the] gravity of their responsibility for [the] formation of [an] effective Greek government resting on [a] foundation which will give it broad national support."(59) In Athens, however, Griswold's tactics were producing results. Prodded by his highly publicized views on government reorganization, the Liberals in the cabinet (Venizelos, Papandreou, and Kanellopoulos) resigned, charging the Maximos-Tsaldaris leadership with being "overwhelmingly right-wing," and demanded instead a government which would "inspire greater confidence abroad and at the same time be more effective domestically." (60) On August 23, the Maximos Government fell, and King Paul (younger brother of George II, who had died on April 1, 1947) called on Tsaldaris, as the leader of the majority party, to form a new cabinet. Four days later, Tsaldaris announced the formation of a narrow Populist Government under his premiership, while his office was telling reporters that he had received "small comfort, indeed, for his plans from Ambassador MacVeagh and Griswold, especially from Griswold." Greek political circles and the press interpreted Tsaldaris' new government as a "defiance of the Americans." (61)

Press accounts of the American role in this latest cabinet crisis were entirely accurate. MacVeagh had called the two antagonists, Tsaldaris and Sofoulis, to his home on August 26 in an effort to work out a compromise. After lecturing them at length on the need to place the national interest above partisan politics, he recommended that Sofoulis, as "senior statesman," assume the premiership, and Tsaldaris become deputy premier, with the disputed Ministries of Public Order, Justice and War going to persons acceptable to both sides. While Tsaldaris appeared willing to consider such a solution, Sofoulis would not, holding out not only

---

office Minister of Security Zervas who, through his strong-arm tactics, "is making more Communists than he is eliminating." Griswold said that he was relying for his information upon the opinions of American reporters and "other Americans who have been in Greece for many, many years." *FR 1947*, V, 294-96. In his reply McGhee wrote that, ". . . in so far as possible, it is highly desirable that you and the Ambassador get together and discuss thoroughly any political questions of this nature and attempt to arrive at as large an area of agreement as you can." He made it clear that Griswold's conflict with MacVeagh was becoming a matter of serious concern within the Department. *FR 1947*, V, 306-307.

for the premiership, but for a cabinet entirely of his choosing. The meeting broke up with the two politicians at loggerheads. (62) Meanwhile, Griswold had also been busy, as MacVeagh telegraphed the Department on August 27:

> Tsaldaris called on me last night and in great agitation handed me memo given him by Stefanopoulos and purporting to be résumé of remarks made to latter by Griswold [on August 25] regarding proposed formation by Tsaldaris of government with Zervas and Gonatas. Memo, allegedly approved by Griswold, said such narrow government would be "inadmissible" because of bad impression on US public opinion and harmful effect in forthcoming GA.[25] Added it would prevent AMAG from authorizing further intervention in support of drachma, since weakness would be due [to] political factors, and would also result in suspension of AMAG construction program and in restriction of imports, except food, pending final evolution [of the] situation. Finally stressed Congressional sentiment in favor of broad government and desirability of forming such government before forthcoming Congressional visits.
>
> On basis this memo, Stefanopoulos told Tsaldaris he could not support proposed government. (Though not party leader, former's attitude likely influence considerable number Populist deputies.)
>
> Tsaldaris demanded to know whether Griswold [was] speaking for US Government in declaring that a Greek Government constitutionally formed and accepted by Parliament would be "inadmissible." Said he [is] confused as to position [of] Griswold, since Department had informed him Griswold [is] "High Commissioner," and if so, asked "Where does Ambassador come in?" Excitedly added, "Does this mean you declare war on us?" I begged him be calm, and telephoned at once for Griswold. Latter did not deny essential accuracy of memo but agreed he had not meant narrow government would be "inadmissible," but only that it would be inadvisable, since it would interfere with effectiveness of US aid program.
>
> At Tsaldaris' urgent request to correct the record, I incorporated this statement of Griswold in brief letter [dated August 26] to Tsaldaris in which I also referred to our policy of non-intervention in details [of] political affairs and reiterated my advice to continue seek broadest possible government. Tsaldaris accepted this oil on troubled waters, and letter contains nothing to indicate support of his efforts as distinguished [from] those of others.
>
> While I of course agree with Griswold as to undesirability of nar-

[25] The General Assembly of the United Nations.

row government and have done and am doing all possible to secure broadening, I feel that any indication that we might fail to support duly constituted government or any threat of applying sanctions if such government not according our wishes, would be inadvisable and believe Department will take same view. (63)

Satisfied with MacVeagh's assurances, Tsaldaris went ahead with his plans. On August 29, a new Populist cabinet, with Tsaldaris as Prime Minister and Foreign Minister, but without Zervas or Gonatas, was sworn in. After the brief ceremony, Tsaldaris indicated to reporters that MacVeagh had agreed to "tolerate" his new government at least for a while. (64) That same evening MacVeagh learned that the right-wing government had been formed at the insistence of the army command, which had threatened to take matters into its own hands. The Ambassador telegraphed on August 30:

Following formation new Government . . . King summoned me to Palace midnight to inform me of developments. Said that both Larissa Corps Commander, who had journeyed Athens for purpose, and Chief of Staff had called on him to say they could no longer answer for Army if some government not immediately formed, and that this had been important motivating factor in acceptance Tsaldaris Government. He thought Tsaldaris had made surprisingly commendable efforts to obtain participation other parties and felt confident he would continue these efforts sincerely realizing present setup unsatisfactory and provisional. Also said that he, the King, would likewise bend every possible effort obtain broadened government soonest. (65)

It was to prove a very "provisional" arrangement indeed. Disturbed over the complexion of the new government and anxious to deal with the apparently growing rift between MacVeagh and Griswold, the Department decided to send Henderson to Athens, where he arrived on August 30. After a round of talks at the embassy, Henderson and MacVeagh saw the principal political figures and the King. MacVeagh reported to the Department that Tsaldaris was "obviously nervous and uncertain as to [the] nature of Henderson's mission," and in a "long and emotional harangue" defended his efforts to secure the cooperation of Sofoulis' Liberals. He was particularly bitter about Griswold's memorandum to Stefanopoulos, which he said had been circulated widely in Athens, and complained that the "apparent American endeavor to split his own party placed him in almost intolerable situation." "Henderson and I," the MacVeagh report continued, "assured Tsaldaris that [the] US Govt. did not propose [to] dictate [the] composition of any Greek

Govt. Said however we felt bound [to] let him know it would be extremely difficult [to] maintain support [of] US public opinion for AMAG if impression should prevail that [the] latter [is] strengthening certain Greek political groups, and thus becoming disintegrating factor, rather than aiding Greece as whole." If an effective government supported by the majority of Greeks could not be formed, "Congress and American people might well refuse [to] expend further energies and resources on aid to Greece. We made it clear that [the] matter is of extreme urgency in view of growing Soviet and guerrilla activity," and because of the impending debate in the General Assembly, "where we would be more vulnerable to criticism if narrow right govt. still in power in Greece. . . ." Henderson suggested to the King that he "bring all leaders together in [one] room and insist they remain till [a] government [is] formed since [the] urgency of [the] matter must preclude further delay." Paul said that he would "try it." At the meeting with Liberal leaders, Mac-Veagh brought along Griswold, in order to exert "maximum pressure," and to "avoid possible recriminations" in the future. (66)

The presence of Henderson had the desired effect upon all concerned. On September 4, it was announced that Tsaldaris would yield the premiership to Sofoulis, but would stay on as deputy premier and Foreign Minister. The new cabinet was sworn in on September 7. Five days later, MacVeagh, exhausted and ill, was provided with a special plane to bring the body of his wife home for burial. (Mrs. MacVeagh died on September 9, at the age of sixty-one.) He was in Washington from September 17th to the 22nd, for consultations at the Department. After travelling briefly back to Athens (from September 22 to October 11), he returned to the United States on October 11. Following further meetings in Washington, he requested and received (on October 28) sick leave.

But even in his absence from his post, MacVeagh's disagreement with Griswold continued to grow. The two men now stood for tactics and outlooks which could not be reconciled. During his trip to Athens, Henderson had clearly taken MacVeagh's side of the argument. The Sofoulis-Tsaldaris cabinet had been MacVeagh's idea; its purpose was to broaden the government and make it more attractive both in Greece and the United States, without, however, humiliating Tsaldaris and the Populists, who continued to represent the majority in parliament. Henderson also felt, as did the Department, that in such a critically important issue as the composition of the Greek Government, the ambassador's views should prevail over those of the chief of AMAG. It was imperative that the American position be expressed with one voice in Athens. Henderson was therefore upset to read, in the September 15 monthly report from AMAG headquarters, a flamboyant account of Griswold's highly personal involvement in the recent cabinet crisis. In a long memorandum to

Under-Secretary of State Lovett, in which he commented favorably on the work of AMAG, he added:

> The section of the report dealing with the political situation repays careful reading because of the clear picture it gives of Governor Griswold's personal approach to these matters. I should like to call especially to your attention Governor Griswold's statement, on page three, that he "determined to try to stop" the formation of an extreme rightist cabinet "by attacking it on two fronts." It appears that he took the initiative in consulting with three of the Greek political leaders with this object in view and, among other things, "urged Mr. Stefanopoulos to lead a fight within the Populist Party against the creation of a restricted rightist government." Governor Griswold states frankly that he used the economic leverage of the Aid Program as a club to induce the Greek political leaders to form a broad coalition government. He asserts that without this club the present Populist-Liberal coalition could not have been formed. In this connection, he states that Ambassador MacVeagh disapproved of some of his actions in discussing political matters with Greek political leaders, but he justifies his policy by saying that the Ambassador had no "club" to use.
>
> I believe we should give careful consideration to the position taken by Governor Griswold with respect to political affairs in Greece. Although I think we are all agreed that the Aid Mission must take a very keen interest in the character of the Greek Government and has every right and duty to present its views, I believe that in questions of major political consequence, such as the formation of a new government, its views should be channeled through the Ambassador and that its members, including the Chief, should refrain from taking the initiative in discussing such questions with Greek political leaders. Without in any way reflecting upon Governor Griswold and his staff, I think it is doubtful that they can be sufficiently versed in the intricacies of Greek politics or American foreign relations to justify them in operating independently or in overriding the views and advice of a veteran and highly capable Ambassador. The question is of more than academic interest since another Greek cabinet crisis may arise at any time, and it would be most desirable to avoid the confusion and unfavorable publicity which resulted from the uncoordinated activities of Governor Griswold and Ambassador MacVeagh during the recent change of government. (67)

Prodded by Henderson's memorandum, and by press accounts of Griswold's high-handed tactics—including an article in the *New York*

Times by Dana Adams Schmidt, entitled "Griswold, Most Powerful Man in Greece"—Lovett telegraphed Griswold on October 17 (telegram number "Gama 340") urging him to correct a public image which the Department viewed as a "most unfortunate misrepresentation of [the] US role in Greece." Lovett was especially perturbed that verbatim statements attributed to Griswold in the Schmidt article were being repeated by the Yugoslav representative in the United Nations, in support of "allegations of US imperialism and responsibility for continued civil strife in Greece." Griswold's press relations office was to be directed "to do all in its power to correct [the] impressions arising from Schmidt's article and to prevent, insofar as possible, [a] recurrence of similar misinterpretations." (68)

Griswold's response to the admonitions contained in "Gama 340" amounted to a blast directed at the Department of State, whose authority over him he clearly refused to accept. He telegraphed on October 24 that in his "considered opinion" it would be "wrong for AMAG or for [the] US Government to attempt to represent to world opinion that AMAG does not have great power or that it is not involved in Greek internal affairs." The Greek Government had accepted the American Mission's "limited but very great powers in many vital fields normally regarded as internal matter[s]" and there was no point in claiming otherwise. After pointing out that "Much stronger and more detailed stories" about the American role in Greece had appeared in the press during Henderson's recent visit in Athens, he lectured the Department on the task confronting the United States in Greece: "[The] Distinction to be observed in my opinion is not [our] involvement or non-involvement [in] Greek internal affairs, but whether [that] involvement would result in serving selfish interest or [would] aid Greek rehabilitation in line with [the] request of [the] Greek Government. . . ." He regarded it as "very necessary that [the] great power of [the] Chief [of] AMAG should be recognized within Greece whether or not he be considered [the] 'most powerful man in Greece.' This opinion on [the] part of [the] Greeks is necessary on [the] basis [of] my experience if good results are to be obtained and US policy and [the] aid program are to be successful." Although AMAG's power had to be employed with tact and discretion, there was no question as to its purpose: "I believe it was [the] intent of Congress that this Mission act discreetly but forcefully to help in the rehabilitation of Greece to the end that Communism would be checked here. Congress also intended and visiting Congressmen have stressed that strict controls over [the] expenditure of American and Greek funds be exercised by the Mission. This means involvement in internal affairs and I see no advantage [in] pretending it is something else." Finally, Griswold offered to try and "correct any impression that AMAG has unlimited power or is involved in [the] details of internal politics," but retorted that the Schmidt article had been based on materials freely obtained from Mission sources, while its direct quotations (attributed to him) had not been "specifically authorized but they represent self-evident truths and I do not consider them significant." (69)

On October 23, unaware of Griswold's impending response to "Gama 340," the Department had sought once again to delineate the responsibilities and authorities of the Ambassador and of the Chief of AMAG. A new directive, drafted with the help of MacVeagh and approved by President Truman, restated the assumption that, at least in the immediate future, the American military involvement in Greece would continue to be on a "restricted and advisory basis," and declared: "The Ambassador is and should be universally recognized as the American representative in Greece charged with dealing with the Greek Government on matters of high policy as defined in Paragraph 4 below. The Embassy should be the sole channel for dealing with the Greek Government or other foreign officials on such matters, except when the Ambassador may approve or request a direct approach by one of the other American officials." After stressing the need for close consultation between the Ambassador and the AMAG Chief, the document provided that in the event of fundamental disagreement between the two, their views would be "jointly brought to the attention of the Department before any action is taken." Paragraph 4 gave a number of specific examples of "high policy decisions" which were to be within the *Ambassador's* exclusive jurisdiction:

a) Any action by United States representatives in connection with a change in the Greek Cabinet; b) Any action by United States representatives to bring about or prevent a change in the high command of the Greek armed forces; c) Any substantial increase or decrease in the size of the Greek armed forces; d) Any disagreement arising with the Greek or British authorities which, regardless of its source, may impair cooperation between American officials in Greece and Greek and British officials; e) Any major question involving the relations of Greece with the United Nations or any foreign nation other than the United States; f) Any major question involving the policies of the Greek Government toward Greek political parties, trade unions, subversive elements, rebel armed forces, etc., including questions of punishment, amnesties, and the like; g) Any question involving the holding of elections in Greece.

To make absolutely certain that the Ambassador's superior position was understood in Athens, the document concluded: "The Greek Government and the British authorities should be informed in general terms of the relative responsibilities set forth in this paper, and it should be made clear to them that the Ambassador is the sole channel for handling high policy questions." (70) For a brief moment it appeared that Mac-Veagh, and the Department behind him, had won.

In part, the new directive on the division of responsibilities among American officials in Athens had been necessitated by a decision of the National Security Council, approved by President Truman on November 3, 1947, to provide the Greek armed forces, down to the level of division commands, with "operational advice." A senior American army officer was to be sent to Greece as Chief of the contemplated Army-Navy-Air Force advisory group. Accordingly, the purpose of the directive of October 23, which was telegraphed to Griswold on November 7 ("Gama 430"), was to establish once and for all the principle that in matters of "high policy," the role of the ambassador was to be superior to that of the Chief of AMAG and of the head of the new military mission. (71)

Griswold's reaction to the new attempt to curtail his authority was a threat to resign. In a long telegram to Secretary Marshall, with a copy addressed to the President and actually transmitted seven hours earlier, he requested a "reconsideration" of the directive, and declared: "Either [these] new instructions show that I no longer have [the] confidence of [the] President and yourself or else, as I hope, [the] new instructions were based on [a] misconception of situation here and without realization of their practical effect." He charged that the new document constituted a "fundamental change in my previous instructions," which had "provided that I should have supreme authority in Greece over all American assistance, both civilian and military, and should determine and supervise the programs of American aid to Greece; that the mission should operate as an entity separate from the Embassy although working in close cooperation; and that the Ambassador should continue in charge of the conduct of 'overall relations' with Greek Government and to have primary responsibility for all aspects of those relations 'which are not directly related to the activities of the Mission'." He also maintained that the new instructions violated the spirit of the report on his authority prepared by the Senate Committee on Foreign Relations as well as the President's own wishes on the matter. He continued:

> New instructions would basically change practical arrangements affecting Mission operations by giving Ambassador right to be sole contact with Greek Government on so-called high policy decisions and relegating Chief of AMAG to administrative and technical contacts with Greek Government. Such arrangements I believe totally unworkable. New instructions would actually establish two heads of

Mission giving senior position and power to Ambassador but without giving him corresponding responsibility for Mission work, whereas Chief [of AMAG] would be left with responsibility but little power of authority. Under new instructions it would not be possible for me to remain here as I could not do effective or efficient work. Economic, political and military questions are all interrelated here and inextricably interwoven with "high policy" questions, although only very rarely with political questions affecting long range relationship between Greece and US.

Ignoring his own recent efforts to undermine the position of the Populist Government in favor of the Liberals, Griswold also argued that the new directive would constitute an "invitation to [the] Greeks to attempt [to] play [the] Ambassador and Chief against each other, and could also subject [the] Ambassador to meeting dissatisfied groups and officials who would defer cooperation with [the] Mission in [the] hope of influencing [the] individual having final authority."

Griswold attempted to downplay the reported personal friction between himself and MacVeagh, and to argue that "increasingly close cooperation" between the Embassy and AMAG had been established. "There was one relatively minor difference between [the] Ambassador and myself," he conceded, "as to [the] degree of pressure which should be put on [the] Greek Government to achieve [the] change in Government desired by [the] Department, [the] Ambassador and [the] Mission. Possibly in violation [of] your Top Secret personal instructions, I employed stronger pressure than [the] Ambassador, fearing [that the] delay [was] dangerous to Mission objectives resulting from normal diplomatic pressure. . . ." Moreover, "the results, I believe, justified this initiative. . . ." On another point, he was especially anxious to reverse the decision to inform the Greek and British authorities of the relative authority of the Ambassador and of the Chief of AMAG: "Such information conveyed [to the] Greek Government would as usual soon be published and would be construed everywhere as [a] split between [the] Embassy and [the] Mission and not merely [a] repudiation of me personally but also [a] repudiation of [the] work of [the] Mission to date. I fear American prestige would be lowered and ability [of the] US Government [to] achieve [the] objectives [of the] Greek aid statute impaired. . . ." Griswold's telegram concluded: "If you believe Mission operations to date have been effective toward achieving [the] intent [of the] Greek aid statute I earnestly recommend that there be no change in previous instructions relating to relations between [the] Ambassador and [the] Chief. If on [the] other hand you believe [the] administration [of] AMAG has been unsuccessful, I then recommend that [the] power and responsibility for all [the] American aid program be placed in Ambassador." (72)

In the face of Griswold's strongly worded refusal to accept a new division of responsibility between himself and MacVeagh, which the Department had recommended and the President approved, there was nothing else to do but refer the matter once again to the highest authority. With Secretary Marshall away from Washington, Under-Secretary Lovett wrote to President Truman on November 15 that because of Griswold's objections ". . . we propose to give further consideration to the question and to discuss it again in the National Security Council." At the same time Griswold was informed that the instructions to which he had objected (contained in "Gama 430") "should be considered as in suspense pending further notice." (73)

Meanwhile, despite the "top secret" classification of the telegraphic exchanges between Washington and Athens on this problem, Griswold's friends and supporters proved to be not only numerous but remarkably well informed about Griswold's complaints. The White House was bombarded with messages of every kind, many of them urging that the matter be settled by recalling MacVeagh and naming Griswold Ambassador to Greece. Rumors began to circulate that if Griswold did not have his way, he would return home to try and run for Vice President on the Republican ticket, in which case he could embarrass the Truman administration by attacking its record in Greece. Such criticism might adversely affect Congressional attitudes toward the Marshall Plan. On November 20, the House of Representatives ordered an investigation of the MacVeagh-Griswold controversy, to be directed by the Republican chairman of the Sub-committee on State Department Appropriations, Representative Karl Stefan, of Nebraska, Griswold's home-state. (74) There was not even a pretense that the investigation would be impartial: Stefan had already joined the ranks of those who had publicly demanded that Griswold replace MacVeagh as Ambassador to Greece.[26]

Unfortunately for MacVeagh, who during these crucial weeks had been hospitalized following major surgery, the Department was rapidly adjusting to the political realities of the situation. On November 18, the MacVeagh-Griswold controversy was the subject of discussion among Assistant Secretaries Norman Armour and John Peurifoy, the Coordinator for Aid to Greece and Turkey, George C. McGhee, and Loy Henderson, representing the Department's Division of Near Eastern and African Affairs. While their formal decision was to raise the matter with the President *before* committing the Department to any particular recom-

[26] Following the decision to withdraw MacVeagh from Greece, the investigation was dropped.

mendation, there was little doubt about the outcome. In their conversation, the four men had in fact narrowed the available options to three: (a) insist on the implementation of the new instructions contained in "Gama 430", (b) attempt to achieve a more flexible arrangement "which would result in a spirit of real cooperation between Governor Griswold and the Ambassador on a basis which would assure the Governor that his prestige will not be weakened or the effectiveness of his work diminished," or, (c) name Griswold Ambassador to Greece. Armour and Henderson preferred the second option, Peurifoy and McGhee the third. There was no support expressed for the first option. (75)

It was left for the White House to cut the Gordian knot. On November 19, Truman decided to withdraw MacVeagh from Greece, to formally cancel the instructions contained in "Gama 430," and to urge Griswold to stay on as Chief of AMAG. At the recommendation of the Department, Truman also agreed not to appoint a new ambassador for the time being, thus leaving career diplomat James Keeley and later Karl Rankin in charge of the embassy. Secretary Marshall was reportedly determined not to permit MacVeagh's successor to be bullied by Griswold. Thus, the next ambassador to Greece was destined to be not Griswold, who retired as AMAG Chief in August 1948, but Henry F. Grady, who had headed the mission to supervise the 1946 Greek elections, and more recently had been chairman of the Cabinet Committee on Palestine and Ambassador to India. Grady took on his duties in Athens only after Griswold's return to the United States. With Griswold out of the picture, it was quickly agreed that in matters of major political importance, the AMAG Chief would defer to the Ambassador's judgment....

On November 20, in a highly complimentary message, Griswold was informed of the President's decision to cancel the instructions in "Gama 430," but not of MacVeagh's withdrawal. Instead, Griswold was told that the condition of the Ambassador's health was such that "it is impossible to determine whether he will be physically able to resume his duties in Greece." (76) Simultaneously, press reports from Washington repeated the Department's public assertions that MacVeagh's health was the only factor preventing his return to his post in Athens. (77) However, several days later, there was speculation in the press that, in view of the Department's cancellation of the directive to Griswold, MacVeagh might not return to Greece. (78) Months later (on February 26, 1948), it was learned in Washington that MacVeagh would soon be named Ambassador to Portugal, replacing John C. Wiley, who had recently been transferred to Iran. (79)

In fact, at Lovett's urging, Truman had approved MacVeagh's transfer to Portugal at the same time that he had decided to withdraw him from Greece. Armour and Henderson had the painful duty of informing

MacVeagh, still recuperating from surgery, of the President's decision. In a state of emotional exhaustion, MacVeagh at first refused the new assignment, but was finally persuaded by his two visitors to accept it.

Embarrassed by the manner in which the whole affair had been handled, MacVeagh's superiors in the Department sought to soothe his feelings. At their urging, Secretary Marshall wrote to Truman on March 8, suggesting that "in view of unfortunate press comments in connection with Ambassador MacVeagh's transfer from Athens to Lisbon," the President might send to MacVeagh a letter "commending him on his exceptionally long and distinguished service in Greece. Such a letter would tend to counteract distorted and unfortunate press comment, rectify any possible injustice to Mr. MacVeagh, and strengthen his position as the new Ambassador to Portugal." Truman's letter, provided by the Department and signed on March 9, 1948, praised the Ambassador for his "scholarly statesmanship and diplomatic judgment," and continued:

> Your broad and farsighted understanding of international developments with respect to Greece helped crystallize American determination to uphold the vital principles at stake in the present Greek situation. Through your knowledge of Greece, and by the exercise of tact, patience and geniality, you were able to adjust many practical difficulties and assure ever closer friendship and cooperation between the Greek and American peoples, thereby laying an indispensable groundwork for our common efforts to preserve Greek independence. . . . (80)

In March 1948, responding to a sympathetic letter from his brother Charlton, MacVeagh wrote that his loyalty to the President and to the Department had prevented him from speaking out to defend himself against a decision in which "I am left to appear as if I had failed in my mission and had been withdrawn in consequence." He concluded:

> The facts are that I tried to carry out the Department's policy in Greece, which was to try and unite the political factions without siding with any, and so far as our aid to Greece was concerned, to make it effective through the cooperation of the Greeks, and not have to wave the big stick and thus both endanger that cooperation and give support to the Communist charge that our "imperialism" is making slaves of the local inhabitants.[27]

[27] The letter continues: "I very much hope that in the implementation of the Marshall Plan, the mistakes made in the guinea pig experiment of Greece will not be repeated on a larger scale, but the auguries don't seem too good. It isn't every smart operator in this country who is able to handle foreign affairs suc-

734 · CHAPTER X

Lincoln MacVeagh served as Ambassador to Portugal from March 1948 until January 1952, when he was named Ambassador to Spain. In 1953, a few months before the completion of his twentieth year in the diplomatic service, he was retired by the Eisenhower administration, and he decided to make his home in Estoril, Portugal. In May 1955, he was married to Mrs. Virginia Ferrante Coats, daughter of Marchese and Marchesa Ferrante di Ruffano, of Naples, Italy. In 1971, after prolonged illness, he was brought to Washington for treatment. He died on January 15, 1972, at the age of eighty-one.

---

cessfully; one does learn something about dealing with alien independent peoples after years of experience at the game, and if we subordinate our experts all around Europe to the interruption and interference and dictation of politically ambitious amateurs, we certainly are heading for disaster. . . ." Copy of (undated) letter in MacVeagh Papers.

APPENDIX A

LIST OF PRINCIPAL NAMES

Titles and positions correspond generally to the time period of this volume.

Acheson, Dean, Assistant Secretary of State, U.S.

Adossidis, Alexander, Director of the Greek Red Cross

Aldrich, Col. Harry, head of OSS in Cairo

Alexander, Gen. Harold, Commander in Chief, Allied Forces in Italy; Allied Supreme Commander in the Mediterranean

Alexandris, Adm. Constantine, Chief of the Greek Navy in Middle East

Allard, Sven, Swedish *Chargé d'Affaires* in Greece

Allen, George V., U.S. Consul in Patras; Deputy Director of NEA; Political Adviser to the U.S. delegation at the Potsdam Conference

Altenburg, Dr. Günther, German Minister to Greece following the surrender of the Greek armed forces

Andrew, Prince, brother of King Constantine I of the Hellenes

Androulis, Pindar, personal secretary of Prime Minister Metaxas

Angelopoulos, Angelos, professor of economics at the university of Athens; Secretary of Finance of PEEA; Deputy Minister of Finance (1944)

Antonescu, Gen. Ion, Prime Minister of Rumania

Antonescu, Mihai, Deputy Prime Minister and Rumanian Minister for Foreign Affairs

Apostolidis, Andreas, Deputy Minister of Finance (1936-1941)

Aras, Tevfik Rüştü, Turkish Minister for Foreign Affairs

Aris, Velouchiotis (Athanasios Klaras) chief *capetanios* of ELAS

Archer, Laird, foreign director of the Near East Foundation; chief of the U.S. Office of Foreign Relief and Rehabilitation; chief of the Balkan Mission of UNRRA

Argyropoulos, Alexander, Director of Economic and Commercial Affairs of the Greek Ministry for Foreign Affairs

Argyropoulos, Pericles, Minister of the Navy (1928-1929); Minister for Foreign Affairs (1929); Ambassador to Spain

Armstrong, Brig. Charles Douglas, head of BLM to Mihailović

Arvanitis, John, Minister of National Economy (1937-1941)

Askoutsis, Nikolaos, Secretary of Transportation of PEEA; Minister of Transportation (1944); Minister of Public Works (1944)

Badoglio, Marshal Pietro, commander of Italian forces in the Ethiopian campaign; supreme commander of the General Staff of the Italian army
Bailey, Col. S. W., senior SOE officer with Mihailović
Bailey, Lt. Stephen, head of SI, OSS for Greece
Baker, Maj. Joseph K., U.S. Military Attaché in Greece (1940-1941)
Bakirdzis, Col. Euripidis, President and Secretary for Foreign Affairs of PEEA; Vice President and Secretary of Food Supplies of PEEA
Balfour, Maj. David, former Orthodox priest and confessor to the Greek royal family; political adviser of the British Embassy to the Greek Government in Cairo
Barbour, Walworth, U.S. Vice Consul in Greece; Counsellor of the U.S. Embassy to the Greek Government in Cairo
Barboza-Carneiro, Julio Augusto, Brazilian Ambassador to Greece
Beaumont-Nesbitt, Maj. Gen. Philip, staff officer for the British Commander in Chief, Middle East, directed the suppression of mutinous Greek troops in the Middle East
Bellm, Col. Newt, head of the Economic Section of USAFIME
Benfield, Brig. K.V.B., Commanding Officer of "Force 133"
Berry, Burton Y., Secretary of the U.S. Embassy in Turkey; Secretary of the U.S. Embassy in Greece
Biddle, Anthony J. Drexel, Jr., U.S. Minister to the Yugoslav Government in London
Blamey, Lt. Gen. Sir Thomas, Commander of I Australian Corps in Greece (1940-1941)
Blunt, Col. J. S., British Military Attaché in Greece
Bodossakis (last name: Athanassiadis, generally known by his first name), prominent Greek industrialist and arms manufacturer
Braden, Spruille, U.S. Ambassador to Argentina
Brewster, Daniel, Secretary of the U.S. Legation in Greece (1940-1941)
Broad, Philip, Counselor of the British Embassy to the Yugoslav Government in Cairo
Caccia, Harold, Political Adviser to the British Embassy in Greece
Calligas, Stephen, personal secretary and interpreter of U.S. Ambassador MacVeagh in Greece
Campbell, Ronald, British Ambassador to Yugoslavia
Cannon, Cavendish W., Secretary of the U.S. Legation in Greece; chief of the Division of South European Affairs, Dept. of State
Capodistria, Count, member of the Greek royal household
Casey, Richard G., British Minister of State in the Middle East
Catherine, Princess, sister of King George II of the Hellenes
Cavallero, Count Ugo, Chief of the Italian General Staff

LIST OF PRINCIPAL NAMES · 737

Chastelain, Gardyne de, SOE agent in Rumania
Christopher, Prince, uncle of King George II of the Hellenes
Chrysostomos, Archbishop of Athens and Primate of Greece
Churchill, Sir Winston S., British Prime Minister and Minister of Defense
Ciano, Count Galeazzo, son-in-law of Mussolini; Italian Minister for Foreign Affairs
Cochrane, Col. Philip G., BML in Cairo
Constantine I, King of the Hellenes (1913-1922)
Craw, Maj. Demos T., U.S. observer attached to the RAF; Asst. Military Attaché for Air in Greece (1941)
Cretianu, Alexander, Rumanian Ambassador to Turkey
Cripps, Sir Stafford, British Ambassador to the Soviet Union
Culbertson, Paul, U.S. representative to the Lend-Lease Administration, representative to the Allied North Africa Economic Board
Cunningham, Adm. Sir Andrew Brown, British Commander in Chief, Eastern Mediterranean Fleet
D'Albiac, Air Vice Marshal John, British Air Officer Commanding in Greece (1940-1941)
Damaskinos, Bishop of Corinth; Archbishop of Athens and Primate of Greece; Regent
Davis, Homer, President of Athens College
Delmouzos, Andreas, Director General of the Ministry for Foreign Affairs
Demertzis, Constantine, professor of law at the university of Athens; Prime Minister of Greece (1935-1936)
Diamantopoulos, Kimon, Greek Ambassador to the United States
Dill, Field Marshal Sir John, Chief of the British Imperial Staff
Dimitrakakis, Stelios, Minister of Justice (1941-1943)
Diomedis, A. N., prominent financier; Governor of the Bank of Greece
Djuvara, Mircea, Rumanian Ambassador to Greece
Donovan, Col. (later Gen.) William J., Pres. Roosevelt's personal representative to assess Britain's needs against the Axis; Director of OSS
Dragoumis, Philip, Minister Director Gen. of Salonica (1932-1933); Director Gen. of Macedonia (1933-1934); Deputy Minister for Foreign Affairs (1944-1946)
Dunn, James C., Director of the Office of European Affairs, Dept. of State
Eaker, Lt. Gen. Ira C. (U.S.), Allied Air Commander, Mediterranean
Earle, George H., U.S. Minister to Bulgaria
Eden, Anthony, British Secretary for War; Foreign Secretary
Eisenhower, Gen. Dwight D., Allied Commander in North Africa; Al-

lied Supreme Commander, Mediterranean; Allied Supreme Commander, Europe

Else, Cpt. Gerald, SI, OSS for Greece

Enis, Akayayen (Enis Bey), Turkish Ambassador to Greece

Erbach-Schonberg, Prince Victor zu, German Ambassador to Greece

Ernst, Philip, clerk of the U.S. Legation in Greece (1936-1941)

Ethridge, Mark, U.S. representative on the U.N. Commission of Investigation in the Balkans

Exindaris, George, Minister of Agriculture (1928); Director Gen. of Macedonia (1933)

Farish, Maj. Linn M., OSS officer with Tito

Fikioris, Petros, Minister of the Air Force (1944-1945)

Fish, Bert, U.S. Minister to Egypt

Fodor, Michael W., correspondent for *The Chicago Daily News*

Forbes, Wing Comm. Lord, British Air Attaché in Greece (1940-1941)

Fortier, Maj. Louis J., U.S. Military Attaché in Yugoslavia (1940-1941)

Foster, Andrew, Secretary of the U.S. Embassy to the Greek and Yugoslav Governments in Cairo

Fotić, Konstantine, Yugoslav Ambassador to the United States

Frederika, Princess (later Queen), wife of Crown Prince Paul (later King) of the Hellenes

Gafencu, Grigore, Rumanian Minister for Foreign Affairs

Gallagher, James W., correspondent for the Associated Press

George II, King of the Hellenes (1922-1924, 1935-1947)

George, Prince, brother of King Constantine I of the Hellenes

Gervasi, Frank, correspondent for the Columbia Broadcasting System

Giles, Maj. Gen. Benjamin F., Commanding General of U.S. Army Forces, Middle East

Goebbels, Joseph, German Minister of Propaganda

Goering, Field Marshal Hermann, Air Minister and Commander in Chief of the German Air Force

Gonatas, Gen. Stylianos, leader of the 1922 coup which deposed King Constantine I; Prime Minister of Greece (1923); in forced retirement following the monarchy's restoration; organizer of the Security Battalions under the auspices of the German occupation authorities

Goodfellow, Col. Preston, head of SI, OSS in Cairo

Gounaris, Dimitrios, leader of the Populist (royalist) Party; Prime Minister of Greece (1921-1922)

Grady, Henry F., U.S. Ambassador, head of the U.S. mission to supervise the 1946 Greek elections; Ambassador to Greece succeeding MacVeagh

Grazzi, Count Emmanuel, Italian Ambassador to Greece

LIST OF PRINCIPAL NAMES

Griswold, Dwight P., Governor of Nebraska; Chief of the U.S. Mission for Aid to Greece
Hadjikyriakos, Adm. Alexander, Minister of the Navy (1933-1935)
Halifax, Viscount Edward Wood, Foreign Secretary; British Ambassador to the United States
Harriman, W. Averell, special representative of Pres. Roosevelt to facilitate aid to the British Empire under Lend-Lease; U.S. Ambassador to the Soviet Union
Hallowell, Lt. Col. Paul, G-2 of USAFIME
Henderson, Loy W., Director of NEA, Dept. of State
Heywood, Maj. Gen. T.G.G., Commanding Officer, BMM in Greece (1941)
Hill, Harry A., Manager of the American Express Co. in Greece, Vice President of the Greek War Relief, Economic Counselor of the U.S. Embassy to the Greek Government in Cairo
House, Charles, head of the American Farm School in Salonica; Executive Director of the American Red Cross in Greece (1940-1941)
Hudson, Maj. Barclay, head of Greek Section, OWI in Beirut, later in Greece
Hughes, Maj. Gen. Ivor T. P., Commanding Officer BML to Greece in Cairo
Hulick, Charles, Secretary of the U.S. Embassy to the Yugoslav Government in Cairo
Hull, Cordell, Secretary of State
Huntington, Col. Ellery C. Jr., chief of the U.S. Military Mission to Tito
Inönü, Ismet, Minister for Foreign Affairs; Prime Minister; President of Turkey
Jackson, Hugh, U.S. Deputy Director General of UNRRA
Jackson, Robert G. A., Australian official, Director of Middle East Supply Center, Senior Deputy Director General of UNRRA
Jevtić, Bogoljub, Yugoslav Minister of Transportation; Director of the wartime Yugoslav Information Center in New York; Ambassador to Britain
Johnson, Herschel, U.S. *Chargé d'Affaires* in Britain
Johnson, John D., U.S. Consul at Salonica
Johnson, Capt. Max S., temporary U.S. Military Attaché in Greece (1940)
Jones, G. Lewis, U.S. Assist. Commercial Attaché in Greece
Joyce, Robert P., head of SI, OSS in Yugoslavia
Kafandaris, George, Minister of Finance (1926-1927, 1933-1934); Deputy Prime Minister of Greece (1945-1946); leader of the Progressive Party
Kanellopoulos, Panayiotis, professor of law at the university of Athens; Deputy Prime Minister and Minister of Defense (1942-1943); Minis-

ter of Finance and Reconstruction (1944); Minister of the Navy (1944-1945); Prime Minister (1945); Minister of the Air Force (1947); leader of the National Unity Party

Karapanayiotis, Byron, Minister of Transportation (1929-1930); Minister of Interior (1930-1931); Minister of the Army (1943-1944)

Kekić, Emil A., Special Assistant, U.S. Embassy to the Yugoslav Government in Cairo

Kemal, Gen. Mustafa Ataturk, President of Turkey

Kent, Lt. Comm. Ralph, Assistant Director of Athens College; Assistant U.S. Naval Attaché to the Greek Government in Cairo

King, Brig. Thomas, New Zealander, BML in charge of supplies for Greece

Kioseivanov, Georgi, Prime Minister of Bulgaria

Kirk, Alexander C., U.S. *Chargé d'Affaires* in Germany; Minister to Egypt and Saudi Arabia; Ambassador to Italy

Knatchbull-Hugessen, Sir Hughe, British Ambassador to Turkey

Kohler, D. Foy, Third Secretary of the U.S. Legation in Greece; Assist. Chief of NEA; Secretary General of the U.S. mission to supervise the 1946 Greek elections

Kondylis, Gen. George, Minister of the Army (1932-1933); Prime Minister of Greece (1935)

Korizis, Alexander, Governor of the National Bank of Greece; Prime Minister (1941)

Kotzias, Constantine, Mayor of Athens; Minister-Governor of Athens (1936-1941)

Koundouriotis, Adm. Paul, President of the Greek Republic (1924-1925)

Krofta, Kamil, Czechoslovak Minister for Foreign Affairs

Lampson, Sir Miles (Lord Killearn), British Ambassador to Egypt

Landis, James M., U.S. Director of Economic Operations in the Middle East and principal civilian representative on the Middle East Supply Center with the rank of Minister

Lane, Arthur Bliss, U.S. Minister to Yugoslavia

Larrabee, Col. Sterling L., U.S. Military Attaché to the Greek and Yugoslav Governments in Cairo

Leeper, Sir Reginald W. Allen, British Ambassador to Greece (1943-1946)

Lehman, Herbert H., Governor of New York; Director of the Office of Foreign Relief and Rehabilitation Operations; Director General of UNRRA

Levidis, Col. Dimitri, Master of Ceremonies of the Greek royal household

Longmore, Air Chief Marshal Sir Arthur, Air Officer Commander in Chief, Middle East

Maclean, Brig. Fitzroy, head of BLM to Tito

LIST OF PRINCIPAL NAMES · 741

Macmillan, Rt. Hon. Harold, Minister Resident, Allied Forces Headquarters, Algiers (1942-1944), Caserta (1944-1945)

MacMurray, John V. A., U.S. Ambassador to Turkey

Maitland, Patrick, correspondent of the London *Times*

Maniadakis, Constantine, Deputy Minister of Public Security (1936-1941)

Maniu, Iuliu, leader of the Agrarian Party and of the United Opposition Parties, plotting to overthrow the regime of Gen. Antonescu, Prime Minister of Rumania

Matthews, H. Freeman, Director of the Office of European Affairs, Dept. of State

Matthews, Sir William, head of the Middle East Relief and Refugee Administration; chief of the UNRRA Balkan Mission

Maugras, Gaston, French Ambassador to Greece

Mavromichalis, Petros, leader of the extreme right wing of the Populist (royalist) Party, Minister of the Army (1946); Minister of Interior (1947-1948); Minister of the Navy (1948-1949)

Mavroudis Nikolaos, Minister for Foreign Affairs (1933) Permanent Deputy Minister for Foreign Affairs (1936-1941)

Maximos, Dimitrios, Minister for Foreign Affairs (1933-1935); Prime Minister of Greece (1947)

Mazarakis, Gen. Alexander, republican officer, in forced retirement following the monarchy's restoration in 1935

McBaine, Lt. Comm. Turner H., SI, OSS in Cairo

McFarlan, M., head of OSS in Turkey

McNeill, Lt. (later Cpt.) William H., U.S. Assist. Military Attaché in Greece

Melas, George, Deputy Minister for Foreign Affairs (1945); Minister of Justice (1948-1949)

Mercati, Count Leonardo, aide to King George II of the Hellenes

Metaxas, Gen. John, Chief of Staff to King Constantine I of the Hellenes; leader of royalist party, Minister of Transportation (1926-1928); Minister of Interior (1932-1933); Minister of the Army (1936); Prime Minister and Dictator of Greece (1936-1941)

Metaxas, Petros, head of the Political Bureau of King George II of the Hellenes

Michalacopoulos, Andreas, Prime Minister of Greece (1924-1925); Minister for Foreign Affairs (1926-1928); Deputy Prime Minister and Minister for Foreign Affairs (1929-1932); Minister for Foreign Affairs (1933)

Mihailović, Gen. Dragoljub-Draža, Serb officer and right-wing resistance leader, Minister of War and Commander in Chief under the Yugoslav Government in Cairo

Molotov, Vyacheslav M., Commissar for Foreign Affairs of the Soviet Union

Moore, Col., U.S. Military Attaché to the Greek and Yugoslav Governments in Cairo

Morgan, Lt. Gen. Sir William D., Supreme Allied Commander, Mediterranean (1946-1947)

Morris, Leland B., U.S. Consul General and First Secretary of Legation in Greece; *Chargé d'Affaires* in Germany

Mowrer, Edgar, correspondent of the Chicago *Daily News*

Moyne, Rt. Hon. Sir Walter, British Resident Minister in Near East

Murphy, Robert D., U.S. Political Adviser to the Supreme Allied Commander, Mediterranean

Murray, Wallace, Director of NEA, Dept. of State

Musulin, Lt. George, OSS officer with Mihailović forces

Mylonas, Alexander, leader of the Agrarian Democratic Party, Deputy Minister of Economics (1928); Minister of Education (1933); Minister of the Navy (1944); Minister of Finance (1945-1946)

Neubacher, Hermann, German Political and Economic Plenipotentiary for the Balkans

Nicholas, Prince, brother of King Constantine I of the Hellenes

Nicholas, Princess, Grand Duchess Helen of Russia, widow of Prince Nicholas

Nicolaidis, Gen. George, Minister of Railroads (1938-1941)

Nicoloudis, Theologos, Minister of Education (1927-1928); Deputy Minister of Press and Tourism (1936-1941)

Norton, Sir Clifford V., British Ambassador to Greece, succeeding Leeper in March 1946

Novikov, Nikolai V., Soviet Ambassador to the Greek and Yugoslav Governments in Cairo (1943-1944)

Othonaios, Gen. Alexander, Greek republican officer, presiding officer in court martial of the "Six" (1922); Prime Minister (1933); in forced retirement following the monarchy's restoration in 1935; Commander in Chief of the Greek Armed Forces (1944)

Paget, Gen. Sir Bernard, British Commander in Chief, Middle East

Palairet, Sir Charles Michael, British Ambassador to Greece, succeeding Waterlow (1939-1941)

Pangalos, Gen. Theodore, member of junta which forced King Constantine to abdicate in 1922; Prime Minister and Dictator of Greece (1925-1926)

Papagos, Gen. Alexander, royalist officer, Minister of the Army (1935-1936); Chief of Staff, Supreme Commander of the Greek Armed Forces

Papademas, Gen. Nikolaos, Deputy Minister of the Army (1936-1941)

LIST OF PRINCIPAL NAMES · 743

Papandreou, George, leader of the Liberal Party, Minister of Education (1930-1932); Minister of Transportation (1933); Prime Minister of Greece (1944-1945); Minister of National Economy (1946); Minister of the Interior (1947)

Papavasiliou, Adm. Ippokratis, Minister of the Navy (1936-1941)

Papen, Franz von, German Ambassador to Turkey

Park, Air Marshal Sir Keith, British Commanding Officer, Air Forces, Middle East

Parsons, Arthur W., Assistant Director of the American School of Classical Studies in Greece; Special Assistant to Ambassador MacVeagh in Cairo, U.S. delegate to United Nations Special Committee on the Balkans

Pasakay, Maj. Turkish Military Attaché in Greece

Paul, Crown Prince, younger brother of King George II, King of the Hellenes (1947-1964)

Paul, Prince, Regent of Yugoslavia

Peter, Prince, cousin of King George II of the Hellenes

Philon, Athanasios, friend of the Greek royal family, Director of the Greek state railroads; Counselor of the Greek Embassy to the United States

Plastiras, Gen. Nikolaos, republican officer, leader of the 1922 coup which deposed King Constantine I, in forced exile after 1935, Prime Minister of Greece (1945)

Popov, Col. Gregori, head of the Soviet Military Mission in Greece (1944-1945)

Porfyrogenis, Miltiadis, socialist leader, Secretary General of EAM, Minister of Labor (1944)

Porter, Paul, head of the U.S. Economic Mission to Greece

Pribichevich, Stoyan, Balkans correspondent of *Time* magazine

Purić, Bozidar, Prime Minister of the Yugoslav Government in Cairo

Rallis, John, royalist leader, Prime Minister of Greece under the Axis occupation

Rallis, Petros, Governor of Macedonia; Minister of Education (1933); Minister of Transportation (1934); Minister of the Interior (1935); Minister of Merchant Marine (1944)

Rankin, Karl, U.S. Commercial and Economic Counselor in Greece; *Chargé d'Affaires*

Rawlings, Adm. Sir Herbert, Commander of the British Navy, Eastern Mediterranean

Reed, Edward L., Counselor of Embassy, *Chargé d'Affaires*, U.S. Embassy to Italy (1938-1941)

Reed, Leslie E., First Secretary of the U.S. Embassy in Greece

Ribbentrop, Joachim von, German Minister for Foreign Affairs

Roussos, George, Deputy Prime Minister of Greece (1943-1944)

Roussos, Petros, Greek communist leader, member of the Central Committee of EAM

Royce, Maj. Gen. Ralph, Commanding Officer, U.S. Forces, Middle East

Sadler, Brig. Percy L., U.S. Deputy Commander of AML for Relief and Rehabilitation in Greece

Sakellariou, Adm. Alexander, Navy Chief of Staff (1936-1941); Minister of the Navy (1941-1942); Minister of Supply (1947)

Saraçoglu, Sükrü, Turkish Minister for Foreign Affairs

Sarafis, Gen. Stefanos, republican officer, in forced retirement following the monarchy's restoration in 1935; Commander in Chief of ELAS

Sariyannis, Gen. Ptolemaios, republican officer, Deputy Minister of the Army (1944)

Scobie, Lt. Gen. Sir Ronald M., Commanding Officer, BMM to Greece

Sedgwick, Alexander C. Shan, correspondent of the *New York Times* in Greece, cousin of MacVeagh

Seitz, Col. Albert B., OSS officer with Mihailović forces

Shantz, Harold, Counselor of the U.S. Embassy to the Greek Government in Cairo

Siantos, George, communist leader, Secretary of KKE's Central Committee, Acting Secretary General of KKE

Simović, Gen. Dusan T., Prime Minister of Yugoslavia following the revolt of 27 March 1941

Smith-Dorrien, Brig. Peter, chief political adviser of BML in Cairo, political adviser to Gen. Scobie

Smuts, Gen. Jan Christian, Prime Minister of South Africa and Minister of External Affairs and Defense

Sofianopoulos, John, leader of the "Union of the Left" Party, Minister for Foreign Affairs (1945)

Sofoulis, Themistoclis, leader of the Liberal Party, Minister of the Army (1928-1930), Prime Minister of Greece (1945-1946, 1947-1949)

Solod, Danill, Counselor of the Soviet Embassy to the Greek and Yugoslav Governments in Cairo

Spiliotopoulos, Gen. Panayiotis, Military Commander of Attica (1944-1945)

Steel, Christopher, British diplomat attached to the Minister of State in the Near East

Stefanopoulos, Stefand, prominent member of Populist Party

Stettinius, Edward R., Under Secretary of State; Secretary of State

Stevenson, Ralph Skrine, British Ambassador to the Yugoslav Government in Cairo

Steinhardt, Lawrence, U.S. Ambassador to Turkey

Stirbei, Prince Barbu, former Prime Minister of Rumania, envoy negotiating Rumania's capitulation to the Allies
Stojadinović, Milan, Prime Minister of Yugoslavia
Subasić, Ivan, former Ban (Governor) of Croatia; Prime Minister of Yugoslavia
Sulzberger, Cyrus, correspondent of the *New York Times*
Svolos, Alexander, professor of constitutional law at the university of Athens, socialist leader, President and Secretary for Foreign Affairs of PEEA; Minister of Economics (1944)
Tambacopoulos, Agis, Minister of Justice (1938-1941)
Thayer, Maj. Charles W., U.S. military representative to Tito
Theotokis, John, royalist leader, Minister of Agriculture (1932-1935); Deputy Prime Minister and Minister for Foreign Affairs (1935); Minister of the Interior (1946)
Tito Marshal (Josip Broz), Yugoslav communist leader, resistance leader, President of the Yugoslav National Committee of Liberation; President of Yugoslavia
Toulmin, Col. John E., head of OSS in Cairo
Tsaldaris, Constantine, leader of the Populist (royalist) Party, Minister of Transportation (1933-1935); Minister for Foreign Affairs (1946); Prime Minister of Greece (1946-1947); Deputy Prime Minister and Minister for Foreign Affairs (1947-1949)
Tsaldaris, Panayiotis, leader of the Populist (royalist) Party, Minister of the Interior (1926-1927); Prime Minister of Greece (1932-1933, 1933-1935)
Tsouderos, Emmanuel, Governor of the Bank of Greece; Prime Minister (1941-1944)
Turle, Adm. Charles E., British Naval Attaché in Greece
Varvaressos, Kyriakos, Governor of the Bank of Greece; Minister of Finance (1932, 1941-1943); Deputy Prime Minister and Minister of Supply (1945)
Venizelos, Eleftherios, Greece's foremost political personality during the 1910's-1930's; Prime Minister (1910-1915, 1916-1920, 1928-1932, 1933)
Venizelos, Sofoclis, leader of the Liberal Party, Minister of the Navy (1943); Prime Minister of Greece (1944); Deputy Prime Minister (1944, 1947); Prime Minister (1950)
Ventiris, Gen. Constantine, royalist officer, Greek Chief of Staff in the Middle East; Commander in Chief (1944-1945)
Vogel, Dr. Georg, Secretary of the German Embassy in Greece (1941)
Voulgaris, Adm. Petros, Commander in Chief of the Greek Navy in the Middle East following the mutiny of April 1944; Prime Minister (1945)

Vukčević, Alexandar, Yugoslav Ambassador to Greece

Wadsworth, George, U.S. Diplomatic Agent and Consul General at Beirut, Lebanon

Waley, Sir David, representative of the British Treasury on the British Committee of Economic and Political Advisers for Greece (1944)

Wallace, David, Press Attaché of the British Embassy in Greece

Warner, Edward, Senior Political Officer of the British Embassy to the Greek Government in Cairo

Waterhouse, E. K., Political Officer of the British Embassy to the Greek Government in Cairo and Athens

Waterlow, Sir Sydney, British Ambassador to Greece

Wavell, Gen. Sir Archibald P., British Commander in Chief, Middle East

Welles, Sumner, Under-Secretary of State

West, Col. Paul, head of Special Operations, OSS in Cairo

Weygand, Gen. Maxime, Commander of the French forces in the Middle East

Wilson, Field Marshal Sir Henry Maitland ("Jumbo"), British Commander in Chief, Middle East; Supreme Allied Commander, Mediterranean

Winant, John G., U.S. Ambassador to Britain

Wines, Maj. Gerald K., Senior U.S. Officer on the Allied Military Mission in Greece

Woodhouse, Col. Christopher M., Chief British Military Liaison Officer in Greece (1943-1945)

Wright, Col. Daniel ("Doc"), U.S. Public Health Service Officer, UNRRA medical officer

Young, Dr. Rodney, American archaeologist at the American School of Classical Studies in Greece; head of the Greek Desk, SI, OSS

Zahariadis, Nikolas, communist leader, Secretary General of the KKE, prisoner at Dachau until 1945.

Zaimis, Alexander, President of the Greek Republic (1929-1935)

Zervas, Gen. Napoleon, military chief of EDES; Minister of Public Order (1947). Initially a republican, he was gradually identified with royalist causes

Zevgos, John, communist leader, Minister of Agriculture (1944)

APPENDIX B

ABBREVIATIONS AND CODE NAMES

AFHQ	Allied Forces Headquarters
AMHQ	Allied Military Headquarters
AML	Allied Military Liaison
ANVIL	Plan for allied invasion of southern France
ATB	Administration of Territory (Balkans) Committee (Allied)
BBC	British Broadcasting Corporation
BEW	Board of Economic Warfare (British)
BLM	British Liaison Mission to resistance groups
BMA	British Military Administration
BSC	Balkans Supply Center (Allied)
CCAC	Combined Civil Affairs Committee (Allied)
CIA	Central Intelligence Agency (U.S.)
C in C	Commander in Chief
CIS	Counter Intelligence Service (British)
DSR	Department of State Records (unpublished)
EAM	*Ethnikon Apeleftherotikon Metopon* = National Liberation Front. Coalition of Greek leftist and republican resistance groups
EDES	*Ethnikos Demokratikos Ellinikos Syndesmos* = National Republican Greek League. Resistance group headed by Col. Napoleon Zervas. Despite its republican origins, it became identified with royalist forces
ELAS	*Ethnikos Laikos Apeleftherotikos Stratos* = National Popular Liberation Army. Military arm of EAM
EKKA	*Ethniki ke Koinoniki Apeleftherosis* = National and Social Liberation. Republican resistance group destroyed by ELAS in the fall of 1943
EON	*Ethniki Organosis Neolaias* = National Youth Organization of the Metaxas dictatorship
EPON	*Enomeni Panelladiki Organosi Neon* = United Panhellenic Youth Organization of EAM
FEA	Foreign Economic Administration (U.S.)
FFI	*Forces Françaises de l'Intérieur* (French resistance)
FO	Foreign Office (British)

748 · APPENDIX B

FORCE 133	SOE forces in the Balkans, with headquarters in Cairo
FORCE 140	British forces for the liberation of Greece
FR	*Foreign Relations of the United States.* Department of State publication appearing in annual volumes and containing major diplomatic documents
G2	Military headquarters section concerned with intelligence
G3	Military headquarters section concerned with plans and operations
GWR	Greek War Relief (U.S.)
JICAME	Joint Intelligence Committee Army, Middle East (Allied)
KKE	*Kommounistikon Komma Ellados* = Communist Party of Greece
MA	Military Attaché
MESC	Middle East Supply Center (Allied)
ML	Military Liaison. Allied command responsible for civil affairs in liberated areas
MO	Morale Operations. Psychological warfare directed at occupied countries
NEA	Near East and African Affairs (Office of), Department of State
NOAH'S ARK	Plan for the liberation of Greece
OG	Operational Group. Allied agents behind enemy lines
OSS	Office of Strategic Services. U.S. intelligence and sabotage service, headed by Gen. William J. Donovan
OWI	Office of War Information (U.S.)
PEEA	*Politiki Epitropi Ethnikis Apeleftherosis* = Political Committee of National Liberation. Provisional government established by EAM in liberated areas of Greece
PPF	President's Personal File
PSF	Personal Secretary's (of President Roosevelt) File
PWB	Psychological Warfare Board (U.S.)
PWE	Political Warfare Executive (British)
RAF	Royal Air Force (British)
SACMED	Supreme Allied Commander Mediterranean
SI	Secret Intelligence (OSS)
SIME	Secret Intelligence, Middle East (British)
SIS	Secret Intelligence Service (British)
SOE	Special Operations Executive. British intelligence and sabotage agency
UKCC	United Kingdom Control Commission

UNRRA	United Nations Relief and Rehabilitation Administration
USCC	United States Control Commission
USAFIME	United States Army Forces Intelligence, Middle East
WSA	War Shipping Administration (U.S.)

NOTES

Notes, Chapter I: "My Passion in Life!"

(1) MacVeagh letter to Roosevelt, November 9, 1932, Personal Secretary's File (hereafter PSF), folder "Greece," Franklin D. Roosevelt Library, Hyde Park, New York (hereafter Roosevelt Library).

(2) *New Canaan Advertiser*, June 15, 1933.

(3) *The Herald Tribune*, June 10, 1933.

(4) MacVeagh letter to Roosevelt, January 31, 1933, PSF, "Greece."

(5) U.S. Department of State unpublished records (hereafter *DSR*), File 123: "MacVeagh, Lincoln," telegram June 2, 1933.

(6) MacVeagh despatch 1, September 22, 1933, *DSR*, File 123: "MacVeagh."

(7) Quoted in *Current Biography, 1952* (New York: H. W. Wilson, 1953), p. 385.

(8) MacVeagh telegram, September 22, 1933, *DSR*, File 123: "MacVeagh."

Notes, Chapter II: 1933-1935

(1) MacVeagh letter to Roosevelt, November 21, 1933, President's Personal File (hereafter PPF), File 1192; Roosevelt letter to MacVeagh, January 16, 1934, PPF, File 1192.

(2) Forrest McDonald, *Insull* (Chicago: University of Chicago Press, 1962), p. 316.

(3) McDonald repeats these allegations, pp. 316-317.

(4) U.S. Department of State, *Foreign Relations of the United States* (hereafter *FR*) *1934*, II: *Europe, Near East and Africa* (Washington, D.C.: Government Printing Office, 1951), 573.

(5) MacVeagh letter to Roosevelt, May 9, 1934, PSF, "Greece."

(6) *FR 1934*, II, 533-49; *FR 1935*, II: *The British Commonwealth, Europe* (Washington, D.C.: Government Printing Office, 1952), 506-10.

(7) MacVeagh letter to Roosevelt, February 12, 1934, PSF, "Greece."

(8) MacVeagh letter to Roosevelt, March 2, 1934, PPF, File 1192.

(9) *FR 1934*, II, 552.

(10) *FR 1934*, II, 554-55.

(11) MacVeagh letter to Roosevelt, August 6, 1934, PSF, "Greece."

(12) MacVeagh despatch 83, December 14, 1933, *DSR*, 868.00/728.

(13) MacVeagh despatch 220, April 11, 1934, *DSR*, 868.00/738.
(14) MacVeagh letter to Roosevelt, May 9, 1934, PSF, "Greece."
(15) MacVeagh letter to Roosevelt, August 6, 1934, PSF, "Greece."
(16) MacVeagh despatch 317, July 18, 1934, *DSR*, 868.00/742.
(17) MacVeagh despacth 367, September 11, 1934, *DSR*, 868.00/746.
(18) MacVeagh despatch 509, January 15, 1935, *DSR*, 868.00/757.
(19) MacVeagh despatch 419, October 18, 1934, *DSR*, 868.00/751.
(20) MacVeagh letter to Roosevelt, December 4, 1934, PSF, "Greece."
(21) Gregorios Dafnis, *E Ellas Metaxe Dyo Polemon, 1923-1940* (Greece Between Two Wars) (Athens: Ikaros, 1955), p. 282.
(22) MacVeagh despatch 561, March 13, 1935, *DSR*, 868.00/815.
(23) MacVeagh despatch 571, March 17, 1935, *DSR*, 868.00/822.
(24) MacVeagh despatch 574, March 18, 1935, *DSR*, 868.00/824.
(25) *FR 1935*, II, 492.
(26) *FR 1935*, II, 493.
(27) *FR 1935*, II, 494.
(28) *FR 1935*, II, 497.
(29) MacVeagh despatch 633, April 24, 1935, *DSR*, 868.00/851.
(30) MacVeagh despatch 634, April 24, 1935, *DSR*, 868.00/852.
(31) MacVeagh despatch 685, June 6, 1935, *DSR*, 868.00/867.
(32) MacVeagh letter to Roosevelt, May 4, 1935, PSF, "Greece."
(33) MacVeagh despatch 686, June 6, 1935, *DSR*, File 123: "MacVeagh."
(34) MacVeagh despatch 881, October 14, 1935, *DSR*, 868.00/917.
(35) MacVeagh despatch 875, October 10, 1935, *DSR*, 868.00/916.
(36) MacVeagh despatch 900, October 26, 1935, *DSR*, 868.00/927.
(37) MacVeagh letter to Roosevelt, October 15, 1935, PSF, "Greece."
(38) *FR 1935*, II, 504.
(39) MacVeagh despatch 915, November 9, 1935, *DSR*, 868.00/934.
(40) MacVeagh telegram 172, November 18, 1935, *DSR*, 868.00/924.
(41) MacVeagh despatch 940, November 21, 1935, *DSR*, 868.00/939.
(42) MacVeagh despatch 946, November 26, 1935, *DSR*, 868.00/940.
(43) *DSR*, File 123: "MacVeagh."

Notes, Chapter III: 1936-1939

(1) MacVeagh despatch 1031, February 8, 1936, *DSR*, 868.00/957.
(2) MacVeagh letter to Roosevelt, February 29, 1936, PSF, "Greece."
(3) MacVeagh despatch 1091, March 10, 1936, *DSR*, 868.00/964.
(4) MacVeagh letter to Roosevelt, April 30, 1936, PSF, "Greece."
(5) MacVeagh despatch 1154, May 2, 1936, *DSR*, 868.00/974.
(6) MacVeagh despatch 1195, May 29, 1936, *DSR*, 868.00/976.
(7) Roosevelt letter to MacVeagh, May 23, 1936, PSF, "Greece."

(8) MacVeagh letter to Roosevelt, June 13, 1936, PSF, "Greece."
(9) *New York Times*, August 7, 1936.
(10) MacVeagh letter to Roosevelt, August 29, 1936, PSF, "Greece."
(11) MacVeagh letter to Roosevelt, November 9, 1936, PSF, "Greece."
(12) MacVeagh despatch 1348, September 19, 1936, *DSR*, 868.00/995.
(13) MacVeagh despatch 1377, October 17, 1936, *DSR*, 868.00/997.
(14) MacVeagh despatch 1523, February 5, 1937, *DSR*, 868.00/1005.
(15) MacVeagh despatch 1447, December 8, 1936, *DSR*, 123 MacVeagh, Lincoln/94.
(16) MacVeagh despatch 1697, May 29, 1937, *DSR*, 123 MacVeagh, Lincoln/118.
(17) MacVeagh despatch 1749, June 25, 1937, *DSR*, 123 MacVeagh, Lincoln/121.
(18) MacVeagh despatch 1795, July 29, 1937, *DSR*, 123 MacVeagh, Lincoln/126.
(19) MacVeagh despatch 2043, January 7, 1938, *DSR*, 123 MacVeagh, Lincoln/154.
(20) MacVeagh despatch 1793, July 26, 1937, *DSR*, 868.00/1012.
(21) MacVeagh despatch 2114, February 18, 1938, *DSR*, 868.00/1032.
(22) MacVeagh letter to Roosevelt, February 17, 1937, PSF, "Greece."
(23) MacVeagh letter to Roosevelt, June 7, 1937, PPF, File 1192.
(24) MacVeagh letter to Roosevelt, November 10, 1937, PSF, "Greece."
(25) MacVeagh despatch 2030, December 30, 1937, *DSR*, 868.0011/23.
(26) MacVeagh despatch 2050, January 9, 1938, *DSR*, 868.0011/24.
(27) MacVeagh letter to Eleanor Roosevelt, January 24, 1938, PSF, "Greece."
(28) MacVeagh despatch 2198, April 4, 1938, *DSR*, 868.00/1036.
(29) MacVeagh despatch 2398, August 3, 1938, *DSR*, 868.00/1048.
(30) MacVeagh despatch 2485, September 27, 1938, *DSR*, 868.00/1053.
(31) MacVeagh letter to Roosevelt, May 20, 1938, PSF, "Greece."
(32) MacVeagh letter to Roosevelt, August 22, 1938, PSF, "Greece."
(33) MacVeagh letter to Roosevelt, November 22, 1938, PSF, "Greece."
(34) MacVeagh despatch 2525, October 24, 1938, *DSR*, 868.00/1058.
(35) MacVeagh despatch 2562, November 14, 1938, *DSR*, 868.00/1060.
(36) MacVeagh despatch 2584, November 24, 1938, *DSR*, 868.00/1061.
(37) MacVeagh despatch 2846, March 6, 1939, *DSR*, 868.00/1079.
(38) MacVeagh despatch 2695, January 23, 1939, *DSR*, 868.00/1069.
(39) MacVeagh despatch 2715, January 31, 1939, *DSR*, 868.00/1073.
(40) MacVeagh despatch 2785, February 20, 1939, *DSR*, 868.00/1075.
(41) MacVeagh despatch 3040, May 15, 1939, *DSR*, 868.00/1086.
(42) MacVeagh letter to Roosevelt, March 6, 1939, PSF, "Greece."
(43) MacVeagh letter to Roosevelt, April 17, 1939, PSF, "Greece."

(44) MacVeagh despatch 3041, May 15, 1939, *DSR*, 868.00/1087.
(45) MacVeagh letter to Roosevelt, July 29, 1939, PSF, "Greece."
(46) MacVeagh letter to Roosevelt, August 21, 1939, PSF, "Greece."
(47) MacVeagh despatch 3334, August 19, 1939, *DSR*, 868.00/1098.
(48) MacVeagh letter to Roosevelt, August 31, 1939, PSF, "Greece."

Notes, Chapter IV: 1939-1940

(1) MacVeagh letter to Roosevelt, September 16, 1939, PSF, "Greece."
(2) MacVeagh letter to Roosevelt, September 26, 1939, PSF, "Greece."
(3) MacVeagh letter to Roosevelt, November 8, 1939, PSF, "Greece."
(4) MacVeagh letter to Roosevelt, December 3, 1939, PSF, "Greece."
(5) MacVeagh letter to Roosevelt, January 17, 1940, PPF, File 1192.
(6) MacVeagh letter to Roosevelt, January 30, 1940, PSF, "Greece."
(7) MacVeagh letter to Roosevelt, February 27, 1940, PSF, "Greece."
(8) MacVeagh letter to Roosevelt, March 26, 1940, PSF, "Greece."
(9) MacVeagh letter to Roosevelt, May 4, 1940, PSF, "Greece."
(10) MacVeagh letter to Roosevelt, May 24, 1940, PSF, "Greece."
(11) MacVeagh letter to Roosevelt, July 2, 1940, PSF, "Greece."
(12) MacVeagh letter to Roosevelt, August 30, 1940, PSF, "Greece."
(13) MacVeagh letter to Roosevelt, September 30, 1940, PSF, "Greece."

Notes, Chapter V: "A Fighting Nation"

(1) MacVeagh letter to Roosevelt, November 6, 1940, PSF, "Greece."
(2) MacVeagh letter to Roosevelt, November 28, 1940, PSF, "Greece."
(3) MacVeagh letter to Roosevelt, December 25, 1940, PSF, "Greece."
(4) MacVeagh letter to Roosevelt, January 19, 1941, PSF, "Greece."

Notes, Chapter VI: "A Gallant Resistance"

(1) *FR 1941*, II, 644-45.
(2) MacVeagh letter to Roosevelt, February 23, 1941, PSF, "Greece."
(3) MacVeagh letter to Roosevelt, March 8, 1941, PSF, "Greece."
(4) MacVeagh letter to Roosevelt, March 25, 1941, PSF, "Greece."
(5) *New York Times*, July 22, 1941.
(6) "Notes on the German Conquest and Occupation of Greece," June 16, 1941, attached to MacVeagh letter to Roosevelt, August 6, 1941, PSF, "Greece."
(7) MacVeagh despatch (unnumbered), July 19, 1941, *DSR*, 868.00/1124, PS/LDP.

Notes, Chapter VIII: Cairo

(1) MacVeagh letter to Roosevelt, December 5, 1943, PSF, "Greece."
(2) MacVeagh letter to Roosevelt, December 13, 1943, PSF, "Greece."
(3) MacVeagh letter to Roosevelt, December 22, 1943, PSF, "Greece."
(4) Roosevelt letter to MacVeagh, January 15, 1944, PSF, "MacVeagh Greece."
(5) MacVeagh letter to Roosevelt, February 17, 1944, PSF, "MacVeagh 1944."
(6) MacVeagh telegram to the Department of State, No. Greek 51, February 18, 1944, 2 p.m., copy in MacVeagh Papers.
(7) MacVeagh letter to Roosevelt, March 17, 1944, PSF, "Greece."
(8) Roosevelt's letter to MacVeagh, April 1, 1944, PSF, "MacVeagh-Greece."
(9) MacVeagh letter to Roosevelt, May 15, 1944, PSF, "MacVeagh."
(10) MacVeagh letter to Roosevelt, June 23, 1944, PSF, "MacVeagh."

Notes, Chapter IX: From Liberation to Civil War

(1) MacVeagh letter to Roosevelt, October 15, 1944, PSF, "MacVeagh-Greece."
(2) MacVeagh letter to Roosevelt, December 8, 1944, PSF, "MacVeagh."
(3) *FR 1944*, V, 147.
(4) *FR 1944*, V, 155.
(5) *FR 1944*, V, 158.
(6) *FR 1944*, V, 160-61.
(7) *FR 1944*, V, 165.
(8) *FR 1944*, V, 161.
(9) *FR 1944*, V, 169-70.
(10) *FR 1944*, V, 171.
(11) *FR 1944*, V, 172-73.
(12) MacVeagh despatch 332, December 28, 1944, *DSR*, 868.00/12-2844.
(13) *FR 1945*, VIII, 98-99.
(14) MacVeagh letter to Roosevelt, January 15, 1945, PSF, "MacVeagh."
(15) MacVeagh telegram, January 10, 1945, *DSR*, 868.00/1-1045.
(16) MacVeagh despatch 585, February 27, 1945, *DSR*, 868.00/2-2745.
(17) *FR 1945*, VIII, 125.

Notes, Chapter X: End of a Journey

(1) Merriam letter to MacVeagh, May 16, 1945, MacVeagh Papers.
(2) MacVeagh despatch 1211, June 22, 1945, *DSR*, 868.00/6-2245.

756 · NOTES, CHAPTER X

(3) Harriman letter to MacVeagh, July 5, 1945, MacVeagh Papers.
(4) MacVeagh despatch 1282, July 4, 1945, *DSR*, 868.00/7-445.
(5) MacVeagh despatch 1333, July 17, 1945, *DSR*, 868.00/7-1745.
(6) MacVeagh letter to Kohler, January 29, 1945, MacVeagh Papers.
(7) *FR 1945*, VIII, 196-97.
(8) *FR 1945*, VIII, 202-03.
(9) *FR 1945*, VIII, 221-22.
(10) *FR 1945*, VIII, 223.
(11) *FR 1945*, VIII, 227-28.
(12) *FR 1945*, VIII, 252-53.
(13) *FR 1945*, VIII, 251-52.
(14) *FR 1945*, VIII, 258.
(15) *FR 1945*, VIII, 276.
(16) *FR 1945*, VIII, 284-88.
(17) *FR 1945*, VIII, 128-31.
(18) For example, MacVeagh telegram 22, July 14, 1945, *DSR*, 868.00/7-1445.
(19) *FR 1945*, VIII, 150-51.
(20) *FR 1945*, VIII, 180-84.
(21) *FR 1946*, VII, 97-99.
(22) *FR 1946*, VII, 126.
(23) MacVeagh memorandum to Henderson, May 2, 1946, *DSR*, 868.00/5-246.
(24) MacVeagh despatch 2945, July 24, 1946, *DSR*, 868.00/7-2446.
(25) *FR 1946*, VII, 186-87.
(26) MacVeagh telegram 983, July 28, 1946, *DSR*, 868.00/7-2846.
(27) Department of State *Bulletin*, September 1, 1946, p. 424.
(28) *FR 1946*, VII, 193-94.
(29) *FR 1946*, VII, 204-207.
(30) MacVeagh despatch 3388, December 5, 1946, *DSR*, 868.00/12-546.
(31) Baxter memorandum, October 8, 1946, *DSR*, 868.00/10-846 CS/V.
(32) MacVeagh letter to Cannon, October 14, 1946, MacVeagh Papers.
(33) *FR 1946*, VII, 235-37.
(34) MacVeagh letter to Henderson, October 19, 1946, *DSR*, 868.00/10-1946.
(35) MacVeagh telegram 1407, October 17, 1946, *DSR*, 868.00/10-1746.
(36) *FR 1946*, VII, 268.
(37) *FR 1946*, VII, 283, fn. 73.
(38) *FR 1946*, VII, 278.
(39) *FR 1946*, VII, 262-63. Also, Memorandum for the President, December 20, 1946, on the impending visit of Tsaldaris, *DSR*, 868.00/12-2046.

NOTES, CHAPTER X · 757

(40) *FR 1946*, VII, 256.
(41) *FR 1946*, VII, 286-87.
(42) *FR 1947*, V, 4-5.
(43) *FR 1947*, V, 16-17.
(44) *FR 1947*, V, 16.
(45) *FR 1947*, V, 28-29.
(46) *FR 1947*, V, 29-31.
(47) Texts of the two British aide-memoires in *FR 1947*, V, 32-37.
(48) *FR 1947*, V, 89-90.
(49) United States Senate, Committee on Foreign Relations, *Legislative Origins of the Truman Doctrine. Hearings Held in Executive Session Before the Committee on Foreign Relations on S. 938* (Washington, D.C.: U.S. Govt. Printing Office, 1973), pp. 32-47, 64-67.
(50) *FR 1947*, V, 142-43.
(51) Text of agreement in *FR 1947*, V, 185-88.
(52) *New York Times*, July 13, 1947.
(53) *FR 1947*, V, 215-16.
(54) *FR 1947*, V, 224.
(55) *FR 1947*, V, 228.
(56) *FR 1947*, V, 252.
(57) *FR 1947*, V, 279.
(58) *FR 1947*, V, 280-81.
(59) *FR 1947*, V, 310.
(60) *New York Times*, August 24, 1947.
(61) *New York Times*, August 27, 1947.
(62) *FR 1947*, V, 316-17.
(63) *FR 1947*, V, 318-19.
(64) *New York Times*, August 30, 1947.
(65) *FR 1947*, V, 320-21.
(66) *FR 1947*, V, 323-27.
(67) *FR 1947*, V, 368-69.
(68) *FR 1947*, V, 370-71.
(69) *FR 1947*, V, 378-80.
(70) *FR 1947*, V, 393-95.
(71) *FR 1947*, V, 391-93, 400.
(72) *FR 1947*, V, 404-07.
(73) *FR 1947*, V, 408, fn. 1.
(74) *New York Times*, November 21, 1947.
(75) *FR 1947*, V, 411-13.
(76) *FR 1947*, V, 416-17.
(77) *New York Times*, November 22, 1947.
(78) *New York Times*, November 25, 1947.

(79) *New York Times*, February 27, 1948.

(80) Papers of Harry S. Truman, Official File, PPF 4220, Harry S. Truman Library. On May 22, 1950, on the third anniversary of Congress' enactment of the aid program to Greece and Turkey, Truman sent MacVeagh another letter of commendation. *Ibid.*

INDEX

Acheson, Dean, 3n, 382, 573, 692, 712, 718
Adossidis, Alexander, 86, 260
Agrarian party, 15
Albania, 27-28, 30, 35, 90, 109, 136-37, 157, 193, 195, 213-14, 216, 218-22, 229, 230, 233, 264-65, 553, 614, 708
Albanian War, vii, 234-348
Aldrich, Col. Henry, 578, 593n, 595-96, 608-609, 633, 641
Alexander, Gen. Harold, 388, 402, 415, 663, 665
Alexander, King of Greece, 13
Alexandris, Adm. Constantine, 494, 501
Allard, Sven, 218, 223, 225, 267, 270, 271, 316-17, 321, 325, 328, 330, 336, 349, 351, 362, 618-19, 624, 633
Allen, George, 41, 160, 388-90, 425
Allied Military Liaison (AML, ML), 485, 516, 524, 538, 542-43, 546, 553-55, 573, 574, 579, 586, 587, 594-99, 601, 603, 607-609, 616, 619, 622, 636-37, 639, 641, 645-47, 649-51, 656, 675, 684-85
Altenburg, Gunther, 358, 360, 362, 364
American Mission for Aid to Greece (AMAG), 717-18, 721, 723, 725-29, 730-32
Anatolia College, 52
Andrew, Prince, 45, 62
Androulis, Pindar, 125, 173, 244, 260, 266, 291, 345
Angelopoulos, Angelos, 512n, 554, 560, 602n, 637, 656n
Antonescu, Gen. Ion, 223, 463, 469-71, 478-80, 483-84, 490, 499, 504, 506, 510-11, 528
Antonescu, Mihai, 479, 490
Apostolidis, Andreas, 51, 245, 247, 344
Aras, Tevfik, 82, 171n
Archer, Laird, 250, 342, 359, 392, 395, 466, 491, 599, 637, 639, 646, 651
Argyropoulos, Pericles, 130, 496
Aris, *see* Velouchiotis
Armour, Norman 731-32

Armstrong, Brig. Charles, 421, 458, 460, 462
Askoutsis, Nikolaos, 512n, 602n, 614, 654, 656n
Ataturk, *see* Kemal
Athanassiadis, Bodossakis, *see* Bodossakis
Athens College, 52
Attlee, Clement, 690n

Badoglio, Marshal Pietro, 246, 258, 470, 497
Bailey, Col. S. W., 458
Bailey, Lt. Stephen, 458-60
Baker, Maj. Joseph K., 225, 234, 236, 239, 242, 246, 249, 257-58, 262, 279, 282, 285, 290, 295, 296, 307, 309, 310, 314, 317-19, 327, 328, 330, 334-37, 340, 345, 347-50, 352, 354-55, 365
Bakirdzis, Col. Euripidis, 466, 479, 504
Baldwin, William, 6
Balfour, David, 546
Balkan Entente (Pact), 27-30, 35, 73, 78-79, 82, 109-10, 113, 130, 133, 135-37, 139-40, 151-53, 155, 177, 179, 185, 186, 189-90, 192-93, 228, 271, 274, 317
Balkan Supply Center (BSC), 467, 483, 501, 524, 534-35, 561, 563-64
Barbour, Walworth, 388, 394, 404, 410, 413, 432, 435-36, 438, 464, 515, 523, 525, 527, 531, 538-39, 592-93, 600, 602, 618, 674, 676
Beaumont-Nesbitt, Gen. Philip, 421
Bellm, Col. Newt, 436-37, 450, 452, 458, 501
Benfield, Brig. K.V.B., 595
Berry, Burton, 250, 336, 340, 348, 351, 428, 607
Bevin, Ernest, 690n
Biddle, Anthony, 497
Blamey, Gen. Sir Thomas, 344
Blunt, Col. J. S., 238, 240, 253, 258, 295, 310
Bodossakis (Athanassiadis), 149, 508, 510-11, 513-15, 552, 559
Bohlen, Charles E., 571

760 · INDEX

Brewster, Daniel, 340
Britain, 12-14, 28, 36, 42-44, 49, 59, 78, 90, 93-94, 110, 113, 117, 137-38, 140-41, 152, 163-65, 168, 173-74, 180, 216, 219, 272-73, 405, 417, 422, 426, 453-55, 506, 522, 531, 549; and Metaxas regime, 112, 121-22, 148-54, 156, 183-84, 185; and Albanian War, 248, 280, 286-87, 296, 300, 302, 305-306, 310-11, 313, 327, 337-48; and Greek monarchy, 56-58, 62, 70, 112, 118, 148-54, 156, 163, 384-85, 390-91, 413, 417, 437, 454. *See also* Churchill; Eden; Leeper; Macmillan; Norton; "Spheres of Influence" Agreement
Broad, Philip, 476, 541
Broneer, Oscar, 51
Bulgaria, 12-13, 28, 30, 35, 49-50, 73, 79, 91, 108-11, 113-14, 133, 135, 137, 140, 156, 159, 165, 172-73, 176-77, 190, 192, 209, 211-12, 224-25, 251-52, 254, 259, 271-72, 280, 708; in World War II, 186, 228, 271, 289, 307, 424, 428-29, 449-50, 453, 464, 467, 469, 483, 578, 587-89, 591, 599-600, 602-603, 623
Byrnes, James, 687, 700n, 706, 710

Caccia, Harold, 163, 636, 656, 677
Cairo Conference, 392-93
Calligas, Stephen, 331, 373, 634, 650, 678
Campbell, Ronald, 306-308, 310, 322
Cannon, Cavendish, 214, 233, 290, 563-65, 571, 578-79, 580-82, 584, 586-88
Caserta Conference, 610, 613-14
Casey, Richard, 393
Cavallero, Count Ugo, 282
Chickering, Gen., 485
Chrysanthos, Archbishop, 143-48, 293
Chrysostomos, Archbishop, 119, 142-46, 293
Churchill, Randolph, 426-27, 433
Churchill, Winston S., 202, 224, 267, 283, 370, 390, 392, 396, 411, 426, 447, 462-63, 477, 489, 493, 502, 504-505, 509-10, 515, 516, 519, 524, 527, 529, 532, 534, 553, 563, 584, 588-89, 593, 604, 612, 617-18, 632, 660-62, 677, 690n; and Albanian War, 250, 257, 327, 333, 352-53, 365; and Greek monarchy, 387, 393, 398, 400, 403, 405-407, 413, 464, 466, 472, 486, 488, 502n, 534, 538, 542, 581, 618, 664-66; and Yugoslav affairs, 405, 408, 426, 428, 433, 435, 437-38, 440-41, 447-48, 460-62, 466, 477, 478, 505, 531, 537, 540, 555, 564-65, 570, 576, 580-82, 584-87, 598, 623-25; and December 1944 uprising in Athens, 654-66, 668, 674. *See also* "Spheres of Influence" Agreement
Ciano, Count Galeazzo, 121, 164, 182, 202, 245
Cochrane, Col. Philip, 622
Communist Party of Greece (KKE), 68, 74, 76, 80, 83-87, 93-96, 271, 389n, 494, 509, 523n, 536, 537, 539, 542, 548, 631, 634, 640, 648, 649, 651-52, 654, 663, 670, 672, 680-81, 683, 694-95, 697
Constantine, King of Greece, 12-14, 41, 65, 72, 75, 104, 118, 134, 626-27
Constantine, Prince (later King of Greece), 207
Counter Intelligence Service, 647-48, 650
Craw, Maj. Demos, 256-58, 262-63, 265-66, 275, 277, 279, 282, 284, 297, 307, 313-14, 323, 327, 329, 330-33, 346, 353, 354, 361
Crete, battle of, 361-62, 364-73, 375
Cretianu, Alexander, 470, 588
Cripps, Sir Stafford, 206-207, 286, 306
Cummings, Homer S., 6
Cunningham, Adm. Sir Andrew, 298, 490, 495, 501
Cyprus, 90, 134, 338

D'Albiac, Marshal John, 308, 322, 327, 331-32, 345, 347, 375
Damaskinos, Archbishop, 143-48, 393-95, 426, 434, 464, 470, 472n, 473, 479, 525, 615-16, 619, 634, 640, 655, 657; regent, 662-66, 668-69, 674, 676, 691n; prime minister, 655, 657
Dardanelles, *see* Turkish Straits
Davis, Homer, 175, 359
Delmouzos, Andreas, 140, 198, 208, 210, 213, 229, 230, 232, 240, 264, 272-74, 276, 299, 302, 647
Demertzis, Constantine, 67, 74-75, 77, 134
Demestihas, Adm. John, 39, 497
Department of State, vii, ix, x, 8, 18, 20, 21, 26, 43, 51, 88, 91, 247-49, 264-

INDEX · 761

66, 286, 357, 379-81, 385-87, 410, 416, 421, 431-32, 436, 440-41, 445-46, 466-67, 540, 626, 630-31, 647, 675, 685, 706, 717-33
Dill, Marshal Sir John, 303, 322-23
Dimitrakakis, Stelios, 487
Diomedis, Alexander, 371-72, 377
Djuvara, Mircea, 176, 190, 238
Dodecanese Islands, 49, 59, 90, 159, 168, 178, 188, 193, 195, 212, 214, 219, 244, 260, 272-74, 577, 681
Dolan, Edward, 6, 7
Donovan, William, 281-92, 295, 296, 298, 379, 424-25, 429, 441, 449, 455, 458-59, 462-63, 583, 633
Dragoumis, Philip, 48, 86, 503, 512n, 529, 539, 560, 655, 664
Dunn, James, 568, 574, 580-82, 585

Eaker, Gen. Ira, 449-50
EAM (National Liberation Front), 389, 394, 411, 422-23, 424, 426, 428-30, 434, 440, 446, 449, 451, 454, 461, 465-67, 470, 472, 480, 483, 484, 486-90, 494, 498, 502-503, 506, 509, 512, 513, 519, 522, 523n, 526, 529, 530, 535-45, 548, 551, 552, 554, 557-58, 560, 562, 566, 572, 575-76, 580, 582, 588-90, 592-93, 596, 601-603, 612, 617, 620-22, 628-31, 634, 642-44, 647-48, 652, 654, 659-61, 668, 672, 676, 695-97
Earle, George, 253-54, 295, 321
Eden, Anthony, 301-309, 312, 319, 321-29, 338n, 393, 398, 400, 402-403, 405, 413, 415, 418-19, 422, 426, 427, 439, 442, 447, 582, 632, 635-36, 647, 665
EDES (National Republican Greek League), 393n, 412, 434, 440, 441, 446, 454, 461, 462n, 580, 597, 602, 609-10, 653
Eisenhower, Gen. Dwight, 402, 411, 415-16, 442
ELAS (National Popular Liberation Army), 389n, 412, 423, 429, 441, 451, 461, 462n, 465-66, 468, 472, 513, 522, 526, 530, 539, 541, 543, 554, 557, 558, 572n, 580, 596-97, 601-602, 609-10, 614, 620, 642, 647, 650, 652-53, 654-60, 663, 672, 680
elections, see Greek elections
Else, Cpt. Gerald, 641, 650
Enis, Akayayen, 168, 192, 224, 230, 237, 252, 270, 290, 292, 296, 298, 316, 326, 339, 341, 356, 366
EON (National Youth Organization), 112, 116, 122, 130, 149, 154, 175, 225, 260-61, 263, 280, 292, 296
EPON (United Panhellenic Youth Organization), 621
Erbach-Schonberg, Prince Victor, 219, 237-38, 270, 276, 293, 299, 321, 325, 328, 349, 354, 356
Ernst, Philip, 340
Ethridge, Mark, 711-13
Eves, Brig., 514
Exindaris, George, 496, 500, 512n, 513, 531, 534, 558-59

Farish, Maj. Linn, 405
Feis, Herbert, 382
Fikioris, Petros, 649
Fish, Bert, 283
Forbes, Wing Comm. Lord, 331, 340
"Force 133," 441, 447, 452, 466, 499, 500, 513, 595, 601, 614
"Force 140," 602
Foreign Economic Administration (FEA), 392, 606
Fortier, Maj. Louis, 187
Foster, Andrew, 388-90, 394, 406
Fotić, Konstantine, 410, 424
Frederika, Princess (later Queen) of Greece, 116-22, 224-25, 383, 388, 395, 399

Gafencu, Grigore, 180, 190, 193, 504
George I, King of Greece, 12
George II, King of Greece, 14, 41, 78, 92, 120, 145-48, 167, 196, 198-99, 228, 245, 262-63, 267, 285, 291, 293, 297-98, 301, 303-304, 313, 320, 324, 332, 337-39, 341-43, 346-47, 356, 360, 366, 383, 388, 401, 409, 426, 429, 430, 434, 440, 449-51, 472, 479, 484-88, 490-92, 494-99, 501, 504, 506, 518, 526, 531, 544-45, 547, 560, 629, 634, 663, 664, 701-702, 704-705, 707, 709-10; personality, 181, 200, 224, 226-27, 496, 544-45, 704, 715; restoration (1935), 42, 48, 50, 52-67, 69-72, 74-77, 118; and Metaxas, 77, 81, 82, 86, 88, 92-93, 96, 98-101, 114, 121-24, 127, 130-31, 138, 154-55, 189, 264, 295-96,

George II, King of Greece (*cont.*)
444, 518, 520, 645; in Albanian War,
243-44, 255, 259-60, 361-74; question
of return after World War II, 361,
363, 370, 372-73, 376-77, 385, 389,
393n, 394, 400-401, 403, 405-406, 411-
12, 414-15, 419-20, 446, 464, 468, 470,
473, 482, 492-93, 495, 526, 534-35,
537-42, 544-45, 547-49, 551, 554, 562,
570, 575, 581, 592, 603-604, 610-11,
617-18, 620, 627, 631-32, 640, 644-45,
647, 655, 660-61, 666, 668, 692, 696,
698-701

Germany, 12-13, 50, 73, 78, 90-91, 107,
109, 135, 138-41, 152, 170, 174-76,
179, 189, 196-97, 209-12, 270, 276-77,
286; and the Balkans, 29-30, 35, 51,
164, 197, 201, 211, 217, 223, 224-25,
229, 231, 270, 279-80, 282, 287, 292,
295, 298, 300-301, 304, 307, 314, 327;
attack on Greece, 239, 241, 250, 259,
263, 269, 270, 275, 284, 290-91, 297,
300-301, 302, 305, 311-13, 338-51;
occupation of Greece, 351-78; withdrawal from Greece, 419, 425, 430,
441, 447, 488, 525, 543, 548, 574, 595,
598-99, 601-602, 604, 610, 614-15,
618, 620-21. *See also* Hitler

Giles, Gen. Benjamin, 475-77, 485, 491,
499, 522, 531-32, 536, 538, 540, 559, 587,
599, 612, 629, 632, 634

Goebbels, Joseph, 134

Goering, Marshal Hermann, 30

Gonatas, Gen. Stylianos, 43, 46, 125,
128, 343, 360, 439, 464, 480, 484,
490, 503, 654-55, 723-24

Goodfellow, Col. Preston, 580

Gounaris, Dimitrios, 14

Grady, Henry, 693, 694n, 732

Grazzi, Count Emmanuel, 171, 172,
191, 193-94, 197-98, 203, 215, 232,
234-38, 270, 294

Great Britain, *see* Britain

Greek elections: 1915, 12-13; 1920, 13;
1926, 15; 1933, 15; 1935, 53-54;
1936, 67-68; 1946, 691-94

Grew, Joseph, 685

Griswold, Dwight, 717-32

Hackett, William, 6
Hadjianestis, Gen. George, 14, 44
Hadjikyriakos, Adm. Alexander, 38-39

Halifax, Viscount Edward, 233, 254,
415, 636

Harding, Comm., 486-87, 493, 499,
505, 507, 509

Harriman, W. Averell, 3n, 491, 532-33,
559, 592, 629-30, 645, 682

Hellowell, Col. Paul, 511-12

Henderson, Loy, xiii, 707, 712, 718,
724-27, 731-32

Heywood, Gen. T.G.G., 257, 285, 288,
339, 344-45, 350, 375

Hill, Harry, 391, 404, 406, 427, 432,
475, 487, 491, 514, 516, 538, 540, 546,
553, 601, 618-19, 621-22, 631, 635-39,
641-42, 645, 656-57, 675

Hitler, Adolf, 30, 34, 96, 111, 114, 136,
157-58, 168, 182, 187, 197, 199, 204-205,
208, 216, 229, 231-32, 251, 253, 267,
268, 273, 287, 307, 308, 317, 324, 326,
328-340, 350, 354, 359, 478, 479, 677

House, Charles, 261, 263-64, 302, 330,
365

Hudson, Maj. Barclay, 597, 611, 630,
640, 674

Hughes, Gen. Ivor, 411, 419, 427, 436-
37, 452, 477, 491, 514, 524, 543, 553,
636, 647

Hulick, Charles, 607

Huling, Wallace, 429-30

Hull, Cordell, 44, 309, 382, 390,
409, 410, 415, 417-18, 422, 427, 439,
453, 497, 520, 566-69, 580-81, 606

Huntington, Col. Ellery, 586

Iatridis, Cpt. Milton, 271
Iceland, viii, 379-81
Inönü, Ismet, 136, 139-40, 156, 238,
307, 308, 397
Insull, Samuel, 18-21, 74
Italy, 27, 29, 42-43, 61, 78-79, 107, 110,
115, 133, 135-37, 164, 172-73, 176,
179, 184, 187, 195, 199, 210, 212, 217;
attack on Abyssinia, 49, 59, 72, 80, 90,
121-22; occupation of Albania, 157-59;
attack on Greece, 161, 165, 166, 168,
213-17, 225, 231-32, 233-35, 245-46;
in World War II, 196-97, 201, 202,
205, 207, 470. *See also* Albanian War;
Mussolini

Jackson, Hugh, 466-67, 606
Johnson, John, 212, 236, 240, 330

Johnson, Cpt. Max, 206, 209, 212
Joint Intelligence Committee, Army, Middle East (JICAME), 425, 433, 436, 529
Jones, G. Lewis, 267, 348, 351
Joyce, Robert, 415-16, 418, 421, 423, 424, 476, 478, 564

Kaclamanos, Dimitrios, 497
Kafandaris, George, 15, 43, 46, 48, 67, 68, 72, 98, 123-24, 126, 359, 446, 482, 503, 529, 601, 664
Kammenos, Gen. Dimitrios, 40
Kanellopoulos, Panayiotis, 68, 360, 390, 496, 501, 512n, 539, 559, 579, 614, 650, 691n, 711, 722
Karamessines, Thomas, 697n
Karapanayiotis, Byron, 417, 434-35, 449, 487, 490, 503, 511, 514, 530, 559
Kartalis, George, 512n, 529, 614, 621
Keeley, James, 732
Kekić, Emil, 600, 607
Kemal, Gen. Mustafa, 14, 113-14, 117, 136-37, 139, 141, 156, 307
Kent, Ralph, 493, 510, 529, 595, 601, 652
Kimissis, Gen. Miltiadis, 43-46, 643
King, Brig. Thomas, 514, 609
Kioseivanov, Georgi, 190
Kirk, Alexander, 188, 384-85, 388-89, 393, 395, 401, 404, 413, 433-34, 499, 579, 596, 607, 621, 624, 632
KKE, see Communist Party of Greece
Knatchbull-Hugessen, Sir Hughe, 306
Kohler, D. Foy, xiii, 218, 233-34, 247, 271, 302, 310, 315, 323-25, 335, 351, 354, 362, 369, 465, 522, 562, 565-66, 572, 573, 578-79, 582, 584, 586-90, 677
Kondylis, Gen. George, 15, 16, 19, 31, 38-40, 42, 46, 48, 53, 54, 56, 58-60, 62-63, 65, 67-70, 72, 77, 86, 125, 127, 134
Korizis, Alexander, 291-92, 297-99, 302-303, 307, 318, 320, 324, 327-28, 332, 337-39, 342, 372, 375
Kotzias, Constantine, 65, 99, 163-64, 183, 189, 215, 316-17, 342, 344, 363

Lambrakis, Dimitrios, 531, 534, 558-59
Lambrianidis, Lambros, 512n, 610, 653
Landis, James, 391-92, 404, 406, 461, 467, 475-76, 481, 501, 504, 522, 523-24, 606
Lane, Arthur B., 176-77, 290, 306, 310, 318, 321-22, 332, 366
Larrabee, Col. Sterling, 429, 430, 432-33, 436, 487, 493, 500, 532, 543, 546, 595, 598, 608, 617-18, 623, 630, 641, 644, 652
League of Nations, 35, 49, 61, 73
Lebanon Conference, 512-16, 520-26, 529-30, 535, 538-41, 544, 547-48, 554, 556, 558, 560-61, 573
Leeper, Sir Reginald, 391, 393-95, 400-401, 404-406, 413, 415-22, 426, 428-29, 434-35, 441, 446, 461, 466, 468-70, 476-77, 479, 484, 486, 490, 492-95, 499, 500-506, 508-513, 516, 521, 525-26, 529-31, 533-34, 536-38, 540, 542-43, 546-47, 550-54, 556-58, 560-61, 568, 579, 588, 593, 606, 620, 624, 634, 636-37, 640, 643, 649, 652-53, 655-57, 662-65, 668, 672, 676-77, 704
Lehman, Herbert, 439, 466, 475, 479, 483, 491, 571, 572, 671
Levidis, Col. Dimitri, 125, 390-91, 395, 398, 400, 450, 498
Liberal Party, 13, 15, 16, 31, 53, 68, 74, 76, 87, 95, 98, 123, 513, 515, 552, 558, 589, 603-604, 628, 644, 650, 657, 663, 693n, 694, 730
Lion of Amphipolis, 52, 198-99
Liossis, Gen. Efstathios, 675
Londos, Dimitrios, 556
Longmore, Marshal Sir Arthur, 283, 285, 332
Loverdos, Spyridon, 27
Lovett, Robert, 726-27, 731-32

Macedonia and Macedonian Question, 11, 13, 30, 32-34, 40, 41, 48, 79, 83, 86, 88, 99, 103-105, 110, 115, 139, 159, 164, 219, 229, 231, 238, 240, 241, 332, 576-77, 600, 611-12, 624
Maclean, Fitzroy, 420-21, 426, 433-35, 437-38, 440, 441, 448, 450, 560, 570, 583, 586
Macmillan, Harold, 467, 471, 476-77, 635-36, 645, 656, 662, 664
MacMurray, John, 168, 208, 310, 331
MacVeagh, Colin, xiii, 4
MacVeagh, Lincoln, vii-xi, xiii, 6-8, 10-11, 14-15, 17, 42-44, 51-52, 66, 88,

MacVeagh, Lincoln (*cont.*)
91, 94, 160, 169-70, 236, 317-18, 374, 382, 662, 665-66, 671-72, 678-79, 683-734; early career, 3-6; letters to Pres. Roosevelt, 3, 7, 17-18, 20-21, 21-24, 25-26, 28-30, 33-37, 49-51, 70-74, 76-80, 89-94, 107-114, 133-142, 155-57, 161-62, 165, 166-69, 173-75, 178-80, 182-83, 184-86, 191-96, 199-200, 203-205, 210-12, 220-22, 227-28, 240-42, 254-55, 267-69, 286-88, 300-302, 311-13, 319-20, 394, 401, 406-408, 414-15, 450-56, 472-75, 517-21, 547-51, 625-28, 659-62, 667-71; appointment to Greece, 6-9, 384-86; appointment to Iceland, viii, 170, 379-81; appointment to the Union of South Africa, viii, 170, 381-87; appointment to Portugal, 732-34; appointment to Spain, 734

MacVeagh, Margaret, 4, 7, 8, 43, 51, 52, 160, 198, 224, 233, 317-18, 340, 343, 347, 352, 354, 358, 382, 395, 608, 633-34, 644, 650, 655, 658, 674, 678, 693, 717, 725

MacVeagh, Margaret Ewen, x, xiii, 3, 4, 8, 51, 160, 198, 224, 247, 317-18, 340, 381

MacVeagh, Virginia, xiii, 734
Mandakas, Emmanuel, 631
Manettas, Gen. Theodore, 16, 128, 343
Maniadakis, Constantine, 96n, 124, 128-29, 130, 149, 183, 278, 295-97, 343-44, 350, 363, 377
Maniu, Iuliu, 462-63, 469-70, 479-80, 486, 499, 504, 506, 510-15, 527-28, 534, 540, 576
Mantzavinos, George, 634
Marshall, George, 379, 529, 713, 718-20, 729, 731, 733
Matthews, H. Freeman, 580
Matthews, Sir William, 491, 524
Maugras, Gaston, 183-84, 197, 199, 206, 294
Mavromichalis, Petros, 45, 56, 61, 62, 98, 698, 701-702, 704, 709
Mavroudis, Nikolaos, 163-64, 171-72, 177, 186, 191, 196-98, 202, 209, 212, 215-17, 223, 232-37, 247, 251, 261-62, 265, 274, 276, 297, 298-99, 300, 302, 306, 310, 318, 334-35, 341-42, 344, 346, 358-59

Maximos, Dimitrios, 8, 16, 19, 20, 25, 27, 28, 30, 41, 65, 79, 86, 92, 358-59, 377, 642-43, 655-57; prime minister, 711, 715-16, 722
Mazarakis, Gen. Alexander, 342-43, 363, 364, 372, 377
McBaine, Turner, 480-81
McGhee, George, 721-22, 731-32
McNeill, Archibald, 6, 7
McNeill, William H., xiii, 546, 652, 693
Melas, George, 217-18, 238, 255, 261-62, 289-90, 328, 377
Mercati, Count Leonardo, 102, 225, 243, 245, 265, 297, 314, 323, 337
Merriam, Gordon P., 679-80
Metaxas, Gen. John, 15-16, 28, 31, 41-42, 46-48, 53, 55, 57, 61, 68, 74, 77, 79, 81-82, 86-87, 172, 176, 177, 181-83, 186, 189-90, 192, 196, 203, 208, 209, 214, 216, 219, 223, 225, 234-35, 240, 243-45, 249-50, 253-55, 259-61, 264-66, 268-69, 272-73, 276, 280, 282, 285-87, 289, 291-94, 301, 634; as dictator (1936-1941), vii, 37, 88, 91, 94-155, 159, 161-67, 189, 200, 208, 229, 248, 260-61, 371-72, 375-76, 464, 509, 537, 626, 668, 683, 693, 703
Michalacopoulos, Andreas, 15, 41, 47, 102, 124-26, 359
Middle East Supply Center (MESC), 439, 504, 563, 565, 611
Military Liaison (ML) *see* Allied Military Liaison
Molotov, V. M., 171n, 245, 249, 252, 380-81, 415, 418-19, 422-23, 424, 442, 477, 479-80, 483, 486, 493, 502, 509, 510-11, 519, 527, 529, 533, 568, 599, 611, 623
Montgomery, Field Marshal Sir Bernard, 708-709
Moore, Col., 415, 421
Morgan, Gen. William D., 688
Morris, Leland B., 8, 32, 271, 362, 370, 698, 700
Moshanov, Stoicho, 591-92
Mountain Brigade ("Third" or "Rimini" Brigade), 602, 638, 643, 644, 653, 656, 659, 669
Moyne, Sir Walter, 461, 464-65, 467-69, 471, 477, 479, 481, 483, 485, 492-93,

499, 501, 504, 506, 510, 515, 522-28, 534-35, 547, 556, 560-61, 565, 578, 586-87, 611, 632, 644, 677
Murphy, Robert D., 410, 562-63, 571
Mussolini, Benito, 27, 30, 34, 49, 59, 80, 90, 96, 110, 117, 134, 136, 157-58, 164, 171, 173, 197, 200, 201, 205, 207-208, 216, 229, 231, 239, 253, 258, 268, 276, 325, 349, 354-55
mutiny in Greek armed forces (April 1944), 482-88, 491-505, 507, 509-10, 511, 513, 518-20, 546, 557, 584, 627
Mylonas, Alexander, 43, 48, 54, 68, 76, 102, 359, 439, 503, 530, 537, 540-42, 544, 582, 589, 599, 604

National Guard (1944), 638, 640, 642, 653-54
National Liberation Front, see EAM
National Popular Liberation Army, see ELAS
National Republican Greek League, see EDES
National Youth Organization, see EON
Neubacher, Hermann, 624
Nicolaidis, Gen. George, 278, 358
Nicoloudis, Theologos, 129-30, 163-64, 183, 254, 278, 344
"Noah's Ark" (Operation), 441, 446, 452, 461, 488, 494, 500, 595, 609
Norton, Sir Clifford, 705
Novikov, Nikolai V., 398, 412, 422, 426, 431, 438, 459-60, 463-65, 469-71, 477-79, 490-92, 494, 496-97, 500, 502, 506, 508, 510-11, 515, 519, 527-28, 534-35, 540, 550, 552-53, 560-62, 568, 572, 576-77, 586, 587, 592, 613, 627, 677

Office of Strategic Services (OSS), 384-85, 409-11, 415, 420-30, 432, 436-37, 441, 449, 452-53, 458, 460, 463-64, 467, 476, 478, 480-81, 488, 490, 494, 499, 503, 514, 520, 525, 528, 529, 536, 562, 578, 585, 593, 595-96, 601, 604, 608-609, 613-14, 621-22, 628, 629, 633, 641, 647, 650, 671, 697n
Office of War Information (OWI), 409, 410, 424, 515-16, 527-28, 536, 539, 546-47, 579, 597, 611, 617, 621

Othonaios, Gen. Alexander, 16, 342, 359, 541, 631, 642, 649
Paget, Gen. Sir Bernard, 468, 495, 496, 499, 505, 511, 513, 536, 543, 547, 602, 611, 615, 617
Palairet, Sir Charles M., 162-65, 167, 173, 183-84, 201, 206-208, 244, 281-82, 284-85, 295-96, 302, 305, 308-11, 315, 321-27, 331-33, 336-37, 339-45, 347, 375, 391, 439
Panayiotakos, Gen., 46
Pangalos, Gen. Theodore, 15, 48, 96, 344, 359, 372, 412
Papademas, Gen. Nikolaos, 297, 344, 358
Papagos, Gen. Alexander, 54, 61, 74, 77, 189, 208, 263, 285, 297, 325, 332, 339, 358, 363, 372
Papanastasiou, Alexander, 14-15, 31, 36, 38, 42-44, 46, 48, 54, 61, 67-68, 76, 98-99, 125, 134
Papandreou, George, 61, 67-68, 76, 124, 359, 370, 377, 385, 482, 487, 503, 504-507, 711, 722; prime minister, 508-14, 519-20, 522, 524-27, 530-31, 534-35, 537, 539-42, 544-46, 548-49, 551-52, 554-60, 562, 566, 581-82, 588-89, 593, 598-99, 603-606, 609, 611-12, 613, 616-17, 620-22, 628-31, 634, 638, 640-47, 649, 652-54, 656-57, 659-60, 663, 668
Papavasiliou, Adm. Ippokratis, 343-44, 358
Papen, Franz, 298
Papoulas, Gen. Anastasios, 43-46
Park, Marshal Sir Keith, 495
Parsons, Arthur W., 388-89, 412-13, 419, 429, 430, 467, 468, 472, 482-83, 488-89, 491, 498-99, 505, 510, 512, 514, 525, 530, 531, 535, 542, 560, 562, 592, 598, 602-603, 605
Paul, Crown Prince of Greece, 65, 102, 115-22, 198-99, 224-25, 244, 278, 281, 293, 297, 346-47, 383, 388, 395, 401, 490, 592, 603-604, 611, 617, 621, 623, 630, 647, 653, 702; King of Greece, 719, 722, 724-25
Paul, Prince Regent of Yugoslavia, 35n, 120, 137, 243, 292, 308, 314, 322-25, 328, 340

PEEA (Political Committee of National Liberation), 465n, 467, 470, 472-73, 479, 482, 484-85, 487, 491, 494, 504, 512, 516, 518, 535-36, 545, 548, 554, 572, 602, 631, 653
"Percentages Agreement," *see* "Spheres of Influence" agreement
Peter II, King of Yugoslavia, 35n, 222, 321, 338, 397, 403-404, 408, 412, 421, 428, 433-35, 438, 443, 445, 447, 450, 454, 461, 468, 498, 517-18, 537n, 539, 541, 550, 570, 597-98
Peter, Prince of Greece, 189, 279, 281, 282, 293, 297, 348-50
Peurifoy, John, 731
Pezmazoglou, George, 16, 360
Pezmazoglou, Steven, 98, 215, 218, 302, 315
Philon, Philon Athanasios, 362, 366-67
Pipinelis, Panayiotis, 709, 710, 716
Pitsikas, Gen. John, 345-46
Plastiras, Gen. Nikolaos, 14, 16-17, 32, 41, 44, 46, 49, 131, 143, 489, 642, 654, 664; prime minister, 666, 669, 672-74
plebiscite: 1935, 53-63; 1946, 669n, 692, 694-95, 698-700
Popov, Col. Gregori, 572n, 580
Populist party, 15-16, 31-32, 36, 41, 53, 63, 68, 75, 76, 86, 95, 513, 556, 655, 665, 693n, 726, 730
Porfyrogenis, Miltiadis, 512n, 516n, 523, 535, 543, 560, 602n, 612, 646, 649, 654, 656n, 680
Porter, Paul, 709, 711-13
Potsdam Conference, 683
Purić, Bozidar, 388-89, 401, 403, 408, 410, 412, 420-21, 423, 428, 442-43, 447, 459-62, 495, 531, 537, 539

Quebec Conference: 14-24 August 1943, 400-401, 442; 11-19 September 1944, 586

Rallis, John, 46, 53, 55, 68, 424, 431, 554, 609, 642-43
Rallis, Petros, 48, 360, 530, 657
Rankin, Karl, xiii, 611, 693-94, 732
Rawlings, Adm. Sir Herbert, 495
Reed, Edward L., 215
Reed, Leslie E., 348, 351-53, 355, 357, 360, 362

Rendis, Constantine, 512n, 559, 589, 599, 604
Reppas, Gen. George, 46, 54, 98
Republican Officers' League, 14-15
Ribbentrop, Joachim, 226, 245, 431
Riggs, Ernest W., 52
Roosevelt, Eleanor, x, 3, 33, 52, 122-23
Roosevelt, Franklin D., vii, x, 3, 5, 7-8, 18, 66, 88, 123, 157-58, 160, 244-45, 248, 259-60, 264, 274-75, 278, 289-90, 292, 316, 327, 340, 359, 379, 380, 382-84, 390, 392, 395-98, 433, 467, 478, 502-503, 505, 509-12, 516, 523, 524, 530, 532, 540, 553, 563, 566, 571, 581-85, 587-89, 590n, 593, 608, 612, 616-17, 625, 638, 643-44, 662, 665-66, 674-77; letters to L. MacVeagh, 18, 24n, 88-89, 182, 269n, 444-45, 507, 651; and King George II of Greece, 393, 396-97, 403-409, 411-12, 414-15, 444-45, 464, 466, 486, 497-98, 507, 538, 542, 544, 547, 560
Roosevelt, G. Hall, x, 3-4, 33, 52, 88, 91, 160, 181, 227, 277, 278
Roussos, George, 427, 449, 487, 489, 491
Roussos, Petros, 512n, 516n, 523, 535
Royce, Gen. Ralph, 436-37, 449, 450, 457-58, 461
Rugman, F., 631
Rumania, 35, 42-43, 73, 78, 79, 91, 135-36, 139, 155, 174, 176-77, 178, 184-85, 210, 215; in World War II, 228, 231, 270, 287, 469-71, 479, 483-84, 490-91, 493, 496, 563-64, 586, 604, 613. *See also* Antonescu; Maniu; Stirbei
Russia, *see* Soviet Union

"Sacred Battalion," 602, 615, 653
Sadler, Brig. Percy L., 499, 553, 594, 598-99, 616-17, 624, 631, 634, 635, 647
Sakellariou, Adm. Alexander, 46, 343, 345, 350
Saraçoglu, Sükrü, 299, 302, 306, 334
Sarafis, Gen. Stefanos, 512n, 513, 530, 534, 536, 560, 610
Sariyannis, Gen. Ptolemaios, 653, 656n
Scobie, Gen. Ronald M., 595, 602, 609-10, 616, 636, 638, 640-42, 647, 649-52, 654, 656, 663
"Security Battalions," 429, 480, 486, 490, 554, 558, 597, 609-10, 620, 654

INDEX · 767

Sedgwick, Alexander C., xiii, 45, 234, 334, 634
Sgouritsas, Christos, 604-605, 608
Shantz, Harold, 465, 469, 472, 475, 478-79, 487, 493, 510, 523, 525, 528, 531, 539, 553, 582, 587-89, 591-93, 596, 605-607, 624, 628, 630-31, 634, 644
Siantos, George, 631, 640, 649, 651, 696
Simović, Gen. Dusan, 321, 338
Skeferis, Pericles, 511
Skinner, Robert P., 8
Skouras, George, 525, 529, 597
Smith-Dorrien, Brig. Peter, 596, 620
Smuts, Gen. Jan Christian, 309, 382-83, 395, 411, 412, 464, 472n, 505, 509, 517, 521, 554-56
Sofianopoulos, John, 512n, 544
Sofoulis, Themistoclis, 15, 48, 54, 67-68, 74-76, 86, 95, 99-102, 123, 125-26, 446, 464, 472, 480, 482, 484, 487, 490, 534, 629, 657, 663, 702, 707n, 711, 720, 722, 724; prime minister, 435-36, 503, 510-11, 528
Solod, Danill, 435-36, 503, 510-11, 528
Soviet Union, 28-29, 36, 115, 167, 170, 172-76, 178-79, 182, 184, 189, 195, 202, 209-11, 226, 228, 230, 252, 261, 270, 276, 280, 286, 306-307, 320, 328, 341, 418-19; and the Balkans, 389, 403, 408, 420-21, 424-25, 432, 436, 454, 455, 483, 491, 493, 505, 511, 517, 520, 531-34, 553, 567-68, 572, 602, 611, 625-26, 629-30, 645; and Greek affairs, 238, 394, 397, 415, 422, 423, 427, 497-98, 503, 505, 510, 519, 550, 602-603, 626-27, 645, 670, 681-83, 713-14. *See also* Molotov; Stalin
Special Operations Executive (SOE), 398-99, 418, 423, 424, 453, 458, 476
Spencer, Comm., 595, 601, 603, 614, 623, 628-29, 631, 634, 637, 643, 657-58
"Spheres of Influence" agreement, 533-34, 550-53, 556n, 560, 562-63, 567-68, 576, 623-24
Spiliotopoulos, Gen. Panayiotis, 609-10, 614, 620
Stalin, Joseph, 121, 268, 396, 423, 478, 515, 524, 532, 623, 626, 666, 682
Stathatos, Cpt. Antonios, 618, 630
Steel, Christopher, 422-24, 465, 469-70, 477, 479, 483-84, 510, 515, 528, 586-87, 591-92, 599, 602
Stefanopoulos, Stefanos, 723-24, 726
Steinhardt, Lawrence, 563, 569
Stettinius, Edward R., 385, 566, 569, 573-74, 581, 584-85, 676
Stevenson, Ralph S., 398, 401, 403-405, 408-10, 412, 420, 422, 423-24, 426-28, 433-40, 442-43, 447-48, 450, 458, 460-64, 466-67, 509, 547
Stirbei, Prince Barbu, 462-64, 468-71, 477, 480-81, 486, 490, 496, 499, 506, 510, 515, 528, 534, 540, 588, 592
Stojadinović, Milan, 113, 186
Stott, Cpt. Donald, 431-32
Subasić, Ivan, 537, 539-41, 555, 559-60, 569-70, 582, 589, 600-601
Sulzberger, Cyrus, 215, 218, 252, 256, 270-71, 273, 315, 326, 334, 336, 341, 409, 509, 542, 556, 567, 593-94
Svolos, Alexander, 504, 512n, 516n, 523-25, 530, 535, 540, 554, 557, 560, 602n, 609, 614, 637, 639, 654, 656, 660-61

Tambacopoulos, Agis, 187, 297, 358
Teheran Conference, 384, 396, 398, 442
Thayer, Maj. Charles W., 585-86
Theofanidis, S., 485, 487
Theotokis, John, 32, 41, 54, 56-58, 63, 67-69, 95, 98, 123, 344, 361, 439, 503
Tito (Josip Broz), 397-98, 402-403, 408, 410, 411, 416, 420-24, 426, 428, 430, 432, 434-43, 445, 447-48, 450-51, 454-56, 473, 476, 478, 481, 497, 506, 509, 517-18, 531-33, 537, 539-41, 549-50, 555, 559, 560, 564-65, 570, 572, 575, 582-83, 585-87, 594, 597-98, 600-601, 610, 623-25, 671
Titulescu, Nicolae, 35, 49, 78
Toulmin, Col. John E., 424, 441, 447, 450, 458-59, 463-64, 466, 481, 488, 525, 528, 529, 532, 536-37, 538, 540-41, 547, 578, 593n, 596-97, 604, 622, 624, 631
Truman, Harry S., vii, x, 674, 679, 691n, 692, 694, 710, 715, 717, 728-29, 732-33; Truman Doctrine, vii, 714-15, 731
Tsaldaris, Constantine, 125, 359, 373, 556, 599, 623, 711, 716, 722; prime minister, 693n, 696, 700n, 707n, 709-10, 722-24

Tsaldaris, Panayiotis, 15-16, 26-27, 31-32, 37, 41-42, 44-46, 48, 53-54, 56, 61, 65, 72, 77, 81, 86, 88, 125, 134, 509
Tsatsos, Themistoclis, 512n, 534, 559, 604, 608, 614
Tsirimokos, Elias, 602n, 614, 619, 621, 656n
Tsolakoglou, Gen. George, 346n, 353, 354n, 357-61, 364, 371, 424
Tsouderos, Emmanuel, 125, 164, 343-46, 370, 377, 383-85, 388-90, 398, 401, 405, 407, 411, 412, 415-19, 422, 423, 425-31, 434-35, 439, 446, 462-68, 470-73, 479-80, 482-88, 490, 492, 494, 497-98, 518-19, 526, 554, 598-99
Turkey, 28, 30, 33-37, 42, 49, 59, 79, 90, 109, 115, 133, 135, 140, 155, 161, 165, 166, 172-73, 176, 190, 192, 195, 211, 219, 224, 230, 237-39, 252, 259, 272, 280, 312, 319-20, 327-28, 331, 459, 569, 578, 628. *See also* Kemal
Turkish Straits, 50, 78, 79, 173-74, 178, 182, 184, 195, 209, 211, 224, 228, 231, 239, 241-42, 253, 280, 284, 296, 302, 307, 320, 506, 511, 517, 601, 682
Turle, Adm. Charles E., 212, 333-34, 649

United Nations Organization, 679, 690, 698n, 705-706, 710-12, 723
United Nations Relief and Rehabilitation Agency (UNRRA), 439, 466-67, 475, 479, 481, 483, 485, 491, 504, 524, 549, 563, 566, 572, 574, 579, 586, 590n, 601, 607-608, 631, 637, 639, 641, 646-47, 650-51, 671, 675, 681, 684-89, 691, 707
United States Army Forces Intelligence, Middle East (USAFIME), 458, 501, 511, 513

Vandenberg, Arthur, 714-15
Varkiza Agreement, 669n, 674, 676, 680, 692, 694
Varvaressos, Kyriakos, 125, 406, 554, 634, 684
Vasiliadis, Adm. Gerasimos, 467, 480, 484, 510, 512n, 534, 598
Velouchiotis, Aris (Klaras, Athanasios), 622, 670
Venizelos, Eleftherios, 11-17, 26-28, 30-32, 36-42, 44, 49, 53, 63-64, 66-67, 70-72, 75, 77, 79, 86, 98, 127, 129, 134, 136, 154, 163, 172, 261, 467, 627, 705
Venizelos, Sofoclis, 405, 417, 435, 449, 470, 480, 483-87, 490-92, 494, 496-506, 508, 510, 512n, 513, 523, 529, 530, 534, 552, 558, 582, 589, 599, 603-605, 676, 711, 722
Ventiris, Gen. Constantine, 617, 621, 653
Villard, Henry S., 719
Vogel, Georg, 351-53, 355-57, 360, 369-71
Voulgaris, Adm. Petros, 435, 487, 500-501, 504, 603; prime minister, 674n, 676, 691n
Vukčević, Alexander, 176, 278-80, 307, 325-26, 348

Wadsworth, George, 395-96, 515, 524
Waley, Sir David, 635, 637, 639, 645
Wallace, David, 334, 405
Warner, Edward, 441, 486, 516, 538
Waterhouse, E. K., 405, 468, 483, 489, 508, 558
Waterlow, Sir Sydney, 55-57, 59, 69, 73, 76, 92, 116, 120, 134, 140-41, 148-54, 162, 164, 173
Wavell, Gen. Sir Archibald P., 283-88, 298, 303, 309, 334, 337, 339, 343-44, 364
Welles, Sumner, 188, 191-92, 566
West, Col. Paul, 424, 429-30, 481, 488, 494, 499, 513, 532, 545, 551, 562, 580, 631, 633
Weygand, Gen. Maxime, 184, 192, 283, 298
Wilson, Field Marshal Sir Henry M., 309, 313, 322-23, 331-32, 334, 337-39, 343, 349-50, 364, 366, 385, 411, 437, 447, 460-62, 466-67, 471, 476, 478-80, 485, 489-91, 501, 504, 523, 527, 543, 570, 579, 587, 596, 602, 610, 615-17, 621, 632, 634, 636, 647, 650, 651
Winant, John G., 393, 403-404, 407, 421, 498
Wines, Maj. Gerald K., 551, 633
Woodhouse, Col. Christopher M., 434, 545, 551, 560, 562
Wright, Col. Daniel, 599

Yalta Conference, 676-77, 679-80, 692, 696
Young, Rodney, 429, 621, 641
Yugoslavia, 27, 35, 73, 78-90, 108-10,

113, 135, 151, 155, 164, 186, 218, 230, 249, 252, 254, 690, 708; in World War II, 243, 259, 261, 275, 286, 289, 313, 316-22, 329, 420-23, 428, 453, 474-75, 509, 531, 533, 549-50, 553, 567-68, 575, 585, 627. *See also* King Peter; Purić; Tito

Zahariadis, Nikolas, 680-81, 695
Zaimis, Alexander, 8, 14, 31-32, 56
Zervas, Gen. Napoleon, 393-94, 429-30, 441, 461, 502, 513, 530, 554, 558, 610, 613-14, 642, 675, 709, 721n, 723-24
Zevgos, John, 602n, 614, 649, 656n
Zolotas, Xenofon, 634

LIBRARY OF CONGRESS CATALOGING IN PUBLICATION DATA

MacVeagh, Lincoln, 1890-1972.
　Ambassador MacVeagh reports.

　Includes bibliographical references and index.
　1. Greece, Modern—History—1917-1944—Sources.
2. Greece, Modern—History—1944-1949—Sources.
3. MacVeagh, Lincoln, 1890-1972.　　I. Iatrides, John O.
II. Title.
DF849.M325　1980　　　949.5'07　　　79-19079
ISBN 0-691-05292-1

Date Due